General Reference Books for Adults

The Bowker Buying Guide Series

General Reference Books for Adults

Authoritative Evaluations of Encyclopedias, Atlases, and Dictionaries

Marion Sader
Editor

Brent Allison

Charles A. Bunge

Patricia J. Rom

Consultants

R. R. Bowker Company
New York & London

Published by R. R. Bowker Company, a division of
  Reed Publishing (USA) Inc.
Copyright © 1988 by Reed Publishing USA
All rights reserved
Printed and bound in the United States of America

Library of Congress Cataloging-in-Publication Data

General reference books for adults: authoritative evaluations of
  encyclopedias, atlases, and dictionaries / Marion Sader, editor:
  Brent Allison, Charles A. Bunge, Patricia J. Rom, consultants.
    p.   cm. — (The Bowker buying guide series)
    Bibliography: p. 587
    Includes index.
    ISBN 0-8352-2393-0
    1. Reference books—Reviews.   2. Encyclopedias and
dictionaries—Reviews.   3. Atlases—Reviews.   I. Sader, Marion.   II. Series.
Z1035.1.G45   1988
028.1′2—dc19   88-10054

Editorial Development and Production
by Visual Education Corporation,
Princeton, NJ

Contents

List of Titles Reviewed

Encyclopedias (pp. 63–147)

Academic American Encyclopedia
Academic American Encyclopedia (Online)
Academic American Encyclopedia (CD-ROM)
Collier's Encyclopedia
The Concise Columbia Encyclopedia
The Encyclopedia Americana
Everyman's Encyclopedia (Online)
Funk & Wagnalls New Encyclopedia
Kussmaul Encyclopedia (Online)
The Lincoln Library of Essential Information
The New American Desk Encyclopedia
New Encyclopaedia Britannica
New Standard Encyclopedia
The Volume Library
The World Book Encyclopedia

Atlases (pp. 163–225)

Ambassador World Atlas
Background Notes on the Countries of the World
Bartholomew Mini World Atlas
Britannica Atlas
Citation World Atlas
Concise Earthbook
Earthbook
Gold Medallion World Atlas
The Great World Atlas
International World Atlas
McGraw-Hill Pictorial Atlas of the World
National Geographic Atlas of the World
The New International Atlas
The New Penguin World Atlas
The New York Times Atlas of the World
The Prentice-Hall New World Atlas
The Prentice-Hall Pocket Atlas of the World
The Prentice-Hall Universal Atlas
The Prentice-Hall University Atlas
Rand McNally Contemporary World Atlas
Rand McNally Cosmopolitan World Atlas
Rand McNally Desk Reference World Atlas
Rand McNally Family World Atlas
Rand McNally Goode's World Atlas
Rand McNally Images of the World
Rand McNally Quick Reference World Atlas
The Random House Concise World Atlas
The Random House Mini World Atlas
Reader's Digest Wide World Atlas

The Times Atlas of the World
VNR Pocket Atlas
The Whole Earth Atlas

General Dictionaries (pp. 239–414)

The American Encyclopedic Dictionary
The American Heritage Desk Dictionary
The American Heritage Dictionary
The American Heritage Dictionary: Second College Edition
The American Heritage Illustrated Encyclopedic Dictionary
Basic Dictionary of English
Chambers Concise 20th Century Dictionary
Chambers Mini Dictionary
Chambers Pocket 20th Century Dictionary
Chambers 20th Century Dictionary
Chambers Universal Learners' Dictionary
The Compact Edition of the Oxford English Dictionary
The Concise American Heritage Dictionary
The Concise Oxford Dictionary of Current English
The Doubleday Dictionary for Home, School, and Office
An English-Reader's Dictionary
Everyday American English Dictionary
The Facts on File Visual Dictionary
Funk & Wagnalls Standard Desk Dictionary (cloth)
Funk & Wagnalls Standard Desk Dictionary (paperback)
Funk & Wagnalls Standard Dictionary
Hugo English Dictionary
The Little Oxford Dictionary of Current English
The Little Webster
Longman Dictionary of American English
Longman Dictionary of Contemporary English
Longman Photo Dictionary
The Merriam-Webster Dictionary
Microsoft Bookshelf CD-ROM Reference Library
Nelson's New Compact Webster's Dictionary
New American Webster Handy College Dictionary
New Century Vest-Pocket Webster Dictionary
Oxford Advanced Learner's Dictionary of Current English
Oxford American Dictionary
The Oxford-Duden Pictorial English Dictionary
The Oxford English Dictionary

The New American Roget's College Thesaurus in Dictionary Form
The Penguin Pocket Thesaurus
The Penguin Roget's Thesaurus of English Words and Phrases
The Random House Thesaurus: A Dictionary of Synonyms and Antonyms
The Random House Thesaurus: College Edition
The Right Word II: A Concise Thesaurus
Roget's International Thesaurus: Fourth Edition
Roget's Pocket Thesaurus
Roget's II: The New Thesaurus
Roget's University Thesaurus
Webster's Collegiate Thesaurus
Webster's New World Thesaurus (hardcover)
Webster's New World Thesaurus (paperback)

Usage Dictionaries and Word Books
(pp. 501–571)

American Usage and Style
Beginner's Dictionary of American English Usage
British/American Language Dictionary
British English, A to Zed
A Browser's Dictionary
Chambers Idioms
Chambers Pocket Guide to Good English
A Concise Dictionary of Correct English
A Dictionary of American Idioms
Dictionary of American Regional English
Dictionary of Collective Nouns and Group Terms
Dictionary of Confusing Words and Meanings
Dictionary of Contemporary American English Contrasted with British English
A Dictionary of Modern English Usage
Dictionary of Problem Words and Expressions
Dictionary of Pronunciation
Encyclopedic Dictionary of English Usage
The Facts on File Dictionary of Troublesome Words
A Handy Book of Commonly Used American Idioms
Harper Dictionary of Contemporary Usage: Second Edition
Homophones and Homographs
Longman Dictionary of English Idioms
Longman Dictionary of Phrasal Verbs

Modern American Usage
Mrs. Byrne's Dictionary of Unusual, Obscure and Preposterous Words
New Dictionary of American Slang
The New York Times Everyday Reader's Dictionary of Misunderstood, Misused and Mispronounced Words
No Uncertain Terms
NTC's American Idioms Dictionary
-Ologies and -Isms: Third Edition
1000 Most Challenging Words
1000 Most Important Words
1000 Most Practical Words
Oxford Dictionary of Current Idiomatic English
The Oxford Guide to English Usage
The Oxford Guide to the English Language
The Penguin Dictionary of Troublesome Words
Practical English
Practical English Usage
Prefixes and Other Word-Initial Elements of English
A Pronouncing Dictionary of American English
The Quintessential Dictionary
Suffixes and Other Word-Final Elements of English
Usage & Abusage
Words on Words

Large Print Reference Books
(pp. 573–585)

Large Print Version of the Little Oxford Dictionary of Current English
The Large Type American Heritage Basic Dictionary
The Merriam-Webster Dictionary for Large Print Users
The Random House Dictionary: Classic Edition
Webster's Concise Family Dictionary
Webster's New Collegiate Dictionary
Webster's New World Large Print Dictionary of the American Language: Second Concise Edition
The Merriam-Webster Thesaurus for Large Print Users
Roget's International Thesaurus
Webster's New World Thesaurus
Hammond Large Type World Atlas

Consultants, Reviewers, and Contributors

Consultants

Brent Allison
Head, Map Library
Humanities/Social Sciences Libraries
University of Minnesota, Twin Cities
Minneapolis, MN

Charles A. Bunge
Professor
School of Library and Information Studies
University of Wisconsin-Madison
Madison, WI

Patricia J. Rom
Director of Library Service
College of Wooster
Wooster, OH

Subject Consultants

Gerald Friedman
Assistant Professor
Department of Economics
University of Massachusetts
Amherst, MA

Robert George
Assistant Professor
Public Law and Jurisprudence
Department of Politics
Princeton University
Princeton, NJ

Clinton W. Hatchett
Astronomical Writer/Producer
American Museum –
Hayden Planetarium
New York, NY

John R. Michener
Principal Investigator
Electron Beam Testing
Siemens RTL
Princeton, NJ

Lynn Nadel
Professor of Cognitive
Science
Department of Psychology
University of Arizona
Tucson, AZ

Reviewers and Contributors

Carole A. Barham
Head Librarian
Columbia High School Library
Maplewood, NJ

W. F. Bolton
Professor of English
Rutgers University
New Brunswick, NJ

April Carlucci
Map Reference Specialist
New York Public Library
New York, NY

Charla A. Coatoam
Literature Specialist
Cuyahoga County Public Library
Mayfield Regional Branch
Cleveland, OH

James A. Coombs
Map Librarian
Southwest Missouri State University
Springfield, MO

Paul Z. DuBois
Director
Roscoe L. West Library
Trenton State College
Trenton, NJ

Michael Dulka
Map Librarian
Dag Hammarskjold Library
United Nations
New York, NY

Keith P. Fleeman
Community Librarian
Little Falls Library
Bethesda, MD

Louise G. Fradkin
Retired, Head Reference Librarian
Trenton State College
Trenton, NJ

Sally G. Gillmore
Head Librarian
Mayfield High School
Mayfield, OH
and
Adjunct Assistant Professor
Kent State University
School of Library Science
Kent, OH

Martin E. Gingerich
Professor
Department of English
Western Michigan University
Kalamazoo, MI

Helen M. Gothberg
Library Consultant
and
Associate Professor
Graduate Library School
The University of Arizona
Tucson, AZ

Diana Hanaor
Formerly Reference Information Assistant
Douglass College Library
Rutgers University
New Brunswick, NJ

Jeannette Handler
Children's Librarian II
Rockville Regional Library
Rockville, MD

William Hoffman
Director
Fort Myers–Lee County Public Library
Fort Myers, FL

David Isaacson
Assistant Head of Reference, and Humanities
Librarian
Dwight B. Waldo Library
Western Michigan University
Kalamazoo, MI

Susan Dye Lee
History Instructor
North Park College
Chicago, IL

Doris Mitchell
Acting Assistant Librarian
Undergraduate Library
Howard University
Washington, DC

Katherine Riley
Adjunct Professor
Department of English
Rutgers University
New Brunswick, NJ

Ann M. Rogers
Library Media Specialist
Evergreen Junior High School
Evergreen, CO

Phoebe Sisco
Reference Librarian
Raritan Valley Community College
Somerville, NJ

Chris Sokol
Monograph Cataloger
Holland Library
Washington State University
Pullman, WA

Teri Wilber
Office of Instructional Technology
University of Delaware
Newark, DE

Editorial Consultants

Sandra Barnard
Chicago, IL

Ester Connelly
ESL Consultant
Consultant, Time to Read
Trenton, NJ

Cindy George
Educational Consultant
Princeton, NJ

Lauren E. Lepow
Princeton, NJ

Gloria R. Mosesson
GRM Associates, Inc.
New York, NY

Princeton Research Forum
Editorial Associates
Princeton, NJ

Tyler W. Wasson
New York, NY

Preface

General Reference Books for Adults is the second volume in the Bowker Buying Guide Series. R. R. Bowker created this series as part of its continuing commitment to provide librarians with useful tools for developing and maintaining their collections, as well as reliable and easy-to-use sources for answers to patrons' queries. The series will give users all the information they need in one place and at one time, in an orderly and accessible form.

A wide range of publications exists to help librarians make collection development and selection decisions. These are useful publications, but they suffer from common weaknesses. For example, works are evaluated individually and with minimal comparison to similar titles; consistent criteria may be applied less rigorously from work to work; and the idiosyncracies and preconceptions of individual reviewers often tend to reduce objectivity. The result is that librarians are without the kind of comparative, consistent, and objective evaluations they need.

General Reference Books for Adults meets this need by reviewing some 215 encyclopedias, world atlases, dictionaries, word books, and large-print reference works that are found in general reference collections. Like those in *Reference Books for Young Readers*, the reviews in this Buying Guide are authoritative, comprehensive, and objective. Moreover, they apply consistent standards and criteria in evaluating each work.

Parts two, three, four, and five contain the reviews that form the core of this guide. Each opens with a chapter titled "What to Look for in . . .," which details the criteria used to evaluate all the titles in that part. The reviews reflect the guidelines that have been established, and follow a common structure. Comments comparing the work in question to others similar in scope and content are an integral part of the reviews. In this way, librarians and patrons are given systematic, clearly organized, comparative reviews that follow consistent criteria.

To be included in this volume, a reference work had to be appropriate for the general reference collection and readily available in the United States as of April 1, 1988.

The books reviewed are all works of a general nature, aimed at and frequently consulted by the lay reader and not requiring or presupposing any specialized knowledge. Moreover, they are suitable for high school students and adults. The first volume in the Buying Guide Series, *Reference Books for Young Readers*, contains evaluations of reference titles written for children and young adults. Some of the titles reviewed here also appeared in *Young Readers*; in all instances, however, the reviews have been updated and revised with the different audience for this guide in mind.

Only in-print titles were reviewed, because only they are easily purchased through normal retail and direct sales channels. Librarians or patrons who wish to purchase out-of-print titles may wish to consult back issues of the journals listed in the bibliography. We have made every effort to identify all appropriate general reference works and have given publishers every opportunity to submit information about their titles. British works are reviewed only if they are readily available for purchase in the United States.

In some cases, publishers have generously provided advance proofs of works that were undergoing revision but were not yet generally available as of the April 1 cutoff date; these updated editions were included to provide the librarian and patron with the most complete information. Some titles, notably encyclopedias, are revised each year. For these volumes, the review may be based on scrutiny of the 1987 edition, but up-to-date statistical information from the 1988 edition, as well as notes on any changes or new features that the publisher has introduced, are included in the review.

Of course, some of the titles included in this volume may go out of print or be revised subsequent to the publication of this guide. Similarly, new titles will be published. We will continue to monitor the activity in general reference books to maintain an up-to-date and comprehensive list of titles so that these changes can be incorporated into future editions of this Buying Guide.

General Reference Books for Adults is divided into five parts. The first offers an overview of general reference books, preparing the reader for the next four parts, which include the product evaluations. Part two focuses on encyclopedias, part three on world atlases, part four on dictionaries and word books, and part five on large-print titles. "Using This Book," which appears on page xv, guides the reader through this volume. A complete list of titles reviewed in this Buying Guide follows the table of contents. A bibliography, list of publishers, and comprehensive index further aid in supporting the text.

Several features provide a useful overview of the field of general reference books, making this guide useful for students in professional library training or as a refresher for practicing librarians. The first two chapters present the history of these reference books as well as offering some guidance on how to choose among them. Each "What to Look for" chapter includes a glossary of terms that defines the specialized vocabulary appropriate to a particular type of reference work. In addition, "What to Look for in Atlases" (chapter 7) includes six pages of generic maps and accompanying text that exemplify the types of maps that atlases may contain as well as illustrate such important cartographic features as scope and projection. Finally, a selected bibliography provides both librarian and patron with a list of resources for further reading in the complex but rich field of general reference books.

A number of special features aid the user in the search for a suitable general reference book. First, comparative charts (in chapter 4) organize the works by type and provide a statistical overview of the size, scope, and price of all titles under review. Second, at the head of each review, a "Facts at a Glance" box conveniently summarizes the relevant information about the title. Third, because it is often impossible for a librarian or patron to actually examine a reference work prior to making a purchase decision, we have included a number of facsimiles of actual pages or partial pages. These facsimiles are annotated to highlight the features of the work under consideration. Thus librarians as well as parents, teachers, and students shopping for general reference books can consult this volume as a consumer guide.

General Reference Books for Adults, then, is designed to be useful on both sides of the reference desk as an authoritative guide. The R. R. Bowker Company has been publishing authoritative books and other professional reference materials for li-

brarians for over 115 years. Among its well-known reference tools are *Books in Print* and *The Reader's Adviser*. The Bowker Buying Guide Series is now taking its place as another demonstration of Bowker's commitment to libraries and librarians. This set of volumes is carefully prepared by professional librarians and subject matter specialists who generously contributed their time and energy. Those who were involved in the preparation of this volume are listed on pages xi–xii along with their current affiliations. In addition, three librarians—Brent Allison, Charles Bunge, and Patricia Rom—acted as consultants, reviewing the lists of titles to be included; advising on the criteria against which the books should be measured; and carefully screening all the reviews to ensure that they were complete, comprehensive, and objective. To these reviewers and consultants, I would like to extend my sincere gratitude.

After the evaluations were created and then reviewed by the consultants, they underwent a painstaking process of revision and checking. This procedure ensures that each review represents a balanced, thoroughly considered judgment. Special thanks are due to Maureen Bischoff, John F. Drexel, and Ann M. Harvey for their editorial guidance throughout this project and to Anita Black for overseeing the production processes. My gratitude is due to Richard Lidz and Dale Anderson without whose calm cooperation, steady support, and rare regard for reference books and libraries this volume could not have been completed.

General Reference Books for Adults presents the most extensive, systematic, consistent, and objective reviews of general reference works gathered into one volume. We are confident that they will prove useful to anyone—librarian or patron—engaged in the important task of selecting an encyclopedia, atlas, or dictionary.

Marion Sader

Marion Sader
Executive Editor
Professional and Reference Books
R. R. Bowker Company
September 1988

Using This Book

General Reference Books for Adults is divided into five main parts: part one, Introduction; part two, Encyclopedias; part three, Atlases; part four, Dictionaries and Word Books; and part five, Large-Print General Reference Books.

The four chapters in part one provide background information on general reference books. Chapter 1, "The History of General Reference Books," outlines the history of these works and describes current trends. Chapter 2, "Choosing General Reference Books," notes the criteria that readers may wish to consider. We recommend that any user of this book begin by reading chapter 2 to reach an understanding of the scope and nature of the works in question. Chapter 3, "Librarians Rate General Reference Books," reports the results of a national survey on behalf of this Buying Guide that asked public and academic librarians about their reference collections. The survey results can be used to supplement the detailed evaluations of individual works that appear in later chapters.

Chapter 4, which closes part one, presents comprehensive charts that compare each title reviewed here on a number of statistical categories. The charts are grouped by type of book and include such information as the edition reviewed, the page and illustration counts, the publisher, and the price. By consulting these charts at the beginning of the selection process, the user can identify titles with similar scope and within a desired price range, thus narrowing choices quickly. The user can then consult the appropriate review in parts two through five, which contain the main thrust of the book; in-depth reviews of encyclopedias, world atlases, general dictionaries, etymological dictionaries, dictionaries of synonyms and antonyms, thesauruses, guides to usage and other word books, and large-print reference books. The initial chapters in parts two, three, and four describe the specific criteria used for evaluating the titles in each part, as well as presenting the structure that the reviews will take. Each "What to Look for" chapter ends with a glossary of terms appropriate to that type of reference work. The atlases chapter (chapter 7) contains an added feature—generic maps that illustrate various features that atlases may contain.

The body of the book consists of the reviews found in chapters 6, 8, and 10 through 15. Each review begins with a "Facts at a Glance" box that lists the essential statistics and editorial data of the title being reviewed. The information summarized includes such data as the work's full title, publisher, and editor; initial copyright date or the edition reviewed; the number of volumes, pages, entries or maps, and illustrations; trim size and binding; price; and sources through which the book can be purchased.

Each review within a category follows a standard format. The subheadings vary from category to category but generally include such essential elements as scope, authority, clarity, objectivity, accessibility, and special features. Criteria that are specific to each type of work, such as quality and currency of entries for dictionaries or scale and projection for atlases, are included when needed. Each review concludes with a summary, which judges the book's overall quality and potential use to readers. In the summary—and throughout the body of the review—comments compare each title to significant related titles when appropriate. For easy identification, all references to titles reviewed in this volume are printed in capital and small capital letters (e.g., WORLD BOOK). Someone considering the purchase of a college dictionary and reading a review of, for example, WEBSTER'S NINTH NEW COLLEGIATE DICTIONARY could thus be directed to read the reviews of such comparable titles as the AMERICAN HERITAGE COLLEGE DICTIONARY and the RANDOM HOUSE COLLEGE DICTIONARY.

Many reviews are enhanced by the inclusion of facsimile pages, reproductions of typical pages or entries annotated to highlight the work's special features. These facsimiles will be of special value to anyone using this guide to comparison shop prior to making a purchase. Readers of this guide should note that facsimiles of encyclopedias and encyclopedic dictionaries are reduced to fit on our pages; a note below the facsimile indicates the amount of reduction. Unless otherwise noted, the remaining facsimiles are reproduced at their actual size. Facsimiles have been selected to illustrate representative samples of the design and editorial features of the various titles. The reproduction process necessarily results in some loss of image quality from the original, especially when converting a color page to black and white. The facsimiles therefore do not represent the quality of the image in the original work, but are meant only as a guide to the general look and features of the book.

The Buying Guide does not include facsimile pages from the atlases reviewed. Color is essential to the maps in these atlases, and black-and-white reproductions do not do justice to these works. In fact, for this reason, atlas publishers were unable to give permission to reproduce their maps in this manner.

General Reference Books for Adults concludes with a bibliography, an alphabetical list of publishers and their addresses, and a comprehensive index. The bibliography includes titles of related reference works and professional journals that regularly review and discuss reference works for librarians. The list of publishers includes all publishers and distributors cited in the reviews; it is current as of April 1, 1988. The index cites page references for all titles reviewed in this volume, as well as for any other titles (such as historically important or out-of-print works) mentioned in the text.

This Buying Guide can be used in a variety of ways. A librarian or lay reader interested in a review of the history and principles of general reference books could read chapters 1 and 2 and then sample reviews of major works. A librarian wishing to evaluate a new dictionary or a new edition of an encyclopedia will probably want to turn right to that review, perhaps consulting the reviews of comparable works and the comments of fellow professionals in chapter 3 as well. A parent or student considering which world atlas to purchase will probably want to start by looking at the comparative chart for atlases to identify titles of interest and then turn to the appropriate reviews.

Whichever method is chosen, we are confident that librarians and patrons alike will find *General Reference Books for Adults* to be authoritative, objective, highly readable, and an indispensable tool in the selection of general reference books.

General Reference Books for Adults

PART ONE
Introduction

Chapter 1
The History of
General Reference Books

General Reference Books for Adults encompasses the major categories of general reference works: encyclopedias, atlases, dictionaries, and other books relating to words and the use of words.

Encyclopedias synthesize knowledge, giving readers a view of what is known about a myriad of specific topics, and present an orderly assembly of the facts essential to an understanding of each topic. Modern encyclopedias are designed to serve as a point of reference from which a reader can proceed to other sources that contain more detailed information. The term *encyclopedia* derives from a classical Greek expression used in describing a "rounded" education, the *enkyklios paideia* (literally a *circle of learning*).

If, at the most basic level, encyclopedias can be characterized as books about *things*, then dictionaries can be described as books about *words*. General dictionaries and their close counterparts, such as thesauruses, etymologies, and dictionaries of synonyms and antonyms, provide information about words as words: They describe the derivation and meanings of words, the relationships words have to each other, and the ways in which words are pronounced, spelled, and used. The term *dictionary* is from the medieval Latin *dictionarium*, which, in turn, derives from the classical Latin *dictio*, "saying or speaking," and *arium*, "a connecting thing or place."

Atlases describe in words and diagrams the surface of the world and its features, both natural and artificial. The maps in atlases are abstract representations of the earth. In addition, atlases use symbols and mathematical scales to depict special features of the earth. The term *atlas* came to be used after early cartographers illustrated the covers of their map collections with pictures of the Titan Atlas who, in Greek mythology, was forced to carry the heavens on his shoulders for eternity after the Olympian gods defeated the Titans for control of the universe. The modern world atlas has a burden, too—the accurate, up-to-date representation of the world, its cities, political boundaries, and salient features.

The history of reference books is closely tied to the development of writing and of printing. The written word is a kind of formalized memory that enables literate people to arrange and record not only the knowledge of individuals but also that possessed by groups, nations, and cultures. The capacity to write, record, and read allows human knowledge to accumulate and to be transmitted over vast spans of time and place.

The compiling of reference works is a response to the same human impulses that created systems of writing. Only by defining and agreeing to an arbitrary collection of signs representing spoken languages and ideas can a permanent record of information be accumulated and passed on—to officials in a neighboring community, to scholars in other countries, or to people in the next generation.

The earliest reference systems were mnemonic aids—pictures and symbols used to prompt the recollection of earlier human experience and acquired information. Contemporary examples of such aids include the rosaries still used by the Buddhist, Catholic, Eastern Orthodox, Hindu, and Muslim faithful to prompt the ordered repetition of a prayer sequence. Such devices as the notched Maori genealogy sticks also make possible the recording of history and other information.

Like these memory aids, Sumerian cuneiform, Egyptian hieroglyphics, and other early writing systems allowed ancient peoples to record genealogies and commercial and political transactions; to represent various aspects of myth, religion, and ritual; and to measure time and to chart the changes in nature. These systems, however, could record only the concrete; the abstract, unseen, and unknowable aspects of thought, of cultural events and their significance, of relations among the living and the dead could not be recorded unless they were first reduced to concrete terms.

The urge to record the most abstract thoughts that language can express led to the development of the alphabet. The first true alphabet, which emerged around 1000 B.C. in the Phoenician city of Byblos, had a liberating effect on the recording of knowledge. By separating language into sounds, the alphabet made it possible to use a finite number of symbols to represent an infinite number of words. More flexible and economical than cuneiform, hieroglyphics, pictograms, or ideograms, an alphabet could be used to record the most abstract statements. As a result, subsequent generations were able to refine the abstract concepts they inherited in light of new as well as accumulated information.

Moreover, a standard alphabet ultimately allowed writers and readers to switch from one language to another with greater ease than did the earlier systems of writing. And, though its creators could not have foreseen it, the alphabet was to be the perfect partner for the printing techniques that would eventually culminate in movable type and the distribution of reading matter in the form of bound volumes.

Encyclopedias

Classification of Knowledge in Ancient Greece and Rome

Improved writing systems resulted in a vastly expanded accumulation of knowledge. Soon the need arose to classify information in order to manage or absorb it easily. Responding to this need, the classical Greeks initiated two systems of classification, methods that were to be important in the making of reference books throughout the coming centuries. The first of these systems was by category, in which a finite number of sets were established to contain information. The second method of classification was by hierarchy, in which knowledge was ranked as either superordinate or subordinate.

Greek philosophers such as Socrates and Plato taught that the good life required thought and that

thought, in turn, required an encompassing knowledge of all things. Books that could contain all known information seemed to be a solution, and the reference work was born.

In his wide-ranging approach to knowledge, Plato may be thought of as the Western world's first truly encyclopedic thinker. Indeed, reference book historian Robert Collison has called him the "father of encyclopedias." It is fitting, therefore, that Plato's ideas were the subject of what was probably the West's first written encyclopedia, a work by his nephew Speusippus (ca. 370 B.C.) that sought to categorize and present the great philosopher's thought. Only a few fragments of this work are extant.

In his writings, Aristotle, the next major classical philosopher, made an encyclopedic attempt at consolidating all of the world's knowledge. Aristotle's comprehensive approach to knowledge and his philosophic emphasis on facts and observation were central to the curriculum of his school, the Lyceum, established in 335 B.C. Both the categorical and the hierarchical classification systems taught in the Lyceum survived in the ideals of Greek education that were spread through the far-flung military conquests of Aristotle's student, Alexander the Great. The Greek idea of the "all around" or general education—the *enkyklios paideia*—survives as the standard for a liberal arts education.

The seven categories of the *enkyklios paideia* developed in the Hellenistic era were divided into three lower categories (grammar, rhetoric, and logic/dialectic) and four higher ones (arithmetic, geometry, astronomy, and music/harmony). These seven areas of study were thought of as the pathways to knowledge; in Latin they were known as the *trivium* and the *quadrivium* and were the foundation of all schooling and university education for centuries. Not only did these seven disciplines become the seven "liberal arts," but they also became the basis for the first true encyclopedias, which appeared in Hellenized Rome.

Roman writers sought to collect existing knowledge and to present it in a readable form, in keeping with the value they placed on acquiring the knowledge necessary for the execution of practical tasks. The first known Roman effort to summarize all useful knowledge was a series of letters from Marcus Porcius Cato (Cato the Censor) to his son. The collection, known as the *Praecepta ad filium* (Advice to His Son, ca. 183 B.C.), survives only in fragments, but it is known that in this encyclopedic work, Cato sought to provide an education for his reader as well as references that could be used in solving practical problems. The *Praecepta* included all the subjects Cato considered essential for the Roman citizen: agriculture, rhetoric, medicine, law, and the art of war.

Another Roman writer, Marcus Terentius Varro, established a more direct link to the *enkyklios paideia*. His *Disciplinae* (The Disciplines, ca. 30 B.C.) consisted of nine volumes, one devoted to each of the seven liberal arts and one each to medicine and to architecture. This work also exists only in fragments.

The earliest *enkyklios paideia* to survive in its entirety was the *Historia Naturalis* (Natural History of General Knowledge, A.D. 77) compiled by Pliny the Elder (ca. A.D. 23–79). The most influential of all the Roman encyclopedias, Pliny's work served as a major source for other encyclopedias for the next 15 centuries. Although the term *encyclopedia*, which first appears in medieval Latin, was never used to describe reference works in the ancient world, the *Historia Naturalis* is often cited as the first *true* encyclopedia.

Pliny's encyclopedia is an immense work. He collected all the information about the natural world he could locate from the writings of 473 Greek and Roman authors. The 37 books that comprise the work divided "all known" knowledge into 2,500 chapters and included such diverse categories as the physical composition of the universe, geography and ethnography, anthropology and human physiology, zoology, minerals and their uses, and painting and sculpture.

Preservation of Knowledge in the Middle Ages

After the fall of the Roman Empire in the fifth century, trade and communications throughout Europe waned, cities declined, and law and order disintegrated. The single unifying force in Europe during the Middle Ages (fifth to fifteenth centuries) was the Catholic Church, which not only provided some social services for the sick and indigent but also fostered learning in monasteries.

In establishing the monastic tradition of scholarship, the early church fathers sought to preserve the learning of the classical pagan world while reconciling it with Christian beliefs and doctrine. During this period, encyclopedias were compiled so that existing knowledge could be interpreted and codified in accordance with orthodox theology. Despite their theocentric purpose, these works fulfilled the traditional goal of the *enkyklios paideia* by recording all known knowledge throughout an era that was largely inimical to it.

In 551, the Roman statesman and writer Cassiodorus withdrew to a monastery and began work on an encyclopedia that was to establish the tone for Christian encyclopedias in the Middle Ages. His *Institutiones divinarum et saecularium litterum* (Institutes of Divine and Secular Literature) presented

encyclopedia entries in order of their perceived importance. Cassiodorus drew clear distinctions between sacred and profane teachings and ranked them hierarchically in his encyclopedia, with Scripture and other religious topics considered first and in detail. Such topics as arithmetic and geometry appeared last and were given only minor attention.

Between 600 and 630, Isidore of Seville (archbishop and saint) compiled an encyclopedia for the education of the newly converted population of Spain. The *Etymologiae* or *Origenes* (Etymologies or Beginnings) was an ambitious collection of 20 books in which Isidore attempted to define and trace the etymology of every term relating to an academic discipline. The books were arranged topically and at the beginning of each major division, Isidore offered a brief historical summary of the subject to be examined. This vast compilation included not only the seven liberal arts but also theology, Church history, languages, nations, cities, animals, and gardening, all organized in hierarchical categories. Because Isidore considered the liberal arts and secular learning to be the true basis of a Christian education, he dealt first with such subjects, then with the Bible and Church teachings, and finally with such practical topics as agriculture, warfare, shipping, and furniture. Isidore's work was highly respected and was reprinted as late as the sixteenth century.

During the next five centuries, European encyclopedias were generally designed to be read by the learned few. (Indeed, few people could read and most had no leisure for such pursuits.) These encyclopedias in the Middle Ages were intended to be read from beginning to end, like textbooks, not to be consulted for specific information as are modern encyclopedias. Because they were intended as tools for professional scholars and the clergy, content was organized to reflect a train of thought, not for ease in usage.

There were, however, four notable departures. At the beginning of the twelfth century, an encyclopedic dictionary called the *Suda* or *Suidas* first used alphabetical order (a practice that was also important for the development of dictionaries) and provided a range of practical information that ensured its popularity for several centuries. At the end of that century, the Abbess of Herrad compiled what is probably the first encyclopedia by a woman, a work intended to educate and edify the nuns of her abbey. The idea of an encyclopedia for readers other than male clerics was taken a step further by Bartholómaeus Angelicus, who designed *De proprietatibus rerum* (1220–40) for the lay reader. Based on Pliny's and Isidore's works, it remained the most popular European encyclopedia for the next 300 years. Also designed for the lay reader was a work by Dante

Alighieri's teacher, Brunetto Latini. Latini wrote the first vernacular encyclopedia in French, which at that time was the language used by the cultured and mercantile classes in Italy. Latini called his work *Li livres dou tresor* (Treasure Books, ca. 1266).

The most authoritative encyclopedia of the period was compiled by Vincent of Beauvais at the request of Louis IX of France (ca. 1244). A Dominican monk, Vincent gathered all the knowledge of the Middle Ages into three comprehensive works: the *Speculum naturale* (Mirror of Nature), the *Speculum doctrinale* (Mirror of Doctrine), and the *Speculum historiale* (Mirror of History). Together with a fourth book, the *Speculum morale* (Mirror of Morals), an anonymous work added after the compiler's death, this encyclopedia is known as the *Speculum maius* (Greater Mirror).

Vincent's portion of the *Speculum maius* consists of 80 books divided into 9,785 chapters, with almost equal space allotted to each of the three sections. In the *Speculum naturale,* Vincent drew on Latin, Greek, Arabic, and Hebrew sources in order to summarize all natural history (including God and the Creation) then known to the West. The *Speculum doctrinale* discussed practical matters as well as scholastic doctrine and philosophy. Intended as a practical handbook for the student or public official, it included the classical curriculum, with chapters ranging from grammar to the art of poetry, from war to mythology. In the *Speculum historiale,* Vincent summarized the first two "Mirrors," recounted the history of the world from the Creation to the Crusade of St. Louis (1254), and predicted the extinction of the human race and the end of the world in the year 2376.

The fourth part of the *Speculum maius* was based principally on the work of St. Thomas Aquinas. In response to the need for standardized clerical training as well as the continuing need to reconcile sacred dogma and sacred thought, Aquinas and his fellow Scholastics attempted to channel all knowledge into rigid, unchanging categories. Because dogma could not brook criticism or questioning, the Scholastics' work took on an authority akin to the Scriptures.

The *Speculum maius* was translated into several languages and was reprinted in its entirety until the end of the nineteenth century. As a repository of fragmentary documents of classical antiquity and a detailed contemporary history of the early thirteenth century, its value is unequaled. In 1485, it was printed by William Caxton as *The Myrror of the Worlde,* the first encyclopedia in English and the first to be produced with movable type.

Early Islamic Reference Works

Clerics in European monasteries were not the only scholars to preserve classical learning during the Middle Ages. Islamic scholars were also collecting and analyzing classical writing as they created encyclopedic reference works. These books served as repositories of knowledge and attempted to reconcile the philosophies of the ancient classical world with Islamic religious teachings.

Like the Roman and Christian encyclopedists, Arabic writers compiled highly structured works, classifying their information into the categories of the scholastic disciplines. The Arabic writers also showed a preference for arranging their work hierarchically.

Early Arabic encyclopedic works include a catalog of sciences by al-Farabi of Baghdad (ca. 870–950), a work that was translated into Latin and read widely in Europe during the Middle Ages. Al-Farabi was aware of the *enkyklios paideia* and divided his work into similar categories: logic (including rhetoric and poetry), mathematics (including optics, astronomy, weights and measures, and mechanics), physics (including botany, meteorology, psychology, and zoology), politics, law, and theology.

The pattern for many later works was set by the first true Arabic encyclopedia, the *Kitab 'Uyun al-Akhbar* (The Best Traditions), written by Ibn Qutayba (828–89). Whereas Cassiodorus began his work with the Scriptures and Isidore of Seville honored the liberal arts, Ibn Qutayba reflected the structure of his own cultural milieu by beginning with power, war, and the nobility, ending with food and women, and placing asceticism and prayers in between.

About a century later, another Arabic encyclopedia, written by the Persian statesman-scholar al-Khwarizmi, drew a clear line between the sacred and the profane. Al-Khwarizmi divided the *Mafatih al-Ulum* (Key to the Sciences, ca. 975–77) into two major categories, distinguishing between the indigenous Islamic sciences (Koranic jurisprudence, theological philosophy, Arabic grammar, secretarial duties, history, poetry, and prosody) and the "foreign" sciences. Although these were not identical to the seven classical disciplines, the "foreign" sciences reflected a synthesis of Greek and Islamic ideas on philosophy, logic, medicine, arithmetic, geometry, astronomy, music, and mechanics.

The Renaissance and Expansion of Knowledge

Literally a "rebirth," the European Renaissance brought with it a ferment of thought and a flowering of culture. The voyages of discovery changed European perceptions of the world and gave rise to new empires. A freer exploration of ideas led to renewed interest in classical literature, in scientific inquiry, in the extension of education, and in an increasing emphasis on the individual.

As European nations began to evolve, the modern sense of nationalism was born. In this period of political upheaval and intellectual achievement, the vernacular languages that had formed from Latin and proto-Germanic roots in the emerging nations of Europe, and that had changed rapidly in the late Middle Ages, continued to take form, gaining in both importance and recognition. During the Renaissance, Latin continued to be used for liturgical and educational purposes, but the many vernacular (or "vulgar") languages of Europe gradually became the accepted means of expression. The individual European vernaculars emerged as the languages of literature and, to a much larger degree than ever before, mediums for scholarly discourse.

The Renaissance was also a time of enormous technological change in which inquiry provoked invention that, in turn, spurred great shifts in patterns of life and learning. For example, with the invention of movable type for printing, books could be produced in quantities and be more widely distributed. As more and more people learned to read and to write, the Church found it increasingly difficult to monopolize the written word and knowledge spread to a wider audience. In this increasingly vigorous and volatile intellectual climate, new kinds of compendiums of knowledge were obviously required.

The English philosopher Francis Bacon (1561–1626) proposed that the new age needed a new kind of reference work, one that took a scientific approach to learning. Bacon conceived of the encyclopedia not as a compendium of all knowledge but as a systematic categorization of knowledge that included only information that could be observed or empirically confirmed. The work that he planned, the *Instauratio magna* (Great Renewal), was to reflect his rational attempts to find the basic forms of nature. The 130 sections of the work Bacon planned were to be divided into three major categories: external nature, man, and man's actions on nature. Only a small part of this encyclopedia was ever written, but Bacon's ideas on the content and structure of such a work exerted a revolutionizing effect both on encyclopedia making and on the categorization of knowledge.

After Bacon, European encyclopedias evolved from repositories of all information available at the time— whether factual or not—into collections of verified knowledge. One of the two works organized on this principle was Johann Heinrich Alsted's *Encyclopedia septem tomis distincta* (Encyclopedia Arranged in Seven Volumes, 1630). Like previous encyclopedias, Alsted's work was arranged topically, but it also included a 119-page index for enhanced accessibility. Thereafter, most general encyclopedias were arranged alphabetically and written in vernacular languages rather than Latin. This reflected the decreasing importance of Latin to a broader base of readership and a realization that the body of knowledge had so expanded that alphabetization was the only sensible way to organize the material.

Forerunners of the Modern Encyclopedia

Public preference for vernacular language and for alphabetically organized encyclopedias was shown by the immediate success of Louis Moreri's *Grand Dictionaire Historique* (1674). Morcri's work, which emphasized geographic and biographical material, was the primary inspiration for encyclopedias that were soon published in England, Germany, the Netherlands, and Switzerland.

A further step toward the format of today's encyclopedias was taken with the publication of the German *Konversations-Lexicon* (Dictionary of Conversation, 1704), which established a pattern for later works by presenting a collection of short, cross-referenced articles by different writers. Prior to this work, encyclopedias were written by their compilers.

Despite its title, the *Lexicon technicum* (1704), compiled by John Harris, was the first modern encyclopedia written in English. Subtitled the *Universal Dictionary of Arts and Sciences,* this alphabetically arranged work contained clear, practical articles written by specialists and contained bibliographies for its more important articles.

In 1728, another outstanding English encyclopedia, Ephraim Chambers's two-volume *Cyclopaedia,* was published. Although this *Cyclopaedia* was designed to be a comprehensive reference work that would also show the relationships between the various areas of knowledge, it included no geographic, historical, or biographical information. It contained scholarly articles from a number of contributors supplemented by systematic cross-referencing, and its design and layout resemble those of present-day encyclopedias. Two other distinguishing features of the *Cyclopaedia* were its 21 large illustrations and its elaborate preface depicting the divisions and subdivisions of knowledge in schematic form.

An important aspect of Chambers's *Cyclopaedia* is the work that it inspired in France. Originally, a Paris publisher named André Le Breton planned to publish the French *Encyclopédie* as a translation and modest expansion of Chambers's work. Philosopher Denis Diderot and mathematician Jean d'Alembert were given the project to complete. In their hands the *Encyclopédie* (1751–65) grew into a gargantuan 28-volume work. Abandoning the idea that an encyclopedia should include entries on all subjects, they endeavored to produce writing of the highest standard in articles that championed rationalism, the scientific method, and republican ideals. The initial subscription to this polemical work was surprisingly large for the time—2,000—and the number of subscribers grew as papal and governmental censorship added to its antiauthoritarian reputation. The *Encyclopédie* is commonly regarded as having played a significant role in helping to ignite the French Revolution (1789).

The next major landmark in encyclopedia making was the *Encyclopaedia Britannica,* conceived by two Edinburgh Scots, Andrew Bell and Colin Macfarquhar, and edited by William Smellie. The first edition (1768–71) was published in three volumes, weighed 12 pounds, and contained 2,659 pages and some 160 copperplate engravings. The *Britannica* favored a monographic approach, featuring long, comprehensive articles, while also including some shorter entries. It was an extremely popular work despite its sometimes startling inaccuracies (such as a description of California as a country in the West Indies). A second edition, edited by William Tytler and published between 1777 and 1784, greatly improved the *Britannica*'s accuracy and extended its scope. The 29-volume 11th edition of the *Britannica* (1910–11) was sponsored by Cambridge University. This edition doubled the number of entries without greatly expanding the work's size by splitting up the lengthy, comprehensive treatises of former editions into shorter, more comprehensible articles. Because of its rich leisurely prose and its outstanding list of contributors, the 11th edition is considered by many to be the finest encyclopedia ever published.

Pirated editions of the *Encyclopaedia Britannica* were printed in the United States as early as 1798, but it was not until the 14th edition (1929) that the *Britannica* was officially published in New York as well as in London. In 1941, the *Britannica* was taken over by a corporation with strong ties to the University of Chicago, and its publishing headquarters were moved to Chicago, where they are located today.

Both the French *Encyclopédie* and the British *Encyclopaedia Britannica* contained extended, learned discussions as well as some short articles. The next major encyclopedia to appear, the *Brockhaus Konversations-Lexicon,* challenged that format. This work began as a German encyclopedia for women and subsequently was taken over by Friedrich Arnold Brockhaus, who published his first edition between 1796 and 1811. Its brief, unsigned articles were written in a popular style, and the *Brockhaus* did not claim to be an encyclopedia of universal knowledge. Instead, it concentrated on subjects of particular interest to Germans, thus becoming the first national encyclopedia. As such, the *Brockhaus* served as a model for later American, British, and European works. This model of a national encyclopedia is still followed by some publishers and has heirs in such works as the 65-volume *Bolshaya sovetskaya entsiklopedya* (Great Soviet Encyclopedia, 1926–47).

The first American encyclopedia was the *Encyclopedia Americana,* published between 1829 and 1833 in Philadelphia. Its editor was a German immigrant, Francis Lieber, who based his work on the seventh edition of the *Brockhaus.* The *Americana* has gone through many revisions and editions since the first 13-volume set was released, and it continues to be published today.

An English translation of the *Brockhaus* provided the format for the *Chambers's Encyclopaedia,* which had no relationship to Ephraim Chambers's *Cyclopaedia* of 1728. The new work was the creation of Robert and William Chambers and was published in Edinburgh between 1859 and 1868. The ten-volume set was issued simultaneously in Philadelphia by J. B. Lippincott & Company.

The subtitle of the Chambers's work, *A Dictionary of Universal Knowledge for the People,* indicates that by the middle of the nineteenth century the multivolume general encyclopedia as a reference book had assumed virtually its present form. In their preface to the first edition, the Chambers brothers wrote:

> The several topics are not handled with a view to the technical instruction of those who have to make a special study of paticular branches of knowledge or art. The information may be characterized as *non-professional,* embracing those points of the several subjects which every intelligent man or woman may have occasion to speak or think about . . . . At the same time, every effort is made that the statements, so far as they go, shall be precise and scientifically accurate.

These are essentially the same criteria as those of today's general encyclopedia makers.

Encyclopedias and Educational Ideas

Encyclopedias for younger readers emerged long after adult encyclopedias had evolved into their modern form. Nonetheless, the first children's encyclopedias reverted to the basic content of the *enkyklios paideia* embraced by Pliny and the early encyclopedists. More important for future encyclopedias, they reflected the new ideas of education that had developed in seventeenth-century Europe and America.

Just before the start of the eighteenth century, a professor at Altdorf University in Germany published the first known encyclopedia for young readers. Johann Christoph Wagenseil's *Pera librorum juvenilium* (Collection of Juvenile Books, 1695) was a collection of essays and stories, literally a set of books intended to serve as a young reader's complete library at a time when almost no children's books were printed. Wagenseil's model of encyclopedist as storyteller was clearly in keeping with the revolutionary educational concepts of John Locke, which governed progressive education in the eighteenth and nineteenth centuries. Locke, in *Some Thoughts Concerning Education* (1693), argued that children should be encouraged to acquire the pleasant habit of reading rather than to store up facts.

By the end of the eighteenth century, the ideas of Jean-Jacques Rousseau were beginning to influence Western society. According to Rousseau, the acquisition of knowledge should, above all, be interesting. Rousseau emphasized this point of view in *Emile* (1762), the chronicle of a boy whose learning was based on his interests. Despite a characteristic tendency to moralize, children's literary classics of the nineteenth century maintained the tradition of instruction through entertaining reading. Thus, as the twentieth century opened, the stage was set for the coalescence of children's literature into a formal encyclopedia. In 1908, the *Children's Encyclopedia* was published in England. Two years later, the Grolier Society issued an American version, *The Book of Knowledge*, subtitled *The Children's Encyclopedia That Leads to Love of Learning*. In keeping with Locke's and Rousseau's ideals of education, these early encyclopedias provided general information in short, interesting segments. Stories, poetry collections, games, and hobby instructions were interspersed among topically arranged articles that described natural phenomena and historical events.

The popularity of the *Children's Encyclopedia* and *The Book of Knowledge* encouraged other publishers to produce youth and school versions of encyclopedias. Like adult encyclopedias, their articles were cross-indexed and arranged alphabetically. *The World Book* (now titled *The World Book Encyclopedia*), written specifically for children of elementary and junior high school age, appeared in 1918. In 1925, *The World Book* adopted a policy of continuous revision and began to publish yearly supplements intended to update each edition.

In 1922, *Compton's Pictured Encyclopedia* took youth encyclopedias a step further, from tools for a general education to those geared for formal education. *Compton's* was designed for student research and included a "Fact-Index" in each volume. It is published today as *Compton's Encyclopedia and Fact Index*. *Britannica Junior* (later *Britannica Junior Encyclopaedia* and now out of print), written for elementary school children, was first published in 1934, also with a policy of continuous revisions. The new 20-volume *Children's Britannica* was issued in 1988.

Finally, in the 1960s, Grolier, Inc. brought youth encyclopedias full circle, publishing its heavily illustrated *Encyclopedia International* (1963, now out of print) for older secondary school students and education-minded adults.

General Encyclopedias Today

Today's general encyclopedias are intended for use by a broad range of people and are sold not only to libraries and to scholarly and academic institutions but also directly to families in their homes. In this sense, encyclopedias have become democratized. The explanation for this democratization of the encyclopedia lies both in the demands of society at large for broad and easily accessible information and in the economic realities of contemporary publishing. Encyclopedias are extremely expensive and time-consuming to produce, and it is essential that publishers recover their substantial investments by the highest volume of sales to the broadest possible market. In addition, today's general encyclopedias are no longer created solely by scholars who present detailed treatises exploring every facet of a topic. Rather, teams of reference book specialists are brought together with scholars for the specific task of synthesizing the ever-expanding body of accessible knowledge.

The makers of the various modern encyclopedias have similar standards as well as similar goals, methods of creating their works, and markets. In general, publishers have elected to avoid polemical articles in favor of ones that codify knowledge in an impartial way. Whenever sensitive and controversial topics are included, reputable publishers go to great lengths to present all sides of the question. Among other standards held by encyclopedia makers today are the inclusion of such items as selected bibliographies, illustrations, cross-references, and separate indexes. The articles themselves are relatively short and written in a straightforward style; the trend toward short articles can be seen in the entries in the *Encyclopaedia Britannica*'s Micropaedia volumes. The similarity in standards and approach common to modern general encyclopedias is largely the result of public demand and of the insistence on quality and content by such professionals as reviewers and librarians.

Throughout the evolution of the encyclopedia form, compilers have tried to satisfy the needs of their age. When the Greeks placed a premium on the ability to think, encyclopedias recorded the thought process; when the Romans learned to value practicality, Cato and Pliny recorded and summarized useful knowledge. When the religious and political temper of the Middle Ages demanded the rationalization of science within an orthodox framework, the encyclopedists complied. When the expanding horizons of the Renaissance called for broader and more accessible materials, writers produced comprehensive vernacular works. And when political questioning became popular, Diderot's work found a receptive audience.

Encyclopedias have also had varied purposes. Initially they were meant to instruct, to lead the reader through the *enkyklios paideia*. Their second goal emerged as the impulse to preserve for future generations the accumulation of all that was known to the current generation of scholars. Third, they were created in an attempt to compile the knowledge of their time into an organized and reasonably accessible form.

As the reading population expanded, more was demanded of the encyclopedia. With knowledge of past ages recorded, readers began to see that their own intellects could guide them in acquiring further knowledge and understanding, if they were given the proper resources. Thus, readers demanded an organized and reliable source of data to use as the basis for self-instruction and further research. Again, the encyclopedists complied. How well the publishers of today's encyclopedias are responding to the needs of the reader is the focus of the reviews in chapter 6 of this book.

Even now, encyclopedia publishers are attempting to anticipate the needs of future users through the application of computers and telecommunications. Fine full-color illustrations and strong graphics have been features of most general encyclopedias for more than 30 years. Today, the use of data processing and electronic text storage has facilitated the revision and updating of encyclopedic works, and several publishers now offer access to their reference titles through online delivery services, software, or laser-read compact discs. In the future, vast data banks may be available to subscribers, including pictures, charts, recordings of music and speeches, and other features.

Dictionaries

Classical Roots of the English Dictionary

The modern dictionary, like the encyclopedia, has its roots in classical Greece and Rome. The earliest word reference books in the West were probably Greek glossaries on the words found in the works of respected authors. What is probably the first such work on record, by Protagoras of Abdera in the fifth century B.C., explained difficult words in Homer's books. Such glossaries became prevalent after the Greek language had changed sufficiently to make many terms unfamiliar or obsolete, and they are common from the first century A.D. onward. Glosses and glossaries that define difficult words in context are still used in modern textbooks. In Shakespeare anthologies, for example, the meanings of archaic terms are provided as glosses. In foreign-language texts and readers, glosses on words as well as fuller, alphabetical glossaries give English synonyms for foreign words that are necessary to understanding.

Latin word books were also being compiled as early as the first century B.C. Works in this period include *De lingua Latina* (On the Latin Language) by Marcus Terentius Varro and what is most likely the first general dictionary in the modern sense, com-

piled by Marcus Varrius Flaccus ca. 20 B.C. This work was later abridged by Sextus Pompeius in his *De verborum significatu* (On the Meaning of Words). Although the word *dictionarius* cannot be found in classical Latin, it appears in medieval Latin as early as A.D. 1225 as a term for lists of words that every educated person was expected to know.

Like the seminal Greek word books, the first such reference works for English speakers were glossaries, in this case bilingual books devoted to equivalents for Latin or French terms. The earliest known English-Latin dictionary was intended as a glossary for children and clerics. Written in manuscript, perhaps as early as 1440, the *Promptorium* was literally a "storehouse" of words to be used in completing translations. The *Promptorium* appeared in print in 1499, a result of William Caxton's earlier introduction of movable-type printing to England. Caxton's interest in glossaries had already been evidenced by his printing of an untitled English-French glossary in 1480.

The first important Latin-English dictionary created in England was a collection of glossaries arranged conceptually by topic. Published in 1500, it was called the *Hortus Vocabularium* (Garden of Words). In 1538, Sir Thomas Elyot's Latin-English glossary was published as the *Dictionary*. In the absence of copyright laws, it was absorbed by Thomas Cooper in his *Thesaurus* (1565), demonstrating a pattern of "borrowing" that has characterized dictionary making throughout its history.

Richard Huloet's *Abecedarium Anglo-Latinum* (1552) brought the bilingual glossary a few steps closer to the form of the modern dictionary by including not only English and Latin equivalents but also their French translations and brief definitions of the English words. Another English-Latin work of the period, *A Shorte Dictionarie for Young Begynners* (1553), introduced the concept of the dictionary as a tool for learning, not just for translation. Its author, John Withal, described his work as a teaching manual for Latin classes.

While the interlingual dictionary increased in scope and purpose, the English language dictionary was beginning to take shape. In 1582, for example, Richard Mulcaster published the *Elementarie,* a list of 8,000 English words, without definitions. Like a multitude of other Renaissance educators, Mulcaster stressed the use of the vernacular as he defended English as an important language in its own right, one that deserved its own dictionary. Mulcaster further expressed the wish that someone "wold gather all the words which we use in our English tung." This task was attempted in 1596 by Edmund Coote who, in his *Englishe Scholemister (English School-Master),* included a lexicon of 1,400 English words and definitions as well as comments on grammar, prayers, and the catechism.

Robert Cawdrey's *A Table Alphabeticall* (1604), based on the *English School-Master,* is generally considered to be the first true dictionary in English. In addition to supplying definitions for 3,000 words, Cawdrey's dictionary included rudimentary etymologies, using symbols to designate which English words were derived from Greek or French. Cawdrey, however, bowed to the glossary tradition by including some entries he referred to as "hard usuall wordes borrowed from the Hebrew, Greeke, Latine, or French. &c . . . gathered for . . . Ladies, Gentlewomen, or any and other unskillful persons."

The next true dictionary, *An English Expositor* by John Bullokar, was registered in 1610 and printed in 1616. It contained twice as many words as Cawdrey's dictionary but actually was less "English" than the *Table* because many of its "hard words" were merely Anglicized forms of Latin words. To increase the usefulness of his work, Bullokar sometimes identified the field in which a word was generally used and included archaisms, which he tagged as "onely used of some ancient writers and now growne out of use." His own work remained in print through 14 editions, the last appearing in 1731.

In 1623, Henry Cockeram borrowed heavily from Bullokar in creating *The English Dictionarie: or, An Interpreter of Hard English Words,* in which he, too, included many ersatz terms coined from Latin. To borrow one of Cockeram's words, the "prodigity" of his listings made this dictionary appear to be what the preface claimed: the most complete dictionary yet published.

An important step in dictionary making was taken by Thomas Blount in *Glossographia: or A Dictionary Interpreting all such Hard Words . . . as are now used in our refined English Tongue* (1656). In this ambitious work, Blount listed, and often cited sources for, words that he had encountered and found difficult in his own reading. The *Glossographia* included scientific and technical terms as well as words that had recently entered the English language, and it attempted to trace the etymologies of all entries.

As has been noted, lexicographers of this period borrowed heavily from previous works, usually without acknowledgment. The first open conflict over this practice arose when Edward Phillips, a nephew of the English poet John Milton, published *The New World of English Words* in 1658. Blount bitterly attacked the work as a plagiarism of his 1656 dictionary. Although Phillips's work was clearly imitative of Blount's, often even repeating Blount's errors, it did introduce one new idea. By claiming that specialists had helped write his dictionary, Phillips introduced into lexicography the practice of enlisting experts on language and its use to support the authority of a dictionary.

An English Dictionary (1676) by Elisha Cole, the most comprehensive dictionary to appear up to this time, featured 25,000 entries, including archaic terms from Chaucer's time and, for the first time in any dictionary, dialectal terms and cant (the secret slang used by thieves and beggars). Nevertheless, like its predecessors, Cole's *Dictionary* mainly included "hard words," not a general vocabulary as dictionaries do today.

Professional Lexicography

With the eighteenth century came the work of John Kersey, who is sometimes regarded as the first professional lexicographer. As the editor of *A New English Dictionary* (1702), Kersey moved away from the "hard words" tradition of English dictionaries toward the concept of a general dictionary by including common as well as difficult or esoteric words. It was a consciously English work that avoided Latin, archaic, or overspecialized words. Although the definitions for its 28,000 entries were often brief to the point of being inadequate, the dictionary was so popular that it remained in print for 70 years.

In his next work, a 1706 revision of Edward Phillips's *The New World of English Words,* Kersey made another departure by listing multiple meanings for words. In a language as polysemous as English, this practice did much to improve the value of dictionary definitions. Kersey also included an impressive list of technical and scientific terms and doubled the size of Phillips's dictionary to 38,000 words.

It then remained for a schoolmaster, Nathan Bailey, to give form to the modern concept of a dictionary as a collection of all recognized words in use at a given time. His 1721 edition of *An Universal Etymological English Dictionary* listed obscene words as well as dialectic, archaic, and literary terms. Bailey, a professional lexicographer and the master of a boarding school, incorporated not only etymologies but also earlier forms of words. Bailey's dictionary was reprinted throughout the eighteenth century and supplementary volumes were issued to add to the 40,000 entries included in the first edition. Later editions added syllabication and syllable stress marks.

Bailey further added to the dimensions of lexicography in his encyclopedic *Dictionarium Britannicum* (1730). Its 48,000 words excluded mere oddities of the language, and like many present-day dictionaries it listed geographic and biographical entries separately. Bailey's collaborators included such specialists as a botanist and a mathematician. This comprehensive work served as the base for one of the most notable and influential dictionaries in English, Samuel Johnson's *A Dictionary of the English Language.*

Dr. Johnson's Dictionary

In the first half of the eighteenth century, a number of notable writers began to express concern with what they felt was a decay in the English language. Jonathan Swift and Daniel Defoe, for example, proposed establishing authoritative standards that would keep English "pure" by halting changes in the language. Joseph Addison proposed that this might be done, if not by an academy, as in France, then with a dictionary that would include literary quotations to illustrate the standard use of the entries. Alexander Pope also proposed such a dictionary.

This challenge was taken up by Samuel Johnson, a critic and poet who had no previous experience as a lexicographer. In 1747, Johnson presented his *Plan of a Dictionary of the English Language* to a potential patron, Lord Chesterfield. In his *Plan,* Johnson seems to agree with Swift and Defoe that the English language was in need of preservation. "The chief intent of [the *Dictionary*] is to preserve the purity and ascertain the meaning of our English idiom," he wrote. While he recognized the changing nature of language in his preface, Johnson's attitude was prescriptive concerning English usage; he objected hundreds of times to uses of words and branded many terms as "low words."

In an effort to include "the whole of the English language," Johnson made liberal use of Nathan Bailey's word stock and added to it words gleaned from legal, medical, and ecclesiastical dictionaries and from his own voluminous reading in literary and scholarly texts. What made Johnson's dictionary both a masterpiece and a landmark in dictionary making was his inclusion of 118,000 amplifying quotations that recorded the usage of words by some of the most illustrious writers of the sixteenth, seventeenth, and eighteenth centuries.

When Johnson's *Dictionary of the English Language* appeared in 1755, it incorporated all of the features of its immediate predecessors—multiple definitions, etymologies, quotations, and stress marks—but used them with a profound intelligence and a new authority. Its reputation as the finest dictionary in the English language remained secure for more than a century in both Great Britain and the United States.

Although Johnson had set out to standardize the English language, he found that the living language refused to calcify and continued to grow. To accommodate these changes, Johnson supervised three revisions of his work during his lifetime, with the fourth edition (1773) receiving particular attention. After his death in 1784, the *Dictionary* was revised by Henry John Todd, and with the 1818 and 1827 editions it became known as the *Todd-Johnson.*

Pronouncing Dictionaries

After the publication of Johnson's masterwork, most dictionary makers concentrated on creating pronouncing dictionaries. Their intention was to satisfy the same fixative urge that lay behind Johnson's *Dictionary.* In particular, the pronouncing dictionaries of the late eighteenth century were meant to oppose the tide of alternative pronunciations presented by Irish, Scottish, and American English.

The first of these pronouncing dictionaries, the *Linguae Britannica,* was produced in 1757 by James Buchanan. William Johnson's *Pronouncing and Spelling Dictionary* followed in 1764. Both works sought to remedy the "manglings" and innovations of "illiterate Court fops, half-witted poets and University boys" that Jonathan Swift had excoriated in his diatribes against the sullying of "pure English." These two works introduced the practice of providing the actual pronunciation of a word in addition to stress marks, and they made use of diacritical marking systems.

The actor and elocution teacher Thomas Sheridan employed both conventions and added phonetic respellings in his 1780 work, *A General Dictionary of the English Language.* Sheridan, who was Irish, particularly hoped that his dictionary would correct the "mistakes" made by "well-educated natives of Ireland."

Although he had advocated language preservation, Samuel Johnson came to modify his views. He recognized that a living language is in constant transition and that no clear choice could be made from among several acceptable pronunciations. In his *Life of Johnson* (1791), James Boswell recorded Johnson's reaction to Sheridan's pronouncing dictionary. When he embarked on his own work, Johnson recalled, "Lord Chesterfield told me that the word *great* should be pronounced so as to rhyme to *state;* and Sir William Younge sent me word that it should be pronounced so as to rhyme to *seat,* and that none but an Irishman would pronounce it *grait.*" Johnson cautioned that if "two men of the highest rank" disagreed, a lexicographer would be out of place in claiming only one pronunciation.

Nevertheless, Sheridan's work gained wide use and, with a later work by another actor, John Walker (1791), was considered authoritative, especially in the United States. The spirit of revolution and a growing pride in American usage had not dimmed a zeal to speak English "properly." Sheridan, incidentally, went on to a lucrative career giving lectures in Ireland on proper English pronunciation.

Noah Webster's American Dictionary

By the time of the American Revolution, the use of dictionaries was well established in American schools. In his *Ideas of the English School* (1751), Benjamin Franklin had recommended that "Each boy should have an English dictionary to help him over difficulties."

Despite his admiration for the English dictionary, Franklin had no use for the chaos that then characterized English spelling. In 1768, he published a paper calling for spelling reform. Franklin's plan was not carried out, but it did inspire a system of American spelling and a dictionary to rival Johnson's—both by Noah Webster.

Noah Webster's first work was the 1783 "blue-backed" *American Speller,* designed for elementary schools. Over 8 million copies of the *Speller* were sold in Webster's lifetime. At a royalty of one cent per copy, the success of the *Speller* gave Webster the financial freedom to devote his life to promoting the spelling, pronunciation, and grammar of American English at a time when it was rapidly acquiring its own distinctive characteristics.

By 1789, Webster had proposed many Americanized spellings. They included dropping the *u* from *-our* words (*colour/color, honour/honor*); changing *-re* endings to *-er* (*fibre/fiber, theatre/theater, centre/center*); substituting *c* for *k* or *ck* (*kerb/curb, musick/music*); and simplifying vowel sounds (*plough/plow, tyre/tire*). These spelling changes might have occurred naturally, but the patriotic Webster felt that decisive action was necessary to encourage a separate American culture. "Our honor," he wrote in *Dissertations on the English Language* in 1789, the year when the first American president was inaugurated and the Constitution came close to final ratification, "requires us to have a system of our own language, as well as government." Webster's first dictionary for schools, the *Compendious Dictionary for the English Language* (1806), satisfied his honor by using American spellings and by including more than 5,000 words that were native to America (such as *canoe*) among its 37,000 entries. To conform to etymology and rules of analogy, however, Webster refrained from such extremes as the substitution of *tuf* for *tough* and *bred* for *bread,* which Franklin had suggested.

For the next two decades, Webster continued to study language usage. In 1828, at the age of 70, he saw the publication of his masterpiece, *An American Dictionary of the English Language.* In this work, Webster showed greater conservatism than in his earlier years, noting that "The body of the language is the same as in England, and it is desireable [*sic*] to perpetuate that sameness."

In 1830, an important rival to Webster's *Diction-ary* was brought out by a man who did not have Webster's reputation as a linguistic reformer and innovator. Joseph Emerson Worcester was a quiet traditionalist but a competent lexicographer, who had worked previously on Webster's *Dictionary.* His *Comprehensive Pronouncing and Explanatory Dictionary of the English Language* and his later *A Universal and Critical Dictionary of the English Language* (1846) were in many ways more authoritative, accurate, and lexicographically correct than Webster's dictionaries. Webster promptly accused Worcester of plagiarism, and what became known as the "war of the dictionaries" began.

Although some learned partisans of Webster and Worcester argued over lexicographical matters, the "war of the dictionaries" was primarily a marketing competition with sales of dictionaries for classroom use as the prize. After Webster's death in 1843, his son-in-law sold Webster's interests to the publishing firm of G. & C. Merriam in Springfield, Massachusetts. Aggressive Merriam sales agents decided the outcome of the "war" by convincing state legislatures to adopt Webster's book and place it, by decree, in all schoolhouses.

Worcester quietly fought back by introducing *A Dictionary of the English Language* (1860), the first dictionary to incorporate illustrations and synonyms, features that were included in most subsequent dictionaries. In 1864, the G. & C. Merriam Company countered with an "unabridged" Webster's that included authoritative etymologies by a noted German scholar, Karl Augustus Friedrich Mahn. After the Webster-Mahn publication, Worcester's publishers gave up their unequal struggle and stopped publishing his books. The Webster-Mahn *Dictionary of the English Language* subsequently became the basis for a long and successful line of American dictionaries, now the Merriam-Webster dictionaries.

The Oxford English Dictionary

While Americans debated the merits of their rival dictionaries, a group of scholars in Great Britain were preparing for a truly monumental dictionary-making project. Now that scientific principles of lexicography had been established, the Philological Society in Great Britain began to call for a full-scale historical dictionary. To that end, the society established an "Unregistered Words Committee." In 1857, the society set about creating a dictionary of "all the words that have formed the English vocabulary from earliest records on" and "all relevant facts concerning their form, sense, history, pronunciation and etymology." The new work was to be called *A New English Dictionary on Historical Principles (NED).*

In 1858, volunteer readers began to compile quotation slips, and in 1862, subeditors began to work under the direction of editor Frederick James Furnivall. In 1879, the task of editing the new dictionary was given to a Scot, James Augustus Henry Murray. Although Murray was later joined by three other editors, he was referred to as the first (chief) editor. For the next half century, Murray shepherded the new dictionary into print. The first copy went to the printer in 1882 and the last portion in 1928.

The final work exceeded 15,500 pages, with three columns of type on each page, and included 1,827,306 of the nearly 6 million quotations that had been submitted to the editors. The size of the work, however monumental, was secondary to the skill and authority of the lexicographers in presenting the full scope of the English language. The authority of the dictionary is such that it has not been revised; instead, supplements have been issued since 1928. The complete work was reprinted in 1933 as a 12-volume set under a new title, *The Oxford English Dictionary,* commonly referred to as the *OED.* Under the leadership of its editor, Robert W. Burchfield, the four-volume *Supplement* to the *OED* was published from 1972 to 1986. A comprehensive historical work in the tradition of its parent volumes, the *Supplement* took 29 years to complete and contains 62,750 words, 5,750 pages, and some 527,000 quotations.

Dictionaries in the Modern Era

After the *OED,* dictionary makers in England and the United States concentrated their efforts less on inclusiveness than on the creation of dictionaries designed for particular audiences. One result of this trend was the introduction in the 1940s of "college" dictionaries for the burgeoning numbers of advanced students. So-called collegiate dictionaries had been published as early as 1898 (Merriam-Webster's), but they were seen as handy abridgments of larger works, not as important works in their own rights. The widely popular Webster's collegiate dictionaries, direct descendants of the Merriam-Webster book, continue to this day with the *Webster's Ninth New Collegiate Dictionary* (1983), based on the unabridged *Webster's Third.*

The first college dictionary that was not an abridgment of a larger work was the *American College Dictionary,* edited by Clarence Barnhart and published by Random House. It quickly became a favorite not only with scholars but also with the general public. Encouraged by its success, the publisher issued *The Random House Dictionary, College Edition* (later called *The Random House College Dictionary*), which contained more entries (155,000) than any previous collegiate dictionary and set a standard for the inclusion of scientific and technical terms. The primary aim of this Random House dictionary and of

its successors was to help the student find the meaning of unfamiliar terms encountered in a lecture or textbook.

English dictionaries, particularly since Dr. Johnson, have tended to be prescriptive, that is, they have attempted to establish certain forms of words, word usages, and pronunciations as acceptable or preferable. Some lexicographers have opposed this practice with the descriptive approach, whereby dictionaries are thought to reflect the changing nature of language by presenting current usage without dictating standard forms. The former approach is traditional; the latter has gained in popularity in the last half of this century. In 1961, for example, the publication of *Webster's Third New International Dictionary* caused a great stir in lexicographic and literary circles due to its descriptive approach to dictionary making. Its stated philosophy recognized the variability of language and the relative quality of usage—it rarely labeled words as informal, slang, or substandard, or designated certain pronunciations as preferred. Numerous critics charged that the dictionary abdicated responsibility and refused to set necessary standards. Today the controversy has largely died away, and it is commonly agreed that dictionaries should ideally tread a sort of middle ground, describing contemporary usages and pronunciations while also suggesting preferred forms.

Controversies over lexical philosophies aside, today's publishers have continued to design dictionaries for specific audiences, and the variety of dictionaries available today is remarkable. Modern dictionaries range from big, unabridged works to small pocket-size volumes. Some are designed specifically for family, for college, or for office use. Others are compiled for nonnative speakers of English and may be published as a series of graded versions with increasing degrees of sophistication.

Whatever their intended market, dictionaries have maintained their traditional role of presenting a working vocabulary in a practical manner. In the articles that follow, our reviewers measure the dictionaries and similar word books by Samuel Johnson's practical standard:

> It is not enough that a dictionary delights the critic, unless at the same time it instructs the learner; as it is to little purpose that an engine amuses the philosopher by the subtilty [*sic*] of its mechanism, if it requires so much knowledge in its application as to be no advantage to the common workman.

Along with the criteria given in this Buying Guide for examining dictionaries, those selecting a dictionary might do well to consider how the dictionary was made. Traditionally, there have been two ways of making a dictionary: by borrowing a word list from another source and constructing revised definitions or adding features such as pronunciation guides, or by collecting citations and constructing a whole new word list. The *Oxford English Dictionary* represents the apotheosis of the latter method. The current market for dictionaries is extensive; however, the market for any specific type of dictionary cannot now support a colossal effort such as the eight-decade process that created the *OED* and its *Supplement*. Some dictionary makers, usually publishers whose major field of publishing is not dictionaries, have therefore reverted to the borrowing of word lists, sometimes buying another publisher's word list and sometimes appropriating an old, out-of-print list. Using a previously published word list, however, is not always a sign of shoddy workmanship. Many dictionary makers, such as Merriam-Webster (which also maintains a large citation file), have used teams of lexicographers, trained definers, consultants, and experts in specific fields to create new, authoritative works with borrowed, carefully edited lists.

As computers become increasingly sophisticated, they inevitably provide ways for dictionary makers to combine both of the traditional methods of constructing dictionaries. Citations as well as word lists can be kept in databases, and if editors, consultants, and other experts have ready access to online databases, new dictionaries can be produced more cost effectively.

The computer revolution has opened another possibility for dictionary makers: the creation of electronic dictionaries accessed directly by the user. Two types of user-accessed computerized dictionaries are coming into use. With the first, the user types in the desired term and the computer displays it. Phonetic searches are being developed to help the user find a word that he or she cannot spell. Another method being researched involves presenting a definition and preferred usage even if a variant of the term is input by the user.

The second type of computerized dictionary being considered is usually linked to a specific piece of text stored in the computer. As the user reads the text on the screen and comes upon an unknown term, he or she can ask for the dictionary entry, read it, and then continue to move along in the text.

In attempting to say just what a dictionary is, some have defined it by comparison with an encyclopedia. A dictionary, they say, explains words, while an encyclopedia explains subjects or phenomena. But while encyclopedias are dictionaries in that they give the meanings of words, dictionaries are not considered encyclopedias. Computerized databases could forever blur these distinctions, however, if an item in the text is looked up not only for dictionary information but also as an encyclopedia entry.

Future dictionary makers will certainly have access not only to new methods of creating dictionaries

but also to new methods of presenting their work to users. As descendants of Samuel Johnson, they will have to seek ways to delight the critic while satisfying the needs of the learner. To do this they will have to find a way to approximate the most practical of all uses of the print dictionary throughout history—the serendipitous learning that occurs when users browse through a volume or get sidetracked while looking up a word.

As reviewers, we look for delight in the dictionaries we review; at the same time, we also seek the match between the needs of the intended user and the "subtilty of the mechanism."

Atlases

The modern atlas is a systematic collection of maps, usually but not always uniform in size and format. An atlas may contain maps of many kinds: political, topographic, transportation, meteorological, or climatic. The maps may also represent such themes as land use, population density, or the distribution of languages and religions.

It is not known when human beings first attempted to represent the surface of the earth symbolically. Among the very earliest recorded maps are Assyrian clay tablets dating from around 3800 B.C. that list properties and describe civil boundaries for administrative purposes such as tax collections. Ramses II commissioned a map of the Nile empire in 1225 B.C., also for taxation purposes, while the earliest surviving papyrus map (1320 B.C.) is one of a Nubian gold mine. Even nonliterate early peoples used utilitarian maps. For example, the cave dwellers in prehistoric southern Europe drew sketches showing hunting spots on cave walls. It is also known that Polynesian navigators constructed maps from the latticed spines of palm branches to show wind and sea currents as references for finding islands, which were represented by seashells.

The first known atlas was made by Ptolemy (A.D. 90–168), a Greek in Hellenic Alexandria. Ptolemy's work, called *Geographike hyphegesis* (Guide to Geography), was published in eight volumes in A.D. 160. It treated the earth as a sphere, contained 27 maps, and listed 8,000 place names. In the eighth volume, Ptolemy offered instructions on mapmaking and discussed the mathematical principles of geography. His work represented an important step toward a scientific approach to geography and cartography. Ptolemy's concept of maps and map collections was surprisingly close to the modern, general atlas ideal. Maps, he said, were "a representation in picture of the whole known world, together with the phenomena contained therein."

The growing influence of the Roman world partially eclipsed Ptolemy's ideas of mathematical geography because the Romans sought practical maps for warfare and administration. The dislocations and decline of learning in the Western world during the first centuries of the Christian era also obscured Ptolemaic ideas of geography. Fortunately, Ptolemy's *Geography* was preserved by the Nestorians, a Christian sect that fled to Persia to escape persecution by the Orthodox Byzantines. There, in the centers of Islamic culture and learning, the science of geography was cultivated by Arab scholars who translated the *Geography* and added to it their own discoveries. Their pioneering use of the compass, for example, enabled Islamic scholars to measure part of the meridian, develop the idea of the 360-degree circle, and reinforce Ptolemy's idea of a spherical earth. Islamic cartographic principles, as well as copies of Ptolemy's *Geography,* were introduced into Europe through the Moors and by refugees who fled to Italy after the fall of Byzantium in the late fourteenth century. In Florence in 1400, Ptolemy's *Geography* was translated into Latin. In 1477, it was printed in Bologna, the first atlas as well as the first classical Greek work to be printed with movable type. The Bologna *Geography* was also the first to use copper-engraved maps instead of woodcuts.

Throughout the fifteenth and sixteenth centuries, cartographers followed Ptolemy's ideal of a map collection as a reflection of contemporary geographic information. As late as 1570, Lafreri, a Roman mapmaker, described his collection of maps as being "arranged in Ptolemy's order." Lafreri, incidentally, was the first cartographer known to have illustrated a collection of maps with the symbolic figure of Atlas supporting the world.

The modern form of the general atlas was introduced in Antwerp in 1570 by Abraham Ortelius. Ortelius was a successful cartographer who had already published a world map in eight sheets in 1565 as well as two-sheet maps of Egypt in 1565 and Asia in 1567. When Ortelius decided to expand his scope by publishing a collection of maps, he noted that all previous collections included maps of varying sizes and formats and often included different authors' contradictory depictions of the same country. In the work he edited and published, Ortelius standardized the format of all the maps included and used only one cartographer for each country. Ortelius's work was titled the *Theatrum Orbis Terrarum* (Theater of the World).

Even before the publication of the *Theatrum,* a Flemish colleague of Ortelius, Gerardus Mercator (who also gave his name to the Mercator Projection map), had outlined a plan for a systematic and comprehensive collection of maps of uniform size and format. Mercator did not live to complete the collection, but he managed to publish two of its three

sections before his death in 1594. His son, Rumold, carried out the project, and Mercator's atlas was published posthumously in 1595 as the *Atlas sive Cosmographicae meditationes de fabrica mundi et fabricati figura* (Atlas, or Cosmographical Meditations Upon the Creation of the Universe, and the Universe as Created). It is the first recorded use of the word *atlas* for a collection of maps.

Although atlases were expensive and available to only a limited number of people, they became common during the sixteenth and seventeenth centuries, the great age of maritime exploration and discovery. The initiative in atlas making was retained by the Dutch, whose efforts reached a zenith in 1662 with the publication of Willem Janszoon Blaeu's 11-volume *Atlas Major*. During this period, Dutch mapmakers also brought out a number of small, or pocket, atlases based on the works of Ortelius, Mercator, and others.

During the eighteenth century, advances in astronomy, mathematics, and meteorology led to the development of increasingly accurate maps. As surveying and triangulation techniques grew more sophisticated, mapmakers abandoned the tradition of decorative, often highly fanciful cartography that had characterized earlier works and concentrated instead on precise instrumental observations. At the same time, the rise of maritime commerce and the nation-state encouraged many European governments to commission meticulous topographical surveys of their territories. The first such national survey was the French *Carte Geometrique de la France,* published in 1794 in 182 sheets and rendered at a scale of 1:86,400. During the nineteenth century, this highly detailed work was followed by similar efforts in England, Spain, Austria, Germany, and many other nations, including Japan.

In addition, Alois Senefelder's development of lithography in 1796 made the duplication of maps easier and less expensive, thus broadening the availability of atlases in the nineteenth century. The late 1800s also saw the first indexed world atlases, published by such firms as Adolf Stieler and Richard Andrée. The increase in an atlas's utility through the addition of an index cannot be overstated. There was also a sharp rise in the publication of "school atlases" during this period. Further nineteenth-century developments were the emergence of international cooperation on standards of measurement, the adoption of a prime meridian, and a proposal for an International Map of the World, all the sheets of which would be drawn on a scale of 1:1,000,000 (1 cm = 10 km).

Mapmaking has advanced rapidly in the twentieth century. Techniques of aerial photography that started during World War I developed into major cartographic tools during World War II, permitting efficient mapping of vast areas with unparalleled accuracy. Also during World War II, military maps, especially aeronautical charts, enabled the filling in of many of the blank spaces on world maps. Since then, developments in photographic emulsions, in lenses, and the science of photogrammetry (taking measurements from photographs) have advanced to such a degree that overlapping strips of film shot from specialized aircraft can be used to create maps showing virtually any feature on the face of the earth. Political and military alliances have also contributed to mapmaking during the twentieth century. The members of the North Atlantic Treaty Organization (NATO), for example, have agreed upon the use of standard map symbols, scales, and formats, and the United Nations has standardized map features while offering technical advice and a clearinghouse service for international cartographic information.

Still further advances have been made possible by techniques of remote sensing coupled with orbiting satellites. Landsat and other satellites equipped with electromagnetic sensing devices have produced countless images of the earth's surface, revealing not only geographic features but such elements as environmental pollution, crop diseases, and the location of mineral deposits. Although these images are not actual maps, they provide new and highly accurate data for the creation of many types of maps.

All of these technological advances in mapmaking have led to the publication of a much more varied, detailed, and sophisticated selection of modern atlases. Because of the almost staggering developments in cartography, the contemporary consumer can reasonably expect much more from any kind of atlas than had ever before been contemplated.

The word *map* comes from the Latin word for *napkin,* and it conjures up images of Roman diners sketching out on a napkin maps of a battlefield or directions to some faraway city in the empire. The image is apt. In choosing whether or not to pocket the napkin drawing for future reference, the diners are assessing the long-term utility of the map. The same process—determining utility—is the overriding factor in choosing an atlas. The reviews in this guide have been written to assist in that process.

Chapter 2
Choosing General Reference Books

This chapter offers suggestions to help public and college librarians clarify their needs for general reference books. It also considers the needs of individual readers who purchase such books for themselves or for a home or office library. These works, particularly comprehensive encyclopedias, large atlases, and unabridged dictionaries, are manufactured to withstand extended use and are often expensive. Thus, while recognizing that no single reference work is capable of satisfying a universal readership, prospective buyers will look for works that can serve as broad a range of users as possible within the confines of specific collections. Since reference books are evaluated according to certain recognized standards, it may be useful to describe each broad category of general reference work and discuss the criteria applied to it.

Encyclopedias

Encyclopedias are found in approximately one out of every four homes in the United States, and the average public library may have anywhere from four to 12 different sets on its shelves. The sale of encyclopedias and the materials that supplement them generates some $500 million in revenues each year; this figure represents both a large investment for the publishers and a substantial expense for the purchaser, especially when the volumes are revised frequently.

Because encyclopedias are costly to write and produce, few new publishers attempt to enter this market. In fact, the number of encyclopedia publishers has been reduced in recent years, and there are now four firms that dominate this market in the United States. These four, whose sales account for more than four-fifths of all encyclopedias sold, are Encyclopaedia Britannica, Inc.; World Book, Inc.; Grolier, Inc.; and Macmillan Educational Company, Inc. Encyclopaedia Britannica not only produces its namesake set, but also *Compton's Encyclopedia* and *Compton's Precyclopedia,* both of which are reviewed in Bowker's *Reference Books for Young Readers.* In 1988 it published a new *Children's Britannica.* Grolier publishes the *Encyclopedia Americana, The New Book of Knowledge* (reviewed in *Young Readers*), and the *Academic American Encyclopedia.*

World Book, with both a multivolume encyclopedia and a two-volume dictionary, enjoys the largest in-home sales share and the highest sales in both dollars and units of these four companies. Encyclopaedia Britannica is a distant second. After the *New Encyclopaedia Britannica* was introduced in 1975, sales increased for a time, but they have since leveled off again. Grolier is in third place, and Macmillan has the least volume and unit sales of the four. The only other American encyclopedia publishers of note are Funk & Wagnalls, which publishes *Funk & Wagnalls New Encyclopedia*, and the Standard Educational Corporation, which produces the *New Standard Encyclopedia.*

Funk & Wagnalls New Encyclopedia is the best-selling set in the supermarket field. Its encyclopedia set is supplemented by a two-volume dictionary. The pattern of supermarket sales usually varies considerably from that of the door-to-door market. As a general rule, the first volume is offered at a greatly reduced price, and subsequent volumes are offered at full price. A complete set purchased in this manner is usually substantially less costly than that of a comparable set purchased through a distributor. For instance, a complete set of 27 volumes of the *Funk & Wagnalls Encyclopedia,* which includes 25,000 entries in 13,000 pages, cost $140 in 1988. By comparison, the 21-volume *Academic American,* priced at $850 for individuals, includes over 28,000 entries in 9,750 pages. The 22-volume *World Book,* costing $599 for individuals, has 18,000 entries in its 14,000 pages. A complete list of the publishers and distributors of all the encyclopedias (as well as atlases and dictionaries) evaluated in this Buying Guide begins on page 591.

In general, when selecting an encyclopedia, prospective buyers should consider three main criteria: depth of coverage, currency, and accuracy. These factors are discussed at length in the section "What to Look for in Encyclopedias." Obviously, multivolume encyclopedias treat their subjects in far greater depth than do one- or two-volume sets. Smaller sets are, however, extremely useful for ready reference information, such as a capsule biography or the geographical features of a country, and most are illustrated with photographs, maps, and charts.

Currency demands frequent revision. However, there is a limit to the value of constantly updating an encyclopedia if substantial information about current or recent events can be located in other, less-expensive reference sources, such as yearbooks, almanacs, and other annuals. Publishers of smaller encyclopedias revise their titles only sporadically if at all. Multivolume encyclopedia publishers keep their works as current as possible by maintaining a regular cycle of continuous revision during which a certain portion of the content (usually around ten percent) is replaced or updated each year. The changes may range from minor updating of existing articles to the creation of entirely new entries about recent events, scientific discoveries, technological accomplishments, political/geographic changes, and biographies. After several years publishers may also undertake a major revision that involves rewriting, adding, or removing hundreds or even thousands of articles and that results in the publication of new editions. Individuals who are thinking about replacing an old set with a revised edition should decide whether the type and amount of changes the publisher announces warrant the cost of replacement.

Buyers expect encyclopedias to be accurate, but no encyclopedia is absolutely error free. Many critics feel that encyclopedias are more often deficient in omitting important information than in making mistakes in the information they do include, particularly in regard to complex or controversial subjects.

A meticulously compiled index is especially important for finding all the information on a given subject in an encyclopedia, especially where the information may appear in several different articles. Ideally, all instances in which the topic is mentioned should be fully indexed. Moreover, a useful index should not require the reader to have a great deal of prior knowledge about the subject. For example, the encyclopedia user wishing to look up information in the general area of restraint of trade, trusts, or antitrust laws will find under these general headings cross-references to articles on other specific topics, such as monopolies and the Sherman Antitrust Act, which may fill in gaps in his or her knowledge and help provide the desired overview of the subject.

Both multivolume and one- or two-volume encyclopedias may range in difficulty of reading and complexity of subject matter from the relatively simple to the fairly difficult. If possible, the prospective purchaser should read several entries to determine if the writing level will suit the reading ability of those who will be using the encyclopedia.

Atlases

Atlases are collections of maps of a specified area— a region, a nation, the lands or oceans of the world, the solar system, the known universe, and so on. This Buying Guide only evaluates world atlases. In a world atlas, the maps can be *political,* showing the boundaries of nations, territories, cities or towns; *physical,* showing natural features, such as shorelines, elevations, and climate; or *thematic,* showing populations, economic features, or other specialized data. When choosing an atlas, the purchaser should examine the scale used to draw each map. The larger the scale, the smaller the ratio—that is, the more details that can be included; however, larger-scale maps also require a larger page size or more pages on which to print them. Although atlases frequently also include photographs, drawings, charts, and explanatory text, it is the quality and quantity of the maps that are most important to the potential user. A special 6-page section in "What to Look for in Atlases" (chapter 7) provides examples of various maps for the atlas buyer's guidance.

Although many world atlases are on the market, most of their maps are produced by a small number of cartographic firms. In the United States, Rand McNally & Company and Hammond Inc. are the two leading mapmakers. The premier cartographers in England are John Bartholomew & Son and George Philip & Son. Bartholomew's maps are the basis for the highly esteemed *Times Atlas of the World,* for example, and Rand McNally's maps are used in *Goode's World Atlas,* an atlas that is found in many public libraries.

In choosing an atlas from among a selection offered by a single publisher, the buyer should be aware that the differences are primarily in format and price; publishers generally use the same basic maps in all their atlases. However, the selection, order of presentation, and number of maps included in a particular atlas may vary widely. Therefore, a number of factors should be weighed in the final purchase decision, including: the nature of the maps; the size of the book, the quality of the paper, printing, and binding; and the additional text, statistical tables, index, and special features.

Dictionaries

Historically, dictionaries began as glossaries of difficult words in various vernacular languages. Contemporary dictionaries are broadly classified, according to the number of entries they contain, as unabridged, semi-abridged, abridged, and paperback or pocket size. The largest unabridged dictionary in existence is the 13-volume OXFORD ENGLISH DICTIONARY (OED), which to date has been augmented by four supplements; it contains 400,000 entries—basically etymologies—and costs about $1,600.

A standard semi-abridged dictionary contains 130,000 to 170,000 entries; an abridged dictionary ranges from 50,000 entries for a concise or desk edition to 130,000 or more for a college dictionary; and a pocket-size dictionary may contain 40,000 to 60,000 entries. Very small pocket-size dictionaries may contain as few as 15,000 entries.

An abridged dictionary omits hundreds, even thousands of obscure, uncommon, archaic, and technical words—and often vulgar or taboo words—as well as certain other features of larger works: The definitions are shorter, the number of meanings for each entry word is reduced, synonyms and antonyms are eliminated, alternate spellings and pronunciations may be omitted. When considering a dictionary, the prospective buyer should bear in mind that the quantity of entries is only one of many factors to consider. Though the number offers a rough guide to a work's scope, it is no measure of its quality or currency. In addition, the number of entries quoted by publishers can vary widely between two dictionaries that appear to be nearly the same size: Some publishers count every form or variant of a word as a separate entry, whereas others count only the main entry word.

An interesting side note to the nature of dictionaries concerns the "Webster's" designation that so many bear. They are named, of course, for the pioneering American lexicographer and philologist Noah Webster. The Webster name is out of copyright and in the public domain—and has been for years. Thus anyone is free to use it in a dictionary title. Since the name carries such weight (for many it is virtually synonymous with the word *dictionary*), some publishers with no actual basis for any connection with the original Webster dictionaries use the name.

Dictionaries are produced by staffs of editors and language specialists who decide what system of symbols is used to clarify pronunciations, how technical words are defined, which new words have entered the standard lexicon, what new meanings have been attached to old words, and other matters. Most new dictionary entries come from files of citations, consisting of continuously updated word lists with examples of use, that editors have culled from current books, periodicals, newspapers, and other sources.

Lexicographers maintain a running debate about whether a dictionary should provide authoritative guidance to correct English or describe current usage, but most try to strike a balance somewhere between the extremes of prescription and description. Most dictionaries concentrate on standard words and meanings but also include colloquial or slang words and usage commonly employed in books, magazines, and newspapers. Certain specialized dictionaries deal specifically with slang, regionalisms, and other specialized kinds of language, and with questions relating to the usage of such language.

Some dictionaries have more components than others, but a standard entry in an abridged dictionary provides the spelling, pronunciation, syllabication, parts of speech, basic definitions, plurals, and inflected forms of each word. In more comprehensive dictionaries, the main entries may also include derivative words, the etymology or history of the word, synonyms and antonyms, and usage labels. Entries may also provide several examples or quotations showing how the word is used in standard written English. Dictionaries may also contain encyclopedic information, which is often found at the back of the book: tables of weights and measures, proofreading marks, biographical entries, geographical entries, a table of alphabets, lists of colleges and universities, maps, and other useful facts.

Generally, only librarians, scholars, teachers, and writers need the breadth of coverage that is found in unabridged dictionaries. The average adult recognizes about 20,000 words and customarily uses far fewer than this number in both writing and speech, so an abridged dictionary will be adequate for most households and offices. For everyday use—a quick check of spelling or meaning—a good desk, paperback, or even a vest-pocket dictionary is usually sufficient. Indeed, in most situations, such shorter works are often easier to consult. College students, however, may require an abridged or a semi-abridged dictionary, depending on their fields of study.

Related to dictionaries are other kinds of word

books such as thesauruses and dictionaries of synonyms and antonyms, which are extensively reviewed in this Buying Guide. The thesaurus, from the Latin and Greek for "treasury," "store," or "collection," is a compendium of words with their synonyms, related words, and sometimes antonyms. The traditional thesaurus arrangement was originated by English lexicographer Peter Mark Roget in his 1852 work *Thesaurus of English Words and Phrases*. In Roget's system, words are grouped according to categories wherein words are accessed by a general table of contents in the front of the book and an index at the back. Many newer thesauruses are published in a dictionary-like alphabetical format, which may be less cumbersome for some readers to use but offers a less comprehensive selection of related words. The dictionary of synonyms and antonyms is closely related to the classic thesaurus, although it is somewhat more restrictive conceptually and generally more pragmatic in outlook. As "Webster's" is often thought virtually synonymous with the word *dictionary*, so "Roget's" is with the word *thesaurus*; the word "Roget's" is also now in the public domain and is often used in titles by publishers.

The range of thesauruses is as wide as that of dictionaries. Some treat an enormous number of words—ROGET'S INTERNATIONAL THESAURUS, FOURTH EDITION, has some 256,000, WEBSTER'S NEW WORLD THESAURUS, some 300,000—while some deal only with a basic vocabulary. Some have extensive lists of synonyms with a full description of many shades of meaning. Some employ numerous sentences to illustrate word usage in context, some are merely lists. Some include antonyms, some do not. And, naturally, the quality of the synonyms and antonyms included varies somewhat from book to book. The reviews in this guide should be helpful in the selection of the appropriate thesaurus or thesauruses for the college or public library or for personal reference collections.

Finally, a comparatively small selection of large-print reference books—many reviewed in part five of this guide—are available from some public libraries, state and other special libraries for the blind or visually handicapped, the Library of Congress, and the American Printing House for the Blind.

Comparing Reference Works

This Buying Guide also has an extensive bibliography that can be consulted for other sources of information on choosing and purchasing reference books of all types. Many of the evaluations in this guide cite critical comments from other publications; an extensive list of periodicals that review reference books appears in the Bibliography.

No matter how many reviews are consulted, there is no substitute for comparing actual copies of the reference books under consideration. It is essential to leaf through the volumes, examine the indexes, read samples of the text, and look at the maps, illustrations, and extra features they offer. The prefaces and other introductory materials should be read, and it is important to look for a statement of purpose, a description of special features, and information about the latest revision. One way to check the currency of a dictionary is to obtain a list of some of the newest words in technology and science, or colloquial or idiomatic expressions that have entered the language, and to check whether or not they are in the dictionaries that are being considered. Likewise, it is possible to compare maps of identical areas in atlases to see how they are handled and whether or not the maps show recent name changes of countries, cities, and other geographical features.

It is also possible to judge which small encyclopedia is easiest to use in terms of locating the material sought and to assess currency by selecting recent topics of general interest, such as arms control or abortion, and seeing whether they are included and how they are handled.

Multivolume encyclopedias are not as easy to compare. Most multivolume sets are sold by sales representatives who make direct presentations to the prospective buyer. The promotional material presented by the sales representative will, of course, describe the sets as advantageously as possible and may not be strictly accurate.

One way to examine a set without pressure is to ask the sales representative to leave a set on a trial basis, for at least a week. This will afford an opportunity for the potential purchaser to examine the set, to arrive at some conclusions based on the criteria outlined in the reviews in this Buying Guide, and to make comparisons with other sets. Always insist that the entire set be left, so that there is ample opportunity to check a full range of articles and index entries to note how cross-references are handled from one volume to another, and to compare with other encyclopedias in school and public libraries. Librarians may also have the opportunity to examine sets on display at library convention exhibits.

Some companies, including Grolier, World Book, and Encyclopaedia Britannica, have what they call "satisfaction guaranteed" policies. Under these, there is a post-purchase examination period (usually 15 or 30 days) during which an order may be cancelled for a full refund. The grace periods and stipulations are specific to various publishers, and since these can change from time to time, this Buying Guide does not include them. Return privileges, of course, carry with them the obligation that the merchandise must be in good, clean, resalable condition.

Encyclopedia Sales Tactics

A substantial percentage of the cost of an encyclopedia set covers the sales representative's commission. It is to be expected, therefore, that a fair amount of "aggressive" selling techniques are employed in such contacts. Quoted in a 1987 *Publishers Weekly* article, Frank Farrell of Grolier notes, "There is an old saying that encyclopedias are sold and not bought." A salesperson's initial contact with a possible buyer may range from price offerings linked to timely "bargains" to a presentation of statistics on the improvement in the family's cultural life and educational standings of its children created by owning an encyclopedia. There was a time when the tactics also included fraudulent claims and promises, including returns and refund privileges that did not exist. However, consumer-protection legislation has curbed such sales practices so that it is relatively rare for the average consumer today to be confronted with them, and it is far easier to redress the grievances occasionally caused by the persistence of such abuses. The Buying Guide will not, therefore, spend time discussing these deceptive practices but will rather focus on the types of questions and "resistance" a prospective buyer may want to offer such a salesperson.

The first step in the selling process is the contact. Salespersons must find a way to meet buyers and to persuade them to set aside some time for a meeting. The approach varies considerably, from simply knocking on the door unannounced and requesting an opportunity to present the set to calling to make a formal appointment to talk with a prospective purchaser. It is often not easy to say no to salespeople at the outset. The initial meeting is, of course, just the beginning of the sales campaign. That campaign usually focuses on two aspects of encyclopedia acquisition—the need for every home to have such a general reference work and the need of the family's children to have it for success in their school work.

The situation is different in the case of sales to schools and libraries. Even if salespeople call on acquisition personnel there, the pressure is different, partly because the purchase must fit into a budget and partly because professional personnel are trained to evaluate encyclopedias. In many cases, salespersons do not call on institutions, since orders are handled directly by the publishers' marketing departments.

Sales personnel must follow certain procedures when selling encyclopedias door-to-door. Prospective customers must be notified in advance that someone will call on them. Furthermore, they must be told the name of the sales representative as well as that of the encyclopedia and the publisher he or she represents.

Consumer-Protection Laws

The Federal Trade Commission is one of the oldest regulatory bodies in the United States. Among its various responsibilities is that of regulating commercial advertising, which, since 1972, has included the requirement that manufacturers substantiate all advertising claims. It also has the responsibility of enforcing consumer-protection laws. Such laws cover purchases, loans, credit approvals, and debt collection. It is worthwhile to discuss briefly the consumer-protection laws that most closely affect encyclopedia sales (and other door-to-door purchases).

1. *The Truth-in-Lending Law.* This is a 1958 statute that requires the seller to inform the buyer of all credit charges involved in the sale, including the total dollar amount of any loan, the finance charges, and the annual percentage rate of interest on the loan. The annual percentage rate is considered the true cost of borrowing money, in contrast to the simple interest rate, which does not reflect total loan costs or finance charges. All contracts for installment payments—a method by which encyclopedias are frequently purchased—must include this information.

2. *The "Cooling-Off" Period.* This 1974 Federal Trade Commission regulation mandates that all purchases from door-to-door salespersons are subject to cancellation within a "cooling-off" period of three business days after signing the contract. This is enforceable even if there is a signed contract and the merchandise has been delivered. This provision is protection for the consumer who is not strong enough to resist a forceful sales approach but who seriously reconsiders when he or she has time and is not under pressure. As additional protection in such circumstances, not only must the salesperson verbally inform the customer about the "cooling-off" period, but a statement about it must appear in at least ten-point type on the sales contract next to the space reserved for the purchaser's signature. A notice-of-cancellation form for the buyer's use if the option to cancel is exercised must be attached to the sales agreement.

   The seller also has some protection in such cases. The decision to cancel must be communicated in writing within the three-day period, either with the notice-of-cancellation form or by letter. In either case, the notice must be postmarked within the three-day period. Certified or return-receipt-requested mail is recommended. The seller is additionally protected by the customer's obligation to return the merchandise in substantially the same condition as that in which it was received.

The seller must return any papers the customer signed, refund any payments made, return any product that might have been traded in as part of the purchase, and pick up the unwanted merchandise within 20 days of receiving the notice of cancellation. Alternatively, if it is mutually acceptable, merchandise may be returned by mail or other common carrier, at the seller's expense.

3. *The Negative-Option Plan.* This plan applies primarily to mail-order sales of books (as well as records, collectibles, and similar products) sold over a period of time. The buyer is permitted to inform the seller each month (or whatever the sales intervals are) whether or not he or she wishes to purchase the next item scheduled to be offered. In addition, the buyer must be informed well in advance—at least ten days—of the item's proposed mailing date. The offering usually comes with a complete description and a form to be used in indicating whether or not the item should be sent. The form also supplies the price and any shipping and handling charges. If the buyer does not return the form or otherwise instruct the seller not to ship the item, it will come automatically at the specified time. If the form has been returned but the selection is nonetheless sent, the customer has the option of returning it. Negative-option plans usually permit the subscriber to cancel after a specified period and/or number of purchases after the first one.

The Federal Trade Commission has considerably strengthened consumer rights in negative-option plans. The seller's notices and promotional materials must clearly spell out how the selection can be declined, how buyers can resign from the plan after they have fulfilled its minimum requirements, the costs of shipping and handling charges, how unwanted selections can be returned, and the annual schedule of notices and announcements.

This regulation applies to encyclopedia purchases, as some publishers use negative-option plans for the yearbooks and educational supplements that accompany the sets.

4. *The Equal Credit Opportunity Act.* This act, which was passed by the Congress in 1975, requires lenders and granters of credit to apply the same standards for granting or denying credit to women as to men. It also grants married women the right to obtain credit in their own name and prohibits lenders from denying women credit if their marital status has changed through death, divorce, or separation. A woman who can prove that she has been unfairly denied credit can use this law to collect up to $10,000 in punitive damages from the vendor who discriminated against her. This is relevant to encyclopedia sales because so many are sold on the installment plan, which involves receiving credits or loans.

5. *The Fair Credit Billing Act.* This 1975 statute offers consumers protection in instances of disputes over billing practices. Creditors must acknowledge consumer complaints within 30 days and process them within 90 days. The creditor is required to investigate the complaint and either issue a corrected invoice or justify his or her original charges. During this 90-day period, consumers have the right to withhold payment of the disputed amount, and creditors may not pursue its payment. And, while the dispute is still pending, they may not bring suit or issue an adverse credit report on the consumer.

6. *The Fair Debt Collection Practices Act.* The purpose of this 1977 statute is to protect consumers against unfair debt-collection practices of creditors and collection agencies. It mandates that creditors may not contact debtors at work or contact their employers, may not use foul or obscene language, may not threaten or harass debtors, may not telephone debtors before 8 A.M. or after 9 P.M., and may not reveal in any way to third parties that they are trying to collect a debt. If the debtor has an attorney, creditors may deal only with the attorney, and if they bring a lawsuit against the debtor, it must be where he or she lives, not in a distant jurisdiction.

These laws were not specifically designed to protect purchasers of encyclopedias and other types of books. However, since abusive practices could occur in any sales situation, prospective purchasers of encyclopedias should be aware of their rights.

World Book, Encyclopaedia Britannica, and Grolier all belong to the Direct Selling Association and subscribe to its code of ethics. Among other things, this code requires sales representatives of the association's 100 member firms to identify themselves as such at the beginning of a sales call and to give clear and accurate information about the company's products, prices, services, and credit terms. Encyclopaedia Britannica and Grolier also have order-verification systems in which nonsales employees contact a buyer after a sale to make sure that he or she understands all the terms of the sale. Both also have customer-service telephone numbers.

Avoiding Unscrupulous Sellers

Although there is far less abuse today than there was in the past, buyers may still occasionally meet an overly aggressive salesperson or a dishonest distributor selling encyclopedias. Here are a few suggestions for avoiding trouble:

- Never admit an encyclopedia salesperson who does not present proper identification.
- Examine the terms of all offers before agreeing to a purchase. Offers that seem too good to be true usually are. Promotional and advertising claims tend to exaggerate, so do not be misled by them. Compare the claims to the facts as presented by objective reviews, such as those in the Buying Guide and in the other reviews and guides listed in Select Bibliography.
- Before you sign a sales contract, read it carefully, and be sure you understand all its terms, including price, extra fees, finance charges, payment schedules, and any other details of the financial obligation you are assuming. If you are unsure of any item, ask the sales representative for an explanation. Be sure that you can afford the monthly payments and the total cost.
- Set a limit to the amount of time you will spend with the salesperson. Any presentation should be completed in less than an hour.
- Make sure you understand all the terms of the firm's "satisfaction guaranteed" period. A firm that does not have one, and that refuses to leave a demonstration set for at least a week, is a firm to avoid.
- Do not sign a blank sales contract or one with some spaces empty, even if the salesperson assures you that he or she will fill in all the blanks according to your understanding at a later time. Be sure you receive a duplicate copy of the agreement as soon as you sign it; it should be identical to the salesperson's copy

and should correctly spell out all the terms and conditions of the purchase, including a description of the merchandise. Make sure that the agreement includes provisions for the three-day "cooling-off" period and that a notice of cancellation is attached to it.
- Negative-option plans frequently include the distribution of one or more expensive add-ons every year. If you know that you will not want these at the time you make the original purchase, be sure to have the salesperson cross out and initial the applicable contract terms. Conversely, you may have the option of selecting the negative-option plan at the time you make the contract. This will entitle you to receive yearbooks and other extras, as specified. If, however, you decide to cancel your participation in this plan at a later date, you may do so by writing to the company. Using certified mail, with a return receipt requested, protects you from a company's claim that it never received your cancellation notification.
- Oral promises are not binding unless they are translated to written form, so make sure that the contract includes any such promises made by the salesperson. If the merchandise comes with a guarantee, be sure to get it in writing when you sign the agreement.
- A delivery obligation, within a reasonable time or a specified period as set forth in the contract, is part of the seller's obligation. The risk of loss or damage from common-carrier shipment is the purchaser's unless the seller also signs a shipping or destination contract, preferably as part of the sales agreement. Both of these put the burden of damage or loss on the seller until the set reaches you and you have signed a receipt for it.
- If you believe that you have been victimized in any of the ways described in this guide—or in any other ways—report this to the Federal Trade Commission, to your local consumer-protection agency, and to your local Better Business Bureau. You may also want to contact Consumers Union, as this group frequently covers such practices in its publications and may thus alert other consumers to potential problems.

Chapter 3
Librarians Rate
General Reference Books

As part of its research effort in preparing this Buying Guide, R. R. Bowker commissioned a survey asking librarians across the country to evaluate and rate particular encyclopedias, atlases, and dictionaries. The survey was mailed to a stratified random sample of librarians in the United States. Recipients of the survey were 199 public, 45 academic, and 6 special libraries—a total of 250 libraries. Returns were received from 89 libraries: 79 public libraries, 8 academic libraries, and 2 special libraries.

A 14-question survey was developed for use by the librarian respondents, using a carefully compiled list of general reference works in the three major review categories (encyclopedias, dictionaries, atlases). The questionnaire focused on these three categories and asked the respondents to consider which works in each of these categories were most useful. Other questions were designed to discover which works were actually in the libraries' collections, which works adults consulted most frequently, and which ones students found most useful. Librarians receiving the survey were asked to rank the order of their choices. Finally, several questions addressed such topics as special needs, computerized reference works, recommendation policies, and the criteria that librarians use when making purchasing decisions.

The results of this specially prepared survey are reported here. Part I of the survey consists of four questions about multivolume encyclopedias; part II, one question on desk encyclopedias; part III, three questions about dictionaries; and part IV, two questions on atlases. Part V presents the results of four questions asking how librarians dealt with general reference information requests.

I. Multivolume Encyclopedias

Multivolume general encyclopedias are those reference works in three or more volumes that serve as the backbone of a library's reference collection. These sets usually represent a substantial portion of the library's reference budget. The average public library reference collection has at least five sets, including duplicates and older circulating editions. Given the importance—and the cost—of multivolume encyclopedias, four of the survey's 14 questions were devoted to this primary category of reference work.

Two encyclopedias garnered the highest percentage of "first choice" ratings. Depending on the intended audience or the subject matter of the research, *The Encyclopedia Americana* and *The World Book Encyclopedia* were consistently the preferred encyclopedia sets, with the *New Encyclopaedia Britannica* a "first choice" in one instance but otherwise consistently a "third choice." A library patron shopping for a home encyclopedia set should not, however, interpret these results as an endorsement of these three sets. A public library serves a wide range of patrons with varying needs, while a home reference collection must suit the needs of a particular individual or family. As always, the reference needs of the user should be considered first rather than any more general criteria (see question 14, page 32).

The four questions on multivolume encyclopedias posed by the survey are shown below. The results are summarized in table 1.

1. Which general multivolume encyclopedias are included in your library's reference collection?

____ ACADEMIC AMERICAN
____ COLLIER'S ENCYCLOPEDIA
____ COMPTON'S ENCYCLOPEDIA
____ ENCYCLOPEDIA AMERICANA
____ ENCYCLOPEDIA INTERNATIONAL
____ FUNK & WAGNALLS NEW ENCYCLOPEDIA
____ MERIT STUDENTS ENCYCLOPEDIA
____ NEW BOOK OF KNOWLEDGE
____ NEW ENCYCLOPAEDIA BRITANNICA
____ NEW STANDARD ENCYCLOPEDIA
____ WORLD BOOK ENCYCLOPEDIA
____ OTHER

As table 1 shows, the *Encyclopedia Americana* appears in virtually every library in the sample (98 percent of all respondents); only one respondent was without this set. *World Book* (92 percent of all respondents) is next in frequency of mention, followed by the *New Encyclopaedia Britannica* (85 percent) and the *Academic American* (84 percent).

The *New Book of Knowledge* (9 percent) and *Funk & Wagnalls New Encyclopedia* (8 percent) are among the sets that are encountered least often. The former is found more often in children's collections. The latter is sold primarily in supermarkets to the home user.

Results showed 12 public libraries own the *Encyclopedia International*, now out of print.

No respondents included the *New Standard Encyclopedia* in their collections.

Because the large majority of respondents were from public libraries, there is little difference between the percentages for all libraries and those for public libraries. Some differences do exist, however, between the public library and the academic and special library results. *New Britannica* appears in all the academic and special libraries but in only 84 percent of the public libraries. *World Book*, on the other hand, is included in virtually all of the public libraries (97 percent), but in only 50 percent of the academic and special libraries. This may be due to the level of the two sets; *World Book* is more appropriate for high school students than more advanced learners. Similarly, the *Merit Students Encyclopedia* (35 percent overall; 39 percent of public libraries), the *New Book of Knowledge* and *Funk & Wagnalls* do not appear in the more advanced libraries.

The average number of encyclopedia titles owned by the respondents was 5.4 sets. The range in public libraries was from two sets to 11 sets; in university and college libraries the range was from two to six sets; in special libraries the range was from one to seven sets.

TABLE 1. Percentage of Respondents Whose Collections Include Selected Multivolume Encyclopedias

Title	All Libraries (%)	Public Libraries (%)	Academic and Special Libraries (%)
Encyclopedia Americana	98	99	100
World Book Encyclopedia	92	97	50
New Encyclopaedia Britannica	85	84	100
Academic American	84	86	75
Collier's Encyclopedia	66	66	75
Compton's Encyclopedia	41	42	38
Merit Students Encyclopedia	35	39	0
Encyclopedia International	13	15	0
New Book of Knowledge	9	16	0
Funk & Wagnalls New Encyclopedia	8	9	0
New Standard Encyclopedia	0	0	0

Due to multiple responses, the totals for respondents equal more than 100 percent.

2. Which general encyclopedia do you recommend that patrons consult first when they are looking for information about the following subjects:

——— HISTORY
——— CURRENT EVENTS
——— BIOGRAPHICAL MATERIAL
——— GEOGRAPHY
——— SCIENCE AND MEDICINE
——— SOCIAL STUDIES
——— NATURE/NATURAL HISTORY

Many respondents did not answer this question completely. Results are based on the number of answers available.

History

37% AMERICANA
22% WORLD BOOK
20% NEW BRITANNICA
3% COLLIER'S

Current Events

31% WORLD BOOK
12% AMERICANA
9% ACADEMIC AMERICAN
2% COLLIER'S

Biographical Material

29% WORLD BOOK
20% NEW BRITANNICA
20% AMERICANA
8% ACADEMIC AMERICAN
2% COLLIER'S

Geography

47% WORLD BOOK
17% AMERICANA
7% NEW BRITANNICA
6% ACADEMIC AMERICAN
3% COLLIER'S
1% MERIT STUDENTS

Science and Medicine

26% WORLD BOOK
13% NEW BRITANNICA
8% ACADEMIC AMERICAN
7% AMERICANA
3% COLLIER'S
1% MERIT STUDENTS

Social Sciences

27% WORLD BOOK
11% NEW BRITANNICA

11% AMERICANA
7% COLLIER'S
4% ACADEMIC AMERICAN
1% MERIT STUDENTS

Nature/Natural History

38% WORLD BOOK
10% NEW BRITANNICA
7% AMERICANA
2% ACADEMIC AMERICAN
2% COLLIER'S
1% MERIT STUDENTS

Some librarians filled in encyclopedia choices to answer this question, but many also commented that they would first refer the patron to a specific topical source. The encyclopedia of choice among public library respondents for these topics was *World Book*, while among the college and university respondents the choice was usually *Americana*. It should be noted that only half of the academic and special library respondents own *World Book*.

3. Which multivolume encyclopedia do patrons consult most frequently?

adults: _____

students: _____

As with question 2, not all respondents answered this question. Those who did respond, however, gave answers consistent with the other results of this survey. Among all librarians, four sets were cited most often as most frequently consulted by adult patrons:

48% WORLD BOOK
29% AMERICANA
16% NEW BRITANNICA
8% COLLIER'S

Responses from public libraries were distributed in similar proportions. Among academic and special libraries, as before, *Americana* and *New Britannica* had the lion's share of the responses (40 percent and 20 percent, respectively), with *World Book* and *Collier's* at 10 percent each.

In regard to students, the results show a much heavier preference for *World Book*:

85% WORLD BOOK
7% AMERICANA
4% ACADEMIC AMERICAN
4% COLLIER'S
3% NEW BRITANNICA

This significant change is due exclusively to a shift in the responses from public librarians; academic and special library results are virtually identical for both parts of the question, but among public librarians, results differed dramatically. The percentage of librarians stating that adult and student patrons most frequently consult *World Book*, *Americana*, and *New Britannica* compare as follows:

Adults

58%	WORLD BOOK
28%	AMERICANA
15%	NEW BRITANNICA

Students

95%	WORLD BOOK
3%	AMERICANA
0%	NEW BRITANNICA

Clearly, according to our respondents, students rely on *World Book*.

An interesting point is that at least three respondents commented that shelf location was a major factor. These three public librarians felt that patrons consulted the encyclopedia set that was "easiest to get to."

---

4. Which multivolume encyclopedia do you generally find most useful for:

adults:_____

students:_____

When asked which encyclopedia they recommended most often for adult and student patrons, librarians responded as follows:

Adults

37%	AMERICANA
28%	WORLD BOOK
19%	NEW BRITANNICA
8%	ACADEMIC AMERICAN
7%	COLLIER'S

Students

63%	WORLD BOOK
22%	AMERICANA
10%	ACADEMIC AMERICAN
7%	COLLIER'S
3%	MERIT STUDENTS
1%	NEW BRITANNICA

These results reflect the proportions found in the answers to question 3, except that the respondents appear to view *World Book* as appropriate for patrons less often than they report that patrons use it. Note that for adults, *Americana* has passed *World Book* as the most frequent mention and that even in

regard to students, librarians cite *Americana* and the *Academic American* more often and *World Book* less often.

While it may appear that librarians prefer *Americana* and *Academic American* more than patrons, these results must be interpreted in light of the responses to question 2. In six out of seven times they were given broad categories, more respondents indicated that they would recommend that patrons consult *World Book* to answer their general reference questions. Only once was *Americana* the recommended set. It must be kept in mind, then, that although respondents cite sources other than *World Book*, the large majority—almost two-thirds—still send patrons with reference questions to that set.

II. Desk Encyclopedias

Desk encyclopedias attempt, in one or two volumes of reasonable dimension and weight, to cover a wide range of topics in far less detail than one would expect from a multivolume encyclopedia. Generally breadth and brevity cannot both be achieved within one or two volumes. The more successful, or at least long-lived, examples provide somewhat less comprehensiveness in exchange for longer entries where needed. In the main, desk encyclopedias are designed for the home or the classroom as adjuncts to the material available in a library's reference collection; still, many librarians do place one or more desk encyclopedias within the reference area.

Question 5 from the survey attempts to discover which desk encyclopedias *patrons* seem to find most useful. (The survey did not require that respondents indicate which titles their libraries had, nor which they, as librarians, found most useful.) Responses are listed in rank order with the associated percentages. Not all respondents answered this question and some answered with more than one choice; thus, the percentages do not always total 100.

---

5. Which of the following desk encyclopedias (i.e., single- or two-volume) do patrons consult most frequently?

_____   CONCISE COLUMBIA ENCYCLOPEDIA
_____   LINCOLN LIBRARY OF ESSENTIAL INFORMATION
_____   NEW COLUMBIA ENCYCLOPEDIA[1]
_____   RANDOM HOUSE ENCYCLOPEDIA[1]
_____   THE VOLUME LIBRARY

Public Libraries

30%	NEW COLUMBIA ENCYCLOPEDIA[1]
18%	LINCOLN LIBRARY
15%	RANDOM HOUSE ENCYCLOPEDIA[1]

9%   CONCISE COLUMBIA ENCYCLOPEDIA
33%   NO RESPONSE

Academic and Special Libraries

40%   NEW COLUMBIA ENCYCLOPEDIA[1]
20%   LINCOLN LIBRARY
10%   CONCISE COLUMBIA ENCYCLOPEDIA
10%   RANDOM HOUSE ENCYCLOPEDIA[1]
60%   NO RESPONSE

Judging from the responses to this question, desk encyclopedias are not major factors in the library reference collection. Thirty-six percent of the respondents indicated that the desk encyclopedias listed were never consulted or that the library had no such titles in its collection. It would appear that library patrons are more ready to consult a multivolume work. These desk encyclopedias are seen as more suitable for the home, office, or classroom.

[1]The *New Columbia Encyclopedia* and the *Random House Encyclopedia* are now out of print.

III. Dictionaries

English-language dictionaries abound, even within the "general" category. The number of available works can overwhelm both librarians and consumers. This fact, along with similarities among titles and apparent provenances, accounts for a good part of the confusion surrounding the question of "best dictionaries." As librarians know, it is not enough to cite "*Webster's*" or "the *American Heritage*" when each of those names may actually refer to a number of various reference works. (Note that the survey list includes general dictionaries only; thesauruses and other special-purpose dictionaries or word-related books were not included.)

In this section of the survey librarians were asked three basic questions concerning dictionaries. In the first, a list was provided. In the second and third, librarians simply wrote in their choices for each user level.

6. Which adult/general dictionaries are included in your library's reference collection?

____   OXFORD ENGLISH DICTIONARY
____   RANDOM HOUSE (UNABRIDGED)
____   WEBSTER'S THIRD NEW INTERNATIONAL
____   WEBSTER'S NINTH NEW COLLEGIATE
____   FUNK & WAGNALLS STANDARD DESK DICTIONARY
____   RANDOM HOUSE COLLEGE DICTIONARY
____   OXFORD AMERICAN DICTIONARY
____   AMERICAN HERITAGE DICTIONARY
____   WEBSTER'S II NEW RIVERSIDE DICTIONARY
____   WEBSTER'S ILLUSTRATED CONTEMPORARY DICTIONARY
____   OTHER

Table 2 shows the responses to this question, comparing the totals for all respondents to those for pub-

TABLE 2. Percentage of Respondents Whose Collections Include Selected Dictionaries

Title	All Libraries (%)	Public Libraries (%)	Academic and Special Libraries (%)
Webster's Third New International	90	91	80
Webster's Ninth New Collegiate	82	82	80
American Heritage Dictionary	80	81	70
Oxford English Dictionary	75	75	80
Random House Dictionary (Unabridged)	72	70	90
Oxford American Dictionary	42	41	50
Random House College Dictionary	38	34	70
Funk & Wagnalls Standard Desk Dictionary	27	25	40
Webster's II New Riverside Dictionary	11	11	10
Webster's Illustrated Contemporary Dictionary	4	5	—

Because of multiple responses, the totals for respondents equal more than 100 percent.

lic libraries and for academic and special libraries. As can be seen, the responses do not differ greatly. More academic and special libraries responded that they had the *Random House Dictionary*—and many more that collections included the *Random House College Dictionary*—than was the case with public librarians. The number of academic and special libraries with *Webster's Third New International Dictionary* and the *American Heritage Dictionary* was slightly lower than the number of public libraries, but still the great majority of such libraries in this sample possessed both titles.

It should be noted that the *Random House Dictionary* cited here was the now-supplanted first edition because the new *Random House Dictionary of the English Language: Second Unabridged Edition* had not been published when the survey was conducted.

---

7. Which dictionaries do patrons consult most frequently?

As with question 3, a number of librarians noted in response to this question that location and ease of access influenced frequency of consultation. Some also noted that abridged dictionaries, because they are easier to handle, were consulted most often. Despite this comment, the title cited most often in response to question 4 was an unabridged dictionary. Responses to this question for all libraries were as follows:

67% Webster's Third New International
35% Webster's Ninth New Collegiate
20% American Heritage
17% Random House (Unabridged)
11% Oxford English

These proportions were maintained among public libraries, but for academic and special libraries *Webster's Third* was cited by only 40 percent of the respondents (still a majority) and the *Oxford English Dictionary* was cited by 30 percent. This more advanced dictionary is clearly more appropriate for patrons at a higher level.

---

8. Which dictionary do you find most useful for:

adults:_____

students:_____

Answers to this question are consistent with answers to the previous two questions. *Webster's Third*

and *Webster's Ninth* are the two works cited most often by librarians. Not surprisingly, *Webster's Third*—an unabridged title—is judged more useful for adults and the abridged *Webster's Ninth* as more appropriate for students. Among the other three dictionaries also cited, the two unabridged titles were mentioned more often than the abridged for adults but less often for students.

Adults

44% Webster's Third
13% Webster's Ninth
10% Random House (Unabridged)
9% Oxford English
6% American Heritage

Students

34% Webster's Ninth
24% Webster's Third
15% American Heritage
7% Random House (Unabridged)
3% Oxford English

IV. Atlases

Despite the plethora of atlases published, many libraries are forced to rely on a very few titles for a wide range of user needs. Library reference budgets are often limited; therefore, it may be difficult to justify purchasing a variety of atlases—political, historical, travel, and the like—for a variety of users. As a result, reference collections in most public libraries rely on one or two good atlases. Most useful are the atlases that can serve both adults and students. These atlases are, of course, supplemented by the map portions of encyclopedias and topical reference works.

The survey asked the librarians two questions about atlases, the first to discover which works were actually in the reference collections and the second to determine which works the librarians found most useful for each level of patron, adult or student. One problem with atlases is that a publisher may present a series of atlases for the librarian to choose from, with differences ranging from number of maps included to size of index—which can lead to confusion in title references for librarians and for consumers.

---

9. Which world atlases are included in your library's reference collection?

_____ Maps on File
_____ Goode's World Atlas
_____ Rand McNally New Cosmopolitan Atlas

_____ RAND MCNALLY NEW INTERNATIONAL
          ATLAS
_____ NATIONAL GEOGRAPHIC ATLAS OF THE
          WORLD
_____ READER'S DIGEST WIDE WORLD ATLAS
_____ HAMMOND GOLD MEDALLION WORLD
          ATLAS
_____ HAMMOND LARGE TYPE WORLD ATLAS
_____ HAMMOND INTERNATIONAL WORLD
          ATLAS
_____ HAMMOND CITATION WORLD ATLAS
_____ HAMMOND AMBASSADOR WORLD ATLAS
_____ UNIVERSAL ATLAS
_____ THE UNIVERSITY ATLAS
_____ PRENTICE-HALL NEW WORLD ATLAS
_____ THE NEW RAND MCNALLY COLLEGE
          WORLD ATLAS
_____ THE NEW PENGUIN WORLD ATLAS
_____ THE TIMES ATLAS OF THE WORLD
_____ OTHER

Table 3 shows the responses to this question. These responses are totaled for all respondents and broken down for public libraries and academic and special libraries.

About two-thirds of all respondents said their collections included the *Times Atlas of the World*, the *National Geographic Atlas*, and *Goode's World Atlas*, the most popular of the smaller-format hardcover atlases. No other atlas was owned by more than 50 percent of all the libraries sampled, although among the academic and special libraries three other titles also achieved that level of representation: the *Hammond Gold Medallion* (60 percent), the *Rand McNally New International* (50 percent), and the *Rand McNally New Cosmopolitan* (50 percent).

10. Which world atlas do you find most useful for:

adults:_____

students:_____

Judging from the responses to this question, the *National Geographic Atlas* is the one title respondents see as suitable for either adults or students. The *Times Atlas* is viewed as a more adult title, with *Goode's* seen as a student-oriented atlas. *Maps on File*, a collection of one-color maps, is cited as valuable for students.

TABLE 3. Percentage of Respondents Whose Collections Include Selected Atlases

Title	All Libraries (%)	Public Libraries (%)	Academic and Special Libraries (%)
The Times Atlas of the World	68	67	80
National Geographic Atlas of the World	66	66	70
Goode's World Atlas	64	63	70
Maps on File	46	47	40
Rand McNally New International Atlas	46	46	50
Rand McNally New Cosmopolitan Atlas	42	41	50
Hammond Gold Medallion World Atlas	36	37	60
Hammond Ambassador World Atlas	34	33	10
Hammond International World Atlas	20	18	40
Reader's Digest Wide World Atlas	16	15	20
Hammond Large Type World Atlas	15	15	10
Prentice-Hall New World Atlas	12	11	20
Hammond Citation World Atlas	11	11	10
The New Rand McNally College World Atlas	11	10	20

Due to multiple responses, the totals for respondents equal more than 100 percent.

Adults

    25%   TIMES ATLAS
    19%   NATIONAL GEOGRAPHIC ATLAS
    10%   RAND MCNALLY NEW INTERNATIONAL

Students

    18%   NATIONAL GEOGRAPHIC ATLAS
    16%   GOODE'S WORLD ATLAS
     7%   MAPS ON FILE

Not surprisingly, the five titles mentioned in response to this question were the five titles cited by most respondents in question 9.

V. General Reference Information

This portion of the survey was designed to question librarians on four points not tracked elsewhere. The first two questions address special user needs for large-print materials and computerized general reference materials. And last, the survey posed two questions to the librarians as consumers and consumer advisors.

11. Does your collection include any general reference books for patrons with special needs (e.g., braille, large print, or foreign-language editions)?

    ____ YES   ____ No

    How often do patrons request such reference works?

    ____ NEVER   ____ SOMETIMES
    ____ RARELY   ____ FREQUENTLY

While 49 percent of the respondents stated that their collection did include books for patrons with special needs, most librarians indicated that such works were used rarely or sometimes:

     5%   NEVER
    43%   RARELY
    45%   SOMETIMES
     7%   FREQUENTLY

More than half of the 45 percent of respondents whose collections did not include reference books for special-need patrons indicated that such works were never requested:

    56%   NEVER
    23%   RARELY
     5%   SOMETIMES
     0%   FREQUENTLY
    15%   NO ANSWER

Three percent of the surveys were returned with no response to this question.

12. Does your library use any encyclopedic databases or other online or CD-ROM encyclopedias?

    ____ YES   ____ No

    If yes, please specify: _____

The responses to this question were:

     8%   YES
    92%   No

All the librarians who responded *Yes* listed *Academic American*, online through *Dialog. Everyman's* was also listed by one library. About half of the *Yes* respondents said that they used it very frequently.

13. Which criteria are most important to you in deciding whether to purchase a particular reference work? Write 1 for most important, 2 for second most important, and so forth.

    ____ PRICE
    ____ CURRENCY
    ____ EASE OF USE (QUALITY OF LAYOUT, INDEXES, CROSS-REFERENCES)
    ____ READING LEVEL
    ____ COMPREHENSIVENESS
    ____ FAVORABLE REVIEWS IN PROFESSIONAL JOURNALS
    ____ OTHER

The librarians responding indicated that the most important criteria in choosing to purchase a particular reference work are:

1. READING LEVEL 41%
2. FAVORABLE REVIEWS 30%
3. PRICE 26%
4. CURRENCY 23%
5. EASE OF USE 23%
6. COMPREHENSIVENESS 20%

Other criteria mentioned were patron demand, relationship to courses offered, and publisher.

14. Do patrons ever ask you to recommend specific dictionaries, encyclopedias, or atlases they should purchase for themselves?

    ____ NEVER
    ____ RARELY
    ____ SOMETIMES
    ____ FREQUENTLY

Do you ever make specific recommendations?

____ YES   ____ No

If No, how do you generally respond to such requests? _____

▬▬▬▬▬▬▬▬▬▬▬▬▬▬▬▬

Responses to this question indicated that the situation occurs, but not often:

3%   NEVER
22% RARELY
60% SOMETIMES
13% FREQUENTLY

Forty percent of the respondents said that they did make specific recommendations and 58 percent said that they did not. Many respondents indicated that they suggest that patrons examine the reference books in the library's collection; many direct patrons to reviews in professional journals as well. Some librarians emphasize the importance of the patron evaluating his or her own needs, purpose, and taste,

and comparing them to specific titles before making a decision. One respondent summed up the process: "We explain that the presence of an encyclopedia in our library is tantamount to some degree of recommendation." Patrons are referred to sources that describe and evaluate encyclopedias.

Librarians are fairly evenly split on how to handle patron requests for recommendations. Most prefer not to recommend specific titles. Of the librarians who offer advice (but do not provide title recommendations), the preferred strategy offered involves: (1) reading reviews, (2) actually perusing the reference works, and (3) considering the consumer's individual and family needs in light of (1) and (2). This is a thumbnail sketch of the strategy recommended by the American Library Association and also by this Buying Guide. Consumers should note that many libraries have an explicit policy prohibiting librarians from advocating one reference book over another. Most librarians can advise and guide consumers in the selection process, but few are permitted to recommend by specific titles.

Chapter 4
Comparative Charts

The comparative charts on the following pages provide basic factual information about every reference book or set evaluated in *General Reference Books for Adults*. Organized for quick and easy reference, the charts break down the works by category. Within each category, works are listed alphabetically by title. The charts include such information as the edition reviewed, the page and illustration counts, the publisher, and the price.

There are two **Encyclopedia** comparative charts. The first of these includes all *multivolume sets*—that is, those with three or more volumes. The second lists titles in the *small-volume* category—works of one or two volumes.

Separate charts are devoted to **Atlases, General Dictionaries, Etymological Dictionaries, Synonym** and **Antonym Dictionaries, Thesauruses,** and **Usage Dictionaries and Related Word Books**. (Because they are qualitatively different from and are not truly comparable to printed reference sources, online and CD-ROM encyclopedias are not included in the charts, nor are large-print reference works.) The data included in the charts have been compiled from fact information request forms, sent to the publishers of respective titles, and in many cases from additional direct contact with publishers. All publication information is current as of April 1, 1988.

One suggested method of utilizing the charts is for the prospective buyer to consult them at the outset of the decision-making process. The various categories in the comparative charts for each type of reference book will help the user to focus on titles that are similar in scope (that is, in size; number of pages; number of illustrations, and so on). The buyer can also locate titles that are priced within a range

that will fulfill other budgetary criteria.

We have made every effort to ensure that this information is complete and up-to-date. When publishers were unable to supply us with precise figures, such as the number of illustrations, we have relied upon their estimates in combination with the careful scrutiny of our reviewers.

It is important to remember that the figures given here are quantitative and not necessarily a reflection of qualitative evaluation. In the category of encyclopedias, for example, the buyer must keep in mind that the sheer number of volumes or contributors does not always ensure a better choice. In all categories, however, the user can limit the number of titles under consideration by careful use of the comparative charts. Once the field has been narrowed, specific reviews may be consulted for additional information.

The date of the edition reviewed is also an important factor in the selection process. The "Edition Reviewed" column reflects the date of the most recent printing, not the date of copyright registration. It is important to stress that a recent printing of a work is not necessarily timely enough for the user's needs. The copyright information, as well as an assessment of whether the most recent printing reflects new revisions or corrections, can be found in the full review of the work. In order to keep pace with the reader's current information requirements (particularly in science and technology), encyclopedias, dictionaries, and atlases should be updated in subject areas that require recent facts and figures. Detailed information on currency can be obtained by consulting that category in each review included in this Buying Guide.

ENCYCLOPEDIAS

Title	Publisher	Edition	Contributors	Volumes	Pages
Multivolume					
Academic American Encyclopedia	Grolier	1988	2,325	21	9,744
Collier's Encyclopedia	Macmillan	1988	4,600	24	19,750
Encyclopedia Americana	Grolier	1988	6,485	30	26,965
Funk & Wagnalls New Encyclopedia	Funk & Wagnalls	1988	1,033	29	13,024
New Encyclopaedia Britannica	Encyclopaedia Britannica	1988	5,000	32	32,330
New Standard Encyclopedia	Standard Educational Corporation	1988	700	17	10,023
World Book	World Book	1988	3,000	22	14,000
Small-Volume					
Concise Columbia Encyclopedia	Columbia University Press	1983	53	1	943
Lincoln Library of Essential Information	Frontier Press	1988	122	2	2,200
New American Desk Encyclopedia	New American Library	1984	31	1	1,305
Volume Library	The Southwestern Company	1986	234	2	2,519

[a] Hardcover unless otherwise indicated; *I* indicates individual price; *L* indicates library price
[b] Paperback

Entries	Words	Illustrations	Maps	Index Entries	Trim Size	Price[a]	
28,700	9,040,000	12,550 color 4,180 b/w	1,080	200,000	8″ × 10″	I	$850.00
						L	650.00
25,000	21,000,000	17,500 color 15,600 b/w	1,600	400,000	8¼″ × 10⅝″	I	$1,399.50
						L	799.00
52,000	30,800,000	3,184 color 19,540 b/w	1,279	353,000	7¼″ × 10″	I	$1,200.00
						L	869.00
25,000	9,000,000	3,332 color 6,000 b/w	317	130,000	6″ × 9″	I, L	$139.81
65,000	44,000,000	6,564 color 19,400 b/w	1,000	186,514	8⁵⁄₁₆″ × 10⅞″	I	$1,349.00
						L	999.00
30,960	6,400,000	2,700 color 9,700 b/w	642	0	6¾″ × 9¼″	I	$699.50
						L	519.00
18,300	10,000,000	24,000 color 5,500 b/w	2,350	150,000	7¼″ × 9¾″	I	$628.00
						L	499.00
15,000	1,000,000	117 b/w	73	0	7¼″ × 10¼″	I, L	$29.95
							I, L	14.95[b]
26,000	3,500,000	145 color 800 b/w	139	26,000	9″ × 11½″	I, L	$149.95
13,000	1,000,000	35 color 225 b/w	225	0	4¼″ × 7″	I, L	$6.95[b]
unspecified	2,500,000	unspecified (several thousand mostly b/w)	200	22,000	9″ × 11″	I, L	$114.95

ATLASES

Title	Publisher	Edition	Pages	Maps	Index Entries	Trim Size	Price[a]
Ambassador World Atlas	Hammond	1988	524	440	148,000	9½″ × 12½″	$45.00
Background Notes on the Countries of the World	U.S. Department of State	1987	160 pamphlets	160	160	8½″ × 11″	$70.00[c]
Bartholomew Mini World Atlas	John Bartholomew & Son; Distributed by Hammond	1987	208	120	20,000	4″ × 6″	$12.95 9.95[b]
Britannica Atlas	Encyclopaedia Britannica	1988	568	301	160,000	11″ × 14¾″	$79.50
Citation World Atlas	Hammond	1988	388	424	25,000	9½″ × 12½″	$27.95 17.95[b]
Concise Earthbook	Graphic Learning International	1987	215	70	20,000	5¼″ × 7¼″	$12.95
Earthbook	Graphic Learning International	1987	327	185	46,000	10″ × 13¼″	$65.50
Gold Medallion World Atlas	Hammond	1987	660	676	148,000	9½″ × 12½″	$75.00
The Great World Atlas	American Map Corporation	1986	352	182	100,000	10¼″ × 13¾″	$39.95
International World Atlas	Hammond	1987	200	265	not available	9½″ × 12½″	$14.95
The McGraw-Hill Pictorial Atlas of the World	McGraw-Hill	1986	178	70	18,500	10¹⁄₁₀″ × 14½″	$22.95
National Geographic Atlas of the World	National Geographic	1981	385	172	155,000	12½″ × 18¼″	$44.95
The New International Atlas	Rand McNally	1986	568	301	168,000	11″ × 14¾″	$150.00
The New Penguin World Atlas	Penguin	1979	96	44	17,000	7½″ × 10″	$9.95[b]

[a] Hardcover unless otherwise indicated
[b] Paperback
[c] Looseleaf binder

(continued on next page)

ATLASES *(CONT.)*

Title	Publisher	Edition	Pages	Maps	Index Entries	Trim Size	Price[a]
The New York Times Atlas of the World	Times Books	1988	244	148	100,000	10½″ × 14½″	$49.95
The Prentice-Hall New World Atlas	Prentice Hall Press	1984	284	100	45,000	8¾″ × 11″	$16.95
The Prentice-Hall Pocket Atlas of the World	Prentice Hall Press	1983	120	55	11,000	4½″ × 7½″	$2.95[b]
The Prentice-Hall Universal Atlas	Prentice Hall Press	1983	404	176	60,000	9″ × 12″	$34.95
The Prentice-Hall University Atlas	Prentice Hall Press	1984	404	176	60,000	9″ × 12″	$27.50
Rand McNally Contemporary World Atlas	Rand McNally	1987	256	216	30,000	9″ × 11″	$9.95[b]
Rand McNally Cosmopolitan World Atlas	Rand McNally	1985	364	325	85,000	11″ × 14½″	$55.00
Rand McNally Desk Reference World Atlas	Rand McNally	1987	528	346	30,000+	6½″ × 9½″	$17.95
Rand McNally Family World Atlas	Rand McNally	1985	256	216	30,000	9″ × 11″	$12.95
Rand McNally Goode's World Atlas	Rand McNally	1986	384	396	36,000	8¾″ × 11″	$22.95
Rand McNally Images of the World	Rand McNally	1983	160	151	0	8¾″ × 11¾″	$24.95
Rand McNally Quick Reference World Atlas	Rand McNally	1987	48	45	4,000	8½″ × 11″	$3.95[b]

[a] Hardcover unless otherwise indicated
[b] Paperback
[c] Looseleaf binder

(continued on next page)

ATLASES *(CONT.)*

Title	Publisher	Edition	Pages	Maps	Index Entries	Trim Size	Price[a]
The Random House Concise World Atlas	Random House	1984	208	120	20,000	6″ × 8⅝″	$7.95[b]
The Random House Mini World Atlas	Random House	1984	208	120	20,000	4″ × 6″	$4.95[b]
Reader's Digest Wide World Atlas	Reader's Digest General Books	1984	240	189	36,000	11″ × 14″	$34.95
The Times Atlas of the World	Times Books	1985	419	123	200,000	11½″ × 18″	$139.95
VNR Pocket Atlas	Van Nostrand Reinhold	1983	236	80	13,500	4½″ × 6⅝″	$8.95[b]
The Whole Earth Atlas	Hammond	1984	256	302	302 same page indexes	8½″ × 11″	$8.95[b]

[a] Hardcover unless otherwise indicated
[b] Paperback
[c] Looseleaf binder

GENERAL DICTIONARIES

Title	Publisher	Edition	Pages[d]	Entries	Illustrations	Trim Size	Price[a]
The American Encyclopedic Dictionary	Salem House	1987	1,936	30,000+	2,500 color photos 1,000 b/w line drawings	7⅜″ × 10³⁄₁₆″	$69.95
The American Heritage Desk Dictionary	Houghton Mifflin	1981	1,184	100,000+	1,500+	6¾″ × 9⁹⁄₁₆″	$10.95
The American Heritage Dictionary	Dell	1985	880	60,000	400+	4¾″ × 6¾″	$4.95[b]
The American Heritage Dictionary: Second College Edition	Houghton Mifflin	1985	1,568	200,000	3,000	6¾″ × 9⁹⁄₁₆″	$18.95
The American Heritage Illustrated Encyclopedic Dictionary	Houghton Mifflin	1987	1,920	180,000	2,300	8½″ × 10⅞″	$55.00
Basic Dictionary of English	Prentice Hall Press	1983	170	4,500	88	4⅜″ × 7¼″	$3.50[b]
Chambers Concise 20th Century Dictionary	Cambridge University Press	1986	1,216	95,000	0	5½″ × 8¼″	$15.95
Chambers Mini Dictionary	Cambridge University Press	1985	640	24,000	0	3″ × 4⅝″	$3.95[b]
Chambers Pocket 20th Century Dictionary	Cambridge University Press	1984	896	33,000	0	4¼″ × 5⅜″	$6.95
Chambers 20th Century Dictionary	Cambridge University Press	1983	1,599	175,000	0	6¼″ × 9½″	$24.95
Chambers Universal Learners' Dictionary	Cambridge University Press	1985	928	45,000	0	5¼″ × 7¾″	$9.95[b]
The Compact Edition of the Oxford English Dictionary	Oxford University Press	1971	5,568[e]	500,000	0	9¼″ × 12″	$195.00
The Concise American Heritage Dictionary	Houghton Mifflin	1980	832	55,000	300	6⅛″ × 9¾″	$7.95

[a] Hardcover unless otherwise indicated
[b] Paperback
[c] Trade paperback
[d] One volume unless otherwise noted
[e] Two volumes
[f] 12 volumes

(continued on next page)

GENERAL DICTIONARIES *(CONT.)*

Title	Publisher	Edition	Pages[d]	Entries	Illustrations	Trim Size	Price[a]
The Concise Oxford Dictionary of Current English	Oxford University Press	1982	1,279	40,000+	0	5¼″ × 8½″	$22.50
The Doubleday Dictionary for Home, School, and Office	Doubleday	1975	906	85,000	970	5⅜″ × 8³⁄₁₆″	$11.95
An English-Reader's Dictionary	Oxford University Press	1985	632	25,000	0	3⅞″ × 6½″	$5.95[b]
Everyday American English Dictionary	National Textbook	1987	400	5,500	0	5¼″ × 7½″	$7.95 $4.95[b]
The Facts on File Visual Dictionary	Facts on File	1986	797	25,000	3,000	7⅛″ × 9″	$29.95
Funk & Wagnalls Standard Desk Dictionary	Harper & Row	1984	880[b]	100,000+	262	7¼″ × 9¼″	$8.95[b]
Funk & Wagnalls Standard Desk Dictionary	Funk & Wagnalls	1984	880[e]	100,000+	262	6¼″ × 8⅞″	gratis
Funk & Wagnalls Standard Dictionary	New American Library/ Meridian	1984	1,011	82,000	0	5¼″ × 8″	$8.95[b]
Hugo English Dictionary	Hugo Language Books	1978	632	30,000	0	2¾″ × 4″	$4.25
The Little Oxford Dictionary of Current English	Oxford University Press	1986	720	25,000	0	4″ × 6″	$9.95
The Little Webster	Langenscheidt	no date	640	7,000+	0	1½″ × 2″	$2.00[b]
Longman Dictionary of American English	Longman	1983	792	38,000	15 pp	5¾″ × 8¾″	$12.95 $7.95[b]
Longman Dictionary of Contemporary English	Longman	1984	1,303	55,000+	0	5½″ × 8½″	$17.95 $13.95[b]

[a] Hardcover unless otherwise indicated
[b] Paperback
[c] Trade paperback
[d] One volume unless otherwise noted
[e] Two volumes
[f] 12 volumes

(continued on next page)

GENERAL DICTIONARIES *(CONT.)*

Title	*Publisher*	*Edition*	*Pages*[d]	*Entries*	*Illustrations*	*Trim Size*	*Price*[a]
Longman Photo Dictionary	Longman	1987	96	2,000+	865	8″ × 10″	$6.95[b]
The Merriam-Webster Dictionary	Pocket Books	1974	848	57,000	0	4⅛″ × 6¾″	$3.95[b]
Nelson's New Compact Webster's Dictionary	Thomas Nelson	1985	314	30,000	0	3½″ × 5¼″	$2.95[b]
New American Webster Handy College Dictionary	New American Library	1981	640	115,000+	0	4¼″ × 7″	$2.95[b]
The New Century Vest-Pocket Webster Dictionary	New Century	1975	304	21,000	300	3″ × 5⅜″	$2.95[b]
Oxford Advanced Learner's Dictionary of Current English	Oxford University Press	1980	1,037	50,000	1,000	5½″ × 8⁷⁄₁₆″	$17.25
Oxford American Dictionary	Oxford University Press / Avon Books[b,c]	1986 / 1980	832 / 832[c] / 1,120[b]	35,000	0	5⅞″ × 9″ / 5¼″ × 8″[c] / 4³⁄₁₆″ × 6⅞″[b]	$14.95 / 7.95[c] / 3.95[b]
Oxford-Duden Pictorial English Dictionary	Oxford University Press	1981	820	28,000+	28,000+	5″ × 7½″	$12.95[b]
The Oxford English Dictionary and Supplement 1 to 4	Oxford University Press	1986	21,133[f]	500,000	0	9½″ × 12″	$1,500.00
The Oxford Mini-dictionary	Oxford University Press	1985	558	20,000	0	3″ × 4¾″	$3.95[b]
Oxford Student's Dictionary of American English	Oxford University Press	1986	714	35,000+	0	5¼″ × 8¼″	$15.95 / 5.95[b]

[a] Hardcover unless otherwise indicated
[b] Paperback
[c] Trade paperback
[d] One volume unless otherwise noted
[e] Two volumes
[f] 12 volumes

(continued on next page)

GENERAL DICTIONARIES *(CONT.)*

Title	Publisher	Edition	Pages[d]	Entries	Illustrations	Trim Size	Price[a]
Oxford Student's Dictionary of Current English	Oxford University Press	1982	769	35,000	0	4½" × 7⁵⁄₁₆"	$6.95[b]
The Pocket Oxford Dictionary of Current English	Oxford University Press	1986	900	49,000	0	4¼" × 7"	$11.95
The Random House American Dictionary: New Revised Edition	Random House	1984	315	30,000	0	2⅞" × 5⅜"	$2.95[b]
The Random House College Dictionary: Revised Edition	Random House	1984	1,600	170,000	1,500	6⁹⁄₁₆" × 9⅝"	$14.95
The Random House Dictionary	Ballantine Books	1983	1,072	74,000	0	4⅛" × 6⅞"	$3.50[b]
The Random House Dictionary: Concise Edition	Random House	1983	1,072	74,000	0	4⅛" × 6⅞"	$5.95
The Random House Dictionary of the English Language: Second Edition, Unabridged	Random House	1987	2,552	315,000+	32 pp in color 2,400 b/w	9¼" × 12"	$79.95
Reader's Digest Illustrated Encyclopedic Dictionary	Reader's Digest	1987	1,920	180,000	2,300+	8⅜" × 10⅞"	$49.96
The Scribner-Bantam English Dictionary	Bantam Books	1985	1,120	56,000+	0	4⅛" × 6⅞"	$3.95[b]
Shorter Oxford English Dictionary	Oxford University Press	1973	2,704[e]	163,000	0	7½" × 10¾"	$150.00
The Thorndike Barnhart Handy Pocket Dictionary	Bantam Books	1985	451	36,000	0	4¼" × 6⅞"	$3.50[b]

[a] Hardcover unless otherwise indicated
[b] Paperback
[c] Trade paperback
[d] One volume unless otherwise noted
[e] Two volumes
[f] 12 volumes

(continued on next page)

GENERAL DICTIONARIES *(CONT.)*

Title	Publisher	Edition	Pages[d]	Entries	Illustrations	Trim Size	Price[a]
12,000 Words	Merriam-Webster	1986	236	12,000	0	6⅞" × 9½"	$10.95
The Universal Webster	Langenscheidt	1958	416	17,000	0	3" × 4¼"	$3.50[b]
Webster Comprehensive Dictionary: Encyclopedic Edition	J. G. Ferguson	1984	1,725[e]	175,000	2,043+	8¼" × 10⅞"	$49.95
Webster Comprehensive Dictionary: International Edition	J. G. Ferguson	1986	1,536[e]	175,000	2,000+	8½" × 11¼"	$39.95
Webster Illustrated Contemporary Dictionary	J. G. Ferguson	1984	1,150	85,000	970	7¾" × 10"	$17.95
Webster's Concise Family Dictionary	Merriam-Webster	1975	848	57,000	0	6" × 9¼"	$8.95
Webster's Dictionary for Everyday Use	Barnes & Noble	1985	446	50,000	0	5⅜" × 7⅝"	$4.95[b]
Webster's New Compact Dictionary for School and Office	Thomas Nelson	1985	313	30,000	0	4½" × 6¼"	$2.95
Webster's New Dictionary and Roget's Thesaurus	Thomas Nelson	1984	992	35,000	300	5⅞" × 9¼"	$9.95
Webster's New Ideal Dictionary	Merriam-Webster	1984	672	57,346	60	6¾" × 8½"	$7.95
Webster's New School and Office Dictionary	Fawcett Crest	1975	888	63,000	0	4⅛" × 6⅞"	$3.50[b]
Webster's New Twentieth Century Dictionary	Prentice Hall Press	1983	2,290	320,000	48 color 2,100 b/w	8½" × 11"	$79.95
Webster's New World Compact Dictionary of American English	Prentice Hall Press	1981	630	38,000	0	3" × 4½"	$4.95[b]

[a] Hardcover unless otherwise indicated
[b] Paperback
[c] Trade paperback
[d] One volume unless otherwise noted
[e] Two volumes
[f] 12 volumes

(continued on next page)

GENERAL DICTIONARIES *(CONT.)*

Title	Publisher	Edition	Pages[d]	Entries	Illustrations	Trim Size	Price[a]
Webster's New World Compact School and Office Dictionary	Prentice Hall Press	1982	540	56,000	0	5¼″ × 8″	$8.95 5.95[b]
Webster's New World Dictionary of the American Language	Warner Books	1984	696	59,000+	200+	4¼″ × 7″	$3.95[b]
Webster's New World Dictionary: The Concise Edition	New American Library	1971	882	100,000	600+	5½″ × 8½″	$8.50[b]
Webster's New World Dictionary: Second College Edition	Prentice Hall Press	1986	1,728	160,000	1,300	7⅜″ × 9″	$16.95
Webster's New World Pocket Dictionary	Prentice Hall Press	1977	316	22,000	0	3″ × 5¼″	$2.95[b]
Webster's New World Vest Pocket Dictionary	Simon & Schuster	1977	188	15,000	0	3″ × 5¼″	$1.95[b]
Webster's Ninth New Collegiate Dictionary	Merriam-Webster	1986	1,568	156,000	573	7″ × 9½″	$16.95
Webster's Third New International Dictionary	Merriam-Webster	1986	2,776	470,000	3,105	9¹⁄₁₆″ × 12⁹⁄₁₆″	$79.95
Webster's II New Riverside Dictionary	Berkley Books	1986	832	55,000	200	4¼″ × 6⅞″	$3.95[b]
Webster's II New Riverside Pocket Dictionary	Houghton Mifflin	1978	256	35,000	0	3½″ × 5½″	$2.95[b]
Webster's II New Riverside University Dictionary	Houghton Mifflin	1984	1,536	200,000	400	6¾″ × 9⁹⁄₁₆″	$14.95
Webster's Vest Pocket Dictionary	Merriam-Webster	1981	380	18,000	0	3⅛″ × 5⅜″	$2.25
Webster's Vest Pocket Dictionary	Thomas Nelson	1985	188	10,000+	0	3″ × 5¼″	$1.25[b]
World Book Dictionary	World Book	1988	2,554[e]	225,000	3,000	8⅜″ × 10⅞″	$69.00

[a] Hardcover unless otherwise indicated
[b] Paperback
[c] Trade paperback
[d] One volume unless otherwise noted
[e] Two volumes
[f] 12 volumes

ETYMOLOGICAL DICTIONARIES

Title	Publisher	Edition	Pages[c]	Entries	Trim Size	Price[a]
The American Heritage Dictionary of Indo-European Roots	Houghton Mifflin	1985	140	13,000	6¾" × 9¼"	$10.95 5.95[b]
The Barnhart Dictionary Companion	Lexik House	1987	varies	1,200 annually	8½" × 11"	$50.00[b] (annual subscription)
The Barnhart Dictionary of Etymology	H. W. Wilson	1987	1,200	25,000+	6¾" × 10"	$59.00
Chambers Wordlore	Cambridge University Press	1984	124	375	5⅛" × 7⅝"	$4.95[b]
Comprehensive Etymological Dictionary of the English Language	Elsevier	1986	844	44,400	7⅝" × 11¼"	$107.50
The Concise Oxford Dictionary of English Etymology	Oxford University Press	1986	552	17,000	5¼" × 8"	$24.95
Dictionary of Changes in Meaning	Routledge, Chapman & Hall	1986	292	1,300+	6⅛" × 9⅛"	$35.00
The Dictionary of Eponyms	Stein & Day	1985	342	3,500+	6" × 9"	$9.95[b]
A Dictionary of the English Language (Johnson's Dictionary)	Times Books	1979 (Facs ed of April 1755 printing)	2,328	40,000	9" × 15¼"	$57.50
A Dictionary of True Etymologies	Routledge, Chapman & Hall	1986	193	1,200	6⅛" × 9⅛"	$22.50
Dictionary of Word Origins	Philosophical Library Rowman & Littlefield	1945 1985	441 441	6,400 6,400	5½" × 8¼" 5" × 8"[b]	$19.95 $7.95[b]
An Etymological Dictionary of Modern English	Dover	1967	856[d]	20,000+	6½" × 9¼"	$17.00[b]

[a] Hardcover unless otherwise indicated
[b] Paperback
[c] One volume unless otherwise noted
[d] Two volumes

(continued on next page)

ETYMOLOGICAL DICTIONARIES *(CONT.)*

Title	Publisher	Edition	Pages[c]	Entries	Trim Size	Price[a]
The Facts on File Encyclopedia of Word and Phrase Origins	Facts on File	1987	590	7,500	8½″ × 11″	$40.00
New Words Dictionary	Ballantine Books	1985	114	388	4″ × 6⅞″	$2.50[b]
Origins	Macmillan	1979	990	12,000	7⁵⁄₁₆″ × 9¼″	$50.00
The Origins of English Words	Johns Hopkins University Press	1984	672	3,000	5⅞″ × 8⅞″	$39.95
Oxford Dictionary of English Etymology	Oxford University Press	1983	1,040	24,000	6″ × 9″	$49.95
Word for Word	Verbatim Books	1982	454	60	6″ × 9″	$60.00
Word Mysteries and Histories	Houghton Mifflin	1986	320	500	6″ × 9″	$16.95

[a] Hardcover unless otherwise indicated
[b] Paperback
[c] One volume unless otherwise noted
[d] Two volumes

SYNONYM AND ANTONYM DICTIONARIES

Title	Publisher	Edition	Pages[d]	Entries	Trim Size	Price[a]
Allen's Synonyms and Antonyms	Barnes & Noble Books	1985	427	12,000	5⅛″ × 8″	$4.95[b]
The Basic Book of Synonyms and Antonyms	New American Library	1986	413	4,000	4¼″ × 7″	$3.95[b]
Choose the Right Word	Perennial Library	1987	736	6,000	7⅜″ × 9½″	$12.95[c]
A Dictionary of Synonyms and Antonyms	Warner Books	1982	384	3,000	4¼″ × 7″	$2.95[b]
Funk & Wagnalls Standard Handbook of Synonyms, Antonyms, and Prepositions	Harper & Row	1984	515	1,700	8½″ × 11″	$13.95
The Merriam-Webster Pocket Dictionary of Synonyms	Pocket Books	1972	441	4,244	4¼″ × 6¾″	$3.95[b]
The Random House Basic Dictionary of Synonyms and Antonyms	Ballantine Books	1984	137	4,000	4¼″ × 6⅞″	$1.50[b]
Reader's Digest Family Word Finder	Reader's Digest	1986	896	10,000	7″ × 9³⁄₁₆″	$21.99
The Synonym Finder	Warner Books	1986	1,361	1,500,000	6½″ × 9⅜″	$21.95
Webster's Compact Dictionary of Synonyms	Merriam-Webster	1987	374	700	4″ × 5½″	$4.95[b]
Webster's New Dictionary of Synonyms	Merriam-Webster	1984	942	8,733	6½″ × 9½″	$14.95
Webster's New World Dictionary of Synonyms	Simon & Schuster	1984	255	4,000	5¼″ × 8¼″	$4.95[b]

[a] Hardcover unless otherwise indicated
[b] Paperback
[c] Trade paperback
[d] One volume unless otherwise noted

THESAURUSES

Title	Publisher	Edition	Pages[d]	Entries	Trim Size	Price[a]
Chambers 20th Century Thesaurus	Cambridge University Press	1986	762	18,000	5⅜″ × 8⅛″	$14.95
The Doubleday Roget's Thesaurus in Dictionary Form	Doubleday	1977	816	17,000+	5⅜″ × 8″	$12.95
Longman Lexicon of Contemporary English	Longman	1982	928	15,000	5⅜″ × 8½″	$19.95 $15.95[b]
Nelson's New Compact Roget's Thesaurus	Thomas Nelson	1986	314	1,000	3½″ × 5¼″	$2.45[b]
The New American Roget's College Thesaurus in Dictionary Form	New American Library	1985	649	20,000+	4¼″ × 7″[b] 5¼″ × 8″[c]	$3.50[b] 7.95[c]
The Penguin Pocket Thesaurus	Penguin	1985	514	882	4⅜″ × 7¹/₁₆″	$3.50[b]
The Penguin Roget's Thesaurus of English Words and Phrases	Penguin	1985	776	990	5″ × 7¾″	$7.95[b]
The Random House Thesaurus	Random House	1985	261	4,500	2⅞″ × 5⅜″	$2.95[b]
The Random House Thesaurus: College Edition	Random House	1984	812	11,000	6⁹/₁₆″ × 9⅝″	$14.95
The Right Word II	Houghton Mifflin	1983	288	approx. 647	4″ × 5½″	$3.95
Roget's International Thesaurus: Fourth Edition	Harper & Row	1984	1,318	256,000	8½″ × 11″	$11.45
Roget's Pocket Thesaurus	Pocket Books	1946	479	1,000	4¼″ × 6¹¹/₁₆″	$3.95[b]

[a] Hardcover unless otherwise indicated
[b] Paperback
[c] Trade paperback
[d] One volume unless otherwise noted

(continued on next page)

THESAURUSES *(CONT.)*

Title	Publisher	Edition	Pages[d]	Entries	Trim Size	Price[a]
Roget's II: The New Thesaurus	Houghton Mifflin	1980	1,088	250,000	6¾″ × 9⁹⁄₁₆″	$11.95
Roget's University Thesaurus	Barnes & Noble	1986	741	80,000	5⅛″ × 8″	$8.95[b]
Webster's Collegiate Thesaurus	Merriam-Webster	1976	976	23,000	6½″ × 9½″	$12.95
Webster's New World Thesaurus	Simon & Schuster	1985	854	30,000+	6½″ × 9½″	$13.95
Webster's New World Thesaurus	Warner Books	1984	530	30,000	4″ × 6⅞″[b] 5½″ × 8″[c]	$3.50[b] 8.95[c]

[a] Hardcover unless otherwise indicated
[b] Paperback
[c] Trade paperback
[d] One volume unless otherwise noted

USAGE DICTIONARIES AND RELATED WORD BOOKS

Title	Publisher	Edition	Pages[c]	Entries	Trim Size	Price[a]
American Usage and Style	Van Nostrand Reinhold	1980	433	3,145	5⅞″ × 9″	$12.95[b]
Beginner's Dictionary of American English Usage	National Textbook Company	1986	280	4,000	5¼″ × 7½″	$7.95 $4.95[b]
British/American Language Dictionary	Passport Books	1984	192	3,200	5¼″ × 8¼″	$7.95[b]
British English, A to Zed	Facts on File	1987	496	5,000	5¾″ × 9″	$35.00
A Browser's Dictionary	Harper & Row	1980	429	1,275	6⅛″ × 9⅛″	$18.45
Chambers Idioms	Cambridge University Press	1982	440	2,500	4½″ × 7″	$7.95[b]
Chambers Pocket Guide to Good English	Cambridge University Press	1986	140	660	4½″ × 7″	$4.95[b]
A Concise Dictionary of Correct English	Littlefield, Adams	1979	166	940	5½″ × 8⁷⁄₁₆″	$1.50[b]
A Dictionary of American Idioms: 2nd Revised Edition	Barron's	1987	480	5,000+	6″ × 9″	$11.95[b]
Dictionary of American Regional English	The Belknap Press of Harvard	1985	903	14,500	8½″ × 11″	$60.00
Dictionary of Collective Nouns and Group Terms	Gale	1985	288	1,800+	5¼″ × 8½″	$65.00
Dictionary of Confusing Words and Meanings	Routledge, Chapman & Hall	1986	267	3,000	6″ × 9″	$22.50
Dictionary of Contemporary American English Contrasted with British English	Humanities Press	1983	404	1,000	5½″ × 8¾″	$35.00

[a] Hardcover unless otherwise indicated
[b] Paperback
[c] One volume unless otherwise noted
[d] Two volumes

(continued on next page)

USAGE DICTIONARIES AND RELATED WORD BOOKS *(CONT.)*

Title	Publisher	Edition	Pages[c]	Entries	Trim Size	Price[a]
A Dictionary of Modern English Usage	Oxford University Press	1986	748	4,350	4⅞″ × 7¼″	$9.95[b]
Dictionary of Problem Words and Expressions	Washington Square Press	1985	369	1,500+	4⅛″ × 6¾″	$4.95[b]
Dictionary of Pronunciation	Cornwall Books	1981	584	58,000	6⅛″ × 9¼″	$19.95
Encyclopedic Dictionary of English Usage	Prentice Hall Press	1987	342	15,000+	6⅛″ × 9¼″	$19.95
The Facts on File Dictionary of Troublesome Words	Facts on File	1984	173	1,093	5½″ × 8½″	$17.95
A Handy Book of Commonly Used American Idioms	Prentice Hall Press	1985	112	1,200+	4″ × 6″	$4.67[b]
Harper Dictionary of Contemporary Usage (2nd Edition)	Harper & Row	1985	672	2,675	6″ × 9¼″	$19.45
Homophones and Homographs: An American Dictionary	McFarland	1986	272	4,200	5⅜″ × 8½″	$29.95
Longman Dictionary of English Idioms	Longman	1985	387	4,500	6″ × 9″	$19.95
Longman Dictionary of Phrasal Verbs	Longman	1986	752	12,000+	5¼″ × 8½″	$18.95
Modern American Usage	Hill and Wang	1986	436	approx. 340	5½″ × 8¼″	$10.95[b]
Mrs. Byrne's Dictionary of Unusual, Obscure, and Preposterous Words	Washington Square Press	1984	237	6,000	4″ × 6¾″	$3.50[b]

[a] Hardcover unless otherwise indicated
[b] Paperback
[c] One volume unless otherwise noted
[d] Two volumes

(continued on next page)

USAGE DICTIONARIES AND RELATED WORD BOOKS *(CONT.)*

Title	Publisher	Edition	Pages[c]	Entries	Trim Size	Price[a]
New Dictionary of American Slang	Harper & Row	1986	650	15,000	7⅜″ × 9¼″	$21.45
The New York Times Everyday Reader's Dictionary of Misunderstood, Misused, and Mispronounced Words	Times Books	1985	410	14,000	5½″ × 8³⁄₁₆″	$18.95
No Uncertain Terms	Facts on File	1984	128	132	5½″ × 8½″	$6.95[b]
NTC's American Idioms Dictionary	National Textbook Company	1988	480	8,000+	6″ × 9″	$9.95[b]
-Ologies and -Isms	Gale	1986	795	17,000+	6″ × 9″	$90.00
1000 Most Challenging Words	Facts on File	1987	334	1,000	6″ × 9″	$22.95
1000 Most Important Words	Facts on File	1982	193	1,000	6″ × 9″	$16.95
1000 Most Practical Words	Facts on File	1983	272	1,000	6″ × 9″	$16.95
Oxford Dictionary of Current Idiomatic English	Oxford University Press	1984	1,225[d]	15,000	5⅜″ × 8½″	$18.95
The Oxford Guide to English Usage	Oxford University Press	1985	256	4,581	5½″ × 8½″	$14.95
Oxford Guide to the English Language	Oxford University Press	1985	574	30,000	5″ × 7¾″	$9.95[b]
The Penguin Dictionary of Troublesome Words	Penguin	1986	173	1,093	5⅛″ × 7¾″	$7.95[b]
Practical English: 1000 Most Effective Words	Ballantine Books	1983	343	1,000	4¼″ × 6⅞″	$2.95[b]

[a] Hardcover unless otherwise indicated
[b] Paperback
[c] One volume unless otherwise noted
[d] Two volumes

(continued on next page)

USAGE DICTIONARIES AND RELATED WORD BOOKS *(CONT.)*

Title	Publisher	Edition	Pages[c]	Entries	Trim Size	Price[a]
Practical English Usage	Oxford University Press	1985	708	639	5½″ × 8½″	$10.95[b]
Prefixes and Other Word-Initial Elements of English	Gale	1984	533	3,000	6″ × 9″	$78.00
A Pronouncing Dictionary of American English	Merriam-Webster	1953	542	42,000 +	6″ × 8¼″	$12.95
The Quintessential Dictionary	Warner Books	1984	422	1,200 +	4⅛″ × 6¾″	$3.95[b]
Suffixes and Other Word-Final Elements of English	Gale	1982	363	1,545	6″ × 9″	$85.00
Usage and Abusage	Penguin	1985	381	3,822	5⅛″ × 7¹³⁄₁₆″	$7.95[b]
Words on Words	Columbia University Press	1980	406	2,500	6″ × 9″ 5¾″ × 9″[b]	$34.00 $12.00[b]

[a] Hardcover unless otherwise indicated
[b] Paperback
[c] One volume unless otherwise noted
[d] Two volumes

PART TWO
Encyclopedias

Chapter 5
What to Look for in Encyclopedias

The value of any encyclopedia depends on the needs of the individual user. No matter how good it may be, no one work can satisfy the needs of all users. Some works are designed for ready reference, others offer sophisticated discussion of complex subjects, and yet others excel in the straightforward presentation of information for the casual browser.

There are a number of criteria by which to assess any given encyclopedia. The importance of each criterion may well differ from reader to reader. Each print encyclopedia reviewed in the Buying Guide is divided into the following sections: Introduction, Scope, Authority, Currency, Accuracy, Clarity, Objectivity, Accessibility, Special Features, Format, Other Opinions, and Summary. (Electronic encyclopedias are evaluated by other appropriate criteria.) This chapter explains the considerations and clarifies the criteria on which each evaluation is based. It also gives the reader a sound basis for forming a personal evaluation of these works.

Facts at a Glance. Beginning each review is a "Facts at a Glance" box, which includes such factual information as the names of the publisher and editor; the number of volumes, pages, and illustrations; the price; and ordering information. This information enables the prospective purchaser to determine immediately if the encyclopedia might be of interest and if it might meet his or her requirements. Information in this box has been provided by the encyclopedia's publisher.

Our reviewers examined the most recent edition of each work available at the time of review. In some cases, however, encyclopedia publishers issued revised editions of their works just prior to this Buying Guide's press date. Therefore, we contacted all en-

cyclopedia publishers again before going to press, to obtain statistical information about these latest editions. This information has now been incorporated into the "Facts at a Glance" section; in addition, the text of each review notes any significant changes that have been made in the latest editions.

Introduction. The body of each review begins with a statement about the intended purpose of the encyclopedia under discussion. In many cases the publisher has provided the Buying Guide's editors with an overview of the set and described some of its highlights. Naturally, publishers present their products in the best possible light. In some instances their claims amount to a sales pitch. Nevertheless, whenever possible we have quoted publishers' statements about their works, since part of the function of the reviews is to examine whether these claims stand up to critical scrutiny.

Scope. This section gives the reader an overview of the work's range and contents. It reports some basic statistics about the encyclopedia, such as the number of words it contains and the average length of a typical article as well as its general maximum and minimum length. This section also describes what sort of subjects are covered and assesses the depth and breadth of coverage of various subject areas. Among other things, this section usually breaks down the encyclopedia's content into broad subject categories (such as humanities, sciences, history, biography, and how-to) by percentage. It also examines the attention paid to non-American subjects in biographical and geographical entries. Serious omissions are identified, as are areas in which the encyclopedia's coverage is particularly strong.

Authority. Many readers assume that an encyclopedia—*any* encyclopedia—is necessarily a trustworthy source of information and that the authors of encyclopedia articles are well qualified to write about their chosen subjects. In reality, however, there is no guarantee that what is printed in an encyclopedia is any more authoritative than the opinion expressed by the average person in the street.

An encyclopedia is the result of a massive collaborative effort involving hundreds—sometimes thousands—of scholars, scientists, writers, editors, researchers, artists, designers, and other specialists and generalists. The excellence of any encyclopedia depends largely on the qualifications and experience of its contributors.

In the context of these evaluations, the word *authority* refers to the reputation of the publisher and the qualifications of the work's editors and contributors. An encyclopedia of questionable authority is unlikely to be a source of sound and comprehensive information. A work whose contributors are known to be well versed in their fields is more likely to provide accurate information.

The section begins with a brief history of the encyclopedia under consideration. Most titles currently on the market had their genesis early in this century, although two (NEW ENCYCLOPAEDIA BRITANNICA and THE ENCYCLOPEDIA AMERICANA) date from the eighteenth and nineteenth centuries, while others are of relatively recent origin. In any event, the current edition often reflects the pedigree and reputation of its earlier editions. Times do change, however, and with them, standards. An illustrious history is not necessarily a warranty that quality has been maintained. Thus the review briefly recapitulates the fortunes and misfortunes of the publisher and its encyclopedias, and determines to what extent the encyclopedia's reputation has altered over the years.

The review also examines the credentials of the contributors and whether or not their contributions are likely to be genuinely authoritative. Name recognition is only one of several factors in determining authority. Often a strong editorial staff may make up for the lack of big-name contributors. Professional writers and editors frequently are able to convey the essence of the subject in a clearer, more direct manner—one more appropriate to the needs of the average reader.

Many academics and other well-known figures are very active in writing or otherwise contributing to encyclopedias. However, the prospective buyer should be alert to the occasional instance when an encyclopedia retains well-known authorities simply for the prestige associated with their names. Often such contributors have had little actual input in the work. Signed or initialled articles offer the reader some assurance that the cited authority has, theoretically

at least, read the article before publication and verified its accuracy or made suggestions for revision.

The reader should note whether the encyclopedia relies heavily on corporations, professional organizations, or government agencies for information. Such practices may cause one to doubt the work's objectivity. The reader should also question the authority of the current edition if many of the contributors are deceased.

Currency. Unlike newspapers, magazines, and specialized journals, encyclopedias are not intended to provide newsworthy information. However, an encyclopedia should reflect current understanding of the subjects it covers and include significant recent developments. This is particularly important in entries on contemporary figures, ongoing events, and scientific subjects. For example, where relevant an up-to-date encyclopedia should report the current general economic and political situation in a given nation, the status of research into a deadly disease, or the death of a world leader. Currency is less of a consideration in areas in which facts have been well established and are unlikely to change substantially from one edition to the next, although encyclopedia editors do take into account recent scholarly findings on such subjects as the Elizabethan period, Greek mythology, and the Russian revolution.

Multivolume encyclopedias are revised and reissued annually. The extent of revision varies from publisher to publisher, and the revision may take one of several forms. Some subjects require more revision than others. Knowledge changes rapidly in the sciences and technology. An article that is current when it first appears may be out of date only a few years later. By its very nature, an encyclopedia can never be entirely up-to-date, although online or "electronic" encyclopedias at least have the potential to come close to this goal.

In examining encyclopedias, readers are advised to pay particular attention to three volatile areas in which currency is a major consideration: (1) science, health, and technology; (2) contemporary biography (especially for political figures, creative artists, and entertainers); and (3) politics and international affairs.

At the same time, encyclopedias must be careful not to make sweeping predictions about the future. Although such forecasts might seem reasonable when the encyclopedia is published, they could prove wildly wrong and embarrassing a few years later. While noting any obvious instances of currency or datedness, our reviewers gave special attention to several specific entries. These subjects include, but are not limited to, **AIDS, Woody Allen, Ronald Reagan, South Africa, Soviet Union, space exploration, sports medicine,** *Titanic*, **video cassette, terrorism,** and the role of **women** in contemporary society. We believe that these entries, because of their volatility and the high degree of interest in each, serve as appropriate benchmarks in assessing an encyclopedia's overall currency. Whenever possible, the reviews also note the number of entirely new articles in the current edition as well as the number of articles substantially revised from the previous edition. Examples of new and revised entries are given. When appropriate, the reviews also comment on the currency of the encyclopedia's illustrations, maps, and statistics.

Accuracy. Because they are widely consulted by nonspecialists, encyclopedias have a large responsibility to present information that is accurate. An encyclopedia that is inaccurate has no value other than as a curiosity. Unfortunately, a printed falsehood often acquires the ring of truth, especially when it appears in a reference book. No reference book, no matter how carefully it is edited, is entirely error free. In the course of compiling an encyclopedia, errors and inconsistencies almost invariably find their way into print. Most errors that do occur are the result of the writer's or editor's uncritical acceptance of a piece of information that, on the surface, seems perfectly plausible. The publisher employs researchers, editors, and subject specialists to help ensure the encyclopedia's accuracy. In a well-edited encyclopedia, any errors or inconsistencies will generally be so slight as to be insignificant.

Apart from honest mistakes, other factors may contribute to an encyclopedia's lack of accuracy. These can include oversimplification, generalization, and imprecise writing. A set's currency may also have a direct bearing on its accuracy.

To determine the general accuracy of each encyclopedia reviewed, the Buying Guide has drawn on the expertise of a number of scholars, scientists, and other subject specialists. Each of these individuals read the entries for a particular subject in all the encyclopedias and assessed their accuracy in each. This process also allowed them to make direct comparisons among the different encyclopedias. The entries reviewed for accuracy include **Henry the Navigator**, **Bill of Rights**, **brain**, **money**, **Saturn**, and **transistor**. By assessing these articles, which cover a wide range of subjects, our reviewers were able to glean some idea of each encyclopedia's overall accuracy in the fields of history, geography, biography, natural history and life sciences, and physical sciences, etc. Additionally, our general reviewers made spot-checks and noted any obvious inaccuracies. Captions were also spot-checked, as were population figures and other readily verifiable statistics.

Clarity. Important as accuracy is, accurate information will be of little value if it is poorly organized or explained in terms that are difficult for the reader to understand. Clarity refers to an encyclopedia's readability as well as to the overall quality of its writing and the internal structure of its entries.

To gauge the clarity of an encyclopedia, the prospective purchaser might want to consider whether the writing is sufficiently flexible to explain both simple and complex subjects in an easy-to-understand manner. Does the writing match the complexity of the subject? Part of the key to clarity is consistency in article structure. For example, do the extended articles begin with a general overview of the subject and then move on to consider more complex details? Do subheads divide the articles into well-defined component parts?

In addition to discussing these aspects of clarity, the Buying Guide also describes the general writing style and its benefits and drawbacks. And each review includes an extended quotation from a single entry, *Titanic*, which will allow readers to compare writing style and clarity from one encyclopedia to another. The *Titanic* was chosen as a representative subject of general interest that required the presentation of historical facts, some technical information, and some informed conjecture. In short, it is the sort of entry that can reveal the encyclopedia's ability to convey information clearly.

Objectivity. People consult encyclopedias primarily to learn particular facts and to get background information on specific subjects. These works are intended to inform, not to persuade, the reader; an encyclopedia article is not the same as a newspaper editorial, and serves its purpose only if it presents accurate information without bias.

The responsible encyclopedia editor filters out contributors' biases, whether they are intentional or unconscious. However, when controversy is part of the subject, it should be noted and explained. Clear distinctions should be made among fact, theory, supposition, belief, doctrine, and evidence.

One way to test the objectivity of an encyclopedia is to examine how it deals with controversial or potentially controversial issues. Does it ever take a particular stance on such issues? In dealing with specific political figures and movements, is there a predominantly liberal or conservative tone or subtext? Or is controversy ignored altogether?

Encyclopedias may reflect other types of bias as well. Readers can ask if contributors ever express personal opinions. If so, how does this affect the overall objectivity of a particular article? Are all sides of an issue presented in articles on controversial topics? Or does the set avoid controversy entirely? And finally, are the encyclopedia's illustrations generally objective?

Our reviewers examined a number of entries in each encyclopedia for objectivity. These subjects include **abortion**, **evolution**, **scientific creationism**, **homosexuality**, **South Africa**, and **Andrew Jackson**. Of course, these are not the only subjects that could be used to test objectivity, but they are representative of the kinds of subjects likely to provoke debate. When warranted, the reviews also note instances of exceptional objectivity or bias in other subjects.

Accessibility. Multivolume encyclopedias contain thousands of pages, tens of thousands of entries, and several million words. With all this material, how can the user locate particular information quickly? How easy is it to locate all the information required? Encyclopedias can provide a number of devices for locating information. The preface generally contains information about the set's finding aids. Many sets contain an introductory section on how to use them.

Most important, however, is the index, which helps users who know what they are after but may not know which subject headings to consult. For example, an index might tell the user that information about Marie Curie would be found not only in the entry **Marie Curie** but also in **Nobel Prize**, **physics**, and **radium**. For a variety of reasons, some encyclopedias (notably the single-volume CONCISE COLUMBIA ENCYCLOPEDIA and NEW AMERICAN DESK ENCYCLOPEDIA and the multivolume NEW STANDARD ENCYCLOPEDIA) dispense with indexes altogether, relying instead on cross-references to supply the desired accessibility. Such substitutes may work to varying degrees, but most reference librarians find that a comprehensive index is still the single most useful finding aid.

Cross-references within articles are also important finding aids. For example, an article on **jazz** may contain cross-references to entries on specific jazz musicians. Without these cross-references, the reader might never have known that other entries could contain pertinent additional information.

Layout and design can also enhance—or hinder—accessibility. The reviews tell whether entries are alphabetized word by word or letter by letter and describe any anomalies in alphabetization. They also describe entry headings, running heads, guide words, pagination, the use of subheads, and inconsistencies of structure in similar articles.

Special Features. Virtually all general reference encyclopedias attempt to enhance their usefulness with a number of special features. The significance of these features may vary according to the user's needs and interests. For example, a reader interested in art history may be concerned with the quality of the encyclopedia's art reproductions. The student of history may want to know about the quality of a set's maps and whether historical maps are included.

The special features most commonly found in encyclopedias include illustrations (photographs, art reproductions, drawings, and diagrams); maps; and charts, graphs, and tables. Readers with special needs may want to check the special features before choosing an encyclopedia. Are the illustrations clear? Are they of adequate quality? Are they appropriate to the text they are intended to supplement?

Similarly, are the maps of good quality and will they be helpful to the reader? (The basic criteria that apply to the maps in the Atlas section of the Buying Guide—see pages 152–57—apply to the maps in encyclopedias as well.) Does the encyclopedia make good use of charts, graphs, and tables?

Our reviewers also point out how the special features are related to the encyclopedia's text. Do the features truly enhance the encyclopedia, or are they merely superficial extras designed to give the set a more sophisticated appeal?

Format. However well the contents of an encyclopedia may measure up, the size, number of volumes, or binding durability may be determining factors for the prospective buyer. The reader should decide carefully in advance, for example, whether or not shelf space is available for a larger-size, multivolume, hardcover set, or whether it might be wiser to limit the purchase to a one-volume edition.

Other Opinions. To balance the assessments of our own reviewers, the Buying Guide includes excerpts from reviews that have appeared in review journals, reference book guides, and other pertinent media. Among the sources from which we have drawn are such publications as *Library Journal* and *American Reference Books Annual*. These excerpts are cited without comment, so that the reader may draw independent conclusions from unbiased accounts.

Summary. Each review concludes with a brief summary in which the encyclopedia's major strengths and weaknesses are reviewed. The summary indicates the readership that the encyclopedia would best serve and the type of library in which it would be an asset. A significant feature of the summary is a general comparison of the work with similar, competitive encyclopedias.

Glossary

In the event that users of this guide are unfamiliar with the terms employed in these reviews, the following glossary is provided:

authenticate To establish as being genuine, accurate, and authentic any article or information contained in an encyclopedia.

authenticator A qualified authority responsible for critically examining an article and ensuring its reliability and authenticity.

completely revised edition Any edition of a previous work which has been critically reviewed, authenticated, revised, brought up-to-date, re-edited, and re-set.

consultant An expert or specialist who provides professional advice, reviews an original entry on a specific topic, and makes recommendations to the **editor**. See also **contributor**; **editor**; **authenticator**.

continuous revision The practice of most encyclopedia publishers in which major and minor changes are made in the content of a publication for succeeding printings. Generally, about 10 percent of a work's contents are revised each year.

contributor A person (whether a consultant, freelance specialist or staff writer) who provides written information for inclusion in a text. See also **consultant**; **editor**; **authenticator**.

cross-reference A finding aid (a word or phrase, often in italics or boldface type) that directs the reader to another related entry or article for additional information. An **external or main entry cross-reference** is found as a separate entry in the main alphabetical sequence; it indicates that information on the topic named in the **entry** term is found under another title. An **internal cross-reference** is found within or at the end of an article.

distribution The system by which general reference works are sold. Marketing or merchandising either by mail order, direct sales, retailers, jobbers, or directly from the publisher.

distributor A person or organization that markets or delivers an encyclopedia for a publisher. See also **vendor**.

edition The entire number of copies of a work printed at one time and having the same (unaltered) content. Note the difference between an annually revised "printing" of a work, which may include only minor additions and changes, in contrast to a **completely revised edition**, or a **revised edition**.

editor The person with responsibility for the contents and organization of a written work.

entry A self-contained article, listed under a subject heading (also called the entry word[s] or title) and dealing with that subject.

entry-specific See **specific entry**.

external or main entry cross-reference See **cross-reference**.

general entry An entry that is broadly focused or deals with a large subject (such as an entire historical period rather than a single historical figure). Often lengthy and discursive, general-entry articles may include interpretations of the subject in addition to specific facts.

internal cross-reference See **cross-reference**.

major revision For reference books, an edition which is changed beyond the regularly scheduled programs between printings. (See **continuous revision**.) A major revision requires re-editing, resetting of type, new illustrations, and more extensive inclusion of new material. The resulting work may be referred to as a **new edition**, as opposed to a **completely revised edition** of a work.

minor revision The slight changes in the content of a reference work usually accomplished in regularly scheduled programs between printings. (See **continuous revision**.) These can include correction of typographical errors, facts, figures, or updates of events.

multivolume As used in this Buying Guide, any encyclopedia in which information is presented in three or more separate books or volumes.

new (e.g., "new encyclopedia") An encyclopedia never before offered to the public and freshly composed from original material based on available data but not specifically on any previous publication. Also, an encyclopedia which has been so completely rewritten, redesigned and re-typeset as to be unrecognizably related to any previous work. See also **new edition**.

new edition A work that has been overhauled, beyond the extent of a **minor revision**, but not so extensively as to be described as a **completely revised edition** or a **major revision**. A new edition would contain new material considerably beyond the standard annual **continuous revision** program. These would include, for example, significant reworking of specific subject areas or categories of information (maps, statistics, etc.) from a previous edition.

online encyclopedia electronic database that can be accessed with a personal computer.

ready reference A phrase describing a reference work that provides concise, easily accessible, factual information.

revise To change or edit material in order to improve it. If material in an encyclopedia has been checked and reviewed, and actual changes are made, it has been "revised"; if the material has been checked and no changes are necessary, it has been "authenticated." See **authenticate**.

revised edition A work that has been changed in some way from an earlier edition. These alterations can range from minor corrections in typography, and updating certain facts and figures, to a **completely revised edition** that entails extensive new research and rewriting. See also **major revision**; **continuous revision**; **minor revision**.

small volume As used in this Buying Guide, any encyclopedia in which information is presented in two or fewer separate books or volumes.

specific entry Refers to an entry that focuses on a single, narrow subject or on a single aspect of a broader subject (such as one historical figure rather than a historical period). Usually concise rather than discursive, entry-specific articles concentrate on the main facts related to the subject.

up-to-date The timeliness or degree of currency of an encyclopedia. Generally, a minimum of 10 percent of the material contained within an encyclopedia should undergo a thorough revision or review in order to be considered current. This is often accomplished through the annual **continuous revision** process.

vendor The service or organization that carries **online encyclopedias** and other electronic databases and communications via computer for subscribers.

Chapter 6
Evaluations of Encyclopedias

Academic American

Facts at a Glance

Full Title: **Academic American Encyclopedia.**
Publisher: Grolier Incorporated.
Editors: Bernard S. Cayne, Editorial Director; K. Anne Ranson, Editor-in-Chief.
Edition Reviewed: 1987. (Statistics apply to 1988 edition.)

Number of Volumes: 21.
Number of Contributors: 2,325.
Number of Entries: 28,700.
Number of Pages: 9,744.
Number of Words: 9,040,000.
Number of Maps: 1,080.
Number of Cross-references: 67,000.
Number of Indexes: 1.
Number of Index Entries: 200,000.
Number of Illustrations: 12,550 color; 4,180 black-and-white.
Trim Size: 8" × 10".

Price: $850 plus shipping and handling for individuals; $650 plus shipping and handling with library discount.
Sold directly by the publisher and door-to-door.
ISBN 0-7172-2016-8.
Revised annually.

I. Introduction

The *Academic American Encyclopedia* is a 21-volume work designed, according to the publisher, to meet four criteria: (1) to provide quick access to definitive factual information; (2) to provide a readily intelligible general overview of a subject that does not compel the reader to grasp intricate subtleties or wade through a drawn out historical analysis; (3) to give readers a starting point for further research by isolating key concepts, outlining the structure of a subject, and directing the reader to more specialized primary and secondary goals; and (4) to help readers visualize or recognize people, places, objects, and processes by means of maps, photographs, and drawings.

This review is based on an examination of the 1987 edition; the 1988 edition was not available at the time of review.

II. Scope

Academic American contains 28,600 articles, the majority of which are of the specific-entry type. More than half of the content is presented in articles that are less than 500 words long.

As an indication of how space is apportioned among different subjects, **Charlemagne** receives about one and one-sixth pages, while **Konstantin Chernenko** is covered in approximately one-fourth of a page. **Ray Charles** is treated in 11 lines, as is **Ty Cobb** (although his entry is accompanied by a photograph). The U.S. **Civil War** is discussed in 19 pages; the entry for **Christianity** is about two pages long; and **China** is the subject of a ten-page article (including a two-page map). Readers should note, however, that the **history of China** is treated as a separate article (nearly seven and one-half pages long). Indeed, because *Academic American* is an entry-specific work, individual aspects of a broad topic are generally covered

Academic American

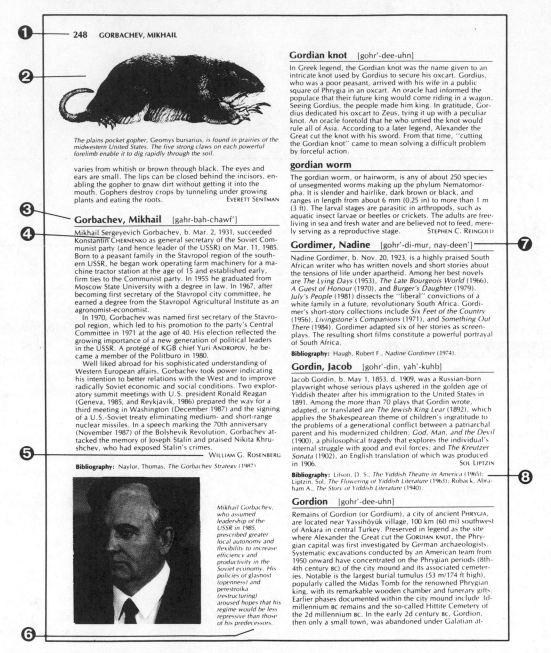

① **248** GORBACHEV, MIKHAIL

The plains pocket gopher, Geomys bursarius, is found in prairies of the midwestern United States. The five strong claws on each powerful forelimb enable it to dig rapidly through the soil.

varies from whitish or brown through black. The eyes and ears are small. The lips can be closed behind the incisors, enabling the gopher to gnaw dirt without getting it into the mouth. Gophers destroy crops by tunneling under growing plants and eating the roots. EVERETT SENTMAN

Gorbachev, Mikhail [gahr-bah-chawf']

Mikhail Sergeyevich Gorbachev, b. Mar. 2, 1931, succeeded Konstantin CHERNENKO as general secretary of the Soviet Communist party (and hence leader of the USSR) on Mar. 11, 1985. Born to a peasant family in the Stavropol region of the southern USSR, he began work operating farm machinery for a machine tractor station at the age of 15 and established early, firm ties to the Communist party. In 1955 he graduated from Moscow State University with a degree in law. In 1967, after becoming first secretary of the Stavropol city committee, he earned a degree from the Stavropol Agricultural Institute as an agronomist-economist.

In 1970, Gorbachev was named first secretary of the Stavropol region, which led to his promotion to the party's Central Committee in 1971 at the age of 40. His election reflected the growing importance of a new generation of political leaders in the USSR. A protégé of KGB chief Yuri ANDROPOV, he became a member of the Politburo in 1980.

Well liked abroad for his sophisticated understanding of Western European affairs, Gorbachev took power indicating his intention to better relations with the West and to improve radically Soviet economic and social conditions. Two exploratory summit meetings with U.S. president Ronald Reagan (Geneva, 1985, and Reykjavik, 1986) prepared the way for a third meeting in Washington (December 1987) and the signing of a U.S.-Soviet treaty eliminating medium- and short-range nuclear missiles. In a speech marking the 70th anniversary (November 1987) of the Bolshevik Revolution, Gorbachev attacked the memory of Joseph Stalin and praised Nikita Khrushchev, who had exposed Stalin's crimes.
WILLIAM G. ROSENBERG

Bibliography: Naylor, Thomas, *The Gorbachev Strategy* (1987)

Mikhail Gorbachev, who assumed leadership of the USSR in 1985, prescribed greater local autonomy and flexibility to increase efficiency and productivity in the Soviet economy. His policies of glasnost (openness) and perestroika (restructuring) aroused hopes that his regime would be less repressive than those of his predecessors.

Gordian knot [gohr'-dee-uhn]

In Greek legend, the Gordian knot was the name given to an intricate knot used by Gordius to secure his oxcart. Gordius, who was a poor peasant, arrived with his wife in a public square of Phrygia in an oxcart. An oracle had informed the populace that their future king would come riding in a wagon. Seeing Gordius, the people made him king. In gratitude, Gordius dedicated his oxcart to Zeus, tying it up with a peculiar knot. An oracle foretold that he who untied the knot would rule all of Asia. According to a later legend, Alexander the Great cut the knot with his sword. From that time, "cutting the Gordian knot" came to mean solving a difficult problem by forceful action.

gordian worm

The gordian worm, or hairworm, is any of about 250 species of unsegmented worms making up the phylum Nematomorpha. It is slender and hairlike, dark brown or black, and ranges in length from about 6 mm (0.25 in) to more than 1 m (3 ft). The larval stages are parasitic in arthropods, such as aquatic insect larvae or beetles or crickets. The adults are free-living in sea and fresh water and are believed not to feed, merely serving as a reproductive stage. STEPHEN C. REINGOLD

Gordimer, Nadine [gohr'-di-mur, nay-deen'] **⑦**

Nadine Gordimer, b. Nov. 20, 1923, is a highly praised South African writer who has written novels and short stories about the tensions of life under apartheid. Among her best novels are *The Lying Days* (1953), *The Late Bourgeois World* (1966), *A Guest of Honour* (1970), and *Burger's Daughter* (1979). *July's People* (1981) dissects the "liberal" convictions of a white family in a future, revolutionary South Africa. Gordimer's short-story collections include *Six Feet of the Country* (1956), *Livingstone's Companions* (1971), and *Something Out There* (1984). Gordimer adapted six of her stories as screenplays. The resulting short films constitute a powerful portrayal of South Africa.

Bibliography: Haugh, Robert F., *Nadine Gordimer* (1974).

Gordin, Jacob [gohr'-din, yah'-kuhb]

Jacob Gordin, b. May 1, 1853, d. 1909, was a Russian-born playwright whose serious plays ushered in the golden age of Yiddish theater after his immigration to the United States in 1891. Among the more than 70 plays that Gordin wrote, adapted, or translated are *The Jewish King Lear* (1892), which applies the Shakespearean theme of children's ingratitude to the problems of a generational conflict between a patriarchal parent and his modernized children; *God, Man, and the Devil* (1900), a philosophical tragedy that explores the individual's internal struggle with good and evil forces; and *The Kreutzer Sonata* (1902), an English translation of which was produced in 1906. SOL LIPTZIN

Bibliography: Lifson, D. S., *The Yiddish Theatre in America* (1965); **⑧** Liptzin, Sol, *The Flowering of Yiddish Literature* (1963); Roback, Abraham A., *The Story of Yiddish Literature* (1940).

Gordion [gohr'-dee-uhn]

Remains of Gordion (or Gordium), a city of ancient PHRYGIA, are located near Yassihöyük village, 100 km (60 mi) southwest of Ankara in central Turkey. Preserved in legend as the site where Alexander the Great cut the GORDIAN KNOT, the Phrygian capital was first investigated by German archaeologists. Systematic excavations conducted by an American team from 1950 onward have concentrated on the Phrygian periods (8th–4th century BC) of the city mound and its associated cemeteries. Notable is the largest burial tumulus (53 m/174 ft high), popularly called the Midas Tomb for the renowned Phrygian king, with its remarkable wooden chamber and funerary gifts. Earlier phases documented within the city mound include 3d-millennium BC remains and the so-called Hittite Cemetery of the 2d millennium BC. In the early 2d century BC, Gordion, then only a small town, was abandoned under Galatian at-

Page shown at 67% of actual size.

① Page number and guide words
② Illustration: Academic American includes 16,730 illustrations, of which 75 percent are in color.
③ Main entry: Academic American contains 28,700 entries, arranged alphabetically, word-by-word. A rule separates the entry title from the article itself.
④ Cross-reference: Academic American contains 67,000 cross-references, printed in capital letters.
⑤ Contributor's credit: Academic American has 2,325 contributors. Seventy-five percent of all articles are signed.
⑥ Caption: Captions in Academic American often add to the information presented in the main text.
⑦ Pronunciation: Foreign or other difficult entry words are followed by phonetic pronunciation.
⑧ Bibliography: More than 40 percent of Academic American's articles include a bibliography.

under separate entries. At the same time, however, there is often a good deal of overlap among different articles. For example, both **space exploration** and **space shuttle** present information about the shuttle, the *Challenger* disaster, and its effects on the American space program.

The publisher has provided the following breakdown of total space allocated to different subject areas: humanities and the arts, 36 percent; science and technology, 35 percent; social science, 14 percent; geography, 13 percent; sports and contemporary life, 2 percent. Thirty-five percent of all entries are biographical, although the percentage of actual pages is much smaller.

Academic American was originally compiled in the United States under the aegis of a Dutch publisher, and its content was written primarily for North American readers. Moreover, as the Preface notes, "the list of entries (and their lengths) reflects the curriculum of American schools and universities." The publisher also remarks, however, that articles on general topics "grant appropriate recognition to the diversity of practice throughout the world." As an indication of the attention given to non-American subjects, a section chosen at random (Volume 7, pages 102–135) includes the following entries: **Elat** (Israeli town), **Elba**, **Elbe River**, **Mount Elbrus**, **Elburz Mountains**, **Elche** (Spanish city), **Eleanor of Aquitaine**, **Eleatic School**, **Electra** (mythology), **Electra** (play), **Elegy Written in a Country Churchyard**, **Elephanta** (island in Bombay harbor), **Eleusinian Mysteries**, **Eleusis**. Note that these amount to only 14 entries out of 93 in this page span. The majority of other entries in this segment are devoted to scientific, technical, or natural subjects that have no particular national orientation. Indeed, this is the pattern for the entire *Academic American*. In general, entries for foreign places and people tend to be brief.

III. Authority

Academic American is the newest encyclopedia on the market; in fact, it is the only adult encyclopedia now in print to have been created since the advent of COLLIER'S ENCYCLOPEDIA in the 1950s.

The set was originally published in Princeton, New Jersey, by the Arete Publishing Company, an American subsidiary of the Dutch publishing conglomerate VNU. The encyclopedia was Arete's first production. *Academic American* has the distinction of being the first set to make use of computer technology in planning, editing, and revising an encyclopedia. This allows the publisher to revise the set quickly and at less expense. Most other encyclopedia publishers have since followed Arete's lead.

As noted, *Academic American* was designed specifically for the American market and is not based on any previous encyclopedia, foreign or domestic. The encyclopedia's editorial staff was American, and the contributors were drawn mainly from American universities. Upon publication, the first edition met with general acclaim for accuracy, currency, and objectivity.

In 1982 the set was acquired by the well-known Connecticut-based publisher Grolier, which also publishes THE ENCYCLOPEDIA AMERICANA. As its title implies, *Academic American* is the product of extensive scholarship. Some 2,300 contributors, many of whom are internationally known authorities in their fields, were drawn mainly from American universities. In addition, the list of entries was prepared by a board of 25 distinguished scholars and other prominent authorities. The editorial staff works under the direction of Bernard S. Cayne, Grolier's Editorial Director, and K. Anne Ranson, the Editor-in-Chief, who served as a Supervisory Editor of the first edition. All in all, the credentials of the contributors appear impeccable; the authority of the *Academic American* appears to be of the highest quality.

IV. Currency

As a fairly new encyclopedia, *Academic American* has an automatic advantage over older encyclopedias in terms of currency. It is revised annually. The 1987 edition features a revision rate of about 11 percent of the total text pages, plus the entire index. More than 130 new articles were added; 55 were replaced; and another 170 received major revision. According to the publisher, "less extensive but nonetheless significant" revisions were made in 1,270 other articles.

As a result of this process, *Academic American* is extremely up-to-date. Most entries on volatile topics include important developments through the end of 1986. For example, the article on **AIDS** includes information about the antiviral drug AZT, which was approved for the treatment of AIDS patients late in 1986. The article also notes that "the first U.S. hospital devoted solely to AIDS treatment and research opened in Houston, Tex., in 1986."

The **South Africa** entry mentions the new constitution of 1984 as well as the abolition of the pass laws and the declaration of a state of emergency in 1986. The article ends with the general comment: "An international campaign to impose economic sanctions against South Africa and encourage foreign-owned businesses to halt investment there gained momentum."

The entry on **Ronald Reagan** was virtually up-to-the-minute at the time the 1987 edition of *Academic American* was published. The article mentions his approval (October 1986) of the tax reform measure, the Iceland summit meeting with Mikhail Gorbachev (also October 1986), and the Democrats' capture of the Senate in the November elections. The article concludes with the statement that "shortly after [the election], Reagan and his aides were embroiled in controversy over revelations of secret arms sales to Iran, some of the profits of which were diverted to the Nicaraguan 'contras.' " **Nicaragua** includes the 1984 election of Daniel Ortega Saavedra and the Reagan administration's support of the contras. The article ends by saying that "Efforts by four Latin American nations . . . to mediate a regional peace settlement made little progress, and no end to the civil conflict or resolution of U.S.-Nicaraguan differences was in sight."

Academic American's coverage of **terrorism** is fairly up-to-date but concentrates on the legal definition and political implications of terrorism rather than on its history. Relatively few specific terrorist incidents are mentioned; the most recent occurred in 1985.

A four-page article on **women in society** reflects contemporary trends and attitudes.

The article **space shuttle** contains three paragraphs that discuss the January 1986 *Challenger* explosion, the inquiry into the disaster, and the possible consequences for the United States space program. Additionally, *Academic American* contains biographical entries for each of the seven crew members killed in the explosion. Other new biographical entries in the 1987 edition include **Corazon Aquino**, **Jerry Falwell**, **Lee Iacocca**, **Jack Kemp**, **Neil Kinnock**, **Daniel Ortega Saavedra**, and **Manuel Puig**.

Academic American also includes up-to-date entries dealing with many aspects of contemporary technology. Among these are an extensive (five-page) article on **video**, plus a number of related topics including **music video**, **video art**, **video camera**, **video display terminal**, **video game**, **video recording**, **video technology**, **videodisc**, **videotape**, and **videotex**. There are also entries on the **compact disc** and **digital technology** as well as for such computer-related subjects as **personal computer**, **computer-aided design** and **computer-aided manufacturing**, **computer crime**, **computer graphics**, the **computer industry**, **computer languages**, **computer memory**, **computer modeling**, **computer networking**, **computer software**, and **computers and privacy**.

For the 1987 edition of *Academic American*, such articles as **common cold**, **computer**, **depression**, **history of Europe**, and **Halley's comet** were entirely rewritten (or replaced by new articles on these subjects) in order to reflect more recent knowledge or revised views. A new article on the **Vietnam War** "reflects the changed perspective that the passage of time has allowed," in the words of the publisher.

Entirely new subject entries include **Chernobyl**, **computers in education**, **childhood diseases**, **literary modernism**, **privatization**, **Progressive Era**, and **Vietnam Veterans Memorial**.

In addition to its up-to-date text, *Academic American* also features an exceptionally up-to-date illustration program. Among new photographs included in the 1987 edition are those of Corazon Aquino, P. W. Botha, the Supreme Court (with new justice Antonin Scalia), the *Challenger* explosion, and Halley's comet. Moreover, *Academic American*'s photographs, apart from those of specifically historical interest, are not dated in any manner. Like its text, the illustrations in *Academic American* are as up-to-date as those in any general multivolume encyclopedia currently on the market.

V. Accuracy

More so than any of its competitors, *Academic American* is geared to the presentation of fact; there is very little speculative or discursive material. The publisher asserts that in order to ensure the encyclopedia's accuracy, "a large team of research editors— all specialists in their field—verified every fact, inference, and conclusion against primary and other authoritative sources in several of the world's largest libraries. . . . "

Academic American is the only encyclopedia reviewed in the Buying Guide that does not succumb to the popular and erroneous claim that **Henry the Navigator** established a school of navigation at Sagres, nor does it depict him as a beneficent patron of Portuguese explorers. Rather, it acknowledges that "his explorations were motivated as much by hatred of the Muslims and hunger for gold as they were by the desire for geographical knowledge."

Our subject specialists also remarked on the high degree of accuracy in most of the articles they examined. **Bill of Rights** includes useful summaries of the first ten amendments, although it does not mention the important concept of "incorporation." The well-written entry on **money**, contributed by a prominent economist, is concise and touches on most aspects of the subject that one would expect in an adult presentation. The article on the **brain** is accurate, although many readers will find it overly technical. The entry does not deal with **cognitive psychology**, **memory**, **perception**, or **problem solving**, but each of these is the subject of a separate article. The entry on **Saturn** is concise and detailed and is careful to note that in astronomy, measurements are not absolute but relative. **Transistors** has an excellent description of how transistors work. There are cross-references to related entries on **semiconductors**, **electron tubes**, **integrated circuits**, and **microelectronics**.

VI. Clarity

A number of critics have claimed that *Academic American*'s text is too advanced for the average user, whether student or adult. (See *Other Opinions*.) Sentences tend to be long, syntax is often unnecessarily complex, and difficult or unusual terms are not always explained in context. These problems are particularly evident in articles on scientific or technical subjects.

A few examples will illustrate. The first sentence in the article **solar system** reads: "The solar system is the group of celestial bodies, including the Earth, orbiting around and gravitationally bound by the star known as the SUN, one of at least a hundred billion stars in our galaxy." In the following sentence, the planets are described as "the Sun's retinue." The first sentence in **electron** reads: "The electron is often described as a particle of ELECTRICITY, a definition that reflects its role as a piece of matter and suggests its relationship to electrical phenomena."

Entries on highly technical subjects also make extensive use of acronyms, formulas, and jargon. Although these are usually explained, they are nonetheless often presented at a level that requires a college-level mastery of the subject. Mathematical and chemical formulas are strewn profusely through such articles. Again, they require the reader to have a fundamental grasp of the discipline and of the terminology used in that discipline and will be of limited use to the average reference book user. For example, the third paragraph of the article on the **electron** quoted above reads as follows:

> Modern measurements have determined the mass of the electron to be 9.1083×10^{-28} grams, about 1/1836 of the mass of the proton. The charge is 4.80×10^{-10} electrostatic units, or 1.60×10^{-19} coulombs. Even more useful to scientists is the ratio of charge to mass, e/m, since this term appears in many calculations. Its value is 1.759×10^{11} coulombs/kg.

While this information may indeed be important to an understanding of the electron, it is presented in a way that is beyond the grasp of the average reader who has little or no previous knowledge of the subject.

The article on the **Titanic**, quoted in its entirety, illustrates the style of a typical (and less technical) entry in *Academic American*:

Titanic [ty-tan' -ik]
The *Titanic*, a British passenger liner, struck an iceberg off Newfoundland on the night of Apr. 14–15, 1912, and sank. The ship, the largest and most luxurious built up to that time, was on its maiden voyage from Southampton to New York, carrying more than 2,200 people; about 1,500 drowned.

Official inquiries determined that the *Titanic* was traveling too fast for the known icy conditions; it rammed the iceberg at a speed of 22 knots (41 km/h; 25 mph). The large loss of life was partly because of the failure of a nearby ship, the *Californian*, to respond to the distress signals, and the insufficient number of lifeboats

on the *Titanic*. The shipwreck, considered by contemporaries the worst in history, prompted international agreements to improve safety procedures at sea. The sunken vessel was located by a team of U.S. and French researchers, using a remote-control submarine, in 1985.

VII. Objectivity

The editors of the *Academic American Encyclopedia* acknowledge that "scholars may differ among themselves even on questions that do not involve social policy." One of the functions of the encyclopedia, therefore, is "to reflect those differences and to consider alternative theories or interpretation as well as opposing points of view. . . ." On the whole, the encyclopedia achieves this aim.

Occasionally, however, *Academic American*'s bias toward scientific and technical subjects affects not only the extent of its coverage of such subjects but also the tone and point of view inherent in this coverage. For example, in its treatment of the evolution-creationism debate, *Academic American* cannot be considered strictly objective. The extensive entry on **evolution** contends that "Exactly how evolution occurs is still a matter of debate, but that it occurs is a scientific fact. . . . It is plausible that all organisms can be traced back to the origin of life from inanimate matter." Similarly, the article on **prehistoric humans** declares that "the human species . . . is related, in descending order of closeness, to apes, monkeys, tarsiers, and lemurs." A much shorter entry on **creationism** notes fundamentalists' objections to evolution and their efforts to mandate the teaching of creationism in public schools. The article distinguishes between religious and scientific grounds for creationism, and notes that " 'creation science' papers . . . have also been reviewed by established scientific journals and rejected for lack of scientific coherency and documentation."

Academic American's discussion of **abortion** is generally objective. The article is broken down into four subsections, which treat "Medical Aspects," "Legal Aspects," "Impact of Legalization," and "Ethical Aspects." This last section briefly recapitulates contemporary arguments both for and against abortion.

The discussion of the history of the **Bill of Rights** takes a somewhat dismissive and sectarian tone in discussing the Federalist argument against the necessity for such a bill.

The two-and-one-quarter-page article on **Andrew Jackson** is evenhanded, neither ignoring nor sensationalizing the controversy that surrounded his political career. He is fairly described as "a man of strong convictions, iron will, and fiery temperament." The main facts relating to his presidency are presented in a straightforward and objective manner.

VIII. Accessibility

The *Academic American* is generally well designed and contains a number of basic finding aids that should make it readily accessible to the average intended user. The Preface, located at the front of Volume 1, describes the set's organization and the different elements involved. However, unlike most other general multivolume encyclopedias reviewed in the Buying Guide, it does not give specific instructions on how to use the set.

Entries are arranged alphabetically, word by word. Names beginning with *Mc* are treated as though they began with *Mac*; the same rule applies to the use of the abbreviation *St.* for *Saint*.

Page numbers are located at the top of each page, flush with the outside margin. Guide words indented from the page numbers indicate the first entry on the left-hand page and the last entry on the right-hand page.

Article headings are printed in 10-point boldface type. A rule separates the heading from the article text.

The main key to *Academic American*'s accessibility is its index, which contains more than 200,000 entries and occupies all of Volume 21. A "Guide to the Use of This Encyclopedia" at the front of the index describes the index's features and explains how to use it. As an indication of the scope and style of individual entries, the reader searching for information about Marie Curie will find the following index entry:

> **CURIE, MARIE AND PIERRE 4:**328
> *illus.*; **5:**391–392 *bibliog.*,
> *illus.*; **15:**286 *illus.*
> polonium **15:**417
> radioactivity **16:**60–61 *illus.*
> radium **16:**68

The set's accessibility is further enhanced by some 67,000 cross-references. These are of three types: cross-reference entries; cross-references within article text, which are printed in small capital letters; and "See also" references that occur at the ends of articles. Both the index and the cross-references are well designed and serve to tie together separate articles on related subjects—particularly crucial in a specific-entry encyclopedia.

IX. Special Features

Of its several special features, *Academic American* has been most highly praised for the excellence of its illustrations. Fully three-quarters of its more than 16,000 illustrations are in color. Among its competitors, only WORLD BOOK, with 29,000 illustrations, can boast a more extensive illustration program.

Altogether, *Academic American*'s photographs, maps, and commissioned artwork occupy one-third of the set's available editorial space. The editors' use of illustrations reflects great care and creativity. The publisher claims that "many of the major articles are so profusely illustrated and extensively captioned that the reader will acquire a basic comprehension of the subject as well as considerable factual information by studying the illustrations and captions alone." While this statement may be dismissed as advertising hyperbole, it is not totally without merit. Very few of the illustrations can be characterized as dull; most are stimulating and will lead to a greater understanding of the subject they illustrate. The publisher's claim that "each [illustration] was carefully selected to explain, support, or expand ideas in the text" is borne out by an examination of the set.

Photographs of individuals have been carefully selected. The publisher notes that "whenever possible the traditional postage-stamp-size 'mug shot' was avoided, and photos that reveal more of the subject's personality were selected." This claim too is generally true.

In addition to excellent photographs, *Academic American* also makes extensive use of commissioned drawings and diagrams. The full-color drawings that accompany many of the entries on specific mammals and birds are particularly outstanding. Readers will also find the full-color illustrations of various aircraft quite useful. Anatomical and technical drawings throughout the encyclopedia are similarly distinguished.

Photographs and drawings alike are supported by captions that not only identify the illustration they accompany but also often provide information not found in the main text. Moreover, the captions often reinforce the text. For example, the caption accompanying the photograph of a sailplane for the article **glider** reads: "The long, thin wings of a glider, or sailplane, enable the craft to remain aloft by soaring on rising air currents. Gliders, the first heavier-than-air vehicles to achieve sustained flight, are flown today both for recreation and as a competitive sport." Captions that accompany technical drawings and cross-section diagrams frequently identify and explain various numbered elements in the illustration.

Academic American contains over 1,000 maps covering all the continents and countries of the world, all U.S. states and Canadian provinces, and nearly 50 of the world's major cities. In addition, there are hundreds of historical and thematic maps. In their clarity, currency, and accuracy of detail, the maps in *Academic American* (created by the cartographers of Rand McNally, R. R. Donnelley Cartographic, Lothar Roth and Associates, and the Arete/Grolier staff) are second to none.

Standardized "fact boxes" accompany entries on individual nations, states, Canadian provinces, and U.S. presidents, presenting important statistical and general information on the subject. These features are well designed and up-to-date. Tables, graphs, and lists accompany other entries where pertinent, providing the reader with an accessible source of basic information.

Foreign or difficult entry words are immediately followed by a phonetic pronunciation. *Academic American* uses a pronunciation system similar to that used by *Time* magazine. For example, the pronunciation for **Agamemnon** is given as *ag-uh-mem'-nahn*; the pronunciation for **Gibraltar** is given as *juh-brawl'-tur*.

Selected bibliographies accompany about 40 percent of all entries. According to the editors, the bibliographies are intended "to furnish a well-chosen list of standard and recently published works to which readers may turn for further information or additional development of particular points of view. Leading textbooks, paperbacks, and recordings are included, as well as occasional periodical references." However, the editors note that "we have not attempted, especially in science, to furnish the most definitive work in the field if, in our opinion, that work would be well beyond the comprehension of the intended reader. . . . [E]very effort has been made to refer to books currently in print." In general, the bibliographies are up-to-date and diverse. However, as they are not annotated, the reader cannot tell which titles might be most appropriate to his or her needs.

X. Format

The 21-volume *Academic American Encyclopedia* comes in one print format and in several electronic formats. (For information on the electronic formats, see pages 70–74). Like the NEW STANDARD ENCYCLOPEDIA and WORLD BOOK, among others, volumes in *Academic American* are arranged by letter. That is (with the exception of entries beginning with A, C, and S, which are spread over two volumes each), entries for each letter are contained within a single volume. Some volumes contain all the entries for two, three, or four letters.

The typeface is also worthy of comment. Apart from FUNK & WAGNALLS NEW ENCYCLOPEDIA, *Academic American* is the only encyclopedia to use a sans serif typeface, which has a lighter, more functional look than the traditional typefaces used by other encyclopedias. Some readers, however, find this typeface more difficult to read. The relatively small 8-on-9-point type size may also discourage readers with impaired vision. Apart from WORLD BOOK, *Academic American* is the only encyclopedia to use a "ragged," rather than a justified, right-hand margin.

Each volume is bound in a durable blue and red McCain Sewn, Lexotone binding that should stand up well to frequent use. The paper quality is good. The encyclopedia's title and the volume number and letter are stamped in gold lettering on the spine and front of each volume. The entire set takes up slightly more than two feet of horizontal shelf space.

XI. Other Opinions

ARBA 81 (Janet H. Littlefield): "[*Academic American*] features higher coverage of the sciences than other general encyclopedias. . . . Orientation of the encyclopedia is international, stressing coverage of Asia, Africa, and South America, as well as North America and Europe. Coverage of geography, especially, is less than in other encyclopedias, necessitating the elimination of many smaller American cities from consideration."

College and Research Libraries, January 1982 (Wendy Pradt Lougee): "*Academic American Encyclopedia* . . . appears to have a competitive edge in terms of currency, contemporary biography, and graphics. It is well researched, well written, and a strikingly attractive set. In comparison to similar multivolume encyclopedias, *AAE* is noticeably more compact. . . . it [is] particularly appropriate for library 'ready reference' collections. . . . The text has a reasonable level of technical and scholarly sophistication, but maintains accessibility as well. . . . Clearly the articles can best serve as aids in definition and as starting places for further investigation. Although *AAE*'s brevity may fail to capture adequately the nuances that only length can bring to a subject, its format does provide quick and easy access to concise information. One must rely, however, on the index and textual cross-references to maintain the integrity of the overall coverage of a topic."

Wilson Library Journal, February 1982 (James Rettig): "*Academic American*'s strengths are its currency, its accessibility, and its graphics. . . . No other English-language, general encyclopedia has graphics comparable to [*AAE*'s]. . . . For ready-reference and fact-finding purposes, *Academic American* is the best of the general encyclopedias. However, as a source for broad industry information or as an overview on any but the narrowest subjects, others—notably BRITANNICA, AMERICANA, and COLLIER'S—are superior even if not as current. . . . Public and academic libraries should have this [set] to complement other encyclopedias."

Library Journal, May 15, 1982: "The *AAE* is a superior, short-article encyclopedia. The *AAE*'s strengths are its objective treatment of controversial subjects, its coverage of science, and its articles on contemporary people and events. The *AAE*'s more than 16,000 photographs, maps, diagrams, and drawings, plus its general layout, make it the most visually pleasing general encyclopedia on the market. . . . Librarians will find it useful for ready reference questions."

ARBA 84 (G. Edward Evans): "None of the other encyclopedias packs as much information into as little space as does *AAE*. . . . Brevity does have a price, however, and [the user] certainly would have to consult other encyclopedias to get a full sense of interrelationships within an area. Users may decide it is better to start with longer articles, such as those in AMERICANA, WORLD BOOK, or COLLIER'S, than to begin with *AAE* and then move on to those other encyclopedias before getting to primary sources. . . . Overall, *AAE* is a sound purchase for . . . undergraduate libraries for use as a ready-reference tool. It cannot be thought of as a replacement for WORLD BOOK, AMERICANA, or COLLIER'S . . . but rather as a supplement to these works. It is a good buy for the money, but it does need to be used with caution."

Booklist (*Reference Books Bulletin*), November 15, 1986: "Because of its recent creation . . . and since it is supported by Grolier's aggressive revision program, *AAE* is one of the most up-to-date encyclopedias in the world. . . . It is hard to find an area where *AAE* is not up-to-date. . . . Because *AAE* is such a new encyclopedia, it is not burdened with a legacy of dated photographs. . . . *Academic American Encyclopedia* remains one of the best English-language encyclopedias for . . . college and adult use. If Grolier continues its program of updating the accurate, excellently illustrated contents, this encyclopedia will be one of the premier works of its kind for many years to come."

XII. Summary

The newest multivolume encyclopedia on the market, and the first to use computer technology in storing and collating information and in typesetting, *Academic American* garners top honors as an up-to-date source of basic factual information. It covers many topics of contemporary interest not included in other encyclopedias, and with noteworthy accuracy. In short, *Academic American* is an outstanding ready-reference encyclopedia, especially in its coverage of science, technology, and contemporary biography.

Many users will find that the science entries are written at too advanced a level to be helpful to the average layperson. However, reference librarians will find it an excellent source of ready-reference answers to specific questions from patrons. The set will be particularly valuable in the reference departments of academic libraries as well as in corporate and other institutional libraries where there is frequent need for a good ready-reference encyclopedia. It is highly factual, accurate, current, and objective, and its outstanding illustrations and maps are a decided plus.

Academic American is not a direct competitor to any other encyclopedia now on the market. Its entries are briefer and less discursive than those in COLLIER'S ENCYCLOPEDIA, THE ENCYCLOPEDIA AMERICANA, and NEW ENCYCLOPAEDIA BRITANNICA. At the same time, its reading level is more difficult than that of WORLD BOOK, although it is visually similar. The prospective purchaser's decision may depend on whether a good "support" encyclopedia is needed to supplement a main encyclopedia. *Academic American*'s excellent coverage of science and technology topics and its currency may be deciding factors. *Academic American* costs $850 to individuals and $650 to institutions—a reasonable price at current market rates.

Individuals wishing to purchase *Academic American* may contact the publisher, Grolier Incorporated, at Sherman Turnpike, Danbury, CT 06816, or telephone (800) 243-7256. Libraries should address their orders to Grolier Educational Corporation at the same address or phone number.

For information about the online and CD-ROM versions of *Academic American*, consult the reviews that follow.

Academic American (online)

Facts at a Glance

Full Title: **Academic American Encyclopedia** (online version).
Publisher: Grolier Incorporated.
Editors: Bernard S. Cayne, Editorial Director; K. Anne Ranson, Editor-in-Chief.
Online Vendors: Bibliographic Retrieval Services; CompuServe; Dialog; Dow Jones News/ Retrieval; IHS Online; InfoMaster; QuantumLink; Startext; The Source; VU/ TEXT.
Copyright: 1987.

Number of Entries: 28,700.
Number of Words: over 9,000,000.
Number of Cross-references: over 67,000.
No index in online version.

Price: Each online service has its own pricing structure. In general, *Academic American* is offered either on a subscription basis or at an hourly royalty rate.
Revised quarterly.

I. Introduction

The online version of the *Academic American Encyclopedia* contains the same text as recent editions of the print version, so the two are closely similar in their contents and approach. (For fuller information, see the review that begins on page 63). But the online version does not include any of the finding devices, notably the index, of the print version. Nor does it include any of the print edition's many illustrations.

II. Accessibility

The online version of *Academic American* is carried by several vendors of online database services, including Bibliographic Retrieval Services, CompuServe, Dialog Information Services, Dow Jones News/Retrieval, and VU/TEXT Information Services. It is also available through services that package access to the vendors, such as InfoMaster (a feature of Western Union's EasyLink), which was used to conduct this review. The user cannot access *Academic American* directly, and without direct access the user's experience of the encyclopedia will depend somewhat on the interface provided by the particular vendor. Some are probably a bit swifter or more flexible than others. For example, BRS, Dialog, VU/TEXT, and The Source all provide full-text searching. The Source also allows users to search by article headings alone. The other services that carry *Academic American* online permit searching by partial or full article headings only. This is the case with InfoMaster.

Accessing information in the *Academic American* usually entails the following steps:

Section I
1. Boot system
2. Load communications program
3. Dial vendor or service
4. Connect, give user ID
5. (Select vendor if a service is used)

Section II
1. Select database
2. Select topic
3. Conduct database search
4. Display text
5. Respond to prompt for next action

With InfoMaster, the final choice takes the user all the way back to II.1, reasonably supposing that the next search may require a different database. The time required between a "hit"(a match between the search string and an entry in the database) and the text display depends on the length of the entry: the lengthier entries take considerably longer. Even for a short entry such as **Ty Cobb**, however, section II takes about two minutes. Section I takes about three minutes, so from cold boot to display of the entry can take at least five minutes, by which time the user is as grouchy as dour old baseball titan Cobb—and with far fewer hits to show for it. However, the reader should note that other online/videotex networks may allow a more expeditious search than is possible with InfoMaster.

III. Locating Information

The index that occupies all of Volume 21 of the print *Academic American* and is crucially important to an entry-specific encyclopedia such as this one is not available in the online version. Rather, with services that do not allow full-text searching, the user locates information on a given topic by searching for the entry title, in effect attempting to reconstruct the table of contents verbatim by guesswork. A search for **Ménière's disease** was unsuccessful when it tried "Ménière" as the search word, and again when it used the Boolean string "ears AND disease." The correct entry titles are **Ménière's disease** and **ear disease**; the latter includes a cross-reference to the former (but not vice versa).

The entire text of *Academic American* resides in the database, so in theory it should be possible to carry out a thorough and efficient electronic search by using logical operators. In actuality, this is possible only with those vendors that offer full-text searching. Otherwise, online searches do not explore the text of the entries, just the entry titles; and they provide a hit only on an absolute match. If the search does not provide a hit, the user must expend at least two minutes retracing the way through a succession of menus back to the desired topic.

IV. Cost

All the while the meter is ticking. As an example, InfoMaster charges 15¢ per minute for connection through a local network node (35¢ for a WATS connection), plus an $8 per topic search fee (waived if no hits are made). That can be a high price for the seven-line entry on **Ménière's disease**, which, like many of the shorter entries, includes no bibliography. Other services have comparable rates. Under an FCC proposal, connection fees would increase by

$4 or $5 per hour. Even at current rates, a hundred average searches of the online *Academic American* will pay for the print version. Grolier reports that *Academic American* online is currently offered "either on a subscription basis or at an hourly royalty rate."

V. Currency

In theory, an online database can readily be updated; that is why the *Oxford English Dictionary* is going online, and why many library catalogs are following suit. Print, whether encyclopedia volume or catalog card, resists change. Electronic databases, by contrast, merge and purge effortlessly.

The publisher claims that "the online edition . . . is updated four times each year and includes information that is not found in the print edition." While this is undoubtedly the case, as of mid-June 1987 the electronic version of *Academic American* actually appeared far *less* up-to-date than the 1987 print version in many areas. For example, it did not mention the following items new in the 1987 print version: the antiviral drug AZT for AIDS; Manuel Puig; the nuclear disaster at Chernobyl; privatization; or President Reagan's approval of the tax reform measure, or his Iceland summit meeting with Mikhail Gorbachev (both October 1986), or indeed anything later than his cancer surgery in July 1985. On the other hand, the online version did mention that "the first U.S. hospital devoted solely to AIDS treatment and research opened in Houston, Texas, in 1986," and it included the entry on **Corazon Aquino** that is new to the 1987 print edition. On the whole, the online version appears to be a blend of the 1987 and earlier print editions.

The advantage of the print edition over the electronic version can be reversed, and perhaps it shortly will. The editors have used advanced computer technology in preparing the print version, so its up-to-date information must exist on electronic media somewhere; the job of transferring it to the online databases should not be too difficult. But the theoretical advantage of electronic information storage and retrieval is not *automatically* realized in practice, as *Academic American* amply showed at the time of this review.

VI. Accuracy, Objectivity, and Clarity

In terms of accuracy and objectivity, the online *Academic American* bears a close resemblance to its justly admired print namesake. But in the matter of clarity the electronic version is at a considerable disadvantage, because it includes no illustrations; Grolier acknowledges that "current technology precludes the delivery of high-quality graphics." The

print version contains 16,730 illustrations, three-quarters in color and many with useful captions. These illustrations occupy one-third of the set's available space, enabling the reader to, in the publisher's words, "acquire a basic comprehension of the subject as well as considerable factual information by studying the illustrations and captions alone." The publisher's further claim that "each [illustration] was carefully selected to explain, support, or expand ideas in the text" only shows how devastating the loss really is, for the online version gives no evidence that the entries were rewritten to compensate for the absence of the illustrations.

Digitizing scanners should enable the publisher to incorporate the graphics into the online database, where modern high-speed modems along with EGA or VGA boards and monitors will enable the user to retrieve and display them. Such developments would help put the online *Academic American* in an advanced technical position comparable to that occupied by the print version.

VII. Summary

The print *Academic American* has been chiefly praised as a ready-reference tool, especially for its index, its graphics, and its inclusion of the latest information. In comparison, the online edition must be judged a crippled version at best. The user in search of ready reference must leap numerous electronic hurdles before even arriving at the database; electronic search methods could, but do not, make up for the loss of the print version's 200,000-entry index; computed at 1,000 words per picture, the nonillustrated online version is some 16,650,000 words' worth less informative than the print edition; and the electronic information is often older than the print.

That said, however, it should be noted that of the three online encyclopedias currently available to library and home subscribers (the other two are EVERYMAN'S ENCYCLOPAEDIA and the KUSSMAUL ENCYCLOPEDIA), *Academic American* is the only one backed by the resources of a major American reference publisher (Grolier). It is likely that the company and its electronic publishing division will continue to update the database and improve accessibility. The system is worthy of buyer consideration.

Individuals and institutions interested in acquiring *Academic American* online may contact any of the vendors listed in "Facts at a Glance" at the head of this review; addresses and phone numbers appear in the list of Publishers beginning on page 591. Since services and charges vary from vendor to vendor, consumers are advised to examine the total package offered by vendors before subscribing to this system.

Academic American (CD-ROM)

Facts at a Glance

Full Title: **Academic American Encyclopedia**
   (CD-ROM version).
Alternate Title: The Electronic Encyclopedia.
Publisher: Grolier Incorporated.
Editors: Bernard S. Cayne, Editorial Director;
   K. Anne Ranson, Editor-in-Chief.
Copyright: 1987.

Number of Volumes: 1 compact disc.
Number of Contributors: 2,325.
Number of Entries: 28,700.
Number of Words: 9,040,000.
Number of Cross-references: 67,000.
Number of Indexes: 1.
Number of Index Entries: 200,000.

Price: $299.
Sold directly by the publisher.
Revised annually.

The CD-ROM version of the *Academic American Encyclopedia*—popularly known as *The Electronic Encyclopedia*—was introduced by Grolier in January 1986. It contains the same text as the 21-volume print edition on one compact disc less than 4¾″ in diameter. However, it lacks the illustrations that are a major strength of the print edition.

Of the libraries surveyed by the Buying Guide (see Chapter 3, pages 25–33), only 8 percent as yet use electronic encyclopedias in either online or CD-ROM format. Indeed, at this point, *Academic American* remains the only general reference encyclopedia available on compact disc.

Overall, very few libraries currently possess the technology necessary to use these electronic information systems. Moreover, contrary to the impression created by computer salespeople, most librarians have found that the CD-ROM format does not provide quick and easy access to specific information. *Academic American* is already one of the most accessible of all print encyclopedias; given the limitations of present computer technology, it would be difficult to improve upon this version.

Once the novelty of the computer has worn off, most patrons express a preference for the print version. Books have the advantage of being portable: the reader can sit down at any desk with a book and take notes, whereas in order to use *The Electronic Encyclopedia*, the user must be at the computer terminal. And as W. F. Bolton, professor of English at Rutgers University and an expert on electronic reference sources, has noted, electronic encyclopedias preclude the serendipitous experiences that are inherent in the use of print encyclopedias.

The Electronic Encyclopedia does possess two advantages over the print edition. Most obviously, with its entire contents contained on one small disc, it takes up much less space than does a multivolume print encyclopedia—in fact, it quite literally takes up next to no space at all. And its price ($299) is considerably less expensive than the library discount price of $650 for the print version. In comparison with *Academic American* online, it is fairly accessible and bypasses many of the problems that make online reference works difficult to use. The user need not go through all the steps of dialing a vendor and selecting the reference information from a menu of different services, as is the case with all online encyclopedias. And there are no online charges. This can represent considerable savings over the long run.

However, the hardware needed to drive and read the CD-ROM version is still prohibitively expensive for most institutions. Unless this equipment is already in place, or unless the institution is already planning to install it to accommodate a wide range of CD-ROM software, the initial investment required will simply be beyond the resources of the average public library. The most advanced research libraries in the country are only now beginning to test or use this technology. In short, the idea of the CD-ROM encyclopedia is tremendously exciting, but its practicability for the typical library's general reference services will remain in doubt for some time.

According to the publisher, the CD-ROM *Academic American* is accompanied by "the Knowledge Retrieval System, a powerful, full-text search and retrieval program that allows the user to search for any word or combination of words in seconds." The system's full retrieval program incorporates Boolean logic and is screen-prompted. Grolier notes further that "search results can be printed out or saved to disk in one of three types of word processing files."

More than one-half of the CD memory is occupied by an extensive index. *School Library Journal* (June-July 1987) reports that this index "allows users to locate a listing of every entry containing a reference to a particular subject. A further refinement allows a user to narrow any topic by employing two search terms to get a display of entries mentioning, for example, both religion and China. Obviously, this capability saves a great deal of time." It also gives the CD-ROM version a distinct advantage over the online version, which does not have this capability, where accessibility is concerned.

For complete information about the contents of *The Electronic Encyclopedia*, see the review of the print edition of the ACADEMIC AMERICAN ENCYCLOPEDIA that begins on page 63.

The Electronic Encyclopedia can be ordered directly from the publisher, Grolier Incorporated,

Sherman Turnpike, Danbury, CT 06816, telephone (800) 243-7256. Grolier can also arrange a demonstration of the system.

Collier's Encyclopedia

Facts at a Glance

Full Title: **Collier's Encyclopedia**.
Publisher: Macmillan Educational Company.
Editors: William D. Halsey, Editorial Director; Bernard Johnston, Editor-in-Chief.
Edition Reviewed: 1986. (Statistics apply to 1988 edition.)

Number of Volumes: 24.
Number of Contributors: 4,600.
Number of Entries: 25,000.
Number of Pages: 19,750.
Number of Words: 21,000,000.
Number of Maps: 1,600.
Number of Cross-references: 13,000.
Number of Indexes: 1.
Number of Index Entries: 400,000.
Number of Illustrations: 1,750 color; 15,600 black-and-white.
Trim Size: 8¼″ × 10⅝″.

Price: $1,399.50 to individuals; $799 plus $20 shipping to libraries ($709 plus shipping for two or more sets).
Sold door-to-door, directly to libraries, and by direct mail.
ISBN 0-02-940301-4.
Revised annually.

I. Introduction

Collier's Encyclopedia is a 24-volume general reference work described by its editors as "a scholarly, systematic, continuously revised summary of the knowledge that is most significant to mankind." Its articles cover "the curricula of colleges and secondary schools." However, while the material is intended to be within the grasp of readers in "the upper grades," the editors state that "an attempt is made to prepare the reader by references to preliminary reading in more elementary related articles." This suggests that portions of the text may be somewhat advanced for many secondary students.

Today, *Collier's* is regarded as one of the "big three" scholarly encyclopedias on the market—the other two being The Encyclopedia Americana and New Encyclopaedia Britannica. As such, it is directly competitive with these two sets.

Because of the large lead time necessary in preparing the Buying Guide, this review is based on an examination of the 1986 edition, the most current edition available at the time of review.

II. Scope

Collier's Encyclopedia contains 25,000 articles and a total of 21 million words, making it just in terms of size the smallest of the "big three." Articles average 840 words, or approximately one and one-quarter pages in the encyclopedia's two-column page format. Actual article lengths vary from short entries such as the five-line **Acheron** to the 75-page overview of the **United States of America**.

As an indication of how space is apportioned among different subjects, **Charlemagne** receives two and one-half pages, **Konstantin Chernenko** gets approximately one-half page, **Grover Cleveland** is accorded two pages, and **Ty Cobb** is given about one-quarter of a page. The article on **China** is 63 and one-half pages, the **U.S. Civil War** is covered in 38 pages, and 8 pages are devoted to **Christianity**.

The articles in *Collier's* cover all of the major academic disciplines as well as practical information of general interest. Geographical, biographical, and historical subjects are treated thoroughly and consistently. In addition, conceptual topics such as **apostasy** and **a priori** are covered, as are practical subjects such as **safety**, which New Britannica totally omits.

Collier's coverage of international subjects, both in the geographical entries and elsewhere, is similarly broad. Articles on major countries include color maps and other illustrations. International political, historical, and cultural figures of importance are discussed either in individual articles or within longer articles accessible through the index.

As an indication of the attention *Collier's* gives to foreign subjects, the entries from **Bartolomé Mitre** to **Mohammed**, inclusive, include the following: **Mitre** (Argentine statesman), **Mitsubishi** (Japanese conglomerate), **Mitsui** (Japanese financial monopoly), **François Mitterrand** (French president), **Miyazaki** (Japanese city), **Moab** (ancient Near Eastern kingdom), **Mobutu Sese Seko** (Zairean president), **Modena** and **Modica** (Italian cities), **Amedeo Modigliani** (Italian artist), **Mödling** (Austrian city), **Jorgen Moe** (19th-century Norwegian writer), **Mogadishu** (Somalian capital), **Mogilev** (Soviet city), and **Mohammed**. This represents 15 entries out of a total 33 in this span.

North America is also particularly well covered, with illustrated articles on each of the 50 states and the Canadian provinces.

Popular subjects of current interest are added to the encyclopedia with each revision. Thus the 1986 edition includes new entries on **Fred Astaire**, **Larry Bird**, and **Stephen Sondheim**. The same edition also

Collier's Encyclopedia

HUSÁK, GUSTAV 409 — ❸

Stardust (1921), *Appassionata* (1926), *Five and Ten* (1929), *Back Street* (1930), *Imitation of Life* (1933), *Family!* (1960), *God Must Be Sad* (1961), and *"Fool, Be Still"* (1964), many short-story collections, and three plays. A number of her books have been made into successful films. Her autobiography, *Anatomy of Me,* appeared in 1958. She died in New York City, Feb. 23, 1968. PHILIP KRAPP

HUS, JAN (HUSS, JOHN) [hʌs, hʊs] (c. 1369-1415), Czech reformer, was born at Husinec, Bohemia, about 1369. He studied at the University of Prague, and in 1396 he took the degree of Master of Arts. Then he devoted himself to the study of theology and in 1404 took the degree of Bachelor of Divinity. After his ordination as a priest, he divided his time between the pulpit and a university chair. He was appointed chaplain at the Bethlehem Chapel in the old town of Prague, where his main duty was his preaching in the Czech language. He lectured at the university, and in 1409 he was elected its rector.

During his university studies, Hus came under the influence of prominent representatives of a reform movement which originated in Bohemia in the latter phase of the reign (1346-1378) of Emperor Charles IV (1316-1378) and made notable progress before 1400. He espoused the cause and supported it ardently. So prominent was his part in disputations and polemics concerning the progress of church reform that he was soon considered the chief spokesman of its adherents. Though the urgent need of reform was widely recognized, opinions differed as to its extent and the means to be adopted. At the beginning, harmony prevailed between reform preachers and church authorities, and they often worked hand in hand. On several occasions Hus was invited by the Archbishop of Prague to preach before the assembly of the clergy and propose a remedy for the evils of the time. When, in addition to his own ideas, Hus began to propagate the tenets of John Wycliffe, an estrangement set in between Hus and the clergy. Aroused by Hus' adversaries, the papal court issued several decrees and finally, in 1411, promulgated a sentence of excommunication against him. In 1412 papal emissaries were dispatched to Prague to raise money for the intended war with the King of Naples by granting indulgences to contributors. Hus' campaign against them was the last straw. A papal bull proclaimed aggravation of the sentence of excommunication and Prague was put under an interdict. As the church authorities seemed determined to enforce the terms of the interdict and to suspend divine services in the populous city, Hus retired to the country seat of one of his followers. Later he decided to go before the general council in Constance in the hope that he would be given a chance to justify his teachings and activities. Soon after his arrival in Constance he was imprisoned. Since he refused to recant he was condemned as an obstinate heretic and burned at the stake on July 6, 1415.

Hus' literary work developed along lines parallel with his public activities. He made use of both Latin and Czech so as to reach academic circles and laymen alike. In addition to learned works that originated in his university lectures, he wrote several treatises in Latin, both during the early phase of his life and during the unrelenting struggle with his opponents. His most important contribution to the defense of the reform program was the book *De Ecclesia* (1413), an English translation of which has been published in New York (1915). Hus' writings in Czech are a remarkable literary supplement to his sermons in the Bethlehem Chapel. They grew in number during his voluntary exile and were intended both for the faithful in Prague and his

ARCHIVES FOR ART AND HISTORY

JAN HUS, late-14th-century-early-15th-century Czech theologian, being led to the stake; the hat bears an inscription denouncing him as the "chief of the heretics." Hus, a former priest, was excommunicated by the church for his unorthodox teachings and writings. — ❺

new followers in the country. Short tracts on matters of general interest preceded a series of works in Czech in which he endeavored to elucidate controversial issues or explain fundamental points of Christian doctrine. Hus' *Exposition of the Faith, the Decalogue and the Lord's Prayer* is the most outstanding example of his knowledge of the people's spiritual needs as well as of his ability to treat subtle theological problems in a popular vein. An important place is to be given to a collection of Czech sermons, *Postilla,* and to a delightful summary of Christian principles, *The Daughter, or Of the Real Knowledge of True Salvation,* dedicated to pious women among his congregation. Letters written in Latin or Czech both in the country and in the jail at Constance contain valuable details concerning his doctrine and life. Often considered as a forerunner of the reformers of the sixteenth century, Hus enjoys high esteem all over the world. His position in Czech spiritual tradition is dominant. He gave his name to a popular movement that permeated social and cultural life, and immensely strengthened the national consciousness of the Czechs. He also contributed greatly to the development of the Czech language and literature. *See also* HUSSITES. OTAKAR ODLOZILIK — ❻

HUSÁK, GUSTAV [hu'sɑk] (1913-   ), Czechoslovak Communist leader, was born near the present Slovak capital of Bratislava on Jan. 10, 1913. He studied and later practiced law in Bratislava and, in 1933, also joined the Communist Party of Czechoslovakia (CPCz). During World War II Husák belonged to the leadership of the illegal Communist Party in the German-dominated Slovak — ❼

Page shown at 70% of actual size.

❶ Contributor's credit: Collier's has more than 4,600 contributors. Virtually all articles are signed.

❷ Main entry: Collier's Encyclopedia contains 25,000 entries, arranged alphabetically, letter-by-letter. Entry words are printed in boldface capitals.

❸ Guide words and page number

❹ Illustration: Collier's contains 17,350 illustrations, of which 1,750 are in color.

❺ Caption: Captions in Collier's not only describe the illustration but also encapsulize information presented in the text.

❻ Cross-reference: Collier's contains 13,000 cross-references. Titles of cross-referenced entries are printed in large and small caps.

❼ Pronunciation: Foreign or other difficult entry words are followed by phonetic pronunciation.

introduced new entries on **Rajiv Gandhi**, **Edward Koch**, and **Desmond Tutu**, among others, thus keeping abreast of world affairs.

Collier's includes a considerable number of longer survey articles that discuss aspects of a general topic that might be treated only as shorter separate entries in other encyclopedias. For example, the article on **American literature** spans 30 pages and includes sections on Herman Melville, Walt Whitman, Henry James, and others. The survey article format will be extremely useful for the reader who requires an overview of American literature, and it provides a convenient alternative to consulting numerous cross-references as a means of studying a broad subject. But since only certain subjects are treated in this manner the reader is not always so accommodated, and the broad entry format does not facilitate locating specific information. (See also *Accessibility*.)

III. Authority

Collier's Encyclopedia is published by the Macmillan Educational Company (MEC), a division of the Macmillan Publishing Company. The company is well known in the reference field and is one of the four leading publishers of general encyclopedias in the United States. Conceived early in the postwar period, *Collier's* first appeared in 1950 and was favorably received. Since that time the encyclopedia has established a strong reputation as an authoritative reference work, particularly in the library market.

Editorial Director William D. Halsey and Editor-in-Chief Bernard Johnston oversee the editing of *Collier's*. They are assisted by a staff of 24 house editors. In addition, the frontmatter lists three advisory boards (Library, Curriculum, and International), giving the credentials and affiliations of each member. The publisher reports that the members of these boards "contributed to the development" of the encyclopedia. The frontmatter also includes a list of senior editors and advisors, classified under the broad subject categories of Biological Sciences, Physical Sciences, Humanities, Regional Studies, and Social Sciences.

Collier's boasts an impressive roster of contributors—some 4,600 in all—drawn mainly from North American and British universities. Among its many notable contributors are agricultural researcher and Nobel laureate Norman Borlaug; child psychologist Bruno Bettelheim; novelist Kingsley Amis; sociologist Lewis Mumford; linguist Mario Pei; economist and Nobel laureate Milton Friedman; historians Barbara Tuchman, Asa Briggs, and A. L. Rowse; and British political figure Shirley Williams. A number of *Collier's* outstanding contributors, such as legal scholar Felix Frankfurter, anthropologist Margaret

Mead, theologian Reinhold Niebuhr, art critic Herbert Read, and aviation engineer Igor Sikorsky, have been deceased for some time; however, this in no way diminishes the authority of their original contributions. (The list of contributors identifies deceased contributors as such.) Lesser-known figures who have contributed to this encyclopedia appear to be respected authorities in their fields as well. Like both ENCYCLOPEDIA AMERICANA and NEW BRITANNICA, *Collier's* list of contributors gives its contributors' academic degrees, professional affiliations, and titles of selected relevant books they have authored.

Most of the articles in *Collier's* are signed; in the cases of extended articles in which different sections were written by separate contributors, each section is signed. Some of the signatures are preceded by "Reviewed by," indicating that the contributor reviewed a prepared article; others are signed with more than one name, indicating joint authorship.

On the whole, the editors have taken meticulous care to ensure the authority of each entry and to faithfully document this authority. The result is an encyclopedia whose authority rivals, and frequently excels, that of ENCYCLOPEDIA AMERICANA and NEW BRITANNICA.

IV. Currency

The editors and publisher of *Collier's Encyclopedia* maintain a laudable policy of annual revision. According to the editors, the last five revisions have averaged about 2,000 revised pages each; this represents an annual revision of about 10 percent, which is standard for the industry. As a result, the 1986 edition is up-to-date to the time of publication in most important factual areas. Ongoing lists such as heads of state and recipients of awards are current to the mid-1980s.

The article on the **Republic of South Africa** reports recent activity there, with information such as "In July 1985 the government proclaimed a state of emergency in large parts of South Africa. Military repression intensified." The article on **Nicaragua** reports events of 1984, explaining that "Intensified U.S. support enabled the counter-revolutionaries to increase their attacks . . ." and mentions the Sandinistas' 1984 presidential victory. The article on **Acquired Immune Deficiency Syndrome (AIDS)** reflects understanding of the disease current at the time the article was written and mentions attempts by researchers in the United States and elsewhere to develop a vaccine.

Inevitably, some portions of the text are not quite up-to-date. For example, the entries on the **Republic of Ireland** and **Northern Ireland** fail to mention the 1985 agreement between Great Britain and the Republic granting the Republic a voice in the government of Northern Ireland. The article on **Margaret Thatcher** fails to mention her 1983 reelection victory, which was a significant event marking widespread support for the Conservative Party at that time. **Papacy** refers to Pope John Paul II only in passing and does not mention the fact that his selection as the first pope from an Eastern bloc country signaled a major development in the history of the Catholic Church. In Volume 10 (page 396) the caption of a photograph of Jean-Paul Sartre and Simone de Beauvoir is written in the present tense although Sartre died in 1980. However, since the encyclopedia is continuously revised, those sections that are less current at present would presumably receive attention in a future revision.

The choice of topics for articles also reflects the editorial goal of maintaining an up-to-date picture of events. New articles on **Mikhail Gorbachev** (general secretary of the Communist Party of the Soviet Union from March 1985), **Ted Hughes** (appointed poet laureate in Great Britain in 1984), and **Shimon Peres** (prime minister in Israel's coalition government in 1984) show the effort to incorporate new figures in the arts and international affairs. The articles on **nuclear fission**, **elementary particles**, and **desalinization** have been completely rewritten for the 1986 edition, presenting new developments in science and technology. However, our reviewers noted some curious omissions. For example, the article **sound recording and reproduction** does not mention digital technology, which was introduced on a wide scale in the early 1980s and is now central to the recording industry. Moreover, the article discusses quadraphonic recording technology as though this were still in vogue; in fact, virtually all record companies had abandoned this process by 1980. The encyclopedia does not contain entries for digital recording or the compact disc.

The statistics reported in the articles, like most other factual material, are generally up-to-date. *Collier's* population figure for the U.S.S.R. dates from 1983—a reasonably up-to-date statistic for a 1986 encyclopedia. The entry's tables for the civilian labor force, industrial production, mineral production, principal exports and imports, and the consolidated state budget all date from 1978. However, given the difficulty of obtaining current economic statistics from the Soviet Union, these tables are not unreasonably outmoded. Population figures for **Africa** and **Afghanistan** date from 1985 and 1983, respectively. However, the figure for **Bhopal** state dates from 1961; the population figure for the city of Bhopal is more recent (1981). The entry does not mention the 1984 industrial disaster at the Union Carbide plant there. The articles on **advertising**, **divorce**, the **electrical industry**, and **frozen foods** all include tables in which

the figures date from 1975, but these are exceptions, and most of the tables are reliably up-to-date.

The vast size of *Collier's Encyclopedia*, set against the pace of changing events in the world, makes the task of updating such a work most challenging. On balance, *Collier's* editors have succeeded in producing a work that is reasonably current, and they have demonstrated their commitment to keeping it up to the same standard in subsequent editions. Readers should be able to turn to this encyclopedia for recent information in most fields with confidence.

V. Accuracy

The articles in *Collier's Encyclopedia* are consistently accurate in reporting information. The careful preparation, editorial review, and frequent revision are evident throughout and generate a high standard of reliability. For example, the long article on **printing** provides a thorough explanation of the typesetting, printing, and binding processes, in sufficient detail to serve as a helpful review for the professional, and with attention to the latest technology and computerization of the industry.

The article on **Ronald Wilson Reagan** covers Reagan's early life and acting career, the major events of his early political career, and details of his presidency through late 1985. The level of detail provided is appropriate, with the most detailed discussion devoted to the years since 1980.

With only one exception, our content reviewers report that the articles they have examined are highly accurate and useful. *Collier's* entry on the **brain** is fairly complete and straightforward, taking into account such important aspects of the subject as the specialized functions of the right and left brain, theories of memory and learning, and neurotransmitters (although the coverage of this last item is not as current as it could be). The article on the **Bill of Rights** is thorough and good. Taking the historical approach, the entry covers the English Bill of Rights, the Virginia Declaration, and the first ten amendments to the U.S. Constitution, illuminating the relationship among the three. Our astronomy consultant reports that, of all encyclopedia articles on **Saturn**, *Collier's* is clearly the best. The article provides a good balance between hard factual information and reasonable speculative information, and should remain accurate and reliable for some time. The encyclopedia's coverage of **transistors** is similarly excellent. The entry provides a good description of different types of transistors, their behavior, and their applications. There are helpful and appropriate cross-references to related entries. However, our consultant also notes that some of the discussion of transistors is likely to be too advanced for the general reader.

Collier's entry on **money** is less reliable than its coverage of the subjects just discussed. It is significantly narrower in scope than the article in NEW BRITANNICA and difficult even for an economist to understand. It contains some serious errors and biases that, on the whole, render it of little value to the general reader. However, such examples are the rare exception rather than the rule. In general, *Collier's* accuracy is second to none, and this encyclopedia maintains a high standard of excellence.

VI. Clarity

According to the Preface, the articles in *Collier's Encyclopedia* "have been constructed according to carefully designed patterns. Typically, such a pattern provides for immediate definition, for simple explanation, and for presentation of the basic facts early in the article." A random review confirms that long articles are indeed often introduced in this fashion. The structure of the articles aids the reader by presenting material in a logical sequence and highlighting specific aspects. This is especially valuable in the survey articles. For example, the article on **chess** begins as described above, with a succinct definition and some general information. This is followed by sections introduced with bold headings on "Rules of Chess," "Notation," "Chess Theory," "A Classical Game," and so on. Whether the reader is looking for an overview of the subject or a specific piece of information, this format should pose little difficulty.

The writing style is generally clear and scholarly but may vary considerably from article to article. Compare this passage from the article on **archaeology**: "Now this may all seem simple and unexciting; but an archaeologist is an outsider to the men and cultures with which he chooses to deal" with a sentence from the article **chord**: "This distinction between several tones heard simultaneously but independently and those perceived as a homogeneous union is the distinction between contrapuntal ('horizontal') and harmonic ('vertical') texture in music." The two *Collier's* articles dealing with evolution (**evolution of man** and **organic evolution**) are both highly technical and may be beyond the grasp of the typical reader. Each assumes that the reader possesses a fairly thorough familiarity with genetics, anthropology, and paleontology.

For the most part, though not always and not consistently, technical terms are defined in context. Individuals are occasionally mentioned by surname only, without identification or an explanation of their relationship to the subject at hand. For example, the article on **T. S. Eliot** includes this statement: "Through Russell he met Clive Bell, who introduced him to members of the so-called Bloomsbury Group." This is the first and only mention of (Bertrand) Russell, who may be unfamiliar to the reader and should perhaps be identified more fully. Minor stylistic inconsistencies also occur; for example in Volume 8 (pages 284 and 285) the captions to the two photographs of the Indonesian capital use different spellings of the city's name, Jakarta and Djakarta. However, such lapses are few, and with the exception of the occasional article, the overall style of this encyclopedia is lucid and easy to follow.

The following extract from **Titanic** illustrates the style of a typical entry in *Collier's Encyclopedia*:

TITANIC, an English ocean liner lost in an extraordinary marine catastrophe. Just before midnight on April 14, 1912, the White Star liner *Titanic* on its maiden voyage from Southampton to New York, while almost 1,300 miles from its destination, struck an iceberg and sank, leaving 1,513 dead. Casualties were particularly heavy among the crew, only 24 percent surviving. None of the ship's band or of the engine crew was saved. Of the 534 women and children aboard 70 percent survived; of the 1,667 men only 20 percent. Among those lost were the ship's captain; the president of the Grand Trunk Railway, Charles M. Hays; the vice-president of the Pennsylvania Railroad, J. B. Thayer; John Jacob Astor IV; Benjamin Guggenheim; George D. Widener; and Isidor Straus, whose wife refused rescue.

When the tragedy occurred the sea was unusually calm and the night was clear and cold. Although the captain had received warnings of icebergs ahead he had decided to follow the prevailing practice of relying on a sharp lookout rather than reducing speed. For this he was severely criticized by a London court of enquiry headed by Lord Mersey. Also castigated was the captain of the Leyland liner *Californian* for refusing prompt aid to the stricken vessel although his ship was less than 10 miles away when distress signals were reported. This most tragic of ship disasters to the largest vessel then afloat (46,328 gross tons), occurring on the ocean's most heavily traveled route, brought investigations on both sides of the Atlantic and resulted in the tightening of the marine laws of the United States and England in matters relating to equipment and practices for the promotion of safety at sea.

VII. Objectivity

Like its major competitors, ENCYCLOPEDIA AMERICANA and NEW ENCYCLOPAEDIA BRITANNICA, *Collier's* is in the main an objective, well-balanced encyclopedia. The Preface states that "to insure objectivity, articles involving key issues are submitted to authorities representing all major points of view." Thus, in areas where controversy exists, it is usually mentioned.

For example, the entry on **abortion** summarizes the main arguments held by those who favor the legalization of abortion and those who oppose it. The article notes that the subject continues to raise controversy, and mentions further legislation and court rulings affecting abortion in the United States during the 1970s and 1980s. The article also deals with other problematic aspects of the subject. For example, it points out that "to what extent, if any, access to legal abortion has led to a deterioration of contraceptive practice is a matter of contention." A section on "Complications and Aftereffects" deals with *psychological reactions*—an area not addressed in the abortion entries of any other encyclopedia.

Collier's articles on **organic evolution** and **evolution of man** mention pre-Darwinian views on these subjects, but allude only briefly to contemporary challenges to evolutionary theory. Neither creationism nor scientific creationism is mentioned by name, and this encyclopedia does not contain an entry under either heading. This is a rare instance in which *Collier's* does not address an alternative viewpoint on a major issue.

Collier's coverage of controversial historical figures is well balanced. For example, the entry on **Henry Kissinger** describes Kissinger's successes in negotiations with the Soviet Union, the People's Republic of China, North Vietnam, Israel, and Egypt, but also notes that his "tenure was flawed by much controversy" in matters concerning Cambodia, Chile, and Angola.

The entry on **Andrew Jackson** gives a full and rounded account of his personality and his career. Early in the article we read that "the gay, headstrong youth often seemed more interested in horse racing, cockfighting, gambling, and girls than in study or his career." Later he is described as "trigger-touchy concerning slights to his 'honor' or to [his wife's] sacred name"; the article also reports that he killed one opponent in a duel, and that he "owned 20 slaves." Jackson's many involvements in political controversy during his presidency are also noted, but his positive achievements are emphasized. A *summation* section states that "most historians rate Jackson not only as a 'great' president but as a 'strong' one. . . . His strength lay in the firmness and decisiveness of his conduct of the office, particularly in instances of conflict with Congress, and in his resistance in the name of 'equal protection and equal benefits' to domination of government by special interests."

VIII. Accessibility

Collier's Encyclopedia is well organized and most specific information can be easily located. Entries are arranged alphabetically in a letter-by-letter system. Names beginning with *Mc* are alphabetized as though they began with *Mac*; names beginning with *St.* are likewise alphabetized as though *Saint* were

spelled out. Entry headings are in bold capital letters, with several levels of subheads in bold or italic type depending on the complexity of the article. Subheads in historical articles are in chronological order; those in articles on authors often identify individual works; still other subheads help to distinguish various aspects of the topic under discussion.

Several special features to the system of organization serve as aids to the reader. Glossaries of technical terms appear at the end of many articles, such as **archaeology** and **archery**. The articles on states include lists of prominent state citizens with brief descriptions of their contributions. Some longer articles, such as **astronomy** and **automobile**, are accompanied by boxes containing a brief explanation of how the article is organized. These aids are useful since the survey article format incorporates a great deal of information in each article.

Subjects are listed under their most familiar names. Thus authors appear under their pseudonyms with cross-references under their real names sometimes, but not always, supplied. The use of familiar names leads to some inconsistencies; for example, the brothers of the French emperor Napoleon I are all discussed in Volume 4 under their surname Bonaparte, whereas the article on the emperor appears under Napoleon I in Volume 17. Decisions such as this are necessary and have been made logically.

There are some 13,000 cross-references (fewer than one per page), appearing at the end of articles or sections of articles, as suggestions for further reading, or following an entry title where the entry itself appears elsewhere. In a sense, the broad entry format makes some cross-references unnecessary by bringing related material together.

Articles on related subjects frequently overlap and information on a similar theme may thus appear in different volumes. For this reason, and because much information appears under a single title in survey articles, the index is an essential element in this encyclopedia. To the editors' credit it is an exhaustive and well-compiled reference, with 400,000 entries annotated to distinguish similar entries and with references to maps, illustrations, and bibliography entries. Readers will find the index indispensable and reliable.

As an indication of the scope and style of individual entries, the reader searching for information about Marie Curie will find the following index entries:

> **CURIE** (Fr. fam.) 7-571a
> **Curie, Eve** (Fr. mus., au.) 7-571c
> **Curie, Irene** (Fr. phys.): see Joliot Curie, Irene
> **Curie, Jacques** (Fr. phys.) 21-223b
> **Curie, Marie** (Pol. sci.) 7-571a; 17-571a, 572c;
> 19-604d, 630b

medicine **15**-653d—*Ill.* **7**-571
Curie, Paul-Jean (Fr. phys.) **7**-571c
Curie, Pierre (Fr. chem., phys.) **7**-571c, 571a;
   17-571a; **19**-604d
magnets **15**-271b
medicine **15**-653d
sound **21**-223a

These are followed by entries for **curie** (measure), **Curie point**, **Curie's law**, **Curie temperature**, and **Curie-Weiss law**. Thus the index is highly specific, and the reader may have to do some close reading to track down every reference to *Curie*.

IX. Special Features

A special feature of *Collier's Encyclopedia* is the annotated bibliography in Volume 24. There are 11,500 titles, numbered and arranged according to subject and in order of difficulty. This will be especially helpful to those using the encyclopedia for research.

The bibliography was compiled by 45 public and academic librarians and academic subject specialists. According to the editors, "the books listed begin at about high school level and progress through college level and beyond. All books have been selected with a view to their availability. . . . Many are books one may expect to find even in smaller libraries or are books that a small library in all probability can borrow from its state agency." Most of these claims are true most of the time. Many of the titles listed are classics that are still widely available; the bibliographies also include a significant number of books published in the 1980s.

Unlike the bibliography in FUNK & WAGNALLS NEW ENCYCLOPEDIA, the *Collier's* bibliography is not arranged by any standard system (e.g., Dewey Decimal or Library of Congress). Rather, the titles appear under very broad subject headings such as philosophy, history, the arts, economics, and general science. All titles are listed in the index.

Altogether, the *Collier's* bibliography is more comprehensive than the separate bibliographies included at the end of selected subject entries in ENCYCLOPEDIA AMERICANA and the NEW BRITANNICA Micropaedia. Like those encyclopedias, however, some of the articles in *Collier's* also include brief bibliographies.

A study guide appears in Volume 24 between the bibliography and the index. It is divided into academic disciplines, and within each field are listed the titles of relevant *Collier's* articles, moving from introductory to advanced material. Many critics and educators question the efficacy of such study guides, which will be useful only to the extent that they are consulted and applied by the user.

The index is a major feature (see *Accessibility*). It takes up the greater part of Volume 24.

There are 17,350 illustrations, of which 1,750 are in color. There are several color transparencies, which are attractive and show relationships between things in a dramatic way. The color plates on subjects such as birds, dogs, paintings, and shells are also beautifully produced and very effective. The black-and-white illustrations are mostly of good quality but, like those in ENCYCLOPEDIA AMERICANA, vary widely in quality. Some of the photographs have reproduced rather dark in the current edition. A small number of photographs appear to be somewhat dated. There is also some repetition of certain subjects in illustrations, while other subjects that could benefit from illustrations are not illustrated at all. For example, there are four photographs of the Appian Way (one each in Volumes 2, 9, 12, and 22), while there is no illustration for the article on **John Singer Sargent**.

Collier's contains 1,600 maps, which were prepared by the well-known cartographer Rand McNally. Articles on continents, major countries, and North American states and provinces include excellent color maps with extensive map indexes. There are also maps with topographic and economic information, rainfall, growing seasons, and other topics of interest. On the whole, *Collier's* maps are of the highest quality, and in many cases surpass those found in competing encyclopedias.

Helpful tables accompany some articles. There are tables on subjects such as "The Growth of the Old Testament," "International Atomic Weights," and "Table of the World's Languages," as well as in entries on individual states, nations, and continents. These tables present a great deal of information clearly and concisely.

X. Format

Collier's Encyclopedia includes 24 volumes of between 700 and 800 pages each (except Volume 24, which is 1,050 pages long). Like ENCYCLOPEDIA AMERICANA and NEW BRITANNICA, *Collier's* is organized in the split-letter system. The black cloth binding with red panels and gold lettering is sturdy and attractive. The trim size is 8¼″ × 10⅝″ and the books are roughly 1⅜″ thick. The entire set takes up approximately three feet of horizontal shelf space. The two-column page layout is augmented with illustrations; the headings, running heads, and page numbers (flush with the outside margin at the top of each page) are bold and legible.

XI. Other Opinions

ARBA 82: "*Collier's* is a relatively up-to-date encyclopedia that is competitive with ENCYCLOPEDIA AMERICANA and the NEW ENCYCLOPAEDIA BRITANNICA. . . . Carefully prepared and edited, . . . *Collier's* is suitable for general adult use, and has features particularly useful to the . . . college student."

ARBA 86: "*Collier's* is one of the best encyclopedias on the market, it is readable and reasonably up-to-date. It is best suited for schools and home use and one can also recommend it for junior college level. Certainly not flashy, *Collier's* is reasonably priced and should be recommended for purchase without any serious reservations."

Booklist, November 15, 1986: "*Collier's Encyclopedia* continues to be one of the most important encyclopedias . . . a systematic program of revision maintains excellence in readability, objectivity, scholarship, and currentness."

XI. Summary

As a well-balanced reference source with good general coverage, *Collier's Encyclopedia* offers excellent value. It is reasonably up-to-date and well written. Strong coverage of academic disciplines makes it a good choice for college students and adults engaged in general research.

The broad entry format makes *Collier's* slightly less suitable for quick-reference use than some other multivolume encyclopedias (notably ACADEMIC AMERICAN ENCYCLOPEDIA), although readers familiar with its index will have little difficulty.

Smaller and less expensive than both ENCYCLOPEDIA AMERICANA and NEW BRITANNICA, *Collier's* yields to neither in authority, accuracy, or currency. It offers scholarly articles in a clear and concise format that will serve many reference needs.

Collier's Encyclopedia costs $1,399.50 to individuals and $799 to institutions. Thus the set is a particularly attractive purchase to colleges.

Individuals wishing to purchase *Collier's Encyclopedia* may contact the publisher, Macmillan Educational Corporation, at 866 Third Avenue, New York, NY 10022, or telephone (800) 257-9500. Institutions may address their orders to the same address or phone (800) 257-5755.

The Concise Columbia Encyclopedia

Facts at a Glance

Full Title: **The Concise Columbia Encyclopedia**.
Publisher: Columbia University Press (hardcover and large-print editions); Avon Books (paperback edition).
Editors: Judith S. Levey and Agnes Greenhall.
Copyright: 1983.

Number of Volumes: 1.
Number of Contributors: 53.

Number of Entries: 15,000.
Number of Pages: 943.
Number of Words: 1,000,000.
Number of Maps: 73.
Number of Cross-references: 50,000.
Number of Illustrations: 117, black-and-white only.
Trim Size: 7¼" × 10¼".

Price: $29.95, cloth; $14.95, paper; $275, large-print.
Sold in bookstores and by direct mail.
ISBN 0-231-05678-8.
No revision policy; no scheduled revision.

I. Introduction

The Concise Columbia Encyclopedia, published in 1983, is a single-volume general encyclopedia. As its title implies, the volume aims to be concise and yet truly encyclopedic—no easy task, given the immense body of knowledge that is condensed into so small a space. In their preface, the editors claim that to achieve this end they have made "scrupulous efforts to avoid distortion and to maintain readability without sacrificing grace of expression." However, they do not give details of their selection criteria, beyond saying that they "did not include articles that would be simply definitions available in a dictionary, nor certain survey articles . . . on subjects whose depth and breadth precludes adequate treatment in a short-entry encyclopedia."

II. Scope

The Concise Columbia Encyclopedia contains 15,000 entries, each an average length of 70 words. Thus the entire volume contains slightly more than one million words.

According to the editors, approximately one-third of the entries are biographical. A spot-check by our reviewers bears this out. Place names and historical topics and events are also given prominent attention, but the *Concise Columbia* covers a wide range of subjects in all the traditional academic disciplines. The jacket blurb also asserts that over 3,000 articles deal with "up-to-date scientific and technical subjects." Relatively few entries relate to contemporary popular culture, and the book scrupulously avoids topics of merely passing interest or ephemeral quality in favor of mainstream subjects in the humanities and natural sciences. Such contemporary figures from the world of sports and entertainment who are included are those whose accomplishments in their fields, from the vantage point of 1982, seemed likely to have more than a passing impact. Among such entries are **Woody Allen**, **Henry Fonda**, **Jane Fonda**, and **Jack Nicklaus**.

The Concise Columbia Encyclopedia

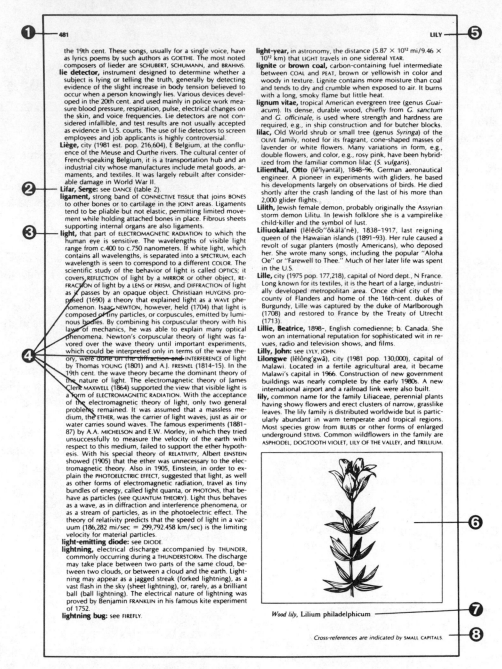

481

the 19th cent. These songs, usually for a single voice, have as lyrics poems by such authors as GOETHE. The most noted composers of lieder are SCHUBERT, SCHUMANN, and BRAHMS.

lie detector, instrument designed to determine whether a subject is lying or telling the truth, generally by detecting evidence of the slight increase in body tension believed to occur when a person knowingly lies. Various devices developed in the 20th cent. and used mainly in police work measure blood pressure, respiration, pulse, electrical changes on the skin, and voice frequencies. Lie detectors are not considered infallible, and test results are not usually accepted as evidence in U.S. courts. The use of lie detectors to screen employees and job applicants is highly controversial.

Liège, city (1981 est. pop. 216,604), E Belgium, at the confluence of the Meuse and Ourthe rivers. The cultural center of French-speaking Belgium, it is a transportation hub and an industrial city whose manufactures include metal goods, armaments, and textiles. It was largely rebuilt after considerable damage in World War II.

Lifar, Serge: see DANCE (table 2).

ligament, strong band of CONNECTIVE TISSUE that joins BONES to other bones or to cartilage in the JOINT areas. Ligaments tend to be pliable but not elastic, permitting limited movement while holding attached bones in place. Fibrous sheets supporting internal organs are also ligaments.

light, that part of ELECTROMAGNETIC RADIATION to which the human eye is sensitive. The wavelengths of visible light range from c.400 to c.750 nanometers. If white light, which contains all wavelengths, is separated into a SPECTRUM, each wavelength is seen to correspond to a different COLOR. The scientific study of the behavior of light is called OPTICS; it covers REFLECTION of light by a MIRROR or other object, REFRACTION of light by a LENS or PRISM, and DIFFRACTION of light as it passes by an opaque object. Christiaan HUYGENS proposed (1690) a theory that explained light as a WAVE phenomenon. Isaac NEWTON, however, held (1704) that light is composed of tiny particles, or corpuscules, emitted by luminous bodies. By combining his corpuscular theory with his laws of mechanics, he was able to explain many optical phenomena. Newton's corpuscular theory of light was favored over the wave theory until important experiments, which could be interpreted only in terms of the wave theory, were done on the diffraction and INTERFERENCE of light by Thomas YOUNG (1801) and A.J. FRESNEL (1814–15). In the 19th cent. the wave theory became the dominant theory of the nature of light. The electromagnetic theory of James Clerk MAXWELL (1864) supported the view that visible light is a form of ELECTROMAGNETIC RADIATION. With the acceptance of the electromagnetic theory of light, only two general problems remained. It was assumed that a massless medium, the ETHER, was the carrier of light waves, just as air or water carries sound waves. The famous experiments (1881–87) by A.A. MICHELSON and E.W. Morley, in which they tried unsuccessfully to measure the velocity of the earth with respect to this medium, failed to support the ether hypothesis. With his special theory of RELATIVITY, Albert EINSTEIN showed (1905) that the ether was unnecessary to the electromagnetic theory. Also in 1905, Einstein, in order to explain the PHOTOELECTRIC EFFECT, suggested that light, as well as other forms of electromagnetic radiation, travel in tiny bundles of energy, called light quanta, or PHOTONS, that behave as particles (see QUANTUM THEORY). Light thus behaves as a wave, as in diffraction and interference phenomena, or as a stream of particles, as in the photoelectric effect. The theory of relativity predicts that the speed of light in a vacuum (186,282 mi/sec = 299,792.458 km/sec) is the limiting velocity for material particles.

light-emitting diode: see DIODE.

lightning, electrical discharge accompanied by THUNDER, commonly occurring during a THUNDERSTORM. The discharge may take place between two parts of the same cloud, between two clouds, or between a cloud and the earth. Lightning may appear as a jagged streak (forked lightning), as a vast flash in the sky (sheet lightning), or, rarely, as a brilliant ball (ball lightning). The electrical nature of lightning was proved by Benjamin FRANKLIN in his famous kite experiment of 1752.

lightning bug: see FIREFLY.

LILY

light-year, in astronomy, the distance (5.87×10^{12} mi/9.46×10^{12} km) that LIGHT travels in one sidereal YEAR.

lignite or **brown coal,** carbon-containing fuel intermediate between COAL and PEAT, brown or yellowish in color and woody in texture. Lignite contains more moisture than coal and tends to dry and crumble when exposed to air. It burns with a long, smoky flame but little heat.

lignum vitae, tropical American evergreen tree (genus *Guaiacum*). Its dense, durable wood, chiefly from *G. sanctum* and *G. officinale*, is used where strength and hardness are required, e.g., in ship construction and for butcher blocks.

lilac, Old World shrub or small tree (genus *Syringa*) of the OLIVE family, noted for its fragrant, cone-shaped masses of lavender or white flowers. Many variations in form, e.g., double flowers, and color, e.g., rosy pink, have been hybridized from the familiar common lilac (*S. vulgaris*).

Lilienthal, Otto (lē'lyäntäl), 1848–96, German aeronautical engineer. A pioneer in experiments with gliders, he based his developments largely on observations of birds. He died shortly after the crash landing of the last of his more than 2,000 glider flights.

Lilith, Jewish female demon, probably originally the Assyrian storm demon Lilitu. In Jewish folklore she is a vampirelike child-killer and the symbol of lust.

Liliuokalani (lēlēō̄o̅o̅̅"ōkälä'nē), 1838–1917, last reigning queen of the Hawaiian islands (1891–93). Her rule caused a revolt of sugar planters (mostly Americans), who deposed her. She wrote many songs, including the popular "Aloha Oe" or "Farewell to Thee." Much of her later life was spent in the U.S.

Lille, city (1975 pop. 177,218), capital of Nord dept., N France. Long known for its textiles, it is the heart of a large, industrially developed metropolitan area. Once chief city of the county of Flanders and home of the 16th-cent. dukes of Burgundy, Lille was captured by the duke of Marlborough (1708) and restored to France by the Treaty of Utrecht (1713).

Lillie, Beatrice, 1898–, English comedienne; b. Canada. She won an international reputation for sophisticated wit in revues, radio and television shows, and films.

Lilly, John: see LYLY, JOHN.

Lilongwe (lēlông'gwä), city (1981 pop. 130,000), capital of Malawi. Located in a fertile agricultural area, it became Malawi's capital in 1966. Construction of new government buildings was nearly complete by the early 1980s. A new international airport and a railroad link were also built.

lily, common name for the family Liliaceae, perennial plants having showy flowers and erect clusters of narrow, grasslike leaves. The lily family is distributed worldwide but is particularly abundant in warm temperate and tropical regions. Most species grow from BULBS or other forms of enlarged underground STEMS. Common wildflowers in the family are ASPHODEL, DOGTOOTH VIOLET, LILY OF THE VALLEY, and TRILLIUM.

Wood lily, Lilium philadelphicum

Cross-references are indicated by SMALL CAPITALS.

Page shown at 68% of actual size.

❶ Page number

❷ Cross-reference entry

❸ Main entry: Concise Columbia contains 15,000 entries, arranged alphabetically, letter-by-letter. Entry words are printed in boldface type, and may be followed by a phonetic pronunciation. (See, for example, the entry for Liliuokalani in the second column.)

❹ Cross-references: Concise Columbia contains 50,000 cross-references, printed in small capital letters.

❺ Guide word

❻ Illustration: Concise Columbia contains 117 illustrations, many of which are annotated. All illustrations are in black-and-white.

❼ Caption

❽ Running foot repeated on every right-hand page reminds users about cross-references. Running foot in corresponding position on left-hand pages reminds users about pronunciation guide in frontmatter.

In their preface, the editors explain that "subjects of approximately equal importance [sometimes] required different treatment. . . . Explanations in some detail proved to be necessary for an understanding of certain technical subjects, and some controversial topics required mention of several points of view. . . . The length of an article does not necessarily indicate the importance of a subject." Entries for complex scientific concepts or major historical movements are generally longer than those for biographical subjects.

As an indication of how space is apportioned among different historical figures, a sampling of biographical entries on a page taken at random (page 240) shows the following: **John Dos Passos** is accorded 10 lines; **Fedor Dostoevski**, 32 lines; **Gerard Dou**, 4; **Abner Doubleday**, 7; **Charles Doughty**, 3; **Sir James Douglas**, 6; **Sir James de Douglas**, 8; **Stephen Douglas**, 15; **William Douglas**, 8; **Sir Alec Douglas-Home**, 6; and **Frederick Douglass**, 10.

The *Concise Columbia* is also notable for its coverage of non-American, non-British topics. For example, out of 19 people and place entries on a random page (page 473), 14 are non-American and non-British. Another random page (page 330) includes such entries as **Gezira** (a region in the Sudan), **Ghana** (separate articles on the ancient African empire and the modern African nation), the **Ghats** mountain ranges in India, the Islamic philosopher **al-Ghazali**, the 20th-century Belgian dramatist **Michel de Ghelderode**, the Belgian city of **Ghent**, the Rumanian Communist leader **Gheorghe Gheorghiu-Dej**, the Florentine artists **Lorenzo Ghiberti** and **Domenico Ghirlandaio**, and the Indian mystic **Aurobindo Ghose**.

As already mentioned, a preponderance of the articles are specific-entry rather than general-survey. However, the encyclopedia does include "articles on many specific aspects of these broad topics." Only rarely does the *Concise Columbia* depart from this scheme, as in the articles on the **French Revolution**, the **Renaissance**, and **Renaissance art and architecture**. Such longer articles tend to be brief chronological sketches, and rely heavily on a system of extensive cross-references. Generally, however, the specific entries are only several sentences long.

With 117 line drawings and 73 maps accompanying nearly 1000 pages of text, the *Concise Columbia* is sparsely illustrated. There are no photographs. The line drawings, many of which are annotated diagrams, pertain almost exclusively to technical subjects (e.g., **circulatory system**, **ear**, **jet propulsion engines**, **reproductive system**), and thus add to the encyclopedia's conciseness. Here the *Concise Columbia* has a distinct advantage over the NEW AMERICAN DESK ENCYCLOPEDIA, which has no illustrations and only rudimentary maps. At the same time, because the *Concise Columbia* does not contain photographs or color illustrations, the publisher is still able to sell the book at a reasonable price.

III. Authority

Over the last half century, the Columbia University Press has established a solid reputation as a leading publisher of both general and topical reference works. *The Concise Columbia Encyclopedia* carries on the tradition of excellence begun in 1935 with the *Columbia Encyclopedia* and continued with subsequent editions of that work, including the celebrated 1963 edition and the extensively revised *New Columbia Encyclopedia* (1975). Some users may also be familiar with the one-volume *Columbia-Viking Desk Encyclopedia* and the 22-volume *Illustrated Columbia Encyclopedia* (1967). All these titles are currently out of print.

The work's joint editors, Judith S. Levey and Agnes Greenhall, bring impressive credentials to the book. Levey, now Editor-in-Chief at Macmillan, held that position at Columbia University Press and has edited a number of other reference works. Greenhall was Senior Editor, Humanities, for the *New Columbia Encyclopedia*; Associate Editor, Humanities, for COLLIER'S ENCYCLOPEDIA; and Managing Editor of *The Columbia Dictionary of Modern European Literature*. The editors were assisted by the reference staff of the Columbia University Press.

Nineteen of the book's 33 consultants are affiliated with Columbia University; most of the remaining consultants hold posts at other universities, museums, or on periodicals. The extent of the consultants' participation is not clear, though the generally high quality and factual accuracy of the individual entries would seem to indicate that the articles were carefully checked by content specialists.

The editors acknowledge that "although the articles have been prepared especially for the *Concise* encyclopedia, much of the information derives from its predecessors—especially *The New Columbia Encyclopedia*." Direct comparison of entries in the two books gives clear evidence that many of the *Concise Columbia*'s articles are basically adaptations of longer articles that appeared in the earlier volume. But about 500 new entries were written especially for this volume, and articles adapted from *New Columbia* have been revised to bring them up-to-date.

The contributors—the actual writers of the articles—are listed in the front of the book. However, their credentials, affiliations, and areas of expertise are not given. All articles are unsigned.

IV. Currency

Published in 1983, *The Concise Columbia Encyclopedia* differs significantly from most other single- and multivolume encyclopedias in that it is not periodically revised, but is rather a one-time publication. This puts it at an automatic disadvantage for currency when compared with other small volume encyclopedias.

The editors claim that "many of our articles reflect the enormous changes that have taken place worldwide during the past five years" (i.e., 1978–83). The preface states that "the articles are up to date as of January 1, 1983," an assertion that seems justified, for the most part. The articles on **Ronald Reagan**, **Margaret Thatcher**, and **South Africa**, for example, include information on those subjects through 1982. One subject conspicuous by its omission, however, is AIDS, which was first identified in 1980.

The publisher's policy of not revising the book periodically does pose certain limitations on the encyclopedia's currency, limitations that will become increasingly apparent with the passage of time. For example, while the article on **nuclear disarmament** ends with mention of the 1982 Strategic Arms Reduction Talks, there can obviously be no mention of President Reagan's 1983 Strategic Defense Initiative—the kind of information that one would expect to be included were the book revised on a regular cycle. Nor can one expect any mention of the Bhopal, *Challenger*, Chernobyl, and Rhine disasters, which would also have to be incorporated in a revision. Thus in terms of currency, the *Concise Columbia* will become increasingly weak in its coverage of current events; however, its coverage of pre-1983 events is reliably up-to-date and, in subject areas where no new findings or interpretations are expected, should remain authoritative.

V. Accuracy

The highly condensed articles that make up the *Concise Columbia* are comprised largely of straightforward statements of facts and figures. Indeed, with its experienced editors and team of distinguished consultants, this reference work sets high standards for factual accuracy. A great deal of meticulous scholarship has evidently gone into the preparation of this volume.

Factual errors do occasionally occur, however. For example, the article on **herpes simplex** reports: "Genital herpes, a type of VENEREAL DISEASE, can be treated with the drug acyclovir." The article does not mention that this drug treats only the symptoms of the infection and that, as of January 1983, genital herpes was incurable.

Our subject specialists note that the *Concise Columbia*'s entries on **money** and **Saturn** are both brief but accurate. The encyclopedia's coverage of the **Bill of Rights** is somewhat cursory, but correct as far as it goes. **Transistors** is brief and discusses only bipolar

transistors; however, it does contain important cross-references to entries on **integrated circuits** and **microelectronics**, which help give the reader a more complete picture of the subject.

On the whole, such sins of omission that occur from time to time seem to be the unavoidable consequence of this encyclopedia's concise approach—in which complex topics must necessarily be reduced to their bare essentials—rather than of editorial carelessness. The *Concise Columbia* can generally be counted on to provide accurate factual information, and the reader need have little hesitation in trusting the facts presented in this work.

VI. Clarity

Many of the *Concise Columbia*'s articles are abridged versions of articles from *New Columbia*. With the average length of an entry a mere 70 words, clarity was obviously a prime concern. The articles are straightforward and to the point. Scholarship is evident in the writing, but the scholarly quality does not intrude on presentation of the subject. The *Concise Columbia*'s straightforward prose presents a clear contrast to THE LINCOLN LIBRARY OF ESSENTIAL INFORMATION, which is sometimes pedantic and tends to rely on generalities in many of its articles. The tone and style of THE NEW AMERICAN DESK ENCYCLOPEDIA is more directly comparable.

In general, entries in the *Concise Columbia* assume that although the reader may have heard of the particular subject, he or she has no previous knowledge of that subject. The purpose of this encyclopedia is to present basic facts about the subjects rather than to give specialist information that may not be available elsewhere. Throughout the work, our reviewers found no condescension or unnecessary explanation.

A few examples will illustrate the style of the entries in the *Concise Columbia*. The entries are quoted in full.

Muses, in Greek mythology, the nine patron goddesses of the arts; daughters of ZEUS and Mnemosyne, a TITAN who personified memory. They were: Calliope (epic poetry and eloquence), Euterpe (music and lyric poetry), Erato (love poetry), Polyhymnia (oratory or sacred poetry), Clio (history), Melpomene (tragedy), Thalia (comedy), Terpsichore (choral song and dance), and Urania (astronomy).

Lena, river easternmost of the great rivers of Siberia, USSR, c. 2,670 mi (4,300 km) long. It flows generally north, then northeast, from a source near Lake BAYKAL to empty into the ARCTIC OCEAN through a delta c. 250 mi (400 km) wide. The river, which is navigable for 2,135 mi (3,436 km) in summer, is frozen at its mouth from Oct. to June.

gadolinium (Gd), metallic element, extracted in oxide form by J.C.G. de Marignac in 1880. This silver-white malleable, ductile, lustrous RARE-EARTH METAL is found in gadolinite, MONAZITE, and bastnasite. It is paramagnetic at room temperature but becomes strongly ferromagnetic when cooled. See ELEMENT (table); PERIODIC TABLE.

Titanic, British liner that sank on the night of Apr. 14–15, 1912, after striking an iceberg in the North Atlantic. The disaster, which occurred on the ship's maiden voyage, claimed the lives of more than 1,500 of the 2,200 people aboard. Many perished because of a shortage of lifeboats. More stringent safety rules for ships and an iceberg patrol were later instituted.

While these entries are straightforward, they require at least a passing familiarity with Greek mythology, Asian geography, chemistry, and modern history, respectively. Some readers may find that they will also need to consult a dictionary. Also, contrary to the editors' stated intention, some of the articles (such as the one on gadolinium) are only one step removed from being dictionary definitions. While these articles are clear and precise as far as they go, they are little more than thumbnail sketches. The article on the **Muses**, for example, neither explains the implications of their parentage nor indicates their mythological and historical significance. The **gadolinium** article gives the reader no idea of the metal's uses, if any. And the **Titanic** entry omits many significant details.

The articles in *The Concise Columbia Encyclopedia* conform to a strict house style. The entire book reads like the work of a single author, or of a handful of experienced authors who are all the product of the same intellectual environment. While this is not necessarily desirable (or even possible to achieve) in a general multivolume encyclopedia, it brings particular benefits to a concise one-volume reference work. For one thing, the articles are structured in such a way that, after using this encyclopedia a few times, the reader knows what to look for and what to expect in an entry. Rarely are these expectations disappointed. While technical terms are not defined in the context of an entry, the reader is frequently directed, via a cross-reference, to a separate entry for that term. On the whole, the entries in the *Concise Columbia* are models of brevity and precision.

VII. Objectivity

In its tone and in the balance with which it presents information on a wide range of subjects, *The Concise Columbia Encyclopedia* is scholarly and objective. The article on **homosexuality** notes that "Medical and psychological research has yielded little evidence that homosexuality is caused by either biological predis-

position or feelings that one belongs to the opposite sex. No theory is conclusive but many have been proposed. . . . " The concluding sentence in **Republic of South Africa** reports that "South Africa's refusal to yield control over Namibia, its creation of bantustans, and its rigid support of apartheid has led to growing international ostracism of the country." The entry on **Ronald Wilson Reagan** gives factual information about his presidency through 1982 without editorial comment.

In articles dealing with political or religious subjects (or subjects that may be the focus of political or religious controversy), the encyclopedia's tone is rigorously neutral. It presents known facts as such, and identifies theory as such. For example, the article on **evolution** describes the concept and dispassionately states the grounds on which it rests. It also notes that "[evolution] has been challenged by those believing in the creation theory of the universe (see CREATIONISM)." The article on **creationism** describes it as "belief in the biblical account of the creation of the world" and notes that its advocates dispute the theory of evolution. The articles make no value judgments on either subject.

As previously noted, the *Concise Columbia* does an admirable job of avoiding, as far as is possible in a work of its size and scope, an undue American bias in its contents. (See *Scope*.)

VIII. Accessibility

With space limitations making conciseness a major concern, the editors appear to have given careful thought to the book's layout and to the arrangement of the articles. A one-and-a-half-page introduction, "How to Use *The Concise Columbia Encyclopedia*," systematically explains all the elements and variations of style that are encountered in the body of this volume. However, the explanations are not as clear as they might be.

All article heads are in boldface type, making them easy to distinguish and identify at a glance. Entries are arranged alphabetically by word. Headnotes indicate the first entry on the left-hand page and the last entry on the right-hand page. Page numbers are located at the top of the page, but flush with the inside, not the outside, margin of the page—a format that makes them less easy to see as the reader thumbs through the book.

Given the number of entries and the complexity of some of the subjects, it was probably inevitable that the arrangement of the entries could not be as obvious or as clear-cut as the user might wish. While the editors have attempted to come up with a logical system for arranging the entries, they have not been entirely consistent, and there are some puzzling exceptions to each rule they have made.

For example, when several items have the same heading, they are arranged in order of persons, places, and things. Thus **McKinley, William** comes before **McKinley, Mount**. However, **Paris**, the city, precedes **Paris**, the character whose abduction of Helen precipitated the Trojan War. The reason for this deviation is unclear, unless the second Paris, being mythological, is classified as a thing rather than as a person. Such apparent inconsistencies mean that the reader may not initially find a particular article where he or she expected to find it, and that it may be necessary to look in other likely locations.

There are several other departures from strict alphabetic order when the encyclopedia deals with proper names. Although most biographical headings are inverted and alphabetized by the subject's last name (e.g., **Bunyan, Paul**), some mythological or folkloric figures are entered with their first name first (e.g., **John Henry**). The rationale for this is not made clear. Names with *de, van, von,* or other prefixes are entered according to what the editors regard as the most common form of the name in general use. Thus the *Concise Columbia* gives us **Beauvoir, Simone de**; **Teilhard de Chardin, Pierre**; and **von Neumann, John**; there are no cross-reference entries for possible variations, such as "**de Beauvoir, Simone**: see BEAUVOIR." This can make certain entries difficult to find and may be frustrating to the reader who is unfamiliar with the common form of a particular name, or when there are several commonly used forms. The reader has better luck finding articles on people who are best known by their pseudonyms: the entry for **Evans, Mary Ann**, for example, refers the reader to **Eliot, George** for information about the famous Victorian novelist.

Names beginning with *Mc* are treated as though they began with *Mac*. A similar rule applies to the use of the abbreviation *St.* for *Saint*.

Members of the same family are generally grouped together under the family name. Monarchs are grouped together under their given name by nationality. Thus the *Concise Columbia* gives us "**Henry**, rulers of the Holy Roman Empire"; "**Henry**, kings of England"; and "**Henry**, kings of France." The individual rulers are treated in succession within the appropriate article.

While such treatment of proper name entries may seem like excessive scholarly scruple, and may occasionally confuse or even intimidate some readers, the system is not difficult to master. The boldface type makes entries easy to spot, and with a little practice in thumbing through the volume, users can find subjects in the *Concise Columbia* as easily as they can find words in a dictionary.

The real key to the accessibility of the *Concise Columbia* is the volume's extensive system of cross-references, of which there are some 50,000. It is this system that helps the book achieve its conciseness. Cross-references occur in the text of individual articles, at the conclusion of articles, and immediately after a heading when the subject is actually discussed under a different heading (such as "**peat moss**: see SPHAGNUM"). In all cases, cross-reference indications are printed in small capitals, making them, like the entry headings, immediately identifiable.

Occasionally some articles seem to be little more than lists of cross-references. The 32-line article on **drugs**, for instance, refers the reader to 29 different articles. There is a danger that an article will rely so heavily on cross-references that the reader will be unable to comprehend the subject without reading the related entries. Also, the potential purchaser should be aware that *The Concise Columbia Encyclopedia* does not contain an index. This is a distinct drawback, especially in light of the inconsistencies in the arrangement of entries as already noted. Without an index, the user has no easy and reliable way of knowing whether a certain topic is included in the *Concise Columbia* or, if it is, on what page it is discussed.

Regardless of these criticisms, however, in the vast majority of cases the use of cross-references greatly enhances the value of a particular article. Indeed, the careful and comprehensive cross-referencing throughout *The Concise Columbia Encyclopedia* is indispensable to the volume's conciseness. And the book's alphabetical arrangement makes it more accessible and far less complicated to the average reader than is the LINCOLN LIBRARY.

IX. Special Features

As a basic single-volume desk encyclopedia, *The Concise Columbia Encyclopedia* does not boast any unusual special features. Many of its features, such as metric equivalents for measurements and pronunciations for some foreign-name entries, are standard for any encyclopedia of this size and scope. The book is significantly enhanced, however, by the clear line drawings that illustrate subjects not easily explained in the text. (For more on the illustrations, see *Scope*.)

Equally helpful are 37 tables that accompany corresponding entries. While some of these tables (e.g., **Constitution of the United States**, **Rulers of England and Great Britain**, **Nobel Prizes**) are fairly standard and will be found in any decent encyclopedia, others are quite surprising and provide interesting factual information not readily accessible in other general reference sources. Among such tables are **African Languages**, **American Indian Languages**, **Dance Companies**, **Music Festivals**, **National Parks of the United States**, and **Shakespeare's Plays**. Many of these tables are by no means all-inclusive and comprehensive, but they do give the reader a handy, compact outline, providing good starting points for further study. Like the text, the tables also make extensive use of cross-referencing.

X. Format

The Concise Columbia Encyclopedia is available in hardcover and paperback. The hardcover edition is priced at $29.95; the paperback, distributed by Avon Books, retails for $14.95. The paperback version is a photo-reduced copy of the hardcover edition, which means that the print in the paperback version is noticeably smaller. The text of both editions is identical. There is also an eight-volume large print edition for $275.

The hardcover edition does have the advantage of a 16-page, four-color world atlas provided by Rand McNally, which appears in the middle of the book. Though the map scales are small and not consistent throughout the atlas, the overall quality of these maps is very good indeed. The paperback edition includes seven maps of the continents. These black-and-white maps, which appear in the back of the volume, are rudimentary and cannot compare in quality to the color atlas in the hardcover version.

The other main difference between the hardcover and paperback versions is durability. While the paperback is half the price of the hardcover edition, it may become worn much more quickly. Libraries will certainly prefer the more durable hardcover edition. Both formats are certainly more suitable for library use than is the format of THE NEW AMERICAN DESK ENCYCLOPEDIA. At the same time, the *Concise Columbia* is easier to handle than the two large books that constitute the LINCOLN LIBRARY.

XI. Other Opinions

Harry E. Whitmore, *Library Journal* (December 15, 1983): "The *Concise Columbia* continues the high standards of its predecessors and is a useful ready reference and supplementary information source. There is no comparable work within its price range."

Wilson Library Bulletin (December 1983): "Giving balanced subject coverage in clear, objective articles, the *Concise Columbia* merits accolades and frequent use as a desk reference."

Reference Books Bulletin (March 1, 1984): "The *Concise Columbia* covers a broad range of historical and contemporary topics. . . . There are some inconsistencies in coverage. . . . Articles include facts and brief explanations; they generally lack the historical coverage and detail found in the *New Columbia*, [but] the level of accuracy is high. . . . The en-

cyclopedia is both current and objective. . . . [It] is a reasonably priced reference tool for all types of libraries and for home use as well . . . an attractive alternative to other . . . one-volume encyclopedias [for] ready reference."

Samuel Rothstein, *ARBA 84*: "For clarity, coverage, ease of use, and low cost, *CCE* ranks very high indeed. It should be a top priority for the home reference library, and even in institutional collections its up-to-dateness and conciseness will make it welcome."

XII. Summary

The Bowker library survey indicates that while many librarians continue to find *The New Columbia Encyclopedia* a useful single-volume reference work, patrons consult *The Concise Columbia Encyclopedia* much less frequently. The book's relatively compact format, reasonable price, and wide availability—it is stocked in many bookstores—would seem to indicate that the *Concise Columbia* is intended primarily for purchase by individuals for use in the home or office, rather than as a major library reference resource. However, it may also be a particularly attractive purchase to small public libraries with limited budgets.

The *Concise Columbia* provides concise, accurate, and fairly accessible answers to such questions as: What islands make up the nation of The Comoros, and where are they located? When did Czeslaw Milosz win the Nobel Prize? What happens in a cell during meiosis? What is a mirage? While it obviously cannot compete with multivolume encyclopedias in providing in-depth discussions of these topics, and indeed contains less detailed information than the competing small-volume encyclopedias, for its size and price it is a remarkable value. Keeping in mind its limitations, it can be highly recommended to any reader looking for a handy desk-top single-volume encyclopedia for ready reference.

The Encyclopedia Americana

Facts at a Glance

Full Title: **The Encyclopedia Americana**.
Publisher: Grolier Incorporated.
Editors: Bernard S. Cayne, Editorial Director; David T. Holland, Editor-in-Chief.
Edition Reviewed: 1987. (Statistics apply to 1988 edition.)

Number of Volumes: 30.
Number of Entries: 52,000.
Number of Pages: 26,965.

Encyclopedia Americana

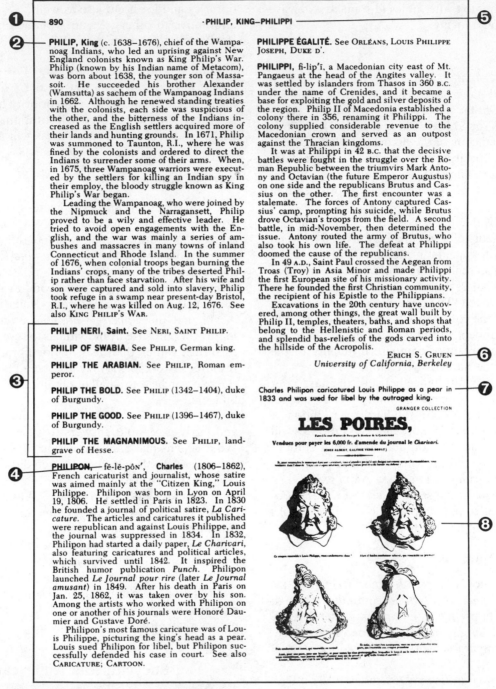

❶ 890   ·PHILIP, KING—PHILIPPI   **❺**

❷ PHILIP, King (c. 1638–1676), chief of the Wampanoag Indians, who led an uprising against New England colonists known as King Philip's War. Philip (known by his Indian name of Metacom), was born about 1638, the younger son of Massasoit. He succeeded his brother Alexander (Wamsutta) as sachem of the Wampanoag Indians in 1662. Although he renewed standing treaties with the colonists, each side was suspicious of the other, and the bitterness of the Indians increased as the English settlers acquired more of their lands and hunting grounds. In 1671, Philip was summoned to Taunton, R.I., where he was fined by the colonists and ordered to direct the Indians to surrender some of their arms. When, in 1675, three Wampanoag warriors were executed by the settlers for killing an Indian spy in their employ, the bloody struggle known as King Philip's War began.

Leading the Wampanoag, who were joined by the Nipmuck and the Narragansett, Philip proved to be a wily and effective leader. He tried to avoid open engagements with the English, and the war was mainly a series of ambushes and massacres in many towns of inland Connecticut and Rhode Island. In the summer of 1676, when colonial troops began burning the Indians' crops, many of the tribes deserted Philip rather than face starvation. After his wife and son were captured and sold into slavery, Philip took refuge in a swamp near present-day Bristol, R.I., where he was killed on Aug. 12, 1676. See also KING PHILIP'S WAR.

❸ PHILIP NERI, Saint. See NERI, SAINT PHILIP.

PHILIP OF SWABIA. See PHILIP, German king.

PHILIP THE ARABIAN. See PHILIP, Roman emperor.

PHILIP THE BOLD. See PHILIP (1342–1404), duke of Burgundy.

PHILIP THE GOOD. See PHILIP (1396–1467), duke of Burgundy.

PHILIP THE MAGNANIMOUS. See PHILIP, landgrave of Hesse.

❹ PHILIPON, fē-lē-pôn′, **Charles** (1806–1862), French caricaturist and journalist, whose satire was aimed mainly at the "Citizen King," Louis Philippe. Philipon was born in Lyon on April 19, 1806. He settled in Paris in 1823. In 1830 he founded a journal of political satire, *La Caricature*. The articles and caricatures it published were republican and against Louis Philippe, and the journal was suppressed in 1834. In 1832, Philipon had started a daily paper, *Le Charivari*, also featuring caricatures and political articles, which survived until 1842. It inspired the British humor publication *Punch*. Philipon launched *Le Journal pour rire* (later *Le Journal amusant*) in 1849. After his death in Paris on Jan. 25, 1862, it was taken over by his son. Among the artists who worked with Philipon on one or another of his journals were Honoré Daumier and Gustave Doré.

Philipon's most famous caricature was of Louis Philippe, picturing the king's head as a pear. Louis sued Philipon for libel, but Philipon successfully defended his case in court. See also CARICATURE; CARTOON.

PHILIPPE ÉGALITÉ. See ORLÉANS, LOUIS PHILIPPE JOSEPH, DUKE D'.

PHILIPPI, fi-lip′ī, a Macedonian city east of Mt. Pangaeus at the head of the Angites valley. It was settled by islanders from Thasos in 360 B.C. under the name of Crenides, and it became a base for exploiting the gold and silver deposits of the region. Philip II of Macedonia established a colony there in 356, renaming it Philippi. The colony supplied considerable revenue to the Macedonian crown and served as an outpost against the Thracian kingdoms.

It was at Philippi in 42 B.C. that the decisive battles were fought in the struggle over the Roman Republic between the triumvirs Mark Antony and Octavian (the future Emperor Augustus) on one side and the republicans Brutus and Cassius on the other. The first encounter was a stalemate. The forces of Antony captured Cassius' camp, prompting his suicide, while Brutus drove Octavian's troops from the field. A second battle, in mid-November, then determined the issue. Antony routed the army of Brutus, who also took his own life. The defeat at Philippi doomed the cause of the republicans.

In 49 A.D., Saint Paul crossed the Aegean from Troas (Troy) in Asia Minor and made Philippi the first European site of his missionary activity. There he founded the first Christian community, the recipient of his Epistle to the Philippians.

Excavations in the 20th century have uncovered, among other things, the great wall built by Philip II, temples, theaters, baths, and shops that belong to the Hellenistic and Roman periods, and splendid bas-reliefs of the gods carved into the hillside of the Acropolis.

ERICH S. GRUEN **❻**
University of California, Berkeley

Charles Philipon caricatured Louis Philippe as a pear in 1833 and was sued for libel by the outraged king. **❼**

GRANGER COLLECTION

LES POIRES,

Vendues pour payer les 6,000 fr. d'amende du journal le *Charivari*.

❽

Page shown at 73% of actual size.

❶ Page number
❷ Main entry: Encyclopedia Americana contains 52,000 entries, the second-largest amount of any multivolume general encyclopedia. Entries are arranged alphabetically, word-by-word.

❸ Cross-reference entries: Encyclopedia Americana contains 40,000 cross-references.
❹ Pronunciation: Foreign or other difficult entry words are followed by phonetic pronunciation.
❺ Guide words
❻ Contributor's credit: Encyclopedia Americana has

6,485 contributors. On signed articles, the contributor's authority is frequently cited.
❼ Caption
❽ Illustration: Encyclopedia Americana contains 22,724 illustrations, of which 3,184 are in color.

Number of Words: 30,800,000.
Number of Maps: 1,279.
Number of Cross-references: 40,000.
Number of Indexes: 1.
Number of Index Entries: 353,000.
Number of Illustrations: 3,184 four-color; 19,540 black-and-white.
Trim Size: 7¼″ × 10″.

Price: $1,200 plus shipping and handling for individuals; $869 plus shipping and handling with library discount.
Sold directly by the publisher and door-to-door.
ISBN 0-7172-0118-X.
Revised annually.

I. Introduction

The Encyclopedia Americana is a 30-volume general reference work written for "a wide range of readers." Today the *Americana* is regarded as one of the "big three" scholarly encyclopedias on the market—the other two being COLLIER'S ENCYCLOPEDIA and NEW ENCYCLOPAEDIA BRITANNICA. To some degree, as its title indicates, the *Americana* is designed to emulate the NEW BRITANNICA and to challenge it as the preeminent encyclopedia in the United States.

This review is based on an examination of the 1987 edition because the 1988 edition was not available at the time of review.

II. Scope

With some 52,000 articles, the *Americana* is one of the most wide-ranging of all multivolume encyclopedias, second only to the NEW BRITANNICA, which contains approximately 11,000 more entries. Like both NEW BRITANNICA and COLLIER'S, the *Americana* includes a mix of general survey and specific-entry articles. As the publisher notes, the short articles are designed for ready reference; "when further expansion is needed," the articles are somewhat longer; and very long articles allow major subjects to be covered at some length. "Many of the short articles are 20 lines or less and are structured to answer specific questions on a subject. Every short article is designed at least to define, describe, and provide the significance of the subject it covers," the publisher adds. On the whole, these claims are justified. In effect, *Americana*'s extended general-subject entries serve much the same function as NEW BRITANNICA's Macropaedia entries, although *Americana* does not segregate these entries from the rest of the text.

As an indication of how space is apportioned among different subjects, **Charlemagne** receives two and one-half pages; **Konstantin Chernenko** gets just over one-half page (including a family photograph); **Ty Cobb** also receives one-half page, with a photograph. The article on the American **Civil War** is 38 pages long; 17 pages are devoted to **Christianity**; and **China** is treated in 106 pages.

Although the set is geared to the American reader, Grolier reports—not without justification—that the *Americana*'s "coverage of foreign topics, such as foreign cities, artists, and politicians, is in most cases at least as great as that of American topics and in some cases greater."

As an indication of the attention *Americana* gives to non-American subjects, the encyclopedia's entries from **Bartolome Mitre** to **Mohammed**, inclusive, include the following articles: **Mitre** (Argentine statesman), **Dimitri Mitropoulos** (Greek-born American orchestral conductor), **Eilhard Mitscherlich** (19th-century German chemist), **François Mitterrand** (French president), **Mixtec Indians**, **Miyagi** (Japanese prefecture), **Miyazaki** (Japanese city), **Mizoram** (territory in India), **Mo Tzu** (ancient Chinese philosopher), **Moab** (ancient Near Eastern kingdom), **Vilhelm Moberg** (20th-century Swedish author), **Mobutu Sese Seko** (Zairean president), **Moche** (Peruvian valley), **Modena** (Italian city), **modernismo** (Latin American literary movement), **Amedeo Modigliani** (Italian artist), **Thomas Mofolo** (African writer), **Mogadishu** (Somalian capital), **Mogilev** (Russian city), **Mohacs** (Hungarian town), and **Mohammed**. These represent 21 entries out of a total of 58 in this span.

III. Authority

The *Americana* has the distinction of being the first encyclopedia published in the United States. The initial volumes were issued in 1829, and the first set was completed four years later with the publication of Volume 13. By 1850 the *Americana* was a standard feature in many American homes—the publishers claim that it was included in Abraham Lincoln's small collection of books.

Since 1930 *Americana* has been published by Grolier, a major publisher of encyclopedias and educational material. Grolier also publishes the ACADEMIC AMERICAN ENCYCLOPEDIA and, for younger readers, *The New Book of Knowledge*.

A staff of eight editors, 16 associate editors, and other researchers and editorial assistants works under the direction of Bernard S. Cayne, Editorial Director (who is also responsible for Grolier's other two encyclopedias) and David T. Holland, Editor-in-Chief. Some 6,460 contributors, most of whom are affiliated with colleges, universities, museums, or professional journals, are listed in the front matter. Articles are signed, and the end-of-article credits frequently cite a major book on the subject by the contributor, thereby establishing the writer's authority. Among well-known names in the contributors' list are Isaac Asimov, Jacques Barzun, Eric Bentley, Asa Briggs, Henry Steele Commager, Norman Cousins, Richard Ellmann, Thor Heyerdahl, Alan Hodgkin, Edward Teller, Carl Van Doren, and Martin Williams. However, a considerable percentage of the contributors have since moved on to institutions other than the ones to which they are identified as belonging, and some, like Van Doren, have been deceased for several years.

According to the Preface, "Distinguished advisors have assisted the editors in organizing the information in their fields into convenient forms of presentation. . . . The advisors have also assisted the editors in choosing leading authorities in each field to write the articles. After the expert is selected . . . he or she is reminded of the need to write for the unspecialized reader. The author is asked not to 'write down,' but to present facts and interpretations in an orderly way and in a direct style, and to explain technical terms when they are used." On the whole, the contributors seem to have adhered to this dictum, although technical terms are not always defined. (See also *Clarity*.)

IV. Currency

Like virtually all general multivolume encyclopedias on the market, the *Encyclopedia Americana* is revised and reprinted annually. While the publisher does not give a specific figure as to the percentage of pages handled in each revision, it does remark that "thousands of pages . . . are revised each year to reflect new developments in the modern world and fresh discoveries about the past." In this process, new entries have been added; outdated existing articles have been replaced by newly written ones on the same subject; major changes have been made within articles when the subject (or human knowledge about it) has changed significantly; and minor revisions have been made when recent developments warrant them.

Among new biographical entries added to the 1987 *Americana* are those for **Benigno Aquino**, **Corazon Aquino**, **Steve Carlton**, **Jane Goodall**, **Antonin Scalia**, **Stevie Smith**, **Alice Walker**, and **Elie Wiesel**. The 1987 edition includes 42 new entries in all. In light of recent or ongoing developments, 71 existing articles were replaced. These include **extinct and endangered species**, **health insurance**, **Hong Kong**, **Ferdinand Marcos**, **Imelda Marcos**, **nuclear energy**, and **Uranus**. Important chapters within the long entries on **Brazil**, **Chile**, and **Colombia** were also replaced. An additional 60 articles underwent major revision; minor changes were made in another 950 entries.

Significant as these revisions are, however, our reviewers found that the *Americana* is not consistently up-to-date. Some articles are very current, while others (sometimes dealing with a closely related topic) are out of date. For example, the article **Afrikaners** ends: "After 1948, the NP [National Party] was in power successively under D. F. Malan (1948-1954), J. G. Strijdom (1954-1958), H. F. Verwoerd (1958-1966), and B. J. Vorster (1966-)." P. W. Botha, who became head of the South African government following Vorster's resignation in 1978, is not mentioned, nor is there a biographical entry for him. Yet he is named in the **South Africa** article, which also describes the main provisions of the 1984 constitution but does not note that international sanctions were applied against the nation in the mid-1980s in an effort to change the government's apartheid policy.

Titanic reports that "on September 1, 1985, the *Titanic* was located on the ocean floor upright and mostly intact by a U.S.–French team of oceanographers." Yet the article on **sound recording and reproduction** makes no note of digital recording or compact discs; in fact, the last innovation it mentions is the introduction of quadraphonic recording, which occurred in 1971. Nor is there any indication that the quadraphonic technique failed to catch on and that the record industry abandoned quadraphonic recording by 1980.

The entry on **Ronald Reagan** is reasonably up-to-date. It mentions the ouster of the Marcos regime and the recognition of the Aquino government in the Philippines (February 1986), the U.S. raids on Libya (April 1986), and the passage of tax reform (October 1986). On the other hand, the entry on **Margaret Thatcher** ends with the Conservative Party's victory in the election of May 1979, providing no information about her subsequent long and often controversial tenure as Prime Minister of Great Britain. Yet the entry on **Great Britain** follows developments during her government through the 1983 election.

Coverage of notable contemporary figures is also uneven. For example, the *Americana* includes entries for **Geraldine Ferraro**, **Gary Hart**, **Barbara McClintock**, and **Brian Mulroney**, but none for Brazilian President Jose Sarney or 1984 and 1985 Nobel (literature) Prize winners Jaroslav Seifert and Claude Simone. The omission of Sarney is particularly curious, since the article on **Brazil** concludes with five paragraphs about his administration. Seifert and Simone are listed in the encyclopedia's roster of **Nobel Prize** winners.

The publisher reports that United States population figures are based on the 1980 census. Those for Canada are based on the 1981 Canadian census. For other nations, the publisher claims that "every effort is made to provide the latest available figures or the most recent reliable estimates." In fact, however, these statistics frequently are not as current as they could be. For example, *Americana*'s entry on the **Union of Soviet Socialist Republics** gives the nation's 1970 census figure (241,720,134) and the 1977 estimated figure (257,900,000). By contrast, the 1987 ACADEMIC AMERICAN gives a 1986 estimate (279,904,000); the 1986 NEW BRITANNICA gives a 1984 estimate (274,492,000); the 1986 COLLIER'S gives the 1983 figure (273,000,000); and the 1987 WORLD BOOK ENCYCLOPEDIA gives a 1987 estimate (283,620,000).

According to the publisher, "the encyclopedia has been engaged in a program through which entire volumes are completely rebuilt. In the rebuild program the alphabetical span covered by an entire volume is examined as though a totally new work were being created." Grolier reports that Volumes 1 through 19 and 21 through 26 have already been "rebuilt" and that "the program is continuing." This undertaking is certainly ambitious, and is made all the more difficult by the sheer size of the set. It remains to be seen if the program will ultimately result in an encyclopedia that is as comprehensively and consistently up-to-date as Grolier's ACADEMIC AMERICAN.

V. Accuracy

With its many distinguished contributors, one can expect a high degree of accuracy in the *Americana*'s articles. Indeed, this is the case more often than not, especially where significant facts are concerned. However, our reviewers did encounter a number of factual errors that cast doubt on the set's consistency.

For example, the article on the **symphony** tells us that Dimitri Shostakovich "wrote 14 symphonies," and refers to "the six symphonies of the English composer Ralph Vaughan Williams." In fact, Shostakovich composed 15 symphonies, while Vaughan Williams wrote nine. The entry for **John Le Carre** reports that this is the nom de plume of David Cromwell, when in fact the author's name is *Cornwell*.

Other distortions or misinterpretations also occur. For example, the entry on **Ty Cobb** asserts that "his father, a respected educator and state senator, was fatally shot by his mother, who supposedly had mistaken him for an intruder." It has been generally established that his mother shot Cobb's father in a fit of rage because of his infidelity. It must be stressed, however, that for the general reader such minor inaccuracies will not detrimentally affect the overall usefulness and reliability of the set.

The *Americana* gives a fuller and more truthful account of Prince **Henry** the Navigator's motives than is found in either NEW BRITANNICA or COLLIER'S:

In 1418 he settled at the Vila do Infante near Sagres, where he built an observatory and attracted to his palace adventurers as well as astronomers and others involved in the study of navigation. . . . Although he had a scientific interest in navigation, he also hoped that these voyages would expand Portuguese trade in African gold and slaves. . . . Henry won lasting fame by encouraging voyages of exploration and the scientific study of navigation, although he himself did not travel farther than North Africa.

Americana's entry on **Saturn** is complete and up-to-date. **Bill of Rights** presents a clear account of that subject, combining the historical and analytical approaches. In contrast to these entries, the article on **money** is poorly written and organized, making it difficult for the average reader to follow. Moreover its errors and biases make it of a significantly lower standard than its counterparts in COLLIER'S and NEW BRITANNICA. The entry on the **brain** also suffers from poor organization and is not up-to-date. Overly detailed in some areas, it is skimpy in others. Among its major omissions, it does not mention the different functions of the left and right hemispheres of the brain, and its discussion of consciousness is also weak. *Americana*'s description of how **transistors** work is also accurate but probably more detailed than it needs to be. For example, the discussion of various wiring configurations used with bipolar transistors will be of interest mainly to the specialist and is more pertinent to an article on electronics than to one limited to transistors. At the same time, the article barely mentions integrated circuits; the reader is referred to the section *microelectronics* in the **electronics** article.

VI. Clarity

According to Grolier, the *Americana*'s "level of readability . . . is as carefully planned and controlled as the content. Each article is written at a level that seems appropriate for those most likely to consult the article. Technical vocabulary is kept to a minimum, and no article is written at a higher level than it need be. . . . Where technical terms cannot be avoided, they are defined when introduced into the text."

However, our reviewers have found that these claims are not always justified. Contrary to the publisher's claim, difficult or technical terms are not consistently explained in context. This is particularly evident in articles on scientific or technical subjects. For example, the first paragraph of **electron** reads as follows:

ELECTRON, an elementary particle carrying a unit negative charge of electricity. The charges of all other particles are positive or negative integral multiples of unit charge of the electron. The rest mass of the electron is 9.11×10^{-28} gram, about 1/1836 the mass of the proton or neutron.

This definition is so abstruse as to be virtually meaningless to the average reader who has little or no previous knowledge of the subject. At the same time, however, it does allow for a more highly sophisticated discussion of this complex subject than would otherwise be possible.

Like NEW BRITANNICA, the *Americana* allows its contributors a good deal of leeway. As in NEW BRITANICA and, to a lesser degree, COLLIER's, many of *Americana*'s nonscience articles are also pervaded by a scholarly and sometimes idiosyncratic writing style. While the writing is often distinguished and rarely "talks down" to the reader, it makes few concessions to the average adult reader. For example, we read in the entry on **Unitarianism** that "In England, in the turmoil of the 17th century, Socinianism made an appeal to several Anglican and Nonconformist circles as a rational, irenic expression of Christianity, tolerant of nonessential variations." Even though Socinianism is defined earlier in the article, this sentence may puzzle many readers. Nor is this an isolated example. Articles by specialist contributors in philosophy, history, and the social sciences often make liberal use of the particular language of that discipline.

The following article, **Titanic**, quoted in its entirety, illustrates the style of a typical entry in *Encyclopedia Americana*:

> **TITANIC**, ti-tan'ik. Shortly before midnight on April 14, 1912, the 46,328-ton White Star liner *Titanic*, on her maiden voyage from Southampton to New York, collided with an iceberg off the Banks of Newfoundland. The night was clear, but apparently there was some surface haze. Two hours and forty minutes after the impact, the magnificent new liner—the pride of the British merchant service, the largest and most sumptuously appointed vessel which had ever put to sea—went down with a loss of more than 1,500 lives.
>
> The root cause of this appalling catastrophe, which was accounted at the time "the most terrible shipwreck in history," was simply bad seamanship. Despite all the urgent warnings of ice, by radio and signal-lamp, the *Titanic*, in hopes of an early arrival in New York harbor, continually increased speed and drove that night into the ice track at over 22½ knots (41.7 km/hr).
>
> The *Californian*, the only vessel in the vicinity, made no attempt to reach the wreck. Her radio operator had gone off duty. The Cunard *Carpathia*, however, on receiving the *Titanic*'s distress call, turned round and steamed at high speed to the rescue of the survivors.
>
> It is to be observed that though the White Star Line was absolved at the British inquiry, in the High Court—and subsequently on appeal—the charge of negligence was upheld, and the company was ordered to pay heavy damages to the relatives of several of those lost.
>
> Some safety measures prompted by the wreck were creation of the International Ice Patrol, provision of lifeboat space for all persons on a ship, and constant radio watch at sea.
>
> On Sept. 1, 1985, the *Titanic* was located on the ocean floor upright and mostly intact by a U.S.-French team of oceanographers.

VII. Objectivity

In describing the encyclopedia's objectivity, the Preface to the 1986 edition of *Americana* quotes the editor of the first (1829) edition: "My wish has been not to obtrude opinions, but to furnish facts." However, as in NEW BRITANNICA, contributors are often allowed considerable latitude in expressing personal opinions or venturing speculative surmises. There is much to be said in favor of this essay-style approach to encyclopedia article-writing. Certainly it makes for more interesting reading and gives the reader a more human perspective on the particular subject than is possible in an article that attempts only to recite facts. It also assumes that the reader is able to exercise critical judgment about the writer's interpretation.

For example, the general introduction to the **United States** article, contributed by a Princeton University historian, is a rather subjective and freewheeling exploration of the contradictions of contemporary American society. The first sentence reads: "The United States entered its third century the richest nation in history, secure in its broadly democratic structure, brilliant in the application of techniques for mastering land, sea, and water—and deeply troubled." Various sections of the article, written by other historians, seem less like standard encyclopedia articles than personal essays in which the historian is at liberty to argue a thesis. Facts are presented selectively; occasionally more attention is devoted to certain points than seems warranted. For example, President Jimmy Carter is characterized as "a 'born-again Christian' " and "a self-proclaimed expert on efficiency in government," and the writer refers to "his ostentatious Baptist faith." While these references may be accurate, they are made in a context that suggests a biased, not necessarily central, point of view.

In many survey articles, speculative statements are not uncommon. For example, we read in **London** that "Great cities rarely change fundamentally in a short time, but those who knew the London of the empire, of extremes of wealth and poverty, and of a concentration on commerce have wondered if they were witnessing a historic transitional period in the life of the 1,900-year-old city." Such speculative remarks may stimulate the reader to think about the subject in a more imaginative way, rather than just trying to memorize facts and figures.

Entries on social issues and scientific concepts occasionally present a one-sided, doctrinaire view of the subject without mentioning other valid points of view. For example, the eleven-and-a-half-page article on **prejudice and discrimination**, while generally accurate, often takes a moralistic, moralizing tone. The article seeks not simply to inform but also to persuade. The four and a half pages it devotes to *sexism* take a strongly feminist view of the issue and imply that those who do not actively share feminist views, goals, or methods contribute to the exploitation of women. The article ends with the exhortation that "contemporary societies must make an attempt to [eliminate sexism]. If this effort is to succeed, it must incorporate all of the available approaches." One may agree or disagree; the point is, this type of writing is more appropriate to a newspaper editorial or political essay than to an encyclopedia, and cannot be considered objective. Such instances of overtly polemical writing in the *Encyclopedia Americana* are relatively rare, however.

The more objective article on **abortion** is divided into two sections of roughly equal length. The first is a discussion of the moral, religious, legal, and political issues surrounding the topic; the second is a discussion of its medical aspects. Under the subhead "The Moral Issue," the article states that "The basic problem is the moral or religious one relating to the rights of the fetus. One answers the question according to the conclusion one wishes to reach. . . ." The article then summarizes the major arguments both pro and con. However, it does not mention the common pro-abortion view that the fetus is part of the mother's body and that women should have the right to control their bodies.

The *Americana*'s comprehensive and well-balanced coverage of **evolution** includes a discussion of pre-Darwinian beliefs and theories. The article notes that "some people have always preferred to believe that the world is stable and unchanging, while others have thought that it is changing." It also reports on post-Darwinian theories of evolution, and on opposition to Darwin both from within and without the scientific community. The article assumes, however, that evolution is "the only scientifically tenable explanation of organic diversity and of adaptedness" and that "species have not always existed in their present state but have evolved from different ancestral species."

A one-page article on **creationism** recounts the history of the movement from Darwin's day through the Scopes trial and up to the present, summarizing the main creationist arguments. While the article is factually sound, the reader might infer from its tone that the contributor, identified as the chairman of the Department of the History of Medicine at the University of Wisconsin, is dismissive of the creationists' claims. The article notes creationists' efforts to pass state laws "requiring a balanced treatment of creation and evolution" in the schools. However, the claim that "they also convinced a majority of Americans that evolution should not be taught exclusively" is unsubstantiated and questionable.

The five-page article on **Andrew Jackson** is highly objective, reporting all the major achievements and controversies in a fair and straightforward manner. The article mentions that the duel in which he killed another lawyer "gave wide fame to Jackson's iron will but also provided his enemies with the claim that he took pleasure in violence and brutality." The entry ends with a paragraph on *Historical Interpretation* of his presidency, noting that "historians have debated the significance of Jacksonian Democracy for many decades" and presenting some major interpretations. The article concludes that "it is likely that succeeding generations will make their own judgments on the Age of Jackson."

VIII. Accessibility

Entries are arranged alphabetically, word by word. When several items have the same heading, they are arranged in the customary order of people, places, and things. Names beginning with *Mc* are alphabetized as though they began with *Mac*; names beginning with *St.* are likewise alphabetized as though *Saint* were spelled out.

According to the publisher, *Americana*'s index of more than 350,000 entries "provides a complete guide to the contents of the encyclopedia." The index is extremely useful and comprehensive. It not only includes entry subjects, but also refers the reader to instances where subjects not covered under their own entries are discussed in other articles.

As an indication of the scope and style of individual entries, the reader searching for information about Marie Curie will find the following index entry:

CURIE, Marie (Fr. phys.) 8-331
   Polonium 22-362
   Radioactivity 23-186
   Radium 23-199

(Information pertaining to Irène, Jacques, and Pierre Curie is indexed under separate entries for each of these individuals.)

The *Americana* makes use of several types of cross-references. In addition to *q.v.* or *qq.v.* notations, articles incorporate "See also" entries within the text or at the end of the article. However, the end-of-article cross-references are sparser and less comprehensive than those found in the NEW STANDARD ENCYCLOPEDIA and in WORLD BOOK. Like all other encyclopedias, *Americana* also makes use of cross-reference entries.

Nevertheless, although the publisher reports some 40,000 cross-references (an average of two per page), our reviewers found that the cross-referencing in the *Americana* is sometimes inadequate. For example, the half-page article on **Mount Everest** contains no cross-references, even though Edmund Hillary and Tenzing Norkay, who are mentioned, receive separate biographical entries. Readers looking for more information under *Norkay*, where the climber's biography might be expected, will not find a cross-reference entry directing them to the entry **Tenzing Norkay**, where his entry is actually located. (In fairness, neither NEW BRITANNICA nor COLLIER'S includes a cross-reference entry under *Norkay*, although WORLD BOOK does.) Without adequate cross-referencing, it is difficult for the lay reader to appreciate the entire scope of a given subject and the interrelationships within that subject.

Structurally, the articles in *Americana* are clearly organized. In long survey articles, readers are aided by a paginated "table of contents" printed on the first page of the article. The contents table for **United States**, for example, shows that the article is organized into eight main sections: introduction, the land, the people, culture and the arts, government, national defense, the economy, and history. These sections are divided further into 30 major subsections; in fact, the article makes use of four levels of subheads. Only NEW BRITANNICA (Macropaedia), NEW STANDARD ENCYCLOPEDIA, and WORLD BOOK provide comparable structure. Such organization makes the articles extremely easy to follow and enables readers to see at a glance the relationships among the different aspects of a complex topic.

IX. Special Features

The Encyclopedia Americana contains a number of standard special features common to most multivolume general encyclopedias, including illustrations, bibliographies, tables, charts, graphs, and maps. There are more than 22,500 illustrations, of which a little more than 3,000—only about 14 percent—are in color. This is a greater number of illustrations, overall, than in COLLIER'S, and almost as many as in NEW BRITANNICA—but the *Americana*'s illustrations are larger than the NEW BRITANNICA'S.

The illustrations are generally adequate but not outstanding. Occasionally hairstyles, dress, automobiles, or other incidental features betray the age of a particular photograph. In this respect, however, the *Americana*'s photos are usually on a par with those in COLLIER'S. The photos bear out Grolier's claim that they have been "carefully chosen to complement the text." More than 5,000 drawings and diagrams, about 10 percent of them in color, were commissioned for the *Americana*. Of particular interest are the simplified schematic diagrams that accompany many of the articles on technical subjects. The *Americana*'s anatomical drawings and diagrams are also clear and useful.

Three hundred of *Americana*'s 1,279 maps are in full color, and many are full-page or double-page in size. Designed by the respected cartographic firm of Hammond, these maps are generally clear, accurate, and up-to-date, and are as fine as those found in any other contemporary encyclopedia. There are maps for the continents, most major countries, and all 50 states as well as many special-purpose topical maps.

Bibliographies are provided for articles "when there are works of value to cite that can be used as a starting point for further study." The publisher claims that works listed in the various bibliographies "are known to be authoritative and are at the appropriate level for the user." For the 1987 edition of *Americana*, important new titles were added to more than 550 existing bibliographies, thereby enhancing these bibliographies' value. Classic texts are still included regardless of their age or current print status. Moreover, many of these (apart from these "classics") are now quite dated and out of print, and may not be available in many public libraries. The bibliographies function as "starting points for further study," but the reader will probably need to consult the library catalog for a more comprehensive listing of pertinent titles.

As previously noted (see *Accessibility*), long survey articles are headed by excellent tables of contents.

X. Format

The 30-volume *Encyclopedia Americana* comes in a standard green McCain Sewn Lexotone II binding, which should stand up well under heavy, repeated use. The volumes, using the split-letter system, are of approximately equal length, generally about 800 pages each. (The shortest, Volume 9, is 761 pages long, while Volume 14, at 965 pages, is the longest.) A single volume does not contain all the entries beginning with a particular letter. For example, Volume 26 contains all the entries from **Sumatra** to **trampoline**, while the next volume contains all the entries from **trance** to **venial sin**. The volume number and the titles of the first and last entries are stamped in clear gold lettering on red bands on the spine.

With a smaller trim size than either COLLIER'S or NEW BRITANNICA, the individual volumes of the *Americana* are fairly easy to handle. However, the entire set takes up nearly four and a half feet of horizontal shelf space, making it physically the longest of all general multivolume encyclopedias.

XI. Other Opinions

ARBA 82 (Susan C. Holte, Bohdan S. Wynar): "In terms of statistics (number of words and articles, quantity of illustrations, number of contributors), *Americana* ranks as one of the most comprehensive general encyclopedia. . . . Readability is quite evident in such areas as medicine and technology, where technical terms are introduced into most of the articles with definitions that are adequate for the nonspecialist."

ARBA 84 (Bohdan S. Wynar): "*The Encyclopedia Americana* is a well-balanced and clearly written authoritative work prepared by an experienced editorial staff, with an excellent index and well-designed illustrations. . . . In spite of certain shortcomings, *Americana* remains a well-edited and comprehensive work, which is highly recommended to all types of libraries as well as for home use."

Booklist (Reference Books Bulletin), November 15, 1986: "Today's *Americana* is international in coverage and scope. It is outstanding for its detailed coverage of U.S. and Canadian history and geography; its biographical, scientific, and technical articles; and its extensive treatment of literature, art, and music of every century. It is written in language easily comprehended by nonspecialists. . . . *Americana* maintains a high level of accuracy and authority. . . . *Americana*'s index is extremely detailed, with citations to illustrations and maps. . . . The 1986 edition lives up to the good reputation for informative, unbiased, authoritative articles established by earlier editions of the *Encyclopedia Americana* and [is recommended] for home and library use. . . ."

XII. Summary

As a comprehensive multivolume reference set, *The Encyclopedia Americana* can be classified in the mainstream of contemporary American reference books. The set will be of interest to a wide range of adults, including those with scholarly interests and those who use an encyclopedia only occasionally for casual reference or browsing.

The *Americana*'s main strengths are its wide scope and its comprehensive and detailed articles. The short specific-entry articles are excellent for ready reference, while the longer survey articles often are more informative than textbooks on the same subject. On the whole, *Americana* provides more information than COLLIER'S; many of its individual entries give more

information than their counterparts in NEW BRITANNICA. Its biographical articles are generally first-rate, and its coverage of science and technology is also outstanding (even though many of the entries in these areas are written at a higher level of complexity than they need to be).

Against these considerable strengths, the potential purchaser needs to weigh *Americana*'s defects. Although particular articles are sufficiently up-to-date, the set is not consistently current, and the user cannot assume that any given article will give a contemporary account of the subject. This lack of currency often adversely affects the set's accuracy. Moreover, the encyclopedia is dotted with many instances of obvious factual errors that, while relatively minor, could and should have been prevented. Certain articles evidence an occasional lack of objectivity and reflect the contributor's personal biases. The inadequate cross-referencing system is a more serious weakness that will prevent many readers from taking full advantage of the wealth of information that the *Americana* does contain. And finally, the preponderance of black-and-white illustrations (of which a number are noticeably outdated) give the set a somewhat drab, unappealing look.

The *Encyclopedia Americana* costs $1,200 to individuals and $869 to institutions. The disparity between the two prices may make the set a much more attractive purchase to libraries than to private collectors.

Individuals wishing to purchase *The Encyclopedia Americana* may contact the publisher, Grolier Incorporated, at Sherman Turnpike, Danbury, CT 06816, or telephone (800) 243-7256. Libraries should address their orders to Grolier Educational Corporation at the same address and phone number.

Everyman's Encyclopaedia

Facts at a Glance

Full Title: **Everyman's Encyclopaedia** (online version).
Publisher: J. M. Dent & Sons, Ltd.
Editor: David A. Girling.
Online Vendor: Dialog Information Services.
Copyright: 1978.

Number of Entries: 50,000.
Number of Words: 8,000,000.
Number of Cross-references: 15,000.

Price: by subscription to vendor and online charges.
Revised infrequently.

I. Introduction

The online version of *Everyman's Encyclopaedia* derives from a respected multivolume British encyclopedia published by J. M. Dent & Sons since 1913–14. The 12 volumes of the most recent print edition (1978) contain almost 9,000 pages, 50,000 entries, and eight million words, along with 5,600 black-and-white illustrations. Most of the 350 contributors are British academics, and the set was clearly designed to meet the needs of British readers.

Revised infrequently—once every ten years or so—the print version of *Everyman's* has been withdrawn from the American market in the face of stiff competition from more up-to-date American encyclopedias. Today the set is something of a rarity in American libraries, although it is available in Canada from Fitzhenry & Whiteside Publishers.

II. Accessibility

Online, *Everyman's Encyclopaedia* is accessible only through Dialog Information Services, a vendor of online database services; a user cannot access *Everyman's* directly. With Dialog, the search routine is in two parts: first, boot the system, load the communications program, dial the vendor, and when connected give the user ID. Second, select the database, give the search word(s), conduct the database search, display the text of the desired entry, and finally respond to the prompt for the next action. Each part usually takes at least two minutes, though the second can take far longer.

The command-driven Dialog search method is complex but very efficient once mastered. It was designed, however, for bibliographical databases such as Georef ("Surveys of worldwide technical literature on geology and geophysics from the American Geological Institute") and the Federal Index, so is only moderately suitable for searching an encyclopedia. A Dialog search makes much use of abstracts, for example, and abstracts do not appear in encyclopedias. As a result, online search of *Everyman's* can seem slow compared with direct consultation of the print edition, even though Dialog uses a well-designed search method and the 12-volume print edition lacks an index.

III. Locating Information

The Dialog search method attempts to match search words, which may be connected by logical operators such as AND, OR, and NOT, with text in the *Everyman's Encyclopaedia* entries themselves, not simply with the entry titles. Because the search method was designed for use with abstracts, the user cannot always narrow the search sufficiently without seeing the full entry. A search for "Ménière's Disease" or "Ménière's Syndrome" found no matches ("hits"), but a search for "Ménière" alone reported several; without abstracts, only by displaying the full entry on the screen could the user see which if any of these would be pertinent. "Ménière" might figure in the title of a lengthy entry, or it might be part of a passing mention. An alternative strategy, search for "ears AND disease," elicited among other things a lengthy entry on the history of grain cultivation.

Copious capitalized cross-references to other entries enable the user to extend the search beyond the target entry. The excellent 2,900-word entry on **Spanish-American Literature** encourages the reader to "see also BRAZIL, CENTRAL AMERICA, MEXICAN AND CENTRAL AMERICAN NATIVE LANGUAGES, PORTUGAL, ROMANCE LANGUAGES, SOUTH AMERICA and SOUTH AMERICAN NATIVE LANGUAGES" generically, along with specific individuals from **Cortes** to **Borges**.

IV. Cost

A search in *Everyman's* via Dialog need not prove costly, assuming the user already subscribes to the vendor's service. If the search makes an immediate hit—that is, if the service reports that it has only one match for the search word(s)—the entry can be displayed and the search concluded in less than a minute, which with Dialog means less than a dollar's cost. The connect time through a local node of Tymnet or Telenet would increase that figure only by pennies (the short entry on **Ronald Reagan** quoted in the following text cost about 57 cents to retrieve).

Search and connect costs rise, however, if the user fails to make a hit or makes more than one and has to renew the search on a more specific set of words or, worse still, has to review a large number of entries on the screen to discover which one is relevant to the search.

When the desired entry has been found, the user can obtain a hard copy in three ways: by ordering it from the vendor; by storing the incoming file in the computer memory (floppy or hard disc) and printing it later when off-line; or by outputting it directly to the home printer. Because most printers cannot keep up with the incoming data, the last option is the least economical, and causes the online charges to burgeon.

V. Currency

The online *Everyman's Encyclopaedia* is not at all up-to-date. In July 1987 the entry on **Ronald Reagan** read as follows in its entirety:

Reagan, Ronald Wilson (1911-), US politician, born at Tampico, Illinois; educated Eureka College (1932). He was a sports announcer in Des Moines, Iowa (1932–37) and a motion picture actor in Hollywood (1937–54), becoming president of the Screen Actors Guild (1947–52 and 1959–60). Later he became a TV actor and producer, and in 1964 he became active in Republican politics in California. In 1966 he was elected governor of California, serving until 1974. He became a possible presidential or vice-presidential candidate in 1968, and again in 1972. He is active in Republican national politics and especially popular among conservatives.

BIOGRAPHY

United States: 19th [sic] Century A.D.
History; North America

The two entries that include material on the space shuttle, **Rocket** and **Space Travel**, make no reference to events after 1976, and their bibliography also stops at that year. The entry on the British **Conservative party** mentions Margaret Thatcher only once:

> The party was again defeated in October 1974 and in February 1975 Heath was defeated in the leadership election by Mrs Margaret Thatcher, who thus became the first woman to lead a major party in Western Europe or North America.

As Mrs. Thatcher has become, since the 1987 British General Election, the senior national leader in the Western alliance, the entry is obviously long out of date.

The encyclopedia also lacks any reference to such current concerns as AIDS, privatization, or Chernobyl. Neither Corazon Aquino nor Armand Hammer have entries. When dealing with timeless topics, such as Thomas Aquinas, the encyclopedia's out-of-dateness is less vital. However, the bibliography for this entry lists no books written after 1962. Judging from the entries scanned in this review, the online version of the mid-1980s is no more up-to-date than the 1978 print edition. Online *Everyman's* severely undermines its authority by its lack of timeliness. Timeliness should be the salient quality of an online reference work.

VI. Accuracy, Objectivity, and Clarity

The academic background of its contributors has served *Everyman's Encyclopaedia* well. To the extent that any entry a decade out of date can be accurate and authoritative, these appear to be. And by the same token, they are objective. At something over 1,200 words, the entry on the **Conservative party** shows the British origins of the work but, allowing for the British viewpoint, it is even-handed, although because of the passage of time certain facts no longer hold true. It concludes:

> The modern Conservative party, while opposed to any extension of state ownership, has not, when in power, repealed the nationalisation acts of its Labour prede-

cessors except in the cases of road transport and steel. Its general economic outlook remains bound up with free enterprise, though it has in fact increasingly acknowledged that in the modern state this must operate within the framework of much state planning. Its progressive policies today differ from those of its principal opponents largely on points of emphasis. Despite its verbal insistence on tradition, the Conservative party has been able to absorb new ideas and policies, and to adapt itself to changing conditions, both domestic and international.

The bibliography for this entry includes books by Hailsham on the right and Harrington on the left, among others.

VII. Summary

Everyman's Encyclopaedia is a large-scale reference work especially valuable for its coverage of British and other European subjects. The astute cross-references adapt it readily to the user's needs. As long as the user makes an immediate "hit" and does not need to output a hard copy directly to the printer, *Everyman's* is relatively inexpensive to use. Unfortunately the version accessible online in mid-1987 was so out of date that information taken from it could be used with confidence only after checking and supplementation elsewhere. The Buying Guide's library survey results indicate that *Everyman's* is not the first choice of public and academic libraries when selecting an online encyclopedia; its lack of currency is no doubt a major factor. Until and unless *Everyman's* undergoes a thorough revision, its usefulness will remain limited.

Individuals and institutions interested in subscribing to the online version of *Everyman's Encyclopaedia* may contact the vendor, Dialog Information Services, Inc., 3460 Hillview Avenue, Palo Alto, CA 94304, telephone (415) 858-2700.

Funk & Wagnalls New Encyclopedia

Facts at a Glance

Full Title: **Funk & Wagnalls New Encyclopedia.**
Publisher: Funk & Wagnalls, Inc.
Editors: Leon L. Bram, Editorial Director; Norma H. Dickey, Editor-in-Chief.
Edition Reviewed: 1986. (Statistics apply to 1988 edition.)

Number of Volumes: 29.
Number of Contributors: 1,033.
Number of Entries: 25,000.
Number of Pages: 13,024.
Number of Words: 9,000,000.

Funk & Wagnalls New Encyclopedia

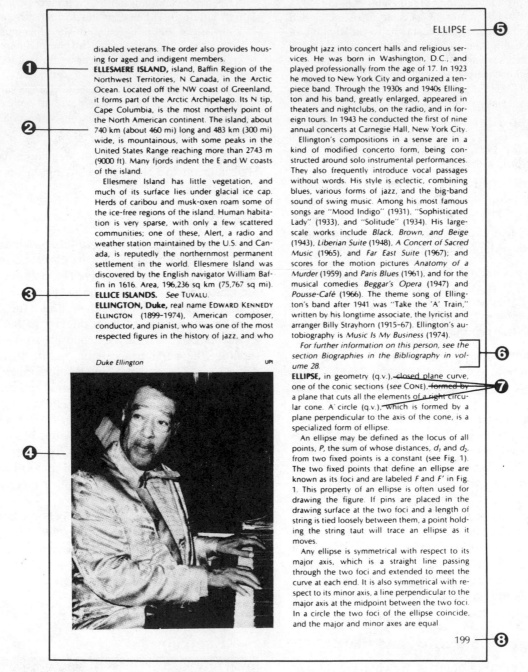

ELLIPSE — ⑤

disabled veterans. The order also provides housing for aged and indigent members.

ELLESMERE ISLAND, island, Baffin Region of the Northwest Territories, N Canada, in the Arctic Ocean. Located off the NW coast of Greenland, it forms part of the Arctic Archipelago. Its N tip, Cape Columbia, is the most northerly point of the North American continent. The island, about 740 km (about 460 mi) long and 483 km (300 mi) wide, is mountainous, with some peaks in the United States Range reaching more than 2743 m (9000 ft). Many fjords indent the E and W coasts of the island.

Ellesmere Island has little vegetation, and much of its surface lies under glacial ice cap. Herds of caribou and musk-oxen roam some of the ice-free regions of the island. Human habitation is very sparse, with only a few scattered communities; one of these, Alert, a radio and weather station maintained by the U.S. and Canada, is reputedly the northernmost permanent settlement in the world. Ellesmere Island was discovered by the English navigator William Baffin in 1616. Area, 196,236 sq km (75,767 sq mi).

ELLICE ISLANDS. *See* TUVALU.

ELLINGTON, Duke, real name EDWARD KENNEDY ELLINGTON (1899–1974), American composer, conductor, and pianist, who was one of the most respected figures in the history of jazz, and who

Duke Ellington   UPI

brought jazz into concert halls and religious services. He was born in Washington, D.C., and played professionally from the age of 17. In 1923 he moved to New York City and organized a ten-piece band. Through the 1930s and 1940s Ellington and his band, greatly enlarged, appeared in theaters and nightclubs, on the radio, and in foreign tours. In 1943 he conducted the first of nine annual concerts at Carnegie Hall, New York City.

Ellington's compositions in a sense are in a kind of modified concerto form, being constructed around solo instrumental performances. They also frequently introduce vocal passages without words. His style is eclectic, combining blues, various forms of jazz, and the big-band sound of swing music. Among his most famous songs are "Mood Indigo" (1931), "Sophisticated Lady" (1933), and "Solitude" (1934). His large-scale works include *Black, Brown, and Beige* (1943), *Liberian Suite* (1948), *A Concert of Sacred Music* (1965), and *Far East Suite* (1967); and scores for the motion pictures *Anatomy of a Murder* (1959) and *Paris Blues* (1961), and for the musical comedies *Beggar's Opera* (1947) and *Pousse-Café* (1966). The theme song of Ellington's band after 1941 was "Take the 'A' Train," written by his longtime associate, the lyricist and arranger Billy Strayhorn (1915–67). Ellington's autobiography is *Music Is My Business* (1974).

For further information on this person, see the section Biographies in the Bibliography in volume 28. — ⑥

ELLIPSE, in geometry (q.v.), closed plane curve, one of the conic sections (*see* CONE), formed by a plane that cuts all the elements of a right circular cone. A circle (q.v.), which is formed by a plane perpendicular to the axis of the cone, is a specialized form of ellipse. — ⑦

An ellipse may be defined as the locus of all points, P, the sum of whose distances, d_1 and d_2, from two fixed points is a constant (see Fig. 1). The two fixed points that define an ellipse are known as its foci and are labeled F and F' in Fig. 1. This property of an ellipse is often used for drawing the figure. If pins are placed in the drawing surface at the two foci and a length of string is tied loosely between them, a point holding the string taut will trace an ellipse as it moves.

Any ellipse is symmetrical with respect to its major axis, which is a straight line passing through the two foci and extended to meet the curve at each end. It is also symmetrical with respect to its minor axis, a line perpendicular to the major axis at the midpoint between the two foci. In a circle the two foci of the ellipse coincide, and the major and minor axes are equal

199 — ⑧

Page shown at 76% of actual size.

① Main entry: Funk & Wagnalls New Encyclopedia contains 25,000 entries, arranged alphabetically, letter-by-letter. Entry words are printed in boldface capitals.

② Measurements are given in both metric and standard systems.

③ Cross-reference entry

④ Illustration: Funk & Wagnalls contains 9,500 illustrations, of which more than one-third are in color.

⑤ Guide word

⑥ Bibliography reference: Many entries are keyed to the encyclopedia's Bibliography, which lists some 9,400 titles in 1,255 subject areas.

⑦ Cross-references: Cross-references are indicated in several ways, including the initials q.v. in parentheses. Other cross-references are distinguished by the words "see" or "see also." In all, Funk & Wagnalls contains some 85,000 cross-references.

⑧ Page number

Number of Maps: 317.
Number of Cross-references: 85,000.
Number of Indexes: 1.
Number of Index Entries: 130,000.
Number of Illustrations: 9,500, of which more than
    one-third are in color.
Trim Size: 6″ × 9″.

Price: $139.81.
Sold in supermarkets; only schools and libraries
    may order direct from distributor. (See page
    591.)
ISBN 0-8343-0072-9.
Revised twice a year, with twice-yearly printings.

I. Introduction

Funk & Wagnalls New Encyclopedia is a 29-volume
work designed primarily for household use. The publisher's promotional brochure boasts that it is "the
wisest investment you'll ever make for your family"
and that it provides "a wealth of information that
doesn't cost a fortune." The brochure emphasizes
the encyclopedia's usefulness as a home study aid
and highlights a number of features, such as "clear,
simple language, thousands of vivid illustrations with
informative captions, and distinguished contributors
and consultants."

While such claims might be regarded as advertising hyperbole, they do indicate the publisher's desire
to challenge other encyclopedias in the lucrative home
encyclopedia market.

Because of the long lead time necessary in preparing the Buying Guide, this review was based on
an examination of the 1986 edition, the most current
edition available at that time.

II. Scope

Funk & Wagnalls New Encyclopedia contains some
25,000 entries at an average length of 360 words, for
a total word count of nine million. Actual article
length varies considerably, from a few lines for minor
biographical entries and geographical locations to
upward of 30 pages or more for general survey articles on continents, nations, and other broad subjects. For example, as an indication of how space is
apportioned among different subjects, **Ray Charles**,
Konstantin Chernenko, and **Ty Cobb** each get about
one-sixth of a page; **Cleveland** (Ohio), one and a half
pages; the article on the American **Civil War** is 11
pages long; **Christianity** is treated in just under 12
pages; and **China** receives 47 pages of coverage. (Individual Civil War battles are accorded separate entries, where they are treated in more depth; subjects
such as Chinese art and architecture, literature, music, and philosophy are also treated in separate entries, where they receive a combined 25 pages of
coverage. For a discussion of article arrangements
and structure, see *Accessibility*.)

In their Preface, the editors write that "the organization and selection of information in all major
areas of knowledge and activity . . . must create a
network of articles interrelated in such a way that no
area is omitted or inadvertently isolated." For the
purposes of compiling the encyclopedia, subjects were
broken down into ten major categories. According
to the publisher, 20 percent of the text space is devoted to history and an almost equal amount to geography. The physical sciences get 12 percent; the
life sciences, 11 percent; and the social sciences, slightly
more than 9 percent. The remaining 25 percent of
text space is accorded to coverage of religion and
philosophy (8 percent), language and literature (6¾
percent), the visual arts (nearly 6 percent), the performing arts (3½ percent), and miscellaneous subjects such as sports, hobbies, and military affairs.
About 40 percent of all entries (*not* text space) are
biographical; in the breakdown given above, the publisher has counted the space in biographical articles
toward the subject area in which the person worked.

From this breakdown, the coverage of literature
and the arts seems rather weak. The publisher claims,
however, that "the subject-area proportions of [*Funk
& Wagnalls New Encyclopedia*] historically reflect
the needs of its users, as demonstrated in the mar-
ketplace since 1971. . . ." Nonetheless, the content
of such survey articles as the **novel**, **music**, and **painting** is sketchy at best. Information given in articles
on particular authors and artists also tends to be
superficial.

The company points to "a concerted effort to increase the scope of the encyclopedia's international
coverage," and claims that although the encyclopedia is still designed primarily for the U.S. and Canadian markets, "every feasible effort has been made
to escape Anglo-American bias." The results of these
efforts are readily apparent. As an indication of the
scope and depth of its coverage of non-American/
British subjects, a random page spread in Volume 1
(pages 260–261) contains the following 15 entries:
Aguadilla (town in Puerto Rico), **Aguascalientes** (city
in Mexico), **Emilio Aguinaldo** (historic Filipino leader),
Lope de Aguirre (Spanish colonial adventurer), **Ahab**
(king of ancient Israel), **Ahad Ha-am** (Russian-Jew-
ish writer), **Ahaggar Mountains** (Algeria), **Ahasuerus**
(Old Testament character), **Ahaz** (king of ancient
Judah), **Ahmadou Ahidjo** (first president of Came-
roon), **Ahithophel** (Old Testament character), **Ah-
madabad** (city in India), **Ahmad Shah** (first emir of
Afghanistan), **Ahmadu** (African Islamic leader), and
Fakhruddin Ali Ahmed (fifth president of India).

With the major 1983 revision, *Funk & Wagnalls*
added "new history articles treating a number of van-

ished ancient African and Asian states" in addition to its coverage of contemporary nations on those continents. Coverage of Islamic religion, culture, and politics has also been greatly expanded. Indeed, the attention to non-American and non-Western subject matter is impressive.

III. Authority

The name Funk & Wagnalls has long been synonymous with encyclopedias and dictionaries. The company originated in 1875, when Isaac Kaufmann Funk, a Lutheran pastor turned editor and publisher, started the firm of I. K. Funk & Co. in New York City. A year later he was joined by clergyman Adam Willis Wagnalls, and the company was renamed Funk & Wagnalls. Originally a publisher of religious books and periodicals, the company issued its first general reference encyclopedia, the 25-volume *Funk & Wagnalls Standard Encyclopedia*, in 1912. This set formed the basis for all subsequent editions, although the firm and the rights to the Funk & Wagnalls name have changed hands several times since the 1940s.

In the early 1950s the publisher began selling the encyclopedia in supermarkets. From a marketing standpoint this practice was highly successful, but it was frowned on by librarians, educators, and other publishers, who tended to regard any encyclopedia sold by such methods as inherently inferior.

In 1971 the company undertook a major revision of the set, issued in 1972 as *Funk & Wagnalls New Encyclopedia*. The set underwent another overhaul in 1983. Every article was studied by staff editors and outside consultants for accuracy, objectivity, and currency, and nearly two-thirds of the content was revised. Outdated articles were dropped or thoroughly rewritten; new articles were commissioned; the number of four-color illustrations was almost doubled; all the maps were revised and most converted to four-color; a new index was created; and a comprehensive bibliography was compiled. The publisher now incorporates ongoing revisions into the set with each biannual printing.

To keep the encyclopedia up-to-date, the firm maintains a large and experienced editorial staff, led since 1974 by Vice President and Editorial Director Leon Bram. Previously Executive Editor of F. E. Compton, Bram has worked in the reference publishing field since 1955.

The Editor-in-Chief, Norma H. Dickey, was Editor-in-Chief of the Bibliography and Index of the spring 1983 edition and has held editorial posts with Macmillan and other educational and reference publishers. For the autumn 1986 edition reviewed here, the credits page lists an editorial staff of 45 people, many of whom have previously worked for such major reference publishers as Columbia University Press, Encyclopaedia Britannica, Grolier, and Macmillan.

In addition to these individuals, Funk & Wagnalls employs a separate staff of some 20 people responsible for the bibliography and index. Barbara M. Preschel, the Index Manager, formerly held the same post on the ACADEMIC AMERICAN ENCYCLOPEDIA and has also taught library and information science. Bibliography Editor Rachel Shor Donner has edited three catalogs for the H. W. Wilson Company.

The frontmatter lists 73 consultants along with their credentials and areas of expertise. Although drawn primarily from the academic community, some are affiliated with museums or professional organizations or are editors of journals. Familiar names include literary biographers Denis Donoghue and Leon Edel and the paleontologist Stephen Jay Gould. The publisher states that the consultants "made recommendations on coverage, proportions, and contributors" in planning the 1983 edition; their participation in the subsequent biannual revisions is unclear.

Many of the 1,000 contributors are prominent academics or practicing specialists. Among the names on this roster are economist and social scientist Kenneth Boulding, heart surgeons Denton Cooley and Michael DeBakey, religion scholar Mircea Eliade, writer-broadcaster Magnus Magnusson, and critic Lionel Trilling. However, the fact that a number of these contributors have been deceased for several years throws some doubt on the extent of the contributors' participation in the autumn 1986 revision. Fewer than half of the articles are signed (with initials only, keyed to the initials given in the list of contributors). The publisher explains that "unsigned articles are either house-written or are house-reviewed and approved texts, the contributors of which are now deceased." The editorial staff includes 11 writers.

IV. Currency

With its policy of ongoing revisions incorporated in each biannual printing, *Funk & Wagnalls* is quite up-to-date. Within already existing articles, the editors make an effort to include recent developments. For example, the entry on **Saturn** is up-to-date in all respects except in its breakdown of the planet's atmosphere, and there only minor revision is necessary. **Union of Soviet Socialist Republics** mentions the 1986 accident at the nuclear power plant in Chernobyl. The entry on **South Africa** concludes: "In the mid-1980s continued unrest and rising black militancy resulted in international pressure, a state of emergency, restriction of press freedoms, and abolition of pass laws." Given the volatility of the situation, this is a fair contemporary assessment. The article also includes a photograph showing two prominent black figures of the mid-1980s, Winnie Mandela and the Reverend Allan Boesak.

However, in articles on other nations, our reviewers did find some examples of important recent developments that went unmentioned. For example, although the article on **Nicaragua** states that in the 1980s "the U.S. . . . began to support an anti-Sandinist guerrilla movement," it does not mention the contras by name, nor does it supply any details about that movement or the nature of the U.S. support, although this information was available at the time. The article on **Northern Ireland** fails to report the significant 1985 agreement between Great Britain and the Republic of Ireland giving the Republic a formal voice in the governing of the province, although this agreement is referred to in both the articles on **Great Britain** and the **Republic of Ireland**.

Evidence of the set's currency is found in articles in other subject areas. For example, **space exploration** not only reports the January 1986 *Challenger* disaster and its cause, but also notes the findings of the Presidential Commission on the tragedy and discusses the implications for the future of the American space program. **History of motion pictures** discusses the impact of cable television and the video rental business on both the film industry and the nature of the movie-watching experience. **Advertising** includes a four-color still photo from a 1986 television commercial that was airing at the time of this review, and the caption describes the commercial. Current public service ads are also depicted.

According to the publisher, "population and economic statistics throughout the set are as current as available international source material allow." However, this is not always the case. For example, the population figures given for the U.S.S.R. are 1983 estimates; those for the United States are from the 1980 census. At the time of publication, more recent accurate estimates were available.

As well as updating existing articles, the publisher has added new articles on subjects that have been the focus of increasing attention in the 1980s. Among these articles are **AIDS**, **employment of women**, **international terrorism**, **sports medicine**, and **video recording**.

While pursuing this aggressive updating policy, the publisher also notes that "despite the desire to present the state of human knowledge in a recognizably contemporary form, the editors in general favor proved topics over 'hot' or trendy ones, preferring to err in the direction of caution rather than of mere topicality. Some ephemeral topics—mostly in the area commonly described as popular culture—that are judged to have journalistic rather than permanent importance are set aside to be treated in the encyclopedia's yearbook until such time as a clearly permanent pattern is discernable." By generally accepted encyclopedia publishing standards, this is a sound practice.

V. Accuracy

Funk & Wagnalls' promotional literature states: "Factual accuracy ranks, along with consistency and balance, as one of the three overriding editorial concerns." In the course of the editorial process, each article undergoes scrutiny by at least six people; in fact, the publisher claims that some articles were reviewed 15 times or more before they were approved for publication.

On the whole, the editors have done an admirable job of ensuring the set's accuracy. Occasional errors do creep in, however. For example, the article on **Gerard Manley Hopkins** refers to him as "a Victorian poet whose work was not introduced to the world until 1981." Here a minor typographical transposition that slipped past the copy editors misleads the reader. Hopkins's work, in fact, was first published in 1918.

A caption in Volume 19, page 188, reads: "Belfast is the focus of political and religious strife between Great Britain and Northern Ireland." This is not quite accurate: the strife is not between Great Britain and Northern Ireland, but between the Protestant and Catholic communities in the province, and between the IRA and their supporters on the one hand and government forces on the other.

The article on **Henry the Navigator** perpetuates the popular but erroneous belief that he "established an observatory and the first school for navigators in Europe." Although Henry supported such efforts, he himself did not found any institutions.

Such instances suggest that although *Funk & Wagnalls* is broadly accurate, specific details are not as precise as they might be. Beyond the question of simple accuracy lies that of comprehensiveness and oversimplification. While this encyclopedia's content is generally accurate, it is not always as thorough as one might wish. For example, the article on **Ronald Reagan**, which is fairly brief, does not name his vice president or cabinet members, or describe any of the controversies that have involved officials in his administration. (See *Objectivity*.)

The general survey articles also present accurate facts, but again the question of comprehensiveness and simplification arises. For example, while **American literature** provides basic factual information about major movements, authors, and works, it rarely discusses a particular aspect of the subject in detail. About Mark Twain, for instance, it makes the sweeping statement that "[his] genius . . . was that he understood the moral realism of childhood," but the statement is never amplified.

Similar lack of detail was noted in two of the entries examined by our subject specialists. **Money**, though reasonably clear and accurate, has a narrow focus and touches on only a few aspects of the subject. **Bill of Rights** is short, omits some basic information, and is potentially misleading.

VI. Clarity

The writing style in *Funk & Wagnalls New Encyclopedia* varies considerably from article to article. Scientific subjects, for example, are usually written at a higher level of sophistication than, say, articles on general interest subjects. In such technical subjects, the encyclopedia uses the so-called pyramid approach, in which the article begins by presenting the most basic facts and works up to more complex information, or begins with a general description of the subject before dealing with specific aspects. Technical terms are usually defined when they are first used; however, the editors sometimes assume that the context provides an adequate definition, and in such cases do not provide a further definition. The reader may be referred to articles on related subjects by means of cross-references. (See *Accessibility*.)

The editors claim to have striven for "an encyclopedia style that was clear, concise, direct, and as lively as possible." However, while the writing in *Funk & Wagnalls* is straightforward, it is generally dry and unlikely to evoke enthusiasm in the indifferent reader. The reader often encounters overuse of the passive voice, vague generalizations and imprecise words, repetition, and choppy sentence structure, as in this paragraph from **South Africa**:

> In general, the rivers of the country are irregular in flow. Many are dry during much of the year. Consequently, the rivers are of little use for navigation or hydroelectric power but are of some use for irrigation.

This awkwardness may be a consequence of the limited space available. In the process of revision, when additional information is added to one part of an article but the overall space allotted to that article is not increased, part of the article may be cut and condensed.

Yet it must be said that some individual entries are very well written indeed. For example, the encyclopedia's articles on the **Strategic Defense Initiative** and on **evolution** present information on those complex subjects in a clear and interesting manner.

The following article, *Titanic* **Disaster**, quoted in its entirety, illustrates the style of a typical entry in *Funk & Wagnalls*:

> *TITANIC* **DISASTER**, one of the worst maritime disasters in history. The British luxury liner *Titanic* of the White Star Line, a 46,000-gross-ton ship, was on its maiden voyage from Liverpool to New York City, when, just before midnight on April 14, 1912, it struck an iceberg about 153 km (about 95 mi) south of the Grand Banks of Newfoundland. Of the more than 2220 persons aboard, about 1513 lost their lives, including the American millionaires John Jacob Astor (1864–1912), Benjamin Guggenheim (1865–1912), and Isidor Straus.
>
> Although the ship had been proclaimed unsinkable because of its 16 watertight compartments, the iceberg punctured five of them, one more than was considered possible in any accident, and the *Titanic* sank in less than three hours. Subsequent investigations found that the ship had been steaming too fast in dangerous waters, that lifeboat space had been provided for only about three-fourths of the passengers and crew, and that another ship, close to the scene, the *Californian*, had not come to the rescue because its radio operator was off duty and asleep. These findings led to many reforms, such as lifeboat space for every person on a ship, lifeboat drills, the maintenance of a full-time radio watch while at sea, and an international ice patrol. The sinking of the *Titanic* has been the subject of several books and films; attempts to retrieve the sunken ship and its treasures were underway in the early 1980s.

VII. Objectivity

During the 1950s and 1960s, Funk & Wagnalls encyclopedias generally ignored controversial subjects or controversial aspects of more conventional subjects. However, since the early 1970s, the editors have made a conscious effort to provide a more balanced view of such subjects. The publisher's press release for the major 1983 revision states that "In the treatment of controversial subjects, *Funk & Wagnalls New Encyclopedia* strives for fairness by presenting all major shades of opinion in as balanced a fashion as possible."

This effort has been largely successful. For example, the article on **abortion** devotes considerable attention to the controversy over its legalization, discussing several court cases challenging its constitutionality, and concluding that "As both proponents and opponents of abortion carry on their fight, it appears that the political and social controversy engendered by legal abortion will concern the nation for years to come."

The article on **evolution** does not take Darwin's account as a necessarily correct view of existence but does assume that living organisms "have been diversified and modified through sustained changes in form and function." The only controversy it describes is that among scientists who have proposed differing theories of evolution. It does not refer specifically to fundamentalist objections to general scientific evolutionary theory, but concludes with the note "For a theological interpretation of the origin of life, *see* CREATION." **Creation** describes the challenges to a literal interpretation of the biblical account of the Creation that have taken place since the Renaissance and notes that contemporary "creationists claim that the evidence for evolutionary science is flawed, that the biblical account of creation can be proved scientifically, and that either both theories should be taught in American schools or neither should be." It also mentions court cases brought by fundamentalists in various states over the teaching of evolution in public schools.

Biographical entries in *Funk & Wagnalls* also cite controversial facts or apparent contradictions when they are pertinent to a balanced understanding of an individual's life. However, except in the cases of extremely significant historical figures, the article generally does not attempt to evaluate the individual's accomplishments.

The article on **Andrew Jackson** presents an even and balanced view of the man, mentioning some controversial aspects of his career: his ownership of large numbers of slaves, his proslavery views, his forcible removal of American Indians from lands that had been promised to them by federal treaties and Supreme Court decisions, his abuse of patronage, his misuse of the presidential veto, and his highhanded attitude toward the banking system. His achievements are also reported.

VIII. Accessibility

On the whole, *Funk & Wagnalls* is a well designed and organized encyclopedia, and includes a number of features that enhance its accessibility. Entries are arranged letter by letter rather than word by word. When several items have the same heading, they are arranged in order of persons, places, and things. Following standard library practice, names beginning with *Mc* are treated as though they began with *Mac*; the same rule applies to the use of the abbreviation *St.* for *Saint*.

Running heads indicate the first entry on the left-hand page and the last entry on the right-hand page. Page numbers are located at the bottom of each page, flush with the outside margin. For pagination purposes, each volume is treated as a separate book: pages are numbered 1 through 448, except for Volume 29, the index volume. The text is printed in two columns per page.

Entry headings are in boldface type, but some readers may find that they do not stand out conspicuously. Moreover, there is no additional space between the end of one article and the beginning of the next; this may make it difficult for some readers to locate a specific entry quickly.

Internally, articles may follow one of several set structures, depending on the length of the article and the nature of the subject. Brief articles (generally one text column or less) are usually written as running text, without subheads. Longer, more detailed biographical entries may contain main heads that break the treatment of the subject into chronological periods and, for extremely significant figures whose

accomplishments may be varied and complex, sometimes include separate subhead sections under which a particular work is discussed. Longer geographical articles—in particular, those treating continents, nations, and states—generally contain both A-heads (main heads) and B-heads (subheads).

As previously noted (see *Scope*), subjects related to a broad survey entry are generally treated under separate, individual entries, not in the survey article. Thus, for example, there are separate entries for **Russia**, **Russian language**, **Russian literature**, **Russian Revolution**, **Russo-Finnish War**, and **Russo-Japanese War**. The article **Russia** includes cross-references to these entries where appropriate.

The most significant finding aid in *Funk & Wagnalls New Encyclopedia* is the index, which takes up all of Volume 29 and contains some 130,000 entries. This means that, on average, there are more than five index entries for every article, or one per every 70 words of text. Each article is cited under its own title as well as under other appropriate headings. The index also contains a number of standardized subheads that are used whenever appropriate in referring the reader to articles on continents and nations, and for certain types of historical events, such as wars. These subheads allow the reader to find the specific page within an article that contains information on the sought-for subject.

In addition to cross-reference entries, several types of cross-references are used within individual articles. Some cross-references are indicated by the abbreviation q.v. (for the Latin *quod vide*, "which see") printed in parentheses immediately after the name of a subject that is treated in a separate article. In other cases, a parenthetical note in the text directs the reader to "*see* . . . [article title]." *See* notations may also be given at the end of an article in the form, "*See also* [article titles]," or "For further information on this topic, see . . . [article titles]." When a person's name is mentioned in an article without life dates following, there is a separate entry for that person.

IX. Special Features

A basic, low-cost general reference work, *Funk & Wagnalls* is not known for outstanding special features. However, it does have a substantial annotated, fairly up-to-date bibliography organized in 1,255 numbered subject areas (corresponding to the Dewey decimal system), plus a separate section for biographies. Altogether, some 9,400 titles, chosen by 21 librarians and subject specialists, are listed. Cross-reference notations at the end of individual articles refer the reader to the appropriate section of the bibliography. For example, the article on **Zaire** ends with the note "*For further information on this topic, see the Bibliography in volume 28, section 1031.*" Section 1031 lists ten books on the region.

Most of the books in the bibliography date from the 1970s, and many are out of print. Some older books that have attained classic status are listed, as are some technical or scholarly books. According to the bibliography editors, "dull treatments of subjects have been avoided as much as possible. Opposing points of view on controversial topics are represented." A brief annotation for each title should help the reader decide whether that book will be useful for the reader's purpose.

Other special features include three-page articles on "How to Use the Library" and on "How to Write a Term Paper," located just before the bibliography in Volume 28. While these articles provide some useful information, they are rather cursory and cannot take the place of a more detailed orientation. Moreover, their value for adults is negligible. The front-matter in Volume 1 includes a profusely illustrated 18-page essay titled "In the Course of Human Affairs. . . ." The essay describes seven general ways of explaining history; while intriguing, it is highly idiosyncratic and has no evident relation to the encyclopedia as a whole.

More than one-third of the 9,500 illustrations in *Funk & Wagnalls New Encyclopedia* are four-color. The color photographs are generally adequate, but it should be pointed out that they have not reproduced well on the paper and in both reproduction quality and overall attractiveness cannot match the photographs in THE WORLD BOOK ENCYCLOPEDIA. Some of the black-and-white photographs are reproductions of color artwork; apart from this drawback, many of the illustrations lack clarity and definition. Still, considering the set's very low price, one cannot expect the kind of illustrations one would find in a "coffeetable" artbook.

The encyclopedia also contains 317 maps, provided by Hammond, which accompany the respective articles on continents, nations, and states. More than 250 of these maps are one-half page or larger (including a significant number of two-page spreads), and these are all in color.

X. Format

Funk & Wagnalls New Encyclopedia is available in only one format—the 29-volume edition. Each volume is 448 pages long, except for Volume 29, which is 496 pages. With a trim size of 6″ × 9″, these one-inch-thick books should be easy to handle by users of all ages. While the binding and cover material is not as sturdy as that used in comparable encyclopedias, it should prove adequate for home use. The entire set will take up a little more than two and a half feet of shelf space.

XI. Other Opinions

Reference Books Bulletin 1983–1984: "[*Funk & Wagnalls New Encyclopedia*] offers excellent value for its price. While certainly not as scholarly and as detailed as ENCYCLOPEDIA AMERICANA, COLLIER'S ENCYCLOPEDIA, or NEW ENCYCLOPAEDIA BRITANNICA, it offers global coverage of all fields of knowledge. . . ."

Reference Books Bulletin (Nov. 15, 1986): "While not as comprehensive as the largest English-language encyclopedias, *Funk & Wagnalls New Encyclopedia* presents facts on people, places, and things in a straightforward manner offering global coverage of all fields of knowledge. . . . The set continues to provide fine value for its price and remains an excellent choice for homes, useful for both adults and older children."

XII. Summary

Even at a higher price than its present $139.81, *Funk & Wagnalls New Encyclopedia* would still be a good bargain. For many families on a restricted budget, it will be the first choice. It is reasonably up-to-date, accurate, objective, and well written.

Where *Funk & Wagnalls* falls short is in the depth of its coverage. Here it certainly cannot compare with such multivolume reference works as NEW BRITANNICA and COLLIER'S—but at a small fraction of their cost, it is not intended to. It will not be the choice of the scholar, and college students will usually consult another set before they consult this one. However, for the adult who consults an encyclopedia as a general source of basic information rather than as a sophisticated research tool, *Funk & Wagnalls* will be quite adequate. And while it is designed primarily for home use, libraries with very small reference budgets may be well satisfied and well served with this set.

Individuals can purchase *Funk & Wagnalls New Encyclopedia* only at supermarkets, one volume per week. Unfortunately, the publisher cannot give out information about when the set will be sold in a particular supermarket, but individual store managers may be able to let interested consumers know ahead of time if and when the set will be available. Otherwise, prospective purchasers should stay alert when they shop and make sure that they begin collecting the set during the first week it is offered.

Schools and libraries may purchase the entire set through a distributor: Proteus Enterprises, Inc., 961 W. Thorndale, Bensenville, IL 60106; (312) 766-5544.

Kussmaul Encyclopedia

Facts at a Glance

Full Title: **Kussmaul Encyclopedia.**
Former Title: Cadillac Modern Encyclopedia (one volume, 1973, out of print).
Publisher: General Videotex Corporation.
Editor: J. Wesley Kussmaul, Editorial Director.
Online Vendor: Delphi (a service of General Videotex).
Copyright: 1981 through 1988.

Number of Entries: 20,000.
Number of Words: 3,000,000.
Number of Cross-references: 50,000.

Price: $49.95 for permanent subscription to Delphi, plus online charges.
Revised irregularly.

I. Introduction

The *Kussmaul Encyclopedia* is an online general reference encyclopedia derived from the single-volume *Cadillac Modern Encyclopedia*, which was published in 1973 and is now out of print. Updated and put into online form in 1980 by J. Wesley Kussmaul, for whom it was renamed, *Kussmaul* is one of several features of Delphi, a service of General Videotex Corporation that provides online information and communications.

II. Accessibility

Delphi is available through many local nodes of packet-switching networks such as Telenet and Tymnet. Subscribers to Delphi can readily read the *Kussmaul Encyclopedia* articles, or "files;" with a home computer or an office terminal. Unlike other online encyclopedias, *Kussmaul* has no available related print version and is accessible through only one online information service.

Because *Kussmaul* is part of the larger Delphi package, subscribers have automatic access to a wide range of information and communications databases. Among these, *The Research Library* (described as "a collection of 200 separate databases with comprehensive information on just about everything") will be of particular interest to library reference departments.

III. Locating Information

First-time Delphi users get a tour of the service from a genial monologuist named "Max"; well-designed menus then take over to locate the "Library" feature of Delphi and within it, the encyclopedia. More experienced users can opt for a faster command-driven path to the feature. In response to the plain English "Search for:" prompts, the user simply enters the subject and the program searches for an article (called here a "file") with that assigned title.

If the program finds more than one title that fits, it displays them all in a numbered list and asks which number the user wants to see. Because the program lists all titles that include the search string, the lists can be surprising: a search for "ear" found the sought-for string along with **ear training**, **Earle, John**, **earth**, and seven other "earth" titles from **earth quake** to **earthworm**, culminating in **earwig**. The effect nicely reproduces the serendipity of leafing through a print encyclopedia and happening on articles only alphabetically akin to the one sought.

If the program cannot match the entire string, it automatically tries again with strings incrementally shortened from the end. Thus when no "Chernobyl" was found, the program tried "Chernoby," "Chernob," and finally "Cherno," which it found in the longer string:

> CHERNOZEM (cher'-no-zem), a black SOIL of alluvial origin rich in humus and with a loose crumbly texture. It is found wherever the original vegetation cover was natural grassland, and it is one of the most productive soils in the world. The largest expanse of chernozem is found in a zone stretching from E. Siberia west to Hungary and Romania and in the U.S. and Canada, where it is coextensive with the former natural prairie grassland from Manitoba south to Texas.

In the same fashion the search word "Aquino" garnered only an article on **St. Thomas Aquinas**, and "privatization" came up with a numbered list of the titles **private bank**, **private enterprise**, **private property**, and **privateering**.

Because the program searches titles rather than full text, the listed search item "Private Enterprise" did not find the phrase where it appeared in the article on **Margaret Thatcher** (see *Currency*).

Most articles in the *Kussmaul Encyclopedia* include several cross-references, set in capital letters. For convenience, these are repeated in a numbered list at the end of the article, enabling the user to pursue the reference by simply typing the desired number. The pursuit involves occasional wild geese: the cross-reference HEARING in the article on **ear** turned out to concern judicial, not sensory, hearing.

Most articles in the encyclopedia do not include bibliographical references.

IV. Cost

Subscription to Delphi costs $49.95; online charges are $16.00 per hour at peak times and $6.00 per hour off-peak (evenings, weekends, and holidays). Use of a local node of Tymnet incurs little or no charge. Delphi is operational 24 hours a day, but even a peak-time search can cost well under a dollar, because the menu and search features of the program are notably brisk, the articles are usually short, and the faster 1,200- or 2,400-baud modems are supported without surcharge.

V. Currency

Wes Kussmaul's original intention to update the *Kussmaul Encyclopedia* by adding current news to the articles inherited from *Cadillac* did not prove practical in the long run. Consequently, in mid-1987 many of the articles were badly behind the times, as the lack of articles on Corazon Aquino, Armand Hammer, Chernobyl, and AIDS suggests.

The article on **Margaret Thatcher**, for example, contains no information after 1981; that on **Ronald Reagan**, none after 1980. The entry **space shuttle** also contains no information after 1981. Among the technical and scientific articles in which the *Kussmaul Encyclopedia* excels, the lengthy article on **superconductivity** is of limited use because it omits any reference to the important research discoveries published during 1986 and 1987. Lack of currency in a rapidly evolving scientific field such as this one is tantamount to lack of accuracy.

VI. Accuracy, Objectivity, and Clarity

The article on **Margaret Thatcher** begins

> THATCHER, MARGARET HILDA (1925-) became the first woman prime minister of Great Britain in May, 1979. A member of the Conservative party, Thatcher espoused the belief that the lessening of inflation of prices and the economic revitalization of Great Britain could be achieved through a policy of reducing government expenditures and tight control of the nation's money supply. Thatcher's steadfastness in pursuing this policy, which is known as monetarism, in the face of a severe economic slump earned her the epithet, "Iron Lady."

The paragraph and especially the second sentence are rather loose. Sharpening the sentence to read "Thatcher believed that price inflation could be lessened and the British economy revitalized through tight control of government spending and the nation's money supply," 24 words instead of 35, would bring the passage back into focus.

The account of Thatcher emphasizes her distinction as a woman prime minister and quotes a popular epithet that also refers to her sex. But the article avoids the more scurrilous politicosexist epithets (such as "Attila the Hen") frequently applied to Thatcher in popular journalism, and uses terms like "steadfastness" and elsewhere "leading challenger," "break

decisively," "embarked boldly," "held firm," that treat the subject as a resolute political leader, not merely as a historical curiosity.

VII. Summary

The *Kussmaul Encyclopedia* is a distinctive online-only general reference work with concise articles on a wide variety of scholarly and general-interest subjects. Without question the most accessible and easiest to use of the online encyclopedias, the user-friendly features inherent in the Delphi system will make it especially attractive for home, office, and library. Although it does not have full-text searching capabilities, its search procedures and cross-references are usually comprehensive enough to enable the user to make the most of its contents.

Although charges vary from vendor to vendor, and direct, consistent comparisons are difficult to make, in the long run *Kussmaul* would seem to be considerably cheaper to access than ACADEMIC AMERICAN ENCYCLOPEDIA online. It may well be substantially more cost-effective to use than EVERYMAN'S ENCYCLOPEDIA online. However, despite the addition of some 2,000 articles not in the 1973 *Cadillac Modern Encyclopedia* on which it is largely based, *Kussmaul* is badly out of date. This unfortunately negates some of its more admirable qualities. Prospective users are also reminded that it contains only about half as many entries as either ACADEMIC AMERICAN or EVERYMAN'S. But subscribers do get automatic access to Delphi's *Research Library*, a useful bonus. Subscribers can even communicate online with Wes Kussmaul himself.

Individuals and institutions interested in the *Kussmaul Encyclopedia* should contact General Videotex Corporation, 3 Blackstone Street, Cambridge, MA 02139. General Videotex's toll-free number is (800) 544-4005; in Massachusetts the number is (617) 491-3393.

Lincoln Library

Facts at a Glance

Full Title: **The Lincoln Library of Essential Information**.
Publisher: Frontier Press.
Editor-in-Chief: William H. Seibert.
Edition Reviewed: 1985. (Statistics apply to 1988 revised edition.)

Number of Volumes: 2.
Number of Contributors: 122.
Number of Entries: 26,000.
Number of Pages: 2,200.
Number of Maps: 139 black-and-white maps; 48-

Lincoln Library

❶ 1126

❷ Literature

TABLE OF CANADIAN LITERATURE

	AUTHORS	REPRESENTATIVE WORKS	
Time	Name	Prose	Poetry and Drama
1724–1789	Frances Brooke	Novel (Emily Montague)	
1739–1824	Alexander Henry	Travels	
1763–1820	Alexander Mackenzie	Travels	
1786–1871	Philippe A. de Gaspé	Novel (Les Anciens Canadiens)	
1796–1852	John Richardson	Novels	
1796–1865	Thomas C. Haliburton	Satire, Humor, History	
1804–1873	Joseph Howe	Essays, Orations	
1809–1866	François X. Garneau	History of Canada (French)	
1816–1876	Charles Heavysege		Dramas (Saul)
1817–1906	William Kirby	Stories	Poems (The U.E.)
1819–1898	William Kingsford	History of Canada	
1822–1893	Charles Sangster		Poems
1822–1879	Octave Crémazie		Poems (French)
1824–1882	Gérin-Lajoie	History (French)	Poems (French)
1825–1868	Thomas D'Arcy McGee	History, Oratory	
1836–1880	James de Mille	Fiction	
1837–1918	Pamphile Lemay	Novels (French)	Poems (French)
1839–1908	Louis Fréchette		Poems (French)
1850–1887	Isabella V. Crawford		Poems
1854–1907	William H. Drummond		Poems (The Habitant)
1856–1904	William McLennan	Habitant Tales	
1858–1918	W. Wilfred Campbell	Essays, Novels	Poems, Poetic Dramas
1860–1937	Ralph Connor (C. W. Gordon)	Novels	
1860–1943	Sir Charles G. D. Roberts	Fiction, Animal Tales	Poems
1861–1899	Archibald Lampman		Poems (Lyrics of Earth)
1861–1929	W. Bliss Carman	Essays	Poems
1861–1944	Frederick G. Scott		Poems
1862–1932	Sir H. Gilbert Parker	Novels	Poems
1862–1947	Duncan C. Scott	Stories	Poems
1869–1944	Stephen Leacock	Essays, Stories, Humor	
1872–1918	John McCrae		Poems (In Flanders Field)
1874–1942	Lucy M. Montgomery	Novels (Anne of Green Gables)	
1874–1958	Robert W. Service	Novels	Rhymes of a Red Cross Man
1875–1924	Albert Lozeau		Poems (French)
1879–1941	Émile Nelligan		Poems (French)
1879–1948	Frederick Philip Grove	Novels (Our Daily Bread)	
1879–1961	Mazo de la Roche	Novels (Jalna)	
1880–1913	Louis Hémon	Novels (Maria Chapdelaine)	
1883–1922	Marjorie L. C. Pickthall	Stories, Novels	Poems, Poetic Dramas
1883–1964	Edwin J. Pratt		Poems (Titans)
1890–1980	Ethel Wilson	Stories, Novels	
1895–1960	Ringuet (Philippe Panneton)	Novels (French)	
1900–	Alain Grandbois		Poems (French)
1903–	Morley Callaghan	Novels (Strange Fugitive)	Poems
1907–	Hugh MacLennan	Novels (Two Solitudes)	
1909–	Gabrielle Roy	Novels (French)	
1909–1957	Malcolm Lowry	Novels (Under the Volcano)	Poems
1912–1943	Saint-Denys-Garneau		Poems (French)
1912–	Irving Layton		Poems (A Red Carpet for the Sun)
1913–1965	Gwethalyn Graham	Novels (Earth and High Heaven)	
1913–	Robertson Davies	Novels (Deptford trilogy)	Plays
1915–	Yves Thériault	Novels, Stories (French)	
1916–	Anne Hébert	Novels (French)	Poems, Dramas (French)
1920–	Pierre Berton	Historical Nonfiction	
1921–	Brian Moore	Novels (Cold Heaven)	
1926–	Margaret Laurence	Novels, Short Stories	
1926–	James Reaney		Poems (Red Heart)
1931–	Mordecai Richler	Novels, Stories	
1934–	Leonard Cohen	Novels	Poems (Let Us Compare Mythologies)
1939–	Margaret Atwood	Novels, Criticism	Poems
1939–	Marie-Claire Blais	Novels (French)	

❸

❹

AUSTRALIAN LITERATURE

In the last thirty years Australian literature has become recognized as a discrete branch of English literature, and has therefore received special critical and scholarly attention. The principal reasons for this new status are an increased output by writers of distinct merit, a noticeably Australian character of atmosphere, location, plot, and language, and the publication or republication of Australian writers' work in Britain and the United States.

Within Australia there is a great awareness of the growth of a distinctly national literature: the Federal Government has established a Commonwealth Literary Fund which, upon the recommendation of an Advisory Board, awards Fellowships to approved writers, subsidizes the publication of works of literary merit, and provides pensions to older writers who have made significant contributions to the nation's literature. In addition, the Fund supports a series of lectures, delivered annually, in each of the Australian universities and colleges, on the subject of Australian literature. Canberra University College now gives a course in Australian Literature and the University of Sydney is about to appoint a professor of the subject. Courses in Commonwealth Literature, including Australian and New Zealand writing, are now being offered in some American universities. All these developments indicate the growing interest in the creative writing produced in Australia.

❺

Colonial Period. The first creative writing produced in Australia was poetry, and that form of literature has been the most common ever since. Michael Massey Robinson (1744–1826), poet laureate to Governor Lachlan Macquarie, composed commemorative birthday odes for George III and Queen Charlotte from 1810 to 1820 and for George IV's birthday in 1821. These odes, printed in the *Sydney Gazette*, the government journal, provide the starting point of Australian literature. Barron Field (1786–1846), a Judge of the Supreme Court of New South Wales, was one of Lamb's "distant correspondents" and his *First Fruits of Australian Poetry* (1819) was the first book of verse published in Australia. In a much quoted letter to the Judge, Lamb refers delicately to the prevalence of hanging at that time.

Page shown at 73% of actual size.

❶ Page number

❷ Running head

❸ Information table: Lincoln Library contains 275 tables and

charts, some of which are a full page or more in length.

❹ Level 1 subhead: Extended articles in Lincoln Library are

usually divided into self-contained sections.

❺ Level 2 subhead

page color atlas of the world.
Number of Index Entries: 26,000.
Number of Cross-references: 8,800.
Number of Indexes: 1.
Number of Illustrations: 800 black-and-white, 145 color.
Trim Size: 9″ × 11½″.

Price: $149.50, hardcover only.
Sold in bookstores, and by direct mail to libraries and other educational institutions.
ISBN 0-912168-12-9.
Generally revised biannually; extent of revisions varies.
Next Scheduled Revision: 1990.

I. Introduction

The Lincoln Library of Essential Information is a two-volume general encyclopedia for the layperson and was first published in 1924. According to the Preface, a main purpose of the *Lincoln Library* is "to embody in two volumes the greatest amount of useful information for the average reader that could reasonably be placed in one work." The Preface goes on to say that "this work contains from twice to many times as much information as the average work of many volumes." This seemingly vast quantity of information has been arranged within 11 subject areas, called "departments," plus a Miscellany department. This approach was chosen for its merits of grouping related material and avoiding repetition. The editors do not explain how the 11 departments (Geography, Economics, History, Government, Education, English, Literature, Fine Arts, Mathematics, Science, and Biography) were chosen.

The *Lincoln Library* is designed for the reader involved in self-education—hence the titular reference to Abraham Lincoln. The topical structure of the work is intended to give the reader a thorough overview of selected branches of learning. The material is "based upon primary sources and . . . has been subjected to intense verification." With its voluminous information, thematic arrangement, and pedagogical outlook, *Lincoln Library* combines many of the functions of reference works and textbooks.

This review was based on an examination of the 1985 edition, as the 1988 revised edition was unavailable at the time of review.

II. Scope

There are approximately 3.5 million words in the *Lincoln Library* and 26,000 entries in the index. Much of the material is organized to proceed from the general to the specific (a survey article on geography is followed by a section on the geography of North America, with subsections on New England, the Middle Atlantic states, and so on). The length of entries or articles varies widely, from two-line entries under **meanings of place names** to a 74-page article on **American history**.

At 333 pages, Biography is the largest department, with over 4,000 profiles arranged alphabetically. History, geography, and the humanities receive broad but not particularly consistent coverage. All of the physical sciences are combined in one department of 289 pages, not much longer than the 223 pages devoted to the fine arts. There are no departments for religion, philosophy, or some of the other social sciences. Thus the coverage of various branches of study is at best uneven.

Within the departments, the choice of subjects receiving detailed discussion is also idiosyncratic. For example, the Science department includes 51 pages on **botany** but fewer than four pages on **microbiology**. The Education department contains 12 pages on **intelligence testing** (with several pages on World War I, U.S. Army test questions reproduced in full), but only six pages are devoted to **modern school systems of world countries**.

As mentioned above, the editors do not outline in the Preface the rationale for selecting material, saying only that "This work . . . offers a vast array of practical information on subjects that are fundamental." In particular, subjects that have grown in importance since the *Lincoln Library* was first compiled in 1924 seem to be sparsely covered. **Computers**, for example, are discussed in less than one page in the Miscellany department; **psychiatry** is also dealt with under Miscellany, appearing between **religious bodies** and **design and drawing**.

While the Biography department emphasizes historical subjects, it also includes some more varied and more current entries than found elsewhere in this encyclopedia. For example, there are entries for such figures as **Yasir Arafat**, **James Baldwin**, and **Robert Dole**. Space seems to be apportioned according to relative importance of the subjects, from four lines for **Jean Baptiste Biot** (1774–1862), a French astronomer and physicist, to 80 lines for **Beethoven**.

The *Lincoln Library* includes photographs, maps, drawings, paintings, and diagrams. Of these, 800 are black-and-white and 145 are in color. There is a detailed 48-page color atlas in Volume 1 that is quite useful, although dated (the nation of Zimbabwe is labeled Rhodesia). The illustrations in the Science and Fine Arts departments are also helpful and informative, while many of the others are less integral to the text. However, the editors make plain in the Preface that "it has not been the aim to provide a heavily illustrated reference work."

III. Authority

The Lincoln Library of Essential Information was first compiled in 1924 under the direction of M. J. Kinsella, founder of the Frontier Press Company. From 1978 to 1981 the work was known as *The New Lincoln Library Encyclopedia*, and it has occasionally appeared in three rather than two volumes. Now in its 43rd edition, the work has reverted to two volumes, and the original title has been restored. Some readers may also be familiar with the *Encyclopedia of World Knowledge*, a 14-volume version of the *Lincoln Library* that was available in supermarkets at one time.

The current editor-in-chief is William H. Seibert, president of Frontier Press. The frontmatter of Volume 1 lists a staff of 15 editors. Also included is a partial list of contributors, with annotations identifying those sections for which each contributor was responsible and specifying whether the individual wrote, reviewed, or revised the material. The contributors' affiliations are also listed; most are (or were) university-level academics in relevant fields from a wide variety of institutions. However, none of the contributors is identified as having been specifically involved subsequent to the 24th edition. Moreover, at least 16 contributors are deceased.

Sources are provided for most of the tables, particularly those involving statistics. The maps in the set's 48-page color atlas were prepared by the well-known cartographic firm of Hammond.

IV. Currency

It is readily apparent that the *Lincoln Library* is badly out of date in some areas. Indeed, this constitutes a serious problem with the encyclopedia as a whole. Although the current edition has a 1985 copyright date, much of the material clearly has remained unchanged from earlier editions. Dated material is not confined to scattered sentences, but rather occupies large blocks of space throughout the encyclopedia. For example, over half of page 899 is occupied by tables of 1967 and 1968 school enrollment statistics.

According to the editors, the *Lincoln Library* is revised continuously and "at each new printing those portions which are affected by the passage of events are thoroughly revised." Yet in many cases new information has simply been added at the end of an article, without any clear relation to the paragraphs that precede it. For example, the Mulroney administration in Canada is mentioned fleetingly under a bold heading **The Trudeau Era**. The Trudeau section ends as follows:

> Trudeau resigned in 1984 and was succeeded for two months by the liberal John Turner. In new elections, Brian Mulroney and the Progressive Conservatives won a landslide victory.

Similarly the article in the Miscellany department on **aeronautics and space exploration** treats in-depth the Apollo missions (including details of handshakes and ceremonial gestures exchanged in the Apollo-Soyuz mission, 1975). The article ends with two brief paragraphs on the space shuttle and a paragraph on The Future in Space. The chart following page 1600, on Recent U.S. Space Flights, lists missions only up to Viking 2 (Sept. 9, 1975). Elsewhere the *Lincoln Library*'s information on the moons of **Saturn** was already out of date some 13 years before the first Voyager mission.

According to our physics reviewer, the article on **transistors** is at least 20 years old. It mentions neither the use of silicon in transistors nor of integrated circuits, and the current dimensions of transistors are far smaller than those described in the article. Similarly, the entry on **money** is filled with anachronisms, and its tables present no data later than 1974.

A few examples will illustrate the fact that the text needs more than updating additions. The following paragraph appears under the heading "Radio and Television in Education":

> A recent invention enables television pictures to be recorded on tape, called "Video tape." This tape is usable for delayed re-broadcasting. Like radio tape recording, it can be edited and used by schools when the recording fits into the curriculum. At the present time, this invention is considered too costly to be practical for extensive school use.

Under the heading **computer** is the following passage:

> Its more sanguine spokesmen foresee the use of the "home computer" by which a person can push a selected button and obtain almost any desired item of information through a telephone circuit . . .

As mentioned above, some of the Biography entries have been more thoroughly updated or more recently written. Biographies for **Ronald Reagan** and **Margaret Thatcher**, for example, are reasonably current up to 1983 or 1984.

Many of the illustrations show signs of age. A page on sports figures includes youthful portraits of Peggy Fleming, James Brown, Gary Player, Arnold Palmer, and Jack Nicklaus. The **sculpture** article, with over 50 illustrations of 20th-century works, includes no pieces more recent than 1972. But sculptors of current importance (Graves, Nevelson, and Christo) are discussed. The Fine Arts section as a whole, however, presents such instructive analyses of works that it is still of value. In general, those illustrations intended as historical documents remain useful.

V. Accuracy

As mentioned, the *Lincoln Library* contains a vast quantity of specific factual information, particularly statistics. The tables were carefully compiled and in general appear accurate up to the time at which they were prepared. The same is generally true of the articles. However, the presence of out-of-date material is at times confusing and frequently misleading. Indeed, this is the source of most of the inaccuracies in this encyclopedia.

For example, entries appear on pages 215 and 663, discussing, respectively, the geography and history of **Rhodesia**. In neither case is there any mention of Zimbabwe. Separate articles about **Zimbabwe** appear on pages 540 and 804. A reader encountering the first two entries mentioned would be unaware of the major political changes in that country since the late 1970s, including the new names of the nation and its capital city. A reader encountering all four references might find them perplexing. Similarly, the information on the **European Economic Community** is incomplete, and no mention is made of the memberships of Ireland, Greece, Spain, or Portugal, all of whom were admitted after the 1957 treaty agreement. The memberships of Great Britain and Denmark are mentioned only in passing elsewhere in the volume.

Several of our content specialists noted serious inaccuracies in entries in their respective fields. For example, the *Lincoln Library*'s 17-sentence entry on **Saturn** contains at least four minor errors and three major ones. It is, on the whole, the least satisfactory article on the subject in all the encyclopedias reviewed in the Buying Guide. Similarly, the *Lincoln Library*'s entry on **money** cannot be considered reasonably accurate. The encyclopedia's information on **transistors** is generally inaccurate because the article is seriously out of date.

VI. Clarity

Entries in the *Lincoln Library* are generally clear if unexciting. The writing varies from the more discursive style used in the background articles to more concise language used to report factual information.

The tone of the articles more often resembles that of a textbook than a reference book. As an example, the introduction to the History department begins as follows:

> The word history is sometimes used to mean all that has happened in the past. In this sense we speak of the history of the earth, of rocks, or of plants, as well as of the history of man. In the narrower sense, however, history is an account of the actions and the fortunes of mankind. Such an account must be based upon reliable records which can be understood and interpreted by the writers of history.

An example of the more condensed language used for specific subjects would be this entry from the section on American history:

> **Ordinance of 1787**. An act of the Congress of the Confederation making provision for the government of the Northwest Territory, providing for religious toleration and popular education, and forbidding slavery in the territory.

The style of the Mathematics department is entirely that of a textbook. Moreover, the language is noticeably dated, as in the following example from page 1479:

> (1) to multiply an integer by 10, 100, 1000, etc.
> Annex to the multiplicand as many ciphers as there are ciphers in the multiplier.
> **Problem**. Multiply 28 by 1000.
> *Solution*.—Three ciphers annexed to 28 gives 28,000, which is the product required.

In a random review of individual pages, certain stylistic inconsistencies were noted. An entry on **John Dewey** (page 860) is written in the present tense. The first heading in the Government department is "Introductory," while the heading beginning the Economics department is "Introduction." The metric system is not used consistently for scientific material. However, these are minor matters and do not tend to distort the sense of the text.

VII. Objectivity

The presentation of the information in *The Lincoln Library of Essential Information* is generally balanced and objective. An attempt is made to mirror the complexity of issues and to represent varying points of view. The biography of **Ronald Reagan** states that "The combination of tax cuts and tremendous increase in defense spending fueled an economic recovery toward the end of his first term. But the federal deficit under Reagan grew to almost 200 billion dollars a year." The article on **South Africa** notes that its government's "policies of racial segregation won the antipathy of much of the world. . . . South Africa became the most prosperous country of southern Africa. Yet political turmoil was constant." The biography of **James Joyce** says of *Ulysses*, "Couched in expressive but often difficult language forms and complicated by the author's erudition, it expressed the thoughts of the characters with a freedom of inhibition unexampled in English literature. Its influence on other authors was widely felt."

The *Lincoln Library* covers a few controversial subjects. There are no articles on homosexuality, racism, contraception, drug abuse, or nuclear disarmament. The article on **evolution** asserts, "This has established practically universal acceptance by the scientific world of the general theory of evolution as a cosmic process." There is no article on creationism. While the omission of these subjects leaves gaps in the comprehensiveness of this encyclopedia, those subjects that are discussed are treated impartially and without distortion.

VIII. Accessibility

The organizational structure of the *Lincoln Library* works well for readers interested in studying one of the large subject areas covered by a department. The encyclopedia begins with an atlas, followed by the subject departments and a comprehensive index. Each department opens with some background material on the particular discipline, followed by articles exploring the subject in detail. Each main article begins with an uppercase heading, with subsections introduced by boldface headings. Glossaries of terms in relevant subject areas are included, with entries appearing in boldface. The tables are organized in logical fashion, often chronological, and are positioned close to relevant text. Where the material is grouped according to national boundaries (as in History and Government), the United States is discussed first, followed by other countries in alphabetical order. Historical subjects are treated chronologically.

The title page of each department provides a table of contents to assist the reader in locating information. The best aid to locating material is the detailed index, which is printed in full at the end of both volumes.

One drawback of the division of the books into departments is that information on a particular subject may be dispersed throughout the two volumes. For example, information on Iran is found in the departments of Geography, Economics, History, Fine Arts, Government, and Miscellany. In order to find this information the reader would consult the index where there are 14 subentries under **Iran**, as well as entries for **Iranians** and **Iran-Iraq War**. This process is avoided in THE CONCISE COLUMBIA ENCYCLOPEDIA and in all the other single and multivolume general encyclopedias, which are arranged alphabetically. A review in *Booklist* (January 1, 1979) noted, "Persons used to the simple alphabetical arrangement of most American encyclopedias will find more disadvantage than advantage in the *Lincoln*'s structure." The *Lincoln Library* system might be useful for a reader wishing particularly to compare the government of Iran with those of Indonesia, Iraq, Israel, and Italy, which are discussed on facing pages.

As noted, the index is the key to locating information in the *Lincoln Library*. Subentries are arranged alphabetically under the main entry, so that references for a single key word are in one place. Cross-references are italicized. Occasionally, related entries are not arranged together. For instance "Let-

ters of Marque" falls between "Letters: Words and Phrases Frequently Misused in" and "Letter Writing." Arrangement of entries beginning with the same word is strictly alphabetical, as in "Adams, John; Adams, John Couch; Adams, John Q."

Some individuals with pseudonyms are listed under their real names while others are listed under their pseudonyms. There is a biography for **Lewis Carroll** and a cross-reference for **Charles Dodgson** but no index entry for Dodgson. Conversely, **Mark Twain** appears under **Samuel Langhorne Clemens**, with a cross-reference under his pseudonym. He is listed under both names in the index. **George Eliot** is treated in the same manner as Lewis Carroll, with no index entry for Mary Ann Evans. Some names beginning with prefixes are listed both under the prefix and under the main portion of the name, as "Da Vinci," "Vinci," "Leonardo da" and "Vinci, Leonardo da." Others appear in only one form, as "Balzac, Honoré de," for which there is no cross-reference.

Names beginning with *Mc* are alphabetized as though they began with *Mac*. The abbreviation *St.* is always spelled as *Saint* in the index; in the Biography department, it is abbreviated but alphabetized as *Saint*. Monarchs with the same name are grouped according to country and in the order of their succession.

While the division of the work into departments results in repetition of some information and separates related material, it also brings some related material together; moreover, frequent reference to the index can aid the reader. Also of help are the cross-references, of which there are some 8,800. These are italicized and often preceded by "see" in the text and in the index. The arrangement of the *Lincoln Library* is complex, but with an awareness of the topical, alphabetical, and chronological systems employed most information can be readily located.

IX. Special Features

The *Lincoln Library* provides several special features not found in similar works. One such feature is the 48-page color atlas of maps of the world. While the scale of the maps is necessarily small, national boundaries are distinguished in color, and small land masses, secondary cities, and provincial boundaries are represented in detailed fashion.

Another feature is the glossaries, called Dictionaries, included in most of the departments. These are alphabetical lists of identifications and definitions of terms relevant to the field. Some of the dictionary entries are longer than some articles in the CONCISE COLUMBIA or THE NEW AMERICAN DESK ENCYCLOPEDIA. There are over 60 dictionaries on subjects such as Art Terms and Subjects; Business, Banking, and Legal Terms; Chemical Substances; Popular

Names of Cities; and Literary Plots, Characters, and Allusions. The Dictionaries are printed in a typeface smaller than that of the text, thus condensing the information further.

One of the *Lincoln Library*'s most useful features is its tables. A great deal of thought seems to have gone into organizing these and positioning them near relevant articles. Subjects treated in tables include abdications; air pollution; cabinet members; bacterial diseases; Federal Reserve System; historical periods, events, and movements in the New World; common logarithms; mythological associations; Nobel Prize winners; Presidents of the United States; and United Nations. As already mentioned, there is a problem with out-of-date information in some of the tables, but others deal with information unaffected by the passage of time. Some tables have been brought up to date, such as the table of Presidents of the United States and the table of Nobel Prize winners (both current to 1984). Like the Dictionaries, the tables are concise vehicles for conveying a great deal of information. In addition, they help to show linear and tabular relationships between facts. According to the editors, "Many, if expanded into descriptive text, would each provide material for a substantial volume."

Yet another special feature is the Review Questions section included at the end of each department. Numerous questions are posed (seven full pages of questions at the end of Economics) to assist the reader in reviewing the material. The questions are challenging, as, for example, "Summarize the history of popular ratification of state constitutions" and "What kinds of words were brought into the English language by the introduction of Christianity?" In the Mathematics section, answers to numerical problems are supplied. According to the Preface, "In all, there are 10,000 such questions, the answers to which, in themselves, constitute the foundations of a liberal education." Only the multivolume WORLD BOOK includes a similar feature.

Bibliographies are included at the end of each department. These have apparently been updated at various times. The references in Geography and History are to works published up to 1966, while the references in Economics date from 1969 to 1976. The Education and English Language departments contain *no dates*—a distinct drawback. Author, title, and publisher are supplied for each work, and works are listed under bold headings corresponding to portions of the text. Neither of the single-volume encyclopedias (CONCISE COLUMBIA, NEW AMERICAN DESK ENCYCLOPEDIA) include bibliographies.

X. Format

The Lincoln Library of Essential Information is available only in a two-volume hardcover edition. The sturdy Black Wolf Grain binding is suitable for school and library use. Both volumes are thumb-indexed for easy access to the subject departments, which are also embossed on the spines in gold.

XI. Other Opinions

Booklist, January 1, 1979 (reviewing the 36th edition, pub. 1974): ". . . those who wish to explore independently the subjects covered in *Lincoln* will find its arrangement effective. Others may find it arbitrary and complicated. . . . The most successfully handled topics are in the sciences, history, and mathematics. . . . The social sciences are less well treated. . . . Because *Lincoln Library* does not treat turbulent and controversial subjects—or those aspects of well-known subjects—its fairness in handling topics of this sort is seldom questioned. . . . Bibliographies are not a strong feature of the *Lincoln Library*. . . . The maps . . . are small but have excellent definition."

William A. Katz, *Introduction to Reference Work*: "The index is detailed enough to overcome the basic problem of arrangement, which is not ideal for ready-reference work. Among its many good features are its several hundred charts and tables, bibliographies, quality illustrations, a good atlas of the world, and broad coverage of general knowledge. The articles are well written and can be easily understood by a junior high or high school student. As the material is arranged under broad sections with over 25,000 different entries, coverage tends to be brief, factual, and unopinionated.

"The difficulty with the *Lincoln* is its revision policy. Although it claims a policy of constant revision, a cursory glance at the 1980 printing will show it is best on current events, but slower on updating standard material in the social sciences, arts, and humanities."

XII. Summary

The Lincoln Library of Essential Information is a basic two-volume general reference work intended for nonspecialists. It is not meant to replace full-scale multivolume encyclopedias, but it may be preferable for readers who do not require a multivolume set.

The *Lincoln Library* is adequate for casual reference work in some subjects and for browsing. Unfortunately, however, the encyclopedia is not of consistently high quality. Much of the content of the 1985 edition, especially in the sciences, was already badly dated when this edition was first issued. This has an adverse effect on accuracy. Moreover, some subjects receive less coverage than they deserve, and many are treated in a superficial manner even for an encyclopedia with concise entries. The *Lincoln Li-*

brary tends to ignore or skate over controversial topics. Locating specific information within the volumes is also a problem.

At $149.50, the *Lincoln Library* is priced reasonably for a volume of its size. It will be most valuable in small libraries where the demand for general reference material is light or where it will be a supplement to larger, more detailed general reference works. It has only one direct competitor, THE VOLUME LIBRARY.

The Lincoln Library of Essential Information is sold by some bookstores. Individuals and institutions can also order the set from the publisher, Frontier Press, at P.O. Box 1098, Columbus, OH 43216, telephone (614) 864-3737.

New American Desk Encyclopedia

Facts at a Glance

Full Title: **The New American Desk Encyclopedia.**
Publisher: New American Library.
Editor-in-Chief: Robert A. Rosenbaum.
Edition Reviewed: 1984.

Number of Volumes: 1.
Number of Articles: 13,000.
Number of Pages: 1,305.
Number of Words: 1,000,000.
Number of Maps: 225.
Number of Illustrations: 35 color.
Trim Size: 4¼″ × 7″.

Price: $6.95.
Sold in bookstores and supermarkets, and by
    direct mail.
ISBN 0-451-14289-6.
Revision of not less than 10 percent every 4 to 5
    years.
Next Scheduled Revision: 1989.

I. Introduction

The New American Desk Encyclopedia is a single-volume general encyclopedia designed to provide quick and convenient ready reference. Available in a compact, mass-market paperback edition, it aims to cover a full range of subjects in a limited amount of space. The publisher claims that this encyclopedia is "the only one-volume pocket-size paperback guide that combines information on all major fields of knowledge with up-to-the-minute coverage of the contemporary world scene."

There is no preface to the book, and thus no explanation of how the subjects were chosen or the entries compiled and edited.

The edition current at the time of this review carried a 1984 copyright.

II. Scope

The New American Desk Encyclopedia contains 13,000 entries and approximately one million words. Thus the average length of an article is 77 words, roughly the same as for the entries in the CONCISE COLUMBIA ENCYCLOPEDIA, although that work contains 2,000 more entries.

Entries are arranged alphabetically, letter by letter. Some entries are only a few lines long, such as those for **Muslims** (two lines) and for the aviatrix **Amelia Earhart** (eight lines). Others go into greater depth and length, including more detailed technical explorations (such as the 106-line entry for **heart**) or historical information (such as the 86-line entry for **immigration**). There are 175 articles about individual countries, as well as separate entries for each of the 50 states of the United States. Geographical entries follow a format distinct from that of other subjects. They are introduced by a list of general facts about the region, such as area and population, as well as a small regional map with the relevant country or state highlighted. The remainder of the article is subdivided by boldface subheadings such as *Land, People, Economy,* and *History.* As a result, these are among the longer articles in the book; taken together, they give the *New American* a consistently broad, but succinct, coverage of political geography.

Many of the brief entries serve primarily as definitions or identifications. Entries for individuals typically supply dates of birth and death, nationality, position or occupation, and the bare outlines of significant activities or accomplishments. Cross-references direct the reader to further information in order to avoid repetition of definitions. All efforts seem to have been made to use the available space in this compact book economically.

In light of the variety of subjects covered, the publisher's claim that the *New American* includes "all major fields of knowledge" is justified. Major historical figures and events are well represented, as are many of their present-day counterparts. As an indication of the *New American*'s range, there are entries for **Mozart, Benjamin Britten, Coriolanus, Fidel Castro,** the **astrolabe,** and the **electron microscope**. Contemporary popular subjects of importance are covered, as in the entries on **bluegrass music** and **Humphrey Bogart**. Issues of current social concern, such as **baby boom,** are also included. While considerable space is devoted to coverage of the United States, international subjects are not neglected (for comparison, the article on **Idaho** is slightly longer than the article on **Iceland**). Although names of people and places predominate, there is excellent coverage of scientific and technical subjects, and wide coverage of other subjects of general interest such as **integration, intelligence, interior decoration,** and **international law**.

New American Desk Encyclopedia

❶ 636   KAHN

parents. Most of Kafka's stories confront his protagonists with nightmarish situations which they cannot resolve or escape from. They reflect his profound sense of alienation, and his inhibitions and shortcomings, particularly in relation to the powerful figure of his father. Kafka died of tuberculosis at age 40. His friend and executor Max BROD ignored his instructions to destroy all his work, and subsequently published Kafka's many short stories and his novels *The Trial* (1925), *The Castle* (1926) and *Amerika* (1927).

❷ KAHN, Louis Isadore (1901–1974), US architect, noted for his work on housing projects and university buildings, particularly the Richards Medical Research Laboratories at the U. of Pennsylvania, where he was a professor.

KAHN, Otto Hermann (1867–1934), German-born US banker and patron of the arts. As a member of the New York Metropolitan Opera Company board he instituted many reforms, and appointed TOSCANINI as principal conductor.

KAISER, Henry John (1882–1967), US industrialist, founder of the Kaiser-Frazer Corporation. He contributed greatly to the Allied war effort in WWII by his development of faster production techniques for ships, aircraft and military vehicles, especially the famous "jeep."

❸ KAISER, title, derived from Latin *Caesar*, sometimes used by rulers of the HOLY ROMAN EMPIRE (800–1806) and the German Empire (1871–1918).

KALAHARI DESERT, arid plain of some 100,000sq mi in S Africa. It lies mainly in Botswana but extends into Namibia and South Africa. The region has low annual rainfall and only seasonal pasture for sheep. It is inhabited only by Bushmen. There is a wide variety of game.

KALININ, Mikhail Ivanovich (1875–1946), Russian revolutionary leader. A loyal Stalinist, Kalinin was chairman of the central executive (now the presidium) from 1919 and a member of the Politburo from 1925.

KALMAR UNION, treaty whereby Denmark, Norway and Sweden were united under Margaret of Denmark and her heirs. It was signed at the Swedish port of Kalmar (1397), which became the Union's political center. The Union endured until 1523.

KAMCHATKA PENINSULA, land area and oblast in the USSR which extends about 750mi S from NE Siberia to separate the Sea of Okhotsk from the Bering Sea. It is largely tundra and pine forest, and has Siberia's highest peak, Klyuchevskaya Sopka (15,584ft) and includes 22 active

volcanoes, along with geysers and hot springs. Its main city is Petropavlovsk-Kamchatsky.

KAMEHAMEHA I (c1738–1819), Hawaiian monarch from 1790, a benevolent despot who united the islands (1810). He encouraged foreign contact and trade, but always sought to preserve the independence of his country and its people.

KAMENEV, Lev Borisovich (1883–1936), Russian politician, an associate of Lenin in exile. As president of the Moscow Soviet 1918–26, he sided with his brother-in-law TROTSKY and with ZINOVIEV against Stalin after Lenin's death (1924). Stalin used the murder of Sergei KIROV as a pretext for arresting Kamenev; he was executed after a "show-trial."

KAMIKAZE ("Divine Wind"), Japanese force of suicide pilots in WWII. Inspired by the ancient SAMURAI code of patriotic self-sacrifice, they deliberately crashed bomb-bearing planes onto Allied ships and installations. They inflicted particularly heavy damage at Okinawa.

KAMPUCHEA, formerly Cambodia, republic in SE Asia, known as the Khmer Republic, 1970–75. Laos lies to the N, Vietnam to the E and Thailand to the W and N.

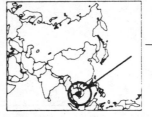 **❹**

Official name: Democratic Kampuchea
Capital: Phnom Penh
Area: 69,892sq mi
Population: 6,000,000
Languages: Khmer; French
Religions: Hinayana Buddhist
Monetary unit(s): 1 riel=100 sen **❺**

Land. About half of Kampuchea is covered by tropical forest; at the center of the country the Mekong R flows from N to S, providing 900mi of navigable waterways. During the rainy season, May-Oct., the river backs up to the Tonle Sap Lake, vastly increasing its size and leaving rich fertile silt, excellent for rice production. There are two mountain ranges, the Dong Rek to the N and the Cardamom to the SW. **❻**
People. About 85% of the population are Khmers, with sizeable minorities of Chinese and Vietnamese, and smaller groups of

Page shown at 108% of actual size.

❶ Page number and guide word
❷ Main entry: New American Desk Encyclopedia contains 13,000 entries, arranged alphabetically, letter-by-letter. Entry words are printed in boldface type.

❸ Cross-references are indicated by words printed in small capital letters.
❹ Location map: New American Desk Encyclopedia contains 225 maps in all.

❺ Nation and state entries include a "fact table" giving basic statistics about geography, population, etc.
❻ Subheads: Nation and state entries are divided into sections by subheads.

Illustrations are not a strong feature of this encyclopedia. In addition to the small black-and-white maps in the geographical articles, there is a 16-page color atlas section with a handful of small maps and illustrations relating to geology, geography, and astronomy. This is located near the beginning of the work and does not illustrate any particular article. There are no other illustrations in the volume.

III. Authority

The current edition of *The New American Desk Encyclopedia* was issued in 1984 by New American Library, a leading publisher of mass-market paperbacks. According to the publisher, the *New American* is a "derivation and adaptation of the *University Desk Encyclopedia*," which was published jointly by E. P. Dutton and the Dutch publisher Elsevier in 1977. That work was never revised and is now out of print. In 1981 a three-volume edition was published by Concord Reference Books as the *Concord Encyclopedia*; this is also now out of print.

The *New American* differs from the *University Desk Encyclopedia* in several respects. It includes half as many entries and half as many words as the older book, which was heavily illustrated and produced in a large hardcover format. Its entries have been updated through 1983 (see also *Currency*), and it costs less than its older cousin did.

The nine-person editorial staff for this edition was headed by Robert A. Rosenbaum, the editor-in-chief. In addition, the credits list 31 contributing editors although their affiliations and areas of specialization are not identified. All of the articles are unsigned.

IV. Currency

As mentioned above, since *The New American Desk Encyclopedia* was first produced in the early 1980s, both the choice of subjects and the content of the articles are generally current to that time. Where articles have been adapted from the *University Desk Encyclopedia* they have often been updated, and subjects missing from the earlier work appear in the *New American*. For example, the article on **Margaret Thatcher** mentions her party's electoral victory in 1983, while the article on **Ronald Reagan** mentions his 1984 election campaign. The article on **South Africa**, however, mentions none of the recent political upheaval in that country, and ends "In 1961 this country became a republic and left the Commonwealth largely because of differences over its apartheid policies." The article on **disarmament** ends with mention of the 1975 arms limitations agreement but makes no mention of either the 1982 Strategic Arms Reduction Talks or Ronald Reagan's 1983 Strategic Defense Initiative, although there is a separate article on the former. The entry on **transistors** is, on the whole, quite dated.

Brevity of the articles sometimes limits the amount of current information, since details beyond a certain level of significance are not included. Thus an article on the **Iraqi-Iranian War** states that "Sporadic fighting, without military distinction, led to a stalemate that continued through the early 1980s." The growing implications of this conflict, for the Middle East and the entire world, are not incorporated in the space available for the entry.

Many subjects that have only recently achieved prominence are covered, as in the articles on **AIDS** and **boat people**. According to the publisher, the *New American* will be revised every four to five years, with at least 10 percent of the material revised each time. The next scheduled revision will appear in 1989. This policy shows a promising intention to keep the encyclopedia more or less up-to-date and to incorporate new material as developments warrant.

V. Accuracy

The majority of the entries in *The New American Desk Encyclopedia* are reliably correct, and the level of detail is consistent. However, because the articles are so brief, unavoidable choices have been made in selecting information to include. On the whole, important facts are given appropriate weight, but occasionally significant information has been omitted. For example, **AIDS** fails to mention the high incidence of the disease in Africa; instead statistics are given for high-risk groups, presumably in the United States although this is not made clear. The article on **Robert Byrd** identifies him as a "U.S. legislator" but fails to mention the state (West Virginia) that he represents. The article on **Isaac Bashevis Singer** mentions his 1978 Nobel Prize for Literature, yet the article on **Saul Bellow** does not mention his (awarded in 1976). There is no entry at all for **Eugenio Montale**, recipient of the 1975 Nobel Prize. These omissions can be misleading for a reader trying to rely upon the encyclopedia's consistent and accurate presentation of information.

The article on **money** contains several mistakes and oversimplifications. The entry on **Saturn** is generally accurate.

On the whole, the inaccuracies noted here are not so significant as to cast doubt upon the *New American*'s overall authority. Since the entries consist largely of salient, well-confirmed facts, this is not a great problem.

VI. Clarity

In order to cover 13,000 subjects in one paperback volume, the articles are extremely condensed. Many of the entries are basically definitions or identifications, with perhaps a small amount of background information. While not dictionary definitions, they may be only a few sentences in length. The entry for **Titanic**, quoted in its entirety, is an example of this:

> TITANIC, 46,328-ton British liner which sank in 1912 after hitting an iceberg on her maiden voyage to New York. At least 1,500 of the 2,200 aboard drowned. After the disaster (caused mainly by excessive speed), lifeboat, radio watch and ice patrol provisions were improved.

Certain complex subjects are treated in longer articles written in a less truncated style. The tone is still direct, scholarly without being pedantic, and easily understood by the average reader. The following passage from the article on **economics** illustrates this:

> Under the influence of KEYNESIAN ECONOMICS., US government policies from the 1950s emphasized increasing demand by both manipulating tax rates and increasing the money supply. However, starting in the 1970s, inflation and a stagnating or decreasing gross national product brought these fiscal policies under question, strengthening the influence of non-Keynesian economists.

Alternate forms of scientific or technical terms are sometimes supplied, which is most helpful, as in the case of "ASPIRIN, or **acetylsalicylic acid**," but technical terms are not always defined in context. The article on **artificial respiration** begins: "the means of inducing RESPIRATION when it has ceased, as after drowning, asphyxia, in coma or respiratory paralysis." Some readers may need to consult a dictionary for the meaning of *asphyxia*. Similarly, the entry for **hunchback** includes the terms *ankylosing spondylitis* and *vertebral collapse* without defining them. The article on **Saturn** uses units of measurement designated as *Mm* and *Gm*, but these are not explained in the list of abbreviations in the frontmatter. In general, the more technical articles are written at a higher reading level than the rest of the *New American*.

As previously mentioned, this encyclopedia contains few illustrations other than its maps. The maps are very small black-and-white outline drawings, with no labeling or scale and with the state or country under discussion colored in black. For regions whose outlines are familiar to the reader these maps give an idea of general location, but for unfamiliar regions they are only marginally helpful.

The lack of illustrations is sometimes a drawback. For example, the text must cope with the task of describing the periodic table of the elements ("arranged in rows and columns to illustrate periodic similarities"). This could be much more clearly depicted with an illustration of the table accompanying the entry.

VII. Objectivity

The articles in *The New American Desk Encyclopedia* are predominantly factual rather than interpretive, and the presentation of facts is generally objective. Information is given emphasis and space in accordance with its relative importance, and multiple points of view are suggested for complex issues. The article on **capital punishment**, for example, states that "Capital punishment has long been a center of debate as to whether it deters serious crime or is only a form of revenge."

There are a few exceptions to this rule, in the form of subjects receiving an insufficient or inordinate amount of space, or biased coverage. One of the longest articles is that on the **women's movement**, which is twice as long as articles on similarly important subjects such as **civil rights** or **slavery**. In discussing legislation concerning women, the article includes this barbed statement: "Chivalrous legislators still exempted them from certain responsibilities of citizenship, such as jury duty and poll and property taxes." The article on **family planning** states that with modern methods of contraception "unwanted PREGNANCY should be a rarity. However, ignorance and neglect have prevented the realization of this ideal." The article does not mention the social and political controversy surrounding this issue, although there is a separate entry treating the **abortion controversy**.

The entry on **evolution** describes several evolutionist theories and gives examples of the process. It concludes that "today, the evidence for evolution is overwhelming and comes from many branches of biology." It also declares that "LIFE probably first evolved from the primeval soup some 3–4 billion years ago, when the first organic chemicals were synthesized due to the effect of lightning." The entry on **creationism** treats the subject in a somewhat dismissive tone. Creationism is identified as a "theory held by fundamentalist Christians that the Earth and living beings were created as described in Genesis rather than through a process of evolution, such as is accepted in modern geology and biology." The article goes on to note that "espousing supposedly nonreligious 'scientific creationism,' creationists of the 1970s pressured textbook publishers and science teachers nationwide into equivocating with regard to the validity of scientific knowledge."

In spite of these examples, the encyclopedia's overall tone is one of balanced objectivity. The *New American* can be consulted for a reasonable presentation of most issues.

VIII. Accessibility

Entries in the encyclopedia are arranged alphabetically, letter by letter. At the beginning of the volume is a helpful section entitled "How to Use *The New American Desk Encyclopedia*," which explains the system of alphabetization in simple terms. This is followed by a section explaining the use of "Subheadings and Cross-References," and a list of abbreviations. However, this list is not comprehensive, since some abbreviations (such as *mp* and *bp*, used in the entries for chemical elements) are not listed.

Entry titles appear in bold capital letters, with subheads in bold upper- and lowercase letters. The editors' notes indicate that subheads are used for divisions of longer entries as well as "subjects that might otherwise appear as entries in their own right in a larger encyclopedia." Guide words showing the first and last entries in each spread provide a quick means of locating articles. According to the editors, "Keywords [entry titles] appear in the form most familiar to the majority of readers. . . . Where the keyword is a pseudonym the real name will appear either in this way or in the text if less well known." Thus there are entries under **George Eliot** and **Mark Twain**, with cross-references under **Mary Ann Evans** and **Samuel Langhorne Clemens**.

As in THE CONCISE COLUMBIA ENCYCLOPEDIA, a complex system of cross-references is provided, which is essential since information on a broad subject is often dispersed under various keywords with little repetition. Cross-references appear either within the articles or at the end of an article, in small capital letters. Some articles contain a considerable number of cross-references (there are 35 in the article on **philosophy**) and they can be distracting, but they are an invaluable and necessary means of locating related material.

This is even more true as *New American*, again in common with the CONCISE COLUMBIA, contains no index. The lack of an index is a disadvantage since, by choosing the wrong keyword, a reader can fail to locate information that may actually exist elsewhere in the volume. An index with subheads listed under major entries might have brought related keywords together to show at a glance all of the entries in a field. However, the logical alphabetical format, the lucid editors' notes on organization, and the extensive cross-references all come to the reader's aid in making information readily accessible.

IX. Special Features

Few special features are incorporated in *The New American Desk Encyclopedia*, which, because of its small size, devotes all available space to subject entries. The rudimentary black-and-white location maps enhance the articles on countries and states but do not provide much detail. The 16-page color section, titled "An Atlas of the Earth and Universe," includes color drawings and maps, and a chart offering information on astronomy, geology, and geography. These illustrations are not linked to the text or mentioned in cross-references, but they are interesting and attractive and the extensive captions are informative. On the whole, the maps and illustrations in the CONCISE COLUMBIA give that desk encyclopedia an advantage over this title.

X. Format

The *New American* is available in paperback form only. This form has the advantages of light weight and low price, since at $6.95 this is the least expensive encyclopedia in this category. It is "pocket-size" ($4\frac{1}{4}''$ × 7") and can easily be held in one hand.

The paper binding is not very durable and would not be suitable for libraries. Nor does the volume lie flat when open. However, it should be sufficiently durable for use by individuals when purchased for personal use.

XI. Other Opinions

The Los Angeles Times Book Review (April 22, 1984): ". . . Adapted from the 'University Desk Encyclopedia,' this truly portable version offers good general coverage of basic reference subjects, plus some rather contemporary entries: not only Archimedes, Atomic Clock, and Maple Syrup, but AIDS, Agent Orange, and the Moral Majority too."

XII. Summary

The New American Desk Encyclopedia is an adequate book of its type but is more suited for ready reference in the home or office than as a library research tool. It offers the benefit of up-to-date information about subjects of both current and general interest. The format is convenient and easy to use.

The small size of this book, however, means that the articles are brief, and few subjects are explored in depth. The fact that there are few illustrations and tables also limits the work's comprehensiveness. By comparison, THE CONCISE COLUMBIA ENCYCLOPEDIA, with a similar number of entries, does include these features, and its format is also more suited to library collections. Still, at $6.95, the *New American* is a good value for readers who want a single-volume paperback reference work for occasional personal use.

The New American Desk Encyclopedia is available in the reference section of many bookstores. Individuals and institutions that wish to order directly should send their request, with $6.95 plus $1.00 to cover postage and handling, to New American Library, P.O. Box 999, Bergenfield, NJ 07621.

New Encyclopaedia Britannica

Facts at a Glance

Full Title: **New Encyclopaedia Britannica.**
Publisher: Encyclopaedia Britannica.
Editors: Philip W. Goetz, Editor-in-Chief;
Margaret Hutton, Executive Editor.
Edition Reviewed: 1986. (Statistics apply to 1988 edition.)

Number of Volumes: 32 (1 Propaedia, 12
Micropaedia, 17 Macropaedia, 2 index).
Number of Contributors: more than 5,000.
Number of Entries: Micropaedia: 84,200 (65,100
articles, 19,100 cross-reference entries);
Macropaedia: 680.
Number of Pages: 32,330.
Number of Words: 44,000,000.
Number of Maps: 1,000.
Number of Cross-references: 25,000.
Number of Indexes: 1 (two volumes).
Number of Index Entries: 186,514.
Number of Illustrations: 6,400 color, plus 164 color
plates; 19,400 black-and-white.
Trim Size: $8^5/_{16}'' \times 10^7/_8''$.

Price: $1,349.00 for individuals, $999.00 with
library discount.
Sold directly by the publisher, through
distributors, at conventions, in selected
bookstores, and in some supermarkets.
ISBN 0-85229-443-3.
Revised annually.

I. Introduction

The *New Encyclopaedia Britannica* is a 32-volume general reference work designed to offer "a truly remarkable range of valuable information . . . in a highly-acclaimed four-part structure." In a brochure accompanying the set, the publisher assures the reader that "your family will find it an invaluable source of reference and learning for years to come."

The largest and most ambitious reference work on the market today (and a direct descendant of the most venerated encyclopedia in the English language), *New Britannica* has inspired both widespread acclaim and vituperous criticism from reviewers, librarians, and general users alike. Many critics have disputed the publisher's claims about accessibility and suitability, while others have expressed admiration for the breadth and depth of learning that the set embodies.

New Britannica aims to accomplish three things: to supply an easy-to-use source of basic facts (the Micropaedia), to provide a scholarly presentation of "knowledge in depth" (the Macropaedia), and to present an organized plan for self-education (the Propaedia). Thus *New Britannica* can be viewed as three (or four, counting the index) distinct but interrelated sets of reference tools, each serving a different but complementary purpose.

This review is based on an examination of the 1986 edition, the edition current at the time of review.

II. Scope

Any useful discussion of the scope of *New Britannica* must first take into account the encyclopedia's unique structure. Otherwise, a count of number of articles, article lengths, number of words, and so forth would be rendered meaningless.

New Britannica's four parts are (1) the Propaedia, or "Outline of Knowledge," one unnumbered volume; (2) the Micropaedia, or "Ready Reference," 12 volumes numbered 1 through 12; (3) the Macropaedia, or "Knowledge in Depth," 17 volumes numbered 13 through 29; (4) the index, two unnumbered volumes.

In the words of Mortimer Adler, who planned its concept and directed its execution, the single-volume Propaedia is intended to provide "an orderly topical outline of the whole of human knowledge, in the form of the circle of learning that is an *en-cyclo-paedia*." The publisher claims that the 744-page Propaedia "sets up major fields of knowledge in an outline sequence that enables you to learn on your own, at your own pace, using the pages of Britannica as your personal tutors."

The ten areas outlined in the Propaedia are (1) Matter and Energy; (2) The Earth; (3) Life on Earth; (4) Human Life; (5) Human Society; (6) Art; (7) Technology; (8) Religion; (9) The History of Mankind; (10) The Branches of Knowledge (logic, mathematics, science, history and the humanities, and philosophy). Each outline is preceded by a prefatory essay or overview by a noted authority in that field. At the end of each section of the outlines are lists of related articles in the Macropaedia and Micropaedia. Finally, the Propaedia also contains a complete list of all contributors to *New Britannica*, giving their credits and credentials.

The 12-volume Micropaedia is the part of *New Britannica* that most closely resembles other standard multivolume general encyclopedias. Its more than 11,800 pages contain some 65,000 specific-entry factual articles, in addition to 19,000 cross-reference entries. When *New Britannica* was first issued in 1974, articles in the Micropaedia were never longer than 750 words. Editorial policy has since changed, however, and some articles are now several times that

New Encyclopaedia Britannica

❶ — Jacob ben Asher 462

full of paradoxes; he punned or sobbed with the same apparent ease. He charmed and influenced many of his contemporaries and toward the end of his life was surrounded by a devoted group of younger and older artists.

❷ — **Jacob ben Asher** (b. 1269?, Cologne?—d. 1340?, Toledo, Castile), Jewish scholar whose codification of Jewish law was considered standard until the publication in 1565 of the *Shulḥan 'arukh* ("The Well-Laid Table") by Joseph Karo.

Little of certainty is known about Jacob's life. In 1303 he immigrated to Spain with his brothers and father, the great codifier Asher ben Jehiel, who became chief rabbi of Toledo. Although Jacob was eminently qualified, he never became a rabbi. Instead, it is likely that he eked out an existence as a moneylender.

Jacob is best known for his code *Arba'a ṭurim* ("Four Rows"; first published in its entirety in 1475 and also known as *Ṭur*), which systematically divided all Jewish law into four "rows," or classes, a new arrangement that became classic. He is therefore called Ba'al ha-Turim (Master of the Rows). His four divisions are: (1) *Oraḥ ḥayyim* ("Path of Life"), dealing with laws governing prayer and ritual; (2) *Yore de'a* ("Teacher of Knowledge"), setting forth the laws concerning things that are permitted or forbidden, such as dietary laws; (3) *Even ha-'ezer* ("Stone of Help"), containing the laws governing family relations, such as marriage and divorce; and (4) *Ḥoshen mishpaṭ* ("Breastplate of Judgment"), epitomizing civil and criminal law. Jacob eliminated all laws and customs that had been rendered obsolete by the destruction of the Second Temple (AD 70).

Revealing a marked indebtedness to his father's code, Jacob's austere digest became, after the Bible, the most popular work among 15th-century Jews and the usual basis for rabbinic decisions. It departed from his father's code and from that of Maimonides by basing the preponderance of its laws on decisions by post-Talmudic rabbinical authorities rather than on the Talmud itself.

❸ — **Jacob ben Machir ibn Tibbon:** *see* ibn Tibbon, Jacob ben Machir.

Jacob ben Zebi: *see* Emden, Jacob Israel.

Jacob Isaac OF PRZYSUCHA: *see* Przysucha, Jacob Isaac ben Asher.

Jacob Joseph OF POLONNOYE, in full JA-COB JOSEPH BEN TZEVI HA-KOHEN KATZ OF POLONNOYE (d. *c.* 1782), rabbi and preacher, the first theoretician and literary propagandist of Jewish Ḥasidism.

Jacob Joseph was a rabbi in the large Jewish community at Shargorod, in Podolia; after he came under the influence of the Ba'al Shem Ṭov, the founder of Ḥasidism, he was expelled (*c.* 1748) from Shargorod. He was subsequently rabbi of Rashkov, Nemirov, and ultimately Polonnoye, where he remained until his death.

As a writer, he contributed significantly to the spread of Ḥasidism. His first and main work was the controversial *Toldot Ya'aqov Yosef* (1780), which not only related the teachings of the Ba'al Shem Ṭov but also criticized traditional Jewish leadership and values. The work thus provoked anti-Ḥasidic sentiment and was burned by some opponents of the movement. Other works include homilies and commentary on books of the Bible, including *Ben Porat Yosef,* on Genesis; *Ẓefenat Pa'ne'aḥ,* on Exodus; and *Ketonet Passim,* on Leviticus and Numbers.

Jacoba OF BAVARIA, Dutch JACOBA VAN BEIEREN, French JACQUELINE DE BAVIÈRE (b. July 25, 1401, Le Quesnoy, Flanders—d. Oct. 9, 1436, Teilingen, near Leiden, Neth.),

duchess of Bavaria, countess of Holland, Zeeland, and Hainaut, whose forced cession of sovereignty in the three counties to Philip the Good, duke of Burgundy, in 1428, consolidated Burgundian dominion in the Low Countries.

Jacoba, the only daughter and heiress of William, count of Zeeland, Holland, and Hainaut, was married in 1415 to John of

Jacoba, 15th-century painting by an unknown artist, in the Rijksmuseum, Amsterdam
By courtesy of the Rijksmuseum, Amsterdam

Touraine, who died two years later. Jacoba's claim to succeed her father, who also died in 1417, was not recognized by the German king Sigismund, who instead supported her paternal uncle John of Bavaria.

After marrying her cousin, John IV, duke of Brabant, in March 1418, Jacoba fought against John of Bavaria in Holland. Her uncle John the Fearless, duke of Burgundy, settled the dispute in 1419, but John of Bavaria gained control of Holland and Zeeland the following year, when the counties were mortgaged to him by John of Brabant.

Disgusted by her husband's actions, Jacoba left for Hainaut and, after repudiating her marriage in 1421, went to England, where she was welcomed by Henry V. In 1422 she married Humphrey, duke of Gloucester, whose intrusion into the Low Countries two years later destroyed the English–Burgundian alliance.

Jacoba returned to Hainaut in 1424 with Humphrey and an army, but Humphrey deserted to England in 1425. Jacoba was subsequently interned by her opponent, Philip the Good, duke of Burgundy, at Ghent.

After Philip had gained possession of Holland and Zeeland (1425), Jacoba escaped and for the next three years contested Philip's power in the Netherlands. Her hopes dimmed, however, after the Pope declared her marriage to Humphrey illegal (Jan. 9, 1428); she made a settlement with Philip on July 3, 1428, in the Treaty of Delft, which maintained Jacoba's title of countess but transferred administration of her three counties (Holland, Zeeland, and Hainaut) to Philip and stipulated that she was not to marry without his consent.

After Philip had mortgaged the revenues of Holland and Zeeland to three nobles of the Borselen family from Zeeland (1430), Jacoba secretly married one of them—Francis, lord of Zuilen and St. Maartensdijk—probably as part of a plot to overthrow Burgundian sovereignty in Holland. Philip then imprisoned Francis (October 1432) and forced Jacoba to abdicate her countship (1433). She later became duchess in Bavaria and countess of Ostrevant (in Bohemia), and was allowed to remarry Francis in 1434. She died childless.

Jacobābād, city and district, Sukkur Division, Sind Province, Pakistan. The city is the district headquarters and is a junction of the Pakistan Western Railway and main roads through Sind. It was founded in 1847 on the site of the village of Khānghar by Gen. John Jacob, the district's first deputy commissioner. Jacob, who laid out the modern city, is commemorated by monuments, and even his horse has been memorialized by a

❹ mud pyramid. The city was incorporated as a municipality in 1875. It is noted for its consistently high temperatures, with readings (May–June) sometimes exceeding 126° F (52° C) in the shade.

❺ Manufactures include cotton carpets (*ghalichah*), lacquered wooden toys and lamps, and embroidery. Grain markets and milling mark Jacobābād's position at the centre of a rice-and grain-cultivating region. The city has several public parks, Victoria clock tower (1887), a municipal broadcasting station, and government colleges affiliated with the University of Sind.

Jacobābād District (area 2,038 sq mi [5,278 sq km]), formerly the Upper Sind Frontier District, occupies an alluvial plain along the Indus River in the east, protected from flood by the Kashmor embankment, and a desolate clay desert (*pakki*) in the west; to the north are the Bugti Hills. Cultivation is by means of canal irrigation. Millet, gram (chick-pea), rice, wheat, and oilseeds are the chief crops; rice is milled locally. Pop. (1981 prelim.) town, 80,000; district, 1,013,000.

❻ **Jacobean age** (from Latin Jacobus: James), period of visual and literary arts during the reign of James I of England (1603–25). The distinctions between the early Jacobean and the preceding Elizabethan styles are subtle ones, often merely a question of degree, for although the dynasty changed, there was no immediate stylistic revolution.

Jacobean builders expressed a marked preference for the rectangular "U" and "H" plans for domestic architecture and insisted that facade elevations be rigidly symmetric. They incorporated elements from Italian Mannerist architecture and also made full use of the stucco strapwork (a decorative design consisting of narrow fillets, or bands, folded, crossed, and sometimes interlaced) of the French school of Fontainebleau (a group of artists, largely Italian, who evolved a distinctive Mannerist style at the court of Francis I).

In architecture the stylistic revolution occurred in 1615, when the King appointed his former masque set designer, Inigo Jones, to the office of surveyor. Elizabeth I had preferred to be entertained at the great houses of her favourites (and at their expense), but James preferred to act as host. Jones was engaged, therefore, in the building or rebuilding of numerous royal houses and other structures in London, not only during the reign of James I but also during that of Charles I (1625–49). The gulf separating the work of Inigo Jones from the earlier architecture of James's reign is too wide to be bridged by the designation "Jacobean style," however, because the style that Jones espoused was entirely new to England, a style based on the theories and works of the Italian architect Andrea Palladio (*see* Palladianism).

During this period, painting and sculpture lagged behind architecture in accomplishments because there was no outstanding practitioner of either. For this reason, a good case can be made for a continuous, if mediocre, Jacobean style in these arts. The chief of the early Jacobean painters was the talented miniaturist Isaac Oliver. Most of the Jacobean portraitists, like the sculptors, were foreign: for example, Marcus Gheerhaerts the Younger, Paul van Somer, Cornelius Johnson, and Daniel Mytens. Their efforts were surpassed by those of the Flemish painters Peter Paul Rubens and

Page shown at 66% of actual size.

❶ Guide words and page number

❷ Main entry: The Micropaedia contains 65,100 entries, arranged alphabetically, word-by-word. In addition, there are 680 entries in the Macropaedia.

❸ Cross-reference entries: The Micropaedia contains 25,000

cross-reference entries. Occasionally, cross-references within Micropaedia articles refer readers to the Macropaedia.

❹ Illustration: New Britannica contains 25,964 illustrations, of which one-third are in color. Many are taken from historical sources.

❺ Metric equivalents of standard measures are given in parentheses.

❻ Caption

length. Nevertheless, the general average remains around 300–400 words, and some Micropaedia articles are as brief as 50 words.

The 17-volume, 23,000,000-word Macropaedia contains more than 17,000 pages and includes in-depth discussions of 680 subjects—an average of 25 pages per article. Actual article length ranges from fewer than three pages for such entries as **Beirut** and **Barcelona**, to 90 pages or more for subjects such as **Australia**, **animal behavior**, and **biblical literature and its critical interpretations**. At 323 pages, the entry for **United States of America** is truly book-length. As the page lengths and subject titles indicate, Macropaedia articles are generally of the broad-entry type.

Whereas the Micropaedia intends to be encyclopedic in its breadth of coverage, entries in the Macropaedia are much more selective, and therefore more arbitrary. (Moreover, the Macropaedia's articles are often written from a highly personal or idiosyncratic viewpoint. See also *Objectivity*.) Mortimer Adler's influence on the Macropaedia may be seen in the coverage extended to philosophy and subjects with some philosophical content. In Volume 24, for example, at least 12 out of 48 entries touch on aspects of philosophy or involve a substantial degree of discussion of theory as well as practice: **metaphysics**, **ancient Middle Eastern religions**, **John Stuart Mill**, **Milton**, **philosophy of mind**, **modernization and urbanization**, **mystery religions**, **motion pictures**, **myth and mythology**, **names**, **Newton**, and **Nietzsche**. Indeed, the Macropaedia is highly philosophical throughout, not merely in the popular sense meaning "thoughtful" or "contemplative" but also in the sense of teasing out various meanings, possible causes, and consequences. The purpose of the Macropaedia is not only to present facts but also to engage in substantial philosophical speculation or to discuss possible interpretations in a philosophical manner. In this sense, Macropaedia articles may be said to resemble university seminars.

The Micropaedia is printed in a format of three columns per page; the Macropaedia has two columns per page. As an indication of how space is apportioned among different subjects, **Charlemagne** is covered in 47 lines in the Micropaedia and three and a half pages in the Macropaedia. **Konstantin Chernenko** receives 49 lines in the Micropaedia; **Ty Cobb** is covered in 34 lines in the same volume. *New Britannica*'s coverage of the **American Civil War** consists of about two-thirds of a page in the Micropaedia, more than eight pages in the Macropaedia article **United States of America**, and several dozen Micropaedia entries on individual figures, battles, and issues. **Christianity** occupies two-thirds of a page in the Micropaedia, but the reader is referred to the Macropaedia, which devotes 115 pages to the subject. The nine-and-a-half-page Micropaedia entry on **China** includes a seven-page table of major Chinese dynasties; the nation and its history receive 222 pages in the Macropaedia.

Britannica encyclopedias have long been noted for their extensive coverage in the areas of geography and biography. The 15th edition maintains this reputation and also provides strong coverage of literature, the arts, and the humanities, while scientific and technological subjects now make up close to two-fifths of the encyclopedia's entries. Although the publisher has not provided the Buying Guide with a percentage breakdown of subject areas covered in *New Britannica*, the cross-reference entry lists in the Propaedia outlines give a good clue to the scope of the encyclopedia's overall coverage. Using the Propaedia's subject classifications, our reviewers arrived at the following approximate breakdown for entries in the Micropaedia:

Matter and Energy (physics, astrophysics, chemistry): 6 percent

The Earth (geology, physical geography, climatology): 4.5 percent

Life on Earth (life sciences, nature): 13.33 percent

Human Life (evolution, heredity, health and disease, behavior and experience): 5.5 percent

Human Society (social and political science): 10.5 percent

Art (literature, fine and performing arts): 17 percent

Technology: 7.5 percent

Religion: 13 percent

History: 23 percent

The Branches of Knowledge: 5.5 percent.

Because a number of entries are classified under more than one subject area, percentages add up to more than 100 percent. Biographical entries have not been counted as a separate category.

With its scholarly perspective, *New Britannica* gives short shrift to fads and to contemporary figures who, from the present perspective, may not be likely to have more than a passing influence on our culture and society. (For example, there are entries for **Elvis Presley** and the **Beatles**, but none for Michael Jackson, who is included in ACADEMIC AMERICAN ENCYCLOPEDIA and COLLIER'S ENCYCLOPEDIA.) This policy is generally a sound one. *New Britannica* also disdains the sort of "how-to" subjects covered in most general multivolume encyclopedias. Presumably such subjects do not fall within the purview of the "Outline of Knowledge" presented in the Propaedia and would conflict with the set's scholarly tone. However, in the view of our reviewers, this intellectual fastidiousness may make *New Britannica* less competitive with THE ENCYCLOPEDIA AMERI-

CANA and COLLIER'S, which otherwise also set high standards of scholarship.

Writing in the *Encyclopedia Buying Guide* (R. R. Bowker, 1981), critic Kenneth Kister pinpointed one of the major strengths of the 1980 version of *New Britannica*: "Considerably more attention is given to non-Western languages and social systems than has ever been attempted by a general encyclopedia." This assessment holds true for the 1986-copyright edition as well. *New Britannica*'s coverage of foreign, non-American subject matter is indeed second to none. While the set may have a predominantly Anglo-American tone, its coverage is by no means Anglo-centric or parochial.

As an indication of the attention *New Britannica* gives to non-American subjects, 74 of the encyclopedia's 150 Micropaedia entries in the span from **Bartolomé Mitre** to **Mohammed** concern foreign subjects. There are too many to list here, but the following examples will give an idea of the range of subjects *New Britannica* covers: **Magnus Gösta Mittag-Leffler** (Swedish mathematician), **Mittenwald** (Bavarian village), **Mmabatho** (town in Bophuthatswana), **Moçâmedes** (province in Angola), **Pavel Mochalov** (Russian actor), **Leone Modena** (Jewish Venetian writer), **Moesia** (a province of the Roman Empire), **Thomas Mokopu Mofolo** (African writer), **Mogi das Cruzes** (Brazilian city), and **Peter Mogila** (17th-century Moldavian theologian).

Note that *New Britannica* contains more total entries in this span than does either AMERICANA or COLLIER'S, and that a higher proportion of them (49.3 percent) deal with foreign subjects.

There is a very small degree of overlap (though not duplication) between the Micropaedia and the Macropaedia, in that particular subjects included in the Micropaedia are also covered in greater detail in the Macropaedia. As already noted, the Micropaedia is intended to be consulted as a source of major facts, while the Macropaedia articles give in-depth, large-scale overviews of broad subjects. (See also *Accessibility*.) Suffice it to say that *New Britannica*'s coverage is exceptionally well balanced and that no other encyclopedia can rival its broad scope.

III. Authority

For many people, the name Britannica is virtually synonymous with encyclopedias. Now in its 15th edition, *Britannica* is the oldest and largest English-language general encyclopedia on the market, and is considered by many to be the most authoritative. This authority derives largely from the set's distinguished history.

The first edition was published in 1768–71 in Edinburgh under the auspices of editor William Smellie, engraver Andrew Bell, and printer Colin Macfarquhar. (For more of *Britannica*'s early history, see Chapter 1: "The History of General Reference Books.") In 1901 a group of American investors purchased the rights to the set, and although it has been published in the United States ever since that time, the *Britannica* has preserved much of its British flavor. Many critics regard the 11th edition, in print from 1910 to 1922, as possibly the most comprehensive and most perfect encyclopedia ever published in the English language (if, indeed, any encyclopedia can be said to approach perfection). In 1936 the editors began the policy, maintained ever since, of annual revision.

The 14th edition was in print from 1929 through 1973. In the late 1950s *Britannica*'s editorial board, under the aegis of businessman and former U.S. Senator William Benton, decided to launch an entirely new edition. The significance of this 15th edition was not simply its unprecedented length, or even the fact that it was an entirely new encyclopedia in which every article was written from scratch. Rather it was the radically different structure of the set, in which the editors attempted not only to list all subjects but to relate all subjects to each other in a grand scheme— in other words, to provide a full circle of learning. The 15th edition was conceived as a comprehensive general reference encyclopedia that would provide a structured pedagogical function akin to that available in a good university. Thus was born the concept of the tripartite encyclopedia: the Propaedia (Outline of Knowledge), the Macropaedia (Knowledge in Depth), and the Micropaedia (Ready Reference and Index). This 30-volume edition cost the publisher an estimated $32 million, not including printing costs, and is said to have involved 2.5 million man-hours. The work was such a radical departure from previous editions that the publisher added the word *New* to the title. Interestingly, the Britannica company managed to keep the development of this massive new edition a secret not only from other publishers but from Britannica's own salespeople as well.

Upon its publication in 1974, the *New Encyclopaedia Britannica* (popularly dubbed *Britannica 3*, because of its three-part structure) generated a good deal of controversy. It was greeted with some scathing reviews not only in professional journals but also in a number of respected mass-circulation periodicals, notably the *Atlantic* and the *New York Times Book Review*. Critics particularly bemoaned the lack of any index in such a complex multivolume work. In response, the publisher undertook a major overhaul of the set in an attempt to make it more accessible. Among other changes, a two-volume index was added, bringing the set to 32 volumes. Several hundred Macropaedia articles were shortened and transferred to the Micropaedia. This extensive restructuring, first evident in the 1985 edition, cost Britannica an estimated $24 million.

While some critics have also called the encyclopedia's accuracy into question, it is hard to deny that among the many contributors to *New Britannica* are some of the world's most distinguished contemporary writers, historians, biographers, and scientists, including a number of Nobel Prize winners. Among the more than 6,500 contributors and consultants of international repute are astronomer Carl Sagan; biologist Sir Peter Medawar; cardiologist Michael DeBakey; historians Frank Friedel and A.J.P. Taylor; novelists Anthony Burgess, Anthony Powell, and Isaac Bashevis Singer; economists Kenneth Boulding, Arthur Burns, and Milton Friedman; musicologist H. C. Robbins Landon; social critics Asa Briggs (Lord Briggs), Jacques Barzun, and Conor Cruise O'Brien; and former U.S. Senator and Secretary of State Edmund S. Muskie. A large majority of the contributors hold prestigious posts at major universities and other important institutions (e.g., museums, observatories, hospitals, journals, newspapers, and professional organizations). Indeed, the lengthy credits in *New Britannica* read like a Who's Who of world intellectuals. (Articles are unsigned, but the writers' initials are given and are keyed to the credits list in the Propaedia.)

As the names above suggest, *New Britannica*'s contributors include a large proportion of British academics—about 25 percent, by one estimate. An examination of the full list of contributors also reveals a sizable proportion of contributors from other parts of the globe. Indeed, the encyclopedia's editorial board maintains formal affiliations with the universities of Oxford, Cambridge, London, and Edinburgh, as well as with the University of Chicago, the University of Tokyo, and the Australian National University.

Philosopher and educator Mortimer Adler served as Director of Planning for the 15th edition and is at present Chairman of the Board of Editors. The overall scheme of *New Britannica* was largely his inspiration. Philip W. Goetz, who served as Executive Editor during the period of *New Britannica*'s genesis, is now Editor-in-Chief. Otherwise, the editorial staff remains anonymous. (During the encyclopedia's development in the early 1970s, some 360 editors were reportedly employed in-house. Presumably that number has dropped considerably.)

IV. Currency

Like most general multivolume encyclopedias on the market, *New Britannica* is revised annually. As already noted, the 1985 revision was a major one, affecting not only individual articles but the entire structure and organization of the encyclopedia. According to the publisher, the 1986 revision involved changes on 2,000 pages in the Macropaedia, 1,300 pages in the Micropaedia, and 800 pages in the Propaedia. Furthermore, the index was entirely revised and reset. Not counting the index and Propaedia, this amounts to roughly a 10 percent revision. The 1986 Macropaedia added one new article (**Humanism**) and revised 79 from the 1985 edition, mostly in the areas of science, technology, and foreign nations and cities. Some 90 new articles were added to the Micropaedia; most of these were biographies, but some covered topics in the sciences and technology.

This rate of revision represents a considerable improvement over the rate of revision between 1974 and 1984, estimated in that period to have been less than 4 percent per year. Nonetheless, the 1986 Macropaedia still cannot be considered sufficiently up-to-date.

For example, articles on nations often end with the advice "For current political history, see the annual issues of *Britannica Book of the Year*." The "Northern Ireland" section of **United Kingdom** (Macropaedia) concludes with a summary of crucial events in 1972 (the shooting of 13 Catholic protestors in Derry by British soldiers, the suspension of the Northern Ireland parliament and the institution of direct rule by Westminster); the article's final sentence reads, "Violence continued for the rest of the decade and beyond." The last election mentioned in **Ireland** (Macropaedia) is that of 1973, and none of the subsequent prime ministers is ever referred to.

South Africa (Macropaedia) is somewhat more current. Here, the "History" section ends with a description of the 1984 constitution. However, the international economic and political pressures against that nation are not mentioned, and the reader is again advised to "see the annual issues of the *Britannica Book of the Year*." The final sentence in **Nicaragua** (Macropaedia) reads: "The forced relocation of 10,000 Miskito Indians in 1982 and the defection of non-Communist revolutionaries from the junta and the FSLN stimulated increased internal opposition to the Sandinistas." Sandinista leader and national president Daniel Ortega is not mentioned, nor are the "non-Communist revolutionaries" identified as the contras. Furthermore, while noting that the United States cut off aid to Nicaragua in 1981, the article does not mention the Reagan administration's overt and covert support of the contras.

Micropaedia entries are generally more up-to-date than those in the Macropaedia. (The publisher sets the Micropaedia on computer tape, thus facilitating revision and resetting.) However, while many individual Micropaedia articles are reasonably up-to-date, our reviewers found that there are too many omissions (both in terms of entries, and of recent developments reported in articles) for this portion of *New Britannica* to be considered consistently current.

Ronald Reagan receives a cursory entry in the Micropaedia (about 300 words). The last of three paragraphs notes his 1984 electoral landslide but does not name his opponent. The article is current as of late 1985 but tends to deal with events and issues in general, not specific, terms: "Reagan presented the Congress with a program of political and economic changes designed to reduce government spending, government activism, and the national inflation rate." It reports his hard line toward the Soviet Union and other communist nations, and his administration's efforts "through military and economic means to counteract what was perceived as the threat of Communist advances in the Middle East and Latin America." However, Lebanon, Nicaragua, and Grenada are not mentioned by name. Nor is there any mention of the record budget deficits that mounted during his administration, or of the controversies surrounding some of his cabinet members and advisors even during his first term.

The Micropaedia entry on **acquired immune deficiency syndrome** was current through 1985, but subsequent developments have already necessitated a thorough revision in future printings. The article also neglects to report the number of individuals affected by the syndrome, nor does it explain (except by implication) how the AIDS virus is transmitted.

Terrorism gives a good historical overview and refers to a number of recent and contemporary terrorist organizations. It also notes the way in which the ubiquitous presence of the mass media has changed the methods used by modern terrorists.

The entry on **Bhopal** includes a paragraph on the 1984 gas leak at the Union Carbide plant that killed or injured several thousand residents.

The Micropaedia also includes up-to-date entries on such subjects of contemporary interest as **sports medicine**, **video disc**, **videotape recorder**, **video telephone**; the cross-reference entry for **video cassette** refers the reader to **cassette**. The digital compact disc is discussed in the article **sound recording**. However, all these articles tend to concentrate on the technical aspects of these subjects and largely ignore their social implications.

The rapidly changing roles of women and adolescents are discussed at some length in the Macropaedia article **social differentiation**, although much of the coverage here relates to conditions in Britain. The article entitled **work and employment** contains little reference to women in the workplace.

The currency of statistics in *New Britannica* varies. As a rule, figures given in the Micropaedia are more up-to-date than those in the Macropaedia. The 1986 Micropaedia entries on the **Union of Soviet Socialist Republics**, **United Kingdom**, and **United States** all give 1984 population estimates. These figures are reasonably current.

As previously noted, *New Britannica* is not entirely consistent in its inclusion or omission of current events and personalities. For example, the 1986 Micropaedia contains entries for such recent or contemporary political luminaries as **Howard Baker**, **Tony Benn**, **Geraldine Ferraro**, and **Helmut Kohl**, but none for (former) Irish prime minister Garret Fitzgerald, former Senator and sometime presidential candidate Gary Hart, Brazilian president Jose Sarney, or longtime British Liberal Party leader David Steel. (See also *Scope*.)

On the whole, *New Britannica* is not the encyclopedia to consult for information about recent trends, issues, and events. Its strength lies rather in the other direction—that of the more obscure movements and figures of history.

V. Accuracy

Britannica encyclopedias have long been venerated as impeccable sources of truth and wisdom. Indeed, in discussing the present (15th) edition, it is often difficult to distinguish between authority and accuracy.

While our content experts have noted occasional errors, omissions, and instances of bias in *New Britannica*, they have found all the entries they have examined to be of exceptional quality.

For example, the Micropaedia article on **Henry the Navigator** gives the fullest, most detailed account of his life and career of any of the multivolume encyclopedias in the Buying Guide. It cuts through many of the myths that surround the man and his career. At one point, the article notes that:

> When Duarte [Henry's oldest brother] succeeded King John in 1433, he did not hesitate to lecture and reprove Henry for such shortcomings as extravagance, unmethodical habits, failure to keep promises, and lack of scruples in the raising of money. This rebuke is not supported by the traditional account of the Navigator as a lofty, ascetic person, indifferent to all but religion and the furtherance of his mission of discovery.

The article clearly delineates the complexity of Henry's motives in sponsoring Portugal's voyages of trade and discovery, and in his dealings with the rest of the royal family.

Our economics consultant reports that the Macropaedia entry on **money**, written by Noble Prize-winning economist Milton Friedman, is far and away the strongest entry on this subject of those in all multivolume encyclopedias. The article is comprehensive in scope and written clearly for the lay reader. Friedman's views, as one might expect, are biased in favor of monetarism, and the editors have let his biases stand, making no serious attempt to treat alternative approaches to monetary policy. Like all other encyclopedia articles on this subject, Friedman's assumes that money circulates within a "closed economy," and does not take into account such major influences as foreign trade and international political considerations. Nevertheless, despite these flaws, the article is recommended to anyone interested in getting an intelligent introduction to money and monetary policy.

New Britannica's Micropaedia entry on **Saturn** is one of the better articles on the subject in all the encyclopedias considered in the Buying Guide. The entry is brief but accurate, complete, and up-to-date in all important respects. However, the longer Macropaedia article on **Saturn** is less satisfactory. Many basic statistics, such as the planet's distance from Earth, its mass, and its albedo (the measure of a planet's brightness), have not been revised in light of recent findings, and are therefore inaccurate.

The Micropaedia entry on **transistors** is accurate as far as it goes; but in the opinion of our reviewer it does not go quite far enough, and there are some crucial omissions. For example, there is no discussion of the different types of transistors, and only one sentence on the development of integrated circuits. Much of the information presented in the Macropaedia entry is very dated and therefore no longer accurate. The article states that bipolar transistors are the only type of transistor (this is no longer true), and it fails to mention any of the applications made possible by integrated circuits. Moreover, the article, written at an advanced level, assumes that the reader is familiar with device physics. On the whole, this article is not sufficiently accurate to be recommended.

The entry on the **brain** in the Micropaedia contains a good deal of material and for the most part is presented in a clear, straightforward manner. However, the first several paragraphs jump from species to species, making it difficult to tell when the writer is talking about the human brain as opposed to the brains of animals. The reference to brain scanning methods is not quite contemporary. The Macropaedia article gives an accurate and detailed account of the structure and function of the brain and the central nervous system. Although the article touches on the function of the different lobes, it fails to mention the specialized functions of the brain's right and left hemispheres. But this is the only notable deficiency in this article.

New Britannica's Micropaedia includes individual entries for the British and U.S. **Bill of Rights** and the French **Declaration of the Rights of Man and of the Citizen**. All three entries are accurate, concise, clearly written, and useful, covering all major points. The article on the U.S. Bill of Rights combines historical and analytical approaches. The entries on the British Bill of Rights and French Declaration of Rights are accompanied by the complete texts of these documents, printed as separate boxes. The text of the U.S. Bill of Rights is printed in the Micropaedia entry **Constitution of the United States of America**.

VI. Clarity

Britannica encyclopedias have long and justly been admired by many readers for the scholarly and often colorful, idiosyncratic qualities inherent in the writing. These same qualities are apparent in *New Britannica*, where the tone continues to be scholarly and the prose can often be characterized as elegant.

The generally high reading level and the sophistication with which difficult concepts are presented may pose a challenge for some readers. Even among college students, one may surmise that only the more advanced will be able to take full advantage of the wealth of information that *New Britannica* offers. Moreover, the longer Macropaedia entries generally require more intellectual stamina and more sustained attention than many students (even at the college undergraduate level) are able to muster. Readers should also be aware that, unlike most general multivolume encyclopedias (notably THE WORLD BOOK ENCYCLOPEDIA), *New Britannica* does not define difficult terms in context. Even highly technical terms and concepts, such as those occurring in physics, are used without comment. The majority of articles are written at a college reading level (and many are suitable for postgraduate students), and it is generally assumed that the reader will already possess some familiarity with the subject and any special terms relating to it.

Another notable quirk (seen by some readers as an annoying affectation but regarded by others with affection) is *New Britannica*'s continued insistence on using British spellings (e.g., *colour*, *theatre*, and *encyclopaedia*). This accounts, in part, for the general public perception that Britannica is still a British publication. A rather high-toned and sometimes willfully archaic writing style (today rarely encountered outside the Oxbridge academic establishment) is also evident in many articles, further contributing to this perception. In other words, much of *New Britannica*—particularly the Macropaedia—reads the way many Americans like to imagine that the British write and speak. While our reviewers do not regard this in itself as a serious drawback, this style frequently stands in the way of clarity. What is the average American reader to make, for example, of this sentence from **Southern Africa** in the Macropaedia:

"Health services were biased toward curative medicine in central hospitals." Or this, from the Macropaedia's article on **birds**: "It is hoped that these developments will encourage taxonomists to abandon some of their more tenacious opinions—*e.g.*, that the crows represent the apex of passerine evolution." Although admittedly these sentences are quoted out of context, surely the observations they are meant to convey could be expressed in a simpler, more straightforward manner.

Elsewhere, articles display a propensity for understatement—another characteristic commonly associated with British English. For example, in **United Kingdom** (Macropaedia), we are told that "Northern Ireland's climate is temperate and maritime: most of its weather comes from the southwest in a series of lows bringing the rain and cloud that often lend character to the landscape." What this means is that the generally overcast skies and frequent rain make everything seem dreary and depressing. One may read this as the writer's personal tongue-in-cheek comment. (See also *Objectivity*.)

And yet many readers will admire *New Britannica*'s elegance and subtlety of argument. In the Micropaedia article on **censorship**, for example, one reads: "Whereas it could once be maintained that the law forbids whatever it does not permit, it is now generally accepted—at least wherever Western liberalism is in the ascendancy—that one may do whatever is not forbidden by law." Such delightful prose and subtle distinctions are rare in modern general reference works, where the demand for utilitarian information usually outweighs concern for the elegance with which that information is presented.

The following article, **Titanic**, quoted in its entirety, illustrates the style of a typical entry in the Micropaedia of *New Britannica*. The reader should be aware, however, that this encyclopedia more than in any other set currently on the market contains a wide variety of styles and that the degree of clarity varies from article to article. No single excerpt can be taken as the norm for the entire set.

> **Titanic**, British luxury passenger liner that sank on April 14–15, 1912, during its maiden voyage, with a loss of 1,513 lives, about 95 miles (150 kilometers) south of the Grand Banks of Newfoundland, after it struck an iceberg. The great ship, at that time the largest and most luxurious afloat, had a double-bottomed hull, divided into 16 watertight compartments. Because four of these could be flooded without endangering the liner's buoyancy, it was considered unsinkable. Shortly before midnight on April 14, however, while steaming at a relatively rapid 22 knots, the ship collided with an iceberg that ripped a 300-foot (90-metre) gash in its right side, ruptured five of its watertight compartments, and caused it to sink at 2:20 AM April 15. Inquiries held in the United States and Great Britain alleged that the Leyland liner "Californian," which was less than 20 miles (32 kilometres) away all night, could have aided the stricken vessel had its radio operator been on duty. Only the arrival of the Cunard liner "Carpathia" 1 hour and 20 minutes after the "Titanic" went down prevented further loss of life in the icy waters.
>
> As a result of the disaster, the first International Convention for Safety of Life at Sea was called in London in 1913. The convention drew up rules requiring that every ship have lifeboat space for each person embarked (the "Titanic" had only 1,178 boat spaces for the 2,224 persons aboard); that lifeboat drills be held during each voyage; and, because the "Californian" had not heard the distress signals of the "Titanic," that ships maintain a 24-hour radio watch. The International Ice Patrol also was established to warn ships of icebergs in the North Atlantic shipping lanes.

Finally, a word must be said about the clarity of the Propaedia. It is no easy task to classify all the information contained in a multivolume encyclopedia of *Britannica*'s scope into a single-volume outline of knowledge. But while admiring the Propaedia's comprehensiveness, our reviewers believe that the publisher's claims for this volume are grossly exaggerated. For the average reader—and even for many of above-average ability and curiosity—the Propaedia will remain difficult to use and to comprehend, and its value will remain limited.

VII. Objectivity

In presenting differing points of view on sensitive issues, *New Britannica* is impeccably objective. The Micropaedia generally presents known facts as such without editorial comment; it is also careful to identify theory, belief, and opinions as such, though it rarely goes into detail in explaining these. The generous space in the Macropaedia affords writers the opportunity to expand upon various theories and suppositions at some length. Here, the writing is often less objective, in the sense that writers can and do indulge their personal tastes and pursue byways and eddies of thought that would not enter a more straightforward encyclopedia. This same subjective quality also informs most of the essays that precede the Propaedia outlines. It should be stressed, however, that in both cases this "subjectivity" is virtually always well informed, not narrow or partisan. The tone of such articles is one of scholarly enthusiasm, not of dry pedantry or of propagandizing.

New Britannica offers an excellent presentation of **sex and sexuality** (Macropaedia), where, under the heading "Psychological Aspects," a full page is devoted to "Effects of Early Conditioning." "Social and Cultural Aspects" of sexuality and "Homosexuality" each receive two and a half pages of thorough and highly objective coverage.

New Britannica approaches the highly sensitive issue of **abortion** in an exemplary manner. The Micropaedia article on the subject makes clear that "whether and to what extent induced abortions should be permitted, encouraged, or severely repressed is a social issue that has divided theologians, philosophers, and legislators for centuries." After a brief overview of attitudes toward abortion in various cultures and at various times in history, the article describes the ongoing debate in the United States and presents lucid summaries of the major arguments, both pro and con. It concludes that "the public debate . . . has demonstrated the enormous difficulties experienced by political institutions in grappling with moral and ethical problems."

The Macropaedia contains extensive, highly technical articles on the **theory of evolution** and **human evolution**. Both articles assume that the "main hypothesis of organic evolution" has been accepted by the scientific community and by society as a whole, although **human evolution** notes widespread opposition to the theory in Darwin's day and remarks that "misconceptions . . . still arise . . . from the use and misuse of the colloquial terms man and human in the discussion of evolutionary origins." **Theory of evolution** contains a brief section on "The Acceptance of Evolution," which mentions the 1925 Scopes trial and states that "in 1968, the United States Supreme Court ruled that anti-evolution laws were unconstitutional." However, subsequent (and ongoing) opposition by certain fundamentalist religious groups to the teaching of evolution in public schools goes unmentioned. Nor are there any articles on creationism or scientific creationism in either the Micropaedia or the Macropaedia.

The 3,000-word Micropaedia article on **Andrew Jackson** is straightforward and generally objective. However, unlike most of the rival multivolume encyclopedias (including Americana and Collier's), the *Britannica* article does not mention his early rambunctiousness—his duels, gambling, and hot temper. Nor does it describe the fierce attacks on Jackson's wife by his political opponents. More important, there is nothing about his ownership of slaves; his policy toward the Indians is alluded to but not fully spelled out in any detail. In recounting his activities as president, the article does deal with the issues of patronage, nullification, and the national bank. It notes quite objectively that the spoils system "did not begin with Jackson, nor did he utilize this practice as extensively as was charged. Jackson removed fewer than one-fifth of all federal officeholders."

VIII. Accessibility

In the past, the main criticisms of *New Britannica* have centered on the set's accessibility, or lack thereof. In 1985, with the introduction of the two-volume index, the encyclopedia's accessibility was improved considerably. Many of the problems the critics had complained about were rectified. (See also *Other Opinions*.)

As previously discussed, both the Macropaedia and the Micropaedia may be regarded as self-contained sets. Entries in each are arranged alphabetically, word by word. Names beginning with *Mc* are treated as though they began with *Mac*; the same rule applies to the use of the abbreviation *St.* for *Saint.*

Running heads (guide words) at the top of each page indicate the first entry on the left-hand page and the last entry on the right-hand page. Page numbers are located next to the guide words.

In the Micropaedia, entry headings are printed in boldface type, and individual articles are separated by a line space. Subheads are used only in longer articles; in such cases, subsections are identified by a word or words in italics at the beginning of a paragraph. Since these words are in the same typesize as the main text, it is difficult for the reader to readily distinguish such subsections.

Macropaedia articles usually begin on a new page; the title is printed in large boldface type. Most Macropaedia entries begin with a brief overview of the subject. A "table of contents" or outline is also usually given near the beginning of the entry, followed by the main article text. Three levels of subheads may be used.

New Britannica contains the most extensive index of any multivolume encyclopedia, with some 186,500 entries spread over two volumes and a total of nearly 420,000 index references. As an indication of the scope and style of individual entries, the reader searching for information about Marie Curie will find the following index entry:

Curie, Marie, *or* Manya Sklodowska (Fr. phys.) **3**:798:3a
    association with Becquerel **2**:35:3b
    discovery of
        polonium **9**:574:2b; **15**:990:2b
        radium **15**:969:1b
    naming of curie **3**:798:3a

Each citation contains three elements, identifying the volume, the page number, and the section of the page on which the item occurs. For example, in the example above, the first reference occurs in Volume 3, page 798, in the upper half of the third column. Several critics reviewing the 1985 *New Britannica*—the first printing to contain the index—noted that the index was by no means comprehensive or consistent. For example, several index entries referred to the Macropaedia but did not note that the subject was also covered in the Micropaedia. In checking these specific examples, our reviewers found that in every case these omissions had been rectified in the 1986 edition, and did not find any other obvious oversights. There is no guarantee that the index is now complete and accurate, but it does seem to have been improved from the 1985 version. Since the entire index is revised and reset annually, we may hope that each successive printing will result in further refinements.

The cross-references also play an important role in enhancing *New Britannica*'s accessibility. The Micropaedia contains some 25,000 cross-reference entries; in addition, both the Micropaedia and Macropaedia contain an unspecified number of "see" cross-references within individual entries.

IX. Special Features

Apart from its unique four-part organization, *New Britannica* does not boast any special features to speak of. Many users consider the Propaedia a special feature, as it contains elements (e.g., the comprehensive outlines of human knowledge) not found in any other encyclopedia. The essays that precede each outline may also be of interest to some readers. The section on "The Human Body" contains two sets of detailed transparent overlays, identifying the principal parts of the male and female anatomy. Mortimer Adler's explication of the Propaedia, "The Circle of Learning," will be useful only to those interested in his epistemological theories.

The publisher claims nearly 26,000 illustrations in the set, of which 6,400 are in full color (in addition to 164 color plates). The prospective purchaser should be aware that the vast majority of these illustrations are little larger than postage-stamp size, and as a whole *New Britannica* is graphically dull. There are no illustrations in the Propaedia (apart from the physiology color transparencies); the majority of illustrations occur in the Micropaedia. In the Macropaedia, a handful of articles, such as that on the **decorative arts**, are accompanied by color plates. But otherwise, many consecutive pages of text go unrelieved by illustrations of any kind. Nevertheless, most photographs and art reproductions for biographical entries are interesting and give an adequate representation of the subject; the same is true for photographs illustrating various flora and fauna. Technical diagrams are also generally clear and functional.

New Britannica contains about 1,000 maps, most of which are in black-and-white and occupy only a fraction of a page. A number of the maps, particularly the historical maps, were not designed for *New Britannica* but have been reprinted from other sources. (For a review of the separate atlas published by Britannica, Inc., see *Britannica Atlas* in the atlas review section of the Buying Guide.)

Like its competitors, *New Britannica* contains extensive bibliographies. These are found at the end of selected articles in the Micropaedia and at the end of each article in the Macropaedia. Bibliographies in the Micropaedia are the exception rather than the rule. The Micropaedia bibliographies are generally quite brief, but they are up-to-date.

Macropaedia bibliographies are often extensive, sometimes running over two entire pages or more. However, all too often they are seriously out of date. For example, an overwhelming majority of titles in the half-page bibliography at the conclusion of **endocrine systems** were published in the 1960s; the most recent are from 1971. A spot check reveals that this is also the case in the bibliographies for **human emotion and motivation**, **human evolution**, and the **theory of evolution**. Incidentally, many of the Macropaedia bibliographies, especially those pertaining to scientific or technical subjects, list foreign-language works without English translations.

It seems to our reviewers that the value of the Propaedia could have been enhanced by the placement of comprehensive bibliographies in this section. However, the publisher has not chosen to arrange the set this way.

For the most part, the bibliographies are highly specialized and will be of more use to the scholar than to the general reader.

X. Format

The 32-volume *New Britannica* comes in a standard heavy-duty simulated brown leather binding with embossed gold lettering on the spine. Colored bands on the spine identify each volume as part of the Propaedia, Micropaedia, Macropaedia, or index. The titles of the first and last entries in the volume are also stamped on the spine, enabling the user to identify and retrieve the pertinent volume easily. Volumes are of roughly equal length (generally from 950 to 1,050 pages each) and therefore a single volume does not contain all the entries beginning with a particular letter. (For example, Volume 8 of the Micropaedia contains the entries **menage** through **Ottawa**; Volume 9 contains **otter** through **Rethimnon**.) The entire set takes up slightly more than four feet of horizontal shelf space.

Macropaedia pages are printed in a two-column format. Micropaedia pages use a format of three columns per page.

XI. Other Opinions

Geoffrey Wolff, "Britannica 3, Failures Of," *Atlantic*, November 1976: "There . . . seems no justification for the segregation of long articles (arranged alphabetically rather than topically) from short, save the economic convenience to [the publisher]."

Newsweek, May 6, 1985: "The addition of a two-volume index is a signal improvement; the new Britannica is far more accessible than its predecessor. And yet, welcome as it is, this index needs work."

ARBA, 1986: "Without question, the restructuring and refinements [reflected in the 1985 revision] have drastically improved the accessibility and convenience of the set. The Micropaedia can now stand alone as an impressive one-stop source of factual information. The Macropaedia's and Propaedia's changes further enhance the set's educational objectives. . . . The real key to this revision, however, is the two-volume index. While applauding the tremendous improvement it brings to the set, we cannot overlook its numerous flaws . . . We found again and again . . . that important references were omitted. . . . *See also* references are used unevenly. . . .

"We might have hoped for more currency. Some [Macropaedia] articles are woefully out-of-date, making the Micropaedia articles which are derived from them also dated. . . ."

"[A]ccessibility and currency [are] two persistent weaknesses in an otherwise outstanding encyclopedia, arguably the very best English-language general adult set available."

Booklist (*Reference Books Bulletin*), November 15, 1986: "The 1986 printing retains the international coverage and impressive list of contributors commended earlier by the Board. . . . While most of the bibliographies in the Macropaedia are current, some need updating . . . illustrations are adequate. . . . [T]he attention to biographies and current topics and additions to the index are evidence that continuous revision remains *NEB*'s policy. It can be recommended to serious . . . readers for its scholarly, exhaustive articles on a wide range of subjects."

Harvey Einbinder, "The New Britannica: Pro: Depth and Detail by Design," *Library Journal*, April 15, 1987: "The primary achievement of the *New Britannica* is to provide an editorial plan that efficiently furnishes factual information and effectively deals with ideas. This has been accomplished by utilizing two sharply separated sets of alphabetic entries supplemented by a two-volume index and a volume that contains a guide to related articles in the set. Although the titles and contents of individual articles will change in future editions, this editorial plan will assist the editors in maintaining the *Britannica*'s position as the leading general encyclopedia in the English language."

Harvey Einbinder, "The New Britannica: Con: The Not-So-Perfect Britannica," *Library Journal*, April 15, 1987: "Twenty years ago I demonstrated in *The Myth of the Britannica* the danger of retaining old articles for decades. Nevertheless, this hazardous policy has been adopted in the 1985 edition, despite an editorial budget of $24 million. . . . Important medical developments are slighted. . . . Similar omissions occur in treating technological subjects. . . . Major advances in mathematics are neglected because the *Britannica*'s mathematical articles consist almost entirely of material taken from the 1974 edition. . . . Much material has been taken from the 1974 edition without critical scrutiny. . . . The large number of old bibliographies diminishes the *Britannica*'s utility as a reliable guide to outside sources of information. Yet its annotated bibliographies are potentially a valuable aid for students and libraries because they contain a convenient, detailed compilation of printed sources on an extremely wide range of subjects. But their utility is severely impaired when they neglect references published in the last decade. . . . The large amount of material taken from the 1974 edition seriously undermines the many outstanding innovations and improvements introduced in the latest edition."

XII. Summary

The product of years of research, writing, and editing, the *New Encyclopaedia Britannica* is without question the most scholarly and formidable general reference encyclopedia currently in print. Its volumes present a greater range and depth of knowledge than any other encyclopedia. For this reason alone, most academic and many large public libraries will find it indispensable for their reference collections.

Certainly, *New Britannica* is unique in its tripartite structure, although most users will find that they customarily consult only one segment of the work. The 12-volume specific-entry Micropaedia fulfills the function of a comprehensive ready-reference work. Yet its contents by no means contain only facts and figures. The Micropaedia is admirably clear, concise, and accurate. The Macropaedia devotes 17 volumes to 680 core subjects, with some of the entries in this part of the encyclopedia running close to book length. The Macropaedia will be most useful to those who desire a detailed overview of these subjects; it is of considerably less value to those seeking facts and figures. It is also less up-to-date than one might ideally wish. The single-volume Propaedia will be of limited value to all but a handful of users.

Despite its two-volume index, *New Britannica* remains arguably the most difficult encyclopedia to use. Patrons unfamiliar with the set may require the assistance of an experienced reference librarian to find the information they need, and even for experienced users the index is not foolproof.

New Britannica not only is a basic reference source but will also be valued as an intelligent browser's encyclopedia. It will be of most interest to college students, writers, and others who not only seek answers to specific questions but also wish to broaden their understanding of a range of complex subjects.

Considering the high costs involved in producing an encyclopedia of such size and complexity as *New Britannica*, this set offers good value. Its price ($1,349 for individuals, $999 for institutions) is only marginally higher than those of its major competitors, COLLIER'S, which has eight fewer volumes, and ENCYCLOPEDIA AMERICANA, a 30-volume set. The yearbook, *Britannica World Data Annual*, will probably be useful for libraries but is less crucial to individuals.

Individuals wishing to purchase *New Britannica* may contact the local distributor listed under "Encyclopaedia Britannica, Inc." in the "Encyclopedia" section of the Yellow Pages. The company offers a modest trade-in allowance on previous *Britannica* editions and on major encyclopedias of other publishers. This offer is available to individuals only, not to institutions.

For library purchases, phone the Britannica Educational Corporation at (800) 554-9862.

New Standard Encyclopedia

Facts at a Glance

Full Title: **New Standard Encyclopedia.**
Publisher: Standard Educational Corporation.
Editor-in-Chief: Douglas W. Downey.
Edition Reviewed: 1986. (Statistics apply to the 1988 edition.)

Number of Volumes: 17.
Number of Contributors: 700.
Number of Entries: 30,960 entries for 17,394 articles.
Number of Pages: 10,023.
Number of Words: 6,400,000.
Number of Maps: 642.
Number of Cross-references: 40,000.
Number of Illustrations: 2,700 four-color; 9,700 two-color or black-and-white.
Trim Size: $6\frac{3}{4}'' \times 9\frac{1}{4}''$.

Price: $699.50, publisher's suggested retail price to individuals; $519.00 with library discount.
Sold only through independent distributors.
ISBN 0-87392-191-7.
Revised annually.

I. Introduction

The *New Standard Encyclopedia* is a 17-volume work designed, in the editor's words, "to provide as much information of interest to the general reader as is possible within an illustrated set selling for a moderate price. . . . For advanced students and for adults who need detailed information, this encyclopedia serves as a general source to consult before seeking out more specialized and advanced works." It can also be used, as the editor reminds us, "for the pleasure and profit that come from just browsing." In short, *New Standard* is conceived as a general reference work for the layperson whose interests may be wide-ranging but not necessarily scholarly.

This review is based on an examination of the 1986 edition, the edition current at the time of review.

II. Scope

The *New Standard Encyclopedia* contains 17,394 articles, in addition to some 13,500 "See" entries that serve solely as cross-references. With a total word count of approximately 6,400,000 spread over its 10,023 pages, the average article length is about 375 words. Actual article length in *New Standard* varies considerably, from a half-dozen lines (45 words) for minor biographical figures to as much as 90 pages for **United States**. As a rule, however, the majority of articles are shorter than the 375-word average.

As an indication of how space is apportioned among different subjects, **Charlemagne** receives about one and one-sixth pages (including a map and bibliography); **Konstantin Chernenko** receives about one-third of a page (including a small photograph); and **Ty Cobb** gets 11 lines (about one-tenth of a page). The article on the **American Civil War** is nine and a half pages long (including maps, illustrations, cross-references, and bibliography); the entry for **Christianity** is shorter than two and a half pages; and **China** is treated in 22 pages.

Because *New Standard* is a specific-entry encyclopedia, individual Civil War battles are accorded separate entries, as are individual figures from the Civil War. The same is true for different Christian religious figures, denominations, movements, and practices, and for specific aspects of a nation's geography. As the Buying Guide reader may infer, there is not necessarily a direct correlation between the length of an article and the relative importance of the subject it covers.

The publisher has not provided the Buying Guide with a percentage breakdown of subject areas. By our reviewers' estimates, roughly one-third of the articles are biographical and about one-fifth deal with geography. Science subjects generally receive adequate coverage, at least in terms of the frequency of science entries (though not necessarily in terms of the space devoted to a particular subject). The arts, literature, religion, and philosophy seem underrepresented both in number of entries and in percentage of space.

As a general-interest encyclopedia for the non-academic lay reader, *New Standard* covers a wide

New Standard Encyclopedia

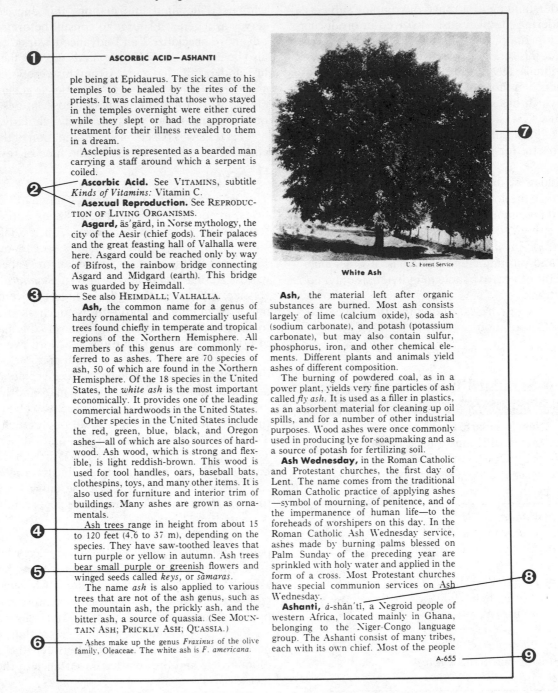

1 ASCORBIC ACID — ASHANTI

ple being at Epidaurus. The sick came to his temples to be healed by the rites of the priests. It was claimed that those who stayed in the temples overnight were either cured while they slept or had the appropriate treatment for their illness revealed to them in a dream.

Asclepius is represented as a bearded man carrying a staff around which a serpent is coiled.

2 **Ascorbic Acid.** See VITAMINS, subtitle *Kinds of Vitamins:* Vitamin C.

Asexual Reproduction. See REPRODUCTION OF LIVING ORGANISMS.

Asgard, äs'gärd, in Norse mythology, the city of the Aesir (chief gods). Their palaces and the great feasting hall of Valhalla were here. Asgard could be reached only by way of Bifrost, the rainbow bridge connecting Asgard and Midgard (earth). This bridge was guarded by Heimdall.

3 See also HEIMDALL; VALHALLA.

Ash, the common name for a genus of hardy ornamental and commercially useful trees found chiefly in temperate and tropical regions of the Northern Hemisphere. All members of this genus are commonly referred to as ashes. There are 70 species of ash, 50 of which are found in the Northern Hemisphere. Of the 18 species in the United States, the *white ash* is the most important economically. It provides one of the leading commercial hardwoods in the United States.

Other species in the United States include the red, green, blue, black, and Oregon ashes—all of which are also sources of hardwood. Ash wood, which is strong and flexible, is light reddish-brown. This wood is used for tool handles, oars, baseball bats, clothespins, toys, and many other items. It is also used for furniture and interior trim of buildings. Many ashes are grown as ornamentals.

4 Ash trees range in height from about 15 to 120 feet (4.6 to 37 m), depending on the species. They have saw-toothed leaves that turn purple or yellow in autumn. Ash trees **5** bear small purple or greenish flowers and winged seeds called *keys,* or *samaras.*

The name *ash* is also applied to various trees that are not of the ash genus, such as the mountain ash, the prickly ash, and the bitter ash, a source of quassia. (See MOUNTAIN ASH; PRICKLY ASH; QUASSIA.)

6 Ashes make up the genus *Fraxinus* of the olive family, Oleaceae. The white ash is *F. americana.*

Ash, the material left after organic substances are burned. Most ash consists largely of lime (calcium oxide), soda ash (sodium carbonate), and potash (potassium carbonate), but may also contain sulfur, phosphorus, iron, and other chemical elements. Different plants and animals yield ashes of different composition.

The burning of powdered coal, as in a power plant, yields very fine particles of ash called *fly ash.* It is used as a filler in plastics, as an absorbent material for cleaning up oil spills, and for a number of other industrial purposes. Wood ashes were once commonly used in producing lye for soapmaking and as a source of potash for fertilizing soil.

Ash Wednesday, in the Roman Catholic and Protestant churches, the first day of Lent. The name comes from the traditional Roman Catholic practice of applying ashes —symbol of mourning, of penitence, and of the impermanence of human life—to the foreheads of worshipers on this day. In the Roman Catholic Ash Wednesday service, ashes made by burning palms blessed on Palm Sunday of the preceding year are sprinkled with holy water and applied in the form of a cross. Most Protestant churches have special communion services on Ash **8** Wednesday.

Ashanti, a-shăn'tĭ, a Negroid people of western Africa, located mainly in Ghana, belonging to the Niger-Congo language group. The Ashanti consist of many tribes, each with its own chief. Most of the people

9 A-655

White Ash — U.S. Forest Service **7**

Page shown at 77% of actual size.

1 Guide words indicate the first and last entries on the page.

2 New Standard contains 13,500 cross-reference entries. The encyclopedia lacks an index and relies on cross-references to provide accessibility.

3 "See also" cross-references: New Standard includes 40,000 cross-references within article text or at the ends of articles.

4 Metric approximations for standard measures are given in parentheses.

5 Italics indicate that a term is defined in context.

6 Endnotes to articles on fauna and flora give scientific classifications.

7 Illustration: New Standard contains 12,000 illustrations, of which 2,700 are four-color.

8 Pronunciations are given for foreign or unusual entry words.

9 Page number

range of subjects not usually found in more scholarly reference works. For example, there are entries for many legal terms, such as **abandonment**, **alias**, **easement**, **negligence**, and **tort**. A large number of corporations, professional associations, government agencies, and public service organizations are also the subjects of individual articles. A random sampling of entry titles taken from Volume 5, pages D286b–D327, will illustrate the extensiveness of general-interest subjects: **drills and drilling**, **driver education**, **driver's license**, **drought**, **drowning**, **drum**, **Drury Lane**, **dry cleaning**, **dry farming**, **dry ice**, **dry rot**, *The Duchess of Malfi*, **ducking stool**, **duckbill platypus**, **duckweed**, **ductility**, **duel**, **dugong**, **duke**, **Duke University**, **Dukhobors**, **dulcimer**, **Dumas**, **dumdum bullet**, **The Dun & Bradstreet Corporation**, **duplicating and copying machines**, **Du Pont Company**, **dust**, **Dust Bowl**, **dust counter**, **dust explosion**, **Dutch elm disease**, **Dutch Reformed Church**, **dwarf**, **dyes and dyeing**, **dynamite**, **dynamometer**.

Compared to competing encyclopedias (FUNK & WAGNALLS NEW ENCYCLOPEDIA, for example) that have taken deliberate measures to increase their coverage of non-American subjects, *New Standard* shows evident weakness in this aspect. Nearly 19 pages are devoted to the state of **South Carolina**, for example, while **South Africa** gets 13 pages.

III. Authority

Although the name *New Standard* and the Standard Educational Corporation may not be as familiar to most readers as those of other encyclopedias and their publishers, the *New Standard Encyclopedia* is by no means a newcomer to the reference publishing market. Its forerunner, the five-volume *Aiton's Encyclopedia*, was published in 1910 and achieved some popularity at the time. It was reissued in an expanded six-volume edition in 1912, under the title *Standard Reference Work for Home, School, and Library*. In 1930 the set, which had by this time expanded to ten volumes, was acquired by the Standard Educational Society (now Corporation), and was retitled *New Standard Encyclopedia*.

As its former title implies, the *New Standard*'s intellectual aims have always been modest, and it has never been regarded as a particularly authoritative source of information. Unlike NEW ENCYCLOPAEDIA BRITANNICA, which has long-established ties with the University of Chicago, or THE CONCISE COLUMBIA ENCYCLOPEDIA and its predecessors, which drew many advisors and contributors from Columbia University, *New Standard* does not rely on a pool of scholars for its authority. Rather, most of the articles are written by an in-house editorial staff; the credits page lists 30 "contributing editors" in addition to 50 other editors, designers, cartographers, and general consultants. In explaining how the encyclopedia has been put together, the foreword notes that "staff members are qualified in their fields by education and experience and are trained in the techniques of encyclopedia writing." This staff works under the direction of Douglas W. Downey, Editor-in-Chief since 1964.

An additional 700 people are listed as "contributors, consultants, advisers, and authenticators"; this list also identifies their credentials and affiliations, as well as the articles on which they have worked. The term "authenticator" is used to describe the subject specialist who is responsible for an article's accuracy. The foreword states that "each article . . . has been reviewed by five or more persons. At least one of these is a recognized authority in the field being covered." However, the term "recognized authority" is vague; the skeptical reader may well ask, "Recognized by whom?" A substantial number of these people are employed by corporate public relations departments, professional organizations, or government agencies. While these individuals may well have a more thorough practical knowledge of their particular subject than do many academics, their objectivity may be called into question. (See *Accuracy* and *Objectivity*.) Only a very small number of these consultants (such as former astronaut Neil Armstrong and linguist Mario Pei) have achieved wide recognition outside their fields of specialization. Simply in terms of name recognition, *New Standard* would seem to have the weakest consulting staff of any encyclopedia on the market today. Moreover, a number of these individuals are deceased.

Apart from the subject notations given in the list of consultants, it is difficult to trace responsibility for individual articles. As the publisher notes, "since each article is the work of several persons, the articles are not signed."

IV. Currency

The *New Standard Encyclopedia* is revised and reprinted annually. Although the publisher claims that 23 percent of the pages in the 1986 edition were revised from the previous edition, it is difficult to judge the extent of actual revision. The publisher states: "Each year major sections within volumes are completely revised; all material is reevaluated and many articles are rewritten or reillustrated to assure a contemporary approach to the subjects involved." However, it is difficult to verify this claim.

According to the publisher, "graphs, bibliographies, and statistics are reviewed for revision at least once every four or five years." While some new articles have been added, most updating seems to be in the form of new figures (e.g., recent death dates) and a sentence or two added to the ends of articles (usually articles on nations) to give the reader some notion of recent developments.

Apparently the galleys of the 1986 *New Standard* were set near the end of 1985. The article on the **United States** (subsection: *History*) concludes by mentioning that "a summit meeting between President Reagan and the Soviet leader was arranged for November, 1985." The article on the **Union of Soviet Socialist Republics** ends with the sentence: "[Chernenko] died in March, 1985, and was succeeded as party chief by Mikhail S. Gorbachev." Again, as the 1986 edition of *New Standard* went to press, it was probably too early to assess how the new leadership might affect Soviet society.

New Standard does include reasonably up-to-date entries on such subjects of contemporary interest as **AIDS**, **compact disc player**, and **Mikhail Gorbachev**. Yet there is no entry for the American filmmaker **Woody Allen**. The entry on **computers** discusses in some detail the growing use of personal computers in the 1980s as well as their applications.

The article on **terrorism**, however, is badly dated. It includes mentions of the Mau Mau, the Irish Republican Army, the Ku Klux Klan, the Mafia, and "various Palestinian groups" as organizations that have used terror tactics but gives no specific historical examples of any terrorist acts perpetrated by these groups. Furthermore, the article gives no sense of the rising tide of terrorism in the 1970s and 1980s, or of the counterterrorist measures taken by various governments. Similarly, the article on **sports medicine**, a booming field in the 1980s, is extremely sketchy and generalized and gives no examples of sports medicine's contemporary applications. There is no entry for **employment of women**; the article titled **affirmative action** does not give the reader a sense of how women's roles in the workplace have changed over the last 20 years or of how these changes have affected the rest of society. Nor does the article include any recent statistics about the number of women now working full time in the United States and other nations. Funk & Wagnalls provides a much fuller and more up-to-date account of all these subjects.

Illustrations (apart from those chosen for historical interest) are sometimes dated. For example, the most recent photos in **advertising** seem to date from the 1950s or early 1960s. (The text of the article itself is badly out of date. The only sentence on the history of television advertising states that "the use of television for advertising purposes began shortly before the end of World War II, and grew rapidly in the postwar period.")

The overall impression one gets is that while many of the articles are up-to-date, revision is spotty and seemingly random.

V. Accuracy

New Standard generally maintains a reasonable standard of accuracy. However, our reviewers note that the set has a tendency to make unsubstantiated generalizations. For example, a caption of a photo in the **Europe** article (Volume 5, page E-246) declares that "Ancient European Civilization reached its apex under Marcus Aurelius. . . ." In the same article, one reads that "No other continent has produced so many great artists, musicians, writers, philosophers, and scientists." In **Stalin**, the terms "Russia" and "Soviet Union" are often used interchangeably, and no distinction is made between Russians and other ethnic groups within the Soviet Union. Such instances of editorial carelessness and generalization are not confined to these articles or to entries in particular subject areas. One can find similar minor but misleading lapses throughout the set. For example, the article on **Henry the Navigator** remarks that the 15th-century Portuguese prince "held an informal school of navigation at his court in Sagres. . . ." This is a popular misconception; although he favored the idea of such a school, he was not personally involved in this work.

Yet in many respects *New Standard* is remarkably informative. The entry on **Ronald Reagan**, for example, presents a good deal of accurate factual information about the man and his presidency. It includes details of his early radio and film careers and his first marriage, although it is vague on his activities as head of the Screen Actors Guild in the late 1940s. It gives an accurate account of his entry into politics, his terms as governor of California, and the major events of his presidency up to November 1985.

New Standard's entry on **Saturn** is generally accurate, although the information it gives about the planet's moons is out of date. The information contained in the several articles on **bills of rights** is, by and large, accurate, but the discussions are too brief to be particularly illuminating. The **money** article is narrower in scope than other encyclopedias' entries on this subject, but the information given (apart from the dated exchange rates) is accurate. The coverage of **transistors** is extremely dated; most important, there is no explanation of how transistors work, while integrated circuits are only mentioned in passing.

VI. Clarity

A major strength of *New Standard*—indeed, perhaps its most attractive feature—is its generally colloquial, nontechnical writing style. While this sometimes resembles textbook style, it is never dry or pedantic. The general-interest survey articles (e.g., **airplane**) in particular should stimulate and satisfy the curiosity of the average reader. Even such complex subjects as the **theory of relativity** are explained in lucid, easy-to-understand language. However, unlike THE WORLD BOOK ENCYCLOPEDIA, *New Standard* does not use a controlled reading level vocabulary.

New Standard contains particularly well written articles in several subject areas. The user will find excellent, well-organized, well-illustrated, and useful articles on certain animals (e.g., **dog** and **horse**), which give detailed breakdowns and descriptions of different breeds. There are also good though brief articles on classical music performers, giving thumbnail characterizations in addition to the standard biographical data. Readers who possess only a rudimentary grasp of science and scientific principles should find the science entries interesting and easy to understand.

The following entry on the **Titanic**, quoted in its entirety, illustrates the style of a typical entry in *New Standard*.

> **Titanic,** a British ocean liner that sank on its maiden voyage in 1912, with a loss of at least 1,500 lives. The 882½-foot *Titanic*, owned by the White Star Line, was the world's largest ship at that time and was considered unsinkable. It was speeding from England to New York with more than 2,200 aboard, including many prominent persons, when on the night of April 14 it sideswiped an iceberg. A 300-foot gash was torn through the hull, and the ship sank within three hours, about 400 miles south of Newfoundland and 1,200 miles east of New York.
>
> The *Titanic*'s lifeboat capacity was slightly less than 1,200 (which, however, was more than regulations required) and in the confusion many boats were lowered half-filled. The liner's distress call was not picked up by the nearby *Californian*, whose wireless operator was asleep. The *Carpathia* heard the call, arrived about two hours after the *Titanic* was struck, and rescued more than 700 persons. Investigations led to strict rules of safety at sea and to iceberg patrols.

VII. Objectivity

New Standard is not afraid to make broad value judgments or to characterize major historical figures when such judgments are supported by historical evidence. For example, the article on **Joseph Stalin** asserts that "[in transforming Russia] from an underdeveloped land into an industrial and military power . . . he drove the Russian people ruthlessly, and millions suffered and died. Although outwardly mild-mannered, Stalin annihilated all opposition and turned Russia into a police state."

Assessing **Andrew Jackson**'s personality, *New Standard* says: "Jackson was neither an original nor a profound thinker, and did not always follow or understand the principles of 'Jacksonian democracy' that bears his name. . . . Jackson's hot temper frequently caused him to act in a hasty or injudicious manner, and he was often swayed by personal prejudices." According to current historical interpretations of the man and his presidency, this is a fair and even-handed assessment.

In many instances, however, articles tend to skim over controversial issues and downplay or ignore disturbing facts. For example, although the article on **drugs** contains a section on "the drug problem," cocaine is not mentioned, and the article does not include any facts or figures about contemporary drug abuse in America.

Often the writers seem to take information provided by official sources at face value, as in the article on **South Africa**. For example, in describing the four ethnic groups differentiated by the South African government, the article reports that "under the policy of *apartheid* ('apartness'), each group is to develop separately, the official goal being a number of autonomous states based on racial and cultural identity." There is no comment on what apartheid means in practice, or on the political and economic inequality that the system is intended to perpetuate. This section simply notes, in describing the "Bantu" population, that "in urban areas they must live in separate communities called townships. In some cases their families do not live with them but reside in the Bantu homelands and states." In the subsection *government*, *New Standard* notes that "the Bantu homelands, called Bantustans, are largely self-governing and some are nominally independent." Later in the *history* section, the article reports that "In 1976 Transkei was granted independence. However, no foreign government recognized it as a separate nation, the feeling being that it was independent in name only." The article concludes with a mention of the new constitution that came into force in 1984, and which "for the first time gave some political power to the Colored and Asian populations." There is no mention of any black political groups, nor are the names of any prominent black leaders given, although the caption to a photo of Desmond Tutu notes that he "was awarded the 1984 Nobel Peace Prize for his outspoken opposition to apartheid. . . ." These statements may be true as far as they go, but certainly they do not tell the whole story, and cannot be considered objective.

A glowing tone pervades many of the articles on individual nations, corporations, professional organizations, and government agencies. For example, the entry on the **Union Carbide Corporation** makes no mention of the 1984 chemical leak at the company's plant in Bhopal, India, that killed and injured hundreds of people.

By the same token, *New Standard* often adopts a negative tone toward many subjects that do not conform to a mainstream American view of contemporary affairs. For example, the entry on **Socialism** generalizes: "All socialists . . . hold certain fundamental beliefs in common. They believe that the existing capitalist society is unjust, that a new society can be created that will improve mankind, and that what is required is a fundamental transformation amounting to a revolution." While some socialists may feel this, certainly the experience of Western European nations with democratic socialist parties in power does not bear this out; in such countries, mixed economies (i.e., a combination of government ownership and private enterprise) have been the rule. The conclusion of the article does note that in the United States "public policy has been influenced to a considerable extent by socialistic ideas, and many early socialist proposals, such as a social security system, have been adopted by the two major political parties." Even this statement, however, is a simplification.

The second sentence in **evolution** states that "some religious groups deny that evolution exists, but most scientists accept it as fact." The article also points out that, contrary to a popular misconception, "the theory states that man and apes had a common ancestor that was neither man nor ape." It acknowledges that "most religious denominations now accept the theory, but in varying degrees" and mentions the ongoing campaign by creationists to teach creationist theory along with evolution theory in public schools. There is no separate article dealing with creationism.

The article on **abortion** fails to mention the intense ongoing debate over the morality of abortion. It simply states that "abortions . . . long were illegal in most of the United States. However, a 1973 decision of the U.S. Supreme Court held that the right of privacy covered a woman's right to end an unwanted pregnancy in the early stages." **Homosexuality** notes that "among psychologists and other experts, much controversy exists as to whether homosexuality is a mental illness" but does not mention the 1974 decision by the American Psychiatric Association to remove homosexuality from its official list of mental disorders.

VIII. Accessibility

New Standard contains a number of basic finding aids that should make it readily accessible to the average intended user. A two-page article in the front matter, "Suggestions on How to Use *New Standard Encyclopedia*," with a section on "Finding What You Want Quickly," explains the arrangement of entries clearly and simply.

Entries are arranged alphabetically, word by word. The single exception to this rule is for hyphenated entry words, which are treated as a single word. When several items have the same heading, they are arranged in order of persons, places, and things or ideas. Following standard indexing practice, names

beginning with *Mc* are treated as though they began with *Mac*; the same rule applies to the use of the abbreviation *St.* for *Saint*.

Nevertheless, despite these standard features, the user will encounter some peculiar entry arrangements. A notable example is the arrangement of articles on national literatures. The reader searching for information on American literature, for example, will find the article not in the A–AND volume, but in the K–L volume under **literature, American**, following the entry for **literature, African**. The following pages contain articles on **literature, Arabic**; **literature, Australian**; **literature, Babylonian and Assyrian**; and so on. However, this type of article arrangement is not consistent for all national and ethnic literatures. For instance, the entry for **literature, Anglo-Saxon** instructs the reader to "See LITERATURE, ENGLISH, subtitle *Old English*"; **literature, Austrian** refers the reader to **literature, German**; **literature, Brazilian** sends the user to **literature, Portuguese**, and so forth. *New Standard* is the only general multivolume encyclopedia currently in print that uses this arrangement; every other encyclopedia reviewed in the Buying Guide contains the articles under their normal headings.

Guide words at the top of each page indicate the first and last entries on that page. Page numbers are located at the bottom of each page, flush with the outside margin. (See also *Format*.)

Entry headings are printed in boldface type. There are 13,500 "See" entries, which serve only as cross-references. In addition, there are 40,000 cross-references within the text. According to the publisher, these cross-references make the set entirely "self-indexing" and dispense with the need for a general index. Regardless of the quality of the internal cross-referencing features, an index would help readers locate information more efficiently. FUNK & WAGNALLS and WORLD BOOK both include full indexes.

IX. Special Features

New Standard includes few special features. Many of the longer articles include bibliographies under the heading "Books about [subject]." While the bibliographies are neither extensive nor definitive, they will help lead the reader to additional basic information on the subject. Unlike those in FUNK & WAGNALLS, the bibliographies in *New Standard* do not key individual titles to Dewey Decimal numbers. However, since *New Standard*'s bibliographies are located at the ends of the relevant articles rather than in a separate volume, they will certainly be much easier for readers to consult than those in FUNK & WAGNALLS.

New Standard's illustrations are of varying quality. Many are too small to give an adequate representation of their subject, and some are outdated. A large number were provided by government tourist agencies or corporate public relations departments; while these photos may be of high technical quality, they do not always give an objective impression of the subject. For example, most of the photographs in *South Africa* were provided by Satour, the official South African tourist authority. Those that illustrate the country's landscape are attractive and accurate; however, those that show people portray an idyllic society.

Most of the 642 maps in the encyclopedia were prepared by the respected cartographic firm of Rand McNally. However, these maps are not of even quality. American states have full-page (and often two-page spread), full-color maps, whereas many articles on large nations are accompanied by half-page (or smaller) two-color maps that show little detail. In addition, so-called fact boxes accompany articles on states and nations, giving basic statistics about those subjects.

X. Format

New Standard Encyclopedia comes in one format— the 17-volume edition. Unlike most general multivolume encyclopedias on the market today, the volumes in *New Standard* are not of equal length. Rather (with the exception of A and S, which are each spread over two volumes), each volume contains all the entries for one, two, three, or four letters (e.g., Volume 7 contains all the entries beginning with H, I, and J, while Volume 17 contains all the entries beginning with W, X, Y, and Z). This means that volumes are not equal in length. Volume 16 (U, V), containing 410 pages, is shortest, while the longest volume, 6 (F, G), contains 716 pages. The main advantage of this system (which WORLD BOOK also uses) is that the user can know immediately which volume to consult to find a particular entry.

Each volume is bound in a bright red Sturdite binding that should stand up to repeated use over a long period of time. The entire set will take up just under two feet of shelf length, making *New Standard* the most compact multivolume encyclopedia reviewed in this section of the Buying Guide.

XI. Other Opinions

Kenneth Kister, *Encyclopedia Buying Guide* (R. R. Bowker, 1981)—review of 1980 edition: "*New Standard* is a decent but not outstanding encyclopedia that can adequately serve the needs of . . . adults, especially those with a limited educational and intellectual background."

Frances Neel Cheney, *ARBA 84*—review of 1983 edition: "[Earlier ARBA reviews of previous edi-

tions] noted that treatment of subjects was satisfactory for home use, with some exceptions, showing much improvement in such areas as technology, literature, and certain aspects of the fine arts; that controversial subjects were handled objectively and that there was good coverage of practical information; that illustrations were adequate and generally well integrated with the text; that difficult words in the text were defined, with separate glossaries as needed; and that there was an adequate revision program. Weak points mentioned were the lack of a general index . . . Also noted were inadequate treatment of certain specific articles. . . .

"In subject emphasis, biographies are well covered, with the exception of some contemporary figures. Geographical entries give more space to some U.S. states than to some foreign countries . . . Science and technology receive adequate treatment. . . .

"However, libraries will continue to prefer encyclopedias that treat their subjects more fully . . . while the increased price [then $559] may make the set less attractive for home purchase."

Booklist (*Reference Books Bulletin*), November 15, 1986: "*New Standard* aims to serve a broad audience. . . . The editors do not use a controlled vocabulary list nor do they subject articles to formal reading-level tests. *New Standard* employs a matter-of-fact, reportorial style throughout. Even in articles on controversial subjects . . . the editors choose merely to summarize opposing viewpoints. *New Standard* has long had a reputation for meeting high standards in both objectivity and accuracy. . . .

"The quality of updating of text varies. . . . As strong as *New Standard* is on recent facts, it is weak in analyzing recent social trends. . . .

"[The] cross-references are integral to the encyclopedia's functioning. . . .

"Overall, the *New Standard Encyclopedia* meets its goal of providing current, accurate basic information about a wide range of topics. . . ."

XII. Summary

While the *New Standard Encyclopedia* is generally well written, its articles easy to comprehend, and its format easy to use, prospective purchasers should carefully consider its deficiencies in currency and objectivity. Families requiring a simple, straightforward source of practical information may be satisfied with this set. On the other hand, they may find that such competing sets as FUNK & WAGNALLS (at a fraction of the cost) and WORLD BOOK (which costs considerably more) will provide them with a somewhat more balanced, objective, and comprehensive overview of the same information.

The Buying Guide's library survey indicates that the *New Standard Encyclopedia* is a rarity in public and academic library reference collections. This is probably because the set is designed primarily as a home reference work and is not perceived by reference librarians as an authoritative research tool.

The *New Standard Encyclopedia* is sold only through independent distributors. Interested individuals should contact Standard Educational Corporation, 200 West Monroe, Chicago, IL 60606, telephone (312) 346-7440. The publisher's suggested retail price for individuals is $699.50. A discount price of $519.00 is available for schools and libraries.

Volume Library

Facts at a Glance

Full Title: **The Volume Library.**
Publisher: **The Southwestern Company.**
Editors: The Hudson Group, Inc. Gorton Carruth, Editor-in-Chief; Hayden Carruth, Managing Editor; Courtlandt Canby, Bryan Bunch, and Lawrence T. Lorimer, Editors.
Edition Reviewed: 1986.

Number of Volumes: 2.
Number of Contributors: 208.
Number of Pages: 2,519.
Number of Entries: not available.
Number of Words: 2,500,000.
Number of Maps: over 200.
Number of Indexes: 1.
Number of Index Entries: 22,000 (estimated).
Number of Illustrations: not available.
Trim Size: 11″ × 9″.

Price: $114.95.
Sold in bookstores and directly by the publisher.
ISBN 0-87197-208-5.
Next Scheduled Revision: 1990.

I. Introduction

The Volume Library is a two-volume general reference encyclopedia intended for "home and school use." According to the publisher, the work is "designed for interested, well-informed people . . . who need a convenient reference book on their home bookshelves." The work's text and illustrations are intended to "provide clear introductions to all major fields of study and bring together in one convenient volume [*sic*] much important and hard-to-find information." The editors add that "Only you, the reader, can decide which of the many attractive features of

the *Volume Library* makes it most useful for your purposes."

The publisher further identifies four broad purposes for which *Volume Library* will be useful: learning, reference, research, and browsing. Thus its function is not only to serve as a general reference: it is also intended as a pedagogical tool in self-education.

II. Scope

The Volume Library contains some two and a half million words and an unspecified number of entries. Because the encyclopedia is arranged topically rather than alphabetically, and because individual subjects within a section tend to be treated as subsections of longer articles rather than as separate entries, there is no way to obtain a consistent count of the number of entries. (This arrangement is similar to that of The Lincoln Library of Essential Information.)

Volume Library is organized into 26 topical departments (called "volumes" by the publisher, although they are not separate volumes in any common sense of the word). These give an indication of the range of subjects covered by the set, and the amount of space devoted to each. These departments, and the number of pages included in each, are as follows. Book One: **Animals** (66 pages), **Art** (66 pages), **Asia and Australasia** (82 pages), **Astronomy and Space** (50 pages), **Business and Finance** (82 pages), **Computers** (50 pages), **Chemistry and Physics** (82 pages), **Child and Family** (66 pages), **Earth Sciences** (82 pages), **Europe** (145 pages), **Food and Agriculture** (51 pages), **Government and Law** (98 pages), **Health and Life Sciences** (82 pages), **Industry and Technology** (104 pages), **Language** (96 pages). Book Two: **Literature** (130 pages), **Mathematics** (114 pages), **Middle East and Africa** (98 pages), **People** [biographies] (178 pages), **Performing Arts** (66 pages), **Plants** (66 pages), **Religion and Philosophy** (50 pages), **Social Sciences** (66 pages), **South and Central America** (82 pages), **Sports and Recreation** (50 pages), **United States and Canada** (146 pages).

The publisher notes that the subjects included in *Volume Library* can be categorized into six broad areas: History and Geography, Social Studies, Arts and Letters, The Sciences, Practical Arts, and Practical Skills.

III. Authority

Although *Volume Library* is not a household name in the reference world, it actually has the longest history of all American small-volume general reference encyclopedias. It was first published in a single-volume edition in 1917 by Educators Association, which subsequently issued the book in annual editions through 1962. As the 1981 Bowker *Encyclopedia Buying Guide* notes, the first editor, Henry Woldmar Ruoff, also compiled the 800-page *Standard Dictionary of Facts* (1908–1927), upon which much of the first edition of the LINCOLN LIBRARY was based. The close resemblance between LINCOLN LIBRARY and *Volume Library* continues to this day.

In 1963 rights to the book were acquired by Cowles Book Company, and it was retitled *Cowles Comprehensive Encyclopedia: the Volume Library*. A few years later this was abbreviated to *Cowles Volume Library*. The Southwestern Company of Nashville, Tennessee, purchased the book in 1970 and brought it out under the original title. In 1985, because its contents had expanded to well over 2,000 pages, *Volume Library* was issued in two volumes to facilitate easier handling.

Southwestern (not to be confused with South-Western Publishing Company of Cincinnati, Ohio, which publishes textbooks) also markets popular how-to books (e.g., cookbooks, home decorating books) and does not have wide recognition in the library reference field.

The frontmatter lists some 200 contributors to the 1986 edition, their credentials, and the subject departments to which they contributed. Our reviewers did not recognize any of the contributors' names. About one-quarter hold positions at universities or institutions, including the Massachusetts Institute of Technology, Princeton University, and the Smithsonian Institution. However, the vast majority are identified simply as freelance writers and editors or are affiliated with corporations or professional and industry associations. These affiliations may affect the objectivity of *Volume Library*. (See also *Objectivity*.)

Based solely on the names and credentials of their respective contributors, *Volume Library* would appear to be neither more nor less authoritative than LINCOLN LIBRARY. However, most of its contributors are living, while a high proportion of LINCOLN LIBRARY's are deceased. And, more significantly, *Volume Library* is edited by a highly experienced staff.

IV. Currency

During the 1970s and early 1980s, *Volume Library* became so severely out-of-date in many subject areas that it could no longer be taken very seriously as a general reference work. Under the aegis of The Hudson Group, however, there has apparently been a concerted effort to substantially revise the encyclopedia. The results of this can clearly be seen.

One notable example is the **Computers** department, which contains a wealth of up-to-the-minute information on different types of computers, their various features and components, and their applications. In fact, this section is as up-to-date as any of the computer and computer-related entries in any of the encyclopedias reviewed in the Buying Guide. The **Computers** department concludes with a highly current and comprehensive "Glossary of Computer Terms" and a bibliography in which virtually all the listed titles were published after 1982.

However, some other departments have been picked up and carried over from the previous editions with only minimal changes. This is evident not only from the content but also from the typeface, graphics, and design, which differ noticeably from those in the newer departments, having a distinctly dated look. (At the same time, the use of a new design in the newer departments may well be a signal that the publisher eventually intends to replace or rewrite all the departments. If this is the case, future editions of *Volume Library* may be consistently current.) Among the most evidently dated departments in the 1986 edition are **Business and Finance** and **Industry and Technology**. Incidentally, in contrast to the **Computers** bibliography mentioned above, the **Business and Finance** bibliography lists two 1975 titles and one 1962 title under "Business and the Computer." Departments on regions of the world (**Asia and Australasia**, **Europe**, **Middle East and Africa**, **South and Central America**, and **United States and Canada**) are generally current through the early 1980s. Population figures for individual nations, for the most part, are for 1980. As a rule, like the LINCOLN LIBRARY, *The Volume Library*'s coverage of recent events in nations is not as consistent as the coverage provided by multivolume encyclopedias.

While much of the set is up-to-date, the revision is uneven. Apart from the aforementioned **Computers** department, and the very up-to-date **Health and Life Sciences**, the editors seem to have concentrated on humanities and social science subjects rather than on science and technology in their revisions. Presumably, these areas will be revised in future editions. At any rate, suffice it to say that *Volume Library* is already far more up-to-date than its main competitor, LINCOLN LIBRARY.

V. Accuracy

Overall, *Volume Library* is a reasonably accurate and reliable reference work. Much of the inaccuracy that does exist in this encyclopedia is a consequence of outdated information. Some of it, however, seems to be a result of lack of adequate research and editorial carelessness. For example, the entry for the American poet **Theodore Roethke** in the **People** department erroneously reports that his poems are "often based on his Pennsylvania childhood. . . ." Roethke actually spent his entire childhood in Michigan, a fact that the briefest of research would have easily uncovered or that an authority on 20th-century American literature would be expected to know. The brief entry for **William Butler Yeats** in the same department rightly describes him as "one of the outstanding figures in 20th-century poetry"; but of the nine works mentioned by title, only two of them are poetry collections, and both are from the early phase of his career. From reading the entry on **Ralph Vaughan Williams**, the reader would not get an inkling of the fact that this 20th-century composer wrote nine symphonies.

While it may be unfair to focus on such isolated examples as these, the fact remains that readers looking up information on these figures would be misinformed in the first instance and underinformed and misled in the second and third.

The brief entry on **Saturn** states that the planet's atmosphere is composed of 80 percent hydrogen and 18 percent helium; these figures are substantially off from the currently accepted figure of 90 percent hydrogen and approximately 8 percent helium. But the reference to the number of moons ("21 or 23") is accurate according to our present knowledge.

The portion of the article on **semiconductors** that deals with **transistors** is generally accurate and up-to-date. It discusses different types of transistors (including integrated circuits), briefly describing the characteristics and applications of each. The importance of silicon and germanium in semiconductors is also noted.

The article on **money** explains the significance of money as a standard medium of exchange. It also describes the private banking system (and how money "grows") in some detail. The Federal Reserve system, monetary policy, and international trade are also among the related subjects covered. This article is highly technical, and portions may be too advanced for many readers. In general, though, *Volume Library* offers a very good and comprehensive treatment of this difficult subject.

Information on the U.S. Bill of Rights is scattered throughout the **Government and Law** department of this encyclopedia, but there is no single entry on the subject. However, the Amendments to the Constitution are printed in their entirety, with brief but helpful marginal annotations.

VI. Clarity

Volume Library contains a fairly wide variety of writing styles, ranging from the scholarly to the popular ("how-to"). There seems to have been little editorial effort to achieve a consistency of tone from depart-

ment to department, although this is not necessarily a negative criticism. Difficult or technical terms are rarely defined in context, but most of the departments conclude with a glossary of commonly used terms in that subject area.

Although most longer entries in *Volume Library* do not formally follow a "pyramid" style, individual articles are usually well organized. Extended articles often use up to three levels of subheads.

Users will find that some departments are exceptionally clear and well written, while others leave something to be desired in this category. **Literature**, for example, is extremely well organized. It begins with a 47-page narrative, **History of Literature**. This is followed by an 80-page **Literature Glossary** containing entries for genres (e.g., **biography**, **epic**, **fairy tales**), classical and mythological characters (e.g., **Charon**, **Circe**, **Furies**), movements (e.g., **angry young men**, **Irish renaissance**, **New Criticism**), and specific literary works (e.g., **The Canterbury Tales**, **The Raven**, **Wuthering Heights**). These brief entries are ideal for ready reference; they are generally sophisticated for their length and indeed are more comparable to similar articles in THE CONCISE COLUMBIA ENCYCLOPEDIA than those in LINCOLN LIBRARY. This department does not contain entries for individual authors; these may be located under **People**.

Volume Library does not contain an entry on the *Titanic*, the subject we have been citing to illustrate the style of typical entries in other encyclopedias. However, the following extract from the encyclopedia's feature on plate tectonics will serve as a suitable indicator of how *Volume Library* deals with a complex, multifaceted subject:

> **Continental drift**. Inspection of a map of the world reveals an apparent fit between the coastlines of Africa and South America. Fossil remains of the same animals have been found on both continents, and both share the same rock formations. Is this just coincidence?
>
> Alfred Wegener, a German scientist, in 1912 proposed a theory of continental drift. According to Wegener, about 200 million years ago all the land on Earth was one large continent, which he called Pangaea. Approximately 180 million years ago, according to Wegener, Pangaea began to break apart to form three separate continents. The large block to the north (which later became Europe, Asia, North America, and Greenland) he called Laurasia. It broke away from the other two land masses, which together he called Gondwanaland.
>
> The northern block of Gondwanaland was to become South America and Africa; the southern block would become Antarctica, Australia, and New Zealand. A small piece broke away between the northern and southern parts of Gondwanaland and began moving northward. According to Wegener's theory of continental drift, this became India. . . .

VII. Objectivity

On the whole, *Volume Library* is an objective and well-balanced reference work. Although space is limited in this two-volume encyclopedia, the combination of survey articles and specific subject entries allows the editors to address a number of controversial topics.

The department **Religion and Philosophy** includes straightforward, evenhanded descriptions of virtually all religions, religious denominations, and sects.

Evolution is discussed in **The Origin of Life and Life Processes**, part of the **Life Sciences** section in the **Health and Nutrition** department. Various hypotheses are described, but scientific creationism is not among them. Nor is there a separate entry for scientific creationism anywhere in *Volume Library*.

Homosexuality is discussed briefly in the **Marriage and Family** section of the **Child and Family** department. The discussion notes that

> Even though many societies (including our own) have discouraged homosexual behavior, it continues to exist. . . . There is no general agreement on what causes homosexuality. Evidence suggests that certain people may have a biological predisposition. Other evidence suggests that a homosexual orientation may be fostered by experiences in early childhood. . . . Most psychologists agree that homosexuality is not an emotional illness but a part of some people's makeup that is unlikely to change.

Addressed primarily to parents and adolescents, the **Child and Family** department in particular largely adopts a textbook tone. Topics discussed include **Child Development** and **Theories of Development; The First Two Years; The Preschool Child; The Grade-School Child;** and **Adolescence**. The writers take pains to avoid offending readers who may hold differing points of view. For example, **Dating and Sex** (part of the **Adolescence** section of this department) contains the following:

> It seems clear that parents must offer their teenage children a clear explanation of their own moral and religious beliefs about sex and dating. They need also to set certain limits on the activities of teenagers, if for no other reason than to express concern for the child's well-being. At the same time, the parent must realize that the child has, in fact, the ability to act according to his own wishes and desires. Moreover, the time is approaching when the child will be an adult who must negotiate the world of sex and dating without any parental intervention. It is the parents' job, then, to offer guidelines and assistance where necessary, with the goal of having the adolescent develop his own rational and coherent set of moral standards.

Clearly this passage is prescriptive, not descriptive. This illustrates the educational, as opposed to strictly reference, function of *Volume Library*.

VIII. Accessibility

Volume Library is a highly accessible and easy-to-use reference work. Accessibility is facilitated by the work's straightforward organization into 26 clear-cut topical departments (see *Scope*), the table of contents, and the 159-page index. Moreover, sections, subsections, and specific entries within individual departments are clearly identified.

There is a thumb index for each department, making it easy for both the casual browser and the serious researcher to locate a particular topical section quickly. (LINCOLN LIBRARY also includes thumb indexes, but has only 13 compared to *Volume*'s 28.) Guide words at the top of each page also alert the reader to the nature of the topical section.

The only major impediment to accessibility is the general lack of cross-references, which are found only in the introductions to individual departments. Printed in small capitals, these tend to direct the reader to general sections elsewhere in *Volume Library* rather than to specific entries.

Volume Library's index contains some 22,000 entries, making it quite comprehensive for an encyclopedia of this size. Entries are arranged alphabetically, letter by letter, regardless of punctuation. Names beginning with *Mac* or *Mc* are arranged as they are actually spelled. Entry words are printed in boldface type, making them easy to locate on the index page. Page numbers are followed by *a*, *b*, or *c*, indicating the column on the page where the pertinent information will be found. The index is preceded by a concise section on "How to Use the Index" and by a list of abbreviations.

IX. Special Features

Perhaps the most noteworthy special feature is the 55-page **Atlas** department, which in comprehensiveness and overall quality rivals some of the atlases reviewed in the atlas section of the Buying Guide. There are 31 four-color maps, the majority of them two-page spreads and many containing insets, as well as two pages of illustrated information on map projections. The cartography was produced by Rand McNally and is up to their generally high standard. Useful indexes for each map are printed on the outside margin of the page on which the map is located. The **Atlas** section is printed on glossy, heavy stock paper.

Volume Library's glossaries are also worthy of comment. They are extensive, accurate, and (especially in the **Health and Life Sciences** department), generally up-to-date. Many of the glossary entries rival the general content entries in the entry-specific single-volume CONCISE COLUMBIA and NEW AMERICAN DESK encyclopedias.

There are an unspecified number of illustrations. Each department opens with a full-page, four-color photograph. These are designed to identify the department rather than to illustrate a particular aspect of the broad subject covered in that department. These photos are clear, dramatic, and up-to-date. Other color photos are included in plates in **Animals**, **Art**, **Astronomy and Space**, **Earth Sciences**, **Performing Arts**, **Plants**, **Sports and Recreation**, and **United States and Canada**. There are also eight pages of **Human Anatomy** color plates in **Health and Life Sciences**. The great majority of illustrations, however, are in black-and-white. Some show signs of age, but most that are intended to illustrate contemporary situations do so. It seems clear that as some of the less up-to-date departments are revised in future editions, old illustrations in these departments will be replaced. At any rate, the illustrations in the 1986 *Volume Library* are already unquestionably more extensive than, and superior to, those in LINCOLN LIBRARY.

X. Summary

The Volume Library is one of two two-volume general reference encyclopedias currently on the market, the other being THE LINCOLN LIBRARY. The two sets have a common origin, and some similarities are still noticeable today.

As its publisher intends, *Volume Library* is an interesting set in which to browse. It also provides answers to some ready-reference questions. In spite of occasional lapses, *Volume Library* gets reasonably good marks in terms of scope, clarity, and currency. It is more accessible than LINCOLN LIBRARY and on the whole maintains a higher degree of accuracy. Neither set is absolutely authoritative, but *Volume Library* does seem to have an edge over its rival. At $114.95, it is significantly less expensive than LINCOLN LIBRARY.

Volume Library is sold in some bookstores. It can also be ordered directly from the publisher, The Southwestern Company, Box 810, Nashville, TN 37202, telephone (615) 790-4000.

World Book

Facts at a Glance

Full Title: **The World Book Encyclopedia**.
Publisher: World Book, Inc.
Editors: William H. Nault, Publisher; Robert O. Zeleny, Editor-in-Chief; A. Richard Harmet, Executive Editor.
Edition Reviewed: 1987. (Statistics apply to 1988 edition.)

Number of Volumes: 22.
Number of Contributors: more than 3,000.
Number of Entries: 18,300.
Number of Pages: 14,000.
Number of Words: 10,000,000.
Number of Maps: 2,350.
Number of Cross-references: 100,000.
Number of Indexes: 1.
Number of Index Entries: 150,000.
Number of Illustrations: 24,000 four-color; 5,000 black-and-white.
Trim Size: 7¼″ × 9¾″.

Price: $599 plus $29 shipping and handling; $499 (including delivery) to libraries.
Sold through local representatives, or direct from World Book, Inc.
ISBN 0-7166-0087-0.
Revised annually.

I. Introduction

The World Book Encyclopedia is a 22-volume general encyclopedia designed, in the publisher's words, to be "an everyday reference tool for librarians, teachers, business and professional men and women, and the general public." It presents "information from the vast reservoir of knowledge about humanity, the world, and the universe . . . in the most accessible and usable form possible." It is also intended to meet a wide variety of "reference and study needs . . . at a level of understanding appropriate to the user."

This review is based on an examination of the 1987 edition, the current edition at the time of review.

II. Scope

World Book contains more than 18,300 entries. With some ten million words spread over more than 14,000 pages, articles in the set average about 550 words. Minor subjects such as **Navajo National Monument** may be treated in only a half-dozen lines (about 45 words), whereas more complex and more important subjects such as **United States history** may have upward of 50 pages. Different facets of some broad subjects are also discussed under separate entries. For example, *World Book* devotes separate articles to the **United States** (38 pages), **United States government** (10 pages), and **United States history** (53 pages.

World Book includes a combination of short, specific-entry articles and longer survey articles. Therefore, information found in a specific-entry article will also be found in a related broad survey entry. For example, the article on **plants** contains a section about

World Book

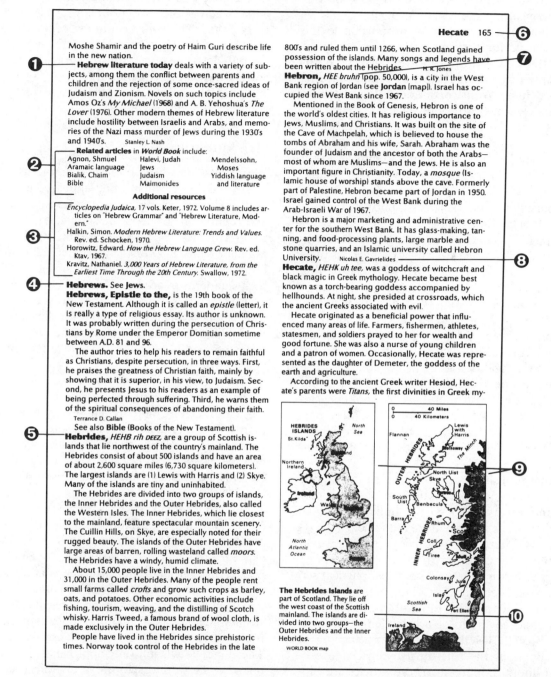

Page shown at 74% of actual size.

From *The World Book Encyclopedia*, 1988 Edition, © 1987 World Book, Inc.

❶ Article subhead

❷ "Related articles" cross-references: Handy lists suggest further readings about related subjects in World Book.

❸ Bibliography: More than 1,600 articles are accompanied by reading lists. Some titles are annotated.

❹ Cross-reference entry

❺ Main entry: World Book contains 18,300 main entry articles, arranged alphabetically, word-by-word.

❻ Guide words

❼ Pronunciations are given for foreign or unusual entry words.

❽ Contributor's credit: World Book has more than 3,000 contributors. All but a few of the articles are signed.

❾ Maps: World Book contains some 2,350 maps, many of which are full-page and in color. In addition, there are more than 29,000 illustrations, with over 24,000 of these in color.

❿ Caption: Captions in World Book often provide specific factual information.

algae. The reader will also find information on this subject by consulting the entry for **algae**.

Article lengths are usually in proportion to the subject's relative importance; only occasionally do article lengths seem out of proportion. The most notable example of this our reviewers found concerns the entry for **Henry Wadsworth Longfellow**, to whom *World Book* devotes three full pages. By contrast, **Emily Dickinson**, a far more significant figure in American literature, is given only a half page; even **Charles Dickens** gets less space than **Longfellow**. (On the other hand, 29 pages are devoted to **Shakespeare**.)

As an indication of how space is apportioned among different subjects, **Charlemagne** receives about two and a half pages (including a map); **Konstantin Chernenko** receives about one-quarter of a page, as does **Ty Cobb**. The article on the **Civil War** occupies 22 pages; the entry for **Christianity** contains about three and a third pages; and **China** is covered in 34 pages.

World Book provides well-balanced if not comprehensive coverage of topics in all major subject areas. While the editors are justly proud of the encyclopedia's readability and of its suitability for use by students, prospective purchasers should be aware that *World Book* is not merely a "school encyclopedia." It covers a wealth of subjects that are not, strictly speaking, part of any school curricula but that will be of interest and importance to students and adults alike.

While the publisher has not provided the Buying Guide with a percentage breakdown of subject areas, our examination of the 1987 set indicates that all major subject areas receive more than adequate coverage and that there are no obvious serious weaknesses in the coverage of any particular area. Topics in geography, history, natural sciences, physical sciences, the arts, literature, and language all receive a fair amount of exposure. In addition, the encyclopedia has good coverage of nonacademic, general-interest subjects. Based on a random sampling of entries throughout the set, the Buying Guide estimates that about 25 percent of the articles are biographies, while an equal number deal with natural history, the natural sciences, or medicine. Some 20 percent discuss nations or geographical features. The remaining articles seem to be divided equally among the other subject areas.

Entries dealing strictly with history seem less numerous than those in other subject areas. However, the reader should note that many of the entries in the biography and geography categories, among others, contain a good deal of historical information. Furthermore, many of the history entries are longer than the 550-word average entry length.

World Book emphasizes American and Canadian history, geography, and culture. For example, more than 23 pages are devoted to the state of **South Carolina**, whereas the nation of **South Africa** is covered in 14 pages. The entire continent of **South America** is dispatched in 17 pages. Individual South American nations do receive generous coverage in their own entries, however: **Argentina** gets 14 pages, **Brazil**, 20, and **Colombia**, 7. This coverage seems quite adequate and appropriate.

III. Authority

World Book has been published in one form or another since 1917, when it first appeared in eight volumes. The encyclopedia quickly grew in both size and reputation. By 1933 the set had been expanded to 19 volumes. No less important, its first editor, Michael Vincent O'Shea, a former education professor at the University of Wisconsin, established high standards of accuracy, clarity, and accessibility. These standards were upheld by his successor, John Morris Jones, who assumed the editorship in the 1940s. Dr. William H. Nault, who succeeded Jones in 1962, has continued to be active in the planning and managing of the set.

World Book was owned by a variety of Chicago-based companies until 1978, when it was bought by the Scott Fetzer Company, an Ohio firm known primarily as a manufacturer of household appliances. Despite this unlikely ownership, however, the encyclopedia seems to operate with a high degree of editorial independence under the aegis of World Book, Inc.

While Dr. Nault serves as Publisher and as General Chairman of the Editorial Advisory Boards, *World Book*'s editorial staff is headed by Robert O. Zeleny as Editor-in-Chief. Some 40 editors are employed in-house, and the publisher also keeps additional art, research, and production staff on hand.

The staff is supported by an extensive and highly structured network of advisors, consultants, and contributors who are scholars or specialists in their fields. These individuals not only approve article revisions but also alert editors to areas in which recent developments necessitate revision or the addition of new articles. In all, the set boasts more than 3,000 authors, authenticators, illustrators, reviewers, and consultants.

The frontmatter lists contributors and consultants, noting their credentials and the articles to which they have contributed. The majority hold impressive posts at major colleges and universities, while others are prominent in professional organizations and publications. Among well-known names on the list are Isaac Asimov, Samuel Eliot Morison, Arthur Schlesinger, Jr., and Werner von Braun. Whereas some other encyclopedia publishers may be seen to use "big names" primarily to give prestige to the product, judging by the credits pages and by the quality of individual articles, the specialists who contributed to *World Book* seem to have been well chosen and to have fulfilled their assignments most conscientiously.

Most articles are signed. Brief, unsigned articles dealing with particular organizations or with historic sites have frequently been authenticated by officials of these organizations. For example, the article **Camp David** was critically reviewed by the Military Office of the White House, while that on the **Camp Fire** organization was critically reviewed by Camp Fire, Incorporated. By and large, this practice does not seem to have affected the objectivity of these articles. (See also *Objectivity*.)

IV. Currency

With its experienced staff and extensive network of consultants and content experts, *World Book* is able to remain admirably up-to-date. The encyclopedia is revised annually. In the period from 1983 to 1988, an average of 5,900 pages (more than one-third of the set) underwent partial or complete revision each year. During this time more than 400 new articles were added to *World Book*, and over 14,900 existing articles were completely or partially revised. Based on a comparison of the revision figures we have received from the publishers of the encyclopedias reviewed in the Buying Guide, *World Book* undergoes a more extensive annual revision than any other encyclopedia now on the market. In the publisher's words, "*World Book* makes revisions in every field of knowledge or activity whenever developments make it appropriate to do so. Every subject in the volume is under continuing surveillance. The revision program is never confined to any one area. . . ."

As well as updating and adding text where necessary, *World Book* also ensures that the statistical information it provides is the most recent available. Population data are always drawn from the most recent census available, the publisher claims; this appears to be true. Furthermore, whenever possible the encyclopedia also gives population figures for 1987 (the year of publication) and projected figures for the near future. For example, **South Africa** reports the nation's 1980 census figures, plus estimates of the 1987 and 1992 population.

Sports tables are updated annually to include the winners of major national and international championship events. Other articles in subject areas in which statistics change rapidly, such as the economy, also receive annual updates. For example, **money** includes a table of currency exchange rates for February 28, 1986.

World Book's comprehensive revision policy is evident in the text of individual articles. The article on

Ronald Reagan, for example, is as current as could be expected for an encyclopedia available for distribution in 1987, mentioning the U.S. air strikes against Libya in April 1986 and the Reykjavik summit meeting that took place in October of that year. Other articles on important subjects are equally up-to-date. **United States history** contains a half-page discussion of events and issues in the 1980s within the subsection "Recent Developments." **Russia** concludes by mentioning the accident at the nuclear power plant in Chernobyl. Information about the Chernobyl accident has also been incorporated into *World Book*'s articles on **nuclear energy** and the **nuclear reactor**.

South Africa describes the constitution adopted in 1984 and renewed outbreaks of violence. It ends: "In July 1985 and again in June 1986, the government declared states of emergency in large black areas. Under the states of emergency, the government was allowed to arrest and hold people without a charge." However, there is no mention of the trade sanctions imposed on South Africa by other nations in an attempt to persuade the South African government to abandon its policy of apartheid. Similarly, **space travel** ends with a mention of the *Challenger* explosion but does not discuss the causes or consequences of the tragedy.

World Book also includes a significant number of new or thoroughly revised articles in science and technology. The articles on **biology** and **chemistry** were revised and reillustrated for the 1987 edition. New articles have been added to deal with such highly specialized subjects as the **artificial heart**, **grand unified theories**, and **Magellanic Clouds**, among others. *World Book*'s coverage of **AIDS** is as up-to-date as that of any encyclopedia reviewed in the Buying Guide.

Spot checks of less significant subjects indicate that revision has not been limited to the more obvious entries. For example, the biographical entry for **Woody Allen** has added the 1986 film *Hannah and Her Sisters* to the list of his pictures. The article on **recording** mentions the compact disc and some of its advantages. And **Statue of Liberty** describes in detail the restoration of the statue, and also includes several photographs and diagrams illustrating how the restoration was carried out.

World Book does include up-to-date entries on such subjects of contemporary interest as **sports medicine** and **terrorism**. **Corazon Aquino** is among the contemporary figures who gets a biographical entry for the first time in the 1987 edition. The six-page article **woman** contains an extensive section on "Woman's Roles Today," which discusses the impact of legislation and the women's liberation movement as well as employment and the roles of women in other countries.

World Book's thorough revision policy applies to illustrations as well as text and statistical material.

Throughout the set, photos are up-to-date; those intended to depict contemporary scenes indeed show no signs of anachronism. In terms of currency, *World Book*'s illustrations are second to none.

V. Accuracy

The same attention to detail evidenced by *World Book*'s revision policy also helps ensure that the facts presented in the encyclopedia are accurate. Contributors, reviewers, and editors have evidently done their jobs well. Our reviewers found few factual errors, and those mostly insignificant.

Among the more notable errors is the statement in **religion** that "Christianity was founded by Jesus Christ. . . ." In fact, Jesus did not found an organized religion; rather, his early followers founded a church based on his teachings.

On a more worldly scale, **Henry the Navigator** states that in planning Portuguese expeditions the 15th-century prince "was aided by mapmakers, astronomers, and mathematicians of many nationalities, whom he gathered together at Sagres. . . ." This is true but fails to mention that Henry sponsored voyages to Africa primarily to extend Portugal's trade rather than to discover new territories or advance European knowledge.

Our subject specialists found that *World Book* entries are generally sound and reliable, if occasionally superficial. For instance, the information in **brain** is well organized and relatively complete, and the illustrations complement the text nicely. **Money** provides an accurate history of U.S. currency, although the exchange-rate table is poorly designed. **Saturn** is reliable, even though it fails to incorporate some recent findings. On the other hand, *World Book*'s accurate entry on **transistors** is marred by some out-of-date information and an obsolete illustration. The encyclopedia covers a wide range of **bills of rights**, but its discussion of the American Bill of Rights is extremely short and not especially useful.

Some articles do display a tendency to stereotype or to make generalizations that, while true in some respects, may oversimplify the truth. An obvious instance of this occurs in the discussion of national cultures and ways of life. This may be a consequence of the editors' attempt to make the articles in *World Book* accessible and interesting to a wide range of readers. (For an example of this, see the reference to **Ireland** in *Objectivity*.)

On the whole, *World Book* remains a remarkably accurate and informative source of information. What it sometimes lacks in depth, it makes up for in breadth.

VI. Clarity

One of *World Book*'s major strengths is its readability. According to the publisher, each article in *World Book* is the result of careful research and "an elaborate procedure of editing, copy editing, and review" designed to ensure "that information is presented in a simple, direct style that meets the most exacting standards of readability."

Additionally, the publisher states that most of the articles are written at a specific reading level, one that is judged appropriate for a wide range of readers and for the particular subject based on *World Book*'s ongoing curriculum analysis and classroom research programs. The encyclopedia's writers and editors use a controlled vocabulary and apply readability guidelines developed by Dr. Edgar Dale, the noted readability specialist. For example, entries on such subjects as **lion**, which would be of interest to children as well as to adults, are written at a grade-school level. This is fine for school students but gives many *World Book* articles a graceless textbook style that some readers will find oversimplified.

Many longer articles use the "pyramid" approach as an aid to clarity. That is, they start out by presenting basic information in easy-to-understand language and gradually build toward more complex concepts and more sophisticated language as the article progresses.

Whatever the drawbacks of this writing method, it does have the decided benefit of helping to make complex subjects comprehensible to the nonspecialist. This is particularly notable in *World Book*'s entries on highly scientific and technical subjects, such as **relativity**, which are usually written in a clear and simple style. This also applies to the more complex general-interest subjects, such as **photography**, and to those entries that deal with aspects of natural history, such as **iceberg**.

The following article, **Titanic**, quoted in its entirety, illustrates the style of a typical *World Book* entry.

TITANIC, *ty TAN ihk*, was a British steamer. On the night of April 14–15, 1912, during its first trip from England to New York City, it struck an iceberg and sank. Experts had considered the ship unsinkable.

The *Titanic* sighted the iceberg just before the crash, but too late to avoid it. The collision tore a 300-foot (91-meter) gash in its hull. The lifeboats held less than half of the approximately 2,200 persons, and took on mostly women and children. The ship sank in about 2½ hours. The liner *Carpathia* picked up 705 survivors.

The *Titanic* had been the largest ship in the world, 882.5 feet (269 meters) long, with a gross tonnage of 46,328. The British inquiry reported 1,490 dead, the British Board of Trade, 1,503, and a U.S. Senate investigating committee, 1,517.

In 1985, researchers from France and the United States found the wreckage of the *Titanic*. The team refused to give the exact location of the ship, but reports indicated it was about 500 miles (800 kilometers) southeast of Newfoundland.

VII. Objectivity

In nearly every respect, *World Book* adheres to high standards of objectivity. The encyclopedia does not avoid dealing frankly with controversy, but neither does it sensationalize or give more attention to unpleasant facts than is necessary to give the reader a fair understanding of the subject. Throughout the set, in articles dealing with controversial or potentially controversial issues, the writers are careful to maintain an impartial tone.

For example, in assessing **Andrew Jackson**'s career and personality, *World Book* does not overlook his flaws but does not draw undue attention to them. It mentions his "hair-trigger temper," his removal of the Indians to the West, and his use of the spoils system but in general portrays Jackson as an energetic, forward-looking president.

World Book's coverage of **South Africa** is admirably objective. The encyclopedia is especially strong in delineating the various complex strands that have formed South Africa's history and its present social structure. For example, the article does not take the government's race classifications at face value, pointing out that each race is not a homogenous community:

> Each group's way of life . . . reflects not only its inherited traditions but also the fact that it must associate with other groups in economic activities. Differences exist within each racial group as well as between the groups. In each group, some people have better jobs and make more money than others. Even in the black, Asian, and Colored communities—which have many very poor people—there are successful executives and professional persons. Political differences also exist within the groups. For example, most whites vote for politicians who support apartheid, but some vote for candidates who oppose the policy. Some blacks would like to drive whites out of the country. Yet other blacks believe in cooperating with whites to build a new society without racial bars.

The article also reports on differences between Afrikaners and English-speaking whites.

Evolution is described as "a process of gradual change," then discussed as the theory that "living things evolved from non-living matter and changed through the ages. . . ." The article also states that "although the theory of evolution is supported by a vast amount of scientific evidence, it is not universally accepted." There are subsections on "Acceptance of Evolution" and "Evolution and Religion." These discussions not only present religious objections to evolution but also note that evolution and religious beliefs are not necessarily incompatible. The article mentions court cases in the 1970s and 1980s in which religious groups sued to have creation theory taught in the public schools.

A separate article on **scientific creationism** notes among other arguments for this belief that existing fossil evidence is incomplete and "fails to show any kind of organism in transition to any other kind of organism." Throughout both these articles, the tone is evenhanded and scrupulously objective: the writers present the case for each argument without passing judgment on its merits. They are careful to distinguish among theory, belief, evidence, and fact.

The encyclopedia is also judicious in its presentation of **abortion**, reporting that "for years, abortion has been an extremely controversial subject. One important aspect of the controversy is whether a woman should be permitted by law to have an abortion and, if so, under what circumstances. Another is whether, and to what extent, laws should protect the unborn child's right to life." A significant portion of the article is devoted to "Arguments Against Abortion" and "Arguments for Abortion"; both cases are presented in an unemotional, well-reasoned manner. The subsection "Abortion Laws" discusses particular legislation and court cases and also describes abortion laws in other countries.

World Book's treatment of **homosexuality** is similarly evenhanded. The article remarks that "causes of homosexuality are not fully understood," and while presenting several theories notes that "the evidence for each of these . . . is contradictory and confusing. Many experts feel that a number of different factors can lead to homosexuality in different people." The article also includes a brief discussion of attitudes toward homosexuality in different cultures.

As noted in the section on *Accuracy*, some *World Book* articles occasionally give the appearance of perpetuating stereotypes. Statements on particular nations or American states sometimes read like tourist brochures. This may be a consequence of the editors' attempt to make the articles in *World Book* accessible and interesting to a wide range of readers. For example, in **Ireland**, under the subsection "Way of Life," we are told that "many of the Irish . . . enjoy visiting their neighborhood *pub* (public house). People gather in their favorite pubs to drink beer and whiskey, talk with friends, and play darts." Yet, while these statements may oversimplify, none of them is untrue, and considering the objectivity evident in *World Book*'s overall presentation, these are minor quibbles.

VIII. Accessibility

World Book is an exceptionally well organized and well designed encyclopedia that contains a variety of useful finding aids. A nine-page article in the frontmatter, "How to Get the Most Out of *World Book*," explains the set's arrangement clearly, simply, and in detail.

Entries are arranged alphabetically, word by word. However, some foreign proper names (such as De Gaulle) are alphabetized as if they were a single word. Unlike most other encyclopedias, *World Book* treats names beginning with *Mc* as they are actually spelled, not as though they began with *Mac*. Some readers may find this system less confusing than the usual library practice of alphabetizing *Mc* as *Mac*. The word-by-word arrangement is also easier for many readers to follow than is the letter-by-letter scheme.

Running heads at the top of each page indicate the first entry on the left-hand page and the last entry on the right-hand page. Page numbers are located at the bottom of each page, flush with the outside margin. Entry headings are printed in large boldface capital letters. Subheads within articles are also printed in boldface type and stand out clearly.

Many longer survey articles in *World Book* are organized into sections called "topical units." The publisher notes that "each topical unit stands on its own as a reference unit within the context of the larger article." Topical units are self-contained and always occupy a complete page or pages for easy reference. Each topical unit is broken down into subsections, identified by subheads. This arrangement enables students to easily find and consult specific information on the aspect of the topic in which they are interested.

World Book's comprehensive index, consisting of more than 150,000 entries, occupies most of Volume 22. As an indication of the scope and style of individual entries, the reader searching for information about **Marie Curie** will find the following index entry:

Curie, Marie Sklodowska [Polish-French physicist] **Ci:950**
Curie, Pierre **Ci:950** *with picture*
Medicine (The Medical Revolution) **M:306e**; *picture on* **M306c**
Nobel Prizes (Physics) **N:340** *with picture*; (Chemistry) **N:342**
Physics *picture on* **P:393**
Radiation (Early Theories and Discoveries) **R:75–76**
Radium **R:98** *with picture*

World Book contains an estimated 100,000 cross-references, which appear in several forms. These include entry cross-references (e.g., RHODESIA. See ZIMBABWE) as well as "see" and "see also" cross-references within the text. All cross-references are printed in small caps and are thus immediately noticeable. Most helpful of all are the lists at the end of many articles under the heading "Related Articles in WORLD BOOK include: . . . ." These enable the reader to tell at a glance what other articles in the encyclopedia may contain relevant information. This feature is unique to *World Book*.

IX. Special Features

World Book contains a number of special features that aim to enhance its accessibility and usefulness. Many of these, however, are directed toward the school student and will be superfluous for the general reader.

Foremost among its features are the nearly 30,000 illustrations, of which 24,000 are in full color, making *World Book* the most profusely illustrated encyclopedia on the market today. Both the color photographs and the commissioned illustrations are of exceptionally high quality. They are generally bright, lively, and interesting; moreover, they bear a clear relation to the articles they are intended to illustrate. For example, the 30-page entry on **architecture** contains 43 four-color photographs (in addition to several black-and-white photos and two-color illustrations) that amply illustrate the wide range of concepts and styles discussed in the text. Most captions are not only descriptive but include specific factual information.

World Book's maps are similarly distinguished. Most state, nation, and continent articles include full-page physical and political maps. Other maps give details of climate, natural resources, economic activity, historic exploration, and shifts in borders. Some of the maps were produced by Rand McNally, while others were prepared in conjunction with *World Book*'s own cartographic staff. Overall, the maps in *World Book* compare favorably with those in all other encyclopedias currently available.

Finally, many *World Book* articles are enhanced by tables, charts, and annotated schematic drawings. "Facts in Brief" tables, located in entries on states, provinces, countries, and continents, provide statistics about government, population, economy, and geographic features. "Tables of Terms" are glossaries that define words or phrases used in technical subjects. "Tables of Important Dates" help the reader to place certain subjects in historical perspective.

X. Format

The pages of the 1988 *World Book* have a distinctive new look. This edition has been entirely reset and printed in a specially designed typeface called World Book Modern. Other changes are: whereas the roman type of previous editions was set in justified (that is, aligned) columns, the columns are now set with a ragged right margin in order to allow equal spacing between words; entry words were printed in all uppercase letters; the current edition uses natural capitalization; and the new design uses four weights of type (regular, medium, demibold, and bold), which permits greater differentiation among different kinds of headings and other typographic elements on the page.

The 22-volume edition of *World Book* is available in three different bindings, known as School/Library, Aristocrat, and Classical. All bindings embody the same production features; there is apparently no substantial qualitative difference between any one binding and another. Regardless of binding style, the books are designed to stand up to heavy use.

Most volumes contain all the entries beginning with one letter; the exceptions are the C and S entries, which are each spread over two volumes. Thus the number of pages in each volume varies. The entire set takes up just over two feet of horizontal shelf space.

(See also *Summary* for information about foreign-language and recorded editions of *World Book*.)

XI. Other Opinions

Booklist (Reference Books Bulletin), November 15, 1986—review of the 1986 edition: "The set is curriculum oriented and has consistently garnered the Board's high praise for readability, authority, accuracy, and outstanding graphics. It is well edited and produced to meet the reference and leisure informational needs of students. . . . It is also an excellent source for adults."

Kenneth Kister, *Best Encyclopedias* (Oryx, 1986): ". . . [A] reference work of prominently high quality. . . . noteworthy for its readability, ease of use, broad and balanced coverage, accurate and up-to-date articles, and appealing illustrations and layout."

XII. Summary

As the Bowker Buying Guide's survey indicates, *World Book* is a popular choice in public libraries. Many patrons prefer it, finding it the least intimidating and easiest to use of all encyclopedias. While *World Book* is not as sophisticated in its content and presentation as THE ENCYCLOPEDIA AMERICANA, NEW ENCYCLOPAEDIA BRITANNICA, or COLLIER'S ENCYCLOPEDIA, it does have considerable strengths. It presents its material in an eminently clear and straightforward manner, concentrating on facts and shunning ambiguity and speculation. It embodies a high degree of accuracy and has acquired an almost impeccable authority. Moreover, on the whole it is more up-to-date than any other multivolume encyclopedia except ACADEMIC AMERICAN. Not surprisingly, *World Book* is the best-selling encyclopedia on the market today.

World Book's price of $599 (plus shipping and handling) to individuals and $499 (including shipping and handling) to libraries compares favorably with the price of other sets on the market—only FUNK & WAGNALLS NEW ENCYCLOPEDIA is less expensive—and adds to its attractiveness.

Individuals and institutions wishing to purchase *World Book* may contact the local distributor listed under "Encyclopedias" in the Yellow Pages, or telephone World Book, Inc., toll free at (800) 621-8202. The publisher offers individuals a discount for trade-ins of previous *World Book* editions.

Consumers should note that foreign-language editions of *World Book* are also sometimes available; these sets may or may not be in print at any given time. Interested individuals may contact the publisher for more information. The American Printing House for the Blind (1839 Frankfort Avenue, Box 6349, Louisville, KY 40206—telephone [502] 895-2405) distributes a massive 219-tape recorded edition of *World Book*, priced at $1,176.

PART THREE
Atlases

Chapter 7
What to Look for in Atlases

Atlases, like encyclopedias and dictionaries, are essential assets to library reference collections. Part Three of this Bowker Buying Guide provides information that will enable reference librarians to make informed decisions when adding atlases to an existing collection. It also gives individuals important information about choosing a work for home or office use.

An atlas is any collection of maps bound together in a book. The reviews in this Buying Guide, however, consider only general world atlases; topical and specialized atlases (such as historical atlases) are not included.

The black-and-white maps on pages 152–57 illustrate the range of features usually found in atlases. They also provide an overview of the various kinds of maps normally included as well as a sampling of the types of projections that atlas readers can expect to encounter.

Even though all general world atlases contain maps that cover all the regions of the world, individual atlases can differ greatly from one another in their content—both in the information shown on the general reference maps and in the choice of any thematic maps. Moreover, a wide range of cartographic techniques is available. Some atlases contain fairly simple maps, while others are more sophisticated and detailed. Many have a variety of special features, such as maps or tables that show population, industrial and agricultural production, energy resources, climate, history or language, while others contain only basic political or physical maps. Therefore, selecting an atlas that meets the needs of a particular user is a more complex process than it might appear at first glance. Every atlas is designed for a specific reader-

ership and purpose. An atlas that does not have the type of maps a reader needs will be of little value to him.

The reviews in this guide assume that most readers are not specialists in the fields of geography and cartography. Therefore, our reviewers describe atlases in more detail than is normally found in reviews that appear in professional journals. The Buying Guide reviews attempt to explain and illustrate specific features of each atlas so that buyers can acquire a balanced view of that work's contents. For the reader's convenience, the reviews follow a set format that includes the following items:

Facts at a Glance. Each evaluation is preceded by a summary of factual information about the atlas, provided by the publishers. This information includes the full title of the work, the publisher, the editor or editorial staff, the copyright date, the publication date of the edition reviewed, the number of pages, and the trim size of the volume. Price, type of binding, and any pertinent information supplied to the Buying Guide on the publishers' revision policy are also included.

In many cases, there is a discrepancy between the atlas's copyright date and its publication date (that is, the edition reviewed). Although some atlases are revised annually, the amount of material revised is often not sufficient to warrant a new copyright. Thus, for example, an atlas may have a 1984 copyright even though it was printed in 1988 and reflects post-1984 revision.

Introduction. This section provides a brief general overview of the atlas reviewed and of its relation to other works by the same publisher, a description of the work's purpose and intended readership, and an identification of the cartographers and consultants and their qualifications. Pertinent statements about the purposes or content by the editors or the publisher are often cited.

Format. The specific purpose of an atlas has a direct influence on the content, physical organization, and arrangement of its maps. Some contain primarily physical maps; others, political maps. (See pages 152–53 for an illustrated explanation of political and physical maps.) In some atlases the maps cover one page; in others, the maps are double-page spreads. The intended purposes of atlases also affect their size. Some are large in order to accommodate large-scale maps of extensive areas; others are small so that they can be carried conveniently. When appraising each atlas's format, reviewers evaluate its ease of handling, the relationship of its size to the type of maps it contains, and the convenience of its size for particular uses.

The bindings used for atlases also affect their uses. If the maps are double-page spreads, for example, the atlas should lie flat when opened, yet without breaking the binding. If it will not lie flat, information may be lost in the gutter (the adjoining inside margins of two facing pages), or the spine may break when users press down on it in an effort to see the information.

Reviewers also describe the map legends used in each atlas, how they are arranged, and which elements or symbols they include. Every atlas should include a legend that explains the symbols used; the explanations are clearer in some atlases than they are in others. The location of the legend is also significant. It should be easy to find and to relate to the map. Most atlases devote a full page before the maps to the legend, while a few also print it on a card that can be consulted beside each open map page. Some legends include all the symbols used; others omit some symbols that the compilers believe are self-explanatory.

Special Features. Many atlases contain a variety of special features. These may include a section of thematic maps; tables of political and socioeconomic statistics; or encyclopedic information, such as descriptions of weather patterns, weather resources, or plate tectonics. The reviewers describe these special features where they exist and comment on their cartographic quality, accuracy, relevancy, and usefulness. (See page 157 for an illustrated explanation of thematic maps.)

Geographical Balance. One extremely important question addressed by the reviewers concerns the adequacy and balance of the atlas's representation of all regions of the world. Some atlases show the United States in great detail while barely representing the Third World; other atlases attempt to use consistent scales for all parts of the world. This is not to say that an atlas with a marked geographical bias is necessarily bad; it all depends on its intended audience. If an atlas does have a bias toward one geographic area and gives it disproportionate coverage, the reviewer comments on whether or not this occurs at the expense of other regions.

Scale and Projections. In order to depict a given area in sufficient detail and with a minimum of distortion, cartographers must choose the scale and projection of each map carefully. The size of the page is often a limiting factor.

The proportional relationship or ratio between the distance or area on the map and the distance or area on the ground is called the *map scale*. It can be represented in three ways: (1) as a simple fraction or ratio, called the *representative fraction* or *RF*; (2) as a verbal or written statement of map distance in relation to earth distance; and (3) as a graphic representation or a bar scale.

The representative fraction is usually written as, for instance, 1:100,000, where 1 always refers to a unit of distance on the map and the 100,000 (or any other number) refers to the number of the same units it takes to cover the same distance on the ground. The written or verbal statement expresses distances in terms such as "one inch equals 64 miles." The graphic representation, or bar scale, is usually a line placed on the map that has been subdivided to show the lengths of units of earth distance.

Many maps include all three types of scale statements. The RF and the verbal statement are used to compare scales of two or more maps in close proximity, while the bar scale is employed to estimate or measure distances on the map itself. Incidentally, the bar scale is the only type of scale statement that remains accurate when the map is enlarged or reduced while being photocopied. (See page 156 for an illustrated explanation of map scale.)

A map projection is the method employed to transfer a curved section of the earth to a flat, two-dimensional plane. Three basic types of projections are in use today: cylindrical, conic, and plane. In order to represent the spherical earth on a flat surface, all methods of map projection involve some shrinking or stretching of certain portions of the earth. The cartographer has a choice of retaining some kinds of comparable angular relationships (bearings or directions) or retaining comparable areas or distances. The projection and scale are chosen according to the information that is to be presented with the least distortion. Some projections can preserve direction and distance only from a single point. Such projections are called *equidistant*. If directions at any point on the projection are preserved (if angles and shapes at any point are as they are on the globe), the projection is called *conformal* (or *orthomorphic*). If a projection preserves comparable areas (only at the expense of conformality and equidistance), it is called *equal-area*. No projection can possess more than one of the three qualities; some possess none.

The earth's grid of lines of latitude and longitude can be projected perspectively or mathematically to give conformal or equidistant representation on a plane, cone, or cylinder. Each property—conformality, equidistance, or equal area—can be attained by projection onto all three projection surfaces. To extend the range of area they cover, or to minimize some of the defects inherent in them, the basic principles are often modified or the characteristics of one are combined with another. (See pages 154–55 for an illustrated explanation of map projections.)

The choice of projection depends on a number of factors, including the purpose of the map, the area covered, and the ease with which the projection can be rendered. The Buying Guide's reviewers indicate whether or not the map scales used are reasonable for the size of the area shown on the map and for the size of the page, as well as to what extent the scales for comparable-size areas are consistent. They also discuss the advantages and disadvantages of the projections used for the various areas mapped and point out any unacceptable or potentially misleading distortions caused by any inappropriate projections.

Accuracy. Comments on accuracy reflect an analysis of place-names and their positioning on the maps. Names must be spelled correctly according to national or international standards, and spellings must be consistent. The introduction of a good atlas will explain to the user its standards of place name spelling.

Place-names must also be located accurately. This can be difficult, particularly when the name of a large area, such as a country or a mountain range, must convey that area's extent as well as its location, or when a number of place-names must appear in close proximity on a map.

Currency. Unless a reader is specifically looking for a historical atlas, the natural assumption is that a recently published atlas has information that is as up-to-date as possible. Any atlas being considered for purchase should be evaluated as to the currency of the political changes it reflects. A recent copyright date does not guarantee the currency of all the information in an atlas. One way the reviewers evaluate recency is by determining whether or not the latest country name changes are used on the maps.

Another is by examining any photographs or text description.

Legibility. Perhaps no element of a map is so important in evaluating its usefulness as the lettering or typefaces used and the manner in which they are positioned. The recognition of a specific named feature, the "search time" necessary to find names, and the ease with which the lettering can be read are all important.

Like all other marks on a map, the type functions as a graphic symbol. By its position within the map's structural framework, it helps to indicate the location of points. By its spacing and layout it indicates, for instance, such features as the linear or areal extent of mountain ranges or the placement of political units. By its arrangement with respect to the latitude and longitude grid, the type can also clearly delineate orientation.

Type style, size, and color can all be used systematically to identify particular categories of landforms or other features. For example, blue type is typically used to identify all hydrographic features, and within that general class, open water may be labeled with all-capital letters and running water by capitals and lowercase characters. Type-size variations can indicate the ordinal characteristics of geographical phenomena, ranking them, for example, in terms of relative area or importance.

In a more subtle way, type size serves as an indication of scale. Size contrasts with respect to other factors, such as line width and symbol size, can give the impression that one map is drawn to a larger or smaller scale than another. If the cartographer has not been careful, this important impression can be lost or even reversed.

Typically, different typeface styles are used to differentiate among various types of geographic information, such as names of physical features and names of populated places. Not only do the typefaces have to be legible, but they must be sufficiently differentiated (by size, upper and lower case, roman or italic style, and so on) so that it is easy for the reader to distinguish among the various types of geographic information.

When many place-names need to be positioned in a small area on the map, the cartographer has to make decisions concerning type size and styles in order to fit all the names in legibly. If he or she does a poor job, the map will look cluttered and individual names will be hard to find. Symbols used to delineate rivers, roads, railroads and so forth also need to be clearly distinguishable from each other.

Accessibility. In determining the accessibility of each atlas, the reviewers evaluated a number of qualities. For example, one of the greatest assets of an

Political Maps

General non-thematic maps in an atlas may be either **political** or **physical** maps. Political maps highlight nations as distinct political entities. They also present information about man-made (artificial) entities on the earth, using a variety of symbols. These symbols are described in a map key or legend, which may be located in the front of the atlas as well as, in an abbreviated form, on each map page.

Typically, political maps depict the following features: 1) Political boundaries (national, and often state or provincial; disputed boundaries or territories may also be indicated). 2) Cities. Depending upon the level of detail and the map scale, these symbols may distinguish the size of the city. Extremely large or densely populated urban areas may be shown by a mark that indicates the actual extent of the area. Otherwise, dots of different sizes or configurations may be used to distinguish different levels of population. Capital cities are frequently marked by a star-shaped symbol. City symbols are invariably printed in black.

Political maps also designate elements of the transportation system: major highways, railroads, and international airports. Sea shipping lanes may be indicated as well. On most four-color maps, colors are used to identify different types of routes. Railway lines are usually gray or black, while roads are customarily red. As with city symbols, these are frequently varied to identify different types of roads.

Physical Maps

Equally important in helping the user distinguish among varying features are the typefaces in which the labels appear. Ideally, different typefaces and type sizes are used to identify nations, provinces, and cities, or other populated areas. Political maps often show limited physical features as well—primarily important bodies of water such as lakes, rivers, and oceans. The presence of extensive landforms such as deserts and mountain ranges is sometimes designated by name labels, but political maps rarely indicate the actual natural boundaries of such areas.

For these, readers turn to physical maps. Some physical maps use color, shades of color, or relief to indicate altitude. Others use color or shading to depict actual land types such as forest, desert, or tundra.

Few maps are purely political or purely physical. Physical maps, for example, may or may not show national borders. Like political maps, they may show roads and cities and distinguish among population centers. As a rule, physical maps are more complex than their political counterparts: they endeavor to interpret the relationship between society and environment.

Projection Types—World Maps

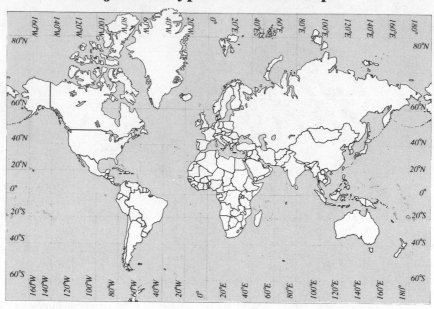

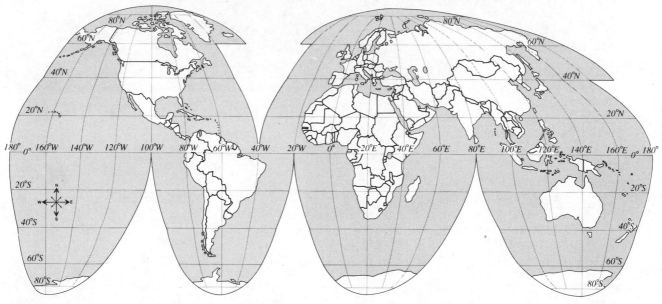

The maps on this page illustrate two types of projections (**Mercator** and **Goode's Interrupted**) and the kinds of distortions that can occur on world maps. Note that virtually all world maps are made from some type of cylindrical projection.

The Mercator projection shows the correct shape of land masses, but distorts their area (that is, their size). This distortion is minimal in equatorial regions, but increases near the poles. As a result, Greenland appears larger than South America. In fact, Greenland's area is only 840,000 square miles, whereas that of South America is 7 million square miles. The Mercator projection is used for ocean navigation because a line drawn between any two points on this map gives the true compass direction from one point to the other.

Many readers will be familiar with the Mercator projection from wall maps of the world. It is one of the cheapest and easiest projections for cartographers to use, and it results in a rectangular map.

A more complex projection for world maps found in a number of atlases is Goode's Interrupted Homolosine projection. Combining the features of two other projections (the **Mollweide Homolographic** and the **Sinusoidal**, or **Sanson-Flamsteed**, projections), it allows fairly faithful representation of both the shape and size of large land masses. Its major distortions— the interruptions—occur in ocean areas. Goode's Homolosine projection is useful for population distribution and other thematic world maps as well as for political and physical world maps.

Projection Types—Regional Maps

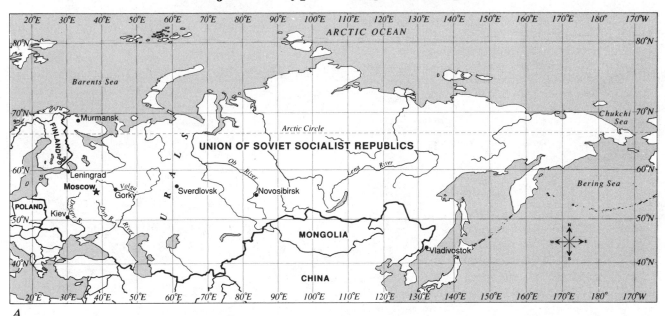

A

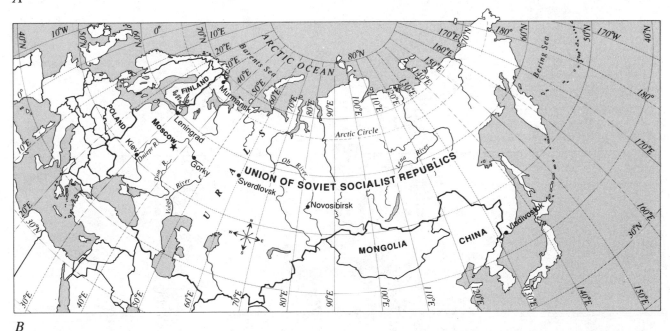

B

The larger the area covered in a map, the greater the distortion will be, regardless of the type of projection used. Thus, while distortions on a map of a continent are not as severe as on a map of the entire world, the choice of projection still affects the accuracy of size, shape, or direction. To produce national and continental maps, cartographers can use conic or plane as well as cylindrical projections. Their preference depends largely on the size, shape, and location of the nation or continent.

Two different projection types are used in the maps on this page. Map A depicts the U.S.S.R. in the Miller projection, a cylindrical projection similar to the Mercator projection. It shows shapes less accurately than does the Mercator projection, but it also distorts sizes less severely. Map B shows the U.S.S.R. in the Lambert azimuthal projection, a plane projection. In this projection, a straight line shows the shortest distance between any two points. This projection is ideal for plotting airline routes. However, both shape and distance are increasingly distorted away from the center of this map.

Large Scale and Small Scale

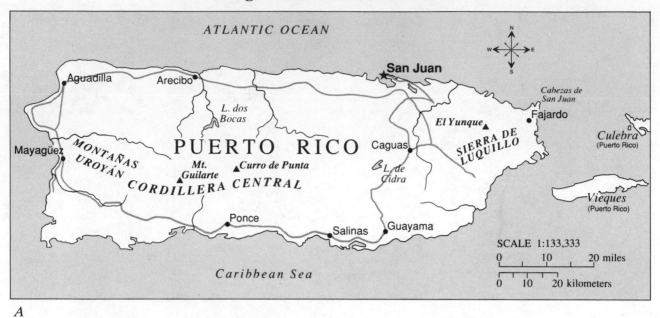

A

B

Readers are often confused by the terms large scale and small scale. These expressions do not refer to the size of a map, but rather to the size of the area that the map covers. The larger the scale, the smaller the area that the map can cover, but the greater the amount of detail that it can include about that area. Different scales are used for different purposes. Each has its advantages and its disadvantages.

The two maps on this page are both the same size, but each is drawn to a different scale. Map A (Puerto Rico) has a scale of 1:333,333, a larger scale than that used for Map B (the Caribbean Sea), which is drawn to a scale of 1:20,000,000.

Map A depicts major towns, roads, and rivers in Puerto Rico, and is therefore useful for anyone needing detailed information about the features of this island only. Map B covers a substantially larger area, allowing the reader to compare the size of Puerto Rico to that of its neighbors and to see the island's location in the Caribbean chain. At the same time, however, it does not render the features of Puerto Rico in as much detail as is possible in the larger-scale map.

Thematic Maps

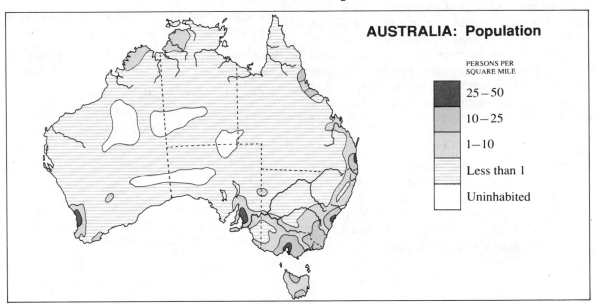

AUSTRALIA: Population

PERSONS PER
SQUARE MILE

25—50

10—25

1—10

Less than 1

Uninhabited

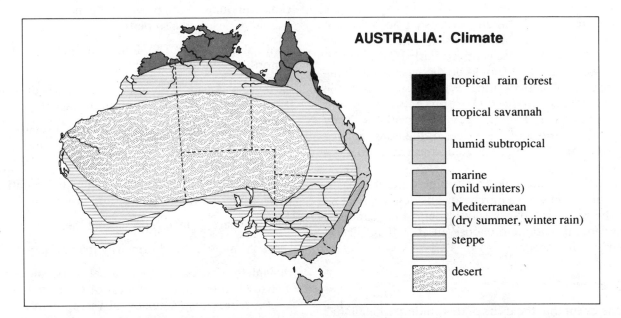

AUSTRALIA: Climate

tropical rain forest

tropical savannah

humid subtropical

marine
(mild winters)

Mediterranean
(dry summer, winter rain)

steppe

desert

Thematic maps present information about particular aspects of geography, the environment, or society. Thematic maps can be used to show agricultural patterns, industry, income, life expectancy, geological structure, military alliances, or a myriad of other topics. An atlas that includes a broad selection of good thematic maps can be a valuable asset to any reference collection.

The two thematic maps on this page are typical of climate and population maps found in many atlases. Generally, such maps are in color, with different colors and patterns representing different features. These black-and-white maps follow the same principles used in color maps, with different types of shading standing in for colors.

It is important to remember that, whereas political and physical maps show specific features in exact locations, thematic maps show prevailing characteristics in less specifically defined areas. In other words, thematic maps generalize about the types of features found in a given area, and present this information in a form that can be readily interpreted by the ordinary reader. By comparing different thematic maps of the same region, the reader can assemble a mental image of the conditions in that region and draw conclusions about the interrelation of various factors, such as climate and population.

atlas should be its index of the place names that appear on its maps. The best index is one that, at a minimum, lists every name that appears on all the general maps. The spelling in the index should be consistent with that on the maps. Ideally, there should also be cross-references to popular or variant name spellings. Most atlas compilers index names to the largest-scale map on which they appear. Sometimes, however, names will be indexed to all maps on which they appear.

After each name in an index, either an alphanumeric (letter/number) grid coordinate or a latitude/longitude reference is used to locate it on the map. The best and most accurate method is latitude/longitude, expressed in degrees and minutes. With the grid-coordinate system, there is usually a one- to four-square-inch area in which to search for the name. Another aspect of accessibility is the indexing of map insets. A good atlas index will also list the place names found in these.

Summary. Certainly every user wants to get the best value possible when purchasing an atlas, but content alone is not necessarily a basis for deciding whether or not an atlas is priced fairly. Overall quality as well as content should be the bases for judging the reasonableness of price. Whenever possible, the reviewers make broad comparisons between the atlas under review and similar competing atlases. They weigh the merits and drawbacks of the atlas and give an overview that can help guide the reader to a decision.

Few buyers are able to examine a number of atlases before making a purchase. The detailed reviews on the following pages should help both librarians and general readers to choose an atlas that will suit their specific needs.

Glossary

In the event that the users of this guide are unfamiliar with the cartographic terms employed in these reviews, a glossary of these terms is provided below:

aerial chart See **aeronautical chart.**

aerial photograph A photograph of the surface of the earth taken downward from the air.

aeronautical chart A map designed to assist navigation in the air.

air photo See **aerial photograph.**

altitude tint See **hypsometric tint.**

ancillary map A small supplementary or secondary map outside the **neat line** of the principal or main map. See also **inset map.**

azimuthal projection See **plane projection.**

bar scale A subdivided line which shows the lengths of units of earth distance.

base map A map used as a framework on which to depict other information.

bathymetric tint A color applied to the area between selected depth contours to depict the physical relief of the floor of a body of water. See also **hypsometric tint.**

bleeding edge An edge of a map to which printed detail extends after the paper has been trimmed.

block diagram A representation of the landscape in either perspective or isometric projection, usually with some vertical exaggeration.

Bonne projection A **conic, equal-area projection** in which distances are true along all parallels and the central meridian.

cadastral map A map which delineates property boundaries. See also **plat.**

cardinal directions The four principal directions: north, south, east, and west.

cartogram A map with areas or distances distorted to promote communication of a concept.

cartographic material Any material representing, in whole or in part, the earth or any celestial body at any scale.

cartouche A panel on a map, often with decoration, enclosing the title, legends, and/or scale.

celestial chart A map representing the heavens.

chart A map designed primarily for navigation.

cholopleth map A map with areal units colored or shaded so that the brightness of each symbolized area represents its numerical value for the distribution mapped.

conic projection Any **map projection** in which the parallels and meridians appear as they would if a cone were laid over a globe and touched it along one or two parallels.

contour A line joining points of equal elevation on a surface.

contour interval The difference in elevation between adjacent contour lines.

contour map A map which uses contour lines to portray relief.

cylindrical projection Any **map projection** in which the parallels and meridians appear as they would if a cylinder were wrapped around the globe, touching it at the equator.

dot distribution map A map in which each discrete dot represents a set number of the objects comprising the distribution displayed on the map.

elevation tint See **hypsometric tint.**

equal-area projection Any **plane** (or **azimuthal**) **projection** that shows land areas in their correct proportions.

equivalent scale See **verbal scale.**

facsimile map A printed reproduction of a map identical with the original.

format The general physical organization of a publication.

form lines Lines, resembling contour lines but drawn without regard to regular spacing, which present the shape of the terrain.

gazetteer A list of geographic names, together with descriptive information and/or references to their geographic location.

geographic coordinates A system which expresses the position of points in terms of latitude and longitude.

geographic pole Either of the two points of intersection of the surface of the earth with its axis, where all meridians meet.

Goode's interrupted homolosine projection An **equal-area projection** that produces an oval-shaped map, often used for world distribution maps.

gradient tint See **hypsometric tint.**

graphic scale A drawing or diagram which enables quantitative measurements to be read. See also **bar scale.**

graticule A network of lines on a map which represents meridians and parallels. See also **grid.**

Greenwich meridian See **prime meridian.**

grid Network of two sets of uniformly spaced parallel lines, one set intersecting the other at right angles. When superimposed on a map, it usually carries the name of the projection used for the map.

hachures Short lines, following the direction of maximum slope, which indicate relief.

hill shading Shading employed to create a three-dimensional impression of relief. See also **shaded relief.**

historical map A map which represents features or phenomena which existed, or which are believed to have existed, in some past period of time.

hydrographic chart A chart designed to assist navigation at sea or on other waterways.

hypsometric layer A uniform tint or shade covering the area between two successive isolines.

hypsometric map See **relief map.**

hypsometric tint A color applied to the area between two selected contours when relief is depicted by a system of layers.

index map An index, usually based on an outline map, which shows the layout and numbering system of map sheets which cover an area.

inset map A separate map positioned within the **neat line** of a larger map.

isoline map A map which represents a continuous distribution by means of lines (called *isolines*) along which values are constant.

key map See **index map.**

Lambert azimuthal equal-area projection A **plane projection** used for mapping polar regions or other circular areas.

Lambert conformal conic projection A **conic projection** that uses two standard parallels instead of the single parallel used in most conic projections. Because distortions of shape and size are minimal, this projection is useful for mapping regions in middle latitudes with extended east-west areas, such as the United States or Asia.

landform drawing A small-scale map showing landforms by the systematic application of a standardized set of simplified pictorial symbols. See also **pictorial relief map.**

Landsat One of a series of Earth-observation satellites in a near-polar orbit designed to cover almost the entire earth, with repeated coverage every 18 days.

landscape map A **topographic map** made to a relatively large scale and showing all details.

latitude Angular distance on a meridian measured north or south of the equator.

layered (relief hair) map A map on which relief is represented by hypsometric layers. See also **relief map.**

layer tint See **hypsometric tint.**

leaf One of the units into which the original sheet is folded to form part of a book, each leaf consisting of two pages, one on each side.

linear scale See **bar scale.**

location map A small-scale map inset in, or placed in the margin of, a map at a larger scale, to show the location of the area represented by the large-scale map.

longitude The angular distance east or west of a reference meridian, usually the **prime meridian.**

map A representation, normally to scale and on a flat medium, of a selection of material or abstract features on, or in relation to, the surface of the earth or another celestial body.

map profile See **profile.**

map projection Any systematic arrangement of meridians and parallels, portraying the curved surface of the earth upon a plane.

map section A scaled representation of a vertical surface displaying both the profile where it intersects the surface of the ground and the underlying structures along the plane of intersection.

marginal information Information which appears in the margin of a map.

marginal map See **ancillary map.**

Mercator projection A **cylindrical projection** that shows correct land shapes but distorts land areas, especially in higher latitudes. Frequently used for world maps.

meridian A great circle arc of 180 degrees terminated by the geographic poles. See also **parallel.**

Miller cylindrical projection A cylindrical projection used for showing the world. As in the **Mercator projection**, distortion increases in higher latitudes.

Mollweide homolographic projection An **equal-area projection** that produces an oval-shaped map, often used for world distribution maps.

natural scale See **representative fraction.**

neat line A line which encloses the detail of a map.

orthophotomap A map with a planimetrically accurate photograph image and some symbolized terrain and man-made features.

outline map A map which presents just sufficient geographic information to permit the correlation of additional data placed over it.

overlay A transparent sheet containing matter, at the same scale as the map to which it is keyed, showing detail that does not appear on the original.

panorama A perspective representation of the landscape in which the detail is shown as if projected onto a vertical plane or onto the inside of a cylinder.

parallel Any line of latitude, running parallel to the equator in an east-west direction. See also **meridian.**

perspective view The representation on a plane surface of the three-dimensional landscape, using lines of projection converging to a central point, as the landscape might appear to the eye. Also called **worm's-eye view.**

photomap A reproduction of an aerial photograph, to which names, symbols, grid lines have been added.

pictorial map A map in which features are represented by individual pictures in elevation, or perspective, rather than by conventionalized cartographic symbols.

pictorial relief map A map on which landforms and other topographic features are shown in their correct planimetric position by pictorial symbols representing their appearance from a high oblique view. See also **landform drawing.**

plane projection Any **map projection** in which the parallels and meridians appear as if the surface of a globe were projected onto a flat surface (a plane) touching the globe at a single point.

planimetric map A large-scale, detailed map, in which the outlines of buildings, roads, and other man-made features are shown to scale with little generalization.

plat A scale diagram of political, subdivision, and property boundaries, as well as some physical features, designed to provide a frame of reference for the purpose of recording ownership of land, mineral claims, or other property rights.

plate A page or leaf containing illustrative matter, with or without explanatory text, that does not form part of either the preliminary or the main sequence of pages or leaves.

prime meridian The meridian on the earth's surface from which longitude is measured. Since 1884, the meridian passing through Greenwich, England, has been recognized as the prime meridian.

profile A scale representation of the intersection of a vertical surface with the surface of the ground.

recto The right-hand page of a book; or the side of a map sheet intended to be read first.

relief The collective elevations or inequalities of a land surface, represented on maps by **contours, hypsometric tints, shaded relief, spot hachures,** etc.

relief map A map produced primarily to represent the physical configuration of the landscape, often with **hypsometric tints**.

remote sensing The measurement of surface characteristics from a distant aerial or satellite platform with an electronic or optical device for measuring or recording electromagnetic radiation.

representative fraction The scale of a map expressed as a fraction or ratio which relates unit distance on the map to distance, measured in the same units, on the ground. Also referred to as RF.

scale The ratio of distances on a map to the actual distances they represent.

schematic map A map representing features in a much simplified or diagrammatic form.

segment A part of a map where, because of physical limitations, the area being portrayed has been divided to fit on the sheet.

shaded relief A cartographic technique that provides an apparent three-dimensional configuration of the terrain on maps by the use of graded shadows that would be cast by high ground if light were shining from the northwest.

sounding The measured or charted depth of water, expressed in feet or fathoms.

spot height A point on a map whose elevation above sea level is noted, usually by a dot and the elevation value.

thematic map A map portraying information on a specific topic, such as geology, agriculture, or demography, rather than general geographic distributions.

topographic map A map designed to portray and identify the features of the earth's surface as precisely as possible within the limitations imposed by scale.

Universal Transverse Mercator (UTM) grid A widely used plane-coordinate system, based on the transverse Mercator projection and employing 60 zones worldwide, extending from 80 degrees south to 84 degrees north, with each zone covering 6 degrees of longitude.

verbal scale The relationship which a small distance on a map bears to the corresponding distance on the earth, expressed as an equivalence, such as 1 inch (on the map) equals 1 mile (on the ground).

verso The left-hand page of a book.

vertical exaggeration The ratio of the vertical to the horizontal scale.

view A perspective representation of the landscape in which detail is shown as if projected onto an oblique plane.

worm's-eye view See **perspective view.**

Chapter 8
Evaluations of Atlases

Ambassador World Atlas

Facts at a Glance

Full Title: **Ambassador World Atlas.**
Publisher: Hammond.
Editors: Martin A. Bacheller, Editor-in-Chief, and the Hammond staff.
Copyright: 1988.
Edition Reviewed: 1988.

Number of Pages: 524.
Number of Maps: 415.
Number of Indexes: 1 master index, plus individual same-page indexes accompanying all map areas.
Number of Index Entries: 100,000 in master index; 48,000 in same-page indexes.
Trim Size: 9½″ × 12½″.
Binding: cloth.

Price: $45.00. 15 percent discount to libraries.
ISBN 0-8437-1244-9.
Revised annually or twice a year as necessary.

I. Introduction

The Hammond *Ambassador World Atlas*, revised in 1988, incorporates the same cartography as Hammond's 1988 CITATION WORLD ATLAS and is identical in trim size. Two additional features and a greatly expanded index, however, make the *Ambassador* edition 136 pages longer. This review considers only those features unique to the *Ambassador World Atlas*; for a complete review, refer to the evaluation of the CITATION WORLD ATLAS on pages 169–72.

The *Ambassador* is intended for readers in grade 9 and above, although it may have more appeal to adult users, primarily because of its indexes.

II. Format

Unlike its companion volume, the *Ambassador World Atlas* is available only in a hardcover edition, although it shares the same convenient 9½″ × 12½″ trim size. Its sturdy binding, durable cover, and heavy paper will stand up to extensive library use.

In format, the arrangement of maps corresponds exactly to that of the CITATION.

III. Special Features

In addition to all the features found in the CITATION, this atlas includes two special sections on weather. The first provides two pages of charts on "Foreign City Weather," listing average daily high and low temperatures for each month, together with the average number of days with rain. These well-organized, highly readable charts furnish useful information not only for travelers but also for students of world geography.

The second section, "U.S. City Weather," lists data on annual precipitation, wind speeds, record high and low temperatures (without dates), the elevations of weather stations, and average monthly temperature. Our reviewers found the information in this section too incomplete to be of significant value either to travelers or students.

The *Ambassador World Atlas* now features 24 pages of model maps. These maps use color and relief effects to give the continents and the ocean floor a three-dimensional appearance. The world model map section helps make this edition of the *Ambassador* more competitive with such works as the BRITANNICA ATLAS, THE NEW YORK TIMES ATLAS OF THE WORLD, and the READER'S DIGEST WIDE WORLD ATLAS, all of which include a special section of similar maps.

IV. Currency

Map contents in the *Ambassador World Atlas* are as current as its 1988 copyright date. According to the publisher, the atlas is updated annually or twice yearly to incorporate changes in political boundaries, place-names, and statistical data.

V. Accessibility

The major difference between the *Ambassador* and CITATION editions is the master index of the place-names in each volume. The *Ambassador*'s index of some 100,000 entries occupies more than 140 pages; the CITATION has 25,000 entries on 24 pages. According to the publisher, the master index cites all place-names found in the atlas, including those not listed in the same-page indexes that accompany the maps. The entries themselves are more complete than those in the CITATION and enable the reader to locate a place-name in only one step. ZIP codes for U.S. cities are also given in the master index, which is a feature that will be useful to users.

In principle, the master index gives a citation for every map on which a given place-name appears, which makes this edition much more accessible than the CITATION. Since each name is given a separate entry for each map, however, this system tends to inflate the total number of index entries. Nevertheless, there are problems. For example, the city of Bombay is listed three times in the master index. The first citation is given as "54/J8," Bombay's correct location on a map of Asia on page 54. The second citation is "2/N5." Although the grid "N5" is correct, this location is actually on page 3, not 2, of a two-page world map. (Bombay's location on a world map on page 1 is not cited in the index.) The final map location is given as "Bombay (harb.), India 68/B7." This gives the mistaken impression that the location is for the harbor rather than for the city itself. Moreover, the grid location "B7" refers to an inset map, not to Bombay's location on the map of India. (Similarly, the same-page index for India gives the single map reference "B7.") Although rare, such lapses pose pitfalls for the reader.

As in the CITATION, four large-scale maps of U.S. cities are not included in either the master index or the table of contents, and are thus effectively lost to users.

A "Gazetteer-Index of the World" appears at the front of the volume. This list, which includes more place-names than does its counterpart in the CITATION, also provides the "Sources of Population Data," thus allowing the user to check the data and reliability of statistics. This feature is important for serious researchers but not necessary for the casual browser.

VI. Summary

The *Ambassador World Atlas* is the largest atlas in Hammond's INTERNATIONAL/CITATION/AMBASSADOR series and is priced accordingly. As does the CITATION, the *Ambassador* contains individual maps of all 50 U.S. states, and a same-page index for each map in the atlas. It also contains thematic maps for different nations and regions, as well as basic population statistics that accompany each main map. These features are all decided pluses, and $45.00 is a fair price to pay for the greater accessibility offered by the *Ambassador* edition—but only if this is the primary world atlas in a library's collection. Users requiring less emphasis on the United States, and/or more information about the physical world, may prefer THE PRENTICE-HALL NEW WORLD ATLAS or RAND MCNALLY GOODE'S WORLD ATLAS.

Background Notes

Facts at a Glance

Full Title: **Background Notes on the Countries of the World.**
Publisher: U.S. State Department; distributed by the Superintendent of Documents.
Editors: Juanita Adams, Joan Reppert Reams, and other State Department officers.
Copyright: 1984–87.

Number of Indexes: 1.
Number of Index Entries: 160.
Binding: series of 160 loose-leaf pamphlets; two-piece notebook binder available separately.

Price: $70.00 for complete set; individual pamphlets $1.00 or $2.00.
Ongoing revision; yearly subscription to revised pamphlets as issued, $32.00.

I. Introduction

Background Notes is not an atlas per se but rather a series of more than 160 "short, authoritative pamphlets about various countries, territories, and international organizations." Each pamphlet in the set combines a number of encyclopedic and atlaslike features and is designed to serve the needs of a wide variety of users, including teachers, librarians, writers, travelers, and businesspeople.

Background Notes is issued by the U.S. State Department, which states that each pamphlet is "written by officers in the Department of State's geographic and functional bureaus" and edited by the department's editorial division, a branch of its Bureau of Public Affairs.

II. Format

Each *Background Notes* pamphlet consists of four or eight 8½″ × 11″ pages devoted to a particular nation. (A few, such as *China*, are 16 pages long.) The self-contained pamphlets are perforated for insertion in a ring binder, and because each follows the same internal format, the entire series can be arranged to form an international atlas-gazetteer.

Each pamphlet provides informative text, a small location or orientation map, and a full national map. All maps are black-and-white and show political rather than topographical detail; the level of detail varies from one map to another.

The text is divided into several sections: "Profile" (including statistics on population, geography, government, and economy), "People," "Geography," "History," "Government," "Political Conditions," "Economy," "Foreign Relations," "Defense," and "Relations with the U.S." A "Travel Notes" sidebar gives pertinent information for travelers to the country. Principal government officials are also listed, as are principal U.S. officials at the American embassy and consulates in the country. In addition, many of the *Background Notes* include a bibliography.

The full-page black-and-white nation map included in each *Background Notes* is suitable for photocopying. All material in the pamphlets is in the public domain and may be reproduced without permission. These political maps show international boundaries, national capitals, major cities and towns, roads, railroads, international airports, and rivers. A handful of maps also depict state or provincial boundaries as well as major natural features other than rivers (for example, mountain ranges and deserts). All maps include a symbol key and scale.

A ring binder is not provided, but the pamphlets can be used with any two- or three-ring notebook binder. Because the complete set of *Background Notes* amounts to roughly 1,000 pages, at least two notebooks are needed to hold the set.

III. Special Features

Apart from the elements just mentioned, *Background Notes* contains no special features as such. However, since much of the information included in the pamphlets—in particular, the lists of government officials, embassies, and consulates—is not available in most general atlases or encyclopedias, these may be regarded as special features. The location or orientation maps, printed on the first page of each pamphlet, which show the nation in relation to its neighbors, are also useful.

IV. Geographical Balance

Because virtually every nation, including such small or little-known countries as Andorra, Bhutan, the Comoros, Liechtenstein, Monaco, Nauru, San Marino, São Tomé and Principe, and the Seychelles, is the subject of an individual pamphlet, *Background Notes* can be said to have excellent geographical balance. Each nation, regardless of its size, is given a fairly detailed map; the size of the map seems to be determined by the nation's size and shape. In general, the maps are large enough to clearly show major cities, roads, and other important features.

The text provides a level of attention appropriate to each nation's importance and to the reader's potential requirements. As mentioned, smaller nations are covered in 4 pages, larger or more complex ones in 8, and a few, such as China, in 16. Nations whose governments are out of favor with the U.S. government (such as Cuba, Kampuchea, and Nicaragua) receive the same dispassionate attention accorded to its closest allies. In cases where relations with the United States are either particularly warm or especially strained, this is noted in the section on U.S. relations. However, the nature of the relationship does not seem to have prejudiced the information presented in the rest of the text.

V. Scale and Projections

Each map in *Background Notes* has been drawn to a different scale. As with the map sizes, scale is determined to a large degree by the size and shape of the nation and by the amount of detail needed to make the map accurate and useful. To determine the relative sizes of several different nations at a glance, the user must consult another source, since *Background Notes* does not contain a world map. However, the orientation map on the first page of each pamphlet is useful for comparing the size of a nation with that of its neighbors.

The map scales are not reported as fractional representations. However, each main map is accompanied by a bar scale that gives both metric and standard measures. The following examples indicate the general range of scales used in *Background Notes* maps: Iran, ⁹⁄₁₀″ = 150 miles; Iraq, ¹⁄₁₀″ = 100 miles; Indonesia, 1″ = 400 miles; Ireland, 1½″ = 50 miles; Italy, 1″ = 100 miles. At opposite extremes of the spectrum are the map of Canada, where 1″ = 500 miles, and San Marino, where ⁴⁄₅″ = 1 mile. Although they exhibit a wide range, the scales are generally appropriate to the size of the country.

The projections used in the various maps are not identified. Because each map covers a single nation, where distortions are not as apparent as in area, continent, or world maps, this is not a serious omission. (It should be noted, however, that optimum projection types vary according to the size and location of the area depicted. For example, an ideal projection for representing an equatorial nation would cause unacceptable distortions if used to represent a nation in the high latitudes.) On the whole, *Background Notes* seems to use projections that cause the least distortion to the area represented.

VI. Accuracy

Background Notes maps reflect official U.S. government policy. Each map carries the disclaimer that "boundary representation is not necessarily authoritative." The maps also note when U.S. government policy differs from the policy of other nations regarding political boundaries. For example, the maps of Finland, Poland, and the Soviet Union remind the reader that "the United States Government has not recognized the incorporation of Estonia, Latvia, and Lithuania into the Soviet Union. Names and boundary representation are not necessarily authoritative." The map of the Federal Republic of Germany includes the German Democratic Republic; the border between the two is shown but is not represented as an international boundary. A footnote on the map comments that the "final borders of Germany have not been established."

Even though the amount of detail is limited by the size and nature of the maps, in all other respects, the information appears to be definitive. Place-names are spelled with consistent accuracy, and spelling follows generally accepted contemporary practice. Anglicized spellings are used for major cities (for example, *Warsaw*) with the vernacular spelling in parentheses (*Warszawa*).

Although all maps in the set are rendered in black-and-white, cartographic detail is clear and is often comparable to that of political maps found in many commercial atlases. Occasionally, nation maps show less detail than the user might wish. For example, while the United Kingdom map shows such major cities as London, Bristol, Birmingham, Manchester, Liverpool, and Leeds, it excludes others such as Portsmouth, Sheffield, Bradford, and York. On the whole, however, users will be well served with the accuracy of the maps.

Since more pages of *Background Notes* are occupied by text than by maps, the accuracy of the text is also an important consideration. The text (including nation statistics) has been compiled by area specialists in the State Department. Our reviewers found the information about people, geography, history, government, political conditions, economy, and other aspects to be highly reliable. Although this material makes no effort to be comprehensive, it nevertheless provides an accurate, well-organized introduction to each nation akin in many respects to that found in a good encyclopedia.

VII. Currency

Background Notes is available as a complete set, but each pamphlet is published separately and updated on an individual basis. The title page of each pamphlet includes the month and year it was published. Because the State Department issues updated versions of approximately 75 *Background Notes* each year, the currency of an entire set will vary. Text and maps are revised to reflect conditions at the time of publication. Institutions and individuals can take out annual subscriptions to all the *Background Notes* pamphlets published during the year. (See also *Summary*.) This revision and subscription procedure helps ensure that a collection's set of *Background Notes* is as up-to-date as possible.

VIII. Legibility

As mentioned, all maps and text in the *Background Notes* series are in the public domain and may be reproduced without permission and at no fee. Although the maps are not specifically designed for photocopying, our tests indicate that most of them will produce satisfactory copies, depending on the quality of the machine.

The maps generally display a high graphic quality. For the most part, place-names are legible, although the small type used for place-names on many maps may discourage some readers, especially those who are visually impaired. It may also adversely affect the quality of photocopies. Similarly, the detail on some of the maps (for example, the Bahamas and Fiji) is also too small to reproduce clearly. Lines representing roads and rivers are faint and may not reproduce on some machines. The dark shading of neighboring nations may also be obscured on photocopies. (The main nation covered on these maps is always unshaded so that place-names and other symbols appear on a plain white background.) Nevertheless, the overall legibility of the maps is adequate for their intended purpose.

IX. Summary

Background Notes is a concise, accurate, and authoritative source of maps and basic information about the world's nations. The series should serve the needs of a wide variety of users. Professors can use the series to supplement geography and political science lectures and to provide definitive national statistics, or to add to their resource collection. Librarians will also find many uses for the series in response to their patrons' ready-reference requests; in addition, libraries will welcome the fact that the pamphlets can be copied without permission. Travelers, writers, and journalists may also find these publications useful for many purposes.

Background Notes are available individually at $1.00 or $2.00 each, depending on the title. The complete set, which costs $70.00, represents a considerable savings over the cumulative price of individual pamphlets. An annual subscription, costing $32.00, ensures that the subscriber automatically receives revised pamphlets upon publication. Roughly 75 titles are updated and reissued each year.

Interested individuals or institutions may order *Background Notes* through the Superintendent of Documents, U.S. Government Printing Office, Washington, D.C. 20402.

Bartholomew Mini World Atlas

Facts at a Glance

Full Title: **Bartholomew Mini World Atlas.**
Publisher: John Bartholomew & Son; distributed by Hammond.
Editors: staff of John Bartholomew & Son.
Copyright: 1987.
Edition Reviewed: 1987 revised edition.

Number of Pages: 208.
Number of Maps: 120.
Number of Indexes: 1.
Number of Index Entries: 20,000.
Trim Size: 4″ × 6″.

Binding: cloth and paperback.
Price: $12.95 (cloth); $9.95 (paperback).
Sold in bookstores, by direct mail, and directly to libraries.
ISBN 0-7028-0704-4 (cloth);
ISBN 0-7028-0703-6 (paperback).
Revised as needed.

I. Scope and Format

The *Bartholomew Mini World Atlas* is a British-made pocket-size atlas distributed in the United States by Hammond. Its contents are identical in every respect to those of THE RANDOM HOUSE MINI WORLD ATLAS. As with that title, this book may be useful for casual ready reference and as a portable pocket atlas for the business traveler, but otherwise it is a poor choice for either library or personal collections.

The *Bartholomew Mini World Atlas* is available in two formats. The deluxe hardcover edition features a padded cover and gilt edges; the title is embossed in gold on the front and the spine. This version is handsome and should prove durable, but $12.95 seems frankly a rather high price to pay for this atlas.

The paperback edition, at $9.95, is really not a bargain either; it costs considerably more than the identical Random House edition, which retails for only $4.95.

For full information about the cartography and other features of the *Bartholomew Mini World Atlas*, consult the review of THE RANDOM HOUSE MINI WORLD ATLAS on pages 214–15.

Britannica Atlas

Facts at a Glance

Full Title: **Britannica Atlas.**
Publisher: Encyclopaedia Britannica.
Copyright: 1988.
Edition Reviewed: 1988.

Number of Pages: 568.
Number of Maps: 301.
Number of Indexes: 1.
Number of Index Entries: 160,000.
Trim Size: 11″ × 14¾″.
Binding: cloth.

Price: $79.50.
Sold door-to-door, by direct mail, and in combination with NEW ENCYCLOPAEDIA BRITANNICA.
ISBN 0-85229-495-6.
Revised every two years.

I. Introduction

The *Britannica Atlas* is a large-size (11″ × 14¾″) general world atlas that was compiled and published in a joint effort with Rand McNally. The contents of this atlas, except for slight variations in the foreword, are taken directly from THE NEW INTERNATIONAL ATLAS, published by Rand McNally.

The maps were compiled by the cartographic firms of Rand McNally & Co. (Chicago), Mondadori-McNally GmbH (Stuttgart), Cartographia (Budapest), Esselte Map Service (Stockholm), George Philip & Son Limited (London), and Teikoku-Shoin Co., Ltd. (Tokyo), under the direction of an eight-member International Planning Conference, and assisted by a team of map advisers and contributors from academic and government institutions. The maps for the "World Scene" section were designed by David L. Burke with the help of a team of contributors from American universities.

II. Format

The *Britannica Atlas* is arranged in six distinct sections: introductory material (contents, index maps, and legend); general reference maps; world thematic maps ("World Scene"); lists of geographic terms and name changes; statistical information; and an index to place-names. The general reference maps occupy nearly 300 pages; the index is 200 pages long.

Almost all of the maps spread across both open pages. Because the pages lie flat without breaking the spine, no information is lost in the gutter.

On maps of the oceans and continents, the colors used correspond to broad ecosystem types such as tundra, grassland, or desert. The regional maps at 1:3,000,000 and 1:6,000,000 use colors to show elevation with hypsometric tints. The regional maps at 1:12,000,000 and 1:1,000,000 show international boundaries with colors, as well as internal political boundaries.

III. Special Features

The main special feature of this atlas is its cosmopolitan quality. The foreword and other text is in five languages: English, German, Spanish, French, and Portuguese. The local spellings of place-names are used on the maps. For names in nonroman alphabets, an internationally accepted transliteration is used. This is a generally sound practice but may cause some confusion for American users. Transliterations for place-names in the Soviet Union in particular will look odd to most Americans. In the case of extremely unfamiliar local names of prominent cities and natural features, English translation is provided.

A glossary, arranged alphabetically by local spelling of place-names, follows the map section. Each term is translated in each of the five languages.

Following the glossary are tables showing place-name changes since 1969; area and population data for continents, countries, and administrative subdivisions; and the population of cities and towns. The international effort is clearly evident, as every country and its capital city are listed, as well as all urban centers with 50,000 or more inhabitants.

The "World Scene" section contains double-page world maps showing 24 subjects related to cultural and physical geography. Among the topics covered in these thematic maps are population, religions, languages, agricultural regions, minerals, energy production and consumption, time zones, climate regions, and natural vegetation. Tables, graphs, and inset maps help describe each subject. This section of world thematic maps is much more extensive and detailed than comparable sections in other atlases.

The index is quite helpful. In addition to listing the page and location of each place-name, it uses symbols to indicate the type of feature (political unit, mountain, swamp, island, and so forth) associated with all names other than populated places.

An especially useful feature is the listing of adjoining map page numbers in the borders of each regional map.

IV. Geographical Balance

The collaborative efforts of an international team of distinguished cartographers, and the cartographic capabilities of respected mapmaking concerns in five countries, have helped ensure that the *Britannica Atlas* is the most balanced atlas on the market today. There is no evident bias toward any region or nation as there is in most U.S., Canadian, and British atlases of otherwise high quality. All areas of the earth receive adequate coverage, with an appropriate level of detail.

V. Scale and Projections

In an effort to provide valid area comparisons of world regions, consistent map scales have been used throughout this atlas. Maps of the oceans are at a scale of 1:48,000,000; continents are shown at 1:24,000,000; and regions are at 1:12,000,000.

Most inhabited areas of the world are mapped at either 1:6,000,000 (for less populous areas such as South America, Africa, and Australia) or 1:3,000,000 (for more populous areas such as Anglo-America, Europe, and parts of Asia). Regions with high population or significant economic activity are shown again at 1:1,000,000, and selected metropolitan areas at 1:300,000.

On all maps, scales are given as ratios and also shown in bar scales (in both kilometers and statute miles).

VI. Accuracy

The *Britannica Atlas* is noted for its precision and accuracy. The 1986 edition had two minor but noteworthy blemishes. The first of these concerned the placement of the nonexistent town of Wansbeck in the north of England. This "town" appeared on both the British Isles map and on the more detailed Dublin-Manchester-Newcastle upon Tyne map, both of which were compiled by the highly respected firm of George Philip & Son. The error has been corrected in the 1988 edition, and Wansbeck, like Brigadoon, has vanished into the mists from whence it came.

The detailed map of the Ukraine now shows Chernobyl. For unknown reasons, this fairly large town had not appeared in previous editions of the *Britannica Atlas*.

Place-names are given in the vernacular. For major cities such as Wien, München, Milano, and Gor'kij, the common English-language name is printed in smaller type immediately beneath or beside the local name label.

Names of cities, towns, rivers, mountains, and other specific political and physical features are printed in their appropriate locations. Even in densely populated areas, it is easy to determine which name is associated with which point. This virtue is especially welcome here, as most of the maps in the *Britannica Atlas* are exceptionally detailed.

The positioning of lettering for physical area names indicates their actual extent and location. Offshore boundaries and territorial demarcation lines are also shown clearly and precisely, and disputed areas are indicated as such. The map of Northern India and Pakistan labels four disputed areas, and annotations name the parties involved and the nature of the disputes.

The editors and contributors have done a remarkable job of ensuring that the statistical tables and thematic maps that appear in this volume are accurate as well as comprehensive.

VII. Currency

The *Britannica Atlas* is one of the few atlases to undergo annual revision, and as a result is remarkably up-to-date. The population figures in the "World Information" table are Rand McNally estimates for January 1, 1988, and are based on "official data, United Nations estimates, and other available information."

The comprehensive revision policy is also evidenced in the maps themselves. For example, a comparison of the 1988 and 1986 editions shows that the cartographer has taken note of urban population changes, upgrading the symbol used for some towns and cities to reflect increased or decreased populations. New place-names have been added to the maps, presumably representing towns whose growth in recent years now merits placement in an international atlas.

VIII. Legibility

Typefaces on the maps are neat and legible, although some users may have difficulty reading the 3-point type used for some small towns and natural features. Place-name categories are easily differentiated by typeface and are explained extensively in the legend. On the maps, land areas are shown in a fairly dark tint, while bodies of water are in shades of blue. Though shaded relief is used extensively, this does not interfere with legibility. Name labels are well placed, and it is easy to identify the features to which they refer.

Political boundaries are pastel colored on the 1:12,000,000 scale maps and red on the other scale maps. One of the drawbacks of this atlas is that on the other scale maps, the province or state names are sometimes placed along the borders, sometimes in the center of the unit, and appear in either red or black type. This is quite confusing, as there is no explanation on the map pages and it is not adequately explained in the legend.

Different symbols are used to indicate the size of cities, and different sizes of type are used to indicate their economic and political importance. These are all readily distinguishable.

IX. Accessibility

To find the location of a place-name, the user can look in the index under its local language spelling or under the English equivalent name. For example, the location of Vienna, Austria, can be found by looking under "Vienna" or "Wien." Most place-names are indexed to the largest-scale map on which they appear.

Degrees of longitude and latitude, rather than the letter-number grid common to other atlases, are used to locate a place. Because the coordinates of each place are given in degrees and seconds in the index, places can be located much more accurately.

X. Summary

Despite its title and the fact that it is sold by Encyclopaedia Britannica, Inc., the *Britannica Atlas* has no direct connection with the NEW ENCYCLOPAEDIA BRITANNICA. Rather, it is a much lower-priced edition of THE NEW INTERNATIONAL ATLAS, published by Rand McNally.

Without question, the *Britannica Atlas* is among the most comprehensive and authoritative large-format world atlases on the market today, rivaling even THE TIMES ATLAS OF THE WORLD. It features excellent geographic balance, an extensive index, and up-to-date thematic maps. Its outstanding, highly detailed general maps present a wealth of information about every region of the globe.

The *Britannica Atlas*, which costs $79.50, would be the flagship atlas of any collection. That said, however, it should be noted that libraries that do not require so comprehensive or expensive an atlas might be just as well served by the NATIONAL GEOGRAPHIC ATLAS OF THE WORLD, THE PRENTICE-HALL NEW WORLD ATLAS, or RAND MCNALLY GOODE'S WORLD ATLAS.

Citation World Atlas

Facts at a Glance

Full Title: **Citation World Atlas.**
Publisher: Hammond.
Editors: Martin A. Bacheller, Editor-in-Chief, and the Hammond staff.
Copyright: 1988.
Edition Reviewed: 1986. (Statistics apply to 1988 edition.)

Number of Pages: 388.
Number of Maps: more than 400.

Number of Indexes: 1 master index, plus 400
    individual map indexes.
Number of Index Entries: 25,000.
Trim Size: 9½″ × 12½″.
Binding: cloth and paperback.

Price: $27.95 (cloth); $17.95 (paper). 15 percent
    discount to libraries.
Sold in bookstores and directly to libraries.
ISBN 0-8437-1258-9 (cloth);
ISBN 0-8437-1253-8 paperback.
Revised annually or twice a year as necessary.

I. Introduction

The Hammond *Citation World Atlas* is a general-reference world atlas. This 388-page volume, featuring more than 400 maps, was edited by the Hammond staff, with an advisory board composed of 13 notable specialists in geography and related fields. The selected list of source materials includes the best available government documents for statistics and place-names, although with a heavy bias toward United States sources. For this edition, Hammond has used new typography and has also added elevation shading to the political maps. Thus, the political maps now incorporate some of the features of physical maps. The *Citation World Atlas* was formerly also available in a deluxe leather binding under the title *Diplomat World Atlas*, and in a washable hardcover binding as *New Horizon World Atlas*. As of April 1, 1988, these titles were no longer in print, and Hammond had announced no plans for reissuing them.

II. Format

Physically, the atlas will hold up well. The sturdy hardcover binding holds the pages firmly and does not crack with repeated use. The paperbound edition of the *Citation* was not examined by reviewers.

The maps in this volume are divided into nine geographic sections: World and Polar Regions, Europe, Asia, Pacific Ocean and Australia, Africa, South America, North America, Canada, and the United States. The largest-scale map for every continent, region, country, province, or state is a political map, followed by smaller-scale thematic maps depicting such topics as population distribution and climate. A physical map is also provided for each region.

Most maps fit on one full page or less. Some maps extend to a second page, but this does not pose a problem, as the contents do not run into the gutter and the pages lie flat when the book is opened. The size of the atlas is ideal for library collections.

Map legends, which appear under the title of each political map, provide bar scales in miles and kilometers and the scale as a fractional representation, but only a few of the symbols that are found on the maps. Symbols used on the political maps (including those for rivers, mountain peaks, marshlands, urban areas, and cities other than capitals) are not described anywhere in the atlas. Although experienced map users will not find this omission a drawback, anyone unfamiliar with the conventions of cartography will require some assistance in interpreting the maps. For example, on the map of Central Africa, users may not be able to identify the unexplained symbol for swamps that is used along the Congo-Zaire border or, on the map of Southern Africa, the dots spread along the southern coast of Namibia. Knowledgeable readers may correctly assume that these dots represent the desert but will be left to wonder why the name Namib Desert extends well beyond the dots along the entire coast.

Each thematic map is accompanied by its own legend, which adequately explains the meaning of the colors and symbols employed.

III. Special Features

The *Citation World Atlas* now features 24 pages of model maps. These new maps use color and relief effects to give the continents and the ocean floor a three-dimensional appearance. The world model map section helps make this edition of the *Citation* more competitive with such works as Britannica Atlas, The New York Times Atlas of the World, and The Reader's Digest Wide World Atlas, all of which include a special section of similar model maps.

Each political map in the *Citation World Atlas* is accompanied by a brief fact table listing the area, population, largest city, and highest and lowest points for every continent. The same information is provided for individual nations, in addition to their capital cities, monetary units, major languages, and major religions. Additional data are provided for the United States. A color illustration of the country's national flag adjoins each fact list. Population figures appear in each political map's list of place-names, as do ZIP codes for U.S. cities. These features will be useful for ready reference.

A two-page introduction clearly explains the scope, organization, and use of the atlas but fails to provide an adequate guide to map reading. In the section entitled "Indexes—Pinpointing a Location," the text and two illustrations are particularly misleading and confusing.

Seven pages of special features appear at the end of the atlas. Airline distances are provided in five separate tables. Two pages of world statistical tables offer useful data on the solar system, the earth, continents, oceans, canals, islands, mountains, rivers, and natural lakes. An illustrated article on map projections by the noted cartographer Erwin Raisz completes the atlas and adds a noteworthy dimension to the work. True geographic awareness requires knowledge of the uses and limitations of map projections. This three-page article is a good, authoritative introduction to the subject. For librarians, these pages of special features are clearly organized for ready-reference work.

IV. Geographical Balance

The *Citation World Atlas* includes maps of all nations, although half of the volume is devoted to the United States and Canada. Canada is covered in 26 pages, for example, and the entire continent of Africa in only 18. Not a single African country is given an individual map. Countries on other continents appear in groups, pairs, or individually. The introduction explains that several nations are shown on a single map if "they are of lesser relative importance" as separate entities. As examples, the following four areas are listed with their largest-scale maps: Ohio (1:1,800,000), Denmark (1:2,300,000), Argentina (1:13,000,000), and Western Africa (1:15,200,000). Geographic imbalance limits the usefulness of the *Citation*, as a world atlas should serve as a primary source of information on those areas least familiar to the user.

V. Scale and Projections

A variety of scales are employed in the *Citation World Atlas* depending on the nation or area depicted. The choice of scales reflects the editors' appraisal of a given area's relative importance, a judgment that may not always coincide with the specific needs of the reader.

The name of the map projection used for each political map appears with the map's title. The projections are the most common ones used to depict areas of the size and shape under consideration. Southeast Asia, for example, is shown on an azimuthal equal-area projection. Smaller areas, such as Scandinavia and the Indian subcontinent, use a conic projection, while many individual countries are shown on the Mercator projection. These projections ensure that the shapes and sizes of continents, countries, and states will be familiar to nonspecialists.

VI. Accuracy

Place-names appear in the local official spellings— a sound practice that conforms to international cartographic trends—with the exception of major names, which follow conventional anglicized spellings. According to the introduction, the complete form of a place-name can be found in the index when there is not sufficient space on the map itself. Likewise, alternate names or spellings of a place appear only in the index, not on the maps. This system can present problems to the reader who consults a map without looking at the index. For example, on the map of Germany, the two German nations are labeled only *West Germany* and *East Germany*. The map nowhere identifies the two by their respective official names, *Federal Republic of Germany* and *German Democratic Republic*. In the maps of China, *Peking* is given preference over *Beijing*, although the majority of names are spelled according to the official Pinyin system.

The placement of names on the maps is accurate. Locations of physical features, such as mountain ranges, are clear when they are labeled, although the physical maps fail to add a generic description to names of physical features. El Djouf, for example, is identified as a desert only in the index, not on the map itself.

VII. Currency

With a few exceptions, most of the *Citation*'s data are as current as its 1988 copyright date. The nation of Brunei is not described as a member of the United Nations, even though it joined the UN in 1984. The Byelorussian SSR is not listed in the gazetteer-index of "grand divisions" and countries, although it is a member of the UN, as is the Ukrainian SSR, which does appear on the list. Changes rendered to the flags of Egypt, Haiti, and St. Vincent prior to or during 1986 are not reflected in the atlas.

VIII. Legibility

Typefaces used on the maps are neat and legible. Place-name categories are clearly differentiated by typefaces, although these categories are not delineated in the legend. Individual maps of the U.S. states (each on one or two pages) have the greatest number and density of place-names, but towns and geographic features are easy to locate. The use of different colors to highlight international and internal boundary lines is an immense help to the reader. In fact, it is the generous and clear use of color that makes this atlas especially suitable for the general reader.

IX. Accessibility

Individual political maps are accompanied by an index of place-names that appear on their pages together with a key to each map's local grid system. Although inset maps of urban areas do not appear in the table of contents, they are included in the individual indexes, but at the expense of their locations on the primary political maps. For example, the index for the map of India refers the reader only to the inset map of Bombay. To find Bombay's location within the country as a whole, the reader must scan the map of India.

A complete index of place-names is found at the end of the volume. This 25,000-item master index cites the larger political division for each entry, with the page number for the largest-scale map on which the place appears. A reader must then turn to the map's individual index (which is not always on the same page as the map) to obtain the precise location. Latitudes and longitudes are not given.

A major fault with this "complete" index is the practice of citing only one map for each place-name, even when the name appears on several maps. Furthermore, four large-scale maps of U.S. cities that appear at the end of the U.S. section are not listed in either individual indexes or the complete index. This incomplete and often cumbersome indexing system limits access to the *Citation World Atlas* and will doubtless prove frustrating not only to the beginning but also to the experienced atlas user.

X. Summary

The *Citation World Atlas* is available in a cloth edition at $27.95 and in paperback at $17.95. These prices are fairly reasonable, given the generous size of the book. However, prospective purchasers should be aware of some major limitations. For one thing, the United States and Canada receive disproportionate coverage. For another, the indexing system hinders accessibility.

This atlas is useful for readers seeking information about political geography. Moreover, now that physical shading has been added to the political maps, and a 24-page section of physical model maps added to the book, the *Citation* also provides more information about physical geography than did previous editions of this title. While the cartography may still be less sophisticated than that found in such comparably priced and sized atlases as RAND MCNALLY GOODE'S WORLD ATLAS and THE PRENTICE-HALL NEW WORLD ATLAS, the *Citation* is an impressive volume.

Concise Earthbook

Facts at a Glance

Full Title: **Concise Earthbook.**
Publisher: Graphic Learning International.
Copyright: 1987 by Esselte Map Service AB, Stockholm.
Edition Reviewed: first edition, 1987.

Number of Pages: 215.
Number of Maps: 70.
Number of Indexes: 1.
Number of Index Entries: 20,000.

Trim Size: 5¼″ × 7¼″.
Binding: cloth.

Price: $12.95.
Sold in stores; also sold to libraries and other educational institutions.
ISBN 0-87746-101-5.
No revision policy.

I. Introduction

The *Concise Earthbook* world atlas is a 215-page, small-format general world atlas that serves as a portable ready-reference source of geographic information. It has 70 color maps, a 48-page statistical section, and a 78-page index. Produced by the well-known Esselte Map Service of Sweden, the American edition is published by Graphic Learning International of Boulder, Colorado. The cartography is similar to that in the larger EARTHBOOK published by the same firm. James E. Davis and Sharryl Davis Hawke are credited as consultants for this edition.

II. Format

Most of the maps in the *Concise Earthbook* are physical, with shading to indicate relief and coloring to indicate the types of land cover, such as tundra, sand desert, or cultivated land. The maps spread over both open pages. The tightly sewn binding prevents the pages from lying flat when opened, but loss of information in the gutter is minimal.

The maps are arranged by continent in a west-to-east, north-to-south order, starting with North America and ending with Australasia. Each continent section begins with a physical map of the continent accompanied by flags of the countries included, then covers the continent in west-to-east, north-to-south order, from the northwest corner to the southeast. Following these are maps of the polar regions, world thematic maps, a section of continent and country statistics, and finally the index.

The maps are preceded by a master legend (called "Reader Information"), which includes a sample map with annotations explaining the meaning of selected symbols and abbreviations, and a table of explanations of symbols and colors used on the maps.

The maps themselves do not include legends. Most of them do include the scale expressed as a representational fraction and a bar scale, but others lack any indication of scale.

III. Special Features

Inside the front cover is a world political map, accompanied by a list of countries and the page numbers on which their map coverage can be found. The countries on each continent map are keyed numerically to flags in the margin, as well as to their location in the statistical section. The maps that include a bar scale also feature an airplane symbol indicating the distance covered by "modern passenger aircraft" in one hour or a half hour.

One feature not found in any other atlas allows the user to compare the latitudes of cities on any map with cities in other parts of the world whose names are printed at their appropriate latitudes in the right-hand margin. Thus, for example, a user looking at the map of North America can see at a glance that Rome is at approximately the same latitude as New York. This feature helps the reader put the rest of the world in perspective. However, only a limited number of off-map names are used, and they are not used consistently. Incidentally, *Ottawa* is frequently misprinted in these marginal notes as *Ottava*.

The section of world thematic maps includes a political, a physical, and a time zone map, in addition to a map showing the location of 21 animals "on the edge of extinction."

The statistical section includes basic statistics (including area, population, population density, and physical feature notes) for each continent. The section also reports the following information for each country: the official name, area, population, annual population growth, life expectancy, literacy rate, capital city with population, other important cities with population, language, religion, and currency. A brief thumbnail description is also included for each.

Inside the back cover is another copy of the world time zone map, accompanied by a table of international telephone dialing codes and toll-free numbers for airlines. Given the volatility of the airline industry, however, this latter information is apt to become out of date quickly.

IV. Geographical Balance

This atlas gives adequate representation to all populated regions of the world. While there is no marked North American or European bias, it is unfortunate that the populous areas of eastern and southern Asia are shown at a scale smaller than that accorded to the populous areas of Europe and the United States. Maps of this small scale cannot comfortably accommodate the number of place-names that this region warrants.

V. Scale and Projections

The map scales are reasonable for the areas represented on the maps and for the page size. For the most part they were well chosen and are consistent for each continent. The notable exception is for the coverage of eastern and southern Asia already mentioned.

Europe and the Middle East are shown at a scale of 1:10,000,000; North America is at 1:13,500,000; South America, Asia, Africa, and Australasia at 1:20,000,000; and the polar regions at 1:60,000,000. The world maps are at 1:180,000,000 and the continent maps are at 1:50,000,000, with the exceptions of Europe at 1:30,000,000 and Asia at 1:75,000,000.

The types of map projections are not indicated, except on the political and time zone maps of the world, and on the South American continent map. Despite this inconsistency, the projections used are appropriate. These maps appear to be on the same projections as those in the full-size EARTHBOOK, which identifies them as the Miller bipolar and the Lambert azimuthal equal-area projections.

VI. Accuracy

The inaccuracies in this atlas are numerous and detract significantly from its usefulness. There are word misspellings, for example (such as *Ottava* for *Ottawa*, as already noted), and dot symbols indicating the location of populated places without an adjacent name label. The names of some physical areas do not accurately indicate their extent, a problem compounded by use of the same type style for physical names and political subunits, and because no explanation is offered in the legend.

The choice of place-names, at least for the United States, is questionable. For example, the town of Champaign-Urbana, Illinois (pop. 100,000) does not appear on the largest-scale maps, while smaller Illinois towns such as Anna (pop. 5,400) and Taylorville (pop. 11,000) do.

In the master legend, six sizes of type and five different symbols are listed for populated places. The symbol for the smallest population category is not used on the maps, however.

These inaccuracies do not appear in the full-size edition, in part because of the larger scale of the maps.

Local spellings are used on the maps for foreign names, with popular, anglicized names in parentheses. The indexing of these names is inconsistent, though. *Cairo* is in the index, even though it is in parentheses beneath *Al Qahirah*. *Aden* is not in the index; its local spelling *Baladiyat Adan* is the only index listing. *Jerusalem* is in the index, but its reference is to a 1:20,000,000-scale map of the Nile Valley and Arabia, while the reference for the city's local name, *Yerushalayim*, is to the 1:10,000,000-scale map of the Middle East.

VII. Currency

In general, the information in this atlas is as up-to-date as its copyright date. It includes recent boundary and place-name changes, including the 1986 boundary claims of Libya. The only bit of out-of-date information is the inclusion of the American bison in the "animals on the edge of extinction" map.

VIII. Legibility

The typefaces on the maps are legible, with the exception of the smallest population category names on the large-scale maps. These are too small and faint to be easily deciphered, particularly when superimposed over relief shading.

Only two styles of type are used: one for populated places and another for all other place-names. These two type styles are quite similar, and differentiating between types of place-names is difficult, particularly where many names are close together.

On the positive side, rivers, roads, railroads, borders, and natural features are clearly distinguishable. Also, the colors used for land cover types are in register and give the maps a high-quality appearance.

IX. Accessibility

The index in this atlas is extensive. Place-names are located by alphanumeric grid coordinates which are integrated into the latitude-longitude grid on the maps. Most of the inset maps have separate grid coordinates, and the names included in them are accurately indexed.

There are many discrepancies and inaccuracies in the index, however, in addition to the ones already mentioned. Names are missing, for example, such as *Manila* and other cities in the Philippines. The Soviet Union cannot be found under any of its common names (*USSR, Russia,* or *Soviet Union*).

There are inaccuracies on the contents page also. French Guiana is not listed at all, for example. Panama is listed with other South American countries but is included in the North American section of flags and statistics. Again, these inaccuracies do not appear in the full-size edition.

X. Summary

Priced at $12.95, the *Concise Earthbook* is fairly expensive for its size and on balance is not as consistent as the RANDOM HOUSE CONCISE WORLD ATLAS, which contains similar features and larger-scale, better-detailed maps. However, libraries may find that the CONCISE EARTHBOOK will serve well as a circulating atlas.

Earthbook

Facts at a Glance

Full Title: **Earthbook.**
Publisher: Graphic Learning International.

Copyright: 1987 by Esselte Map Service AB, Stockholm.
Edition Reviewed: first edition, 1987.

Number of Pages: 327.
Number of Maps: 185.
Number of Indexes: 1.
Number of Index Entries: 46,000.
Number of Illustrations: 240, color.
Trim Size: 10″ × 13¼″.
Binding: cloth.

Price: $65.50.
Sold in stores and directly to schools and libraries.
ISBN 0-87746-100-7.
No revision policy.

I. Introduction

Earthbook is a general world reference atlas that includes a 96-page encyclopedic section on earth science. The book is designed to be more than simply a collection of maps; part of its purpose, in the publisher's words, is to raise its users' "geographic consciousness."

The publisher claims, not without cause, that "the environmental maps in this atlas bring the representation of the Earth's surface much closer to reality" and that the "new form of cartography" used in this volume "represents the surface of the Earth at a level of detail never achieved before in an atlas of this kind."

Earthbook's text and cartography were prepared by the well-known Esselte Map Service of Stockholm, Sweden. Base material for the large-scale United States maps was supplied by the U.S. Geological Survey. The atlas was printed in Sweden and published by Graphic Learning International in Boulder, Colorado.

II. Format

Earthbook is divided into three distinct sections of approximately equal length: "The Encyclopedia of the Earth," "The World in Maps," and the glossary and index. The encyclopedic section is discussed in part III here, while the index is evaluated in part IX.

The atlas's maps are contained in the "World in Maps" section, which is about 120 pages long. Instead of the hypsometric tints that many atlases use to show elevation, the physical maps in *Earthbook* use color to indicate the type of environment, with plastic relief effects showing elevation. Thus, for example, deserts are represented by tan, forests by green, and arable land by yellow. A master legend at the beginning of "The World in Maps" explains all the environments that are represented, with photographs and locator maps enhancing these explanations. A comprehensive key that includes all the symbols used on the maps appears on the endpapers. The maps themselves do not contain legends, but most do have a bar scale and/or a representative fraction scale. Some maps, however, lack scale statements and even titles.

Earthbook is small enough for users to handle easily but large enough to provide large-scale maps covering broad areas. The book itself is well made. The sewn binding is loose enough to let the atlas lie flat when opened but strong enough to stand up to heavy use. The two halves of two-page spread maps join accurately, and no information is lost in the gutter.

III. Special Features

The main special feature of this atlas is the 96-page section of reference material called "Encyclopedia of the Earth." It is divided into four sections: air, water, earth, and fire. These correspond to the four classical elements, as identified by the ancient Greeks. Each section begins with a basic description of the element, then discusses its dynamics and interactions, and ends with a description of man's impact on and use of it. The text, photographs, and illustrations are well done and do a wonderful job of describing the current state of the planet.

There is a special section of thematic maps for each continent which includes, in addition to a general map, maps showing political divisions, population distribution, relief, rainfall and ocean currents, temperature and winds, climate, soils, organic (agricultural) production, and inorganic (energy and mineral resources) production.

The bar scales on the general continent maps feature an airplane symbol and a time unit (e.g., one hour). Unfortunately this is not explained. The same symbol is used in the CONCISE EARTHBOOK, where the legend explains that it indicates the distance covered by "modern passenger aircraft" in the time unit specified.

There is also a section of thematic maps of the world, which includes maps on the themes of environment types, climate, oceans, population, political divisions, energy, and ethnology.

IV. Geographical Balance

Although its cartography is Swedish, *Earthbook* was designed specifically for sale in the United States and has a marked bias toward this country. The United States maps are the largest-scale maps in the atlas. They are prominently listed first in the contents and

have a separate legend of symbols and colors inside the back cover.

Adequate representation is given to the rest of the world; the extensive coverage given to the United States is not at the expense of other regions. It is unfortunate, however, that the populous areas of Asia are not shown at the same scale as the populous areas of Europe.

V. Scale and Projections

In general, the map scales and projections used were well chosen for the size of areas represented in relation to the page size. All areas of the world are shown at the consistent scale of 1:10,000,000, with the exceptions of the polar regions, which are shown at 1:30,000,000, and Oceania, which is shown at 1:27,000,000. Europe and the Middle East are shown again at the larger scale of 1:5,000,000 and the United States is shown again at 1:3,000,000.

Each continent is shown on a two-page spread at a scale of 1:25,000,000, with the exception of Europe, which is at 1:15,000,000. The largest-scale map of the world is at a scale of 1:90,000,000; the smallest scale is 1:220,000,000.

Map projections are identified only on the general continent maps. The projections used are Miller's bipolar for North and South America, Miller's stereographic for Africa, Lambert's conformal conic for Europe, Lambert's azimuthal equal-area for Asia and Australasia, Mercator for Oceania and the small-scale world maps, azimuthal equidistant for the polar regions, and Van der Grinten for the large-scale world maps. These projections are appropriately chosen, as they are the same as or similar to those used for the same areas by other atlas producers.

There are a few unfortunate cases of inappropriate scale choice. The coverage of the populous areas of Asia already mentioned should be at 1:5,000,000 for comparability to the Europe maps. Oceania is shown at 1:27,000,000 to make it fit on the page, compromising the amount of detail that could be shown. The largest-scale coverage of New Zealand is on a 1:10,000,000-scale map which also includes the southeastern portion of Australia and a lot of empty space (in the form of the Tasman Sea). The only incidence of misleading distortion caused by the use of the "wrong" projection is on a world physical map depicting the ocean floor, which uses the Mercator projection.

VI. Accuracy

Generally, the information in this atlas is accurate. Place-names are spelled correctly and consistently and are positioned accurately.

There are discrepancies concerning "local" and "generic" names, however. For countries, the generic name is listed first, with the local name below it in parentheses, while for cities, the local name is first and the generic name is in parentheses.

It is unfortunate that political unit names are sometimes shown with compact letter spacing and other times with expanded spacing. The names of physical features are also shown with expanded lettering and use the same type style, making it hard to differentiate between political and physical names.

Other inaccuracies include the listing of Panama in the contents as a South American country rather than a Central American country; the presence on the 1:3,000,000-scale map of California of a permanent lake in Death Valley National Monument, rather than the dry lake bed that actually exists there; and the presence of what appears to be a strip of prairie west of St. Louis on the 1:10,000,000-scale map of the United States. This prairie, which does not actually exist, does not appear on the 1:3,000,000-scale map of the area.

VII. Currency

The information in this atlas is as up-to-date as its copyright date. Recent boundary and place-name changes are included, such as the 1986 boundary claims of Libya, and Panama's joint ownership of the Panama Canal. The publisher claims that *Earthbook*'s maps are more current than all of the competition."

The text, illustrations, and photographs in the "Encyclopedia of the Earth" section are up-to-date and contemporary. Nothing in this atlas gives it a dated appearance.

VIII. Legibility

In general, the typefaces on the maps are legible. The exception is the names for the smallest population category on all large-scale maps other than the 1:3,000,000-scale United States maps. The type used for these names is too small and faint, particularly when superimposed over relief shading.

While many sizes of type are used, there are only two styles of type—one for populated places and another for all other names. As already mentioned, the same style is used for both political and physical names, making it difficult to differentiate between the two. Similarly, some of the colors used to depict types of environment are quite similar, making it hard to differentiate between them.

On the positive side, rivers, roads, railroads, and borders are clearly distinguishable. Also, the use of color to depict types of environment gives a much higher quality appearance to the maps than do the traditional hypsometric tints, which show the low-lying Sahara desert in green.

IX. Accessibility

The index in this atlas is extensive and includes all names on the maps. Place-names are located by alphanumeric grid coordinates, which are integrated into the latitude-longitude grid on the maps. Most of the inset maps have separate grid coordinates, and the names on them are accurately indexed. Both "generic" and "local" name spellings are listed in the index, but they are listed separately, with no cross-referencing.

Unfortunately, there are discrepancies and inaccuracies in the index. Names of U.S. cities are identified by state, but foreign cities are not followed by the name of the country in which they are located. There is also no note indicating what type of feature the names correspond to. The result is that the same name appears in the index two or more times, forcing the user to peruse the list in order to locate the right one. This happens on almost every index page.

Another problem with accessibility is that the grid boundaries on the large-scale Europe maps are quite large, so that the user has an 8- to 14-square-inch area in which to search for the name. For most of Europe, quite a few names are packed into each grid square.

X. Summary

At $65.50, *Earthbook* is more expensive than such comparable volumes as THE GREAT WORLD ATLAS, THE NEW YORK TIMES ATLAS OF THE WORLD, and THE PRENTICE-HALL UNIVERSAL ATLAS. However, despite its flaws, *Earthbook*—the newest atlas on the U.S. market—is impressive and should find a place in many libraries. Its most distinctive features are its extensive, well-organized, clearly written, and generously illustrated "Encyclopedia of the Earth" section and its maps, which show not only where places are located but what the actual environment is like.

Gold Medallion World Atlas

Facts at a Glance

Full Title: **Gold Medallion World Atlas.**
Publisher: Hammond.
Editors: Martin A. Bacheller, Editor-in-Chief, and the Hammond staff.
Copyright: 1986.
Edition Reviewed: 1986. (Statistics apply to 1987 edition.)

Number of Pages: 660.
Number of Maps: 652.
Number of Indexes: 1 master index, plus individual same-page indexes accompanying all map areas.

Number of Index Entries: 100,000 in master index; 48,000 in same-page indexes.
Trim Size: 9¼″ × 12½″.
Binding: leather (hardcover).

Price: $75.00.
ISBN 0-8437-1248-1.
Sold directly to libraries and educational institutions; not sold to the general public.
Revised annually.

I. Introduction

The *Gold Medallion World Atlas* is the largest and most expensive of the several world atlases published by Hammond. As such, it draws on the same stock of maps that make up the AMBASSADOR, CITATION, and other Hammond world atlases reviewed in this Buying Guide. Unlike those atlases, however, this volume is sold only to the library and educational markets; it is not sold to individuals.

II. Format

Page for page, the first 484 pages of this 660-page atlas are identical to the same pages in the Hammond AMBASSADOR WORLD ATLAS and CITATION WORLD ATLAS. These pages are made up of contemporary political, physical, and thematic maps (with same-page indexes accompanying the political maps) and a master index which also includes statistical tables. (For full information about these maps and indexes, consult the review of the CITATION WORLD ATLAS on pages 169–72.)

The remainder of the *Gold Medallion World Atlas* is occupied by four supplementary sections: a 12-page encyclopedic feature entitled "Environment and Life," a 48-page "Atlas of the Bible Lands," a 48-page "World History Atlas," and a 62-page "United States History Atlas." These last three sections are in fact separate Hammond books that have been added to this volume.

The leather binding is handsome and sturdy. The pages are sewn into the spine. However, on two-page spreads, facing halves of a map do not always meet accurately, and on some pages information seems to have been lost in the gutter area. The atlas is thumb-indexed, and the pages are gilt-edged.

III. Special Features

The 12-page "Environment and Life" encyclopedic section focuses on the interrelation of living things and their surroundings, man's impact on the environment, and the consequences of pollution. However, this section is by no means comprehensive, and

it does not begin to match similar sections in EARTH-BOOK, THE PRENTICE-HALL UNIVERSAL ATLAS, and other large-format atlases.

The "Atlas of the Bible Lands" contains 27 maps retracing events described in the Old and New Testaments, six reference maps, and a gazetteer-index. The "World History Atlas" has 93 maps depicting events from 3000 B.C. to A.D. 1980, two physical maps of Europe, and a population distribution map of the world. The "United States History Atlas" contains 64 maps covering events from the voyages of discovery to the 1984 presidential election, a list of presidents, and a two-page index. At least seven of the maps in this section are duplicated in the world history section.

These supplemental atlases provide a wealth of additional historical-geographical information under one cover, and they obviate the need for consulting separate historical atlases for this information. However, they do not necessarily make the *Gold Medallion* a better atlas, but only one that contains more features than the AMBASSADOR.

IV. Geographical Balance

As with the AMBASSADOR WORLD ATLAS, the geographic coverage in this atlas runs clockwise around the world, starting with Europe and moving to Asia, Australasia, Africa, South America, and North America. These regions are followed by large-scale maps of Canada and the United States. The arrangement of countries within each continental section generally runs west to east or north to south, depending on the shape of the continent. Canadian provinces are arranged east to west, south to north, and the U.S. states are arranged alphabetically.

There is a noticeable bias toward the United States, which receives disproportionate coverage at the expense of the rest of the world. Africa, for example, is treated in only four maps, and not a single African country is given its own map. European and Asian countries are mapped individually, in pairs, or in groups. South American countries and Australian states get better treatment, as most are shown on separate maps. Note also that the maps of U.S. and Canadian states and provinces are more detailed (because they are drawn to a larger scale) than those of countries outside North America.

V. Scale and Projections

The scale and projection of most political maps is stated in the title box for each map. The scale is expressed as a bar in both miles and kilometers, as well as a ratio. A bar scale accompanies each topography map, inset map, and vegetation/relief map. In the thematic atlas sections, scale is expressed as a bar scale on most maps.

For European countries, the map scales range from 1:1,140,000 to 1:6,150,000, with the average scale at 1:3,200,000. For Asia, the range is 1:1,325,000 to 1:19,100,000; the average is 1:10,000,000. For Africa, the range is 1:13,800,000 to 1:15,200,000; the average is 1:14,450,000. For South America, the range is 1:3,650,000 to 1:14,700,000; the average is 1:7,650,000. For Australian provinces, the range is 1:3,000,000 to 1:14,100,000; the average is 1:9,310,000. For Canadian provinces, the range is 1:1,900,000 to 1:8,550,000 (excluding the Northwest Territories); the average is 1:4,050,000. For U.S. states, the range is 1:610,000 to 1:4,400,000 (excluding Alaska); and the average is 1:2,110,000. In the U.S. section, every map has a different scale; therefore, size and distance comparisons cannot be made from map to map.

VI. Accuracy

The locations and extent of physical features, large and small, are clear on the topography maps. However, it is difficult to determine the extent of large physical features such as deserts and mountain ranges on the political maps. Although place-name labels show the general location of these physical features, no shading or other type of physical relief depiction is used.

The placement of cities and physical features such as lakes, rivers, and peaks on the political maps is fairly accurate. Inset maps of cities, populous regions, and islands accompany most political maps, and give an accurate portrayal of these areas.

VII. Currency

The copyright date of the 1986 edition is 1985, and the copyright date of the historical atlas supplements is 1984. The publisher claims that this volume is revised annually and sometimes twice a year. While this may be true for the maps, it does not seem to be so for the index. For example, while the African nation of Burkina Faso is so labeled on the maps, this name is not found in the index; instead, there the country goes under its former name of Upper Volta. Other political name changes—some made as long ago as 1981—have also not been recorded in the index to correspond with those changes on the maps. In the "Atlas of the Bible Lands," one of the photo captions refers to Transjordan, a term that is found nowhere in the text or on the maps and has not been used for that region since the 1960s.

Apart from these cases—minor quibbles, except where the index is concerned—the *Gold Medallion World Atlas* is sufficiently up-to-date.

VIII. Legibility

Typefaces on the maps are neat and legible. Place-name categories are clearly differentiated by type-faces but are nowhere explained, as the atlas lacks a master legend. The locations of specific towns are easily determined, except where there is a high density of place-names. Unfortunately, an empty circle resembling the letter *o* is used as the symbol for populated places. Names are placed directly to the left or right of this symbol, which sometimes blends in and appears to be part of the name.

Political boundary lines are highlighted in different colors, which is a great help in determining boundaries and identifying the nations that lie on either side of them.

IX. Accessibility

Each political map is accompanied by an index that not only lists all places on that map but also reports the population of each town. These indexes are quite handy and mean that the reader does not have to flip back and forth between a map and the master index.

Alphanumeric references in the indexes guide the user to latitude/longitude grid squares of four inches or less on the maps. However, references are sometimes made to inset maps, even though they have a different latitude/longitude grid. This makes it difficult to locate names in insets.

Metropolitan area maps of Washington, D.C., New York, Chicago, and Los Angeles follow the political maps, but these are not listed in the table of contents, nor are the names that appear on them indexed.

The master index appears after the political map section. Listings for each place-name include the political entity of which it is a part, the page number, and the alphanumeric grid reference. For U.S. cities, ZIP codes are also given.

The master index also reports variant spellings of names as well as alternate names. Names that appear on more than one map are indexed to all maps of their parent political and physical units. Note, however, that this master index does not contain entries for any of the three thematic map sections. One minor but annoying problem with the master index is that, for maps that spread over two pages, only left-hand page numbers are given, even for place-names which appear on the right-hand page.

The *Gold Medallion World Atlas* contains a comprehensive two-page table of contents that lists not only the different sections of the book but also all the maps in each section. This is one of the most thorough and useful tables of contents in any atlas reviewed in this Buying Guide.

X. Summary

The Hammond *Gold Medallion World Atlas* is the largest, most comprehensive atlas in the Hammond line, and it is sold only to libraries. Although billed as a "deluxe" volume, with a leather cover and gilt-edged pages, its political and topographical maps are identical to those found in Hammond's AMBASSADOR WORLD ATLAS. Its special historical maps have been picked up from other Hammond publications.

At $75.00, the *Gold Medallion World Atlas* is reasonably priced and is significantly less expensive than several other large-format titles, including THE TIMES ATLAS OF THE WORLD and THE NEW INTERNATIONAL ATLAS, both of which have fewer pages, although their contents are more sophisticated. On the other hand, the *Gold Medallion* is costlier than the popular NATIONAL GEOGRAPHIC ATLAS OF THE WORLD.

The major drawbacks of this atlas are its outdated master index and the inadequate coverage (both in scale and in number of maps) that it gives to the world outside North America. All those other large-scale maps give much more detailed coverage of these other areas. Moreover, because its contents duplicate those found in other Hammond titles, libraries that already have some of those titles may find that this volume is largely superfluous.

The Great World Atlas

Facts at a Glance

Full Title: **The Great World Atlas.**
Publisher: American Map Corporation.
Editor: Vera Benson, Director of Cartography, American Map Corporation, in cooperation with Kartographisches Institut Bertelsmann.
Copyright: 1986 by RV Reise- und Verkehrsverlag GmbH, Munich.
Edition Reviewed: first edition, 1986.

Number of Pages: 352.
Number of Maps: 182.
Number of Indexes: 1.
Number of Index Entries: 100,000.
Number of Illustrations: 55 color.
Trim Size: 10¼″ × 13¾″.
Binding: cloth.

Price: $39.95.
Sold in bookstores, by direct mail, and directly to libraries.
ISBN 0-8416-2001-6.
Revised periodically.

I. Introduction

The Great World Atlas, published in the United States by American Map Corporation, is a new (1986) large-format atlas. It is designed to "inform and instruct us about our world and how we have imposed our presence on it" by integrating traditional carto-graphic elements with modern satellite imagery. The cartography is by the respected Kartographisches Institut Bertelsmann of West Germany, and the book is printed in West Germany.

II. Format

Maps in *The Great World Atlas* are printed in either single pages or two-page spreads. A variety of formats is used; but physical maps, which number close to 70, predominate, compared to 123 physical maps in THE TIMES ATLAS OF THE WORLD. These are interspersed with almost 50 metropolitan area maps. Twenty-eight thematic maps depict political, geographic, economic, demographic, and cultural information. Fifteen pages of statistical maps and charts provide graphic and textual information on such topics as "Human Rights and Work" and "Mineral Resources and Energy."

The more traditional maps and charts are complemented by 16 single- and double-page satellite images of selected regions, accompanied by descriptive text. These images are intended to be used in conjunction with the maps; for instance, one compares the vegetation types in the Denver area image with a physical map of the same area that shows relief. Or, as the introduction suggests, by comparing the image with a climate map, the reader might better understand the reasons for the presence or absence of vegetation. The thematic maps (including climate maps), however, are on a continental or world scale, whereas the satellite images cover only a relatively small area (9,072 to 12,544 square miles).

This atlas has an attractive four-color jacket. Most readers will have no trouble handling this volume, though it is larger and considerably heavier than the average book. It is somewhat smaller than THE TIMES ATLAS OF THE WORLD. The heavy semiglossy pages are bound in a sturdy, attractive hardcover format which is both sewn and glued for durability. The book lies flat when open. Maps fit comfortably on the page; the page size allows a good deal of detail at a medium to small scale while enough area is shown to preserve context. Neat lines contain the maps except on the inner page edge of double-page maps, where unfortunately there is no inner margin to prevent some small loss of detail in the gutter.

The table of contents is arranged so that continent, page, area, and scale can be seen at a glance. The "Key to Map Coverage" outlines the section of the continent covered by each map, including page numbers of maps, inset maps, and satellite images. Scale is indicated by the color of the outline. This device is very useful for obtaining an overview of the extent of coverage of various areas.

There is a master legend employing 45 symbols, including various natural landscape features, transportation structures, boundaries, capitals, six population levels of urban areas, 11 type styles, altitudes and depths (all given in meters on the maps), and a conversion diagram for meters and feet. There are 19 supplemental symbols for the metropolitan area maps.

III. Special Features

The feature that distinguishes this work from other atlases is its collection of 17 natural-color satellite images of selected areas of the world. From San Francisco to the French Riviera to Iceland, these spectacular photographlike views show geological formations, urban areas, water pollution, vegetation, and agricultural patterns. They are accompanied by informative and lucid explanations that point out specific features, keyed by number to the photograph. Unfortunately, the numbers on the map indicating features referred to in the accompanying text are small and are often difficult or even impossible to pick out from the background. A distinguishing outline or colored background surrounding each number, or even larger numbers, would have made them readily visible. These images are one of the best features of the atlas and readers will find them attractive and interesting. But although these colorful satellite images contribute a great deal to this atlas, the overall scheme of images and maps is not as valuable as in RAND MCNALLY IMAGES OF THE WORLD, in which each image corresponds to a map of the same area depicting and labeling features in detail. However, the Rand McNally volume is a quite different type of book and is not really an atlas at all, as it is *all* images, whereas here the images/satellite section serves as an adjunct to this comprehensive atlas.

A "Description of Map Types and Scales" discusses and illustrates the characteristics of the physical, political, metropolitan, and thematic maps, as well as the significance of their scales. Projections used in the atlas are also illustrated and clearly explained. An interesting feature of the index is a list of motor vehicle nationality letters that are used to differentiate identical place-names located in different countries.

IV. Geographical Balance

Coverage is relatively equal for all parts of the world, although the United States is intentionally favored with slightly larger-scale maps. The statistical maps and charts provide significant information about Western, Soviet bloc, and Third World nations alike. The detailed major city maps interspersed throughout the atlas depict not only large U.S., Canadian, and European cities but also such cities as Singapore, Jakarta, Lagos, Kinshasha, and Johannesburg.

V. Scale and Projections

Scales are relatively uniform for similar geographic units, allowing the reader to compare different areas easily. The world physical map is at a scale of 1:27,000,000. With the exception of the polar regions, continents are depicted at 1:13,500,000 (South America, Asia, and Africa being shown in two parts at this scale, and in one part at smaller scales). Larger areas, such as the Pacific Ocean and most of the thematic maps, are shown at scales from 1:54,000,000 to 1:162,000,000. Individual map scales are noted in the table of contents.

Scales are generally presented in fractional, verbal, and bar scale format, the last calibrated in both kilometers and miles.

Five chiefly true-to-area projections are used in the atlas. Their attributes and the types of maps for which each projection is used are explained in a special section (see *Special Features*).

VI. Accuracy

Vernacular name spellings are preferred over conventional anglicized forms; for example, *Bucharest* appears in parentheses on the map following the vernacular *Bucuresti*. Both forms have entries in the index.

Symbols and names are properly placed on the maps. Natural features are accurately represented by relief, symbols, and names. Terms describing the type of feature are frequently given in the vernacular.

A multilingual list of abbreviations of geographical names and terms is grouped by general feature type, such as "mountains." It would have been helpful if all such foreign terms were also provided in English, but only those that have been abbreviated appear on the abbreviations list.

Some German spellings have not been translated into English; for example, on the physical maps of South Africa, the Cape of Good Hope and Orange Free State are labeled in the vernacular Afrikaans, *Kaapland* and *Oranje-Vrystaat*, but on the political map of Africa they are in German, *Kapland* and *Oranjefreistaat*. Likewise, *Cambodia* is preferred over the more recent form *Kampuchea*; in the index *Kampuchea* is followed by *Kambodscha* (the German spelling of *Cambodia*) as the preferred form, rather than *Cambodia*. There is no index entry for *Kambodscha*.

VII. Currency

Information in the atlas is generally current with its 1986 publication date. The sole exception is the city maps, which appear to be less up-to-date than the national and regional maps. For example, the map of Philadelphia still shows Connie Mack Stadium, which was torn down some years before this atlas was published. On the same map, Drexel University is anachronistically and incorrectly labeled *Rexel Inst. of Tech*. A few anachronisms were also noted on other city maps. These are minor flaws, however, and do not detract from the general currency of this atlas.

VIII. Legibility

The cartography is excellent. Typefaces are dark, very clear, and easy to read. Seven easily distinguishable variations are used. Urban concentrations are differentiated by six population categories of typeface and symbol. Although most maps are filled with names and symbols, they are never cluttered. Boundaries, transportation lines, and rivers are clearly distinguishable from one another, as are natural features.

Three relief shading schemes are used, depending on the map scale. Larger-scale maps show more levels of altitude relief, but the gradation among some of the colors is too slight to distinguish readily. Color quality, however, is excellent. Colors are abundant and in register throughout the atlas. Altitude and depth numbers are quite legible.

IX. Accessibility

This work contains over 100,000 entries in one index, about half the number of entries found in THE TIMES ATLAS OF THE WORLD. All names that appear on the metropolitan area, country, regional, and world maps fall within the scope of the index.

The index is easy to use, with page references indicating alphanumeric grid coordinates, but not latitude and longitude. Grid sections on the maps are small enough so that using a coordinate citation to pinpoint a name is very easy.

Index entries consist of official and variant forms of names, renamings, and other secondary name designations. These forms may be followed by the names as they appear on the maps, if they are different; for example, "Moscow = Moskva."

It is not specified but the entries in the index usually refer to the largest-scale map on which a place appears, if it appears on more than one map. In some cases, however, for no apparent reason, the smaller-scale map is cited. For example, Kirillov, USSR, appears on a 1:4,500,000 map and a 1:13,500,000 map, but the latter page is cited rather than the former. A similar situation exists for Levkosia (Nicosia), Cyprus.

Our reviewers noted some errors in the index entries; for example, the town of Truth or Consequences, New Mexico, is not on the map cited in the

index. Other places in this part of New Mexico are also listed as being on the same map, but the coordinates given do not even exist on this map in the southern part of the state. Luckily, these places do appear on another map of the same scale, though they are not cited in the index.

A few inset maps are included, and these are clearly labeled.

X. Summary

The overall quality of *The Great World Atlas* outweighs its occasional shortcomings. This atlas, at $39.95, is less than one third the price of THE TIMES ATLAS OF THE WORLD, which contains no satellite images, although THE TIMES ATLAS does not suffer the drawback of some lost information in the middle of double-page maps, and it does contain a few more special features. *The Great World Atlas* is significantly less expensive than EARTHBOOK, which it resembles in size, purpose, and cartographic quality. Both atlases are highly sophisticated and provide a good deal of geographic information. The satellite images, high-quality cartography, special features, and overall organization make *The Great World Atlas* a good purchase for library and home collections.

International World Atlas

Facts at a Glance

Full Title: **International World Atlas.**
Publisher: Hammond.
Editors: Martin A. Bacheller, Editor-in-Chief, and the Hammond staff.
Copyright: 1986.
Edition Reviewed: 1986 (1987 statistics).

Number of Pages: 200.
Number of Maps: 265.
Number of Indexes: No master index, but same-page indexes accompany all map areas.
Trim Size: 9½″ × 12½″.
Binding: cloth.

Price: $14.95. 15 percent discount to schools and libraries. Sold in bookstores, by direct mail, and directly to libraries.
ISBN 0-8437-1237-6.
Revised annually.

I. Introduction

The current edition of the Hammond *International World Atlas* was published in 1986. The smallest (in number of pages) of the atlases in Hammond's hardcover AMBASSADOR/CITATION/INTERNATIONAL series, its contents were taken entirely from the Hammond CITATION WORLD ATLAS. The reader should refer to the evaluation of that title on pages 169–72 for a complete description of the maps.

II. Format

The *International World Atlas* is a slimmer version of the CITATION. It measures 9½″ × 12½″, a convenient size for desktop work. The binding is sturdy and will withstand regular use in schools and libraries.

The arrangement of maps corresponds exactly to the CITATION's format. The main difference, which is discussed more fully in this chapter, is the elimination of the United States state maps and the master index.

III. Special Features

The same features that accompany the maps in the CITATION WORLD ATLAS appear here. Other features of the CITATION which appear in separate sections have been eliminated outright or reduced in length. The CITATION's one-and-a-half-page introduction has been cut to one page in the *International*. This cut was minor and will have no significant impact on the atlas's use.

IV. Geographical Balance

With the elimination of the 50 state maps of the United States from the CITATION, this atlas is—in theory—a more balanced international world atlas. This cut in itself is not a problem, but it has created the unusual situation of Canada's having more coverage and detailed maps than does the United States (Canada has 26 pages; the United States, 5). Readers will find this atlas useful for research on non-U.S. countries, but they will have to look elsewhere for information at the state level for the United States.

V. Currency

As with other Hammond atlases, the contents are as current as the copyright date. This particular title is updated annually but, as usual with Hammond atlases, the copyright is only changed every few years.

VI. Accessibility

The *International World Atlas* lacks a master index, leaving users to depend upon the same-page indexes that accompany each individual map. As in the CITATION WORLD ATLAS, these indexes are somewhat incomplete, for in order to find a specific place-name, the user must first know the name of the country or region in which the place is located. For example, a user who wants to find the town of Chichicastenango on a map would have to know that it is in Guatemala, or else consult another source. An index entry for Chichicastenango occurs only under the Guatemala—Cities and Towns index on the page where the map of Central America is located. Clearly, the elimination of the master index makes the atlas much more difficult for the average reader to use. It also makes this atlas less desirable than its many competitors that do include comprehensive master indexes.

The "Gazetteer-Index of the World" at the front of the volume is identical to the one in the CITATION WORLD ATLAS.

VII. Summary

While the title *International World Atlas* may sound impressive, it is somewhat misleading, implying a more detailed and more extensive work than this atlas really is. Does eliminating the maps of individual U.S. states make a world atlas more "international" in character? Our reviewers think not. Moreover, the absence of a comprehensive master index is a major drawback. For the average person who consults an atlas, such an index is essential; without it, the user is reduced to hit-and-miss search techniques when trying to find a specific place on a map.

The *International World Atlas* costs $14.95. Libraries and individuals alike, however, will be better served by other Hammond titles—in particular, the AMBASSADOR WORLD ATLAS and the CITATION WORLD ATLAS, which both include a master index and also make use of more modern and sophisticated cartography.

McGraw-Hill Pictorial Atlas

Facts at a Glance

Full Title: **The McGraw-Hill Pictorial Atlas of the World.**
Publisher: McGraw-Hill.
Editor: John Woodward.
Copyright: 1986 by Salamander Books Ltd., London; maps, 1986 by George Philip & Son Ltd., London.
Edition Reviewed: first U.S. edition, 1986.

Number of Pages: 178.
Number of Maps: 70.
Number of Indexes: 2.
Number of Index Entries: 18,500.
Number of Illustrations: 140 four-color.
Trim Size: 10¹⁄₁₀″ × 14½″.
Binding: cloth.

Price: $22.95.
Sold in bookstores and directly to libraries.

ISBN 0-07-054455-7.
No revision scheduled.

I. Introduction

The McGraw-Hill Pictorial Atlas of the World is a large-format illustrated atlas combining maps, text, and photographs to present the reader with "one of the most compendious surveys of today's world." Of British origin, this new and original work is the result of collaboration among a number of authorities in several fields. The maps were provided by the respected cartographic firm of George Philip & Son. Dr. John Salt, lecturer in geography at University College, London, served as geographical consultant. The text was written by four free-lance authors: Jack Tresidder, Norman Barrett, Arthur Butterfield, and Keith Lye, all experienced journalists with wide-ranging background in geographical studies. Most of the photographs are credited to national tourist agencies and to stock photo houses (most notably, The Image Bank). The book was edited by John Woodward. Incidentally, the book's title is somewhat misleading, for McGraw-Hill serves only as the *American* publisher and distributor and has had no input in the atlas's content, which has not been in any way modified for the American market.

The editor believes that "no longer can nations stand isolated; they will always be influencing, or being influenced by, their place on the map." Because "new problems such as overpopulation, pollution, and the decline in natural resources have taken on a global significance . . . a comprehensive and up-to-date atlas is as essential to the general reader as it is to the student of geography." The *Pictorial Atlas* is therefore not simply a collection of maps, but it is part atlas, part geographic encyclopedia.

II. Format

In its size and design, *The McGraw-Hill Pictorial Atlas* resembles a coffee table book. Its trim size (10¹⁄₁₀″ × 14½″) is virtually identical to that of THE NEW YORK TIMES ATLAS OF THE WORLD, but with 110 fewer pages, it is considerably thinner and lighter. The book's size allows the maps, photographs, and text to be presented in a handsome, uncluttered manner. The semiglossy paper is good quality, and there is no significant show-through. The book is well bound; the pages are both glued and sewn and lie almost flat when the book is open.

Like conventional atlases, the *Pictorial Atlas* organizes its contents by continent. The great majority of the maps are four-color political reference maps, with relief used to depict elevation. There is a continent map at the beginning of each section; the remaining maps show individual countries, groups of adjacent countries, or large regions within a single country. Map sizes vary. Some occupy a full page, some are from one half to three quarters of a page, and yet others are spread across two pages, occupying the top three quarters of the spread.

Running text describes each country individually. Each self-contained country section begins with a fact box that gives information about the country's area, population, language, economy, climate, and other aspects. The text, which makes up approximately one third of the book's content, is frequently divided by subheads and deals with such subjects as "Land and Climate," "Economy," "People," "Government," and "History."

As its title implies, *The McGraw-Hill Pictorial Atlas* is richly illustrated. Captioned four-color photographs show geographic landforms and social activities generic to particular countries and regions. More so than the map sizes, photo sizes vary. Some occupy a third of a page, while others are postcard size or smaller. Regardless of size, all photographs are strategically placed within the section that covers the country or region they are intended to illustrate.

III. Special Features

The two most significant special features in this atlas are the text and photographs. The text is written for the lay reader who may have no previous knowledge about the geography or history of the country in question. The text tends to summarize facts rather than discuss particular topics in depth; the purpose is to give the reader a context for understanding and interpreting the maps and the countries they depict. This is as it should be in an atlas of this kind. While the writing style is not particularly elegant and tends toward generalizations, it is concise, straightforward, and easy to follow. As an indication of the style of these text entries, the first paragraph of the section on **West Germany** reads as follows:

> Before 1800 the German people were divided into more than 300 states. But, after the defeat of Napoleon, the number of states was reduced to 39, including Prussia. Between 1814 and 1871, these states were loosely confederated. Following the success of Germany in the Franco-Prussian War (1870–1871), a federated German empire, or *Reich*, was established with the King of Prussia as its *Kaiser* (emperor). The united Germany rapidly expanded its military power, and colonised overseas territories.

The text for West Germany begins opposite a full-page political map of Germany and Switzerland. The entry is accompanied by a one-third-page photo of Neuschwanstein Castle, a one-third-page photo of the Black Forest, a one-sixth-page photo of Heidelberg, and a small shot of skyscrapers in Frankfurt.

For the most part, the photographs have been well chosen to represent particular aspects of geography and society. They are generally attractive and sometimes dramatic. In virtually all cases, they emphasize positive aspects of the country they are illustrating and serve to whet the appetite of the armchair traveler; in this respect, they do not necessarily depict the country as the native may see it. The five photographs that illustrate the text on the United Kingdom, for example, show a view in the Lake District, a panoramic aerial shot of London, the beach at Hastings, a Scottish fishing village, and the Malvern Hills; the reader does not get any impression of the urban industrial areas where four fifths of the nation's population resides.

The maps are also accompanied by graphs showing average monthly temperature, barometric pressure, and precipitation for selected cities. Unfortunately for American readers, these graphs report the figures in centigrade, millibars, and millimeters, respectively; nonmetric equivalents are not given.

There are about 20 thematic maps throughout the book. The most common thematic maps show population density, minerals, and industries in individual continents and also in some countries.

IV. Geographical Balance

Part of the purpose of *The McGraw-Hill Pictorial Atlas* is to represent the interrelation of different areas of the world, and to give the reader a global rather than a national or regional perspective for viewing the world's problems and opportunities. Insofar as the maps, text, and illustrations deal with every part of the world, the *Pictorial Atlas* succeeds.

As in virtually all British atlases, the United Kingdom and Western Europe lead off the coverage of individual nations, and the text and map coverage of these areas tends to be slightly more detailed than that of other regions of the world. Text describing small or lesser developed countries, such as Nepal, Bhutan, and Sri Lanka, is usually only a few paragraphs in length and is not broken down into topics by subheads. Even such major Third World countries as the Philippines, Indonesia, and South Korea receive relatively cursory treatment in comparison with the industrial nations of the West. Still, the fact that there is some text for *every* country of the world cannot be discounted. Even frigid Greenland, with its tiny population of 52,000, is given a text entry, and the excellent photograph accompanying this text gives a fascinating insight into how the people of this icebound island live.

V. Scale and Projections

The cartographer has tried to ensure a consistency of scale wherever possible. For example, most maps in the Europe section are drawn at 1:2,500,000 or a similar scale, while 1:10,000,000 and 1:16,000,000 are common scales for maps of other regions of the world. This consistency is made possible by the large pages of the atlas, and by the fact that the maps are not all the same size. These scales work well and allow for the representation of an appropriate amount of detail. Scales are given in both representative fractions and in bar scales; the bar scales show both miles and kilometers.

The map projections are also well chosen for minimum distortion. The individual projections have been selected with consideration for the size of the area being mapped, and its latitude. The projection type is labeled on each map.

VI. Accuracy

George Philip maps have a reputation for accuracy, and the maps they have provided for this atlas are no exception. Place-name spellings are in the local forms given in the latest official lists and generally agree with the rules of the Permanent Committee on Geographical Names and the United States Board on Geographic Names. For well-known places, such as *Torino* and *Roma*, English-language names are labeled parenthetically.

Names of cities, towns, and other specific places are printed adjacent to the symbols that represent them and are accurately located.

Disputed boundaries are drawn to show the de facto situation. This does not imply international recognition of territorial claims, but rather it indicates actual control of disputed territories, such as obtains in Jammu and Kashmir.

Our reviewers noted no inaccuracies in the text or in the fact boxes that precede the entry for each nation. The captions, too, accurately describe the illustrations that they accompany.

VII. Currency

As an entirely new work first published in 1986, *The McGraw-Hill Pictorial Atlas* was up-to-date at the time of this review. According to the introduction, in preparing the maps for this atlas, the cartographer revised coastlines, rivers, boundaries, administrative divisions, railways, roads, and airports to reflect current conditions. (However, the southeast Asian nation of Kampuchea is identified by its former, more familiar name, *Cambodia*.) Information reported in the text appears to be consistently up-to-date, and the photographs are also contemporary.

The publisher has not announced any plans for revision.

VIII. Legibility

Most of the maps in the *Pictorial Atlas* contain a great deal of information, and the type size for the smallest towns is quite small indeed. Despite this, however, the print is very legible, and reading the printed information on the maps will be difficult only for those who are visually impaired.

The publisher notes that "the style of colouring chosen for the maps takes advantage of new developments in cartographic design and production. The inclusion of a hill-shading to complement the political colouring brings out clearly the character of the land and relief features without impairing the detail of names, settlement, and communication." This is indeed the case.

IX. Accessibility

The design format of the *Pictorial Atlas* greatly enhances this work's accessibility. Each map is individually numbered; both the number and the name of the area covered are highlighted in large print at the top of the appropriate page. Each map is listed in the table of contents.

The *Pictorial Atlas* contains two indexes. The first of these, two pages long, contains references to the text only. The second, 31 pages long, contains references to the maps. Both indexes are comprehensive.

In the map index, an open square after a name signifies that the name refers to an administrative division of a country, while a solid square indicates the name of a country. Names of rivers are also followed by a special symbol.

Each index entry includes the number, in boldface type, of the map on which that feature or place is found. The latitude and longitude of each place or feature is also included. Grid references are not given, but they are not necessary.

X. Summary

The McGraw-Hill Pictorial Atlas of the World is a new work from England that combines the features of a conventional atlas, a gazetteer, and an illustrated geographic encyclopedia in an attractive and accessible format. The maps, drawn by George Philip & Son, are relatively large-scale and convey a good deal of information. The text gives an overview of every nation, although it does not discuss particular topics in great depth. The photographs are attractive and contemporary but are generally selected to emphasize the positive aspects of each nation or region; they would be equally appropriate to travel brochures.

This work has no direct competitors among the general reference atlases currently available. THE NEW RAND MCNALLY COLLEGE WORLD ATLAS does contain a gazetteer, with statistics and descriptions of each nation, but its format is quite different; it lacks the wide range of illustrations found in the *Pictorial Atlas*, and it is less up-to-date.

While *The McGraw-Hill Pictorial Atlas* is a well designed book with good maps, informative text, and attractive color photographs, it really does not provide information that cannot be readily obtained in a good encyclopedia or geographical dictionary. It will be most popular as a gift item, and it will make enjoyable browsing for the armchair traveler. In the library, it will probably be more appropriate for the circulating geography collection than for the general reference collection.

National Geographic Atlas of the World

Facts at a Glance

Full Title: **National Geographic Atlas of the World.**
Publisher: National Geographic Society.
Editors: Wilbur E. Garrett, Editor; Joseph Judge, Associate Editor.
Copyright: 1981.
Edition Reviewed: fifth edition, 1981.

Number of Pages: 385.
Number of Maps: 172.
Number of Indexes: 1.
Number of Index Entries: 155,000.
Number of Illustrations: 36 four-color.
Trim Size: 12½" × 18¼".
Binding: cloth.

Price: $44.95.
Sold through direct-mail advertising.
ISBN 0-87044-347-X.
Revised every ten years. Next scheduled revision 1991–92.

I. Introduction

The *National Geographic Atlas of the World* is a folio-sized (12½" × 18¼") general world atlas. It was compiled by National Geographic Society staff, with the help of scientific contributors and geographic consultants from American universities, cartographic consultants from U.S. and foreign government agencies, and editorial consultants from government, academic, and private organizations, all of whom are named on the copyright page of the volume.

II. Format

The atlas contains seven types of information: encyclopedic descriptions of the universe, solar system, and planet Earth; physical maps of continents and ocean floors; thematic maps of the world; political/physical maps of the United States and foreign countries; statistical data; a glossary; and a place-name index.

There is a handy "Key to Atlas Maps" inside the front and back covers, which consists of a world map showing the page number and coverage of each physical and political/physical map. A card containing map symbols, table of contents, and metric conversion tables is stored in a pocket attached to the inside back cover. This card is intended to help interpret the political/physical maps.

Almost all of the maps are double-page spreads with no margins. Unfortunately, information is lost in the gutter because the pages do not lie flat when opened. Librarians will quickly find that readers will break the spine while attempting to see that information.

III. Special Features

Annual updates to this atlas, which are formatted so that they can also be stored in the back cover pocket, are automatically sent to atlas owners. These describe changes in political boundaries, flag designs, and place-name spellings.

The encyclopedic section begins with the society's unique graphic description of the size and scope of the known universe, called "The Universe Through Time and Space." This is the same graphic issued with the June 1983 issue of National Geographic's magazine. It is followed in the atlas by maps of the heavens, and graphic descriptions of the solar system and earth's near-space environment, atmosphere, and crust. These are all depicted in an easy-to-understand fashion.

The world thematic section features a two-page text and three maps of resources: one of food, one of energy, and one of minerals. Each includes three small inset maps showing related subjects.

Each section of political/physical maps is preceded by two to four pages of text describing the history of each U.S. state or foreign country, depending on the map content, and tables listing its area, population, capital, and economy. For U.S. states, state nickname and date of admission to the Union are included. For foreign countries, the official language(s), religion, and literacy rate are listed.

Two to four pages of urban regional insets follow each section. These are not detailed street maps, but they do locate suburbs, outlying towns, and main roads.

The statistical data section includes geographic comparisons; airline distances; a time zone map; metric conversion tables; monthly climatic data for 320 places around the world; 1980 populations of U.S. cities;

"latest estimate" populations of foreign cities; and a list of foreign terms (glossary).

IV. Geographical Balance

This atlas has a fairly good geographical balance. Of the 168 pages of political/physical maps, 40 pages are devoted to North and Central America (28 of these to the United States), 32 to Europe, 28 to Asia, 12 to Africa, 10 to South America, 10 to the oceans, and 6 to Australasia and Antarctica.

The maps of heavily populated and/or industrialized regions are shown in the larger scales and the Third World is shown with smaller scales. This typical but unfortunate treatment of underdeveloped countries might result from the lack of large-scale source maps.

V. Scale and Projections

The scale expressed as a representative fraction, the map projection, and a bar scale appear below the title of each map. A variety of map scales and projections are used and are apparently determined by what it takes to fit the named area onto the two-page spread with the most detail and least distortion. The variety of projections and scales creates a problem because they are misleading about relative size and shape when comparing two areas. Fortunately, there are other ways to compare area, such as the statistical data in this atlas or a terrestrial globe.

VI. Accuracy

Names on the maps are placed quite accurately. Although there is no generic description of foreign terms for physical features on the maps themselves, they are easily interpreted with the general legend and glossary.

International boundaries, shown with dotted lines and tasteful pastel colors, are designated as either defined or undefined. The claims of both nations are shown where boundaries are in dispute.

The maps in the world thematic section are valuable only for conveying general information. No statistical information is attached to the symbols used. For example, one can see that South Africa is a source of diamonds, but the volume of production is not given.

VII. Currency

With the exception of changes that occurred as the atlas was going to press, the data is as current as its 1981 copyright date. The annual supplements keep the atlas up-to-date, although no means are provided to coordinate the new information into the existing text.

VIII. Legibility

The legibility of the maps in this atlas helped to establish the National Geographic Society's fine cartographic reputation. The typefaces are neat, legible, and clearly differentiate place-name categories. The society's subtle portrayal of shaded relief and use of color only at boundaries greatly enhances place-name legibility.

IX. Accessibility

The gazetteer, or place-name index, occupies the last third of the atlas. The listing for each place includes the larger political division it belongs to, the page number, and alphanumeric coordinates for the largest-scale map on which the place appears, and if applicable, the same for an urban regional map or physical map.

Latitudes, longitudes, populations, and elevations are not listed for place-names in the index. Latitude and longitude lines are printed on the maps, so the coordinates of a particular place can be interpolated. Elevations are not given. Different sizes of type are used for towns, but there is no explanation of the population categories to which they correspond, if that is indeed the intent. There is no means in this atlas of determining the elevations of towns.

X. Summary

The *National Geographic Atlas of the World* is priced at $44.95, which is very reasonable considering the wealth of information packed within its covers. There are some drawbacks, such as the loss of detail in the gutters and the absence of some kinds of information. On the whole, the general reference maps convey more political than physical information. These weaknesses, however, are more than offset by this atlas's many strengths.

The *National Geographic Atlas* competes effectively against THE NEW YORK TIMES ATLAS OF THE WORLD, the RAND MCNALLY COSMOPOLITAN WORLD ATLAS, and the READER'S DIGEST WIDE WORLD ATLAS. It is a useful supplement to the RAND MCNALLY GOODE'S WORLD ATLAS and other medium-sized atlases when a large-page atlas is required.

New International Atlas

Facts at a Glance

Full Title: **The New International Atlas.**
Former Title: International Atlas.
Publisher: Rand McNally.
Editors: Russell L. Voisin and Jon M. Leverenz.
Copyright: 1986.

Edition Reviewed: 1986.

Number of Pages: 568.
Number of Maps: 301.
Number of Indexes: 1.
Number of Index Entries: 168,000.
Trim Size: 11″ × 14¾″.
Binding: leather (hardcover).

Price: $150.00. 25 percent library discount.
Sold in bookstores and through other outlets; also sold directly to libraries.
ISBN 0-528-83086-4.
Revised annually.

I. Scope and Format

The New International Atlas, published by Rand McNally, is identical in content to the BRITANNICA ATLAS. The only differences are the binding, paper, and price. *New International*'s heavy stock paper, gilt-edged pages, and leather binding place it in the deluxe category, both in physical quality and in price. At $150, it is twice as expensive as the BRITANNICA ATLAS.

The New International Atlas can hold pride of place among general reference atlases in any public or academic collection. While it is slightly more expensive than the oversized TIMES ATLAS, many American users will prefer *New International*'s cartography and its more extensive, more modern-looking thematic maps. And even though it is several times more costly than the other major large-format atlases, including EARTHBOOK, THE GREAT WORLD ATLAS, NATIONAL GEOGRAPHIC ATLAS OF THE WORLD, and THE NEW YORK TIMES ATLAS, this price is justified by *New International*'s greater sophistication and variety of contents.

For a full description of the maps and other features of this atlas, see the review of the BRITANNICA ATLAS on pages 167–69.

The New Penguin World Atlas

Facts at a Glance

Full Title: **The New Penguin World Atlas.**
Former Title: The Penguin World Atlas.
Publisher: Penguin Books.
Editor: Peter Hall.
Copyright: 1979.

Number of Pages: 96.
Number of Maps: 44.
Number of Indexes: 1.
Number of Index Entries: 17,000.

Trim Size: 7½″ × 10″.
Binding: paper.

Price: $9.95.
Sold in bookstores.
ISBN 0-14-051-096-6.
No scheduled revision.

I. Introduction

The New Penguin World Atlas, which was compiled by Oxford University Press, is a revision of the 1974 *Penguin World Atlas*. The new edition is designed to be "even more accessible to the general reader." The volume presents physical, economic, and political data. Peter Hall, editor of the atlas, is professor of geography at the University of Reading. The maps themselves were prepared by the Oxford University Press.

II. Format

The atlas contains 44 physical maps superimposed with political information. Twenty-nine of these are two-page spreads. The paperback volume is slim, easy to hold, and will stay flat when opened. The text paper is of good quality and opacity and the cover stock is of normal weight for paperback volumes. The binding is sturdily sewn and should stand up well to normal use.

Each map has a title and an indication of scale, projection, and elevation (in meters). A legend is provided for most, but not all, maps and typically includes symbols for boundaries, roads, railways, airports, canals, seasonal rivers and lakes, marshes, salt pans, ice caps, sand deserts, and national parks. Ocean maps show currents.

Maps extend to page edges without neat lines. Two-page maps tend to lose detail and information in the gutter.

III. Special Features

Several continental maps show rainfall, bedrock geology, minerals, and population on a very small scale (for example, 1:110,000,000 for Eurasia and 1:190,000,000 for Africa). Inset maps represent population density and power resources of the British Isles, as well as monsoon rainfall in India and neighboring countries. These special maps do not have much detail but are useful for an overview. Also included is an easy-to-read two-page table listing capital cities, population, and other statistics for the world's states and dependencies. Another page lists populations of major urban areas and basic geographic figures for the continents, such as land areas, longest rivers, highest peaks, and largest lakes.

IV. Geographical Balance

The publisher states that maps have been selected to "focus maximum attention on those parts of the world likely to attract the average reader's interest." This includes primarily the British Isles, Western Europe, and North America. Special coverage is supposed to be provided for those parts of the world "likely to appear in the world news," such as the Middle East and southern Africa, but neither of these areas has above-average coverage in terms of numbers of maps or amount of detail except for the Suez Canal, whose map is at a 1:1,500,000 scale. Coverage of most of South America and the eastern USSR is disappointingly sparse. There is no map of Antarctica in its entirety.

V. Scale and Projections

Scales are noted in the table of contents as well as on each map. Scales vary widely, ranging from 1:1,500,000 for certain areas, such as the Suez and Panama canals, to the 1:165,000,000 world map (the table of contents lists this scale as 1:163,000,000). Scales are roughly consistent for areas of comparable size, although the bias toward Great Britain and Europe means that these areas are represented at somewhat larger scales than are others.

Throughout the atlas, distances on bar scales are given in kilometers only, never in miles. This may limit this atlas's usefulness for American readers who are not fully conversant with metric measurement.

Projections are identified on most maps. In all, seven standard projections have been used.

VI. Accuracy

Geographic names appear in their conventional anglicized forms when these exist. For example, *Moscow* is used rather than the vernacular Russian *Moskva*. The alternate vernacular name is frequently given in parentheses on the map, and a cross-reference appears in the index from the alternate name of the familiar one.

Names and their locations are for the most part accurate, although some inconsistent spellings are given for West Germany. For example, the town of *Giessen* is incorrectly spelled *Geissen* on the main map on page 24 and in the index (thus hindering the reader who looks for it under its correct spelling in the index), but it is spelled correctly on the map on page 20. Likewise, *Schwabisch Hall* is incorrectly spelled *Schwarbisch Hall* on the map on page 24 and in the index. Both German nations are labeled with their official names rather than simply *West Germany* and *East Germany*.

VII. Currency

The New Penguin World Atlas carries a copyright date of 1979 and shows no evidence of subsequent revision. Nor has the publisher announced any plans for future revision. Therefore, this atlas is obviously not as up-to-date as most of the other atlases reviewed in this Buying Guide, which all carry later copyrights.

This lack of currency is reflected immediately in the population tables at the beginning of the book. The publisher states that the statistics given here are "based on the latest available United Nations figures," but obviously this is no longer the case.

Lack of currency is also reflected in certain place-names. For example, although Zimbabwe is labeled with its current name, the capital, now called *Harare*, is identified by its old name of *Salisbury*. Burkina Faso appears as *Upper Volta*, and all Chinese place-names are spelled in the Wade-Giles style of transliteration rather than in the Pinyin style that has generally superseded it. But the country formerly known as *Cambodia* is labeled by its more current appellation, *Kampuchea*. The label *Ho Chi Minh City* is followed by *Saigon* in parentheses.

VIII. Legibility

None of the maps appears cluttered with too many place-names; in fact, there is even enough space for additional place-names on most maps.

Typefaces are legible and are differentiated to indicate various sorts of political and physical features. Although these distinctions are not explained in any legend, most of them become obvious as one uses the atlas. Some differences in typeface are not clear, however. For instance, on some maps most town and city names are slightly italicized, but others (apparently the largest) are not. On other maps, only names of natural features are italicized. The various city symbols used do not make the distinction any clearer, as they are also not explained. Mantua and Cremona in Italy, for example, are represented on page 25 with what appears to be the same symbol; *Mantua*, however, is printed in heavy italics and *Cremona* is in a thinner, regular typeface.

Various boundaries, roads, railways, canals, and rivers are clearly distinguishable from one another. Natural features, shaded relief, and spot heights are likewise clear. Elevations are in meters. Colors are sufficiently strong and in register.

IX. Accessibility

The index endeavors to list every name shown on the maps, unlike some small atlases that omit some less important names. The index is easy to use, although abbreviations are not explained. Alphanumeric grid coordinates are included for easy place location. Latitude and longitude are not given in the index but do appear on the maps. The grid areas are too large on some maps, which may make finding a particular place difficult. To pinpoint the small city of Herisau, Switzerland, for example, one has to comb an area of 4¾" × 7" spanning two pages.

Numerous inset maps supplement the main ones. Most have no title, but they are clearly marked with latitude, longitude, and indication of scale. Inset maps are indexed.

X. Summary

The New Penguin World Atlas is a good, concise paperback atlas. Its high-quality cartography, large physical map format, and pleasing visual impact make it worthy of consideration. However, it does not contain as much information as the smaller-format VNR POCKET ATLAS, nor is it as easy to interpret as THE RANDOM HOUSE CONCISE WORLD ATLAS, both of which are less expensive. Its British orientation, disproportionate coverage of the British Isles and Europe, outdated information, and metric bar scales will keep it from being the first choice among paperback atlases for American collections.

New York Times Atlas of the World

Facts at a Glance

Full Title: **The New York Times Atlas of the World.**
Publisher: Times Books.
Editors: Janet Christie, Alison M. Ewinton, et al.
Copyright: 1986 by John Bartholomew & Son Limited, and Times Books Limited, London.
Edition Reviewed: second revised edition, 1988.

Number of Pages: 244.
Number of Maps: 148 reference maps.
Number of Indexes: 1.
Number of Index Entries: 100,000.
Trim Size: 10½" × 14½".
Binding: cloth.

Price: $49.95.
Sold in bookstores and other outlets; also sold directly to libraries.
ISBN 0-8129-1626-3.
Revised periodically.

I. Introduction

The New York Times Atlas of the World is a large-format general world atlas prepared by the British cartographic firm of John Bartholomew & Son Limited in association with *The Times* of London. Despite its title, this atlas is connected with the *New York Times* in name only. The publisher is Times Books, a subsidiary of Random House; the book is distributed in the United States by Harper & Row. In Britain, this atlas is sold as *The Times Concise Atlas of the World*, a title that points up the fact that this book is a "junior" version of the massive TIMES ATLAS OF THE WORLD.

II. Format

Although it is large-sized ($10\frac{1}{2}'' \times 14\frac{1}{2}''$), this atlas is relatively thin (one inch), lightweight, and easy to handle. The West German binding is excellent. The pages open flat, and there is a very narrow margin in the gutter to ensure that no information is lost.

The atlas opens with a 40-page introductory section (see *Special Features*), followed by 148 pages of full-color general reference maps.

The majority of the maps are physical, and many are spread over two pages. In addition, the atlas contains many large-scale insets of cities, islands, and areas adjacent to the main maps. The extensive index, along with a glossary and two statistical tables, occupies 96 pages.

The legend is located at the beginning of the general map section. It lists all the symbols used for boundaries, transportation, lake types, landscape features, and man-made features. It also keys all the lettering types used in the atlas, gives principal abbreviations, and includes the symbols used in the city inset maps. The individual maps themselves do not contain legends, but they do include information about the scale, map projection, and a hypsometric tint elevation bar graph.

III. Special Features

The introductory section opens with two pages entitled "geographical comparisons," in which small one-color outline maps show the relative sizes of the major oceans and seas, inland waters, drainage basins, continents, and islands. These small maps are accompanied by statistics on area in both square miles and square kilometers. Separate statistical tables report the heights of important mountains and long rivers on each continent.

The seven regional physical maps in the introductory section are generalized depictions that use color and relief to portray various geographic features, and they are drawn in projections that give the impression of viewing the earth from space. The few name labels on these maps identify major physical features such as rivers, mountain ranges, large bodies of water, islands, and geographic regions. Unfortunately, there is no accompanying legend to iden-

tify the scale, projection, or types of environmental features shown in these maps.

These maps are followed by two pages of detailed star charts. The remainder of the introductory section is occupied by encyclopedic features on the universe, the solar system, the moon, space flight, the Earth's structure, climate, vegetation, minerals, energy, food, population, patterns of human settlement, and map projections. Here the well-written text is profusely illustrated with accurate, up-to-date maps, diagrams, and photographs. While some of these pages may be of little interest to the general user, the thematic maps that accompany the pages on climate, vegetation, minerals, energy, food, and population provide a wealth of useful information. The feature on map projections is a condensed version of a feature that appears in THE TIMES ATLAS OF THE WORLD. This feature explains the processes by which different projections are achieved and the distortions that they involve.

The statistical data on states and territories of the world at the back of the book list the capital or main city, the area, and the population (generally as of 1984). The table on metropolitan areas lists the major metropolises in each continent, with their populations.

IV. Geographical Balance

The New York Times Atlas of the World gives adequate representation to all areas of the world. Great Britain, Europe, the United States, and Australia receive particularly close and detailed attention, but not at the expense of other regions.

The general reference maps begin with Europe, then move to Asia, Africa, North America, South America, Australasia, and finally Antarctica. Maps of the oceans and their islands are located in geographical sequence between the continents they separate.

Traditionally, atlas maps cover each continent in a north-to-south, east-to-west pattern, so that maps of adjacent areas are generally on adjacent pages. In this atlas, however, the maps for the individual regions of the United States are arranged in a geographically counterclockwise order, starting with the northeast and ending with the southeast. In consequence, the map of the southeast United States is 11 plates away from the map of the northeast United States.

V. Scale and Projections

John Bartholomew & Son has taken great care to ensure that every map gives large-scale coverage to its subject. Many different scales are used, but each continent is covered at fairly consistent scales.

Areas within Europe are mapped at scales of 1:300,000 to 1:5,000,000, with 1:3,000,000 a common standard. The United States and populous areas of Canada are represented at 1:300,000, with larger-scale maps at 1:500,000 for metropolitan areas and smaller-scale maps for less-populated areas at 1:6,000,000. For Asia, Africa, South America, and Australasia, the most common scale is 1:6,000,000. However, some areas on these continents are mapped at the smaller scale of 1:12,000,000. The scales of the numerous city inset maps range from 1:60,000 to 1:1,200,000, with most at 1:300,000. The scales of the island and subregion inset maps range from 1:210,000 to 1:12,000,000, with most at 1:1,000,000. An Anglo-European bias is evident in the insets, as the largest scales are used for European cities and for areas formerly associated with the British Empire.

A variety of projections were used in preparing the maps in this atlas. For large- and medium-scale maps of mid- and high-latitude areas, conic projections were preferred. The Mercator projection was used for maps of equatorial areas. Most small- and medium-scale maps are in the Lambert azimuthal equal-area projection. Some maps, however, use another appropriate projection that allows the area depicted to fit neatly on the page. In virtually all instances, the projection that was chosen minimizes distortion and permits the user to make size and distance measurements over any part of the map.

VI. Accuracy

Place-name spellings are consistent with those recognized by the local authorities. Where necessary, names have been transliterated according to the current systems of transliteration (such as Pinyin for Chinese). For well-known locations, English-language conventional names of local spellings are labeled parenthetically.

Names of cities and other specific locations are printed in appropriate locations. Even in heavily populated areas, it is easy to determine which name is associated with which point—a virtue that many other atlases do not embody. The positioning of lettering for physical area names indicates their actual extent and location. Name labels and designated international boundaries always reflect the situation on the ground at the time of publication, even in areas where sovereignty and boundaries are contested. In such areas, boundaries are shown as either undefined, as cease-fire lines, or as part of a demilitarized zone. When the size of the contested area is substantial, as it is along the Indo-Chinese border, the boundary claims of both nations are shown.

On the negative side, Bartholomew's use of hypsometric tints to depict elevation (green for low-lying areas, fading to beige, brown, gray, and white for higher elevations) gives a false impression of the environment. This discrepancy is particularly noticeable for low-lying deserts.

VII. Currency

The New York Times Atlas is remarkably up-to-date for its 1986 copyright. Place-name labels and boundary lines reflect the 1986 world situation. The text, illustrations, and photographs in the encyclopedic introductory section are also contemporary.

VIII. Legibility

Although a variety of typefaces and sizes are used in this atlas, a simple system makes it easy for the user to differentiate physical and political place-names. Country names and their subdivisions are shown in uppercase letters. With the exception of country and state capitals, city names are printed in upper- and lowercase letters. All physical place-names are in italic type; those denoting extended regions are in all uppercase print, while names for more limited features are in upper- and lowercase lettering.

The cartographers have achieved a good balance between map scale and the number of place-name labels, so that for the most part the maps are not cluttered. (The maps of the eastern United States, on which labels for populated places obscure most other information, are a rare exception.) The detail of linear features, such as rivers, roads, and railroads, is also well balanced with map scale. The symbols for these features are well delineated and distinguished from one another, as are those for boundaries. At the same time, it is fairly easy to distinguish national borders from state and provincial borders.

IX. Accessibility

The index of *The New York Times Atlas* is quite extensive, containing about 100,000 place-names. Each name is indexed with a page number and alphanumeric grid reference. The grid references generally refer to the largest-scale map containing that place-name; in some cases this is an inset map. Occasionally, however, the reference is to the general map, even when a larger-scale inset shows the place in greater detail.

As previously mentioned, there are inset maps on almost every general map page in this atlas. All have their separate latitude-longitude grid, but few have separate grid coordinates. Most use the same grid coordinates as the main map, even when their latitude-longitude grid does not match the alphanumeric grid coordinates.

City name listings in the index include the country (and in some cases, the state or province) in which they are located. Physical names are identified by type of physical feature, such as mountain, lake, or desert. Unlike the index in THE TIMES ATLAS OF THE WORLD and many other general world atlases, the index in *The New York Times Atlas* does not report the latitude and longitude of each place. For the serious geographer, such an omission is a drawback, but it should not affect the layperson's use of this atlas.

The alphanumeric grid coordinate references refer to grid areas of four square inches or less. While the maximum number of place-names within one grid square is close to 50, most squares contain fewer than 20 names. Thus, the user should not have to hunt through a forest of names to find the one he or she is seeking.

X. Summary

At $49.95, *The New York Times Atlas of the World* is expensive by comparison to such competing volumes as the NATIONAL GEOGRAPHIC ATLAS OF THE WORLD, THE GREAT WORLD ATLAS, the READER'S DIGEST WIDE WORLD ATLAS, and the AMBASSADOR WORLD ATLAS, but less expensive than EARTHBOOK and THE TIMES ATLAS OF THE WORLD. In overall quality, however, it rivals any atlas on the market today, at any price. Its potential drawbacks—the use of hypsometric tints for elevation, the lack of latitude-longitude coordinates in the index, and a slightly British perspective—are minor in comparison with its strengths. Produced to the highest standards by meticulous cartographers, *The New York Times Atlas of the World* is well worth its cost and will be an important title in any atlas collection.

Prentice-Hall New World Atlas

Facts at a Glance

Full Title: **The Prentice-Hall New World Atlas.**
Publisher: Prentice-Hall.
Editors: B. M. Willett and Harold Fullard.
Copyright: 1984 by George Philip & Son, Ltd.
Edition Reviewed: first edition, 1984.

Number of Pages: 284.
Number of Maps: 100.
Number of Indexes: 1.
Number of Index Entries: 45,000.
Number of Illustrations: 200 color.
Trim Size: 8¾" × 11".
Binding: cloth.

Price: $16.95.
Sold in bookstores and supermarkets, also by direct mail and newspaper and magazine advertising.

ISBN 0-13-695867-2.
No scheduled revision.

I. Introduction

The Prentice-Hall New World Atlas is a general reference atlas first issued in the United States in 1984. It is intended for high school through adult readers. The maps have been provided by George Philip & Son, a leading British cartographic firm, which also produces atlases under its own name in the United Kingdom. The publishers state that this atlas has been designed to provide a compact and convenient reference book which is easy to handle and consult.

II. Format

The atlas contains political maps with shaded relief, the majority of which are two-page spreads, in the general reference section. There is an adequate though not generous gutter along the spine edges of the pages. There is also a large section of world thematic maps, most of which are on single pages.

With pages 8¾" × 11", the atlas is a convenient size and allows for maps with a fair amount of detail.

There is a master legend at the front of the reference section. Each map in this section includes a bar scale and a representative fraction scale, and a scale showing relief (elevation) coloring used. Each thematic map includes a clear, well-located legend.

The volume has a well-finished cloth binding, and a sewn spine. The map section is produced on heavy paper; the index is on lighter weight matte paper with poor opacity. The volume is sturdily produced. It also has an attractive full-color jacket.

III. Special Features

The atlas begins with a 48-page section of world thematic maps, which includes: "Chart of the Stars"; "Solar System"; "Time"; "Atmosphere and Clouds"; "Climate and Weather"; "Earth from Space"; "Evolution of the Continents"; "Unstable Earth"; "Making of Landscape"; "Earth: Physical Dimensions"; "Distances"; "Water Resources and Vegetation"; "Population"; "Languages"; "Religion"; "Growth of Cities"; "Food Resources"; "Nutrition"; "Mineral Resources"; "Fuel and Energy"; "Occupations"; "Industry"; "Transport"; "Trade"; and "Wealth." Each section includes one or several clear, well-made maps, which are often supplemented by graphs, text, and photographs.

The reference maps section covers 128 pages and generally includes political relief maps, with several solely political or physical maps for each continent.

IV. Geographical Balance

This atlas was produced in Great Britain by a British cartographer; thus, its marked European bias is to be expected. Of the 128 pages of reference maps, 52 are of Europe; 18 are of Asia; 16 of Africa; 8 of Australia/Oceania; 20 of North America; and 7 of South America. There are maps of administrative divisions of Great Britain, a detail not repeated for other countries. Maps of Europe also appear most consistently at the largest scale available in the atlas, 1:2,500,000, as compared to 1:6,000,000 to 1:10,000,000 for Asia; 1:8,000,000 for Africa; 1:4,500,000 to 1:12,000,000 for Australia/Oceania; 1:6,000,000 to 1:12,000,000 for North America; and 1:8,000,000 to 1:16,000,000 for South America. The thematic world maps also frequently include insets of Europe that are the same size as the world maps; however, this actually presents a clearer picture of what would otherwise be an overcrowded map.

V. Scale and Projections

The atlas uses a wide range of scales, 1:1,000,000 to 1:50,000,000. The choice of scales is appropriate to the size of the pages and provides maps of good detail. There is fairly good consistency in presenting adjacent areas at similar scales, particularly in the maps of Europe, Africa, Canada, and the United States. However, the range of scales for Asia, at 1:1,000,000 to 1:20,000,000, may be too wide and may confuse some users about the relative sizes of areas.

Although not confusing, the presentation of South America in northern and southern halves at 1:16,000,000, with an enlarged map of central South America at 1:8,000,000, is an unfortunate inconsistency.

Many of the maps are drawn using a conical projection with two standard parallels, an excellent choice for equal-area representation with a minimum of distortion. Other projections used in the atlas, such as Bonne, Lambert's equivalent azimuthal, and Mercator, are less frequently seen. However, they are adequate for their purposes, with the exception of the Hammer equal area and Mollweide's homolographic projections, used for the world and Pacific Ocean maps, respectively, which are unusual and distortive.

VI. Accuracy

Place-names are consistently presented in their respective languages, with English versions given in parentheses for important or otherwise unrecognizable place-names. New version (Pinyin) Chinese place-names are used consistently. Great care is evident in placing names in their proper locations, clearly adjacent to appropriate symbols.

VII. Currency

Recent name changes (*Belize, Vanuatu, Vietnam, Zimbabwe*) are presented correctly, although Kampuchea is labeled *Cambodia*.

Text and photographs are contemporary, and should not appear dated for some time.

VIII. Legibility

Typefaces are legible and sufficiently varied to distinguish different types of features and sizes of towns. Most of the maps are clear and show good detail without appearing overcrowded. The relief colors are well distinguished, although print in mountainous areas is occasionally hard to read. Color reproduction is excellent and in register.

The typeface used in the index is very small and may prove difficult for many readers.

IX. Accessibility

The table of contents covers seven pages. It is divided into continents and includes a list of maps, their pages, and scales; a numbered inset on each two-page spread showing the regions listed in the contents pages; and an appropriate photograph. It is a worthwhile feature but contains a serious flaw: it includes only the maps in the main reference section. Although the main title of the thematic maps section is given at the top of the table of contents, there is no listing of topics or page numbers. The same is true of the index. In addition, each of the three sections (thematic maps, main maps, index) is paginated separately (a frequent problem in atlases), so there is virtually no access to the thematic maps and index, and the situation is confusing.

There is a 96-page index, including 45,000 entries, and a table of recent name changes of places in India, Iran, Mozambique, and Zimbabwe. The index is prefaced with a short but sufficient explanation of its use, and a list of abbreviations. Symbols are included with entries for rivers, countries, and administrative subdivisions. Unfortunately, countries are not given in entries for cities, towns, and so forth, unless they are needed to distinguish between identical entries. Entries give page numbers and latitude and longitude in degrees and minutes. A spot check shows that even small towns on the maps are included in the index, and entries in the index were found on the maps with reasonable ease, although some confusion resulted when the place-name appeared in an inset instead of in the main map.

There are several clearly labeled, easily distinguished insets.

X. Summary

The Prentice-Hall New World Atlas is an attractive, well-designed volume. The opening section of thematic maps is a valuable asset, and the general reference maps are very good indeed. However, the coverage has a distinct British-European slant, and the atlas lacks detailed maps of the United States.

This atlas is appropriate for college and public libraries that require a medium-sized British atlas to supplement their collections. It is also a good choice for personal collections. Although it is a fairly new title, *The Prentice-Hall New World Atlas* is an authoritative alternative to the well-established RAND McNALLY GOODE'S WORLD ATLAS, which costs six dollars more. In short, at $16.95, this work is a splendid value.

The Prentice-Hall Pocket Atlas of the World

Facts at a Glance

Full Title: **The Prentice-Hall Pocket Atlas of the World.**
Publisher: Prentice-Hall.
Editor: Harold Fullard.
Copyright: 1983.

Number of Pages: 120.
Number of Maps: 55.
Number of Indexes: 1.
Number of Index Entries: 11,000.
Trim Size: 4½" × 7½".
Binding: paperback.

Price: $2.95.
Sold in bookstores and through direct mail and magazine and newspaper advertising.
ISBN 0-13-697045-1.
No scheduled revision.

I. Introduction

The Prentice-Hall Pocket Atlas of the World is a basic collection of maps in a handy pocket-size format. Created by George Philip & Son, the respected British cartographer, the maps combine both physical and political features. Although the current edition is published under the aegis of Prentice-Hall, the content has not been modified for the American market.

II. Format

A political map format is used throughout, with some physical features identified by name or symbol. There are 14 one-page maps and 41 two-page maps.

The atlas is easy to hold and flip through, though it does not lie flat by itself when opened. The paperback binding is sewn and the text paper is good quality and reasonably opaque. The attractive full-color cover is standard cover stock. The cover is also scored to minimize damage to the binding from repeated use. All in all, it is a well made book for its type. The book's size is suitable for the kinds of maps included.

Legends are sparse. Instead of a master legend in a small atlas such as this, each map has an inset containing a title (a feature lacking in many pocket atlases), a scale, and a few symbols. The majority of legends show symbols for railways, canals, and altitudes only. Several legends indicate oil pipelines, and a few show other miscellaneous symbols. Principal roads—a feature not usually shown on pocket atlas maps—are indicated in the legends for maps of New Zealand and the central Middle East, although there is no apparent reason why only these two maps were chosen for this feature.

Maps are contained within neat border lines. Two-page maps are separated in the center by a small margin so that nothing is lost in the gutter of the book. Some effort has been made to ensure that words spanning two pages are not inconveniently cut in half, but this is not always true.

III. Special Features

The only special feature is a small-scale map that provides an adequate overview of world air routes. The table of contents lists the scale for each map, thus enabling the reader to compare scales at a glance. The individual map legends give scale not only in ratio and bar scale form, but also in miles per inch, a useful aid found in very few atlases.

IV. Geographical Balance

Western Europe is somewhat better represented than the rest of the world, with generally larger-scale maps. Japan's map is at a 1:8,500,000 scale, although Japan is bigger and has almost double the population of Italy, which has a larger-scale map at 1:6,000,000.

V. Scale and Projections

Scales vary throughout the atlas, from the smallest-scale world air routes map (1:250,000,000) to the largest-scale map, the Suez Canal (1:1,000,000). Continental maps of Asia and Africa are represented at much smaller scales (1:60,000,000 and 1:45,000,000, respectively) than are Europe and Australia, continents much smaller in size (1:27,500,000 and 1:22,500,000, respectively). Scales are given in fractional, verbal, and bar form; bar form scales are in miles and kilometers.

An unusual feature for an atlas of this size is the inclusion of the map projection under the legend inset. In all, ten projections are used, generally well chosen for the area represented. On the world map, the continents and other land areas would have been more accurately represented had a projection other than Mercator been used. Greenland is smaller than South America, not larger as it appears to be in the Mercator projection. The world map also fails to show the Pacific Ocean south of the Aleutian Islands between about 185°E and 135°W, an area that encompasses Hawaii and several other islands. Although this area is shown on another map, it is misleading to omit it from a "world" map.

VI. Accuracy

It is convenient for the average American reader that place-names are given in conventional anglicized spellings. Although no symbols are used to denote natural features, such as mountains, deserts, or plateaus, many such areas are indicated by their names on the maps. Some names include the generic term to describe the feature, but many do not; the lack of both a generic term and a descriptive symbol on the map and in the index may leave a reader with no idea about the type of feature shown. El Djouf, for example, a desert in Mauritania, is not described or symbolized as such on the map or in the index, although the list of index abbreviations includes *des.* for "desert."

Placement of names on the maps is generally accurate, although the town of Rehoboth is located in two different places on the map of Namibia on page 74 and indexed for only one placement.

VII. Currency

Geographic names are relatively current with the 1983 publication date of this atlas. *Cambodia*, however, is referred to by that name, rather than by *Kampuchea*, its official name since 1979, which appears widely in many other atlases.

VIII. Legibility

In general, colors are adequate and in register, but a few of the maps have a "washed out" appearance; their colors and print are somewhat weak. A few maps, such as that of eastern France, Switzerland, and northwest Italy (pages 20–21), appear slightly cluttered because numerous places are shown and the print is not very dark. Close inspection, however, reveals this map to be accurate and remarkably full of information, considering the small page size. However, not all areas of the world enjoy such detailed coverage as this.

Typefaces are differentiated for various place categories, but no legends indicate what these are. In most cases, the experienced reader can deduce from typeface and location to what a particular name refers and can judge the comparative sizes of towns and cities by symbols and typeface. Capital cities are not distinguished from other cities, either on the maps or in the index.

Rivers are drawn and labeled clearly. Borders are also drawn clearly but again, because there is no legend, the reader must deduce whether some boundaries are local or national. The map of Germany and Austria, for example (pages 16–17), is confusing as both West and East Germany are colored the same shade of tan, with the word *Germany* spanning both parts. They only indications that they are somehow separate are the *West* and *East* labels and a fine-line yellow border. Some readers could be misled into thinking that these are not actually two autonomous countries.

Other than rivers and a few other symbols which appear on the maps without explanation, physical features are distinguishable only when they are labeled with a name. Readers familiar with standard map symbols may be able to recognize some of the unexplained symbols used on these maps, but inexperienced readers could not. Elevations are not depicted, although most map legends have a statement that appears to indicate height in feet for the highest area on it.

IX. Accessibility

This atlas index contains about 11,000 entries, compared with 20,000 for a similar size pocket atlas such as THE RANDOM HOUSE MINI WORLD ATLAS. The index is adequate, though not all names shown on the maps are indexed. The Eifel mountains in West Germany, for example, are not indexed, although the Ardennes mountains, 50 miles to the west in France, are. A bigger deterrent to easy use is the index format, which is not only presented in small, hard-to-read type, but in columns in which the reference page precedes the name so that it almost appears to "belong" to the item in the column to the left. The locations on the maps are indicated by letter designations (Bd, Ce, and so on) rather than by the more commonly used alphanumeric grid system. Latitude and longitude are not given.

X. Summary

The Prentice-Hall Pocket Atlas, which costs only $2.95, has much to recommend it—not least the low price. For their small size and scale, its maps are of remarkably high quality. The book is well organized, and there is no extraneous text material to distract from the main purpose of this book—to be a pocket-sized handy reference atlas. That said, however, one should realize that this book is not really appropriate for a public library reference collection, although it would be a cheap addition to a circulating collection. This atlas will best serve the traveler (whether businessperson or tourist) who wants a convenient pocket-sized world atlas for casual reference. Those seeking a slightly larger paperback atlas with more detailed maps might choose THE RANDOM HOUSE CONCISE WORLD ATLAS, THE RANDOM HOUSE MINI WORLD ATLAS, or the VNR POCKET ATLAS, although all of these cost several dollars more.

The Prentice-Hall Universal Atlas

Facts at a Glance

Full Title: **The Prentice-Hall Universal Atlas.**
Publisher: Prentice-Hall.
Editor: Harold Fullard.
Copyright: 1983 by George Philip Raintree, Inc.; text George Philip & Son, Ltd.; maps and index George Philip & Son, Ltd.
Edition Reviewed: 1983.

Number of Pages: 408.
Number of Maps: 176.
Number of Indexes: 1.
Number of Index Entries: 60,000.
Number of Illustrations: 48.
Trim Size: 9″ × 12″.
Binding: cloth.

Price: $34.95.
Sold in bookstores, by direct mail, and directly to libraries.
ISBN 0-13-697094-X.
No scheduled revision.

I. Introduction

The Prentice-Hall Universal Atlas is a comprehensive general-reference world atlas suitable for both home and library use. The cartography was prepared by the noted British mapmakers George Philip & Son. It is the largest in the line of atlases published in the United States by Prentice-Hall that includes THE PRENTICE-HALL UNIVERSITY ATLAS, THE PRENTICE-HALL NEW WORLD ATLAS, and THE PRENTICE-HALL POCKET ATLAS.

II. Format

At 9″ × 12″, *The Prentice-Hall Universal Atlas* is a convenient size for standard library shelves and is easy to handle. Moreover, this size allows for maps with a fair amount of detail. The maps are printed on heavyweight semiglossy paper with excellent opacity; the index is on heavyweight matte paper. The volume itself has a well-finished hard cover, a sewn spine, and an attractive four-color jacket. The binding is loosely sewn so that the pages lie flat when open, but with repeated use the pages may begin to fall out altogether. The volume therefore may need to be rebound for library collections.

The atlas opens with a 30-page section of statistical information, followed by 48 pages of encyclopedic text and thematic maps. (See also *Special Features*.)

A full-page legend occupies the first page of the general-reference map section. The bulk of the book is occupied by 176 pages of general physical relief reference maps that also include political information. These maps are arranged by continent; each continental section begins with general political, physical, and climate maps showing the entire continent. There are also occasional special maps showing administrative subdivisions and population distribution for particular nations. Though inset maps are relatively few, they are clearly labeled and easy to distinguish.

Finally, in addition to the 140-page, 60,000-item index, there are tables of recent place-name changes, Chinese place-names, and a glossary of geographical terms.

Each section of the atlas is paginated separately.

III. Special Features

The special features in this atlas are the introductory statistical tables, the encyclopedic section "The Universe, Earth & Man," and the brief back-of-the-book glossary and place-name tables.

Collectively, the statistical tables function as a sort of almanac. They provide comprehensive information about U.S. states, cities, and towns; cities outside the United States; national population figures; world climate; and national economic figures.

"The Universe, Earth & Man" includes detailed thematic maps supplemented by text, graphs, diagrams, and photographs. A wide variety of geography topics are covered. Among these are the solar system, time, atmosphere and clouds, climate and weather, evolution of the continents, making of landscape, water resources and vegetation, language, religion, growth of cities, fuel and energy, industry, transport, and wealth. In concept and execution, this section is similar to the encyclopedic features in the EARTHBOOK and THE NEW YORK TIMES ATLAS OF THE WORLD.

The one-page list of recent place-name changes gives information about changes that have occurred in recent years as the result of political upheaval in Angola, Iran, Madagascar, Mozambique, Vietnam, and Zimbabwe. The single-page list of Chinese place-names lists the Pinyin designations of principal places with the Wade-Giles equivalents. These lists are not necessary to a comprehensive atlas, but they will be helpful to readers who are in doubt about current or former names of places in these countries. The two-page glossary of geographical terms is a list of geographical words that are found in the place-names on the maps; each is followed by the name of the language it is in and by the English meaning. This feature is useful in helping readers decipher place-name labels.

IV. Geographical Balance

The Prentice-Hall Universal Atlas was produced in Britain by a British cartographer, and the content of the American edition is identical to that of the edition sold in the United Kingdom. Thus, the atlas's Anglo-European bias is not unexpected. Of the 176 pages of reference maps, 70 are of Europe; 27 of Asia; 17 of Africa; 12 of Australia and Oceania; 24 of North America; and 9 of South America. Maps of continental Europe also appear most consistently at a scale of 1:2,500,000. Generally, the scales range from 1:1,000,000 to 1:20,000,000, with Great Britain shown at 1:1,000,000. (See also *Scale and Projections.*) One full-page thematic map in the Europe section shows North Sea oil and gas fields and includes a table that breaks down United Kingdom oil and gas production from each of these fields. Other detailed full-page thematic maps represent the geological structure, climate, and population distribution of the British Isles, while there are also two facing political maps of the British Isles that show the old counties and the new (post-1974) administrative counties of the United Kingdom. Such maps will interest Anglophiles, but they are hardly necessary to a general world atlas. There is a similar full-page political map showing the departments of France, but there are no similar maps for other countries, apart from a quarter-page political map of the 48 contiguous U.S. states.

This emphasis on Great Britain and Europe does not mean, however, that the rest of the world is ignored. The user can expect to find good, detailed maps of all parts of the world, though usually at smaller scales than the maps of Great Britain and Europe.

V. Scale and Projections

The Prentice-Hall Universal Atlas uses a wide range of scales from 1:1,000,000 to 1:50,000,000. However, the scales are appropriate to the size of the pages, and they provide maps of good detail. Moreover, there is fairly good consistency in presenting adjacent areas at similar scales for easy comparison, partic-

ularly in the maps of Europe, Africa, Canada, and the United States.

As previously mentioned, the maps of European countries are drawn in the largest scales. Maps in the Asia section range from 1:1,000,000 to 1:20,000,000, with most at 1:6,000,000; Africa ranges from 1:8,000,000 to 1:15,000,000, with most at 1:8,000,000; Australia/Oceania from 1:3,500,000 to 1:8,000,000; North America from 1:3,000,000 to 1:15,000,000, with most at 1:6,000,000 and 1:7,000,000; and South America at either 1:8,000,000 or 1:16,000,000.

Many of the maps are drawn using a conical projection with two standard parallels, an excellent choice for equal-area representation with a minimum of distortion. Other projections used in the atlas are not as common; these include the Bonne, Lambert equivalent azimuthal, and Mercator projections, which are all adequate for their purposes. However, the Hammer equal-area and Mollweide's homolographic projections used for the world and Pacific Ocean maps, respectively, are unusual and create somewhat more distortion than some alternative projections would have caused.

VI. Accuracy

Place-names are presented consistently, in the official language of the country in which they are located, with English versions of important or potentially unrecognizable place-names given in parentheses. The cartographers have evidently taken great care in placing names in their proper locations and clearly adjacent to the appropriate symbols. In short, *The Prentice-Hall Universal Atlas* is an accurate and authoritative world atlas.

VII. Currency

Most recent name changes (such as *Belize, Vanuatu, Vietnam,* and *Zimbabwe*) are reflected in this atlas, although Kampuchea is still labeled as *Cambodia.*

In a somewhat dated practice, traditional Wade-Giles names, rather than the newer Pinyin transliterations, are used in the China maps and in the index.

U.S. statistical data is based on the 1980 census. World economic tables are dated 1981. World population figures are dated 1970 through 1981.

Text and photographs are contemporary and should remain so for some time.

VIII. Legibility

Typefaces throughout the atlas are legible and sufficiently varied to distinguish different types of features and sizes of towns, although place-name labels for the smallest towns are very small indeed. Most of the maps are clear and show good detail without appearing cluttered. The relief colors are well differentiated, although print in mountainous areas is occasionally hard to read. Color reproduction is excellent and in register.

The typeface used in the index and the world economic tables is small and may prove difficult for some readers.

IX. Accessibility

The accessibility of *The Prentice-Hall Universal Atlas* is greatly enhanced by a detailed and well-organized four-page table of contents. The general-reference map section is divided by continents, with each map listed individually along with its scale. The table of contents also lists the thematic maps and statistical tables that appear in the front of the volume. This is an advantage, as the various sections of the book are paginated separately.

The index includes 60,000 entries and is prefaced with a short but adequate explanation of its use and a list of abbreviations. Symbols are included with entries for countries and administrative subdivisions. Unfortunately, the entries for cities do not include the country names unless they are needed to distinguish between different places with identical names. Entries give page numbers and latitude and longitude in degrees and minutes. A spot check shows that even small towns on the maps are included in the index. Entries in the index were found on the maps with reasonable ease, although some confusion results when the place-name appears in an inset map instead of on the main map.

X. Summary

At $34.95, *The Prentice-Hall Universal Atlas* is reasonably priced and provides good value for the money. It is accurate and accessible and features first-rate cartography, although it is no longer as up-to-date as it might be. This atlas, which won the Best Reference Book Award at the 1983 Nice Book Fair, will be a likely choice especially for public and academic libraries that do not need the very largest (and most expensive) world atlases, such as the EARTHBOOK, the NATIONAL GEOGRAPHIC ATLAS OF THE WORLD, THE NEW INTERNATIONAL ATLAS, or THE TIMES ATLAS OF THE WORLD, or that want a smaller but still comprehensive and authoritative atlas to supplement these.

Prentice-Hall publishes another edition of this atlas, minus the statistical tables and encyclopedic features, as THE PRENTICE-HALL UNIVERSITY ATLAS, at a lower price.

The Prentice-Hall University Atlas

Facts at a Glance

Full Title: **The Prentice-Hall University Atlas.**
Publisher: Prentice-Hall.

Editors: Harold Fullard, H. C. Darby et al.
Copyright: 1984 by George Philip & Son, Ltd.
Edition Reviewed: twenty-first edition, 1984.

Number of Pages: 404.
Number of Maps: 176.
Number of Indexes: 1.
Number of Index Entries: 60,000.
Trim Size: 9″ × 12″.
Binding: cloth.

Price: $27.50.
Sold in bookstores, by direct mail, and directly to libraries.
ISBN 0-13-698259-X.
Revised periodically.

I. Scope and Format

The Prentice-Hall University Atlas is a general-reference atlas produced in Britain by the English cartographers George Philip & Son. Sold in England as *The University Atlas*, this map collection was first issued in 1939 and has since been through 21 editions. Over this time, significant changes have been made in content and design. Today *The Prentice-Hall University Atlas* is one of the finest atlases of its kind.

Page for page, the maps and index in the *University Atlas* are identical to those in THE PRENTICE-HALL UNIVERSAL ATLAS. The only difference in content is that the *University Atlas* does not include the 30-page section of statistical tables and the 48-page section of encyclopedia features ("The Universe, Earth & Man") found at the beginning of the UNIVERSAL ATLAS. This results in a book that costs $7.45 less than the larger volume. Libraries that require a quality medium- or large-format atlas with maps and index will be satisfied only with the *University Atlas*; those that need an atlas that also includes comprehensive statistical tables and encyclopedic features on geography should choose the UNIVERSAL ATLAS.

For complete information about the cartography and other aspects of this atlas, see the review of THE PRENTICE-HALL UNIVERSAL ATLAS on pages 196–98.

Rand McNally Contemporary World Atlas

Facts at a Glance

Full Title: **Rand McNally Contemporary World Atlas.**
Former Title: *Worldmaster.*
Publisher: Rand McNally.

Copyright: 1987.
Edition Reviewed: 1987.

Number of Pages: 256.
Number of Maps: 216.
Number of Indexes: 1.
Number of Index Entries: 30,000.
Number of Illustrations: 16 color.
Trim Size: 9" × 11".
Binding: paperback.

Price: $9.95.
Sold in bookstores, by direct mail, and directly to
libraries.
ISBN 0-528-83146-1.
Revised annually.

I. Scope and Format

The *Rand McNally Contemporary World Atlas* is a
paperback edition of the RAND McNALLY FAMILY
WORLD ATLAS. The contents are identical; the sole
difference is the binding and price. At $9.95, the
paperback version costs only $3.00 less than the hard-
cover edition, which is not a substantial enough savings to warrant purchasing the paperback instead of
the hardcover title.

Although, like its hardcover equivalent, the paperback contains a good 32-page thematic map section, the general-reference maps are heavily weighted
toward coverage of the United States at the expense
of other regions, and the maps are poorly laid out
and cluttered in their detail. The same reservations
that apply to the FAMILY WORLD ATLAS apply to
this atlas. For full information about the cartography
and other features of the *Contemporary World Atlas*,
consult the review of the RAND McNALLY FAMILY
WORLD ATLAS on pages 204–6.

Rand McNally Cosmopolitan
World Atlas

Facts at a Glance

Full Title: **Rand McNally Cosmopolitan World
Atlas.**
Publisher: Rand McNally.
Copyright: 1981.
Edition Reviewed: 1985.

Number of Pages: 364.
Number of Maps: 325.
Number of Indexes: 2.
Number of Index Entries: 85,000.
Number of Illustrations: 60 color.
Trim Size: 11" × 14½".

Binding: cloth.

Price: $55.00.
Sold in bookstores, by direct mail, and directly to
libraries.
ISBN 0-528-83149-6.
Revised annually.

I. Introduction

The *Rand McNally Cosmopolitan World Atlas* is an
oversized, comprehensive atlas with a number of special features. Along with the READER'S DIGEST WIDE
WORLD ATLAS, it is one of Rand McNally's medium-
priced large-format atlases, although not quite as large
or comprehensive as the same publisher's deluxe NEW
INTERNATIONAL ATLAS. Unlike those two other titles, however, the *Cosmopolitan World Atlas*'s general-reference maps are predominantly political,
whereas the general-reference maps in THE NEW
INTERNATIONAL ATLAS and the READER'S DIGEST
WIDE WORLD ATLAS emphasize physical features.

II. Format

With a trim size of 11" × 14½" and a thickness in
excess of one inch, the *Rand McNally Cosmopolitan
World Atlas* is physically a formidable volume, and
one that should prove durable. It has a heavy cover,
a sewn spine, and pages large enough to hold detailed
maps. The dust jacket is attractive, and the cover
itself, which is simulated leather with the title embossed in gold lettering, gives this atlas a high-quality
appearance. The medium-weight nonglossy paper on
which the maps are printed provides good color reproduction and opacity. The feature section at the
front of the atlas is printed on semiglossy paper.

The contents are divided into eight sections entitled "Human Patterns and Imprints," "Environment Maps," "United States Travel Maps," "Reference Maps and Global Views," "United States
Metropolitan Area Maps," "United States Geographical Information," "World Geographical Information," and "Index to World Reference Maps."
Several of these sections are discussed under *Special
Features.* In a departure from standard practice, the
general-reference map section includes double-page
spreads of text that precede the maps for each continent (and often for subregions within a continent).

Most of the maps in the atlas are heavily colored
political maps with shaded relief. The majority of
these are single-page maps, usually with a generous
border on all sides. The environment maps, some of
the thematic maps, and a few of the reference maps
are two-page spreads. With these, the tight binding,
combined with a lack of sufficient gutter space along

the spine, causes an unfortunate loss of some information in the gutter.

There are map legends for each of the thematic maps, but only one master legend is included for all the U.S. travel maps and the world reference maps. There is no legend for the U.S. metropolitan area maps.

III. Special Features

The 33-page feature, "Human Patterns and Imprints," which opens the atlas, is a discussion of worldwide patterns of human settlement, industrialization, and environmental concerns, written by Marvin W. Mikesell, professor of geography at the University of Chicago. The feature relates these issues to a global perspective and is profusely illustrated with maps, graphs, and four-color photographs. (Note, however, that some of the photographs lack captions.) This section is somewhat comparable to similar features on world geography in the EARTH-BOOK and THE NEW YORK TIMES ATLAS OF THE WORLD, although it is less encyclopedic in form, written rather as an extended essay. The thematic maps in this section are well presented, and they support and clarify the text. In the "World Reference Maps" section proper, there are well-illustrated features on map projections, latitude and longitude, and scale.

The continental environment maps in the next section are identical to those found in the RAND MCNALLY GOODE'S WORLD ATLAS and the READER'S DIGEST WIDE WORLD ATLAS. Together with the legend and introductory text, these first-rate maps occupy 16 pages.

The U.S. travel maps, which together with their legends and introductory matter take up 12 pages, are in actuality road maps with physical relief effects. These maps, as one might expect given Rand McNally's experience in producing road atlases, detail major interstate highways and some state routes clearly. However, the value of such maps to a general world atlas is questionable.

Following the extensive section of general-reference maps, which occupies the center of the book, is a section of U.S. metropolitan area maps. Only 12 U.S. metropolitan areas are included; 8 of these are on the East Coast or in the Northeast, 2 are in the Midwest, and 2 are on the West Coast. These maps, which also appear in THE NEW INTERNATIONAL ATLAS and the READER'S DIGEST WIDE WORLD ATLAS, give good overviews of the cities they cover, but again they do not necessarily enhance this book's prestige as a *world* atlas.

Finally, there are two sections of statistical tables. "United States Geographical Information" gives contemporary and historical population statistics on towns, cities, and states. "World Geographical Information" includes not only population figures but also statistical information on the world's lakes, rivers, mountains, islands, and oceans.

IV. Geographical Balance

The *Cosmopolitan World Atlas* contains maps representing all areas of the world; to the atlas's advantage, it includes good political maps of the Arctic, Antarctic, Atlantic, and Pacific oceans. However, like the statistical tables and the city maps already discussed, the world reference maps are strongly weighted toward coverage of the United States, Canada, and Europe. This is evident both in the number of maps devoted to each region and in the scales at which the maps are presented. (See also *Scale and Projections*.) There are 29 pages of European maps; Mediterranean countries (such as Spain, Italy, and Greece) are covered in both the main Europe section and in a subsection on the Mediterranean. The continents of Asia, Africa, and South America are each covered in 10 pages, with Australia and Oceania covered in 5 pages. On the other hand, there are 68 map pages for North America. Fifty of these are devoted to the United States. Most states are covered singly in full-page, large-scale maps; a few smaller states are mapped in pairs. There are 14 pages of Canada maps, but only 4 maps of Central America and the Caribbean. The disparity of scales is discussed in the following section of this review.

In short, in terms of its international coverage, the *Cosmopolitan World Atlas* is heavily biased—perhaps unacceptably so. Of large world atlases on the market today, only the Hammond AMBASSADOR WORLD ATLAS and the GOLD MEDALLION WORLD ATLAS (also Hammond) embody the same degree of geographical imbalance.

V. Scale and Projections

Each map is labeled with its scale as a representative fraction, verbal statement, and bar scale, a comprehensive feature and one ideal for any atlas. The scales are generally adequate to present a fair amount of detail on the large pages. However, as noted earlier, the United States, Canada, and Europe maps are drawn to the largest scales, while Third World areas are generally drawn to much smaller scales. For example, the maps of U.S. states are from 1:700,000 to 1:4,000,000, while scales of the Canadian provincial maps vary from 1:1,900,000 to 1:4,200,000. Europe, Asia, and Australia/Oceania have regional maps at 1:16,000,000. The remaining maps of Europe are at scales of 1:200,000 or 1:400,000, with the exception of the various maps of the USSR and the Mediterranean, which are at 1:8,000,000 or 1:28,000,000. Asia is covered at either 1:800,000 or 1:16,000,000. Australia/Oceania includes only one map of southeastern Australia and New Zealand, at 1:8,000,000, with several insetlike maps of major Pacific islands at various scales. Several sections of this area have no representation at scales larger than 1:16,000,000. All of South America is covered at the scale of 1:8,000,000, while all of Africa is at 1:11,400,000. This consistency within regions is admirable, but it means that the Africa maps especially omit much detail. Moreover, because like-size areas in different continents are presented at different scales, the reader is apt to get a false impression of their relative sizes.

The *Cosmopolitan World Atlas* uses standard conic, sinusoidal, and azimuthal projections, which are well chosen. These projections minimize distortion and provide equal-area representation. The projection is identified on each map. The explanation of map projections at the beginning of the world reference section should help readers understand the advantages and drawbacks of each projection type.

VI. Accuracy

Place-names are spelled correctly and consistently, and each is printed in the appropriate location. Great care has been taken to ensure that each place-name clearly identifies the proper location symbol.

There is some inconsistency in the presentation of anglicized and vernacular versions of names. The map of Italy shows many larger towns and cities labeled with their anglicized names, with the Italian names in parentheses, whereas the map of Spain labels Seville *Sevilla* only.

Physical features are well represented, considering that these are essentially political maps. The shaded relief shows the location of mountain ranges, although it does not give an accurate indication of altitude.

VII. Currency

Recent name changes (such as *Belize, Kampuchea, Vanuatu, Vietnam,* and *Zimbabwe*) have been taken into account on the appropriate maps. But the maps of China use the old Wade-Giles system of transliteration rather than the Pinyin system that has generally superseded it and is used in most other Rand McNally atlases. However, there is a one-page Pinyin/Wade-Giles conversion chart to aid readers.

The U.S. statistical tables present 1980 census figures, which are the most recent available both at the time of the book's publication and at the time of this review. However, at least half of the population figures in the world data tables date from the early 1970s, with some as old as 1962 even though more recent figures had been made public at the time of publication.

A major revision was scheduled for 1988, but that book was not available for review when this Buying Guide was compiled.

VIII. Legibility

The typefaces used throughout the atlas are clearly legible. Apart from a few of the U.S. state maps, the maps are not cluttered. There is a good variety among the typefaces used for different types of features. Place-names for political and physical features are clearly distinguishable from one another, as are boundary lines. The shaded relief is visible but does not interfere with the print that is superimposed on it. Peaks are plainly marked with name and elevation.

IX. Accessibility

The accessibility of the *Cosmopolitan World Atlas* is enhanced by a complete and comprehensive two-page table of contents. Every map and table is listed in the contents. However, the pagination is somewhat confusing, with some of the sections paginated individually and some with letter prefixes or suffixes. It almost appears as if these individual sections were added as separate entities—perhaps picked up from other Rand McNally publications—and, for the sake of printing economy, never fully integrated into the volume.

The 82,000-entry index to the world reference maps give page and alphanumeric grid locations. Physical features and places of interest are printed in italic type, and the feature is identified as a mountain, a lake, and so forth. Political names are printed in roman type, with a descriptive term (town, city) and country or state abbreviation. There is an abbreviation key and an explanation of the index at the beginning of the index. This text explains that the index includes "all important names that appear on the reference maps." In addition, some names not appearing on the maps are listed in the index with an asterisk. A spot check shows that only one in 20 names on the maps does not appear in the index; the pages and grid locations given are accurate.

A separate 3,000-entry index follows the U.S. metropolitan area maps, listing cities, towns, neighborhoods, and local area names that appear on the 12 city maps, and giving page and grid coordinates. The individual state maps, in particular, contain many insets that show important metropolitan areas or extensions of areas covered by the main map. The insets are well placed and clearly distinguishable from the main maps.

X. Summary

The *Cosmopolitan World Atlas* costs $55.00, which is not unreasonable for a large, well-made atlas of this type. As in most Rand McNally atlases, the cartography is good (if not outstanding) and authoritative. The book is also highly accessible, despite some odd pagination, and the indexes are comprehensive and easy to use. The special features are, for the most part, well designed and interesting.

However, when compared to atlases of similar scope and price, such as the EARTHBOOK, THE GREAT WORLD ATLAS, the READER'S DIGEST WIDE WORLD ATLAS, and THE NEW YORK TIMES ATLAS OF THE WORLD, the *Cosmopolitan*'s weaknesses become apparent. Foremost among these is the volume's lack of geographical balance. What purports to be a world atlas is, in effect, a U.S. atlas with maps of other parts of the world. Some of the special features, interesting as they may be, are really not germane to a world atlas. In short, while this atlas looks quite impressive from the outside, its contents do not measure up to those of most of its competitors in this size and price category.

Thus, the *Rand McNally Cosmopolitan World Atlas* will not be the first choice of libraries seeking a large-format world atlas; all of the titles mentioned above will be preferable. Collections that require a somewhat smaller, lower-priced but very authoritative atlas will be quite satisfied with RAND MCNALLY GOODE'S WORLD ATLAS or one of the larger atlases on the Prentice-Hall list.

Rand McNally Desk Reference World Atlas

Facts at a Glance

Full Title: **Rand McNally Desk Reference World Atlas.**
Former Title: The New Rand McNally College World Atlas.
Publisher: Rand McNally.
Copyright: 1987.
Edition Reviewed: 1987.

Number of Pages: 528.
Number of Maps: 346.
Number of Indexes: 1.
Number of Index Entries: 30,000.
Number of Illustrations: 60 black-and-white; 1 color.
Trim Size: 6½″ × 9½″.
Binding: cloth.

Price: $17.95.
Sold in bookstores, by direct mail, and directly to libraries.

ISBN 0-528-83287-9.
Revised periodically.

I. Introduction

The *Rand McNally Desk Reference World Atlas* combines a variety of maps with text and statistical tables in a format designed for ready reference. The book itself resembles a so-called desk or college dictionary rather than a traditional atlas, thus reinforcing the "desk reference" image that the publisher is trying to create. This work is in fact a reprint of THE NEW RAND MCNALLY COLLEGE WORLD ATLAS, a work last revised in 1985. Apart from minor changes in some of the tables in the back of the book, really only the title has changed. Thus, this cannot be considered a new work.

II. Format

Maps make up less than half of this volume. The bulk of the book is occupied by special tables, lists, and text. (See *Special Features*, below.) There are seven types of maps, with some printed on one page and others spreading across two facing pages. On the two-page spreads, map information extends into and is lost in the gutter because the tight binding prevents the pages from lying flat when the book is open.

The general-reference maps show political and cultural information. The only physical features shown are bodies of water and spot heights of selected mountain peaks. Physical relief is shown in the section of environmental maps of continents. There are also sections of world thematic maps, metropolitan area maps, world and U.S. historical maps, and road maps. While they are small, the book's maps are sufficiently detailed for the ready-reference purpose for which this atlas is intended.

A master legend precedes the sections of general reference, metropolitan area, and road maps. The maps themselves include only a bar scale and map projection statement (except the road maps, which are all drawn at the same scale and in the same projection). In the historical and thematic sections, each map has its own legend. The symbols used on the maps are all explained adequately.

III. Special Features

The special map sections in this atlas are entitled "Thematic Maps of the World," "Historical Maps of the World," and "Historical Maps of the United States." The subjects covered by the world thematic maps are climate, vegetation, land use, soils, population, and language. The maps, which are two-page spreads, are fairly detailed for their scale (about

1:130,000,000) and represent from 7 to 33 different types of features.

The environmental maps of the continents show ten categories of man-made and natural types of land use, and likewise they are quite detailed maps for their small scale. The section on world history contains one- and two-page maps depicting 21 historical situations ranging from the ancient world to post–World War II. The U.S. history section contains one- and two-page maps depicting 8 historical situations ranging from the colonial period to 1970. Each map is accompanied by a short text.

The special tables and lists include "Largest Metropolitan Areas of the World," "United States City and County Populations and Zip Codes," "Colleges and Universities of the United States," and "Major Military Installations of the United States." The tabular information is easy to read and contains a wealth of detailed information.

The "Largest Metropolitan Areas of the World" includes 257 areas with populations of 1,000,000 or more grouped by continent. The next table lists approximately 25,000 U.S. cities and counties, including places with as few as 250 people. Most population figures are from the 1980 census; Rand McNally estimates are given where census data is not available. The cities are arranged alphabetically, not state by state.

"Colleges and Universities of the United States" lists accredited four-year colleges and universities with 100 or more students. The colleges and universities are arranged in alphabetical order by state and include the city location and fall 1982 enrollment figures. "Major Military Installations of the United States" are arranged alphabetically by state and include city locations.

The special text material includes "Gazetteer of the World," "Guide to Major World Cities," "Guide to Major United States Cities," and "Glossary of Map Terminology." All of these are presented in concise, easy-to-comprehend formats. The "Gazetteer of the World," which describes the world's countries and includes photos, drawings, tables listing political subunits, and statistical information, resembles a geographic encyclopedia. Population figures are "recent estimates based on UN statistics." Dates of other statistics range from 1975 to 1979.

Each entry in the guides to major world and U.S. cities includes the altitude, average temperatures, travel information (such as airport transportation, hotels, restaurants), and sources of additional information. The lists are arranged alphabetically by city. The world city list also includes English-language publications and banking hours. In addition, the U.S. list gives for each city the area code, time zone, trade exhibition facilities, and phone numbers for time and weather.

IV. Geographical Balance

There are 89 pages of general-reference maps in this 528-page atlas, 44 of which are for the United States. There is a marked disproportionate coverage of North America, as virtually every U.S. state and Canadian province has its own map. The only foreign country with its own map is Italy; all other nations are mapped in pairs or groups. Coverage of the world is in a clockwise arrangement around the globe, with Europe on 11 maps; Asia on 5; Africa on 3; Australia/New Zealand on 2; and South America on 5. Oceania is represented only on the world maps.

V. Scale and Projections

A variety of projections and scales are used on the maps, but there is consistency. For example, the European maps (except Scandinavia) are all in a conic projection at a scale of 1:6,000,000. Asia is represented in Lambert conformal conic and polyconic projections at scales ranging from 1:11,400,000 to 1:26,000,000, with most at 1:22,800,000. Africa is covered in sinusoidal projections at a scale of 1:22,800,000. Australia is shown in the Lambert azimuthal equal-area projection at 1:22,800,000. South America is on an oblique conic conformal projection at 1:11,600,000. Canadian provinces are mapped in oblique cylindrical projections at scales ranging from 1:6,150,000 to 1:2,800,000, while U.S. states are on a Lambert conformal conic projection at scales ranging from 1:1,000,000 to 1:5,850,000. In all cases, the scale is indicated on the inset maps.

The metropolitan maps of the world are drawn at a scale of 1:367,000. The environmental maps are in Lambert azimuthal equal-area projections, with most at a scale of 1:32,000,000. The exceptions are Europe, which is shown at 1:20,500,000, and the United States, which is at 1:16,000,000. The travel maps are on the Albers conical equal-area projection, at a scale of 1:4,740,000. The world political maps are at 1:133,000,000 on Miller cylindrical and 1:100,000,000 on a polar azimuthal equidistant projection. Both distort drastically, but taken together they give the reader an accurate idea of the earth and its landforms.

The world thematic maps are drawn in either Goode's interrupted homolosine equal-area projection or Robinson's projection. These are good choices, because readers are comparing areal distribution of phenomena on these maps, and these projections minimize distortion.

VI. Accuracy

The cartographic information in this atlas appears to be quite accurate. Place-names in foreign countries are spelled according to the currently accepted English translations. Chinese names are the exception, however, as they are the old Wade-Giles transliterations (*Peking*, *Canton*, and so forth), with the new Pinyin spellings (*Beijing*, *Guangzhou*, and so forth) given beneath each name in smaller print. Place-names are labeled accurately, and the lettering of physical place-names stretches over the extent of the feature named.

Considering the small scale of the maps, political boundaries, rivers, and coastlines are delineated quite accurately. One inaccuracy our reviewers noticed was that a portion of far western Kentucky is shown as part of Tennessee. Another concerns the boundary dispute among India, Pakistan, and China in the Jammu and Kashmir region, where China's line of control is not shown.

VII. Currency

For the most part, the information in this atlas is as current as its 1987 copyright date. In a few cases, however, redesigned national flags and place-name spelling changes are not reflected. Harry S Truman reservoir in west central Missouri, which was created in 1979, does not appear on the general-reference map. It does appear, but is not named, on the road map.

The photographs in the gazetteer and at the beginning of each section are contemporary. The text descriptions of places are up-to-date. In general, this atlas is modern.

VIII. Legibility

The typefaces on the maps are quite legible and sufficiently differentiated, so that the different categories of names are easily distinguishable. However, the profusion of labels gives the maps a cluttered appearance. There are simply too many names for the small scale of the maps.

Linear symbols for roads, rivers, and boundaries are clearly distinguishable, but there are problems with the use of color. Different colors are used for different political units, and they are rather garish. Furthermore, where an aqua color is used, rivers and political names (which are printed in blue) are hard to distinguish. In most places the two symbols used to delineate boundaries are out of register.

IX. Accessibility

The reference map index lists "all the important names," most of which are political units, in a single alphabetical sequence. Each place-name is identified with its U.S. state or country, the map index key, and the page number of the largest-scale map on which it appears. Places that are shown both on the main map and on an inset on the same page are indexed to both. The insets have a separate key grid. Of the physical place-names that appear on the maps, only the "most important" are listed in the index. Each of those entered is followed by a descriptive term to indicate its nature.

X. Summary

At $17.95, the *Rand McNally Desk Reference World Atlas* is currently the only atlas that contains a variety of ready-reference features in a desk-size format. However, its maps are neither as well designed nor its facts as up-to-date as one might normally expect from a Rand McNally atlas. Until the volume is revised, therefore, this title can be recommended only with reservations.

Rand McNally Family World Atlas

Facts at a Glance

Full Title: **Rand McNally Family World Atlas.**
Former Title: **Worldmaster.**
Publisher: Rand McNally.
Copyright: 1984.
Edition Reviewed: 1985 revision.

Number of Pages: 256.
Number of Maps: 216.
Number of Indexes: 1.
Number of Index Entries: 30,000.
Number of Illustrations: 16 color.
Trim Size: 9″ × 11″.
Binding: cloth.

Price: $12.95.
Sold in bookstores, by direct mail, and directly to libraries.
ISBN 0-528-83145-3.
Revised as needed.

I. Introduction

The *Rand McNally Family World Atlas* is a medium-sized general-reference atlas designed primarily for home use; the jacket copy describes the work as "a must for every home library." The cartography, produced by the experienced Rand McNally staff, is identical to that found in THE NEW RAND MCNALLY COLLEGE WORLD ATLAS.

II. Format

With a trim size of 9″ × 11″ and a thickness of less than one inch, the *Rand McNally Family World Atlas* is a convenient size for both home and library shelves. The volume is in fact virtually identical in size to the RAND McNALLY GOODE'S WORLD ATLAS, although the contents of the two books are quite different. The maps are printed on fairly lightweight paper, with good nonglossy color reproduction but poor opacity, so that there is a fair amount of show-through of dark colors. The book has a sewn spine with a heavy, well-finished cover. The binding is scored so that it opens easily and lies flat.

According to the publisher, the atlas contains 216 maps. While this sounds like a generous selection, in fact the number of full-page maps is significantly less. The *Rand McNally Family World Atlas* relies heavily on inset maps, and more than half of the 216 maps in this book are indeed insets. Many of these are very small, some only about one tenth of a page. Some pages have as many as four insets, which leaves little space for the main map. This type of layout gives many of the pages a cluttered look and will be confusing to many readers.

A master legend precedes the political map section. Although straightforward, it does not include actual population figures for the different-sized city symbols. There is no map key on any of the individual reference map pages.

III. Special Features

The atlas begins with a 26-page section entitled "Today's World in Maps." Each continent is given introductory text, a global view showing relief, a location map, and several small thematic maps. The thematic maps include subjects such as rainfall, vegetation, population, minerals, and energy. Each continent is covered by six or eight maps.

The next section, "The Political World in Maps," includes 90 pages of political maps. "World Tables and Facts" includes 9 pages of political information, comparisons, and populations, while "United States Tables and Facts" covers 34 pages and includes for the most part populations of cities, towns, counties, and states.

A table of abbreviations precedes the 75-page index.

IV. Geographical Balance

North America, South America, and Africa fare best in the opening section of thematic maps, each with eight maps, as compared to six each for Europe, Asia, and Australia/Oceania.

In the main section of political maps, a North American bias is evident. North America has 57 pages of coverage, of which 9 are on Canada and 45 are on the United States. Europe has 12 pages; Asia, 6 pages; Africa, 4 pages; Australia/Oceania, 2 pages;

and South America, 6 pages. Each U.S. state and Canadian province is given a full page, with the space-saving exceptions of 12 states which appear two on a page.

V. Scale and Projections

Only bar scales are given for most maps, making comparison of areas difficult. The scales of maps in the main political section range from approximately 1:950,000 to 1:52,000,000. These very small scales are inappropriate for the size of the pages and the amount of detail the maps attempt to show. The maps are crowded and cluttered in appearance, and difficult to use. The individual state maps vary widely in scale. Texas actually looks smaller than New Jersey, as each fills the page on which it appears. This distortion may be misleadng to younger readers.

The thematic maps are small but usable, although several have such wide margins that they could have been made larger. They would then have been able to cover more area or, even better, to have been reproduced in a larger, more readable scale.

The standard azimuthal, conic, and cylindrical projections have been used, and no serious distortions in shape or area caused by projection are evident. However, a polar azimuthal projection is used to show the North Pole and air distances, and a Miller cylindrical projection is used for the map of the world; both result in considerable distortion at their edges.

VI. Accuracy

Place-names appear to be spelled accurately, with anglicized versions given preference over vernacular spellings, which are included in parentheses for important entries: for example, *Riyadh (Ar Riyad)*, *Ruse (Ruschuk)*, *Rio Grande (Rio Bravo del Norte)*, and so on. Considerable care is evident in printing names in proper correlation to their symbols. This is always important, but all the more so when the maps are of such small scale and include so many place-names.

Except for rivers and lakes, most physical features are labeled but not represented on the maps by any symbols or relief. Borders are fairly clear. They are somewhat heavier than usual on most maps, but this makes them easy to locate.

VII. Currency

Recent name changes (*Belize, Vanuatu, Kampuchea, Vietnam, Zimbabwe*) are represented correctly.

As in the RAND McNALLY COSMOPOLITAN WORLD ATLAS, the figures given in the "Populations of Foreign Cities and Towns" table are not recent. At least half of the figures are from the early 1970s, with some as early as 1962. The revision of this atlas is inconsistent, as the population figures in the "World Political Information" table are 1984 estimates, and comparisons between the two sources of figures show considerable differences. U.S. figures are from the 1980 census.

VIII. Legibility

Typefaces are clear and sufficiently varied to distinguish between political units and physical features.

Because they are relatively small, most of the maps appear very cluttered. Print size is also quite small, of necessity, thus adding to the confusion. On the U.S. state maps, county borders are represented by a blue broken line over a gray solid line; often, these colors are not in register, which further detracts from the appearance of the maps and adds to the confusion. Adults with poor eyesight may have trouble with the size of the print; all readers, with the cluttered appearance.

Though fairly dark, the colors reproduce well.

IX. Accessibility

The table of contents is clear and comprehensive, making it easy for users to locate particular maps and tables.

The index includes over 30,000 entries and gives page and alphanumeric grid locators. The grid squares are small enough for easy location. However, the marginal grid markings are very small and light and are themselves hard to see and keep in view. The introduction to the index is thorough and concise, and it states that "all important names that appear on the reference maps" are included. A spot check shows that most of the smaller towns on the maps do not appear in the index, which is consistent with their not being important enough for inclusion. Each entry includes a descriptive term, such as *co* for county, *is* for island, and so on, for entries other than cities and the state or country. Several entries cite appearances of names on both main maps and insets.

Abundant insets show important urban areas or extensions of areas from the main maps. The insets are clearly distinguishable from the main maps; however, because they are tucked into much of the available space on pages, their inclusion adds to the clutter.

X. Summary

The *Rand McNally Family World Atlas* is intended for the home rather than the library market. The book is well made and at $12.95 is inexpensive for its size. These factors alone, however, cannot recommend it, for they are outweighed by considerable drawbacks. The preponderance of U.S. maps, the dearth and small scale of the maps of non-U.S. re-

gions, and the cluttered pages and confusing layout all make this atlas a questionable value at any price. Home and public library collections alike would be better served by the clear maps and excellent special features of the RAND MCNALLY GOODE'S WORLD ATLAS or by THE PRENTICE-HALL NEW WORLD ATLAS, even though both of these volumes are more expensive than the *Family World Atlas*.

Rand McNally Goode's World Atlas

Facts at a Glance

Full Title: **Rand McNally Goode's World Atlas.**
Publisher: Rand McNally.
Editors: Edward B. Espenshade, Jr., and Joel L. Morrison.
Copyright: 1986.
Edition Reviewed: 17th edition, revised second printing, 1986.

Number of Pages: 384.
Number of Maps: 396.
Number of Indexes: 1.
Number of Index Entries: 36,000.
Number of Illustrations: 43 color.
Trim Size: 8½″ × 11″.
Binding: cloth.

Price: $22.95.
Sold in bookstores and directly to libraries. 25 percent library discount.
ISBN 0-528-83127-5.
Major revisions on reference maps for each printing; statistical thematic maps revised every four years.

I. Introduction

The *Rand McNally Goode's World Atlas* is a comprehensive medium-sized (8½″ × 11″) reference atlas. It is edited by Edward B. Espenshade, Jr., professor emeritus of geography at Northwestern University, and Joel L. Morrison, senior consultant affiliated with the United States Geological Survey. The atlas, which still carries the name of its original compiler, the American cartographer J. Paul Goode, is now in its 17th edition. The first edition was issued in 1922.

II. Format

Goode's World Atlas is printed using a good medium-weight paper which provides excellent color reproduction and opacity. The spine is sewn, and the binding is well finished and durable. It has an attractive full-color jacket. The size of the atlas makes it easy to handle and convenient to store, but it also leads to overcrowding on its maps and elimination of worthwhile detail. Many maps are two-page spreads, but a gutter along the spine edge makes reading their centers easy. Maps often "escape" their neat lines and this, combined with the many insets, gives some pages a cluttered look, as, for example, on page 200. Full legends appear only at the beginnings of the "Regional" and "Major Cities" sections, requiring awkward consultation. Scale, relief, and population symbols conveniently appear on most pages.

The atlas is divided into six distinct sections: "Introduction: Maps and Imagery," "World Thematic Maps," "Major Cities," "Regional Section," "Plate Tectonics and Ocean Floor Maps," and "Geographic Tables and Indexes."

III. Special Features

Each of the six sections of *Goode's World Atlas* may be considered a special feature.

"Introduction: Maps and Imagery" (nine pages) contains a basic discussion of maps and mapmaking, including map scales and projections, and recent technological advances. The text is brief, basic, and good, but it is also fairly technical and might be difficult for the layman to read and/or comprehend. For example, the explanation of Mercator projection says in part: "Thus, for every point on the map, the angles shown are correct in every direction within a limited area. To achieve this, the projection increases latitudinal and longitudinal distances away from the equator." Without an explanation of latitude this is hardly clear.

"World Thematic Maps" (52 pages) includes maps on a wide variety of subjects, including political and physical maps, climate, weather, vegetation, soils, population, health, economics, industry, agriculture, minerals, and transportation. Many of these maps are accompanied by statistical graphs. The thematic maps are an excellent ready source of basic information.

"Major Cities" (28 pages) includes 62 maps of the world's most populous metropolitan areas, all depicted at the same scale and in a standardized and comparable format.

The "Regional Section" (160 pages) is divided into standard continental areas. A selection of thematic maps precedes the general physical/political maps of each area. Many insets highlight important population centers throughout this section. "Plate Tectonics and Ocean Floor Maps" (seven pages) includes text, diagrams, and maps.

"Geographic Tables and Indexes" (126 pages) has an unusual feature in an atlas—for the most part, entries have a pronunciation key, which is missing only with repetition of a first part. For example, when a word like *Valley* or *Pine* is repeated, the phonetic spelling is not given twice, although frequently it appears in the second entry, not the first. There are also tables of political information, comparisons, principal cities, and foreign geographical terms. The pronouncing feature of the index is both unusual and quite helpful.

IV. Geographical Balance

This atlas is heavily weighted toward the United States and Canada. Of 160 pages in the "Regional Section," 60 represent North America, 37 Europe, 25 Asia, 7 Australia, and only 14 show Africa and 8 South America. The "Major Cities" section is slightly better; 14 of the 62 maps show U.S. or Canadian cities, and several more unusual cities are represented, such as Brazzaville, Manila, and Teheran. The thematic maps preceding the North America regional section are far more extensive than those in any other section.

V. Scale and Projections

Scales for the most detailed maps in the "Regional Section" are 1:4,000,000, which provides a good overall picture, although at the cost of some detail. Conic projections, which represent areas equally and with a minimum of distortion, are used for the majority of maps in this section. The world thematic maps generally use a Goode's homolosine equal-area (condensed) projection, which is standard in this type of map. One unfortunate problem occurs in the "Landforms" map, where the interruption, which removes the center portion of the Atlantic Ocean to save space on the page, actually causes the deletion of the Mid-Atlantic Ridge, which is precisely the type of feature being shown on this map. Most of the small world thematic maps try to show more detail than their scales will allow with clarity. A few of these maps require insets to show adequate detail; this is confusing. All "Major Cities" maps are at the scale of 1:300,000, making comparison easy. However, this scale allows little detail beyond major through routes, extent of urbanization, boundaries, and some local names. A larger scale would show less of the cities' surroundings but could give greater detail more clearly presented.

VI. Accuracy

Considerable effort is evident in the positioning of place-names in their proper relationship to symbols. Unfortunately, confusion and overcrowding occasionally result from the small size and large scale of maps, combined with the variety of information the cartographers are trying to include, often in several different typefaces, such as the names (sometimes in two languages) of countries, cities, towns, rivers, physical features, regions, states, and so forth. A few problems in accuracy appear. One problem is an inconsistent use of conventional and new forms in Chinese names. The capital of China is given as Peking (Beijing), with preference to the Wade-Giles form, whereas another label says Xizang (Tibet), giving preference to the new Pinyin form. On two maps the English resort towns of Torquay and Torbay appear as one city. The New York City metropolitan map lists *Passaic Expwy* as an alternate name for Interstate 80, although this name is not in common usage locally.

VII. Currency

Rand McNally's excellent revision policy includes major revisions of the reference maps for each printing, and revisions of the statistical thematic maps every four years as new data become available. This assures that the most recent geographic information will appear in each printing of the atlas. In spot checks, recent name and/or boundary changes for the following were shown correctly in the atlas: Salisbury, Rhodesia, now *Harare*, *Zimbabwe*; North Vietnam and South Vietnam, now *Vietnam*; Cambodia, now *Kampuchea*; British Honduras, now *Belize*.

VIII. Legibility

The typefaces used on the maps are legible; however, their size, combined with the range of information being portrayed, sometimes results in an overcrowded map which is difficult to read. The use of shaded gradient tints enhances the depiction of relief, but it also hinders the readability of the print. The city maps portray roads with a yellow line against a dark background. This is unusual and can confuse readers, as roads are more generally depicted in a dark color against a lighter background. This is also inconsistent with road symbols used on the regional maps, which show roads in red against a light green or light brown background.

IX. Accessibility

The extensive index refers to pages and gives latitude and longitude for locating places. Having coordinates appear here provides valuable additional information; however, this requires some practice for locating places. A brief explanation of latitude and longitude would have been a welcome addition. It must be noted that the presentation of coordinates in an alternate style, for example *53.37 N* rather than *53° 37′ N*, requires some familiarity with this system, or some practice on the part of a new user. The detailed table of contents is an important and necessary asset, as many insets may appear out of strict geographic order, and most thematic maps appear two on a page.

X. Summary

Rand McNally Goode's World Atlas is an excellent quick-reference source with particularly helpful features in the thematic maps and pronouncing index. Public, academic, and research libraries will find that *Goode's* makes an excellent supplement to larger atlases such as THE NEW INTERNATIONAL ATLAS, THE NEW YORK TIMES ATLAS OF THE WORLD, and THE TIMES ATLAS OF THE WORLD. Home users will also be well served by this atlas and may prefer its format.

In either case, the volume's price of $22.95 is quite reasonable for the amount of information provided, making this an excellent value. Its longevity (17 editions since 1922) is a clear indication that it has found acceptance by a substantial buying public. In short, few atlases of this size are in *Goode's* class. THE PRENTICE-HALL NEW WORLD ATLAS is one title that may prove a less expensive, high-quality alternative, but although its thematic maps are good, they are much less extensive than *Goode's*.

Rand McNally Images of the World: An Atlas of Satellite Imagery and Maps

Facts at a Glance

Full Title: **Rand McNally Images of the World: An Atlas of Satellite Imagery and Maps.**
Former Title: *Diercke Weltraumbild-Atlas.*
Publisher: Rand McNally.
Editor: Christopher Mueller-Wille.
Copyright: 1983.
Edition Reviewed: 1983.

Number of Pages: 160.
Number of Maps: 151.
Number of Illustrations: 112 satellite images (photographs).
Trim Size: 8¾″ × 11¾″.
Binding: cloth.

Price: $24.95; 25 percent discount to libraries.
Sold in bookstores and by direct mail.
ISBN 0-528-63002-4.
No scheduled revision.

I. Introduction

Rand McNally Images of the World: An Atlas of Satellite Imagery and Maps is a compilation of high-altitude photographs and corresponding maps of areas of agricultural, geologic, industrial, and urban development interest throughout the world. It is a specialized work, intended for college students, geographers, researchers, and lay readers with an interest in satellite imagery, and it should not be mistaken for a traditional atlas. Its editor states that "its concept of clearly focused regional emphasis makes it a perfect companion to other atlas and geographic texts, as well as a valuable, independent fact-providing and fact-finding volume."

II. Format

Each two-page grouping contains one or more large satellite-image photographs and one or more corresponding maps, depicting the same area with emphasis on a particular theme, such as delta environments, flooding, economy, and so forth. In a relatively few cases, photographs bleed into the page gutters, thus losing some of the image.

The paper stock is lightweight and glossy, and this glossiness enhances the photographic printing. Color reproduction is excellent. Although the pages are sewn and reinforced with headbands and footbands, the full-color paper-over-boards binding appears to be weak. The front endpapers and cover were already torn in our review copy. The volume will probably not hold up well with moderate use.

III. Special Features

Three sections of introductory text discuss "Concepts and Technical Foundations of Remote Sensing," "Uses and Applications of Spaceborne Remote Sending," and "Image Processing and Cartographic Preparation." Although the text is fairly technical, these well-illustrated sections provide a solid basic knowledge of satellite imagery. The introduction concludes with a glossary of foreign terms, abbreviations, a metric conversion chart, and a table of imagery sources and dates of photographs used in the volume.

The subjects of photo/map groupings consist of: coastal forms/estuaries/land reclamation (13 groupings); geology/tectonic structure/natural catastrophes/natural events (6 groupings); vegetational succession/vegetational and climatic zonation (7 groupings); agriculture/agricultural development (8 groupings); irrigation agriculture/oases/arid lands (10 groupings); subarctic and arctic zones/tundra/taiga (6 groupings); industrial production and energy/mineral extraction (8 groupings); and urban agglomerations (9 groupings).

An appendix includes nine images of Munich, West Germany, which illustrate different data collection and reproduction techniques. This might have been better integrated into the introductory material, which deals with the technical aspects of satellite photography.

IV. Geographical Balance

The geographical balance is somewhat weighted toward Europe, with 34 groupings, as compared to 20 for North America, 24 for Asia, 10 for Africa, 4 for Australia, and 5 for South America. However, this should not be considered a serious problem as the purpose of this atlas is not to attempt to represent the entire world, but rather to use a variety of images to illustrate the versatility of satellite photography and to show different types of Earth environments. The editor states that photographs for inclusion were selected on the basis of quality.

V. Scale and Projections

Scale information appears for most maps and photographs in the form of representative fractions.

The photographs are given larger scales, with ones usually of 1:1,500,000 or larger. The scales of the urban photographs for New York, Washington, D.C., and San Francisco are particularly impressive. At 1:50,000, the reader can clearly see the World Trade Center, the White House, and the towers of the Golden Gate Bridge.

The scales of the maps are often smaller, and there are many examples of maps at scales more than half that of the corresponding photographs. In fact, most of the groupings have photographs and maps that are not at the same scale. This makes it difficult to interpret the photographs, a task already unfamiliar to most readers. Only rarely is a box provided on a map to outline the area shown in the photograph, and the photographs are never labeled with the area shown on the map.

Several examples of photographs and corresponding maps are presented in a misoriented fashion; that is, with north-south alignments that do not match. Although this does not seriously hamper the reader's ability to interpret the photograph, it is careless and should have been avoided.

Projections used for the maps are not stated; however, given the purpose of the volume, this is not troublesome.

VI. Accuracy

Two obvious inaccuracies are present. On the map of New York City, one of the most detailed maps in the atlas, ferry lines that did not exist at the time of publication are incorrectly shown crossing the Hudson River. On the photograph of California a straight line represents the state's border. An inexperienced reader might interpret this to mean that this man-made feature actually occurs in nature, particularly as no other photograph includes any superimposed label. Although neither is a glaring error, they bring into question the accuracy of depictions of other less-familiar areas.

A more subtle but also more frequent inaccuracy is the presence of several maps that do not properly match their corresponding photographs. This is often caused by misorientation or greatly differing scales and may cause difficulty in interpreting the photographs. Examples include the groupings for the Rhone Valley, France (page 38); Fujiyama, Japan (page 63); Elburz Mountains, Iran (pages 64–65); and Argolis, Greece (page 93).

VII. Currency

It is difficult to judge the currency of the material, as the volume does not present the standard benchmarks against which to judge. Most of the photography was done in the 1970s, which is sufficiently recent for the stated purpose of depicting thematic features of the Earth's surface. Similarly, only major changes in satellite technology would cause the introductory materials to become outdated. It was copyrighted in West Germany in 1981 and in 1983 when the American edition was published. There probably were no revisions between the two dates.

VIII. Legibility

The volume boasts excellent color reproduction. The photographs are very well reproduced, and the maps are clearly legible. Symbols used on the maps are well differentiated, easy to interpret, and appropriate to the purpose of each map.

IX. Accessibility

The detailed table of contents takes up two pages, and the two color-coded index maps that appear early in the volume indicate the subject and geographic coverage provided in the atlas.

Unfortunately, there is no index. However, there are illustrated introductory sections: "Concepts and Technical Foundations of Remote Sensing," "Uses and Applications of Spaceborne Remote Sensing," and "Image Processing and Cartographic Preparation."

X. Summary

Despite some problems, *Rand McNally Images of the World* is a handsome volume which is well worth its $24.95 price, if only for its uniqueness. However, besides this, it is an excellent value and would be well used as a text that illustrates new ways to learn about our planet, for example, as required additional reading for college students in geography and geology courses. Although it has little reference value for general public libraries, it does provide much worthwhile, and often hard-to-find, satellite imagery in one place. It is particularly recommended for geography, aerospace, and other science collections. It will also make for fascinating browsing for anyone

interested in different and revealing perspectives of our planet.

Rand McNally Quick Reference World Atlas

Facts at a Glance

Full Title: **Rand McNally Quick Reference World Atlas.**
Publisher: Rand McNally.
Copyright: 1986.
Edition Reviewed: 1987.

Number of Pages: 48.
Number of Maps: 45 map pages.
Number of Indexes: 1.
Number of Index Entries: 4,000.
Trim Size: 8½″ × 11″.
Binding: paperback.

Price: $3.95.
Sold in bookstores and by direct mail.
ISBN 0-528-83226-3.
Revised annually.

I. Introduction

The *Rand McNally Quick Reference World Atlas* is a concise, notebook-size paperback atlas intended for general ready-reference consultation. And though most atlases of this type are designed specifically for students, the *Quick Reference Atlas* is unique in that its maps are purposely "adult."

II. Format

The *Quick Reference Atlas* has a simple format. Of its 64 pages, fully 47 are occupied by political general-reference maps with shaded relief. The majority of these maps are two-page spreads, allowing for relatively large-scale coverage of extended areas with good detail. Unlike Rand McNally's CONTEMPORARY WORLD ATLAS and FAMILY WORLD ATLAS, the *Quick Reference Atlas* makes judicious use of inset maps, which greatly enhance its utility.

The atlas's cover is made of heavy-coated paper, and the pages are securely stapled. There is no spine, so the book is flexible. The pages open fully, and a sufficient interior margin prevents the loss of information in the gutter.

III. Special Features

While the *Quick Reference Atlas* contains relatively few special features, those it does include are well designed and present useful ready-reference information. The inside front cover contains a list of principal countries and regions of the world, including their areas in square miles, populations, and population per square mile. The inside back cover lists principal cities of the world and their populations. There is a world map with a graph showing comparative land areas and populations.

IV. Geographical Balance

Of the 47 pages of maps in the atlas, more than one third (16 pages) show the United States. These maps are also presented at the best scales used in the atlas (1:4,000,000). Of the remaining maps, the geographical representation is fairly well distributed, although Africa receives only four pages and South America only three pages.

V. Scale and Projections

Scales are given on every map in the forms of representative fraction, verbal statement, and bar scale. Each map also contains a small diagram showing area represented in square miles.

The scales used in the atlas, ranging from 1:4,000,000 to 1:40,000,000, with most at 1:16,000,000, do not allow the depiction of a great deal of detail, but they do result in a clear map that avoids cluttering and overcrowding. By presenting maps of adjacent areas at the same scale (for example, Africa on several pages all at 1:16,000,000), the editors have given a degree of consistency.

Standard conic, azimuthal, and sinusoidal projections are used to show equal-area representation with a minimum of distortion. Projections are identified on each map. There is a statement on each map that "elevations and depressions are given in feet," but no keys or legends indicate these.

VI. Accuracy

Greater care could have been given to the placement of names on maps in order to provide a clearer connection with the appropriate city symbols. There are several examples in urban areas of confusion in determining which names match which symbols. In addition, on the 1:4,000,000 map of the northeastern United States, the symbol for Burlington, Vermont, is incorrectly the same size as those for its much smaller neighbors, Essex and Winooski. Although symbols are available on the legend for cities of 1,000,000+ population, most large urban areas are represented instead by a red area that shows the extent of urbanization, a practice that introduces occasional distortions. For example, on the 1:12,000,000 U.S. map, Miami appears to occupy the lower third of Florida's east coast.

VII. Currency

Population figures in the "World Political Information" table are estimates for 1985. Recent name changes, such as *Belize*, *Zimbabwe*, *Vanuatu*, and *Kampuchea*, are represented correctly. There is a small table converting conventional Wade-Giles Chinese place-names to the new Pinyin versions. However, the presentation of Chinese place-names on the maps themselves is inconsistent. For example, the capital city is identified as *Peking (Beijing)*, but *Xizang (Tibet)* is the way the former Himalayan nation is labeled.

VIII. Legibility

Typefaces are legible and clear, with sufficient differentiation to distinguish political units from physical features. However, names printed over dark relief shading are difficult to read. Only the Western Europe map suffers from serious overcrowding. Colors are varied and well produced, without giving the appearance of overcoloring.

IX. Accessibility

Accessibility is not a major concern in a 64-page book. The 10-page, 3,500-entry index is quite sufficient. Each place-name entry is preceded by the number, in boldface, of the page on which it appears. The place is located not by alphanumeric grid coordinates but by latitude and longitude figures, rounded to the nearest degree. A list of abbreviations of geographical names and terms at the head of the index assists the reader in deciphering the abbreviations that appear in the index.

X. Summary

The *Rand McNally Quick Reference World Atlas*, priced at $3.95, provides excellent value as a convenient ready-reference resource. It is sufficiently detailed for casual home and office use, although the volume itself probably will not stand up well to heavy library use, and most library users will prefer more substantial volumes. Readers seeking a sturdier ready-reference atlas may prefer THE RANDOM HOUSE CONCISE WORLD ATLAS or the VNR POCKET ATLAS, although both of these have smaller pages (and thus smaller maps) and are more expensive. For a basic (if small) selection of world maps that combine physical and political features, however, readers will be just as well served by the *Rand McNally Quick Reference World Atlas* as by such more expensive titles as the CITATION WORLD ATLAS, the RAND MCNALLY COMTEMPORARY WORLD ATLAS, the RAND MCNALLY FAMILY WORLD ATLAS, or THE WHOLE EARTH ATLAS, none of which uses shaded relief to show physical features.

The Random House Concise World Atlas

Facts at a Glance

Full Title: **The Random House Concise World Atlas.**
Publisher: Random House.
Editors: staff of John Bartholomew & Son.
Copyright: 1984 by John Bartholomew & Son Ltd.
Edition Reviewed: 1984.

Number of Pages: 208.
Number of Maps: 120.
Number of Indexes: 1.
Number of Index Entries: 20,000.
Trim Size: 6″ × 8⅝″.
Binding: laminated paper.

Price: $7.95.
Sold in bookstores and directly to schools and
 libraries.
ISBN 0-394-74007-6.
Revised as needed.

I. Introduction

The maps contained in *The Random House Concise World Atlas* were compiled by John Bartholomew & Son, the same respected Edinburgh-based cartographers responsible for THE TIMES ATLAS OF THE WORLD and its junior version, THE NEW YORK TIMES ATLAS OF THE WORLD. The *Concise World Atlas* is intended to provide the general reader with basic physical and political maps of the world in a convenient and inexpensive format.

II. Format

The *Concise World Atlas* consists predominantly of physical maps of regions and countries, interspersed with smaller-scale political maps of the continents. Over half of the maps are two-page spreads, but these are generally separated by a narrow space so that the contents are not swallowed in the gutter. In the center of a few maps, however, names are cut off and boundary lines and other features do not match exactly. Each map is contained within neat lines. Occasionally, part of a map spills over the neat line in order to show an important detail that might otherwise be cut off.

There is both a print and graphic table of contents. Every continent but Antarctica is shown in outline form overlaid with index maps that are labeled with page numbers.

The atlas opens fully but does not lie flat, and an unacceptable amount of information is lost in the gutter. The size is adequate for the types of maps included and is convenient both for desktop use and storage on library shelves. The sewn laminated paper binding is sturdy. Pages are heavy and nonglossy.

A master legend is located near the front of the atlas; the relatively small page size precludes a legend on each map. The symbols describe various types of boundaries, transportation elements, and landscape and miscellaneous features. The legend ranks eight levels of population centers and uses various typefaces to describe political and other features. The only features described in the atlas that relate to economic geography are oil and gas fields and pipelines.

Two British usages in the legend may be drawbacks for the general American reader: the numbers describing various sizes of population centers are printed with a space instead of a comma to denote thousands. Also, elevations are recorded in meters only, and there is no indication to show that *m* means "meters."

III. Special Features

Three special two-page thematic maps complement the political and physical maps. The world physical map, at a 1:150,000,000 scale, is very general but does show major air travel routes. On the same two pages is a comparative cross-sectional diagram of major mountain peaks and their elevations. The world time zones map, a desirable atlas feature, has a slightly larger scale with national boundaries delineated. Major ocean shipping lanes are also shown. However, the use of 24-hour clock readings rather than "A.M." and "P.M." might be a drawback for many American readers.

The world environment map, at a larger scale than the previous two maps, shows general relief, river systems, vegetation, major ocean currents, continental and ice shelves, and a few extreme weather records. Eight vegetation types are shown in color and are explained succinctly in a legend. Specific rainfall figures are not given.

Two two-page bathymetric maps show the Atlantic Ocean in its entirety and most of the Pacific Ocean, with special emphasis on the maritime boundaries of Australasia. The latter map includes only those areas between about 45°N and 55°S. Some of the other maps provide information about the parts excluded from this map, but part of the area directly south of the Bering Strait, including the southwestern Aleutian Islands, is omitted from this atlas.

IV. Geographical Balance

Most of the world is well represented in this atlas, although there are gaps such as those already noted.

There is slightly better coverage of the United States and Western Europe than of any other regions, both in terms of scale size and number of maps. Great Britain has six pages of maps while all of Africa has only seven. Most countries appear in groups, although that is not a major disadvantage in an atlas of this size.

V. Scale and Projections

Various scales are used throughout the atlas, presented both as representative fractions and as bar scales (kilometers and miles). The capital letter *M* is used after the representative fraction to denote "million," but nowhere is this explained. The use of 1:2.5M in place of 1:2,500,000 with no explanation might be confusing to American readers.

In general, densely populated areas have been selected for detailed representation. The slight Anglo-American geographical bias, however, leads to such instances as a two-page map of New Zealand at 1:5,000,000 and a one-page map of the Philippines (which has a larger population and total land area) at 1:10,000,000. The smallest scale used (least detailed) is the 1:150,000,000 world physical map. The largest is 1:2,500,000, used for Europe, parts of the United States, and Israel and Lebanon. The most typical scale is 1:20,000,000.

Town and city symbols are generally clear. It is ambitious for an atlas of this size to distinguish between towns above and below 10,000 inhabitants, and in fact, the distinction between these two symbols is often difficult to see on the maps.

Projections are not specified, although they appear to be standard ones suitable for the areas represented.

VI. Accuracy

Names of countries appear in their conventional anglicized forms. Other place-names are usually spelled according to the official language(s) of each country. Alternate spellings are included in parentheses for places commonly known by conventional spellings. On the map of Central European Russia, for example, *Warsaw* appears in parentheses as the alternate name for *Warszawa*. However, *Warsaw* as an alternate spelling does not appear on the larger-scale map of east-central Europe. Similarly, the Carpathian Mountains appear on the former map only as *Carpathians* but on the latter only as *Carpatii Orientali*.

Names are generally well placed on the maps. Generic terms describing physical features do not always appear together with the proper name, nor are symbols or shading always sufficient to indicate the nature of a physical feature. For example, the map of England gives no indication as to what kind of feature The Weald is. This information can be found in the index, however.

VII. Currency

Place-names and international borders are up-to-date. A notable exception is the use of *Cambodia*—both on maps and in the index—in place of the currently universally accepted *Kampuchea*, which was adopted by the government of that country in 1977. However, this atlas does use the name *Zimbabwe*, which was adopted in 1980.

VIII. Legibility

Typefaces on the maps are legible and sufficiently differentiated to distinguish categories. The number of place-names that appear is suited to the size of the map to avoid a cluttered appearance. Major transportation routes, physical features, and borders are clearly marked and distinguishable from one another.

Nine levels of shading, for which the key appears in the introductory section, indicating relief above sea level are sharp and easily distinguishable. Six levels of shading are used for below-sea-level elevations, but the color for one category did not match the legend, so differences between it and the next elevation are not easily apparent. Colors are registered and consistent throughout.

IX. Accessibility

The 20,000-entry index lists only the vernacular spellings, if used, of place-names; there are no cross-references from common conventional spellings. The reader who is not familiar with the vernacular spellings might not find in the index such major places as Copenhagen (København), Vienna (Wien), and Sardinia (Sardegna). Names in the index are followed by the name or abbreviation of the country in which they are located. The names of physical features are clarified by one of 21 categories. The index is extensive, although the countries of Mauritius and Zimbabwe have been omitted from the index (but not from the maps). Because the index is otherwise so complete, it would appear that these are typographic oversights and do not reflect intent.

The index indicates map page number and on the page, location by the alphanumeric grid system. Latitude and longitude coordinates are not used. Perhaps to save space, not all occurrences of a place are listed in the index. The map listed for Papua New Guinea, for example, actually shows less of that country than does another unindexed map at the same scale. The contents feature of numbered areas of an inset map correlated with the printed text is a helpful ready-reference guide.

There are over 20 inset maps, each clearly marked, including indication of scale.

X. Summary

At $7.95, *The Random House Concise World Atlas* compares favorably with similar-sized atlases, such as the CONCISE EARTHBOOK. The cartography is first-rate. The maps are clear and uncluttered, and the level of detail is just right for the page size and the scales used. Both physical and political features are represented. The atlas's shortcomings—primarily, its Anglo-European bias—are negligible in comparison with its strengths. Its manageable size—slightly larger than the typical pocket atlas—makes *The Random House Concise World Atlas* a good choice for both library and personal collections.

The Random House Mini World Atlas

Facts at a Glance

Full Title: **The Random House Mini World Atlas.**
Publisher: Random House.
Editors: staff of John Bartholomew & Son.
Copyright: 1984 by John Bartholomew & Son Ltd.
Edition Reviewed: 1984.

Number of Pages: 208.
Number of Maps: 120.
Number of Indexes: 1.
Number of Index Entries: 20,000.
Trim Size: 4″ × 6″.
Binding: laminated paper.

Price: $4.95.
Sold in bookstores and directly to schools and
   libraries.
ISBN 0-394-74008-4.
Revised as needed.

I. Introduction

The Random House Mini World Atlas is a smaller, more compact version of THE RANDOM HOUSE CONCISE WORLD ATLAS. Some minor deletions have been made because of space considerations. For complete information about the basic material common to both atlases, see the review of THE RANDOM HOUSE CONCISE WORLD ATLAS that begins on page 212 of this Buying Guide.

II. Format

Format and pagination are the same as in the CONCISE version, but the maps differ; what were physical maps in the CONCISE version have been rendered here as simple political maps. Shaded relief is not shown and shaded ocean depths are shown on only a few maps. Everything is on a reduced scale from the CONCISE version; dimensions have been reduced by 2¾ inches in height and 2 inches in width to produce a compact, easily held size. As a result, there is less content of several symbols from the master legend; for example, maritime boundaries and roads have been eliminated. The only landscape-feature symbols retained are rivers and permanent and seasonal lakes.

The neat borders enclosing the maps in the CONCISE version have been omitted, so that maps extend to the edge of the page and much of the content is lost in the gutter of the book. This was not a major problem in the CONCISE atlas, but it will frustrate any serious atlas user. Occasionally a name has been cut in half at the page edge, which leaves the reader wondering what is missing.

The table of contents lacks the extremely useful index maps found in the CONCISE atlas.

III. Special Features

The special features of the *Mini World Atlas* are essentially the same as those in the CONCISE version, which are described in detail on pages 212–14 of this Buying Guide.

IV. Geographical Balance

Like THE RANDOM HOUSE CONCISE WORLD ATLAS, this volume gives greater and more detailed coverage to Europe and the United States than to other regions of the world. Given the limited size of this atlas, however, the balance is adequate.

V. Scale and Projections

The CONCISE atlas presents most scales in both fractional and bar scale form. Because the same base maps are used in both versions, however, the scale of maps in the *Mini* atlas is necessarily reduced in order to incorporate the same information onto a smaller page. Thus, the representative fraction scales no longer apply to the scaled-down version and have, therefore, been omitted. However, since these are still relevant, bar scales calibrated in kilometers and miles remain for most of the maps. The four world maps have only fractional scales in the CONCISE version, which means that no scales appear at all for these maps in the *Mini* version. Most users will find this a drawback.

VI. Accuracy

The accuracy is the same as in the CONCISE version, on the whole acceptable, particularly for an atlas this small.

VII. Currency

The currency is the same as in the CONCISE version, usually reflecting place-names and borders current in the early 1980s.

VIII. Legibility

Despite the reduction of typefaces to accommodate the smaller page size, names remain legible and the various typefaces and borders are still easily distinguished. Names of natural features are shown. Colors are good and in register.

IX. Accessibility

A few place-names that appeared in the CONCISE version have been omitted, but these tend to be located at the page edges. Papua New Guinea, for example, lost several towns on its eastern coast. This would not be a significant problem except that the indexes for both versions contain the same entries, resulting in blind index references in the *Mini* atlas. The town of Finschhafen in Papua New Guinea, for instance, is listed in both indexes but appears on the indicated map only in the CONCISE atlas.

X. Summary

John Bartholomew has tried to adapt an existing small atlas to an even smaller format rather than produce a new atlas with features and scale more suitable to the reduced format. The publisher describes *The Random House Mini World Atlas* as "small enough for ready reference, detailed enough for essential information," but THE RANDOM HOUSE CONCISE WORLD ATLAS is not much bigger or much more expensive and is a good deal more useful. The PRENTICE-HALL POCKET ATLAS OF THE WORLD is almost as small as the *Mini* atlas, is reasonably good, and costs less. The *Mini* atlas could be useful for basic reference and easy desk-drawer storage, but its flaws make it a poor choice for either library or personal collections.

Reader's Digest Wide World Atlas

Facts at a Glance

Full Title: **Reader's Digest Wide World Atlas.**
Publisher: Reader's Digest.
Copyright: 1984 The Reader's Digest Association, Inc.; contains material originally copyrighted by Rand McNally and by Encyclopaedia Britannica.
Edition Reviewed: 4th printing, July 1984.

Number of Pages: 240.
Number of Maps: 189.
Number of Indexes: 1.
Number of Index Entries: 36,000.
Number of Illustrations: 17 color.
Trim Size: 11″ × 14″.
Binding: cloth.

Price: $34.95.
Sold in bookstores, by direct mail, and directly to libraries.
ISBN 0-528-83148-8.
Revised periodically.

I. Introduction

The *Reader's Digest Wide World Atlas* is a large-format reference atlas published by Reader's Digest in cooperation with Rand McNally. This work is in effect a concise yet comprehensive edition of Rand McNally's NEW INTERNATIONAL ATLAS, from which it draws many of its maps, charts, and tables. Other material in this atlas is derived from the RAND MCNALLY GOODE'S WORLD ATLAS and from the RAND MCNALLY COSMOPOLITAN WORLD ATLAS.

II. Format

The *Reader's Digest Wide World Atlas*'s trim size of 11″ × 14″ places it in the large-format category. It has a sewn spine and a heavy, durable, simulated cloth (laminated paper over sturdy boards) binding, plus an attractive full-color dust jacket printed on coated stock. The heavyweight pages are nonglossy with good color reproduction. The book, lightweight and easy to handle in spite of its size, in general has a sleek, modern appearance.

The atlas contains five types of maps: large-area small-scale physical representations, political maps with shaded relief, political maps of metropolitan areas, environment maps showing land use and vegetation types, and world thematic maps. Most of the maps are two-page spreads with generous borders and minimal but adequate gutters. The contents are divided into two parts, the first of which contains the general-reference maps, while the second contains the thematic maps and statistical material. The physical maps, which occupy 104 pages, are most useful for general reference; all the other maps in the book can be considered as feature maps. (See also *Special Features.*)

There is a master legend for the world and metropolitan area maps at the beginning of the political maps section. This legend gives clear examples of various symbols that appear on different maps of different scales. A small legend appears on each of the environment maps, and separate legends appear on the thematic map pages.

III. Special Features

The first part of the book, the general maps section, includes 12 pages of continental physical maps which show the Earth (including the ocean floor) as if viewed from space. These maps use colors to depict natural features, with a combination of color and relief effects to illustrate elevated areas. The same maps appear in THE NEW INTERNATIONAL ATLAS, as do the 21 pages of metropolitan regional maps that follow the main political reference maps.

"The Planet Earth in Space" is a six-page illustrated feature with capsule encyclopedic descriptions of the planets in the solar system, a solar system map (with data on the planets), and a two-page spread on the moon. This feature is interesting but does not add much to the value of this atlas.

The 16 pages of environment maps in "The World in Theme Maps" section are taken from the RAND MCNALLY GOODE'S WORLD ATLAS, although in this book they are reproduced at a larger size. The 22-page "World View" section is a collection of thematic maps taken from THE NEW INTERNATIONAL ATLAS. These maps cover such subjects as population, energy production and consumption, climate, natural vegetation, and soil types. The data in this section was prepared by Encyclopaedia Britannica. Six pages of ocean floor maps were also taken from THE NEW INTERNATIONAL ATLAS.

The five-page "World Political Information" table gives the area, population, population density, form of government, capitals and largest cities, and predominant language for each continent, country, province, and state. There is also a table of the largest metropolitan areas of the world.

Taken together, the special features included in this atlas are not inconsiderable, but the very same features are also found in one or more other atlases that will be mentioned in this review.

IV. Geographical Balance

The *Reader's Digest Wide World Atlas* is geographically weighted toward the United States, Canada, and Europe, although not quite as heavily as most other Rand McNally atlases. Of the political maps, 20 pages represent the United States; 10, Canada; 6, Mexico, Central America, and the Caribbean; 8, South America; 24, Europe (including the USSR); 18, Asia; 12, Africa; and 6, Australia and Oceania.

Scales too are skewed in favor of the United States, Canada, and Europe, giving these areas more detailed coverage than other parts of the globe. Although the larger-scale maps of South Africa, the Philippines, and Japan are useful, the omission of some regions and the repetitive coverage of others raise serious questions about the volume's balance. (See also *Scale and Projections*.)

The metropolitan area maps include 18 North American cities, 7 Latin American cities, 10 European cities, 7 Asian cities, and 2 Australian cities. There are no maps for any cities in Africa, even though this continent has 7 cities with populations of over 2 million (including one, Cairo, with over 5 million). However, the 44 metropolitan area maps do present a good selection of foreign cities, including Athens, Hong Kong, Seoul, Tehrān, and Tokyo-Yokohama.

V. Scale and Projections

Each map, with the exception of the environment maps, is labeled with the scale given in three forms: as a verbal statement, as a representative fraction, and in a bar scale. This is an excellent feature, for it makes the maps accessible to readers who may be familiar with only one of the three forms of representation.

Scales used for maps in the political section generally range from 1:3,000,000 to 1:12,000,000, which are good choices for the size of the pages. Unfortunately, some regions are represented at smaller scales than they might have been and are thus not really shown to advantage. For example, neither of the polar regions is represented adequately in the main political map section. Only two areas of South America are included at a scale (1:6,000,000) larger than the one used for the two maps that together depict the entire continent (1:12,000,00), leaving some parts of the continent depicted only on that small-scale map. Rio de Janeiro, for example, one of the continent's most important cities, shows up only on the 1:12,000,000 maps. Conversely, there are several instances where one area is covered on a number of maps. The Saudi Arabian peninsula is included in the 1:12,000,000 map of India-Pakistan-Southwest Asia, on the 1:12,000,000 map of eastern North Africa, and on the 1:6,000,000 map of the Middle East. The 1:6,000,000 map of Northern Europe includes Scandinavia and the northeastern USSR and is followed by a map of southern Scandinavia at 1:3,000,000, while several pages later there is a 1:3,000,000 map showing the Baltic and Moscow regions. Yet southern India is not shown at a scale larger than 1:12,000,000, nor is Australia or most of China.

The metropolitan area maps are all drawn at a

standard scale of 1:300,000, allowing for easy comparison among cities. However, this scale prevents the maps from showing much detail beyond major roads, parks and points of interest, extent of urbanization, boundaries, and rivers.

Standard conic and azimuthal projections arc uscd to provide equal-area representation with a minimum of distortion. The political maps of Africa are drawn in stereographic projections which are unusual but acceptable. Unfortunately, the special features do not include any discussion of scale, projections, or mapping techniques.

VI. Accuracy

Place-names are spelled correctly and consistently in the vernacular, with the English version given in parentheses when necessary. Although it is not a major flaw, the care in placing town and city names clearly adjacent to the appropriate symbol is not always evident here, particularly on the Central European maps. Here, the inexperienced user will not always be able to tell which place-name goes with which location. But this type of inaccuracy is certainly the exception rather than the rule in the *Wide World Atlas*.

Like THE NEW INTERNATIONAL ATLAS, which uses the same cartographic base on the physical maps, the *Wide World Atlas* depicts the nonexistent town of Wansbeck on its map of England. This, however, may be a copyright protection device.

VII. Currency

Most recent place-name changes (such as *Belize, Zimbabwe, Vietnam,* and *Kampuchea*) have been incorporated. In one insignificant instance, Vanuatu is labeled with its former name, *New Hebrides*, on the world physical map, although it is called *Vanuatu* elsewhere. Population figures in the "World Political Information" table are current as of 1984, an indication that these figures are updated with each revision.

VIII. Legibility

Although some of the place-name labels are very small, they remain legible. Several typefaces and colors are used to differentiate city sizes and different kinds of features on the maps. These are well chosen and consistent, and in general the maps are neither cluttered nor confusing. On occasion, however, as in the maps showing the Himalayas, the heavy relief effects can obscure the small print.

International borders are clear and well marked. However, state/provincial borders are often difficult to make out, as they are light pastel colors against a light gray background.

Color reproduction is good, although there are some minor examples of colors out of register. Unlike the physical maps in the BRITANNICA ATLAS and THE NEW INTERNATIONAL ATLAS, which are otherwise identical with the *Wide World* maps, the *Wide World* maps do not use color tints to represent different elevations. Rather, the background color is light gray. Needless to say, these maps have an attractive, sophisticated appearance.

IX. Accessibility

The two-page table of contents is thorough, well designed, and easy to use.

The index includes 36,000 entries and lists page numbers as well as latitude and longitude. A good introduction explains how to use the index. Entries are given in the official vernacular, with helpful cross-references to English versions and to former names. A somewhat overinclusive list of abbreviations and symbols (of which there are 81) is provided to help the reader identify the type of feature or political unit for each entry. Curiously, the city listings in the index do not include the name of the country or state in which the city is located unless two or more cities have the same name. For example, the 13 entries for Albany (12 cities and one river) include the state or country of each city, although the river is identified only as a river without any location. Absecon, New Jersey, is listed only as Absecon; Aberystwyth, Wales, identified simply as Aberystwyth. This practice is a drawback in an otherwise excellent index.

Just as in the index of the RAND McNALLY GOODE'S WORLD ATLAS, latitude and longitude figures here are not presented in their standard form with degree and minute symbols (for example, 54° 15′N 2° 35′E), but rather as numbers with periods separating the degree from the minute figure (54.15N, 2.35E). This departure from the norm may be confusing for some readers who might incorrectly interpret the period as a decimal point.

X. Summary

The *Reader's Digest Wide World Atlas* is a handsome, well designed, up-to-date volume with good cartography and a number of useful special features. At $34.95, it is one of the least expensive large-format atlases available.

Unfortunately, there are some disadvantages that may offset these pluses. The uneven coverage of different parts of the world, both in terms of numbers of maps and choice of scales, makes this volume less appealing than it might otherwise be. Moreover, because the two contents largely overlap, this atlas will be superfluous for collections that already include THE NEW INTERNATIONAL ATLAS. Readers who have GOODE'S WORLD ATLAS will also gain little from the addition of this volume. In the final analysis, the *Wide World Atlas* can be recommended only for libraries and individuals that have limited budgets and do not already have or expect to acquire another large-format atlas.

The Times Atlas of the World

Facts at a Glance

Full Title: **The Times Atlas of the World.**
Publisher: Times Books.
Editors: John C. Bartholomew, H. A. G. Lewis, et al.
Copyright: 1985 by John Bartholomew & Son Limited and Times Books Limited.
Edition Reviewed: seventh comprehensive edition, 1985.

Number of Pages: 419.
Number of Maps: 123.
Number of Indexes: 1.
Number of Index Entries: 200,000.
Trim Size: 11½" × 18".
Binding: cloth.

Price: $139.95.
Sold in bookstores, by direct mail, and directly to libraries.
ISBN 0-8129-1298-5.
Revised periodically.

I. Introduction

The Times Atlas of the World is an oversized, general world atlas. In terms of trim size and thus the sizes of its maps, it is the largest atlas currently on the market. It is compiled jointly by *The Times* newspaper of London and the British cartographic firm John Bartholomew & Son. The first *Times* atlas was published in 1895, with German cartography; completely new editions were issued on several occasions over the ensuing 90 years, all with cartography provided by Bartholomew. The present edition, the seventh, was published in 1985.

This atlas derives its authority from several dozen cartographers, geographers, scholars, and government departments from around the world. Among official bodies contributing to it were the American Geographical Society, New York; Esselte Map Service, A.B., Stockholm; Institute Géographique National, Paris; the British Meteorological Office; NASA; the National Geographic Society, Washington, D.C.; Rand McNally & Company; the Royal Geographical Society, London; the United States Geological Survey, Washington, D.C.; and the Academy of Sciences of the USSR, Moscow. Overall editorial direction was provided by John C. Bartholomew, while H. A. G. Lewis served as geographical

consultant to *The Times*. Needless to say, *The Times Atlas* is one of the most authoritative world atlases, if not *the* most authoritative world atlas available today.

The version sold in the United States (published by Times Books, a division of Random House, and distributed by Harper & Row) is identical to the British edition published by Times Books, Limited, London. Other editions are available in French, German, and Dutch. A concise edition is available in the United States under the title, THE NEW YORK TIMES ATLAS OF THE WORLD.

II. Format

With a trim size of 11¾" × 17¾", *The Times Atlas of the World* will not fit on standard-size shelves but will have to be stored in the oversized-book section of the library. The volume is nearly two inches thick, is relatively heavy and unwieldy, but is very well made. The pages lie flat when open, and there is a narrow interior margin so that no map information is lost in the gutter. The binding is durable, and the book should stand up well to heavy library use.

The atlas contains primarily physical maps of regions and political units. Unlike the maps in virtually every other atlas, which are four-color, the maps in *The Times Atlas* are eight-color, which allows for exceptional subtlety and level of detail. The majority of the maps are double-page spreads. Many contain large-scale insets of cities, islands, or adjacent areas. The maps are contained within neat lines, though occasionally part of a map will spill over its neat line into the margin in order to show important information that would otherwise be cut off. This is a sound and useful practice.

A full page containing all the symbols and abbreviations precedes the main map section. In addition, the legend and abbreviations are duplicated on a separate, laminated, 5½" × 16" card for easy reference. Both forms of the legend include all the symbols used for boundaries, transportation, lake types, landscape features, and man-made features. Styles of lettering and symbols used in the city inset maps are also included.

The individual maps themselves do not contain legends. However, the scale, map projection title, and a hypsometric-tint elevation bar graph appear on each map.

The contents are divided into three main sections: 46 pages of special features; 123 plates of general reference maps and several thematic maps; and a glossary and index-gazetteer.

III. Special Features

The special features in *The Times Atlas of the World* are not as extensive as one might expect to find in an atlas of this size; the editors have apparently decided that the primary function of this atlas is to present clear, large, general-reference maps, and that since encyclopedic information can be readily found elsewhere, its inclusion would be superfluous.

A five-page table of "States and Territories of the World" leads off the special features. This table lists the name, area, and population of every country (and its states or provinces) and also gives the number of the map plate on which each area is represented.

A two-page feature on "geographical comparisons" includes outline maps showing the relative sizes of the major continents, oceans and seas, drainage basins, inland waters, and islands. For each outline map, area statistics are given in both square miles and square kilometers. There are also tables listing mountains and their heights and rivers and their lengths.

There is a two-page encyclopedic feature on the universe, illustrated with both black-and-white and four-color telescope photos and other illustrations. Three star charts (for the northern sky, southern sky, and equatorial zone) appear on the next two pages. These are followed by a four-page encyclopedic feature on the solar system, again illustrated with telescope and space-probe photographs and with schematic drawings. There are also three maps of the Earth's moon and two pages of encyclopedic material on space flight. The latter deals not so much with the history of manned space missions as with the mapping, meteorological, and related applications of space technology. Other features deal with earth science (four pages) and map projections (three pages). Fourteen pages of schematic physical maps represent the Earth, including the ocean floor, as viewed from space.

Double-page thematic maps on world minerals, climatology, climate and food potential, vegetation, mankind, food, and energy are included at the beginning of the main reference map section. These pages also include statistical charts and graphs.

This material is extremely well written, well illustrated, and authoritative. It is identical or very similar to special features found in THE NEW YORK TIMES ATLAS OF THE WORLD which, however, also contains additional encyclopedic features not included here.

IV. Geographical Balance

Although produced by British cartographers primarily for the British and U.S. markets, *The Times Atlas of the World* does not betray an undue British or U.S. bias. On the contrary, although Western Europe and the United States are the subjects of more maps than most other regions, the rest of the

world is covered in admirable detail. As an indication of the *Times Atlas*'s geographical balance, Australia and New Zealand are covered in 10 pages, Japan in 4 (including a map of the nation in relation to the Asian mainland), China in 8, India in 8, the USSR in 20, Great Britain in 10 (including a double-page metropolitan map of Greater London), and France in 12 (including a two-page map of Paris and its environs). Altogether, 72 pages are devoted to Europe (excluding the Soviet Union), while Africa gets 24 and Latin America, 14. There are 10 pages on Canada and 26 on the United States.

The order of the maps is opposite to the north-to-south, west-to-east arrangement commonly found in American-made atlases. Rather, the general-reference maps begin with Australia and Oceania, then move to Asia, Europe, Africa, North America, South America, and Antarctica. Maps of the oceans (with insets of midocean islands) are placed in geographical sequence between the continents they separate.

V. Scale and Projections

The exceptionally large pages of *The Times Atlas* allow not only for larger maps than in any other general-reference atlas, but also for maps of larger scale. In the foreword, the editors state that they have aimed for a standard range of scales for the maps but have departed from this when a particular area was best covered by a particular scale. As a rule, the more densely populated or strategically important the region, the larger the scale at which it is represented.

Most European countries are mapped at scales ranging from 1:500,000 to 1:1,250,000; the political map of Europe is drawn at 1:2,500,000. The largest consistent scale for regions in Australia, Asia, Africa, and South America is 1:5,000,000, although some individual maps are drawn at larger scales, up to 1:200,000 (for example, India, Plains, Nepal, Mt. Everest). The scales of inset maps range from 1:12,000 to 1:35,000,000. Most island and city insets are at 1:250,000, so their sizes can be accurately compared. London and Paris are each mapped at 1:100,000.

A number of different projections are used in this atlas. Great care has apparently been taken in selecting projections that minimize distortion and permit distance and size comparisons for all areas on the particular map. Conic projections are used for large- and some medium-scale maps of mid- and high-latitude regions. The Mercator projection is used for maps of equatorial areas. For most small- and medium-scale maps, the Lambert azimuthal equal-area projection is used. Other projections are used when necessary in order to allow a certain area to fit on the map pages.

VI. Accuracy

The Times Atlas of the World is unfailingly accurate and authoritative. Place-names are spelled correctly and consistently, according to the principles and practice of the British Permanent Committee on Geographical Names. Place-name labels appear in the official language of the country shown; English versions are also given when space permits.

The names of cities and other specific places are printed in their proper locations. The names of general physical areas give adequate representation of their actual extent and location.

Disputed or undefined international boundaries are shown as such. Boundary lines and place-names of disputed areas reflect the situation on the ground as closely as possible. In such cases, the maps show the de facto rather than the de jure situation. Thus, in this respect also *The Times Atlas of the World* is objective and accurate.

Unlike virtually all other world atlases on the market today, *The Times Atlas* uses hypsometric tints (rather than color or layer tints) to depict elevation. In this system, green is used for lowlands, gradually shifting to beige, brown, gray, and finally white as elevation increases. This system is not inaccurate, but it can give readers a misleading impression of environment types. For example, low-lying deserts appear as green in this atlas, but they certainly are not green in real life. In order to get an accurate impression of the environment, readers must pay close attention to the subtle markings used to indicate such features as glaciers, ice caps, lava fields, deserts, dunes, marshes, flood areas, swamps, and the like.

VII. Currency

The information contained in *The Times Atlas* is up-to-date to within a year of 1985, its publication date. All major political name changes in effect at that time are accurately given. By and large, population figures in the "States and Territories of the World" table date from the early to mid-1980s.

The cartographers have taken advantage of satellite and computer technology in compiling the maps. Thus, certain features in relatively unpopulated areas of the globe are depicted with a level of accuracy hitherto impossible.

The illustrations and photographs in the encyclopedic features are contemporary and include satellite imagery of the surface of Venus and the moons of Jupiter and Saturn.

VIII. Legibility

Most of the maps use two basic lettering styles in order to distinguish the names of physical features from those of political and cultural features. The various lettering substyles are shown in the legend, allowing the reader to determine country names, major administrative divisions, administrative centers, airports, historic regions, physical regions, physical features, ocean bottom features, and tribal names.

The cartographer has achieved a good balance between the map scale and the number of place-names on any given map so that each map can be as detailed as possible without being cluttered. Only on maps of heavily populated regions is it difficult to locate the name of an individual town.

Rivers, roads, railroads, and pipelines are all clearly distinguishable, as are boundaries. And it is fairly easy to distinguish national borders from state and provincial borders.

IX. Accessibility

The three-page table of contents is thorough, well designed, and easy to use. It is divided into two sections. The first section lists each item in the front matter (the special features) individually and also gives the page numbers for the index and its component parts. Each general-reference map is then listed by plate number, with the number itself printed in large red numerals. The map name is printed in boldface and the scale is given. Inset maps, if included on the main map, are also listed in roman type.

Endpaper maps of the world (front) and North America and Europe (back) are overlaid with interlocking plate outlines keyed by plate number and scale. With this simple and useful device, the reader may discover on which plate inside the book a given area of the world appears.

The index is extensive, containing more than 200,000 entries. As far as our reviewers can determine, every name appearing on the maps is listed in the index. Index entries include both an alphanumeric grid location and latitude/longitude coordinates rounded to the nearest minute. This means that the reader can determine the actual locations of specific towns to within half a mile. While the maximum number of names within any given grid is close to 50, most grids contain fewer than 20. Using the index and alphanumeric coordinates, it is quite easy to find specific place-names on the maps.

More than half the maps contain insets, and almost all insets have separate grid coordinates. Large-scale city inset maps, however, do not have separate grid coordinates, nor are the names on these maps indexed.

The index database is coded on magnetic tape so that the index can be easily updated for each revised edition.

X. Summary

The Times Atlas of the World has long been considered the most definitive general-reference world atlas available. Its maps convey a greater level of detail at larger scales and on larger pages than do the maps of any other atlas. Moreover, it is admirably up-to-date, and thus, in many cases, *The Times Atlas* can be relied upon to provide information that is simply not available in most other atlases. In short, *The Times Atlas* will be the atlas of first and last resort in any collection in which it is included.

At $139.95, *The Times Atlas of the World* comes close in price to the most expensive atlas on the market, THE NEW INTERNATIONAL ATLAS, which sells for $150.00. And *The Times Atlas* is certainly well worth the price. The only significant drawback is the use of hypsometric tints, which are found in few other atlases, to indicate elevation. These tints can cause confusion because the colors do not correspond to actual environment types, and in some cases seem to contradict the environment.

The Times Atlas of the World has no direct competitors, although Rand McNally's 568-page NEW INTERNATIONAL ATLAS comes close in accuracy, authority, and sophistication. Apart from this title, however, such atlases as the EARTHBOOK, THE GREAT WORLD ATLAS, and the NATIONAL GEOGRAPHIC ATLAS OF THE WORLD all present impressive maps in a large format, but they have certain drawbacks that keep them from being in the league of *The Times Atlas*. Those who want the benefits of Bartholomew's cartography in an almost equally authoritative form but cannot afford *The Times Atlas* should investigate THE NEW YORK TIMES ATLAS OF THE WORLD, which is a condensed version of this atlas. THE NEW YORK TIMES ATLAS maps are not quite as large-scaled or as detailed, but the atlas itself is still in the large-format category.

VNR Pocket Atlas

Facts at a Glance

Full Title: **VNR Pocket Atlas.**
Publisher: Van Nostrand Reinhold.
Editors: RNDr. Jiří Novotný, Cartographic Editor, and Marie Pánková, Technical Editor.
Copyright: 1981 by Kartografie, Prague.
Edition Reviewed: first U.S. edition, 1983.

Number of Pages: 236.
Number of Maps: 80, including insets.
Number of Indexes: 1.
Number of Index Entries: 13,500.
Trim Size: 4½" × 6⅝".
Binding: laminated paper.

Price: $8.95.
Sold in bookstores and by direct mail.
ISBN 0-442-29661-4.
No scheduled revision.

I. Introduction

The *VNR Pocket Atlas* is a concise pocket-size book of 236 pages that provides 80 full-color maps as well as information on the political, economic, and physical geography of the world. Designed for students and the general reader, it was published in 1983 by Van Nostrand Reinhold, using maps and text prepared in 1981 by Kartografie of Czechoslovakia and printed in Czechoslovakia.

II. Format

The *VNR Pocket Atlas* measures 4½" × 6⅝" and fits easily in a student's pocket or book bag. Its sturdy paperback binding opens flat without cracking and should withstand heavy use, although like any paperback, the corners of the cover can quickly become dog-eared. The matte-finish text stock has good opacity.

Maps cover one or two pages except for 11 gate-fold pages for maps of the world, Northern and Central Africa, and several other areas. Political maps, which predominate in the work, are far more detailed than physical maps. Most maps are not contained within neat lines and bleed to the edges of the page. The master legend at the front of the atlas includes symbols for cities, boundaries, railway lines, train ferry routes, ten types of physical features, relative sizes of cities, relief above sea level, ocean depths, and typographic conventions for place-name categories. Metric measurements are used throughout the atlas, supplemented with a simple metric conversion table at the front of the book.

Each two-page map spread is interspersed with an additional two pages of text that provides a succinct description of the history, political administration, geography, population, and economy of each continent and nation. Much of the statistical data is organized in convenient tabular form, which facilitates access. A color illustration of each nation's flag appears in the text pages. Although not intended as a substitute for an encyclopedia or comprehensive almanac, the text is nevertheless remarkably informative and furnishes far more data than do many larger atlases.

III. Special Features

In addition to the text material described, the *VNR Pocket Atlas* includes a number of special maps and tables. A world time zone map identifies not only standard time zones but also those zones that vary from the standard. Tabular data about the planets provides such information as mean distance from the sun, sidereal period, diameter, mass, rotational period, and number of satellites. The sky maps of the Northern and Southern hemispheres include codes for the spectral classes and magnitudes of stars. There is also a table of satellites (some of it outdated since the *Mariner* and *Voyager* flights), a map of the moon, a map of Mars, and statistical data about the Earth.

Two interesting physical maps of Antarctica and the Arctic show routes taken by more than 20 polar expeditions, as well as the location and nationality of recent scientific research stations.

IV. Geographical Balance

In terms of coverage, the *VNR* atlas is decidedly biased toward the United Kingdom. European and English-speaking nations in general receive more coverage than do other areas, with an average of half a page of text per country. Many countries in Asia, Africa, Central America, and Oceania, however, receive as little as one sixth of a page of text. The United Kingdom enjoys by far the most coverage, with 14 pages of maps and text. The Soviet Union also reaps a bumper harvest, with nine pages of text and map material.

V. Scale and Projections

Although map projections are not identified in the *VNR Pocket Atlas*, our reviewers found them appropriate for the size of the maps and the areas represented.

In an atlas of such small dimensions, map scales tend to be small of necessity. Each map labels the scale as a representative fraction and a bar scale, shown in both meters and miles. By far the smallest-scale maps (those showing largest area and least detail) are those of the world (1:150,000,000). Many large regions are rendered at 1:50,000,000 (for example, North America or Australia and the Pacific) or 1:65,000,000 (for example, Asia and Europe). Australia, South America, Canada, China, and similar areas are shown at a scale of 1:25,000,000, whereas individual nations or small groups of countries range from 1:3,500,000 (England) to 1:10,000,000 (Scandinavia). The choice of scales is appropriate and enables the reader to make ready comparisons among various parts of the globe.

VI. Accuracy

Place-names are generally spelled according to the official language of the country. Alternate conventional anglicized spellings for well-known places are listed on many maps and appear in the index with a cross-reference to the vernacular spelling. Physical and political features are accurately represented and labeled, although the Laurentian Plateau in Canada is misspelled *Laurentin* both on the map and in the index.

West Berlin is listed in the text with its own entry, separate from West Germany. It is merely described as being "administered by the Senate," with no explanation that this is the West German Senate, or that it is a state of West Germany.

VII. Currency

The maps and text are relatively current with the 1983 publication date. The latest date cited for statistics is 1982, although the average date for national statistics, such as population, is about 1978; 1970 rather than 1980 figures for U.S. population are given, but the date cited for the name of the U.S. president is 1981. The use of what has by now become badly dated statistical information undermines the value of this portion of the book, particularly for students of economic geography and current events.

VIII. Legibility

Typefaces on the maps are legible and serve to differentiate among place-name categories. Although there are only a few small-scale physical maps, several types of natural features are shown, identified either by symbol or typeface. However, because deserts, lowlands, plateaus, and plains are all labeled in the same typeface, the reader can easily become confused, especially when the map does not label the type of feature. If the name is in English or has been anglicized, the generic English term is usually provided—for example, the Great Victoria Desert. If the name is given in the vernacular, however, the generic English term is often omitted. For example, the Deccan Plateau in India is described on the physical map of India only as "Deccan." The reader must consult the index to learn that Deccan is a plateau.

Physical maps label some cities and altitudes but not international boundaries. On political maps the five types of political boundaries are often difficult to distinguish because, like rivers, they are printed in blue. Town and city symbols, however, are very easy to distinguish. Six symbols are used for towns and cities of Great Britain and five for the rest of the world. Colors are strong and are in register, although they are not always used to advantage. For example, on the maps of Africa and southern Africa, the bordering nations of Botswana, Zimbabwe, Zambia, Malawi, Tanzania, Kenya, and Uganda are all shaded pink, even though as many as eight colors and shades are used elsewhere and could have been used for clearer differentiation.

States or provinces are shown on the political maps for selected countries. For some countries they are labeled directly; on others, they are indicated by numbers, with the individual names in an inset legend.

Type size ranges from 8 points to as small as 3 points, which will test the eyesight of even those with perfect vision. Yet, compared with their counterparts in THE PRENTICE-HALL POCKET ATLAS, political maps in *VNR* are much more legible, primarily because there is less background detail. Legibility becomes a noticeable problem in the text pages, where dense blocks of small type discourage the eye; in the index the near-flyspeck type presents serious obstacles to efficient use.

IX. Accessibility

The table of contents lists each map alphabetically and refers the reader to text page, map number, and the page on which the map can be found. The system is not without its pitfalls. Because maps bleed to the edge of the page, only text pages are numbered, which can make locating maps a nuisance. Moreover, it is left to the reader to figure out that map numbers are given on text pages; the running head on the left-hand page usually refers to the map on the preceding page; the running head on the right-hand side to the map on the following page. Even then, the running heads may trip the unwary reader. The text material for Yemen, for example, appears on a page with the running head "map 25" (Southeast Asia), whereas Yemen is located on maps 26 and 28. The table of contents refers the reader to map 28 only; likewise, Singapore is found on more than one map but is listed only once in the table of contents. This system is sure to defeat all but the most persistent reader.

The comprehensive 49-page index lists all geographical names used in the maps in alphabetical order, followed by the map rather than the page number. Alphanumeric grid coordinates are used for locator references, but these also present pitfalls. Since there are no neat line borders on the maps, the letter and number coordinates fall on the maps themselves and are not always easily located mixed in with place-names, and so on. Text entries are not indexed.

Many index entries are accompanied by one of 25 abbreviations for such features as channels, hills, lakes, rivers, reservoirs, swamps, and volcanoes. The index is preceded by a clear explanation of entry notations and abbreviations.

Although all main entries are in the vernacular form, cross-references guide the reader from well-known conventional anglicized versions to the vernacular.

X. Summary

The *VNR Pocket Atlas* is a well designed, highly portable ready-reference atlas that is very easy to use. It includes a surprisingly large amount of useful information for such a small book.

Most of the maps, of course, are at a very small scale and cannot convey the level of detail found in most larger atlases. It is only the small type size that allows the *VNR Pocket Atlas* to present as much information and detail as it does, but many readers will find this type a strain on the eyes. These readers may prefer THE RANDOM HOUSE CONCISE WORLD ATLAS, although that atlas does not present nearly so much statistical information about individual countries. The *VNR Pocket Atlas* will meet a variety of reference needs, but its high price of $13.95 may deter many prospective purchasers.

The Whole Earth Atlas

Facts at a Glance

Full Title: **The Whole Earth Atlas.**
Publisher: Hammond.
Copyright: 1984.
Edition Reviewed: New Final Census Edition.

Number of Pages: 256.
Number of Maps: 302.
Number of Indexes: 256 same-page indexes. Same-page indexes for each map.
Trim Size: 8½″ × 11″.
Binding: paperback.

Price: $8.95. 15 percent library discount.
Sold in bookstores and directly to libraries.
ISBN 0-8437-2499-4.
Revised annually.

I. Introduction

The Whole Earth Atlas is a paperback collection containing mostly political maps, with some smaller thematic and topographical maps as well as brief statistical tables. The pages in this volume duplicate many of those found in the 1986 edition of the Hammond CITATION WORLD ATLAS. However, the maps in this edition do not include the elevation relief effects now found in the CITATION's political maps. Nor does *The Whole Earth Atlas* include any of the physical model maps that are now in CITATION.

II. Format

The Whole Earth Atlas measures 8½″ × 11″, a smaller trim size than that of the CITATION. The binding appears secure, considering that this is a paperback book, and the laminated cover should be reasonably durable. The book can be made to lie fairly flat when opened if the reader presses the center of the page with his or her hand; otherwise, as with virtually all paperbacks, there is a tendency for pages to flop over. The potential user should be aware that many of the maps bleed to the center so that text is lost in the gutters, and place-name labels near the gutters are often difficult to read.

In general, the map arrangement follows the one used in the CITATION atlas. This is not always the rule, however. For example, the section on North America begins with Canada, and is then followed by Mexico, Central America, the West Indies, and finally the United States. Atlas users normally expect to find the maps of Canada and the United States in adjacent sections. The selection of maps is not as generous or as well balanced as the selection in CITATION. (See also *Accessibility* and *Geographical Balance*.)

III. Special Features

The front and back inside covers of the book contain a total of 11 "World Statistical Tables." Among these tables are "Elements of the Solar System," "Dimensions of the Earth," "Oceans and Major Seas," "Largest Islands," "Principal Mountains of the World," and "Longest Rivers of the World." These tables are handy, but they do not include any information that cannot be found in a good world almanac.

Like the other Hammond atlases reviewed in this Buying Guide, *The Whole Earth Atlas* includes thematic maps that accompany every general reference map. There are two basic types of thematic maps: topography; and agriculture, industry and resources. These are located either on the same page, the facing page, or the succeeding page as the general reference maps to which they correspond.

A limited number of other thematic maps are provided, though without any consistency. For example, there are population distribution and vegetation maps for the United States and Canada. There are two historical maps for Poland, one showing the country in 1938 and the other in 1945. Along with the general reference map of the Soviet Union there is a special map entitled "U.S.S.R.—Railroads and Navigation," which at a glance provides interesting information that is not readily available elsewhere in such a simple format.

The general reference maps are also accompanied by brief statistical tables that give basic data, such as areas, population, capital, monetary unit, and major language and religion for each country. Each country's flag is also depicted.

IV. Geographical Balance

Some of the general reference maps found in the CITATION atlas are not included in this volume. Among the notable omissions are the relief and other thematic maps of continents, as well as the provincial maps of Australia. There are only two maps each for Africa and South America. By contrast, there is a single map for virtually every U.S. state. In fact, literally half the pages in the book are given over to coverage of the United States. As a consequence, *The Whole Earth Atlas* is not so much a world atlas as a United States atlas that includes maps of other parts of the world.

V. Scale and Projections

The maps in this atlas are in effect reduced versions of the ones that appear in the CITATION (minus the elevation shading). As a result, the map scales are smaller. This reduced scale is reflected in the bar scales that accompany the maps. Unlike the CITATION atlas, however, *The Whole Earth Atlas* does not give representative fractions for its individual maps.

The map projections remain the same. As is the case in the CITATION, they are well chosen to represent the size and shapes of the areas shown without any unacceptable distortion.

VI. Accuracy

Like the other Hammond atlases reviewed in this Buying Guide, *The Whole Earth Atlas* generally maintains a high level of accuracy. Place-names are printed in the correct local official spellings. Given the relatively small scale of many of the maps, the locations of place-name labels and the points they identify are reasonably accurate.

VII. Currency

As this Buying Guide went to press, Hammond announced that it was preparing a revised version of *The Whole Earth Atlas*. That edition will supersede this 1984 edition, but it is yet uncertain how extensive the revision will be. An advance copy was not available at the time of this review.

The publisher's blurb on the jacket of the 1984 edition states: "Every map has been completely updated to reflect recent population information and such vital information as the birth of new nations, shifting boundaries, . . . name changes and new flags. . . ." However, in this edition, Kampuchea is still identified by its former name, *Cambodia*; similarly, Burkina Faso is still called *Upper Volta*. But *Kalâtdlit Nunât*, the official Innuit name for Greenland, is given in parentheses as part of the Greenland place-name label. (This spelling, curiously, differs significantly from the spelling given in other atlases such as EARTHBOOK. But this is a very minor point.)

VIII. Legibility

Typefaces here are even smaller than they are in the CITATION WORLD ATLAS. This presents a problem throughout the atlas, particularly on small scale maps with many name labels and political and physical markings, such as that of South America: Southern Part. On such maps, the profusion of names and of typefaces and sizes makes it difficult for the reader to pinpoint individual towns and to identify the precise feature to which a particular name refers.

IX. Accessibility

As the comments above make clear, the small print and cluttered appearance of the maps make the use of this atlas difficult for visually-impaired and sharp-eyed users alike. Accessibility is made even more difficult by the absence of a master index and of a table of contents. Instead, individual maps are accompanied by same-page indexes. In lieu of a contents page, we are given a "Gazetteer-Index of the World" which lists continents, countries, and U.S. states alphabetically, and includes the page numbers on which each of these places is found in the atlas. But neither the same-page indexes nor the gazetteer-index can make up for the lack of a master index and a contents page. With limited accessibility, this atlas is suitable only for the most casual purposes.

X. Summary

The Whole Earth Atlas is an abridged version of Hammond's CITATION WORLD ATLAS, in a large (8½" × 11") paperback format. It remains to be seen how extensive the changes in the next edition will be, and whether they will eliminate the many shortcomings that make the present edition a questionable value.

The major drawbacks in the current version are the poor accessibility and the minute print on the maps. Moreover, with half the maps devoted to the United States, this volume does not give the reader a balanced view of the world.

The Whole Earth Atlas costs only $8.95, which is a reasonable price. However, libraries will be much better served by the more expensive CITATION WORLD ATLAS, which includes more (and larger, more sophisticated) maps, a 24-page model map section, and a table of contents and master index.

PART FOUR

Dictionaries and Word Books

Chapter 9
What to Look for in Dictionaries and Word Books

Readers consult general dictionaries and word books in search of a wide range of information. Many people only need to locate definitions or to ascertain correct spelling; others regularly seek synonyms, word histories, and guidance on pronunciation or usage. If a dictionary is the sole reference source that is owned or used habitually, the presence of special features—tables, charts, lists, biographical or geographic names that make it a more encyclopedic work—may become especially important.

Readers also consult dictionaries in a variety of contexts. The dictionary needs of a college student are quite different from those of the student of English as a second language (ESL). The recreational reader or crossword-puzzle addict will consult a more streamlined work than will a serious reader, a writer, or a scholar. The journalist requires a dictionary of superb currency; a novelist may prefer a volume that emphasizes historical meaning and usage.

Because of the differing needs of readers, the selection of general-purpose dictionaries becomes a complicated process. Furthermore, general-purpose dictionaries are more complex and individual than may be readily apparent. Today most dictionaries range beyond the basic purpose of presenting an alphabetical register of the words and meanings of a given language. The reviews in the Buying Guide, therefore, describe the similarities and differences of the individual works and evaluate the features they offer in addition to the main vocabulary and definitions.

Chapter 2, "Choosing General Reference Books,"

describes the broad classifications and basic features of dictionaries and word books. But in selecting specific titles, readers of this guide will want to

- know how the reviewers, consultants, and editors approached the task of evaluation;
- be aware of the specific issue of *currency*, especially of scientific and technical words, in dictionaries and in word-related books; and
- understand how the dictionary and word-book reviews in this guide are presented, as well as the kinds of features that reviewers commonly selected for comment or illustration.

General Approach to Dictionary Evaluations. The reviews were prepared with an overriding awareness of each dictionary's intended purpose and readership and give a balanced view of a work's contents and features. This will help readers of the Buying Guide to select dictionaries that meet a wide range of reference needs.

Currency of Scientific and Technical Words. One aspect of dictionaries is featured prominently in review periodicals and in publishers' promotional materials: the *currency* of words and meanings, how up-to-date a work is. The Buying Guide evaluates how currency affects the quality and usefulness of a dictionary's overall vocabulary. The most obvious signs of a dictionary's currency are found among the scientific and technical terms included. Increasingly, publishers emphasize the *quantity* of new scientific and technical words or phrases and meanings included in their dictionaries—even in concise or paperback editions. Accordingly, prospective buyers tend to seek examples of such words in assessing the latest edition of a work. The current emphasis on scientific and technical currency influences the choices made by the editors of a general dictionary about which terms they consider to be most frequently used or needed by general readers.

In evaluating currency, the reviewers have tried to judge the dictionaries from the perspective of *general* use; that is, how clear the definitions of scientific and technical terms will be to readers who do not have special knowledge of the fields the terms cover. We notice, for example, a trend in some college dictionaries toward defining terms (for example, in biochemistry and mathematics) in formal scientific terms rather than in language that can be readily understood by a general reader. (Many such definitions are, of course, written by specialists.) Nevertheless, many dictionaries do make a strenuous effort to define all words clearly and to discriminate among meanings, so that general readers can readily understand them. Other dictionaries reveal that editors have chosen to include definitions that are as precisely scientific as possible, even if the result is that a general reader must embark on an elaborate search for definitions of several additional terms used to define the first word. Dictionary editors, of course, face an increasingly complex task as the technical language in many professions increases substantially each year. Take the field of computer technology, for example, where the quantity of so-called mnemonics (aids to memory) in the form of acronyms (BASIC is one) invented for software, firmware, and hardware may well negate the original point of their use. Choosing which terms to include among all the coinages and changes in meanings is difficult for lexicographers.

To be considered current, a dictionary must include many new words and reflect changes in meanings. Thus, general dictionaries that are current—even those described as concise or condensed—should include both a noun and a verb definition of *program*, as it is used in computer science. Few dictionaries, as yet, include the acronym *AIDS*, which emerged into the general vocabulary in about 1982. But by the late 1990s, a dictionary that did not include *AIDS* would certainly not be considered current.

In many cases, the reviews in this guide give examples of scientific and technical definitions, to show a work's currency or lack of updating. When considering any dictionary for purchase, however, buyers should conduct a search for a sample of words from medicine, science, and technology to judge whether the inclusions and defined senses of such words are up-to-date enough and presented in the most useful way for the intended reader. The user can also con-

sult the comparative charts in chapter 4 for basic factual information about every reference book or set evaluated in this Buying Guide.

In addition to reviews of general dictionaries, chapters 11 through 15 of the Buying Guide evaluate other kinds of word-related books that are often used by general readers. Perhaps the most familiar of these is the thesaurus. Most readers associate the name *Roget* with a work they might consult in the search for synonyms.

Dr. Peter Mark Roget, English physician and lexicographer, published his *Thesaurus of English Words and Phrases* in 1852. *Thesaurus* means "treasury"; and indeed Roget developed what he called a "classed catalog of words" to "supply my own deficiencies." He wrote that he found his work "of much use to me in literary composition," as have many subsequent generations of writers.

Roget organized his thesaurus according to broad conceptual classifications, within which words of similar meaning are grouped. One group succeeds another because its words are related or contrasted to those of the previous group. Later thesauruses either modify this pattern or abandon it altogether. Some thesaurus editors have revised and expanded Roget's classification system in order to include additional words and phrases, such as Americanisms, slang, and coinages that have entered the language since Roget's time. Other editors have adopted a dictionary format, which is initially easier to use than the classic thesaurus format with its necessary index or copious cross-referencing. However, many readers still prefer the categorical classifications that encourage profitable browsing.

Prospective thesaurus buyers should also be aware that the terms *thesaurus* and *dictionary of synonyms* are sometimes used interchangeably but often represent distinct types of reference work. A thesaurus is a useful tool if you know the meaning of a term and are endeavoring to find the best word to capture it. While many "thesauruses" simply list synonyms (and sometimes antonyms), others define and discriminate among them. Similarly, a "dictionary of synonyms" is, strictly speaking, an alphabetically arranged collection of brief essays discriminating among words that are close in meaning by pointing out subtle differences. However, some works that define themselves by this phrase provide only unembellished word lists. Works in both categories may also contain additional features, such as illustrative sentences or quotations, that individual buyers may especially value.

Other word-related books evaluated are dictionaries of etymology and other sources concerned with word histories. While some of these are best used in scholarly study, others are engagingly written for the nonspecialist reader with an interest in language. Also included are usage dictionaries and related word books. This category contains such diverse but generally useful items as dictionaries of pronunciation, dictionaries of American slang, and dictionaries of "misunderstood" and "troublesome" words. For the many language questions that general dictionaries are not designed to answer, such word books are invaluable resources. This guide enables prospective buyers to assess their individual strengths and applications.

The Structure of Reviews. For the convenience of readers of this guide, each review of a dictionary or word book is divided into numbered sections, so that the evaluations of specific features are readily accessible. There are two basic formats for the reviews:

Dictionaries
   I. Introduction
  II. Authority
 III. Comprehensiveness
 IV. Quality and Currency of Entries
  V. Syllabication and Pronunciation
 VI. Special Features
VII. Accessibility
VIII. Graphics and Format
 IX. Summary

Word Books and Large-Print Works
   I. Introduction and Scope
  II. Format
 III. Quality and Currency of Entries
 IV. Accessibility
  V. Summary

A special note: In the reviews of word books and large-print works, the opening section is entitled "I. Introduction and Scope." Information included in this section embraces three dictionary review categories, "Introduction," "Comprehensiveness," and "Special Features."

The following paragraphs explain some considerations and detail the criteria for each section of the dictionary and related word-book evaluations that appear in chapters 10 through 15. Describing the criteria will highlight some of the features of general dictionaries and word books and will give the prospective purchaser a sound basis for making an evaluation of the works reviewed.

In some cases, the evaluations of dictionaries or word books consist of only the "I. Introduction and Scope" section. This short-format review provides a sketch of the title listed and a cross-reference to a full review that appears under another title listing in the Buying Guide. The short-format review is used when a book is a slightly different version of a work reviewed fully in another edition, for example, or

when a book is an exact or close replica of a title that exists in another format (such as a paperback edition and a hardbound edition from the same publisher).

Facts at a Glance. Each evaluation is preceded by a section of factual information about the dictionary provided by the publishers. This information includes the full title of the work and occasionally alternate or previous titles; the publisher's formal name; the compiler or editor, and, in some cases, the senior lexicographic staff; the date of the edition reviewed; the number of definitions or entries as specified by the publisher (where publishers have not given this information, there is an estimate of the number of main boldface entry words based either on a hand count or on the sampling procedures described in the "Federal Specification—Dictionaries, English": G-D-331D, 28 June 1974); the number of pages; the number of indexes; the number and a brief description of the kinds of illustrations; the trimmed-page size of the volume(s); the kind of binding (occasionally more than one binding is listed); for multivolume works, the number of volumes; and the price(s). This is followed by a general note on where the dictionary is sold; and by the ISBN (international standard book number) or an order number for large-print works, if available.

Introduction. This section provides an overview of the edition of the dictionary reviewed, a brief description of the work's purpose and intended readership, and its relation to other general dictionaries by the same publisher. Pertinent statements about the purposes or content from the introduction or preface are often included.

In addition, a brief description is usually included on the size of the vocabulary, the approach taken by the dictionary's compilers to the vocabulary and other lexicographic features, and any additional features.

Authority. This section briefly summarizes the reputation of the dictionary's publisher and may mention other dictionaries currently or previously published by the same publisher. If the work is a revision of an earlier edition, critical opinions of the original work may be cited, if they are considered useful to readers of this guide.

Information is provided on the editors, the publisher's lexicographic staff, and whether that staff has been involved in the preparation of other dictionaries. (Every dictionary of quality needs to have experienced lexicographers and editors, as well as the advice and expertise of language scholars.)

Information is also supplied on the academic, linguistic, and lexicographic qualifications, or other expertise, of consultants. If there are special sources for vocabulary, etymologies, usage, or other features, which might include citation files or a previous dictionary's word bank or databases, this information is noted. Brief descriptions of the authority of a dictionary give buyers some basis on which to judge its contents. Buyers should keep in mind, however, that although there are many dictionaries on the market whose original staffs and consultants were extremely authoritative, these have not been well revised or updated in accordance with the original work's standards. In general, an authoritative reputation can guide the buyer in the initial selection of a work and may be a final deciding factor, but it should not take the place of a thorough assessment of a work's contents.

Comprehensiveness. In these reviews, the category of comprehensiveness is viewed from several perspectives. One is the relative comprehensiveness of the vocabulary, linguistic data, and information on the history and use of language as measured against well-known works such as the multivolume OXFORD ENGLISH DICTIONARY, WEBSTER'S THIRD NEW INTERNATIONAL, WEBSTER'S NEW TWENTIETH CENTURY DICTIONARY, or the unabridged RANDOM HOUSE DICTIONARY OF THE ENGLISH LANGUAGE. A second view is the relative comprehensiveness of a dictionary when compared to another in the same—or a similar—category.

The reviewers have not criticized dictionaries for a lack of comprehensiveness, however, when that is not appropriate to either the category of a work or its purpose. For instance, a pocket dictionary intended for quick checks on spelling, hyphenation, and basic meanings of an everyday core vocabulary may be sufficiently comprehensive for those purposes without extensive lists of synonyms or usage notes. Many general readers will need no more than brief etymologies, even in works with more extensive vocabularies.

The specific features considered under this section are the inclusion of etymologies and their treatment, lists of combining forms, quotations and usage examples, and notes and prescriptive guidance on use. Synonym treatment is also occasionally discussed in this section (in addition to the information in the definitions section).

Readers' needs are a prime consideration here and, of course, vary widely. Etymologies are of interest not only as background to the meanings of words but as part of social and cultural history. Usage examples and prescriptive guidance are particularly important for users who write extensively. Synonym lists and discrimination of meaning and usage in context are also important to writers and to readers seeking to increase their vocabularies.

This section includes a generous number of brief examples of the various features; these are used to offer both criticisms and compliments. In addition, the section often includes comments on the currency of the dictionary's vocabulary (in addition to the information in section IV, which describes the entries in detail), with examples of words included or omitted in the dictionary's lexicon.

Quality and Currency of Entries. This section characterizes the entries and the definitions included in a dictionary—their extent, quality, variety, and usefulness. The reviewers also assess whether or not the entries will meet the needs of intended readers.

Some of the questions that reviewers asked about each work were: Are the definitions generally accurate and to the point? Are they adequate, given the intended scope of the work, or too concise? Are the meanings carefully discriminated and are special senses labeled when necessary? Are useful cross-references included?

Reviews describe the general sequence of information in the entries (main word, pronunciations, parts of speech, labels, etymologies, and so forth) and note how senses and homographs are ordered. In part, the sequence of information presented in dictionaries depends on custom: a bold main entry word is usually followed by its respelled pronunciation; thereafter, the sequence varies considerably. Buyers will want to look at the sequence of information given in several short and longer entries, to judge whether or not such items as the part of speech, field label, or word history (etymology) can be located easily. When etymologies, for example, are not considered an important feature for the intended reader, they are often shortened or placed at the end of an entry, or sometimes omitted. Buyers should also check on the discriminated senses of words: Are they numbered within entries or otherwise clearly differentiated? Are phrases or sentences given that illustrate how different meanings are used? Are homographs (two words spelled alike but with different etymologies and meanings) omitted, or run into an entry, or are they numbered and placed as separate entries?

Other questions answered by the reviews include: Are the meanings of words defined in historical order or is current usage placed first? Buyers will need to consider which order will best serve their needs. While historical order is well suited to scholarly research, an emphasis on current usage will aid the business writer, for example, or the journalist. Reviews often indicate whether synonyms are used to define meanings, are separately listed, and are exemplified, discriminated, or cross-referenced.

Entries for a given word differ markedly from one dictionary to the next. One expects a pocket dictionary to provide briefer definitions and to omit such features as etymology or synonyms; one would expect an unabridged dictionary to provide detailed information in all areas. However, even within a given dictionary category differences among entries are noteworthy. For example, here are entries for the word **heuristic** from two highly respected unabridged dictionaries:

¹**heu·ris·tic** \'(h)yu̇'ristik, -yü'-, -tēk\ *adj* [G *heuristisch*, fr. NL *heuristicus*, fr. Gk *heuriskein* to discover; akin to OIr *fūar* I have found] **:** providing aid or direction in the solution of a problem but otherwise unjustified or incapable of justification ⟨∼ techniques⟩ ⟨a ∼ assumption⟩ ⟨even vague and dubious assertions can render good services to empirical research as a ∼ stimulus —Edgar Zilsel⟩; *specif* **:** of or relating to exploratory problem-solving techniques that utilize self-educating techniques (as the evaluation of feedback) to improve performance ⟨a ∼ computer program⟩ — **heu·ris·ti·cal·ly** \-tək(ə)lē, -tēk-, -li\ *adv*
²**heuristic** \"\ *n* -s [G *heuristik*, fr. NL *heuristica*, fr. fem. of *heuristicus*] **1 :** the science or art of heuristic procedure **2 :** heuristic argument

(from *Webster's Third New International Dictionary*)

heu·ris·tic (hyo͞o ris′tik *or, often,* yo͞o-), *adj.* **1.** serving to indicate or point out; stimulating interest as a means of furthering investigation. **2.** encouraging a person to learn, discover, understand, or solve problems on his or her own, as by experimenting, evaluating possible answers **or** solutions, or by trial and error: *a heuristic teaching method.* **3.** of, pertaining to, or based on experimentation, evaluation, or trial-and-error methods. **4.** *Computers, Math.* pertaining to a trial-and-error method of problem solving used when an algorithmic approach is impractical. —*n.* **5.** a heuristic method of argument. **6.** the study of heuristic procedure. [1815–25; < NL *heuristicus,* equiv. to Gk *heur(iskein)* to find out, discover + L *-isticus -ISTIC*] —**heu·ris′ti·cal·ly,** *adv.*

(from *The Random House Dictionary of the English Language: Second Edition Unabridged*)

To begin, the reader notices differences in the placement of information. In WEBSTER'S THIRD NEW INTERNATIONAL DICTIONARY, for example, the etymology is placed at the beginning of the entry; in the RANDOM HOUSE DICTIONARY OF THE ENGLISH LANGUAGE: SECOND EDITION UNABRIDGED it appears at the end and includes the date of the word's entry into English. The latter dictionary defines the word as both an adjective and a noun within a single entry; the former provides separate entries for the two parts of speech. WEBSTER'S THIRD shows two definitions for **heuristic** (*adj.*), while RANDOM HOUSE shows four, one of which is a specialized meaning in computer science and mathematics. On the other hand, WEBSTER'S THIRD provides four illustrative phrases, one of which is a quotation, in contrast to RANDOM HOUSE'S one. Thus, the reader requiring specialized definitions of words would find RANDOM HOUSE preferable; the reader seeking fully illustrated general definitions would turn to WEBSTER'S THIRD.

In the case of semi-abridged dictionaries, entries also show considerable variation:

heu·ris·tic (hyo͞o ris′tik) *adj.* [< G. *heuristisch* < Gr. *heuriskein,* to invent, discover: see EUREKA] helping to discover or learn; specif., designating a method of education or of computer programming in which the pupil or machine proceeds along empirical lines, using rules of thumb, to find solutions or answers—**heu·ris′ti·cal·ly** *adv.*
heu·ris·tics (-tiks) *n.pl.* **1.** heuristic methods or procedures **2.** [*with sing. v.*] the art or practice of using heuristic methods or procedures

(from *Webster's New World Dictionary: Second College Edition*)

heu·ris·tic (hyo͞o-ris′tĭk) *adj.* **1.** Of or relating to a usually speculative formulation serving as a guide in the investigation or solution of a problem: *"the historian discovers the past by the judicious use of such a heuristic device as the 'ideal type' "* (Karl J. Weintraub). **2.** Of, relating to, or constituting an educational method in which learning takes place through discoveries that result from investigations made by the student. **3.** *Computer Sci.* Relating to or using a problem-solving technique in which the most appropriate solution of several found by alternative methods is selected at successive stages of a program for use in the next step of the program. —*n.* A heuristic method or process. [< Gk. *heuriskein,* to find.] —**heu·ris′ti·cal·ly** *adv.*

(from *American Heritage Dictionary: Second College Edition*)

heu|ris|tic (hyu̇ ris′tik), *adj.* serving to find out or discover; leading to or stimulating investigation or research: *heuristic teaching. What methods will lead students to become more inquisitive, flexible, heuristic, which, in turn, would lead to scientific creativity?* (New York Times). [< Greek *heur-,* root of *heurískein* to find + English *-ist + -ic*] —**heu|ris′ti|cal|ly,** *adv.*
heu|ris|tics (hyu̇ ris′tiks), *n.* **1** the study or use of discovery procedures in science. **2** a heuristic approach or procedure: *The rules are not necessarily rules of logic; various strategies, or heuristics, may be available for different types of problems* (Scientific American).

(from *World Book Dictionary*)

Once again there are differences in the placement of such information as etymology and in the kind and quantity of information provided. For example, the AMERICAN HERITAGE DICTIONARY: SECOND COLLEGE EDITION entry shows three senses for **heuristic** (*adj.*), one of which is the specialized computer science sense; each of the other two dictionaries offers a single sense. And while that single definition in the WEBSTER'S NEW WORLD DICTIONARY: SECOND COLLEGE EDITION refers to computer programming, the WORLD BOOK DICTIONARY definition does not. WEBSTER'S NEW WORLD and WORLD BOOK both provide separate entries for the noun form, which they show in the more usual plural form; AMERICAN HERITAGE shows the adjective and noun forms in a single entry and elaborates less on the noun than do the other two. The illustrative phrases and sentences also reveal significant differences. WEBSTER'S NEW WORLD provides none. AMERICAN HERITAGE offers a full-sentence quotation in elaboration of one adjectival sense. In WORLD BOOK, full-sentence quotations illustrate both noun and adjective forms, and both quotations are taken from respected general sources. As with the unabridged dictionaries, to select the best work for their purposes prospective buyers of a semi-abridged volume must consider which features are important to them. The reviews describe these kinds of features to help convey to the buyer the quality as well as the style of the definitions and to guide in purchase selection.

Reviewers also examined the methods of conveying usage information. They often comment on prescriptive guidance, such as the explanations of how to use grammar or disputed words, in the main vocabulary. They assess the usefulness of context, field, style, and temporal labels. All in all, the reviewers have attempted to present a balanced judgment of each work's entries.

Syllabication and Pronunciation. How the main entry words and variants are divided into syllables, and the system or practice this is based upon, are briefly noted in this section. Because readers often seek guidance on hyphenation of words, a dictionary needs a clear system that conforms to current printing practice. Prospective buyers should know, for example, that WEBSTER'S THIRD follows a different pattern for hyphenation and word breaks from that used in most other works, including RANDOM HOUSE and WEBSTER'S NEW WORLD DICTIONARY: SECOND COLLEGE EDITION, for example. Where the latter

dictionaries permit the breaking of the word **about** (a·bout), WEBSTER'S THIRD does not. WEBSTER'S THIRD breaks **England** (En·gland) and **English** (En·glish) differently from most other works, which follow the patterns *Eng·land* and *Eng·lish*.

The information given on the pronunciations is often more detailed than that given on syllabication because each dictionary varies in how it respells words for pronunciations and conveys the sounds of spoken language. Most adult dictionaries use a range of symbols from the International Phonetic Alphabet for English (IPA) rather than just alphabet respellings (see the chart for the IPA Phonetic Alphabet and the Trager-Smith Phonemic Alphabet). However, some other systems are used, as in the OXFORD

The International Phonetic Alphabet and the Trager-Smith Phonemic Alphabet for Standard American English

	IPA Symbol	Sound Represented	Trager-Smith Symbol
Consonants	[p]	*p*arson, u*p*	/p/
	[b]	*b*ill, sla*b*	/b/
	[t]	*t*ry, po*t*	/t/
	[d]	*d*ark, en*d*ure	/d/
	[k]	*c*at, qui*ck*	/k/
	[g]	*g*aze, pi*g*	/g/
	[f]	*f*law, enou*gh*	/f/
	[v]	*v*ain, re*v*eal	/v/
	[θ]	*th*in, *th*rough	/θ/
	[ð]	*th*is, *th*erefore	/ð/
	[s]	*s*eal, re*c*eive	/s/
	[z]	*z*ebra, ea*s*ed	/z/
	[ʃ]	*sh*ip, *s*ure	/š/
	[ʒ]	mea*s*ure, sei*z*ure	/ž/
	[tʃ]	*ch*urch, *ch*atter	/č/
	[dʒ]	*j*ud*g*e, *j*angle	/ǰ/
	[m]	*m*ain, sta*mm*er	/m/
	[n]	*n*eon, differe*n*t	/n/
	[ŋ]	si*ng*, a*n*xious	/ŋ/
Liquids	[l]	*l*eap, rumb*l*e	/l/
	[r]	*r*anch, sc*r*atchy	/r/
Glides	[j]	*y*et, uni*v*ersity	/y/
	[w]	*w*ander, q*u*ick	/w/
	[h]	*h*elp, thresh*h*old	/h/
Vowels	[ɪ]	*i*ndex, p*i*t	/i/
	[ɛ]	*e*ver, tr*e*mble	/e/
	[æ]	*a*fter, c*a*n	/æ/
	[ə]	*a*bout, ros*e*s	/ə/
	[ʌ]	*ju*st, th*u*nder	/ə/
	[ɑ]	*f*ather, b*o*ther	/a/
	[ʊ]	b*oo*k, p*u*t	/u/
	[o]	(no example in English)	/o/
	[ɔ]	l*a*w, bl*o*nde	/ɔ/
	[a]	*au*nt (some dialects)	—

(continued)

	IPA Symbol	Sound Represented	Trager-Smith Symbol
Diphthongs	[i]	*see*, cl*ea*n	/iy/
	[ɛɪ]	w*ay*, bl*a*me	/ey/
	[aɪ]	f*ly*, b*i*nd	/ay/
	[ɔɪ]	n*oi*se, b*oy*	/ɔy/
	[u]	m*oo*n, bl*ue*	/uw/
	[oʊ]	t*oe*, m*o*tor	/ow/
	[aʊ]	h*ow*, r*ou*nd	/aw/
	[ɛh]	y*eah*, *e*ver	/eh/
Post-Diphthong	[ɚ]	f*ear*, f*air*, f*ar*, t*our*	/hr/
[r] *or* /ɾ/			

Chart from *How Language Works* (p. 41) by Madelon E. Heatherington.

AMERICAN DICTIONARY (see the chart for this pronunciation key).

Each review describes the system used and indicates whether or not there are adequate pronunciation charts and keys and clear explanations of the phonetic symbols. The reviews also explain a dictionary's method of recording acceptable alternate pronunciations; and they describe information given on regional variations in pronunciations.

If pronunciations are important to users, then buyers need to examine carefully the respellings and symbols to see if they are suited to the intended readers' needs and knowledge of phonetics and diacritical marks.

Pronunciation Key

a *as in*	act, bat, marry	ng *as in*	bring, singer, thank
ă *as in*	ago, suitable, metal	o *as in*	odd, box, hot
ah *as in*	father, calm	ŏ *as in*	official, lemon, ardor
ahr *as in*	arm, cart, bar	oh *as in*	oat, bone, sew
air *as in*	air, dare, scary	ohr *as in*	board, four, hoarse, adore
aw *as in*	all, walk, saw	oi *as in*	oil, join, toy
ay *as in*	age, came, say	oo *as in*	ooze, soon, too, rule
b *as in*	boy, habit, rib	oor *as in*	poor, tour, sure
ch *as in*	chin, teacher, beach	or *as in*	bored, for, horse, adorn
d *as in*	dog, ladder, head	ow *as in*	out, mouse, now
e *as in*	egg, bed, merry	p *as in*	pin, caper, cap
ĕ *as in*	taken, nickel, lawyer	r *as in*	red, carry, near
ee *as in*	eat, meat, see, key	s *as in*	sit, lesson, nice, cellar
eer *as in*	ear, beer, tier	sh *as in*	she, ashen, rush
f *as in*	fat, effort, puff	t *as in*	top, butter, hit
g *as in*	get, wagon, big	th *as in*	thin, method, path
h *as in*	hat, ahead	*th as in*	this, mother, breathe
hw *as in*	wheat, nowhere	u *as in*	up, cut, come
i *as in*	if, give, mirror	ŭ *as in*	suppose, circus, feature
ĭ *as in*	pencil, credible	ur *as in*	her, fir, burn, hurry
ɪ *as in*	ice, bite, fire, spy	uu *as in*	book, full, woman
j *as in*	jam, magic, edge	v *as in*	van, river, give
k *as in*	king, token, back	w *as in*	will, awoke, quick
l *as in*	leg, alley, tell	y *as in*	yes, you
m *as in*	me, common, him	z *as in*	zebra, lazy, tease
n *as in*	no, manner, tan	zh *as in*	vision, pleasure

Key from the *Oxford American Dictionary* (p. ix).

Special Features. Dictionary publishers frequently emphasize the so-called special features of a dictionary, in addition to its main lexicon or vocabulary. A few dictionaries include the kind of reference matter that might be found in an encyclopedia; others have separate "encyclopedic" supplements; some contain almanac-type listings.

The purpose of this section is to point out the additional kinds of information available and to assess its quality, currency, and usefulness to the readers for whom the work is intended. Reviews often note when special features seem to be merely tacked on to a dictionary or when they do not match the quality or currency of the main vocabulary.

Among the other items found in dictionaries that may be reviewed in this section are lists, charts, and tables in the main vocabulary related to entry words (for example, alphabets, kinds of animals, or insects); essays on the spoken and written use of language, its varied pronunciations, or its history; style manuals; examples of forms of address and of letters; and appendixes of information, such as measurements, symbols, and signs. Special, additional information can be helpful to readers whose everyday research needs can thus be met by a single volume.

Readers' needs for such additional material will vary. In general, biographical and geographic lists are useful for quick checking of unfamiliar names or places, although readers should not rely on the dates in such sections because dictionaries are rarely revised as frequently as almanacs or encyclopedias. Entries for specific countries, especially those in the Third World, are also not current in many dictionaries. Full, up-to-date separate listings of abbreviations are always useful to general readers, especially because abbreviations and acronyms are used with increasing frequency.

Accessibility. In brief, accessibility means the ease with which a reader can locate the required information within a dictionary. The reviews describe how information is placed on a dictionary's pages and point out the specific aids to finding the information in entries appearing in the main lexicon as well as in the introductory and supplementary sections.

This section describes, for example, the sequence and the methods of alphabetizing words. Letter-by-letter sequence is usual. Other features that help a reader find words are noted, such as the guide words at the top of pages and thumb indexes. Pairs of guide words at the top of pages are useful in finding the range of entries on a dictionary's page. In larger dictionaries, readers may find thumb-index tabs helpful in getting to the general alphabetical vicinity of a sought-for entry quickly. In small volumes, readers may find thumb indexes unnecessary. Buyers should be aware that tabs with more than one letter of the

alphabet on them guide a reader only to the approximate center of the range of entries between the listed letters.

Each review includes a description of any introductory material or guides to using the contents of a dictionary. These are important sections and should be well spaced on the page and should have clear headings and specific instructions with examples.

In addition, reviews comment on the accessibility of material in appendixes, such as biographical and geographic listings, and abbreviations lists. Occasionally a review will mention the accessibility of additional tabular or chart material that appears within the main vocabulary at specific entries and note when such material is indexed, a useful accessibility feature, especially when extensive charts or tables supplement the vocabulary.

Graphics and Format. The illustrations, general appearance, and physical format are important features of any dictionary. Because a dictionary must stand up to frequent use, a sturdy binding and good-quality paper, preferably with high opacity (so text does not show through from one side of a page to the other) are necessary. Durability is especially important for any dictionary that will be consulted by many library patrons or used extensively in the home. All these features are assessed in this section, as well as the suitability of format—whether paperback, desk size, or over-sized—to the work's contents and purpose.

The reviews occasionally provide fairly extensive descriptive assessments of illustrations and captions, tables, and charts in relation to the definitions. For example, do the illustrations help a reader to understand specific meanings or are they merely decorative? Reviews also assess whether or not illustrations attempt to clarify difficult discriminated meanings that might not be easy to understand from a definition and whether or not captions and labels add information. Signs and symbols are judged for clarity.

The general appearance of the typeface of various elements, such as the main entry word, run-on entries, guide words, and text, is described. These basic elements need to be clear and readable. Reviews describe whether or not there are sufficient margins and enough leading (white space between text lines) to make reading relatively easy. In cases where the specific format or size of a dictionary is important, reviews offer notes, for example, on whether or not a so-called pocket dictionary will actually fit into a pocket or whether the size of a large-print text can be read easily by visually impaired readers.

Summary. The summary of each dictionary's evaluation coordinates the main points made in each section of the review, often making brief comparisons with similar works. The strengths and weaknesses of the volume reviewed are balanced and a general judgment as to its overall quality and specific usefulness is given. The buyer may wish to compare the general characteristics and qualities of several dictionaries by reading their review summaries first and then proceeding to the entire reviews of those that seem likely to be of most value to the potential reader.

Facsimile Entries. Facsimiles that show representative entries, illustrations, and occasional special features of the dictionaries and word books reviewed in the Buying Guide have been included. These will help buyers to judge the type of features and qualities they may specifically require in a dictionary and to comparison-shop prior to making a purchase. The facsimile examples were chosen from as wide a range of titles as possible so that Buying Guide readers could acquire an overview of the whole category of general dictionaries. Each facsimile contains explanatory captions, keyed by number to specific items, that identify particular features of a dictionary.

Publishers often include partial or extensive full-page facsimile illustrations with labels in the introductory material and sometimes on the back of a dictionary's dust jacket. These are valuable guides to a work's format and content for buyers who have a chance to inspect titles before purchase.

Above all, the reviewers, consultants, and editors of this guide have attempted to provide as much information as possible on the qualities and characteristics of the dictionaries reviewed, within the space limitations. No dictionary is perfect, but many are superior in some way to others in a similar category. The reviews, in effect, attempt to define and describe each dictionary in as helpful a manner as possible for potential buyers.

The following glossary contains terms relating to dictionaries and word books that are used in the reviews and that may be unfamiliar to some readers.

Glossary

abridged (dictionary) A category of dictionary based on size; a dictionary of about 55,000 to 130,000 entries; **condensed**, shortened, or reduced from a larger or longer work.

addendum(a) A supplement to a book.

antonym A word that has an opposite or contrary meaning to another. See also **synonym**.

authority The experience, expertise, and reputation of a dictionary or word book's publisher, **lexicographers**, editorial staff, and consultants, as well as a work's generally acknowledged quality and crit-

ical reputation (if the edition reviewed is not the first).

basic vocabulary The fundamental words of a language that must be learned.

bidialectic Referring to the use of two dialects of a language.

bilingual Using or being able to use two languages.

circular or **circularity** In **lexicography**, the defining of a **main entry** word or term using the same word or a **variant** form—a technique that is best avoided in definitions.

citation The source of **definition**s; quotations in the context of actual usage in newspapers, magazines, journals, and books that provide a basis for defining new words and new meanings or senses of words; citations are also used to establish the approximate date of a new word or meaning's appearance in the general **vocabulary**.

citation file Also called citation database. A collection of illustrative quotations, usually from newspapers, magazines, or books with a wide reading public, in the context of actual usage used to develop lexical matter. See also **citation**.

cognate words Words that are related through the same origin or are derived from a common original form.

coinage The invention of words.

college (dictionary) Often called a collegiate or **semi-abridged** dictionary, a category of dictionary usually containing from 130,000 up to 170,000 entries, desk size and directed toward the vocabulary needs of the college community; also, it has fewer entries than an **unabridged** dictionary but more than a **desk** dictionary.

collegiate (dictionary) See **college (dictionary)**.

colloquial Informal style of expression; a phrase or term that may not be considered appropriate in standard formal contexts; a label used in some dictionaries for words or phrases considered informal.

compact See **condensed**.

concise (dictionary) See **abridged** or **condensed**.

condensed Also **concise**, **abridged**. Shortened definitions or versions of a text; *compact* is sometimes used as a description in place of *condensed* or to describe a dictionary with a smaller physical format than a **desk** volume but larger than a standard paperback.

connotation The attributes of a word or phrase derived from use and custom; the associated emotional or attitudinal meaning of a word or phrase. See **denotation**.

core vocabulary The central or most important words in a language.

corrigenda In a book, a list of errors with their corrections.

cross-reference A key word or phrase directing the reader from one **entry** (word or phrase) in a dictionary to another.

definition Information a reader must have to understand the meaning of a word. A definition tells what a word means rather than describing its concept or illustrating its use.

denotation The exact, or literal, meaning of a word or phrase.

desk (dictionary) A category of dictionary containing 50,000 or 60,000 to 100,000 words, conveniently sized for home or office use; sometimes called an **abridged** or **concise** dictionary.

dictionary A reference work that lists words and idiomatic phrases in alphabetical order, describes their meanings, and often provides other information related to words, such as **usage**, **pronunciation**, **etymology**, **synonym**s; a work that serves as a record of, and often a standard for, the language it describes.

discrimination(-ed) The careful distinguishing of the various meanings and **usage** of words; separating and identifying the subtle shades of the meanings of **synonym**s and **antonym**s.

entry A word or phrase identified or defined in a dictionary, usually printed in boldface type; also the paragraph or more of information contained under an alphabetically placed word or phrase that may include subentries and **cross-reference**s. See also **headword** and **run-on entry**.

entry term The key element that comprises the dictionary **entry**. Also called a **main entry**.

ESL English as a second language—the study of English by a nonnative speaker.

etymology The study of word origins, their history, and their development.

etymon A **root word**, from the Greek for "true meaning."

field label A qualifying term that restricts a word's meaning to its use in a scientific, technical, or applied field, such as physics, biology, engineering, law, music, philosophy, and so forth; a term for the field of work or study in which a word or phrase has a special meaning; used for identification and clarification.

finding aid Any device that helps a reader to find information in a dictionary or thesaurus, such as **guide words**, **thumb index**, or printed **thumb tabs**. **Cross-references** are often considered such aids.

glossary An alphabetically listed **vocabulary** of specialized terms, with brief definitions. A glossary is usually restricted to one subject or field of information.

guide word A word at the head of a column or a page that repeats the first or the last **entry** on that page. Guide words often appear in pairs at the top of a page, indicating the first and last entries on that page.

headword The alphabetized form by which the word or expression that is being defined is identified; it indicates preferred spelling, capitalization, and **syllabication**. See also **entry**.

homograph(s) Words that are spelled the same way but often pronounced differently and that have different meanings and different **etymologies**.

homonym See **homophone**.

homophone(s) Sometimes called a **homonym**. Words that are written differently and that often have different meanings, but which sound alike.

idiom An expression, the meaning of which cannot be worked out from its separate parts; an expression, usually of two or more words (an idiomatic phrase), that functions as a single unit and that conveys a distinct meaning in a specific language.

inflected form The alteration of a word to show a change in grammatical function (such as number, person, or tense).

inflection Changing a word in some way according to the rules of grammar.

IPA International Phonetic Association; also International Phonetic Alphabet. IPA designates a complex phonetic pronunciation system (often used in **ESL**, **bidialectic**, and **bilingual** dictionaries as well as in general dictionaries).

key See **pronunciation key**.

label A brief caption for an illustration; in **lexicography**, a tag word that indicates a specific application of a word or phrase. See also **field label**, **style label**, **usage label**.

lexicographer One who compiles or writes a dictionary or **lexicon**.

lexicography The process of writing or compiling a dictionary.

lexicology The study of a language's **vocabulary**, meanings, and changes in form, sense, and use.

lexicon A dictionary; the set (collection) of all the words and **idioms** of a language; also refers to a dictionary's main alphabetical **vocabulary**; often, a dictionary of an ancient language (a Greek *lexicon*).

linguistics The science of language; the study of the nature and structure of human speech and communication.

main entry Where the core information that defines or describes a word or term is contained.

meaning That which the language in general, or a word in particular, represents or expresses.

nonstandard A label used in some dictionaries to indicate **usage** or words not considered acceptable in all circumstances or that are regionalisms, slang, colloquialisms, vulgarisms, or taboo words.

phonemic Notation of the smallest speech units that may be pronounced differently by different people. The phonemic alphabet, developed by George L. Trager and Henry L. Smith, Jr., is referred to as the Trager-Smith or T-S system. See chart preceding this glossary on pages 232–33.

phonetic Notation of actual speech sounds with a distinct set of symbols, each representing a particular sound or articulation. American English has about 45 distinctive speech sounds. See chart preceding this glossary on pages 232–33.

pronunciation The way words sound when spoken and the way these sounds are symbolized in the dictionary, either in a **phonetic** or a **phonemic** system.

pronunciation key A short guide to **pronunciation** used in a particular dictionary.

provenance label Indicates a group responsible for the **coinage** of a word or phrase.

received pronunciation or **RP** Standard British English pronunciation that reveals no regional variation; often called "BBC [British Broadcasting Company] English" because for many years RP was the required pronunciation for news announcers.

respelling Spelling a word again using letters and symbols to represent a **phonetic** alphabet.

root word A term derived from the Greek for true meaning.

RP See **received pronunciation.**

run-on entry Also called *run-on derivative* or *run-on*. A word created by adding or dropping suffixes (such as *-ly*, *-er*, *-tion*, *-ness*, *-ity*, *-ment*, etc.), the meaning of which is understood from the form of the word to which it is added; usually a subordinate entry to the **main entry**. See also **entry.**

semantic Pertaining to the meaning(s) of a language; the study of languages' meanings and their historical change.

semi-abridged (dictionary) A general category of dictionary having approximately 130,000 to 170,000 entries. Sometimes this is called a **college dictionary.**

standard A label that refers to words or **usage** generally recognized and accepted as correct by all educated *native* speakers of the language.

style label A term that denotes a context (social or cultural) of **usage.**

syllabication Word division; the division of a word into syllables to show spelling, hyphenation at the end of lines of writing or printing, or **pronunciation**; usually denoted by a centered period, a space, or other symbol.

synonym A word that can be substituted for another word that is very close in meaning. **Discrimination** of synonyms involves describing the context in which words with near but not exact meanings are used. See also **antonym.**

synonym study See **synonymy.**

synonymy Equivalence in meaning; a list of synonyms; also, a so-called *synonym study* or descriptive paragraph in which synonyms are defined and discriminated by meaning from one another.

thumb index or **thumb tab** A **finding aid** in dictionaries and other reference books; thumb-size notches cut in the fore edges of a book's pages, usually reinforced with labeled tabs that indicate the sections of a volume.

Trager-Smith system See **phonemic.**

unabridged (dictionary) Not **condensed**; a category of dictionary of over 300,000 entries that provides full coverage of the **lexicon** of a language that is in general use; quotations are provided to support **definition**s and to illustrate context and varieties of **usage**.

usage How a language is actually used; the ways people write or speak a language; also, more loosely, a prescriptive indication of how to use or when to use designated grammar, meanings, **idioms**, or other forms of language.

usage label Information given in dictionaries to identify special or restricted use of a particular word or phrase; usage labels can show cultural, regional, scientific, technical, temporal, or other restrictions of a word.

variant A slight difference in the form of a word, such as a different spelling or **pronunciation**.

vocabulary A **glossary** or **lexicon**; a list of words arranged and defined in alphabetical order; all the words and **idioms** of a language.

WNI rule Refers to *words not in*; a general principle that all words used in a **definition** should be included in the dictionary itself.

word history See **etymology**.

Chapter 10
Evaluations of Dictionaries

The American Encyclopedic Dictionary

Facts at a Glance

Full Title: **The American Encyclopedic Dictionary**.
Publisher: Salem House.
Edition Reviewed: © 1987.

Number of Volumes: 1.
Number of Entries: over 30,000.
Number of Pages: 1,936.
Number of Illustrations: 2,500 color photographs;
   1,000 illustrations and maps in color.
Trim Size: 7⅜″ × 10³⁄₁₆″.
Binding: hardcover.

Price: $69.95.
Sold in bookstores; also sold to libraries and other
   educational institutions.
ISBN 0-88162-231-1.

I. Introduction

The copyright line in *The American Encyclopedic Dictionary* states that the text is "derived from the Oxford Illustrated Dictionary" and that the illustrations and captions were "compiled in association with Oxford University Press" by an Australian firm, Bay Books Pty Ltd. The text has been Americanized both in spelling and, presumably, in content, since many American words, phrases, abbreviations, place names, and biographies are included as entries. The introductory section states that "this new work attempts to combine in a form that can be easily and pleasurably used the essential features of dictionary and encyclopaedia." Over 30,000 entries give the "meanings of words in common or not-so-common currency," including "hundreds of entries on famous people and places, animals and plants." The entries are illustrated with 2,500 color photographs plus 1,000 illustrations and maps. The book is intended for a general readership, primarily in homes and offices, and, according to the introduction, contains up-to-date scientific and technical terms but omits most obsolete words and phrases, as well as most etymologies.

In addition to the main alphabet, the volume contains a four-page introductory section entitled "How to Use the Dictionary," a three-page listing of abbreviations used in the dictionary, and four pages of brief appendixes.

II. Authority

The vocabulary of the *Oxford Illustrated Dictionary* was based on THE CONCISE OXFORD ENGLISH DICTIONARY, a smaller version of the famous OXFORD ENGLISH DICTIONARY. The renowned dictionary staff of the Oxford University Press worked on this volume, although no criteria are given for the choice of entries or illustrations.

III. Comprehensiveness

The American Encyclopedic Dictionary presents a wide variety of words and subjects in very brief entries with as many as three or four illustrations per page. A typical sequence of entries appears on page 668, beginning with **Freud, Sigmund** and ending with **frill**. In between, we find: **Fri.** (abbrev. for *Friday*); **friable** (including **friability** and **friableness**); **friar** (in-

The American Encyclopedic Dictionary

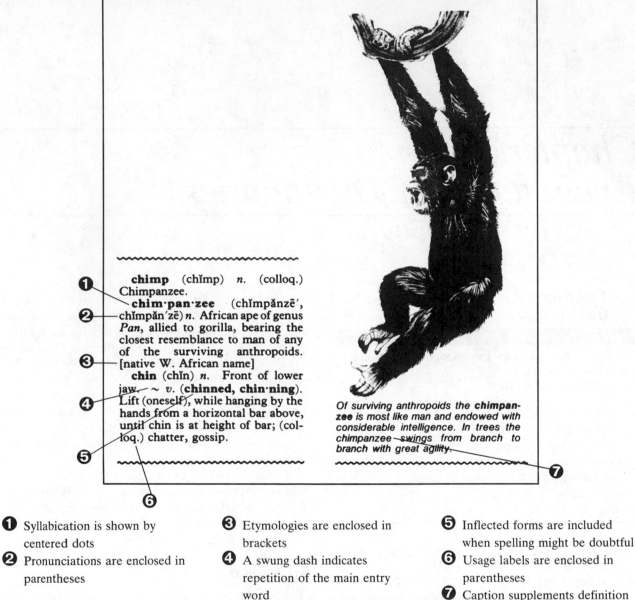

chimp (chĭmp) *n.* (colloq.) Chimpanzee.

chim·pan·zee (chĭmpănzē′, chĭmpăn′zē) *n.* African ape of genus *Pan*, allied to gorilla, bearing the closest resemblance to man of any of the surviving anthropoids. [native W. African name]

chin (chĭn) *n.* Front of lower jaw. ~ *v.* (**chinned, chin·ning**). Lift (oneself), while hanging by the hands from a horizontal bar above, until chin is at height of bar; (colloq.) chatter, gossip.

*Of surviving anthropoids the **chimpanzee** is most like man and endowed with considerable intelligence. In trees the chimpanzee swings from branch to branch with great agility.*

❶ Syllabication is shown by centered dots

❷ Pronunciations are enclosed in parentheses

❸ Etymologies are enclosed in brackets

❹ A swung dash indicates repetition of the main entry word

❺ Inflected forms are included when spelling might be doubtful

❻ Usage labels are enclosed in parentheses

❼ Caption supplements definition

cluding the subentries **Gray Friars**, **Austin Friars**, **Black Friars**, **White Friars**, and **friary**); **fricassee**; **fricative**; **Frick, Henry Clay**; **friction** (including ~**coupling**, ~**tape**, **frictional**, and **frictionally**); **Friday** (including **Good**~, **man**~, and **girl**~); **fried**; **friend** (including ~**at court**, **F**~, **Society of Friends**, **friendship**, and **friendless**); **friendly** (including **friendliness**); **friendship**; **frieze**[1], **frieze**[2]; **frigate** (including ~**bird** and **magnificent**~); **Frigga, Frigg**; **fright**; **frighten** (including **frightened at**); **frightful** (including **frightfully** and **frightfulness**); **frigid** (including **F**~ **Zone**, **frigidly**, **frigidness**, and **frigidity**).

The page also contains a full-color illustration of two frigate birds, one with its throat pouch inflated. (Curiously enough on the right-hand page of this double-page spread is a full-page, full-color photograph of a member of the same species with its throat pouch inflated. A spot check did not reveal other repetitions of this kind, however.)

This double-page spread makes for more dramatic use of illustrations in comparison with the double-page spread covering the same range of words (between *Freud* and *frill*) in THE AMERICAN HERITAGE ILLUSTRATED ENCYCLOPEDIC DICTIONARY. However, the latter volume contains 54 main entries (not counting subentries) as compared to the 19 found in *The American Encyclopedic Dictionary*. The AMERICAN HERITAGE entries are also brief, but they are informative and are written at a higher language level. The space in that work, therefore, has been devoted to providing more information (in smaller type), with less emphasis on the illustrations. (See elsewhere in the Buying Guide for a review of THE AMERICAN HERITAGE ILLUSTRATED ENCYCLOPEDIC DICTIONARY.)

Animals, birds, cities, mountains, plants, insects, machines, buildings, and ethnic costumes are well covered in illustrations, and the vocabulary includes such entries as **Manicheism, Dow-Jones average, torque, shofar, Gullah, black hole, pièce de résistance, fuck, data bank, hard hat, Malthusianism, Sir Laurence Olivier, hanky-panky, DNA, Georgia O'Keeffe, OPEC, "Dixie," Anwar el Sadat, Te Deum, Sacajawea, Mr. Micawber, blast-off, Oneida Colony, and Pap smear.**

IV. Quality and Currency of Entries

Entries defining words are very brief and precise and are expressed without using the infinitive *to* for verbs, for example. Synonyms are the chief means used to describe nouns, sometimes with semicolons rather than numbers to indicate different meanings. A typical entry is:

> **grasp** (grăsp, grähsp) *v.* Clutch *at,* try to seize; seize and hold firmly with the hand; get mental hold of, comprehend. ~*n.* Fast hold, grip; control, mastery; mental hold, comprehensiveness of mind. **grasp′a·ble,** *adj.* **grasp′ing** *adj.* (esp). Greedy, avaricious. **grasp′ing·ly** *adv.*

The entry word appears in boldface, slightly indented. Pronunciations are included, as well as parts of speech, but very few entries show an etymology (sources *are* given for unexpected etymologies or for words derived from proper names), and illustrative phrases or sentences are almost never used.

Abbreviations are included among the main entries, which are listed alphabetically, letter by letter. Words having the same spellings but different meanings are listed separately, with superscript numbers, for example, the word **bay,** which has five entries. Brief labels are given in parentheses for fields, historical usage, opposite meanings, or sources (such as the Bible). Irregular plurals are spelled out.

Encyclopedic entries vary in length and in the amount of detail included, but they are usually cursory paragraphs of 50 words or less. Geographical entries supply no population figures, *sometimes* pinpoint location of cities, and *sometimes* include history and lore, for example:

> **New Orleans** . . . City and port on Mississippi in Louisiana, 100 mi. (160 km) N. of Gulf of Mexico; noted for French architecture and Creole cuisine of early settlers; birthplace of jazz music.

However, the geographical entry for **Paris** reads:

> **Paris** . . . Capital city of France, on the Seine River.

Biographical entries as a rule provide minimal information, for example:

> **Pierce, Franklin** (1804–1896). Fourteenth president of U.S., 1835–7.

Or, somewhat more detailed, the entry following **Pierce,**

> **Piero della Francesca** (1420?–1492). Italian painter and mathematician; famous for frescoes in the church of St. Francis at Arezzo, *The Legend of the Holy Cross.*

The entries are not as up-to-date as the copyright promises. Ronald Reagan is listed as president of the United States (1981) and Margaret Thatcher as the British prime minister (1979), but Sandra Day O'Connor is not listed as a Supreme Court justice (1981), nor is Brian Mulroney as the Canadian prime minister (1984). A surprising number of current terms are also omitted, for example, *ultrasound, AIDS, ozone layer, amniocentesis, CAT* (computerized axial tomography), *supply side, synthesizer* (keyboard instrument), *Alzheimer's disease,* and *Burkina Faso* (formerly Upper Volta).

Readers will note, despite the Americanized spelling, the frequent inclusion of British pronunciations and meanings, for example: under **pop[1]** . . . a reader will find a British idiom that might be unfamiliar:

> **pop off,** (slang) die suddenly; speak or write emotionally.

Other distinctly British usages are found occasionally in the volume. The definition at **bowl[2]** covers the sport of bowling on a green but not the American sport, although that appears under **bowling.** The small chart of professional boxing weights will confuse Americans because the weights are listed as

> fly 8st
> bantam 8st 8lb
> feather 9st

and so forth. Neither the definition of **boxing,** nor that of **boxer,** nor the chart itself notes that "st" is an abbreviation for a British unit of weight equivalent to 14 pounds (although that definition is found under the entry for **stone**).

British subjects also appear in photographs American children, for example, carry schoolbooks to school not in **satchels,** as the illustration implies, but in book bags.

The volume is heavily weighted in dictionary entries over encyclopedic entries. All entries are precise, but many are so brief as barely to define the words or identify the subjects described.

V. Syllabication and Pronunciation

Syllabication is indicated by centered dots in main entries, and pronunciation is by phonetic respelling and use of a few, widely recognized symbols; for example: ā, ē, ī, ō, ū, ōō for the long vowel sounds in *mate, mete, mite, mote, mute, moot*, respectively. A clear, brief guide to pronunciation appears in the introductory section to the volume, but there are no shorter, convenient keys on text pages themselves.

VI. Special Features

Aside from the many illustrations, there are no special features other than the appendixes and the initial letters appearing at the beginning of each new letter section of the alphabet. These letters, designed (according to the information provided at occasional letters such as *A* and *G*) by Albrecht Dürer, are accompanied by several other forms of the letter used through history in different alphabets.

The appendixes, mere listings of information, are "Presidents of the United States of America"; "Prime Ministers of Canada since 1867"; "Rulers of England and the United Kingdom"; "Prime Ministers of Great Britain"; "Weights and Measures"; and "The Chemical Elements."

VII. Accessibility

Guide words appear at the top left and right corner of each double-page spread showing the first word on the left-hand page and the last word on the right-hand page. The very brief introductory section is adequate for the use of the volume. A table of contents is provided, and page numbers appear at the top center of each page. There is no thumb index, presumably because it might have obstructed some of the illustrations.

VIII. Graphics and Format

The full-color illustrations—photographs, drawings, and diagrams—in the volume are numerous and well printed. Their range is very wide, and they are well chosen to clarify words or subjects or to give a pictorial indication of place. Many helpful outline maps are included. Illustrations are frequently labeled, and a brief caption in italics describes in one or two sentences all the illustrations on one page. (Many illustrations fill an entire page, and the caption is found on the opposite page.) Unfortunately, captions are sometimes difficult to locate, as they are not separated sufficiently from the surrounding text, despite their appearing in italics. While the illustrations are excellent in themselves, they seem to overwhelm the entries. This obvious discrepancy may lead readers to expect more information than it is possible to include in an encyclopedic dictionary. Nevertheless, our reviewers believe that each page is a satisfactory graphic mixture of three columns of large-size type and illustrations. The book will give pleasure to those who enjoy gaining information—brief as it is—through pictures. But as THE AMERICAN HERITAGE ILLUSTRATED ENCYCLOPEDIC DICTIONARY demonstrates, it is possible to combine a far greater number of longer entries (180,000 to the 30,000 of *The American Encyclopedic Dictionary*) with a large number of illustrations in approximately the same amount of space.

The volume is sturdily bound but may not be durable enough for extensive library use. There is some show-through on the paper, but not enough to disturb either the text or the illustrations.

IX. Summary

The American Encyclopedic Dictionary does combine, pleasurably, features of the dictionary and the encyclopedia, but at a cost, chiefly the brevity of the entries, which leaves the reader dissatisfied and craving more information. The volume is deficient in some current information that might reasonably be expected to appear in a book with a 1987 copyright. Lavish as the volume may at first appear, it was perhaps prepared mainly for family browsing and quick reference. The size of the type and the generous white space tend to support this. If libraries intend to supply their readers with an illustrated encyclopedic dictionary, they would be better advised to purchase the excellent—and less costly—AMERICAN HERITAGE ILLUSTRATED ENCYCLOPEDIC DICTIONARY (reviewed elsewhere in the Buying Guide).

The American Heritage Desk Dictionary

Facts at a Glance

Full Title: **The American Heritage Desk Dictionary.**
Publisher: Houghton Mifflin.
Editors: Fernando de Mello Vianna, Editor-in-Chief.
Edition Reviewed: © 1981.

Number of Entries: more than 100,000.
Number of Pages: 1,184.
Number of Illustrations: more than 1,500 black-and-white photographs and line drawings.
Trim Size: 6¾″ × 9⁹⁄₁₆″.
Binding: cloth.

Price: $10.95.
Sold in bookstores and other outlets; also sold to libraries and other educational institutions.
ISBN 0-395-31256-6.

The American Heritage Desk Dictionary

❶ Pronunciations are enclosed in parentheses

❷ Inflected forms, abbreviated where possible, are set in boldface type

❸ Idiomatic expressions, set in small boldface type and preceded by the boldface italic subheading — *idioms*, are defined after the main entry

❹ Usage labels are italicized

❺ Synonyms are discussed in a separate note headed by a boldface italic *Syns*

❻ Cross-references are set in boldface type

❼ Etymologies are enclosed in brackets

❶ **deem** (dēm) *tr.v.* To judge; consider; think: *We deem it advisable to wait.* —See Syns at **believe.** [Middle English **demen**, from Old English *dēman.*] ❻

❷ **deep** (dēp) *adj.* **-er, -est. 1.** Extending far downward below a surface: *a deep hole.* **2.** Extending far backward from front to rear, or inward from the outside: *a deep closet.* **3.** Far distant down or in: *deep in the woods.* **4.** Extreme; profound; intense: *a deep silence.* **5.** Very much absorbed or involved: *deep in thought.* **6.** Showing much thought or feeling: *a deep understanding; a deep love.* **7.** Difficult to understand or penetrate: *a deep mystery.* **8.** Rich and vivid: *a deep red.* **9.** Low in pitch: *a deep voice.* **10.** Coming from or located at a depth: *a deep sigh.* —*adv.* **1.** Far down or into: *dig deep.* **2.** Well on in time; late: *work deep into the night.* —*n.* **1.** A deep place, esp. one in the ocean. **2.** The most intense or extreme part: *the deep of night.*

❸ —*idioms.* **in deep.** *Informal.* Completely committed. **the deep.** *Poet.* The ocean. [Middle English *dep*, from Old English *dēop.*] —**deep′ly** *adv.* —**deep′ness** *n.* ❼

❺ — **Syns: deep, esoteric, heavy** (*Slang*), **profound** *adj.* Core meaning: Beyond an average person's understanding (*a deep book*).

I. Introduction

The American Heritage Desk Dictionary, published in 1981, is the second largest of the dictionaries in the American Heritage "family." The publishers describe the desk version as "an entirely new comprehensive dictionary for home, school, and office . . . that reflects the basic lexicographic approach" of THE AMERICAN HERITAGE DICTIONARY (AHD). The main features of that approach were: a) an attempt to place the most current central meaning of a word first in a definition and then to add other meanings in logical sequence; and b) guidance on using words according to "educated" speech with "grace and precision." Both approaches are evident in this desk dictionary and in its "Usage Notes," based on the opinions of the celebrated Usage Panel for the original AHD.

The vocabulary in the desk volume consists of more than 100,000 entries, plus 2,500 biographical and geographic entries. According to the publisher, the synonym paragraphs reflect the extensive work that went into the preparation of the ROGET'S II: THE NEW THESAURUS (1980), published by the same company.

The desk dictionary's design and page layout differ from the other American Heritage dictionaries, although similar, extensive use is made of photographs. In this desk volume, photographs and diagrams are larger, printed more clearly, and hence are more useful.

II. Authority

Houghton Mifflin's lexicographic staff prepared this volume under the guidance of Fernando de Mello Vianna, who was also Editor–in–Chief of the publisher's respected ROGET'S II: THE NEW THESAU-RUS. The American Heritage family of dictionaries not only is well known but has generally received excellent reviews.

Considerable effort has been made to reflect contemporary usage and meaning in this volume, as in other American Heritage dictionaries. In appearance, this desk dictionary is a model of contemporary, accessible design; the many photographs are generally appropriate for the entries, placed as close to them as possible, and provided with a clear caption in boldface.

III. Comprehensiveness

For an abridged work with a typeface large enough to be read with ease, *The American Heritage Desk Dictionary* is sufficiently comprehensive for most users as a general, everyday reference. The dictionary does not have the extensive number of scientific and technological terms included in THE AHD: SECOND COLLEGE EDITION. There are, for example, fewer medical terms and the level of some of them, such as *levulose* (defined here as fructose) are over-simplified. Students requiring a specialist vocabulary in the sciences and technology will be better served with a textbook or special glossary.

A comparison of a representative segment of entries from **paprika** to **parachute** shows that the SECOND COLLEGE EDITION includes 22 separate entry words, while the desk dictionary has nine. In the SECOND COLLEGE EDITION, however, seven of the 22 separate entries are variants of **par, par-,** or **para,** while in the desk dictionary several of those diverse meanings are included under the entries for **par** *n.* and **para-** or **par-.** Neither the desk dictionary nor the CONCISE AMERICAN HERITAGE DICTIONARY (reviewed later in this Buying Guide) include the following entries between **paprika** and **parachute**:

Papuan *n.*, **papule**, **papyrika**, **papyrology**, **para-aminobenzoic acid**, **parabiosis**, **parablast**, or **paraboloid**. This more specialized and scientific terminology is included in the AHD: SECOND COLLEGE EDITION.

Although *The American Heritage Desk Dictionary* is comprehensive for an abridged dictionary, some words in frequent current use, such as *videocassette* and *aerobics*, are missing.

IV. Quality and Currency of Entries

A typical entry includes the following information: boldface syllabication, pronunciation with abbreviated variations given in parentheses, italicized abbreviation of the part of speech, definitions, variant word forms with the parts of speech indicated, usage information for some entries, and etymology or source.

In general, definitions are concise and easy to understand. Frequent italicized short examples (phrases or brief sentences) follow immediately after many of the meanings. These examples are often helpful, lively, and contemporary. For example, see:

> **fend** *tr. v.* To keep off; repel. *He used an oar to fend off the sharks*

or

> **a·bol·ish** *tr. v.* To do away with; put an end to: *We must abolish sexism.*

When such examples are quotations, the author is cited.

The order of defined meanings tends to present the most widely used meaning first, as in:

> **ab·ra·ca·dab·ra** *n.* **1.** A word once held to possess magical powers to ward off disease or disaster. **2.** Jargon; gibberish.

The terms in the etymologies are spelled out in full as, for example, the one for **abracadabra**:

> [Late Latin, from late Greek **abrasadebra**, a magic word used by an ancient religious sect.]

Where necessary, words that are, in fact, short forms are noted. **Graph**, for example, is defined as "short for graphic formula." Synonyms are listed after the appropriate meaning or cross-referenced. For **lapse**, the cross-reference is "—See Syns at **error**." Then, at **error**, a synonym list appears which includes a fuller definition of **slip-up**:

> (*Informal*) *n. Core meaning:* An unintentional deviation from what is correct, right, or true (*an error in judgment*).

The "core meaning" is derived from the first definition of a word appearing in ROGET'S II: THE NEW THESAURUS, and differs from the main entry for **slip-up**:

> *n. Informal:* An error; oversight; mistake.

The insertion of the core meanings for selected synonyms is one method used by *The American Heritage Desk Dictionary* to condense material. But it also helps the user who is searching for a more complete definition of the word or a synonym.

Several other features are especially helpful, including the identification of homographs, listing of prefixes and suffixes, and listing of plural forms of verbs.

Homographs, words that have distinctly different meanings but that are spelled alike, such as **lark**, a bird, or **lark**, a carefree adventure, are included as separate numbered entries. Prefixes and suffixes (**-ish**, etc.) are also separate entries with definitions and etymologies. For more complete spelling reference, plural forms of words follow main entry words, but are *also* listed separately if they are variant forms. Compare "**lar·ynx** *n.* pl. **larynges** or **-ynxes**" with the separate entry, "**laryn·ges** *n.* A plural of **larynx**." Similarly, prefixes and prefix variant forms appear as separate bold entries: "**laryng-**. Var. of **laryngo-**."

Idiomatic usage is clearly labeled and defined, with multiple meanings when necessary. For the entry **large**, under the label **—idioms.**, the idiomatic phrase "**at large**" has four defined meanings followed by a definition of "**by and large**."

The usage notes following definitions seem up-to-date and useful in the desk dictionary. Under the entry **chair**, for example, a usage note appears:

> **chair, chairman, chairperson**. These three nouns are interchangeably used to refer to one who presides over a group. The terms chair and chairman can also be used as verbs,

that is absent in the SECOND COLLEGE EDITION.

A comparison of specific definitions, from the desk edition and the AHD: SECOND COLLEGE EDITION may be of special interest to potential buyers.

From the *Desk Dictionary*:

> **fem·i·nism** *n.* **1.** A doctrine that advocates the political, social, and economic equality of men and women. **2.** Activity undertaken in support of the doctrine of feminism.

From the SECOND COLLEGE EDITION:

> **fem·i·nism** *n.* **1.** A doctrine that advocates or demands for women the same rights granted men, as in political and economic status. **2.** The movement in support of feminism.

From the *Desk Dictionary*:

> **rac·ism** *n.* Racial prejudice or discrimination.

From the SECOND COLLEGE EDITION:

> rac·ism *n.* **1.** The notion that one's own ethnic stock is superior. **2.** Discrimination or prejudice based on racism.

As the reviewer for *American Reference Books Annual 1983* commented, "Naturally, this variant [the desk dictionary] relies heavily on *AHD* . . . the reductions in entries and definitions produced some cases of circularity [but] on the whole, a solid piece of work. . . ." The vocabulary and phrasing of many entries in the desk dictionary does rely on the AHD: SECOND COLLEGE EDITION, as a comparison of one brief segment of entries (chosen at random)—from **paprika** to **parachute**—shows. Some entries in the desk version have been shortened by omission of secondary meanings, or a few words. In the desk dictionary, **paprika** is defined as "A mild, powdered seasoning made from sweet red peppers." In the AHD: SECOND COLLEGE EDITION, that is the first meaning, followed by a second, which is omitted in the desk version: "A dark to deep or vivid reddish orange."

Another representative entry, **Pap test**, shows how the two dictionaries define an entry from a specialist field such as medicine. In the desk dictionary **Pap test** is defined:

> A test in which a smear of bodily secretion is immediately fixed and examined to detect cancer in an early stage. Also called **Pap smear**. [Invented by George Papanicolaou (1883–1962), American scientist.]

In the SECOND COLLEGE EDITION, **Pap smear** is a separate entry word, and the definition of **Pap test** is more detailed and includes a field label:

> *n. Med.* A test in which a smear of a bodily secretion, esp. from the cervix or vagina, is immediately fixed and examined for exfoliated cells to detect cancer in an early stage or to evaluate hormonal condition. [After George Papanicolaou (1883–1962), its inventor.]

The preceding comparison shows that the desk version is especially helpful for readers who need a quick, understandable definition but not the scientific detail implicit in a phrase such as "exfoliated cells."

V. Syllabication and Pronunciation

As in other American Heritage dictionaries, centered bold dots divide syllables in all the main entries: **mor·a·to·ri·um**. Hyphens in compound words are retained, but syllable division is not, if a word in a compound appears elsewhere as a separate entry: an example is "**bituminous coal**." Syllable divisions follow modern printing and editorial practice.

Pronunciation symbols are given for all main entries and for other forms as required. The pronunciation key appears in a large chart with a good explanation at the front of the dictionary. The symbols used are "designed to enable the reader to reproduce a satisfactory pronunciation with no more than a quick reference to the key." A shortened form of the key is printed at the bottom of each page of the dictionary for quick reference. The system of symbols is common to all the American Heritage dictionaries, and the publisher states that "all pronunciations given are acceptable in all circumstances," meaning in formal as well as in informal circumstances. If more than one pronunciation is listed for a word, the first is assumed to be more common:

> **pan·zer** (păn′zər, pän′sər, pänt′sər).

In addition, there are clear notes on special symbols that may be less familiar, such as the schwa (ə). Primary and secondary stress is indicated with bold and lighter face marks: "păn′ta-mīm′."

VI. Special Features

Tables are located at the end of the dictionary's entries and include: a "Guide to the Metric System," a "Periodic Table of Elements," proofreaders' marks, symbols and signs, and alphabets.

Following the tables are separate sections of approximately 2,500 very brief biographical and geographic entries. Its main competitor, WEBSTER'S NINTH NEW COLLEGIATE DICTIONARY, boasts a combined total of 18,000 biographical and geographical entries. Biographical entries here include appropriate part-of-speech labels (**Chaucerian** is identified as both an adjective and a noun). The names of popes and kings, such as Pius and George, differentiated only by Roman numerals, are listed as separate entries. Variant spellings are entered for geographic names. Neither section is current for dates or population figures after the early 1980s. Thus, for example, state leaders Gorbachev, Kohl, and Mulroney are excluded, and artist Andy Warhol and writer Saul Bellow suffer a similar fate.

The ready accessibility of the special features at the end of the desk dictionary make it useful for quick reference for the general reader; however, for more in-depth research, specialized sources would need to be consulted.

A brief list of standard abbreviations is included at the end of the book. In addition, there is an extensive, separate listing of abbreviations used in the dictionary's entries, including field labels, abbreviations used in the etymologies, and those used in the biographical and geographic entries. This gathering together in one place of all abbreviations used in the dictionary is an excellent idea, providing users with an easily accessible reference page.

Other special features, conveniently explained in "How to Use Your Dictionary" at the front of the volume, include:

(1) *Synonym Studies,* both short and long paragraphs listing parts of speech, core meaning, and giving examples;

(2) *Usage Notes*, based on the opinions of the Usage Panel for the original AHD whose members are listed at the front of the desk edition. These notes are not, the publisher says, "prescriptions. . . . Rather they reflect standard American English as it is written and spoken by educated users today." The publisher also indicates that these notes "are designed to help you express yourself fluently, clearly, and concisely in formal and informal settings—and in such a way as to avoid criticism"—clearly, a rather large claim;

(3) *Alphabet Letter Histories*, which appear on the first page of each alphabetical sequence, tracing the 3,000 or so years of a letter's past. These are condensed versions of a feature in the AHD: SECOND COLLEGE EDITION; in the desk volume, they are more a narrative than an orthographical history.

Another feature is the eight-page "Manual of Style" with four main sections: punctuation, capitalization, use of italics, and business letters. There are brief examples covering most typical problems in the first three sections and four styles of business letter formats used in current correspondence. A similar handbook of style may be found in WEBSTER'S NINTH NEW COLLEGIATE DICTIONARY.

VII. Accessibility

All entries, including compound words, are arranged in strict letter-by-letter alphabetical order. The two-column format with boldface main entries—printed in a readable size overhanging the text—makes this dictionary easy to access. Inflected forms of a word, numbers preceding definitions with an entry, cross-referenced words, and labels for phrasal, modifying, and idiomatic examples (—**phrasal verbs**, —**modifier**, —**idiom**.) are printed in sans-serif bold type and are easily found within entries. Synonym lists are placed in separate paragraphs following the main body of an entry.

The use of easily readable type plus the listing of special features such as synonyms and idiomatic examples within each entry makes it easier for a user to find cross-references and variant forms of words.

A special effort has been made in the "How to . . ." section to define what a dictionary is and to explain what its various parts are intended to do—in general and in this desk version in particular.

A brief contents appears immediately after the title page and lists all the tables in the appendix except for "Symbols and Signs" (presumably an oversight). The separate biographical and geographic entries follow the tables, and the list of abbreviations is handily located at the end of the book.

VIII. Graphics and Format

The quality varies among the over 1,500 captioned illustrations, all in the main vocabulary. Some pictures appear "muddy," but most are clear and useful. The size of the illustrations ranges from 2¼ inches wide and 1½ inches high to slightly larger. This means that the objects in the pictures are much easier to see than in other illustrated American Heritage dictionaries. Furthermore, the white, relatively opaque paper makes the photographs seem even clearer in contrast.

The schematic drawings of human anatomy are clear, with many small, but readable labels. The line drawings of flowers and of birds are exceptionally detailed. Many photographs are excellent (for example, that of screech owls). Generally, the pictures have been cropped well, so that the detail intended to illustrate an entry is readily apparent (there are, of course, exceptions, such as the **hookah**, which cannot be seen in one photo). Occasionally drawings and up-to-date photographs illustrate several kinds of a defined object (for example, **nail** and **triangle**) or variations in meaning (**afghan rug** and **afghan hound**). There are neither portraits in the biographical section nor maps in the geographic section.

The overall design of the dictionary is attractive—with the notable exception of the "Style Manual" at the front of the book. This displays too much distracting white space between letters. To be fair, the design of the "Style Manual" is a minor drawback in an otherwise easy-to-read and attractive book.

IX. Summary

The American Heritage Desk Dictionary is a useful, everyday reference for those who may not require the additional special features or more technical definitions of the larger volume, THE AMERICAN HERITAGE DICTIONARY: SECOND COLLEGE EDITION. Many colleges, offices, and households will find this a good choice because access is easy, the typeface is readable, the paper quality is good, and the binding is sturdy. Furthermore, the generous number of illustrations, spaced well in the two columns of entries, give the pages an open and more accessible look than is usual in desk dictionaries. It has more than twice the number of illustrations of WEBSTER'S NINTH, although it has less main entries (100,000 compared with WEBSTER'S 160,000).

In addition to its physical features, the simplified definitions are clear and well written. The paragraphs on synonyms will be especially useful for writers. Readers with more specialized requirements will need a more extensive dictionary, however. A bonus for general users is the condensed introductory matter on how to use this dictionary as well as on the most common writing problems, such as capitalization of words.

Though buyers may also wish to have a look at WEBSTER'S NINTH NEW COLLEGIATE, *The American Heritage Desk Dictionary* is generally recommended for individuals, businesses, and public libraries, as a concise, accurate, desk-top reference, where extensive research is not commonly pursued.

The American Heritage Dictionary

Facts at a Glance

Full Title: **The American Heritage Dictionary**.
Publisher: Dell Publishing Co.
Editors: Susan Moldow (Dell); Mark Boyer, Kaethe Ellis, Dolores R. Harris, and Anne H. Soukanov (Houghton Mifflin).
Edition Reviewed: © 1983; 1985 printing.

Number of Definitions: about 60,000.
Number of Pages: 880.
Number of Illustrations: over 400 black-and-white photographs and drawings.
Trim Size: 4¾" × 6¾".
Binding: paperback.

Price: $4.95.
Sold in bookstores and other outlets; also sold to libraries and other educational institutions.
ISBN 0-440-10068-2.

I. Introduction

The 1983 Dell paperback edition of *The American Heritage Dictionary* (*AHD*) is based on the AMERICAN HERITAGE DICTIONARY: SECOND COLLEGE EDITION, published in 1983 by Houghton Mifflin. The preface to the Dell edition states that "it is an independent reference work embodying in smaller form the additions of the parent book." This refers to the general and technical words that were added to the AHD: SECOND COLLEGE EDITION to reflect more current vocabulary and use. The vocabulary and length of entries in the Dell edition are more like those in the desk-size CONCISE AMERICAN HERITAGE DICTIONARY, although there are some differences. (The etymologies and word sources, for ex-

ample, are even shorter in the paperback than in the CONCISE AHD.)

The Dell edition, however, readily serves as a portable, simplified version of its much larger parent dictionary. Although the type size is very small, entries are suitable for most readers. Some brief usage notes, based on the opinions of the *American Heritage Dictionary*'s Usage Panel, are included. There are approximately 60,000 definitions and more than 400 photographs and line drawings. Separate biographical and geographic entries appear at the back of the book.

II. Authority

Dell, a publisher of several quality paperback imprints, began publishing paperback editions of the American Heritage family of dictionaries in 1970, a year after the original AMERICAN HERITAGE DICTIONARY appeared. As with the previous paperbacks, this edition was prepared by Houghton Mifflin's *AHD* staff. Even though no paperback abridgment can substitute for its larger parent work, the Dell dictionary's editors have produced carefully condensed or rewritten definitions that are generally reliable. Given the size limitations of the format, this dictionary manages to retain a family resemblance to the respected parent work.

III. Comprehensiveness

The 60,000 definitions advertised are not the equivalent of main entries. The number of main entry words is slightly over 31,000. The remaining number are secondary definitions that are run into the main entries. The quantity of entries and definitions is sufficient for most everyday reference purposes.

Separate lists of words derived from combined forms do incorporate more vocabulary and spellings. Placed on the lower half of pages and separated from the text by rules, these lists include the common compound words formed from **de-**, **dis-**, **-mania**, **non-**, **over-**, **-phobia**, **re-**, and **un-**. The word lists for **-mania** and **-phobia** also include brief meanings.

The publisher claims that the dictionary includes "10,000 new words and meanings from business, science, and technology." But a comparison of all entries between **paprika** and **parachute** (a sample segment chosen arbitrarily) from the paperback and from the college edition shows that the paperback *excludes* most current and more advanced medical, chemical, economic, and geographic words, and also omits taxonomy and field labels. In this sample section, there are 14 *more* main entry items in the college dictionary than in the paperback. The paperback entries in this sample sequence include **paprika**, **Pap test**, **papyrus**,

par, **para**, **para-** or **par-**, **parable**, **parabola**, **parachute** (all these words are in the college edition, too). The following college edition entries are omitted in the paperback edition: *Pap smear*, *Papuan*, *papule*, *papyri*, *papyrology*, several forms of *par-/para-*, *para-aminobenzoic acid*, *parabiosis*, *parablast*, *parabolic*, and *paraboloid*. College and general adult users may need a larger dictionary for science and technology entries.

The approximately 1,000 biographical entries and 1,500 geographic entries may serve for minimal quick reference in everyday contexts. The list of abbreviations needs revision. It includes a selected range, from those most frequently encountered, such as **a.k.a.** (also known as), to some not so frequent, such as **LOOM** (Loyal Order of Moose). Some areas of abbreviations are not well covered: the titles of **Mdm.** (Madam) and **Mr.** (Mister) are included, but not *Mrs.* or *Ms.*

IV. Quality and Currency of Entries

The entries appear in strict letter-by-letter alphabetical order. The general sequence of information in the entries is: boldface main word; pronunciation(s); part of speech; inflected form(s); stylistic or field label; definition (numbered, when necessary); very brief etymology or source; other parts of speech; verbal phrases; and idioms. A cross-reference is substituted in some cases for a definition: "**par·a** *n.* See table at **currency**. [Turk.]." The definitions are generally clear, and often considerably shorter than in the parent work. Occasionally, a definition or explanation of the source words for entries, such as **gerrymander** and **hobby**, is omitted, and hence the sources are of little value. In other cases, only the source language is cited; for example, [F.] French or [G.] German. However, the shortened usage notes are sometimes less confusing than the extended examples in the larger work. One example of improvement in the Dell edition is the briefer explanation of **who**. Because it is more concise, the explanation makes the difference between **who** and **whom** clearer.

There are fewer stylistic and field labels in the paperback. Regional *area* labels are simplified to one term: "regional." Poetic use of words such as **o'er** is labeled. Some meanings of a few words are labeled *Chiefly Brit.* when appropriate, but this is not indicated in the "Guide to the Dictionary." Some field labels such as *Math.* or *Mus.* (music) are included. Special use in a field is indicated, if necessary, in the definitions. Words or senses that are idiomatic or capitalized in special senses are labeled and briefly defined. Entries for verbs such as **be** include a chart of tenses.

The first definition of a word is the "central meaning about which the other senses can be logically organized," according to the "Guide to the Dictionary." This order is not necessarily historical or the most current. Chemical symbols are included as separate entries and are also labeled within entries. The synonym paragraphs, which had examples in the larger work, are cut to occasional brief lists, but the synonyms do appear as separate entry words.

The publisher states that new words and meanings from business, science, and technology are included, but some words in current use are not entered, such as *heuristic*, *modem*, and *mainframe*, as well as computer science meanings for the terms *disc*, *disk*, or *floppy*. **Software** is included. As already noted, most advanced terms in the sciences are absent.

As simplified or rewritten, the definitions may be more useful or immediately accessible to a wider audience. An example is the entry **papyrus**. In the college edition, the first entry reads:

> **pa·py·rus** 1. A tall aquatic sedge, *Cyperus papyrus*, of southern Europe and northern Africa.

The Dell paperback version reads:

> **pa·py·rus** 1. A tall, grasslike water plant of northern Africa.

V. Syllabication and Pronunciation

All main entries are divided into syllables by centered dots, as in **hin·ter·land**, in keeping with current printing practice. As in the parent work, entries consisting of more than one word are not broken into syllables or given pronunciations if the separate words appear as main entries themselves.

Pronunciations, based on the parent work's clear, phonetic system—intended to reflect "educated" speech—follow all main entries and are given for other word forms as needed: see the entry for "**sto·ic** (stō·ĭk) *n.*," as well as for its adjective form "*-adj.* Also **sto·i·cal** (-ĭ-kol)." Most readers will find them easy to use. Additionally, the pronunciations are briefly but clearly explained in the "Guide to the Dictionary" that precedes the alphabetical entries, where a pronunciation key with clear notes on the symbols used appears. Two lines of this key appear throughout the dictionary at the foot of left-hand pages. This feature is handy and useful for readers. Primary and secondary stresses are marked, and variant pronunciations are included, as in "**il·lus·trate** (il′ə-strāt′, i-lus′trat′)."

VI. Special Features

The dictionary includes nine tables at appropriate alphabetical entries. These are a table of alphabets, books of the Bible, months of three principal calendars (Gregorian, Hebrew, Moslem), currency (five and one third pages long), a periodic table of the elements, a guide to the metric system, proofreaders' marks, Roman numerals, and symbols and signs.

The 1,000 biographical entries appear in a separate appendix, illustrated with 41 portraits. Seven of the portraits are of women; three are of blacks. The usefulness of such a section is questionable, and some of the identifying information is less than helpful: St. Bede's traditional epithet, "The Venerable," is omitted; James Boswell, biographer of Samuel Johnson, is listed as Scottish lawyer and writer; W. H. Auden is listed as an author but not as a poet.

The geographical section has no maps. Entries, including capital cities, are identified briefly, although some of the most recent name changes have not been included, such as Burkina Faso for Upper Volta. Population figures are given but are not current. Pronunciations are included.

VII. Accessibility

The dictionary's inside back cover has an "Easy Reference Index" that shows at a glance on which page each letter of the alphabet begins. All main entries, including prefixes such as **ab-** and **post-**, appear in alphabetical order, letter by letter. Particles such as **dis-**, **-phobia**, and others appear in the main lexicon, and the separate lists of compound words from which they derive are printed close by.

Italicized, succinct examples of usage are readily apparent within definitions. See, for example, under the phrasal verbs of the main entry **call**:

> **call off**. **1.** To cancel or postpone. **2.** To recall; restrain: *Call off your hounds!*

Variant forms of words are printed in bold type and are easy to distinguish in the entries.

A pair of guide words is located at the top of each page, representing the first and last main entries: **culvert|curium**. Readable page numbers appear at the top of each page near the inner margins. When a usage note follows a definition, it is printed as a separate paragraph with the word **Usage** in bold type. The brief table of contents and "Guide to the Dictionary" are easily located at the front of the work. The 8½-page guide contains clearly labeled short sections that provide an overview of the dictionary and explain the parts of definitions and the information they contain. It is easy to leaf through the guide to find, for example, the list of abbreviations used in etymologies. All style labels are noted in the guide, but the one sentence explaining the field labels is not accompanied by a list or examples (users might be interested to know, for example, that both **cricket** and **baseball** terms are included).

In general, the small type in which this edition is printed requires more concentration in scanning for the required head entry word than is usual in dictionaries with larger type.

VIII. Graphics and Format

The entries are printed in two columns with adequate margins. The main entry words are printed in sans serif bold type overhanging the small-size text set in Times Roman. The illustrations are generally good—often better, in fact, than those in the parent dictionary. It is interesting, for a change, to see **embryo** illustrated with a cow embryo rather than a human one. There are slightly over 300 photographs, and small, useful line drawings are scattered throughout the word list; some illustrate, for example, three different meanings of a word, such as those for **fluke**, **graft**, **spring**, and **splice**. The pictures have been chosen with care to illustrate words that may not be immediately recognizable from a written definition.

The captions often contain additional, useful historical or other specific information. However, some—photoreduced along with the illustrations—are flyspeck size. **Mallet**, **oil well**, **tooth**, and **thalamus** are examples of clear line drawings with almost unreadable tiny labels.

The general appearance of the dictionary is pleasant, and the pictures help to make the text look less dense on the pages. The paper is good-quality newsprint stock; there is some show-through of text and pictures as in most dictionaries, but this is not obtrusive. In repeated use, ink rubs off the page onto the fingers. The attractive cover design, in a rich dark blue with red and white, emphasizes the "American Heritage" of the title. For a paperback, the laminated cover is sturdy. And even after extensive use, with deliberate "cracking" of the spine to facilitate opening the pages, the text signatures did not become detached from the spine (which is about 1½" thick). This dictionary should stand up to repeated use by an individual fairly well; libraries may want to rebind the work for their paperback collections.

IX. Summary

Dell's *The American Heritage Dictionary* is widely available, very popular in terms of sales figures, and is a handy, much-condensed paperback version of a respected college dictionary. Users should be aware that the publishers' claims to include extensive, up-to-date vocabulary in the sciences and technology are not readily apparent in the paperback. This is good value for a circulating library's paperback collection. It is also useful in the home when readers need brief guidance on spelling and meaning, or in some cases on usage and pronunciation—and particularly when price and size are primary considerations.

The American Heritage Dictionary: Second College Edition

Facts at a Glance

Full Title: **The American Heritage Dictionary: Second College Edition.**
Publisher: Houghton Mifflin.
Editors: Mark Boyer, Pamela B. DeVinne, Kaethe Ellis, et al.
Edition Reviewed: © 1985.

Number of Volumes: 1.
Number of Entries: 200,000.
Number of Pages: 1,568.
Number of Indexes: 1.
Number of Illustrations: 3,000 black-and-white photographs and line drawings.
Number of Maps: 152.
Trim Size: 6¾" × 9⁹⁄₁₆".
Binding and Price: Cloth, thumb indexed (price: $15.95). Deluxe edition, kivar bound (price: $18.95). Large-format edition (price: $24.95).

Sold in bookstores and other outlets; also sold to libraries.
ISBN 0-395-32944-2.

I. Introduction

The 1985 printing of the *Second College Edition* of *The American Heritage Dictionary* is substantially the same as the 1982 version, which was the "first complete revision" of the dictionary since its original publication in 1969. The *Second College Edition* acknowledges the *AHD*'s original purpose, in the words of former editor William Morris, "to create a new dictionary that would not only faithfully record our language but also add the sensible dimension of guidance toward grace and precision in the use of our language."

The basic lexicon of some "200,000 precise definitions" (according to the book jacket), appropriate for an abridged, or desk, dictionary, is intended for "the well-informed, contemporary adult." The *AHD*'s contemporary emphasis is apparent in the entries, definitions, and reference sections; in the special articles on language as it is used, spoken, and structured; and in the choice of members for the Usage Panel, representing the arts and sciences, entertainment, business, industry, and politics.

More than 10,000 general vocabulary words and 5,000 scientific and technical terms were added to the *AHD* in 1982. The illustrations now number several thousand and include photographs and line drawings. Separate biographical and geographic sections appear at the back of the work, with approximately 5,000 new entries apiece.

II. Authority

Houghton Mifflin publishes a complete line of dictionaries derived from the *AHD*. The original edition and its successors were well received, were recommended by librarians and other knowledgeable reviewers, and have since become standard—and popular—dictionaries. Like its predecessors, the *Second College Edition* is known for distinguishing nonstandard, regional, dialect, slang, idiomatic, colloquial, vulgar, and obscene usages from standard, or educated, use.

Many eminent writers, language scholars, and men and women from a wide variety of fields are associated with this dictionary. The name of William Morris, editor of the original *AHD* and its *New College Edition*, no longer appears, but two of the original staff, Anne D. Steinhardt (editor, definitions) and Kaethe Ellis (editor, biographical and geographic entries), are still listed. The credentials of the more than 50 editorial staff members are not provided, although those of the Usage Panel, chaired by Edwin Newman, and of the consultants are. Among the well-known members of the Usage Panel, Maya Angelou, Isaac Asimov, Daniel J. Boorstin, Dr. Robin Cook, Vine Deloria, Jr., S. I. Hayakawa, Ishmael Reed, Gloria Steinem, and William Zinsser are only a sampling. The panel members, according to the dictionary's introduction, responded to usage questions, and "after careful tabulation and analysis" of their responses, the staff editors prepared more than 400 usage notes.

Listed among the special staff consultants are Geoffrey Nunberg of Stanford University and Dwight Bolinger, both of whom contributed introductory essays on issues concerning the use of language. Lee Pederson of Emory University wrote the opening article, a survey of the historical and cultural backgrounds of American speech and writing.

III. Comprehensiveness

As a standard college and adult desk dictionary, the *AHD* is comprehensive enough to serve most general purposes. The range of words included from specialized fields, such as medicine and computer science, is more than adequate for general needs.

Along with the emphasis on contemporary vocabulary, definitions, and usage, the prescriptive features of this dictionary are a distinguishing mark; they are clear and useful, and they add a considerable amount of lexicographic and stylistic information to the work. These features include labels for stylistic, field, and geographic usage; notes on preferred current usage; a "Style Manual" that is functional and brief; and short essays describing American language and its use in speech and writing. Additionally, guidance on syllabication, pronunciation, spelling var-

The American Heritage Dictionary: Second College Edition

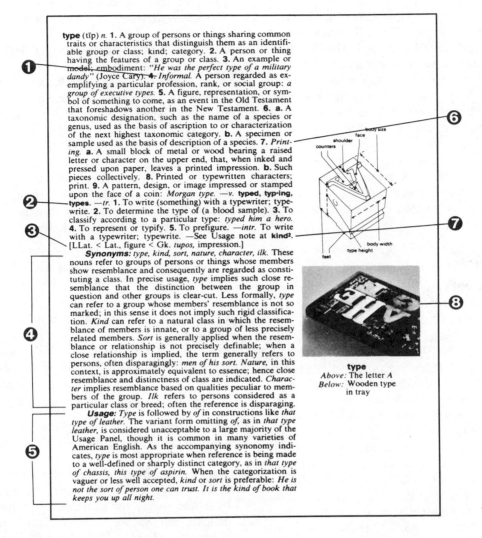

type (tīp) *n.* **1.** A group of persons or things sharing common traits or characteristics that distinguish them as an identifiable group or class; kind; category. **2.** A person or thing having the features of a group or class. **3.** An example or model; embodiment: *"He was the perfect type of a military dandy"* (Joyce Cary). **4.** *Informal.* A person regarded as exemplifying a particular profession, rank, or social group: *a group of executive types.* **5.** A figure, representation, or symbol of something to come, as an event in the Old Testament that foreshadows another in the New Testament. **6. a.** A taxonomic designation, such as the name of a species or genus, used as the basis of ascription to or characterization of the next highest taxonomic category. **b.** A specimen or sample used as the basis of description of a species. **7.** *Printing.* **a.** A small block of metal or wood bearing a raised letter or character on the upper end, that, when inked and pressed upon paper, leaves a printed impression. **b.** Such pieces collectively. **8.** Printed or typewritten characters; print. **9.** A pattern, design, or image impressed or stamped upon the face of a coin: *Morgan type.* —*v.* **typed, typ-ing, types.** —*tr.* **1.** To write (something) with a typewriter; typewrite. **2.** To determine the type of (a blood sample). **3.** To classify according to a particular type: *typed him a hero.* **4.** To represent or typify. **5.** To prefigure. —*intr.* To write with a typewriter; typewrite. —See Usage note at **kind².** [LLat. < Lat., figure < Gk. *tupos,* impression.]

   Synonyms: type, kind, sort, nature, character, ilk. These nouns refer to groups of persons or things whose members show resemblance and consequently are regarded as constituting a class. In precise usage, *type* implies such close resemblance that the distinction between the group in question and other groups is clear-cut. Less formally, *type* can refer to a group whose members' resemblance is not so marked; in this sense it does not imply such rigid classification. *Kind* can refer to a natural class in which the resemblance of members is innate, or to a group of less precisely related members. *Sort* is generally applied when the resemblance or relationship is not precisely definable; when a close relationship is implied, the term generally refers to persons, often disparagingly: *men of his sort. Nature,* in this context, is approximately equivalent to essence; hence close resemblance and distinctness of class are indicated. *Character* implies resemblance based on qualities peculiar to members of the group. *Ilk* refers to persons considered as a particular class or breed; often the reference is disparaging.

   Usage: Type is followed by *of* in constructions like *that type of leather.* The variant form omitting *of,* as in *that type leather,* is considered unacceptable to a large majority of the Usage Panel, though it is common in many varieties of American English. As the accompanying synonymy indicates, *type* is most appropriate when reference is being made to a well-defined or sharply distinct category, as in *that type of chassis, this type of aspirin.* When the categorization is vaguer or less well accepted, *kind* or *sort* is preferable: *He is not the sort of person one can trust. It is the kind of book that keeps you up all night.*

type
Above: The letter *A*
Below: Wooden type in tray

❶ Usage labels are italicized
❷ Inflected forms are shown in small boldface letters
❸ Etymologies are enclosed in brackets
❹ Distinctions among synonyms are discussed under the boldface italic subheading *Synonyms*
❺ Usage notes appear after the boldface italic subheading *Usage*
❻ Field labels are italicized
❼ Cross-references are set in boldface type
❽ Illustrations elaborate on text definitions

iants, and synonym nuances is easy to understand, as are the brief etymologies.

   The list of general abbreviations in current use and the separate geographic section with its locator maps are both helpful, although some geographical place names have not been updated; for example, *Burkina Faso* appears as **Upper Volta**, and *Harare,* the capital of Zimbabwe, appears as **Salisbury.** The biographical section can serve only as a quick reference because of the brevity of its entries, some of which are cryptic at best; see "**Grasso, Ella.** 1919–81. Amer. public official," and "**Onassis . . . 2. Jacqueline Lee Bouvier Kennedy.** b. 1929. Amer. socialite and editor."

IV. Quality and Currency of Entries

The general order for entries is: boldface word; pronunciation; part of speech; inflected forms; stylistic or field label (if applicable); the definitions themselves; notes on word form, source, or etymology in square brackets; variant form(s); part(s) of speech of the variant forms (with label, such as *—idiom* or *—phrasal verb*). Examples are interspersed in the entries as appropriate. Synonyms and usage notes follow in separate paragraphs; both often include extensive examples. The usage notes contain prescriptive opinions of the Usage Panel.

The definitions present "the most prevalent, contemporary sense of meaning of a word first." This emphasis on currency is not, however, as claimed by the publisher, "unique" to the *AHD*; the feature is also used in, for example, THE RANDOM HOUSE COLLEGE DICTIONARY. In general, the definitions are understandable and accurate and cover an accepted range of meanings. Occasionally, the necessity for being concise leads to cursory definitions that assume background knowledge on the part of the reader; however, the intended readership *is* designated as "well-informed."

When a word has more than one sense, the succeeding definitions are ordered analytically, rather than historically or by frequency of use, and go from a central meaning to related or separate senses. A short example is:

> cyn·i·cal *adj.* **1.** Scornful of the motives or virtue of others. **2.** Bitterly mocking; sneering.

Italicized words, phrases, or sentences are often used to demonstrate a particular meaning; the sources of some, but not all, examples are cited.

One entry from the 1982 edition, cited by ALA *Booklist* (August 1983), was "**channel bass** *n.* A fish, the red drum." It has become less clear in the revised *Second College Edition:* "**channel bass** *n.* The red drum." A reader who does not realize that *bass* refers to a fish will have to look up "**red drum** *n.* A food fish, etc." or remain puzzled. Although few entries are as brief as **channel bass**, some do suffer from brevity. **Blue point**, for example, is defined as a noun (an oyster), but not as an adjective referring to a type of domestic cat. Although cross-referenced to **who**, **whom** is defined merely as "*pron.* The objective case of **who**." The use of *whom* is troublesome for many people. Even though there are good usage examples under the **who** main entry word, with explanations of the grammatical difficulties, readers would be more readily served with some guidance at **whom**.

Brevity appears to be the culprit in other representative cases of less than satisfactory definitions. There is a tendency toward circularity, a hazard in all dictionaries where space is at a premium. The definition of **black comedy**, for example, reads, "Comedy that uses **black humor**," which requires the reader to consult the entry **black humor** to complete the definition. Similarly, **mesmerism**, defined in the first instance as "Hypnotic induction believed to involve animal magnetism," is not clarified by looking up "**animal magnetism** *n.* **1.** Hypnotism or mesmerism." Another problem involves the presumed knowledge of contexts that are not explained. For example, the entry "**Bunyanesque** *adj.*" refers to John Bunyan's allegorical style as well as to Paul Bunyan. John Bunyan's work *The Pilgrim's Progress* is not mentioned, and it is arguable whether the majority of readers today will grasp the meaning of *Bunyanesque* from the word *allegorical* in the brief definition.

The claim that words are first defined according to their "most prevalent, contemporary sense" is broadly accurate. For example, the first definition of **believe** (transitive verb) is given as "To accept as true or real." **Skirmish** is first defined as "A minor encounter in war between small bodies of troops, often as part of larger movement" and then as a "minor or preliminary conflict or dispute." But there are enough instances of first definitions that seem unlikely to strike the reader as current to suggest that the claim needs qualification. Compare the sequence of definitions for **ben·e·fit of clergy**:

> *n.* **1.** Exemption from trial or punishment in a civil court given to clergy in the Middle Ages. **2.** The authorized sanction of a religious rite: *cohabiting without benefit of clergy*.

Or **skinny**, first defined as "Of, pertaining to, or resembling skin" and then as "very thin." And will readers consider "parched with the heat of the sun" the most prevalent or current definition of **torrid**?

V. Syllabication and Pronunciation

Entry words as well as inflected and derived forms are divided into syllables, indicated by centered dots: **fly·a·way**. The syllables represent the "established practice of printers and editors" in breaking words that fall at the end of a printed line. Entries of more than one word, for example, **dust jacket**, are not divided into syllables if the divisible word or words appear elsewhere as a separate entry, as does **jack·et**.

Pronunciations of words are also divided "for the sake of clarity" according to phonetic rules. The division of syllables (marked by stress marks and hyphens), which is according to pronunciation, often differs from written division, as in **or·di·nar·y** (ôr′ dn-ĕr′ ē).

There is an admirably clear description of the pronunciation symbols, which should be "familiar to the reader untrained in phonetics." Pronunciation is thus relatively easy to determine. The editors state simply that the pronunciations recorded are "exclusively those of educated speech," not those of social dialects, although the guide to pronunciation recognizes the "great variety" of American speech sounds and regional intonations. A table of sound-speech correspondences is included with an explanation to help readers find words they can pronounce but cannot spell:

sound: **church** *spelling:* **cz** *sample word:* **Czech**.

Additionally, a formal pronunciation key lists word spellings with both the *AHD* symbols and those of the International Phonetic Alphabet (IPA), noted as being "widely used by scholars." Three common French sounds (**feu, tu**, and bo**n**), three common German sounds (schö**n**, **ü**ber, i**ch**), and one Scottish sound (lo**ch**) are also keyed. So too are primary stress (indicated by a boldface stress mark) and secondary stress (a lightface mark): *bi'*o-mass'. For quick reference, two-line examples of keyed pronunciations are printed at the bottom of each dictionary page.

VI. Special Features

The *AHD*'s special features range from usage notes and a substantial list of abbreviations to the periodic table of the chemical elements. The right-hand front endpaper lists, alphabetically, 23 reference features, including the tables (of alphabets, calendars, the elements mentioned above, currency, geologic time, Morse code, proofreaders' marks, Roman numerals, signs and symbols, subatomic particles, taxonomy, and common weights and measures). It also directs the reader to the "Explanation of the Color Definitions," an illustrated mini-essay accompanying the entry **color** that explains the technical basis of terms such as **hue, lightness**, and **saturation** and describes the color-naming system developed at the National Bureau of Standards.

An index list appears on the left-hand back endpaper. Included are the main sections of the dictionary, the items in the frontmatter (for example, the "Style Manual" and Usage Panel), and the formal titles of tables. Appendixes include A-to-Z biographical entries with 217 small but excellent portraits (including those of 25 American minority group members). Syllabication and pronunciation of names is indicated. Historical dynasties are included and variant spellings of names are listed. The section of A-to-Z geographical entries contains 152 clear, small locator maps of countries and islands. Entries are identified as city, lake, and so forth. Population figures are included; U.S. towns and cities follow 1980 U.S. census figures, but the populations given for countries predate reliable 1983 estimates. Occasional tidbits of identifying historical information are included, as are variant spellings, alternate names (**Porto** *Portuguese* **Oporto**), and former names (**Belgian East Africa** for *Rwanda* and *Burundi*). Adjectival and noun forms of geographic names are noted. Additionally, there are lists of four-year and two-year colleges and universities (the latter lists institutions with as few as 20 students and includes technical and vocational schools, as well as selected "for-profit" business schools [Katherine Gibbs is one]).

The "Style Manual" is concise and gives clear, brief directions with examples, but the sample footnote and bibliographic styles should not be relied on—especially by college students: the examples are outdated, and the editions of the standard style manuals recommended in the section have been superseded by new editions with significant changes.

Four special articles give an excellent view of contemporary thought about language. Professor Lee Pederson's opening essay, "Language, Culture, and the American Heritage," is notable for its succinct and authoritative overview of the diversity in the American language. Included in the essay is brief, useful information on topics such as Gullah, bilingualism, social dialects, and regional variants in pronunciation. The essay-debate—between Dwight Bolinger (for) and William F. Buckley (against)—on "Resolved: The prevailing usage of its speakers should be the chief determinant of acceptability in language." is perhaps more informative on the current state of rhetorical argument than it is on the set topic. Many readers will find Henry Kučera's superb essay "The Mathematics of Language" a pleasure to read even if their main field of interest is not mathematics or language.

VII. Accessibility

Familiarity with alphabetizing is the only knowledge required to use the *Second College Edition* of the *AHD*. All entries are listed in strict letter-by-letter alphabetical order. Each letter section of the dictionary is preceded by a full page showing graphic examples of the letter, a device that also provides helpful spatial separation of letters. The thumb-index tabs available in one edition are attractive and sturdy.

Alternate spellings are generally treated thoroughly, thereby saving the reader from confusion and needless speculation. They appear as variants in an entry and also alphabetically as entry words. For example, there is the entry "**na·if** or **na·ïf** *adj. & n.* Variants of **naive**"; then its main entry, "**na·ive** or **na·ïve** also **na·if** or **na·ïf**," is followed by the definitions. Inflected forms of a word are printed in boldface and are easily found, even in longer entries. Sometimes cognate words, for example, **naiveté** for **naive**, are referred to under the synonym example (*unaffected* in the case of **naiveté**) and then also appear as an entry. Words spelled alike that have different etymologies are listed as separate entries with superior numbers, making them easy to scan.

In 13 pages, the "Guide to the Dictionary" explains in clear language how to find specific information within an entry. The heads and subheads in the guide are in large type, which is fortunate because there is no key or outline for the section, and therefore a reader has to leaf through it to discover where to find synonyms, cross-references, undefined forms of a word, or the abbreviations and labels used in the dictionary.

At the top of each page, a pair of guide words separated by a vertical line, for example, **interferometer | internal**, indicates the first and last entry words on the page. One word of each pair extends into the white space of the illustration column and is readily visible. This adds to the ease of finding a word and, when the dictionary lies open, allows the reader to see at a glance the inclusive contents of a double-page spread. Small page numbers are printed at the top of the text near the inside margins.

The location of pictures in the outside margins on each page is a handy way for a reader to check whether he or she is close to locating a required word.

On the left-hand back endpaper there is a brief index, in larger type than the text, to the special sections and the tables in the dictionary.

VIII. Graphics and Format

The *Second College Edition* has several notable graphic elements. The sturdy white paper does not crease or tear easily, an important feature in a dictionary that must sustain frequent use. As with many other dictionaries, there is noticeable show-through of text and pictures, although this is more obvious in the *AHD* because of the illustrations column on each page.

For a desk dictionary, the *AHD* devotes an unusual amount of space to illustrations. These are printed in the outside margin of each page and contribute to a feeling of space. Frequently, the pictures illustrate the different meanings of a word. (There are photographs, for example, of an Afghan rug and an Afghan hound.) An estimated three fifths of the illustrations are photographs, which adds a contemporary feeling to the pages. Perhaps as many as a third of the photographs, however, show too much surrounding detail, making it difficult to determine which object is intended to illustrate the entry. The bird drawings by George Miksch Sutton are outstanding; line drawings of plants and medical subjects vary in quality; the many photographs of tools and mechanical devices add interest to a usually dull category of dictionary illustration; geometric and architectural drawings are clear. There is little question that the illustrations enhance the *AHD*'s value as a reference source. One reviewer quibbled that some illustrations are placed too far away from relevant entries on a page, although many have brief captions.

Useful, and decorative, features include the separate page preceding each letter of the alphabet with large examples of how the letter is printed in different typefaces, accompanied by a brief orthographical history.

All entries, inflected forms, variant forms and spellings, numbers for different meanings, as well as the word *Usage* preceding the paragraphs explaining usage, are printed in bold sans serif, an easy-to-read typeface. Main entry words overhang the text for easier visual access. The guide words are printed in a larger bold sans serif face. The text is printed in a two-column format, allowing for a third, narrower column for all illustrations. Although the typeface is small, there is sufficient white space between lines for readability. A farsighted person, however, might not find the text comfortable to read.

IX. Summary

The American Heritage Dictionary: Second College Edition, as claimed, "covers the vocabulary ranging from the language of Shakespeare to the idiom of the present day." Although some definitions are cursory, its coverage of contemporary language—especially the developments of the 1970s in the sciences and technology—is extensive. The quantity of illustrations adds an extra dimension to the dictionary, as do the paragraphs on contemporary usage in the entries.

The *Second College Edition* is attractively and sturdily bound; its pages lie flat when opened; and it feels substantial but not uncomfortably heavy when picked up. The heavy endpapers are solidly reinforced.

Numerous recognizable and some world-famous names are associated with the *Second College Edition*; many, but certainly not all, are experts in the fields of language and lexicography. This dictionary has been recommended by reliable reviewers as a good desk reference in each succeeding edition. ALA *Booklist* concluded its mostly favorable review of the 1982 edition: "*The American Heritage Dictionary* continues, in its College Edition, to be a credit to its publishers, editors, and contributors. . . ." In his *Dictionaries: The Art and Craft of Lexicography* (1984, p. 74), Sidney I. Landau provided an interesting highlight: in 1969 "the *AHD* reintroduced taboo words . . . excluded from general dictionaries . . . since the eighteenth century. This was an important and courageous step in reporting the actual usage of commonly used words, and every other college dictionary with the exception of *World* soon followed suit." *Library Journal*, in a short review (1 November 1982, p. 2086), wrote: "Although this dictionary has been published in a number of editions . . . the same high standards prevail as in previous editions . . . labeling is firmer and more precise . . . the volume generally fulfills its stated purpose and will meet the needs of most dictionary users."

The reader may want to compare the *AHD: Second College Edition* with WEBSTER'S NINTH NEW COLLEGIATE DICTIONARY, another widely used dictionary for the same readership. One main difference between these two excellent reference works lies in the use of extensive marginal illustrations by the *AHD*. The *AHD* also places greater emphasis on contemporary usage and scientific terms. WEBSTER'S, however, appears to offer more precisely worded definitions and a more accessible vocabulary, for example, in mathematics. WEBSTER'S is also more linguistically advanced and uses a complicated set of symbols for pronunciation, features that some readers may find difficult to master. The two dictionaries have similar, useful introductory and appendix material, with WEBSTER'S providing, in addition, a Language Research Service for individual written inquiries. Readers who want a more descriptive approach to language will be better served by THE RANDOM HOUSE COLLEGE DICTIONARY. Its pages, however, are not as well designed or as easy to read as those of *The American Heritage Dictionary*.

Regardless of whatever other dictionaries are in their general reference collections, virtually all libraries will want to have one or more copies of *The American Heritage Dictionary*. For the reader who wants a dictionary that distinguishes educated from other use and that provides guidance to usage as well as generally solid definitions—standard, scientific, and technical—the *Second College Edition* of *The American Heritage Dictionary* is a good choice at a reasonable price.

The American Heritage Illustrated Encyclopedic Dictionary

Facts at a Glance

Full Title: **The American Heritage Illustrated Encyclopedic Dictionary**.
Publisher: Houghton Mifflin.
Editors: Pamela B. DeVinne (Houghton Mifflin); David Rattray (Reader's Digest).
Edition Reviewed: © 1987.

Number of Entries: 180,000.
Number of Pages: 1,920.
Number of Illustrations: 2,300 four-color illustrations.
Number of Maps: 175.
Trim Size: 8½″ × 10⅞″.
Binding: hardcover.

Price: $55.00.
Sold in bookstores and other outlets; also sold to libraries and other educational institutions.
ISBN 0-395-44295-8.

I. Introduction

The American Heritage Illustrated Encyclopedic Dictionary attempts to combine the word usage function of the dictionary and the informational function of the encyclopedia in one large volume, adding numerous illustrations besides. The nearly 2,000 pages of the book present a wide selection of words and phrases, both up-to-date and archaic, mainly from North American English (the U.S. and Canada), but also from all the sources of global English, as well as many biographies, geographic entries, and concepts from the worlds of science, technology, industry, politics, history, art, and literature. More than 200,000 meanings are supplied with "such traditional features as word origins, usage notes, illustration quotations, and synonyms[,] . . . several hundred illustrated feature articles, and 2,300 four-color pictures," states the preface. Because of space restrictions, definitions are short, although the boxed articles on various subjects and people often fill several paragraphs. Illustrations range from diagrams to photographs to intricate drawings and maps, and are extremely well chosen and helpful in illustrating or explaining the subject material.

A six-page section entitled "How to Use This Dictionary" precedes the lexicon. It includes a detailed guide to the entries with a numbered and labeled key and a list of abbreviations.

II. Authority

The American Heritage Illustrated Encyclopedic Dictionary is the newest in the line of American Heritage dictionaries edited by the eminent Houghton Mifflin dictionary staff and adapted and developed from the publisher's own lexical databases. Special features have also been contributed by the *Reader's Digest*, who will publish a mail order edition of the same dictionary. (See the brief review in this guide of the READER'S DIGEST ILLUSTRATED ENCYCLOPEDIC DICTIONARY.) No criteria for the choice of features, however, have been provided.

III. Comprehensiveness

The American Heritage Illustrated Encyclopedic Dictionary covers an extremely broad range of vocabulary and topics. A small sample of entries includes **fiber optics, Marshall Field, kiss of life, free will, joint resolution, eutrophic, blastoff, oddball, Guido Cavalcanti, Joe DiMaggio, flow sheet, ad nauseam, mercantilism, basso profundo**, and **Bermuda Triangle**. Special illustrated features appear in boxes and include: the Milky Way, the Pascal triangle showing probability, "Unchanging Zones and Currents in the Ever-moving Sea," keyboard instruments, the spinal

American Heritage Illustrated Encyclopedic Dictionary

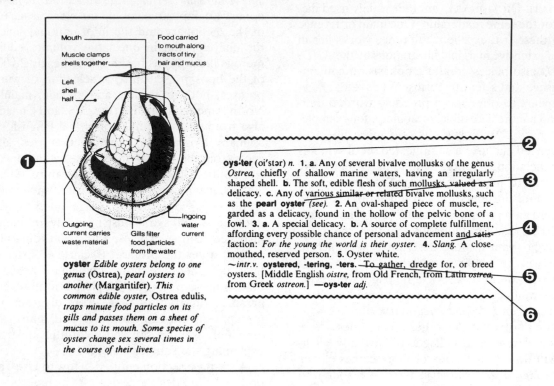

oyster *Edible oysters belong to one genus (Ostrea), pearl oysters to another (Margaritifer). This common edible oyster, Ostrea edulis, traps minute food particles on its gills and passes them on a sheet of mucus to its mouth. Some species of oyster change sex several times in the course of their lives.*

❶ Captioned illustrations present further information

❷ Syllabication is shown by centered dots

❸ Cross-references are set in boldface type

❹ Usage labels are italicized

❺ Inflected forms are given when spelling might be doubtful

❻ Etymology is enclosed in brackets

cord, apples, abbeys, fly-tying, Victoriana, the laser, and relativity, among other topics.

Impressive as this scope of coverage may be, THE RANDOM HOUSE DICTIONARY OF THE ENGLISH LANGUAGE: SECOND EDITION, UNABRIDGED is far more generous with its biographic and geographic entries. Between **barcarole** and **barfly**, the *American Heritage Illustrated* includes six such entries, while the RANDOM HOUSE, UNABRIDGED has eleven; between **Marconi** and **margarine**, the *American Heritage Illustrated* has seven non-definition terms, while the RANDOM HOUSE, UNABRIDGED has 23. More significant than the numbers, however, is the choice of entries: *American Heritage Illustrated* omits *Marcuse* and *Margaret of Navarre*, while admitting **Margaret Rose**, sister of Queen Elizabeth II.

IV. Quality and Currency of Entries

Generally speaking, entries fall into either the dictionary class, providing pronunciations, parts of speech, definitions—including the most current ones—illustrative phrases or sentences, word origins, synonyms, and sometimes lengthy usage notes, or the

encyclopedia class, providing information about the word or phrase, or giving the required geographic or biographical description. Abbreviations are included among the main entries, which are listed alphabetically, letter by letter. So-called four-letter words appear to be omitted. Words having the same spellings but different meanings and etymologies are listed separately with raised numbers. An example is the word **bay**, which has five separate entries. Plurals are spelled out when they are irregular; verb inflections and principal parts are spelled out in shortened form. Alternate forms appear after the part of speech, or in such a case as

foetus. Variant of **fetus**

the word receives a separate entry if its place in the alphabetical listing is more than ten words away from the original (**fetus**, in this case).

Definitions are labeled historically (*Archaic* or *Obsolete*), geographically (by area or region), for field of knowledge (*Music*, *Chemistry*, for example), style (*Informal*, *Slang*, and *Nonstandard*), and foreign language. Cross-references are shown in boldface.

A typical entry appears as follows:

adult (ə-dŭlt′, ăd′ŭlt) *n.* **1.** One who has attained maturity or legal age. **2.** A fully grown, mature organism, such as an insect that has completed its final stage of metamorphosis.
~*adj.* **1.** Fully developed and mature. **2.** Pertaining to, befitting, or intended for mature persons: *adult education.* **3.** Sexually explicit; pornographic. Used euphemistically: *adult films.* [Latin *adultus*, past participle of *adolescēre*, to grow up. See **adolescent.**]—**a·dult·hood** *n.*

A typical usage note appears for the entry

al·ter·na·tive . . . **1.** The possibility or necessity of choosing only one of two or more things, courses of action, or the like. . . .

Usage: *Alternative* is widely used to denote simply "one of a set of possible courses of action," but many traditionalists continue to insist that its use be restricted to situations in which only two possible choices present themselves. In this stricter sense, *alternative* is incompatible with all numerals (*there are three alternatives*), and the use of *two*, in particular, is held to be redundant (*the two alternatives are life and death* would be unacceptable to traditionalists). Similarly, traditionalists reject as unacceptable sentences like *there is no other alternative* on the grounds that it is equivalent to the simpler *there is no alternative.*

An encyclopedic entry in general reads more simply. For example:

Cavan (kăv′ən). County in the Republic of Ireland, in Ulster. It is a predominantly hilly region, infertile and boggy with many lakes. The county town is also named Cavan.

quantum theory *n.* A mathematical theory of physical systems that was developed to account for several physical phenomena that could not be explained by classical mechanics. It postulates that a system can gain or use energy only in discrete amounts (quanta). Further developments led to the theory of **wave-particle duality** (see) and were formalized in quantum mechanics.

Kandinsky (kăn-dĭn′skē), **Wassily** (1866–1944). Russian abstract painter, who worked in Germany. He considered form and color capable of spiritual expression. Kandinsky was appointed professor of the Bauhaus School in Weimar (1922). He was a member of the *Blaue Reiter*, a group of German expressionist painters.

Some words seem to fall somewhere between the strictly dictionary or the encyclopedic entry. For example:

al·sike clover (ăl′sĭk′, -sīk′) *n.* A plant, *Trifolium hybridum*, native to Eurasia and widely cultivated for forage, having compound leaves and pink or whitish flowers. [After *Alsike*, town in Sweden, where it was first found.]

The entries are up-to-date in many areas, including slang, biography and geography; for example: **AIDS**; **modem**; **databank**; **access** (verb); **blow one's mind**; **snort** (cocaine); **glitz**; **retrorocket**; **Gorbachev, Mikhail Sergeevich** (1985, elected General Secretary of the Communist Party); **Redford, Robert**; **Pavarotti, Luciano**; **Burkina Faso**, and **Harare** (cap. Zimbabwe). Undated population figures for countries throughout the world are supplied. A random check with other sources shows that figures usually—but not always—correspond with the 1980 census figures or estimated population figures; however, a precise date would have made the information more useful to the reader.

Since the encyclopedic entries are so concise, the briefer ones are often indistinguishable from dictionary definitions. For example:

Lent (lĕnt) *n.* The 40 weekdays before Easter (beginning on Ash Wednesday), observed as a season of penitence. [Middle English *lente*, *lenten*, originally "spring," Old English *lencten*, probably from Germanic *lang-* (unattested), LONG (referring to the lengthening days of spring).]

Morse code *n.* A system of communication in which letters of the alphabet and numbers are represented by patterns of short and long signals, which may be conveyed as sounds, flashes of light, written dots and dashes, or the waving of flags. Also called "Morse," "Morse alphabet." [Invented by Samuel MORSE.] See feature, next page.

The information as presented is very clear, but because of its conciseness the user may often need to do further research or have previous knowledge to fully understand an entry. For example, the sample entry on **quantum theory** demands some knowledge of physical systems and mechanics to understand it. However, with some common sense and judicious use of the cross-references provided, the user will generally find the definitions clear and useful.

V. Syllabication and Pronunciation

Syllabication is indicated by centered dots in main entries. Pronunciation is given in 44 simplified IPA symbols, primarily for vowels, and including the schwa (ə). Six additional symbols are given for foreign words. Primary and secondary stress marks are used. A full table of symbols appears in "How to Use This Dictionary" in the front matter of the volume, and a convenient, brief pronunciation key appears in a shaded gray box either in the left or right margin of nearly every double-page spread in the dictionary.

VI. Special Features

One hundred and ninety-five boxed essays appear in full color throughout the volume, in a variety of partial or full-page formats. These consist of brief, illustrated discussions of topics that particularly benefit from the lavish use of illustrations, diagrams, or photographs as aids to descriptions or definitions. For example, at **engraving:** an engraving by Albrecht Dürer is reproduced and is accompanied by five brief paragraphs describing various types of engraving used in printing from a metal plate—line, drypoint, etching, aquatint, and mezzotint; at the entry **hail:** a picture of a thundercloud over land is marked with labels and directional arrows to show how hail is formed; at **keyboard instruments:** eight drawings illustrate the history of the instrument from the clavichord to the synthesizer; for **sun:** a cutaway drawing of the sun discloses the inner layers of its structure. Other featured topics include: flags of the world, abbeys, Palladian architecture, the zodiac, volcanoes, the solar system, clocks, leaf shapes, Pieter Breughel, and deserts, among others. While the amount of information provided in the features is somewhat limited, this is adequately compensated by photographs and artwork. Nevertheless, the features deliver the kind of helpful introduction to a topic that is satisfactory for identification or recognition of the material involved and for the first steps in gaining some knowledge that can lead to further reading or research. Overall, the features provide a varied and broad-based survey of knowledge about the world that will be extremely useful—and interesting—not only for the general adult reader, but for the whole family.

VII. Accessibility

The introductory material on how to use the encyclopedic dictionary is adequate, but quite brief for so large and ambitious a volume. The two-page "Reading the Entries" section, however, with highlighted sections in bright blue and 40 numbered directions in the key, is very detailed and clear. The volume contains no table of contents, but one is not necessary. An index to the features is also not provided, though this would have been most helpful in tracking down topics the reader may mistakenly search for under a different heading. Large, boldface type guide words to first and last entries are provided on each page, and page numbers are helpfully placed in the upper outside corners of each page. No thumb index has been provided, which is a pity in such a large, alphabetically arranged volume.

VIII. Graphics and Format

The entry words in boldface overhang the text, which is printed in small, but very legible type with adequate white space between the lines. Each large page contains two columns of text and wide outer margins in which the smaller illustrations referring to entries in the lexicon appear. There are one or more illustrations on nearly every page (as well as the pronunciation key) and sometimes an illustrated feature as well. Even with all these elements, the pages do not appear jumbled or overcrowded. The illustrations—all of them in full color—usually appear on the same page and near the definition referred to; otherwise, the definition has a "see" reference to an illustration's location, for example, "see **Morse code.**" The illustrations are all captioned in bold type with a sentence or more of information, and specific labels for parts of objects when necessary.

There are also 175 simply and clearly drawn maps showing the world and many individual countries in their surrounding regions. These appear at the appropriate places in the alphabetical listing. The maps range in size from the four-column spread over two pages used for the world, to about one-quarter of a column used for Venezuela. The binding is sturdy, and the pages are topsewn; however, a stand would be helpful to hold this heavy volume, and librarians may find rebinding necessary.

Finally, much care has been taken to make this large illustrated volume attractive, from the quality of the color printing to the quality of the paper, which is thin but allows almost no see-through.

While there are some double-page spreads with no color on them, the volume gives the impression of sumptuousness both in number and quality of illustrations. It is an extremely impressive achievement in reference bookmaking.

IX. Summary

This new and ambitious one-volume illustrated encyclopedic dictionary should serve large numbers of users, both in libraries and in the home. Its dictionary side lives up to its family name, and the encyclopedic entries, while brief, are sufficient for ready reference. The illustrations, both in the volume's margins as well as in the feature boxes, are first-rate, both in choice of subject and reproduction. Sturdy enough for normal use in the home, the volume would benefit from use of a bookstand and possibly rebinding for the library. Libraries already holding standard unabridged dictionaries and basic reference works like *Webster's Biographical Dictionary* and *Webster's New Dictionary of Geography* will find the *American Heritage Illustrated* a colorful, though not vital acquisition. Home buyers and small libraries may benefit from at least browsing through THE RANDOM HOUSE DICTIONARY OF THE ENGLISH LANGUAGE: SECOND EDITION, UNABRIDGED, before settling on the purchase of this work.

Basic Dictionary of English

Facts at a Glance

Full Title: **Basic Dictionary of English**.
Publisher: Regents Publishing Company (Prentice Hall Press).
Compiler: G. Capelle.
Illustrator: P. Kneebone.
Edition Reviewed: © 1983.

Number of Volumes: 1.
Number of Words: 4,500.
Number of Pages: 170.
Number of Illustrations: approximately 88 black-and-white line drawings.
Trim Size: 4⅜" × 7¼".
Binding: paperback.

Price: $3.50.
Sold to educational institutions.
ISBN 0-88345-542-0.

I. Introduction and Scope

The *Basic Dictionary of English*, a monolingual dictionary designed for use by beginning students of English as a Second Language, was first published in Paris by Hachette in 1980. The foreword of the dictionary states that the words included are among those defined by the Council of Europe as being at the "threshold level" (the level at which nonnative speakers of English begin to acquire a core English vocabulary), and that the "definitions are based on an elementary level vocabulary and common defining words." Many words have been selected from standard secondary texts, and less common meanings as well as more complex inflections are omitted. The foreword notes that the advantage of an all-English dictionary for foreign language students is in making the student infer the meaning of the word from the context in which it is used, as opposed to understanding English through a word-by-word translation.

II. Authority

Prentice-Hall publishes this dictionary, which was copyrighted by the Regents Publishing Company in 1983. Hachette, which produced the first edition, is a respected publisher of pedagogical and literary works in France.

III. Comprehensiveness

The dictionary is clearly and simply put together; the information given about words is brief. Most of the entries consist of basic or core words in the English vocabulary. Holidays, plants, and animals are included. Personal names do not appear, nor are there many place names. **Britain**, **France**, **Australia**, and the **United Kingdom** are entered, but the United States is not. Separate entries for homographs are rare. The foreword to the dictionary states that the verb form of an entry is always given first, even if it violates the alphabetical order. The noun form of the word follows, with adjectives and adverbs given last within the entry paragraph; noun plurals are not given separate entries when they are formed by irregular means.

For each main entry word the following information is provided: The entry word, followed by pronunciation which appears between brackets; next follows the part of speech designation in abbreviated form. Definitions, preceded by a boldface black dot, are not detailed. Derived forms of the main entry word, combined form, and idiomatic expressions are included within the paragraph and are marked by a boldface black diamond. Synonyms are not included, although many of the definitions make use of synonymous words; specific antonyms are included and are marked by the sign ≠.

When words or specific meanings are restricted to either American English or British English use, the designations (*U.S.*) or (*Brit.*) follow. A number of other abbreviations are used within the entry paragraph and are identified under the "List of Abbreviations" in the foreword. At the end of each definition a sentence in italics illustrates its use. Examples of typical entries are shown below:

please [pliːz] v. tr., intr. • give or have satisfaction: *Are you pleased with your new car? It's impossible to please everybody at the same time.* ◆ **please** interjection • (polite form = if you please) *Come in, please. Please take me with you. May I have some water, please.* ◆ **pleasant** [ˈpleznt] adj. • giving pleasure, agreeable: *We had a pleasant evening at John's house. What a pleasant surprise!* ◆ **pleased** [pliːzd] adj. • glad; feeling or showing satisfaction: *I'm very pleased to meet you.* ◆ **pleasing** [ˈpliːzɪŋ] adj. ◆ **pleasure** [ˈpleʒə] n. U. • feeling of happiness, satisfaction: *I had the pleasure of meeting him last year in England.*

bonny [ˈbɔni] adj. (G.B.) • healthy, pretty: *What a bonny baby!*

poor [puə] adj. • ≠ rich: *Poor people are often very generous.* • small in quantity, ≠ rich: *This country is poor in minerals.* • low in quality: *The soil in this region is very poor.* • unfortunate, helpless: *The poor girl has lost all her money.*

There are cross-references for different forms of verbs that are formed by irregular means. This is of considerable help to the intended user because English has so many irregular verbs. Examples of how such cross-references are handled are:

won [wʌn] v. pret. p.p. → win.

won't [wəunt] aux. mod. → will.

Basic Dictionary of English

❶ Phonetic symbols in brackets are from the International Phonetic Alphabet (IPA)

❷ Definitions are preceded by a boldface black dot

❸ Examples of usage are italicized

❹ Related forms are preceded by a boldface black diamond

❺ Line drawings illustrate definitions

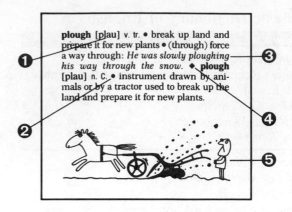

The aim of the *Basic Dictionary of English* is to keep the information easy to use and uncomplicated. This may explain the omission of etymologies from the entry text, although this information could be useful to those learning the language.

IV. Quality and Currency of Entries

Some entries are quite lengthy while others give only very brief information. The definitions are adequate for their purposes, although in many cases synonymous words are used in place of defining phrases. This weakness is offset by the fact that almost every meaning of an entry is illustrated by a simple sentence appropriate for a beginning speaker of English. Some entries, however, are not used in a sentence and supply only the briefest information; for example:

prop [prɔp] adj. • support.

porch [pɔːtʃ] n.C. • roofed doorway.

There are a number of entries that are defined only through the use of the word in a sentence. For example, "**pole** . . . *The North Pole*." Other examples include: "**pardon** . . . *I beg your pardon*," and the noun form of **park** "*Shall we go and play in the park today?*"

Although the foreword states that verbs are entered first, in the case of **park**, the noun precedes the verb, possibly because this is a homograph. The use of such variations, however, is not explained in the foreword to the dictionary. There are also inconsistencies in the way words are entered. For instance, although there are almost no abbreviations in the dictionary, **a.m.** is entered but *p.m.* is not. **British** is found under the entry **Britain**, but **German** is the main entry, and ♦ **Germany** is located within the entry paragraph.

Some definitions are of little help. Take **goose** as a case in point: The oversimplified definition is "big white bird." (There *is* an illustration of a goose that

helps somewhat.) Some definitions may confuse the reader. One such example is **jut**, which is defined as "to go or be out of sth." "Sth" is an abbreviation that means "something," a meaning few readers will grasp unless they check it in the front of the book. Most American dictionaries would define **jut** as "to stick out or protrude."

V. Syllabication and Pronunciation

Syllabication is not given. Each part of speech is provided with full word pronunciation using the International Phonetic Alphabet as it appears in the first thirteen editions of Daniel Jones's *English Pronouncing Dictionary*. The pronunciations given are those for British rather than American English, and the symbols used for vowels are different from those most commonly used in dictionaries published in the United States. The pronunciation key appears in the foreword and is not repeated in the lexicon.

VI. Special Features

Within the foreword, there is an explanation of how American English and British English differ in pronunciation. In addition, there is an appendix that lists synonymous terms that differ in use in the United States from that in Great Britain. A few examples are *bonnet* versus the U.S. *hood* (of a car), *lorry* versus *truck*, and certain variances in spelling such as *behaviour* versus *behavior* and *programme* versus *program*.

VII. Accessibility

There are no guide words, but none are really needed in this small dictionary. The use of boldface type and italics, plus a variety of symbols, makes it easy to locate information in this dictionary. There is also a generous amount of white space between entry-word paragraphs so that the pages are easy to scan.

VIII. Graphics and Format

There are a number of black-and-white line drawings in the dictionary, surrounded by white space that helps to make the pages look open and accessible. For example, the illustration for the entry **pin** shows a **safety-pin** in the nose of an individual; a picture of a **skirt** with feet below is paired with a gentleman doffing his hat. These cartoonlike drawings are not all that helpful in enhancing definitions; however, they often illustrate, in an amusing way, jokes or cultural conventions that are common in English (especially British English) but that may not be familiar to non-native speakers. The cartoon for **heart** shows a man's face locked behind bars in a woman's heart. A **typist** is shown before his machine dressed in white tie and tails in the pose of a concert pianist.

The book is a small format paperback. It opens easily and lies fairly flat, but does not appear to be glued well at the spine; there was evidence in the review copy that pages in the center would soon loosen. The inner margins are very close to the spine, preventing rebinding and making it necessary to break the covers back fully in order to read all the text.

IX. Summary

The *Basic Dictionary of English* is not really suitable for library purchase. It would serve little reference use that many other small dictionaries would not serve better, including the NEW AMERICAN WEBSTER HANDY COLLEGE DICTIONARY. The use of British pronunciation in the dictionary would be a problem for foreign speakers in the United States. Although the publisher has succeeded in making the dictionary "basic," the inconsistencies in the way information is presented are a drawback. AN ENGLISH READER'S DICTIONARY would be a better choice for an adult beginning speaker or reader of English.

Chambers Concise 20th Century Dictionary

Facts at a Glance

Full Title: **Chambers Concise 20th Century Dictionary.**
Publisher: W. & R. Chambers; published in the United States by Cambridge University Press.
Editors: G. W. Davidson, M. A. Seaton, J. Simpson, and E. M. Kirkpatrick.
Edition Reviewed: © 1985; 1986 printing.

Number of Entries: 95,000.
Number of Words: 124,000.
Number of Pages: 1,216.
Trim Size: 5½″ × 8¼″.
Binding: cloth.

Price: $15.95.
Sold in bookstores, other outlets, and through direct mail; also sold to libraries and other educational institutions.
ISBN 0-521-6000-6.

I. Introduction

The *Chambers Concise 20th Century Dictionary* is an abridged version of its parent work, CHAMBERS 20TH CENTURY DICTIONARY. It contains about half the number of entries as in the larger work. With 95,000 entries and more than 124,000 words, it can be classified as a desk-sized dictionary. It has nine appendixes, three of which differ from those in the larger dictionary. The preface states that this is "a reliable medium-sized dictionary of modern English which accurately records the language of the 1980s." It is intended for use in schools and colleges, at home, and in the office.

II. Authority

The *Chambers Concise* has been edited by the same experienced staff of editors and lexicographers who worked on the parent dictionary. Although the preface claims that this is "a truly comprehensive dictionary of international English," the user should be aware that the slant is primarily toward British usage. This is true of the entire family of Chambers dictionaries.

III. Comprehensiveness

The *Chambers Concise* contains many of the new words included in the larger volume, such as: **househusband**, **futon**, **zero option**, and **brain death**; however, *tofu* and *zowie* are not included. The meaning of **surrogate mother** is not provided in the parent work, which was published in 1983, but is included in the *Chambers Concise*, published in 1985. It gives a very clear definition:

> a woman who bears a baby for another, esp. childless, couple, after either (artificial) insemination by the male, or implantation of an embryo from the female.

This difference indicates that *Chambers Concise 20th Century Dictionary* is not just an abridgment of the larger work, but includes the addition of new words and definitions as appropriate.

A comparison of the two dictionaries shows that obscure words and definitions have been left out of the smaller volume. The main entry word **dove** is an example: in the more comprehensive work there are three numbered entries—the first is a pigeon; the second is Scottish for half asleep or stupefied; and the third entry is the past participle for *dive* (as used

Chambers Concise 20th Century Dictionary

❶ Bracketed etymologies show derivation of main entry words

❷ Pronunciations are italicized

❸ Cross-references are boldfaced

❹ Derivatives are run into the main entry and boldfaced

❺ Common foreign phrases with source language and pronunciations are included in the main alphabetical listing

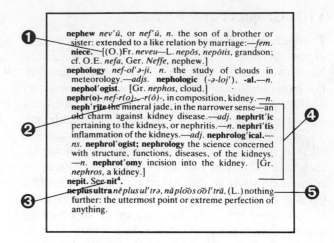

in the United States). In the concise version of Chambers there is only the first entry. Another entry that has been omitted in the concise dictionary includes a second definition for **kite** or **kyte**, which is also of Scottish derivation and means a paunch or belly. The number of cross-reference entries has also been reduced in this medium-sized work.

The concise edition does include many scientific terms and other unusual words, such as **dividivi**, which is defined as

the curved pods of *Caesalpinia coriaria*, imported for tanning and dyeing.

There are also entries for **chloasma**, a skin disease; **Elzevir**, any publication of the Dutch family of printers by that name who worked between 1592 and 1681; **meprobamate**, a drug used as a sedative and muscle relaxant; and **scammony**, an Asian plant.

Many of the literary references have been omitted from this abridged version of the CHAMBERS 20TH CENTURY DICTIONARY. For example, in the entry for **furfur** the notation referring to Burns is not included. However, some literary sources such as Milton, Shakespeare, Spenser, and the Bible are used and appear among the "List of abbreviations used in the dictionary." Most abbreviations per se appear in a separate appendix rather than in the lexicon.

The practice of grouping words formed from the same root under one main entry word is carried out in this dictionary as it is in the parent work. Lengthy entries can pose a difficult problem in locating terms in the parent work, but in *Chambers Concise* the paragraphs following a main entry word are somewhat shorter. The root entry word **homo-** rates the equivalent space of two columns in the parent volume and only about one-and-a-half columns in the concise work. Still it remains a challenge to locate a word like **homosexual** that falls near the end of an entry.

Cross-references are found in about the same frequency as in the more comprehensive work. For ex-

ample, **flotsam**, which is defined, refers to **jetsam** (also defined), which in turn has a "see" reference back to **flotsam**. Slang words are included and labeled, as are some trade names including **Coke**® for **Coca-Cola**. Since this is a British publication, it is somewhat surprising to find a good number of American–English words included. **Preppy**, for example, appears with the U.S. definition

vaguely denoting the values, mores, dress, etc., of a class of people who (might wish to seem to) have attended a (U.S.) preparatory school.

Yuppies, on the other hand, do not rate an entry.

IV. Quality and Currency of Entries

Although this dictionary is called a concise work, there are many definitions given for each entry, including occasional more up-to-date entries than could be included in the parent dictionary, published at an earlier date. It retains the current vocabulary of the parent dictionary, including such terms as **AIDS, modem, palimony**, and **videocassette**. But some entries of more obscure use are omitted, as are more lengthy descriptions of etymological origins. For example under **haiku** the *Chambers Concise* defines the word as

a Japanese poem in three lines of 5, 7, 5 syllables, usu. comical. [From Jap.]

The CHAMBERS 20TH CENTURY DICTIONARY begins with that definition and adds

developed in the 17th cent., incorporating a word or phrase that symbolizes one of the seasons.—Also **haikai** (*hī'kī*) orig. a linked series of haiku forming one poem (short for *haikai na renga*, linked comic verse), and **hokku** (*hö'kŏŏ*) orig. the first half-line of a linked series of haiku. [From Jap.]

As has been noted, overall entries are often shortened. In general, definitions are clearly stated, and the use of synonymous word definitions and circularity are usually avoided. The use of labels identifying the grammatical forms follows the same practice as in the CHAMBERS 20TH CENTURY DICTIONARY.

V. Syllabication and Pronunciation

The same method of syllabication and pronunciation is used in the *Chambers Concise* as in the CHAMBERS 20TH CENTURY DICTIONARY, which involves a somewhat complicated system of respelling and the use of diacritical marks. This method is explained in the "Detailed Chart of Pronunciation" in the preface. There is also a page of notes on American English pronunciation. Some readers may find all this more elaborate than necessary; however, they should have no trouble understanding the system.

VI. Special Features

Chambers Concise 20th Century Dictionary opens with a very brief preface and guide to using the dictionary and pronunciation chart, notes on American English, and a list of abbreviations used in the dictionary. In addition, it has nine appendixes. These include: list of abbreviations, symbols, etc.; some useful conversion tables; SI metric units of measurement; mathematical symbols; Roman numerals; the Greek alphabet; some geographical facts; international clothing and shoe sizes; and ISO paper sizes. Six of these can be found in the parent work.

VII. Accessibility

Cross-references are used appropriately and do help the reader locate words that have variant spellings. Guide words appear at the top of each double column. There is a contents page, but no thumb index, which might be useful in a desk-sized dictionary.

VIII. Graphics and Format

Like the parent volume, there are no illustrative sentences or phrases in this dictionary, which can be a drawback in defining some words clearly. For example, the verb *materialise, -ize* is defined as "to render material: to cause to assume bodily form: to reduce or to regard as matter . . .", etc. It would be helped by adding such an illustrative sentence as, *When he built his own sailboat his dream materialized.*

The concise dictionary is not as well bound as the larger dictionary, which is sewn. For library circulation, it would require rebinding. The cover is made of cloth-covered boards. The page layout, design, and paper weight are the same as in the parent dictionary. The whiteness of the paper makes the type easy to read.

IX. Summary

Chambers Concise 20th Century Dictionary has many of the same excellent features of scholarship, as well as the international approach to the English language, as the parent work on which it is based. Since it was published somewhat later, the concise edition includes some newer words or definitions of words. It has many scientific and technical terms, but the fascinating compendium of unusual and archaic terms included in the parent volume is omitted. For a library needing this international approach to the English language, but not desiring the more comprehensive CHAMBERS 20TH CENTURY DICTIONARY, it is a good option.

Chambers Mini Dictionary

Facts at a Glance

Full Title: **Chambers Mini Dictionary.**
Publisher: W. & R. Chambers; published in the United States by Cambridge University Press.
Editor: E. M. Kirkpatrick.
Edition Reviewed: © 1978; 1985 printing.

Number of Entries: 24,000.
Number of Words: 38,000.
Number of Pages: 640.
Trim Size: 3″ × 4⅝″.
Binding: paperback.

Price: $3.95.
Sold in bookstores and by direct mail; also sold to libraries and other educational institutions.
ISBN 0-521-60003-0.

I. Introduction

Chambers Mini Dictionary is described in its preface as a "brand-new, really 'pocket' dictionary." This mini dictionary is physically about half as large as most pocket dictionaries, yet it contains 38,000 definitions.

II. Authority

The authority for this smallest of the series of four Chambers dictionaries is the same as for the others (see, for example, the review of CHAMBERS 20TH CENTURY DICTIONARY).

III. Comprehensiveness

Obviously this tiny volume is not as comprehensive as either full-size cloth dictionaries or even the many other paperback pocket dictionaries now available.

Chambers Mini Dictionary

❶ Main entry words include stress marks and indicate long vowel sounds

❷ Regional labels are italicized

❸ Pronunciations are enclosed in brackets

❹ Cross-references are set in boldface type and preceded by an italic *see*

❺ Related forms are run into the main entry and set in boldface type

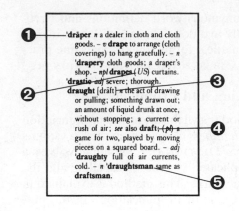

It contains, however, extensive examples of word usages and, despite its British origins, a significant number of American terms and spellings.

IV. Quality and Currency of Entries

The definitions are quite brief but easily understood. The number of compounded words is limited, but a few are given, such as under the main entry word **house: houseboat, housebreaker, household, householder, housewarming, housewife,** and **household word.** All parts of speech are included as well.

Separate entries are given for homographs, such as **bow** and **bow** or **tear** and **tear.** Alternative spellings of words are accessed through *see* references. For example, we find the following entry: **hur′rah, hur′ray, hoo′ray** with a cross-reference from **hoo′ray.** Alternative spellings for U.S. and British words, such as *catalog* and *catalogue*, can be located in the appendix; however, these few words may be overlooked because there is no table of contents in the dictionary. Illustrative phrases and sentences are used when necessary to clarify meaning. A typical entry is the word *decree:*

> **de′cree** *n* an order or law; a judge's decision. - *v* to give an order: - *pt* **de′creed**

In comparing this entry to that for *decree* in CHAMBERS UNIVERSAL LEARNER'S DICTIONARY, note that the *Mini* has no pronunciation and fewer definitions, omitting, for example, the more specialized *decree nisi.*

Abbreviations are not included in the main alphabet, but a few may be found in the appendix, including **CIA** and **DJ.** There seems to be little reason to include these abbreviations in the appendix rather than in the main alphabet because they are few in number and are not noted in a table of contents, and they may be easily overlooked.

V. Syllabication and Pronunciation

Syllable stress and pronunciation are given for many entries. Only primary stress is noted, and pronunciation appears only for some words in brackets following the entry word, for example, "[′hundrəd]" for **hundred.** A pronunciation key that uses a modified IPA system appears in the front of the book.

VI. Special Features

There is a very brief guide to using the dictionary in the front of the book and some all-too-brief appendix material in the back. Appendixes include a list of abbreviations, some foreign words and phrases (21 listed), and a few comparisons of British and American spelling.

VII. Accessibility

Guide words at the top of each column facilitate searching for entry words. The use of boldface type makes it easy to locate word variations within the paragraph following the main entry word.

VIII. Graphics and Format

There are no illustrations in this small paperback dictionary. There is good visual contrast between the white paper and the small, but readable type; there is ample white space on the page; and the paper is sufficiently heavy to avoid much see-through. The binding is stitched, which is an unusual feature for any paperbound reference work of any size and means that the book will stand up to considerable use. Because of its size, it does not lie flat when opened, but then it is intended more as a handbook in the true sense of that word.

IX. Summary

This is a very handy dictionary for quick reference for definitions and spellings. Its size and British emphasis would not make it suitable for library use in the United States.

Chambers Pocket 20th Century Dictionary

Facts at a Glance

Full Title: **Chambers Pocket 20th Century Dictionary.**
Publisher: W. & R. Chambers; published in the United States by Cambridge University Press.
Editors: G. W. Davidson, M. A. Seaton, and E. M. Kirkpatrick.
Edition Reviewed: © 1984.

Number of Entries: 33,000.
Number of Definitions: 50,000.
Number of Pages: 896.
Trim Size: 4¼″ × 5⅜″.
Binding: cloth.

Price: $6.95.
Sold in bookstores and by direct mail; also sold to libraries and other educational institutions.
ISBN 0-521-60001-4.

I. Introduction

The *Chambers Pocket 20th Century Dictionary* is one of the Chambers family of dictionaries. According to the preface, "a wide selection of the words most likely to be met with in everyday life" are included in its concise form. The *Chambers Pocket* contains 33,000 entries, consisting of some 50,000 definitions.

II. Authority

W. & R. Chambers Ltd., of Edinburgh, is a respected British publisher of dictionaries and other reference books. This edition is a handy, comprehensive dictionary which, however, has not been adapted for American usage. This is a British publication, with a British vocabulary and British spellings, distributed in the United States by Cambridge University Press.

III. Comprehensiveness

The preface claims that *Chambers Pocket* contains "a wide selection of words used in everyday life," and then goes on to say that the volume "reflects, as far as its scope allows, the latest trends and de-

velopments in science and in the world at large." Everyday language is indeed well represented in the dictionary, and although such words as **ergonomics**, **fibreglass**, **reggae**, **satellite**, **pressurize**, and **Frisbee**® are included, the selection of words representing trends in science and in the world at large seems after a spot check neither extensive nor very technical and, in fact, appears quite idiosyncratic. Neither geographic nor biographical entries are included. For the American user who is unaware of its British slant, such British terms as **lift**, **pavement**, **boot**, **bonnet**, **pram**, **Life Guards**, **National Trust**, **Open University**, and **sleeping policeman** will cause puzzlement. An American reader, however, who chooses it for its British usage will find it just what is wanted. The occasional inclusion of Americanisms, such as **Pullman**, **Santa Claus**, and **pawpaw** seems merely quixotic.

IV. Quality and Currency of Entries

Boldface, main entry words overhanging the text are followed by pronunciations in italics, and parts of speech. Definitions are in roman type and are numbered. They may be interspersed with italicized example phrases or sentences to show how a word is used. Different forms of the entry word follow in a boldface list below the main definition. These different forms—nouns, verbs, adjectives—may also have numbered meanings and may include word phrases or idioms. The etymology appears last in italics within brackets.

Here is an example of a typical entry:

> **prepare** *pri-pār′*, *v.t.* **1** to make ready. **2** to train, equip (for). **3** to make (someone) ready, fit, to bear a shock.—Also *v.i.*:—*pr.p.* **prepar′ing**.
> **preparation** *prep-à-rā′sh(ò)n*, *n.* **1** the act of preparing. **2** study of work for a lesson in class (often shortened to **prep**). **3** the state of being prepared **4** something mixed and prepared for use (e.g. face cream).
> **prepar′ative** (*-par′*) *adj.*
> **prepar′atory** *adj.*
> **prepared′** *adj.* **1** ready **2** willing
> **preparatory school** (often shortened to **prep school**) one which prepares pupils for a public school (*def. 2*).
> **preparatory to** before (doing something)
> [L. *prae*, before, *parāre*, to make ready.]

This is a clear, concise, easy to understand entry, with good examples of word usage. However, note that even this example of an ordinary, English-language word has specific British usages, such as "public school."

Even with its 1984 copyright date, this dictionary lacks some common, up-to-date terms, such as *AIDS*, *Alzheimer's disease*, or *ozone layer* (**ozone** is defined as **1** [usu. *humorous*] fresh sea air. **2** a form of oxygen). It does include **bit**, **byte**, **program**, and **database** as computer terms; as well as **blastoff**, and **gay** (homosexual).

V. Syllabication and Pronunciation

Syllabication is not indicated in the entry word but does appear in the phonetically respelled pronunciations. It is shown with a hyphen or a stress sign (accent). For example:

    chloroform *klor'ö-förm*

A pronunciation guide appears on the right-hand front endpaper.

VI. Special Features

Special features include front endpaper lists of abbreviations used in the dictionary and the pronunciation guide, a brief preface explaining the scope of the dictionary and certain spelling rules. Following the lexicon, a six-page list of abbreviations in everyday use and back endpaper listings of the metric system and the ranks in the British Armed Forces appear.

VII. Accessibility

The dictionary has boldface guide words on the left and right at the top of every page, making the dictionary very easy to use. There is no table of contents and no thumb index; however, the latter is not usual in a dictionary of this size.

VIII. Graphics and Format

Perhaps too bulky for the American idea of pocket-sized, this is, nevertheless, a very neat, handy-size dictionary, that is sturdily bound in cheerful red with a matching dust jacket. The page is divided into two columns and has boldface, overhanging entry words that are easily seen. The type is small, but it is quite legible, with adequate white space. The paper is nearly opaque and is the basis of a very pleasant and readable page.

IX. Summary

It is a pity that this neatly packaged dictionary has not been adapted to American usage, or revised in an edition for the American reader. While some current words are missing and the vocabulary has some quaint choices of entries, this is a suitably comprehensive concise dictionary. Americans, however, would be ill-advised to choose a British dictionary such as this without having some special requirement to do so.

Chambers 20th Century Dictionary

Facts at a Glance

Full Title: **Chambers 20th Century Dictionary**.
Publisher: W. & R. Chambers; published in the United States by Cambridge University Press.
Editor: E. M. Kirkpatrick.
Edition Reviewed: © 1983.

Number of Entries: 175,000.
Number of Definitions: 250,000.
Number of Pages: 1,599.
Trim Size: 6¼" × 9½".
Binding: hardcover.

Price: $24.95.
Sold in bookstores and other outlets; also sold to libraries and other educational institutions.
ISBN 0-521-32539-0.

I. Introduction

Chambers 20th Century Dictionary is the most comprehensive in the Chambers family of dictionaries, which also includes, in order of decreasing size: CHAMBERS CONCISE 20TH CENTURY DICTIONARY, CHAMBERS UNIVERSAL LEARNERS' DICTIONARY, and CHAMBERS MINI DICTIONARY. This mid-sized, semi-abridged dictionary is a British publication that covers words from all corners of the English language. While its lexicon is predominantly British, it includes a wide range of American, Australian, Scottish, and South African words.

This single volume contains 250,000 definitions, which makes it roughly a British equivalent of THE AMERICAN HERITAGE DICTIONARY or WEBSTER'S NINTH NEW COLLEGIATE DICTIONARY. The 1983 edition was expanded to contain 10 percent more new material as well as additional appendixes. The dictionary is intended as an "authority for those who work with words—student and scholar, writer, publisher, journalist and librarian." The preface to the dictionary notes that not only current words and definitions are included, but also those for literary, unusual, archaic, technical, and scientific terms.

Except for the addition of new words and meanings, the editors of the dictionary, which was originally published in 1901, have "made very few radical changes." Readers familiar with the CHAMBERS 20TH CENTURY will note that some humorous definitions deleted from the 1972 edition have been restored.

Chambers 20th Century Dictionary prides itself on its usefulness to Scrabble® players; it is the reference dictionary for the National Scrabble Championship and the National Scrabble Club Tournament.

Chambers 20th Century Dictionary

❶ Pronunciations are italicized

❷ Usage labels are italicized and enclosed in parentheses

❸ Derivatives are run into the main entry and set in boldface type

❹ Field labels are italicized and enclosed in parentheses

❺ Cross-references are boldfaced

❻ Etymology, enclosed in brackets, appears at the end of the main entry

❶ ❷ ❸ ❹ ❺ ❻

ivory *ī'və-ri, n.* dentine, esp. the hard white substance composing the tusks of the elephant, walrus, hippopotamus, and narwhal: an object of that material, as a billiard-ball, a piano-key, a dice: a tooth or the teeth (*slang*).—*adj.* made of, resembling, or of the colour of, ivory.—*adj.* **i'voried** made like ivory: furnished with teeth (*slang*).—*n.* **i'vorist** a worker in ivory.—**i'vory-black** a black powder, originally made from burnt ivory, but now from bone; **ivory gate** (*myth.*) see **gate**[1]; **i'vory-nut** the nut of Phytelephas or other palm, yielding **vegetable ivory** a substance like ivory; **i'vory-palm**; **i'vory-por'celain** a fine ware with an ivory-white glaze; **ivory tower** (*fig.*) a place of retreat from the world and one's fellows: a life-style remote from that of most ordinary people, leading to ignorance of practical concerns, problems, etc.; **i'vory-tree** the palay.—**show one's ivories** (*slang*) to show the teeth.   [O.Fr. *ivurie* (Fr. *ivoire*)—L. *ebur, eboris*, ivory; Coptic *ebu*, elephant, ivory.]

II. Authority

The *Chambers 20th Century Dictionary* has been in print, in various editions, for most of this century, and over the years has acquired an excellent reputation in the U.K. Most of the Chambers dictionaries are published by W. & R. Chambers, Ltd., Edinburgh, and are distributed in the United States by Cambridge University Press. This dictionary is now also published for the first time in this edition by Cambridge in the United States. Noted for its long history of scholarly book publishing, Cambridge University Press is, according to the book's flyleaf, the world's oldest publishing house, which also makes it the oldest in the English language. This edition was edited by E. M. Kirkpatrick and a staff of editors and lexicographers.

III. Comprehensiveness

Entries appear in boldface type and overhang the text. The pages are double column. The entries are arranged in alphabetical order, letter by letter. Words derived from the same root have been grouped together under one main entry word. This practice is intended as a space-saving device, but it can make locating a word difficult. In some cases, however, this practice is facilitated by the use of cross-references, such as: "cole-slaw. See cole." Under **cole**, we find that it is another name for cabbage and thus can also locate several other combined forms of the word, such as **cole-garth**, **cole-seed**, and **cole-wort**.

Synonyms and antonyms are not included, but etymologies are provided at the end of the entry and appear in italics between square brackets. The use of a dash before a language source indicates that a word was originally derived from this source. An example is the etymology for *coin*:

[Fr. *coin*, a wedge (see **quoin**), also the die to stamp money—L. *cuneus*, a wedge.]

Literary sources are given for some words as in the examples which follow:

furfur . . . (*Browning*, **furfair**) n. dandruff, scurf . . . , and **easle, aizle** . . . (*Burns*) n. hot ashes. . . .

There are few abbreviations included in the dictionary, although **I O U** [*sic*] was located, but most are appended in a separate list in the back of the dictionary. There are slang words such as

cosh n. a bludgeon . . . lead pipe . . . or the like, used as a weapon.—Also *v.t.*

Other slang expressions include **haymaker**, a wild swinging blow; **second banana**, a vaudeville performer who played a secondary role; and **goner**, meaning a person who is either dead or beyond recovery.

Proper nouns can be located in the dictionary and are capitalized in the entry word, such as **Camberwell Beauty**, a large butterfly; **Camembert**, the cheese; and the flower **Camellia**, which would not be capitalized in an American English dictionary. Personal names are not included except for gods and goddesses of Greek, Roman, or other origins. First names and their origins are in an appendix. Place names are excluded, but words such as **Londoner** can be located as well as **French**, **German**, and so on.

The following main entry shows the standard format:

carpenter *kär'pint-ər, n.* a worker in timber as used in building houses, etc.—*v.i.* to do the work of a carpenter.—*v.t.* to make by carpentry: to put together or construct, esp. clumsily.—*n.* **car'pentry** the trade or work of a carpenter.—**car'penter-bee'**, **-ant'** a bee or ant that excavates its nest in wood. [O.Fr. *carpentier*—L.L. *carpentārius*—*carpentum* a car, from root of **car**.]

The practice of grouping words under main entry words means that many run-on, combined forms of words and idioms are included: **out** and the prefix **out-** (given a separate entry) take up almost seven columns including brief lists at the bottom of three pages; the coverage is similar for **over**.

Trade names appear in this Chambers dictionary, occasionally with cross-references. For example, we can find **Coca-Cola**® and **Dictograph**.® There is a cross-reference from **Coke** to **Coca-Cola**.® There are many scientific and technical words: **total allergy syndrome** and **CAT scanner**, identified as short for **computed axial tomography scanner**, are two of the many terms to be found.

IV. Quality and Currency of Entries

Many words have more than one definition, and each definition appears as a separate entry. They are arranged in historical order with superscript numbers so that the reader can see at a glance the historical development, or as the preface states, "a potted history of the word." Many unusual definitions are provided for words. **Carte**[1] is defined as "the fourth position of the wrist in fencing," and **carte**[2] as "bill of fare: a playing-card (Scot.): a *carte-de-visite*." Definitions are graphic, such as the one for **carrion**: "the dead and putrid body or flesh of any animal; anything vile."

There are many fascinating words in Chambers to delight anyone who loves language. **Hobbledehoy**, a youth who is neither man nor boy; **fringillaceous**, pertaining to finches; and **frigorific**, which means freezing, are a few examples. Every page has at least one or more words that cause the reader to pause. In addition to the many unusual words that can be found in Chambers, there are a number of newer coinages, including **house-husband**, **brain death**, **palimony**, and approximately fifteen definitions under the word **video** such as **videotex**, **videotape**, and **videocassette**. **Bit** and **byte** are included as computer terms; in addition to the usual definition for **bit**, there is an added note that it is the contracted form of "binary digit."

Definitions are clearly stated, and synonymous words and circularity are avoided as means of defining words. There is no attempt to avoid the controversial. One of the definitions of **gay** is homosexual; **bitch** is defined not only as a female dog, wolf, and fox but also a malicious woman; and various vulgar sexual terms and expletives are defined.

Definitions are labeled as appropriate, such as "(*slang*)", or "(*coll*)" for colloquial as in the case of **ain't**, or "(*vulg.*)" for vulgar, but there is no attempt to provide prescriptive notes on word use other than these notes. For example, a prescriptive dictionary would note the difference in use for the words *further* and *farther*. Under the main entry for **farther**, the reader is told that it is the same as **further**. Some

definitions are slightly humorous, such as the one defining *back* as "the hinder part of the body in man, and the upper part in beasts."

There are two weaknesses in the definitions found in *Chambers 20th Century Dictionary*. One is the lack of descriptive sentences that would help to clarify the use of words like **homograph**, **homogram**, and **homonym**; the other is the lack of illustrations. For example, a **cucking-stool** ("a stool on which . . . culprits were placed . . . to be pelted by the mob") is probably something like the early American stocks, but a picture would help to clarify this definition. In spite of such problems, however, the dictionary definitions are on the whole very clear and straightforward, and can be understood by any educated American adult. They will also be valuable for college students of English literature.

V. Syllabication and Pronunciation

Pronunciation is a combination of both respelling and diacritical marks for vowels and consonants. In the introductory materials to the pronunciation chart in the front of the dictionary there is a notation that

> Respelling is a rough method of showing pronunciation compared with the use of phonetic symbols, but it has two merits—it is intelligible to a large number of people who do not know phonetic symbols, and it allows for more than one interpretation so that each user of the dictionary may choose a pronunciation in keeping with his speech.

This note should not, however, lead the reader to believe that the pronunciation chart will not be needed, for it is. The dictionary devotes five pages to charts and notes on pronunciation. There is also a very brief pronunciation guide of limited usefulness at the bottom of even-numbered pages, and a note on odd-numbered pages to see the chart in the front.

Syllabication appears within the pronouncing word and is marked either by an accent mark to show stress or a dash. *Decomposition* is pronounced "*di-kompə-zish'ən*" meaning to decay; however, it is pronounced somewhat differently for the second definition, meaning the compounding of things: "*de-kompə-zish'ən*." Alternate pronunciations can also be found for **tomato**, **oblique**, **mathesis**, and many other words. Pronunciations are provided for other grammatical forms of the main entry word as well.

When hyphenation of compounded words occurs at the end of a line, the equal symbol is used to distinguish it from the ordinary hyphen indicating a line break.

VI. Special Features

There is a guide to using the dictionary in the front of the book, but it is quite brief and only minimally helpful; the publisher expects that users will be familiar with dictionaries and their vagaries. Appended to the back of the book are the following lists: phrases and quotations from Latin, Greek and modern languages; a list of abbreviations, symbols, etc.; musical terms, signs and abbreviations; some English personal names; Greek and Russian alphabets; Roman numerals; some conversion tables; some physical constants; and SI metric units of measurement. Mathematical symbols rate a page, as does a chart of paper sizes used in Britain for standard book printing, stationery, posters, and wall charts.

All of these tables are useful to a degree—given the fact that they are shortened and could be located in more detail in other sources. The list of abbreviations will not be of much use to Americans, as it deals mostly with names of interest to the British. For example, **CB** is given as the "Companion of the Order of the Bath."

VII. Accessibility

A table of contents helps the user find the main parts of the dictionary. Guide words at the top of each column are helpful in finding the root word, but the practice of grouping many word combinations under the root word makes it difficult for the reader to locate these derivatives. Take the words *homograph*, *homogram*, and *homonym*, for example. All three words appear under the root **homo-** along with dozens of other words beginning with this prefix.

Cross-references are used for variant spellings of words, such as "**attap**. See **atap**." or "**paddymelon**. See **pademelon**.," or yet another variation, "**Pahlavi**. Same as **Pehlevi**." Both spellings are given in the main entry word that is referenced. There is no note in the section called "Using the Dictionary" to indicate any preference in spelling by the order given in which it appears. Some variant spellings have to do with national variations in the English language, and thus we find "**colour**, also, esp. in U.S., **color** . . . ," and also "**diarrhoea**, (U.S.) **diarrhea**. . . ." The volume is not thumb-indexed.

VIII. Graphics and Format

The two-column pages are very full; the print is clear, black, and readable, though small. The lack of illustrations in the dictionary has already been noted; however, the omission is not a major detractor from what is a very scholarly and useful dictionary. The book is sturdily bound with a cloth cover; paper is off-white and thin, but there is no appreciable show-through.

IX. Summary

Every library that can afford to buy *Chambers 20th Century Dictionary* for its reference shelf should do

so. It will be especially useful to college and university students studying English literature and to all readers of British books and periodicals. For example, this dictionary will tell the reader that the Chaucerian verb **clepe** means "to call: to name"; that a **garda** is "an Irish policeman" and that the plural is **gardai** and that the expression **gone for a Burton** is airman's slang for "drowned, dead, absent, missing, no longer in existence." The reader can also learn the interesting etymology of **grog-shop**, the connotative meaning of **Harley Street**, and the sort of gesture that someone makes when he or she makes a **Harvey Smith**.

Chambers is full of many new, archaic, unusual, scientific, and technical words—more than will be found in American abridged dictionaries. This will make the dictionary especially appealing to writers in many fields.

The definitions are of excellent quality, and the authority of the dictionary is unquestioned. Although there are many British and other English-language words not commonly used in American speech and writing, their inclusion makes *Chambers* even more useful for some purposes. Where else, other than a crossword puzzle dictionary, can the reader go to find that **peenge** is Scottish for "to whine like a peevish child"? Scrabble® players and all word lovers will find *Chambers* not only a useful reference, but a book to sit down and read—just for the enjoyment of the richness of the English language.

Chambers Universal Learners' Dictionary

Facts at a Glance

Full Title: **Chambers Universal Learners' Dictionary.**
Publisher: W. & R. Chambers; published in the United States by Cambridge University Press.
Editor: E. M. Kirkpatrick.
Edition Reviewed: © 1980; 1985 printing.

Number of Entries: 45,000.
Number of Words: 55,000.
Number of Pages: 928.
Trim Size: 5¼" × 7¾".
Binding: paperback.

Price: $9.95.
Sold in bookstores and in other outlets; also sold to libraries and other educational institutions.
ISBN 0-521-60008-1.

I. Introduction

Chambers Universal Learners' Dictionary is part of the Chambers family of dictionaries, the most comprehensive of the four being the CHAMBERS 20TH CENTURY DICTIONARY, and the smallest, the CHAMBERS MINI DICTIONARY. The *Universal Learners'* falls in the middle with 45,000 entries. The preface of this dictionary states that it has been "created for learners of English who already have some knowledge of English and who are at the stage of requiring particular help with how to use the language." To assist such a reader, many examples of usage have been included. Such examples do not appear in either the CHAMBERS 20TH CENTURY DICTIONARY or the CHAMBERS CONCISE 20TH CENTURY DICTIONARY. "The aim of the dictionary is to provide comprehensive information in as simple a form as possible." The vocabulary is basically British English but includes some American spellings and usages.

II. Authority

The *Chambers Universal Learners' Dictionary* has been prepared by the same staff of editors and lexicographers that prepared the companion volumes in the Chambers family, with E. M. Kirkpatrick serving as the primary editor of the work. Pronunciations were the responsibility of Professor David Abercrombie and Alan Kemp of the Department of Linguistics, University of Edinburgh.

III. Comprehensiveness

The *Universal Learners'* really cannot be compared with the CHAMBERS 20TH CENTURY DICTIONARY or the CHAMBERS CONCISE 20TH CENTURY DICTIONARY because it serves a different purpose. The emphasis of this dictionary is on providing clear and accurate definitions, in simple language, with many examples of usage. Especially thorough are the labels to indicate "correct" usage. For this reason there has been little attempt to include the newer "trendy" vocabulary words, such as *house-husband* or *surrogate mother*. Nevertheless, some recent terms, such as **blast off**, **data processing**, and **program** (in the sense of instructions to a computer) are included. These give the vocabulary a broader, more useful base than might be expected in an entry list of 45,000 words.

IV. Quality and Currency of Entries

Definitions are concise and easy to understand. They are fully clarified by the use of illustrative sentences following the definition. The definitions generally do not make use of synonymous terms in explaining a word. More than one meaning is usually given when appropriate, and circularity is avoided. Take the main entry word **area** as an example.

    area . . . 1 *ncu* ["noun countable or uncountable"] the extent or size of a flat surface: *This garden is twelve*

square metres in area. 2 *nc* a place; part (of a town etc): *Do you live in this area?* 3 *nc* a subject, activity or topic: *Do you have any experience in this area?; an area of dispute.*

The preceding entry is more complete in terms of definitions than the same entry in CHAMBERS 20TH CENTURY DICTIONARY; the one definition omitted is that of area code for U.S. telephones. Different meanings or senses of a word are arranged in numerical order based on frequency of use, with the most common meaning first.

Main entry words are in boldface type and overhang the double-column text. Pronunciation follows in brackets. The abbreviations for the labeling system are explained in the preface of the book; these labels are in parentheses and are italicized. Some examples include (*Amer*) for American spelling, use, or pronunciation. Other examples are (*sl*) for slang, (*ironic*), (*offensive*), and (*vulg*) which stands for vulgar. The difference between *offensive* and *vulgar* is illustrated using the word **nigger** as an example of what is offensive speech, and **cunt** for what is considered vulgar. Some readers will no doubt wince over the use of the latter word and wonder whether the publisher could not have found a suitable but less vulgar example. Altogether, there are 22 usage labels.

Next comes the part of speech. The symbols used to denote grammatical designation are more detailed than those used in most American dictionaries—or in most American schools. For example, phrasal verbs are labeled *vt fus*, verb transitive fused; *vt sep*, verb transitive separate; *vt oblig sep*, verb transitive obligatorily separated; and *vt usu sep*, verb transitive usually separated. The *vt oblig sep* label is illustrated (as are the others), with the sentence: "He pushes his young brother around, *not* He pushes around his young brother." An adult learner can thus absorb how a phrasal verb such as **push around** is used by native speakers of English. Definitions of the main entry word are numbered; numerals are in boldface type. The italic sentence or phrase that follows illustrates the use of that particular definition. There are no synonyms or antonyms given, and the etymology of words is omitted. A typical example is

    decree [di'kri:] *nc (formal)* **1** an order, edict or law: *The king issued a decree forbidding hunting on royal land.* **2** (*legal*) a ruling of a court of civil law. - *v* - *pt, ptp* **de'creed** - *vt (formal)* to order, command or decide (something): *The court decreed that he should pay the fine in full.*
    decree nisi ['naisai] (*legal*) (*not in Scotland*) a decree of divorce which becomes effective after a certain period of time unless anyone who has a right to object to it does so: *She was granted a decree nisi.*

All forms of a word in addition to run-on words and combined forms are indented in block format under the main entry word. They are in boldface type, and each entry begins on a new line, which makes them easy to find. There are some cross-references; for example, **deduct** and **deduce** have *see also* notes because they are similar but not the same in meaning. Verb forms that are spelled so differently as to fall in another part of the alphabet are also cross-referenced, such as **are** *see* **be**.

Homographs, that is, words having the same spelling but different roots and meanings, are listed separately. For example, **bail**[1] a sum of money used to free a person from jail and **bail**[2] meaning one of the crosspieces laid on top of the wicket in cricket are given separate entries. **Bail**[3] meaning to clear water out of, say, a boat with a bucket is cross-referenced to **bale**[2], the usual British spelling of the word.

Abbreviations do not appear as main entries in the lexicon, but some are given in an appendix. No personal or geographic names appear in the lexicon either, but countries and nationalities are listed in a separate appendix that includes both noun and adjectival forms.

V. Syllabication and Pronunciation

Nearly five pages at the front of the dictionary are devoted to pronunciation. The introduction to this section states:

> The variety of English pronunciation that has been used as a model in this dictionary is that which is commonly known as **Received Pronunciation** or **RP**. The symbols used for the transcriptions are those of the alphabet of the International Phonetic Association (IPA). . . . The particular style of transcription used in this dictionary is that which is known as the "simplified" or "extra-broad" IPA transcription of English, devised by Daniel Jones and recommended by him for use in teaching English to foreign learners.

The words used to illustrate the sound of the pronunciation symbols are, for the most part, quite simple, but there are two which may be troublesome to a beginning speaker of English. They are *avant-garde* and *raison d'être*. Primary stress on a syllable is denoted by placing an accent mark (') just before the syllable; secondary stress, also placed before the syllable, is a somewhat different accent mark (,). Whenever there is a change of pronunciation or stress for a derivative word, this is also given. French vowel symbols are given for *ã, ẽ,* and *õ*. Syllabication is not indicated, which is a questionable decision on the part of the publishers for a learners' dictionary.

VI. Special Features

The preface material contains a fairly extensive guide on using the dictionary, including a pronunciation key, information about American pronunciation, and labels and abbreviations used in the dictionary. In addition there are a number of appendixes. These include the following: numbers, fractions and numerical expressions; geographical names, nationalities and languages; ranks in the British armed forces; musical notation, weights, and measures; the solar system; the English alphabet; abbreviations and symbols; and some common affixes (that is, prefixes and suffixes) and combining forms. These appendixes are very brief, and most of the information could be found in an almanac. For non-English speakers the appendix table that lists cardinal numbers and their ordinal equivalents is helpful, as is the appendix that lists prefixes, suffixes, and combining forms.

VII. Accessibility

There are guide words at the top of each column to help the reader locate the main entry word. And since all defined words are in boldface, and the paragraphs are not overly long, it is not difficult to locate sought-for words. There is a detailed table of contents, but no thumb index—a not unusual occurrence in paperback dictionaries.

VIII. Graphics and Format

The double-column page has adequate margins, and the type is clear, if small, with enough white space for easy reading. The paper is of high quality for a paperback and has almost no show-through. The flexible vinyl cover is glued over a sewn binding, which is unusual for a paperback reference book. Pages lie flat and will not easily come loose from the binding. The book will stand up to normal library use.

IX. Summary

The *Chambers Universal Learners' Dictionary* is a good choice for an ESL reference work, although users may also want to consider the OXFORD STUDENT'S DICTIONARY OF AMERICAN ENGLISH or the LONGMAN DICTIONARY OF AMERICAN ENGLISH for a more American vocabulary. The *Chambers* vocabulary is broad for the size of the dictionary and very accessible to learners. The format corresponds to the purpose of the volume and will withstand normal library or home use.

The Compact Edition of the Oxford English Dictionary

Facts at a Glance

Full Title: **The Compact Edition of the Oxford English Dictionary.**
Publisher: Oxford University Press.

Editors: James A. H. Murray, Henry Bradley, W. A. Craigie, C. T. Onions.
Edition Reviewed: © 1971; 22d printing.

Number of Entries: 500,000, plus 62,000 in the Supplement.
Number of Pages: 5,568 (2 volumes, plus one-volume Supplement).
Trim Size: 9¼″ × 12″.
Binding: hardcover.

Price: $195.00 (two-volume *OED* only); $75.00 (Supplement only); $270.00 (all three volumes).
Intended Readership: adults.
Sold in bookstores and other outlets; also sold through direct mail and to libraries and other educational institutions.
ISBN 0-19-86117-X.

I. Introduction and Scope

The *Compact Edition of the Oxford English Dictionary* (*OED*) is a micrographic reproduction of the full text of the original 1933 OED. That work is well known as the preeminent historical dictionary of the English language. It traces word forms and meanings from their earliest appearance in English onward through extensive quotations. The work is of inestimable value to readers seeking accurate and detailed information about word origins, derivations, and histories. However, the OED lacks a number of features found in many good general dictionaries, such as syllabication and biographical and geographical terms. American readers should also be aware that the work incorporates British spelling and pronunciation.

The two-volume photoreduced *Compact OED* has been available since the early 1970s; in early 1988 Oxford issued the SUPPLEMENT TO THE OXFORD ENGLISH DICTIONARY in a single micrographically reduced volume. The complete *Compact OED* and Supplement can now be purchased in a three-volume set. Those who already own the *Compact OED* may purchase volume III separately.

The single-, two-, and three-volume sets are all packaged in a sturdy dark blue slipcase. The top of the case has a small drawer that contains a Bausch & Lomb 4.5× magnifying glass. The glass is necessary for reading the text pages, each of which contains four micrographically reduced pages of the OED. The work's paper is high-quality coated stock. The print is exceptionally small, and reading it, even under magnification, is extremely tedious. However, for occasional home or office use by the reader in need of a historical dictionary, this set serves very well, and librarians may wish to recommend it to interested patrons.

Most libraries will prefer to purchase a set of the full-sized OED with its four supplemental volumes (reviewed in this Buying Guide). However, smaller libraries with limited budgets and shelf space, or those which receive few requests for the OED, may find this set appropriate for their collections.

The Concise American Heritage Dictionary

Facts at a Glance

Full Title: **The Concise American Heritage Dictionary**.
Publisher: Houghton Mifflin Company.
Editors: Staff of *The American Heritage Dictionary*.
Edition Reviewed: © 1980.

Number of Definitions: about 55,000.
Number of Pages: 832.
Number of Illustrations: nearly 300.
Trim Size: 6⅛″ × 9¾″.
Binding: hardcover.

Price: $7.95.
Sold in bookstores and other outlets.
ISBN 0-395-24522-2.

I. Introduction

The Concise American Heritage Dictionary retains many features that are characteristic of the parent work from which it has been abridged, the *American Heritage Dictionary of the English Language* (1969), edited by William Morris. The preface to the *Concise* summarizes these as "several innovations in lexicography, principally in the areas of design and illustration, guidance on matters of usage, and etymology." And the tracing of words to their Indo-European roots in the etymologies, a much praised feature of the parent work, has been kept as a separate appendix for this dictionary.

The *Concise* is heavily abridged from the original and contains about 55,000 entries. The definitions have also been specially revised to be simpler and easier to read, and the typeface and the nearly 300 illustrations are larger. Biographical and geographic entries are included in the main alphabet.

A paperback edition of this work, called simply THE AMERICAN HERITAGE DICTIONARY, is published by the Dell Publishing Company and is reviewed elsewhere in this Buying Guide.

II. Authority

The Concise American Heritage Dictionary is published by Houghton Mifflin, publisher of the American Heritage family of dictionaries and other respected language reference books. The dictionary was prepared by the *American Heritage Dictionary* editorial staff, none of whom are listed in the current printing.

The preface explains that the more than 100 usage notes in the text "are derived from the deliberations of the American Heritage Panel on English Usage over a period of four years." No formal list of the panel's members appears, but the back cover mentions that they include some of "America's most famous writers, editors, and speakers—including Isaac Asimov, Cleveland Amory, Barbara W. Tuchman, David Ogilvy, the late Walter W. (Red) Smith—led by Edwin Newman, the distinguished commentator and writer."

As in the other American Heritage dictionaries, the etymologies are based on those prepared for the parent work by Professor Calvert Watkins and other members of Harvard University's linguistics department.

III. Comprehensiveness

The *Concise* has an acceptable number of entries for an abridged everyday dictionary and does not claim to be "comprehensive." A brief comparison of the number of entries between **largess** and **lasagna** shows that the *Concise AHD* has 12 entries compared to the AMERICAN HERITAGE DESK DICTIONARY's 18. The words not in the *Concise* are **larghetto, laryng-, laryngeal, larynges, laryngo-** or **laryng-,** and **laryngoscope.** In the section of entries from **paprika** to **parachute**, the *Concise* and the DESK both have nine entries, eight of them alike: for the ninth entry, DESK includes the adjective **parabolic**, and *Concise* includes the abbreviation **par** (which is not labeled as an abbreviation, incidentally).

All words have etymologies or sources; there is also a generous use of short examples and quotations with attributions, but only 100 words have usage notes.

Lists of compound words formed from **de-, dis-, non-, over-,** and **re-** are included, and so are English meanings for a list of words combined with **-mania,** such as **heliomania** (sunbathing) and **sitomania** (food). There are also a considerable number of illustrations with caption labels, as well as charts and tables that add to the reader's understanding of words (see the section below on "Special Features" of this dictionary).

In general, the dictionary is very complete for a concise edition, although many *advanced* scientific and technical terms are excluded from the *Concise*, as they are from the DESK. In the *Concise*, fewer meanings are included and these are considerably rewritten and condensed.

IV. Quality and Currency of Entries

The publisher's claim that the definitions have been "selected, and rewritten or edited, to be as accurately lucid and useful as possible" is generally true. The reviewer of the *Concise American Heritage Dictionary* for *American Reference Books Annual 1982* stated that this dictionary "approaches language sensibly" but cited an example of "inevitable inconsistencies and lapses"; for example, "The entry *prior* is labeled an adjective, its accepted usage; but in the definition of *premature*—'occurring . . . prior to the customary or correct time'—*prior* functions in its prevalent but questionable role as a preposition."

The information in the entries follows the usual *American Heritage Dictionary* sequence: bold main entry word divided into syllables; pronunciation(s); part of speech; inflected forms; definitions, numbered when necessary and often accompanied by short examples of use; brief etymology, source, or indication that an entry is a short form—"**em·cee** . . . [short for *M(aster of) C(eremonies)*.]"—and alternate forms and their parts of speech. In some cases, variant forms or spellings follow the entry word. Field or style labels occur before meanings, but apart from the label "*Informal*" these appear less frequently than in other abridged versions of the parent work. Synonyms are not labeled or listed. All this information under each entry is helpful to users, since they do not have to search in the appendixes or in other reference books for specifics.

A comparison of several definitions between the entries for **largess** and **lasagna** from the AMERICAN HERITAGE DESK DICTIONARY and the *Concise* reveals considerable differences in how these abridged works define terms. In almost all cases, the language of the *Concise* is simpler and more direct. Taxonomy is omitted, only the most common field labels are included, and the etymologies or sources are stripped to the bare bones, for example:

> **lar·rup** *v. Informal.* To flog; thrash; beat. [?].

In the DESK DICTIONARY, the etymology for **larrup** is "[Orig. unknown.]," rather than a bracketed question mark. Compare "**lark**^{2} *n.* A carefree romp or prank" from the *Concise* with "**lark**^{2} *n.* A carefree adventure or harmless prank" from the DESK. Or **larva**, defined in the *Concise* as

> **1.** The wingless, often wormlike form of a newly hatched insect. **2.** The newly hatched stage of any of various animals that differ markedly in the adult form, as a tadpole.

In the DESK version, **larva** is defined as

> **1.** The wingless, often wormlike form, such as a caterpillar, of a newly hatched insect before undergoing metamorphosis.

2. The newly hatched, earliest stage of any of various animals that undergo metamorphosis, differing markedly in form and appearance from the adult.

As these examples show, the *Concise* is a dictionary that can be understood by readers with unsophisticated, or limited, vocabularies.

The order of defined meanings is not necessarily the historical order, as explained in the "Guide to the Dictionary." Rather, it is the central meaning with other meanings added in logical order. This order is clearer for the reader. The guide specifically notes that the organization of meanings under an entry "seeks to clarify the fact that, despite its various meanings, the entry is a single 'word' and not a number of separate words that happen to be spelled the same way." This goal is usually achieved in the simplified definitions of the *Concise*, as the example for **larva** shows. Occasionally the condensation does leave out a useful sense, but the *Concise* is sometimes more efficient at including senses than the slightly larger AMERICAN HERITAGE DESK DICTIONARY. For example, under the prefix **para-**, which is widely used, the *Concise* includes the meaning of "subsidiary to," whereas the DESK does not.

Since this dictionary's most recent copyright date is 1980, many words in common use today are also not included. The omission of advanced technical terms and of words such as *aerobics*, *byte*, and *videocassette* limits the overall usefulness of this dictionary.

V. Syllabication and Pronunciation

Syllables in the *Concise*'s entry words are divided by bold centered dots, as in other American Heritage dictionaries: **da·ta** or **pro·cess·ing**. However, when words in phrasal entries also appear as separate entries, they are not divided: **data processing**; another example is **cir·cu·la·tory system**, but the adjective *circulatory* does not appear as a main entry. The breaking of words into syllables follows standard editorial and printing practice.

The pronunciation also follows the standard American Heritage system and is intended to help readers reproduce a satisfactory pronunciation acceptable in "all circumstances," although the editors acknowledge that regional sounds will vary. A brief key to pronunciations, with a typical word that demonstrates the sound accompanied by *The American Heritage Dictionary* sound symbol, appears in the "Guide to the Dictionary." Two lines of this pronunciation key appear at the bottom of each page in the dictionary. Special vowel sounds, such as the *schwa* (ə) in **telegraph** (tĕl′ə-graf′), and *l* and *n* (the syllabic consonants) are explained, as are nine foreign sounds common in English, including the French

sound of *gn* in compiègne. Primary and secondary stress are shown with bold and lighter face stress marks: **beau′ti·fi·ca′tion**. These pronunciation guides are very useful to the reader who takes the time to read them, as are the pronunciation guides at the bottom of each page.

VI. Special Features

Within the alphabetical sections of the *Concise* are numerous excellent charts, lists, and tables presented in larger formats than in the other American Heritage dictionaries. These include a table of alphabets (Arabic, Hebrew, Greek, and Russian), a list of 26 common bacteria (clearly illustrated, with Latin names), books of the Bible (Hebrew Scriptures, Douay, King James Version, and New Testament, accompanied by a handsome facsimile of a page from a fourteenth-century Spanish Hebrew text), the Braille alphabet, months of three principal calendars (Gregorian, Hebrew, and Moslem), a table of currencies (with exchange rates for August 1975), a periodic table of the elements, international code flags, Morse code, a full-page chart of geologic time scales, a chart of the Indo-European family of languages, the manual alphabet, a table of measurement units, proofreaders' marks, Roman and Arabic numerals, and even a chart of the 24 basic Germanic and two later English alphabetic runes, plus symbols and signs. Since there is no table of contents, and no appendixes, readers who are used to finding these tables at the back of a dictionary (where they are placed in many other dictionaries) may have difficulty finding them within the alphabetical listing—until they become familiar with the text.

Apart from these, two other features are the opening "Guide to the Dictionary" and the alphabetic listing of Indo-European roots, a feature of the original *American Heritage Dictionary*. The guide has helpful subheads for its explanatory paragraphs, for example, "Idioms," but rather surprisingly the whole section has not been revised so that its language matches the simpler definitions and text in the *Concise*. The etymologies of the parent work traced words to their Indo-European roots. This material is placed in an appendix in the *Concise*. There is no question that it is scholarly and excellent lexicographic material, but it does seem too advanced for the level of the *Concise*'s definitions, which were specially revised, according to the publisher, to be easy to read.

Usage notes, which were featured in the original *American Heritage Dictionary* and its subsequent college editions, are much condensed here and accompany the most basic words such as **affect**[1] *v.*, **comprise**, **convince**, **foot**, **help**, **influence**, **who**, and so forth. A particularly useful note distinguishes the use of **bimonthly** from **semimonthly**. The majority of definitions feature very brief, italicized examples of a word's use.

VII. Accessibility

At first glance, the most notable feature of this dictionary is the generous size of its typeface, which is a relief from the eye-straining print in many dictionaries. Also, the generous white space between lines makes scanning the text and head words easier. In addition, the pair of guide words at the top of each page is printed in large bold type. This is helpful, since the dictionary is not thumb-indexed. For readers with some visual impairment, this dictionary could be useful.

All entries occur in letter-by-letter alphabetical order. This includes compound words, biographical names, geographic entries, and standard abbreviations. For example: **kt.**, **Kuala Lumpur**, **Kublai Khan**, **kudos**. Alternative spellings and inflections are printed in boldface type. In the definitions, cross-references are indicated by bold type:

net·ton. See **ton**.

New Greek. Modern Greek.

mold[3] *n.* Also chiefly Brit. **mould**.

mould. Chief Brit. Variant of **mold**.

The five-page "Guide to the Dictionary" is printed immediately before the main entries and has clear subheads for its explanatory paragraphs such as "Idioms," "Numbers and Letters," "Main Entry Words Having Meaning Only in a Phrase," and so forth. The pronunciation key list is easily deciphered, and the explanatory notes are clear. A list of abbreviations and symbols appearing in the dictionary's etymologies faces the first page of entries for the letter **Aa**.

The appendix of Indo-European roots appears after **Zz** entries and includes a brief explanation of the root entries.

Special charts and tables, such as currencies, appear in the main alphabetic sections, but are not listed elsewhere. There is, in fact, no table of contents, a regrettable omission.

VIII. Graphics and Format

Although there are only approximately 300 illustrations, many of them photographs, they are large enough to see clearly and are generally excellent. In its original 1979 review of the *American Heritage Dictionary* abridged versions, *Library Journal* noted that the publicity on the illustrations (especially for the paperback abridgment) was "more a promotional gimmick than a vocabulary aid." In the case of this hardbound abridgment, the opposite is true. The pictures, especially those with extensive labels such as

the anatomical drawings, add considerably to the reader's understanding of words. There are even clear line drawings for the entries **beef**, **lamb**, and **pork** that label cuts of meat.

The maps are large enough to show geographic locations and areas clearly; capital cities are indicated on them with bold stars. The portraits are also large and clear, although only 2 women (Elizabeth I and Queen Victoria) appear out of 70. Charts, tables, and lists such as Morse code are well designed. The heavy white paper and sturdy binding with plain dark blue laminated cover are attractive and will withstand heavy use.

IX. Summary

The *Concise* is a very thorough, as well as reliable, dictionary for its size, in some areas providing more information than is generally needed. It is easy to use, and many readers will appreciate the large, informative pictures, as well as the larger type. Readers should be aware, however, that the current edition does not have a large vocabulary of highly scientific or technical words and that some dates, such as population figures in the geographic entries or recent death dates in the biographical, are either not current or absent. While usage is explained and demonstrated, the dictionary is less prescriptive in its condensed form here than in other versions; only basic style labels such as *informal* and *poetic* are included, and the special field labels are less evident.

To describe it briefly, the *Concise American Heritage Dictionary* is a much condensed, easier-to-read variation of the respected AMERICAN HERITAGE DICTIONARY: SECOND COLLEGE EDITION. For a "budget-priced dictionary," as the publisher calls it, the work offers good value for the money.

The Concise Oxford Dictionary of Current English

Facts at a Glance

Full Title: **The Concise Oxford Dictionary of Current English**.
Publisher: Oxford University Press.
Editor: J. B. Sykes.
Edition Reviewed: © 1982.

Number of Entries: over 40,000.
Number of Pages: 1,279.
Trim Size: 5¼" × 8½".
Binding: cloth.

Price: $22.50.
Sold in bookstores; also sold to libraries and other educational institutions.
ISBN 0-19-861131-5.

I. Introduction

The Concise Oxford Dictionary of Current English is a British desk dictionary widely available in the United States. Over 1,200 pages long, it contains more than 40,000 main entries, with a total of about 75,000 "vocabulary items including derivatives, compounds, and abbreviations." While predominantly a dictionary of the language written and spoken in Great Britain, this edition includes information about American spelling, definitions, idioms, and usage.

II. Authority

This is the seventh edition of a work originally conceived and compiled by the redoubtable brothers H. W. and F. G. Fowler and first issued by the Oxford University Press in 1911. The current edition was edited by J. B. Sykes, the English lexicographer who also edited the sixth edition (1975) and has contributed to other Oxford dictionaries. The publisher notes that in preparing this edition, Sykes drew on the material assembled for the Supplement to THE OXFORD ENGLISH DICTIONARY. *The Concise Oxford Dictionary* thus bears the mark of authority that has made Oxford a major force in lexicography for many years.

III. Comprehensiveness

With 40,000 main entry words and 75,000 "vocabulary items" defined, *The Concise Oxford Dictionary* is a fairly comprehensive dictionary for its size. However, such comparable works as THE AMERICAN HERITAGE DESK DICTIONARY and CHAMBERS CONCISE 20TH CENTURY DICTIONARY contain more entries.

The Concise Oxford Dictionary does contain a great many words that are specifically British that one would not encounter in a typical American concise desk dictionary. Among entries that are designated as exclusively British are **beanfeast, champers, ha'p'orth, Hodge, ironmonger, linhay,** and **Purbeck stone.** Briticisms also abound among entries for abbreviations and acronyms. Page 148 alone contains **CBE** (Commander of the British Empire), **CBI** (Confederation of British Industry), **CC** (Companion of the Order of Canada, County Council, or Cricket Club), **CCF** (Combined Cadet Force), **C.Chem.** (chartered chemist), and **CEGB** (Central Electricity Generating Board), all designated as specifically English.

British spellings are given preference, but American alternates are noted. Moreover, *The Concise Oxford Dictionary* also systematically includes words and definitions that are specifically American, and designates these as such. For example, it includes **intermission** ("interval in theatre performance"), **intern** ("advanced student or recent graduate residing in hospital and acting as assistant physician or surgeon; teacher undergoing practical training"), **interstate, IRS,** and **Ivy League.** This enhances the dictionary's utility for American as well as for British users.

The dictionary's comprehensiveness is extended by including defined compounds, derivatives, and idioms within a main entry. The use of the swung dash (~) to stand for the main entry word in these instances saves a considerable amount of space, enabling *The Concise Oxford Dictionary* to include more vocabulary items than might otherwise be possible. For example, the entry **lion** provides definitions not only for this word on its own, but also includes the following: **~in the way** or **path, ~'s mouth, ~'s provider, ~'s share, ~ (-heart), ~hearted, ~hunter, the British L~, ~and unicorn, twist the ~'s tail,** and **L~s.**

IV. Quality and Currency of Entries

Main entry words are printed in boldface type, or in boldface italic if not yet naturalized in English. Alternative spellings are given in boldface immediately after the first entry word, which is the preferred spelling. Generally, the part of speech is the first item in the entry, and any irregular inflections are also noted. Usage and field labels are included where necessary. An abbreviated etymology is given at the end of the entry.

Definitions in *The Concise Oxford Dictionary* are usually arranged in the order in which the word is most commonly used today; such is also the case in THE POCKET OXFORD DICTIONARY, which is in part derived from this work. Note, however, that the most common meaning in Britain is not necessarily the most common meaning in the United States. Readers may sometimes have reason to doubt that the definitions are arranged by frequency of use rather than on historical principles; witness, for example, the first definition of **pen:**

> quill-feather with quill pointed and split in two, for writing with ink; similar instrument of steel, gold, etc., fitted into rod of wood, plastic, etc.

The British flavor of this dictionary is evident in numerous entry words and in many of the definitions. For example, the definition for **infield** reads:

> 1. farm land around or near homestead; arable land; land regularly manured and cropped. 2. (Cricket) part of the ground near the wicket, fieldsmen stationed there; (Baseball) area between the four bases, four fielders stationed on its boundaries.

The following typical entry shows how *The Concise Oxford Dictionary* discriminates between British and American spellings:

‖**ar′dour**, **ar′dor*, (*-er*) *n.* fierce heat; warm emotion; fervour, zeal, (*for*), [ME f. OF, f. L *ardor -oris* (*ardēre* burn; see -OR)]

Published in 1982, the current edition of *The Concise Oxford Dictionary* obviously does not include words of very modern vintage that have found their way into more recently revised dictionaries. Absent words include *AIDS*, *modem*, and *yuppie*. On the other hand, such words as **ayatollah**, **byte**, **cruise missile**, **hype**, **microchip**, and **sushi** are included. In short, *The Concise Oxford Dictionary* is not absolutely up to the minute but nonetheless does contain a fair smattering of words of the 1980s. By no means is this dictionary obsolete.

V. Syllabication and Pronunciation

Syllabication and pronunciation are indicated in the main entry word itself by means of word breaks, primary stress marks, and diacritical marks. Phonetic respellings are given in parentheses only when necessary, and then only to show that part of the pronunciation that would not be apparent from the original spelling. For example:

foo′tball (-awl)
gē′osphēre
prĭ′soner (-zn-)
probā′tion | **arў**

Note that this scheme does not indicate all word breaks. This omission will be a decided weakness for many American users.

There is a four-page section on pronunciation in the dictionary's introduction. Here the editor declares that "the pronunciation given in this dictionary is the standard one 'without any accent', associated especially with Southern England (sometimes called 'Received Pronunciation')." Thus, *The Concise Oxford Dictionary* provides little help to readers seeking guidance on how a word is pronounced in the United States. With that limitation in mind, however, it must be said that this dictionary will be helpful to anyone desiring guidance on "correct" English pronunciations. Moreover, the introduction contains extensive information on the pronunciation system. Fifty-nine different sounds are represented in the phonetic respelling key, listed with their IPA equivalents.

VI. Special Features

Like other dictionaries in the Oxford series, *The Concise Oxford Dictionary* seems to rely heavily upon abbreviations and symbols. While this may intimidate some readers and confuse others, these generally enable the dictionary to present a great deal of information in a relatively limited space. A complete list of the abbreviations and symbols used in the dictionary is located on the front and back endpapers.

Prominent among the special features is the identification of words and definitions that are uniquely British or American. Two parallel vertical lines precede British terms, while an asterisk precedes American ones.

The other special features are found in two appendixes. One contains tables of British and American weights and measures with their metric equivalents. The other appendix lists the Greek and Russian alphabets, with English transliteration.

VII. Accessibility

The Concise Oxford Dictionary includes a brief but handy table of contents. Boldface guide words at the top of each page indicate the first and last main entry words on that page. Readers will have to get used to the fact that idiomatic phrases, compounds, and derivatives are embedded within the main entries and, as noted previously, are not main entries themselves. In such instances, the use of the swung dash may also increase the difficulty of locating the desired expression. For example, the reader looking for *horse-chestnut* will have to search halfway through the long **horse** entry before finding it as ~**-chestnut**.

VIII. Graphics and Format

With a trim size of $5\frac{1}{4}'' \times 8\frac{1}{2}''$ and a thickness of $2''$, *The Concise Oxford Dictionary* fits conveniently into the desk dictionary category. The paper is thin but there is minimal show-through. The book is sturdily bound and includes the standard Oxford dictionaries dust jacket (dark blue with a red and green diagonal band).

Each page is divided into two columns. The interior and outer margins, as well as those at the top and bottom of the page, are narrow but sufficient, and the book will lie flat when opened.

Main entry words are in boldface type and overhang the text, making them easy to see. Compound words, variant forms, and idioms within the main entry are printed in semi-bold type, which is also easily distinguishable. Previous editions of *The Concise Oxford Dictionary* were printed in 10-point type; for this edition, 8-point type is used, which some readers will not find as easy to read. There are no illustrations.

IX. Summary

The Concise Oxford Dictionary is a desk-size dictionary and, as such, is the mainstay among all the single-volume dictionaries published by the Oxford University Press. It is generally authoritative, although no longer as up-to-date as one might wish. Perhaps its major strength is the way in which it distinguishes between British and American spellings and definitions, presenting both clearly and concisely. (Its pronunciations, on the other hand, are wholly British.) Ultimately, however, it will be preferred by the British rather than the American reader; only Americans with a special interest in British spellings, definitions, and pronunciations might want this as a concise desk dictionary. Such readers would be better served by purchasing the CHAMBERS CONCISE 20TH CENTURY DICTIONARY which has a greater number of entries (95,000) and a more current vocabulary.

The Doubleday Dictionary for Home, School, and Office

Facts at a Glance

Full Title: **The Doubleday Dictionary for Home, School, and Office**.
Publisher: Doubleday.
Editor: Sidney I. Landau, Editor-in-Chief.
Edition Reviewed: © 1975.

Number of Entries: 85,000.
Number of Pages: 906.
Number of Illustrations: 970 black-and-white line drawings, maps, tables, and charts.
Trim Size: 5⅜" × 8³⁄₁₆".
Binding: hardcover.

Price: $11.95: thumb-indexed, $12.95.
Sold in bookstores and other outlets; also sold to libraries and other educational institutions.
ISBN 0-385-04099-7;
ISBN 0-385-03368-0.

I. Introduction

The Doubleday Dictionary was designed as a general-purpose dictionary, compact in size but comparable "in coverage of the general vocabulary with much larger dictionaries," states the preface. With its 85,000 entries it fits somewhere in between concise dictionaries of about 55,000 entries and abridged works of 100,000 words and up. To achieve compactness, many obsolete and archaic terms have been excluded, etymologies have been condensed, and technical terms are included only when their meanings cannot be deduced from general definitions of words already appearing in the lexicon.

When first published in 1975, *The Doubleday Dictionary* claimed to be the only entirely new dictionary of its size, but other new dictionaries of a comparable

size soon appeared, including THE SCRIBNER-BANTAM ENGLISH DICTIONARY in 1977 and THE OXFORD AMERICAN DICTIONARY in 1980. As of April 1988, a revised edition of *The Doubleday Dictionary* had not been announced.

II. Authority

Doubleday & Company is a well-known publisher whose titles include several special-feature dictionaries (such as crossword puzzle dictionaries). Sidney I. Landau, editor in chief of *The Doubleday Dictionary*, is a prominent authority on dictionaries and editor of THE DOUBLEDAY ROGET'S THESAURUS and several Funk & Wagnalls dictionaries, including their STANDARD DESK DICTIONARY. He notes in the preface that the staff "had the use of an extensive citation file" of usage quotations.

The five distinguished members of the Dictionary Advisory Committee were Albert H. Marckwardt, its chairman, professor emeritus of English and linguistics, Princeton University; Harold B. Allen, professor emeritus of English and linguistics, University of Minnesota; S. I. Hayakawa, president emeritus, San Francisco State University; Rudolph C. Troike, former director of the Center for Applied Linguistics, Washington, D.C.; and H. Rex Wilson, associate professor of English (linguistics), University of Western Ontario. These scholars' names often appear on dictionaries incorporating Funk & Wagnalls lexicographical material.

III. Comprehensiveness

Because the stated original purpose of *The Doubleday Dictionary* was to provide general vocabulary coverage comparable to much larger dictionaries, the buyer needs to weigh this claim, as well as the relative comprehensiveness of this compact, midsize work, against the claims of other dictionaries of similar size and, now, more up-to-date vocabularies.

One technique used by the editors was to omit entries for technical terms that could be understood from component words. Terms such as **data processing** and **software**, however, are included because their technical meanings cannot be gleaned by combining the definitions of **data** with **processing** or of **soft** with **ware**. A random check of other words that an up-to-date dictionary of this size should include shows that **bit**, for example, and computer science meanings for **program** are included. Missing words include *ayatollah, baud, blue point* (a variety of oyster and of Siamese cat), and *byte*. Some definitions need additional meanings, such as **Orthodox**, which refers here only to the Eastern Orthodox Church.

A comparative check of more difficult and not commonly used words shows that *The Doubleday*

Dictionary compares well with others in its class. For example:

> **sternutation** . . . n. **1** The act of sneezing. . . .
>
> **osculate** . . . *v.t. & v.i.* **1** To kiss. . . .

Occasionally, *The Doubleday Dictionary* provides fuller coverage with more extensive examples. The following is an example, from assorted entries for **gob·ble·dy·gook**:

WEBSTER'S NINTH NEW COLLEGIATE DICTIONARY
n.[irreg. fr. *gobble, n.* (1944)]: wordy and generally unintelligible jargon

THE RANDOM HOUSE COLLEGE DICTIONARY
n. language characterized by circumlocution and jargon: *the gobbledygook of government reports* . . . [fanciful formation from GOBBLE[2]]

THE AMERICAN HERITAGE DICTIONARY: SECOND COLLEGE EDITION
n. unclear wordy jargon. [Coined by Maury Maverick (1895–1954).]

The Doubleday Dictionary
n. Informal Involved, pedantic, and pompous talk or writing. Also gob'·ble·de·gook[1]. *Gobbledygook* usually refers to wordiness, the unnecessary use of long words, and a stuffy style often encountered in bureaucratic memoranda. "The writer is disposed to regard as contrary to efficient office procedure the utilization of governmental communications apparatus to conduct nongovernmental business," for example, means "Don't use our phones to conduct your personal business."

Perhaps unfairly, many earlier reviews of the dictionary expressed reservations about its claims to comparison with larger works. For example, *Library Journal* (15 January 1975) wrote that "a random survey of their entries (not only in the text but also in the useful gazetteer and biographies sections) does support their claim that they have truly reexamined the language. . . . Definitions, however, are another matter: their efforts to cram much into little result in a terseness which defeats the major purpose of a dictionary. . . . Recommended for limited purposes." The *Wilson Library Bulletin* (April 1975) noted that "the 'how to use' material is well done, and there are brief sections on usage, punctuation, and Canadian English. Definitions are very brief."

IV. Quality and Currency of Entries

The vocabulary used in the definitions is appropriate for the general user. In general, the definitions are slightly fuller in *The Doubleday Dictionary* than in other compact dictionaries of a similar size.

The basic sequence of information is: main entry word; pronunciation; part of speech; inflected or alternative forms, or comparative forms of adjectives and adverbs; definitions (numbered and labeled when appropriate, or cross-referenced to a main entry variant spelling or synonym, as in "**barrel organ** HAND ORGAN"); etymologies; run-in derivatives; and occasional synonym lists appended to entries:

> **event** . . . **-Syn. 1** occurrence, happening, episode, incident.

Brief guidance on usage appears in definitions as illustrative phrases or prescriptive instruction:

> **who** . . . **1** Which or what person or persons: *Who* is she? . . . **3** That: used as a relative to introduce a clause: the man *who* mows our lawn.

No guidance appears at **whom**, unfortunately.

Meanings are ordered according to frequency of use, not semantic evolution, as in **sabotage**:

> *n.* **1** A wasting of materials or damage to machinery, tools, etc., by workmen to make management comply with their demands. **2** The destruction of bridges, railroads, supply depots, etc., either by enemy agents or by underground resisters. **3** Any deliberate effort to obstruct plans or aims.

The restrictive labels in this dictionary are useful and they indicate (a) usage: *Slang, Informal* (for colloquial use), and *Nonstand.* (for usage not accepted as standard by most native speakers of English); (b) localization: *Regional* for a particular U.S. region, *Brit.* (British), *Can.* (Canadian), *Austral.*, and occasionally *U.S.* when a meaning of a word differs from that understood in the larger English-speaking world. Fields and subjects, for example, *Med.* (medicine), *Ecol.* (ecology), and *Geom.* (geometry), are used. Language of origin, *French, German,* and *Latin*, is indicated for words often italicized in writing that have not been Anglicized: for example, **Weltschmerz** [G, lit., world pain], **par excellence** [F, lit., by way of excellence].

In a selected segment of entries, **paprika** to **parachute**, the Doubleday and Scribner-Bantam dictionaries each contain 11 entries, with some minor differences. The Doubleday work uses **Pap smear**; Scribner-Bantam, **Pap test**. The Scribner-Bantam includes geographic entries, such as **Papua New Guinea**, while the Doubleday lists geographic terms in a separate alphabetical appendix.

THE SCRIBNER-BANTAM ENGLISH DICTIONARY includes **papule**; *The Doubleday Dictionary* does not, but it adds the abbreviation **par.**, defined, and the combining form **para-**[2], defined separately from the prefix form entered as **para-**[1]. Etymologies for both are included selectively, for example, in the Scribner-Bantam work, **para-** [Gk = besides]; in Doubleday, **para**[1] [Gk, *para* besides] and **para**[2] [<Ital. *parare*

defend]. The Doubleday etymologies, although brief, include the source word as well as the language.

The following comparisons of the definitions for **helix** will give the reader a sense of the style and fullness of the Doubleday work:

The Doubleday Dictionary
　1 *Geom.* A curve lying on the surface of a cone or cylinder and cutting each element at a constant angle greater than 0° and less than 90°. **2** Any spiral. **3** *Anat.* The spiral cartilage of the external ear. **4** *Archit.* A small volute.

THE AMERICAN HERITAGE DICTIONARY: SECOND COLLEGE EDITION
　1 *Math.* A three-dimensional curve that lies on a cylinder or cone and cuts the elements at a constant angle. **2.** A spiral form or structure. **3.** *Anat.* The folded rim of skin and cartilage around the outer ear. **4.** *Archit.* A volute on a Corinthian or Ionic capital.

OXFORD AMERICAN DICTIONARY
　a spiral with a diminishing circumference (like a corkscrew) or a constant circumference (like a watch spring).

THE SCRIBNER-BANTAM DICTIONARY
　Anything in the shape of the thread of a screw or a spiral.

V. Syllabication and Pronunciation

Syllables are indicated by centered dots to show where words may be hyphenated at the end of a line: **pa·trol**. In general, words in phrases or in special terms are not syllabicated if the words appear separately in the vocabulary as main entries: **patrol wagon**. Exceptions, however, do occur; *rheumatoid* is not a separate syllabicated entry, nor is it divided in **rheumatoid arthritis**. A reader will have to judge its correct syllabication from **rheu·ma·tic** and similar entries.

A "Pronunciation Key" appears on the right-hand front endpaper and following the preface. The pronunciations use the letters of the alphabet and the more familiar diacritical marks for vowels (â, ä, ē, ī, ō, ô, o͝o, o͞o, û, yo͞o), plus th for *th*is, a superscript ʰ (whale ʰwāl) and superscript ʸ (**due** dʸo͞o), and the schwa (ə) for the five unstressed vowel sounds in *a*bove, sick*e*n, clar*i*ty, mel*o*n, and foc*u*s. There are brief but useful instructions on pronouncing six foreign sounds frequently encountered in English: à *ami*, oe *peu* or *schön*, ü *vue* or *grün*, kh *ach* or *loch*, ṅ indicating a preceding nasal sound, and ' a voiceless *l* or *r* as in the French *débâcle* (dā·bä′kl') or a consonant *y* pronounced as a separate syllable with a slight schwa sound following, as the French *fille* (fē′ʸ). A handy, brief reference chart of vowel signs appears at the bottom of each right-hand page in the book. This chart also explains the signs < derived from ; ? origin uncertain or unknown.

VI. Special Features

The introductory material includes two essays and an article on punctuation that are regularly reprinted in other dictionaries derived from *The Doubleday Dictionary* and from former Funk & Wagnalls dictionaries now published by J. G. Ferguson, formerly a part of the Doubleday publishing operation.

Professor Marckwardt's interesting and informative opening essay on usage appears in several other works that incorporate *Doubleday Dictionary* entries, including the WEBSTER ILLUSTRATED CONTEMPORARY DICTIONARY and the WEBSTER COMPREHENSIVE DICTIONARY (international and encyclopedic editions). His useful analysis of some of the well-known objections to the use of *hopefully* is also included. The article on punctuation by Professor Allen and that on Canadian English by Professor Wilson also appear in the dictionaries cited above (see reviews of them in this book for further description).

Other special features are the separate gazetteer, which includes all U.S. and Canadian towns and cities with a population over 15,000, and a list of post office ZIP codes. As would be expected in a book with a 1975 copyright date, American population and world population figures are not current, and some country names are not up-to-date. Most readers would be better served by a current reference tool for this information.

VII. Accessibility

All main words, including abbreviations, appear in strict letter-by-letter alphabetical order. The lower-case form of a word usually precedes the capitalized form, but abbreviations show the most common form first. In the following representative sequence of main entries, note the two entries for **loyalist** and for **Ltd.**, for example:

> **loy·al·ist, Loy·al·ist, loy·al·ty, loz·enge, LP, Lr, L.s.c., LSD, £.s.d., Lt., l.t., l.tn., Ltd., ltd., Lu, lub·ber.**

Main entry words are printed in bold type overhanging the text. Within entries, inflected and alternative forms of words, idioms, and run-in derivations appear in smaller bold type. Two boldface guide words appear at the top of each page with a centered page number.

A contents page lists the features including the appendix of measures and weights, which is also reprinted on the back endpapers, the alphabetical gazetteer and the separate biographies, as well as the special essays on language by the chairman and two advisory committee members, the pronunciation key, and a half-page note on the "Formation of Plurals and Participles." Preceding the "Guide to the Dictionary" is a page containing a sample column of text with exceptionally clear call-out labels that point to the special terms used in the guide's eighteen numbered sections. The instructions, running little more than two pages, are clear; their brevity certainly makes them accessible to many readers. The examples given in the guide are short but sufficient. A "List of Abbreviations and Symbols Used in This Dictionary" precedes the main word list vocabulary and is also printed along with the pronunciation key on the front endpapers.

An edition with thumb-index tabs is available; there are no index tabs to the gazetteer or biographical sections.

VIII. Graphics and Format

The dictionary includes 970 black-and-white line illustrations, including tables, charts, and some 50 locator maps within the 863-page main vocabulary. The maps range in size from $\frac{3}{4}'' \times \frac{3}{4}''$ to $3\frac{1}{4}'' \times 4\frac{1}{2}''$. In general, the pictures are well selected to illustrate less familiar terms or meanings. For example, "ac·co·lade . . . 2 *Archit.* A curved ornamental molding" is accompanied by a clear drawing. Pictures are labeled with a cross-reference to a numbered meaning (*def.* 2) or to a numbered homograph (spats[4]). Cross-references to pictures are preceded by centered dots.

Fal·lo·pi·an tube. . . . • See OVARY.

Mathematics, anatomy, and mechanical diagrams are especially clear, and many have useful labels (**airplane** has 16, for example). A generous proportion of drawings illustrate several varieties of a term: there are three kinds of **adze** shown and three different **acorns**. Smaller, explanatory drawings of the **date line**, **meridians**, and a **Mercator projection** will be useful to many readers.

The tables and charts, which are useful but not always up-to-date, include the Braille alphabet, a chess game in progress, constellations, chemical elements, geologic time scale, comparative grades in the United States Armed Services, the Jewish calendar, phases of the moon, and the teeth of an adult human, as well as a periodic table of elements, a table of planets, proofreader's marks, a temperature conversion table, and signs of the zodiac. (More description of these appears in the section *Graphics and Format* in the review of the WEBSTER COMPREHENSIVE DICTIONARY.)

The general typography in *The Doubleday Dictionary*'s two-column text is clear and pleasantly free of distracting gimmicks. The margins are adequate, and there is sufficient white space between lines of text, although the print is *very small*. Most earlier reviews commented on the text size unfavorably; buyers will want to consider this factor.

The ivory paper is sturdy and the pages lie flat when the dictionary is opened, but in the copy examined by this Buying Guide's reviewers, some signatures separated from the spine's reinforcement. Although the dictionary is hardbound in gold and black simulated leather paper, the meager reinforcement at the spine, despite its top headband, will not withstand even moderate library use without rebinding. The rounding of the spine allows too flexible a gap; hence the dictionary's bottom and top spine edges develop noticeable fraying and some cracks after even a few sessions of use. If the dictionary is for the home, buyers will want to consider how much use it will need to sustain.

IX. Summary

The Doubleday Dictionary faces strong competition from dictionaries with a more up-to-date vocabulary, especially in scientific and technical terms. There are many readers, however, who do not require the level of scientific and technical definition, written in special terminology by specialist definers, that appears increasingly frequently in larger, newer dictionaries. Many dictionary users will find the size of *The Doubleday Dictionary*'s general vocabulary more satisfactory than those of many smaller desk dictionaries. Moreover, the writing style of the definitions and the less complex lexicographic apparatus make this dictionary accessible. These factors make this a suitable candidate for the home and office, though readers will want to examine the page carefully to judge whether or not the type size is readable.

Librarians will probably want to turn to one of the larger, newer dictionaries, such as the AMERICAN HERITAGE DICTIONARY: SECOND COLLEGE EDITION or WEBSTER'S NINTH NEW COLLEGIATE DICTIONARY.

An English-Reader's Dictionary

Facts at a Glance

Full Title: **An English-Reader's Dictionary: Second Edition, Revised and Enlarged.**
Publisher: Oxford University Press.
Compilers: A. S. Hornby and E. C. Parnwell.
Edition Reviewed: © 1969; 1985 printing.

Number of Entries: 25,000.
Number of Pages: 632.
Trim Size: $3\frac{7}{8}'' \times 6\frac{1}{2}''$.
Binding: paperback.

Price: $5.95.
Sold in bookstores; also sold to libraries and other educational institutions.
ISBN 0-19-431116-3.

I. Introduction

An English-Reader's Dictionary is for a very special group of learners, those who do not have an adequate bilingual dictionary to help them learn English. Readers will also be students who have completed an elementary course in English and can read books written in everyday language, write straightforward compositions, and speak English in a natural conversation.

An English-Reader's Dictionary, with only 25,000 vocabulary entries, is for home use and has been compiled with the needs of ESL students in mind. There are 15,000 example phrases and sentences and practical explanations in plain English.

II. Authority

Oxford is a reliable publisher, and the two compilers are respected lexicographers. A. S. Hornby was chief compiler of the OXFORD ADVANCED LEARNER'S DICTIONARY OF CURRENT ENGLISH, on which this is based.

III. Comprehensiveness

The definitions are concise and stated in simple terms with particular attention to the use of structural words such as *for*, which also receives examples. Sometimes an American English usage is referred to the British use, such as **elevator** = **lift**, but this is not consistent throughout. The American term **trunk** is not equated with the British term **boot**, nor is **apartment** cross-referenced to **flat**.

Following the stated purpose, there are no etymologies, quotations, usage notes, or synonyms. These features would not be helpful for the intended reader.

IV. Quality and Currency of Entries

An English-Reader's Dictionary was last revised in 1973 so that its currency is of the early 1970s. Examples of some commonly used current words found in the *ERD* are **computer**, **radar**, and **spaceship**. Missing are words such as *Cold War*, *memory* (in a computer), and *Third World*, although **Old World** and **New World** are defined.

V. Syllabication and Pronunciation

This dictionary uses the IPA phonetic transcription. The main entry words are syllabified with dots. The key to pronunciation is given in the "Notes" section in the frontmatter.

VI. Special Features

With the exception of "Common Prefixes and Suffixes" and "Irregular Verbs," the special features appended to the dictionary are not especially useful. "Abbreviations" is far too short—there is no *ibid*, no *CEO*, no *GI*, no *ICBM*—abbreviations which native users may take for granted but are a stumbling block to the ESL student. "Geographical Names" is an incomplete list of countries with their pronunciations (for example, where are Kampuchea and Namibia?). Associated adjectives and the country's languages would have rendered the list more useful.

VII. Accessibility

Main entry words are in boldface type and overhang the text. The definitions are numbered in boldface type. Entries are arranged alphabetically, letter-by-letter. Italics are used for the example sentences. There is no table of contents; however, the small size of this dictionary makes it easy to use without this feature.

VIII. Graphics and Format

Well-done line drawings are used to illustrate some definitions. They are properly placed next to the definitions being illustrated. The margins are adequate for such a small book and the typeface, while small, is readable. The paper is an ivory newsprint quality with no show-through of the text.

The book lies flat when used, but it is not suitable for rebinding. Perhaps because the publishers wished to keep the cost of the dictionary within the reach of all students, the graphic design of the book is rather unattractive.

IX. Summary

For a foreign student learning English, this seems a serviceable dictionary. Although this paperback is suitable as a student's personal copy, it is not for school and library collections. They would be better served by the OXFORD ADVANCED LEARNER'S DICTIONARY OF CURRENT ENGLISH which, coincidentally, can also be a step upward for the more advanced learner.

Everyday American English Dictionary

Facts at a Glance

Full Title: **Everyday American English Dictionary**.
Publisher: National Textbook Company.
Editors: Richard A. Spears, Linda Schinke-Llano, Betty Kirkpatrick.
Edition Reviewed: © 1984; 1987 printing.

Number of Entries: 5,500.
Number of Pages: 400.

Everyday American English Dictionary

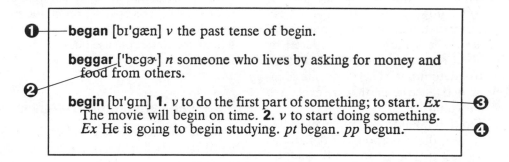

① Irregular forms receive separate entries referring readers to the main entry

② Pronunciation is indicated by the International Phonetic Alphabet (IPA)

③ Examples of usage are introduced by the italic abbreviation *Ex*

④ Principal parts of verbs are spelled out, in roman type, at the end of the definition

---

Trim Size: 5¼" × 7½".
Binding: hardbound; paperback.

Price: $7.95 (hardbound); $4.95 (paper).
Sold in bookstores and other outlets; also sold to libraries and other educational institutions.
ISBN 0-8325-0335-5 (hardbound);
ISBN 0-8325-0337-1 (paper).

I. Introduction

The preface to the *Everyday American English Dictionary*, described as "A Basic Dictionary for English Language Learning" on the cover and published in 1984, states that the work is intended to serve as either a portable dictionary or an educational text for use by students of English as a Second Language. According to the publishers, it will aid students in learning to speak and write English well and will also teach "the basic methods of finding dictionary information with ease and confidence." However, the selection of entries, the notes to the instructor, and the accompanying workbook all suggest that the primary use of the work will be in connection with *formal* ESL instruction.

There are 5,500 dictionary entries, geared to the vocabulary level at which second-language students can begin to read works in English independently. The work focuses on the language associated with daily living experience and provides basic "survival word lists."

II. Authority

The dictionary is published by the National Textbook Company, which has gained recognition as a pub- lisher of books for ESL programs. The work is partially based on *Chambers First Learners' Dictionary*, published by the British firm of W. & R. Chambers. Richard A. Spears, the editor, is an associate professor of linguistics at Northwestern University and a specialist in lexicography, ESL, American culture, and several areas of linguistics. The associate editor and primary writer of the companion workbook is Linda Schinke-Llano, a lecturer in linguistics at Northwestern University and an ESL specialist. Betty Kirkpatrick, editorial director and dictionaries editor at Chambers, served as a consulting editor on the work.

III. Comprehensiveness

The scope of the work is purposely limited to words that the beginning and intermediate ESL student is likely to encounter in everyday life. However, the word list more closely reflects the vocabulary of ESL texts at this level than the spoken or written vocabulary the student may actually need. For example, although **cash** and **charge** both appear in the word list, there is nothing in these entries that will enable the student to make sense of the common question "Cash or charge?" Idioms are also excluded. While these omissions will not undercut the dictionary's value as a classroom text, they do limit its usefulness as a portable dictionary for independent use by the nonnative English speaker.

IV. Quality and Currency of Entries

Typical entries include the entry word in boldface, a pronunciation guide in brackets, an italicized part-of-speech abbreviation, and the definition(s). When more than one meaning of a word is given, boldface numerals precede each definition, and the part-of-speech designation follows each numeral. In about 10 percent of the entries, an illustrative sentence follows the definition. The sentence is introduced by the signal *Ex.* For irregular verbs, inflected forms are given after the definitions. The forms are identified with abbreviated tense labels that are explained in the front of the volume.

Although the book is intended for use in everyday situations as well as in the classroom, its definitions are not well designed to teach "survival" English. For example, a "survival" definition of **egg** would be "something that one buys, cooks, or eats"; this work defines **egg** as

> an oval object with a thin shell which holds a baby bird, fish, or reptile.

Similarly, the higher-level word **summon** would first be encountered in daily living in its inflected form *summons.* In this dictionary, only **summon** is included; it is defined as

> to send for someone.

The definitions are written with a controlled vocabulary, and terms used in the definitions are given their own main entries. However, in some cases the student looking up a secondary word will be baffled by an inadequate definition. For example, **pasta** is defined as

> foods made from flour paste, such as macaroni, spaghetti, lasagne, and ravioli.

The student seeking a definition of the word **paste**, used in this entry, will find the unhelpful phrase:

> a thick white glue used to stick paper and other things together.

When more than one definition is given for a word, the dictionary appears to follow the pattern of adult native language dictionaries that list definitions in order of historical use rather than in order of frequency of use. **Patch**, for example, is defined first as

> a small piece of ground.

The sense of a cloth patch for clothing follows, and the verb form is defined last. **Patter**, in itself a questionable choice for inclusion, is defined first as

> to tap lightly and quickly

and then as

> the sound of light tapping.

ESL students and new speakers of English would be better served by an ordering based on frequency.

An ESL dictionary is not expected to adhere to the standards of currency usual in a dictionary for native speakers. However, this dictionary's failure to cover some common conversational applications of words, as well as specific idiomatic usage, limits its usefulness. Overall, the work's entries render it adequate for classroom use but not for independent use in everyday life.

V. Syllabication and Pronunciation

Syllable breaks are not shown in either the entry word or the phonetic respelling provided as a pronunciation guide. Although stress marks indicate stressed syllables, the absence of full syllabication is a serious drawback, especially in a work designed to help its readers speak English correctly.

The dictionary uses International Phonetic Alphabet (IPA) phonetic transcriptions to indicate pronunciation. Standard American English pronunciations are given, and no variants are provided. A full pronunciation guide appears in the introductory section of the volume. This guide lists sample words showing the various ways each sound may be spelled. Exercises in the companion workbook will also help the student learn correct pronunciation. There are no abbreviated pronunciation keys within the word list, an omission that—like the absence of syllabication—will prove inconvenient to the reader.

VI. Special Features

The volume's introduction addressed "To the User" provides keys to abbreviations and to pronunciation. A section addressed "To the Instructor" explains the work's organization, selection of entries, and pronunciation system. It also provides a table of irregular verbs, with their past tenses and past participles.

An appendix at the back of the book lists U.S. states with their postal abbreviations, capitals, and largest cities. U.S. presidents through Ronald Reagan are listed, with their dates in office. There are also listings of U.S. national holidays (excluding Martin Luther King, Jr., Day and Presidents' Day), cardinal and ordinal numbers, and common fractions. Also included in the appendix is a map of the United States, showing states and capitals. Large secondary cities are shown, as are surrounding bodies of water and neighboring countries.

The 40-page companion workbook gives a series of lessons and exercises that can be used for building vocabulary, as well as for practice in using the dictionary. Topics covered include alphabetizing, pronunciation, parts of speech, irregular plurals, verb forms, synonyms and antonyms, and others. Well-designed practice exercises in each section require students to use the dictionary to locate correct answers. A number of the exercises valuably require students to write full-sentence answers. The workbook significantly enhances the dictionary's value as a text for formal ESL instruction.

VII. Accessibility

Two large, boldface guide words appear on each spread, indicating the first and last words entered on the spread. A ruled line sets off the guide words, along with the page number, at the top of the page, so page numbers are easy to spot. This is important because the workbook often refers to page numbers.

Within the entry, neither entry words recurring in illustrative sentences nor inflected forms are italicized or boldfaced: the reader will therefore find these difficult to distinguish from other parts of the entry. Another confusing feature is the absence of periods after abbreviations. Nonnative speakers might naturally attach an *n*, *v*, or *Ex* to the beginning of an unfamiliar word.

Because no table of contents is provided, the volume's appended special features may be overlooked.

VIII. Graphics and Format

The dictionary is very readable, with only one column of type on each page. Main entry words appear in boldface overhanging the text. Both the dictionary and the workbook are paperbound, with heavily varnished and colorful covers. The paper is off-white, with no distracting show-through. The typeface in both books is larger than usual for books of this genre, and the layout of each page is inviting and easy to read. Refreshingly, the answer lines provided in the workbook are long enough and separated with enough leading for the student to write in the answer easily.

IX. Summary

Despite the claims of the publisher, the *Everyday American English Dictionary* is not well designed to be used independently by non-English speakers in everyday situations, and its use would be best limited to ESL classrooms. There the perplexities caused by difficult definitions and differences in the senses of words could be explained by the teacher; and the deficiencies of the book—incomplete definitions, lack of syllabication, and so on—could be compensated for and its easy-to-read reference format put to good use.

The dictionary and workbook would also be suitable for native speakers who need basic or remedial classes and would benefit from learning dictionary skills and doing workbook exercises. Therefore, libraries and adult schools serving ESL and remedial student populations will want to consider this work.

The Facts on File Visual Dictionary

Facts at a Glance

Full Title: **The Facts on File Visual Dictionary**.
Publisher: Facts on File Publications.
Editor: Jean-Claude Corbeil, Editor in Chief.
Graphics Staff: Sylvie Lévesque, Francine Giroux, and Emmanuelle Rousseau.
Edition Reviewed: © 1986.

Number of Entries: 25,000.
Number of Pages: 797.
Number of Illustrations: 3,000 black-and-white drawings.
Number of Indexes: 3.
Trim Size: 7⅛" × 9".
Binding: Laminated paper over boards.

Price: $29.95.
Intended Readership: General adult, educators, and students.
Sold in bookstores and other outlets; also sold to libraries and other educational institutions.
ISBN 0-8160-1544-9.

I. Introduction

The Facts on File Visual Dictionary, according to its preface, "is the first basic dictionary of terminological orientation, comprising within a single volume . . . thousands of more or less technical terms" and providing a "reliable modern terminology" for the objects, devices, machines, and tools of daily life—in a visual format. The purpose of the *Visual Dictionary,* according to Jean-Claude Corbeil, the editor, is to graphically "portray the many elements of everyday life in an industrial, post-industrial or developing society . . . which one needs to know to buy an object, discuss a repair, read a book or a newspaper, etc." The 25,000 terms and concepts, illustrated by 3,000 technical drawings, are arranged within 28 thematic chapters.

Since all the terms and ideas selected can be graphically presented, no abstract words, adjectives, adverbs, or nouns are included.

The *Visual Dictionary* is intended for "the active member of the modern industrial society who needs to be acquainted with a wide range of technical terms from many assorted areas, but not to be specialist in any."

According to the introductory section, some 4,000 to 5,000 references were used in researching and documenting the dictionary, including a variety of dictionaries, encyclopedias, catalogs, and technical documents. Jean-Claude Corbeil, the editor in chief, is a linguistic specialist. He and his team of Canadian "terminologists" and graphic artists designed this

The Facts on File Visual Dictionary   **VEGETABLE KINGDOM**   ❸

mushrooms

structure of a mushroom

cap ———————   ——————— scale

                                                                            ❹

gill ———————   ——————— spores

ring ———————   ——————— stem

❶

volva ———————

mycelium ———————

hypha ———————

                                                    poisonous mushroom

                                                         fly amanita

edible mushrooms

                        truffle   delicious lactarius

green russula

edible gyromitra   **deadly mushroom**

❷

                                                    cep

oyster mushroom

                                              amanita virosa

chanterelle   morel   cultivated mushroom

65

Reprinted by permission of Editions Québec/Amerique Inc.

❶ Visual definition of term   ❸ Subject heading
❷ Examples of different varieties   ❹ Identification of parts

unique reference work following the methodology of systematic and comparative bilingual (French/English) terminological research developed in Quebec in the 1970s. The book was first published in Canada. American English, based on various Merriam-Webster dictionaries and on the 1983 unabridged RANDOM HOUSE DICTIONARY OF THE ENGLISH LANGUAGE, has been used throughout the dictionary.

II. Format

The *Visual Dictionary* is divided into three sections:

- An extensive table of contents, listing all the chapters divided by subcategories. For example:

  SPORTS
      Team Games
          Baseball
              Field, catcher, player, bat, glove
          Football
              Playing field . . . , scrimmage . . .
              uniform . . .
          Rugby
              Field, team, ball
          Soccer
              Field, ball. . . .
      Water Sports . . .

- Illustrations depicting the entries
- Three alphabetical indexes (general, thematic, and specialized), which provide three different ways to access the text.

In a series of wide-ranging sections, including **ASTRONOMY, GEOGRAPHY, VEGETABLE KINGDOM, ANIMAL KINGDOM, FOOD, HOUSE, CLOTHING, MUSIC, SPORTS, WEAPONS,** and **SYMBOLS,** black-and-white drawings illustrate various terms and "notions."

Each section, for example, **SPORTS**, is introduced by a title page. The pages following are headed with large boldface guide words repeating the section title or a category within it. For example, under **SPORTS**, the headings are **Team Games, Water Sports, Winter Sports,** and so forth. On each page in the section, the subject of the category is presented graphically under a somewhat smaller boldface heading. For example, under **Team Sports: Baseball,** a schematic of a baseball playing field is drawn with each player's position indicated and labeled. Other categories show much more detailed drawings of humans, plants, animals, or objects, with labels for every part shown. Under **Leisure Sports: Mountaineering,** there is a human figure outfitted with, among other things, helmet, helmet lamp, snow goggles, rucksack, rope, and hammer. In another section, **DO-IT-YOURSELF,** pages of drawings show tools for carpentry, plumbing, painting, and so forth, with labels providing the name of each tool and its parts.

The general and category indexes are each arranged in four alphabetical columns with page references; italics indicate an illustration, and bold type designates a chapter heading. The general index includes all of the terms in the *Visual Dictionary* in alphabetical order. The thematic indexes list the words and terms alphabetically by sections (e.g., **Architecture, Communications, Health, House, Transporta-**

tion, **Weapons**). The specialized indexes place all of the elements or objects depicted on each page within subcategories such as **Athletics, Automobile, Domestic Appliances, Electricity, Men's Clothing, Microcomputer, Skiing.** For example, under **Microcomputer**, 87 concepts and terms related to microcomputers are listed, including **cursor, light pen, joystick, peripherals, input, ROM,** and **computer room**. Where terminological variation exists (that is, where different words are used for one idea), the most frequently used or best-known terms have been selected.

III. Quality and Currency of Entries

Published in 1986, the *Visual Dictionary* is very up-to-date. In the section **HOUSE FURNITURE**, illustrations include an automatic drip coffee maker, a food processor, and a microwave oven. In the **COMMUNICATIONS** section, the items depicted include a disc camera, a VCR, a video camera, a telephone-answering machine, and telecommunication satellites. Microcomputer systems are shown under **OFFICE SUPPLIES**. The category **ENERGY** includes graphic representations of various contemporary energy sources, including wind, solar, and nuclear power.

The illustrations are presented from a modern-day perspective (especially clothing, cars, and personal articles) and are simple, accurate, and conceptually clear. Technical graphics were selected because "they stress the essential features of a notion and leave out the accessories."

IV. Accessibility

The *Visual Dictionary* is easy to use in several different ways. Most readers will find that browsing through its intriguing pages will expand one's vocabulary. Basically, however, the *Visual Dictionary* is the book to consult to find out what something is called. Starting with an image in mind, the user would search out the probable appropriate theme in the table of contents and find the reference to an illustration. Turning to that illustration, he or she would find the word. If the user had a word and wanted to know what it looked like or in what category or categories it belonged, he or she would look up the word in one of the indexes and find a reference to the illustrations for the word.

The organization of this dictionary, therefore, allows users to look up an image to find its name or to determine the nature or function of an object in an appropriate context.

Occasionally, there is some confusion in the placement of words or in the illustrations. Some words do not appear where they would be expected: there are no fruits or vegetables listed under **Food**; they are listed in the general index under **Vegetable Kingdom**. A roulette table and a slot machine seem odd choices to include under **Parlor Games**. There are no cross-references between sections. But these are minor quibbles and will not lessen this work's usefulness.

V. Summary

Highly recommended by the *Book Report* (February 1987) and *Library Journal* (December 1986), the *Facts on File Visual Dictionary* was also named an "Outstanding Reference Source of 1986" by the American Library Association (RSAD) and a "1986 Reference Book to Remember" by the New York Public Library (*Adult and Reference Sources*). It is a unique reference source for public libraries or for college and even high school libraries. Especially useful for foreign students needing to find the English terms for an object, it is also an excellent resource for educators, and—as the publisher states—for "curious minds of all ages." The *Facts on File Visual Dictionary* will be a valuable addition to any reference collection.

tion on geographical entries (including population figures based on the 1970 census) as well as pages of weights and measures, special signs and symbols, and abbreviations used within the dictionary. These pages do not appear in the paperback edition. On the other hand, while the paperback edition contains a lengthy table of words beginning with the prefix **non**, this does not appear in the hardcover edition. The omission of this table in the hardcover edition occurs, perhaps, from the need to reorganize some pages in order to create two volumes out of one. The parent volume, in this case, was the paperback edition from which the hardcover edition was photographed. Only the front matter has been reset.

The hardcover edition has a sturdy, attractive binding with gold lettering, but the paper is rougher, and the type and page sizes have been reduced a little too much, giving the work a rather cramped look.

For a full evaluation of the content, see the review of the Harper & Row edition of FUNK & WAGNALLS STANDARD DESK DICTIONARY in this guide.

Funk & Wagnalls Standard Desk Dictionary (cloth)

Facts at a Glance

Full Title: **Funk & Wagnalls Standard Desk Dictionary**.
Publisher: Funk & Wagnalls.
Editor: Sidney I. Landau, Editor-in-Chief.
Edition Reviewed: © 1984.

Number of Entries: over 100,000.
Number of Pages: 862; 2 volumes.
Number of Illustrations: 262 black-and-white drawings.
Trim Size: 6¼″ × 8⅞″.
Binding: cloth.

Price: Copies gratis with the purchase of Volumes 2 and 3 of FUNK & WAGNALLS NEW ENCYCLOPEDIA.
Available only in supermarkets as premium for buying NEW ENCYCLOPEDIA.

I. Introduction and Scope

This two-volume edition of the *Funk & Wagnalls Standard Desk Dictionary* has, with a few minor differences, the same contents as FUNK & WAGNALLS STANDARD DESK DICTIONARY published in one volume in paperback by Harper & Row. In the front matter, the hardcover edition has added a brief sec-

Funk & Wagnalls Standard Desk Dictionary (paperback)

Facts at a Glance

Full Title: **Funk & Wagnalls Standard Desk Dictionary**.
Publisher: Harper & Row.
Editor: Sidney I. Landau, Editor-in-Chief.
Edition Reviewed: © 1984.

Number of Entries: over 100,000.
Number of Pages: 880.
Number of Illustrations: 262 black-and-white drawings.
Trim Size: 7¼″ × 9¼″.
Binding: paperback.

Price: $8.95.
Sold in bookstores and other outlets; also sold by direct mail and to libraries and other educational institutions.
ISBN 0-06-091142-5.

I. Introduction

Based on the considerably larger *Funk & Wagnalls Standard College Dictionary* (now out of print), this paperback edition of the *Funk & Wagnalls Standard Desk Dictionary* was designed, according to the editors, to provide "an up-to-date survey of the English language . . . including many scientific and technical

Funk & Wagnalls Standard Desk Dictionary
(cloth)

❶ Syllabication of main entries is indicated by centered dots

❷ Inflected forms are listed when spelling is irregular

❸ Idiomatic expressions are set in small boldface letters and preceded by a dash

❹ Usage labels are italicized

❺ Synonyms are introduced by the boldface abbreviation *Syn.* and are numbered to correspond with the relevant definitions

❻ Homographs appear as separate, numbered entries

❼ Cross-references appear in small capitals

❽ Field labels are italicized

❾ Derivatives are set in small boldface type, preceded by a dash, and are syllabicated and stressed

❿ Etymologies appear in brackets at the end of each entry

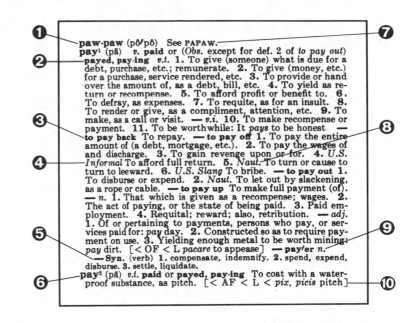

terms seldom found in dictionaries of comparable size." This desk edition contains over 100,000 entries, occasional black-and-white illustrations, selected idioms and figurative expressions (including common slang terms and meanings), usage notes, etymologies, and synonym and antonym analyses.

Among the supplementary material appended to the main vocabulary are a glossary of "Common Computer Terms"; "A Pronouncing Gazetteer" that lists such geographic features as the states and major cities of the United States, the countries and major cities of the world, other political divisions of the world, population figures, and general locations; a biographical section; an extensive list of abbreviations and acronyms; and a "Secretarial Handbook" that includes basic rules of grammar and syntax, and quick-reference material for business correspondence. Funk & Wagnalls publishes a hardcover edition of this work which is also reviewed herein.

II. Authority

The respected American lexicographer Sidney I. Landau, who edited the WEBSTER COMPREHENSIVE DICTIONARY and WEBSTER ILLUSTRATED CONTEMPORARY DICTIONARY, served as editor-in-chief of this work. Although it is published by Harper & Row,

this dictionary has a recognizable relation to other Funk & Wagnalls works and represents the efforts of an advisory staff of distinguished linguistic scholars, notably Albert H. Marckwardt, Professor of English and Linguistics, Princeton University.

III. Comprehensiveness

The word list in the *Funk & Wagnalls Standard Desk Dictionary* reflects the vocabulary found in most general reading. The work has a 1984 copyright date, but does not include many technical, scientific, and media-generated words or meanings that have passed into general usage by the mid-1980s, including *biofeedback*, *bioenergetics*, *grid lock*, *palimony*, *workaholic*, and *zero-based*. However, such terms as **biorhythm**; **Dolby**; **downer**; **gay**, as the word relates to homosexuality; **meltdown**; plus a generous amount of computer terms (**floppy disk**, **modem**, **down load**, **mouse**, and **bubble memory**) are included.

Biographical and geographic entries also reflect the 1984 copyright date; such names as *Chernobyl*, *Deng Xiaoping*, and *Gorbachev* are not included. In general, the biographical and geographic entries are brief and in the format usually associated with almanac and atlas entries. Readers can use these only for checking an unfamiliar name or for quick checks on pronunciation, spelling, and location. The entry for **Renoir**, for example, cites the dates of his birth and death, his nationality, and his broad topic area: "1840–1919, Fr. Impressionist painter." The entry for **Seine** merely states, "river, NE France; 482 mi. long."

IV. Quality and Currency of Entries

Definitions are concise and occasionally supplemented by synonym and antonym analyses in paragraph format.

Multiple definitions are listed with the most commonly used meaning first. Consider the following entry example:

> **au·then·tic** (ò·then′tik) *adj.* **1.** Authoritative; reliable. **2.** Of undisputed origin; genuine. **3.** *Law* Duly executed before the proper officer. Also **au·then′ti·cal**. [< OF < L < Gk. < *authentēs* the doer of the deed] —**au·then′ti·ca·ly** *adv.*
>   —**Syn. 1.** true, veritable. **2.** real, legitimate, authorized, accredited. —**Ant.** spurious, counterfeit, fictitious, false.

Note that a semicolon divides subtle senses within a particular meaning ("Authoritative; reliable").

Although space limitations will always be the bane of abridged dictionaries, the abridgment process does not have to mean that comprehensive definitions and concrete meaning must be sacrificed, as is often the case here. Users may be disappointed with the greatly telescoped definitions in the *Standard Desk Dictionary*—particularly when one considers the large format of this dictionary. Certainly readers will tend to expect to find more extensive definitions than those found in most of the smaller standard paperback dictionaries.

Another limiting feature of this dictionary is the lack of verbal illustration to help clarify the subtle shades of meaning among the various definitions. For instance, consider the meanings for the entry **cough**: "**1.** To expel air from the lungs in a noisy or spasmodic manner . . . **2.** To expel by a cough . . ." These meanings do not adequately convey that something without lungs can "cough," as in "the engine coughed and died"—a figurative meaning that should be discriminated.

Not only do the definitions often lack a concrete quality, but they occasionally fail in comprehensiveness as well. For example, the definition for **celibacy** is given as "the state of being unmarried, esp. in accordance with religious vows"; however, the sense of the word as meaning "complete sexual abstinence" is omitted.

V. Syllabication and Pronunciation

The boldface entry words and their variant or inflected forms are divided into syllables by centered

dots: "**par·a·chute** . . . **-chut·ed**, **-chut·ing**." Pronunciations, shown as phonemic respellings, are given in parentheses following the main entry words. These respellings are particularly easy to use, as each symbol is used for only one sound or for closely clustered sounds, and no sound is shown by more than one symbol. In cases where variant pronunciations are given, the preferred pronunciation is offered first, and only syllables that differ from the preferred pronunciation are shown in the alternate pronunciations: **by-pass** (bī′pas′, -päs).

A pronunciation key precedes the main text of the dictionary and appears in an abridged form on the bottom of each right-hand page. This simplified pronunciation and the quick-reference key make this dictionary very accessible to the reader.

VI. Special Features

In addition to the occasional tables and graphs found in the main text (for example, a periodic table of the elements appears under the listing for **element**; under the entry for **Hebrew or Jewish calendar** there is a chart spelling out the months of the calendar), there are several supplementary sections. The "Common Computer Terms" glossary deserves special attention; it provides five full pages of entries that pertain to computer technology. Many of these terms are not included in other paperback dictionaries.

A "Pronouncing Gazetteer" provides pronunciation guides and brief descriptions of geographic place names and physical features. A separate section of "Biographies" lists key "people of the past and present." As in the gazetteer, the biographical glossary entries are too brief and nonspecific to be of much value, except as pronunciation aids.

A "Secretarial Handbook," comprised of rules of grammar and syntax, as well as guidance on letter writing, is also included. The handbook concentrates on rules of punctuation and usage that a secretary may refer to in transcribing, as opposed to writing, business communications. For quick reference, a forms-of-address subsection may also prove useful.

The "Abbreviations and Acronyms" section is lengthy and fairly current, providing information that is not easily gained in comparable dictionaries. While all of these features could prove useful for quick reference, other sources would provide the depth needed for serious studies.

VII. Accessibility

Dense type and the absence of word and picture illustrations may initially intimidate the reader, but experience and intelligent use of the dictionary guide soon make it more accessible. There are no graphic representations of typical entries; instead, the explanatory material is divided into 14 parts listed at the head of the guide. At the end of the guide there is a fine table of English spellings for those who may have heard a word but are unsure of its spelling. Abbreviations are fully explained immediately before the dictionary text.

Access to the supplementary material is facilitated by a complete listing on the contents page. Dictionary entries are straightforward, with homographs indicated by small superscript numerals following each entry: **miss**[1] . . . **miss**[2] **Miss** . . . . Synonym and antonym paragraphs are introduced by the abbreviations **syn.** and **ant.** and distinctions among the words in a single synonym/antonym analysis are numbered to correspond to the various senses of the main entry.

VIII. Graphics and Format

On the whole, *Funk & Wagnalls Standard Desk Dictionary* does not boast outstanding graphics. Its illustrations are small, indistinct, and sparse. In many cases, poor reproduction quality makes the key identifying characteristics of illustrated items indistinguishable.

The typeface is adequate, but has a somewhat heavy, old-fashioned look (quite different from the lean, modern typeface used in FUNK & WAGNALLS NEW ENCYCLOPEDIA). Margins are narrower than one might like, but at least print is not lost in the gutter. The designer could have made a more generous use of white space. The paper is of good quality, and is opaque.

The book lies flat when opened to one of the middle pages, but not when opened to a page near the front or back of the book. The pages are sewn, rather than glued. The laminated paper cover is attractive and appears to be stronger than the covers of many ordinary paperbacks. However, as a rule, paperback volumes of this size rarely stand up to heavy use over a prolonged period.

IX. Summary

For home use or as a reader's dictionary for occasional word checking, the *Funk & Wagnalls Standard Desk Dictionary* is a reasonable value for the price. Its major strength is the comprehensiveness of the word list; its major weaknesses are the limited scope of the definitions and the lack of examples of contextual use. Therefore, its primary value will be to users who are interested in a rapid, cursory identification of a term. Buyers who particularly need a dictionary that reflects today's general computer terminology may find this edition a worthwhile reference source, but those who want a more erudite and up-to-date dictionary will still want to look elsewhere.

Funk & Wagnalls Standard Dictionary

Facts at a Glance

Full Title: **Funk & Wagnalls Standard Dictionary**.
Publisher: New American Library/Meridian.
Editors: Patrick Barrett, Carol Cohen, and Norman Hoss.
Edition Reviewed: © 1980; 1984 printing.

Number of Entries: 82,000.
Number of Pages: 1,011.
Trim Size: 5¼" × 8".
Binding: paperback.

Price: $8.95.
Sold in bookstores and other outlets.
ISBN 0-452-00677-5.

I. Introduction

The *Funk & Wagnalls Standard Dictionary* is derived from an earlier edition of the larger FUNK & WAGNALLS STANDARD DESK DICTIONARY. Although billed in the preface as a "completely re-edited and reset version . . . containing hundreds of new words and meanings," it in fact has not been revised since 1980, and many of the "words and meanings" referred to above can no longer be considered "new."

There are significant differences between these two titles. For example, although the *Standard Dictionary* is smaller, it includes an essay on the differences between Canadian and American English and provides tables for foreign alphabets and weights and measures (including British/Canadian measurements). These features are not present in the FUNK & WAGNALLS STANDARD DESK DICTIONARY. On the other hand, the biographical listings found in the desk edition's "Pronouncing Gazetteer" are omitted from the same section in the *Standard Dictionary*. Nor does this volume include the updated section on "Common Computer Terms." The desk edition's "Secretarial Handbook" section appears in slightly different form under the title "Basic Style Manual."

II. Authority

As noted, the *Funk & Wagnalls Standard Dictionary*, published by New American Library under the Meridian imprint, is based on the 1980 edition of Harper & Row's FUNK & WAGNALLS STANDARD DESK DICTIONARY and other dictionaries in the Funk & Wagnalls "Standard" dictionary series. Among the editorial staff who assisted in the revision are Patrick Barrett and Carol Cohen, supervisory editors; the late Norman Hoss, chief revising editor; and Martin

Apter, Myrna Breskin, Robert Haycraft, Geoffrey Horn, and Ruth Koenigsberg. (Sidney I. Landau, who was editor-in-chief of a number of other Funk & Wagnalls dictionaries, is not listed in the credits for this book.) None of these individuals is a well-known lexicographer. There is no indication that the entries are based on any established citation file.

III. Comprehensiveness

Apparently, the *Funk & Wagnalls Standard Dictionary* not only has borrowed its word lists but also draws its definitions and basic entry format from its Harper & Row counterpart. Consider the following entry in the Harper & Row desk edition:

> **les·son** (les′ən) *n.* **1.** An instance or experience from which useful knowledge may be gained. **2.** A division or portion of a course of study. **3.** An assignment to be studied or learned, as by a student. **4.** A reprimand; reproof. **5.** A portion of the Bible read or designated to be read at a religious service.—*v.t. Rare* **1.** To give a lesson or lessons to; instruct. **2.** To admonish; rebuke. [<OF<L *lectio, -ionis* a reading]

Note how the entry has been pared down from the desk version in this same example entry in the *Funk & Wagnalls Standard Dictionary*:

> **les·son** (les′ n) *n.* **1.** An instance or experience from which useful knowledge may be gained. **2.** An assignment to be studied or learned, as by a student. **3.** A reprimand; reproof. **4.** A portion of the Bible read or designated to be read at a religious service. [< L *lectio, -ionis* a reading]

In the above example, one noun meaning has been deleted from the desk edition (definition 2), the transitive verb definitions have been excluded, and the etymology citation is slightly different in the *Standard Dictionary* entry. Otherwise, the entries are identical.

As in the desk edition, usage and label aids have been provided in the *Standard Dictionary* to supplement what the editors refer to as "bare-bones" definitions—those meanings not "adequate to give a reader confidence in using a word or phrase." But the editors trim down the entries by excluding the synonym and antonym studies that are found in the desk edition. For example, the definitions for the entry **authentic** are identical in both dictionaries, including one particular sense that is designated by the restrictive *Law* label (in this case, **authentic** means "duly executed before the proper officer"). However, unlike the desk version, the *Standard* does not include the alternative adjective distinction *authentical*, nor does it provide a synonym and antonym paragraph. This omission may limit the dictionary's usefulness, especially for those users who rely on a

dictionary to be something more than a lexicon. For instance, synonym and antonym paragraphs can be important tools for students of English who have not fully assimilated the rich variety of language usage or developed the ability to distinguish the more subtle nuances of word meanings.

IV. Quality and Currency of Entries

The basic ordering of an entry is as follows: the syllabified boldface entry term, slightly overhanging the text; the pronunciation guide in parentheses; the part-of-speech label in italics; the partially spelled, boldface inflected or truncated terms, preceded by a dot (when the base word remains unchanged) or the fully rendered inflected or truncated term (when irregular); a boldface numeral if more than one definition is included; an italicized restrictive label, where applicable; boldface variant forms, preceded by a dash; and word etymologies in brackets.

Multiple definitions are listed with the most commonly used meanings first. But the lack of verbal illustrations to help amplify abstract and subtle shades of meaning will be a serious drawback for inexperienced users.

This dictionary's 1980 copyright date limits the inclusion of many of the technical, scientific, and media-generated words and meanings of the 1980s. Although entries appear for such established terms as **biorhythm**, **Dolby**, **downer**, and **gay**, as the word refers to homosexuality, such recently coined terms as *meltdown*, *biofeedback*, *grid lock*, *palimony*, *workaholic*, and *zero based* are not offered in the *Funk & Wagnalls Standard Dictionary*.

Users who require a technically up-to-date dictionary should be aware that the useful glossary of new computer terms appended to the revised version of the desk edition (which lists such current words as *floppy disk*, *modem*, *down load*, *mouse*, and *bubble memory*) is not given in the *Standard Dictionary*. The glossary of geographical entries is identical to the one given in the desk edition but, again, reflects only those notable almanac and atlas entries prior to the 1980 copyright date.

V. Syllabication and Pronunciation

As in the desk edition, the boldface headwords and their variant or inflected forms are divided into syllables by centered dots. Phonemic respellings are given in parentheses immediately following the entry term. In addition to a standard pronunciation key preceding the main text of the dictionary, a "Table of English Spellings" delineates various possible spellings for the sounds of the English language, and shows how these sounds are represented in the International Phonetic Alphabet—for example, the sound *ou* is listed, its equivalent IPA symbol *au* is provided, and the word examples *out*, *bough*, and *cow* are offered. Thus, a user might check under all three of these sounds when a particular spelling is uncertain. Unfortunately, neither the pronunciation key nor the table is duplicated anywhere else in the text. Because this omission makes cross-checking pronunciation symbols and spelling guides difficult, requiring the user to flip back and forth between pages, it defeats the purpose of providing an aid for poor spellers and for those who are unfamiliar with phonetic symbols.

VI. Special Features

In addition to the "Guide to the Dictionary," an essay on the pronunciation, spelling, and vocabulary of Canadian English, and the pronunciation and spelling keys preceding the main text, there are several glossaries and tables appended to the main listings. An extensive alphabetical list of abbreviations and acronyms is identical to the one found in the FUNK & WAGNALLS STANDARD DESK DICTIONARY. These entries are followed by "A Pronouncing Gazetteer," which includes brief descriptions of geographical place names and physical features; however, the *Standard Dictionary* excludes the separate "Biographies" section that is included in the desk edition.

Several tables of foreign alphabets (Arabic, Hebrew, Greek, Russian, and German) are listed. Although perhaps interesting, these tables seem to serve no practical function. Their inclusion is particularly puzzling in light of the severe abridgment that must inevitably occur in any compact dictionary, especially one of this size and scope. When so much other essential information must be sacrificed, it is not clear why the editors choose to insert such peripheral information.

Apparently, the section called the "Basic Style Manual" is a marketing attempt to appeal to a broader or more "academic" audience than the almost identical "Secretarial Handbook" found in the desk edition. In addition to covering the same basic material provided in the handbook, such as capitalization, punctuation, forms of address, and rules of grammar and syntax, the "Basic Style Manual" merely omits the information that pertains to business correspondence and opts, instead, for several brief paragraphs on manuscript preparation. Although users may occasionally refer to this section as a quick reference guide, because of the complexity of the information, this material would be better gleaned from a good, comprehensive writer's handbook.

The "Proofreaders' Marks" table is also not inclusive enough to merit serious consideration. Those who wish to learn the standardized proofmarking system would profit from a more comprehensive treatment. Like the encyclopedic information that fills the back matter of many paperback, portable dictionaries, the three-page tables of weights and measures may prove helpful for users who want quick access to and comparisons of British and American measurement equivalents but will probably be ignored by the majority.

VII. Accessibility

Boldface guide words are positioned at the top outer corner of each page to help isolate a word search to facing pages. Geographical listings and abbreviation entries are separate, alphabetically arranged glossaries. Homographs are indicated by small, raised numerals following the entry word.

VIII. Graphics and Format

The sparse and poorly reproduced drawings in the FUNK & WAGNALLS STANDARD DESK DICTIONARY have been completely omitted from this dictionary. The typeface is very small and cramped, which, combined with the uneven inking of the text and a large amount of show-through, makes this dictionary difficult to read. However, the space around the margins is generous; despite the curvature of the spine, the words toward the inner margin are easily visible to the eye when the book is flattened. The paperback binding is of a poor quality, will crack easily, and will not withstand extensive or rough use. The pages in our review copy were already quite yellowed.

IX. Summary

The primary value of this dictionary lies in its portable size, its simple definitions, and the overall comprehensiveness of its word list in comparison with those of other paperback dictionaries. However, this 1980 edition is seriously outdated and will not serve readers who seek a dictionary that reflects today's technical and computer terminology. Nor will it be of much value to users who require verbal illustrations, synonym and antonym paragraphs, and more complete definitions. At best, this dictionary will provide readers with correct spellings and the most rudimentary definitions of 82,000 words. It will not serve readers who have a more than casual interest in the English language, and it will add little to a library reference collection. WEBSTER'S NEW WORLD DICTIONARY is a better choice for readers in search of a more current, portable dictionary.

Hugo English Dictionary

Facts at a Glance

Full Title: **Hugo English Dictionary.**
Alternate Title: Hugo Pocket Dictionary: English.
Publisher: Hugo's Language Books Ltd.;
   distributed by Rowman & Littlefield.
Compilers: D. M. Caswell and R. Batchelor-
   Smith.
Edition Reviewed: © 1973; 1978 printing.

Number of Entries: approximately 30,000.
Number of Pages: 632.
Trim Size: 2¾″ × 4″.
Binding: paper over boards.

Price: $4.25.
Sold in bookstores.
ISBN 0-85285-049-2.

I. Introduction

The *Hugo English Dictionary* (cover and spine title),
also called the *Hugo Pocket Dictionary: English*, is
a very small hardbound pocket dictionary, first published in Great Britain in 1973. According to its preface, this edition was produced "in reply to the great
demand for a really compact edition similar to Hugo's world-famous range of foreign language dictionaries, and has our many years of experience . . .
behind it." The *Hugo* is designed, according to the
preface, for "students both young and old, English
and foreign; businessmen and office secretaries, and
as a handy book in the home." Buyers should note
that British spellings and meanings are the base of
this work.

II. Authority

Hugo's Language Books Ltd. is a London publisher
known for its bilingual dictionaries, phrase books,
language course books, language cassettes, and other
language-learning aids.

III. Comprehensiveness

The *Hugo's* vocabulary is somewhat limited owing
to the constraints of its size; however, the editors
state that "every effort" was made to include "the
most important words in use today."

   Its size and early 1970s copyright date notwith-
standing, Hugo is quite current and comprehensive,
including such terms as **feminist**, **terrorist**, and **guru**.

IV. Quality and Currency of Entries

This handy dictionary, much smaller than those usually called "pocket-size," contains common words
and phrases with brief, succinct definitions. British
spellings and usage are, of course, used throughout
(**licence**, **colour**, **sceptic**, **centre**). Usage labels are
provided when necessary:

for slang	**cop** *n* (*sl*)
for medical	**functional** *a* (*med*)
for colloquial	**hanky-panky** *n* (*coll*)
for music	**metronome** *n* (*mus*)

The part of speech is identified for each entry word
as well as for each derivative word. As is common
in most British dictionaries, derivatives are given as
subentries or, as the preface states, "hung on" to the
main entry words, as in the following examples:

   fragment *n* piece broken off; unfinished part; *a* **fragmentary** incomplete; *n* **fragmentation** separation into
   fragments.

   rational *a* reasonable, sensible; *ns* ["nouns"] **rationalism** doctrine that reason is only source of knowledge;
   rationalist; *v* **rationalize** give rational explanation of;
   ns **rationalization**. . . .

Definitions, though quite brief, are clear, and an
attempt has apparently been made to include all *common* uses and derivatives of the selected words. In
order to save space, pronunciation, etymology, illustrative examples, and spelling variations are omitted from the *Hugo*.

V. Syllabication and Pronunciation

Words are not divided into syllables, nor are any
pronunciations given.

VI. Special Features

Because the *Hugo* is intended to be a compact pocket-
style dictionary, it is a streamlined basic reference
work. Therefore, except for a list of abbreviations
preceding the lexicon, there are no appendixes,
graphics, supplementary material, or other special
features.

VII. Accessibility

With its small size, *Hugo* is easy to handle. The use
of boldface type for entries, and for guide words and
page numbers—set off from the text by a rule at the
top of each page—as well as ample margins and
smooth, ivory paper, make it easy on the eyes, despite the small typeface.

VIII. Graphics and Format

There are no illustrations in the *Hugo English Dictionary*. For its size, the margins, especially the gut-

Hugo English Dictionary

❶ Related words, in boldface, follow main entry

❷ Past tenses and past participles are given for irregular verbs

❸ Usage labels are italicized and enclosed in parentheses

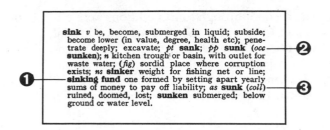

ter, and white space are more than adequate. The paper is a good-quality stock with little show-through. The binding is sturdy, and the cover is a turquoise wipe-clean vinyl over solid binder boards. It should stand up well to extensive use.

IX. Summary

The *Hugo English Dictionary* is a handy and well-crafted compact dictionary. Given its small size and limited features, it provides the general user, businessperson, or traveler with clear, concise definitions for most common words and phrases. The greatest drawback of this dictionary is its obvious British slant. The *Hugo* does not, as do some British dictionaries, present American variations in spelling and usage. American readers looking for the correct spelling of certain words (*color, maneuver*) might have a problem with the British variants (**colour, manoeuvre**). In addition, some British terms and colloquial definitions included are not used in the United States (for instance, "**mangel-wurzel** *n* large kind of beet").

The *Hugo* compares favorably with other pocket edition dictionaries, including THE LITTLE OXFORD DICTIONARY (British), THE RANDOM HOUSE AMERICAN DICTIONARY (American), THE THORNDIKE-BARNHART HANDY POCKET DICTIONARY (American), and WEBSTER'S NEW WORLD HANDY POCKET DICTIONARY (American), in terms of vocabulary size, treatment, and arrangement. American travelers to the United Kingdom and other countries where British English is better known than the American version will find this book useful. Other readers who need a pocket dictionary should select an American work such as the Merriam-Webster WEBSTER'S VEST POCKET DICTIONARY or THE THORNDIKE-BARNHART HANDY POCKET DICTIONARY.

The Little Oxford Dictionary of Current English

Facts at a Glance

Full Title: **The Little Oxford Dictionary of Current English: Sixth Edition.**
Publisher: Oxford University Press.

Editor: Julia Swannell.
Edition Reviewed: © 1986.

Number of Volumes: 1.
Number of Entries: 25,000.
Number of Words: 34,000.
Number of Pages: 720.
Trim Size: 4" × 6".
Binding: paper over boards.

Price: $9.95.
Sold in bookstores and by direct mail; also sold to libraries and other educational institutions.
ISBN 0-19-861188-9.

I. Introduction

The Little Oxford Dictionary of Current English is part of the Oxford dictionary series published in England by Oxford University Press and now sold in the United States as well. In terms of size and number of entries, this title is the second smallest work in the series, the smallest being THE OXFORD MINIDICTIONARY. *The Little Oxford Dictionary* closely resembles THE POCKET OXFORD DICTIONARY, which is the next largest work in the series. Many of its definitions are identical, or nearly so, to those in the POCKET OXFORD; others have obviously been condensed from those in the larger work. Both dictionaries also use the same typographic conventions. But *The Little Oxford Dictionary* has fewer entries and also lacks the basic etymologies found in the POCKET OXFORD edition.

This is a wholly *English* dictionary; its spellings, pronunciations, and definitions clearly reflect its origins. The work has not been revised for the American market. However, the current (sixth) edition, published in 1986, places special emphasis on quick and easy reference and contains many new American terms that were not in the previous edition.

II. Authority

Published by the highly reputable Clarendon Press of Oxford University, the dictionary's first edition appeared in 1930 under the editorship of George

Ostler. The second through fourth editions were edited by Jessie Coulson, a member of the editorial staff of the *Oxford English Dictionary*. Julia Swannell edited the fifth and also the current sixth edition, with the assistance of members of Oxford University Press's Oxford English Dictionary department.

III. Comprehensiveness

The book jacket lists among the work's important features its broad range of contemporary English and the special attention paid to the vocabulary of new technology. The computer-related definition of **bit** is included; some terms dealing with the new video technologies are not. Also well represented are popular new words and phrases, such as **ageism**, **aikido**, **allergenic**, **futon**, **privatize**, **surrogate mother**, **tofu**, and **user-friendly**.

Foreign words that are not fully assimilated into English appear as main entries in bold italics, and their language is noted in abbreviated form in square brackets; for example, [F] for French.

Parts of speech are indicated immediately following the entry word. There are some usage labels, such as *colloq.* for colloquialisms and *sl.* for slang words. Field labels, such as *law*, are provided to identify other specialized word uses. Irregular inflected forms are provided. For example, under **lie** (*v.i.*) appears this clarification of inflections:

(*past* **lay**: *p.p.* **lain**: *partic.* **lying**).

Similarly, the forms **better** and **best** are listed under **good**.

There are no illustrative phrases or sentences to enhance definitions such as can be found in many other pocket dictionaries. For Americans seeking to understand unfamiliar British usages, this omission is a drawback. Etymologies, synonyms, and antonyms are excluded, but these omissions are not unusual in a work of this scope.

IV. Quality and Currency of Entries

The definitions are concise and clearly written. Senses of words are arranged by frequency of use in Great Britain and are numbered consecutively. Specialized uses are introduced by an abbreviated, italicized label. For example, the third entry for the noun **bill** indicates that the word historically (*hist.*) meant

weapon with hook-shaped blade.

The verb form as well as phrases and compound words are listed under the first and most common sense; these include **bill of exchange** and **billposter**. Adjectives are most often defined by the use of syn-onymous words rather than a sentence or phrase of definition. For example, **steely** is defined as

of or like steel; inflexible, obdurate.

V. Syllabication and Pronunciation

The work uses the International Phonetic Alphabet to indicate pronunciations, and it adds marks for nasalization and an *x* for the Scottish *ch*, as in **loch**. The pronunciation key appears at the front of the volume. Set off by slash marks, pronunciation is noted immediately following the entry word for most but not all words. For example, **bleach** is pronounced, but **bleak**, **bleed**, and **bleep** are not. Accent marks indicate stressed syllables within the pronunciations, but syllabication is not noted. This omission is a drawback for student readers of the dictionary. The pronunciations provided are those of southern England, not standard American English. Only the preferred form of pronunciation is given.

VI. Special Features

The dictionary's introduction provides a helpful explanation to the reader on how to use the contents effectively. Also provided at the front of the book are a full pronunciation key, a list of abbreviations, and a note on proprietary terms and trademarks. There are three appendixes: I. "Some points of English usage"; II. "Countries of the world and related adjectives"; and III. "The metric system of weights and measures." These features take up only ten pages and are especially useful.

VII. Accessibility

Main entry words appear in boldface type and overhang the text; capital letters are used as appropriate, as for abbreviations and proper nouns. Subsenses are easily located with their boldface numbers, and run-in entries and compounds also appear in boldface.

The dictionary has paired bold guide words at the top of each double-columned page, with a centered page number. This is helpful because some of the work's cross-references cite page numbers. A table of contents lists the dictionary's special features, so the reader will not overlook them.

VIII. Graphics and Format

There are no illustrations provided in this dictionary. The overall layout of each page is good for a book of this size. The margins are narrow, but the typeface is strong and clear. The board cover, stitching, and headband make this a sturdy volume that would withstand travel and frequent consultation.

IX. Summary

The Little Oxford Dictionary is a handy pocket-size work that will serve well as a quick reference source for concise British definitions of words in the basic English lexicon. It is fairly up-to-date and is easy to use. Those who require a small British dictionary will find this a good buy. That said, however, it should also be pointed out that in libraries where there is frequent demand for good British dictionaries, this title is not sufficiently comprehensive to be considered as a first choice; this cannot be the *only* British dictionary in a good collection. For such collections, a larger, more comprehensive volume such as THE CONCISE OXFORD DICTIONARY, CHAMBERS 20TH CENTURY DICTIONARY, or CHAMBERS CONCISE 20TH CENTURY DICTIONARY will also be needed.

The Little Webster

Facts at a Glance

Full Title: **The Little Webster (Langenscheidt Lilliput Webster English Dictionary).**
Publisher: Langenscheidt, New York.
Compiler: Sidney Fuller.
Edition Reviewed: © by Langenscheidt KG, no date.

Number of Entries: more than 7,000.
Number of Pages: 640.
Trim Size: 1½″ × 2″.
Binding: paper with flexible vinyl cover.

Price: $2.00.
Sold in bookstores and other outlets; available directly from the publisher.
ISBN 3-468-96519-2.

I. Introduction

The *Little Webster* dictionary, also known as the *Langenscheidt Lilliput Webster English Dictionary*, is a diminutive novelty dictionary. Despite its miniature size, however, it is the product of serious lexicography. Moreover, there is a deliberate rationale behind the word selection. "Most dictionaries," explains the preface, "contain a large number of words which are known to the reader and which he rarely needs to look up. In order to gain as much space as possible for words which we felt the reader might really need to look up, we decided to leave out as many words of this simple kind as we could." As a result, this dictionary "has room to explain an unusually large number of relatively rare and difficult words." In fact, these claims are true.

II. Authority

The *Langenscheidt Lilliput* dictionary has been in print since the early 1900s. This edition is the only one of the publisher's volumes devoted exclusively to the English language. The 15 other small-size works are bilingual (English-French, English-German, and so forth).

III. Comprehensiveness

Given its stated rationale for eliminating common words, the word list takes on a decidedly different character from those of most dictionaries. For example, here is a list of all of the words defined on one randomly selected page: **fatigue, fatuous, faun, fauna, feasible, feature, febrile, feces, fecund.** This list of relatively rare and difficult words eliminates such common words as *fault, favor, feast,* and *February*.

IV. Quality and Currency of Entries

Most small dictionaries, according to the preface, provide definitions in "words similar or nearly equal in meaning to the head entry," based on the theory that the user will know at least one of the words. *The Little Webster*, where possible, has used words in the definition that are simpler than the main entry word, clear, and easy to understand. For example,

> **roustabout** dock worker
> **zombi(e)** dead person said to be brought to life by witchcraft

When a definition will not fit on one line, the last word may be set flush to the right margin of the previous or succeeding line, where another entry also occurs. For example,

> **ev′·er·y·where** in or to every
> place   [*etc*]. **-ion**
> **e·vict′** force to leave (land,

This is sometimes confusing to the reader. Word forms are occasionally included; etymology, synonyms, and antonyms are not.

Because of the criterion for selection and the lack of a copyright date, it is difficult to evaluate the word list's currency.

V. Syllabication and Pronunciation

Syllabication is indicated by a dot between syllables of the main entry words. Stressed syllables are indicated. Pronunciation is clarified using only the macron to denote long vowel sounds and by phonetic respelling. There is no pronunciation key.

VI. Special Features

The special feature of this dictionary is its unusually diminutive size.

The Little Webster

❶ Boldface main entry words receive both syllabication, indicated by centered dots, and stress marks

❷ Irregular plurals are given

❸ Derivatives are indicated by boldface, truncated forms

❹ Pronunciations are enclosed in parentheses

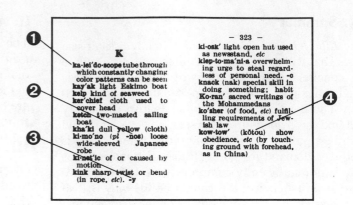

VII. Accessibility

Access is by alphabetical order; to save space, there are no guide words. When searching for a word users must, therefore, stop every few pages and read a main entry word to locate their place. Page numbers are centered at the top of each text page.

VIII. Graphics and Format

This lilliputian dictionary is the size of a fat matchbox—1½″ × 1¾″ × ¾″; therefore, the typography and design are as simple as possible. The main entry is in bold print; the definitions are indented one space and run across the entire page. The printed text on each page runs 1″ horizontally and 1½″ vertically; the ⅛″ margins and gutter provide a generous amount of white space given the book's size. The entries are in small type that is clearly printed on a smooth white paper. The cover is wipe-clean flexible dark blue plastic with gold lettering.

IX. Summary

The *Little Webster* dictionary is not merely a novelty gift item; it also provides clear, concise definitions for 7,000 relatively rare and difficult words. As the editor states, it tells the user "things he does not know and wants to know." By no means is this an essential purchase for either individuals or librarians. But it will make for useful and pleasant browsing.

Longman Dictionary of American English

Facts at a Glance

Full Title: **Longman Dictionary of American English: A Dictionary for Learners of English**.
Publisher: Longman.
Editors: Arley Gray, Della Summers, Adrian Stenton, and Leah Berkowitz.

Edition Reviewed: © 1983.

Number of Entries: 38,000.
Number of Pages: 792.
Number of Illustrations: 15 pages of black-and-white drawings.
Trim Size: 5¾″ × 8¾″.
Binding: cloth and paper.

Price: $12.95 (cloth); $7.95 (paper).
Sold through magazine and newspaper advertising.
ISBN 0-582-906113 (cloth);
ISBN 0-582-79797-7 (paper).

I. Introduction

The *Longman Dictionary of American English* is designed for individuals whose native tongue is not English but who possess an intermediate or advanced fluency in the English language. It is intended to help these users become less dependent upon bilingual dictionaries. It does so by giving not only literal definitions but also connotative values and usages of words and expressions in English.

II. Authority

Longman is a highly regarded publisher of texts for ESL instruction as well as for the training of ESL teachers. Consultants for the project include Virginia French Allen, William Crawford, and other recognized authorities in the field, representing major U.S. centers for ESL research and instruction.

Both the selection of main entry words and the controlled vocabulary used in the definitions are based on the publisher's established list of words most frequently used in spoken as well as written English.

III. Comprehensiveness

The dictionary's word list is appropriate for the student of English at the intermediate and advanced levels and for high school and college students using

English in mainstream (as opposed to bilingual or remedial) content courses. The list contains a balance of words that students will encounter in formal and informal speech and reading. The jargon of language instruction, used in the introductory exercises and the "Study Notes," is incorporated into the word list.

The list provides full coverage of standard "survival" words and expressions common to ESL texts. It gives equal attention to the words that students will encounter in the speech and writing of native speakers. The work includes over 5,000 idioms and figurative expressions. For example, the expressions **lay off**, **psych out**, **brand new**, and **mess up** are given, as are such words as **mess**, **junket**, **snack**, **tease**, and (sports) **fan**. The financial-transaction definitions for **credit**, **interest**, **deposit**, and **reduce** are included, enhancing the work's practical value.

Variant forms and comparable and contrasting forms are given and illustrated, expanding the range of the word list still further.

IV. Quality and Currency of Entries

The information is ordered within entries according to the following basic sequence: entry word or phrase; pronunciations, set off by virgules; the part-of-speech label; British spelling or other variant, as appropriate; boldfaced inflected forms, when irregular or requiring consonant doubling; a boldfaced numeral, when more than one meaning is defined; the grammar code (explained in the introduction); definition; illustrative sentence or phrase, in italics; synonyms; boldfaced run-ins; cross-references to related words, "Study Notes," and illustrations; and sometimes a paragraph of usage notes, also cross-referenced. Many entries also include cross-references for comparison of words that are logically equal in deep structure but not interchangeable in surface structure, for example, HOMEWORK and HOUSEWORK.

An important feature of the entries, second in importance to the well-controlled vocabulary, is the usage instructions. Codes and symbols are used to show such language features as noun countability and the objects of phrasal verbs. These points of syntax are essential to native-level language use. Step-by-step instructions in the introduction and a series of thorough "Study Notes" explain the use of these guides. Both the introduction and the "Study Notes" are cross-referenced in the entries.

Another key feature of the entries is the extensive use of illustrative phrases and sentences, at a ratio of 55,000 illustrations of context for 38,000 entry words.

The work's currency is strong in the area of contemporary idiom, as is appropriate to an ESL dictionary.

V. Syllabication and Pronunciation

Entry words are syllabified by centered dots; inflected forms and run-ins are not syllabified.

Each entry word is followed by a pronunciation guide enclosed within virgules. The guide takes the form of a respelling in the International Phonetic Alphabet (IPA). In international ESL instruction, the IPA is the pronunciation code of choice. Students initially instructed by U.S.-educated teachers without professional ESL training may not have encountered the IPA symbols. However, foreign-born or educated students and those who have used standard ESL beginning texts will find the symbols familiar. In any case, the symbols are fully explained in the introduction, where a full pronunciation key is provided. In acknowledgment of the sometimes tenuous links between English pronunciation and spelling, "Spelling Notes" are provided that outline the varying ways in which a sound may be spelled.

VI. Special Features

A thorough introduction explains the work's features. It is based on the assumption that the literate student will know how to use a general dictionary, and it builds on this knowledge with careful directions for using a study dictionary of usage. Also included is a 38-page "Dictionary Skills Workbook," which is cross-referenced throughout the text. The workbook provides exercises for using the dictionary to illustrate the features of grammar and usage that are discussed. Answers are provided at the end of the section.

Affixes are explained, and separate listings for prefixes and suffixes are appended in a section called "Word Building." Explanations and examples are given for ways to change a word's meaning and/or part of speech by using affixes. This is a key skill for the student to master in gaining linguistic fluency. Also provided is a listing of irregular verb forms.

VII. Accessibility

Boldfaced guide words are provided for each spread and are set off by rules. The work is heavily cross-referenced, and the "Spelling Notes" offer tips to aid students in finding words they may never have seen or may have only partially heard.

Homographs are listed separately and are designated by superscript numerals following the entry word.

VIII. Graphics and Format

The entries are easy to read with their clear typeface and adequate leading. The paper is bright white with no show-through. The margins are narrow, but the entry words are clearly legible, printed in a larger type, boldfaced, and overhanging the text.

There are no illustrations for individual entries. However, concepts in the "Study Notes" are illustrated with line drawings, and 15 full-page drawings are provided. These drawings are in the realistic cartooning style used in most adult ESL texts. They identify objects related to everyday experience and travel. For example, one illustration features items and fixtures in a clothing store; another shows a doctor's office. The illustrations are captioned with the most common spoken variant for each object. The illustration pages are placed adjacent to the page where the relevant main entry appears—that is, the entry for the location (airport, kitchen) or general grouping (electronic items, car parts) illustrated. All the captions are themselves main entry words, and cross-references to the drawings are provided in their entries.

IX. Summary

The *Longman Dictionary of American English* serves both as a dictionary of the English language and as an instructional text for intermediate and advanced students of English as a second or foreign language. As such, it can be used either as a personal general reference dictionary by nonnative English-speakers or as an auxiliary text for formal instruction.

Although this dictionary presupposes the inherent diligence of the ESL student, it can also be useful for native speakers of English. It is recommended for public and academic libraries serving patrons who are pursuing the study of English as a second or foreign language.

Longman Dictionary of Contemporary English

Facts at a Glance

Full Title: **Longman Dictionary of Contemporary English.**
Publisher: Longman.
Editor: Paul Proctor, Editor-in-Chief.
Edition Reviewed: © 1984.

Number of Entries: over 55,000.
Number of Pages: 1,303.
Trim Size: 5¾" x 8¾".
Binding: cloth; paper.

Price: $17.95 (cloth); $13.95 (paper).
Sold in bookstores; also sold to libraries and other educational institutions.
ISBN 582-52571-3 (cloth);
ISBN 582-55608-2 (paper).

I. Introduction

The *Longman Dictionary of Contemporary English* is a completely new dictionary designed especially for users for whom English is a foreign language. Using a core vocabulary of 2,000 words, it defines some 55,000 words and, by means of a unique coding system, analyzes the meaning and grammatical behavior of each word. Usage notes, illustrations, detailed labeling, and British and American pronunciation help to fulfill the editors' goal of providing "an invaluable help to the learner who wishes to communicate naturally in speech."

II. Authority

Longman is an established name in the field of lexicography. In recent years this publisher pioneered an encyclopedic dictionary *Longmans English Larousse* and a thesaurus dictionary Longman Lexicon of Contemporary English, both of which were well received.

The *Longman Dictionary of Contemporary English*'s controlled vocabulary was selected from *A General Service List of English Words* (Longman 1953, reprinted 1977) and examples and usage notes were compiled using the files of *The Survey of English Usage* at University College, London. Director of the Survey, Professor Randolph Quirk, was also chief linguistic adviser for this dictionary.

III. Comprehensiveness

The editors have incorporated the spellings, pronunciation, and vocabulary of British and American usage, and have also given coverage to English from other parts of the world.

As well as colloquial, idiomatic, and technical words, full main entry word treatment is given to phrasal verbs like **make up** and **leave behind**, compounds like **inkstand** and **seabed**, and prefixes and suffixes like **pre-** and **-ism**.

There are no etymologies or biographical entries and only an uneven representation of abbreviations (**IRA** but no *PLO*). Geographical adjectives are listed within the text, with fuller treatment of the name of the country, its language, and money in an appendix at the back.

Every entry contains details of pronunciation, definition, and usage, and these are supplemented by a system of grammatical coding. These letter and number codes describe the syntactic behavior of the word: [U] refers to uncountable nouns such as **colour-blindness** and **collusion** that take a singular verb and are not usually used with *a/an* or *one*; [U9] shows that the uncountable noun also needs a descriptive phrase— **jurisdiction** *over us*.

A 40-page introductory guide covers every aspect of the dictionary's use and includes a large-type explanatory chart and the complete International Phonetic Alphabet (IPA). Eight appended tables cover nationality, weights, military ranks, and two of particular use to the new user of English, a table of irregular verb forms and another giving variant spellings of the same sound, enabling the user to find a word which has been heard but not seen before.

IV. Quality and Currency of Entries

The *Longman Dictionary of Contemporary English* is remarkably accurate and lucid, despite its self-imposed constriction of a 2,000-word defining vocabulary listed in full at the end of the book. Of course there are occasions where the quality of the definition suffers from the limitation. Thus, though *developing* would seem fundamental to the concept of **darkroom**, this dictionary only gives a cross-reference to this meaning; likewise, since neither *mental* nor *hospital* is in the basic list, the definition for **nuthouse** is given in the form of a cross-reference to MENTAL HOSPITAL. However, given this generous cross-referencing, the advantages to the neophyte user of a controlled vocabulary far outweigh the disadvantages.

Multiple senses of a word are entered separately with raised numbers after them, historically ordered. If two words differ because one is treated with a capital letter—**renaissance** and **Renaissance**, for example—these also receive individual entries.

Variant spellings, where applicable, are given after the main entry word—**caftan, kaftan; colour,** *AmE* **color; generalize, -ise**—and it is also possible to look up **color** and **kaftan** and find them with cross-references. Pronunciation uses IPA and, once again, variants are given for British and American usage divided by a double bar—**new** nju ‖ nu.

The more common parts of speech such as *nouns* and *adverbs* are supplemented by two lesser knowns—*determiners* like **many** and *predeterminers* like **such**. Most dictionaries simply classify these as *adjectives*. There is also an expanded labeling system used when a word or phrase is limited in some way. To the categories *informal* and *formal*, the *Longman Dictionary of Contemporary English* adds *not formal*—words like **send-off** unsuitable on ceremonial occasions; *taboo*—words like **come** (*n.*) and **shit** to be avoided when talking to strangers and children; *appreciative*—words like **forward-looking**; and *pompous*—words that sound foolishly overimportant like **pen** (*v.*). These lesser known word types and labels, however, appear only rarely.

Usage notes are appended to many entries in an attempt to resolve problems arising from uncertainty and difficulty in the use of English. Following the entry on **habit**, a usage note clarifies the differences

between **habit, custom** and **practice; un-** is contrasted with **non-**; and the rules governing use of **should, would,** and **ought** are explained after the **should** entry. THE OXFORD GUIDE TO THE ENGLISH LANGUAGE has a more systematic approach to usage and includes a fine list of careless phrases like "sort of" and another of confusable spellings like "any one" and "anyone."

The *Longman Dictionary of Contemporary English* expands definitions with excellent illustrative examples and line drawings. **Head** receives no less than 26 examples. There are times when all the best usage notes and examples in the world are no substitute for a good picture. The drawings in the *Longman Dictionary of Contemporary English* usually demonstrate the differences between members of the same class—breeds of dogs and values of musical notes—but they are also used to show component parts of a whole—players' positions in a sport or signs of the zodiac.

V. Syllabication and Pronunciation

Syllabication and pronunciation are given at the beginning of each entry. International Phonetic Alphabet (IPA) symbols are used, and though there is no handy IPA key on each page, there is one on the inside cover of the dictionary. Where there is a difference in British and American pronunciation, the British form is given first in full and the American form follows after a double bar.

    sched·ule . . . ʃedju·l ‖ skedʒʊl, -dʒəl

VI. Special Features

Certainly the most unusual feature of the dictionary is its grammatical coding system which gives a description of the syntactic behavior of the words. While intended for teachers and students of English as a second language, the wealth of information would also be useful to the native English speaker.

Listing the 2,000 defining words and providing unambiguous tables of spelling and family relationships are again features that may be of primary interest to those learning the language, but could prove equally useful to others.

VII. Accessibility

Accessibility is one *raison d'être* for the *Longman Dictionary of Contemporary English*. The introduction states "It is in no way a difficult work . . . it is the belief of the editors and publisher that simplicity of description is not at all incompatible with presentation of complex and intricate patterns of language." To this end, definitions are written using simpler words than the one to be defined and there are few abbreviations.

Large-type guide words appear at the top of each page and variant spellings may be found either alongside the main entry or in alphabetical position with a cross-reference. Access to the tables at the back of the book is facilitated by a table of contents at the beginning.

VIII. Graphics and Format

This dictionary is a chunky 1,300-page volume clearly printed and sturdily bound. It is divided into three main sections: a 40-page introductory guide, the 1,280-page dictionary itself, and 20 pages of tables. Where appropriate, black-and-white illustrations accompany the text and are cross-referenced: e.g., at the end of the entry for **tropic** there is a note "see picture at **globe**."

IX. Summary

The Longman Dictionary of Contemporary English successfully combines the functions of a dictionary and usage guide for a limited though nonetheless important audience—students of English as a foreign language. The language usage component should probably be supplemented by the OXFORD guide mentioned above or the HARPER DICTIONARY OF CONTEMPORARY USAGE which shows by discussion and example the standards of linguistic usage adhered to by those who know the language well. The dictionary component stands on its own—as an easy-to-use guide.

As the reviewer concluded in *American Reference Book Annual* (Vol. 11, 1980) "the simplicity and clearness of definitions and the emphasis on contemporary spoken English make this a desirable acquisition for most libraries."

Longman Photo Dictionary

Facts at a Glance

Full Title: **Longman Photo Dictionary**.
Publisher: Longman.
Compilers: Marilyn Rosenthal and Daniel Freeman.
Editors: Joanne Dresner, Executive Editor, and Penny Laporte, Project Editor.
Illustrator: Joseph DePinho.
Photographer: John Edelman.
Edition Reviewed: © 1987.

Number of Entries: over 2,000.
Number of Pages: 96.
Number of Indexes: 2.
Number of Illustrations: 865.
Trim Size: 8" × 10".
Binding: paperback.

Price: $6.95.
Sold in bookstores; also sold to libraries and other educational institutions.
ISBN 0-8013-0004-5.

I. Introduction and Scope

The *Longman Photo Dictionary*, a vocabulary and conversation book that presents contemporary North American language, life, and culture through a series of photographs, is directed at English as a second language students. It contains more than 2,000 vocabulary words in over 80 different semantic categories. According to the authors, this visual dictionary in oversize paperback format may also be used for alphabetizing, word games, listening practice, dictation, storytelling, categorizing, writing practice, composition, debates, discussions, and group work. Depending on the level and needs of students, listening, speaking, reading, and writing skills activities may be drawn from each unit.

In the *Photo Dictionary*, photographs depicting modern American culture are presented in units that show concrete objects, such as "Men's and Women's Wear," "Fruit," "The Supermarket," "The Laundry Room," and "Tools"; activities, including "Action at School," "Action at Home," and "Winter Sports"; and places, such as "The Beach," "The Waterfront," and "The Airport." Other units include "Emotions," in which male and female mimes express 25 emotions, and "The Family," which presents an abbreviated Kennedy family tree with each family member identified by name and letter of the alphabet to show his or her place within the family and relationship to the other members. For example, Rose and Joseph are identified as mother and father, husband and wife, parents, grandparents, grandmother and grandfather, in-laws, and so on.

Words are presented in realistic contexts, designed to help non-English-speaking students learn the vocabulary needed for everyday life, such as eating in a fast-food restaurant, going to the dentist or the bank, shopping, watching or participating in sports, and functioning in other common modern-day situations.

II. Format

In the over 80 semantic units in the *Photo Dictionary*, a variety of full-color photographs are labeled and accompanied by lists of vocabulary words that describe the pictures. In some units a photograph of a scene is labeled, as in "The Dining Room," with its table, chairs, plate, spoon, fork, centerpiece, wineglass, water glass, napkin ring, and chandelier. In other units a series of photographs is used. For example, "Action at Home" shows 19 photographs of various family members in a variety of situations: Dad brushing his teeth, Mom washing her face, Dad in the shower, Mom watching television, Little Sister in a bubble bath. A unit called "Opposites" uses 24 photographs to show pairs of opposites: Grandma reading to baby is labeled old/young; a pair of young twins, one with chocolate smeared on its face, the other clean, illustrates clean and dirty; hot tea is contrasted to iced tea for hot and cold; and a cheetah and turtle represent fast and slow.

Each unit also has a "Mini Practice" designed to provide students with conversation practice, to help them describe the scenes, and to allow them to use the new vocabulary to communicate about their own lives.

III. Quality and Currency of Entries

Most of the photographs are colorful, sharply focused, and of excellent quality. Some, however, are very small in size. The objects used in the units are familiar and have obviously been selected to present the full range of modern American culture. Models are dressed in contemporary style and are representative of all ages. Various racial and ethnic groups are also represented. It is evident that the compilers were careful to be nonsexist in their selection of photographs. Both males and females are shown throughout, with some pictures depicting individuals in nontraditional roles. An attempt has been made to show people with unisex clothing and hairstyles (especially children) so that the sex of the model is not clear, insuring that gender is not an issue.

"Mini Practices," or teaching activities, are included in each self-contained unit, and ESL teachers are encouraged to use the units in a variety of ways according to the needs of a specific teaching situation.

In the unit on women's wear the practice consists of a few sentences to read and then some questions to answer. Other units use a similar format (the numbers refer to photographs):

What's she wearing?	11 She's wearing a *yellow sweatshirt*.
What's she wearing?	14 She's wearing *flowered shorts*.
What's she wearing?	13 She's wearing a _____.
What's she wearing?	12 She's wearing _____.
What's she wearing?	9 She's wearing _____.
What's she wearing?	8 She's wearing a _____.

The language in the exercises is conversational and vernacular in style.

According to the authors, the units are self-contained and are not presented in a development fashion. Therefore, teachers can combine units, such as "Numbers" and "Money and Banking," to suit their teaching needs.

IV. Accessibility

The *Longman Photo Dictionary* includes an introduction, a table of contents, a word list, and a grammar index. The latter is more useful to teachers than to students. The dictionary is attractively put together and can be used effectively by students browsing through the eye-catching photographs. The typeface is easy to read, and the "Mini Practices" are set off clearly at the end of each unit.

V. Summary

The *Photo Dictionary* is an unusual English-language adult picture dictionary for speakers of English as a second language. It presents word lists and photographs arranged under a variety of topics in near-magazine format, which makes it an excellent choice for ESL students of all ages. It is definitely the leading work for beginning students, preferable to the more complex OXFORD-DUDEN PICTORIAL DICTIONARY and FACTS ON FILE VISUAL DICTIONARY. The compilers have successfully achieved their goal of providing a ". . . basic resource of language and culture to be used on various levels as either a main or supplementary text." The introduction notes that they hope "the photographs will excite you and your students and move you to emote and discuss each topic at hand." They have clearly succeeded in producing a useful workbook that should do just that.

The Merriam-Webster Dictionary

Facts at a Glance

Full Title: **The Merriam-Webster Dictionary**.
Publisher: Pocket Books.
Editor: Henry Bosley Woolf, Editor-in-Chief.
Edition Reviewed: © 1974; 39th printing.

Number of Entries: 57,000.
Number of Pages: 848.
Trim Size: $4\frac{1}{8}'' \times 6\frac{3}{4}''$.
Binding: paperback.

Price: $3.95.
Sold in bookstores and other outlets; also sold to libraries and other educational institutions.
ISBN 0-671-53088-7.

I. Introduction

This is a photoreduced paperback edition of WEBSTER'S CONCISE FAMILY DICTIONARY, prepared by the lexicographic staff of the Merriam-Webster Company. In the preface, the editors state that this edition was published to meet "the needs of those who want an up-to-date record of present-day English in compact form." With its core vocabulary of some 57,000 words, this Pocket Book edition has been selling steadily for 14 years, at this writing. While the work is no longer "up-to-date," as the preface still claims, it is a condensed, but substantial paperback compilation equivalent to the category of dictionaries normally labeled "concise" in hardback.

II. Authority

Pocket Books, now a paperback publishing division of Simon & Schuster, Inc., has published the current edition of this dictionary, by arrangement with G. & C. Merriam Co. (now Merriam-Webster Inc.), since 1964. It was prepared by Merriam-Webster's staff of lexicographers, using the publisher's own continuously updated citation files that then numbered some 11,500,000 entries. The Editor-in-Chief, Henry Bosley Woolf, and the staff—from senior editors to typists, as well as the librarian—are credited.

III. Comprehensiveness

The *Merriam-Webster Dictionary* has about 2,000 more entries than THE CONCISE AMERICAN HERITAGE DICTIONARY, and about 3,000 fewer than THE AMERICAN HERITAGE DICTIONARY paper edition. The *Merriam-Webster Dictionary*'s 57,000 entries include an estimated 36,000 main vocabulary words, with the remainder being variant spellings, variant forms, and run-on entries. Under **doghouse**, for example, the run-on entry is "**—in the doghouse**: in a state of disfavor."

A large number of main entries contain self-explanatory single words or sequences of words as definitions. Multiple definitions and senses are handled fairly extensively for a condensed work. In a 1979 review of this edition, a *Library Journal* reviewer correctly noted that although "the definitions are normally very brief and verbal illustrations few and far between . . . synonyms are fairly plentiful, however, as are helpful cross-references."

Included within the main entries are common abbreviations such as the two-letter postal state codes, the languages used in the etymologies, symbols of chemical elements, and so forth.

The opening notes indicate that etymologies are given for "a number" of words, but not how these sparse selections were chosen.

Within the alphabetical entries, ten common prefixes have additional lists of undefined compound words showing hyphenation where appropriate. At the entry for **anti-** there are 22 words listed; **non-** has a list of 224 additional combinations.

IV. Quality and Currency of Entries

The definitions, based on citations in Merriam-Webster's extensive files, present condensed meanings of what the preface calls "the core of the English language."

The explanatory notes detail the information and typographic conventions used in the entries with examples. The overall sequence of information in the entries is main boldface entry, pronunciation(s), part of speech, etymology, inflected forms, and definitions. An example of the method used to teach pronunciation is given in the explanatory notes: **vol·ca·no** \vȯl-'kā-nō\. The symbols between the reversed virgules show the pronunciation, which is based on the key inside the back cover. The definitions include necessary labels (temporal, regional, or stylistic): **kick in** *vb* **1**: CONTRIBUTE **2** *slang* : DIE. Entries often contain more than one definition of a single sense, frequently a synonym, as in ²**flat** *n* **1** : a level surface of land : PLAIN. Usage examples are shown at the appropriate senses within angled brackets: ³**flat** *adv* **1** : FLATLY **2** :EXACTLY < in one minute~>. Multiple meanings in entries are numbered and variant forms follow with pronunciations for appropriate syllables and with parts of speech.

Several additional labels are used, such as *often cap* (for capitalization), *abbr* (for all abbreviations appearing as main entries), and the spelling out in full of some parts of speech: *indefinite article, conjunction, past of* ("¹**lit** . . . *past* of light"), *pron, objective case of*, and so forth.

The definitions, in general, are good for quick reference, and the use of synonym cross-references will appeal to many readers. A comparison of a randomly chosen segment of entries, **paprika** to **parachute**, shows that the *Merriam-Webster Dictionary* contains 11 entries to the 9 included in this segment in the paperback AMERICAN HERITAGE DICTIONARY. There are minor differences in the entries. The Merriam-Webster work contains no etymologies in this section, whereas all entries have abbreviated ones in the American Heritage work. Merriam-Webster's contains **Pap smear** in addition to **Pap test** (defined much more simply than in the other dictionary). Merriam-Webster's other addition is an entry for **pap·ule** . . . *n* : a small solid usu. conical lesion of the skin.

Because these two paperbacks are similar in size, length of definitions, and have vocabularies relatively similar in length, as well as authoritative reputations, the following representative comparison of an entry may help demonstrate the difference between THE AMERICAN HERITAGE DICTIONARY (based on a larger *college* dictionary) and the *Merriam-Webster Dictionary*.

From the *Merriam-Webster Dictionary* paperback:

pa·rab·o·la \pə-'rab-ə-lə\ *n* : a curve formed by the intersection of a cone with a plane parallel to its side—**par·a·bol·ic** \,par-ə-'bäl-ik\ *adj*.

From THE AMERICAN HERITAGE DICTIONARY paperback:

pa·rab·o·la (pə-răb′a-lə) *n.* A plane curve formed by the locus of points equidistant from a fixed line and a fixed point not on the line. [<Gk. *parabolē*.]—**par·a·bolic** (par′-ə-bŏl′ ĭk) *adj.*

In general, the *Merriam-Webster Dictionary*'s definitions are simpler and more accessible to readers who may not be especially familiar with technical and scientific language.

The dictionary does not include the many terms that have gained popular currency within the last decade. The word **aerobic** (*adj.*) is in, but not the prevalent noun *aerobics*; *ayatollah*, *baud*, *byte*, and *mainframe*. But established, standard terms are, such as the computer sense of **bit**, **program** as a verb form used in computer science, and even **immunosuppressive** with an example of use: ⟨~techniques for kidney transplants⟩.

The general definitions are helpful with only minor exceptions (the noun **killing**, for example, needs an additional sense besides "a sudden notable gain or profit"). These clear definitions are adequate for most general purposes.

V. Syllabication and Pronunciation

Entry words are divided into syllables by centered dots, indicating the point(s) where a hyphen may be inserted at the end of a line of print or writing. The explanatory notes print an example of the three ways that **res·er·va·tion**, for example, can be hyphenated. Single letter syllables at the front or end of words are not divided by dots because printers rarely break words at syllables such as the *a* in **abet**, the *o*'s in **oleo**, or the *y* in **tributary**. Syllable divisions are shown for the first, but not the succeeding homographs: ¹**of·fi·cial**, ²**official**. Inflected and variant forms, as well as run-in entries, are divided: ¹**old** . . . —**old·ish**.

The dictionary employs a useful typographic convention—the stacked, double hyphen (=) to distinguish those words in the definitions that fall at the end of a line but that are normally hyphenated. In pronunciations, syllable division is shown by a normal hyphen. The following example shows syllable division in a main entry, in an entry's pronunciation, and with the double hyphen:

pitch·fork ′pich-,fork *n* : a long=handled fork used esp. in pitching hay.

The pronunciations are derived from the system used in WEBSTER'S THIRD NEW INTERNATIONAL

DICTIONARY, although simplified. Based on the symbols used in the scholarly International Phonetic Alphabet (IPA), the pronunciations are, relatively, much more sophisticated than the condensed vocabulary definitions. Readers unfamiliar with IPA symbols or the pronunciations in the larger Merriam-Webster dictionaries will need to study those used here carefully before they become as easy to use as the vocabulary.

A brief explanation of the pronunciation respellings with clear examples appears in the explanatory notes at the front of the dictionary. The notes indicate that the chart of pronunciation symbols is "printed inside the front and back covers," but it is only printed on the inside back cover of the paperback. In addition, there is no pronunciation key at the bottom of each page.

Merriam-Webster pronunciation editors base the given pronunciations on a continuously updated citation file, and the publisher indicates that "all of the variants fall within the range of acceptable variation." Occasionally, area labels, such as *Brit.* (British) or *Southern*, indicate special regional pronunciations.

The pronunciation chart contains brief examples of explanations of fifty symbols based on alphabetic letters and three standard diacritical marks: ă, ä, and à plus *th*, and a superior ⁿ and ʸ. The symbols are keyed to short words with corresponding boldface letters: "zh . . . vision, pleasure." In addition, five special symbols are used. These include the syllable hyphen and reversed virgules, or slant lines, enclosing pronunciations: **may·fly** \'mā-flī\. Stress marks precede syllables. A "high-set mark" shows primary stress; a "low-set mark" indicates secondary stress: **pol·i·ti·cian** \,päl-ə-'tish-ən\. Parentheses enclose letters or symbols for sounds that are sometimes not pronounced: **leg·horn** \'leg-,(h)òrn\.

There is no question that even in simplified form these pronunciations are authoritative (with minor errors such as a primary stress mark on the last syllable of **po·et·ic** \pō'et-'ik\). The range of diacritical marks, however, coupled with other typographic symbols plus various ligatures, such as oe, œ̄, ue, ūe, will make the pronunciations less accessible for many casual users.

VI. Special Features

Immediately following the main vocabulary, there are seven short reference lists. The first is an 11-page dictionary of foreign words and phrases often encountered in English speech and writing. Latin and French phrases predominate (mostly aphorisms and mottoes—all U.S. state ones are included); but German, Greek, Italian, Spanish, and even the Chinook

al-ki, Japanese **sayonara**, and Russian **nyet** appear. Pronunciations are included for each phrase and a key to the symbols appears on each double-page spread.

There are also lists of nations of the world (with pronunciations and outdated population figures), population of places in the U.S. (with 12,000 or more inhabitants as of 1970—also outdated), plus brief outdated population lists of U.S. states, Canadian places, provinces, and territories. The ten groups of common symbols and signs (astronomy, business, mathematics, medicine, apothecaries' measures and weights, miscellaneous, reference marks, stamps, and weather) are clear and useful. However, much of this supplementary material is outdated.

VII. Accessibility

The main text is printed in very small type. The main entry words are in clear bold type overhanging the text, which is printed in two columns. The entry words as well as the variant forms of words and run-on entry words and phrases appear in bold type and are easy to distinguish on a page. Each letter of the alphabet begins with a large capital letter enclosed in a bold decorative square. Two boldfaced guide words appear at the top outer margin on each page; readable page numbers appear at the top inner margins. The inner, top, outer and bottom margins are generous.

The explanatory notes appear in separate sections with appropriate subheads and are readily accessible at the front of the book. There is no separate list of the appendix sections, although these are mentioned in the preface. The text entries also refer to the metric system tables, which appear on pp. 440–41, almost in the center of the book. The weights and measures equivalent tables are found in the *W* vocabulary at **weight**. It is unlikely that readers will use these tables unless they find them by chance or perseverance.

VIII. Graphics and Format

This paperback has no illustrations apart from the separate signs and symbols lists. These are generously spaced out on the pages and are easy to read. The opening explanatory notes are similarly well spaced. The text appears to be a reduction of about 30% of the text size in the WEBSTER'S CONCISE FAMILY DICTIONARY. There is noticeable blurring of letters and some of the diacritical marks in the pronunciations cannot be distinguished. When multiple lines in successive entries run to the full column width, the text appears uncomfortably dense on a page. The bold figures for numbered meanings and bold colons

preceding definitions are visually helpful. Within definitions, small capital letters indicate cross-references and are readily apparent.

The book's design, in general, is clear. The newsprint quality paper reveals scant show-through. The dictionary is excellently bound; pages open easily and seem to withstand use even when the spine is cracked.

IX. Summary

As a review in *Library Journal* (15 November 1979) pointed out, for years this work has been one of the leading, authoritative abridged paperback dictionaries and "many consumers will continue to buy Merriam-Webster, if for no other reason than that it represents the best known name in American lexicography."

With its excellent core definitions, this is a useful, smaller dictionary to have at hand, especially for people who prefer a dictionary with less lexicographical apparatus and who do not require etymologies for most words.

As is typical of Merriam-Webster dictionaries, the explanatory notes are especially good. The separate alphabetical listing of foreign words and phrases is also useful. However, this fine dictionary, printed in 1974, is dated; many new ideas and terms are absent.

Microsoft Bookshelf CD-ROM Reference Library

Facts at a Glance

Full Title: **Microsoft Bookshelf CD-ROM Library Version 3.1.**

Contents: One single CD-ROM disk which includes: *The American Heritage Dictionary, Roget's II: Electronic Thesaurus, Bartlett's Familiar Quotations, The 1987 World Almanac and Book of Facts, The Chicago Manual of Style 13th Edition, Houghton Mifflin Spelling Verifier and Corrector, U.S. ZIP Code Directory, Houghton Mifflin Usage Alert, Business Information Sources* and a collection of *Forms and Letters*; User's Guide and Quick Reference Guide.

Publisher: Microsoft Corporation.
Edition Reviewed: © 1987.

Hardware Requirements:
Computer: IBM-PC, XT, AT (or compatible system).
Memory: 512K for a hard disk system
640K for a dual floppy system.

CD Drives: CD-ROM Drive and MS-DOS CD-ROM Extensions.

Price: $295.00 for one CD-ROM Disk, software, User's Guide and Quick Reference Guide. $50.00 for CD-ROM Extensions sold separately. Sold by Microsoft Corporation.

I. Introduction

Microsoft Bookshelf CD-ROM Reference Library is a collection of ten popular reference sources on a single CD-ROM disk. The sources included are THE AMERICAN HERITAGE DICTIONARY, *Roget's II: Electronic Thesaurus*, *Bartlett's Familiar Quotations*, *The 1987 World Almanac and Book of Facts*, *The Chicago Manual of Style: 13th Edition*, *Houghton Mifflin Spelling Verifier and Corrector*, *U.S. ZIP Code Directory*, *Houghton Mifflin Usage Alert*, *Business Information Sources*, and a collection of *Forms and Letters*. It is marketed as a tool for writers and is primarily designed to be used as a memory resident program with a word processing package. Currently, it is compatible with many of the most popular word processors including Microsoft Word and Word-Perfect.

II. Accessibility

Bookshelf requires an IBM PC, XT, AT or compatible system with 640K system memory for a floppy system, or 512K for a hard disk system. A CD-ROM drive, MS-DOS CD-ROM Extensions (software), and DOS 3.1 or higher are also required. The documentation states that use of a mouse or hard disk will increase the efficiency of using *Bookshelf*, although this is not a prerequisite for use.

It is Microsoft's intention to sell the CD-ROM Extensions to CD-ROM drive manufacturers so that they will be included with drives that are sold. In the meantime, and for those who have already purchased CD-ROM drives, the Extensions must be purchased separately. The suggested source is Meridian Data Inc., 4450 Capitola Rd., Capitola, CA 95010, (408) 476-5858.

The installation and setup of *Bookshelf* was rather difficult, at least when using a Sony 100 CD-ROM drive. In fact, the presence of the two peripherals suggested by the Microsoft Corporation as increasing *Bookshelf*'s efficiency, a mouse and a hard disk, generated some hardware conflicts that greatly complicated this procedure. Since the documentation for installation and setup provided with the software did not give enough information to solve problems such as these, several calls to the Microsoft Corporation were required to successfully complete installation.

III. Locating Information

Once installed and loaded into the computer's memory, *Bookshelf* is very easy to use. There is an online tutorial provided to teach users how to use *Bookshelf* which includes several practice searches for each of the reference sources. Two print manuals, a *User's Guide* and a *Quick Reference Guide*, contain additional information on using *Bookshelf*. All of these resources were more than adequate for instructing users on *Bookshelf*'s operation.

Bookshelf can be used as a stand-alone application or as a memory-resident program, meaning that once loaded into the computer's memory, it can be accessed from other programs without leaving the original application. With a simple keystroke (ALT-LEFT SHIFT key), *Bookshelf* is activated and a menu bar listing all ten reference sources appears across the top of the screen. This top level menu is the starting point each time you enter *Bookshelf*. Choosing a source from this menu will reveal a sub menu with additional options. After selecting a specific reference tool, a browser menu bar appears at the top of the screen which includes options specific to that reference. All of the menus operate in the same manner, allowing movement between options via the cursor keys, and selection of options via ENTER or ALT-key combinations. Short cuts, or "hot keys" as Microsoft calls them, are available to allow for a quick choice of the most frequently used option. For example, while in *Bookshelf*, pressing ALT-D immediately initiates a word search in the Dictionary. The combination of "hot keys" and menus allow both novice and experienced users to use *Bookshelf* easily and efficiently.

The ten tools in *Bookshelf* are of two general types: "quick lookup" (*Thesaurus, Dictionary, Spell Check, Usage Alert, ZIP Code Directory*) and reference tools (*Manual of Style, World Almanac, Bartlett's Quotations, Business Information Sources*, and *Forms and Letters*).

The "quick lookup" tools all operate in the same manner. A quick search of a word can be initiated using one of the ALT-key combinations. In the *Thesaurus, Spell Check*, or *Usage Alert*, a replacement word can be selected and automatically inserted in a document.

The *Dictionary* can be searched in this same manner to locate a definition of a word. In addition, it is possible to perform a keyword search through all definitions to locate a common term or terms. There is also quick search access to a biographies section and a geography section.

The *ZIP Code Directory* is the most inflexible of the quick lookup tools. To find a ZIP code, street address, city, and state must all be provided, even though the street name may not be necessary to determine the ZIP code. Once the ZIP code is found, the user has the option to automatically insert it in a document.

The reference tools allow more sophisticated searching and editing. Limited Boolean searching is provided (phrases, AND, OR); however, truncation and the logical operator NOT are unavailable. Three boxes are provided in which to enter search terms. Multiple words separated by spaces and typed in one box are treated as phrases and are searched in the order they are typed. If the terms are separated by commas, they are logically "ORed." The logical operator AND is used between terms typed in separate boxes. The search unit (chapter, section, article, paragraph) can also be user defined. Once the search has been conducted and the results displayed, the user can "zoom in" or "zoom out" to the next narrower or broader search unit.

These tools provide a "cut and paste" feature that allows users to save text found in one of these references and insert it into their document, with copyright information automatically inserted. Because of a special feature to hide columns in tables, sections of tables retrieved in the *World Almanac* may be saved and easily inserted into a document.

The *Manual of Style* can also be searched using Boolean logic and search terms but a more efficient search results if the table of contents or general index is used.

Forms and Letters is a large database of sample business forms, personal forms, and business letters which can be saved, copied to a word processor, and customized. The table of contents is the most efficient way to search this source.

One of the major problems encountered while using *Bookshelf* was a confusion about how the ENTER, TAB, and spacebar keys operate. Most of the time, ENTER is used to make a choice or select an option. However, sometimes the user is required to press the spacebar to make a selection, and pressing ENTER will only perform *Bookshelf*'s pre-selected option. In addition, the TAB key is used to move between options when entering information for a search. If by mistake the user presses ENTER, a search will be initiated prematurely. The operation of these keys may tend to frustrate experienced computer users because it is a departure from keystroke conventions used in other software packages.

Another problem was speed of execution. An IBM Personal System 2 Model 30 with 640K without a hard disk was used for this review. On this particular system, response time was rather slow. (A hard disk should speed up the program's execution.) For example, it took three to four seconds to activate *Bookshelf*, approximately five seconds to check words in the *Dictionary* or *Thesaurus*, and approximately eight to ten seconds to check the spelling of a single word in the *Spelling Verifier*. Asking for a spelling check of an entire screen took much longer (minutes, rather than seconds). Use of a RAM disk, which the documentation indicated was a preferred option, did speed up operation but the performance of *Bookshelf* was erratic for reasons that could not be determined.

IV. Cost

Microsoft Bookshelf has a suggested retail price of $295. As mentioned previously, MS-DOS CD-ROM Extensions are also required and cost $50 if they must be purchased separately. In addition, *Bookshelf* will also be available as part of a package offered by Amdek Corporation. This package will include an Amdek Laserdrive 1, the interface board and cable, and the MS-DOS CD-ROM Extensions, as well as *Microsoft Bookshelf.*

V. Currency

The information in *Bookshelf* is taken from the most recent editions of the ten reference sources. Copyright dates of most of the sources are 1986 or 1987. Reviewer documentation provided by the Microsoft Corporation stated that Microsoft "recognizes the time-sensitive nature of many of the resources in *Bookshelf* and is planning to offer annual updates." No further information regarding cost or mechanism for providing updates was given. Performing comparative searches in the printed sources versus the CD-ROM sources revealed no differences in the currency of these two versions.

VI. Accuracy and Quality of Entries

In general, the information in the *Bookshelf* sources appeared to be as accurate and complete as that in the printed sources. In some cases, *Bookshelf* sources provided less information. For example, the *Dictionary* does not provide pronunciations, a list of abbreviations, or illustrations. However, at times the *Bookshelf* sources seemed to provide more information than the printed versions. In many cases, the *Thesaurus* provides more possible synonyms than the printed version and displays them in the same grammatical case as the search term entered by the user.

VII. Summary

Overall, *Microsoft Bookshelf* is an impressive product. It is a powerful tool that is easy to master and to use. Improved documentation for installation and setup and increased speed of execution would enhance its utilization. Expanded searching features, such as availability of truncation and the Boolean NOT operator, would provide more sophisticated searching capabilities.

The sources available on *Bookshelf* are not meant to replace the print sources, and, in fact, many are adaptations for the electronic medium. However, the unique way that these sources can be used with a word processor create exciting possibilities for future CD-ROM applications.

Nelson's New Compact Webster's Dictionary

Facts at a Glance

Full Title: **Nelson's New Compact Webster's Dictionary**.
Publisher: Thomas Nelson.
Editor: Laurence Urdang.
Edition Reviewed: © 1978; 1985.

Number of Entries: 30,000.
Number of Pages: 314.
Trim Size: 3½″ × 5¼″.
Binding: paperback.

Price: $2.95.
Sold in bookstores and other outlets; also sold to libraries and other educational institutions.
ISBN 0-8407-5979-7.

I. Introduction and Scope

Except for the new foreword and the heavy flexible binding, *Nelson's New Compact Webster's Dictionary* is the same book as WEBSTER'S NEW COMPACT DICTIONARY FOR SCHOOL AND OFFICE (see the more complete review elsewhere in this guide). Although the pages have been photographically reduced in size, they appear open and inviting, and the text is well printed on good quality white stock. With its bright red, wipe clean vinyl cover, this small dictionary will be useful for quick personal reference—its vocabulary is larger than, for example, either the Merriam-Webster or the Nelson editions entitled *Webster's Vest Pocket Dictionary* and it is slightly less expensive than WEBSTER'S II NEW RIVERSIDE POCKET DICTIONARY.

New American Webster Handy College Dictionary

Facts at a Glance

Full Title: **New American Webster Handy College Dictionary**.
Former Title: The New American Webster Dictionary.
Publisher: New American Library.

Editors: Albert and Loy Morehead, Philip D. Morehead, and Andrew T. Morehead.
Edition Reviewed: © 1981.

Number of Entries: more than 115,000.
Number of Pages: 640.
Number of Indexes: 2.
Trim Size: 4¼″ × 7″.
Binding: paperback.

Price: $2.95.
Sold in bookstores and other outlets; also sold to libraries and schools.
ISBN 0-451-12537-1.

I. Introduction

The *New American Webster Handy College Dictionary* first appeared in 1951 and has had numerous successive printings. An expanded edition was published in 1972. According to the introduction, the work "supplies the spelling, syllabication, pronunciation, and meaning of the most useful words in the English language as it is spoken in the United States." This revised and updated edition contains more than 115,000 definitions and includes abbreviations, geographical names, foreign words and phrases, and forms of address.

II. Authority

The dictionary was prepared and edited by an organization that calls itself the "National Lexicographic Board." This group has no apparent formal connection to recognized scholarly associations or to those groups within the government that promote language studies. The late Albert H. Morehead is listed as chairman and general editor. A large number of consultants and their positions are listed; most are affiliated with universities, but companies such as Corning Glass Works and General Electric are also represented. The consultants' fields are wide-ranging and include art education, theology, sports editing, bacteriology, and electronics. No information is given on the criteria for inclusion of words or on any sources used to compile the work.

III. Comprehensiveness

Comprehensiveness is not a primary criterion for a small pocket dictionary; however, users' expectations for comprehensiveness will be met in part by this dictionary's inclusion of special feature listings at the back of the volume, such as a gazetteer, an abbreviations list, forms of address, and weights and measures, plus signs and symbols.

Within the main word list, some slang and colloquialisms and a few abbreviations are included.

Particularly full coverage is given to irregular verbs. For example, under **be** appear the following forms:

> *present indicative:* **I am**; **you are** (*Archaic*, **thou art**); **he is**; **we, you, they are**; *pret.* **I, he was**; **we, you, they were**; *p.p.* **been** ʿbin): **be′ing**.

Biographical entries appear rarely in the dictionary. A few historically significant people, such as **Caesar**, are entered; names of gods and goddesses and of literary figures are not. Some proper nouns are entered, such as names of movements (**Black Power**), trade names (**Magicube**), and holidays (**Shrove Tuesday**).

No etymology is given, and regularly formed inflections do not appear. Illustrative sentences or phrases are not provided.

IV. Quality and Currency of Entries

Definitions are brief and to the point. Entries include italicized part-of-speech abbreviations, pronunciation, and usage labels. A representative entry is the following:

> **die** (dī) *v.i.* [**died, dy′ing.**] **1.** cease to live; expire. **2.** come to an end. **3.** (with *away* or *out*) fade away. **4.** (with *for*) (*Colloq.*) desire keenly.—*n.* **1.** an engraved stamp used for impressing a design. **2.** any of various mechanical devices, as a tool for cutting the threads of screws. **3.** sing. of *dice*.

Definitions are generally more concise than those in the comparable WEBSTER'S NEW WORLD COMPACT SCHOOL AND OFFICE DICTIONARY. For example, under **contempt**, the first definition listed in the COMPACT is: "the feeling of a person toward someone or something he considers low, worthless." In the *Handy College Dictionary*, the first meaning reads: "the act of despising." For a second definition, the COMPACT lists "the condition of being despised"; the *Handy College Dictionary* provides "a feeling of disdain." In both dictionaries, the final meaning listed is the word's specialized usage in law. The COMPACT's definition is "a showing of disrespect for the dignity of a court (or legislature)"; the *Handy College Dictionary*'s is "defiance of a court, etc." Although the *Handy College Dictionary* provides very brief definitions, they are adequate for a work of this size. For many entries, several meanings are listed.

Homographs, such as **fair** (beautiful) and **fair** (bazaar) are generally grouped within a single entry. This practice is likely to prove confusing for users, who may expect to find homographs separately listed.

The volume's size and scope limit its inclusion of new words, although a number do appear. Included in the word list are **byte**, **videodisc**, **tofu**, and **afterburner**; excluded are, for example, *surrogate mother* and *videocassette*. While such omissions might be expected of a compact dictionary, purchasers will have to determine whether this level of currency meets their needs.

V. Syllabication and Pronunciation

Pronunciation is given in parentheses immediately following the entry word. The key to pronunciation is located at the front of the volume in the guide to the dictionary, and there is also an abbreviated guide at the bottom of each page. All of the symbols are standard ones, except for three not commonly found in small dictionaries: **ngg** as in *finger*, **nk** as in *ink*, and **kh** as in *blockhouse*. One German and two French sounds are indicated. Only one pronunciation is given for each entry word, and it is based, according to the editors, on "normal conversation rather than . . . formal speech."

Syllabication is indicated in the entry word with stress marks or centered dots. A single accent mark indicates primary stress, and paired accent marks indicate secondary stress, as in **smor′gas·bord″**. These procedures are similar to those used in other dictionaries.

VI. Special Features

For a dictionary of its size, the *New American Webster Handy College Dictionary* has a number of interesting features. It includes a five-page guide to the use of the dictionary, which presents rules for forming inflections. Appended to the lexicon is a list of abbreviations, which adds considerably to the few included in the main word list. Its wide range of entries includes **AP** (Associated Press), **BLT** (bacon, lettuce, and tomato sandwich), **SALT** (strategic arms limitation treaty), **Thurs.** (Thursday), and **ult.** (last month). While the list itself may be helpful to students, having some abbreviations located only in the main word list (not all appear in *both* places) may be inconvenient and misleading for the user.

Also included in the volume is a pronouncing gazetteer with population figures from the late 1970s and early 1980s. There is a three-page list of foreign words and phrases, including many from the Latin. Each entry provides pronunciation, a language label, and a translation. Other features are a list of forms of address, tables of weights and measures (including a metric conversion chart), and a list of signs and symbols. This last includes symbols used in punctuation, business and finance, weather, mathematics, medicine, and other fields.

VII. Accessibility

The boldface type makes entries fairly easy to locate; however, the fact that the dictionary does not provide separate entries for homographs and does not set main entry words overhanging the text requires more painstaking searching for words. Guide words on each page indicate the first and last entries on the page. These are set in boldface but rather small type.

Occasionally, an alternative spelling is noted at the end of an entry. Under **catalog**, for example, appears "Also **cat′a·logue″**." For the most part, however, alternative spellings are not given. The guide to the dictionary notes that "The user of this dictionary may rely upon finding a correct way to spell his word, but it will not necessarily be *the only* correct way." Given the limited scope of the dictionary, this should suffice.

VIII. Graphics and Format

Entry words are set in boldface, flush with succeeding lines of the entry. This format may pose problems, since it is always easier for the eye to locate words when entries overhang the text. Pages are double-column, and the layout and spacing are very tight. The paper is stock newsprint, but it is sufficiently heavy so that type from one side does not show through to the other. Pages separate easily from the volume's binding, and this paperback is unlikely to withstand heavy use.

IX. Summary

For the limited, quick reference use expected of a small pocket dictionary, the *New American Webster Handy College Dictionary* stands up well. It is concise, current, and inexpensive. The guide to the dictionary is unusually good for a small paperback, and the appendixes are useful. The binding and paper are not adequate for library use, but the paperback edition is useful in the home or office. In comparison, WEBSTER'S NEW WORLD COMPACT SCHOOL AND OFFICE DICTIONARY provides a better format for locating words easily, includes etymologies and personal names, and usefully places all abbreviations in the main word list. The COMPACT, which is more expensive than the *Handy*, has better-quality paper and is sturdy enough to withstand moderate library circulation. Nonetheless, the *Handy College Dictionary* will be preferred by many as an up-to-date, popularly priced, small-size dictionary.

New Century Vest-Pocket Webster Dictionary

Facts at a Glance

Full Title: **New Century Vest-Pocket Webster Dictionary.**
Publisher: New Century Publishers.
Editors: Arthur Norman and Robert E. Allen.
Edition Reviewed: 1975.

Number of Entries: Approximately 21,000.
Number of Pages: 304.
Number of Illustrations: Approximately 300.
Trim Size: 3″ × 5⅜″.
Binding: paperback.

Price: $2.95.
Sold in bookstores; also sold to libraries and other educational institutions.
ISBN 0-8329-1536-X.

I. Introduction

The *New Century Vest-Pocket Webster Dictionary* is a small, brief-entry-format dictionary similar in size and purpose to other "vest-pocket" books such as THE RANDOM HOUSE AMERICAN DICTIONARY, Simon & Schuster's WEBSTER'S NEW WORLD VEST POCKET DICTIONARY, and Merriam-Webster's VEST POCKET DICTIONARY.

According to the preface, dictionary users "rarely or never look up the meaning or spelling of common, everyday words like *be, and, is, not, of, or,* etc." Therefore, in order to make the best use of limited space, many such words are not included in this edition. They are also omitted, states the publisher, in order to make room "for thousands of modern terms and definitions not usually included in a dictionary of this size"—many of these inclusions, however, are now out-of-date.

II. Authority

Although this dictionary was revised by two English professors, no information is given about any previous edition of this work, nor are the original editors identified. Moreover, no information is provided regarding the word lists or sources used in compiling the work. In short, its authority is questionable.

III. Comprehensiveness

The *New Century Vest-Pocket Webster Dictionary* contains some 21,000 main entries, a relatively large number for so small and compact a book. However, owing to space limitations, the entries are far from comprehensive. Verbal illustrations have been omitted, and discriminated meanings for the same word are not identified by numerals.

The *New Century Vest-Pocket Webster Dictionary* has not been updated since 1975. Therefore, the statement made in the preface that certain common terms were excluded for the purpose of adding recent terms is no longer of much significance. Examples of recent but common technological words that are not included are *videocassette, video disc, video tape, modem, database, data bank* (although **data pro-**

cessing is included), and *disc/k drive*. The only reference to **disc** applies to a phonograph.

IV. Quality and Currency of Entries

A typical entry appears in the following sequence in the *New Century Vest-Pocket Webster Dictionary*: boldface, syllabified entry word; pronunciations in parentheses (when given); italicized part-of-speech label; principal verb form endings in parentheses (where appropriate); synonymous meanings, divided by commas, plus the various definitions, divided by semicolons; and any idioms or colloquialisms. Note the entry format in the following examples:

> **odd** *a.* not paired with another, single; left over; not exactly dividable by two; strange; -ɪ·ᴛʏ *n.* strangeness; strange person or thing; -s *n. pl.* difference in favor of one against another; advantage

> **o'cean** *n.* vast expanse of salt water that covers the greater part of the globe

> **op·pro'bri·um** (ə·pro'bre-əm) *n.* disgrace, shame; ᴏᴘ·ᴘʀᴏ'ʙʀɪ·ᴏᴜs *a.*

Some arbitrary decisions have been made regarding the "common, everyday words" not listed in the *New Century Vest-Pocket Webster Dictionary*. As noted above, the simple entry **odd** is included, but there is no listing for **fast**, whereas most abridged paperback dictionaries offer several entries for **fast** and note its homograph distinction.

Definitions are often inadequate. For example, the definition for **extrasensory** merely states: "gotten by some means other than normal senses (as *extrasensory perception*." This gives little indication of *what* is "gotten by . . . other than normal senses," nor does the example "extrasensory perception" help to further qualify the meaning in any substantial way.

V. Syllabication and Pronunciation

Entry word syllabication is indicated by centered dots, except where stress is shown by an accent mark. Only problematic pronunciations are phonetically respelled (see **opprobrium**, in the previous section, as compared to **odd** and **ocean**). A "Key to Pronunciation" in the front section of the book describes the 41 phonetic symbols used in this dictionary. According to the editor, the key is based on the Midwestern dialect.

VI. Special Features

In addition to the pronunciation key, the front matter provides an explanatory page that clearly outlines the structure of the book's definitions and gives an annotated example of all entry components. There is also a listing of the 22 abbreviations used in the dictionary.

Appendixes include short essays that provide rules for punctuation, abbreviations and contractions, capitalization, spelling, and letter writing. By and large, this section is too general and condensed to substantially assist users. The back matter also contains a 2-page map with time zones indicated and 20 pages of statistical tables on such subjects as population, food, industrial production, United States and world cities, U.S. presidents, and weights and measures. Many of these statistics are badly outdated and of little practical value, while others remain marginally useful.

VII. Accessibility

Entries are reasonably accessible. Boldface guide words at the top outer corner of each page indicate the first entry on the left-hand page and the last entry on the right-hand page. No thumb indexes or other finding aids are provided. Alternate spellings of words are included as part of the main entry heading (**crit'i·cize**, **crit-i·cise**).

VIII. Graphics and Format

The print in this pocket edition is extremely small, and it is almost impossible to read the supplementary back sections without the aid of a magnifying lens.

The black-and-white line drawings that are scattered throughout this dictionary are too small and rudimentary to be of much value. Often these illustrations are irrelevant simply because the definition is not stated clearly enough to show the intent of the drawing; in other instances, it is impossible to tell what detail in the illustration actually represents the defined word.

IX. Summary

The *New Century Vest-Pocket Webster Dictionary* is a book of dubious value. Even for a vest-pocket book, its entries are limited in scope and detail. The definitions are at best rudimentary, at worst misleading. On top of this, the dictionary has long been outdated. Readers requiring a dictionary in this format will be much better served by Wᴇʙsᴛᴇʀ's Vᴇsᴛ Pᴏᴄᴋᴇᴛ Dɪᴄᴛɪᴏɴᴀʀʏ, published by Merriam-Webster.

Oxford Advanced Learner's Dictionary of Current English

Facts at a Glance

Full Title: **Oxford Advanced Learner's Dictionary of Current English**.

Publisher: Oxford University Press.

Editors: A. S. Hornby with A. P. Cowie and A. C. Gimson.

Oxford Advanced Learner's Dictionary of Current English

❶ IPA pronunciation is enclosed by virgules

❷ Syllabication is shown by centered dots

❸ Arrows denote cross-references

❹ Stress marks appear in examples as well as entry words

❺ A swung dash indicates repetition of main entry word

❻ Usage labels are enclosed in parentheses

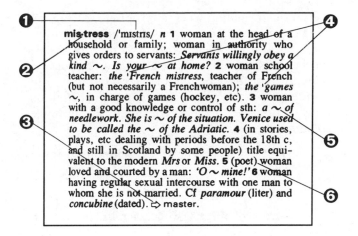

Edition Reviewed: © 1974; 14th printing revised and reset, 1980.

Number of Entries: 50,000.
Number of Pages: 1,037.
Number of Illustrations: 1,000 black-and-white drawings.
Trim Size: 5½″ × 8⁷⁄₁₆″.
Binding: hardcover.

Price: $17.25.
Sold in bookstores; also sold to libraries and other educational institutions.
ISBN 0-19-431101-5.

I. Introduction

The *Oxford Advanced Learner's Dictionary of Current English* is for the foreign student of English, which accounts for the unusual and somewhat misleading title. Advanced here means a student who has already mastered the rules of grammar and pronunciation, and has a large enough vocabulary "to read and understand English of moderate difficulty." This dictionary has been designed primarily for a nonnative speaker of English who is gaining competence in British English and "who wants to develop further his knowledge of how English words, compounds and idiomatic expressions are used, what they mean, how they are pronounced and how they are spelt." American meanings and spellings are also covered.

This work, reviewed in its fourteenth printing, is an abridged dictionary of over 100,000 items that include 50,000 main entry words and derivations, 11,000 idiomatic expressions, and illustrative phrases and sentences. It is for a serious student, and for use in home, classroom (from high school through graduate school), and library.

II. Authority

Oxford has about 60 dictionaries bearing its name, all with high standards of scholarship, carefully written and researched. The *Oxford Advanced Learner's Dictionary*, first published in 1948, lists A. S. Hornby as its general editor and compiler. Hornby has been a leading writer and teacher of the English language. He is a renowned lexicographer, grammarian, and experienced teacher of English, three necessary areas of expertise in compiling a student dictionary.

This edition is a revised, updated, and reset impression of the 1974 third edition.

III. Comprehensiveness

The *Advanced Learner's Dictionary* claims to be a dictionary "of the English language as it is written and spoken today [meaning the late 1970s] by educated British men and women" and to have up-to-date vocabulary, including literary and technical English. Examples of current words are **radar, disc jockey, detente, acupuncture, memory** (as a unit of a computer), **parthenogenesis, punk rock,** and **gay** (slang meaning). Not included were *amniocentesis,* computer terminology such as *data base, disc, random access memory* (RAM, also not in the abbreviation appendix) and other acronyms used with computers, as well as commonly used terms such as *cold war* and *big bang.*

Etymologies and quotations are not given, but they are not within the intended scope of this dictionary. The helpful features are the usage notes, example phrases and sentences that illustrate sentence patterns and contexts, the appendixes, the cross-references shown by use of an arrow, and the 29 pages of introductory material.

IV. Quality and Currency of Entries

The definitions are clear and concise. Words are entered under the British spelling with cross-references to American spelling when appropriate. Definitions give both British and American meaning and usage. Scientific and technical words and phrases are defined enough to allow the reader to get a sense of the word and the meaning of the material; but, for a reader who really needs a more detailed definition, other dictionaries must be consulted. For example, **belladonna** is defined as

> (drug prepared from) poisonous plant with red flowers and black berries

parthenogenesis is briefly treated:

> reproduction of offspring without fertilization by sexual union

plaque is only defined as a

> flat metal or porcelain plate fixed on a wall as an ornament or memorial

The dental definition of *plaque* as a thick, sticky material made up of bacteria and other substances that accumulate on teeth and gums is not given.

Multiple definitions for a word are numbered showing the different meanings or usages. The introduction notes that "Definitions are listed in order of meaning from the most common or most simple to the most rare or most complicated."

In the segment from **paprika** to **parachute**, this work has four intervening entries: **papyrus**, **par**, **parable**, and **parabola**. *The Thorndike Barnhart Advanced Dictionary* (1973) has 16 intervening entries and The American Heritage Dictionary: Second College Edition has 21 intervening entries. Of the words omitted from the *Advanced Learner's*, the largest percentage are scientific or medical words, and a few geographic entries. The compilers must have felt that these were not needed for the general reader. However, **para** is omitted as a prefix and as a combining word in both the main body and in "Appendix 3 • Affixes."

V. Syllabication and Pronunciation

The *Advanced Learner's Dictionary* uses the International Phonetic Alphabet (IPA) as a guide to pronunciation. The only IPA key in the dictionary is placed on the inside front cover. British pronunciation is given for each word and, when the American pronunciation is very different, the "General American" pronunciation is also shown.

VI. Special Features

The special features are a strong point of this dictionary. The "Key to Entries" clearly explains how to read each entry and the introduction includes sections on writing and speaking English, grammar, and style. All of these will be particularly helpful and interesting to nonnative users of English. The appendixes have a less even quality. "Affixes," "Irregular Verbs," "Numerical Expressions," "Weights and Measures," "Books of the Bible," and "Works of Shakespeare" are comprehensive and easy to follow. "Geographical Names," "Abbreviations," and "Punctuation" show a decidedly British bias. We find the abbreviation **TUC**, but not *AFL-CIO*, **MP** but no *GOP*. Likewise, "Geographical Names" includes every English county, and "Punctuation" guidelines invariably choose very British illustrative examples. A phrase in apposition is exemplified by "Queen Elizabeth II, a very popular monarch, celebrated her Silver Jubilee in 1977."

Some biographical information is included, if it is part of a definition such as **Queen Victoria**, under the entry for **Victorian**. Mythological and Biblical names are defined, for example, **Mercury** and **Moloch**.

VII. Accessibility

Main entry words, compounds, and variant spellings are in boldface type and are easily found. American forms appear both alongside the main entry word— **centre** (U.S. = **center**)—and in their own alphabetical position with a cross-reference—**cen'ter**/sĕnt(r)/ *n* (U.S.) = **centre**. Sample sentences are liberally distributed—**hold** and its associated idioms like **hold water** and **hold one's own** receive more than 40 illustrative examples. Italics are used for the sample sentences.

There is no thumb index, probably because the side margins are so narrow, but the dictionary would have been easier to use if there had been one. The contents page lists the prefaces, introductory materials, and appendixes as well as the information found on the inside of the front and back covers.

VIII. Graphics and Format

The general format of the dictionary's two columns of text is tight looking and very unappealing. The ivory-colored paper is thick, so there is no see-through, but the total effect is somewhat dreary. The book does not lie flat and its margins are extremely narrow.

Despite the cover claim that the dictionary is "fully illustrated," photographs and line drawings are not generously supplied, are frequently not alongside their associated entry words, and do not receive any cross-references. Both line drawings and photographs are of poor quality and much too small to serve any explanatory purpose.

IX. Summary

This dictionary lives up to its scope and purpose. It gives the student clear definitions, aids in usage for formal and informal words and phrases, slang, and idiomatic phrases. It will be helpful for reading, formal course work, writing, and conversation. For a foreign student who will be using American publications and/or studying and living in the United States, there are other publications that should be looked at, such as Hornby's OXFORD STUDENT'S DICTIONARY OF AMERICAN ENGLISH, the LONGMAN DICTIONARY OF CONTEMPORARY ENGLISH, and Maclin's *Reference Guide to English: A Handbook of English as a Second Language*. The dictionary, as bound, will not withstand heavy library use.

Oxford American Dictionary

Facts at a Glance

Full Title: **Oxford American Dictionary**.
Publishers: Oxford University Press (hardcover edition); Avon Books (paperback editions).
Editors: Eugene Ehrlich, Stuart Berg Flexner, Gorton Carruth, and Joyce M. Hawkins.
Copyright: © 1980; 1986 printing (Oxford).

Number of Entries: 35,000.
Number of Pages: 832 (hardcover and trade paperback editions); 1,120 (mass market paperback edition).
Trim Sizes: 5⅞″ × 9″ (hardcover); 5¼″ × 8″ (trade paperback); 4³⁄₁₆″ × 6⅞″ (mass market paperback).

Price: $14.95 hardcover; $7.95 trade paperback; $3.95 mass market paperback.
Sold in bookstores, in supermarkets, and directly to libraries.
ISBN 0-19-502795-7 (Oxford, hardcover);
ISBN 0-380-51052-9 (Avon, trade paperback);
ISBN 0-380-60772-7 (Avon, mass market paperback).

I. Introduction

The *Oxford American Dictionary*, first published in 1980 by Oxford University Press (and issued simultaneously in two paperback editions by Avon Books), was designed to give Americans a concise desk dictionary whose authority matches that of Oxford's British dictionaries. Unlike the many other dictionaries published by this firm, the *American Dictionary* embodies an American lexicon and uses American spellings. Thus, although it bears the Oxford imprint, the *Oxford American Dictionary* stands apart from the rest of the Oxford dictionaries reviewed in this Buying Guide, being the only Oxford dictionary designed specifically for Americans.

II. Authority

The *Oxford American Dictionary* is based primarily on the *Oxford Paperback Dictionary* (not available

in the United States). Apart from Joyce Hawkins, who compiled that work, its chief editors are American and are not on the staff of Oxford University Press. These editors include Stuart Berg Flexner (editor of THE RANDOM HOUSE DICTIONARY OF THE ENGLISH LANGUAGE, among many other works), Eugene Ehrlich (lecturer in English and comparative literature at Columbia University), and Gorton Carruth, former editor at Funk & Wagnalls. All are eminently qualified for their task and bring wide experience in language studies and reference books to the *Oxford American Dictionary*.

III. Comprehensiveness

According to the publisher's jacket blurb, "the *Oxford American Dictionary* contains all the words an American is likely to hear or read in the home, office, or school." Given that it contains only 35,000 entries, however, this claim is not to be taken seriously. Indeed, the "Publisher's Note" at the beginning of the dictionary acknowledges that "this *Oxford American Dictionary* is not intended to be comprehensive or to be a substitute for an encyclopedia or larger dictionary."

The count of 35,000 entries is somewhat misleading because many derivative words and phrases are included under these main entries. Therefore, the dictionary covers a wider range of vocabulary than the number 35,000 indicates. Biographical and geographical names are included as entries, but again there is no attempt to be all-encompassing. In preparing this edition, the editors omitted a number of British words that are little used in America, but retained others, such as **Oxbridge** and **pence**, that are occasionally encountered in the United States.

When it was issued in 1980, the *Oxford American Dictionary* was intended to be a dictionary for the eighties. However, it has not been revised since its initial publication and now shows its age. For example, while it includes such common modern terms as **ayatollah and gridlock**, it does not include *AIDS*, *compact disc*, or *yuppie*.

IV. Quality and Currency of Entries

The *Oxford American Dictionary* presents "the most common current meanings, spellings, and pronunciations" and thus is more suited for everyday practical use than for the scholar. The editors have endeavored to provide "concise and precise definitions presented in a straightforward way." Words used in defining difficult or technical entry words are generally much simpler than the entry word itself. For example, the first definition for **psychology** is "the study of the mind and how it works."

Oxford American Dictionary

❶ Pronunciation is enclosed in parentheses

❷ Inflected forms are set in boldface type and are enclosed in parentheses

❸ Syllabication is shown by centered dots

❹ Idiomatic expressions are introduced by an open square

❺ Usage notes are introduced by an open triangle, set on its side

❻ Usage labels are italicized and enclosed in parentheses

❶ ❷ ❸ ❹ ❺ ❻

> **hope** (hohp) *n.* 1. a feeling of expectation and desire combined, a desire for certain events to happen. 2. a person or thing or circumstance that gives cause for this. 3. what one hopes for. **hope** *v.* **(hoped, hop·ing)** to feel hope, to expect and desire, to feel fairly confident. ☐**hoping against hope,** hoping for something that is barely possible.
> **hope·ful** (hohp-fŭl) *adj.* 1. feeling hope. 2. causing hope, seeming likely to be favorable or successful. **hopeful** *n.* a person who hopes or seems likely to succeed, *young hopefuls.* **hope′ful·ness** *n.*
> **hope·ful·ly** (hohp-fŭ-lee) *adv.* 1. in a hopeful way. 2. it is to be hoped, *hopefully, we shall be there by one o'clock.* ▷Many people regard the second use as unacceptable.
> **hope·less** (hohp-lis) *adj.* 1. feeling no hope. 2. admitting no hope, *a hopeless case.* 3. inadequate, incompetent, *is hopeless at tennis.* **hope′less·ly** *adv.* **hope′less·ness** *n.*
> **hop·head** (hop-hed) *n.* *(slang)* a drug addict.

The dictionary does not use synonyms to define words "unless they help distinguish shades of meaning." Occasionally, a simple sentence or phrase is included to show how a word might be used in context; such examples are printed in italics. For instance, the brief entry for **qualitative** includes the phrase *qualitative analysis.* There are no etymologies, although literal translations are given for words of foreign origin.

As an example of a typical entry in the *Oxford American Dictionary*, consider the following:

> **dis·en·chant** (dis-en-chant) *v.* to free from enchantment, to disillusion, *they are disenchanted with the government.* **dis·en·chant·ment** *n.*

Idiomatic phrases and derivative or compound words are included within the entry for the word from which they derive and are printed in boldface type. As an example, the entry for **grace** includes **be in a person's good graces, days of grace, grace note,** and **with good grace.** Again, however, the *Oxford American Dictionary* does not attempt to be comprehensive in its inclusion of idioms and derivatives.

V. Syllabication and Pronunciation

Main entry words and their inflected and variant forms are divided into syllables by centered dots, showing the acceptable division of the word in writing, typing, or printing. Derivative words within an entry include a stress mark to indicate different emphasis in similar words.

The pronunciation is indicated by a system of respelling that includes diacritical marks where necessary. This system is quite simple and easy to use. Just as the British Oxford dictionaries give standard English pronunciations, so the pronunciations in the *Oxford American Dictionary* are standard American English.

VI. Special Features

The most notable feature of the *Oxford American Dictionary* is its usage notes, which are included for about 600 potentially troublesome entries. These give clear guidance for the reader who is not sure of proper usage. The editors proudly point out that this dictionary "distinguishes between good and bad English" and claim that it "sets high, somewhat conservative standards in usage." This is generally true. For example, although the second sense of the word **disinterested** is given as "uninterested, uncaring," the usage note for this word remarks that "careful writers regard [this] use as unacceptable because it obscures a useful distinction between *disinterested* and *uninterested.*" The usage note for **contact** observes that "careful writers do not use *contact* as a verb. Instead of *contacting* someone, they *call* or *write* or *visit* him." Another usage note emphasizes the distinction between *fewer* and *less.*

Usage notes are indicated by the symbol ▷. A special index lists all the entries that include usage notes.

Many entries also carry usage labels. The *Oxford American Dictionary* identifies *informal, slang, old* (for archaic), and *contemptuous.*

VII. Accessibility

The excellent design of the *Oxford American Dictionary* enhances its accessibility. (See also *Graphics and Format.*) Entry words are printed in boldface type, and in a different typeface from the main text, and overhang the text. Different senses of a word are numbered but run-on in the text. Different parts of speech, derivative words, and idiomatic words and phrases are all included under the main entry but are printed in the same boldface type as the main entry word, enabling the reader to find them with ease.

Guide words, printed flush with the outside margin at the top of each page, indicate the first and last entry word on the page.

VIII. Graphics and Format

The *Oxford American Dictionary* is available in three formats: hardcover, trade paperback, and mass market paperback. The hardcover edition will be the first choice for library collections. Individuals may settle for the small mass market edition, but the larger trade paperback edition, with bigger print, better paper and printing quality, and a more durable binding, is well worth the extra few dollars.

The typeface is large and easy to read, especially in the hardcover and trade paperback versions. Although not designed specifically for the visually impaired, these versions will have extra appeal for people who have trouble reading small print. The page design is clear and uncluttered, with ample white space and margins. Entry words are printed in boldface and overhang the text. The absence of illustrations is not a drawback.

Curiously, the pronunciation key is included in the introductory text. It would have been more accessible on a page by itself. Regrettably, neither the key nor an abbreviated version of it is repeated at the foot of each two-page spread, as is the normal practice in many dictionaries of this size.

IX. Summary

The *Oxford American Dictionary* is the first Oxford University Press dictionary designed specifically for Americans. With only 35,000 entries, it cannot be considered the first or only choice for either library or individual collections. Also, it is now becoming seriously outdated, and at the time of this review Oxford University Press had not announced any plans to revise the work.

Despite these drawbacks, however, the *Oxford American Dictionary* still has much to recommend it. It offers basic and clear if unsubtle definitions that can be easily understood by the average reader. Moreover, it contains some 600 authoritative usage notes whose conservative stance will be applauded by grammarians. These notes make the *Oxford American Dictionary* particularly useful to those readers (and writers) whose knowledge of correct usage may be shaky but who want and will accept guidance in this area. The clear print and excellent page design (particularly in the hardcover and trade paperback editions) is an added bonus.

The *Oxford American Dictionary* does not compete against other Oxford dictionaries. It is sufficiently different from the titles that originated in the U.K. that many libraries may want to have both this book and another Oxford work, such as the CONCISE OXFORD DICTIONARY. It is most closely comparable to THE AMERICAN HERITAGE DESK DICTIONARY and WEBSTER'S NEW IDEAL DICTIONARY, although the comparison is not clear-cut. In any event, this book, ideally suited for everyday use by ordinary Americans, makes a useful supplement to other, more comprehensive dictionaries. The pity is that it is not more comprehensive and up-to-date.

The Oxford-Duden Pictorial English Dictionary

Facts at a Glance

Full Title: **The Oxford-Duden Pictorial English Dictionary.**
Publisher: Oxford University Press.
Editor: John Pheby.
Edition Reviewed: © 1981.

Number of Entries: over 28,000.
Number of Pages: 820.
Number of Illustrations: over 28,000 in black and white plus 6 color plates.
Trim Size: 5″ × 7½″.
Binding: paperback.

Price: $12.95.
Sold in bookstores; also sold to libraries and other educational institutions.
ISBN 0-19-864155-9.

I. Introduction and Scope

The Oxford-Duden Pictorial English Dictionary was first published in 1981. According to the work's foreword

> There are certain kinds of information which can be conveyed more readily and clearly by pictures than by definitions and explanations alone: an illustration will help the reader to visualize the object denoted by the word and to form an impression of the way in which objects function in their own technical field or in the everyday life of English-speaking countries.

Thus the work is designed to be useful to the native speaker expanding a technical vocabulary as well as to the learner of English as a second language. For either, the work can be a practical supplement to a good general dictionary.

It should be noted that the vocabulary is British in slant, but that American forms are shown in parentheses, preceded by the abbreviation *Am.*: for example,

grocer's shop (grocer's, delicatessen shop. *Am.* grocery store, delicatessen store), a retail shop (*Am.* retail store)

Although the British form is given first, both forms are indexed, and the work's British origin should cause few problems for the speaker or learner of American English.

Over 28,000 objects are named and illustrated in the dictionary. The subjects include "typical scenes in domestic and working life, recreation and sport, flora and fauna, industry, the arts, science, and technology." These are arranged by categories, such as "Atom, Universe, Earth," "Man and His Social Environment," "Nature as Environment, Agriculture and Forestry," and so forth. This arrangement enables the reader to use the book as "a key to the vocabulary of a subject." An alphabetical index lists all the words illustrated, so words can also be accessed as they would be in a conventional dictionary.

The work is based on *The Oxford-Duden Pictorial German-English Dictionary*, published in 1980. The current work is the product of "numerous modifications of the text and illustrations of the original work . . . , especially regarding the depiction of everyday objects and situations."

II. Format

The illustrations grouped within the broad categories are numbered. Each page or double-page spread shows a list, printed in a two-column format, of words associated with a particular subject. The words are numbered with boldface numerals, each of which corresponds to a numbered item in the illustration. The numbers in the illustration are circled when they refer to the name of an entire construct rather than one of its components. For example, under **Dining Room**, 33 items are named and pictured; these include such objects as a **placemat**, a **wineglass**, and a **coffee cup**. The number 27, referring to the **coffee set**, is circled; numbers for its parts (**coffee pot**, **sugar bowl**, and so forth) are not. In the list, words that refer to an item whose component parts are also named appear in boldface, and they arc usually preceded by the inclusive numerals for the component items. For example, the first item listed under **Dining Room** appears as **1–11 dining set**. Items 1 through 11 include **dining table**, **table leg**, **table top**, and so forth. Synonyms for listed words are often given in parentheses after the words: for example, **masked ball** (masquerade, fancy-dress ball).

The alphabetical index is printed in a three-column format. Each word and phrase entered is followed by a boldface numeral indicating the scene in which the item is pictured and a lightface number referring to the item within the picture. Homonyms and uses of the same word in different fields are distinguished by italicized section headings:

groove *Iron Foundry etc.* **148** 59
groove *Sawmill* **157** 6

groove *Ball Games* **291** 29
groove *Winter Sp.* **301** 39
groove *Music. Instr.* **326** 13
groove *Art* **334** 27

The abbreviations used for subject fields are explained on the first page of the index.

The dictionary is physically well designed. The typeface used in the lexicon is large and clear; that used in the index, although smaller, is readable. White space is used advantageously throughout the work to make it attractive and easy to use. Although the good-quality paper allows some show-through of text and illustrations, this is not a serious drawback. However, some of the illustrations are small in size so that the embedded numbers may be more difficult for the user to follow. The paperback is exceptionally sturdy and can be opened flat with no danger of loss of pages; it will hold up well to heavy use.

III. Quality and Currency of Entries

The dictionary is remarkable in its range of subjects and the detail and quality of its illustrations. Its value to the learner of English as a second language lies in its excellent coverage of everyday scenes and items. For example, the learner who needs an English vocabulary to negotiate family clothing purchases will find five double-page spreads devoted to the topic: **Children's Clothes**; **Ladies' Wear I (Winter Wear)**; **Ladies' Wear II (Summer Wear)**; **Underwear, Nightwear**; and **Men's Wear**. Under **Children's Clothes** alone, 68 items are named and pictured, including both names of garments (**playsuit**, **snow suit**, **culottes**) and names of their parts (**pompon**, **front zip**, **inset pockets**). However, the American user of the dictionary will not find an entry for electric range. That entry can only be found under its British equivalent, **cooker**.

The native English speaker will benefit from the work's comprehensiveness and detail, particularly in more technical fields. For example, the 68-item illustrated vocabulary on beekeeping will assist a novice interested in pursuing this subject. Homeowners attempting to communicate with the plumber or roofer will similarly find extensive vocabularies to describe their problems and preferences. Not only will the reader find vocabularies applicable to daily life and leisure time; a great many sections are devoted to highly technical occupations, such as the production of synthetic fibers and of nuclear energy.

In addition to identifying Americanisms, the entries provide some usage information; 11 abbreviations are explained at the front of the volume. These identify, for example, terms for male (*m.* bull) and female (*f.* cow) animals and their young (*y.* calf).

The black-and-white line drawings in some cases depict coherent scenes. **Office I**, for example, shows the interior of a modern receptionist's office, with its furnishings and machines. Other illustrations depict discrete items: **Office III** pictures a range of office equipment, such as **paper clips**, **correcting fluid**, and a **desk diary**. The drawings are uniformly clear and carefully detailed, regardless of whether their subject is everyday life or the most specialized field. In addition to the line drawings, the volume contains six superbly reproduced color plates. One of these illustrates **Color** itself; four others depict butterflies, birds (two plates), and deep-sea fauna. A sixth color plate depicts human organ systems. These plates are a valuable addition to the book.

IV. Accessibility

The work is well designed to facilitate accessibility. A detailed table of contents shows the broad category headings in boldface. Listed beneath these are the titles and numbers of the drawings. The easy-to-use alphabetical index lists all the words depicted in the volume as well as their variants. At the top of each page within the lexicon, bold running heads display the picture name and number. Within the index, two boldface guide words appear on each double-page spread, indicating the first and last words on the spread.

V. Summary

The Oxford-Duden Pictorial English Dictionary is an excellent, easy-to-use pictorial dictionary. Although some Briticisms are not translated into American usage, its vocabulary includes a wide range of both everyday and technical language; its drawings and color plates are detailed, attractive, and useful.

For the English-language learner, this work will serve as the perfect complement to a good ESL dictionary. Some beginning ESL students, to be sure, will find its wealth of information overwhelming. These students would initially be better served by a smaller, simpler pictorial dictionary, such as the LONGMAN PHOTO DICTIONARY, which contains exercises that can be used in the language classroom. The FACTS ON FILE VISUAL DICTIONARY is another work that would be useful for ESL students. Its larger illustrations with fewer labels would be less daunting. However, once the student reaches the intermediate level, the *Oxford-Duden* would be the appropriate choice.

For the native speaker the work also has considerable value, enabling users to expand their vocabularies in many previously unfamiliar areas. The work bears comparison in this regard with THE FACTS ON FILE VISUAL DICTIONARY, which illustrates a comparable number of words and is also highly useful and well designed. The FACTS ON FILE work is limited in value for the learner of English as a second language because it depicts fewer scenes of everyday life and because its size prevents it from being conveniently portable. While the native speaker will find THE FACTS ON FILE VISUAL DICTIONARY valuable because it was written for an American audience, the easier portability and lower price of the *Oxford-Duden* will make it more attractive to some. It will be useful for larger public and college and university libraries.

The Oxford English Dictionary

Facts at a Glance

Full Title: **The Oxford English Dictionary** and **Supplement**, Volume 1 A–G; **Supplement**, Volume 2 H–N; **Supplement**, Volume 3 O–Scz; **Supplement**, Volume 4 Se–Z.

Former Title: A New English Dictionary on Historical Principles.

Publisher: Oxford University Press.

Editors: James A. H. Murray, Henry Bradley, W. A. Craigie, C. T. Onions.

Supplements Editor: Robert W. Burchfield.

Editions Reviewed: © 1933, 1971 printing; supplements, © 1972, 1976, 1982, 1986.

Number of Entries: 500,000.

Number of Pages: 21,133 (12 volumes); Supplement, Volume 1, 1,331; Supplement, Volume 2, 1,300; Supplement, Volume 3, 1,579; Supplement, Volume 4, 1,454.

Number of Illustrative Quotations: 2,354,806.

Trim Size: 9½″ × 12″.

Binding: hardcover (12 volumes plus 4 supplements).

Price: $1,500.00; single supplement volumes, $150.00.

Sold in bookstores, through other outlets, and by direct mail. Also sold directly to libraries.

ISBN 0-19-861101-3;
ISBN 0-19-861115-3;
ISBN 0-19-861123-4;
ISBN 0-19-861124-2;
ISBN 0-19-861136-6.

I. Introduction

The Oxford English Dictionary (*OED*) is certainly by far the largest, and for some uses the best, dictionary in the world. It is a historical dictionary, in which word forms and meanings are traced from their earliest appearance in English onward through extensive quotations. Its record of the history and

The Oxford English Dictionary

❶ Etymology is enclosed in brackets

❷ Quotations, arranged chronologically, illustrate word histories

❸ Field labels are italicized

❹ Cross-references are set in small capitals

❺ Dates, in boldface type, and sources are cited for all quotations

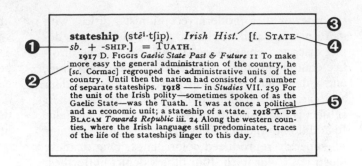

meaning of English words between about 1150 and the present is incomparable. The work is of greatest value to readers seeking accurate and detailed information about word origins, derivations, and histories. However, it is not a dictionary in the conventional sense, lacking many features found in general dictionaries, such as syllabication and biographical and geographic terms. American readers should be aware that the work incorporates British spelling and pronunciation; it does not serve as an accurate guide to the language current in the United States. The origins of the *OED* date from 1857, when the Philological Society adopted a proposal for a dictionary "on historical principles." (The Philological Society, founded in 1842, is a part of the School of Oriental and African Studies, London, and is dedicated to the study of the structure and history of languages.) The first volume, on the letters *A* and *B*, was completed in 1888, under the title *A New English Dictionary on Historical Principles* (the present title was substituted in 1895). The tenth and final volume of the original set, on letters *V–Z*, appeared in 1928.

From the early years of the project, users noted gaps in the published volumes, especially overlooked words or early uses. Many of their observations were published in journals such as *Notes and Queries*, while others were sent directly to the dictionary's Oxford offices. A supplemental volume to the original ten, published in 1933, was the first outcome of these contributions. More thorough correction came in four additional supplemental volumes published 1972–86, which subsumed the entries of the 1933 volume. The 1933 volume remains useful, however, not only for its lengthy history of the project (to which account add K. M. Elizabeth Murray, *Caught in the Web of Words: James A. H. Murray and the Oxford English Dictionary* [1977]) but also for its bibliography of the works from which the citations were taken, which explains the sometimes cryptic references in the lexicon.

The *OED* has no competitors, but several abridged editions have been issued. Condensed from the original are the Shorter Oxford English Diction-

ary on Historical Principles (two large volumes), The Concise Oxford Dictionary of Current English (one large volume), and the Little and the Pocket Oxford Dictionary of Current English (each one small volume). Also available is an unabridged edition called The Compact Edition of the Oxford English Dictionary, which photographically reduces four pages onto one and requires the use of a magnifying glass, which is provided with it. In addition, the *OED* is now available on compact disc; see pages 324–27 for further information about this format.

Some so-called Oxford dictionaries (such as the Oxford American Dictionary, 1980) are formed on a different plan. The *OED* is unique and preeminent, while the abridgments are neither. For most users, the *OED* itself will always be the English dictionary of preference and greatest value for the history of word forms and meanings.

II. Authority

The *OED* has received kudos in virtually every book about the English language: Baugh and Cable, for example, call it "the greatest dictionary of any language in the world" (*A History of the English Language*, 3d ed., 1978). A major enterprise of a major international press, it has earned knighthoods for two of its editors. But the publishers' and editors' authority stems ultimately from the collection of citations on which they worked.

The Philological Society's plan was to incorporate the materials of earlier dictionaries, notably Samuel Johnson's (1755 and later editions), and to add citations from all writers before 1500 and "as many as possible of the more important writers of later times." (The Early English Text Society was founded in 1864 chiefly to provide reliable editions of medieval English writings for the new dictionary.) By 1884 about 1,300 readers had ransacked over 5,000 British authors for some 3½ million citations, a collection that subsequently grew to 6 million. For the post–World

War II supplements, readers culled a further 1½ million citations, with which several large specialized word collections were merged.

Despite its huge size and scope, the *OED* remains too selective for some periods and some regions, so projects that take the *OED* as a model have been founded to record the English of those somewhat neglected times and places more fully. These works include *A Dictionary of American English on Historical Principles* (four volumes, 1936–44) and *A Middle English Dictionary* (1952– in progress).

The authority of the *OED*, then, rests on the long-standing solidity of the enterprise, the lexicographical leadership of its large and distinguished editorial staff, and the comprehensive collection of materials assembled for it. But this same collection, and the scrupulous work needed to arrange it into the definitions, have made revisions inevitably infrequent.

III. Comprehensiveness

The intent of the *OED*'s editors has been to include all words and meanings that have come into English since 1150. However, according to the introduction to the first volume, the limits of the lexicon were extended further for the scientific and technical vocabulary than for the vocabulary of slang. Victorian notions of words fit to print were narrow, and in 1888 the scientific vocabulary was not yet the growth industry it is today. For example, the editor omitted *appendicitis* from the first volume because the Regius Professor of Medicine told him the word was too specialized. When appendicitis delayed Edward VII's coronation in 1902, the word emerged from scientific speciality into popular use, and **appendicitis** appeared in the 1933 supplement.

Even the later volumes of the original 10 included only a few citations dated after 1915. When the volume containing the letter *G* appeared in 1901, for example, it was too late to include the verb *garage*, first recorded the same year (the use of the word as a noun is first recorded from 1902); the volume for *Pa-* appeared in 1905 lacking *paprika* (recorded from 1898).

The post–World War II supplements have brought the collection of citations up-to-date and have extended the dictionary's coverage into the English of the countries once part of the British Empire (including the United States) and into the candid vocabulary of a liberated age, including **switch-hitter** in both the sporting and the sexual senses. Thus the *OED* is now reasonably comprehensive, but only if the user reads both the original entry and the entry in the supplement. For example, for the first entry on **album**, only the original volume gives the etymology, pronunciation, and four senses with illustra-

tive quotations ranging from 1651 to 1878; only the supplement gives a fifth and sixth sense, along with another use for the fourth sense and further illustrative quotations dating from 1918 to 1967. Thus the reader must always consult two volumes: the appropriate volume from the original set and the matching supplemental volume.

IV. Quality and Currency of Entries

An entry may take only a couple of lines, or it may be voluminous. Such is the case of the verb **set**, for example, which occupies 550 column-inches, with a further 30 column-inches in the supplemental volume. Each entry falls into two main parts. The first gives the word's status along with its spoken and written forms; the second gives the definitions, along with their illustrative quotations.

The first part of each entry begins with a leading symbol, if required (restricted to ‖ for "not naturalized" and a dagger for "obsolete"); entry word in boldface; pronunciation, if any, within parentheses; an abbreviation for the part of speech (if the word is unmarked, it is a noun); specialized uses, such as *Mus*[*ic*], *Bot*[*any*]; status labels such as *Obs*[*olete*], *rare*, *nonce-w*[*or*]*d* [a word coined to suit one particular occasion]; and a chronological list of spelling and inflectional forms.

Not every entry includes all these features. The entry for **andante** is short; **game** is longer:

‖**Andante** (anda·nt*e*, ăndæ·nti), *a* and *sb. Mus.*

Game (g*θ*ⁱm), *sb.* Forms: α. 1–5 **gamen**, 1 **gǫmen**, 3–5 **gamin, -yn**, ?5 **gamon**, (4, 6 *pl.* **gamnes**), 4–5 **gammen, -in, -yn**, ?5 **gammon**, 3–5 **gomen**, (4 *pl.* **gomnes**), 4 *Kent.* **gemen**; β 3–6 **gamme**, 4–5 (9 *dial.*) **gam**, 3–4 **gome**, 4 *Kent.* **geme**. 6 *Sc.* **gemm**, 3– **game.**

The numbers indicate dates by centuries: 1–5 means from before the 12th century through the 15th, 9 the 19th. The last item shows that the spelling **game** first occurred in the 13th century, when the word was already hundreds of years old. The other items show that the new spelling did not become standard until the 16th century.

The second part of the entry begins with the etymology in brackets. The etymological comments on **andante** and **game** are:

[It., pr. pple. of *andare* to go.]

[Com. Teut.: OE. *gamen*, *gǫmen* str. neut. = OFris. *game*, *gome*, OS., OHG. *gaman* (MHG. *gamen*) joy, glee, ON. *gaman* (Sw. *gamman*, Da. *gammen*) game, sport, merriment; regarded by most Germanists as etymologically identical with Goth. *gaman* neut., participation, communion, f. *ga*-prefix, together, 'com-'

(see Y-prefix) + root of MAN. If this explanation be correct, the OTeut. accentuation (as in a few other nouns formed with *ga-*) has been preserved because the word had already in the prehistoric period ceased to be apprehended as a compound.]

Next come the definitions (with occasional editorial comments such as "This word [the obsolete word **agemate**] is worth reviving"), including illustrative quotations. The *OED* definitions attempt to discriminate all shades of meaning in separate sections, which are further divided, as necessary. They separate **album** into two entries (marked with superscript "1" and "2"). These words, though historically related, are substantive homographs in English, different words with the same written form. The first has the plural **albums** and stems from Latin for "a blank tablet used for entries." The second is marked with a leading ‖ as "not naturalized" and a trailing *Obs.* as "obsolete"; it stems from the Latin for "white."

The first entry discerns four meanings, treated in numbered paragraphs that follow the word's sense development chronologically:

> 1. *Rom. Antiq.* A tablet on which the prætor's edicts and other public notices were recorded for public information; afterwards extended to other lists. . . .
> 2. A blank book in which to insert autographs, memorial verses, original drawings, or other souvenirs. According to Johnson 'a book in which foreigners have long been accustomed to insert the autographs of celebrated people.' . . .
> 3. 'A book in which visitors enter their names.' Webster. (This in England is called a *Visitors' Book*.) . . .
> 4. A book for reception of photographic cartes and views, or of postage-stamps, crests, or other things which are collected and preserved; a scrap-book. . . .

Each of these definitions is illustrated with two or more quotations, of which the first is the earliest among the citations and the last often the most recent (as of 1884). The second homograph, used only in obsolete technical senses, receives briefer separate treatment in the original volume, and none at all in the supplements.

For **album**[1], the postwar supplement adds an attributive use to the fourth sense and gives illustrative quotations for it. As is often the case, one quotation is itself a definition: "Album papers and boards are cover papers, or double thick pasted board . . intended for photographic albums" (such definitions sometimes are flagged "See quot."). The supplement then gives two new numbered senses:

> 5. *attrib.* passing into *adj.* Applied to verses of a sort or quality suitable for inclusion in an album (often with disparaging implication). . . .
> 6. A long-playing gramophone record or a set of such records. . . .

The complete entry gives more than just the sense development of **album**: It also subsumes remarks of earlier lexicographers, in this case the two best known; points to Anglo-American differences in use; observes changes in the syntax of the word; and, in **album**[2], notes that the word is Latinate and obsolete.

The total of the original and supplement entries on **album**[1], including pronunciation, is about six column inches. Even with the advantage of the *OED* as one source, an unabridged dictionary such as THE RANDOM HOUSE DICTIONARY OF THE ENGLISH LANGUAGE (1966 and later editions) gives a scant column inch to **album**, containing a bare five-word etymology, no syntactic observations, no currency labels, and only four numbered definitions, the senses current in present-day English. As a result, RANDOM HOUSE does not show how the word was used in the past and hence does not explain how the modern word came to have its present-day panoply of senses. On the other hand, the reader seeking only the current meaning of **album** in the *OED* must wade through two separate volumes and several out-of-date meanings, each with its illustrative quotations.

Yet the *OED* entries on **album** are relatively short. The longer entry on **ache** differs from the **album** entry in giving a brief history of the word's forms, both the spellings (including **ake** and the late Scottish variant **yake**) and the inflections (including the medieval forms **ook** and **akede** for the past tense). The entry states that the verb and the noun were originally spelled and pronounced differently, and that modern English combines the sound of the verb and the spelling of the noun for both parts of speech.

For a word like **abroad**, the *OED* divides the adverb from the preposition in a single entry under **A** and **B**, respectively. It divides **A** into five numbered senses, the first of which it further divides into four, designated **a** through **d**, distinguishing the meaning "Widely asunder" ("The angry Northerne winde Will blowe these sands like Sibels leaues abroad," Shakespeare) from "Widely apart" ("At his coming he did bend to us a little, and put his arms abroad," Bacon).

The entry **at** is characteristic of the dictionary's longer entries. Following the material on pronunciation, part of speech, forms, etymology, and syntax, the editor comments:

> *At* is used to denote relations of so many kinds, and some of these so remote from its primary local sense, that a classification of its uses is very difficult. Only a general outline can be here given; its idiomatic constructions with individual words must be looked for under the words themselves, e.g. AIM, ANGRY, APT. . . . The arrangement of the senses here adopted is:—I. Local position. II. Practical contact, engagement, occupation, condition, etc. III. Position in a series or graduated scale, rate, price, etc. IV. Time, order, conse-

quence, cause, object. V. In other adverbial phrases. VI. With the infinitive mood. VII. Followed by other prepositions.

Under each of the sections designated by a Roman numeral, the entry divides by Arabic numeral and further divides by lowercase roman letter. These strategies become essential in a particularly long entry such as the verb **set**, which has 154 definitions, the last (**set up**) divided into 44 shades of meaning, concluding with a "key to phrases and idiomatic uses" as a finding aid to the entry.

Such an analysis is a structure imposed inductively by the editors on the collection of citations, although to the reader the citations appear subordinate to the analysis. So the long entry on the noun **game** (the *OED* has separate entries on the adjective and on the verb) includes the general sense I, "Amusement," etc.; a division numbered 3, a specific amusement or diversion; and a further division designated **b**, "Amorous sport or play. *Obs.*" This sense is accompanied by six illustrative quotations from 1230 to 1601 (Shakespeare). Of sense I.3.b, the postwar supplement says "Delete . . . *Obs.* and add later examples; *spec.* signifying sexual intercourse." The examples are from the novelist Graham Greene (1938) and the periodical *Mademoiselle* (1964).

The *OED* division of the historical citations into hierarchies of sense enables the reader to assemble the evidence for the meaning or range of meanings available at any time. The division also provides the reader with an overview of the word's history and development. And an entry like **at** or **game** shows amply that no word has a single "true meaning." Instead, each word has a range of related meanings from which the careful writers of every age have selected and among which careful readers of the present must find their way.

Sometimes the editors seem to have been too hasty or too brief. Under the protean word **gentile**, for example, a few instances of the older spelling **gentle** are given. And in winnowing the millions of citation slips gathered in the course of preparing the work for publication (only a third of these were actually published), the editors sometimes fell under the spell of Shakespeare, including only his use of a word to illustrate the usage of his century: the entry for **betide** (*Richard III*, II.i.6) is typical. Yet the user who wants to explicate Shakespeare's word needs above all to know how his contemporaries used it, so the *OED* citation of Shakespeare's line alone is of little help.

The *OED* pauses rarely for cross-references and hardly at all for synonyms. Some alternative spellings are cross-referenced to the main article (**albocore**, obs. variant of ALBACORE), and some formations are related to their constituents (**albuminize** . . . (see AL-

BUMEN) + -IZE), but the longer the entry, the fewer such cross-references. The *OED* has no systematic discussions of synonyms or antonyms.

The abbreviated status labels in the original *OED* were chiefly historical: "*arch*[*aic*]," "*obs*[*olete*]," "*euphem*[*istically*]," "*colloq*[*uially*]." The postwar supplements add "*vulg*[*ar*]" to the list of labels and the comment "*taboo*" to the entries as the occasion requires. (In both the original *OED* and the supplements, the lengthy "List of abbreviations, signs, etc." occurs only at the beginning of the volume, not on each page.) Some of the labels, attached to the entries in Britain between 1888 and 1928, are inaccurate for a present-day American user: **avocado**, for example, is now scarcely "*alien*."

On many controversial usages the *OED* throws only indirect light, as is appropriate for a historical dictionary. For example, a reader concerned about the use of **infer** to mean "suggest" can find that Thomas More in the 16th century and James Mill in the 19th were among those who used it as a synonym for "imply," but the original *OED*, where the information occurs, makes no comment on the use. The postwar supplement does comment ("This use is widely considered to be incorrect, esp. with a person as the subject"), but it also gives examples from respected writers from 1813 to 1973. Similarly, the original *OED* gave **hopefully** only to mean "with hope"; the postwar supplement adds

> **hopefully**, *adv.* Add : **2**. It is hoped (that); let us hope. (Cf. G. *hoffentlich* it is to be hoped.) orig. *U.S.* (Avoided by many writers.)

V. Syllabication and Pronunciation

The *OED* is a British dictionary, so some of its spellings (**ætiology**, **armour**) are not a reliable guide for Americans.

The *OED* gives no guidance to syllabication: An entry like **e:choloca·tion** shows only that the main stress is on the fourth syllable, the secondary stress on the first. The entry does not tell how to divide the word.

The pronunciations are those of "the educated speech of southern England," transcribed in a fairly narrow (detailed) notation that shares many symbols with the International Phonetic Alphabet. The system is decoded near the beginning of each volume (but not on every page). American users will not be much the wiser for having deciphered the transcription and learned that **clerk** has the *a* of *father*, and even British users may find the 100-year-old versions of words like **gooseberry** (rhyming with *who's merry?*) old-fashioned and unfamiliar (modern Britons usually pronounce the word in only two syllables, the first with the vowel of *foot*). Fortunately **acrasy** is marked *obsolete*, so its complete lack of any hints for pronunciation should cause users no difficulty.

One irksome typographical convention in the *OED* is the printing of all main entry words with an initial capital. The reader thus has no way of knowing, without reading further in the entry, whether the word is capitalized in actual practice. The postwar supplements capitalize only as usage requires.

VI. Special Features

The *OED* contains no biographical or geographical material either in its main vocabulary (like THE AMERICAN HERITAGE DICTIONARY) or in separate lists (like WEBSTER'S NINTH NEW COLLEGIATE DICTIONARY), except where the word has become part of the common language (for example, **Alzheimer's disease**, **Bolton twill**), and it contains no encyclopedic material such as tables of measurements or monetary values.

The *OED* has no special features outside its main lexicon. But the main lexicon, with its abundance of dated illustrative quotations analyzed into hierarchies of meaning, is an integral feature that no other dictionary can match. Indeed, some readers use the *OED* as a virtual quotation dictionary.

VII. Accessibility

The *OED* guide words atop the first and third column of each page designate the first and last entries on that page. The dictionary has no thumb index; however, the inclusion of such a feature would accomplish little in a dictionary where the user may have to search 12 large volumes before a difficult passage from long ago and far away finally yields its meaning. Second-hand editions of the full set can sometimes still be found with the oak cabinet with which they were once sold, but the postwar supplements will not fit in the shelves under the lectern. For intensive use readers commonly arrange the volumes in alphabetical order around a large table that they circumambulate as their searches direct.

The CD-ROM version solves many of these problems. But the print edition does not yield its riches without something of a struggle.

VIII. Graphics and Format

The *OED* has no pictures, maps, diagrams, or charts. It is printed in clear type, with no show-through and adequate margins, on sturdy paper. The volumes are strongly bound in the blue buckram the Oxford University Press uses for many of its reference books. Hundred-year-old copies of Volume I are still fine and firm.

The format is dictated by the nature of a dictionary "on historical principles": the display of the citations in chronological order, organized by sense relations. The adoption of this format virtually without change by other more specialized dictionaries attests to the success of its design. However tiring the *OED*'s physical embodiment may become, the constant user is rarely impatient with the intellectual arrangement of the dictionary. The conceptual format, at least, is highly accessible.

IX. Summary

The *OED* is uniquely useful for its intended purpose: tracing the evolution of the meanings of English words through dated citations. If that is what a user needs, no other dictionary will be nearly so useful. On the other hand, the *OED* is almost useless for some of the needs that dictionaries often have to meet. Prospective buyers should not let the *OED*'s fame cause them to pay its considerable price expecting to be able to put it to the many uses that a good general dictionary can serve. On the other hand, those whose writing, reading, or general interest in words makes a historical dictionary useful will find the *OED* a source of endless information and entertainment.

The first editor of the *OED* wrote that "the circle of the English language has a well-defined centre but no discernible circumference," because the common literary and colloquial vocabulary shades off into the special scientific, technical, slang, dialectal, and foreign. For the outer reaches of those vocabularies, specialized dictionaries are essential. But for the history and meanings of the central vocabulary, the *OED*'s cornucopia of classified quotations is peerless.

The Oxford English Dictionary on Compact Disc

Facts at a Glance

Full Title: **The Oxford English Dictionary on Compact Disc Version 3.8.**

Contents: Two 4.72″ CD-ROM disks: volume 1: Disc A–N, volume 2: Disc O–Z; software on two double-sided double-density diskettes (14 files); User's Guide (looseleaf binder, 148 pages); packaged in 2⅜″ × 9¼″ × 8⅛″ box.

Publisher: Tri Star Publishing.

Edition Reviewed: © 1987 by Oxford University Press.

Hardware Requirements:
Computer: IBM-PC, XT, or AT (or clones).
Memory: minimum recommended 640KBs.
Monitor: monochrome or color (supported with either a CGA or EGA interface).
CD Drives: Hitachi, Philips, Sony or Sony with an Online Controller.

Printer: Any printer supported by the DOS
PRINT.COM file.

Price: $1,250.00 for two CD-ROM Disks,
software, user's guide (excludes hardware). As
of May 1988, the OED will be available on one
compact disk. The price will be $950.00. The
two-disk version will still be available.
Sold by Tri Star Publishing.
ISBN 0-944674-00-3.

I. Introduction

The Oxford English Dictionary on Compact Disc offers the same wealth of information that has made
the print *OED* a classic of the English language, and
supplements this with the flexibility of online retrieval software. The result is a revolutionary reference tool that was unimaginable some sixty years
ago when the print version was completed. The *OED
on Compact Disc* (*OED-CD*) gives the user instant
access to any information included in the 12-volume
OED, regardless of sequence or position.

II. Accessibility

The *OED-CD* is available as a single purchase directly from its CD-ROM publisher, Tri Star. The
OED-CD package consists of two compact disks, two
double-sided double-density floppy diskettes, and a
User's Guide. This software can be used at any local
workstation consisting of a desktop IBM computer
and compact disk drive, as specified in "Facts at a
Glance," above.

System Start-Up

The installation of the software required to begin
execution of searches on either a hard or floppy disk
system is clearly described in the User's Guide and
is partially prompted on the screen. The user makes
simple online menu selections or responds to prompted
questions through specified keyboard strokes. The
desired compact disk must be inserted into the drive;
a change of disk currently requires repeat of some
start-up steps. To execute the program, the user is
asked to identify the "User Profile" to be used for
the session. At this point the search panel screen
appears.

These installation and execution steps take only
seconds to accomplish from the time the computer
is booted, assuming no complications occur. Actual
start-up time depends on hardware specifications and
the user's familiarity with DOS (operating system)
commands if problems occur. As of May 1988, the
single compact disk version will feature the High
Sierra standard for data. This will enable virtually

any CD-drive to run the product that supports the
MS-DOS CD-ROM extensions.

According to Tri Star, several additional features
intended to enhance the accessibility of the *OED-
CD* were scheduled to be available as of April 1988.
The 3.8 version reviewed here did not include these
features. The improved version is said to include:

- the ability to access either the A–N or the
  O–Z disk without rebooting the system
- the ability to store a query created while
  using one disk and to apply it to the same
  disk at a later time or to the other disk
  without having to rekey it
- the automatic identification and initialization
  of the CD drive

Screen Displays

The *OED-CD* software provides access to all functions through a menu selection system. The majority
of functions used for a search utilize two (search and
display) screen panels.

The search panel may consist of up to seven visible
sections. A search statement is developed in the *query
box*, above which a *message window* may contain
computer-generated notes about errors or status of
the execution. The *search panel menu* provides options to be used in development of the query or to
employ other utilities such as Help, Writing Notes,
or Editing User Profiles. Additional options may appear in a boxed *sub-menu*. Up to 16 query statements
and execution results are saved in a user profile and
are listed in the *saved queries window*. Information
on the *key functions* and *text windows* that apply to
the menu option being executed are also shown.

The *display panel* is used to view entries that have
been called up; it contains six sections. A *display
panel menu* is used to change entries and to access
areas within the entry, and is sometimes extended
to a *sub-menu*. A window for computer-generated
messages may appear as in the search panel. An *entry
window* displays the actual *OED* entry in the central
portion of the screen. Among other screen display
niceties are a continuous display of the main entry
word lemma during scrolling of an entry, and highlighting in the entry of the "occurrence term" on
which the search query is matched. *Key functions*
and *text windows* also appear on the display panel.

III. Locating Information

The first step in the automated search process is to
develop the query statement, which contains three
basic elements: the index specifier, the search term,
and the Boolean operators. The index specifier identifies one of eight indexes, corresponding to a field

in the *OED* entry. These allow for searching for the main entry word or bold lemma (LE); the etymology (ET); the sense (SE); the usage label (LA), which may specify parts of speech, topics, or geographical locations; the elements in the quotation fields of the quoted date (QD); author (QA); work (QW); and text (QT). During a search the computer matches the search term (specified within quotation marks) in the query statement and terms in the index lists. Right-hand truncation using a minimum three-letter stem can be used here to generate a prefix listing of an index. Use of three Boolean operators (OR, AND, and ANDNOT) allows retrieval of more specific items when searching more than one index or terms within one index.

Although the query statement must contain the proper syntax for a successful search, letter casing is virtually unimportant and punctuation and additional blank spaces are ignored except within the quotation marks.

Among the several methods provided in the *OED-CD* software to identify variables in the query statement is the option to access lists of words, symbols and dates that make up the different indexes. By accessing the index list, all forms of an inconsistently quoted author's name, such as "Shakespeare," can be marked to assure complete retrieval. Index list access within the quoted date list permits the user to retrieve entries even if the exact date is not known; a date range of up to 20 years may be specified, as can "ante" and "circa" marked date ranges. These search parameters may take long to execute and may require more memory than the computer has, but are powerful features of the *OED-CD* system. Previously saved queries can also be used within a new query. Retrieving a saved query is quicker than its original execution since the actual search does not occur again, only already stored locations of entries from the user profile disk file are recalled.

A successful search may result in one or multiple entries (occurrences). Several menu options are available in the display panel to give quick access to different parts of a single entry as well as to other entries in the list. Since one page of the printed *OED* is equivalent to approximately 15 to 20 screens on the monitor, some entries may require hundreds of screens in order to be viewed in their entirety. Among the options for reviewing entries is the "Bookmark" menu option, which provides a means to place and save for future use—a locating mark on entries of greatest interest within an entry list. Another interesting option, especially useful in long entries, is the structure "Map" menu option. This provides, within a window, a summary of the sense fields and the ability to move directly to the desired sense.

Print and store functions enable the user to print out entries immediately or to save portions of an entry in a file for later printing. For special characters, either a code is printed or for those printers with an EGA (Extended Graphics Adapter) interface, the actual characters are depicted as precisely as possible. An electronic note pad is available in both the search and the display panels; notes in the latter may be printed.

IV. Currency

The *OED-CD* version 3.8 replicates information in the original Oxford English Dictionary. Apparently, the later *OED* supplements are not included. A check of the quoted date index reveals that 1928 is the latest specified quotation year, with four occurrences.

V. Accuracy and Clarity

The CD product is accurate in replicating information from the original print *OED*, as we learned from a random comparison of a few entries. The only noticeable differences are the use of coded notations for special characters, the omission of italicization, and the use of both color (with appropriate hardware) and of indentations. The CD displays are altogether easier to scan.

However, as with the print version, an entry display from the *OED-CD* may be confusing to the untrained eye. The complexity of notations and numerous abbreviations found within a label are accurately replicated. Codes are provided for special characters (such as accents) in the *OED* for which computer keyboards do not have keys; these codes may be reviewed online but initially may be confusing, as for example in the depiction of pronunciations of "at" ("%t, a <<breve>> t" in the online display, compared to "ae t, ăt" in the print entry). In addition, background information about the search or about key functions that appears on the screen may distract the novice user. The error statements, prompts, and summaries are clear, concise and easily understood.

VI. Documentation

The well-written user's guide offers clear, accurate concise documentation to use the system. The lack of an index, which may at first frustrate the user who is trying to return to a specific reference in the guide, is partially offset by the easily retrieved online help screens. One particularly helpful online display summarizes the applications of the function keys. A similar summary in the form of a template to place over the keyboard would be a useful addition for the new or infrequent user.

VII. Summary

Just as the print *OED* is not appropriate for the casual dictionary user looking for a current meaning of a word, so the CD version is not a quick reference tool. All the sophistication required of a reader to appreciate the *OED*, plus a basic computer literacy, are prerequisites for the *OED-CD* user. However, just as the lure of the *OED* seduces the serious student of the English language, so the expanded search ability of the *OED-CD* stimulates the imagination of both the serious reader and the literary trivia enthusiast. It takes only an hour or so for a new user to learn how to retrieve specific entries; however, several days of serious study are probably necessary before one is able to use the *OED-CD* to its full capacity.

A closing example illustrates the potential of the *OED-CD*, impossible to match in the *OED*. The reviewer wanted to know what law terms are quoted by Dickens. A search query utilizing the Boolean "AND" to join search terms within the quoted author (QA) and label (LA) indexes (i.e., QA = "Dickens" AND LA = "Law") resulted in 13 matches (including **cite**, **defendant**, **detainer**, **hue and cry**, and **jury**) in a matter of minutes.

With the introduction of further refinements to ease the changing of disks and possibly extending coverage to include the *OED* supplements, as well as current updates, the *OED-CD* could become the definitive dictionary of the automated age. Meanwhile, the first release is quite revolutionary. It is highly recommended for large public and academic libraries where the necessary hardware is in place and where there is serious research in literature, the humanities, and the arts.

The Oxford Minidictionary

Facts at a Glance

Full Title: **The Oxford Minidictionary**.
Publisher: Oxford University Press.
Editor: Joyce M. Hawkins
Edition Reviewed: © 1981; second printing 1985.

Number of Entries: 20,000.
Number of Words: 50,000.
Number of Pages: 558.
Trim Size: 3″ × 4¾″.
Binding: plastic over paper.

Price: $3.95.
Sold in bookstores; also sold through magazine and newspaper advertising.
ISBN 0-19-861138-2.

I. Introduction

This minisized abridged dictionary is intended for use by adults as well as upper junior high and high school students. The dictionary's compiler states in the preface that it is "the smallest member of the Oxford family of dictionaries and is written for those who need a compact guide to the spelling and meaning of the commonest words of the English language today." *The Minidictionary* defines current words and is not to be confused with smaller editions of the monumental OXFORD ENGLISH DICTIONARY (OED). This small dictionary contains 20,000 entries and nearly 30,000 vocabulary items.

II. Authority

The Oxford Minidictionary is published in the United States by Oxford University Press (New York) but was prepared and printed by OUP in Great Britain. The editor, Joyce M. Hawkins, is a distinguished member of the OXFORD ENGLISH DICTIONARY staff. In addition, Dr. R. M. Burchfield, Chief Editor of the *OED* department of Oxford University Press, was a contributor to the dictionary, as were several other of his *OED* staff colleagues.

III. Comprehensiveness

Many colloquial words are included, which is unusual for a volume this small. Also, special meanings are indicated for Irish, Australian, South African, Indian, Scottish, and U.S. usage. It is well to keep in mind that this is a British publication, so many of the special definitions reflect this slant. Words such as *ain't* and *kitsch* do not appear in the dictionary, nor do newer words related to technology, such as *videocassette* or *videodisc*. Nothing in the introductory materials suggests how words were chosen for this dictionary.

Some abbreviations appear in the *Minidictionary*, but *VCR*, for example, is not among them. Actually, very few technical terms are included, even words in common use long before 1981, which is the date of the first edition of this dictionary. Etymologies are not given nor are there word illustrations, synonyms, or antonyms. There is an occasional cross-reference from a variant form of a word, such as **smelt**[1] *see* **smell**, and there are quite a few run-in entries. Common terms of foreign origins are included, such as **non sequitur** meaning "a conclusion that does not follow from the evidence given." No biographical or geographical entries are found within the main vocabulary, which, as is the case with other excluded categories of words, is not surprising in a dictionary of this length.

IV. Quality and Currency of Entries

Definitions are, as the preface states, both common and current; they are also clear and concise but necessarily limited because of the small size of the dictionary. A drawback for American readers is that the definitions reflect everyday British usage, as well as British spelling: **lino** for *linoleum* and **colour** not *color*. Secondary senses of words are almost never given, nor are definitions illustrated by sentences or phrases. Phrases and hyphenated compound words are separated by a swung dash (~) instead of repeating the entry word. For example, for the word **down**, there is "~and out," and for **kith**, "~ and kin." This space-saving device is usually not difficult to read, but its use points up the extreme brevity of the entries. Occasionally, however, it is confusing: for example, the entry **hell n.** is followed by the subentry

> ~ **-bent** a. recklessly determined. ~ **for leather**, at great speed.

Those unfamiliar with the phrase "hellbent for leather" would not necessarily understand that the immediately preceding subentry ~-**bent** should be used to complete the phrase rather than the original entry **hell** alone.

V. Syllabication and Pronunciation

The preface of the dictionary notes that the pronunciation given is for the standard speech of Southern England. The International Phonetic Alphabet (IPA) is used with nasalization for foreign words as in the French language and *x* for Scottish words ending in *ch* and pronounced as a *k*, as in *loch*. Primary stress marks are also indicated. Pronunciation appears between slash marks after the entry word and is indicated only where the editors feel it is needed. This means that very often the pronunciation symbols are limited to only one syllable, such as "/ˋsai-/" for **sinecure**. This is not a particularly clear method of indicating pronunciation.

VI. Special Features

At the front of *The Oxford Minidictionary* there is a pronunciation guide, a list of abbreviations used in the dictionary, and a brief note about proprietary terms. At the end of the vocabulary, a list of "Independent Countries of the World" shows both noun and adjective forms. The final back pages are left blank for notes. A few sentences in the preface provide some help with using the dictionary, but more explanation would be helpful.

VII. Accessibility

Words are listed in alphabetical order and appear in boldface type overhanging the text. Specialized uses are labeled clearly, such as "(*colloq.*)" for **kerfuffle**, a colloquial word meaning "fuss or commotion," or the Australian definition of the word **squatter** meaning "sheep-farmer." Each page has two boldface guide words at the top and a centered page number. Each letter section is preceded by a large bold capital letter. All of these features make the dictionary easy to use.

VIII. Graphics and Format

There are no illustrations in the dictionary, the lack of which does not detract from its usefulness—as a quick-reference source. The typeface is small and fairly easy to read, but the margins are very narrow and there is little white space. The paper is thin, but print from the opposite side does not show through. This little volume is primarily intended for personal use and would not stand up well to library use.

IX. Summary

Although *The Oxford Minidictionary* is a good small volume, it is difficult to see it serving any real purpose for most American users. For individual use, few Americans will need a quick-reference source based on British spelling, pronunciation, and usage of this type, and libraries with a need for such a dictionary will want a more comprehensive version.

Oxford Student's Dictionary of American English

Facts at a Glance

Full Title: **Oxford Student's Dictionary of American English**.
Publisher: Oxford University Press.
Editors: A. S. Hornby, with Christina A. Ruse, Dolores Harris, and William A. Stewart (American editors).
Edition Reviewed: © 1986, second edition.

Number of Words and Phrases: over 35,000.
Number of Pages: 714.
Number of Illustrations: 142 in black and white.
Trim Size: 5¼" × 8¼".
Binding: cloth; paperback.

Prices: $15.95 (cloth); $5.95 (paper).
Sold in bookstores; also sold to libraries and other educational institutions.

Oxford Student's Dictionary of American English

❶ IPA pronunciation is enclosed by virgules

❷ Stress marks appear in examples as well as entry words

❸ Syllabication is shown by centered dots

❹ A bracketed *C* denotes countable nouns

❺ A swung dash indicates repetition of main entry word

❻ Idiomatic expressions, set in boldface italic type, are defined after the main entry word

❼ Arrows indicate cross-references

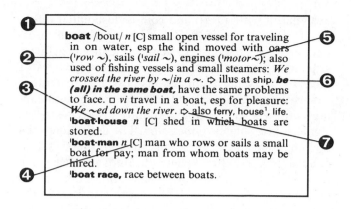

ISBN 0-19-431140-6 (cloth);
ISBN 0-19-431194-5 (paperback).

I. Introduction

The preface to this small dictionary states that it is "an American adaptation of the *Oxford Student's Dictionary of Current English*, with some inclusion of advanced level material from the *Oxford Advanced Learner's Dictionary of Current English*, somewhat expanded to serve learners of American English through the Intermediate level." Some pains have been taken to distinguish between British and American English, implying that users already will have had some experience with British English; however, it will be a useful work for *any* adult student of English as a second language. With a vocabulary of over 35,000 words and phrases, it focuses on common words heard in conversation and read in written material every day by a learner in the United States, with the exclusion of technical and literary terms. Sample verbal illustrations frequently show usage distinctions or clarify difficult points of spelling, pronunciation, and meaning. Occasional black-and-white drawings and photographs help to illustrate entries.

The introductory material includes a 30-page "Dictionary Workbook," which tells "all about the different types of information available" and includes practical exercises. Completing these may require the help of a knowledgeable instructor.

II. Authority

Not only is this work an adaptation of the original *Oxford Student's Dictionary of Current English*, but material from the OXFORD ADVANCED LEARNER'S DICTIONARY OF CURRENT ENGLISH has also been incorporated. The *Oxford Student's Dictionary of American English* was compiled by the highly reputable Oxford University Press staff, and the Amer-

ican editors, who adapted the earlier A. S. Hornby *Current English* for this work, are Dolores Harris and William A. Stewart.

III. Comprehensiveness

In the words of the editors, "there has been no attempt [in this dictionary] to include the considerable body of slang, which varies from place to place and is always changing." Further, because this dictionary serves the dual purpose of acting as a lexicon and as a learning tool, this edition should not be judged wholly on how inclusive or up-to-date entries are. Readers will want to be aware that the following are *not* included: the noun sense of *aerobics*; *crack*, as the word refers to cocaine; *Dolby*; *freebase*; *fast track*; *sitcom*; *meltdown*; *gridlock*; and *modem*. The slang term **hippie (hippy)** is included, but the more recent term *yuppie (yuppy)* is not.

Other current listings seem to have been selected arbitrarily. For example, such computer and technical terms as **data processing**, **data bank**, **programming** (as it relates to the computer), **video recorder**, and **video tape** are included; but *database*, *video cassette*, *video disc/k*, and *disc/k drive* are omitted. **Gay**, in its homosexual sense, is included. The dictionary is not completely successful in its attempt to home in on "everyday" language.

IV. Quality and Currency of Entries

The typical entry is presented as follows: the boldface entry word divided into syllables, overhanging the text at the left of each column; the pronunciation(s), enclosed in diagonal bars; the italicized part-of-speech label; and in the case of noun entries, stylistic usage labels. [C] stands for "countable" and indicates that a noun has both a singular and plural form; [U] indicates an "uncountable" noun, one that does not have a plural form; [C,U] indicates that a noun can be used either as a countable or uncountable word. Thus, **kumquat** is designated with a [C]; **kinship** is designated with a [U]; and **coin** is designated with a [C,U]. In the case of irregular verb entries, the present participle, the past participle, and inflected forms appear in parentheses. In the case of adjectives or adverbs, irregular comparisons appear in parentheses. Boldface numerals introduce the various meanings and, when applicable, boldface lowercase letters signal subtle shades of meaning. The definitions then appear, followed by verbal instructions in italics; language labels in italics, when indicated; an open, small box symbol (⊏) to denote when a main entry word changes from one part of speech to another, where applicable; idiomatic expressions in bold italic type, listed alphabetically; and occasionally, an arrow sign (⇒), indicating cross-references to other entries (the word cross-referenced appears in sans serif type).

Consider the following main entry with its subsidiary entries:

> **boat** /bout/ n/ [C] small open vessel traveling in on water, esp the kind with oars ('row ~), sails ('sail~) engines ('motor~); also used of fishing vessel small steamers: *We crossed the river by ~/in a~.* ⇒ *illus at* ship *be (all) in the same boat* have the same problems to face □ *vi* travel in a boat, esp for pleasure: *we~ed down the river.* ⇒ *also* ferry, house[1], life.
>   'boat·house . . .
>   'boat·man . . .
>   'boat·race . . .
>   'boat·swain . . .

As a space-saving device, note that the editors insert a swung dash or tilde (~) rather than repeatedly restate the main entry word; this shortcut is especially useful in the longer entries.

It will take the user some time to become familiar with the various labels, symbols, abbreviations, and different typefaces used throughout this dictionary. This reference guide is obviously not designed for a novice to the use of a dictionary. For instance, a user will need to know how to find a key or an explanation to understand the meaning of such symbols as the bracketed *C*, the tilde, the arrow, and the numbers in parentheses in the example shown. Although this information can be gleaned from the introductory "Using the Dictionary" section, and a chart of symbols and abbreviations used in the volume appears on the inside back cover, specific material is not easy to locate. However, this dictionary was *never* meant to act as a quick-and-handy reference guide, but as a *learning* device. Regular users are forced to become familiar with the information section of the book, and to refer to it frequently.

Definitions are listed in order of meaning, from the most common or simple sense first to the most uncommon or complex meaning. As in the example shown, word derivatives are alphabetically listed in conjunction with the main root word entry (**boat-house**, **boatman**, **boat race**); whereas **boatswain** is listed as a separate entry, and overhangs the text as do other main entry words.

Derivatives are not as fully defined as their root word and tend to restate the previous derivative, as in the following example:

> **im·mo·bile** /i′moubəl/ *adj* not able to move or to be moved; motionless.
>   **im·mo·bil·ity** /ˌimou′bɪləti/ *n* [U] state of being immobile.
>   **im·mo·bi·lize** /i′moubəˌlaiz/ *vt* make immobile.
>   **im·mo·bi·liz·ation** /i′moubəˌli′zeiʃən/ *n* [U].

Note that there is no meaning given for the noun **immobilization**: this may cause confusion to users.

V. Syllabication and Pronunciation

Entry word syllables are indicated by boldface centered dots. The phonetic symbols in this dictionary are the ones designated by the International Phonetic Association, although the shift from British to American English necessitated some changes in the use of certain symbols and in the indication of stress and length. These changes are detailed in the preface, following a brief discussion on converting British to American spelling, or vice versa. Pronunciations and spellings are not presented in key form on the lexicon's pages. A chart of phonetic symbols does appear on the inside front cover. Since pronunciation is one of the most significant differences between British and American English, this omission may detract from the usefulness of this work.

VI. Special Features

Generally, the appendixes are functional and help to educate the reader about some of the subtler nuances that differentiate American English from British English, particularly from a pragmatic, "everyday" perspective. For instance, one appendix discusses how numerical expressions are handled in American English, pointing out the discrepancies with British English. Appendixes on dates, the time of day, and money serve the same function. The list of names and postal abbreviations of the states will be helpful to readers as a quick reference. The appendix on the Greek alphabet is introduced by a brief statement that relates the Greek alphabet to mathematical symbols and to use for honorary societies.

VII. Accessibility

Guide word pairs, divided by a diagonal bar, appear in the upper, inner margin of each page—for example, **cow/craft**; **craftsman/crawl**. These guide words are not much larger than the entry words themselves. This small size, combined with their close proximity to the inner margins of the book, makes them difficult to read; users must turn the pages individually and spread the book flat to see them clearly. There are no thumb tabs or other location devices to help the user find specific terms.

VIII. Graphics and Format

The black-and-white line drawings scattered throughout the volume are well conceived and labeled and quite attractive. Some illustrations fill a considerable amount of the page—for example, one drawing not only depicts various types of fruit but labels the different parts (skin or peel, core, seed, pip—a Briticism for seed, as in the illustrated orange—rind, section, and so on). Another drawing diagrams several flowers and their parts in a similar manner. The editors have also included photographs, some of which depict uniquely "American" scenes—for example, one photograph shows a duplex house (for the entry **duplex**); another pictures the Washington Monument (for the entry **monument**). However, in many instances, the illustration captions, which are set in small boldface capitals not appreciably larger than the entry words, are placed at the side of the column very close to entry words and it is hard to see them easily.

This dictionary (the paperback edition was reviewed) has a sturdy sewn binding that should withstand extensive use. Although the inking is generally sharp, the typeface is small but readable. The paper is thin but fairly white and of good opacity, so that there is little show-through.

IX. Summary

Despite the complicated coding system and lack of easily accessible pronunciation keys, the *Oxford Student's Dictionary of American English* is a handy, portable reference work and learning tool with simply stated definitions in language readily understandable by learners—both those who have already learned some degree of British English and may be bidialectical or those who are newcomers to American English. Buyers should be aware, however, that the dictionary is not completely up-to-date in its vocabulary, particularly in everyday American slang words.

In comparison, the LONGMAN DICTIONARY OF AMERICAN ENGLISH provides a greater number of illustrative phrases and sentences, while the *Oxford* has more line drawings and photographs throughout the text. The LONGMAN DICTIONARY is designed to function effectively as a self-study tool, while the *Oxford* demands an instructor in a classroom setting for best usage. However, for those learners who are serious about acquiring formal American English, this would be an excellent choice. Librarians serving a population of teachers and learners of English as a second language will want to consider this work for their collections.

Oxford Student's Dictionary of Current English

Facts at a Glance

Full Title: **Oxford Student's Dictionary of Current English.**
Publisher: Oxford University Press.
Editors: A. S. Hornby, with Christina A. Ruse.
Edition Reviewed: © 1978; 1982 printing.

Number of Entries: 35,000.
Number of Pages: 769.
Trim Size: 4½" × 7⁵⁄₁₆".
Binding: paperback.

Price: $6.95.
Sold in bookstores; also sold to libraries and other educational institutions.
ISBN 0-19-431114-7.

I. Introduction and Scope

The *Oxford Student's Dictionary of Current English* is adapted from the OXFORD ADVANCED LEARNER'S DICTIONARY (reviewed elsewhere in this Buying Guide). This sturdy paperback edition omits most of the introductory section on grammar and style while retaining the graphic sample entries. Six of the parent volume's ten appendixes are also omitted.

Most of the main entries, however, remain intact: between **frieze** and **frisk**, the *Student's Dictionary* leaves out **frippery** and **Frisbee** and all 24 entries between **pistachio** and **pivot** are the same in both works. Many of the illustrative word examples and all of the pictorial illustrations have been deleted from this condensed *Oxford Student's Dictionary of Current English*. These examples are particularly helpful to the non-native English audience for whom both dictionaries are written. Therefore, libraries considering purchase should opt for the OXFORD ADVANCED LEARNER'S DICTIONARY for this reason alone. As a first monolingual dictionary for personal use, however, the *Oxford Student's Dictionary of Current English* is a handy, well-presented reference tool.

The Pocket Oxford Dictionary of Current English

Facts at a Glance

Full Title: **The Pocket Oxford Dictionary of Current English: Seventh Edition.**
Publisher: Oxford University Press.
Editor: R. E. Allen.
Edition Reviewed: © 1984; 1986 printing.

Number of Entries: 49,000.
Number of Pages: 900.
Trim Size: 4¼" × 7".
Binding: hardcover.

Price: $11.95.
Sold in bookstores; also sold to libraries and other
   educational institutions.
ISBN 0-19-861133-1.

I. Introduction

The Pocket Oxford Dictionary, part of the Oxford
dictionary series published by Clarendon Press, is a
nominal abridgment of the CONCISE OXFORD DIC-
TIONARY. As such, it occupies an intermediate position between that dictionary and the still smaller
LITTLE OXFORD DICTIONARY OF CURRENT ENG-
LISH. At some 900 pages in length, however, it is a
substantial reference work in its own right. Although
the current edition is about 150 pages shorter than
the sixth edition (1978), it not only has a larger trim
size but is also noticeably thicker and heavier than
its predecessor. Both in size and in content, *The
Pocket Oxford Dictionary* is weightier than the term
"pocket" normally suggests—at least to American
readers, who would find it better described as a
smaller-size desk dictionary.

It should be noted that although this volume includes "American" words and also gives American
spellings as well as British ones, where these differ,
The Pocket Oxford remains primarily a dictionary of
the English language as it is written and spoken in
the United Kingdom. (The edition sold in the United
States is identical to that sold in the United Kingdom,
and has not been modified for American users.)

II. Authority

The first edition of *The Pocket Oxford Dictionary*,
issued in 1924, was the result of more than seven
years' labor by the redoubtable Latin scholars F. G.
and W. H. Fowler. In creating the work as, osten-
sibly, an abridged version of the CONCISE OXFORD
DICTIONARY, their goal was to "keep to the principle
that a dictionary is a book of diction, concerned primarily with words and phrases as such," and to achieve
"the task of making clear the idiomatic usage of
words."

The Pocket Oxford Dictionary has been revised
and reissued periodically, most recently in the seventh edition (1984). The sixth edition (1978) was
edited by Dr. J. B. Sykes with assistance from several
distinguished lexicographers including Robert W.
Burchfield, Chief Editor of the Oxford English dictionaries, and Julia Swannell, Editor of the fifth and
sixth editions of the LITTLE OXFORD DICTIONARY
OF CURRENT ENGLISH. The current edition, said by
the publisher to be "the most thorough and far-
reaching revision yet of the smallest of the dictionaries originally conceived by the Fowler brothers,"
was edited by R. E. Allen, again with the assistance
of the Oxford English Dictionary Department. Suffice it to say that this pocket volume remains perhaps
the most authoritative dictionary of its kind.

III. Comprehensiveness

Writing in the preface, editor R. E. Allen notes that
in preparing the seventh edition "The choice of vocabulary has been thoroughly reconsidered with many
items no longer current in general English omitted
in favour of the many new items clamouring for attention from day to day. Particular attention has been
paid to the language of computers and the information sciences and in general to those technical
terms such as *acid rain* and *fibre optics* that are ever
more forcefully thrust upon us in everyday life."

Indeed, in addition to the two terms cited above,
the dictionary includes a generous selection of contemporary words. One will find such acronyms, for
example, as **AID** ("artificial insemination by do-
nor"), **AIDS**, **BASIC**, **FORTRAN**, and **PASCAL**. At
the same time, however, the work continues to include such quaint slang expressions as **heebie-jeebies**,
collywobbles, and **guttersnipe** that find slim portion
in the language spoken in the United States today.
Many of the entries are for words common in British
but not in the American vocabulary: **Borstal**, **pram**,
pavement, **sus**. In many instances, compound and
derivative words listed under a main entry have application strictly to British English—for example,
the entry for **home** includes such compounds and
derivatives as **at-home**, **Home Counties**, **home farm**,
Home Guard, **home help**, **Home Office**, **Home Rule**,
and **Home Secretary**. The word **homely** is first defined as "simple, plain, unpretentious," and only second as "*US* (of facial appearance) unattractive."

Given these quibbles, however, it must be admitted that *The Pocket Oxford Dictionary*, covering
49,000 words and phrases (including many idioms),
is quite comprehensive for a dictionary bearing the
appellation "pocket."

IV. Quality and Currency of Entries

Entries in *The Pocket Oxford Dictionary* are unusually comprehensive for a smaller desk dictionary.
Different senses of the same word are given "in order
of comparative familiarity with the most important
and current senses first" and those that are evidently
less so arranged in descending order thereafter. Thus,
the currency of definitions is a main feature.

When appropriate, usage and subject labels are included in the entries. In addition to the standard labels found in many dictionaries (indicating slang or colloquial usage), this edition introduces two new usage labels. Words that are considered offensive by members of a particular ethnic or religious group are labeled with a boldface **R** (for racially offensive). The boldface capital letter **D** indicates a disputed use that, although widely encountered, is not generally approved by grammarians and word specialists. Subject or field labels indicate when a word is used in music, law, a particular science, and so forth. The label *US* alerts the reader to words, spellings, and definitions that are peculiar to the United States. This last feature has little utility for the American user, especially as there is no equivalent designation for those words, spellings, or definitions that are unique to the United Kingdom. (Note, however, that specifically Australian and New Zealand terms, such as **sheila**, are included and so labeled.)

Compound and derivative forms of an entry word, as well as idiomatic phrases, are given within the main entry. Etymologies are given in highly abbreviated form at the end of entries.

The following entry, quoted in full, indicates the style of a typical entry in *The Pocket Oxford Dictionary:*

> **narrow** /ˈnˆaeˆrˆəˆʊ/ **1** *a.* of small width in proportion to length; not broad; confined or confining (esp. *fig.*: *within narrow bounds*); careful, exact; with little margin (*narrow escape*); narrow-minded. **2** *n.* (usu. in *pl.*) narrow part of a sound, strait, river, pass, or street. **3** *v.* make or become narrower, lessen, contract. **4 narrow boat** canal boat; **narrow-minded** intolerant, prejudiced, rigid or restricted in one's views; **narrow seas** English Channel and Irish Sea. [OE]

Note that *The Pocket Oxford Dictionary* relies heavily on abbreviations in order to achieve its conciseness and comprehensiveness. Until or unless they have mastered these abbreviations, some users may find it difficult to interpret the entries. Even for readers who know what they mean, the plethora of abbreviations may remain an annoyance.

V. Syllabication and Pronunciation

Syllabication is not indicated in the entry word but does appear in the phonetically respelled pronunciations. Whereas previous editions used conventional respelling pronunciation, the current edition utilizes the International Phonetic Alphabet (IPA). The editor justifies this switch by saying that the IPA affords "greater precision and consistency" and also enables "guidance on pronunciation to be more valid internationally."

Apart from the IPA syllabication and pronunciation system, which may be unfamiliar to some readers, American users must also be aware that *The Pocket Oxford Dictionary* gives the British, not American, pronunciations of its entry words. This pronunciation is commonly known as *Received Pronunciation* (RP), the standard pronunciation of educated speakers in the south of England. The most obvious (but by no means the only) difference between British and American pronunciation concerns the pronunciation of *a* sounds, as in the words **rather**, **basket**, and **repatriate**, to name but three.

VI. Special Features

The Pocket Oxford Dictionary boasts several unusual special features, not all of which will be of use to the typical American reader. The appendixes include a table of weights and measures, featuring both British and American weights and measures (where these vary) and their metric equivalents. The Greek and Russian alphabets are also shown, with the English transliteration for each letter. A table of the principal countries of the world gives the proper name for an inhabitant of each country, the capital, and monetary unit. The counties of the United Kingdom and the states of the United States are listed in separate tables. Another list names the books of the Bible. There is also a three-page section on the use of punctuation marks that uses the British system of single quotation marks.

VII. Accessibility

The Pocket Oxford Dictionary includes a brief but handy table of contents. Boldface guide words at the top of each page in the main section of the book indicate the first and last entry words on that page. Readers will have to get used to the fact, however, that idiomatic phrases and compound words are generally embedded within main entries. Thus, for example, the reader looking for the definition of *public address system* will find it in the entry **public**. This entry contains not only expressions beginning with the word **public**, but also expressions such as **in public**, which one might expect to find under the entry **in**.

VIII. Graphics and Format

With a trim size of 4¼ inches × 7 inches and a thickness of 2 inches, *The Pocket Oxford Dictionary* is somewhat larger than the typical pocket dictionary. Each page is divided into two columns. Entry words are in boldface and overhang the text, making them easy to see. Compound words, variant forms, and idioms within the main entry are also printed in boldface. The type is small but legible, and the white space is adequate for a book of this size. The paper is thin and there is show-through, which may annoy some readers. The book is sturdily bound, however, and includes a dust jacket.

IX. Summary

Although this edition of *The Pocket Oxford Dictionary* makes a number of concessions to the contemporary language and the contemporary reader, it is still predominantly British in its orientation. Its treatment of vocabulary, spelling, definitions, pronunciation, and usage will serve the British user very well. Unless American readers have a special need for an authoritative British dictionary of this size, they would do better to choose an American paperback dictionary, such as Dell's edition of THE AMERICAN HERITAGE DICTIONARY, or a WEBSTER'S NEW WORLD edition.

The Random House American Dictionary: New Revised Edition

Facts at a Glance

Full Title: **The Random House American Dictionary: New Revised Edition**.
Publisher: Random House.
Editor: Stuart B. Flexner, Editor-in-Chief.
Edition Reviewed: © 1984.

Number of Entries: 30,000.
Number of Pages: 315.
Trim Size: $2\frac{7}{8}'' \times 5\frac{3}{8}''$.
Binding: paper with flexible vinyl cover.

Price: $2.95.
Sold in bookstores and office supply stores; also sold to educational institutions; and licensed to Wang Laboratories for a variety of software formats and widely used by Wang sublicensees as a spelling checker.
ISBN 0-394-52900-6.

I. Introduction

The Random House American Dictionary: New Revised Edition, the smallest dictionary in the Random House line, contains some 30,000 entries. Its tiny size, identical to that of THE RANDOM HOUSE THESAURUS: A DICTIONARY OF SYNONYMS AND ANTONYMS, puts it in the "vest-pocket" category. The publisher describes it as "a handy reference book for the student or business person who requires a small format dictionary offering reliable guidance in spell-

ing, pronunciation, and word meanings, plus a host of useful and up-to-date encyclopedic supplements."

II. Authority

The dictionary's primary editor, Stuart Berg Flexner, is an experienced, highly regarded lexicographer, as was its editorial consultant, the late Jess Stein. Both worked on a number of Random House dictionaries, including the 1966 edition of *The Random House Dictionary of the English Language: Unabridged Edition*—Flexner as Senior Editor and Stein as Editor-in-Chief.

III. Comprehensiveness

With only 30,000 entries included in the dictionary, many common words are excluded. For example, while the new unabridged RANDOM HOUSE DICTIONARY OF THE ENGLISH LANGUAGE has 65 entries between **dizzy** and **do**, *The Random House American Dictionary* has none.

Few proper names or abbreviations are listed. Names of nations are not included as entries, but some words relating to continents and countries are. Thus, **African**, **French**, **German**, and **Russian** can be found, but not *Africa*, *France*, *Germany*, or *Russia*. Idioms, synonyms, and antonyms are not given; nor are etymologies. However, entries do identify part of speech, and some include usage labels (such as *informal*). Alternative spellings are given where appropriate, but phonetic pronunciations are given only in rare instances.

IV. Quality and Currency of Entries

As is the standard practice in vest-pocket dictionaries, definitions in *The Random House American Dictionary* are compressed, often into a single word or phrase. For the most part definitions in this dictionary are succinct and to the point. As far as is possible within the limitations of the vest-pocket format, multiple meanings are given. Word forms are always given, and variations of the word are found at the end of the entry.

Brief as the definitions usually are, they remain clear and direct. For example, **caffeine** is identified as a noun and defined as "chemical in coffee, etc., used as stimulant." **Myopia** is defined simply as "nearsightedness," while **visible** is labeled as an adjective and given three definitions: "1. capable of being seen. 2. perceptible. 3. manifest."

The dictionary's coverage of technologically current terms is uneven. Although **byte**, **videodisk**, and **videocassette** are included, *cursor* and the computer-related meanings of *file* and *program* are not.

V. Syllabication and Pronunciation

Dots indicate syllabications, and diacritical marks distinguish phonetic values in main entry words. If further pronunciation guides are needed, they follow the main entry word in parentheses. For example: **ar·te′sian** (-zhən) **well**.

The dictionary lacks a pronunciation key, but readers who are familiar with standard pronunciation symbols should have no difficulty.

VI. Special Features

Despite its very small size, *The Random House American Dictionary* also contains 22 useful tables in a ready-reference appendix. Among these are "Major Nations of the World," "World Time Differences," "Distances Between U.S. Cities," and "The Metric System." More directly relevant to language and grammar are such features as "Forms of Address," "Rules of Spelling," "Rules of Punctuation," and "Words Most Often Misspelled." These features enhance the value of this dictionary for readers.

VII. Accessibility

In general, accessibility is not a problem in this little dictionary. Entries are arranged alphabetically, letter by letter. Two guide words at the top of each page identify the first and last entries on the page.

The sole reservation concerns the type size, which can only be described as minuscule. A user with less-than-perfect vision will probably experience some difficulty in locating a particular word and in reading the print, and extended reading would doubtless cause severe eye strain.

VIII. Graphics and Format

Entry words and variant forms and endings are printed in boldface, distinguishing them from the definitions, which appear in the same type size but in light print. Although the print is extremely small, the typeface is otherwise legible. Entry words overhang the text by one character space. A thin vertical line divides each page into two columns, giving the book a look of clean organization. There are no illustrations. The red, white, and blue cover of the book is flexible, washable vinyl.

IX. Summary

The Random House American Dictionary is intended as a vest-pocket dictionary for quick reference by an individual rather than for research. Because it has 30,000 entries, a fairly large number for a dictionary of this size and format, the print is uncomfortably small. Public libraries will require larger, more comprehensive dictionaries. However, the definitions are concise, and the work will be useful to individuals who need a handy reference of this size, in book format or as part of a computer software package.

The Random House College Dictionary: Revised Edition

Facts at a Glance

Full Title: **The Random House College Dictionary: Revised Edition**.
Publisher: Random House.
Editors: Jess Stein, Editor-in-Chief Emeritus; Stuart B. Flexner, Editor-in-Chief; Leonore C. Hauck, Managing Editor; P. Y. Su, Senior Defining Editor.
Edition Reviewed: © 1984.

Number of Entries: 170,000.
Number of Pages: 1,600.
Number of Illustrations: 1,500.
Number of Maps: 200.
Trim Size: 6⁹⁄₁₆″ × 9⁵⁄₈″.
Binding: cloth.

Prices: $15.95 (thumb indexed); $14.95 (plain).
Sold in bookstores and other outlets; also sold to libraries and other educational institutions.
ISBN 0-394-43600-8.

I. Introduction

The Random House College Dictionary: Revised Edition is based on the first edition of the unabridged *Random House Dictionary of the English Language*. Thus, it is one of the major dictionaries of its kind. In the words of editor emeritus Jess Stein, *The Random House College Dictionary* is designed "to give the user the information he wants and needs as reliably, clearly, and quickly as possible." Stein also makes a claim for this work as "the most complete and authoritative dictionary of its kind ever published"—a claim that may be exaggerated, given the excellence of several other college dictionaries on the market, notably the AMERICAN HERITAGE DICTIONARY: SECOND COLLEGE EDITION and WEBSTER'S NINTH NEW COLLEGIATE DICTIONARY.

Like its unabridged parent, *The Random House College Dictionary* attempts "to provide the user with an exact record of the language he sees and hears." It can therefore be considered a descriptive dictionary. However, as Raven I. McDavid, professor of English at the University of Chicago, writes in his introductory essay "Usage, Dialects, and Functional Varieties," "this does not mean an abandonment of standards."

The Random House College Dictionary: Revised Edition

❶ Syllabication is indicated by centered dots

❷ Usage labels are italicized

❸ Discussion of synonyms (and sometimes antonyms) is introduced by the boldface subheading —*Syn.*; synonyms and antonyms are numbered to correspond with the appropriate definition above

❹ Field labels are italicized

❺ Etymology is enclosed by brackets

❻ Cross-references are set in small capitals

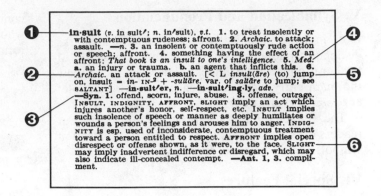

II. Authority

The editor in chief, Stuart B. Flexner, has long been associated with a variety of respected general and special dictionaries, most recently of the revised, unabridged edition of THE RANDOM HOUSE DICTIONARY OF THE ENGLISH LANGUAGE. Noted lexicographers Jess Stein and Laurence Urdang have also contributed to this work. Other members of the editorial and consultant staffs are listed along with their credentials. Among the more than 200 consultants from a wide variety of fields are Craig Claiborne, Erik Erikson, Andreas Feininger, Toni Morrison, Richard Sennett, and James D. Watson.

Random House, a major trade book publisher, is no stranger to the reference book field; in 1947 the firm published the *American College Dictionary*. In the past ten years, through the use of electronic data processing, the firm's dictionary editors have been able to research "texts of every written material imaginable—newspaper and magazine articles, stories, textbooks, novels, even specialized texts ranging from parts catalogs through articles in technical and scholarly journals to court decisions." Tape recordings of radio and television programs have been analyzed for pronunciation.

III. Comprehensiveness

The editors' goal in preparing this dictionary has been to provide "judicious selectivity." Such contemporary words as **AIDS**, **ayatollah**, **chemotherapy**, **modem**, **Heimlich maneuver**, and **freebasing** are included; however, other current terms such as *Alzheimer's disease*, *laparoscopy*, *redshirt*, and *arthroscope* are not. Curiously, every breed of dog checked by the reviewers was provided, but only **Siamese** and **Manx** cat breeds were found. Cats are

so generally excluded that **blue point** is defined as an oyster but not as a type of cat. However, although the general selection sometimes appears limited in certain subject areas, the dictionary is more than adequate in its coverage of present-day American English.

The editors have also provided excellent usage notes and synonym lists. The entry **because**, for instance, includes a long usage note that explains the difference in meaning among its synonyms **as**, **since**, **for**, **inasmuch as** and gives an example for the proper use of each synonym. Each synonym in the dictionary is cross-referenced, and synonyms are provided whenever possible. The reader, therefore, has the greatest chance of choosing the proper word. Quotations from literature and the sciences are not included. But, in view of the extensive usage notes and synonym lists, this is not a serious drawback.

Etymologies are included at the end of each entry, allowing the reader to concentrate on spelling, definitions, and usage, which are probably the most frequently used features of the dictionary. The etymologies are well prepared. Words are carefully traced from one language and time period to another. The etymology key and language abbreviation table are conveniently placed on the front endpaper. The bibliographic entries are extensive (numbering some 700) but far from comprehensive.

The appendixes provide useful reference material. For example, the list of "Signs and Symbols" contains, among others, the signs of the zodiac, mathematical symbols, and musical notation.

IV. Quality and Currency of Entries

Entries consist of main entry word (in boldface), pronunciation, part of speech, restrictive label (if applicable), inflected forms, definitions, etymology, and synonyms. Antonyms and usage notes for many words are included.

High school seniors and graduates should be able to understand the definitions with little difficulty. The definitions are thorough, detailed, and descriptive. The entry **farm**, for example, includes reference to "farm teams" in baseball, as well as historical and obscure meanings. The entries **wave** and **vector** explain the scientific meanings in intelligible and precise language. The entry **double-time** includes the number of paces a marching troop takes in one minute at this speed. The **fandango** is described as a "lively Spanish or Spanish American dance . . . performed [while] playing castanets," and the **Charleston** is described as "vigorous."

The most common part of speech is listed first, and for each part the definitions are numbered in order of frequency. Idiomatic meanings and phrases are defined. When necessary, a definition is clarified by a sentence that demonstrates its use. For example, the definition of **whiz** includes one sentence to clarify its meaning as a sound and movement and another sentence for the colloquial meaning ("expert at a particular activity").

V. Syllabication and Pronunciation

Syllabication is provided as a guide for both pronunciation and written word breaks. Main entries are syllabicated by centered dots "according to the usual American principles of word division, as observed . . . in printing and typing." Pronunciations are syllabicated to provide "a visual aid in sounding out a word." For quick reference, a shortened pronunciation table is included at the bottom of every page. The table refers to the full key printed in large type on the front flyleaf. In place of the International Phonetic Alphabet symbols, 47 phonetic symbols with six diacritical marks are used.

The guide to the dictionary explains both syllabication and pronunciation, although it assumes a full understanding of phonetics on the part of the reader. While it will not always be necessary to consult the pronunciation guide, some symbols such as the schwa (ə), "th" variant, and a, ā, ä, and â may require further explanation, which can be found in the key. The pronunciation most frequently used among educated speakers is given first. Permissible variants are also included.

VI. Special Features

The work has a number of special features that merit discussion. Most important are the prefix tables for **re-**, **pro-**, **well-**, **un-**, **over-**, and so on that appear in their respective alphabetical sections. The periodic table of elements is included, as is the International Phonetic Alphabet. The appendixes include a list of U.S. and Canadian colleges and universities, a list of English given names, and a manual of style. The final endpapers contain weight and measurement tables and a list of five foreign alphabets and their transliterations.

Entries for plants and animals include the Latin names, and entries for chemical elements include symbols, atomic weights, and numbers. Biographies are also included within the alphabetical list. Aside from U.S. presidents, the twentieth-century names listed include **Camus**, **DiMaggio**, **Einstein**, **Garbo**, **Giraudoux**, **Heifetz**, **Hitler**, **Fulbright**, **Van Doren**, **Van Vechten**, and others. Each entry includes birth and death dates and a brief descriptive phrase. These biographical entries are useful mainly for spelling purposes. Finally, the guide to the dictionary includes a few essays on language that will be of interest to scholarly readers.

VII. Accessibility

The volume includes a brief but useful table of contents that directs readers to the dictionary's charts, special features, and items in the appendixes. The dictionary is also thumb-indexed (two letters per tab). Each thumb tab is midway between the letters. There are no tabs for the introductory material or the appendixes.

Page numbers are centered at the top of the page between the two columns. There are also two guide words at the top of each page, allowing the reader to see at a glance the range of entries on the particular page.

Variant spellings are cross-referenced to the most common spelling. This permits the user to establish the preferred spelling and to distinguish misspellings from variants.

VIII. Graphics and Format

The volume contains approximately 1,500 illustrations, all clear black-and-white line drawings or diagrams. Definitions for many entries such as **graph**, **geodesic dome**, **lantern**, and **water gauge** are graphically explained through illustration. Some other entries, such as **cross** and **vault**, include multiple illustrations for various types of the item. Illustrations do not always show variations, however. The entry for **column**, for example, illustrates the parts of a Roman column but not the five orders; they are depicted at the entry **order** but without cross-reference. Informative maps are included for a variety of geographic regions and countries, both modern and historical.

The dictionary has a bold red dust jacket that describes some of its more important features. The cover is also red with gold letters on the spine. The hardback curvature spine is tight and durable enough to withstand repeated use in a library or at home. There is sufficient gutter margin to permit the reader to see the full page without straining the binding. The paper is white but rather thin, with some show-through. The publisher has used a variety of type-faces within each entry: boldface, italic, roman. Each is clear and precise but small.

IX. Summary

The Random House College Dictionary: Revised Edition is, on the whole, a very good dictionary. The definitions are substantial and easy to understand. The usage notes, synonym lists, graphics, and special features will prove helpful to the everyday user.

Its drawbacks are few and relatively minor but should be mentioned. Most significantly, the relatively small typeface and mediocre paper quality make the contents of this dictionary less attractive than those of THE AMERICAN HERITAGE DICTIONARY and WEBSTER'S NINTH NEW COLLEGIATE DICTIONARY, both of which are better designed and easier on the eye. The cluttered appearance of its pages makes *The Random House Dictionary* look more formidable than it really is and may deter some users.

Nevertheless, while it does not quite match the quality of its rivals in either content or design, *The Random House Dictionary* still has much to recommend it. Because it not only supplies a variety of definitions for each entry but also contains information on usage and etymology as well as other encyclopedic information, this authoritative dictionary deserves a place in the home, the office, and the reference collection of academic and public libraries alike.

The Random House Dictionary

Facts at a Glance

Full Title: **The Random House Dictionary**.
Publisher: Ballantine Books.
Editors: Jess Stein, Editor-in-Chief; P. Y. Su.
Edition Reviewed: © 1983.

Number of Entries: approximately 74,000.
Number of Pages: 1,072.
Trim Size: 4⅛" × 6⅞".
Binding: paperback.

Price: $3.50.
Sold in bookstores and other outlets; also sold to libraries and other educational institutions.
ISBN 0-345-32298-3.

I. Introduction

The Random House Dictionary is a paperback edition of the hardcover RANDOM HOUSE DICTIONARY: CONCISE EDITION and is, according to the publisher, "based on" the first edition of THE RANDOM HOUSE DICTIONARY OF THE ENGLISH LANGUAGE. Originally published in 1978, it was "intended to meet the needs of those who want up-to-date, comprehensive, reliable information" in a compact format. However, it has apparently not been revised since 1983.

II. Authority

The Random House Dictionary was prepared by Random House's permanent lexicographic staff under the direction of Stuart Berg Flexner and the late Jess Stein, both distinguished lexicographers. Flexner, noted for his studies of American slang, was also a moving force behind the OXFORD AMERICAN DICTIONARY. Random House has an established reputation as a leading dictionary publisher. Ballantine, which publishes this paperback edition, is a division of Random House.

The publisher notes that in compiling this dictionary, its staff lexicographers were assisted by "many hundreds of scholars, educators, and specialists"; none, however, are identified.

III. Comprehensiveness

The Random House Dictionary contains slightly over 74,000 entries, compared to 60,000 in the Dell AMERICAN HERITAGE DICTIONARY, 57,000 in the MERRIAM-WEBSTER DICTIONARY, and 82,000 in FUNK & WAGNALLS STANDARD DICTIONARY. The word list was compiled from the Random House citation file, which is based on such sources as books, periodicals, special vocabulary lists, and radio and television broadcasts. The publisher claims that among these entries are "thousands . . . not found in any other paperback dictionary." This book, however, has not been revised since 1983.

Given the 1983 copyright, this paperback still provides reasonably adequate coverage of contemporary American English. Many computer terms, such as **floppy disk**, **mainframe**, and **modem** are included. The computer language **COBOL** is listed, but **FORTRAN** is excluded. There is an entry for **videodisc**, but none for *compact disc*. *AIDS* is not included in this dictionary, nor is *CAT scan*. Other words entered in *The Random House Dictionary* include **chemotherapy**, **ophthalmoscope**, **nosh** (Yiddish), and **joie de vivre** (French).

The "Guide to the Dictionary" in the front matter notes that usage labels, usage notes, etymologies, and synonyms are given for many of the entries. For example, the entry for **among** includes a long usage note that compares the word to *between*; the entry for **alright** states that the word is usually unacceptable and refers readers to alternatives. The entry for **Negro** reports that "Many people today consider Negro to be derogatory and offensive, preferring the use of *black*." Usage labels in other entries may note slang, archaic, and informal expressions. These notes and labels are standard features and provide the reader with genuine aids to proper and accurate use of the language. (Field labels, however, are not included.)

Etymologies are included only intermittently and, in fact, are not given for most entries. (An etymology key is printed on the inside of the back cover.) The same holds true for synonyms.

IV. Quality and Currency of Entries

As already mentioned, definitions in *The Random House Dictionary* are concise and economical but by no means simplistic. Many entries include a phrase or sentence to illustrate different meanings of a particular word.

The "Guide to the Dictionary" in the front matter explains clearly how entries are arranged: "Definitions within an entry are individually numbered in a single sequence, regardless of the groupings according to part of speech. In general, the most common part of speech is listed first, and the most frequent meaning appears as the first definition for each part of speech." Idiomatic expressions are entered in boldface type under the main entry word to which they are most closely related, following the definitions for the main entry word.

The following is representative of the entries in *The Random House Dictionary*:

> **de·liv·er** (di·liv′ər), *v.t.* **1.** to carry (letters, goods, etc.) to the intended recipient. **2.** to give into another's possession or keeping. **3.** to utter or pronounce: *to deliver a speech.* **4.** to strike or throw: *to deliver a blow.* **5.** to set free. **6.** to assist in bringing forth young. **7.** to assist at the birth of.—*v.i.* **8.** to give birth. **9.** to provide delivery service.—**de·liv′er·er**, n.

This entry compares favorably with entries for the same word in WEBSTER'S NEW WORLD DICTIONARY and WEBSTER'S II NEW RIVERSIDE DICTIONARY.

Other entries are equally detailed. The word **go**, for example, has 61 separate definitions. Fifteen definitions are given for **hot**, including:

> **4.** having or showing intense or violent feeling: *hot temper.* **5.** lustful or lascivious. **6.** violent, furious, or intense: *the hottest battle of the war.* **7.** absolutely new: *hot from the press.* **8.** *Slang.* following very closely: *hot*

pursuit. **9.** *Slang.* extremely lucky: *a hot crap shooter.* **10.** *Slang.* sensational or scandalous: *a hot news story.* **11.** *Slang.* stolen recently. **12.** actively conducting an electric current: *a hot wire.*

The idiomatic expression **make it hot for** is listed for definition number 14, but the slang term **hot air** is a separate entry. Homographs, such as **content**[1] (matter contained in a book or speech) and **content**[2] (satisfied) are listed as separate entries, distinguished from one another by superscript numbers.

The Random House Dictionary, with a 1983 copyright date, can no longer be considered absolutely current. In 1988, this dictionary could benefit from some revision, given Random House's commitment to high-quality dictionaries, and the fact that in 1987 Random House issued a new (second) edition of the unabridged *Random House Dictionary of the English Language*.

V. Syllabication and Pronunciation

Entry words are divided into syllables by centered dots. Pronunciation is given immediately following the entry word. A full-page pronunciation key in the front matter spells out the dictionary's pronunciation system. The system makes use primarily of phonetic respelling, with a minimum of diacritical marks. Long and short vowels are indicated by the traditional marks; the *schwa* (ə) is also used to indicate the sound of vowels in unaccented syllables. Altogether, the dictionary makes use of 45 different symbols.

As a sample of pronunciation respellings that occur in *The Random House Dictionary*, consider:

> **a·ban·don** (ə ban′dən)
> **ac·tu·al** (ak′ch‾o‾o əl)
> **de·lin·quent** (di ling′kwənt)
> **flau·tist** (flô′tist, flou′-)

There is also a pronunciation key for foreign sounds, employing seven symbols. These apply mainly to French words (such as **fait accompli**), but also to German, Italian, Spanish, and Scottish pronunciations. Unlike WEBSTER'S NEW WORLD DICTIONARY, for one, *The Random House Dictionary* does not include an abbreviated pronunciation key on each two-page spread.

VI. Special Features

The Random House Dictionary includes a number of special features that are standard in many paperback dictionaries. Foremost among these is a 20-page "Basic Manual of Style" appended to the lexicon. The manual attends to such matters of usage as punctuation, division of words, abbreviation, capitalization, and footnotes and endnotes. This section will be particularly useful to students as a quick reference source on style.

Other special features include a three-and-a-half page table of common signs and symbols (used in astronomy, mathematics, medicine, religion, and other fields), proofreaders' marks, forms of address, and weights and measures. These basic, straightforward features all provide useful ready-reference information and enhance the value of this dictionary, especially for students.

VII. Accessibility

Entry words are set in boldface type, making them readily accessible. Inflected forms, variant spellings, and idioms are also printed in boldface, which makes them immediately distinguishable from the rest of the text. The number preceding each definition is boldface as well. Note, however, that main entry words overhang the text by only one character.

Guide words at the top of each page indicate the first and last entry on that page. The table of contents makes the special features accessible at a glance.

VIII. Graphics and Format

In graphics and format, *The Random House Dictionary* is a match for any other paperback dictionary currently before the public. The book has been thoughtfully designed to enhance accessibility. The typeface is clean, and the type itself large and dark enough to avoid straining the reader's eyes.

The paperback book itself is fairly sturdy although, as one would expect from any paperback with more than 1,000 pages, the spine will break down with regular use, and after a while pages will begin to break away. In this respect, *The Random House Dictionary* is virtually identical to WEBSTER'S NEW WORLD DICTIONARY, WEBSTER'S II NEW RIVERSIDE DICTIONARY, and other books in paperback format.

IX. Summary

Were it not for the fact that it is significantly out-of-date, *The Random House Dictionary* would be a first-rate paperback reference work. Its definitions are concise but also express the nuances of meaning that make English such a rich and varied language. Readers seeking a paperback dictionary for personal use, however, will be better served by THE AMERICAN HERITAGE DICTIONARY or THE MERRIAM-WEBSTER DICTIONARY.

The Random House Dictionary: Concise Edition

Facts at a Glance

Full Title: **The Random House Dictionary: Concise Edition**.
Publisher: Random House.
Editors: Stuart Berg Flexner, Editor-in-Chief; Jess Stein, P. Y. Su.
Edition Reviewed © 1983.

Number of Entries: approximately 74,000.
Number of Pages: 1,072.
Trim Size: $4\frac{1}{8}'' \times 6\frac{7}{8}''$.
Binding: hardcover.

Price: $5.95.
Sold in bookstores and other outlets; also sold to libraries.
ISBN 0-394-51200-6.

I. Introduction and Scope

The Random House Dictionary: Concise Edition is a hardcover edition of THE RANDOM HOUSE DICTIONARY's paperback edition. Except for the different bindings, copyright dates, and extraneous information on the covers and flyleaves of the paperback, these two dictionaries are identical. Although the *Concise Edition* bears a later copyright date than its paperback sibling, our reviewers are unable to find any revisions or additions in this version.

With its red, simulated-leather cover embossed in gold with the title and the Random House logo, the *Concise Edition* would seem to be specially designed for library collections. Certainly the hardcover format is much more durable than the paperback. However, this format also presents several problems not evident in the paperback. The pages do not lie flat when the book is opened. The inner margin is scant, and the text tends to spill into the gutter. In short, the cover looks impressive, but this version offers nothing that is not available in the less expensive and more handy paperback edition.

For complete information about the contents of this dictionary, consult the review of THE RANDOM HOUSE DICTIONARY in this Buying Guide.

The Random House Dictionary of the English Language: Second Edition, Unabridged

Facts at a Glance

Full Title: **The Random House Dictionary of the English Language: Second Edition, Unabridged**.
Publisher: Random House.

*The Random House Dictionary of
the English Language*

❶ Usage labels are italicized

❷ Synonyms are introduced by the
abbreviation —*Syn.* and are
numbered to correspond with the
appropriate definition

❸ Field labels are italicized

❹ Idiomatic expressions are set in
boldface type and run into the
main entry

❺ Etymology, enclosed in brackets,
includes date of first recorded
use; cross-references to entries
that contain relevant
etymological information are set
in small capitals

❻ Cross-references are set in
boldface type

blink (blingk), *v.i.* **1.** to open and close the eye, esp. involuntarily; wink rapidly and repeatedly. **2.** to look with winking or half-shut eyes: *I blinked at the harsh morning light.* **3.** to be startled, surprised, or dismayed (usually fol. by *at*): *She blinked at his sudden fury.* **4.** to look evasively or with indifference; ignore (often fol. by *at*): *to blink at another's eccentricities.* **5.** to shine unsteadily, dimly, or intermittently; twinkle: *The light on the buoy blinked in the distance.* —*v.t.* **6.** to open and close (the eye or eyes), usually rapidly and repeatedly; wink: *She blinked her eyes in an effort to wake up.* **7.** to cause (something) to blink: *We blinked the flashlight frantically, but there was no response.* **8.** to ignore deliberately; evade; shirk. —*n.* **9.** an act of blinking: *The faithful blink of the lighthouse.* **10.** a gleam; glimmer: *There was not a blink of light anywhere.* **11.** *Chiefly Scot.* a glance or glimpse. **12.** *Meteorol.* **a.** ice blink. **b.** snowblink. **13. on the blink,** not in proper working order; in need of repair: *The washing machine is on the blink again.* [1250–1300; ME *blinken* (v.), var. of *blenken* to BLENCH¹; c. D, G *blinken*] —**Syn. 1.** See **wink**¹. **8.** overlook, disregard, avoid, condone. **9.** wink, flicker, twinkle, flutter.

Editor: Stuart Berg Flexner, Editor-in-Chief.
Edition Reviewed: © 1987.

Number of Entries: over 315,000.
Number of Pages: 2,552.
Number of Illustrations: 32 pages in color; 2,400 in
black and white.
Trim Size: 9¼″ × 12″.
Binding: cloth.

Price: $79.95.
Sold in bookstores and by direct mail; also sold to
libraries and other educational institutions.
ISBN 0-394-50050-4.

I. Introduction

According to the editor, the main purposes of *The Random House Dictionary of the English Language: Second Edition, Unabridged* are

(1) to provide the user with an accurate, accessible guide to the meanings, spellings, pronunciations, usage, and history of the words in our language . . . ; (2) to provide a scrupulously up-to-date dictionary of record . . . ; (3) to bring to the user the results of the most recent, authoritative research and knowledge from scholars and experts in all fields, edited with care.

With over 315,000 entries in 2,500 pages, *The Random House Dictionary of the English Language* is one of only three dictionaries today that are described by their publishers as "unabridged." (The other two are WEBSTER'S NEW TWENTIETH CEN-

TURY UNABRIDGED DICTIONARY and WEBSTER'S THIRD NEW INTERNATIONAL DICTIONARY.) However, comprehensive as these works may be, none of them is unabridged in the strictest sense, since none contains all the words in the English language. But although *The Random House Dictionary* is the smallest of the three in terms of number of entries, it clearly meets its own definition of **unabridged**:

a dictionary that has not been reduced in size by omission of terms or definitions; the most comprehensive edition of a given dictionary.

II. Authority

The first edition of this volume, published in 1966, has earned a solid reputation for being generally reliable and easy to use. The American Library Association's Subscription Books Committee, for example, although noting that this edition would not "completely serve the needs of those who require an unabridged English-language dictionary," nevertheless praised it for having an "up-to-date vocabulary, explicit definitions, useful general reference features, and an appealing format" (*Booklist*, 1 April 1967, p. 807).

Stuart Flexner, the Editor-in-Chief of the second edition, was one of the senior editors under Jess Stein for the first edition. Flexner has a distinguished reputation as a lexicographer; his NEW DICTIONARY OF AMERICAN SLANG is a very useful standard reference work and his other books about American language such as *I Hear America Talking* (Simon & Schuster,

1977) and *Listening to America* (Simon & Schuster, 1982) are noted for their readability as well as their scholarship. Although Random House has not been in the dictionary business as long as Merriam-Webster, it has compiled a large computerized citation file which facilitated the extensive revisions made in this second edition, including 50,000 new entries and 75,000 new definitions. The editors have received guidance in labeling regional words from consultants working on the *Linguistic Atlas of the United States* and the DICTIONARY OF AMERICAN REGIONAL ENGLISH (DARE).

Hundreds of specialists have been used as consultants for one or both editions of this dictionary, including, to name just those most prominently listed: Arthur J. Bronstein (pronunciation), Thomas J. Creswell (usage and synonyms), Eric A. Hamp (etymology), Raven I. McDavid, Jr. (usage and dialects), and Virginia McDavid (usage and synonyms). The variety of subjects and disciplines represented by the consultants is also impressive; for example: cookery, astrology, Celtic mythology, high fidelity, falconry, alcoholic beverages, hunting, lunar geography, surveying, motion pictures and television, and many more highly specialized fields, as well as broader disciplines and subjects, such as physics, anatomy, criminal law, and languages.

Among the people listed as consultants for one or both editions are some names that are apt to be recognized by the general public: Theodore Bernstein (usage notes), J. Desmond Clark (archaeology), Henry Steele Commager (American history), Nat Hentoff (jazz), and Jack Valenti (motion pictures).

III. Comprehensiveness

This dictionary includes many entries of current terms, constituting the broad scope of new words in use today. None of these terms is present in the first edition or in WEBSTER'S THIRD, although all of them are in the latest supplement to WEBSTER'S THIRD, entitled 12,000 WORDS. There are scientific terms that have entered everyday vocabulary like **AIDS virus**, **cardiopulmonary resuscitation**, **dopamine**, **intensive care unit**, and **mammogram**; technical jargon with broad applications like **end user**, **glitch**, and **zero-base budgeting**; slang like **bag lady**, **flaky**, **nerd**, **uptight**, and **whacked-out**; words for new concepts, states, or activities in our lives (or new words for old ones) like **latchkey child**, **personhood**, **quality circle**, **released time**, **stir-fry**, **theme park**, **Vietnamization**, **yellow rain**, **Harvey Wallbanger**, **jet lag**, **Op-Ed**, and **X-rated**; and words borrowed from other languages that seem to have become firmly rooted in English, like the Yiddish **kvetch**. The dictionary is also heavy on contemporary acronyms and abbreviations such

as **FOBS** ("Fractional orbital bombardment system"), **RDD** ("random digit dialing"), **PET** ("positron emission tomography"), and **ZIP + 4**.

Etymological notes are generally quite precise in designating origins in other languages and earlier forms of English words; however, they also admit puzzling or unknown derivations when necessary, as in

nerd . . . [1960–65, *Amer.*; obscurely derived expressive formation].

A detailed, but clearly explained system of symbols and abbreviations is used in the etymologies to designate numerous relationships, such as descent from one language to another, different historical periods of the same language, sequence in sense or meaning shifts, derived formations, and cross-references.

Unlike WEBSTER'S THIRD, this volume does not include quotations from published sources to illustrate the meanings of words. Instead, as in the first edition, the illustrative sentences have been composed by the dictionary's staff. Previous reviewers have criticized this practice as being an artificial representation of language use, but on the other hand some of the quotations used in WEBSTER'S THIRD have also been criticized for not representing typical or common usage. It is difficult to generalize about this feature because one should not judge the illustrative sentences apart from the definitions they accompany. Furthermore, some idioms, for example, require more explanation than a general dictionary, or an illustrative sentence in one, is expected to provide. For example, the expression **kill with kindness** is defined as "to overdo in one's efforts to be kind" and illustrated with the sentence "*The aunts would kill their nephews and nieces with kindness.*" Although the sentence is appropriate, the expression may still make no sense to an English-language student encountering such hyperbole for the first time; and there is no reference to Shakespeare's *Taming of the Shrew*, where this idiom is first recorded. (But, on the other hand, our reviewers did not find this idiom in WEBSTER'S THIRD.)

More so than either the first edition or WEBSTER'S THIRD, this work adheres to the so-called descriptive school of lexicography, which asserts that a dictionary should report how the language is typically used rather than dictating how it should be used. In general practice, most dictionaries steer a middle course between prescription and description. One can hardly trust a dictionary to provide guidance about proper usage unless one also trusts it to be an authoritative source of unbiased information about those words. In his preface to the first edition, editor Jess Stein defended the descriptive approach:

Since language is a social institution, the lexicographer must give the user an adequate indication of the attitudes of society toward particular words or expressions, whether he regards those attitudes as linguistically sound or not. . . . He does not need to express approval or disapproval of a disputed usage, but he does need to report the milieu of words as well as their meanings.

The second edition carries this descriptive approach a step further, as reflected in the essay, "Usage: Change and Variation," in the frontmatter. "A professionally prepared contemporary dictionary is authoritative in that the information it contains is based upon actual usage, but . . . it does not try to shape or legislate usage," write contributors Thomas J. Creswell and Virginia McDavid. "Language practices keep changing, and what was favored yesterday may be condemned today. . . . Specific judgments are always subject to modification as practice and opinion change." The classics scholar William Arrowsmith, however, has pointed out the danger of this approach in his review of *The Random House Dictionary* in the *New York Times Book Review*, January 3, 1988: "The lexicographer's descriptive practice, combined with the user's prescriptive expectations, must inevitably make the present appalling plunge of English toward sloppiness, vulgar chic and desperate imprecision more and more precipitate. If present usage is increasingly barbarous, why should this barbarism be embalmed and hailed by lexicographers?"

Besides including generally noncontroversial labels for subject, such as *Chemistry*; region, such as *Canadian*; or time, such as *obsolete*, *archaic*, *rare*, and *older use*; the second edition also employs these stylistic labels: *informal*, *nonstandard*, *slang*, *vulgar*, *disparaging*, *offensive*, *facetious*, *baby talk*, *literary*, *eye dialect* (for example, **wimmin** for *women*), and *pronunciation spelling* (**gonna** for *going to*).

Unlike THE AMERICAN HERITAGE DICTIONARY, with its much disputed practice of reporting in percentage form the judgments of language experts about controversial usages, *The Random House Dictionary* offers brief essays of considered advice. For example, the usage note for **disinterested** explains that the word originally meant "not interested" but that it can now mean either "impartial" or "uninterested," depending on the context. Again, however, Arrowsmith takes vigorous exception to this permissiveness:

> Surely there is good reason for retaining, not vacuously dissolving, the difference between "tortuous" and "torturous," "precipitous" and "precipitate," "populist" and "egalitarian," "nauseated" and "nauseous," "sanitarium" and "sanitorium." Why have different words if they all mean the same thing?

IV. Quality and Currency of Entries

One of the most important conventions of this dictionary is its ordering of multiple meanings: the most frequently encountered meanings precede the less common ones; these are followed by specialized senses and, finally, by any rare, archaic, or obsolete senses. This convention differentiates it sharply from WEBSTER'S THIRD, its most important competitor, which lists the older meanings of a word *before* the newer ones. There is a considerable difference, for example, between the first definitions in WEBSTER'S THIRD for **hustler** as "a pickpocket's accomplice" or "one who obtains money by fraudulent means" and the first definition in *The Random House Dictionary* as "an enterprising person determined to succeed."

Generally speaking, this dictionary's definitions, while they are not as extensive and detailed as those in WEBSTER'S THIRD, are usually easier to understand. For example, a French term fully assimilated into English, **déjà vu**, is defined as follows in *The Random House Dictionary*:

> 1. *Psychol.* the illusion of having previously experienced something actually being encountered for the first time. 2. disagreeable familiarity or sameness: *The new television season had a sense of déjà vu about it—the same old plots and characters with new names.* [1900–05; < F: lit., already seen] [.]

WEBSTER'S THIRD, however, while noting an alternative English spelling (*déjà vue*) that *The Random House Dictionary* misses, says in its entry for this term only that it is French for "already seen" and supplies a cross-reference to the entry for **paramnesia**. If it is more accurate to direct the user from a French term used in English to its presumed English equivalent, then the absence of such a cross-reference is an example of *The Random House Dictionary*'s lack of completeness. However, since many nonpsychologists are wont to use **déjà vu**, but very few of them use **paramnesia**, it can be argued that WEBSTER'S THIRD is less helpful in this case as a record of actual usage than is *The Random House Dictionary*. The two works define **paramnesia** in equivalent words, but WEBSTER'S THIRD's definitions do not encompass the second sense of *The Random House Dictionary*'s definition. By giving the user to understand that **déjà vu** and **paramnesia** are equivalent, WEBSTER'S THIRD either ignores or fails to recognize that these terms may have different meanings.

Generally speaking, definitions of abstract things, such as **energy**, "the capacity for vigorous activity; available power," are as clear in *The Random House Dictionary* as are definitions of concrete things, such as **hat**, "a shaped covering for the head, usually with a crown and brim." However, some of the definitions of scientific terms may be too technical for the layperson, as, for example, this definition:

> **AIDS** (ādz), *n. Pathol.* a disease of the immune system characterized by increased susceptibility to oppor-

tunistic infections, as pneumocystis carinii pneumonia and candidiasis, to certain cancers, as Kaposi's sarcoma, and to neurological disorders; caused by a retrovirus and transmitted chiefly through blood or blood products that enter the body's bloodstream, esp. by sexual contact or contaminated hypodermic needles. Cf. **AIDS virus**. [1982; a(cquired) i(mmune) d(eficiency) s(yndrome)] [.]

On the other hand, it might be argued that any further translation of technical language into nontechnical language would distort an essential core of meaning exhibited here in a combination of medical and common words.

As is evident in the definition of **déjà vu**, this volume does provide some guidance to the figurative and connotative as well as the literal and technical meanings of words. Although it recognizes "only" 119 meanings for the verb **set** (some of these are phrases, as in **set about**) as compared to many hundreds of senses defined in the OXFORD ENGLISH DICTIONARY (which is a different kind of dictionary altogether), *The Random House Dictionary* can be trusted to define most of the senses of a word that the general user will need.

V. Syllabication and Pronunciation

Syllabication is indicated by centered dots, which are easily distinguished from hyphens. Primary and secondary stress marks are easy to distinguish from each other. Although the introduction's pronunciation notes are extensive, they are much easier to understand than the much more detailed guide to pronunciation in WEBSTER'S THIRD. In *The Random House Dictionary*, every right-hand page in the lexicon contains a concise pronunciation key, located at the bottom of the last column. Although it is somewhat awkward to turn to the more detailed pronunciation chart inside the front cover, that chart is more useful than the concise key because it is in larger type and includes more examples of words illustrating each sound.

Instead of the International Phonetic Alphabet, this dictionary uses a system of "orthographically motivated" diacritical marks. This means that instead of using different symbols to convey, for example, the differently sounded stressed vowels in **divine** and **divinity**, it represents both of these vowels by a form of the letter *i*. When there is more than one pronunciation for a word, these "are listed in order of frequency, insofar as that can be determined, although the difference in frequency may be minimal." Special labels are occasionally used for nonstandard pronunciations, but unless so labeled "all pronunciations given should be considered standard and may be used freely in all social circumstances." For some regionally limited pronunciations, however, one might want more explicit guid-

ance than is provided. For example, this dictionary shows **tomato** as being pronounced with either a long or a short *a* (with the long *a* variant listed first), but many, if not the majority of Americans, regard the second pronunciation as affected. Although this edition does not provide guidance for **tomato**, it does a commendable job in a pronunciation note for **aunt**. The note explains that while most Americans outside the East pronounce this word to rhyme with **rant**, New Englanders and eastern Virginians often pronounce it with a broad *a*. The explanation suggests that Easterners have maintained closer cultural ties with the British and therefore have retained what many Americans would regard as a British pronunciation.

VI. Special Features

Like the first edition, this edition devotes a considerable amount of space to special encyclopedic supplements, located at the end of the lexicon, which include: a list of signs and symbols; a directory of colleges and universities; the Declaration of Independence; the U.S. Constitution; concise bilingual French, Spanish, Italian, and German dictionaries; a basic style manual; a list of word pairs commonly confused, another list of words commonly misspelled, and a 32-page color atlas. These features will certainly represent an added inducement to some home users who do not own an encyclopedia, but they will be considered superfluous by most libraries. Probably the most often consulted of these supplements will be the signs and symbols, which have come to be conventional parts of most abridged as well as unabridged dictionaries.

The body of the dictionary itself also contains numerous proper name entries, so that geographic names, famous people, and titles of works of art, literature, and music are interspersed with the general vocabulary. Forty-five "boxed features," or special charts and tables, such as the Books of the Bible, Geologic Time Divisions, and Proofreader's Marks, are also found in their appropriate alphabetical positions in the text. Entries are current enough to note, for example, the death in 1986 of James Cagney and the designation of counterrevolutionaries in Nicaragua as **contras** or **Contras**. The map of Nicaragua, similarly, reflects an awareness of contemporary political and geographic facts, since it labels the "Costa de Mosquitos," the coastal region inhabited by the **Miskito** (or **Mosquito**) Indians who have been sometimes caught between the clashing **Sandinistas** and **Contras**.

The essays at the beginning of the volume are accessible to a general audience without compromising scholarly authority. The essence of the late Raven I. McDavid, Jr.'s excellent essay in the first edition, "Usage, Dialects, and Functional Varieties," has been preserved and complemented by the revised essay, "Usage and Variation," by Thomas J. Creswell and Virginia McDavid, mentioned previously. The three essays on the history of English, dialects, and pronunciation are also valuable. The pages instructing the user on how to interpret the entries is mercifully concise without sacrificing essential detail. Boldface type, italics, and highlighting, as well as dexterous use of examples, make these notes a pleasure rather than a chore to read.

VII. Accessibility

Alternative spellings of words are easily located because they are in boldface type. Boldface guide words follow the conventional format of indicating the first word on a page at the top of the left column and the last word on a page at the top of the right column. The sequence of information in the entries is: main entry in boldface type; pronunciation in parentheses; part of speech designated by common abbreviations; inflected forms (if they are irregularly formed); definitions, with senses for words with multiple meanings presented in the order of frequency of use; idioms; subject field, usage, and style labels where considered necessary and useful; etymologies; and end-of-entry notes at some words, which may contain synonym lists (10,500 such lists are included) and synonym-differentiating paragraphs (900 of these); antonym lists; usage notes; pronunciation notes; and regional variation notes.

The dictionary employs an ample system of cross-references to direct the user from partial to full entries, from narrower to broader ones, or to related ones.

The separate supplements at the end of the volume and the "boxed features" within the text are prominently listed in the table of contents.

VIII. Graphics and Format

Approximately 2,400 illustrations and small maps (separate from the atlas) clarify the meanings of some words. These illustrations are noteworthy for their clarity of line, lack of clutter, and size—each is a column wide, and each of the three columns on a page is a generous $2^{10}/_{16}''$ wide. Generally speaking, the illustrations are used to good purpose to represent objects that many people would have trouble understanding without a visual aid, such as a **dihedral angle**, an **emu**, or a **Florence flask**. Other illustrations are of questionable value, however, such as a **downhill skier** and a **cactus** that only shows one variety (the **saguaro**). Each illustration examined by this reviewer is conveniently located directly before or after the word or term it represents. Each is labeled, and some include brief factual captions.

One of the most appealing features of this dictionary is its attractive physical design. While the first edition was $12'' \times 9''$, the second is $12'' \times 9\frac{1}{2}''$. The extra half inch allows for more white space between entries and columns. This advantage combines with the sharp distinction between the boldface and regular type and the fact that the typefaces are considerably larger and easier to read than those in WEBSTER'S THIRD, for instance, to produce a dictionary that invites prolonged consultation or browsing. The paper is of good quality ivory stock with very slight show-through of text. Main entry words are printed in boldface overhanging the text. The book is quite sturdily bound, but it is recommended that such a literally weighty tome (12 pounds) be used with a dictionary stand. This volume should withstand steady library use.

IX. Summary

The Random House Dictionary of the English Language: Second Edition, Unabridged is the first wholly revised dictionary to appear on the market since the mid-1960s. In effect, it is a new work, with more than 50,000 new words and 75,000 new meanings that were not in the first edition, for a total of more than 315,000 entries. About one third of these entries are proper names, so that in fact the vocabulary of ordinary words is little more than 200,000.

If a user puts a premium on the number of words contained in an unabridged dictionary, then WEBSTER'S THIRD, with over 460,000 entries, will be preferable. However, comparisons of the quality of these dictionaries involve more difficult judgments than a simple comparison of the number of words included. On balance, WEBSTER'S THIRD provides more detail for many of its entries than does *The Random House Dictionary*. Insofar as this contributes to precision and ease of comprehension, again, WEBSTER'S THIRD would seem to be preferable. Sometimes, however, the shorter, less detailed definitions in *The Random House Dictionary* are easier to understand than the longer, more detailed definitions in WEBSTER'S THIRD.

The most controversial and problematic aspect of *The Random House Dictionary* is its descriptive—some would say permissive—approach to the English language, which is apparent on several levels. In terms of the lexicon, this dictionary includes many words, such as **chocoholic** and **rad** (meaning "radical"), that cannot be fairly said to have entered the mainstream of the language and may be just the vogue words of a limited number of people. Moreover, many definitions in *The Random House Dictionary* are not as exact or as subtle as those given in WEBSTER'S THIRD or WEBSTER'S NEW TWENTIETH CENTURY UNABRIDGED DICTIONARY. And finally, *The Random House Dictionary*'s approach to usage does not enjoy the sanction of grammarians but rather mirrors that of "mature, socially responsible, literate adults." Users who prefer a measure of prescription in their dictionaries will be better served by WEBSTER'S NEW TWENTIETH CENTURY, although this dictionary is much less up to date than *The Random House Dictionary*. The two-volume WORLD BOOK DICTIONARY, which actually has more general vocabulary entries once one subtracts *The Random House Dictionary*'s proper name entries, should also not be overlooked as a reasonable alternative.

Libraries that can afford both WEBSTER'S THIRD and *The Random House Dictionary* are advised to own both, not simply because some users prefer one over the other, but because neither source alone is a comprehensive record of the English language. Libraries with limited budgets and home users who cannot afford both dictionaries will need to weigh carefully a variety of not always comparable considerations. Some users will simply want the most up-to-date unabridged English language dictionary available and will prefer *The Random House Dictionary*, finding it inconvenient to search the addenda section of WEBSTER'S THIRD as well as consulting its main text. Some users may find the dates of a word's entry into the language, provided with many of the second edition's entries, a very useful feature, one not usually present in WEBSTER'S THIRD's entries. The latter's smaller type and relative paucity of white space may cause some readers eyestrain. Some users may prefer the illustrative sentences composed by the Random House staff to the quotations from published sources provided in WEBSTER'S THIRD. Home users may find that the encyclopedic supplements and numerous proper names in the body of the dictionary add to the volume's usefulness, while others might be disappointed that a sizable portion of the information in this dictionary can be found—usually in greater detail—in a general encyclopedia.

In short, though *The Random House Dictionary* is not an unabridged dictionary in the same sense as is WEBSTER'S THIRD, it still remains a very useful and accessible source, a respectable, authoritative, attractive, user-friendly companion. For better and for worse, it may turn out to be the most influential English-language dictionary of the 1990s.

Reader's Digest Illustrated Encyclopedic Dictionary

Facts at a Glance

Full Title: **Reader's Digest Illustrated Encyclopedic Dictionary**.
Publisher: The Reader's Digest Association.

Editor: David Rattray et al.
Edition Reviewed: © 1987.

Number of Entries: 180,000.
Number of Pages: 1,920; 2 volumes.
Number of Illustrations: more than 2,300.
Trim Size: $8\frac{3}{8}'' \times 10\frac{7}{8}''$.
Binding: hardcover.

Price: $49.96.
Sold by direct mail only.
ISBN 0-89577-267-1 (Volume, I A–K);
ISBN 0-89577-268-X (Volume II, L–Z).

I. Introduction and Scope

The *Reader's Digest Illustrated Encyclopedic Dictionary* is a two-volume edition of THE AMERICAN HERITAGE ILLUSTRATED ENCYCLOPEDIC DICTIONARY. The contents of both are identical in every respect except for the omission in the former of a map showing language families of the world. Otherwise, the two volumes of the *Reader's Digest* are somewhat easier to handle than the single volume of the *American Heritage* edition. The elaborate gold-stamped reinforced bindings, along with a slightly heavier paper, would seem to make the *Reader's Digest* dictionary the more durable edition. The *Reader's Digest Illustrated Encyclopedic Dictionary* is available only by mail, at a somewhat lower price than the *American Heritage* edition. For full information, see the review of THE AMERICAN HERITAGE ILLUSTRATED ENCYCLOPEDIC DICTIONARY.

The Scribner-Bantam English Dictionary

Facts at a Glance

Full Title: **The Scribner-Bantam English Dictionary**.
Publisher: Bantam Books.
Editor: Edwin B. Williams.
Edition Reviewed: © 1979; 10th printing, 1985.

Number of Entries: over 56,000.
Number of Pages: 1,120.
Trim Size: $4\frac{1}{8}'' \times 6\frac{7}{8}''$.
Binding: paperback.

Price: $3.95.
Sold in bookstores and other outlets; also sold to libraries and other educational institutions.
ISBN 0-553-24974-6.

I. Introduction

The Scribner-Bantam English Dictionary is a mass-market paperback book containing over 80,000 definitions in over 56,000 main entries. The publisher, Bantam Books, claims with some justification that this is "the largest paperback dictionary of its kind." As such, it competes against such paperbacks as THE AMERICAN HERITAGE DICTIONARY, THE MERRIAM-WEBSTER DICTIONARY, THE RANDOM HOUSE DICTIONARY, and WEBSTER'S II NEW RIVERSIDE DICTIONARY.

Although it concentrates on American English, the Scribner-Bantam lexicon includes meanings from other English-speaking countries. According to the publisher, this dictionary "leans towards being prescriptive." Publisher Charles Scribner, Jr., remarked in his foreword to the first edition that "the style of the definitions is a writing lesson in itself, and it also demonstrates how American English at its best can combine lucidity and power." Thus, *The Scribner-Bantam English Dictionary* is intended not merely to inform and instruct but to do so with elegance and grace.

II. Authority

This is the first general English-language dictionary that either Scribner's or Bantam has published. General Editor Edwin B. Williams, lexicographer and former chairman of the Department of Romance Languages at the University of Pennsylvania, headed the distinguished staff of academics and lexicographers, listed in the frontmatter, that created this work. There is no mention of a citation file or of any word lists, and literary and scientific quotations are not included as examples of usage in the entries. Instead, the editors state that this dictionary "is based on all the English language dictionaries in print, on other printed and spoken sources and on consultation with authorities in many fields."

III. Comprehensiveness

According to the publisher, this dictionary has "more information than in any other dictionary of its kind . . . including new words and technical-scientific terms appearing in no other dictionary." The range of the dictionary is indeed wide and should well serve the general adult user. However, because it has not been revised since 1979, the vocabulary omits many commonly used words found in other dictionaries of more recent date. It does contain a large number of biographical and geographic entries within the main vocabulary, which is a very useful feature. However, once again, the information is not up-to-date, or in the case of population figures, not dated at all. The dictionary also contains many abbreviations, chemical elements, foreign words and phrases, and slang terms (excluding the notable four-letter ones), as well as an excellent emphasis on synonyms, with distinctions between fine shades of meanings, and antonyms.

IV. Quality and Currency of Entries

Definitions are arranged according to frequency of use. They are often short and incomplete, and they rarely include a sentence to illustrate meaning. The definition of **bluepoint**, for example, refers to oysters but not Siamese cats. The entry for **orthodox** refers to the Eastern Orthodox Church but not to Judaism. The definition of **graph**, for example, is difficult to understand because the sense of a graph as a tool for making comparisons is vague:

> **graph** . . . *n* **1** diagram or curve representing the successive values of a changing quantity; **2** written symbol of a sound; **3** diagram expressing a mathematical relation *vt* **4** to represent by a graph.

The words **who** and **whom** are not defined in a way that makes their proper usage clear. **Whom** is defined as "objective case of *who*." The entry for **who** includes "*colloq* whom, as *who did you speak to*?" The proper use of *who* and *whom* is troublesome enough for many people without the obfuscation that these definitions provide.

Variant spellings are usually cross-referenced, although some are included in the same entry. Synonyms are provided in many entries. They flesh out the definitions and offer a rich bounty of alternative choices for readers. Over 150 subject labels, numerous usage labels, and other qualifying terms are a genuine aid. Antonyms are also provided, but less frequently than synonyms. And, finally, the etymologies are unobtrusive and sufficient for readers who do not require a rigorous history of words. Many everyday words, such as *aerobics, ayatollah, redshirt, modem, mainframe, floppy disk, bit, byte, database,* and *sonogram*, are omitted—the dictionary is simply not up-to-date for the 1980s.

V. Syllabication and Pronunciation

At the front of the book, there is "A Guide to the Dictionary," where the editors provide a detailed, thorough discussion of syllabication. A long and thorough explanation of pronunciation also appears in the guide, followed by a pronunciation key. They help the reader to understand the respellings that are used.

VI. Special Features

Special features include, in the frontmatter, the lengthy "Guide to the Dictionary," pronunciation key, and a list of abbreviations used in the dictionary entries. The backmatter includes a list of principal languages of the world and a chart of Indo-European languages, a foreign alphabets chart, proofreaders' marks, weights and measures. Roman numerals, and forms of address. A list of pronunciation symbols is the final item and would have been better placed in the frontmatter with the pronunciation key. Entries for plants and animals include the scientific names, and entries for chemical elements include atomic weights, numbers, and symbols.

VII. Accessibility

A contents page is provided to the main sections of the volume. The guide to the dictionary is well organized, but the reader must have a rigorous knowledge of grammar to appreciate it fully. Guide words listing the first and last entries on each page are included. Variant spellings are usually cross-referenced, although some are included in the same entry.

VIII. Graphics and Format

The two-column, concise page is well designed for a paperback edition. The print is small, but clear, with adequate white space. The paper is satisfactory, but the binding is not. This is a very bulky paperback, and pages began to fall out of our review copy after only two days of use. As a circulating dictionary, this book would not survive even occasional use in the library, not to speak of a half-dozen tosses into a book-return repository.

IX. Summary

The Scribner-Bantam English Dictionary was conceived in the mid-1970s, and its aims were certainly ambitious. In the late 1980s, however, it is no longer competitive. It fails to include many words now established in the lexicon, and even its definitions of traditional words are not always adequate. Were it more up-to-date, and its binding more secure, it could perhaps lead the paperback dictionary field. For the time being, however, readers looking for a paperback desk dictionary will be better served by THE AMERICAN HERITAGE DICTIONARY or THE MERRIAM-WEBSTER DICTIONARY.

Shorter Oxford English Dictionary on Historical Principles

Facts at a Glance

Full Title: **Shorter Oxford English Dictionary on Historical Principles: Third Edition**.
Publisher: Oxford University Press.
Editor: C. T. Onions.
Edition Reviewed: © 1973.

Number of Entries: 163,000.
Number of Pages: 2,704; 2 volumes.
Trim Size: 7½″ × 10¾″.
Binding: cloth.

Price: $150.00 (plain); $160.00 (thumb-indexed).
Sold in bookstores and through other outlets; also sold to libraries and other educational institutions.
ISBN 0-19-861126-9 (plain);
ISBN 0-19-861127-7 (thumb-indexed).

I. Introduction

The third edition of the *Shorter Oxford English Dictionary on Historical Principles* appeared in 1973, one year after the completion of the first supplement to the OED. It retains C. T. Onions's preface to the first edition (1932) of the abridgment which states that the aim of this work is to "present in miniature all the features of the principal work." It includes about two-thirds of the words included in the original OXFORD ENGLISH DICTIONARY (OED), and "presents, therefore, a quintessence of those vast materials."

It is intended to be a key to the great Oxford dictionary, for those individuals or libraries possessing it, and, "for those who do not it will form the only possible substitute."

The introduction to this edition states that the vocabulary is "designed to include all words in regular literary and colloquial use, together with a selection of those which belong to the terminology of the arts and sciences and those which are current only in archaic or dialectal use, as well as of words now obsolete but of importance during some period of our literature."

Following the introduction, a disclaimer notes that the dictionary includes "some words which are or are asserted to be proprietary names or trade marks."

II. Authority

Dr. G. W. S. Friedrichsen, a colleague of C. T. Onions, is responsible for the revisions of all word etymologies in the third edition, which, as with previous editions, is published by the respected Clarendon Press. A "Publisher's Note" (dated 1972) indicates that Friedrichsen's work was an eight-year undertaking. Other reviewers have examined previous editions and printings of the *Shorter Oxford English Dictionary* and have drawn various conclusions: that the changes here are "relatively few, and more often than not, supplementary, or remedial" (*RQ*; Summer 1974, p. 364); that the "revised etymologies and the additions of this third edition are not superficial changes" (*Choice*, July/August 1974, pp. 740–41); and that a "comparison of etymologies in the 1970 printing with those in the 1973 printing shows that many, but not all, have been revised" (*American Reference Book Annual*, 1975, pp. 553–54).

In addition to Dr. Friedrichsen, the publisher acknowledges N. S. Doniach "for his assistance with the etymologies of Arabic and Hebrew words."

The *Oxford Dictionary of English Etymology* (1966) is named in the introduction as the source for revised and rewritten etymologies in this edition. Also, "in many cases matter from the *Oxford English Dictionary* which had been omitted in the earlier editions of [the *Shorter Oxford*] has been restored."

III. Comprehensiveness

The main lexicon of this volume draws from the *OED* with revisions and rewritings of etymologies as mentioned above. The "Addenda" of some 375 pages consist of

> (1) words not recorded in the body of the dictionary, and (2) further senses and constructions of words already treated.

Volume I of *A Supplement to the Oxford English Dictionary* (1972) is the "Addenda's" main source for words beginning A–G. The remainder, H–Z, are "based on the material in the O.E.D. files that will in due course be included in Volumes II and III of the Supplement to the O.E.D." Now, of course, we know that the completed supplement comprises four volumes.

Naturally the "current" words included in the 1972 "Addenda" will seem familiar if not old hat to most readers. **Airport**, for example, came into use in 1919 and is defined as "An aerodrome, esp. with customs facilities, to which aircraft resort to take on board or set down passengers, or load and unload freight;" under **Amphetamine**, 1938, the chemical basis for its name is given, followed by a short definition and the note that it is "popularly known as an ingredient of 'pep pills' 1955." **Apartheid**, 1947; **Bagel**, 1932; and, **Beatnik**, 1958, are other new words. **Bourbon** falls under the second, or "further senses," category above, and a fourth meaning is noted:

> whiskey of a kind originally made in Bourbon County, Kentucky . . . orig. *United States* 1846.

Caftan is given a second meaning, "a wide-sleeved, loose-fitting shirt or dress worn in Western countries 1965." Most supporting quotations in the "Addenda" are undocumented.

In addition to etymologies (which are given in square brackets), the dictionary includes illustrative quotations selected from the *OED*. Where the history of a word or meaning has been treated extensively in the *OED*, the reader is referred "by means

of the abbreviation N.E.D. [New English Dictionary] (or O.E.D.) to the fuller statement there given."

Usage is indicated by labels such as literary, colloquial, slang, dialectal, local, archaic, vulgar, and by subject or area, such as Art, Natural History, and Mathematics.

Because the *Shorter Oxford* does not include, at this time, the material from the new supplements to the *OED*, it cannot be considered completely comprehensive and current.

IV. Quality and Currency of Entries

Not all features of all words are included under each article or entry (either because of lack of necessity or space), but the general arrangement in the main lexicon is as follows: the "catchword," capitalized and in boldface, preceded where appropriate with the mark † (obsolete) or ‖ (alien); the pronunciation (unless the word is obsolete); the part of speech; the "indication of the modern currency of the word," (literary, colloquial, etc.); variant spellings and their pronunciation; the historical appearance of the word (O.E., M.E., late M.E., or by an exact date); the etymology in square brackets; an indication that the word is specific to a certain discipline "if it is entirely so restricted;" the meanings, "numbered or lettered, with specification of their status and with the date of their first appearance, or if they are obsolete, an indication of their last known occurrence." After each group of meanings there is normally a block of quotations "with dates or indications of authorship, numbered according to the senses which they exemplify;" idiomatic phrases or "attributive uses and combinations conclude the article, unless there are derivatives of minor importance . . ."

Many, if not most, of the abridged articles are adequate for general readers and students. Scholars and students of literature will find it frustrating at times. For example, in the text of the *General Prologue* of the *Canterbury Tales*, the word **crop** ("the tendre croppes") has the obsolete meaning of shoots or young sprouts (*OED* 2. 1188, *crop*, sb., II.3). This meaning has been excluded from the *Shorter Oxford*, and the word's third meaning reads, "The head of a herb, flower, tree, etc.; a cyme." The illustrative quotation corresponding to this meaning is an abridgment of the *OED*'s.

V. Syllabication and Pronunciation

The key to pronunciation immediately precedes the main lexicon of each of the *Shorter Oxford*'s volumes. The pronunciations given are

> those in use in the educated speech of southern England (the so-called 'Received Standard'), and the keywords given are to be understood as pronounced in such speech.

This will automatically present difficulties for many American users. A description of the phonetic system used in the dictionary appears in the introduction. Varieties of pronunciation are said to be recorded "as fully as possible" but not generally for dialectal, colonial, or American varieties. The entry **schedule** does, however, give the U.S. pronunciation immediately after the standard.

Pronunciation is enclosed in parentheses directly after the entry words. The entry words themselves are not stress marked and are universally capitalized. Most of the symbols are the same as those used in the International Phonetic Alphabet.

Syllabication is indicated by a centered dot (·) for the main stress, and a (:) for a secondary stress. Speakers of American English will find a significant divergence from what they are accustomed to in both the pronunciation and syllabication guidelines used by the *Shorter Oxford*.

VI. Special Features

The only special feature of the *Shorter Oxford* edition, is the "Addenda" that includes material gleaned from the first supplement to the OED and from the working files of the additional supplements published after 1972. Integral to the purpose of these volumes is, of course, a dedication to the recording of English as each word appears in the language. The year of entry for each meaning of every word included is noted, when available, and appropriate quotations are listed, where the limits of space allow.

A list of "Authors and Books Cited" appears after the introduction.

This is not intended to be an encyclopedic dictionary: it includes no biography/geography sections or tables of weights and measures.

VII. Accessibility

British spelling (**armour** as opposed to *armor*), a potential problem for some American audiences, is used. There are few cross-references. Two guide words, in uppercase bold type, appear above the first and third columns of each three-column page. "See" references are printed in small uppercase letters.

The volumes examined were thumb-indexed. The paper is sturdy and the print is clear. A variety of typefaces are used for the many features of the entries, making them easy to understand.

While not as preeminent a work as the *OED*, the *Shorter Oxford*, given its abridged two-volume size, is much easier to handle.

VIII. Graphics and Format

The *Shorter Oxford* contains no graphic illustrations, maps, diagrams, or tables.

The two-volume set is sturdily bound in navy blue buckram with gold lettering. The smooth white paper allows a minimum show-through of text. The margins, while not generous, are adequate, especially considering there are three columns to a 7½-inch by 10¾-inch size page.

Main entry words are indented one space so that each "article" has the appearance of a paragraph. The typeface variety is engaging and easy to read.

The volumes of the *Shorter Oxford* are handsomely designed, substantially constructed, and should last a lifetime.

IX. Summary

The Shorter Oxford English Dictionary on Historical Principles represents an admirable effort on the part of its editors and publisher. Libraries that cannot afford the complete *OED* and its supplements will want to include this in their collections. For those on a limited budget, THE COMPACT EDITION OF THE OXFORD ENGLISH DICTIONARY might be a better choice, since it is not an abridgment of the original OED but a micrographic edition that comes with a magnifying glass. It is, however, awkward to use and in most cases the average public library user or college student will likely be satisfied with the *Shorter Oxford*.

All libraries that own the *OED* should also own the *Shorter Oxford*. It provides a convenient starting point for the reader who, interested in the etymology of English language words, can subsequently refer to the larger work if questions are not satisfied by the shorter version. This title's major weakness is that it includes in its "Addenda" only the first (and bits of the others) supplement to the *OED*.

The price is reasonable enough so that any library not owning the *OED* can afford this shorter version. In spite of the fact that it is an abridgment, the *Shorter Oxford* retains the essence and unique significance of the OXFORD ENGLISH DICTIONARY ON HISTORICAL PRINCIPLES, which has no equal.

The Thorndike Barnhart Handy Pocket Dictionary

Facts at a Glance

Full Title: **The Thorndike Barnhart Handy Pocket Dictionary**.
Publisher: **Bantam Books.**
Editors: Clarence L. Barnhart, Editor-in-Chief; W. Cabell Greet and Allan P. Hubbell.
Edition Reviewed: © 1953; 1985 printing.

Number of Entries: 36,000.
Number of Pages: 451.

Trim Size: 4¼" × 6⅞".
Binding: paperback.

Price: $3.50.
Sold in bookstores and other outlets.
ISBN 0-553-25664-5.

I. Introduction

The Thorndike Barnhart Handy Pocket Dictionary is a paperback abridgment of *The Thorndike Barnhart Comprehensive Dictionary*, which has been out of print for many years. Its lexicon is made up of 36,000 words that were deemed "most frequently used" at the time this dictionary was first published—1951. In the words of editor Clarence L. Barnhart, it was designed to be useful to the "writer who seeks a quick reminder of a correct spelling, to the speaker who wishes to verify the acceptability of a pronunciation, or to the beginner in the use of dictionaries who wants a small but trustworthy aid to the most effective use of English."

II. Authority

For some years, the Thorndike Barnhart paperback was considered an outstanding smaller dictionary. Its editor, Clarence L. Barnhart, was editor of *The Thorndike Barnhart Comprehensive Desk Dictionary*, *The American College Dictionary*, and the Thorndike Barnhart series of dictionaries (which currently includes THE WORLD BOOK DICTIONARY and the SCOTT, FORESMAN BEGINNING and INTERMEDIATE DICTIONARIES). The 27 members of the General Editorial Advisory Committee for the original edition were all distinguished experts in the field of language and linguistics.

The preface describes the methods of compiling the vocabulary and presenting its meanings that have made this work useful throughout its life. Specifically, the editors and lexicographers endeavored to explain all entries in simpler terms than the word being defined; they avoided complex constructions; they took care to order meanings of words according to their importance; and they gave "all the specific information essential to a reader's understanding." Today's buyer, however, is advised to approach this once-authoritative compact dictionary with caution because its vocabulary is seriously dated.

III. Comprehensiveness

With 36,000 entry words, this dictionary is slightly more than one-half the size of the Pocket Books edition of THE MERRIAM-WEBSTER DICTIONARY. It omits etymologies and uses compact phrases or short sentences to indicate use: "**known** . . . *Washington is known as a general*." These are justifiable practices for the beginning dictionary user but may not serve a more knowledgeable user who wants a quick reference tool. No additional lists of combining forms are included. Synonym lists are brief: for example, "**ex·treme** . . . **—Syn**. *adj*. **1**. immoderate, excessive." Inflections and variant forms are well covered.

IV. Quality and Currency of Entries

Along with the basic vocabulary, all technical terms, proper names, geographical names, and abbreviations appear in the main lexicon. Homographs are shown by superior numbers following the bold entry words: **mint**[1] and **mint**[2], to remind the reader, as the guide to using the dictionary states, "to look at the other entries spelled in the same way if you do not find the information you are seeking under the first one."

The definitions are simple and brief, but many betray the dictionary's lack of currency. Three factors combine to date the dictionary's vocabulary and definitions: the style and choice of words used to define; the acquiring of new, common meanings for many words; and the entrance of new words into frequent, everyday use. The *Handy Pocket Dictionary* reveals its age in each respect. For example, definitions are needed for *busing* (or *bussing*) and *data bank*, just two of the missing terms cited earlier by the Bowker *Dictionary Buying Guide* (1977). Computer meanings for a term as common as *program* are absent. **Farrier**, a term for blacksmith, is not one of the 30,000 words that might be considered most common in the American vocabulary today. It is also surprising to find **commute** still specially labeled "*Am*." (for an Americanism), since the word is as current in the large cities of Great Britain as in the United States.

Other examples of terms or definitions that need to be updated, redefined, or omitted (in the case of archaic verb forms), especially in a very compact dictionary, are "**as·a·fet·i·da** *n*. gum resin used in medicine"; "**chaise** *n*. a lightweight carriage"; "**durst** *v*. pt. of dare"; **ell**, which is defined only as a measurement with the example, "give him an inch and he'll take an ell (much)"; "**Kenya** *n*. British colony and protectorate in E. Africa"; "**Martian** . . . -*n*. an inhabitant of Mars"; "**mayst** *v*. *Archaic*. may"; "**Zionism** *n*. a plan or modern movement to colonize Jewish people in Palestine."

Below the title in bold type, the paperback's jacket still carries the words: "New Revised Edition." Readers should note that this phrase refers to the 1955 edition.

V. Syllabication and Pronunciation

Words with more than one syllable are divided by centered dots: **got·ten**. The guide to using the dictionary notes that syllabication is determined partly by pronunciation and partly by a word's root and affixes. When more than one pronunciation is given, they ordinarily follow each word: **reb·el** (n. adj. reb|el; v. ri·bel|).

According to the editors, the pronunciations are "those customarily heard from educated speakers of English in the United States," with occasional variants "sometimes not recorded elsewhere," such as **hom·i·cide** (hom|ə·sīd, hō|mə-).

An explanation of the 43 symbols used in representing the sounds of English appears in the guide to the dictionary. Since the larger number of these sounds do not require special symbols, the editors explain, only 13 special diacritical marks are employed. This allows for an abbreviated pronunciation key that is easier to use than those in many other dictionaries. The short vowel sounds are not marked; the five long vowels are marked ā, for example. The 8 remaining symbols appear as fär, cāre tėrm, ôr, tħ as in *th*en, put, rüle, and the schwa for the vowel sound "uh" as in about (ə·bout). The "ng" sound in drink is represented as dri*ng*k in the pronunciations. An abbreviated key to vowel sounds appears at the bottom of each right-hand page as a handy quick pronunciation guide for the reader.

VI. Special Features

Two clear tables, one of weights and measures and one of common signs and symbols (astronomy, chemistry, commerce, mathematics, and miscellaneous), appear after the lexicon. There are four pages of guidance on letter writing with small labeled samples of letters.

Preceding the vocabulary is a "Handy Guide to Writing English" that includes three brief but useful sections on capitalization, writing numbers, and punctuation. The latter is divided into "Punctuation That Terminates, . . . That Introduces, and . . . That Unifies." There follows a two-page chart of special forms of address, which will be useful to many readers. Opposite the first page of the main entries, is a "Common Spellings of English" chart that compares symbols of sounds with appropriate words; for example, *hw* for *wh*eat and *sh* for o*c*ean.

VII. Accessibility

Information is readily accessible in this compact dictionary. Words appear in letter-by-letter alphabetical sequence. The order of information given under each main entry word is clearly listed in the first paragraph of the guide:

(1) the word spelled in boldface type, (2) the pronunciation, (3) part of speech, (4) any irregular inflected forms (plural, past tense, etc.), (5) definitions of its meanings arranged under the appropriate parts of speech, (6) derivatives consisting of main entries, or their roots, plus the common suffixes, (7) synonyms keyed to the definitions, and (8) usage notes . . . .

The preliminary and appendix matter is brief and clearly indicated in the complete table of contents. The opening section, "How to Use This Dictionary," is a clear, numbered guide to finding information.

Under the section "How to Find a Word," instructions with useful examples are given for locating main and subordinate entries, derivatives, homographs, cross-referenced words, and idioms.

Two bold guide words with a centered page number appear at the top of each page. Printed on each right-hand page is a useful mock thumb index tab, or "speedy word finder," consisting of a pair of letters:

fe
fi

This shows the first letters of the first and last main entries on each double-page spread.

VIII. Graphics and Format

The text is printed in two columns of small but readable type with generous white space (for the dictionary's size) between lines. The pages appear much less cramped than in many other paperback dictionaries. The paper is good-quality newsprint. Some ink adheres to the fingers when the pages are handled repeatedly.

The binding appears to hold together even when the spine is creased in use. The white laminated cover with plain black type is utilitarian but attractive. On the back cover, there appears a facsimile of a column of the vocabulary with eight identifying labels for special features of the definitions. The red arrows criss-crossing from the call-outs to the entry words are visually appealing although they obscure the matter being highlighted.

IX. Summary

The Thorndike Barnhart Handy Pocket Dictionary was once a model of the lexicographer's art. However, this work has not been revised in more than 30 years, and it is now thoroughly outdated. Readers seeking a good, up-to-date paperback dictionary will be much better served by The AMERICAN HERITAGE DICTIONARY or THE MERRIAM-WEBSTER DICTIONARY, among others.

12,000 Words

Facts at a Glance

Full Title: **12,000 Words**.
Publisher: Merriam-Webster.
Editors: Frederick C. Mish et al.
Edition Reviewed: © 1986.

Number of Entries: approximately 12,000.
Number of Pages: 236.
Trim Size: 6⅞″ × 9½″.
Binding: cloth.

Price: $10.95.
Sold in bookstores; also sold to libraries and other
   educational institutions.
ISBN 0-08-779207-0.

I. Introduction and Scope

Two purposes are served by this supplement to
WEBSTER'S THIRD NEW INTERNATIONAL DICTION-
ARY: to record new words and meanings that have
entered the English language since the publication
of that dictionary in 1961 and, according to the preface,
to enter "older words that for various reasons had
been passed over in the earlier editing." It is important to recognize that this is not simply a dictionary of new words; it is a *supplement* to the latest
unabridged WEBSTER'S, which is also the most recent
Addenda section of that dictionary. Users who own
a copy of WEBSTER'S THIRD printed in 1986 or later,
therefore, will not need to purchase *12,000 Words*
because this 236-page book is exactly the same as
the most recent 56-page Addenda section. Earlier
Addenda sections were added in 1966, 1971, 1976,
and 1981. Users should note that they will find this
section in the front of the book, after the prefatory
material and immediately before the body of the text.

12,000 Words supersedes previous compilations of
these addenda: *6,000 Words*, published in 1976, and
9,000 Words, published in 1983. Users should be
careful to observe the publisher's admonition in the
preface: Like the Addenda section

> . . . *12,000 Words* cannot be self-contained; the reader
> will find it necessary to consult another dictionary for
> terms—especially technical terms—which are unfa-
> miliar.

Although some readers will probably find it convenient to use *12,000 Words* by itself as a list of new
words, they will be frustrated if they do not realize
that some entries require one to refer to the unabridged main text. For instance, a very naive user
might assume that the entry for **bad** in the contemporary slang sense of "good" or "great" had somehow supplanted the main sense of the word, which,

of course, is not true: the asterisk at the end of the
entry indicates that this is a new meaning of an old
word and that the other meanings will be found in
the unabridged edition.

Since this is a supplement to the mammoth unabridged edition, those who do not require the comprehensiveness and detail of this source may be confused by it. On the other hand, readers who expect
WEBSTER'S THIRD to continue, in its supplements,
to maintain its reputation as an objective record of
our language will not be disappointed.

The editorial staff has gathered the words for this
supplement from regular reading of periodicals and
of books, both fiction and nonfiction. Citations are
kept **in-house** (itself an entry in *12,000 Words*) on
both 3 × 5 cards and in an electronic database. New
words have to be in use for several years and in a
variety of sources before the editors consider them
for inclusion. Conservatives will welcome this practice of waiting to enter a word until it is more than
simply **trendy** (defined here as "very fashionable" or
"faddish"); liberals will welcome Webster's inclusion
of every level of language—from taboo to technical.

II. Format

Readers familiar with WEBSTER'S THIRD will not have
to adjust to a new format to use this supplement.
For the sake of convenience, a condensed version of
the very detailed explanatory notes of the parent
volume is printed in *12,000 Words*. In order to obtain
the full benefit of this source, it is, of course, incum-
bent upon the user to read these notes. Even in their
condensed form, an extraordinary amount of information concerning the conventions employed in the
dictionary is provided.

This source is physically pleasing and easy to use.
The typeface is easy to read (even for a middle-aged
reviewer with bifocals), larger than the type in the
Addenda section of the parent volume, and the text
is printed on good quality ivory colored stock, with
virtually no text showing through from the other side
of the page. Margin space is sufficient and the main
entry words are separated clearly from the rest of
the text in boldface type. Variant forms of words,
such as **antifeminism** in the entry for **antifeminist**, are
also set in boldface. The book is sturdily bound and
should be able to endure relatively persistent use—
long enough, in other words, until there is a successor
to *12,000 Words* or one acquires a new printing of
WEBSTER'S THIRD.

III. Quality and Currency of Entries

This dictionary is current enough to include **AIDS**
and **Watergate**, but not *Irangate* for the Iran-Contra
affair or *glasnost* for the new Soviet openness policy.

12,000 Words

❶ A swung dash indicates repetition of main entry word

❷ Etymology is enclosed in brackets; "more at" cross-references indicate location of further etymological information

❸ Examples of usage are enclosed in angle brackets

❹ Cross-references are set in small capitals; *herein* indicates a cross-reference to an entry in *12,000 Words* rather than in *Webster's Third*

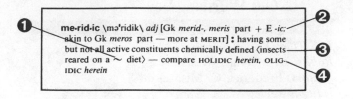

It is quite appropriate that more time elapse before *Webster's* decides which terms are likely to be permanent additions to our language.

There is an impressively broad sweep to *12,000 Words*: words from all levels of usage and a considerable variety of professions and occupations are included. One finds words borrowed from foreign languages, like the Polish **babka**, neologisms based on earlier words, like **bachelorette**, Briticisms like **back of beyond**, colloquialisms like **bad-mouth**, slang like **bad**, scientific terms like **bacteriocin**, technical jargon that has achieved some popular use, like **battered child syndrome**, acronyms like **AIDS**, abbreviations like **BCD**, terms of unknown origin like **barf**, terms that have been in use for some time before 1961 but have taken some time to be recognized by *Webster's*, like **mayo**, and numerous other types of words.

IV. Accessibility

12,000 Words is reasonably straightforward to use. Many of the pronunciations can be figured out without reference to the pronunciation symbols, although sometimes such a practice could be risky. Alternate spellings are placed in boldface type. Guide words are prominently printed at the edge of each page. The order of each entry is: main entry (a word or phrase), including an asterisk for a reference to a new sense of a word already entered in WEBSTER'S THIRD; pronunciation; functional label (part of speech and/or such designations as suffix, symbol, trademark); inflected forms; capitalization; etymology; a designation of usage status (used sparingly, as expected in a dictionary which is primarily descriptive rather than prescriptive); definitions, and cross-references.

V. Summary

Readers who are concerned about having the latest supplement to WEBSTER'S THIRD (and who do not

have a 1986 or later printing of that dictionary) should purchase this book. Readers who are committed to having thorough access to new words in English will need *12,000 Words* plus a number of other dictionaries, such as THE NEW DICTIONARY OF AMERICAN SLANG (1986), the latest supplement to the OXFORD ENGLISH DICTIONARY, vol. 4. Se-Z (1986), and a variety of glossaries and dictionaries of technical and specialized terms restricted to particular subjects or disciplines. Libraries may also want to consider a quarterly, THE BARNHART DICTIONARY COMPANION (reviewed in chapter 11), whose first number was published in 1982, which continues the practice of defining a manageable sample of new words in our common, working vocabulary.

Librarians will want to note that the entries in *12,000 Words* differ in sometimes significant respects from the *Dictionary of New English Since 1963* and the *Second Barnhart Dictionary of New English*, which will be in most collections. These Barnhart works do not include pronunciation unless the editors think the average reader will have trouble understanding this, and they have kept the definitions simple, "generally relying on carefully selected quotations to supply details and complex explanations that in standard dictionaries would be covered in the definition" (*Barnhart Dictionary of New English Since 1963*, p. 19). So while *12,000 Words* uses illustrative quotations sparingly but always provides a definition, the Barnhart sources almost always provide at least one dated quotation, but do not always include a definition. These quotations are often rather lengthy, so that enough context is provided to allow the reader to get a clear focus on how the word or term is typically used.

Not surprisingly then, when *12,000 Words* and one of the Barnhart sources both cover the same word or phrase, the reader will sometimes be better served by one dictionary rather than the other, or will benefit most from using both. For example, *12,000 Words* defines **paparazzo** as "a free-lance photographer who aggressively pursues celebrities in order to take candid photographs" and indicates that the word is borrowed from an Italian dialect word meaning buzzing insect. *The Barnhart Dictionary of New English Since 1963* defines this word as "an aggressive free-lance photographer who pursues celebrities to take their pictures wherever they go." One of the three quotations provided is:

> They are the *paparazzi* of the London picture market, a wheeling horde of newly self-styled impresarios of the arts, past masters of the cooly imperceptible bid, fur-coated, felt-hatted, and above all, undercapitalized. (Benita Egge, *The Sunday Times* [London] 13 April 1969, p. 60)

Because distinctly different entries are not uncommon, most libraries will want to retain the Barnhart works and also include the Webster's *12,000 Words* to be thorough about keeping up with new words and meanings. It is not only that one source may contain a word or phrase the other has missed, but sometimes that one source does a better job when both include the same entry.

The Universal Webster

Facts at a Glance

Full Title: **The Universal Webster: An English Dictionary.**
Publisher: Langenscheidt.
Editors: Sidney Fuller and R. Fuller.
Edition Reviewed: ©1958.

Number of Entries: 17,000.
Number of Pages: 416.
Trim Size: 3″ × 4¼″.
Binding: flexible vinyl cover.

Price: $3.50.
Sold in bookstores and by direct mail; also sold to educational institutions; available directly from the publisher.
ISBN 0-88729-190-2.

I. Introduction

The Universal Webster: An English Dictionary is designed for use in finding brief, current definitions of words commonly used in the English language. The method of selection, according to the preface, was "flexible, favoring those words which constitute modern and general usage, and the rarer words essential to a full understanding of the richness of the English literary language."

II. Authority

Langenscheidt has long been known for publishing foreign-language dictionaries. Where all Langenscheidt's other dictionaries carry the foreign language boldly printed on the spine, this one carries the word "Webster."

III. Comprehensiveness

Words selected were limited by the size of this small dictionary but include, according to the preface, "words in the everyday use, as well as modern technical terms, and the names of plants, animals and minerals, which are essential to every dictionary. In addition, [the editors] incorporated the more difficult words which a reader of English is likely to come across in newspapers and books, and which for the most part are of Latin or French origin." Thus the user finds the word **caoutchouc**, defined as "(pure) rubber," between **canyon** and **cap**. Since the dictionary has not been revised since 1958, it contains none of the new words of the last 30 years, notably those of computer terminology—not even *computer*.

IV. Quality and Currency of Entries

The different meanings listed in the definitions are separated by semicolons, but not numbered. Phrases are frequently used to give a clear understanding; sometimes single words are used, for example:

> **fizzle** make a hissing or bubbling sound; fail after a good start.
> **smart** *a* quick; active; clever; stylish; *v* feel stinging pain.

Occasionally, in the interest of space, part of a definition is either raised a line or dropped a line and appears squeezed in at the end of another definition. While this is typographically indicated, it gives rise to confusion and some humorous readings:

> **fiancé** *m*, **fiancée** *f*, (-sa)
> one engaged to be
> married [ulous failure
> **fiasco** complete or ridic-
> **libretto** (*pl* -tos) text of
> **lice** pl of louse [opera

The abbreviations *Am* [sometimes US] or *Br* indicate American or British usage. **Lorry, perambulator**, and **snicker** are identified as British. Occasional entries, such as **chore, cowboy, depot**, and **streetcar**, are labeled and defined in an American sense only. Etymology, synonyms, and antonyms are not given, and parts of speech and illustrative sentences are infrequently used—not surprisingly in such a small work. Run-on entries are found at the end of the definitions. As already indicated, the dictionary is badly out of date.

V. Syllabication and Pronunciation

The main entry word contains the syllabic division if it is more than one syllable. This is shown by using a dot or by an accent mark ('). For the most part, pronunciation is omitted. A simplified pronunciation key using respellings is provided at the beginning of the dictionary.

VI. Special Features

In addition to the brief introductory notes and the pronunciation key, there is a two-and-a-quarter page appendix with nine measures and weights tables, including apothecaries' fluid measures and avoirdupois weight.

VII. Accessibility

Access is alphabetical. Derivative words come at the end of the definition, but are not defined, for example, **penny**; **-iless**. Irregular verb forms precede the definitions. Guide words appear at the top of each page.

VIII. Graphics and Format

Each page consists of two columns with a vertical line separating them and a horizontal one at the top of the page that sets off the two guide words in bold type and the page number. Main entry words are in boldface type overhanging the text by one space. There are no illustrations. The print is very small, to accommodate the small size of the dictionary, but clear. The cover is a bright yellow, flexible, washable vinyl. This small work is ¾″ thick and could be easily carried in a pocket or a purse.

IX. Summary

There are drawbacks to this dictionary. It is dated, and the print is very small. In some cases, the printing is uneven and the bold face main entries blend with the definitions; this makes it difficult to tell where the main entry ends and the definition begins. *The Random House American Dictionary* provides far easier access because of its bolder format and crisper, albeit even smaller, print. Librarians will have little use for this dictionary.

Webster Comprehensive Dictionary: Encyclopedic Edition

Facts at a Glance

Full Title: **Webster Comprehensive Dictionary: Encyclopedic Edition.**
Former Title: *Funk & Wagnalls Comprehensive Dictionary: Encyclopedic Edition*; also *Funk & Wagnalls Standard Dictionary: Comprehensive International Edition.*
Publisher: J. G. Ferguson.
Editors: Richard Dell and E. Russell Primm.
Edition Reviewed: ©1984.

Number of Entries: 175,000.
Number of Pages: 1,725; 2 volumes.
Number of Illustrations: 2,043 black-and-white drawings, including maps; and two 16-page inserts of black-and-white and full-color photographs.
Trim Size: 8¼″ × 10⅞″.
Binding: hardcover.

Price: $49.95.
Sold door-to-door, by direct mail, and as a premium.
ISBN 0-89434-045-X.

I. Introduction

This two-volume "encyclopedic edition" of the *Webster Comprehensive Dictionary* can be generally categorized as a semi-abridged dictionary. It has been published in several editions with various titles, but its base is the *Funk & Wagnalls Standard Dictionary of the English Language*, first published in 1958. The word "Standard" in the title (registered as a trademark) was intended to reflect the dictionary's emphasis on the words considered standard in American speech and writing in the consensus of many authorities. Nonstandard words and usages are, therefore, rigorously labeled as *dialect, slang, U.S. colloq.* (colloquial), *Irish colloq.*, and so forth; vulgar and terms considered "taboo" are excluded.

According to the introduction, the dictionary is designed "to serve the practical and professional needs of all who speak or use the English language." The editors and lexicographers also attempted "to meet the needs of foreign users and those in other parts of the English-speaking world who want to be at home with American literature and its idioms."

The three major objectives of the *Webster Comprehensive* staff were first, "to present the fundamental facts and characteristics of the language, accurately, fully, and interestingly . . . [and second] to present adequately the significant contributions to English made in the United States, with requisite definitions, usage notes, and discriminative comment," as well as other areas of speech such as dialect and Australian and Canadian English. Their third goal was "to secure the widest possible coverage of both the established word stock of English and of rapidly expanding vocabularies of the arts, sciences, trades and professions." The guiding principle in defining was "to formulate a definition that can substitute for the word itself in the context in which the user reads or hears it." The appendixes and the numerous lists and charts within the main vocabulary are intended to expand this large dictionary's function as a general reference source.

II. Authority

The current edition of the *Webster Comprehensive Dictionary* lists its original, distinguished three-member editorial board; Albert H. Marckwardt, Professor Emeritus of English and Linguistics, Princeton University; Frederick G. Cassidy, Professor of English. University of Wisconsin; and James G. McMillan, Professor of English, University of Alabama. Its original editor-in-chief, Sidney I. Landau, is no longer credited. Listed with the editorial staff are numerous lexicographers, several of whom later created the next generation of American dictionaries. The list includes the *Webster Comprehensive* Consulting Editor William Morris (later editor of THE AMERICAN HERITAGE DICTIONARY) and Laurence Urdang (later editor of several Random House dictionaries and other reference works).

The 28-member Editorial Advisory Board, chaired by Allen Walker Read, professor of English, Columbia University, includes many distinguished scholars: Albert C. Baugh of the University of Pennsylvania, Arna Bontemps of Fisk University, Margaret Bryant of Brooklyn College, and Frederick Pottle of Yale University, among others.

III. Comprehensiveness

At approximately 175,000 entries with extensive lists, charts, and tables of reference matter within the main A to Z vocabulary, the *Webster Comprehensive Dictionary* encompasses the vast majority of words, phrases, abbreviations, and names that general readers would normally encounter. Many more recent specific and technical word combinations (especially the neo-Latin combinations) are not included.

There are extensive additional lists of words and particles forming combinations in English that are useful for spelling purposes and that indicate the form of two-word phrases. The lists indicate whether such combining elements as **air-**, **bed**, **corn**, **fellow**, **folk**, **heart**, and so forth, are written with or without hyphens.

A brief comparison of the number of entries in J. G. Ferguson's one-volume WEBSTER'S ILLUSTRATED CONTEMPORARY DICTIONARY from **paprika** to **parachute** shows that WEBSTER'S ILLUSTRATED contains 11 main entries in that section, whereas the *Webster Comprehensive Dictionary: Encyclopedic*

Edition has 36 main entries. Of the additional entries, 6 are geographic terms, 1 is biographical, and 11 are from specific scientific fields and carry restrictive labels (pathology, biochemistry, biology, mathematics, psychiatry, chemistry, and anatomy).

The etymologies are full; foreign words from which English words derive are given meanings so that readers can sense the evolution of language; cross-references within etymologies also are included. For example:

> **par·a·ble**, *n.* A comparison: simile; specifically, a short narrative making a moral or religious point by comparison with natural or homely things; the New Testament *parables*. See synonyms under ALLEGORY.

The etymology then reads:

> [⟨OF *parable* ⟨LL *parabola* allegory, speech ⟨L comparison ⟨Gk. *parabole* a placing side by side, a comparison *para*-beside—*balein* throw. Doublet of PALAVER, PARABOLA, PAROLE.]

Under the mathematical term, **parabola**, the etymology reads:

> [⟨Med. L ⟨ Gk. *parabole*. Double of PALAVER, PARABLE, PAROLE.]

The dictionary's etymological information will increase the reader's understanding of how scientific and non-scientific language are intertwined, and thus enhance knowledge of the actual workings and nuances of speech and writing.

Within the vocabulary, there are more than 24 major charts and tables, as well as numerous additional lists and illustrated, labeled charts that all add considerably to the dictionary's value as a general reference source.

IV. Quality and Currency of Entries

The definitions, in the main, are well written, understandable, and full. There are also synonym lists for numerous main entry words, including selected cross-references to other main entries: under **error**, there are ten synonyms plus cross-references to DELUSION and FOIBLE. Many words have longer lists of synonyms with discriminated meanings plus antonyms: **equivocal** is an example, with 13 synonyms and usage phrases, two comparative references (CLEAR, PRECARIOUS), and 15 antonyms.

The sequence of information under the bold main entry words is: syllabicated word or phrase, pronunciation (with variants when necessary), cross-reference to another main entry if no further information follows, part(s) of speech, plural or restricted forms with variant spellings in order of preferred use and pronunciations. An example is:

> **co·dex** (kō′deks) *n. pl.* **co·di·ces** (kō′də·sēz, kod′ə-).

Restrictive field and usage labels precede a definition if the restriction applies to all senses of a word; otherwise labels follow a specific numbered definition. The labels qualify, as the editors state, "a word in terms of its relationship to standard English."

Phrasal usages and idiomatic phrases appear where appropriate in definitions:

> **gaul·the·ri·a** . . . **2** Oil of wintergreen; also called oil of **gaultheria**.

Collateral adjectives, frequent in English, as the editors explain, because of the "grafting of Norman French and late Renaissance Latin idioms onto earlier English," are labeled and preceded by a bold diamond:

> **arm** . . . ♦ Collateral adjective: *brachial*.

The more extended usage notes, apart from those in the definitions are also similarly marked:

> **la·dy** . . . **2** Female; a *lady* doctor. ♦ Lady is here a genteelism, as it is in such compounds as *saleslady*. *Woman* is the more appropriate word to indicate the feminine gender. . . .

As is usual in semi-abridged dictionaries, there is extensive and varied lexicographic information provided for entries. The dictionary's explanatory notes show that 36 different kinds of basic information are provided, including the items described above plus homophones and homographs, as in

> **lox**[1] (loks), *n*. Smoked salmon [⟨Yiddish ⟨G *lachs* salmon]
> **lox**[2], LOX (loks), *n*. Liquid oxygen.

Etymologies explain derivation and the creation of, for example, English blends and doublets; for example, as in

> **jour·nal** . . . [⟨OF ⟨L *diurnalis*. Doublet of DIURNAL.]

The extensive system of cross-references, not only for synonyms and etymologies, but to other selected items in the supplementary material and to charts and tables in the main vocabulary, increases the likelihood that readers will acquire a fuller sense of word meanings. For example:

> **in·de·pen·dence** . . . See synonyms under LIBERTY, WEALTH. See DECLARATION OF INDEPENDENCE.

The "compare" references at the end of some entries also point to definitions that will aid the reader in discriminating meanings. Examples are: **Indian tobacco** . . . Compare LOBELINE and **Orthodox Judaism** . . . Compare CONSERVATIVE JUDAISM, REFORM JUDAISM.

Trademarks and names are described, chemical and mathematical formulas are included in definitions in many cases, and there are many main entry abbreviations as well as ones appended to definitions, as for books of the Old Testament.

Biographical and geographical entries, as well as their derived adjectives, are defined, but many need updating. For example, "**Iran** A kingdom of SW Asia" is, in fact, now a republic (correctly identified as such in the dictionary's gazetteer); **Iraq** is also a republic, not a kingdom as the main vocabulary defines it. Geographical definitions in the main vocabulary for **Nauru**, **Papua New Guinea**, **Rwanda and Burundi**, and **Zimbabwe** are outdated.

Within the main vocabulary, several other kinds of definitions are useful. First names are briefly defined and their language of derivation is indicated: the Spanish **Ruiz** and the English **Rufus** are included, and so are Italian, French, and German names, plus diminutive, masculine, and feminine versions. Latin mottoes that have become familiar are given standard English translations: such as "**secundam naturam** *Latin* According to nature" or "**ars poetica** *Latin* The art of poetry." The main entries also include good definitions of mythological and folkloric terms and names (**Rumpelstiltskin**) and even famous streets, such as the **Rue de la Paix**.

Occasional definitions read oddly:

> **Shake·spear·i·an·ism** *n*. **1** An expression peculiar to Shakespeare

or omit a standard sense, as in **blue point**, defined as a variety of oyster, but not a variety of domestic cat. In general, a real effort seems to have been made to define technical or scientific words so that they are relatively accessible to non-specialists.

> **par·a·a·mi·no·ben·zo·ic acid** *Biochem*. A colorless crystalline compound. $C_7H_7NO_2$, forming part of the vitamin B complex. Present in yeast and also made synthetically: source of several local anesthetics.

Although this dictionary covers scientific and technological terms extensively, there are instances in which the definitions need updating even for a general reader. **Steroid** has a formal biochemical definition but no cross-reference to **anabolic steroid**; the definition of **mnemonic** as an adjective is "Designed to aid memory" and that of mnemonics as a noun is "The science of memory improvement," but there is no mention of the word's current use in either computer science or psychology. Certain terms are not included, such as *artificial intelligence* (**artificial language** is an entry, but has no computer meaning included) and *modem*. As a combining form, **brady-** is included, but not, for example, *bradykinesia*. Also, **bibliotherapy** is included with a definition under the restrictive label **Pathol.** (pathology), but since this term is used in the fields of psychology and library science, one expects further definition.

In rechecking some entries that were criticized as not being up-to-date in earlier editions of the *Webster*

Comprehensive Dictionary, our reviewers found that the text has been revised. **Busing** now includes a second meaning that encompasses its intent to achieve racial balance; **data bank** has been added to the entries; *deep space* is still missing; but **aesthete, aesthetic** now includes a philosophic sense; the definition of **radiation** has been extended beyond the field of particle radiation; and although *renovascular* is still not in, the combining forms **ren-** and **reni-** are. Apparently, a small proportion of the entries are revised as each new edition appears. Readers who require more contemporary definitions will need to consult either a special topic dictionary or a general work such as Webster's Ninth New Collegiate or Third International, or the unabridged second edition of *The Random House Dictionary*, or Webster's *12,000 Words*.

V. Syllabication and Pronunciation

Syllables in main entries are divided by centered dots that indicate conventional hyphenation at the end of a line. Run-on entries and variant forms are also syllabicated, although primary and secondary stress marks supplant syllabic dots:

> **in·fat·u·ate** *vt.* **·at·ed. ·at·ing** . . . —**in·fat′u·at′ed** *adj.*— **in·fat′u·a′tion** *n.*

No syllables are shown for words or elements in phrasal entries that appear elsewhere, as shown in **graph·ic** and **graphic arts**.

Pronunciations appear immediately after a main entry. They are also given when necessary for inflected and variant forms that appear within entries. The editors state that "all pronunciations shown are valid for educated American speech." (An exception noted is that normal American pronunciation is given for **flam·boi′ant** at the entry for **flamboyant architecture**, which—as a standard art history term—should have a French pronunciation without the heavy stress on the middle syllable.) When alternate pronunciations occur, the first is that used most widely and frequently, if known; otherwise pronunciations are equally acceptable.

According to the editors, the method of recording pronunciations "is suited to the purposes of a dictionary where the aim is to provide reference rather than extensive linguistic data." The explanation of the pronunciations used states that they "have been compiled by editors trained in phonetics and acquainted with the facts of the spoken language." Where there are *major* regional variations in pronunciations, the first pattern recorded is that of the largest region of speakers in the "great Midwestern section" of the country.

The symbols used are simple letters of the alphabet with standard diacritical marks such as the macron for long vowels, ā (pāy). The breve is only used for the vowel sound in *book* (bŏŏk) to avoid confusion, the editors write, with the vowel sound in *pool*. The schwa ə has been borrowed from the International Phonetic Alphabet (IPA) for unstressed neutral vowels regardless of spelling: **broil·er** (broil′ər) and **vin·di·ca·tion** (vin′də kā′shən). A brief pronunciation key is printed opposite the first page of the main vocabulary with an explanation of the most common foreign sounds used in English, a clear description of how to pronounce them, and notes on accent. In general, readers will have little trouble with the clear symbols. Those requiring more guidance will be able to use the *Webster Comprehensive* and IPA coordinating list of symbols at the front of the work quite easily.

VI. Special Features

The encyclopedic material includes extensive reference matter within the main lexicon. There are also six reference charts and tables and 16 larger supplementary sections at the end of volume two. Many of these are almost identical in content to those in the Webster Illustrated Contemporary Dictionary.

The quality and usefulness of these special supplementary features varies. They have not been recently revised, in general, and much of the material duplicates information given within the main dictionary text. The gazetteer, for example, overlaps the fuller geographical entries in the main dictionary (where the black and white locator maps appear).

"Abbreviations Commonly in Use," arranged in five columns per page of small type, lists some foreign abbreviations and explains capitalizations of abbreviations, as in proper names such as **Mt. Vesuvius**. There are some notable omissions, however: *AIDS* is not included, nor is *AIA* for *American Institute of Architects*; at the entry "**f.f.a., F.F.A.** free foreign agent; free from alongside" there should also be *FFA* for *free fatty acid*.

A list of 16,000 quotations under 182 main subject headings, with 30 cross-referenced terms, ranges from ABILITY to YOUTH. Because such additional information is useful to readers who consider a large, two-volume dictionary as a source for more than just spellings or definitions, it is unfortunate that the information here has not received the revisions needed to make it complete and up-to-date.

VII. Accessibility

At the front of volume one, a table of contents lists the sections of information on how to use the *Webster*

Comprehensive, the various usage essays in the first volume, the appendix sections to volume two, and the titles of the 16 "Special Supplementary Features" that follow the appendixes. The range of entries in the main dictionary is given: for volume one—**A** through **NAME** and for volume two—**NAME-DAY** through **Z**.

The explanatory matter in front of the dictionary is clear and detailed. A useful single page of sample entries contains 36 labels keyed to the main kinds of information available so that a reader has a visual guide to the location of specific items. This is followed by paragraphs of specific guidance on each part of the information in the entries, from syllabication to taxonomic labels to cross-references for doublets in the etymologies.

A useful small chart of the pronunciation symbols makes them easier to read than is the case in many dictionaries. A two-line pronunciation key, including the foreign language symbols and those in the etymologies, is given at the foot of each right-hand page.

The text is printed in small type in three columns per page with enough white space to make reading relatively easy. The entry words, in strict letter-by-letter alphabetical sequence, are printed in bold type overhanging the text. At the top of each page, two bold guide words are printed with a centered page number.

There is no index to the numerous additional lists, charts, and tables in the main dictionary, which are not easy to find in leafing through the work. The lists of particles and words that are combining forms stand out because they are printed in small bold type. The location of variant forms and phrasal entries is explained in the introductory matter and they are printed in bold face within entries, as are run-on entries (words derived from the entry word with the addition of a suffix or prefix).

Apart from the main dictionary, there are certain kinds of information available that the reader will only stumble on by chance, such as the map of major regional speech areas and a table of regional pronunciations, the list of words misspelled most frequently, and even the topics covered in the photographic inserts.

VIII. Graphics and Format

Black-and-white line drawings are scattered throughout the main dictionary in a proportion of one illustration to about 90 entries. The majority of drawings are clear and many captions contain further information, adding to the "encyclopedic" nature of the *Webster Comprehensive*. An attempt has been made to illustrate less familiar meanings and to provide cutaway drawings or cross sections, especially for mechanical objects and for anatomical terms.

There are two large companion drawings of 33 **Beneficial Insects** and 52 **Injurious Insects**, clear enough to be used for identification purposes, for example. Other informational charts and tables are: foreign alphabets (Arabic, Hebrew, Greek, Russian, German), tables of constellations and of chemical elements, of comparative grades in the United States Armed Services, of mathematical and of meteorological symbols, International Morse Code (including its alpha, numeric, and punctuation symbols), a table of major planets, a list of presidents (ending with Gerald R. Ford), proofreaders' marks, standard time in principal cities, a table of principal stars and of Fahrenheit to Celsius conversion. There is a major wars of history chart with names of the contestants, notable battles, and sites of treaties, which includes the Vietnam War.

The photograph pages, half in full color, printed as two separate sections on glossy paper, come from the publisher's archives—they are several decades old, but are interesting from an historical point of view.

Volume two contains an appendix with a large type double-page spread of the metric system and equivalent units (with a ruler illustrating centimeters and inches and a thermometer illustration °F and °C) and a two-page table of weights and measures.

The design of the book in general is attractive and readable, except for the special features printed in a wide assortment of typefaces and with page formats that are often incompatible with the main dictionary.

The dictionary's paper is white and almost opaque; the binding is reinforced and sturdy; the spine has a thickly woven head- and footband. Despite the relative bulk of these volumes, they can be handled with ease and all pages lie flat when opened.

IX. Summary

The *Webster Comprehensive Dictionary: Encyclopedic Edition* was originally published in 1958 as *Funk & Wagnalls Standard Dictionary of the English Language* and has been revised on several subsequent occasions. With 175,000 entries, this work's comprehensiveness is unquestionable. The longer entries contain extensive synonyms, collateral adjectives, and etymologies, as well as full definitions for multiple senses of main entry words. The generous reference materials within the main vocabulary are also quite useful. Moreover, this dictionary manages to convey a feel for the English language, its evolution, and its variety that most college dictionaries do not. The two-volume format is accessible.

Webster's Comprehensive Dictionary:
International Edition

❶ Syllabication is shown by centered dots

❷ Synonyms are listed and distinguished from one another following the italic subheading *Synonyms*

❸ Cross-references are set in small capitals

❹ Homographs receive separate, numbered entries

❺ Inflected forms are set in boldface type

❻ Etymologies are enclosed in brackets

---

❶ **de·file¹** (di·fil′) *v.t.* **·filed, ·fil·ing** **1** To make foul or dirty; pollute. **2** To tarnish or sully the brightness of; corrupt the purity of. **3** To sully; profane (a name, reputation, etc.). **4** To render ceremonially unclean. **5** To corrupt the chastity of. [<OF *defouler* < *de-* down (<L *de-*) + *fouler* trample; infl. in form by ME *filen* soil, OE *fȳlan* < *fūl* foul] — **de·file′ment** *n.* — **de·fil′er** *n.* **❺ ❻**

❷ —*Synonyms:* befoul, contaminate, corrupt, infect, pollute, soil, spoil, stain, sully, taint, tarnish, vitiate. The hand may be *defiled* by a touch of pitch; swine that have been wallowing in the mud are *befouled*. *Contaminate* and *infect* refer to something evil that deeply pervades and permeates, as the human body or mind. *Pollute* is used chiefly of liquids; as, water *polluted* with sewage. *Tainted* meat is repulsive; *infected* meat contains germs of disease. A *soiled* garment may be cleansed by washing; a *spoiled* garment is beyond cleansing or repair. Bright metal is *tarnished* by exposure; a fair sheet is *sullied* by a dirty hand. We speak of a *vitiated* taste or style; fraud *vitiates* a title or a contract. See ABUSE, **❸** CORRUPT, POLLUTE, VIOLATE. *Antonyms:* clean, cleanse, disinfect, hallow, purify, sanctify.

❹ **de·file²** (di·fil′, dē′fil) *v.i.* **·filed, ·fil·ing** To march in a line or by files; file off. — *n.* **1** A long narrow pass; a gorge between mountains. **2** A marching in file. [<MF *défiler* < *dé-* down (<L *de-*) + *file* FILE¹ (def. 3)]

If there is a weakness, it is lack of currency. This is especially noticeable in the supplementary materials, in the omission of secondary meanings acquired by words in recent decades, and even in the absence of a "contemporary" tone in the articles and language. Scientific and technical terms that the user might be most likely to look up are often not there, or are defined in an out-of-date way. For contemporary definitions of such terms, the reader will need to consult a more current source, such as THE RANDOM HOUSE DICTIONARY OF THE ENGLISH LANGUAGE: SECOND UNABRIDGED EDITION.

Still, within its limits, the *Webster Comprehensive Dictionary* remains authoritative. It will be valuable for any collection requiring a comprehensive dictionary with a solid core lexicon and definitions that can be readily understood by the nonspecialist user. The books themselves are sturdily bound and will stand up well to heavy library use.

Webster Comprehensive Dictionary: International Edition

Facts at a Glance

Full Title: **Webster Comprehensive Dictionary: International Edition.**
Former Title: *Funk & Wagnalls Standard Dictionary: International Edition.*
Publisher: J. G. Ferguson.

Editors: Richard Dell and E. Russell Primm.
Edition Reviewed: © 1986.

Number of Entries: 175,000.
Number of Pages: 1,536; 2 volumes.
Number of Illustrations: more than 2,000 including maps.
Trim Size: 8½″ × 11¼″.
Binding: hardcover.

Price: $39.95.
Sold door-to-door, by direct mail, and as a premium.
ISBN-0-89434-054-9.

I. Introduction and Scope

The *Webster Comprehensive Dictionary: International Edition* is identical in content to the WEBSTER COMPREHENSIVE DICTIONARY: ENCYCLOPEDIC EDITION, except that it omits more than 200 pages of supplementary reference material and a 16-page section of photographs found in the latter. The omission of these sections is not a drawback, and makes the *International Edition* less expensive. For full information about the contents of the *International Edition*, see the review of the ENCYCLOPEDIC EDITION, which precedes this one.

Webster Illustrated Contemporary Dictionary

Facts at a Glance

Full Title: **Webster Illustrated Contemporary Dictionary: Encyclopedic Edition.**

Former Title: The Illustrated Contemporary Dictionary: Encyclopedic Edition.

Publisher: J. G. Ferguson.

Editors: Sidney I. Landau, Editor-in-Chief; Richard Dell and E. Russell Primm.

Edition Reviewed: © 1984.

Number of Entries: 85,000.
Number of Pages: 1,150.
Number of Illustrations: 970, including 8 pages in full color.
Trim Size: 7¾″ × 10″.
Binding: hardcover.

Price: $17.95.
Sold door-to-door, by direct mail, and as a premium.
ISBN 0-89434-049-2.

I. Introduction

The *Webster Illustrated Contemporary Dictionary*, formerly *The Illustrated Contemporary Dictionary*, was first published in its current format in 1975 and has since been revised and updated. Its lexicographic base includes material from THE DOUBLEDAY DICTIONARY (© 1975) and from Funk & Wagnalls dictionaries, copyrighted from 1958 to 1977, especially the retitled two-volume WEBSTER'S COMPREHENSIVE DICTIONARY.

The editors state in the preface that the dictionary was designed "to provide a compact, easy-to-use, accurate, and modern desk dictionary for home, school and office use." The preface also claims that the approximately 85,000 entries include "fuller coverage" than the original edition of contemporary general and scientific language. Many distinct British, Canadian, and Australian terms and usages are included. Accordingly, numerous obsolete and archaic terms have been omitted (the publishers do not indicate the extent of these) and the etymologies have been shortened. Thus the dictionary has broadened its base in the contemporary, everyday language of English as it is used around the world and has become more accessible to the general reference book reader.

A small editorial committee of preeminent language scholars advised the editors during preparations for the first edition of this work and wrote the introductory material on language and its use. The late Professor Albert H. Marckwardt of Princeton University wrote in his article on "Usage" that the "editors of this dictionary have assumed that it will be used principally in the United States, by persons who are familiar with American English. Only rarely have they felt it necessary to identify features of the language which are characteristic of this country. For example, the past participial form *gotten* is identified in a note as an American usage, and the peculiarly American use of *integrate* as used in 'to integrate schools' bears the label *U.S.*"

In addition to the articles on usage in this dictionary, there are 17 reference tables, charts, and other items, such as the Declaration of Independence and a list of the presidents of the U.S. in the supplementary matter following the main vocabulary.

The approximately 970 illustrations include simple black-and-white line drawings for selected entries, and a tipped-in, 16-page section of much older photographs, on special topics such as costumes, gems, and reptiles.

II. Authority

J. G. Ferguson and Company, a former subsidiary of Doubleday, are established publishers of premium and subscription reference books, among them the two-volume WEBSTER'S COMPREHENSIVE DICTIONARY in different editions. Their one-volume *Webster Illustrated Contemporary Dictionary* was prepared under Editor-in-Chief Sidney I. Landau, author of *Dictionaries: The Art and Craft of Lexicography* (Scribner's, 1984) and the former editor of Funk & Wagnalls dictionaries and THE DOUBLEDAY DICTIONARY. The name "Webster" on this dictionary has no connection to Merriam-Webster dictionaries and is used, presumably, because marketers believe the name is synonymous with "dictionary" to many American readers.

The advisory committee for all these dictionaries was chaired by Albert H. Marckwardt, Professor Emeritus of English and Linguistics at Princeton University; its other three members were Professor H. Rex Wilson (English—linguistics) of the University of Western Ontario, who contributed the Canadian terms; Harold B. Allen, Professor Emeritus of English and Linguistics, University of Minnesota; and Rudolph C. Troike, formerly Director of the Center for Applied Linguistics, Georgetown University.

III. Comprehensiveness

The approximately 85,000 entries in letter-by-letter alphabetical order comprise 863 pages of this desk dictionary, which is in the mid-range between, for example, THE SCRIBNER-BANTAM ENGLISH DICTIONARY (with somewhere between 60,000 and 80,000 words) and THE AMERICAN HERITAGE DESK DICTIONARY (which claims over 100,000 entries). In a review of the 1982 edition, *American Reference Books Annual* criticized the editors for claiming the *Webster Illustrated Contemporary Dictionary* as "totally new" when it first appeared in 1975 since "it incorporates material from considerably earlier sources now under copyright by the present publishers." However, later in *ARBA 84*, it was suggested that it "should prove quite useful within its intended scope," citing updated vocabulary and the features including a gazetteer and other appendixes. The appendix material contains a sizable amount of additional information that students and teachers, especially, may find useful to have readily at hand in a classroom.

IV. Quality and Currency of Entries

Entries appear alphabetically by letter. Within entries, the sequence of information is: bold main word(s); pronunciation(s), generally given in order of their widest use; part of speech; inflected or variant forms and/or comparative variant forms of adjectives and adverbs—small capitals indicate a cross-reference to another entry, and some synonym cross-references appear immediately after a part of speech; variant British spelling follows if it differs from the U.S. form; then definitions appear, numbered when appropriate. Homographs are entered separately with small superior numbers: **gauntlet**[1] as a glove with armor and **gauntlet**[2] as in *running the gauntlet*. Idiomatic phrases are included, often with italicized usage examples (under the third meaning of **par**, for example, "**3** An accepted standard with which to compare variation: *not feeling up to par*"). Clear etymologies follow, then additional inflected forms. Synonym lists are appended to entries: for example, under **paramount**, the words are, "—**Syn.** chief, foremost, preeminent, supreme." In addition, six combining word forms have extensive lists of compound words following their entries. These are: **in-**[1], **multi-**, **non-**, **over-**, **re-**, **un-**[2].

The dictionary draws on the same lexicographic base as the larger two-volume *Webster Comprehensive* dictionaries published by J. G. Ferguson. A comparison shows that the approach and vocabulary are similar, with the definitions carefully revised or condensed in the one-volume *Webster Illustrated Contemporary Dictionary* and many special field-labeled definitions omitted. For example, a representative definition is:

> **par·a·chute** *n.* An apparatus of lightweight fabric that when unfurled assumes the shape of a large umbrella

and acts to retard the speed of a body moving or descending through air.

The entry in the larger WEBSTER COMPREHENSIVE DICTIONARY reads:

> **par·a·chute** *n.* **1** A large, expanding, umbrella-shaped apparatus for retarding the speed of a body descending through the air, especially from an airplane[,]

which is followed by **2**, a specialized zoological definition, and an aeronautical phrase "—**pilot parachute**." Comparing the same word with another dictionary, similar in purpose and general length of entries, THE AMERICAN HERITAGE DESK DICTIONARY shows:

> **par·a·chute** *n.***1.** A foldable umbrella-shaped device used to slow the fall of persons or objects from great heights. **2.** A similar device used to slow speeding vehicles.

The etymologies at the end of definitions in the *Webster Illustrated Contemporary* are shorter, for example, "[<F < PARA + *chute* fall]," than in the WEBSTER COMPREHENSIVE DICTIONARY: "[<F < *para* PARA-[2] + *chute* fall]," although both typically contain cross-references in small capital letters.

There are five categories of labels employed in the *Webster Illustrated Contemporary* which help the user to know exactly how to use or how *not* to use a word. These appear where entries or particular senses of words have a restricted application. The categories are: (1) level of usage such as *Slang* or *Informal* (colloquial); (2) localization—*Regional* for the U.S., *Brit.* (British), *Can.* (Canadian), and *Austral.* (Australian); (3) field or subject such as *Mus.* (music) or *Ecol.* (ecology); (4) language or origin such as *Latin* or *Spanish* for words that are not yet anglicized; (5) *Nonstand.* (nonstandard) for words or usages not accepted as standard by most native speakers.

Included in the lexicon are such common abbreviations as "**lb., lbs., L.C., L/C, l/c, lc., LD, L.D.**," trade names, and combining forms such as "—**sophy.**" These are helpfully repeated in the list of abbreviations in the appendixes.

The definitions are adequate and well written, in general—with only minor exceptions. The first definition of **boarder**, for example, is misleading: *n.* **1** "A person who receives regular meals, or meals and lodging, for pay." Insert the words "in return" before "for pay" and the meaning of the definition is clear.

A random check for words that are currently much used shows that the following are included with clear definitions: **aerobics, ayatollah, immunosuppressive** (but not *AIDS*), **modem**, and **software**. There is no noun sense given for **heuristic** (a term currently used in education, psychology, rhetoric, and so forth).

And although there is usage guidance at the entry **who**, there are no specific examples of how to use **whom** in the *main* dictionary.

V. Syllabication and Pronunciation

Small dots divide all the bold main entry words into syllables except when phrasal words appear elsewhere as entries: "**Eng·lish**" and "**muf·fin**" are syllabicated, but not "**English muffin**." The dots indicate where it is acceptable to hyphenate words.

Immediately after the dictionary's preface, a simple, easy-to-understand pronunciation key appears. Each of the 42 main alphabetic symbols has two examples. The superscripts *h* and *y* represent sounds commonly pronounced in some regions but not in others, for example: *Tues·day* (t^{y}o͞oz′dā) or *whale* (^{h}wāl). The schwa (ə) represents unstressed vowel sounds, with five examples given. Foreign sounds encountered in English are described with brief guidance on pronouncing them, a useful instruction for the student or traveler. Included are four distinct pronunciations occurring in French and German words (à as in *ami*, œ as in *peu* or *schön*, ü as in *vue* or *grün*, ṅ as in *brun*), plus the *kh* sound that is similar in German and Scottish words:

> kh as in German *ach*, Scottish *loch*. Pronounce a strongly aspirated (h) with the tongue in position for (k) as in *cool* or *keep*.
>
> Additionally, the symbol ′ represents the voiceless *l* or *r* in French: *debacle* (dā·bä′kl′) or the French sound of *y* as a consonant when it is followed by a slight schwa sound in a separate syllable, as in *fille* (fē′y′). Primary stress is indicated by a heavy symbol ′ and secondary stress by a lighter face ′: **e·lec·tion·eer** (i-lek′shən·ir′).

Throughout the A to Z entries, a two-line short-form of the pronunciation key, with an explanation of two symbols in the etymologies (<derived from; ? origin uncertain or unknown), appears at the foot of all right-hand pages as a handy, quick reference for the reader.

VI. Special Features

Special features are an important part of this dictionary. The three opening essays by editorial committee members are excellent. Professor Marckwardt explains "Usage" as "one of many kinds of social behavior" and the "role of the dictionary" from the points of view of a) lexicographers who seek to record the language and b) readers who expect to find prescriptive guidance "relative to spelling, pronunciation, word division and word meaning, or grammatical form." He also describes various approaches to style, ranging from "rigid" reliance on standards (via the nineteenth century) to "nervous reluctance" to label any usage as "nonstandard." He even explains the grammatically unsound objection to *hopefully* as a verb phrase modifier, as in "Hopefully, the project will be finished by the end of the year." *Hopefully* modifies the whole clause not just the verb phrase in standard usage. Professor Allen details punctuation usage thoroughly, and Professor Wilson's brief article on Canadian English is enlightening.

Much of the more than 250 pages of reference material in the *Webster Illustrated Contemporary* does not date readily, which is a plus: for example, given names (male and female), Greek and Latin elements, guidance on vocabulary and spelling (part of this material is duplicated in the dictionary's preliminary material), some 1,600 quotations organized under guide words, an essay on "The World's Religions," mythology, vital facts about U.S. presidents (including Ronald W. Reagan) and vice-presidents (including George H. Bush), the texts of the Declaration of Independence and the U.S. Constitution, with lists of signers of both documents.

Other sections need updating, especially the long essay on "The Library Research Paper": the advice is excellent for students, but the footnote style and the specimen bibliography are obsolete. The extensive abbreviations list needs updating, for example, "**E.R.A.** Educational Research Association; Emergency Relief Administration (ERA)" should include the Equal Rights Amendment. The table of signs and symbols is also in need of revision. Obviously, the editors have made some ongoing changes in the extensive gazetteer and biographical section, but many changes from the 1980s are not in the gazetteer: since 1981, **Antigua** has been *Antigua and Barbuda*, **St. Christopher and Nevis** became independent in 1983, and **Upper Volta** changed its name in 1984 to *Burkina Faso*. U.S. population figures are based on the 1980 census: those for Canada date from 1978; others are not based on even reliable estimates from ca. 1983. The biographical section contains some 1980s updating—John Lennon's death date and the inclusion of Sandra Day O'Connor. Standard figures are clearly identified and the major works of many authors are cited.

Among the illustrations in the main section of entries are many charts and tables, including the Braille alphabet, a list of constellations by groups, a good diagram of a solar eclipse, a table of chemical elements, a table of geological time scales with life forms, a chart of comparative grades in the U.S. Armed Services, the Jewish calendar, eleven types of leaf, almost two pages of weights and measures, phases of the moon, a table of comparative U.S. and British values (1 million to 1 decillion), a periodic table of the elements, an out-of-date table of planets (Neptune has three satellites, not two; Pluto's mass, diameter, and rotation are not current figures, etc.), proofreaders' marks, a temperature conversion table plus a zodiac with labels and an illustration of terrestrial zones. These features are all available in other reference sources, but their inclusion here gives the dictionary's encyclopedic appellation some weight and genuine usefulness.

VII. Accessibility

Access to this dictionary is good in general. A contents page, printed in a larger typeface than the text, immediately follows the title page and lists (1) the preliminary sections that guide a reader in using the work, (2) the main dictionary, and (3) the supplementary, encyclopedic material. The contents do not indicate whether the special material is in the form of charts, tables, or essays, but nevertheless will help readers locate material.

Especially helpful is a two-column guide to terms used in the *Webster Illustrated Contemporary*, preceding the "Guide to the Use of the Dictionary." The right-hand column shows a segment of entries with 20 labels printed opposite, keyed in with a ruled line to the individual parts of entries so that a reader can recognize the typographical conventions used for run-on derivatives or cross-references to maps and so forth. (Under Switzerland, for instance, the reference "·See map at ITALY" appears.)

The chartlike format of the pronunciation key makes the symbols appear more accessible than is often the case in dictionaries. The 18 numbered short sections that explain the terms used in the dictionary contain good, short examples, and the brief pronunciation key on every right-hand page assures quick reference ability.

Throughout the main entries, page numbers are centered above each page of text; and a large, bold guide word is printed at the top outer edge of each page.

VIII. Graphics and Format

The larger format of this desk dictionary accommodates two columns of text per page, each column approximately 2¾-inches wide by 8¾- to 9¼-inches deep. Entry words are in clear, sans-serif bold type and the text is small but readable. The top and side margins are adequate, but the text runs uncomfortably close to the bottom of the pages, and the inner margins seem narrow. The dictionary lies flat when opened. There are no thumb index guides, but the paper is heavy enough to sustain riffling through the pages without creasing or tearing.

Of the almost 900 black-and-white line drawings, most are very clear, especially the illustrations for music, architecture, anatomy, and math (the last two have labels with lines directed to the appropriate area to be identified).

In general, the illustrations attempt to picture an unfamiliar or confusing sense of words. There is also a special 16-page section of photographs printed on glossy paper that are exceptionally outdated, especially those in the sciences. The same pages are among those appearing in WEBSTER'S COMPREHENSIVE DICTIONARY. The reproductions of the seven wonders of the world and bridges of the world are very old-fashioned, indeed, but constitute a historical record. This section could benefit from updating and redesigning, or an explanation of the time periods being illustrated. As it stands, it serves only as a quaint relic or curio for those users who enjoy a glimpse into the past.

IX. Summary

The *Webster Illustrated Contemporary Dictionary*, edited by the noted lexicographer Sidney I. Landau, is a revised version of *The Illustrated Contemporary Dictionary: Encyclopedic Edition*, published in 1978 by the same publisher, J. G. Ferguson. It also includes material from the 1975 *Doubleday Dictionary* and from several Funk & Wagnalls dictionaries.

For its size and age, this desk dictionary has a solid base of good definitions, and its lexicography is authoritative. Many of the more contemporary words it includes are carefully defined and will be readily comprehensible to the general reader. The extensive supplementary material includes a gazetteer, biographies, quotations, a grammar and usage handbook, and other special features that will be of interest to the general reader as well as to writers. Unfortunately, however, some of these features are now somewhat dated.

Like the other Ferguson dictionaries reviewed in this Buying Guide, this book has an excellent library binding. It should stand up well to heavy use.

Webster's Concise Family Dictionary

Facts at a Glance

Full Title: **Webster's Concise Family Dictionary**.
Publisher: **Merriam-Webster**.
Editor: **Henry Bosley Woolf**.
Edition Reviewed: © 1975.

Number of Entries: 57,000.

Number of Pages: 848.
Trim Size: 6″ × 9¼″.
Binding: cloth.

Price: $8.95.
Sold in bookstores and other outlets; also sold to libraries and other educational institutions.
ISBN 0-87779-039-6.

I. Introduction and Scope

This dictionary's lexicon is identical to that of the paperback MERRIAM-WEBSTER DICTIONARY, except for the printing of pronunciation symbols at both the front and back. For an evaluation of the contents, see the review of THE MERRIAM-WEBSTER DICTIONARY.

The dust jacket of *Webster's Concise Family Dictionary* indicates that the text is set in "larger print for easier use." The print *is* larger than that in standard dictionaries, such as WEBSTER'S NINTH NEW COLLEGIATE, but it is still smaller than the type size used, for example, in most trade books. In the review copy, an unacceptable number of letters appeared broken or smudged. In many of these cases, it appeared that a quantity of ink had "lifted" from the pages before they were fully dried. Consumers should, therefore, check the printing they buy, especially by surveying the left-hand margin of the text columns where the superior numbers for successive homographs readily show these flaws.

Potential buyers should also keep in mind that this dictionary, like its paperback edition, dates from the mid-1970s; otherwise, the size of the print and the generally authoritative approach to the lexicon (although it is much condensed) may make this edition useful for those who have some visual impairment.

Webster's Dictionary for Everyday Use

Facts at a Glance

Full Title: **Webster's Dictionary for Everyday Use**.
Publisher: Barnes & Noble.
Edition Reviewed: © 1981; 1985 edition.

Number of Entries: over 50,000.
Number of Pages: 446.
Trim Size: 5⅜″ × 7⅝″.
Binding: paperback.

Price: $4.95.
Sold in bookstores and other outlets.
ISBN 0-06-463330-6.

I. Introduction and Scope

This paperback edition of a 1958 dictionary, originally compiled by John Gage Allee, professor of English philology at George Washington University, is a thoroughly out-of-date work that will be of little use to anyone. The shoddy printing and cheap paper combine with the other less-than-useful elements to produce a work that exemplifies the abuse of Webster's name when it is attached to a dictionary simply for marketing purposes.

Webster's New Compact Dictionary for School and Office

Facts at a Glance

Full Title: **Webster's New Compact Dictionary for School and Office**.
Publisher: Thomas Nelson.
Editor: Walter C. Kidney; prepared under the direction of Laurence Urdang.
Edition Reviewed: © 1985; revised edition.

Number of Entries: 30,000.
Number of Pages: 313.
Trim Size: 4½″ × 6¼″.
Binding: hardcover.

Price: $2.95.
Sold in bookstores and other outlets; also sold to educational institutions.
ISBN 0-8407-4081-6.

I. Introduction

Webster's New Compact Dictionary for School and Office, originally published in 1978 and issued in a revised edition in 1985, is a quick-reference dictionary. As the title suggests, it is readily portable. This dictionary is also available in a smaller format under the title NELSON'S NEW COMPACT WEBSTER'S DICTIONARY.

II. Authority

The title page credits Walter C. Kidney as editor, but adds that the dictionary was "prepared under the direction of Laurence Urdang." Urdang's credentials as a linguist and lexicographer are well-known, and one expects a dictionary bearing his name to be highly reputable. However, the full extent of his involvement in this work is not revealed, and a degree of skepticism about the dictionary's authority may be in order.

III. Comprehensiveness

Webster's New Compact Dictionary for School and Office is by no means intended to be comprehensive.

Rather, as the "Foreword" notes, this dictionary is designed to provide "fingertip answers to the most frequent language puzzlers: spelling, hyphenation, and pronunciation." The parts of speech are identified, and some usage and field labels are included, but there has been no apparent effort to apply them with any regularity. Biographical and geographical names are not included, nor are synonyms, antonyms, or etymologies given.

IV. Quality and Currency of Entries

In the interest of space, the definitions given in *Webster's New Compact Dictionary* are rudimentary. They are not necessarily succinct or clear, and do not always provide enough information to convey the essence of the word being defined. For example, **carrier** is defined as "**1.** thing or person that carries. **2.** aircraft carrier." Both definitions verge on circularity; the first gives no notion of the kind of "thing" a carrier might be (a bag, for example), while the second merely gives the full form of the expression for which it may be used as an abbreviation. Curiously, there is no entry for "aircraft carrier"; the dictionary defines **aircraft** as "flying craft." Some definitions are unduly broad and imprecise. **Cantor** is defined as "singer at a Jewish service." The definition for **destroy** ("damage so as to eliminate") in no way conveys any of this word's connotative sense.

Definitions of this sort send the reader on a frustrating wild goose chase through the dictionary. For example, the reader looking up the meaning of **handgun** will find merely "pistol." The definition for **pistol** is "small hand-carried firearm"; **firearm** is inadequately defined as "weapon operated by explosives." There are no cross-references.

Webster's New Compact Dictionary is by no means consistent in its inclusion of commonly used words that have only recently entered the vocabulary. The reader will search in vain for such current terms as *access* in its computer sense, *acid rain, compact disc, VDT,* or *videocassette.* He or she will, however, find the computer terms **bit, byte,** and **diskette,** as well as such foreign words as **ayatollah.**

V. Syllabication and Pronunciation

Syllabication and pronunciation are indicated by the conventional method of dots and diacritical marks. Full phonetic pronunciation is given only in rare instances, however. Presumably, those words for which pronunciation is given are ones that may be expected to cause difficulty for many readers. However, there seems to be no particular method underlying the choice of such words. For example, phonetic pronunciation is not provided for such potentially troublesome words as **cynosure, dahlia,** or **ubiquity,** but is provided for

conflict, partial, and **spoor**. A more serious drawback is the absence of any pronunciation key.

VI. Special Features

Webster's New Compact Dictionary contains a minimum of special features. It does include tables of weights and measures, metric equivalents, wedding anniversary symbols, birthstones, and states and territories of the United States (with post office abbreviations and capitals).

VII. Accessibility

Entry words are arranged alphabetically, letter by letter. Guide words indicate the first entry on left-hand pages and the last entry on right-hand pages.

VIII. Graphics and Format

Whatever its other deficiencies, *Webster's New Compact Dictionary* is a well-designed book. Entry words, printed in boldface type, overhang the main text. Variant forms and related words are also printed in boldface, while part-of-speech labels are italicized. The print is legible throughout.

The book is printed in two columns per page; each page is numbered at the center of the bottom margin. There are no illustrations.

IX. Summary

Webster's New Compact Dictionary for School and Office is intended primarily for quick reference. It provides spellings, some pronunciation guidance, and basic definitions—but not much more. Its definitions are often reduced to a single word, and are rarely longer than a brief phrase. Multiple meanings of a word are seldom given; the definitions that are given are frequently inadequate.

The bright red cover, with its embossed gold lettering, gives this dictionary an attractive appearance, and the graphics and format are appealing for a book of this size. However, even at its low price, this dictionary is no bargain. Readers seeking a simple compact dictionary might be better served by WEBSTER'S NEW WORLD HANDY POCKET DICTIONARY.

Webster's New Dictionary and Roget's Thesaurus

Facts at a Glance

Full Title: **Webster's New Dictionary and Roget's Thesaurus**.
Publisher: Thomas Nelson.
Editor: American Heritage Dictionary staff.
Edition Reviewed: © 1984.

Webster's New Dictionary and Roget's Thesaurus

❶ Pronunciations are enclosed in parentheses

❷ Usage notes are introduced by the boldface italic subheading *Usage*

❸ Usage labels are italicized and enclosed in parentheses

❹ Synonyms are grouped by parts of speech

❺ Inflected forms appear in small boldface type

❻ Etymologies are enclosed in brackets

❼ Cross-references to list of Indo-European roots are set in boldface type

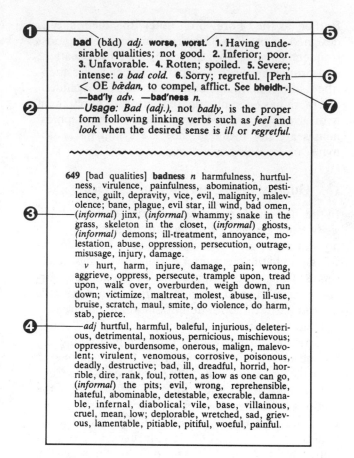

Number of Entries: approximately 35,000.
Number of Pages: 992.
Number of Indexes: 2.
Number of Illustrations: 300 black-and-white drawings.
Trim Size: 5⅞″ × 9¼″.
Binding: hardcover.

Price: $9.95.
Sold in bookstores; also sold to educational institutions.
ISBN 0-8407-4115-4.

I. Introduction and Scope

Subtitled "The two most used reference books in one convenient volume," this dictionary combines a desktop dictionary with an abbreviated form of *Roget's Thesaurus*. The dictionary part of the volume is based on *The American Heritage Dictionary of the English Language*, edited by William Morris, and the source is the CONCISE AMERICAN HERITAGE DICTIONARY, published in 1980. The thesaurus is based on NELSON'S NEW COMPACT ROGET'S THESAURUS, copyrighted in 1978. (Reviews of the two separate volumes used as sources appear elsewhere in this volume.) It is curious that the name "Webster" was used in the title as opposed to "American

Heritage," which is also a respectable name in publishing and more accurately reflects the volume's parentage.

The age level for the dictionary is approximately junior high school through adult. The dictionary follows a format established by *The American Heritage Dictionary of the English Language* and includes usage notes and etymology along with illustrative photographs and line drawings. A list of Indo-European roots appears in the appendix.

The thesaurus is based on Roget's classification system rather than being in alphabetical order. Checking a word's synonyms thus becomes a two-step process as it is always necessary to refer to the index. This makes it more difficult or cumbersome for young people to use, and even some adults may prefer the alphabetical format. The editor, Laurence Urdang, comments that the thesaurus is the only abridgment of *Roget's Thesaurus* available. He further notes in the preface to the thesaurus that all of the 1,000 main entry words have been retained but that "all antiquated words and phrases have been removed." The thesaurus has been modernized to reflect the "newest developments" in language.

II. Format

The dictionary and the thesaurus are paged separately. The dictionary makes up the first 820 pages of the book, and the thesaurus the last 156 pages. The dictionary is arranged in alphabetical order with boldface entries. Attractive black-and-white photographs and line drawings make up the illustrations. Most of the photographs are of famous people, and most of the line drawings are of maps. A useful guide to the dictionary precedes this section.

The thesaurus is made up of several sections. The first is the editor's preface, which unfortunately neglects to provide a clear statement on how best to use Roget's rather complex organization system. Next follows a one-page plan of the classification and a tabular synopsis of categories under which words are entered and then the thesaurus itself. An extensive index which lists every word in the thesaurus appears at the end of the book. Main entry words are in boldface type. Each word is assigned a number that indicates its position in the thesaurus.

The debate over whether Roget's classification system or the alphabetical arrangement of words in a thesaurus is preferable will probably never be settled. For the average reader, alphabetical order means ease of use, while for those who understand the advantages of the classification system, this type of arrangement does not make a great deal of sense—they will want the "real thing."

III. Quality and Currency of Entries

Although the combined volume carries a 1984 copyright date, the database for the dictionary is from 1980. Most of the words included are those of everyday speech, with personal and place names included. There are few words beginning with *video* other than the word **video** itself; nor will the reader find words such as *futon* and *tofu*. Even though these words have been around for some time, they have too recently become a part of everyday speech to be found in this dictionary.

The thesaurus, too, primarily makes use of everyday language. Gone are those wonderful impressive-sounding words that college students like to sprinkle throughout their term papers. For example, under the noun **experiment** the synonyms are: *test, trial, examination, proof, assay, procedure; experimentation, research, investigation,* and *analysis*; gone are *docimasy, probation, crucible,* and *trial balloon* and its French equivalent *ballon d'essai.* However, the entry for **misanthropy** does include *incivism* and *misogynist.*

IV. Accessibility

The dictionary part of this book is easily accessible with dual guide words at the top of each page which is printed in two columns. The layout and design of the dictionary make it easy to read. The end of the dictionary, however, runs right into the thesaurus,

and a thumb guide or an edge marking of some type to indicate where the dictionary ends and the thesaurus begins would have made it easier and more practical to separate the two volumes.

The thesaurus itself is in a smaller and lighter typeface than is the dictionary. It is not as easy to locate words in the thesaurus as it is in the dictionary, partly because of the system of organization, but also because of the layout and design of this part of the book. The index to the thesaurus is in five columns per page and in a lighter typeface than that found in the dictionary.

V. Summary

The idea behind the *Webster's New Dictionary and Roget's Thesaurus* is basically sound. It would be especially useful as a desk dictionary for students who could work back and forth between the two volumes with comparative ease. The organization of the thesaurus is somewhat cumbersome but helpful once a student catches on to how to follow and use it. The basic problem is that the editors have not provided a good guide to using this part of the book. The vocabulary is down to earth, and the usage notes in the dictionary section are particularly helpful to students.

In spite of these drawbacks and the lack of currency in certain areas, this book would make a nice graduation gift for those going to college. Certainly the two-for-one price is right. However, it is difficult to see a need for this type of dictionary in the reference section of a library. Every library will need at least one or more unabridged thesauruses, and most libraries will have the unabridged and/or the concise dictionaries published by American Heritage. This duplication of contents in one volume would therefore serve no particular library need except possibly as a circulating volume.

Webster's New Ideal Dictionary

Facts at a Glance

Full Title: **Webster's New Ideal Dictionary.**
Publisher: Merriam-Webster.
Edition Reviewed: © 1984.

Number of Entries: 57,346.
Number of Pages: 672.
Number of Illustrations: 60 black-and-white drawings.
Trim Size: 6¾" × 8½".
Binding: cloth.

Price: $7.95.
Sold in bookstores and other outlets; also sold to libraries and other educational institutions.
ISBN 0-87779-249-6.

Webster's New Ideal Dictionary

❶ Syllabication is shown by
   centered dots

❷ Cross-references are set in small
   capitals

❸ Pronunciations are enclosed by
   reversed virgules

❹ Homographs appear as separate,
   numbered entries

❺ Line drawings illustrate
   definitions

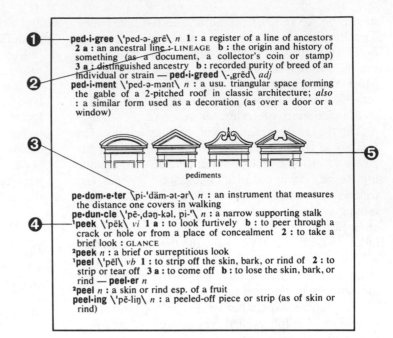

ped·i·gree \'ped-ə-,grē\ *n* **1** : a register of a line of ancestors **2 a** : an ancestral line : LINEAGE **b** : the origin and history of something (as a document, a collector's coin or stamp) **3 a** : distinguished ancestry **b** : recorded purity of breed of an individual or strain — **ped·i·greed** \-,grēd\ *adj*

ped·i·ment \'ped-ə-mənt\ *n* : a usu. triangular space forming the gable of a 2-pitched roof in classic architecture; *also* : a similar form used as a decoration (as over a door or a window)

pediments

pe·dom·e·ter \pi-'däm-ət-ər\ *n* : an instrument that measures the distance one covers in walking

pe·dun·cle \'pē-,dəŋ-kəl, pi-'\ *n* : a narrow supporting stalk

¹**peek** \'pēk\ *vi* **1 a** : to look furtively **b** : to peer through a crack or hole or from a place of concealment **2** : to take a brief look : GLANCE

²**peek** *n* : a brief or surreptitious look

¹**peel** \'pēl\ *vb* **1** : to strip off the skin, bark, or rind of **2** : to strip or tear off **3 a** : to come off **b** : to lose the skin, bark, or rind — **peel·er** *n*

²**peel** *n* : a skin or rind esp. of a fruit

peel·ing \'pē-liŋ\ *n* : a peeled-off piece or strip (as of skin or rind)

I. Introduction

According to the preface, this concise dictionary, with definitions based on the authoritative WEBSTER'S THIRD NEW INTERNATIONAL DICTIONARY, aims at reaching the casual user who may need it for "daily reading and writing . . . the person searching for a meaning, a pronunciation, or a syllabication." This suggests a person who is not a student or a writer already in possession of a collegiate dictionary having a larger vocabulary and more elaborate lexicographic features, or who does not have the use of an office word processor or electronic typewriter with built-in dictionaries.

II. Authority

Webster's Ideal has the reputation of its publisher behind it, and that is a very good reputation indeed. Merriam-Webster has been making dictionaries since 1843 when it acquired the copyright of Noah Webster's dictionary. It is best known perhaps for its unabridged dictionaries, most recently its WEBSTER'S THIRD NEW INTERNATIONAL DICTIONARY upon which all its subsequent dictionaries are based. In compiling *Webster's Ideal*, Merriam-Webster's staff culled approximately 13 percent of the entry words in its unabridged dictionary, choosing those most likely to be looked up in a person's "daily reading or writing," omitting "obsolete, rare, and highly technical words and obsolete meanings of common words," and simplifying the definitions. Pronunciation and word division are also based on WEBSTER'S THIRD.

Within the scope the Merriam-Webster staff has set itself, *Webster's New Ideal Dictionary* is accurate and authoritative.

III. Comprehensiveness

Most of the words in *Webster's Ideal* are current at least as of 1968, the principal copyright date, although enough less-familiar entries are included, such as **olio** (defined as "HODGEPODGE, MEDLEY") and

> **omnium gatherum** . . . *n*: a miscellaneous collection of a variety of things or persons: HODGEPODGE

to question the preface's statement that obsolete words and meanings have been omitted. In addition, **Sputnik** is included as a common noun meaning "satellite." So too are some rather technical words for parts of the body such as **glottis** and **aorta**, as well as **springe** and **thegn** (a variant of **thane** that is entered separately); these latter two are presumably included because they are likely to be encountered in literary reading (for example, in Thomas Hardy and Shakespeare). Overall, however, the word choices seem to be wisely made for the intended audience hypothesized.

In order to streamline the definitions, the editors have included no etymologies, illustrative quotations, or usage notes of a prescriptive kind. They do point out when a word is commonly used in the plural, as in the first meaning of **heaven**, or when it has a limited or special use, such as the musical term **allegro**. Various definitions include cross-references in the guise of near synonyms set in small capital letters. Occasionally, these comprise the definition, as in:

global 1: SPHERICAL **2:** WORLDWIDE.

In most instances, readers should check the synonymous word at its own main entry; VOCABULARY, for example, is given as a synonym under the second meaning of **phraseology** and defined in its second meaning as "a sum or stock of words employed by a language, group, individual, or work or in a field of knowledge." Hence, casual readers and writers should be aware that it is ambiguous to use the two words interchangeably, that "I do not like your vocabulary" is not the same as saying, "I do not like your phraseology."

Readers who want to know the meaning of a word they have just read, or writers who want to look up a word they intend to use to see if they have the right one, should find this dictionary adequate for their needs.

IV. Quality and Currency of Entries

Definitions in *Webster's Ideal* are derived from those in WEBSTER'S THIRD and as a consequence are generally accurate and clear. Since they are somewhat simplified and reduced for the general and possibly more casual user, more sophisticated readers may not consider the definitions complete. Older meanings, for example, have not been included; and consequently, for instance, a reader of Jane Austen (or even of Logan Pearsall Smith) may not find the meaning of **pique** that a particular sentence requires. But the definitions, as they are, are straightforward and, in the main, entered chronologically.

Slang terms are included, but they are not labeled as such. The meaning of **cooler** as jail and of **pigeon** as an easy mark or dupe, for example, are both here but the slang definition is not indicated. In addition, this dictionary does not use any illustrative quotations to define words by means of a context. Occasionally, however, once the definition of a word has been established, a second entry will give a kind of illustration. For example, the verb form of **keynote**, appearing after the noun has been defined, includes the explanations, "1: to set the keynote of 2: to deliver the keynote address at," but that is as close as the volume comes to a contextual illustration. Despite the incompleteness of some definitions and the lack of many of the helpful features described above, *Webster's Ideal* should satisfy the audience for which it is intended.

V. Syllabication and Pronunciation

Merriam-Webster's system of pronunciation is slightly different from that of other dictionary publishers. It borrows from the International Phonetic Alphabet (IPA), making liberal use of the schwa (ə) and many of the standard symbols most readers are accustomed to. A useful pronunciation key appears in the frontmatter of the book and in simplified form at the bottom of each page, so that readers should have little trouble in learning the system. This dictionary does, however, place primary and secondary accent marks *before* the syllables rather than after in contrast to the usual practice. When a syllable is pronounced by some speakers and not by others, this is placed in parentheses. The pronunciation at **factory**, for example, is noted as

\\'fak-t(ə-)rē\\

meaning that some speakers pronounce the middle syllable and some do not. Although some words receive notations of more than one pronunciation, most receive only one and that usually is as if the word were pronounced alone and out of any context. For example, **irritable** is given the pronunciation that is heard when someone asks, "How do *you* pronounce i-r-r-i-t-a-b-l-e?" rather than the pronunciation actually given in ordinary speech. A comparison with the pronunciation of this word given in WEBSTER'S THIRD illustrates the difference:

WEBSTER'S THIRD NEW INTERNATIONAL DICTIONARY:
    \\'irəd - əbəl\\

Webster's New Ideal Dictionary:
    \\'ir-ət-ə-bəl\\

Centered periods are used in the boldface entry words to show where a word may be divided in writing or printing. This practice is the same as that in WEBSTER'S THIRD and in Merriam-Webster's other dictionaries. That is, all syllables are not marked, only those where a publisher would ordinarily divide a word. For example, syllables designated by a single letter at the beginning or end of a word are not marked nor are single letters at the end of an English prefix. This is illustrated by the use of **semi·fi·nal** rather than *sem·i·fi·nal*, or **ane·mia** rather than *a·ne·mi·a*.

It might interest potential buyers of *Webster's Ideal* that many publishers and printers, including the United States Government Printing Office, do not accept Merriam-Webster's authority for word division.

VI. Special Features

The backmatter of *Webster's Ideal* comprises several lists and tables as well as the texts of the Declaration of Independence and the United States Constitution. There, too, are lists of common abbreviations, English given names with their pronunciations, populations of United States cities (1980 census), tables of chemical elements (the symbols of which are also in the list of abbreviations), weights and measures, decimal equivalents of metric measures and fractions, standard time around the world, Jewish years from 1973 to 1992, and the dates for Easter to 1992.

A list of common foreign words and expressions, fuller than the foreign words included in the main word lists of most collegiate dictionaries, is also included in the backmatter. But using it is not so simple as one might think because many common foreign words are in the main section that are not in this special list. Therefore, a reader may have to look in both to find the particular expression he or she wants. For instance, in the main section are: **apropos**, **et cetera**, **ibidem**, **jeu d'esprit**, **nom de guerre**, **nom de plume**, **nota bene**, **status quo**, **vide**, and **videlicet**; but in the special section: *à la francaise*, *amor patria*, *amor vincit omnia*, *et in Arcadia ego*, *ex libris*, *semper fidelis*, and *Wanderjahr*. It would have been handier if all foreign expressions had been placed in the special list, but readers will usually find what they are looking for with only minor inconvenience. And, finally, a few common foreign terms are not included at all.

Nowhere in *Webster's Ideal* is *sic* included, not even in the abbreviations, although other expressions containing it are listed in the special section. Similarly, neither *e.g.* nor *exempli gratia* is given anywhere. The list of abbreviations does include *et al*, *etc*, *et seq*, and *viz* along with *ib* and *ibid*.

VII. Accessibility

Webster's Ideal is relatively simple in format and easy to use. After a contents page and a half-page preface are three pages of explanatory notes and a one-page key to pronunciation. This dictionary is not thumb-indexed, but large-print, boldface guide words are at the top left and right of each page. In the main list boldface entry words are followed by a pair of reversed virgules (\   \) within which are printed their pronunciations in phonetic symbols; variant pronunciations are separated from the first by commas and are not to be considered inferior, only variant. The same is true of variant spellings, which are joined to the boldface entry word by an italicized *or*. A writer may use any of them with equal assurance of correctness, as **judgment** *or* **judgement**. British spellings are not included in this dictionary. After the pronunciation or after the entry word, if no pronunciation is given, there appears an italicized abbreviation of the part of speech—each part of speech of any given word has its own entry—and any usage note in italics such as "*often cap.*" Words usually capitalized, however, are capitalized in the boldface entry, a departure from Merriam-Webster's practice in its unabridged dictionary.

In the definitions proper, each sense of a word with more than one meaning is introduced by a boldface Arabic numeral, and closely related aspects of one sense are separated by a semicolon and "*also*" or "*esp.*" In addition to words and their definitions and pronunciations, the dictionary includes a number of charts or lists in its main vocabulary section. For example, across from **Bible** is a list of the books of the Old and New Testaments in the Douay and Authorized versions and also the books of the Protestant Apocrypha. In another example, the page following the entry **number** includes a table of numbers showing the cardinal, ordinal, Arabic, and Roman numbers up to a million. These special tables are not cited in the contents and are more or less stumbled upon while using the dictionary.

VIII. Graphics and Format

Webster's Ideal is a sturdily bound, attractive book. Its print is small but easy to read, with plenty of white space between words; pages have ample enough margins all around and a line between columns. The paper is a good-quality, smooth white stock, heavy enough to eliminate bothersome show-through of text. Since definitions are kept short, there are no long columns of solid print; and in each case the definitions on any page are varied enough—italics, boldface, small capitals, dashes, colons—to make a pleasing appearance and easy reading. Entry words stand out prominently in boldface overhanging the text.

The illustrations, simple black-and-white line drawings, are clear and helpful. Very few pertain to words with more than one sense, but those few are clearly numbered. The designer must have been fond of music and swords because of the approximately 60 illustrations, three at least are swords and half a dozen or more are musical.

This is a handsome cloth book that should stand up to hard wear and frequent use.

IX. Summary

Within the limits its editors have set for it, *Webster's Ideal* is a good dictionary. It is superior, for example, to WEBSTER'S NEW AMERICAN DICTIONARY (1970), which indicates syllabication only in its pronunciations. When Merriam-Webster's editors chose to omit technical terms, however, they made their dictionary less useful than it otherwise might have been, since those constitute many of the terms that a casual reader is most likely to look up. There is also the minor inconvenience of not knowing whether to look up a word such as **nyet** in the main word list or the special foreign words and phrases section. And for the derivations of words, advice on usage, or older definitions, another dictionary must be consulted.

Nevertheless, the dictionary buyer who is looking for simple definitions, standard spellings, and platform pronunciations in a fairly portable but sturdy form at a low cost will find *Webster's New Ideal Dictionary* a worthwhile investment.

Webster's New School and Office Dictionary

Facts at a Glance

Full Title: **Webster's New School and Office Dictionary**.

Alternative Title: Webster's Super New School and Office Dictionary.

Publisher: Fawcett Crest.

Editor: Thomas Layman.

Edition Reviewed: © 1974; 1975 edition.

Number of Entries: 63,000.
Number of Pages: 888.
Trim Size: 4⅛" × 6⅞".
Binding: paperback.

Price: $3.50.
Sold in bookstores and other outlets; also sold to libraries and other educational institutions.
ISBN 0-449-20939-3.

I. Introduction

The introduction to *Webster's New School and Office Dictionary* states that this is a revision of the original World Publishing Company edition which has "for several decades served as a helpful, economical reference book on language." The revision cited, however, was done in 1974. The book contains over 63,000 entries; its special features include a gazetteer, tables of weights and measures, a perpetual calendar, and a listing of U.S. and Canadian holidays.

II. Authority

Originally published by World, a well-known publisher of reference books, this dictionary made its first appearance in 1943. The 1974 revised edition appeared under a William Collins + World imprint. Collins is a respected British publishing house with many quality reference books to its credit. The edition reviewed was published as a paperback in 1975 by Fawcett Crest.

III. Comprehensiveness

The vocabulary in the *Webster's New School and Office Dictionary* incorporates, according to the introduction, more entries "than in any other pocket-sized paperback dictionary," including "specialized terms in the sciences and arts [and] new terms frequently encountered in newspapers, magazines, and books." However comprehensive the dictionary may have been in 1974, it has to take a back seat today to other dictionaries such as Dell's THE AMERICAN HERITAGE DICTIONARY and Warner's edition of WEBSTER'S NEW WORLD DICTIONARY OF THE AMERICAN LANGUAGE—especially in respect to technological and other terms in current usage.

Following the introduction, the *Webster's New School and Office Dictionary* contains a pronunciation key and a list of abbreviations used in the dictionary. Main entries in the word list contain few abbreviations (other than **Mr.**, **Mrs.**, **Ms.**, and **WASP**) and few biographical entries, except for some religious entries and some related adjectival terms, such as **Shakespearean** and **Freudian**. The gazetteer's entries and population figures date from the early 1970s. No formal etymological information is offered, but entries frequently provide several numbered definitions, with parts of speech and usage labels. The synonyms and antonyms included are not labeled.

IV. Quality and Currency of Entries

Entries are in alphabetical order, letter by letter, and include: main entries in boldface type that overhang the text; respelled pronunciations with simple diacritical marks in parentheses; parts of speech, irregular plural forms of nouns, and past and present participle forms of verbs; and numbered definitions with usage labels. The source of unassimilated foreign words appears after the part of speech, for example: **machismo** . . . , *n.* [Spanish]. Definitions, although brief, differentiate clearly among meanings and are generally accurate. Slang or informal labels appear in brackets, as do rare, archaic, or special field terms. For example:

> **di·rect** (di-rēkt′), *adj.* 1. straight; not circuitous. 2. open; straightforward. 3. of lineal descent. 4. immediate; close. 5. complete. 6. in the exact words: *v.t.* 1. to aim, turn, or point. 2. to guide or show. 3. to point out or determine with authority. 4. to address (a letter, etc.). 5. to supervise the action of (a play, motion picture, etc.): *v.i.* 1. to act as a guide. 2. to be a director: *adv.* directly. — **di·rect′ness,** *n.*

Example phrases are not given, and synonyms are not labeled but may be used as definitions. Prefixes and suffixes appear in their proper alphabetical place in the main vocabulary.

V. Syllabication and Pronunciation

Syllables are indicated by centered dots: **sew·er·age**. A pronunciation key follows the introduction, and a brief, two-line guide with examples, separated from the text by a rule, appears on the bottom of each page in the lexicon.

VI. Special Features

The gazetteer, "A Dictionary of Geography," appears following the main vocabulary, with brief, but adequate entries for cities, countries, rivers, and other features of the world. Lists of the largest cities and metropolitan areas in the United States (with 1970 population figures) are given, as is a list of principal foreign cities (with population figures that need updating).

VII. Accessibility

Bold main entry words that overhang the text, guide words at the tops of pages, and a contents page help to make the information in the dictionary accessible to the reader. However, the format, in general, is poorly designed for ease of reading.

VIII. Graphics and Format

This paperback has a cheerful bright yellow cover that will appeal to readers of all ages browsing in bookstores or at newsstands. The text, however, is printed in extremely small type, and entry words in the copy reviewed were often smudged or blurred. The diacritical marks in the pronunciations were often impossible to decipher. In addition, the poor quality of paper allows for considerable show-through of text. This dictionary is, in fact, extremely difficult to read.

The pages are very crowded, with little white space in the outer margins, between the two columns of text, or in the gutter. The print on some pages can only be read when the book is forced open by bending back the spine. This will quickly render the book unusable.

IX. Summary

There are a number of other paperback dictionaries with more up-to-date entries, better page design and printing, and more readable text than the *Webster's New School and Office Dictionary*. The narrow gutter margins that necessitate bending of the spine make it unsuitable for any library circulating paperback collection. Those who need a mass-market-size, personal paperback dictionary for quick reference should consider the Webster New World Compact School and Office Dictionary.

Webster's New Twentieth Century Dictionary

Facts at a Glance

Full Title: **Webster's New Twentieth Century Dictionary of the English Language: Unabridged, Second Edition.**
Publisher: **Prentice Hall Press.**

Editor: Jean L. McKechnie.
Edition Reviewed: © 1983.

Number of Entries: 320,000.
Number of Pages: 2,290.
Number of Illustrations: 48 pages in full color; approximately 2,100 black-and-white line drawings.
Number of Maps: 16.
Trim Size: 8½" × 11".
Binding: cloth.

Price: $79.95.
Sold in bookstores and by direct mail; also sold to libraries.
ISBN 0-671-41819-X.

I. Introduction

Webster's New Twentieth Century Dictionary of the English Language: Unabridged Second Edition is one of only three American "unabridged" dictionaries currently available. Clearly, the publisher, Prentice Hall Press, intends this volume to compete against THE RANDOM HOUSE DICTIONARY OF THE ENGLISH LANGUAGE: SECOND EDITION, UNABRIDGED, and WEBSTER'S THIRD NEW INTERNATIONAL DICTIONARY, the two leaders in this field. Prentice Hall's unabridged dictionary is intended for "the general reader"; the same can be said for its two main rivals. However, although it resembles these two books in size and format, and bears the Webster name, *Webster's New Twentieth Century* cannot be viewed as a rival to these dictionaries in the authority and currency of its content.

II. Authority

The genealogy of *Webster's New Twentieth Century Dictionary* can be traced to Noah Webster's *Compendious Dictionary of the English Language* (1806). Since that time, the dictionary has appeared under a variety of titles. The earliest date on the copyright page of the current edition is 1955; this work was long a mainstay in the list of the reputable World Publishing Company (later Collins + World, now defunct).

The current edition is published by Prentice Hall Press, a division of Simon & Schuster and a respected reference publisher. The title page notes that the work has been "extensively revised by the publisher's editorial staff under the general supervision of Jean L. McKechnie," but, contrary to the standard practice of most dictionary publishers, none of the lexicographers and editors is listed by name. Upon close inspection, it would appear that this dictionary has simply been repackaged by Prentice Hall Press, with pages reproduced from the old plates, and with min-

Webster's New Twentieth Century Dictionary of the
English Language: Unabridged

❶ Synonyms are discriminated in a
paragraph headed *Syn.* —

❷ Usage labels are enclosed in
brackets

❸ Etymology is enclosed in
brackets

❹ Inflected forms are set in regular
Roman type

çälm (käm), *n.* [Fr. *calme*; LL. *cauma*, the heat
of the sun; Gr. *kauma*, from *kaiein*, to burn;
probably from the period of rest, during mid-
day.] lack of motion, agitation, or disturb-
ance; stillness; tranquillity; quiet.
   The soul as even as a *calm.*   —Shak.
çälm, *a.*; *comp.* calmer; *superl.* calmest,   1.
still; quiet; at rest; undisturbed; not agitated;
not stormy.
   Calm is the morn without a sound.
                              —Tennyson.
   2. undisturbed by passion; not agitated or
excited; quiet; tranquil, as the mind, temper,
or attention.
   People are generally *calm* at the misfortunes
of others.   —Goldsmith.
   Syn.—tranquil, placid, quiet.—*Calm*, when
applied to the mind, implies that the person
remains unagitated, even though there may
be considerable care and anxiety; *tranquil*
implies that the mind is serene and free from
anxiety. *Quiet*, when applied to the disposition, implies that the person is naturally silent
and undemonstrative. *Placid* is nearly allied
in sense to *tranquil*, but denotes a more cheerful and settled state.
çälm, *v.t.* and *v.i.*; calmed, *pt., pp.*; calming,
ppr. to make or become calm (often with
down).
çal′må·tive, *a.* calming; soothing; sedative.
çal′må·tive, *n.* a calmative medicine.
çälm′ẽr, *n.* one who or that which calms.
çälm′ly, *adv.* in a calm manner; quietly.
çälm′ness, *n.* the state of being calm; repose.
Çal′muck, *n.* same as *Kalmuck.*
çälm′y, *a.* calm; quiet; peaceful; tranquil.
   [Poetic or Archaic.]

imal editorial changes. (The most recent date listed on the copyright page of the current edition is 1983.)

According to the introduction, "the staff was fortunate in having available for its use the resources and files of *Webster's New World Dictionary of the American Language*, an advantage which made possible the elimination of much of the back-breaking work involved in the recasting of new, up-to-date definitions." But it is difficult to tell how recent these "resources and files" are, what they consist of, and when the current edition was prepared (and by whom). In short, the evidence for authoritativeness in this dictionary is at worst weak and at best ambiguous.

III. Comprehensiveness

With 320,000 entries in 2,129 entry pages, *Webster's New Twentieth Century Dictionary* would seem to live up to the claim in the editors' introduction that readers will find most of the words that they "will ever be likely to investigate." The editors further assert that the criterion for inclusion was "the probability of usefulness to the reader." However, neither the sheer number of entries in itself nor the probability of a word's usefulness guarantees comprehensiveness. Certainly this dictionary is less comprehensive than the 470,000-entry WEBSTER'S THIRD, and although it contains about 5,000 more entries than the RANDOM HOUSE UNABRIDGED, the *New Twentieth Century Dictionary* does not attempt to be as all-inclusive as that volume.

This is not to say that the *New Twentieth Century* does not contain many words that are part of the contemporary vocabulary. For example, it does include entries for such modern terms as **samizdat**, **quadraphonic**, **glitch**, **cloning**, **urbanology**, **ecocide**, **rollover**, **nerd**, and **Watergate**. **Access** is presented as a verb, in its computer-related sense, as well as in its more traditional noun form. But there is no entry for *AIDS*, perhaps the most significant word to have entered the English language in the 1980s.

Unlike WEBSTER'S THIRD and RANDOM HOUSE UNABRIDGED, not to mention most modern abridged dictionaries, *Webster's New Twentieth Century Dictionary* does not include common, profane four-letter words. Moreover, the common slang definitions of such words as **bastard** are not included. Whether this is a deliberate choice reflecting a prescriptive attitude toward the language, or simply a sign of the dictionary's lack of currency, it is impossible to say.

Whereas the RANDOM HOUSE UNABRIDGED prides itself as a compendium of the contemporary language, *Webster's New Twentieth Century* seems most useful in defining rare, obsolete, and archaic words. For example, on one page taken at random there are individual entries for **puissance**, **puissant**, and **puissantly**, not to mention **puisne** and **puisny** (archaic terms meaning, and pronounced, "puny"). The editors defend this practice of including obsolete, archaic, and rare words with the rationale that such terms "are likely to be encountered in the earlier standard literature." However, words that are now "rare" are not always labeled as such. For example, there are eight separate entries for the word **haw**; only one sense of one of these is labeled "obsolete," but in fact many are no longer in common use.

Webster's New Twentieth Century will tell the reader what was going on when Esau **sod** porridge, what Ian Watt means when he talks about "the new **gelastics**" as a style of writing, and that **nice** once meant "very particular, fastidious, difficult to please or satisfy, very careful, refined," not to mention "ignorant, foolish, wanton, coy, shy." It will also give definitions for some contemporary terms from the fields of computers, finance, and medicine. But these are by no means as comprehensive as are those in the RANDOM HOUSE UNABRIDGED and WEBSTER'S THIRD.

IV. Quality and Currency of Entries

According to the introduction, the editors have aimed "to construct definitions that would be accurate, clear, and simple, and would yet contain sufficient information or explanatory notation so that their meanings would be thoroughly understood by the general reader." On the whole, definitions are clear, accurate, and straightforward.

Of the three unabridged dictionaries, *Webster's New Twentieth Century* is without question the most prescriptive in its approach to vocabulary and definitions. This is not a negative criticism, but simply an observation that the dictionary makes distinctions that will please the purist or anyone seeking guidance on usage. For example, the definition for **irregardless** is quite succinct: "regardless: a substandard or humorous redundancy." The first definition given for **disinterested** is "not influenced by personal interest or selfish motives; impartial; unbiased"; the word's second sense, "uninterested; indifferent," is labeled "colloquial."

Unlike virtually every other reputable dictionary, abridged as well as unabridged, *Webster's New Twentieth Century Dictionary* does not present the different senses of a word in any consistent order. Multiple definitions of a word are arranged neither in chronological order (that is, oldest definitions first) or in the order of their most common contemporary usage. The editors' introduction explains that

> any effort to arrange each entry so that the prevailing current meaning is given first is doomed to failure, since for most words there are a number of senses, on different levels and in different fields, that have equal currency. The editors have therefore allowed practicality to determine their practice. Where the historical order of senses seemed advisable, this order has been followed; where one meaning flows logically into another or others, this too has been indicated.

Not only are different senses of a word given in this way, but when a word can be used as a different part of speech, it receives a separate entry, even when the different parts of speech are closely related. This in fact inflates the number of entries in the dictionary (320,000). To take a simple example, the word **beat** appears as an entry word seven times. First it is a transitive verb with 16 different senses, the first of which is to "strike or hit repeatedly; to pound." The second entry for **beat** is as an intransitive verb with nine different senses, the first of which is "to strike, hit, or dash repeatedly and, usually, hard." The next entry shows it as a noun with 13 different senses, of which the first is "a stroke; a striking; a blow." The remaining four entries are unrelated to the first three.

By comparison, the RANDOM HOUSE UNABRIDGED goes to the opposite extreme, treating all the definitions for **beat** (it gives 58) under a single entry. WEBSTER'S THIRD NEW INTERNATIONAL follows much the same course as the *New Twentieth Century*. It gives the transitive and intransitive verb forms under one entry, the noun ("a single stroke, blow, or pulsation . . .") under another, with four more entries for unrelated meanings of the word. THE WORLD BOOK DICTIONARY, like the RANDOM HOUSE UNABRIDGED, treats all the definitions under one entry, although the different senses for each part of speech are numbered independently. It must be said that, simply as a comment on how these different arrangements affect the user, *Webster's New Twentieth Century Dictionary* is the easiest in which to look up and find the distinct senses of this word. (See also *Accessibility*.) While this arrangement may not be the most lexicographically sound, it is sensible. However, it does inflate the number of entries.

Entries generally consist of the entry word in boldface, overhanging the text, followed by an abbreviation that identifies the part of speech. This is sometimes followed by an etymology, in brackets, with the definition or definitions of the word given next. The different numbered senses of a word do not run into the text, as in the RANDOM HOUSE UNABRIDGED and WEBSTER'S THIRD, but each begins on a different line. Usage labels (such as "Dial." for dialectic and "Brit. Dial." for British dialect, "Obs." for obsolete, and "Rare" for rarely used terms) follow individual definitions where appropriate.

Occasionally, entries include illustrative quotations. Unfortunately, when these do appear they do not always seem well chosen. For example, according to *Webster's New Twentieth Century*, one of the meanings of **pique** is "to stimulate; to excite to action; to arouse; to provoke;" this definition is followed by a not very helpful quotation from the minor late-seventeenth- to early-eighteenth-century poet Matthew Prior, "*Piqued* by Protogene's fame,/From Cos to Rhodes Appelles came." Even when the quotations are from major writers, they rarely shed light on the word they are intended to clarify. What does the line "Somewhat *duller* than at first/ I sit (my empty glass reversed)," from Tennyson, tell us about the word **dull**? And what is added to the meaning of

dull as "blunt; not keen or pointed; having a thick edge" by Shakespeare's "The murderous knife was *dull* and blunt"? By comparison, quotations in WEBSTER'S THIRD are invariably more apt and give the reader a more precise context for the particular sense of the word being defined.

A number of the entries include synonym lists. For example, the entry for **defraud** gives "cheat, deceive, rob, cozen, dupe." However, there does not seem to be a rationale for including synonyms in some entries and not in others.

Where appropriate, entries may also include idiomatic phrases. The second entry for **back** (meaning "the part of the body opposite to the front", among other things) lists and defines such idioms as *behind one's back*, *to be on one's back*, and *to turn one's back on*.

The following is fairly typical of entries in *Webster's New Twentieth Century Dictionary*:

> **dē·fȳ′**, *v.t.*; defied, *pl.*, *pp.*; defying, *ppr.* [ME. *defien, diffyen*; OFr. *defier,* to distrust, repudiate, defy, from hyp. LL. *disfidare,* from L. *dis–,* from, and *fidus,* faithful.]
> **1.** to repudiate; to recoil from. [Obs.]
> **2.** to challenge (someone) to a fight; to provoke by daring a combat. [Archaic.]
> > I once again
> > *Defy* thee to the trial of mortal fight.
> > —Milton
> **3.** to dare (someone) to do or prove something.
> **4.** to brave; to offer to hazard a conflict by resisting or opposing boldly or openly; as, to *defy* the arguments of an opponent.
> **5.** to resist completely; to baffle; to foil.

Unavoidably, technical words are sometimes defined in technical terms that may be beyond the comprehension of the average reader. For example, the dictionary defines **aardwolf** as "a digitigrade, carnivorous quadruped, *Proteles lalandi*, of South Africa, somewhat like the hyena and the civet." Generally, however, definitions will be comprehensible to the adult reader.

V. Syllabication and Pronunciation

Syllabication is indicated by primary and secondary accent marks and by centered dots in the boldface entry word. Stress marks and pronunciation symbols are also incorporated into the entry word. Where necessary, pronunciation is indicated by respelling in parentheses immediately following the entry word, as are any alternative pronunciations.

Webster's New Twentieth Century Dictionary uses a unique system of letters and diacritical marks to indicate pronunciation. Among the unusual features of this system is the use of a dot under double *o* as in mọọn, fọọd, etc., rather than the usual long vowel

mark (moon). The hard *c* sound (as in *cat*) is written ç; the *shun* sound in such words as nation, tension, mortician, Melanesian, and Martian is written as *tion*, *sion*, *ciăn*, *siăn*, and *tiăn*, respectively. In other words, the phonetic key depends not only upon the pronunciation of the word but also upon its spelling. This system is not difficult to follow, but it will be confusing at first for readers who are familiar with other, more prevalent, systems.

A brief, helpful pronunciation guide is included at the bottom of every page.

VI. Special Features

The introductory matter includes a four-page "Outline History of the English Language," a brief overview in essay form by linguist Harold Whitehall. The essay is headed by a chart that traces the various branches of the Indo-European language family. Whitehall addresses orthography and pronunciation, vocabulary, and grammar and morphology, although he omits post-1475 English, finding "the varied and flexible instrument used by Shakespeare, Milton, and eventually, by ourselves . . . altogether too gigantic to be compressed neatly into mnemonic schedules."

Nineteen "supplements," many of which are fairly common in abridged as well as unabridged dictionaries, are found in the back of *Webster's New Twentieth Century Dictionary*. Among these are biographical and geographical dictionaries, a dictionary of foreign words and phrases, forms of address, tables of weights and measures, and special signs and symbols. The "Pronouncing Dictionary of Biography" lists some 6,000 names, each with a brief identification and dates. This section would seem to be better on ancient figures than on modern, although it appears to have been updated through 1978. Nevertheless, it is by no means comprehensive, and many readers will quibble with some of the inclusions and omissions. The list of "Principal Geographic Features of the World" is not entirely up-to-date.

The Declaration of Independence and the U.S. Constitution are printed in their entirety. However, as these documents are readily available in other reference sources, their presence here does not really add much to this dictionary.

The dictionary also includes two 16-page sections of color plates; the first of these is located in the "g" section, the second in the "r." Each plate covers aspects of a particular subject, such as airplanes, human anatomy, cats, state flowers, styles of painting, the solar system, and state flags. The realistic color illustrations are competent, but one wonders why certain subjects have been covered and others excluded.

A 16-page color atlas section features Hammond maps. Several of the maps, however, are out of date.

For example, the two-page Africa map shows the *Central African Empire*, not the *Central African Republic*; *Upper Volta*, not *Burkina Faso*, and *Rhodesia* (with *Zimbabwe* in smaller type in parentheses), and *Salisbury*, not *Harare*. One does not select a dictionary for its maps, but these do not do much to enhance this dictionary; those in the RANDOM HOUSE UNABRIDGED are larger, more detailed, and more current.

VII. Accessibility

Because of their physical size and the sheer number of entries and amount of information that they contain, unabridged dictionaries as a rule appear more difficult to access than are abridged dictionaries. However, the editors of *Webster's New Twentieth Century Dictionary* have used fairly standard dictionary form in arranging the information, and this volume is not nearly as difficult to use as it might at first appear. Guide words at the top left and right of each page indicate the first and last entry words on that page. Entry words, in boldface type and overhanging the text, are easy to locate on the page.

The fact that the different senses of an entry word are defined in no particular order (that is, neither chronologically nor by most common current use) can cause a good deal of confusion for readers who are used to dictionaries in which a particular order is followed.

VIII. Graphics and Format

Like its major competitors, *Webster's New Twentieth Century Dictionary* makes use of black-and-white line drawings to supplement its entries. With some 2,100 altogether, or an average of one per page, this dictionary is less profusely illustrated than any of its rivals. Many of its pages have no illustrations at all; others may have from one to four. The editors' claim that they have selected illustrations that show the function, relative size, and actual appearance of the item is occasionally given the laugh: the cod (*Gadus morrhua*), for example, is displayed against a background of mountains and clouds with a gull in the distance. By any measure, the illustrations in this dictionary are far inferior to those in THE WORLD BOOK DICTIONARY. However, the drawings are almost always inserted at the word or sense of a word that they are intended to illustrate.

The book is physically well-designed. Typefaces are easy to read and the print large for an unabridged dictionary—superior to that of WEBSTER'S THIRD if not the RANDOM HOUSE UNABRIDGED. The paper is rougher and thicker than in most dictionaries but is white, with minimal show-through. Margins (including the gutter margins) are reasonably wide, indentations are well used, and there is sufficient white space on the page. The binding, a plasticized coating over cardboard, is far less sturdy than that of the competing volumes, but seems reasonably durable and makes this the most lightweight of the unabridged dictionaries. It will probably withstand normal library use for several years.

IX. Summary

Webster's New Twentieth Century Dictionary is distinctly old-fashioned, containing a higher proportion of archaic and obsolete words and definitions than either WEBSTER'S THIRD INTERNATIONAL or the RANDOM HOUSE UNABRIDGED. It also takes a decidedly prescriptive approach to vocabulary and usage. Those who find the RANDOM HOUSE UNABRIDGED (and WEBSTER'S THIRD, for that matter) too trendy or permissive in its approach to the English language will find much to admire in *Webster's New Twentieth Century Dictionary*.

However, this dictionary's claims to be up-to-date are exaggerated. The 1983 revision seems to have involved little more than adding a few new words and rewriting some definitions, and the results do not make this dictionary modern or innovative. In technical fields, especially, it falls behind even most contemporary collegiate dictionaries.

More significantly, it is far less authoritative than WEBSTER'S THIRD INTERNATIONAL, which lists for the same price. There is no attempt at consistency in the way definitions are ordered, a flaw that would seem to act against this work's otherwise prescriptive approach and that will certainly cause confusion for the general reader.

Given the fact that it competes against two impressive, authoritative, and up-to-date (if imperfect) unabridged dictionaries, $79.95 seems rather a high price to pay for *Webster's New Twentieth Century Dictionary*, and this title cannot be considered as a first choice for dictionaries in this category. Libraries really need not consider it at all. Most individuals will be served as well or better by a good abridged dictionary such as the AMERICAN HERITAGE DICTIONARY: SECOND COLLEGE EDITION or WEBSTER'S NINTH NEW COLLEGIATE DICTIONARY. Those who desire an authoritative, comprehensive dictionary that covers rare and archaic words will probably want to splurge on THE COMPACT EDITION OF THE OXFORD ENGLISH DICTIONARY.

Webster's New World Compact Dictionary of American English

Facts at a Glance

Full Title: **Webster's New World Compact Dictionary of American English**.
Publisher: Prentice Hall Press.

Editor: David B. Guralnik, Editor-in-Chief.
Edition Reviewed: © 1981; fifth printing.

Number of Entries: over 38,000.
Number of Pages: 630.
Trim Size: 3″ × 4½″.
Binding: paperback.

Price: $4.95.
Sold in bookstores; also sold to libraries and other educational institutions.
ISBN 0-671-41802-5.

I. Introduction

According to its preface, *Webster's New World Compact Dictionary of American English* is intended for those people who "need a simple, accurate, modern aid to a sound working knowledge of the language." Of the more than 38,000 entries, about 22,000 are main entries.

II. Authority

The editors based this compact dictionary on WEBSTER'S NEW WORLD DICTIONARY OF THE AMERICAN LANGUAGE: SECOND COLLEGE EDITION. The parent dictionary, also edited by David B. Guralnik, is well recognized as an authoritative dictionary.

III. Comprehensiveness

In addition to commonly used words, the preface states that the dictionary "contains hundreds of newer terms and newer senses of established terms not to be found in other dictionaries of similar scope." And indeed, such words as **ICBM**, **closed circuit**, **hardware** (the computer-related definition), and **zero population growth** are included; but *floppy disc* and *database*, for example, are not. When slang is used, the definition is coded, as in: "**croak 2.** [Sl.] die."

IV. Quality and Currency of Entries

The definitions have been reduced to the minimum number of words possible that still allow for clarity. Many abbreviations, prefixes, and suffixes are listed in the lexicon, and idiomatic phrases are found in the definitions. Parts of speech are abbreviated and are found just following the main entry. Many colloquialisms are identified. Parts of speech are not given for foreign terms such as **bon jour** or for abbreviations such as **AM** and **A.M.** Examples of these very brief definitions are:

> **liberal arts** literature, philosophy, history, etc.
> **lib′er·al′i·ty** *n.* [*pl.* -TIES] **1.** generosity **2.** tolerance
> **lib′er·al·ize′** *v.* make or become liberal

Words or terms requiring more than a descriptive word or phrase are given longer definitions.

> **Lent** *n.* period of 40 weekdays before Easter.

As previously mentioned, many new words and phrases have been included, although there are omissions that size alone cannot explain, for example: the verb **program**, in the sense of planning a computer program for, is included, while no verb form for **access** appears at all.

V. Syllabication and Pronunciation

Syllabication is indicated by dots and bold and light stresses between syllables in the main entry word. An abbreviated pronunciation key is provided just prior to the guide to the use of the dictionary, but pronunciations (in parentheses) are given infrequently—only when deemed necessary.

VI. Special Features

There are 21 pages appended to the dictionary that provide a variety of useful information; abbreviations; information on countries and the United States; national parks of the United States; the presidents of the United States; and weights and measures.

VII. Accessibility

Entry words are arranged alphabetically, letter-by-letter. Guide words at the top of each column indicate the first and last words appearing on each page. Meanings within definitions are numbered in bold print.

VIII. Graphics and Format

Main entries overhang the definitions and are easy to find. The main entry and subentry words and part-of-speech abbreviations are in bold print. Each page contains two columns separated by a vertical black rule. There are no illustrations. The book is small and has an inch-thick spine. The flexible cover is covered with strong reinforced paper.

IX. Summary

This small dictionary is more useful than many others. It contains numerous new terms, and it provides slang and colloquial meanings for many of the words. However, the limited size necessarily limits the number of main entries and the depth and completeness of the definitions. Thus, while this is acceptable as a personal quick reference dictionary, public libraries should probably pass this one up.

Webster's New World Compact School and Office Dictionary

Facts at a Glance

Full Title: **Webster's New World Compact School and Office Dictionary**.
Publisher: Prentice Hall Press.
Editor: David B. Guralnik, Editor-in-Chief.
Edition Reviewed: © 1982; 12th printing.

Number of Entries: 56,000.
Number of Pages: 540.
Trim Size: 5¼" × 8".
Bindings: cloth; paperback.

Prices: $8.95 (cloth); $5.95 (paperback).
Sold in bookstores and other outlets; also sold to libraries and other educational institutions.
ISBN 0-671-41822-X (cloth);
ISBN 0-671-44882-X (paperback).

I. Introduction

As the title suggests, this is a condensed version of the WEBSTER'S NEW WORLD DICTIONARY: SECOND COLLEGE EDITION intended for use in the home, office, and the classroom. The 56,000 entries are about average size for smaller dictionaries of this type, but its physical format is somewhat larger than the typical "pocket" dictionary. According to the foreword, the words entered have been carefully selected to include all the commonly used words that make up the basic vocabulary of English. In addition, the foreword states that many frequently encountered specialized terms are listed as well as abbreviations, foreign words, and phrases.

II. Authority

The primary authority for this work is WEBSTER'S NEW WORLD DICTIONARY: SECOND COLLEGE EDITION, originally published jointly by William Collins and World Publishing, with the well-known lexicographer, David B. Guralnik, as Editor-in-Chief. According to the editor, the database for the dictionary was created and maintained by the publisher's own lexicographic staff. Many printers use the WEBSTER'S NEW WORLD system of hyphenation (for end-of-line word breaks) as a standard, which may be of special interest to editors, typists, and compositors.

III. Comprehensiveness

The *Webster's New World Compact School and Office Dictionary* gives brief etymological notes, but they are not nearly as detailed as in the parent work.

As a rule only the last language prior to a word's entrance into English is noted. The practice of marking Americanisms is not used in the compact edition, as it is in the college edition. The use of a double dagger signifies a foreign word, such as **maitre d'hôtel,** but **faux pas** is not marked because it has become a part of standard English.

Biographical and geographical names are omitted from the main alphabetical listing of words. However, some personal names are included, such as Greek and Roman gods and goddesses, including **Poseidon** (Greek) and **Jupiter** (Roman). There are a surprising number of literary figures included for a compact dictionary; **Faust**, **Juliet** and **Ali Baba** are examples of only a few.

Other features are the inclusion of parts of speech, usually abbreviated and in boldface type. Few slang terms are to be found in the dictionary, but there are quite a number of abbreviations.

IV. Quality and Currency of Entries

Main entry words are in letter-by-letter alphabetical order. Definitions are easy to understand and brief, but not so brief as to be almost meaningless, which is often the case with small dictionaries. They would be appropriate for high school and bright junior high school students as well as college students and adults. Occasionally an archaic word turns up, such as **yclept**, **ycleped** meaning "to call." **Yarmulke** or **yarmalke**, the skull cap worn by Jewish men, is included, but for the most part the words in this dictionary are those known by almost any well-read college graduate. A few current words are included, such as **videocassette**, but *futon* and *byte*, for example, are not in the dictionary.

Two, three, and sometimes more meanings are given for many words. When there is more than one meaning, they appear in chronological order, as in the parent volume. Meanings under the main entry words are separated by boldface Arabic numerals. The entry for **gauge** is an example of the definitions provided in this dictionary:

> **gauge** . . . **1.** a standard measure **2.** any device for measuring **3.** the distance between the rails of a railway **4.** the size of the bore of a shotgun—*vt.* **gauged, gauging 1.** to measure the size, amount, etc. of **2.** to estimate; judge . . .

A comparison of the number of definitions for **gauge** with the *Second College Edition* shows that there are 13 in the latter including a number of specialized meanings for the noun, and six meanings for the verbs. There are few specialized entries or meanings in the *Compact School and Office Dictionary* in spite of the claims made in the dictionary foreword. Homographs are given separate, numbered entries.

V. Syllabication and Pronunciation

Pronunciation and syllabication are given immediately following the entry word and appear in parentheses. The key to pronunciation appears on the inside of the front cover; it follows the same format as the parent dictionary but excludes a key to foreign sounds. Along with the key are a few explanatory notes on some of the more complex symbols from the International Phonetic Alphabet (IPA). The print on this page is not as crisp as it should be, and some symbols such as *ch*, *zh*, and *g* (the nasal sound of the *-ng* in *sing*) and the like are blurred. There are no abbreviated pronunciation keys at the bottom of the pages of the lexicon, which is something of a disadvantage for readers who may seek pronunciation guidance for unfamiliar words.

Syllables in the main entry words and run-on entries are separated by black dots. Heavy accent marks indicate the stressed syllable, and a lighter accent mark indicates secondary stress. For example: **coronation** is pronounced

(kôr′ ə nā′shən).

VI. Special Features

Webster's New World Compact School and Office Dictionary has a number of special lists and tables appended to the back of the book. These include tables of weights and measures with a separate table of metrics and notes on how to convert U.S. measures to metric. There is a three-page manual on the correct use of punctuation marks that may be useful to students and others. Less useful is a list of presidents and vice presidents of the United States (including Reagan and Bush) giving their dates of office, a five-page dictionary of geographical entries, and brief lists of principal cities of the United States (with 1980 census population figures) and foreign countries.

VII. Accessibility

Main entry words are in letter-by-letter alphabetical order. The boldface entries overhang the text which is printed in two columns of readable text. Compared to many small dictionaries, the pages of *Webster's New World Compact* are clearly designed and hence the words are very easy to locate. There are no thumb guides, but none are really needed. Paired guide words at the top of double-column pages facilitate thumbing through the dictionary.

Alternate spellings of words are provided such as **catalog** and **catalogue**. When the alternate spelling of a word falls some distance away in the alphabet, a cross-reference is used, such as "**kerb** . . . *Brit. sp.* of CURB (n.3)." In this way, the reader is referred

from a British spelling of the word to the third meaning under the main entry **curb**, which is the stone or concrete curbing along a street. Words derived from the formation of other English words are also noted, such as **movie** which clearly shows the word's derivation in bold brackets following the part of speech:

[<MOVING PICTURE] a motion picture.

VIII. Graphics and Format

There are no illustrations in this dictionary; given its size and purpose, they would serve little use. The typeface is clear, but the margins are very narrow. Page 350 of the review copy had a skewed margin so that it almost ran off the edge of the paper. In spite of its somewhat larger size for a compact dictionary, this paperback does not lie flat when opened, but it has an extra sturdy binding. Although it could not be rebound, the price is modest so it can be easily replaced.

IX. Summary

Webster's New World Compact School and Office Dictionary is a handy quick reference guide to words, their spelling, pronunciation, and meanings, as well as their parts of speech. The appended materials are for the most part useful, and although limited; the dictionary of geography can be an aid to the correct spelling of place names. In addition, it has a more readable, less cluttered format than many paperback dictionaries. Although mostly useful for home reference, this could be purchased for circulation in public libraries.

Webster's New World Dictionary of the American Language

Facts at a Glance

Full Title: **Webster's New World Dictionary of the American Language**.
Publisher: Warner Books.
Editor: David B. Guralnik.
Edition Reviewed: © 1984.

Number of Entries: over 59,000.
Number of Pages: 696.
Number of Illustrations: over 200 black-and-white drawings.
Trim Size: 4¼″ × 7″.
Binding: paperback.

Price: $3.95.
Sold in bookstores and other outlets.
ISBN 0-446-31449-8.

I. Introduction

This abridged, illustrated pocket-size dictionary contains over 59,000 entries. According to the foreword, the editors' intent was "to incorporate as much useful information as possible within the available space." This work therefore includes "illustrative examples . . . , idiomatic expressions, affixes and combining forms, and other features not generally included in a paperback dictionary of this size." Among other unusual features is the inclusion of brief etymologies for most entries. A revised edition, the work includes "thousands of new terms and newer senses of established terms not found in the first edition."

II. Authority

The 1984 dictionary is an expansion and updating of a paperback dictionary first published in 1958. The current edition is based on WEBSTER'S NEW WORLD DICTIONARY: SECOND COLLEGE EDITION, first published in 1970. The work was prepared under the supervision of the Editor-in-Chief, David B. Guralnik, by members of the permanent staff that developed the *Second College Edition*. Their selection of entry words was determined on the basis of the word's "frequency of occurrence within our vast citation file and from various word-count lists."

III. Comprehensiveness

The dictionary is unusually comprehensive for a volume of its size. In addition to many new words added during revision, the work incorporates selected biographical and geographical entries. Biographical entries are provided for a number of historical figures, such as **Napoleon I, Carry Nation**, and **José de San Martín**. The geographical entries include world countries (with area, location, and population); major cities of the world and U.S. cities of over 100,000 inhabitants (with location and population); and other geographical landmarks. The date of the population figures is not indicated. Common abbreviations also appear as main entries. For example, **ERA** is defined both as "earned run average" in baseball and as "Equal Rights Amendment." Abbreviations listed include those for U.S. states, government agencies, chemical elements, and many others.

Brief etymologies are provided for most entries. Inflected forms are noted when they are irregular or might cause spelling difficulties. Also provided are usage labels with such identifications as slang, colloquial, archaic, poetic, dialectic, and British. Run-in entries are provided only when their meaning is readily understood on the basis of the main entry word's meaning.

Definitions of various prefixes, suffixes, and combining forms are also noted as separate entries, and lists of compound words are occasionally subsumed under affixes. For example, 64 compound words are listed under the prefix **in-** (meaning "no, not, without, non-"). Synonyms and antonyms are not provided in the dictionary. However, this omission does not detract from the volume's overall comprehensiveness and usefulness to students and adults.

IV. Quality and Currency of Entries

In general, the foreword's claim that the work provides "clear but brief" definitions is accurate. The definitions also succeed in making subtle distinctions when necessary. Multiple meanings of a word and separate entries for homographs are typically given. For example, each of the words **fast**, **mint**, **mark**, **press**, **maroon**, and **ball** has two separate entries; **desert** and **row** have three apiece; and **bay** has five. Most of these entries offer more than one sense of the word.

Each of the multiple senses in an entry is introduced by a boldface numeral. Slang and colloquialisms are given after more standard senses of the word and are identified with bracketed labels. Although the dictionary's obvious space limitations preclude the use of whole sentences to illustrate meanings, bracketed illustrative phrases occasionally appear to clarify distinctions among a word's senses. For example, the sense of **fast** as "nonfading" is clarified by the inclusion of the phrase "[*fast* colors]," and the meaning "ahead of time" is exemplified by "[a *fast* watch]." A representative entry is:

> **fat** (fat) *adj.* **fat′ter, fat′test** [OE. *fætt*] **1.** containing fat; oily **2.** *a)* fleshy; plump *b)* too plump **3.** thick; broad **4.** fertile [*fat* land] **5.** profitable [a *fat* job] **6.** plentiful —*n.* **1.** an oily or greasy material found in animal tissue and plant seeds **2.** the richest part of anything **3.** superfluous part — **chew the fat** [Slang] to chat — **fat′ly** *adv.* — **fat′ness** *n.*

The entries' incorporation of multiple meanings and useful distinction among them make the dictionary especially valuable.

The dictionary is current in its inclusion of new words and new senses. Among the entries are such technical and popular terms as **afterburner**, **AIDS**, **database**, **gay** (homosexual), **palimony**, **program** (computer sense), **videodisc**, **Watergate**, and **word processing**.

V. Syllabication and Pronunciation

Syllabication is indicated in main entry words by centered dots and, for words whose pronunciation is given in shortened form, by centered dots and stress marks. Pronunciation is given in parentheses immediately following the entry word; it is omitted or abbreviated for some compound main entry words. For example, pronunciation is given for **soft**, but not for such successive entries as **softball** and **soft sell**. For **software**, pronunciation appears as (-wer′).

A phonemic key appears in the introductory "Guide to the Use of the Dictionary," and an abbreviated pronunciation key appears at the bottom of all right-hand pages. This feature is not always provided in comparable dictionaries, and it will be useful to students. Although standard American English pronunciation is emphasized, some entries also provide variant pronunciations. For example, variant pronunciations are offered for **February** (feb′rə wer′ē, feb′yoo-), **boundary** (bound′drē, -dər ē), and **octave** (äk′tiv, -tāv). In most cases, the form given first is that most frequently used by American English speakers. Readers will find the inclusion of acceptable regional variants helpful.

VI. Special Features

The volume's introductory "Guide to the Use of the Dictionary" is clearly written and detailed and will be useful to students. It is followed by a list of abbreviations used in the dictionary.

VII. Accessibility

The dictionary's entries are alphabetized letter by letter. At the top of each page appear two boldface guide words, indicating the first and last entries on the page. These guide words are helpfully printed in larger type than that used for the entries. Alternative spellings of entry words are easily found. When they are alphabetically close, they are given in boldface after the main entry word (**theater, theatre**). When they are not close (**aegis** and **egis**), cross-references in small capitals are provided from the less to the more frequently used.

VIII. Graphics and Format

Over 200 black-and-white line drawings are spread through the entire volume, so several pages can be turned before an illustration appears. These drawings tend to look cramped on the page, and the decision to illustrate one entry as opposed to another seems arbitrary. For example, **cogwheel** is pictured, but on the same page **colander**, which is equally hard to visualize, is not illustrated. The work's illustrations will be of minimal use to its readers.

The print in this dictionary is quite small, and the entries themselves seem cramped on the page. Although the generous gutter margin makes the pages more readable, the book does not lie flat and is cum-

bersome to hold. The binding also tends to tear when the book is pressed open, which means that this dictionary cannot withstand heavy use.

IX. Summary

Webster's New World Dictionary of the American Language is a large-size paperback distinguished by the quality and comprehensiveness of its entries. Its lexicon is more extensive than those of the leading mass-market paperback dictionaries, including THE AMERICAN HERITAGE DICTIONARY, THE MERRIAM-WEBSTER DICTIONARY, THE SCRIBNER-BANTAM DICTIONARY, and WEBSTER'S II NEW RIVERSIDE DICTIONARY. On the other hand, the book is physically cumbersome, has small print and cluttered pages, and suffers from poor illustrations.

All in all, however, it remains a good buy for individuals who need a paperback desk dictionary. It also merits a place in the public library's paperback reference collection.

Webster's New World Dictionary of the American Language: The Concise Edition

Facts at a Glance

Full Title: **Webster's New World Dictionary of the American Language: The Concise Edition.**

Alternative Title: The 100,000 Entry Edition: Webster's New World Dictionary of the American Language.

Former Title: Webster's New World Dictionary: The Concise Edition.

Publisher: New American Library.

Editor: David B. Guralnik.

Edition Reviewed: © 1971.

Number of Entries: 100,000.
Number of Pages: 882.
Number of Illustrations: over 600 black-and-white drawings.
Trim Size: 5½″ × 8½″.
Binding: paperback.

Price: $8.50.
Sold in bookstores and other outlets; also sold to libraries and other educational institutions.
ISBN 0-452-00886-7.

I. Introduction

This paperback edition of *Webster's New World Dictionary of the American Language: The Concise Edition* is based on and includes material from the 1970 edition of WEBSTER'S NEW WORLD DICTIONARY: SECOND COLLEGE EDITION. The foreword indicates that the work came into being as a result of "the warm reception given its predecessor, the College Edition," and that it is designed for "professional and business people, secondary-school students, office workers, new speakers of English, and others who want a comprehensive and contemporary dictionary but who have less need for the extensive etymologies, highly technical terms, many rare and obsolete senses, and certain other features found in the College Edition." The jacket copy states that this is "a special edition for the college student . . . ." It has 100,000 entries, making it more inclusive than WEBSTER'S NEW WORLD DICTIONARY OF THE AMERICAN LANGUAGE, which is also based on WEBSTER'S NEW WORLD DICTIONARY: SECOND COLLEGE EDITION.

II. Authority

The dictionary was prepared under the supervision of David B. Guralnik, general editor. The permanent lexicographic staff that developed WEBSTER'S NEW WORLD DICTIONARY: SECOND COLLEGE EDITION, helped to prepare the work. Entries were selected "on the basis of how frequently they occur in contemporary newspapers, magazines, and general books of fiction and nonfiction."

III. Comprehensiveness

Many entries include idiomatic phrases. For example, under **house** are listed **bring down the house**, **keep house**, **on the house**, and **set** (or **put**) **one's house in order**. Under **snap** appear **not a snap** ("not at all"), **snap (a person's) head off**, **snap one's fingers at**, and **snap out of it**. Although some of these idioms are no longer current, their inclusion is generally an asset, especially for students and non-native American English speakers.

The word list includes a limited number of biographical and geographical entries. Their currency is limited by the work's 1971 date; population figures provided for U.S. cities are based on the 1970 census. Also incorporated into the word list are abbreviations for chemical elements, U.S. states, government agencies, academic degrees, and many others. Foreign words and phrases often used in an English context are included and identified with a double dagger (‡). For example, entries are provided for **auf Wiedersehen**, **fait accompli**, and **quid pro quo**. Obsolete and archaic terms are included only if they are frequently found in the Bible or in standard literary works.

Most entries include brief etymologies, which the editor believes "help one to a clearer understanding of the current meaning of these words." Some entries

include illustrative phrases. Derived forms appear within entries when they are easily understood on the basis of the entry word's meaning. When inflected forms are irregular or potential spelling problems, these are provided. Specialized usage is identified with field labels, such as *in chemistry*, *in medicine*. Usage labels identify colloquialisms, slang, obsolete and archaic terms, poetic diction, dialect, and Briticisms.

IV. Quality and Currency of Entries

Each boldface main entry word is followed by pronunciation in parentheses and an italicized part-of-speech abbreviation. Where provided, the word's etymology follows, in brackets. The dictionary's definitions are concise, and multiple senses receive good coverage. Each sense is numbered, and illustrative phrases often enhance the clarification of distinct senses. Senses are ordered from the earliest in use to most recent. A representative entry begins as follows:

> **com·mand** (kə-mand′, -mänd′), v.t. [<OFr. <LL. <L. com-. intens. + mandare, to commit], 1. to give an order to; direct with authority. 2. to have authority over; control. 3. to have and be able to use: as, to command a large vocabulary. 4. to deserve and get; require as due: as, his knowledge commands respect. 5. to control (a position); overlook. v.i. to be in authority or control; act as commander.

The foreword indicates that the editors have made an effort to provide coverage of words recently introduced into the language. However, the work's 1971 date limits its currency. The foreword's examples of newer words—**desegregation**, **automation**, **einsteinium**—are no longer highly topical or unfamiliar. The word list includes such such terms as **analog computer**, **digital computer**, **program** (computer sense), **spacecraft**, and **space station**. However, among the words excluded are *byte*, *file* (computer sense), *gay* (homosexual), and *videocassette*.

V. Syllabication and Pronunciation

Syllabication is indicated in main entry words by centered dots and, in inflected forms, by centered dots or stress marks. Pronunciation is given in parentheses after the main entry word. When that word recurs in a subsequent entry or in a phrase or hyphenated compound, the pronunciation is not repeated. A full key to pronunciation appears in the introductory "Guide to the Use of the Dictionary," and an abbreviated key is helpfully provided at the bottom of all right-hand pages.

The pronunciations given are "those observed among literate speakers of General American English." Regional variants are provided for some words, such as greasy (grēs'i, grēz'i) and route (ro͞ot, rout). The form listed first is the one more frequently used, in most cases.

VI. Special Features

The volume's "Guide to the Use of the Dictionary" is clear and detailed and will be useful to students. It is followed by a list of abbreviations and symbols used in the dictionary. At the back of the work, several other special features are appended. A seven-page list of common given names provides pronunciation, language of origin, and meaning. Other features contribute substantively to the dictionary's value as a reference source. These include a chart of forms of address; tables of weights and measures; signs and symbols used in such fields as astronomy, biology, and commerce; a brief guide to punctuation; and a chart of the Indo-European family of languages.

VII. Accessibility

Two boldface guide words appear at the top of each page, indicating the first and last entries on the page; they are helpfully printed in larger type than that used for the entries. A table of contents lists all special features and ensures that they will not be overlooked. When alternative spellings are alphabetically close, they appear in boldface together at the beginning of the entry (**theater, theatre**). When they are not close (**aegis** and **egis**), each is entered separately, and the less common form is cross-referenced to the more common.

VIII. Graphics and Format

The black-and-white line drawings that illustrate the work are small, and the poor printing often obscures even the little detail they attempt to portray. For example, the four labels for the drawing of a flintlock are unreadable. The illustrations appear next to their entries; they are captioned with main entry words and, at times, additional information, such as sizes for pictures of animals. In most cases, the drawings add little to the definitions.

The dictionary's print is small and cramped on the page, but readability is enhanced by the use of boldface main entry words that overhang the text. When the spine is cracked the book lies flat, and the pages do not separate easily from the binding. The book will hold up better than most paperbacks to heavy use.

IX. Summary

Webster's New World Dictionary of the American Language was a valuable reference source when it appeared in 1971. Its definitions remain clear and detailed, and it provides a wide range of linguistic information, including etymology and usage and field labels. However, it is now significantly outdated; the poor illustrations and graphics are additional drawbacks. Although it is an unusually sturdy paperback, its shelf life is limited.

A preferable alternative for many readers and for library acquisitions is THE CONCISE AMERICAN HERITAGE DICTIONARY. This work is not as current as its 1980 date would suggest, and it comprises just over half the entries contained in the work reviewed here. On the other hand, the book is a hardcover volume, well illustrated, exceptionally easy to read, and less expensive than this paperback edition of *Webster's New World Dictionary*.

Webster's New World Dictionary of the American Language: Second College Edition

Facts at a Glance

Full Title: **Webster's New World Dictionary of the American Language: Second College Edition**.
Publisher: Prentice Hall Press.
Editors: David B. Guralnik, Editor-in-Chief; Samuel Solomon, Mitford M. Mathews, and William E. Umbach.
Edition Reviewed: © 1986.

Number of Entries: 160,000.
Number of Pages: 1,728.
Number of Illustrations: 1,300 black-and-white drawings.
Trim Size: 7⅜" × 9".
Binding: cloth.

Price: $16.95 thumb-indexed; $15.95 plain.
Sold in bookstores and other outlets; also sold to libraries and other educational institutions.
ISBN 0-671-41809-2 (thumb-indexed);
ISBN 0-671-41807-6 (plain).

I. Introduction

Webster's New World Dictionary of the American Language: Second College Edition is the revised second edition of a work of the same title, which was first published in 1953. The second edition initially appeared in 1970, and the work has been updated biennially. As one of four major American abridged "college" dictionaries, *Webster's New World* competes directly against THE AMERICAN HERITAGE DICTIONARY: SECOND COLLEGE EDITION, THE RANDOM HOUSE COLLEGE DICTIONARY, REVISED

Webster's New World Dictionary of the American Language: Second College Edition

❶ Field labels are italicized

❷ Syllabication is shown by centered dots

❸ Synonyms are discriminated in a separate paragraph introduced by the boldface italic abbreviation *SYN.*

❹ Examples of usage are enclosed in italic brackets, with the word being illustrated set in italics

❺ Etymology is enclosed in brackets

❻ Inflected forms are given in boldface type

❼ Usage labels are enclosed in brackets

❽ Cross-references appear in small capitals

❾ Antonyms are listed following the boldface italic abbreviation *ANT.*

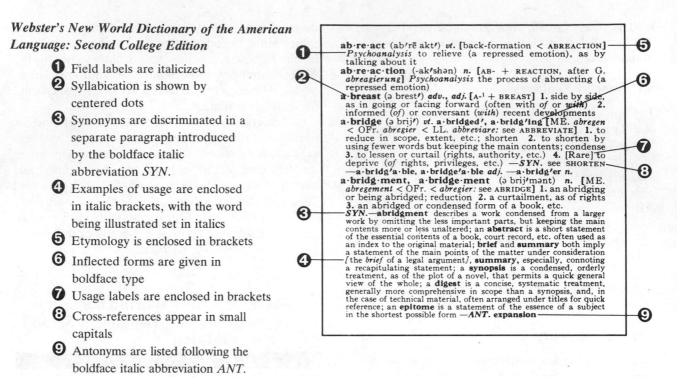

EDITION, and WEBSTER'S NINTH NEW COLLEGIATE DICTIONARY.

Defined by its publisher as "the world's most up-to-date and authoritative desk dictionary," the work contains 160,000 entries. The revised edition contains more than 20,000 new words reflecting current usage. The publisher believes the work to be the most comprehensive source among college dictionaries for Americanisms: it "identifies more than 14,000 words and meanings that first became part of the English language in the United States." The work is also the first general dictionary to explain the origins of American geographical names.

II. Authority

The dictionary is published by Prentice Hall Press, a division of Simon & Schuster. Many outstanding writers, language scholars, and expert subject consultants contributed to the work. David B. Guralnik, Editor-in-Chief, has had a long and distinguished career as a lexicographer and publishing executive, first at World Publishing and more recently at Simon & Schuster. Other editorial luminaries include Samuel Solomon, Mitford M. Mathews, and William E. Umbach. Mathews is well known as the editor of the *Dictionary of Americanisms*.

III. Comprehensiveness

The work is highly comprehensive in its inclusion of new words and of American place names and other Americanisms, identified by stars preceding the entry word or one or more of its senses. Words identified as Americanisms include **bonanza**, **carrying**

charge, **cuchifrito**, **Fletcherism**, **liftoff**, and **released time**. The date of entry into the language is not noted, but sometimes additional historical information is given. For example, under **Cooper's hawk** appears a bracketed note that the bird was named after William Cooper, a nineteenth-century ornithologist. Many students will find this feature of the dictionary interesting and enriching.

Foreign words are included and are signaled by a double dagger (‡); for example, ‡ **mirabile dictu**. Abbreviations are incorporated into the main word list, as are biographical and geographical entries. Biographical entries are sufficiently current to include **Ronald Reagan**. They provide dates, a brief note of identification, and other names by which the figure was known. For example, the entry for **De La Warr** appears as follows:

> Baron (*Thomas West*) 1577–1618; 1st Eng. colonial governor of Virginia (1610–11); called *Lord Delaware*.

Geographical entries include countries, major cities, mountains, lakes, rivers, and other geographical landmarks. Information given includes location; date admitted to the Union (for U.S. states), capital city and area in square miles (for states and countries); and population. Also given for U.S. states are traditional and postal abbreviations and origins of the state name. Population figures are as up-to-date as one would expect to find in a dictionary and more recent than those provided in a well-known almanac, but their dates are not specified in the volume. A representative entry for a U.S. state is that given for **Vermont**:

[< Fr. *Verd Mont* (1647), green mountain] New England State of the U.S.; admitted, 1791; 9,609 sq. mi.; pop. 511,000; cap. Montpelier; abbrev. **Vt., VT—Ver·mont′er** *n.*

Usage labels helpfully identify slang, colloquialisms, and other restricted usages. Field labels, such as *Linguis.* (linguistics) and *Baseball*, identify other special senses. Synonyms are provided for many entries, and they are carefully and usefully discriminated. For example, the synonym paragraph under **error** begins as follows:

> **Syn.—error** implies deviation from truth, accuracy, correctness, right, etc. and is the broadest term in this comparison [an *error* in judgment, in computation, etc.]; **mistake** suggests an error resulting from carelessness, inattention, misunderstanding, etc. and does not in itself carry a strong implication of criticism [a *mistake* in reading a blueprint]; **blunder** implies stupidity, clumsiness, inefficiency, etc. and carries a suggestion of more severe criticism [a tactical *blunder* cost them the war]. . . .

This feature is particularly useful for college students and writers.

Etymology is provided for many entries. The introductory guide indicates that etymology "has been made a strong feature of this dictionary because it is believed that insights into the current usage of a word can be gained from a full knowledge of the word's history." Etymologies appear in brackets after the entry's pronunciation. They indicate derivations that go back to the Latin and Greek, unlike many abridged dictionaries, which show only the more recent history of the word.

Other inclusions in the dictionary are scientific names of plants and animals, idiomatic phrases, and inflected forms. Illustrative phrases or sentences appear only rarely. Excluded are trade names and vulgarisms.

IV. Quality and Currency of Entries

Many entries present multiple senses of the entry term. Main senses are identified by boldface numerals; subsenses are designated by italicized lowercase letters. Senses are grouped by part of speech and numbered consecutively within each part-of-speech grouping. Historically earlier senses appear before more recent ones, with specialized, restricted, and technical usages appearing last. A representative entry containing senses and subsenses begins as follows:

> **re·ac·tion** (rē ak′shən) *n.* **1.** a return or opposing action, force, influence, etc. **2.** a response, as to a stimulus or influence **3.** a movement back to a former or less advanced condition, stage, etc.; countertendency; esp.

such a movement or tendency in economics or politics; extreme conservatism **4.** *Chem. a)* the mutual action of substances undergoing chemical change *b)* a process that involves changes within the nucleus of an atom *c)* the state resulting from such changes

Definitions are clearly stated. For example, **soteriology** is defined as

> spiritual salvation, esp. that believed in Christian theology to have been accomplished through Jesus.

Technical terms are also clearly and simply defined; the definition provided for **magnetohydrodynamics** is

> the science that deals with the interaction of a magnetic field with an electrically conducting fluid, as a liquid metal or an ionized gas.

Although usage notes and labels are provided, some entries fail to make careful usage distinctions. For example, the dictionary may leave users confused about the frequently misused terms **further** and **farther**. Under **farther** appears the cumbersome cross-reference:

> In sense **2** of the *adj.* and senses **2** and **3** of the *adv.*, FURTHER is more commonly used.

THE AMERICAN HERITAGE DICTIONARY does a much better job of clarifying the distinction between the terms, noting that "farther" is normally used to refer to actual distance, "further" to degree and time, and providing illustrative sentences.

The dictionary's currency is among its strong points. New words incorporated into the word list include, for example, **AIDS, byte, futon, mascon, tofu, videodisc,** and **videotex**. However, unlike WEBSTER'S NINTH NEW COLLEGIATE DICTIONARY, the work does not list dates of new words' entry into American English. Definitions are also up-to-date. For example, **tofu** is defined as

> a bland, custardlike food, rich in protein, coagulated from an extract of soybeans and eaten in soups, in various cooked dishes, etc.

In comparison, WEBSTER'S NINTH cross-references **tofu** to **bean curd**, which it defines as

> a soft vegetable cheese prepared by treating soybean milk with coagulants (as magnesium chloride or dilute acids).

Although WEBSTER'S NINTH is more precise, it is less reflective of current American dietary uses of the product.

V. Syllabication and Pronunciation

Syllabication and pronunciation follow standard dictionary procedures and will present few difficulties to readers. Syllabication is indicated by centered dots in the entry word and, in inflected forms, by centered dots or stress marks. Pronunciation appears in parentheses after the entry word. Boldface accent marks indicate primary stress; lighter accents show secondary stresses. Located inside the front cover, the full pronunciation key comprises 43 symbols for English sounds and ten for foreign ones. An abbreviated key appears at the bottom of all right-hand pages within the word list.

According to the volume's introductory guide, the pronunciations presented "are those used by cultivated speakers in normal, relaxed conversation." Alternative pronunciations are provided. The first listed is not necessarily the most preferred, but it may be "the one most frequent in general cultivated usage" if the variants are not equally frequent. Occasionally, usage notes (*now rarely, occasionally*) reveal pronunciation restrictions.

VI. Special Features

A six-page guide to the use of the dictionary is clearly written, although the guide's format impedes readability. Headings are indented and italicized, and minimal white space separates subsections. Information would be easier to locate if headings were boldface and white space were more generously used.

On the inside of the front cover, there appears a map and explanation of U.S. regional dialects. Two special articles follow the guide to dictionary use: "Language and the Dictionary," by Charlton Laird, and "Etymology," by William E. Umbach. Appended at the back of the volume are listings of colleges and universities in the United States and Canada. These are based on "the latest information which has been supplied by the institutions themselves," and they include information on general size of enrollment, location, date founded, source of financial control, and degree programs offered.

Another useful feature is the guide to punctuation, mechanics, and manuscript form, with a discussion of the use and form of footnotes. The volume also includes a chart of proofreaders' marks and sample copy that would be helpful to the writer who needs to proof galleys. Finally, the volume includes tables of weights and measures and a listing of signs and symbols used in fields such as astronomy, commerce and finance, and medicine and pharmacy.

VII. Accessibility

Entries are arranged alphabetically, letter by letter. Homographs, such as **bat** (club), **bat** (animal), and **bat** (wink) are given separate entries, distinguished by superscript numbers. The abbreviated pronunciation key that appears at the bottom of right-hand

pages also helpfully explains the symbols that identify Americanisms, foreign terms, and hypothetical etymologies, as well as the symbol meaning "derived from."

Identical biographical surnames, and geographical names that share an identical element, are grouped together under a single entry. For example, under **Washington** as a geographical entry are listed the state, the U.S. capital, and the lake and mountain of the same name. Under the biographical entry **Washington** are listed, alphabetically, Booker T. and George. Because of the subentries' brevity, the eye picks up the boldface secondary entries. The practice permits the inclusion of more names than could be listed in an abridged dictionary if each were given a separate entry.

The work is available in both thumb-indexed and plain editions. In both, two boldface guide words at the top of each page indicate the first and last entries on the page. Cross-references also enhance accessibility, enabling users to locate additional information about words and their synonyms and antonyms. Small capitals make cross-references easy to locate within entries.

Alternative spellings are provided. When they are alphabetically close, they appear together in boldface type at the beginning of an entry (**catalog, catalogue**). The spelling listed first is the more frequently used but is not to be taken as the more "correct." When variant spellings are not alphabetically close, they are cross-referenced, with the full entry provided under the spelling more frequently used.

A detailed table of contents at the front of the volume lists all special features, including the 12 subsections of the guide to dictionary use.

VIII. Graphics and Format

The dictionary is illustrated with line drawings that are of sufficient size and detail to help define the word they depict. They appear adjacent to their entries and are captioned with main entry words and, in some cases, with additional information. For example, the illustration for **cycloid** shows three different examples of this complex geometrical figure, with each separately captioned. Line drawings are provided for most plants and animals listed, and their captions include indications of size. A full page of drawings is devoted to examples of leaf forms. Small maps are provided for some geographical entries. These are limited in detail but are useful in aiding the user to locate the country depicted.

Main entry words appear in boldface type overhanging the text on double-column pages. For both the entry word and the entry itself, the type is larger than that in other college dictionaries. However, in the review copy, print on some pages was much lighter than that in the rest of the volume. The dictionary is sturdily bound and will hold up well to heavy use.

IX. Summary

Webster's Ninth New Collegiate Dictionary and The American Heritage Dictionary: Second College Edition are the two top recommended dictionaries in the abridged college class, but *Webster's New World Dictionary of the American Language: Second College Edition* is not without considerable merit. To compare the two Webster dictionaries, definitions in Webster's Ninth are truly descriptive and very detailed, but the shorter *New World* definitions are somewhat easier to understand. Both the Webster dictionaries have the same number of entries, including many up-to-date words, but the *New World* has more current definitions. Webster's Ninth provides dates for the words' entry into English; the *New World* does not. The *Ninth*'s introduction is longer and clearer than the *New World*'s poorly formatted guide to the use of the dictionary, and in pronunciation, the Ninth's 59 symbols and five-page explanation is more detailed than the *New World*'s system. Ample listings of synonyms with valuable differentiations among meanings are provided by both Webster's.

Definitions in *Webster's New World* fall somewhere in between the descriptive kind in Webster's Ninth and the prescriptive kind in The American Heritage Dictionary: Second College Edition in which correct usage is all-important. Where the *New World* stands out is in its comprehensive coverage of Americanisms. Both the American Heritage and the Random House College Dictionary: Second College Edition have superior illustrations to those in the *New World*, but the latter has larger type. The *New World* is also slightly higher-priced than the other college dictionaries.

Webster's New World Pocket Dictionary

Facts at a Glance

Full Title: **Webster's New World Pocket Dictionary**.
Alternate Title: *Webster's New World Handy Pocket Dictionary*.
Publisher: Prentice Hall Press.
Editor: Samuel Solomon, Supervising Editor.
Edition Reviewed: © 1977.

Number of Entries: 22,000.
Number of Pages: 316.
Trim size: 3″ × 5¼″.
Binding: paperback with a slip-on vinyl cover.

Price: $2.95.
Sold in bookstores.
ISBN 0-671-41826-2.

I. Introduction

Webster's New World Pocket Dictionary, also called *Webster's New World Handy Pocket Dictionary* by its publisher, was first published in 1964. The current edition was issued in 1977. The book has no preface or introductory remarks. The words included appear to be those that were in common use when this edition was first published, but no criteria for word selection are given. There are some 56,000 words included, with about 22,000 main entry words, accompanied by very brief definitions.

II. Authority

A notice on the copyright page states: "This book is based upon and includes material from *Webster's New World Dictionary, Second College Edition* . . . and *Webster's New World Dictionary, College Edition*." Both dictionaries have solid reputations, although the editions cited as sources for this pocketbook's entries are now outdated (the latest copyright dates listed are 1976 for the first source and 1968 for the second).

III. Comprehensiveness

The overall number of words included is extensive for such a small, compact work. But many meanings in this book do not reflect either current or common usage, and there are many important main entry words missing, as well as important additional meanings missing for those that *are* included. For example, **hardware** has only one definition: "Metal articles, as tools, nails, etc.," which ignores the word's widespread meaning in the field of computers. **Computer** is defined as "(electronic) computing machine."

A brief sample of the kinds of words that do not appear in this pocket dictionary is: *compact disc, hijack, homosexual,* and *infrastructure*. The prefixes **in-** and **un-**, however, both have additional useful lists of combined word forms that will help the reader in quick spelling checks.

IV. Quality and Currency of Entries

The definitions reflect meanings that were contemporary with the dates of publication. The selection of entries, in general, should be revised to make room for more current words and meanings. For example, **access** is defined as a noun only.

Webster's New World Vest Pocket Dictionary

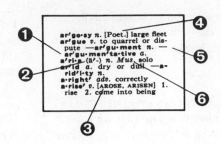

❶ Syllabication and primary and secondary accents are shown for all entries

❷ Pronunciations of doubtful words or syllables appear in parentheses

❸ Irregular inflected forms appear in small capitals within brackets

❹ Usage labels are enclosed by brackets

❺ Related forms are listed at the end of the main entry

❻ Field labels are italicized

Entries are ordered as follows: boldface main entry word divided into syllables followed by part of speech; inflections, variant forms, and plural forms; brief numbered definitions; with additional labeled parts of speech run-in to the entry. Definitions are cursory, often only a single word, and occasionally illustrative. Colloquial and slang terminology is sometimes given as well as common idioms such as "**in the light of**, considering" at the end of the entry for **light**. Word forms are given, but etymology, synonyms, and antonyms are not.

V. Syllabication and Pronunciation

Syllabication is indicated in the main entry by a dot separating the syllables. Primary and secondary stress is indicated by dark and light accent marks. A very brief pronunciation key is found at the beginning of the book, but the symbols rarely appear as guides to words in the main alphabet. They are, however, quite simple and can be used easily.

VI. Special Features

Immediately preceding the main alphabet is a page of rules for spelling and for forming plurals. At the back of the book are punctuation rules, a list of abbreviations (which also needs updating: *a.k.a.*, for example, is not included), weights and measures, a perpetual calendar, names of U.S. states and cities with 1970 population figures, nations of the world with unspecified population figures, facts about the earth, traditional gifts for wedding anniversaries, birthstones, and a list of the members in the "Hall of Fame of Great Americans." Some of this material may be useful, but it is also found in more detail and currency in almanacs.

VII. Accessibility

Words are entered in letter-by-letter alphabetical order. Guide word pairs with a centered page number appear at the top of each page. This small book is very easy to leaf through quickly, and the bold main entry words overhanging the text can be scanned easily.

VIII. Graphics and Format

Each page is divided into two columns by a thin vertical rule. The guide words are separated from the text by a horizontal rule. All main entry words, inflected forms, additional parts of speech, and idiomatic phrases are in clear, but small bold sans-serif type.

The print size of the text is very small and relatively hard to read. The paper is a rough white sturdy stock with little show-through. The book will fit comfortably into a pocket, and it has a flexible, washable red vinyl slip jacket for additional protection and durability. Altogether, the book's format is a neat and practical package.

IX. Summary

Despite its practical format, *Webster's New World Pocket* (or *Handy Pocket*) *Dictionary* will not be the first choice in paperback pocket dictionaries. Too many words in everyday use are either not included or need to have meanings added that reflect current usage.

Webster's New World Vest Pocket Dictionary

Facts at a Glance

Full Title: **Webster's New World Vest Pocket Dictionary**.
Editor: Clark C. Livensparger.
Publisher: Simon & Schuster.
Edition Reviewed: © 1977.

Number of Entries: 15,000.
Number of Pages: 188.

Trim Size: 3″ × 5¼″.
Binding: paperback.

Price: $1.95.
Sold in bookstores and other outlets.
ISBN 0-671-41829-7.

I. Introduction and Scope

Webster's New World Vest Pocket Dictionary is a truncated version of WEBSTER'S NEW WORLD POCKET (or HANDY POCKET) DICTIONARY. The number of main entries for this vest pocket work has been reduced from the pocket dictionary by about one-half. The appendix for this edition contains somewhat less information than the pocket work, and this paperback is considerably less attractive than its parent pocket edition. Like its parent dictionary, *Webster's New World Vest Pocket Dictionary* does not reflect current usage and would not be a user's first choice.

Webster's Ninth New Collegiate Dictionary

Facts at a Glance

Full Title: **Webster's Ninth New Collegiate Dictionary**.
Publisher: Merriam-Webster.
Editor: Frederick C. Mish, Editor-in-Chief.
Edition Reviewed: © 1986.

Number of Entries: 156,000.
Number of Indexes: 1.
Number of Pages: 1,568.
Number of Illustrations: 573 black-and-white drawings.
Trim Size: 7″ × 9½″.
Binding: hardcover.

Prices: $14.95 (hardcover); $15.95 (thumb-indexed); $16.95 (deluxe).
Sold in bookstores; also sold to libraries and other educational institutions.
ISBN 0-87779-506-8 (plain);
ISBN 0-87779-509-6 (thumb-indexed);
ISBN 0-87779-510-X (deluxe).

I. Introduction

Webster's *Collegiate* dictionary has the distinction of being the best-selling dictionary in the United States, with more than one million volumes sold each year. It superseded the equally popular *Webster's Eighth* in 1983. According to Editor-in-Chief Frederick C. Mish, "every entry and feature of the last edition has been reexamined so that this [Ninth] Collegiate offers . . . much that is new and useful while preserving the best features of preceding editions." Notable among the features new to this edition are brief usage paragraphs to provide guidance on words whose usage is confused or disputed.

With nearly 160,000 entries and 200,000 definitions, this is a comprehensive abridged work. It is intended, states Mish, "to serve the general public as its chief source of information about the words of our language." That language is, of course, American English.

Webster's Ninth goes through several printings each year. Although the work is on a ten-year revision schedule—the tenth edition is due out in 1993—new words and definitions are incorporated into the text in reprintings as conditions warrant.

II. Authority

Merriam-Webster is the highly respected publisher of WEBSTER'S THIRD NEW INTERNATIONAL DICTIONARY, the authoritative unabridged work on which the *Ninth Collegiate* is based. The publisher has a permanent, trained staff of lexicographers and linguistic experts. In addition, Merriam-Webster maintains a citation file of words used in context that numbered some 13,000,000 when this dictionary was in preparation. This file was established two years after publication of the firm's original collegiate dictionary in 1898 and contains citations from 1890 to the present.

In the dictionary's opening essay on language, there is an extensive list of the authoritative historical source works used in preparing *Webster's Ninth*. Another section in the essay, titled "Semantics in the Dictionary," explains (with precise examples) the methods used by the editors to define and write entries. This reveals the behind-the-scenes work that maintains the high reputation of *Webster's Ninth Collegiate*, a book directly descended from Noah Webster's *American Dictionary of the English Language* (1828).

III. Comprehensiveness

The preface to the dictionary states that "the treatment of words of the A–Z vocabulary section is as nearly exhaustive as the compass of the work permits."

The main vocabulary includes synonyms with subtly distinguished meanings. There are thorough etymologies, a generous amount of labels, including *ISV*, which is used by the editors to indicate "international scientific vocabulary," and dates of first recorded usage. The following examples show the form of an etymology, dating, labeling, and the form of a usage citation.

Webster's Ninth New Collegiate Dictionary

❶ Dates of first recorded use are enclosed in parentheses

❷ Usage labels are italicized

❸ Synonyms are discriminated in a separate paragraph introduced by the boldface italic abbreviation *syn*

❹ Etymologies are enclosed in brackets

❺ Examples of usage are enclosed in angle brackets

❻ A swung dash indicates repetition of the main entry word

❼ Cross-references are set in small capitals

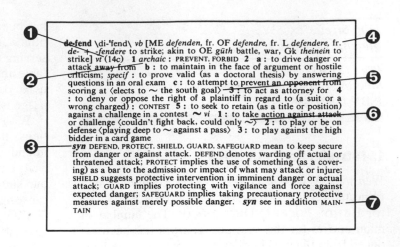

¹mole *n* [ME, fr. OE *māl*; akin to OHG *meil* spot] (bef. 12c) : a pigmented spot, mark, or small permanent protuberance on the human body; *esp* : NEVUS.

ke·tone *n* [G *keton*. alter. of *aceton* acetone] (1851)

ke·to·ste·roid *n* [ISV] (1939)

sci·en·tize . . . (1917) : to treat with a scientific approach <the attempt to ~ reality, to name it and classify it —John Fowles>.

Authoritative and relatively extensive guidance, based on the publisher's staff expertise and enormous citation files, is given in usage notes for disputed or difficult words such as **hopefully** or **whom**. For example:

hopefully *adv* (1639) **1**: in a hopeful manner **2**: it is hoped

usage Only the irrationally large amount of critical fire drawn by sense 2 of *hopefully* requires its particular recognition in a dictionary. Similar use of other adverbs (as *interestingly*, *presumably*, *fortunately*) as sentence modifiers is so commonplace as to excite no notice whatever. While it still arouses occasional objection, *hopefully* as a sentence modifier has been in use at least since 1932 and is well established as standard.

The dictionary also contains six additional reference sections and a style handbook.

IV. Quality and Currency of Entries

Reviews of the definitions in the *Ninth Collegiate* when it first appeared in 1983 were favorable. The American Library Association's *Reference Books Bulletin* review (p. 31, 1983–84) of the dictionary said: "Definitions are precise and clear, with excellent synonym and usage notes. . . . Spot-checking suggests adequate currentness." Other reviews noted that the redesigned page layout allowed for the addition of "thousands" of new words and definitions, plus synonyms with discriminated senses, cross-referenced to analytical definitions, and new usage paragraphs.

All main entries appear in alphabetical sequence, letter by letter. Numerals, for example, are alphabetized as if they were spelled out. The basic sequence of information in the vocabulary is boldface main entry divided into syllables; pronunciations; part of speech, variant forms and inflections with pronunciations when necessary; the etymology is followed by the date of first recorded use; then definitions, numbered and including cross-references in small capital letters as well as sample citations in angle brackets. The senses of a word are historically ordered. The sample below shows the sequence and an example of a numbered homograph:

-para- \par-a*comb form* [*para*chute] **1** : parachute <*para*trooper> **2** : parachutist <*para*spotter>.

Run-on entries to the main entries, such as derivatives or phrases (defined when necessary) are preceded by a hyphen and may include pronunciation and part of speech. Under **para·bi·o·sis**, for example, the run-on entry is:

— **para·bi·ot·ic** \-'ät·ik*adj* — **para·bi·ot·i·cal·ly** \-i-k-(ə-)lē *adv*.

Because *Webster's Ninth* emphasizes descriptive information, rather than prescriptive guidance, its labeling system, although extensive, is not as obvious as, for example, that in THE AMERICAN HERITAGE DICTIONARY: SECOND COLLEGE EDITION. *Webster's Ninth* status labels include regional labels, for words or senses specific to areas of the U.S. or of the English-speaking world. Temporal labels are *obs* for obsolete, and *archaic*.

Stylistic labels are *slang*, *nonstand* for nonstandard, and *substand* for substandard. *Substand* refers to use that is "disapproved of by many" or that differs substantially from that used by "the prestige group of the community" (for example, **ain't**), according to the publisher. Words generally considered vulgar are so explained within definitions. Some special subject labels are given (for example, football terminology), but generally special usage particular to a field or profession are explained in the definitions.

A randomly selected segment of entries from **paprika** through **parachute** shows 22 main entries in *Webster's Ninth*, 23 slightly different main entries in that segment in THE AMERICAN HERITAGE DICTIONARY: SECOND COLLEGE EDITION. A comparison of definitions for a general term from each work reveals that usually discriminations are more precise in the *Ninth Collegiate*.

From the *Webster's Ninth* compare "**par·a·ble** . . . *n* . . . : COMPARISON: *specif* : a usu. short fictitious story that illustrates a moral attitude or religious principle," with *The AHD: Second College Edition*'s "**par·a·ble** . . . *n*. A simple story illustrating a moral or religious lesson." In other cases, such as the definition for **parachute**, the *AHD* is more scientific; in **parabola**, both dictionaries are precisely scientific and both use mathematical diagrams as illustrations.

V. Syllabication and Pronunciation

The points where words may be hyphenated at the end of a line are shown for all main entries, variant forms, and inflections by centered dots: "**mach·i·nate** . . . *vb* **-nat·ed: -nat·ing** . . . — **mach·i·na·tor** . . . *n*." No division is indicated for single letter syllables at the beginning or end of words (**aboard**, **slithery**), nor for succeeding homographs (**-machines**). Within the definitions, where a hyphen within a word is normally used, a double-stacked hyphen is used at a line end: as in the compound adjective salmon=pink.

Syllabication in the pronunciation transcriptions is shown by hyphens: **nest·ed** \nes-təd\. The pronunciation system is clearly explained in the "Guide to Pronunciation" preceding the main vocabulary, where the distingishing marks and special symbols are printed in large bold type. Three pages of "English Spelling and Sound Correspondences" follow, including a list of 25 letters and combinations that are often silent. The editors explain that these correspondences "are by no means exhaustive, but they should enable the user who is uncertain of the spelling to find most words in this book." They also add that "knowing the first five letters of almost any word will get the user to within a few inches of the right place in even the largest unabridged dictionaries." The spelling guide list is organized by the pronunciation symbols for vowels and diphthongs and for consonants; students used to simpler systems will need to spend a considerable amount of time becoming familiar with the extensive range of symbols before the list is useful.

The pronunciation symbols used in the transcriptions are based on the scholarly International Phonetic Alphabet (IPA); many of these will not be familiar to American students in either high schools or colleges, who generally do not receive extensive instruction in the usc of various pronunciation systems. *Reference Books Bulletin* briefly summed up the *Ninth Collegiate*'s pronunciations in the review quoted earlier: "Linguistic data are very precisely displayed, with extensive (possibly to some users forbidding) use of symbols and abbreviatons."

VI. Special Features

Among the additional features of *Webster's Ninth* are a handy list of common abbreviations normalized to one form; a list of the symbols for chemical elements, and a considerable dictionary of foreign words and phrases in common use that are not Anglicized or Americanized. These A to Z entries contain pronunciations and indicate source language. The phrases and words range from frequent Latin, Greek, and French mottoes, including those of the U.S. states, to German, Spanish, Russian, and other words. There are 42 pages of biographical names with death dates up to about 1984–85. Edwin Meese, for example, is listed as U.S. Attorney General as of 1985; Sandra Day O'Connor is listed as an American jurist but not as a member of the Supreme Court. An extensive geographical list, with useful cross-references and alternative name forms, including U.S. populations based on 1980 U.S. census figures and 1976 Canadian figures. The political information is generally up-to-date—for example, Harare is identified as the capital of Zimbabwe, but foreign populations are now outdated.

The remaining items are a list of colleges and universities, with ZIP codes that could, in many cases, be mistaken for enrollment figures; and a clearly designed style handbook with enough examples to be useful. The section on "Documentation of Sources" lists the 1982 *MLA* (Modern Language Association) guidelines but not the association's *Handbook for Writers of Research Papers* (1984, 2d ed.); otherwise, the samples of note style are up-to-date. They even compare the shorter citation style used in many professional fields with that of the humanities. A list of the various forms of address for officials and others is appended. A thorough index lists the charts and tables in the main vocabulary, the reference matter at the back of the book, and even the subsections of the style handbook.

Like THE AMERICAN HERITAGE DICTIONARY: SECOND COLLEGE EDITION, *Webster's Ninth* includes usage notes in its entries for some words whose usage is problematic, such as *disinterested, hopefully,* and *media*. These notes are generally descriptive, citing different uses of the word in question but rarely passing judgment on one use or another.

Webster's Ninth is the first abridged dictionary to give dates for the earliest known use of each entry word. Because definitions in this dictionary are arranged in historical order, the date that is given pertains only to the first sense of the word, which is the oldest. While this feature may have little practical application for the general user, it will be of interest to those who are intrigued by the history of words.

VII. Accessibility

The boldface main entries only slightly overhang the text but can be easily distinguished from the main text. Bold variant forms appearing within or appended to entries can also be seen. Main entries appear in strict alphabetical sequence and homographs are preceded by small bold superior numbers:

> **drug**, *n* . . . **¹drug** *vb* . . . **²drug** *dial past of* DRAG.

The etymologies following parts of speech are printed within square brackets, which sets them apart from the text. Clear bold page numbers appear at the outer top of margins and two bold guide words separated by a bold bullet appear next to them:

> **796 neutron star · newt . . . New Testament · niello 797.**

Thumb index tabs are available with the cloth-bound edition. One of the most useful aids to accessibility is the brief, but excellent index at the back of the book. This lists specifically the many additional charts and tables within the main lexicon, as well as useful items from the front guide to the dictionary, such as "Labels, Functional," and in the style handbook at the rear, such as "Virgule, use of."

The pronunciation symbols are handily printed in bold type on the inside back cover, and a four-line pronunciation key, separated from the text by a bold rule, is printed at the foot of each right-hand page's column.

VIII. Graphics and Format

Scattered sparsely throughout the vocabulary, the 573 captioned black-and-white line drawings are generally precise and attractive. They are also large enough so that details are not obscured, even for those illustrations with numbered labels keyed into captions (a **bird**, a human **ear**, a **fish**, a **horse**, and others).

The small but readable text is set two columns per page. The page width of *Webster's Ninth* was expanded about one-quarter of an inch from that in the eighth edition, which allows a slightly wider text column.

An illustrative feature at the front of the book is a double-page spread of sample text from the dictionary with some 46 labels indicating where the features (such as etymology, or inflections, or usage illustrations in angled brackets) appear in entries. The sample text is printed in gray tone so that the items intended to help the reader find the required information, printed in solid black, can be easily spotted.

The smooth, white paper reveals minimal show-through of text in the vocabulary section, but in the introductory section where white space abounds, show-through is obvious. The book is sturdily bound and in general a very handsome example of reference book production.

IX. Summary

When *Webster's Ninth New Collegiate* first appeared in 1983, *Library Journal* wrote: "this is probably the best abridged dictionary available." *American Reference Books Annual* (ARBA 84) agreed: "Webster's Collegiate line is directed toward students, office employees, and home users, but, as it is one of the finest abridged dictionaries available, no respectable collection would be without it." Summing up the consensus on the work, *Reference Books Bulletin* (p. 31, 1983–84) said: "Rich not only in current English in general use but in the vocabulary of the scientific and particularly the humanistic disciplines and infused with a sense of history, *Webster's New Collegiate Dictionary* continues, in its ninth edition, to live up to its solid—and well-deserved—reputation."

Webster's Ninth has few serious rivals. THE AMERICAN HERITAGE DICTIONARY: SECOND COLLEGE EDITION probably comes closest in authority and comprehensiveness. It takes a more prescriptive approach to language, and therefore makes a good contrast to the more descriptive *Ninth*. Public and academic libraries will want to have copies of both dictionaries; for individuals, the choice may come down to a subjective matter of taste.

Webster's Third New International Dictionary

Facts at a Glance

Full Title: **Webster's Third New International Dictionary of the English Language, Unabridged.**
Publisher: **Merriam-Webster.**
Editor: Philip Babcock Gove, Editor-in-Chief.
Edition Reviewed: © 1986.

Webster's Third New International Dictionary of the English Language: Unabridged

❶ A swung dash indicates repetition of the main entry word

❷ Usage labels are italicized

❸ Homographs appear as separate, numbered entries

❹ Etymology is enclosed in brackets

❺ "More at" cross-references lead to further etymologies of cognates

❻ Examples of usage are enclosed in angle brackets

❼ Cross-references are set in small capitals

❽ Synonym list is introduced by the boldface abbreviation *syn*

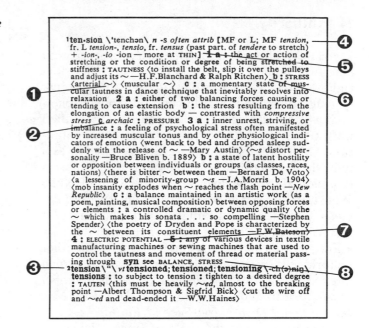

Number of Entries: 470,000.
Number of Pages: 2,776.
Number of Illustrations: 3,105 black-and-white drawings; two color plates.
Trim Size: 9¹⁄₁₆″ × 12⁹⁄₁₆″.
Bindings: blue Sturdite; cloth.

Price: $79.95 (blue Sturdite); $89.95 (cloth). Sold in bookstores; also sold to libraries and other educational institutions.
ISBN 0-87779-201-1 (blue Sturdite);
ISBN 0-87779-206-2 (cloth).

I. Introduction

Webster's Third New International Dictionary is widely recognized as the most authoritative general American dictionary of its kind. Indeed, it may fairly be argued that it is the only dictionary that fully merits the label *unabridged*. Nonetheless, a certain amount of controversy attended its publication in 1961. In fact, when *Webster's Third* first appeared, a prospective buyer might well have been greeted by the bookstore clerk with, "How often is one able to buy a controversial dictionary?" By now, of course, that controversy has died away; but because of it, a number of publishers who had not previously considered producing a large dictionary, such as Random House and Houghton Mifflin, decided to do so in the mid-1960s. They no doubt received encouragement from the numerous scathing reviews of *Webster's Third*

that appeared in such influential publications as the *New York Times*, *Time*, *Life*, and *The Atlantic*. Although there had also been some favorable reviews, many reviewers pounced on the editors at Merriam-Webster for what they saw as permissiveness in language, as well as for omitting the biographical section and the gazetteer that had been included in the previous edition.

Most serious users of dictionaries are, of course, familiar by now with the innovations in dictionary making employed by the editors at Merriam-Webster and recognize the superiority and good sense of their methods; but newer users looking into *Webster's Third* for the first time should be reassured that with practice and a little patience they, too, will discover the advantages of its system.

According to Philip Gove, the Editor-in-Chief, *Webster's Third New International Dictionary* is for all adults as well as some younger users:

[It has been] prepared with a constant regard for the needs of the high school and college student, the technician, and the periodical reader, as well as of the scholar and professional.

Gove also indicates that a good dictionary is important to anyone interested in language and culture as well as in looking up words:

[*Webster's Third*] is offered to the English-speaking world as a prime linguistic aid to interpreting the culture and civilization of today. . . . [It] will supply in full measure that information on the general language which is required for accurate, clear, and comprehensive understanding of the vocabulary for today's society.

II. Authority

Merriam-Webster's authority rests on its history (the firm bought the unsold copies and the copyright of Noah Webster's dictionary when the great lexicographer died in 1843) and on modern scholarship—the editors had access to over 10 million illustrative citations in formulating their definitions. Merriam-Webster's sterling reputation as a publisher of dictionaries and other reference works is undeniable. The firm's 1847 revision of Noah Webster's *American Dictionary of the English Language* became its first "unabridged" dictionary. It was followed in 1864 by another revision formally known as the *Unabridged* and by a number of other unabridged dictionaries: *Webster's International Dictionary* in 1890, *Webster's New International Dictionary* in 1909, and, in 1934, *Webster's New International Dictionary, Second Edition* (a book revered by some as the bible of English language usage, at least in America). In addition, Merriam-Webster has published numerous biographical, geographical, and college dictionaries. Its smaller dictionary based on *Webster's Third* is now in its ninth edition—WEBSTER'S NINTH NEW COLLEGIATE DICTIONARY. Besides the volumes mentioned above, Merriam-Webster currently publishes a thesaurus and a dictionary of synonyms, as well as other standard reference works.

The other base on which the authority of *Webster's Third* rests, its modern scholarship, is also irreproachable. Its editors are justly proud of the more than 6 million citations collected between 1934 and 1961 as evidence of the way in which words are accurately used. The remainder of the 10 million citations available to them consists of those in THE OXFORD ENGLISH DICTIONARY, Sir William Craigie's four-volume *Dictionary of American English*, and Mitford M. Mathews's dictionary of *Americanisms* (1966). As soon as *Webster's Third* was published, the staff at Merriam-Webster began collecting new examples of language usage for the next revised edition, which ought to be published sometime in the next few years. As a matter of fact, many of these have been added to the main word list in various printings since 1961 or are now in the 55 closely printed pages of addenda in the current printing (see also the review of 12,000 WORDS: A SUPPLEMENT TO WEBSTER'S THIRD NEW INTERNATIONAL).

It was this very wealth of citation, of examples of the way in which words are actually employed in contemporary usage, that formed the basis for many of the negative assessments of *Webster's Third*'s authority. What some critics objected to in the practice of creating a dictionary entry from actual usage was the editors' apparent abandonment of their role as legislators of language. How were we to know how to use or pronounce a word unless a dictionary told us? But the Merriam-Webster editors saw their role as describers, rather than as prescribers, of the language.

Critics objected, for instance, to the very admission into this dictionary of the word **irregardless** because, they said, it is a nonword. However, the word had been cited in the previous edition, and in *Webster's Third* it is labeled *nonstand* (nonstandard) and is said to derive from *irrespective* and *regardless*, which explains why people use it. Obviously the editors did not enter the word on the same standing as that of other words but acknowledged and accurately described its widespread use in the language.

In refuting criticisms of the authority of *Webster's Third* in a May 1962 article in *The Atlantic*, Bergen Evans asserted that the negative reviewers had confused the meaning of *authoritative*, which this dictionary certainly is, with *authoritarian*, a kind of lexical dictatorship that its editors did not consider appropriate. In summary, Mario Pei was quite accurate when, in a *New York Times* article, he said of *Webster's Third*: "It is the closest we can get, in America, to the Voice of Authority."

III. Comprehensiveness

Dictionary users are more likely to find a word in *Webster's Third* than in any other "unabridged" dictionary published in America today. They must, however, be willing to use the addenda of new words and meanings and also must be patient enough in some cases to undertake a more complex search. They can find the meaning of *alveoloplasty*, for example, by looking up the combining forms, or of *vestibuloplasty* by adding the meaning of **plasty** to the meaning of **vestibule 2d**. *Frenectomy* combines **frenum** and **-ectomy**. Of course, other scientific and technical terms are there as entries in their own right, especially if they have moved over into common speech. **AIDS** is in the addenda and so is **AWACS**, for example. **Cosmonaut** has been added to the main lexicon since the first printing, and the religious meaning of **charismatic** is now in the addenda, as is **clearway**. The word **gelastic**, for example, not found even in the recent second unabridged edition of THE RANDOM HOUSE DICTIONARY, is a main entry in this dictionary. Most of the terms rising out of the computer industry are included, although *mouse* in this sense is not in either the main section or the addenda. And, as might be expected, it contains a good many slang terms that have intruded into the language in the past 50 years, terms prompting valiant efforts on the part of the editors to keep abreast of recent developments. All in all, the editors have done an excellent job of keeping up with current words and meanings.

Etymologies have been thoroughly and carefully prepared by Charles R. Sleeth. They are placed immediately after the pronunciation, so that one of the first things one learns about a word is its derivation. Generally, these are not repeated for subsequent meanings of a word, unless of course the word is derived differently. The word **boom**, for example, is first derived from Dutch for its meanings related to tree or beam; but as a sound, it is labeled [imit.] for imitative. Abbreviations for languages that appear in the etymologies are explained in the frontmatter of the book.

A common problem facing lexicographers is how to account for the derivation of many scientific terms, which, though often formed from an ancient language or two, are mostly of modern coinage. Sleeth solves the problem by using the label *ISV* (International Scientific Vocabulary) when he cannot be certain of the original language. The care with which Sleeth has assigned his derivations may be illustrated by his treatment of **namby-pamby**. This expression derives from the "nickname given to Ambrose Philips," an eighteenth-century English poet. Sleeth attributes it to "some satirists of his time." Although it was specifically Henry Carey whose poem "Namby Pamby" ridiculed Philips's verses, the cautious etymologist suggests that the word may have been in the air before Carey wrote his poem. Carey may simply have been the one to fix the word in print. In general, from a nonexpert's point of view, Sleeth seems to have done an accurate and careful piece of work.

A number of critics have expressed annoyance with the editorial decision to limit the kinds of usage advice in *Webster's Third*, but in fact there is quite a bit of advice. It uses three kinds of status labels: temporal labels—*obs* (obsolete), *archaic*, and the like; stylistic—*slang*, *substand* (substantial), *nonstand* (nonstandard), and the like; and regional—*dial* (dialect), *Brit* (British), *South (Southern)*, *Austral* (Australian), and the like. The dictionary contains more than a thousand synonym articles clarifying commonly confused words, all cross-referenced. There seems to be no pattern for these, just a judgment call by the editors, but they are very helpful. They include an astonishing array of illustrative quotations taken from a wide variety of authors. On page 1,197, for instance, a page chosen at random, under synonyms for **irritable** appear citations from Lyle Saxon, F. A. Swinnerton, Arthur Schlesinger, Pearl Buck, Charles Kingsley, Samuel Butler, C. S. Lewis, V. L. Parrington, Arnold Bennett, Harriet Beecher Stowe, W. H. Wright, and Aldous Huxley. On the same page under **irritate** are illustrative quotations from D. H. Lawrence, Green Peyton, Edith Wharton, W. J. Locke, C. S. Forester, W. A. White, Louis Auchincloss, J. F. Powers, Ann Bridge, and the WPA's *American Guide Series: Connecticut*. Some readers might feel overwhelmed by so many citations, but others will signally value this feature. In order to guide the reader, carefully defined distinctions of the words listed precede the citations, and each citation illustrates one meaning of the word. Clearly, a reader can find any level of refinement in meanings desired.

In addition to these relatively lengthy synonym articles, in many entries, cross-references to other related words appear in small caps, often making up a complete meaning. For **fix up**, for example, one finds CONTRIVE, DEVISE, FURNISH, EQUIP, SUPPLY, and ACCOMMODATE listed as meanings and directing readers to these entries. In fact, this system of etymologies, citations, status labels, synonym articles, and cross-references in *Webster's Third* will help readers to become as familiar with the past and present life of a word as they wish.

IV. Quality and Currency of Entries

According to Dr. Gove in his preface, his editors "have held steadfastly to the three cardinal virtues of dictionary making: accuracy, clearness, and comprehensiveness." And they have been generally successful, particularly if a user is willing on occasion to look up some of the words in a definition. "Somewhat paradoxically," says Gove, "a user of the dictionary benefits in proportion to his effort and knowledge. . . ." Thus, because the clarity of a definition means something different to different readers, editors cannot always be clear and concise at the same time. Then there is that old bugbear of the lexicographer, the word too simple to put in simpler terms. Critics sneered at the definition of **door** in *Webster's Third*, which takes up nearly half a column, although none of them offered a better one. But the definitions here are straightforward, concise, and comprehensive. Obviously not everyone will grasp at once that **CAT Scan** (Computed Axial Tomograph) is "a sectional view of the body made by computer tomography." Technical terms sometimes lead us to other technical terms and, depending on our education and knowledge, to still more technical terms, as in

> **tomography** . . . a technique of medical roentgenography by which details in one plane of body tissue appear clear and sharp while details of adjoining planes are blurred.

There is an inevitable trade-off between technical accuracy in definitions and their accessibility to a general audience. *Webster's Third* has opted for the first—but looking up **roentgenography** and learning it is "photography by means of X rays" should end the search for most people. If this information is something they really want to know, most readers will not find this search too onerous.

Definitions supply all the important senses of a word in historical order with the oldest first. This principle of ordering must be kept in mind; otherwise the hurried reader may take an older or obsolete meaning for a current one. On the other hand, the illustrative quotations seem to have no regular order. In one of the meanings of **par**, for example, Osbert Sitwell and A. C. Cole are both cited ahead of William Cowper; and on the next page under the first meaning of **parade** Charles Dickens is sandwiched between James Hilton and Margaret Biddle. For some words, of course, where all their senses are current, historical presentation of their meanings may have little significance for many readers, especially since the Merriam-Webster editors have not dated their quotations. However, since the smaller edition, Merriam-Webster's Ninth New Collegiate Dictionary, includes dates for entries, the next version of *Webster's Third* may also date its entries, particularly considering that the 1987 edition of The Random House Dictionary now does so.

V. Syllabication and Pronunciation

This dictionary's attempt to bring some logic to bear on the problem of syllabication and word division incurred the displeasure of a number of users. Among those leveling serious criticism of its treatment of word division was the United States Government Printing Office, which asserts (in the introduction to *Word Division: Supplement to United States Government Printing Office Style Manual*, 1984) that *Webster's Third* had "adopted a new pattern of word breaking which caused changes in the division of many words." Apparently sufficient disagreement on this question exists to make Merriam-Webster's editor say, "Division, from whatever necessity, presents a problem that has no positive solution." In any case, word division practice in *Webster's Third* makes more sense than in most dictionaries, where often a single letter, if pronounced as a syllable, at the end of the word is marked as appropriate for word division. The word **britannia**, for example, is so marked in The Random House Dictionary; but as Merriam-Webster's editor points out, if there is room for the hyphen there is room for the letter; moreover, a single letter beginning a line is confusing and unsightly. Another difference is that *Webster's Third* avoids dividing words where a letter from one element of a compound would be placed with the other element. For example, it divides **cardiovascular** only after the *o*; whereas The Random House Dictionary shows divisions after the *i* or after the *o*.

All readers, however, should examine the frontmatter of *Webster's Third* even though most users at best only browse through this material in most dictionaries. Even a quick skimming of the article on word division may eliminate surprises when encountering it in the main word list. The opening lines of this article are reassuring and worth quoting:

> The centered periods in boldface main entries indicate places at which a hyphen may be put as the last character in a line of print or writing when the rest of the word must be put at the beginning of the following line. We have made an effort to insert the periods only at places where hyphens would actually be used by publishing houses whose publications show a conscientious regard for end-of-the-line divisions.

Writers and typists who look up words in *Webster's Third* for the purpose of word division will not find very much difference from other dictionaries. For example, when they want the divisions for **irrevocable** they may find it exasperating to first have to look up **revocable**, but they will soon not find this inconvenient. And that is where reading the article on word division is most helpful. However, a writer preparing a manuscript for a publisher should ascertain what the house preference is with regard to this.

The pronunciation style is a different matter and will take some getting used to for those who have become familiar with the old dictionary style. The most immediately disconcerting practice is that of placing the accent marks *in front of* the syllables receiving emphasis rather than behind them. Another—and this takes a bit longer to adjust to—is the effort the editor has made to accommodate a wide variety of pronunciations. Where most dictionaries supply one or two, *Webster's Third* gives four or five. A simple word like **launder**, given two possible pronunciations in The Random House Dictionary, receives five here. Two of them, it is true, are marked *dial* for dialect. But a reader seeking specific guidance may find such an array of possibilities distracting. The editors made another choice some dictionary users have found mildly frustrating: they have placed the pronunciation key inside the front and back covers and on one page in the frontmatter and have chosen not to print abbreviated versions of it at the bottoms of the pages. This is less of a nuisance than one might imagine. The key is fairly easy to learn and uses most of the familiar symbols, some adopted from the International Phonetic Alphabet, the most obvious of which is a sophisticated use of the schwa. Here again, a user new to this dictionary would be wise to read Edward Artin's full-scale discussion of his principles of pronunciation in the frontmatter.

Despite these unfamiliar and unusual characteristics, *Webster's Third* manages very well to give an accurate picture of American speech. In his preface Gove sets forth some of his aims:

> This edition shows as far as possible the pronunciations prevailing in general cultivated conversational usage, both informal and formal, throughout the English-speaking world. It does not attempt to dictate what usage should be. It shows a wide variety of acceptable pronunciations based on a large file of transcriptions made by attentive listening to actual educated speech in all fields and in all parts of the country—the speech of those expecting to be completely understood by their hearers.

Thus, as in usage, *Webster's Third* does not prescribe any absolute or correct pronunciation. This means that users trying to find out how to pronounce an unfamiliar word will find recorded the pronunciation(s) used by educated people. Gone is the rule, in this volume at least, that most of us heard as we were growing up that the first pronunciation listed in a dictionary is the "preferred" one.

VI. Special Features

Webster's Third contains no special sections, but it does have 51 tables or charts (some of them quite small) that contain a good bit of encyclopedic information.

Individual articles that appear in the frontmatter of *Webster's Third* might be considered special features. In addition to the articles on word division and pronunciation, there are articles on spelling and punctuation to rival those in a handbook, as well as pages of special symbols and forms of address. Too, there is the 55-page addenda of new words and meanings to keep the dictionary up to date. And incidentally, although biographical sections and a gazetteer have been omitted from this dictionary, quite a bit of that kind of information is included in its generic senses. For example, readers looking up *Papua* would undoubtedly turn to the page on which **papuan** appears and would find, in general, what they are looking for. A person wanting more information would consult an atlas or encyclopedia anyway. One critic claimed that a person interested in Psyche could find her only as a synonym for **cheval glass**, but in actual fact she can be found under **psyche**: "in Greco-Roman mythology a beautiful maiden personifying the soul who was loved by the god of love Eros." For readers who need to have at hand more information or readier access for proper nouns, Merriam-Webster publishes a biographical dictionary and a geographical dictionary.

VII. Accessibility

Readers should find *Webster's Third* easy to use. It is thumb-indexed, guide words give the first and last words on each page, and entries are listed alphabetically letter by letter (that is, with no accounting for abbreviations or white space in compound words as in some listings). Numerals are spelled out as if they were words, words derived from *mac* or *mc* are treated as if all were *mac*, and *st.* or *ste.* is spelled out. Homographs receive distinguishing superior numbers and, whether related or not, are listed historically, with the oldest use first. Alternative spellings of words have their own entries, which means one needs to know the correct or closely approximate spelling before looking a word up. **Colour**, for example, comes three pages after **color**. **Inflexion** has its own entry, but one might spot these variant spellings in the etymologies at **color** and **inflection**. That is, readers might have to run a finger down the list of a good many words to find the British spelling if they do not already know it. Variant American spellings, however, appear in boldface along with the first entry, as in **advertise** . . . also **advertize**.

After the boldface entry word, at least initially, appears first the pronunciation of the word, then functional labels and inflectional forms, and then, since all main entries are in lowercase, a capitalization label where necessary. Next, the etymology is given, followed by status labels where deemed appropriate and, in order, subject labels and subject guide phrases. After a colon come the different senses of that word, each separated by boldface arabic numerals and, in some cases, each with verbal illustrations set between angle brackets. Other meanings of the word have their own entries. Cross-references and "see also" notes may appear after each sense or meaning; and in many entries synonymy paragraphs, some quite lengthy, appear as the last item of information.

VIII. Graphics and Format

The dictionary has seven full-page illustrations of such things as color (the only color illustrations in the book), constellations, muscular and skeletal systems of man, and trees. It is also lavishly illustrated in the main word list. One can hardly open the book without finding an illustration on one of the two pages. These illustrations are usually helpful and adequately detailed. However, one does wonder occasionally why a familiar object like a **faucet**, which comes in many forms anyway, is illustrated instead of the next word, **fauchard**, which is "a long-handled medieval weapon with a convex edge."

Webster's Third is a large, handsome, well-designed book. In educational institutions and libraries its size should cause no storage or usage problems, but most homes may not have a convenient table or shelf, since the opened book takes up half an average-size desk top. Conscious of this difficulty, Merriam-Webster advertises on the dust jacket a piece of furniture called a "dictionary table" that would solve the problem.

Bindings are sturdy and should last a long time. The pages are of durable, good-quality white stock that is heavy enough so there is no show-through of text at all. The type is clear and, though small, easy to read; main entry words are in boldface type overhanging the text. Margins, including the gutter margin, are quite wide. Generally the white space on a page seems ample, except perhaps for entries like **go** that run more than a whole column. Even these, however, are entirely readable because of the use of boldface numerals to mark the different senses.

IX. Summary

Despite the original negative criticism of *Webster's Third*, this is now generally considered to be the best dictionary of its kind in the world. (THE OXFORD ENGLISH DICTIONARY is not competition; that is another kind of dictionary.) This is not to say that it is the best dictionary for everybody. THE RANDOM HOUSE DICTIONARY OF THE ENGLISH LANGUAGE: SECOND EDITION, UNABRIDGED may have greater appeal for the general public. *Webster's Third* is perhaps more useful to scholars than it is to general users because of its thorough scholarship, its comprehensiveness, and its technical accuracy. Certainly, schools, libraries, business offices with large clerical staffs, college department offices, university offices, government offices—indeed, any office where communication in English is important—all should have at least one copy of *Webster's Third*. Also, if money were not a consideration, it should be the first choice for anyone seeking a general, unabridged dictionary. Even were a new edition to appear in the next few years, this dictionary, purchased now, would not go out of date in the purchaser's lifetime.

Anyone who wants to study the language as it is actually used and not as someone decrees it should be used, who wants to learn as much about a word in as concise a form as possible—in short, anyone who wants a comprehensive unabridged dictionary of the English language—wants *Webster's Third*.

Webster's II New Riverside Dictionary

Facts at a Glance

Full Title: **Webster's II New Riverside Dictionary**.
Publisher: Berkley Books.
Editors: Houghton Mifflin lexicographic staff.
Edition Reviewed: © 1984; 1986 printing.

Number of Entries: 55,000 definitions.
Number of Pages: 832.

Number of Illustrations: 200 black-and-white drawings.
Trim Size: 4¼″ × 6⅞″.
Binding: paperback.

Price: $3.95.
Sold in bookstores: also sold to libraries and other educational institutions.
ISBN 0-425-09169-4;
ISBN 0-425-08298-9.

I. Introduction

Described as a "user-oriented dictionary, designed for today's school and business needs," this abridged, pocket-size paperback contains over 55,000 entries and, according to the publisher, includes "hundreds of new words not found in any other dictionary." Other features include style and usage guides; word history paragraphs and synonym lists; foreign words and phrases; abbreviations and acronyms; measurement and monetary tables. According to the editors, the purpose of the *Webster's II New Riverside Dictionary* "is to mirror what our language is and to convey that information in a form appropriate to an inexpensive, fully portable dictionary."

Buyers should note that this Berkley paperback appears in two identical editions with the same price, but different covers and different ISBNs.

II. Authority

Based on the first edition of WEBSTER'S II NEW RIVERSIDE UNIVERSITY DICTIONARY, this 1984 paperback abridgment was compiled by Houghton Mifflin's editorial staff. Its lexicon is drawn from Houghton Mifflin's extensive database of citations.

III. Comprehensiveness

Compared to similar paperback dictionaries, this work offers a variety of the new science, medical, computer technology, and general words of the 1980s. Some of these terms include: **biofeedback**, **video disc**, **videocassette**, **gay** (homosexual), **punk rock**, **fast-track**, **freebie**, and **AIDS**. However, obviously not all of the "25,000" new words cited in the semi-abridged university dictionary have been transferred to this paperback. Among the words not listed are *palimony*, *Dolby System*, *snow* (argot for "cocaine" or "heroin"), *vidicon*, *freebase*, *grid-lock*, *modem*, and *reggae*.

Word etymologies and many of the idiomatic expressions found in the university dictionary are also omitted from this edition. Many of the word history paragraphs found in the hardcover copy are given in this abridged edition. These appear at the end of the entry, and are designated by a triangle, as in the following example:

> **pi·o·neer** . . . ▲ *word history:* The word *pioneer* is derived from the French *pion*, "foot soldier." *Pioneer* orig. denoted a soldier whose task was to prepare the way for the main body of troops marching to a new area. . . .

Although they appear in fewer entries than in the parent dictionary, some word synonym lists are included. These synonyms are printed in small capital letters and are introduced by a star, as in the following example:

> **mur·der** . . . ☆ **syns**: KILL, KNOCK OFF, LIQUIDATE, RUB OUT, SLAY, WASTE, WIPE OUT, ZAP.

A variety of language labels are provided to identify a specific orientation or other qualifying sense of a meaning, including for example, subject and geographic labels, plus nonstandard, informal, archaic, and slang designations. Phrasal verbs are introduced by boldface dashes, and are defined in alphabetical sequence, as in the following case:

> **give** . . . —**give away** . . . —**give in** . . . —**give out** . . . —**give up**.

Inflected forms are either partially or fully delineated (depending on their number of syllables), and immediately follow the pronunciation of the entry word.

IV. Quality and Currency of Entries

Entry words are printed in boldface type overhanging the text columns. When entries have more than one sense, they are ordered according to clusters of related subsenses, rather than by their frequency of occurrence or by their historical meaning. These multiple senses are numbered sequentially in boldface, and subsenses are indicated by boldface letters—for example:

> **gate**[1] (gāt) *n.* **1. a.** An opening in a wall or fence. **b.** An often hinged structure that closes or blocks a gate. **2.** . . .

A boldface colon separates two or more elements within a particular sense of a definition:

> **in·eq·ui·ty** . . . **1.** Injustice: unfairness.

Compared with other paperback dictionaries of its size and scope, the *Webster's II New Riverside Dictionary* has much to offer. Readers will find that the definitions are generally clear and concise. Although the essential meanings of the words are provided, the definitions themselves are less comprehensive than those in the hardcover edition. Other features are also either omitted or trimmed down in this work. Compare, for example, the following entries—the first is found in the hardcover dictionary, the second in the paperback edition:

> **cough** (kôf. kŏf) *v.* **coughed, cough·ing, coughs** [ME *coughen.*]—*vi.* **1.** to eject air from the lungs loudly and suddenly. **2.** To produce a noise similar to that of coughing <The engine coughed and died.>—*vt.* To expel by coughing <coughed out phlegm>—**cough up**. *Slang.* To relinquish (e.g., money), often reluctantly.—*m.* **1.** an act of coughing. **2.** A condition marked by frequent coughing.

> **cough** (kôf, kŏf) *v.* **1.** To eject air from the lungs suddenly and loudly. **2.** To make a noise similar to that of coughing. **3.** To expel by coughing.—**cough** *n.*

Although illustrative phrases are provided in many of the definitions, unfortunately, the exemplification of some abstract senses of words ("To make a noise similar to that of coughing") is excluded in this condensed version.

V. Syllabication and Pronunciation

Syllables are separated by boldface centered dots, not only in the entry word, but in the inflected and derived forms as well, when indicated. However, syllabication of compound words is not duplicated: **dif·fer·en·tial**, but **differential calculus**, if words in the compound appear as main entries.

Pronunciations are given immediately after the entry word and are enclosed in parentheses. Based on the International Phonetic Alphabet (IPA), a pronunciation key appears in the front of the book: however, this key is not shown on any other page of the dictionary, even in a simplified form. This lack of a key throughout the dictionary may limit the paperback's usefulness, but should not prove troublesome for those familiar with basic dictionary phonetics.

VI. Special Features

The appendix includes "A Concise Guide to Style and Usage," an abridged version of the guide found in the hardcover edition. The sections on capitalization, italicization, punctuation, clichés, and redundant expressions are identical to the original, but omit the section entitled "Problems in English Usage." Although the guide in this paperback edition provides some general usage rules for quick reference, it is too cursory to be of great value. Measurement and currency tables are given within the dictionary's main vocabulary, under their corresponding letters in the alphabet.

VII. Accessibility

Boldface pairs of guide words at the top outer corner of each page indicate the first and last entry on that page. Words that have the same spelling, but are derived from a different etymology, are represented by superscript numbers which alert the user to other listings of the word. These aids, along with the fact that entry words are printed in boldface and overhang the text, make it easy for the user to locate specific entries.

VIII. Graphics and Format

The 200 black-and-white line drawings are fairly large and well-rendered. A rectangular border outlines each illustration, making these drawings easy to distinguish on the page. The paper is a newsprint typically used in paperbacks, and the book is not well-bound—placing the book flat, with its pages open, too often will tear them away from the spine; but, the generous amount of margin space, particularly at the gutter, means that this dictionary is easy to hold and read, even though the typeface is quite small.

IX. Summary

The *Webster's II New Riverside Dictionary* provides current, concise, and clear definitions. Its small size will fit conveniently on the most cluttered desk top, but the non-durable binding is a consideration for prospective buyers who plan to use a dictionary often. For the modest price, this dictionary should serve the casual user for a number of years. However, the limitations of its format make it less satisfactory for library collections.

Webster's II New Riverside Pocket Dictionary

Facts at a Glance

Full Title: **Webster's II New Riverside Pocket Dictionary.**
Former Title: The Pocket Dictionary.
Publisher: Houghton Mifflin.
Editors: Fernando de Mello Vianna, Anne D. Steinhardt, and Pamela DeVinne.
Edition Reviewed: © 1978.

Number of Entries: 35,000.
Number of Pages: 256.
Trim Size: 3½" × 5½".
Binding: paperback.

Price: $2.95.
Sold in bookstores; also sold to libraries and other educational institutions.
ISBN 0-395-41822-4.

I. Introduction

Webster's II New Riverside Pocket Dictionary is a pocket-sized reference source of surprising scope and depth. It includes pronunciations, inflected forms, variants, and irregular plurals. The volume also contains several special features: a guide to the use of the dictionary and appended features covering punctuation, proofreaders' marks, weights and measures, the metric system, and U.S. states.

II. Authority

Editors of the volume are members of Houghton Mifflin's permanent lexicographic staff. Editorial Director Fernando de Mello Vianna has also served as an editor for the American Heritage dictionaries.

III. Comprehensiveness

With its 35,000 entries, the dictionary is considerably more comprehensive than the comparable WEBSTER'S VEST POCKET DICTIONARY. The work includes variant spellings, indicating whether two spellings are equally frequent or one is preferred. Inflected forms of verbs, adjectives, and adverbs are provided when they are irregular or may pose spelling difficulties. Irregular plurals are shown; regular plurals appear when there is an irregular variant or when the regular plural is liable to be misspelled. Part-of-speech labels are provided, as are additional grammatical labels indicating, for example, verb forms and tenses, comparatives and superlatives, and noun genders.

Excluded from the dictionary are etymologies, synonyms, abbreviations, and biographical and geographic entries. Only the omission of abbreviations is likely to present problems for the student or adult user of the work.

IV. Quality and Currency of Entries

Entries include the boldface, syllabified main entry word: pronunciation in parentheses: italicized part-of-speech abbreviations: boldface variants and inflected forms, as appropriate: and definition(s). Homographs receive separate main entries, with each distinguished by a superscript number.

Definitions are clear and concise. Multiple senses are frequently provided and are introduced with boldface numerals. Indeed, this work's entries often define more shades of meaning than would be expected of so compact a dictionary. A representative entry is the following:

> **a·bove** (ə-būv′) *adv.* **1.** Overhead. **2.** In a higher place, rank, or position. —*prep.* **1.** Over. **2.** Superior to. **3.** In preference to. —*n.* Something that is above. —*adj.* Appearing or stated earlier.

In comparison, WEBSTER'S VEST POCKET DICTIONARY lists only one adverbial and two prepositional senses for the word.

Webster's II New Riverside Pocket Dictionary

❶ Pronunciations are enclosed in parentheses

❷ Syllabication is shown by centered dots

❸ Inflected forms are given, in boldface, when irregular or when their spelling might be doubtful

❹ Derivatives, set in small boldface type, are run into the main entry

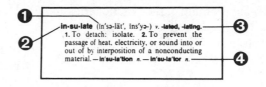

As is appropriate for a work of this size and scope, many technical and specialized terms are excluded. The word list includes current entries such as **astronaut**, **ecology**, **gay** (homosexual), and **program** (computer science sense). However, **computer** is listed only as a variant of **compute**, which is defined as "To calculate." Examples of words excluded, in part because of the dictionary's 1978 date, are *file* and *data* in their computer sense, *videodisc*, and *videocassette*.

V. Syllabication and Pronunciation

Syllabication is indicated in main entry words by centered dots and in inflected forms by centered dots or stress marks. Pronunciation follows a system of 45 symbols that are explained at the front of the volume in the guide to the dictionary's use. Sample words in the pronunciation key show the sound under consideration in boldface type. The symbols should not present difficulties to students or other readers.

VI. Special Features

The number of special features provided is unusual for a pocket dictionary. In addition to a brief, clear introductory guide to the use of the work, the volume includes several appended features. A brief guide to punctuation usefully covers the most important rules governing the dash, exclamation point, comma, period, colon, question mark, quotation marks, semicolon, brackets, apostrophe, and parentheses. A chart lists and illustrates the use of proofreaders' marks. Tables of weights and measures incorporate both customary U.S. and metric units, and a guide to the metric system and metric conversion table are provided. Finally, the volume includes a list of U.S. states that notes capitals, dates of admission to the Union, and population, although the date for the population figures is not indicated.

VII. Accessibility

Alternative spellings appear in boldface type. If the variants are used with roughly equal frequency, they appear together at the beginning of the entry (**ax.**

axe). If one form is distinctly preferred, it is listed as the main entry; the variant appears after the pronunciation (Also **the·a·tre**).

Words are especially easily located with the dictionary's "Rapid Word Finder" system, which is explained on the volume's opening page. According to this system, each letter of the alphabet is assigned a number (A–1, B–2, and so on; *X*, *Y*, and *Z* have no numbers but are instead grouped together). The user refers to the chart on the first page to determine the number corresponding to the first letter of the word he or she is seeking. At the top outer margin of each page within the word list appears the appropriate letter-number designation in prominent white on a black background. The user will find it quicker to seek a number, according to this system, than to seek a letter section through the use of guide letters or guide words alone. However, each spread also is headed by two boldface guide words, indicating the first and last entries on the spread.

A table of contents at the front of the volume lists the dictionary's special features and ensures that they will not be overlooked.

VIII. Graphics and Format

Boldface main entry words overhang the text. Type is small, but readable and larger than that of WEBSTER'S VEST POCKET DICTIONARY. Adequate margins and white space also contribute to readability. Paper permits minimal show-through of text. When the spine is cracked to open the book flat, the pages do not separate from the binding. This paperback is sturdy enough to hold up well to frequent use.

IX. Summary

Webster's II New Riverside Pocket Dictionary sweeps the vest pocket dictionary field. It not only contains more entries than its best-known rival, WEBSTER'S VEST POCKET DICTIONARY, but also defines more senses of its entry words. Moreover—no small consideration—it has larger print and is easier to read. This book may be extremely useful for writers on the go; it can also supplement larger dictionaries in a home or office reference collection. This is altogether an admirable little book.

Webster's II New Riverside University Dictionary

Facts at a Glance

Full Title: **Webster's II New Riverside University Dictionary.**
Publisher: Houghton Mifflin.
Editors: Anne Soukhanov, Kaethe Ellis, Kerry W. Metz, and David Pritchard.
Edition Reviewed: 1984.

Number of Entries: 200,000.
Number of Pages: 1,536.
Number of Illustrations: 400 black-and-white.
Trim Size: 6¾" × 9⁹⁄₁₆".
Binding: cloth.

Price: $14.95.
Sold in bookstores; also sold to libraries and other educational institutions.
ISBN 0-395-33957-X.

I. Introduction

Webster's II New Riverside University Dictionary is designed specifically with the college community in mind. As the dust jacket states, this dictionary is "not only the latest, most up-to-date dictionary . . . [but] also the most distinctive"; it contains 200,000 definitions, which include 25,000 new words from business, technology, science, and general use, plus a variety of special features.

A sampling (but by no means an exhaustive list) of what readers will find in *Webster's II* includes: an informative explanatory diagram of the major elements of this dictionary; 300 "word history" paragraphs throughout the entries describing the origin and development of the words in the English language; two types of usage guides (brief notes included in the actual definitions, plus a section in the front of the book that explains in greater detail the more confusing and complex questions about usage); over 900 synonym paragraphs in the entries; a style guide that contains over 100 rules for capitalization, punctuation, and italics; a diction guide that lists clichés and redundant expressions; guides for writing business letters and school research papers; a section on forms of address; an encyclopedic section with biographic and geographic names, abbreviations, foreign terms, measurement tables; and signs and symbols charts; and 400 detailed line drawings.

II. Authority

An impressive editorial staff and management team of Houghton Mifflin helped to compile *Webster's II*, including Senior Editor Anne H. Soukhanov; Coordinating Editor Kaethe Ellis; Publisher Howard Webber; Director of Editorial Operations Margery S. Berube; Senior Editor, Usage Dolores R. Harris; Editor, Pronunciation Pamela B. DeVinne; Editor, Word Histories and Etymologies Marion Severynse; and numerous contributing editors, database keyboarding staff, and special assistants.

According to the dust jacket, before compiling this dictionary, the editors first "conducted extensive research through the Gallup Organization to find out what features people really want in a dictionary." Drawing from the Houghton Mifflin electronic lexical database, in addition to a number of unique features they ascertained as important, the editors also have stylized the lexicon in *Webster's II* to avoid stereotyping by sex. For example, the definition for **housekeeper** is "one hired to perform the domestic tasks in a household," which avoids identifying the job with either sex.

Certain offensive words are omitted that, according to the preface, "do not inform so often as they raise questions about the access to the lexicon, particularly by young people." For example, *cunt*—which appears as an entry in the WEBSTER'S NEW WORLD DICTIONARY: SECOND COLLEGE EDITION and THE RANDOM HOUSE COLLEGE DICTIONARY—is omitted from *Webster's II*. Slang (vulgar) definitions for the entries *screw* and *bang* are not provided in *Webster's II*, but are given in WEBSTER'S NEW WORLD and THE RANDOM HOUSE COLLEGE.

III. Comprehensiveness

Such recently popularized words as *crack*, in its cocaine sense, *Chernobyl*, *New Age*, *NutraSweet*, *posslq*, and *yuppie* will not be found in *Webster's II;* however most new words of the 1980s are represented in this contemporary edition. The range of current terms in science, medicine, computer technology, and street or media-generated words represented in this dictionary include: **AIDS, biofeedback, Dolby System, fast-track, freebase, gridlock, modem, palimony, punk rock, reggae, snow,** in its cocaine or heroin sense, **vidicon.**

The etymology of most words, inserted in brackets, is placed immediately before the definitions. Exceptions include words that are formed solely from other words, prefixes, and suffixes that are main entries. For example, the entry **blue law** is a term made from two words whose etymologies are provided separately; to avoid redundancy, the etymology is not listed under this entry. All etymological symbols and abbreviations used throughout the text are given on a separate page in the frontmatter of the dictionary.

Webster's II New Riverside University Dictionary

❶ Etymology is enclosed in brackets

❷ Related forms that require no definition are set in boldface type and run into the main entry

❸ Synonyms are listed after the boldface abbreviation *syns*

❹ Word histories appear after selected entries

❺ Examples of usage are enclosed in angle brackets

❻ Usage labels are italicized

❼ Cross-references appear in small capitals

rich (rĭch) *adj.* **-er, -est.** [ME *riche* < OE *rīce.*] **1.** Having extensive material wealth. **2.** Having great value or worth. **3.** Magnificent : luxurious. **4. a.** Abundantly supplied. **b.** Abounding, esp. in natural resources. **5.** Extremely productive. **6.** Containing a large amount of choice ingredients, as butter, sugar, or eggs <a *rich* pastry> **7. a.** Pleasantly full and mellow <a *rich* voice> **b.** Warm and strong in color. **8.** Containing a large proportion of fuel to air. **9.** *Informal.* Very funny. **—rich'ly** *adv.* **—rich'ness** *n.*

☆ **syns:** RICH, AFFLUENT, LOADED, MONEYED, WEALTHY *adj.* *core meaning:* having a large amount of money, land, or other material possessions <a *rich* politician> **ant:** poor

▲ word history: The close connection between wealth and power can be seen in the semantics of the word *rich.* The Old English ancestor of *rich, rīce,* meant basically "powerful," although it also meant "wealthy" and "of high rank." In Old English times it was likely that a person would possess either all three attributes or none. In Middle English the sense "wealthy" came to predominate because Old French *rich,* which meant "wealthy," was also in use as an English word. Both the French word and the English word have a common Germanic ancestor, which is a borrowing through Celtic of Latin *rex,* "king." There are many English words related to *rich,* among them *realm, reign, regime,* and *rajah.*

In addition to etymologies, "word history" paragraphs are supplied for words whose origins are especially interesting. According to the editors, certain words were chosen "because their development illustrates common and important linguistic processes and, it is hoped, an understanding of their development will provide a better appreciation of language as a living and ever-changing human phenomenon." The entry for one such word follows:

blue·stock·ing (bloo'stŏk'ĭng) *n.* [After the *Blue Stocking* Society, a nickname for a chiefly female literary club of 18th-cent. London.] A scholarly or pedantic woman.**—blue'stock'ing** *adj.*

▲ word history: The term *bluestocking* seems always to have been one of contempt and derision, for it originally signified one who was informally and unfashionably dressed in blue worsted rather than black silk stockings. Such informal wear was common at literary and intellectual gatherings in 18th-century London, which were scornfully dubbed "bluestocking" societies by those who preferred parties where they could play cards and indulge in other idle amusements in their best and most fashionable clothes. Since the literary gatherings were organized and attended primarily by women, the term *bluestocking* was transferred, sneer and all, to any woman with pretensions or aspirations to literature and learning.

Numerous labels indicated within the entries help to identify a specific topic, field orientation, or other qualifying sense of a meaning, for example: subject labels; stylistic and geographic labels; "nonstandard," "informal," "slang," "obsolete," "archaic," and "chiefly Brit." designations, as well as regional distinctions. Following is a sampling of some of these designations:

co·da . . . *Mus.* A passage bringing a movement or composition to a formal close.
Di·an·a . . . *Rom. Myth.* **1.** The goddess of chastity, hunting, and the moon. **2.** The moon.
ev·er·more . . . **1.** *Archaic.* Forever: always.

hay·seed . . . *Slang.* A bumpkin: yokel.
lib·ber . . . *Informal.* A proponent of liberation.
med·al·ist . . . **Chiefly Brit. var. of** MEDALIST.

Cross-references provide additional information within an entry, and at the same time help to avoid unnecessary duplication. When two terms are synonymous, a full definition is given for the most frequently occurring term; the second term, alphabetically listed as an entry in the text, is defined by its synonymous term, set in small capital letters, which is then followed by the appropriate sense number of the first term. For example, note how cross-referencing is handled in the following entry: "**rat · fink** . . . n. Slang. RAT 3"; the meaning of **ratfink** is then defined under the following sense of the word **rat**: "**rat** . . . **3.** *Slang.* One who is despicable and sneaky, esp. one who betrays or informs on one's associates." Cross-referencing is also used to designate variant forms, for example, "**fore·swear** . . . v. var. of FORSWEAR." In a third case, cross-referencing directs the user to tabular data located elsewhere in the dictionary; directional cross-references occur at entries for the Bible, letters of various alphabets, monetary units, and the months of principal calendars, for example, "**ru·pee** . . .— See table at CURRENCY."

Entry variants are set in boldface type and are of two kinds: equal variants and secondary variants. An italicized *or* between two variant forms means that they are almost equally used, whereas a distinct preference for one variant form over the other is indicated by an italicized *also*: "**sau·terne** *or* **Sau·terne**," but, "**rav·el·ing** *also* **rav·el·ling**."

Verb phrases and idiomatic expressions are introduced by boldface dashes and are defined in alphabetic order as subentries, for example: "**give** . . .— **give away** . . .—**give back** . . .—**give in** . . .—**give off** . . . —**give out** . . . —**give over** . . .—**give up** . . . —**give way.**" Boldface, syllabified run-on entries also are introduced by a dash, for example: "**crys·tal·lize** *also* **crys·tal·ize** (krĭs′tə-līz′) *v.* **-lized, -liz·ing, -liz·es** *also* **-ized, -iz·ing, -iz·es**."

Usage notes are offered for those terms that have traditionally presented problems to speakers and writers, and they are designated by the heading **usage** before the specific sense of the terms to which it applies. Synonymous terms of various entries that are considered of special interest to users are presented in clusters following the entry, or particular sense of the word. These synonyms are rendered in small capital letters and are followed by the appropriate part-of-speech label, as well as an italicized *core meaning* heading introducing the shared denotation of the word cluster. For the entry word **post**[3], for example,

> **syns**: POST, ENTER, INSERT, RECORD, REGISTER *v. core meaning*: to place on a list or in a record <*posted* the names of the major contributors>.

IV. Quality and Currency of Entries

Definitions are clear and concise and will be adequate for most users. The entry words are printed in boldface type. When entries have more than one sense, they are ordered according to clusters of related subsenses, rather than by frequency of occurrence or by their historical context. In this manner, the various senses are better perceived as a structured unit. These multiple senses are numbered sequentially in boldface, whereas subsenses are introduced by boldface letters, as in the following example:

> **churl** (chûrl)*n.* [ME < OE *ceorl*, peasant] **1.** A rude boor. **2.** A miser: niggard. **3. a.** A ceorl. **b.** A medieval English peasant.

Note that a boldface colon separates two (or more) elements within the senses of the definitions.

Verbal illustrations, particularly useful to exemplify subtle shades of meaning, are enclosed by angle brackets.

> **di·vine** . . . Inspired by or devoted to a deity < *divine* worship > . . . Supremely pleasing < a *divine* little house in the country >.

Explanatory phrases, especially helpful to exemplify function words, interjections, or intensives, are introduced by dashes.

> **by** . . . —Used in multiplication and division < 3 *by* 5 > . . .—Used with measurements < a section 4 *by* 8 feet >.

V. Syllabication and Pronunciation

Boldface centered dots are used to separate the syllables of the entry word as well as its inflected and derived forms (when applicable); however, this dictionary does not show syllabication in compound words following an entry word that is already syllabified, for example, **cor·re·la·tion** and **correlation coefficient**. Pronunciations are also syllabified, but they follow phonological rules rather than the traditional word division method.

The pronunciations, based on the International Phonetic Alphabet, are given immediately after the entry word, enclosed in parentheses. When more than one stress mark is indicated, the strongest stress is indicated by a boldface mark. Variant pronunciations are given when necessary, and they follow the variant forms. Although a full pronunciation key is given in the frontmatter, a short key is provided beneath the inside columns of each pair of facing pages.

A boldface dagger shown at the left of an entry indicates that at least one sense of an entry is limited to a particular region or regions of the United States:

> †**you-all** (yo͞o′ôl′) *also* y′all (yôl) *pron. Southeastern U.S.* You. —Used in addressing two or more persons or referring to two or more persons, one of whom is addressed.

VI. Special Features

Most dictionaries provide a large assortment of special features, and *Webster's II* is no exception. Although "A Concise Guide to Style, Usage, and Diction" is informative, this section is not comprehensive enough to cover all usage and style problems; however, basic conventions of American capitalization, punctuation, italization, and diction (including lists of clichés and redundant expressions) are discussed. The more subtle usage problems that most college-age students will encounter can be better served by a good grammar handbook.

This same reservation applies to both the "Student's Guide to Typewriting Research Papers," and "Business Letter Styles" sections. The information in these is helpful but not exhaustive, which limits their usefulness. However, the "Forms of Address" section is especially comprehensive and will undoubtedly come in handy for users from time to time.

The sections in the back of the dictionary—"Abbreviations," "Biographical Entries," and "Geographical Names," as well as a briefer "Foreign Words and Phrases" section—are extensive and up-to-date and will prove invaluable. Also included in the backmatter are comprehensive measurement tables, including scientific measurement and a metric conversion chart, and on the last page, a half-page listing of "Signs and Symbols."

VII. Accessibility

Pairs of guide words are printed together at the top outer corner of each page and are divided by a bullet.

The word to the left is the first entry listed on the page, and the word to the right is the last word. The volume is thumb-indexed for easy use. However, the pages are of very thin paper, which makes it cumbersome to thumb through the sections to find words quickly. Homographs are conveniently noted by superscript numbers immediately following an entry.

VIII. Graphics and Format

There are 400 distinctive black-and-white line illustrations in *Webster's II*. The large size, combined with the rectangular border outlining each of these drawings, helps to make the graphics stand out on a page. Obviously quantity has been sacrificed for quality, since 400 illustrations in a book of 200,000 entries are relatively few.

The typeface used in this dictionary is very small and requires close scrutiny to discern the printing; however, the even inking and the generous margins help to make it fairly easy to read. Overall, this book has an attractive, sturdy quality so that most users will be able to enjoy it for many years.

IX. Summary

Webster's II is hard to fault on any count. It is comprehensive and contemporary in orientation, its definitions are clearly given and exemplified, and it offers a fountain of information not always found in other reference books of this size and scope. This dictionary is best suited for adult use or university-level study. And overall, this well-bound, sturdy volume should prove of lasting value for its $14.95 price.

Webster's Vest Pocket Dictionary

Facts at a Glance

Full Title: **Webster's Vest Pocket Dictionary.**
Publisher: Merriam-Webster.
Edition Reviewed: © 1981.

Number of Entries: 18,000.
Number of Pages: 380.
Trim Size: $3\frac{1}{8}'' \times 5\frac{3}{8}''$.
Binding: cloth (flexible simulated leather).

Price: $2.25.
Sold in bookstores and other outlets; also sold to libraries and other educational institutions.
ISBN 0-87779-190-2.

I. Introduction

The publisher describes *Webster's Vest Pocket Dictionary* as an "extremely concise reference to those words which form the very core of the English vo-cabulary." Despite its small, handy format, the work bears a distinct family resemblance to the larger, highly respected dictionaries in the Merriam-Webster family. The brevity of the vest pocket work's definitions will provide readers from junior high to adult level with a resource for quick, reliable checks on meaning or spelling.

II. Authority

This pocket dictionary belongs to the highly respected Merriam-Webster family of dictionaries, and bears many resemblances to its larger companions. Readers should be aware that, unlike some other so-called Webster pocket dictionaries available in màss market outlets and chain stores, this is an authoritative, albeit brief, book.

III. Comprehensiveness

A rough estimate of the contents is that there are somewhere between 18,000 and 20,000 bold main entries plus 20 additional lists of words formed from the most common prefixes, such as **anti-**, **mini-**, **super-**, and **un-**. There are also many additional variant spellings, inflected forms, and run-in entries giving a term or phrase related to main entries: for example, **sugar cane** under **sugar**, **eyeball**, **eyelashes**, and **eyelid** under **eye**.

IV. Quality and Currency of Entries

For quick reference, these very condensed definitions provide, in general, the denotative meaning of words as defined by the editors of WEBSTER'S NINTH NEW COLLEGIATE DICTIONARY: "the direct and specific part of meaning which is sometimes indicated as the total of all referents of a word and is shared by all or most people who use the word." This is illustrated by the entries for **mnemonic** ("*adj*: assisting memory") and **parameter** ("*n*: characteristic element").

Although secondary meanings are infrequent, essential ones are included, such as "**chin·a** *n* **1** : porcelain ware **2** : domestic pottery." In that case, the second definition covers typical everyday usage. More specialist or technical and scientific terms are usually excluded, although the third meaning of **program** is given as "coded instructions for a computer." There are other useful inclusions such as "**pro·bate** *n* : judicial determination of the validity of a will."

The lists of undefined words created by the addition of suffixes include a considerable range of words that one is likely to encounter in normal speech and writing. Under **in-**, for example, there are two brief definitions: "**1** not **2** lack of" followed by 201 words using the prefix.

The order of information under a main entry word is a simplified version of the sequence in the larger

Merriam-Webster dictionaries: main entry (with variant spelling) printed in bold type and syllabicated, pronunciation(s), part of speech, inflected forms, definition, and other forms of the word and run-in entries. All entries appear in alphabetical order, including homographs of different origins indicated by superior numbers:

> [1]**lark** *n* : a small songbird
> [2]**lark** *vb* or *n* : romp

Homographs with similar origins are run-in to the main entry; succeeding ones are indicated by a swung dash ~.

V. Syllabication and Pronunciation

Main entries are syllabicated with centered dots to show where a hyphen may be used when breaking a word.

A page of pronunciation symbols, based on the system used in the larger Merriam-Webster dictionaries, is printed immediately opposite the first page of *A* entries. There are brief explanations and sample words for special symbols such as the η indicating the *n* sound in "si**ng**, si**ng**er, fi**ng**er i**nk**," for example.

Primary stress is shown by a bold mark ' before the syllable; secondary stress is shown by a ' mark. All pronunciations appear between sets of back slashes after the bold entry: **im·por·tant** \'im'portənt\. Differences in pronunciations, where a syllable may not be uttered in some cases, are indicated by placing the letter(s) in parentheses, as: **lour** \'lau(')r\.

VI. Special Features

Immediately after the main vocabulary there are four pages of abbreviations, shown in one form, but with a note explaining that they often occur in other forms. There is also a short but clear "Handbook of Style"—a slightly pretentious title for the brief numbered information on how to use punctuation symbols from the apostrophe to the virgule, a section on italicization (5 numbered points) and on capitalization (22 numbered points), plus two short paragraphs on the plurals of English words. There are useful short examples of all these items given in brackets, as

> 15. Personifications are capitalized. <She dwells with Beauty.—John Keats.>

VII. Accessibility

Although the typeface is minute, the main entry words are printed in boldface overhanging the text. They can easily be located, as can the variant forms and run-in entries, also printed in bold type. At the top of each page toward the outer margin, two guide words are printed in bold type. A bold page number is centered over the inner column of text. Because the book is so small, it is easy to leaf through the pages to find a required word.

The main vocabulary is printed in two columns of text, with generous inner margins. There is sufficient white space so that the text does not appear dense on the pages.

VIII. Graphics and Format

There are no illustrations, but the design of the book is attractive and the boldface vocabulary words stand out from the entry text. Occasionally the diacritical marks in the pronunciations are difficult to distinguish; this is particularly true of the umlauted vowels: ä and ü.

The paper is a smooth, white coated stock with minimal show-through.

IX. Summary

This small dictionary fits easily into pockets and handbags. It is derived from authoritative larger works and contains sufficient vocabulary with the most basic definitions to be useful as a check on meaning and spelling. The cloth cover is a reinforced wipe-clean simulated leather. The pages are well glued to the cover, yet they can be opened wide. Of its kind, this is a very good dictionary for quick reference. Along with WESBSTER'S II NEW RIVERSIDE POCKET DICTIONARY, it is the best of the vest-pocket dictionaries.

Webster's Vest Pocket Dictionary

Facts at a Glance

Full Title: **Webster's Vest Pocket Dictionary: Revised Edition.**
Publisher: Thomas Nelson.
Editor: Walter C. Kidney; revised edition prepared under the direction of Laurence Urdang.
Edition Reviewed: © 1985; 3rd printing.

Number of Entries: over 10,000.
Number of Pages: 188.
Trim Size: 3″ × 5¼″.
Binding: paperback.

Price: $1.25.
Sold in bookstores and other outlets.
ISBN 0-8407-5991-6.

I. Introduction

Webster's Vest Pocket Dictionary: Revised Edition (published by Thomas Nelson and not to be confused with the dictionary of the same title published by Merriam-Webster) is an even more compact dictionary than Nelson's WEBSTER'S NEW COMPACT DIC-

Webster's Vest Pocket Dictionary: Revised Edition

❶ Field labels are italicized

❷ Both primary and secondary stress marks appear in boldface main entries

❸ Syllabication is shown by centered dots

❹ Derivatives are run into the main entry

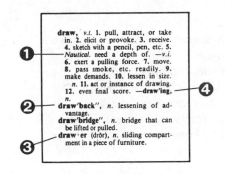

TIONARY. About 10,000 main entry words are defined very briefly. The dictionary is paperback and it fits easily into a shirt pocket or purse.

II. Authority

The dictionary was edited by Walter C. Kidney and its most recent revision was "prepared under the direction of Laurence Urdang," according to the title page. Urdang is the highly acclaimed linguist and lexicographer who has edited and written many books about the English language.

III. Comprehensiveness

No criteria for selection of main entry words is given, but these are words frequently used in everyday conversation. Slang, highly technical, unusual and difficult words are not included. The main entry words have definitions that are identical to those found in WEBSTER'S NEW COMPACT DICTIONARY, although this edition has fewer entries. The basis on which words were eliminated is not explained, but it appears that less common everyday words were omitted. Occasionally a new word has been added. For example, in the list of words beginning with "da," seven words were deleted and one word added to the words that are found in the WEBSTER'S NEW COMPACT DICTIONARY. Words deleted were *damper*, *damsel*, *dapple*, *dastard*, *dated*, *davenport*, and *daytime*. The word added was **daffodil**. Biographical and geographical names, as well as synonyms, antonyms, and etymologies, are not included.

IV. Quality and Currency of Entries

Succinct, bare-bones definitions are often only one or two words, yet they convey a sense of the meaning of the word. For example:

    gargantuan, *adj.* gigantic.
    gargoyle, *n.* fantastic waterspout.
    garish, *adj.* vulgarly showy.

Word forms are not given although variations of the word are found in the run-on entries. The compact design of this small dictionary does not allow for expanded definitions. However, the definitions given provide a clear meaning of the word. The vocabulary contains many words in current use, such as **gay** (referring to *homosexual*), and words pertaining to computers, such as **bit**, **byte**, **database**, **program** and **modem**.

V. Syllabication and Pronunciation

Dots for syllabication and diacritical marks to distinguish phonetic values are used in the main entry word. If further pronunciation guides are needed, they follow the main entry in parentheses. For example: **as·so·ci·ate** (əs sośhē ət). However, this rarely occurs. There is no pronunciation key to explain the symbols.

IV. Special Features

In addition to its small size, which is in itself a special feature, the dictionary has tables of weights and measures, metric equivalents, birthstones, and traditional and modern gift ideas for wedding anniversaries.

VII. Accessibility

For those with vision problems, this dictionary will be difficult to read. The print used in the definitions is minuscule. Even those with excellent sight will not want to use this volume for prolonged periods of time.

    Access to the material is through guide words located at the top of each page and through a letter-by-letter arrangement of the main entry words. In one case, an error occurs when **corpse** is listed before **corps**.

VIII. Graphics and Format

Entry words and related words are in small bold type, the parts of speech are abbreviated in italics, the definition is indented two spaces and is in a very small type font. Each small page is divided into two columns with an average of 28 words per column. There are no illustrations.

IX. Summary

Webster's New Pocket Dictionary is more current than most other pocket dictionaries. With the inclusion of words such as **ayatollah** and **database**, the dictionary keeps pace with political and technical words that have entered the mainstream of everyday usage. This little dictionary is useful for both its clarity and its currency, for occasional personal use, but not for libraries.

The World Book Dictionary

Facts at a Glance

Full Title: **The World Book Dictionary.**
Former Title: *The World Book Encyclopedia Dictionary.*
Publisher: World Book.
Editors: Clarence L. Barnhart and Robert K. Barnhart; Sol Steinmetz, Chief General Editor (Barnhart Books); Robert O. Zeleny, Editor-in-Chief (World Book).
Edition Reviewed: © 1988.

Number of Entries: 225,000.
Number of Pages: 2,554; 2 volumes.
Number of Illustrations: 3,000 in black-and-white.
Trim Size: 8⅜″ × 10⅞″.
Binding: hardcover.

Price: $69.00 (and various other prices when sold with *World Book Encyclopedia*).
Sold to libraries, other educational institutions, and door-to-door.
ISBN 0-7166-0287-3.

I. Introduction

The World Book Dictionary, a two-volume work containing more than 225,000 entries, is part of the Thorndike-Barnhart dictionary series. It is prepared in cooperation with World Book, Inc., which publishes the work. This semi-abridged dictionary is designed specifically to complement WORLD BOOK ENCYCLOPEDIA, but it also stands on its own. Because of its extensive lexicon, and because it is intended to suit the needs of a wide range of readers, it can even be considered a reasonable alternative to one of the three unabridged dictionaries currently on the market, as will be explained below.

In addition to giving careful attention to new words and phrases as well as to those which are well established, *The World Book Dictionary* also includes a generous selection of foreign words and phrases and selective etymologies. There are more than 3,000 illustrations to help clarify definitions.

II. Authority

This dictionary was first published in 1963 under the supervision of lexicographer Clarence L. Barnhart and was the largest work in the Thorndike-Barnhart series. It was based on the principles prepared and applied by linguist Leonard Bloomfield and psychologist Edward L. Thorndike.

In 1976, *The World Book Dictionary* was revised to include new words and meanings that had developed over the first decade of the dictionary's publication. Subsequently, it has been revised annually to reflect what the editors call our "living language"—the working vocabulary of the most common words and meanings in the English language.

The excellence of the Thorndike-Barnhart tradition is clearly visible in this edition. In addition to the editors, more than 150 consultants in over 70 fields of knowledge, who constitute an international advisory committee of distinguished linguists, phoneticians, and scholars, helped in the dictionary's preparation. (These authorities are listed by name and professional affiliation along with titles of their books.) Although the firm of Barnhart Books, Inc., undertook the primary editorial work, WORLD BOOK ENCYCLOPEDIA editors evaluated the dictionary and designed the educational frontmatter found in *The World Book Dictionary*; thus, it is specifically meant to be used as an adjunct to that encyclopedia.

More than 3 million examples gathered in over 25 years constitute the extensive quotation file used to update *The World Book Dictionary*. This is large, although not quite as extensive as Merriam-Webster's file.

III. Comprehensiveness

The World Book Dictionary is generally more comprehensive than other semi-abridged compilations. In fact, its high entry count makes it comparable to THE RANDOM HOUSE DICTIONARY OF THE ENGLISH LANGUAGE. It includes a large assortment of foreign words and phrases not typically found in the main lexicons of many college-level or desk dictionaries, as well as a selection of British terms, such as **beggar-my-neighbor**, **brickie**, and **Civvy Street**. Many of these terms are unlikely to be encountered by most Americans in their everyday reading. This extensive vocabulary, however, does make *The World Book Dictionary* at least partially competitive with the unabridged dictionaries for those readers who want a major dictionary that has a more accessible text and less formal lexicographic apparatus.

The examples often consist of quotations from public figures and actual writing examples. For instance, under the entry for **chafe**, one example of a figurative meaning is taken from the *Wall Street Jour-*

The World Book Dictionary

❶ A bold asterisk indicates that the entry word is illustrated

❷ Syllabication is shown by a vertical line between syllables

❸ Field labels are italicized

❹ Etymology is enclosed in brackets

❺ Cross-references are set in boldface type

❻ Examples of usage are italicized, with sources cited for specific quotations

❼ Usage labels are italicized

*Gothic (goth′ik), *n., adj.* —*n.* **1** a style of architecture using pointed arches, flying buttresses, and high, steep roofs. It was developed in western Europe during the Middle Ages from about 1150 to 1550. **2** the East Germanic language of the Goths. It is known chiefly from the translations of the Bible by Bishop Ulfilas in the 300's. **3** *Printing.* **a** Often, **gothic**. *U.S.* a square-cut style of type without serifs or hairlines. **b** *British.* black letter.
—*adj.* **1a** of or having to do with Gothic architecture: *a Gothic cathedral.* **b** of or having to do with the period during which Gothic architecture flourished: *Gothic art, a Gothic manuscript.* **2** of the Goths or their language. **3** *Figurative.* uncivilized; crude; barbarous: *O! more than Gothic ignorance* (Henry Fielding). **4** having to do with or characteristic of a style of fiction using grotesque and supernatural elements and often medieval settings or details to produce horror and romance: *a Gothic story. The Grecian splendor of the old novels and the Gothic horror of the new ones are products of the same psychology* (Saturday Review). **5** *Obsolete.* Germanic.
[< Late Latin *Gothicus* < *Gothī*; see etym. under **Goth**] —**Goth′i∣cal∣ly,** *adv.*

*Gothic
definitions 1, 3a

Gothic architecture

The World Book Dictionary
Gothic type

nal ("Missing such sales *chafes* retailers"). In another case, one meaning for the entry **alight** is illustrated by a quote from Mark Twain ("I *alighted* on just the book I needed in the library. . . . we *alighted* upon a sign which manifestly referred to billiards.").

Synonym studies immediately follow the particular definition that they are meant to amplify, and are preceded by the boldface label "SYN." in slightly smaller type than the paragraph of text. For example, following one meaning under the entry word for **excuse** is the following synonym list:

SYN.: justify, extenuate, exculpate.

Farther down, following another definition under the same entry, is the following note: "SYN.: justification." In some cases, the reader will be referred to another entry for a synonym study: under the entry word **ethical**, a note refers the user to the synonym study under **moral**.

Regional labels are used to indicate dialectic differentiations. English-speaking variations (Australian, British, Canadian, Scottish, and the United States) are also identified. Language labels are used to designate foreign terms; informal, obsolete, slang, figurative, poetic, and substandard usage; prefix and suffix entries; professional terms (such as those from biochemistry, medicine, and photography); trademark names; and the distinction *unfriendly use*, which applies to terms that belittle or insult.

Boldface run-on forms are syllabicated and are shown at the end of the definition. Abbreviations are included alphabetically among the regular listings. Usage notes are indicated by boldface arrows. The bracketed etymologies rely on two basic symbols: the angle bracket (⟨), which means "derived from" or "taken from," and the plus symbol (+), which means "and," and as in the following example:

cap∣ro∣lac∣tam . . . [⟨capro(ic) acid + lactam].

The many new words and technical terms found in the *World Book Dictionary* include **AIDS**, **biorhythm**, **cliometrics**, **crack** (as the term relates to cocaine), **data processing/base/bank**, **disk drive**, **Dolby**, **downer**, **freebie** or **freebee**, **freebase**, **fritz out**, **fast track**, **floppy disk**, **gofer**, **grid lock**, **gay** (in its homosexual sense), **modem**, **New Wave** (but not *New Age*), **posslq**, **program** (in its computer-related sense), **palimony**, **reggae**, **sitcom**, **videocassette/disk**, and **Yuppie**, **yuppie**, or **yuppy**. Such recently coined terms as *visually handicapped* or *hearing impaired* have not been added. Overall, the level of currency is comparable to that of THE RANDOM HOUSE DICTIONARY.

IV. Quality and Currency of Entries

The definitions are exceptionally clear, readable, and inclusive. The basic ordering of an entry is as follows: the syllabicated boldface entry term overhanging the text; the pronunciation in parentheses; the part-of-speech label in italics; partially spelled inflected terms, preceded by a hyphen, and also printed in boldface type; definitions, preceded by boldface numerals (and sometimes lowercase letters) when more than one definition is given; verbal illustrations in italics, when necessary; alphabetized idioms noted after the meanings to which they refer; etymology in brackets; synonym studies; and usage notes, when applicable, in italics.

The definitions are listed with the most commonly used meaning first. Consider, for example, the following entry:

e|mit (i mit′), v.t., -mit|ed, -mit|ting. **1** to send out; give off; discharge. *The sun emits light and heat. Volcanoes emit lava.* SYN.: exclude, expel, eject. **2** to put into circulation; issue. **3** to utter; express: *The trapped lion emitted roars of rage.* **4** to issue formally (as proper currency). [⟨Latin *ēmittere* ⟨*ex-* out + *mittere* send]

Definitions of less familiar, more specialized words such as **chaetopod** are often written at a sophisticated level:

chae|to|pod (kē t ə pod), **n.** any one of a group of annelid worms, having the body made up of more or less similar segments provided with muscular processes bearing setae. [⟨Greek *chaitē* a seta + *poús, podós* foot].

The definition of **chaetopod** assumes that the reader will either know what *annelid* and *setae* mean or be capable of looking up their definitions. This might present difficulties for those with reading problems who may not have the incentive to locate two definitions or to tie them in together—a necessary process if a user wants to find a comprehensive meaning for the first entry word consulted. For the most part, however, the complexity of the definition is appropriate to the needs of the reader most likely to be researching that term.

Usage notes are given for words about which there is widespread confusion even among well-educated writers. These notes should help to clear up confusion about usage, but they tend to be descriptive rather than prescriptive, so that in the end the writer is often left to his or her own judgment. For example, the usage note appended to the entry for **disinterested** reads as follows:

▶**Disinterested** and **uninterested** can be used to make a useful distinction of meaning. *Uninterested* means having no concern about the matter and paying no attention: *I find it difficult to entertain anyone so uninterested in everything I suggest doing.* In careful usage, *disinterested* means having no reason or desire to be anything but strictly impartial and fair: *A judge should be disinterested.* Increasingly, however, *disinterested* is being used with the meaning of *uninterested.* Because of this, it is wise to make sure that context makes the intended meaning of *disinterested* unmistakable.

The usage note for **hopefully** is slightly more ambiguous:

▶**Hopefully** in the usage "it is to be hoped that" has been avoided by some writers who were perhaps unaware of this long-established pattern of adverbial use in English as *doubtlessly, surely,* and *absolutely.*

V. Syllabication and Pronunciation

The World Book Dictionary presents syllabication in an innovative way. The syllables of entries are separated by light vertical lines. Phrase entries that are syllabified in their own alphabetical place in the dictionary are not divided:

cer|e|bral and cor|tex; but **cerebral cortex**.

Pronunciations are given in parentheses following the main entry word. In cases where several pronunciations are possible, the preferred pronunciation is provided first, and only the syllables that differ from that preferred pronunciation are shown. For example, the entry **criss|cross** lists its two variant pronunciations: "kris′krôs" and "-kros′."

A simplified pronunciation key based on the International Phonetic Alphabet (IPA) is given on the final page of the guide to the dictionary and on the first page of the second volume. An abridged form of this key is also found at the bottom outer corner of every right-hand page, except in rare cases where an illustration supplants the key, as at the beginning of the letter *E.* In addition to the various diacritical marks that help to highlight specific word sounds, a boldface accent emphasizes the primary stress of each word, and, when needed, a light accent indicates syllables that have secondary stress.

VI. Special Features

A notable feature of *The World Book Dictionary* is its lengthy and comprehensive introduction, printed on buff paper. The frontmatter is divided into four sections. "Using Your Language," the first section, contains ten chapters: "Where English Comes From" describes the origin and development of the English language; "Making Words" identifies the three elements that go into forming words (roots, affixes, and combining forms) and provides three full-page listings of prefixes, suffixes, and combining forms, their particular meanings, and word examples; "Learning to Spell Correctly" gives general spelling hints and offers spelling rules along with exceptions to the rules; "Common Misspellings" lists a full page of frequently misspelled words; "Parts of Speech" describes the basic elements and rules of each part of speech; "Capitalization" gives rules for using capital letters; "Punctuation" provides examples of the use of each major punctuation mark; "Choosing the Right Word" shows how various shades of meanings among words color language; "Writing and Spelling Traps" identifies the most commonly confused words in the English language (for instance, **advice**, **advise**; **beside**, **besides**; **council**, **counsel**, and so on); and "Increasing Your Word Power" provides hints for improving vocabulary and gives vocabulary inventory lists arranged by reading level, from third grade through college.

The second section, entitled "How to Write Effectively," provides the following subsections: "Improving your Writing"; "Writing Term Papers"; "Preparing an Outline"; "Documenting Research Reports"; "Writing Book Reports"; "Preparing Manuscripts," which also lists proofreaders' marks; "Letter Writing"; and "Using the Right Forms of Address," which tells how to address, both in speaking and writing, such titled persons as the president of the United States, governors, reigning kings and queens, foreign ambassadors to the United States, Roman Catholic priests, rabbis with doctorates, and so on.

The third section, "Using Different Languages," provides tables of different alphabets (Braille, hand language, International Morse Code, among others); lists the "International Phonetic Alphabet"; and describes systems of "Codes and Ciphers" and "Signs and Symbols" (those found in chemistry, plumbing, mapping, traffic, computer programming, boating, and so on). It also explains the purpose and development of "Slang and Jargon"; provides tables for converting measurements, including wire, lumber, time, surface or area, weight and mass measurements, among others; and gives the origins and meanings of first names.

Beginning on page 113 of the introductory material is the fourth and last section, "Using This Dictionary," a guide to the general features and format of *The World Book Dictionary*. Although this section appears in the table of contents, placing the material at the end of the extensive introductory and instructional matter effectively buries this much needed information. It is also difficult to find quickly even though it immediately precedes the lexicon.

In most cases, nevertheless, students and adults will find ample use for much of the special frontmatter. However, some sections (many pertaining to grammar and writing) cover too much material in too few pages to be of great value; users who need more than a general survey will be better served by more comprehensive, topical reference books. Overall, most readers will learn a great deal by simply browsing through the 124-page introductory section, even if many parts are more inclusive than a typical reader will ever need. The danger is that the sheer length of this section will intimidate some readers.

What sets this introduction apart from other dictionaries is its clear writing and built-in adjustments for different reading levels, a technique that is also a special feature of the main lexicon. In a short review, it is very difficult to characterize this technique—and its success—effectively; however, compare part of the entry for the word **dirty** (likely to be looked up by the youngest reader) with the definition for **disaccharide** (a chemical term likely to be looked up by adults):

> **dirty** . . . **-adj. 1** soiled by dirt; unclean; *dirty* hands.

> **disaccharide** . . . *n.* any one of a group of carbohydrates, such as lactose, maltose, sucrose, and various other sugars, which hydrolysis changes into two simple sugars (monosaccharides): *Ordinary table sugar and milk sugar belong to the disaccharide class of sugars* (Science News Letter). . . .

Both levels of definition are clear and are amplified by well-chosen illustrative usage.

VII. Accessibility

Attractive thumb indexes help readers to locate specific sections of this dictionary. Boldface guide words appear at the top outer corner of each double-page spread. When the book is opened, the guide word on the left-hand page denotes the first listing on the spread, the guide word on the right-hand page indicates the last entry shown. There are three columns of text per page.

When two or more spellings of the same word are used almost interchangeably, the words appear as a single entry and are joined by "or":

> **chan|nel¹** (chan′əl), *n., v.,* **-neled, -neling** or (*especially British*) **-nelled, -nelling**.

When there is a preferred spelling, the alternate spelling is shown at the end of the preferred-spelling entry word's paragraph; alternate spellings are also cross-referenced to the preferred spelling—for example: "**co|or**. . . . Also, *especially British*, **colour**"; the entry for **colour** is then presented in its own alphabetical placement as a separate heading. Cross-references are also given for related etymologies, illustrations, equivalent terms, usage notes, synonyms, and subentries that occur under other main entries. Homographs appear as separate entries and are indicated by superscript numerals immediately following the entry word: **crew**[1] and **crew**[2]. Users should find it easy to understand the etymologies in the *World Book Dictionary*, since these do not rely heavily upon complex abbreviations:

> **game**[1] . . . [Old English *gamen* joy]
>
> **isologous** . . . [⟨*iso-* + Greek *lógos* word, relation + English *-ous*]
>
> **parabole** . . . [⟨Greek *parabolē*. See etym. of doublets **palaver**, **parable**, **parabola**, **parole**.].

VIII. Graphics and Format

This dictionary offers an easy-to-read modern computer-set typeface (sans-serif Spectra for the main text and sans-serif Roma for the supplemental material), with generous white space. It is printed on high-quality, uncoated white paper, except for the introductory section, which is printed on buff.

Because of this dictionary's length (more than 2,500 pages), it is divided into two volumes: A through K and L through Z. The binding is exceptionally sturdy and will withstand heavy use. When either book is opened, the center margin is generous enough to prevent the text from disappearing into the gutter.

The more than 3,000 black-and-white line drawings are extremely well conceived and rendered. In virtually all cases, they will help the reader to understand and visualize the object that the entry is defining. For example, the entry for **carburetor** is accompanied by an annotated diagram of the same. For **caricature**, there is a drawing of George Bernard Shaw by *New York Review of Books* caricaturist David Levine. Beneath the definition for **clef** we see the treble clef, the bass clef, and three C clefs. The entry for **clerestory** includes a drawing of the side of a church, with the clerestory pointed out. What makes the illustrations in *The World Book Dictionary* so valuable is that the reader is never in any doubt about what is being depicted. Rarely is there any extraneous detail to distract or confuse the reader. And, simply as illustrations, these pictures add to the visual appeal of the pages.

IX. Summary

The World Book Dictionary has much to recommend it. Although not advertised as such, it is in effect an unabridged dictionary and in this and other regards can be considered in the same class as THE RANDOM HOUSE DICTIONARY OF THE ENGLISH LANGUAGE, WEBSTER'S NEW TWENTIETH CENTURY DICTIONARY, and perhaps even WEBSTER'S THIRD NEW INTERNATIONAL DICTIONARY. Its 225,000-word lexicon is well chosen, more selective than that of RANDOM HOUSE but just as useful, if not more so, for the general reader. The definitions are clear and precise, while the etymologies are pithy but do not confuse the reader with a plethora of symbols and abbreviations. *The World Book Dictionary* also follows the venerable practice of quoting sentences from newspapers, periodicals, and books to help clarify particular definitions; these illustrative sentences are indeed carefully chosen.

The pages themselves are well designed. The reader's eye is drawn immediately to the entry words. The typefaces are eminently readable, and there is ample white space. If there is any objection, it is that the two-volume format can be an inconvenience for the reader who needs to look up several words at one time. But given the general excellence of the content, this is a minor drawback. In short, *The World Book Dictionary* is a model of the lexicographer's craft. At $69.00, this title will be a valued addition to any general reference collection.

Chapter 11
Evaluations of
Etymological Dictionaries

The American Heritage Dictionary of Indo-European Roots

Facts at a Glance

Full Title: **The American Heritage Dictionary of Indo-European Roots.**
Publisher: Houghton Mifflin.
Editor: Calvert Watkins.
Edition Reviewed: © 1985.

Number of Entries: 13,000.
Number of Pages: 140.
Number of Indexes: 1.
Trim Size: 6¾" × 9¼".
Binding: cloth; paperback.

Price: $10.95 (cloth); $5.95 (paperback).
Sold in bookstores; also sold to libraries and other educational institutions.
ISBN 0-395-37888-5 (cloth);
ISBN 0-395-36070-6 (paperback).

I. Introduction and Scope

This title is a revised edition of what was previously the Appendix of Indo-European Roots in *The American Heritage Dictionary of the English Language* published in 1969. It is now published separately for the first time as a companion to THE AMERICAN HERITAGE DICTIONARY: SECOND COLLEGE EDITION. The editor, Calvert Watkins, states in the Preface that there have been many new findings in Indo-European studies since 1969, and that a thorough revision has been necessary to include the addition of many new roots. The Preface states, "Few entries in the dictionary have escaped revision. Old etymologies have been revised and brought into line with current thinking, and new etymologies have been proposed where it seemed proper to do so. The introductory essay has also been revised. . . ." The dictionary of Indo-European roots is intended for use by the general public, and is not for etymologists.

The Introduction tells us that early-nineteenth-century scholarship defined a family of languages as Indo-European if they had similarities which are assumed to be a continuation of a single prehistoric language known as Indo-European or Proto-Indo-European. Named after the geographical extremities of the distribution of the languages, the Indo-European family is but one of many language families, and English is but one of its many members.

Watkins points out that language has a traceable history unlike many other cultural phenomena and that most of us could trace the roots of our English language more precisely than we could our biological ancestry. English, as a direct descendant of Indo-European, is traced from prehistoric Common Germanic, one of whose dialects was West Germanic which ultimately became Old English. Through the last thousand years of documented history, the English language has borrowed extensively from other languages; however, the small amount of Old English vocabulary remains the core of our language; more than fifty percent of the roots of Indo-European are somehow represented in modern English. Watkins gives an extensive explanation of how the "compar-

The American Heritage Dictionary of Indo-European Roots

❶ An asterisk denotes a reconstructed (hypothetical) form

❷ The abbreviation *Pok.* identifies a page reference to Julius Pokorny's *Indogermanisches etymologisches Wörterbuch*

❸ Boldface cross-references are to other Indo-European roots in the dictionary

❹ Small capitals denote cross-references to etymologies in the *American Heritage Dictionary: Second College Edition*

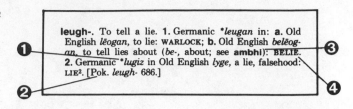

leugh-. To tell a lie. **1.** Germanic **leugan* in: **a.** Old English *lēogan*, to lie: WARLOCK; **b.** Old English *belēogan*, to tell lies about (*be-*, about; see **ambhi**): BELIE. **2.** Germanic **lugiz* in Old English *lyge*, a lie, falsehood: LIE². [Pok. *leugh-* 686.]

ative method" can reconstruct languages spoken before the written word was available. Using as an example the concept of **daughter-in-law**, he traces the word in several languages (cognates) to the prehistoric Indo-European root word. Although none of the languages in the family retain the original word intact, the alterations—seen through cultural practices—are in themselves fascinating.

In the extensive Introduction there are explanations of pronunciation, grammar, and syntax indicating that inflection—variations in the endings of words—showed differences in meaning and relationship within a sentence. With a few exceptions, all Indo-European words were inflected so that the structure of these words became the "root" plus one or more "suffixes" and an "ending." The root was the basic idea which the suffix could modify, and the root plus the suffix(es) became the "stem." Stems were the basic dictionary of Indo-European. Using as an example the English word *love*, which can be a noun or a verb as well as the base for **lovely**, **lover**, and **beloved**, Watkins explains how a single root could produce a number of derivative stems. The stems are thus grouped under the root (which is the base):

> **dail-.** To divide. Northern Indo-European root. **1.** Germanic **dailjan* in Old English *dælan*, to share: DEAL¹. **2.** Germanic **dailaz* in Old English *dāl*, portion, lot: DOLE¹. **3.** Germanic prefixed form **uz-dailjam*, "a portioning out," judgment (**uz-*, out; see **ud-**), in Old English *ordāl*, lot, apportionment: ORDEAL. [In Pok. *dā-* 175.]
>
> **daiwer-.** Husband's brother. Latin *lēvir*, husband's brother: LEVIRATE. [Pok. *dāiur* 179.]

The dictionary is arranged alphabetically by root.

II. Format

The paperback edition reviewed here is a sturdily bound oversize paperback. The typeface, though not large, is readable and printed on good quality white stock. Margins are adequate, and the dictionary text is printed in two wide columns per page. Boldface type for the roots (which are slightly extended into the margins), is easy to spot, as are the English words in all capitals. Unfortunately, the 10,000 English word index is quite difficult to read as is the Table of Indo-European Sound Correspondences which follows it. However, a diagram of the Indo-European Family of Languages at the end of the book is written in a much larger and clearer type.

III. Quality and Currency of Entries

In spot checking the revised 1985 edition with the 1969 edition, virtually all of the entries checked had some slight revision, either in wording or in the addition or deletion of variants. Although Watkins states that new roots have been added to this edition, he does not give examples of these. The definitions given for the roots are clear and concise: **leubh-.** To care, desire, love; **sen-¹.** Old; **peg-.** Breast; and **ker-⁴.** Heat, fire. Variants are as clear as possible, although some knowledge of words, and also some interest in the subject, are necessarily prerequisites for the best use of this work. In comparison with another similar dictionary, DICTIONARY OF ENGLISH WORD-ROOTS by Robert W. L. Smith, the *American Heritage Dictionary of Indo-European Roots* is superior. In length of entries, explanation of variants, and extent of introduction, Watkins is authoritative, whereas Smith's compilation simply gives the root with several English derivative words. Smith's roots do not strictly correspond to those of the *American Heritage Dictionary of Indo-European Roots*, and in some cases there is no similarity whatsoever. Smith gives no justification for his conclusions, and one can only guess at his sources from the bibliography, as no footnotes or citations per entry are to be found. This book, however, cites abbreviated references to the standard authority in the field, Julius Pokorny's *Indogermanisches etymologisches Wörterbuch* (Bern, 1959).

IV. Accessibility

The Indo-European roots are listed alphabetically in boldface type at the head of each entry, followed by one or more variants denoted by numbers, also in boldface type. Basic definitions immediately follow the entry forms and variants; different parts of speech are separated by a semicolon. English words derived from the roots are in all capitals, and correspond to an index in the back of the book of all English words in the root text. Thus one can look up the known word in English and be referred to the root in the text.

There is a table of contents listing the main sections of the book, and guide words (roots) at the top of each page make the book very handy for the user.

V. Summary

This is a scholarly work on a scholarly topic, but its extensive introduction and guide ensure that a somewhat obscure subject is understood by a willing and intelligent reader. Watkins succeeds in convincing the reader of its importance, usefulness and historical significance, and the dictionary text is presented in an understandable, authoritative manner.

This title is recommended for public and academic libraries as well as for home use. It is especially recommended for libraries not owning the 1969 edition of the *American Heritage Dictionary*, of which the unrevised version of this dictionary was a part. Even for those owning the 1969 edition, this book is recommended as easier to use in this format than the heavy, oversize complete dictionary, and the revised introduction (which leads one more gently into the labyrinth of etymology) and revised dictionary text are also considerations in favor of purchase. And obviously, owners of THE AMERICAN HERITAGE DICTIONARY: SECOND COLLEGE EDITION will want this, as a companion to that edition. Libraries not owning any books on Indo-European word roots should consider this volume, whose format and authority leave its few competitors far behind.

The Barnhart Dictionary Companion

Facts at a Glance

Full Title: **The Barnhart Dictionary Companion: A Quarterly to Update General Dictionaries.**
Publisher: Lexik House.
Editor: Clarence L. Barnhart.

Editions Reviewed: © 1982, 1983, 1984, 1985, 1986, 1987.

Number of Entries: Currently, over 1,200 per year.
Indexes: each issue is indexed; one cumulative index per year; companion index (vols. I–IV, 1982–85) with supplementary listing by subject areas, etymology, and word elements.
Trim Size: 8½″ × 11″.
Binding: paperback (6 annual volumes—4 issues per volume).

Price: $50.00 a subscription per year; back issues $12.50 each; companion index, $45.00.
Sold by subscription; academic and public library discount available; classroom discounts for teachers (minimum subscription of 10 copies). ISBN 0736-1122.

I. Introduction and Scope

The Barnhart Dictionary Companion has the explanatory subtitle "a quarterly to update general dictionaries." A typical issue of 32 to 44 two-column pages lists and illustrates some 300 "new words and meanings of current importance." It also contains comments from the editor and letters from readers, book reviews, and a cumulative index.

A comment from the editor (vol. V, no. 1, Spring 1986, pp. 42–43) states the journal's mission more fully:

> One of the developments we are exploring is the measurement of the obsolescence of words. We have 1,338 articles that contain the word *gasohol*. . . . The word now appears to be going out of use. But it may only be sleeping until our next oil crisis. . . .
>
> Unfortunately this information is not widely available. As a matter of fact much of it is not recorded at all in the standard dictionaries. Our two records of standard English—the historical record in the OED and its [s]upplements (1882–1986) and the descriptive record in Webster's New International Unabridged (1961)—are revised so infrequently that they are inadequate and incomplete in the amount of information given. Consequently, they are much less successful in keeping up with the growth of our vocabulary. . . .
>
> A reference source giving information on current words has been missing in our libraries. . . . Moreover, the information given about new words should be much fuller than that given in traditional dictionaries where space is at such a premium.

The Barnhart Dictionary Companion sets out to be that reference source and to give that information.

The Barnhart Dictionary Companion

❶ A *w* within a circle indicates that the entry is a new word, as opposed to a change in meaning or usage

❷ Examples of usage are followed by specific source citations

❸ Date of first recorded use is given if known

❹ Level of usage and frequency of use appear in parentheses

❺ Etymology is discussed

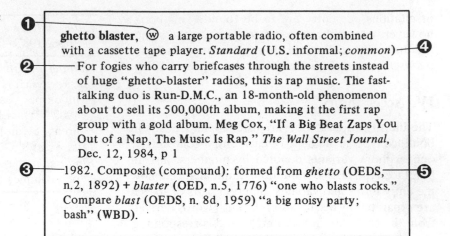

ghetto blaster, Ⓦ   a large portable radio, often combined with a cassette tape player. *Standard* (U.S. informal; *common*)

For fogies who carry briefcases through the streets instead of huge "ghetto-blaster" radios, this is rap music. The fast-talking duo is Run-D.M.C., an 18-month-old phenomenon about to sell its 500,000th album, making it the first rap group with a gold album. Meg Cox, "If a Big Beat Zaps You Out of a Nap, The Music Is Rap," *The Wall Street Journal*, Dec. 12, 1984, p 1

1982. Composite (compound): formed from *ghetto* (OEDS, n.2, 1892) + *blaster* (OED, n.5, 1776) "one who blasts rocks." Compare *blast* (OEDS, n. 8d, 1959) "a big noisy party; bash" (WBD).

II. Format

The bulk of each issue is devoted to the "Changing English" section that is the raison d'être of *The Barnhart Dictionary Companion*. Each boldface entry word is followed by a pronunciation guide, an italicized abbreviation for the part of speech, and a circled superscript symbol for status (new word, new meaning, or changed usage). The definition includes reference to the sources of the word and to other words formed from them. It concludes with a usage label, such as "nonstandard," and a frequency label.

One or more illustrative quotations follow the definition, usually drawn from current newspapers and magazines of wide circulation. The quotations are, when necessary, divided into classifications such as "Transferred Use" or "Figurative Use." In the interest of providing adequate context, the quotations are often lengthy. As the example below shows, however, the context sometimes goes far beyond adequacy.

The entry ends with discussion of the date and pattern of innovation ("blend," "closed compound") and cross-references to related entries in the *The Barnhart Dictionary Companion*. A relatively brief example is **anti-skating**:

anti-skating, *n.* Ⓦ *Often attributive.* Also written **anti-skating.** resistance to improper horizontal movement by the tonearm of a phonograph across a record. *Standard* (used especially in contexts dealing with phonograph design; *infrequent*)

Other points to be checked out periodically include the alignment of the stylus (you can do this with a strong magnifying lens), the correct amounts of vertical tracking force and of anti-skating, and the condition of the stylus tip (this requires a microscope). Norman Eisenberg, "The Trouble With Stereo Systems," *The Washington Post* (Nexis), Jan 16, 1977, p E5

1977. Composite (prefixation): formed from *anti-* (OED,

prefix 4, 1654) "against———" + *skating* (OED, n., 1723) "The action of the verb to skate" [Compare *skate*: v. 1b, 1755: "*transf.* To slide or guide along, to move lightly or rapidly"].

Reprinted in each issue are the list of abbreviations, a pronunciation key, and the valuable "Key to Changing English." Almost all the abbreviations are of dictionary titles: *The Barnhart Dictionary Companion* defines a new word, meaning, or usage as one not recorded as a main or separate entry in "the two great dictionaries of record," WEBSTER'S THIRD NEW INTERNATIONAL DICTIONARY and the OXFORD ENGLISH DICTIONARY, in any of the three chief new word dictionaries, or in any of the four American college dictionaries or their one British equivalent.

The pronunciation key pairs a "newspaper" style ordinary-alphabet guide with a more precise set of phonetic symbols adapted from *The Barnhart Dictionary of New English* (1973). Thus **baladeur**, "a French term for a portable radio and/or cassette player," is both "bah lah DUHR" and /ba la'dœr/.

The tabular "Key to Changing English" explains the etymological terms employed in the definitions, not only the distribution into usage levels such as "standard" and "nonstandard," or into frequencies such as "common" and "infrequent," but also the classification into patterns, subdividing such labels as "Loan word" into "borrowing," "loan translation," and "folk etymology," and defining each one. This key takes fully a column in each issue, but it is space well used. From it the reader can gain a good view of the ways that English vocabulary keeps changing.

III. Quality and Currency of Entries

The Barnhart Dictionary Companion claims to be "the only quarterly newsletter devoted to updating general dictionaries." Currency is its rationale. It uses Nexis and ASAP (machine-accessible editions of magazines and newspapers) "to investigate the candidates for entry in well over 14,000,000,000 words of text." These vast electronic resources also enable the editors to judge the frequency of new words and meanings from written sources. But they do not permit the editors to monitor spoken English as a native or a familiar second language, so at best the publication can report only changes reflected in the written language employed in popular publications. *The Barnhart Dictionary Companion* is more current than the dictionaries it sets out to update, but like them, "while it is hastening to publication, some words are budding, and some falling away," as Samuel Johnson observed in 1755.

The language of popular journalism provides a representative but not exhaustive sample of changing English. Among the topics to which journalists increasingly turn are science, technology, and medicine, so these topics account for a large proportion of the "additions to the standard working vocabulary of English" that the journal lists. The editor confronted the problem of such terms in his column for the Winter 1984 number, concluding that he had no alternative to including any of the millions of "latent" scientific terms when they became "important in daily life."

Nonetheless, many readers will find entries for terms—**giant black hole** or **frozen black hole**, **eclipsing binary X-ray pulsar** or **angiotensin-converting enzyme**, **ice-minus** or **Max-Q**—that seem to open the door to millions more latent terms than the standard working vocabulary of English is likely to find room for.

The Barnhart Dictionary Companion is unlike even the dictionaries it seeks to update in the space it gives to entries of two or more words. Yet some of these, like **emerging technology**, seem to demand an entry no more than does "railway porter," which Sir James A. H. Murray long ago barred from the OXFORD ENGLISH DICTIONARY because it was self-explanatory and because it would provide a precedent for no end of other two-word terms to clog the pages of his book.

Even scientific terms at the margin of the standard vocabulary sometimes receive enigmatic definition in *The Barnhart Dictionary Companion*. For **adrenoreceptor** the editor provides "the location in a cell where adrenalin takes effect," but the only illustrative quotation for the word refers to "a circulating substance called alpha-2-adrenoreceptor." The definition gives a where; the quotation gives a what. The correct definition would be closer to "Something at the location [not necessarily in a cell] where adrenalin takes effect that responds to it and passes the response along," a what *in* a where.

IV. Accessibility

Each number of *The Barnhart Dictionary Companion* ends with an index that has collected the entries for the current year. A separately bound index of the first four volumes, 1982–85, is also available, listing not only the entries but also the "formative elements" in them: for **-acy** it gives *moderacy*, *mullahcracy*, and *quiet diplomacy*. Other sections of the separate index volume list subjects (science and technology, social sciences, and so forth), etymological sources (such as words of foreign origin), and processes of word formation (back formation, clipping, and others).

V. Summary

The Barnhart Dictionary Companion chronicles the changes in the membership and meaning of English vocabulary as an interim record while the standard reference dictionaries are between editions. It enjoys the advantages of a large machine-accessible database under the scrutiny of an experienced lexicographer. The database is not all-embracing, the editorial treatment sometimes carries thoroughness to a fault, and even a quarterly cannot keep up with all the changes in present-day English. But for its important purpose, *The Barnhart Dictionary Companion* is the only game in town.

Barnhart Dictionary of Etymology

Facts at a Glance

Title: **Barnhart Dictionary of Etymology**.
Publisher: H. W. Wilson.
Editor: Robert K. Barnhart.
Edition Reviewed: © 1987.

Number of Entries: over 25,000.
Number of Pages: approximately 1,200.
Trim Size: $6\frac{3}{4}'' \times 10''$.
Binding: hardcover.

Price: $59.00.
Sold in bookstores and other outlets; also sold to libraries and other educational institutions.
ISBN 0-8242-0754-9.

I. Introduction and Scope

Since this book is being published beyond the cutoff date for this Buying Guide, the following is a preview, rather than a thorough review, based on an evaluation of typewritten manuscript pages of the front and back matter and galleys of the pages for

Barnhart Dictionary of Etymology

❶ Pronunciations, in parentheses, are included for difficult or unusual words

❷ An asterisk indicates a hypothetical form

❸ Date of first recorded use is given if known

❹ Cross-references are set in small capitals

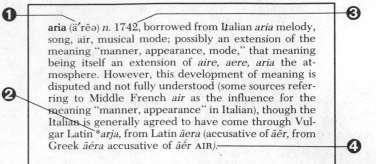

aria (ä′rē∂) *n.* 1742, borrowed from Italian *aria* melody, song, air, musical mode; possibly an extension of the meaning "manner, appearance, mode," that meaning being itself an extension of *aire, aere, aria* the atmosphere. However, this development of meaning is disputed and not fully understood (some sources referring to Middle French *air* as the influence for the meaning "manner, appearance" in Italian), though the Italian is generally agreed to have come through Vulgar Latin *arja, from Latin *āera* (accusative of *āēr,* from Greek *āéra* accusative of *āér* AIR*).*

the letter *A*. In the words of the publisher in the preface, the purposes of this dictionary are

> . . . to make examples of the development of English an understandable subject for those with no specialized knowledge of language study. We also hope this work will serve as a ready reference for language scholars, and that it will contribute to greater interest in serious study of language, but our chief purpose remains to explain to students of English how our present-day language has evolved.

These "students of English" who the publisher hopes to serve might include some high school students, but the larger audience will be college students and adults who are interested in more etymological detail than general dictionaries usually provide.

This dictionary will include over 25,000 entries that trace the "origins of the basic vocabulary of modern English." A special emphasis is placed on the development of the language from the point of view of modern English. In addition to the main entries, two scholars have contributed prefatory essays. Einar Haugen has written a concise, very readable "Short History of the English Language," and Ralph L. Ward has contributed an article explaining, with a minimum of technical jargon, how Proto-Germanic forms and Indo-European roots have played a very important part in the evolution of English.

II. Format

The typeface is clear, with main entries and their associated back formation words and phrases highlighted in boldface type, for example: **abuse** and **abusive** are both included in one entry. Margin space is satisfactory, although there is not much white space between lines of text. It is, of course, impossible to evaluate the physical state of the eventual bound book on the basis of these galleys and typewritten pages.

III. and IV. Quality, Currency, and Accessibility of Entries

The typical entry in this dictionary is written clearly and is considerably easier to interpret than those of other general etymological dictionaries, which often use so many symbols and abbreviations that the general reader sometimes has to exhibit considerable patience to crack these codes. A few standard abbreviations for parts of speech (n., v., etc.) are used, as well as a brief list of abbreviations for standard dictionaries to which frequent mention is made (e.g., *DA* for *Dictionary of Americanisms*), but when a word is attributed to Middle French or Medieval Latin, for instance, these language names are written out, not abbreviated as MF or ML.

Although some of the entries in this dictionary contain brief definitions, since the purpose is to trace the history of words, the editors quite properly don't always include definitions—probably because it can usually be assumed that an etymology seeker already knows the meaning of his word.

A typical entry includes an abbreviation indicating part of speech, year or range of years indicating the earliest usage date the editors have discovered for the word, a description of all living prefixes and suffixes in English, and an indication of some closely related words (such as **abdication** for **abdicate**). An extensive network of cross-references indicates associations of cognate words and suggests sometimes remote connections among various words. Pronunciation is given only for hard or unusual words, sometimes for words with several pronunciations, or for pairs or a series of homographs with different pronunciations. The language periods designated are considered standard by most linguists, and are defined in the explanatory notes, for example, Middle English extends from 1100 to 1500.

One does not expect a selective dictionary of 30,000 words in our basic vocabulary to pay a great deal of attention to current words or to new meanings for old words—partly because some of these words have yet to prove themselves durable and partly because many new words are restricted to a limited use by a particular social group or in a particular geographical region. Nevertheless, to take just one example of a fairly recent word, the existential sense of the word **absurd**, dating back to 1954, borrowed from the French *l'absurde*, is noted as well as the much earlier sense, going back to 1472, from Middle French through Latin.

It should also be noted that the assigned dates of origin of words in this dictionary often represent a revision of designations in such authorities as the OXFORD ENGLISH DICTIONARY. Since it is usually difficult to ascertain an exact year for a word's origin, words like "about," "probably," "before," and "after" are used quite frequently.

When a word has multiple meanings, such as **arm** meaning a limb of the body and *arm* meaning a weapon, each has a separate numbered entry.

When there is some dispute about the origin of a word, this is discussed—occasionally at some length—in terms quite accessible to the nonlinguist. Some of the entries seek to teach as well as to inform, so, for example, we learn that the adjective **Aryan**, now usually replaced by *Indo-European*, began to die out during the 1940s "because of the repugnance of its use associated with Hitler's racism of the 1930's and 1940's."

V. Summary

Although all the major unabridged and many abridged English language dictionaries provide some etymological information, this dictionary is the first scholarly general vocabulary etymological dictionary in some years. As noted earlier, this source is also distinctive because it places a special emphasis on words of American origin. Random comparisons of some of the entries in this source with four highly regarded general, scholarly etymological dictionaries suggest that this new dictionary will probably join them as a standard source. (These sources are Ernest Klein's COMPREHENSIVE ETYMOLOGICAL DICTIONARY OF THE ENGLISH LANGUAGE (1966); C. T. Onions's THE OXFORD DICTIONARY OF ENGLISH ETYMOLOGY (1966); Walter W. Skeat's *An Etymological Dictionary of the English Language*, Oxford University Press, revised edition, 1909; and Ernest Weekley's AN ETYMOLOGICAL DICTIONARY OF MODERN ENGLISH. One should not view the *Barnhart Dictionary of Etymology* as replacing any of these other sources, for sometimes, of course, the user may not find an etymology in one source that is in another, or may prefer a discussion of a word in another source to Barnhart. Barnhart is distinctive, however, for being current, for sometimes revising etymologies made by other sources, and for being written in a quite accessible style. Frequent users of other etymological dictionaries that make extensive use of abbreviations and symbols are not inconvenienced because they have mastered the codes, but the general user will be especially pleased with the *Barnhart Dictionary of Etymology* because it uses very few abbreviations

and special symbols. Based on the materials previewed, it can be assumed that this dictionary will be quite useful in public and academic libraries, and will also appeal to some home users.

Chambers Wordlore

Facts at a Glance

Full Title: **Chambers Wordlore**.
Publisher: W. & R. Chambers; distributed in the U.S. by Cambridge University Press.
Compiler: David Hilliam.
Illustrator: David Wilson.
Edition Reviewed: © 1984.

Number of Entries: 375.
Number of Pages: 124.
Number of Illustrations: 28 black-and-white drawings.
Trim Size: 5⅛″ × 7⅝″.
Binding: paperback.

Price: $4.95.
Sold in bookstores and other outlets; also sold to libraries and other educational institutions.
ISBN 0-521-60016-2.

I. Introduction and Scope

The object of this collection of word origins is to whet the general reader's appetite for etymology. Suitable for the person who has ever asked the question, "I wonder where that word came from?" and as an introduction to derivations, the book has 375 entries written in an unintimidating and informal style. For those whose curiosity is stirred, it includes a brief list of books for reference and further reading.

Wordlore makes no claim to completeness and provides no credentials for the compiler, David Hilliam, who has chosen to include words and expressions with an amusing history. For example, the word **nickel** is attributed to disappointed German miners who called it "*Kupfernickel*" or "copper devil" when they were confused by nickel's similarity to copper. **Sideburns** are said to have been named after General Ambrose Burnside, a Civil War commander. Each entry tells a story—how the word entered the language and how its meaning sometimes changed.

II. Format

This is a thin paperback, its binding strong, its large-size typeface very readable and clear. There are two to five entries to a page, each one 50 to 100 words in length. Twenty-eight pleasant line drawings decorate the text.

III. Quality and Currency of Entries

Hilliam's style is eminently appealing. He wants his readers to enjoy themselves. There are no citations for the etymologies, and, therefore, readers are cautioned always to check etymologies for themselves by reading several sources, and he invites readers to "raise a point with me" or send him some of their own derivations.

Considerable overlap is inevitable with existing popular etymological works, such as Morton Freeman's *The Story Behind the Word* (Philadelphia: ISI Press, 1985) and *The Private Lives of English Words* by Louis Heller, Alexander Humez, and Malcah Dror (Detroit: Gale, 1984), both of which include many of the same words and associated anecdotes. These are, however, more academic and thorough in their approach than is *Chambers*.

Jeans, **punk**, **Frisbee**, and **Falkland Islands** reflect Hilliam's desire to appeal to a contemporary audience; neither **Frisbee** nor **Falkland Islands** is included in the CONCISE OXFORD DICTIONARY OF ENGLISH ETYMOLOGY. A sizable proportion of the words whose true origin is quite well documented have also acquired a folk etymology: **cushy**, it is said, arrived via British soldiers returning from India where they had picked up the Hindustani word, *khushi*, meaning "pleasure"; **tabby**, we are told comes from Attabiy, a suburb of Baghdad where taffeta with tabbylike markings was manufactured.

IV. Accessibility

Wordlore is not a standard reference work, and this explains the absence of a pronunciation guide, guide words, and an index. Easy accessibility is guaranteed, however, since there are so few entries to the page and they are in large capital letters.

Although the book is British in origin, it is international in its choice of words. And the expressions and words that are decidedly British, such as **What the Dickens!**, **macintosh**, and **telly**, are nonetheless immediately recognizable.

V. Summary

Wordlore appeals to our innate "word wonder" curiosity. It is meant neither as an integral element of a serious reference collection, nor as a key source of information for professors and professionals. It is more appropriate for a library's circulating collection than for its reference collection. This volume cannot be classified as an essential addition to smaller or scholarly collections.

A Comprehensive Etymological Dictionary of the English Language

Facts at a Glance

Full Title: **A Comprehensive Etymological Dictionary of the English Language.**
Alternative Title: **Klein's Comprehensive Etymological Dictionary of the English Language: Unabridged, One-Volume Edition.**
Publisher: Elsevier Science Publishing Company.
Compiler: Ernest Klein.
Edition Reviewed: © 1971; 1986 printing.

Number of Entries: approximately 44,400.
Number of Pages: 844.
Trim Size: 7⅝″ × 11¼″.
Binding: cloth.

Price: $107.50.
Sold in bookstores; also sold to libraries and other educational institutions.
ISBN 0-444-40930-0.

I. Introduction and Scope

A Comprehensive Etymological Dictionary of the English Language was first published in two volumes in 1966 and 1967, the product of the author's lifelong interest in philology and his own dissatisfaction with the etymological dictionaries available at that point. Its over 44,400 entries now fill 844 pages, and the one-volume edition, like its predecessor, aspires to be both an easily accessible reference work for scholar and lay reader alike, as well as a document of the "history of human civilization and culture condensed in the etymological data of words" (p. x).

In the autobiographical introduction, Ernest Klein gives eloquent voice to his own commitment to philological study in the face of tragic world events and personal loss. A leader in the prewar European Jewish community, Klein lost his family in the Holocaust, and he eventually immigrated to Canada in the early 1950s. A professional rabbi as well as a linguist, Klein paints a picture of himself reminiscent of those nineteenth-century minister-philologists who yoked together the study of God's word with the analysis of human speech. The "comprehensive" quality of Klein's dictionary is thus grounded in several areas: in its inclusion of loan words from the Semitic languages; its concern with cognates from the Eastern branches of the Indo-European family (including Tocharian); and its consideration of words from recent scientific and technological discoveries—discoveries (Klein implies) that have shaped postwar life into a world whose intellectual adven-

A Comprehensive Etymological Dictionary of the English Language

❶ Etymology is separated from definitions by a dash

❷ An asterisk denotes a hypothetical form

❸ Cross-references are set in boldface type

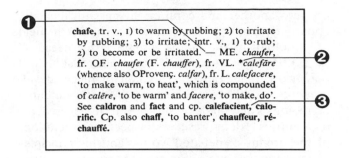

chafe, tr. v., 1) to warm by rubbing; 2) to irritate by rubbing; 3) to irritate; intr. v., 1) to·rub; 2) to become or be irritated. — ME. *chaufer,* fr. OF. *chaufer* (F. *chauffer*), fr. VL. **calefāre* (whence also OProvenç. *calfar*), fr. L. *calefacere,* 'to make warm, to heat', which is compounded of *calēre,* 'to be warm' and *facere,* 'to make, do'. See **caldron** and **fact** and cp. **calefacient, calorific.** Cp. also **chaff,** 'to banter', **chauffeur, réchauffé.**

tures lead to the search for truth and the betterment of living.

The comprehensiveness of this dictionary, of course, also stems from its sheer mass of words. Terms are often drawn from science and literature, from the arts and technologies, from mythology and history. The dictionary also includes the etymologies of names and places (both factual and mythological). In addition to its inclusion of over 750 loan words of Semitic origin, the book includes tables of pronunciation and transliteration for Hebrew, Aramaic, and Arabic, a feature that in its own right makes the dictionary an invaluable guide to the interpretation of those languages by Western readers.

The republication of the dictionary in the one-volume format has made it more accessible to the lay reader, although a potential buyer might want to compare it with another recent work directed at that same audience. Eric Partridge's ORIGINS: A SHORT ETYMOLOGICAL DICTIONARY OF MODERN ENGLISH (first published in 1968) is a characteristically idiosyncratic compilation of about 20,000 words in current English usage. Its wit and erudition contrast sharply with the bland and at times uncritical tone of Klein's entries. Take but one example, that for **salmagundi:**

Klein:

> n. hotchpotch.—F. *salmigondis,* fr. *salmigondin,* a word coined by the French satirist Francois Rabelais (1490?–1553).

Partridge:

> a mixture of pickled herring and chopped meat: EF-F *salmigondis:* [of obscure origin]: Webster cfs It *salame,* salt meat (L *sal,* salt), and It, from L, *condire,* to pickle (cf CONDIMENT): I suggest that Rabelais's *salmigondin* is one of his verbal fantasias and that, in it, he playfully, arbitrarily mutilates the LL *salimuria* (Gr *halmuris*), sea salt, hence, brine, hence a pickle.

The differences between Klein and Partridge, exemplified in these entries, are clear. Partridge attests a range of information drawn from modern and classical languages; he juxtaposes his research against his own playful verbal fantasy (signaled in his phrase

"I suggest") and calls into question the Rabelaisian origin of the term. Klein, however, simply reports received information without comment.

As a work of scholarly Indo-European philology, Klein's dictionary is now superseded by the recent paperback publication of Calvert Watkins's The AMERICAN HERITAGE DICTIONARY OF INDO-EUROPEAN ROOTS. This work offers an alphabetical arrangement of the roots themselves, with their descendants in the Modern English and Germanic languages, together with an alphabetical appendix of English words discussed in those entries. For readers of a less academic orientation, there is the lively ORIGINS OF ENGLISH WORDS by Joseph T. Shipley (Baltimore, 1984), a work similar in organization to Watkins's dictionary, but rich with evidence from literary texts, anthropological documents, and social rituals. Both at the level of individual entry and governing method, these two works offer a degree of sophistication and precision unmatched by Klein's work.

II. Format

The dictionary is arranged alphabetically, with entries arranged in three columns per page. The main entries are in boldface and overhang the text, making each entry easily distinguishable. The text, while for the most part eminently readable, occasionally appears clotted when words in italic and roman come thick and fast in the small type of the entries. Greek words appear in the Greek alphabet, while words from the Semitic languages are transliterated according to the principles set out in the dictionary's introduction.

The book is bound in a medium-weight paper, through which it is at times possible to see the printing on the backs of pages. Its binding is durable, and it is well sewn in signatures, so it lies flat when open.

III. Quality and Currency of Entries

In the introduction to the dictionary, Klein avers: "In most cases etymologies given up by serious science long ago are still wandering out of one dictionary into another and continue living with tenacity, apparently ignoring the truths established in the field of philology in the course of the latter decades" (p. ix). By this statement, Klein implies that his will be a work that does take account of recent developments, and that will revise previously outdated etymologies and interpretations. But in certain of his own entries, Klein preserves suspect interpretations of the origins of debated words, and his principles of selection and exposition are hard to abstract from these entries. One example is the notorious word *quiz*, a word whose origins remain obscure and mired in folk etymology and anecdote. Klein's etymology reads as follows:

> Of uncertain origin. According to Crowther's Encyclopaedia of Phrases and Origins, p. 110, this word owes its existence to a wager laid down in 1780 by Daley, the manager of a Dublin theater, who bet that he would introduce a new word into the English language. The new word was written on the walls of most houses in Dublin. Everywhere on the streets people tried to find out the meaning of the mysterious word never heard before. The word was *quiz*.

Klein's version of the etymology differs markedly—both in tone and substance—from the entry in THE OXFORD ENGLISH DICTIONARY written nearly a century ago.

> Of obscure origin: possibly a fanciful coinage, but it is doubtful whether any reliance can be placed on the anecdote of its invention by Daly, a Dublin theater manager. . . . The anecdote is given by Stuart in his *Walker Remodelled* 1836, but it is omitted in the ed. of 1840. The very circumstantial version in F. T. Porter's *Gleanings and Reminiscences* (1975), 32 gives the date of the alleged invention as 1791; but this is later than the actual appearance of the word and its derivative *quizzity*.

Clearly, Klein's entry fails to take account of the suspicions raised against his story by the *OED*; and he similarly neglects to investigate the origins and afterlife of the story itself. As in the entry on **salmagundi** quoted on page 423, Klein appears to rely on unquestioned information received from sources either out of date or transparently uncritical of the anecdotal nature of the evidence.

Another kind of problem with the dictionary lies in its offerings of purely philological data on words whose meanings and social force have changed radically in the past century. For a work that aspires to the "history of . . . culture," such lapses may lead the user to question the general utility of the book. Two examples may suffice to illustrate this lapse.

> **protocol**, n. —MF, *prothocole* (F. *protocole*), fr ML, *protocollum*, fr. Late Gk. πρατόχολλαν, "the first leaf gluded to the papyrus roll," which is compounded of Gk. τρῶιος, "first," and χόλλχ, "glue."

> **diplomacy**, n. —F. *diplomatie*, fr. *diplomate*; introduced into English by Edmund Burke (1729–97).

For the first example, **protocol**, Klein glosses over the ways in which this term entered the English diplomatic vocabulary in the late nineteenth century and its status early in the twentieth century as an affectation. As the *OED* states, in an entry probably compiled in the first decade of this century, "The word does not appear to have at any time formed part of the English legal or general vocabulary; . . . used only in reference to foreign countries and their institutions. . . ." The *OED* stigmatizes the word as a loan term inappropriate to the English vocabulary; its editorial remarks say something about language use and attitudes toward language change at the turn of the century, attitudes that should be as much a part of the "history of . . . culture" as Indo-European etymologies are. With **diplomacy**, Klein rightly calls attention to its first appearance in the writings of Burke (although he probably garners this information from the citations in the *OED*). But he fails to explore the logic of the coinage: *diplomacy*, from *diplomat* and *diplomatic*, is most likely coined by analogy with *aristocracy*, from *aristocrat* and *aristocratic* (see the *OED*, s.v. **diplomacy**). Here, as elsewhere, it is not enough simply to attribute a coinage to a time or individual; the etymologist needs to explore the bases of analogy that give rise to coinages, and in turn, that yoke such coinages together into semantic fields or groups. It is in such fields or groups of words that "the history of human civilization and culture condensed in the etymological data of words" is inscribed.

IV. Accessibility

The dictionary is relatively easy to use. Guide words at the top of each page make locating the entries simple. A list of addenda and corrigenda qualify and augment some 50 entries in the book.

V. Summary

A Comprehensive Etymological Dictionary can be an easily accessible reference work on English etymology for the lay reader. While lacking the precision and the wit of Partridge, it nonetheless provides the user with a distillation of the gathered work on the philology of English words. Its hefty price tag, however, renders it as extravagant to those who are not indulgent or dedicated readers. For much less, one could purchase Partridge's book and supplement it with the AMERICAN HERITAGE DICTIONARY OF INDO-EUROPEAN ROOTS dictionary by Watkins and the ORIGINS OF ENGLISH WORDS by Shipley. Together with the *OED*, these works would constitute a fine philological library. The one-volume edition of Klein's work would find its best home on the public or college library reference shelf, as one of the first works the student could turn to in the exploration of the English vocabulary, and as the stimulus to more advanced (and in some cases more accurate) study of the history of the language.

The Concise Oxford Dictionary of English Etymology

Facts at a Glance

Full Title: **The Concise Oxford Dictionary of English Etymology.**
Publisher: Oxford University Press.
Editor: T. F. Hoad.
Edition Reviewed: © 1986.

Number of Entries: 17,000.
Number of Pages: 522.
Trim Size: 5¼″ × 8″.
Binding: cloth.

Price: $24.95.
Sold in bookstores and other outlets; also sold to libraries and other educational institutions.
ISBN 0-19-861182-X.

I. Introduction and Scope

This dictionary is a concise version of the OXFORD DICTIONARY OF ENGLISH ETYMOLOGY (*ODEE*) and covers the origin, function, and development of approximately 17,000 English words compared with 24,000 in the parent work. Despite the abridged size and format, it retains the assiduous scholarship of the parent work, and as such will be chiefly useful to those wanting to check an etymological or linguistic point. Those engaged in research may wish to use the larger work.

The editor, Professor T. F. Hoad of Oxford University, intended "that each entry should give a concise statement of the route by which its headword entered the English language together with, where appropriate, a brief account of its development in English." Hoad usually fulfills his promise, though his concern for conciseness occasionally leads to incomplete explanation. **Admiral** is derived, we are told, from the Arabic word *amir* = commander; reference to the *ODEE* expands and explains the *al* element to have come from *amir al ma* = commander of the water. The entry for **book** suffers from a similar abridgment: it is usually taken to be a derivative of the German *Buch* meaning both *book* and *beech*. Why "beech"? *The Concise Oxford Dictionary of English Etymology* (*CODEE*) fails to give the

ODEE explanation that beech wood was the material upon which runes were inscribed.

II. Format

In keeping with the Oxford tradition, this is a beautifully bound and presented work. There are 30 to 40 boldface entries per double-column page, varying in length from two to ten lines, depending on the number of related and derivative forms. Complete etymologies of prefixes and suffixes (**anti-, pro, -itious,** and **-le,** for example) are included in the text. Each main entry is followed by roman numerals indicating the century in which the word was first recorded. This apparently basic etymological information is not found in either of the Oxford etymologies' main competitors, ORIGINS: A SHORT ETYMOLOGICAL DICTIONARY OF MODERN ENGLISH, edited by Eric Partridge, and Klein's COMPREHENSIVE ETYMOLOGICAL DICTIONARY OF THE ENGLISH LANGUAGE. The *CODEE* gives definitions only where meanings are not readily ascertainable and it does not give pronunciations. Early spellings are followed by etymological details; derivatives appear at the end of the entry.

III. Quality and Currency of Entries

Each *CODEE* entry displays all the impeccable scholarship of those in its parent work. Some *ODEE* entries have, of course, been omitted in this concise edition. Between **milli** and **mine**, the *CODEE* loses 3 of the 15 entries in the *ODEE*—*milliary, miminy-piminy,* and *mina*—and of the 15 between *phthisic* and *pianoforte*, the *CODEE* omits *physeter*. However, for the majority, the linguistic histories remain intact.

Personal and mythological names, medical terms, and technical terms included in the Klein work, do not appear in the *CODEE*. Today, more than in previous times, researching some of the developments in forms and sense of these scientific terms is one of the more useful and important functions of etymology, yet, *myxedema, podocarpus, sipylite,* and many others discussed by Klein do not show up in either of the Oxford etymologies. Innumerable cross-references (in small capital letters) are given to words, and elements of words, that are analyzed in the dictionary. At the end of the entry for **roster**, for example, there is a cross-reference to = ER.

IV. Accessibility

Although examples given on the dust jacket of words provided with etymologies (**zenith** is one) make the *CODEE* seem highly accessible, this is not always the case. The entry for **zenith** is one example of an entry that is difficult to comprehend:

The Concise Oxford Dictionary of English Etymology

❶ Homographs receive separate, numbered entries

❷ Roman numerals indicate century in which a word or sense first appeared in English

❸ An asterisk indicates a hypothetical form

❹ Cross-references are set in small capitals

elder¹ tree of genus *Sambucus*. OE. *ellærn*, ME. *eller*, *eldre*, corr. to MLG. *ellern*, *elderne*, *elhorn*, *alhorn*, prob. orig. an adj. formation.
elder², eldest compar. and superl. of OLD. OE. *eldra* (WS. *ieldra*) = OS. *aldira*, OHG. *altiro*, *eltiro* (G. *älter*), ON. *ellri*, Goth. *alþiza* :- Gmc. *alþizan-, f. *alþaz OLD; see -ER³. OE. *eldest* (WS. *ieldest*) = OHG. *altist* (G. *ältest*), ON. *ellztr*, Goth. *alþista* :- Gmc. *alþistaz*; see -EST. Superseded, except in special uses, by *older* and *oldest* (*alder*, *-este* XIII). As sb. *elder* was used in OE. and later for 'parent, ancestor', from *c.*1200 for 'one's senior' or 'superior in age', from XIV rendering L. *senior* and *senatus*, by Tindale used to tr. N.T. Gr. *presbúteros* PRESBYTER; in the Presbyterian and other bodies, title of an office believed to corr. to that of elder in the apostolic church.

zenith point of the sky directly overhead, point of the horizon at which a heavenly body rises *XIV*; highest point or state *XVII*. ME. *cenyth senith, cinit*, obscurely = Arab. *samt* in *samt ar-ra's* 'path over the head' (*samt* way, *al* the ,*AL-, ra's* head)

American Reference Books Annual (1987, p. 402) found that the *CODEE* had sacrificed clarity for brevity and criticized the constant need to refer to the list of 375 abbreviations in order to decipher information in the entries. While the parent work, the *ODEE*, had a helpful summary of the history and sources of the English language, this was dropped from the concise edition. The summary, together with an outline of some of the typical changes, would have helped the novice unravel the mystique that surrounds so many of the entries. This volume truly represents a case of not telling a book by its cover.

V. Summary

The *CODEE* or its parent work would seem to be an essential component of a library's reference collection. While they may be beyond the interests of the general reader, the Oxford etymologies (concise or full) are standard specialized works for those linguists, writers, and teachers who need detailed information about word origins. The browser still has quite a few less academic etymological works to choose from, including WORD MYSTERIES AND HISTORIES and the NEW WORDS DICTIONARY.

Dictionary of Changes in Meaning

Facts at a Glance

Full Title: **Dictionary of Changes in Meaning.**
Publisher: Routledge, Chapman & Hall.
Compiler: Adrian Room.
Edition Reviewed: © 1986.

Number of Entries: over 1,300.

Number of Pages: 292.
Trim Size: 6⅛″ × 9⅛″.
Binding: hardcover.

Price: $35.00.
Sold in bookstores; also sold to libraries and other educational institutions.
ISBN 0-7102-0341-1.

I. Introduction and Scope

This dictionary documents English words "whose meanings have changed over the years, whose senses have shifted in some way since they first entered the English language," according to its introduction. The histories of over 1,300 words are presented from first use to the present, with many illustrative quotations. Written by a well-known British linguist and author of reference works, the book is angled toward a British audience, but its selection of words in general usage is of interest to American word lovers and amateur linguists. As listed in the Introduction, a number of criteria have been established for the categorization of the words in this book. Among these are: a functional transfer of meaning; a narrowing of meaning; and an expansion of meaning, etc.

Besides the word list, the volume contains a fascinating 14-page introduction by the compiler, which includes a brief history of the English language and a classification of the ways in which the meanings of words have changed over the centuries. A brief bibliography ends the volume.

II. Format

Entries in the dictionary are presented in a well-designed and spacious two-column-per-page format, with entry words printed in boldface on a line above the entry, along with a brief definition of the current meaning of the entry word in parentheses. The var-

Dictionary of Changes in Meaning

❶ Main entry is set in boldface type and is followed by its current meaning

❷ Examples of usage are given

❸ Etymology is discussed

❹ Cross-references are set in boldface type

---

❶ **lord** (noble rank or its bearer, 'peer of the realm', ruler)

The present form of the word is a much reduced and distorted version of the Old ❸ English original, which was *hlāford* (and even earlier *hlāfweard*), meaning literally 'loaf ward', 'keeper of the bread' (compare modern English 'breadwinner'). This expressed the basic relation of a head of the household to those who ate his bread, and thus the primary and earliest sense of 'lord' was 'master', 'ruler' and even '**husband**' ❹ (which also see). The fourteenth-century *Cursor Mundi* states that whoever hits his thane (servant) with a stick:

❷ If he [the thane] liue ouer a dai or tuin,
The lauerd sal vnderli na pain.

(That is, if he lives on for one or two days, the master shall undergo no penalty.) The rank of 'lord' arose in the fourteenth century, and the designation for a peer followed a hundred years later. For a similar word, see **lady**.

---

ious meanings of the word are then presented in chronological order. Most of the illustrative quotations are taken from the OXFORD ENGLISH DICTIONARY, many of them from Chaucer, Shakespeare, the Bible, Johnson's DICTIONARY, the Book of Common Prayer, Caxton, Pepys, and Dickens. Pronunciations and syllabications are not given, and there are no formal etymologies. Cross-references appear in boldface.

The book is sturdily bound, and the paper is of high quality. There is generous white space, which makes the text easier to read.

III. Quality and Currency of Entries

Currency is not of primary consequence in this dictionary, and to give an idea of the content and quality of the entries, it may be best simply to quote several:

gang (group of people working together, both legitimately and criminally)
In the twelfth century, a 'gang' was simply a 'going' or 'journey,' with such expressions as 'a days gang' in common use to indicate the length of a journey, as in the *Cursor Mundi* of the early fourteenth century:

Thre dais gang, na mare ne less,
We must weind in to wildirness.

In the fifteenth century, 'gang' came to mean 'road' or 'way,' although mainly in dialect usage. Meanwhile, a secondary dialect sense of the word had developed, from the fourteenth century, to mean 'set of articles' such as a 'gang' of shrouds on a ship, of horses, or of

teeth. This is the meaning that developed into the now common 'company of people,' especially workmen, thieves and the like, with this sense found from the seventeenth century. Pepys recorded in his *Diary* in 1668: 'Home to dinner with my gang of clerks'.

shambles (scene of chaos or disorder)
As originally current in English, in the fifteenth century, the 'shambles' was a meat market, with the word the plural of 'shamble', a special kind of table or stall on which meat was placed for sale. From this sense, the word passed fairly naturally the following century to mean 'slaughterhouse'. And it was also in the sixteenth century that this sense in turn was transferred to mean 'scene of carnage'. Hence the modern 'shambles'. Around Britain traces of the original meat market remain in some towns where there is still a building or street called 'The Shambles' today (such as at York, Nottingham, Chesterfield, Chippenham and Devizes).

sly (cunning, furtive)
As originally used and understood in the twelfth century, 'sly' meant 'skilled', 'clever' (compare **artful**, **crafty** and **cunning**, for example), and the adjective was quite often coupled with a synonym, such as 'wise and sly' or 'quaint and sly' (with '**quaint**', which see, here meaning 'skilled' also). In the following lines from Bishop Grosseteste's *Castel off Loue* (1320), 'sly' is coupled with 'crafty' itself:

So slye and crafty they shull byn alle,
That they shull do all thyng that in here
hert doth falle.

But the modern 'bad' sense of the word appears early, and was the one to prevail, so that the 'clever' meaning, apart from one or two poetic usages, was virtually extinct by the end of the fifteenth century.

The compiler states in the introduction:

> Just as it has obviously not been possible to include *all* words in the English language that have undergone a change of meaning, so it has not proved always easy, or even desirable, to give all the former senses of a word.

What Room has done, however, is to give us an interesting choice of words that illustrate many kinds of change in the language and to make readers aware of the infinitely flexible and adaptable nature of the English language. The book should prove highly informative, as well as irresistible, to browsers in the lore of language.

IV. Accessibility

A contents page is provided for the major sections of the book, and guide words in the upper outside corners and page numbers in the corresponding lower corners prove helpful. The entry words appear in an alphabetical listing, so an index has been omitted.

V. Summary

This is a highly useful and entertaining dip into the history of English words that will appeal to linguists and amateurs alike. The book contains Room's personal selection of English etymologies which illustrate the historical panorama of the language. It does not, however, include all the formal attributes of complete dictionary entries, and, therefore, cannot be considered a final authority. A serious user would turn to THE OXFORD ENGLISH DICTIONARY itself. The volume deserves a place in libraries able to afford the expense, probably in the circulating collection, but some librarians may decide that it is a tempting extravagance that must be forgone.

A Dictionary of the English Language

Facts at a Glance

Full Title: **A Dictionary of the English Language**.
Publisher: Times Books; distributed by The Ayer Company.
Compiler: Samuel Johnson.
Edition Reviewed: 1979 facsimile edition of April 1755 printing.

Number of Entries: 40,000.
Number of Pages: 2,328.
Trim Size: 9″ × 15¼″.
Binding: laminated paper over boards.

Price: $57.50.
Sold by direct mail and directly to libraries and other educational institutions.
ISBN 0-7230-0228-2.

I. Introduction and Scope

Dr. Samuel Johnson's famed *Dictionary of the English Language* has always been considered a classic work of lexicography and, moreover, is highly regarded for its literary value. Through the eighteenth and well into the nineteenth century, it remained, as Robert W. Burchfield writes in the introduction to this facsimile edition, "a primary work of reference for scholars and writers of the day until it came to be superseded by the great dictionaries of Charles Richardson and Noah Webster, and in due course by the *Oxford English Dictionary* itself."

Dr. Burchfield, Chief Editor of the Oxford English Dictionaries, further points out the work's idiosyncrasies: "More than most contemporary or later dictionaries, [Johnson's dictionary] displays a cluster of personal beliefs and precepts that stand far from the kind of objectivity that lexicographers count among their primary aims. Dr Johnson is insular, prescriptive, and unscientific." But in spite of its lapses, Johnson's dictionary was significant, and remains so, because it is "in the whole tradition of English language and literature the *only* dictionary compiled by a writer of the first rank." Perhaps its chief characteristic, and the one that gives the volume its enduring value, is its copious quotations from the works of important pre-1750 authors to illustrate the definitions.

While its flaws as a dictionary are readily apparent, its authority should not be underestimated. Indeed, although it has little practical use as a dictionary today, Johnson's work is consulted by scholars as a primary source in etymology.

II. Format

This facsimile edition of Johnson's *Dictionary of the English Language* is an oversized book with a trim size of 9″ × 15¼″ and a thickness of 3″. At 12½ pounds, the volume is unwieldy and requires a large desk or dictionary stand for consultation. The text is printed in two columns per page. As this is a facsimile of the original, which was printed in 1755, the print is not the best. (Even in its day, the first edition did not represent the best printing job possible.)

Although this dictionary was first published more than 230 years ago, the format of the entries will not be unfamiliar to the modern user. Entry words are printed in large capital letters on their first appear-

A Dictionary of the English Language

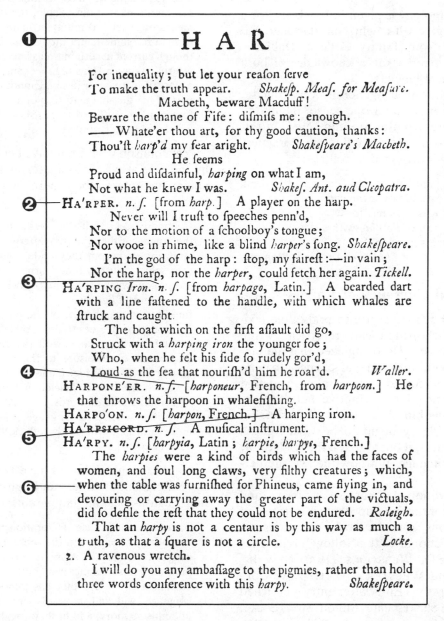

❶ ── **H A R**

> For inequality; but let your reason serve
> To make the truth appear.   *Shakesp. Meas. for Measure.*
>   Macbeth, beware Macduff!
> Beware the thane of Fife: dismiss me: enough.
> ──Whate'er thou art, for thy good caution, thanks:
> Thou'lt *harp'd* my fear aright.   *Shakespeare's Macbeth.*
>   He seems
> Proud and disdainful, *harping* on what I am,
> Not what he knew I was.   *Shakes. Ant. aud Cleopatra.*

❷ ──HA'RPER. *n. s.* [from *harp.*]   A player on the harp.
> Never will I trust to speeches penn'd,
> Nor to the motion of a schoolboy's tongue;
> Nor wooe in rhime, like a blind *harper's* song. *Shakespeare.*
> I'm the god of the harp: stop, my fairest:──in vain;
> Nor the harp, nor the *harper*, could fetch her again. *Tickell.*

❸ HA'RPING *Iron. n. s.* [from *harpago*, Latin.]   A bearded dart
with a line fastened to the handle, with which whales are
struck and caught.
> The boat which on the first assault did go,
> Struck with a *harping iron* the younger foe;
> Who, when he felt his side so rudely gor'd,

❹ Loud as the sea that nourish'd him he roar'd.   *Waller.*
HARPONE'ER. *n. s.* [*harponeur*, French, from *harpoon*.]   He
that throws the harpoon in whalefishing.

HARPO'ON. *n. s.* [*harpon*, French.]──A harping iron.

HA'RPSICORD. *n. s.*   A musical instrument.

❺ HA'RPY. *n. s.* [*harpyia*, Latin; *harpie, harpys*, French.]
> The *harpies* were a kind of birds which had the faces of
> women, and foul long claws, very filthy creatures; which,
❻ when the table was furnished for Phineus, came flying in, and
> devouring or carrying away the greater part of the victuals,
> did so defile the rest that they could not be endured.   *Raleigh.*
> That an *harpy* is not a centaur is by this way as much a
> truth, as that a square is not a circle.   *Locke.*

2. A ravenous wretch.
> I will do you any ambassage to the pigmies, rather than hold
> three words conference with this *harpy*.   *Shakespeare.*

❶ The "guide word" at the top of each column consists of three letters, indicating the beginning of the first entry in a left-hand column or the last entry in a right-hand column

❷ Entry words are printed in capitals and small capitals and overhang the text

❸ A part-of-speech label follows the entry word

❹ A concise etymology is given in brackets

❺ Definitions are usually concise but are sometimes highly subjective as well

❻ An outstanding feature is the inclusion of literary quotations to illustrate entry words; the entry word is italicized within the quotation, and the source of the quotation is cited

ance. (When entry words are verbs, they are printed in their infinitive form: for example, **To DENIGRATE**, not *denigrate*; **To GLIDE**, not *glide*.) A stress mark indicates the syllable on which the main accent falls.

The entry word is immediately followed by a part-of-speech label. Readers unfamiliar with eighteenth-century practice will be surprised to learn that Johnson's abbreviations for the parts of speech are the same abbreviations that we still use today—for example, *n.* for *noun*, *v.* for *verb*, *adj.* for *adjective*, and so forth.

The word's etymology is given in brackets. For a writer who was largely self-taught—his doctorate was an honorary one from Trinity College, Dublin—Johnson displays a remarkable knowledge of both modern and classical language.

Johnson's definitions are generally very concise. When a word has more than one sense, the definitions for the different senses are numbered. In this respect, Johnson again anticipated modern practice.

A typical entry is arranged as follows:

> **To TI′PPLE** v. n. [*tepel*, a dug, old Teutonick.] To drink luxuriously; to waste life over the cup.
>
> > Let us grant it is not amis to sit,
> > And keep the turn of *tippling* with a slave,
> > To reel the streets at noon.
> > > *Shakesp. Ant. and Cleopatra.*

III. Quality and Currency of Entries

"Every other author may aspire to praise; the lexicographer can only hope to escape reproach," wrote Johnson in his preface. He recognized that the language was in a continual state of change, that no dictionary could be considered complete, and that definitions could never be definitive but only approximate. Yet, within these limits, Johnson believed that a dictionary ought to be what we call "prescriptive"; that is, it ought to tell the reader how the learned use language, not how the average person uses it.

The great innovation of Johnson's dictionary, and the source of its continuing importance, is its use of pertinent quotations from the works of famous authors. (Notable dictionaries that follow this practice today are the OED, WEBSTER'S THIRD NEW INTERNATIONAL, and WEBSTER'S NINTH NEW COLLEGIATE DICTIONARY.) Entry after entry is enriched by quotations from Shakespeare, Milton, Swift, Locke, Bacon, Dryden, Sidney, Spenser, the Bible, and other sources. Johnson's rationale was that "the chief glory of every people arises from its authors," and that the works of pre-Restoration (1660) writers in particular represented "*the wells of English undefiled.*" He resisted the temptation to quote living writers, although he greatly admired many of his contemporaries. Obviously, Johnson's dictionary does not reflect the current state of the language, but rather the language spoken and written by educated Englishmen prior to the mid-1700s.

Most contemporary lexicographers, particularly those who adhere to a descriptive approach (such as that followed in compiling THE RANDOM HOUSE DICTIONARY OF THE ENGLISH LANGUAGE: SECOND EDITION UNABRIDGED), would disagree with Johnson's thoughts on currency:

> Nor are all words which are not found in [this dictionary], to be lamented as omissions. Of the laborious and mercantile part of the people, the diction is in a great measure casual and mutable; many of their terms are formed for some temporary or local convenience, and though current at certain times and places, are in others utterly unknown. This fugitive cant, which is always in a state of increase or decay, cannot be regarded as any part of the durable materials of a language, and therefore must be suffered to perish with other things unworthy of preservation.

Yet Johnson would not have been at all surprised by the rate at which computer and financial terminology has entered the general language in our own day:

> Commerce . . . as it depraves the manners, corrupts the language; they that have frequent intercourse with strangers, to whom they endeavour to accommodate themselves, must in time learn a mingled dialect, like the jargon which serves the traffickers on the *Mediterranean* and *Indian* coasts. This will not always be confined to the warehouse, or the port, but will be communicated by degrees to other ranks of the people, and be at last incorporated with the current speech. . . . Those who have leisure to think, will always be enlarging the flock of ideas, and every increase of knowledge, whether real or fancied, will produce new words, or combinations of words. . . . As by the cultivation of various sciences, a language is amplified, it will be more furnished with words deflected from their original sense. . . .

Neither would Johnson have been astonished at the enrichment of American English by the influx of non-English-speaking immigrants:

> There is another cause of alteration more prevalent than any other, which yet in the present state of the world cannot be obviated. A mixture of two languages will produce a third distinct from both, and they will always be mixed . . . . He that has long cultivated another language, will find its words and combinations croud upon his memory; and haste or negligence, refinement or affectation, will obtrude borrowed terms and exotick expressions . . . . No book was ever turned from one language into another, without imparting something of its native idiom . . . .

IV. Accessibility

Entry words are in capital letters and overhang the text. Guide words of a sort are printed in large type at the top of each column: only the first three letters of the last entry word in the column are printed. This practice is not as helpful as the contemporary practice of citing the first or last entry word in its entirety. Johnson's dictionary does contain some of the other finding aids that make modern dictionaries accessible. The overhanging entry words, printed in large capital letters, are one such device. Another is the numbered sense discrimination of different meanings of the same word. Here, too, Johnson and his printers had the foresight to begin each separate definition of a word flush to the left-hand side of the column, rather than running all the definitions directly after one another in the text.

Readers who are unfamiliar with printing conventions of the period may at first be perplexed by the use of the old style *s*, which looks like an *f*.

V. Summary

Although it is now an historical document, Samuel Johnson's *Dictionary of the English Language* remains one of the most valuable sources of information on the English language and its multifarious changes. At the very reasonable price of $57.50 this facsimile edition will be especially useful for academic and public libraries with large collections of works on language and literature, and where research into these is ongoing. Johnson's preface alone, in his witty, expansive, but precise prose, should be required reading for all lexicographers and etymologists, and will be enjoyed by anyone interested in the development of language and words.

The Dictionary of Eponyms

Facts at a Glance

Full Title: **The Dictionary of Eponyms: Names That Became Words**.
Former Title: Human Words.
Publisher: Stein and Day.
Compiler: Robert Hendrickson.
Edition Reviewed: © 1972; 1985 paperback edition.

Number of Entries: more than 3,500.
Number of Pages: 342.
Trim Size: 6″ × 9″.
Binding: paperback.

Price: $9.95.
Sold in bookstores; also sold to libraries and other educational institutions.
ISBN 0-8128-6238-4.

I. Introduction and Scope

An "eponym" is defined in the introduction to this interesting book as "a real or mythical person from whose name the name of a nation, institution, thing, etc., is derived . . . ." This work claims to be the most complete book of its kind with more than 3,500 definitions, etymologies, and miniature biographies. The compiler states in the introduction that he has tried "to include the story of every real person, group

of people, or animal endowed with human characteristics whose name has become part of the language." Fictional or mythological eponyms are not included except where the fictional character is supposedly based on a real person.

A three-and-a-half page bibliography of resources is listed at the end of the book providing authority for the information about the eponyms. These works range from *Who's Who*, the *New York Times' Index*, and *Webster's Biographical Dictionary* to specialized dictionaries which include the *Dictionary of American History*, *Gluttons and Libertines*, Brewer's *Dictionary of Phrase and Fable*, and *A Dictionary of the Underworld*, just to name a few. Robert Hendrickson, the author of this treasure chest of fascinating words and their histories has written a number of other word books, and his articles have appeared in *Time*, *The New York Times*, *Reader's Digest*, *Saturday Review*, and other periodicals.

The Dictionary of Eponyms was originally published in a hardcover edition in 1972 by Chilton Book Company with the title, *Human Words*. This paper edition is a reprint of the original work and has not been revised.

II. Format

Names are entered in boldface type and are capitalized; entries overhang the double columns of text. Other names within the descriptive paragraphs are capitalized. Guide words at the top of each page aid the reader in locating entries.

The cover is a well-illustrated paper one, and the pages are of heavy, off-white stock.

There is a brief introduction in the front of the book, and an addendum and bibliography appended to the back. The addendum includes seven-and-a-half pages of 300 eponyms that are not included under the main alphabet because of space limitations, with brief information about each. A typical example is:

> **Cochise**—pertaining to S.E. Arizona Indian culture—named after Cochise County, Arizona, which honors the Apache leader Cochise (1815–74).

Some entries are shorter:

> **Parrot guns**—American inventor Robert Parrot (1804–77).

III. Quality and Currency of Entries

The entries included range from the common, such as **doubting Thomas** or a phrase such as **keeping up with the Joneses**, to the more obscure. Examples of the latter include a person such as Count D'Orsay, a nineteenth-century French dandy, who designed the pump that was to become the model for women's footwear; or **Malpighian**, a seventeenth-century Ital-

The Dictionary of Eponyms

❶ Possible derivations are discussed

❷ Cross-references are italicized and appear in parentheses

❸ Main entry word is italicized in text

Booze, Boozer Every *boozer* or *boozehound* in America is related to E. G. or E. S. Booze of either Philadelphia or Kentucky, *circa* 1840. Mr. Booze was a distiller who sold his *booze* under his own name, the whiskey often flowing from bottles made in the shape of log cabins. The relationship is a tenuous one, though, *booze*, probably having its roots in the Middle English verb *bousen*, to drink deeply, which comes from an earlier German word. But the English use *booze* only for beer and ale and there is no doubt that the labels on our Mr. Booze's bottles influenced the American use of the word for hard liquor and strengthened its general use. Today *booze* most often signifies cheap, even rot-gut whiskey. Those log cabin bottles, incidentally, cashed in on the United States presidential campaign of 1840, when Tippecanoe and Tyler, too, General William Henry Harrison and John Tyler, ran against Van, Van The Used Up Man, President Martin Van Buren (see *O.K.*). General Harrison and cohorts reminded the voters a thousand times that he had been born in a log cabin, a fact which the bottles commemorated, and Mr. Booze's *booze* probably tasted good to the Whigs, if not the Democrats. Anyway, Harrison did so well with the ploy that Daniel Webster publicly regretted that he hadn't been born in a log cabin.

ian physiologist for whom a family of ornamental tropical plants are named along with other anatomical terms, such as *Malpighian corpuscle* and *Malpighian layer*. States named after American Indian tribes are also given.

The reader can find names of many flowers and fruits, such as the **Dorothy Perkins Rose**, the **McIntosh** or **Jonathan apple**, and **marigold**. Entries are fairly lengthy with about five appearing on each double-page spread. The entry for **Shakespearian** (not the more usual *Shakespearean*) runs about three columns in length. A typical entry provides both factual and anecdotal information, and dates are indicated in parentheses as appropriate. The entry below is an example of one of the shorter ones:

Jackknife The ubiquitous American *jackknife*, which dates back in use to the early eighteenth century, may be based on the earlier Scottish *jocktelig* and that clasp knife possibly takes its name from that of its original maker, a Frenchman named Jacques de Liege. A respected Scottish historian traced the word to this source in 1776, but modern scholars have been unable to confirm his derivation. The word has long been used as a

synonym for "to double up," as the body does in a *jackknife dive*, in allusion to the way the knife's big blade folds into the handle.

Hendrickson is good about including alternative points of view. Take **Eggs Benedict**, for instance, which is a dish supposedly named after Samuel Benedict who ordered it specially prepared for him one morning at the Waldorf to help ease a severe hangover. The dictionary also adds that there is another story that it was created by Oscar of the Waldorf and New Yorker Mrs. Le Grand Benedict. However, Oscar is credited with having confirmed the former version.

There are many comparatively obscure words and phrases included in this dictionary: **Cut a Dido** meaning to play a prank; **Jamie Duff** the name of a professional mourner; **Oslerize** for to kill men over forty; plus lists of nations and cities named after people. There are other, better known names, too, such as **Machiavellian**, **Jughead**, **Jack the Ripper**, and **Father Damien**. This dictionary also covers quite a number of Biblical names.

IV. Accessibility

Primary access is through the alphabetization of entries. There are also a few cross-references included; for example, from state names, the *see States* reference leads the reader to **States Named for Indian Tribes**. There is also a see reference from **Stapelia** to **Raffles**. Because the cross-references are sparse some explanations are difficult to locate. For example, if you are looking up a **John B** hat, the term's derivation is in the dictionary, but you will only find it under **Stetson**.

A number of the entries have multiple listings, such as **Byerly Turk**, **Darley Arabian**, and **Godolphin Barb**, which are all included in one heading. There are no cross-references among the names of these oriental stallions who started the line of thoroughbred race horses we have today. Another example is **Johnnycake** and **Kickapoo Joy Juice** which appear in a single entry. **Jersey**, **Jersey Cow**, **Jersey Cream** are less of a problem when not given separate entries, but **Jezebel**, **Jehu**, and **Jumping Jehoshaphat** are.

V. Summary

The Dictionary of Eponyms is a book that serves both as enjoyable reading and as a reference source. Its use will depend mainly on the size of the library.

Many of the words can be found in the *Dictionary of Americanisms*, THE OXFORD ENGLISH DICTIONARY, Mencken's *American Language*, and even the AMERICAN HERITAGE DICTIONARY. However, there is a distinct advantage to having these eponyms grouped together in one source. Where, for example, except in a special collection of poetry, can one find four examples of **Clerihew** such as these?

> Sir Humphry Davy
> Abominated gravy.
> He lived in the odium
> Of having discovered sodium.

or

> Alfred de Musset
> Used to call his cat Pusset.
> His accent was affected.
> That was to be expected.

The dictionary would be more useful for reference work if it were expanded and updated, and if it either had an index or better cross-references. In spite of these shortcomings, this will be a useful work to include in the reference collections of those libraries, as an earlier review (*ARBA*, 1986, p. 410) noted, "not owning the original or wishing to add a copy to their circulating books . . . . this is a reasonably priced resource that will delight browsers, history enthusiasts, and word lovers everywhere." Hendrickson has done a thorough job of culling other reference tools for the librarian, and we are indebted to him for his full and lively explanations as to the origin of words that are eponyms.

A Dictionary of True Etymologies

Facts at a Glance

Full Title: **A Dictionary of True Etymologies**.
Publisher: Routledge, Chapman & Hall, distributed by Methuen.
Compiler: Adrian Room.
Edition Reviewed: © 1986.

Number of Volumes: 1.
Number of Entries: 1,200.
Number of Pages: 193.
Trim Size: 6⅛″ × 9⅛″.
Binding: cloth.

Price: $22.50.
Sold in bookstores; also sold to libraries and other educational institutions.
ISBN 0-7102-0340-3.

I. Introduction and Scope

As its title implies, this dictionary aims at correcting popular misconceptions about the origins of certain English words. Its 1,200 entries would appear to have self-evident origins, but in fact have more complex ones: **Jerusalem artichoke** derives not from the city but from the Italian word for sunflower, *girasole*; and **pantry** has nothing to do with pots and pans, but comes from *paneterie* meaning a bread store in French.

Room, a linguist and author of many language reference titles (including *Room's Classical Dictionary* and *Place Names of the World*), has written an authoritative yet highly readable work; and though slanted toward the British reader, it will also appeal to the American browser and student linguist alike.

II. Format

A Dictionary of True Etymologies is a hardcover, meticulously presented work. There are two columns and five to ten boldface entries per page, each with a brief definition in parentheses so the reader knows which meaning of the word is being dealt with: **bang** refers here to the hairstyle, not to the loud noise; **top** refers to the spinning toy, not a highest point. Both popular and scholarly etymologies are then presented. There is no index or pronunciation guide. A seven-page introductory essay explains the development of etymological red herrings, and an extensive bibliography of dictionaries and books about the English language appears at the end of the book.

III. Quality and Currency of Entries

Though there are many etymological dictionaries presently available that offer both scholarly and popular etymologies, Room is exclusively interested in exposing false etymologies. So much so, in fact, that he gives only speculative answers to the inevitable question: "Then what is the true origin?" Take the two words **massacre** and **masturbate**. The first word, **massacre**, he says is not related to *mass*, but perhaps to an Arabic word meaning *slaughterhouse*; the second word, **masturbate**, shows no evidence to support the common misconception that it comes from Latin *manus* (hand) and *stirpare* (to defile). Generally, the compiler is interested more in what is not, than what is, known about a word.

Room debunks myths about an enormous variety of common words, ranging from **Canary Islands** and **Ku Klux Klan** to **Dixieland** and **Viking**. Most of the words, though not the names, can be found in THE OXFORD DICTIONARY OF ENGLISH ETYMOLOGY, where for comprehensiveness and scholarship, the serious linguist should still go.

Some of the entries, like **ditty bag**, **fogey**, **hoity-toity**, **mouldwarp**, and **latchet**, seem a little dated or obscure. There are few technical or current words. Perhaps their very currency has meant they haven't had a chance to evolve or be subjected to an analysis of correct (or incorrect) derivation with which Room is primarily involved.

Room's style strikes a good balance between concise information and chatty narrative. Consider the following two consecutive entries:

> **guppy** (kind of small West Indian fish)
> The little fish, also known as 'millions', and frequently found feeding on mosquito larvae in controlled conditions in school 'biolabs', is not so called because it gulps or goes 'glup', as some fish do, but because specimens of it were first presented to the British Museum in the nineteenth century by the Rev. R. J. Lechmere Guppy, President of the Scientific Association of Trinidad.

> **gusto** (relish, enthusiasm)
> The word does not derive from 'gust', as if such a burst of enthusiasm was like a gust of wind, but is Italian (and Spanish) for 'taste'. The term was in use in English from the seventeenth century.

IV. Accessibility

The *Dictionary of True Etymologies* is very easy to use with its entries in boldface, the double spacing between each explanation, and the italicized foreign words. The absence of an index and pronunciation guide in no way detracts from the work, though it is worth noting that its main competitor, the American Heritage WORD MYSTERIES AND HISTORIES, is both indexed and illustrated. WORD MYSTERIES covers much of the same ground as Room's book but is geared to the American reader. Room's volume, also interesting and entertaining for the American reader, however, contains words relatively unknown here, for example, **batty**, **geezer** (an old man), **bawbee** (a Scottish coin), **Orangemen** (Irish loyalists), **Pommy** (an Australian term for a British person), and **pumps** (light shoes). In all fairness, though, Room also discusses the etymology of **gringo**, **ketchup**, and **woodchuck**, which are relatively unknown in Britain.

V. Summary

Room has written an amusing and interesting work with both scholarly and popular appeal. Libraries already owning the American Heritage volume or the better-known *Morris Dictionary of Word and Phrase Origins* (now out of print) might pause before buying a not altogether essential work. But as an entertaining exploration of the oft-misleading byways of the English language, this book is a fine supplement to any collection.

Dictionary of Word Origins

Facts at a Glance

Full Title: **Dictionary of Word Origins.**
Publisher: Philosophical Library.
Editor: Joseph T. Shipley.
Edition Reviewed: © 1945.

Number of Entries: approximately 6,400 entries (including approximately 4,400 cross-references).
Number of Pages: 441.
Trim Size: 5½" × 8¼".
Binding: hardcover.

Price: $19.95.
Sold in bookstores and by direct mail.
ISBN 8022-1557-2.

I. Introduction and Scope

The *Dictionary of Word Origins* was compiled to provide both the histories of individual words and the history of the evolving English language itself. Joseph T. Shipley chose for inclusion words "that have origins at once interesting and enlightening." He omitted current slang (as of 1945) but included "some picturesque new words" that he felt illustrated the constant change in our language.

The work is significantly less comprehensive than the one-volume etymological dictionary by Eric Partridge, ORIGINS: A SHORT ETYMOLOGICAL DICTIONARY OF MODERN ENGLISH, which has about 29,100 entries. The *Dictionary of Word Origins* is prefaced by a set of brief, glib explanatory notes that add little to the reader's understanding of word origins.

Three appendixes follow the main text. The first lists doublets, that is, the pairs of words "that have arrived in our language by different routes from the same source." Of the 127 pairs entered, only 68 are explained in the text; the author invites the reader to look up the remainder in the NED (*A New English Dictionary on Historical Principles*, which was the precursor to the OED and appeared between 1884 and 1928). The second appendix lists words whose origins are in proper names; the third presents the sources and meanings of selected given names. While these appendixes are interesting for the browser, they add little to the dictionary's primary purpose.

II. Format

The work's entries are alphabetized letter by letter on double-column pages. The main entry word appears in boldface and is followed by an indented paragraph that makes the entry word stand out more clearly. Main entries vary in length from a few lines to an entire column. Within the entry paragraph the main entry word and its inflected forms are italicized, as are the words in other languages through which its origins are traced. However, when a word has several meanings and a long history, the explanations are not numbered as in other etymological dictionaries. This is inconvenient, especially for the reader seeking a cross-reference. Cross-reference entries themselves (about 65 percent of all entries) are so numerous that they are likely to annoy many readers. The format for such entries appears as follows:

> **renegade**
> *See* runagate.

The work's type is adequate in size and clarity, but some pages show uneven inking or broken letters, which distracts the reader. There is ample white space, and the paper permits minimal show-through. The hardcover book is sturdy and will stand up well to heavy use.

III. Quality and Currency of Entries

The author's style is discursive and uneven. Humor and punning characterize some entries:

> **dough**
> *See lady*. (The use of *dough* to mean money comes from the fact that it's what every woman kneads.)

Other entries incorporate unexplained—and, for many readers, inaccessible—allusions:

> **disaster**
> . . . how the conjunction of stars affects your fortune. . . . In Shakespeare's *Julius Caesar*, Brutus is reminded that our fate lies "not in our stars, but in ourselves"—which becomes the central theme of Barrie's *Dear Brutus*.

The word histories and definitions checked against other etymological dictionaries are usually accurate but never as clear or as straightforward as those of Partridge's ORIGINS or of Ernest Klein's COMPREHENSIVE ETYMOLOGICAL DICTIONARY OF THE ENGLISH LANGUAGE. The best-written entries are those that are informative without any attempt at humor; these, however, are not the majority.

In the case of Shipley's "picturesque new words," such as **blurb**, **brunch**, **Chinaman's chance**, **jeep**, and **quisling**, the work's entries are neither as clear nor as interesting as those found in the *Morris Dictionary of Word and Phrase Origins* (now out of print). Obviously, they are no longer "new."

This dictionary might entertain and profit the reader with training in linguistics. It is also suited to the casual reader who appreciates anecdotal linguistic information. However, for the nonspecialist seeking etymological information, this work is all too often baffling, potentially misleading, and certainly no longer current.

IV. Accessibility

Two boldface guide words appear at the top of each page, indicating the first and last entries on that page. The absence of a table of contents may result in readers' overlooking the volume's three appendixes.

The author's style of writing results in some problems of accessibility. For example, under the entry **Dora** appears a discussion of acronyms; however, there are no cross-reference entries under **acronyms** or **initials** to direct the reader to this information:

> **Dora**
> As a girl's name, *Dora* might be short for Gr. *Theodora*, gift of God; or just Fr. *d'or*, golden. It was quite otherwise, however, when England declared War in August, 1914; being at once the name of the *Defence of the Realm Act*—drawn from its initials.
> Initials have recently been a favorite way of referring to parties, bureaus, and other creations of human officialdom; when they can be formed into words, they have a chance of entering the language. Thus *Waac*, from *Women's Auxiliary Army Corps*, in the United States, 1942; the first *A* was dropped when the Corps became a regular part of the Army. . . .

V. Summary

The *Dictionary of Word Origins* is not suitable for general library acquisition unless a comprehensive collection of etymological dictionaries is sought. For home use, this work will not merit its expense for most readers, who would be better served by a work such as Partridge's ORIGINS. There are two newer etymological dictionaries that should be considered in place of Shipley's: THE CONCISE OXFORD DICTIONARY OF ENGLISH ETYMOLOGY edited by T. F. Hoad, published in 1986 by Clarendon Press, or its parent work, the OXFORD DICTIONARY OF ENGLISH ETYMOLOGY, published in 1966 and still in print. WORD FOR WORD by Edward C. Pinkerton, published by Gale in 1982, is written in an interesting and understandable style and was highly recommended for all academic libraries as well as medium and large public libraries by *RQ* (Fall 1982, pp. 100–101).

Dictionary of Word Origins

Facts at a Glance

Full Title: **Dictionary of Word Origins**.
Publisher: Rowman & Littlefield.
Editor: Joseph T. Shipley.
Edition Reviewed: © 1945; reprinted 1985.

Number of Entries: approximately 6,400 entries (including approximately 4,400 cross-references).
Number of Pages: 441.
Trim Size: 5″ × 8″.
Binding: paperback.

Price: $7.95.
Sold in bookstores and by direct mail.
ISBN 0-8226-0121-4.

I. Introduction and Scope

This paperback version of Shipley's DICTIONARY OF WORD ORIGINS is based on the 1967 edition issued by Littlefield, Adams & Company. It was reprinted in 1979 and 1982, and the current Helix Books edition was printed in 1985. Although frequently reprinted, the work has not been updated or revised and remains identical with the hardcover edition, reviewed in this guide.

An Etymological Dictionary of Modern English

Facts at a Glance

Full Title: **An Etymological Dictionary of Modern English**.
Publisher: Dover.
Compiler: Ernest Weekley.

Edition Reviewed: © 1967.

Number of Entries: over 20,000.
Number of Pages: 856; 2 volumes.
Trim Size: 6½″ × 9¼″.
Binding: paperback.

Price: $17.00 (each volume $8.50).
Sold in bookstores and by direct mail.
ISBN 0-486-21873-2 (vol. 1).
ISBN 0-486-21874-0 (vol. 2).

I. Introduction and Scope

When *An Etymological Dictionary of Modern English* was written in 1921 as an outgrowth of the author's *Romance of Words* (1912), he claimed it to be "the most complete etymological dictionary in existence." While that was a true statement in 1921, it is not now.

This paperback is a reproduction of the 1921 London edition now in two volumes. Volume one contains a five-page biographical memoir of Weekley by his son, Montague Weekley, a nine-page informative preface followed by three pages of abbreviations, a three-page bibliography of dictionaries, and a short 18-item bibliography of the most quoted early texts.

Weekley, an established linguistic scholar with a widespread reputation and a "gifted popularizer of English etymology," was a witty savant, and any educated, well-read person using this dictionary will appreciate his sense of humor and fine turn of words. Weekley's aim was to "supply the help which many word lovers, as distinct from philological experts, are still seeking." His choices are personal preferences, and he is very clear in the preface as to what he included and excluded.

The vocabulary was taken roughly from the *Concise Oxford Dictionary* (1911), collated with the vocabulary of *Cassell's New English Dictionary* (1919) and is thus strictly British. Included are English words made up of native as well as foreign elements—the words that Weekley felt constituted the whole of the literary and colloquial vocabulary. He was a bit snide with scientific terms, although undoubtedly accurate, stating that they "are often coined with complete indifference to linguistic laws and the real meaning of words," . . . and he excluded everything that the *New English Dictionary* "quotes only from technical treatises and dictionaries." He felt that an intelligent reader could find enlightenment by looking up the elements of scientific words and terms.

Definitions are not given except for brief indications to help the reader distinguish homonyms or to understand the frame of reference of unfamiliar words.

Weekley does trace the meanings of every word as well as its form to show the variations in meaning and the process by which the word became part of the living English language.

The selected quotations are quite successful in illustrating usage and obsolete pronunciation, and in their general interest. Some of the quotations, too, have considerable historical interest. All show the author's keen mind and humorous bent.

Weekley's dictionary is approximately half as long as the more scholarly COMPREHENSIVE ETYMOLOGICAL DICTIONARY OF THE ENGLISH LANGUAGE (1967) of Klein. For example, between the entries *amour* and *ampère* in Klein there are six entries, while in Weekley there are none. And as is true with most of his entries based on personal names, Klein's meaning and explanation for *ampere* is clearer.

> **ampère**, n., a unit of force of the electric current.— named after the French physicist André-Maril *Ampère* (1775–1836).

Weekley's states the mere facts:

> **ampère** Unit of electricity. Adopted by Paris Electric Congress (1881) from name of F. electrician (†1836). Cf. *ohm, volt*.

In many other cases, though, Weekley's style is very personal and easily read, for example:

> **freaked** App. coined by Milton, who may have had *freckle* and *streak* vaguely in mind.
>
> The pansy freaked with jet (*Lycidas*, 144).

II. Format

Entries in the *Etymological Dictionary* are arranged alphabetically with two columns per page. The main entry is in boldface and overhangs the text, making each entry easily distinguishable. The text type is easy on the eyes, and there is ample white space to set it off. The quotations are printed in small type but are still legible and should not be a problem to read. Italics are used for words in a foreign language, and the Greek alphabet is used for Greek words. Cross-references are used only when necessary, and they can be found easily.

The book is bound in heavy, laminated paper, lies flat when open, and is well sewn.

III. Quality and Currency of Entries

There is of course no question of currency in this volume. A few easy-to-understand examples of definitions will best show the literary and philosophical perspective of the compiler, as well as the scholarly restraints he placed on the entries for the sake of reader interest and enjoyment.

> **caveat** [leg.]. L., let him beware, from *cavére*. Init. word of certain legal cautions. Cf. schoolboy *cave* (imper.) and proverb. *caveat emptor*, let the purchaser look out for himself.
>
> **gibbon.** Ape. F. (Buffon), said to be an Indian word. Skeat suggests that this "Indian word" is E. *Gibbon*, dim. of *Gilbert* (see *gib*). The *NED.* does not record *gibbon* in sense of ape before Buffon, but the tombs of the *Gybbon* family at Rolvenden (Kent), dating from c. 1700, are surmounted by an ape's head, the family crest. King John had a falcon named *Gibbon*.
>
> **start.** ME. *sterten* (Kentish), AS. *styrtan*, to move with a bound. WGer.; cf. Du. *storten*, Ger. *stürzen*, to precipitate, rush. From sport. sense (c. 1600) comes gen. idea of beginning, setting out (c. 1800). Hence *from start to finish*. Trans. in to *start a hare* (Chauc.), also common in naut. lang. in sense of fracturing, etc.

> Wrong is often a good starter, but always a bad stayer (D. Lloyd George, May 24, 1918).

> **Tycoon.** Title by which the Shogun of Japan was described to foreigners. Jap. *taikun*, from Chin. *ta*, great, *kiun*, prince.

One is tempted to add *caveat lector*, beware, Reader: for sheer fascinating reading, this book is difficult to put down.

IV. Accessibility

There is no need for a thumb index in this paperback edition. Guide words appear at the top of each column on every page, and a list of abbreviations is provided in the frontmatter, as well as other useful information. The text is, in general, easily accessible.

V. Summary

The *Etymological Dictionary* is inexpensive, well printed, and easy to use. It is a well-researched, scholarly work, and though written in the somewhat stilted style of the period, it is still quite enjoyable and readable. The Greek alphabet will present some problems for many contemporary readers, but it will not keep a general reader from understanding the history or meaning of a word. This book is a curio for any well-read, educated reader with an interest in language; it would make an excellent gift for anyone with a love of words.

Although the inclusion of the word "Modern" in the title may mislead some readers, this classic should be added to any college or university library's collection of up-to-date etymological dictionaries if the original is not already in the collection. And large public libraries may wish to include this paperback set in their circulating collections as well.

The Facts on File Encyclopedia of Word and Phrase Origins

Facts at a Glance

Full Title: **The Facts on File Encyclopedia of Word and Phrase Origins**.
Publisher: Facts on File.
Compiler: Robert Hendrickson.
Edition Reviewed: © 1987.

Number of Entries: 7,500.
Number of Pages: 590.
Trim Size: 8½″ × 11″.
Binding: cloth.

Price: $40.00.
Sold in bookstores and other outlets; also sold to libraries and other educational institutions.
ISBN 0-8160-1012-9.

I. Introduction and Scope

The Facts on File Encyclopedia of Word and Phrase Origins is an oversize reference book tracing the origins of some 7,000 words and phrases. The publisher calls it "the most comprehensive book ever published on the subject." The compiler, Robert Hendrickson, has written more than 25 books, including many on language and literature.

The entries include words and expressions used in everyday life, such as **money**, **budget**, **brunch**, and **electricity**; literary figures, terms, and allusions, such as **whodunit** and **Robinson Crusoe**; historical figures and terms, such as **noblesse oblige**, **no man's land**, and **Molotov cocktail**; terms from folklore or expressions of folk wisdom, such as **Kris Kringle** and **There but for the grace of God go I**; and names of famous people, places, and products such as **Chippendale**, **Chisholm Trail**, and **Heinz's 57 varieties**. The majority of entries are idioms of one sort or another, such as **to put in one's two cents' worth** and **to play a hunch.**

II. Format

The Facts on File Encyclopedia of Word and Phrase Origins has a simple and straightforward format. This oversize (8½″ × 11″) book has the appearance of a coffee-table volume, but in fact contains no illustrations or any other lavish features. The text, however, does not have the open appearance customarily associated with such books. There is ample white space between entries and adequate leading between lines. The two-column format also includes generous inner margins. The typeface, while not unusually large, is clear and easy on the eyes. The book lies flat when open—another plus for library or home desk browsing or consultation.

III. Quality and Currency of Entries

This *Encyclopedia of Word and Phrase Origins* seems intended for the general reader interested in language rather than for the scholar or linguist. Entries are well written and lively but by no means exhaustive. Hendrickson frequently cites his sources, but this is not done in an academic fashion; occasionally, the information in the entries is largely speculative, with little apparent effort to bring new scholarly findings to light. This, however, is not necessarily a drawback if a reader does not expect or require a definitive etymological work.

The *Encyclopedia of Word and Phrase Origins* is a treasure-trove of fascinating tidbits and little-known facts. For example, one learns that, contrary to popular belief, Winston Churchill did not originate the phrase **iron curtain**, nor did Dr. Joseph Ignace Guillotin invent the **guillotine.** Hendrickson also provides persuasive and interesting, if not fully documented, anecdotes about such expressions as **all gussied up**, **flashy**, and **flea market**. Among other facts, we learn that Franklin Roosevelt's famous description of December 7, 1941, as "a date which will live in infamy" was written in the first draft as "a date which will live in world history." In other entries, we are told how the **Brooklyn Dodgers** got their name (and their nickname, the **bums**), why a hollow bullet is known as a **dumdum bullet**, why there are twelve inches to a foot and twelve people on a jury (both appear under **twelve**), and why some scholars believe that the country names *Ireland* and *Iran* derive from the same source.

Not all entries are this informative, however; some merely state the obvious and shed little additional light on their subjects. For example, we are told that the slogan **workers of the world, unite!** "comes from the first page of *The Communist Manifesto* (1848) by Karl Marx and Friedrich Engels." The entry for **born on the wrong side of the tracks** gives a purely conventional explanation of this expression. For **between the cup and the lip there's many a slip** we are informed that "no one knows where this common phrase originated, though it has been traced back to the 16th century. It means of course that anything can happen between the making of plans and their fulfillment." And in another entry we are told that "anyone parading in his *birthday suit* is stark naked. The phrase, first recorded in 1771 but probably older, simply means that someone is wearing nothing, just what he or she wore at birth."

Many of the words and phrases in this work can be traced back hundreds of years—sometimes to an-

The Facts on File Encyclopedia of Word and Phrase Origins

❶ Etymology is discussed in a paragraph

❷ Cross-references are set in boldface type

❸ Date of first recorded use is given if known

---

goldbacks.   (*See* **greenbacks**.) ————————❷

❶———**goldbrick.**   Con men working Western mining properties toward the end of the 19th century sometimes sold gullible investors lead or iron bricks coated with gold paint, representing them as the real thing. One Patrick Burke of St. Louis is recorded as having paid $3,700 for such a "gold" brick in 1887. This all-too-common confidence scheme gave the name *goldbrick* to any swindle or fakery. Later, soldiers picked up the expression and used the phrase *to goldbrick* in its present meaning of avoiding work or shirking duty. The phrase is first recorded in 1914——❸ in this sense, applied to army lieutenants appointed from civilian life.

---

cient Rome and to the Bible—and most are still in common use today. Hendrickson does include some terms of more recent origin, such as **No-tel Motel**, **Ginnie Mae**, and **do a number on**. However, contemporary scientific, technical, and computer terms are few and far between.

IV. Accessibility

Its simple format makes *The Facts on File Encyclopedia of Word and Phrase Origins* a reasonably accessible work. Words and phrases are usually entered under their most common form, although readers may find that they have to search for a particularly long or complex entry under several of its variant forms. Cross-reference entries are provided for some terms, but these are by no means comprehensive. There is no index, but since the arrangement of the entire book is alphabetical, this would have been largely redundant unless it included common variant forms of entry terms. Guide words at the top of each page indicate the first entry on the left-hand page and the last entry on the right-hand page.

V. Summary

Those who require a more scholarly book may want to examine Klein's A COMPREHENSIVE ETYMOLOGICAL DICTIONARY OF THE ENGLISH LANGUAGE. While *The Facts on File Encyclopedia of Word and Phrase Origins* is neither scholarly nor comprehensive, it does provide a wealth of information about the strange and wonderful language we have inherited, in a large format that will encourage use by library patrons. Highly anecdotal, the book is also richly entertaining, and will fit nicely in most nonspecialist public library collections.

New Words Dictionary

Facts at a Glance

Full Title: **New Words Dictionary**.
Publisher: Ballantine Books.
Editors: Harold LeMay, Sid Lerner, and Marian Taylor.
Edition Reviewed: © 1985.

Number of Entries: 388 with 15 cross-references.
Number of Words: approximately 18,720.
Number of Pages: 114.
Trim Size: 4" × 6⅞".
Binding: paperback.

Price: $2.50.
Sold in bookstores; also sold to libraries and other educational institutions.
ISBN 0-345-32461-7.

I. Introduction and Scope

The *New Words Dictionary* was compiled to help the reader understand the meaning of some of the new words, expressions, and acronyms that have been coined by the media, politicians, sports commentators, professionals in specialized fields, and others. Although some of the words and expressions are not *new*, their meanings and nuances have been altered or changed completely. Many of these words may some day find a permanent place in our language and be included in the standard dictionaries, while others will be used for a short time and then disappear.

This informal dictionary was created to fill the gap between the time a word comes into common usage and its acceptance into a standard dictionary. *New*

Words is selective in what has been included and makes no attempt to be complete or precise. The authors are very straightforward about their purpose and make no claims that this little dictionary is a scholarly work. They want to help people understand what they read and what they hear in the media.

The words, expressions, and acronyms were taken from newspapers, magazines, books, pamphlets, catalogues, and labels. The editors listened to radio and television, conversations in train stations, rock concerts, sports arenas, and conventions, and also consulted experts in many fields. Many slang words are included that are found in newspapers such as the *New York Times* and the *Wall Street Journal* and heard on television programs such as *60 Minutes*. They have excluded many medical expressions and computer words, unless such words or terms have entered the mainstream of popular language. Prison language was omitted since it is not often printed in mass media and is not in widespread use. Many of the words will already be familiar to most readers, but the editors state that they guarantee that no one will know all of the words and expressions. They were eclectic in their selection, choosing words that were in common use at the time this dictionary was being written, 1984–1985.

A few of the expressions that are defined have been in use for many years and could have been omitted to allow for additional newer entries. Examples are **Fannie Mae**, in use since 1953 and defined in standard dictionaries as early as 1963 as an acronym **FNMA**; **Freddie Mac** and **Ginnie Mae** both in use since 1975; and **Sallie Mae**, cited as first used in 1972 in the HARPER DICTIONARY OF CONTEMPORARY USAGE. It is interesting to note the many familiar nouns that now have new meanings, such as **camel**, **caramel**, **coyote**, **gorilla**, and **legs**. Some nouns have become verbs with new meanings, such as **rapture**; or have acquired meaning as an adjective, as the word **keys** has. Examples of expressions that have new meanings or nuances are **cattle show**, **cafeteria plan**, **first strike**, **human resources**, and **zoo plane**.

The scope of *New Words* meets the intentions of the editors, and for a limited number of entries (388) gives a good overview of current popular usage.

II. Format

The *New Words* uses a straightforward alphabetical arrangement with definitions running from three to 14 lines, with an average definition running about four and one-half lines. All entries are in boldface type and are followed by the part of speech in parentheses. Some words have their pronunciation given phonetically. The definition section is followed by an index of abbreviations and acronyms, and then by 18 broad subject areas such as **Arts**, **Entertainment**, **Lifestyle**, and **The Media**. When appropriate a word or expression is listed under more than one subject group.

The book is not well-made and will not stand up to heavy use. A library should consider permabinding it before adding it to the collection.

III. Quality and Currency of Entries

With a few exceptions, all entries are for words currently in popular use. Some entries have a short history of how the word or term came into being. When a source is cited, a complete citation is not given. However, for the purpose of this book, as a guide to the general reader, this is not a drawback.

IV. Accessibility

The arrangement is easy to use. There are so few pages that a thumb-index is not needed. There are 15 cross-references.

V. Summary

The *New Words Dictionary* is inexpensive, easy to use, and fulfills its stated purpose. The definitions are breezy, witty, and clearly written. It fills a need for an inexpensive dictionary for current popular words. For those who want a more scholarly reference work, there are other choices such as HARPER DICTIONARY OF CONTEMPORARY USAGE (1985), *Newswordy* by Ken Dachman (Simon & Schuster, 1985), the POCKET OXFORD DICTIONARY OF CURRENT ENGLISH (7th ed., 1984), Merriam-Webster's 12,000 WORDS (1986), as well as the now out-of-print *Second Barnhart Dictionary of New English*, which some libraries may still possess.

The Origins of English Words

Facts at a Glance

Full Title: **The Origins of English Words: A Discursive Dictionary of Indo-European Roots.**
Publisher: Johns Hopkins University Press.
Compiler: Joseph T. Shipley.
Edition Reviewed: © 1984.

Number of Entries: 3,000.
Number of Pages: 672.
Number of Indexes: 1.
Trim Size: 5⅞" × 8⅞".
Binding: cloth.

Price: $39.95.

Sold in bookstores and through direct mail; also
  sold to libraries and other educational
  institutions.
ISBN 0-8018-3004-4

I. Introduction and Scope

Indo-European (IE) is the name given to a hypothetical reconstructed common ancestor language that was never recorded but is believed to be the progenitor of the Celtic, Germanic, Italic, Hellenic, Tocharian, Balto-Slavic and Indo-Iranian language groups. English, once a minor branch of Germanic (Anglo-Saxon), is now the largest "in vocabulary, in number of native speakers, and in the extent of its use around the world."

In the introduction to his *Origins of English Words*, Joseph T. Shipley, also the author of DICTIONARY OF WORD ORIGINS and *Dictionary of Early English*, presents a succinct history of the English language from its earliest Anglo-Saxon form to its intermingling with the language of the Celts, Danes, and Normans. He describes how philologists traced families of languages back through common roots and discovered consistencies in consonant shiftings (the *p* sound in Latin *pater* to the *f* sound of German *Vater* and English *father*, is one example), and how it came to be that different roots may, in Modern English, have opposite meanings (*cleave,* for example). He discusses how readily English, "perhaps because of its early blending," continues to add words, often unaltered, from languages not even included in the IE group, such as Japanese (*karate*) and Afrikaans (*apartheid*).

The author notes that while not all English words can be traced back to an inferred IE root, many can be. This book attempts to list "the most productive of these roots" and to note the "various and frequently diverse English words into which they have been fashioned." Shipley's aim is to "illuminate our living language and give impetus to its further growth."

II. Format

A short chapter under the heading "Frequent Word Forms and Transformations" precedes the main text and provides summary information on vowel and consonant shifts (Grimm's Law is outlined, but not Verner's); confounded sounds ("*l.r.* alternations are found from 'China to Peru' "); metathesis, or the transposition of a sound (the Old English *bridd* becomes *bird*); verbal forms; lost sounds; echoic words; and other considerations in the study of language development. The "Notes on Usage" chapter explains how the figurative use of a word "may continue in a language along with the original," literal sense (*pluck,* for example) and how the richness of English vocabulary is the result of words coming into English "by different journeys from one root," to give us doublets such as *regal* and *royal*, or even multiple variants such as *dais, desk, disc,* and *dish*.

The remainder of the book—its bulk—is arranged in a two-part dictionary format. The Indo-European roots comprise the body of the text, and are alphabetically listed. The root word, in lowercase bold type, overhangs the text. Roots that lead to significantly diverse modern words are listed separately and given Roman numerals to differentiate them; **kel**, for example, has 11 entries: for example, **kel I**: warm; **kel VI**: hollow; to cover; to hide. Each entry is followed by discussion and etymological background in paragraph form.

The second part, an "Index of English Words," lists word forms and foreign phrases used in English, each followed by the root(s) under which it appears." This 183-page index section has two columns of Modern English words per page. There may be one or several references for an index word. Under **crayfish**, the reader is referred to the roots **gerbh, kar**, and **kueit**.

As is the case with most dictionaries, the print is rather small, and the inner margins are narrow, but there is a lot of information in this attractive 672-page clothbound volume.

III. Quality and Currency of Entries

As noted in the introduction, the original Indo-European words "were fashioned to denote material objects or specific events that impinged directly upon the senses, or immediate emotions." It is postulated that centuries went by before these terms "were extended from physical to mental activity, from the concrete to the abstract," and ultimately were perhaps given "figurative uses and applications." The entries reflect this and are presented in an interesting and readable style.

One of the most prolific roots covered is **gn, gen**. Shipley treats this as one root, contrary to some scholars (and to the editors of THE AMERICAN HERITAGE DICTIONARY OF INDO-EUROPEAN ROOTS) because "it defies partition." Its two meanings, to know and to beget, "continue to entwine through the linguistic change." The explanatory text of this entry first shows that this root is an example of the consonant shifts inherent in Grimm's Law, as briefly described in the introductory chapters. "Thus the [Greek] *k* shift turns it to [English] *know*, and *know* may refer to mental or carnal knowledge." This ample and pleasantly rambling entry includes quotes from the Bible, Shakespeare, a 1622 Massinger-Dekker play, and a digressive note on Coney Island. Shipley postulates that the rabbit "may have gotten its earlier name *coney* from its prolific nature." Coney Island, New York, was named after the rabbits that were hunted there. Also covered in this four-page entry is the evolution of the root in Sanskrit (*yoni*), Latin ("*progeny* down the *generation* with the *genitals*, rarely by *parthenogenesis*"), Greek, and German. It is replete with quotes from Chaucer to John Creasey, and covers an abundance of cognate words believed to stem from **gn, gen**—from *agnostic* to *androgenous*, *cunnilingus*, and *uncouth*. The text notes:

> The association of these two sets of meanings [to know, to beget] in one root shows the early sense of their essential unity: knowledge is power; to know how, to produce; to ken, to kindle.

Multiple senses of a word are given separate entries. The index, under *deer*, leads the reader to **dheu I** and **dheu II**. Under **dheu I** ("to smoke; dust; hence rise, fly about, like dust") we are told that

> From smoke, breath, as noticeably on cold days . . . came *deer*, which first meant any animal, as in King Lear iii, 4:
>
>> But mice and rats and such small deer
>> Have been Tom's food for seven long year.

This quote, like many used by Shipley, is also found in the OXFORD ENGLISH DICTIONARY (OED).

Dheu II, to be worn out, die (an extension of **dheu I**) doesn't mention *deer* in the entry. *The American Heritage Dictionary* (1969), under *deer*, leads the reader to the first of three entries for *dheu* in its Indo-European roots appendix. Meaning number 4 under *dheu-1*:

> Suffixed extended form **dheus*-o- in Germanic **diuzam*, breathing creature, animal, in: a. Old English *déor*, animal: DEER . . . .

So Shipley's dictionary is not a replacement for a straight Indo-European dictionary, but a discursive, erudite, and often amusing companion.

IV. Accessibility

Immediately preceding the body of this dictionary is a list of the abbreviations for the languages referred to in the text. The Indo-European root entries are in lowercase bold type, overhanging the text. Both cognate words and *see* references are in italics. Many of the quotes that illustrate usage are set off from the text as extracts, thus enhancing readability.

Guide words, again in lowercase bold, appear at the top outer margins of each double-page spread and indicate the first and last entries of that spread.

The "Index of English Words" in the back of the book includes proper nouns, common nouns, verbs, and compounds (**trigger-happy**, for example). Multiple senses of the same root are given separate entries, and are distinguished by Roman numerals. An example of an index entry is:

> secret: *KerIII, SekVI, Sue.*

A paragraph preceding the bibliography refers to the author's book *In Praise of English* (1977) for those who wish to learn more about word development than is offered in the brief introductory chapter in this volume. The bibliography itself is one and a half pages and unfortunately omits publishers and place of publication.

V. Summary

The Origins of English Words is not a definitive Indo-European dictionary, nor does it pretend to be. Rather, as the author states in his introduction, it is a selected list of the most productive roots. Shipley's discursive writing style is entertaining and the cognate words he chooses to describe are good illustrations for the study of word development.

This is an impressive piece of scholarship, and, being neither stuffy nor staid, its lively presentation makes it accessible to a wide range of readers. Librarians may also wish to look at the equally reliable AMERICAN HERITAGE DICTIONARY OF INDO-EUROPEAN WORD ROOTS. Both works are important etymological sources; medium to large public libraries as well as all college and university libraries will want at least one of these in their collections.

Origins: A Short Etymological Dictionary of Modern English

Facts at a Glance

Full Title: **Origins: A Short Etymological Dictionary of Modern English: Fourth Edition.**
Publisher: Macmillan.
Author: Eric Partridge.
Edition Reviewed: © 1966; reprinted 1979.

Number of Entries: 12,000.
Number of Pages: 992.
Trim Size: 7⁵⁄₁₆″ × 9¼″.
Binding: hardcover.

Price: $50.00.
Sold in bookstores; also sold to libraries and other educational institutions.
ISBN 0-02-594840-7.

I. Introduction and Scope

First published in 1958, this etymological dictionary by the late distinguished English philologist Eric Partridge, now in its fourth edition, is still widely regarded as the standard short work in the field. Intended for the general reader as well as the erudite scholar, the work provides, as stated by the publisher, "information on the evolution and development of the 12,000 most commonly used words in English."

Partridge says in the foreword to the book that the system he devised enabled him, "with the aid of cross-references, not only to cover a very much wider field than might have seemed possible but also, and especially, to treat all important words much more comprehensively and thoroughly." However, Partridge hardly touches on medical or technical terms. For *laser*, *radar*, and *anorexia*, we must turn to Klein's COMPREHENSIVE DICTIONARY OF THE ENGLISH LANGUAGE. Dialect and slang words are also not covered. However, many words from the standard English spoken in the United States, as well as in Canada, South Africa, Australia, New Zealand, India, and Pakistan have been included.

The work also includes a lengthy list of abbreviations, a list of prefixes, a list of suffixes, and a list of compound-forming elements that will enable the user to discover the etymology of many words not included in the dictionary.

II. Format

Though called a "short dictionary," this is a weighty volume of close to 1,000 pages. Sturdily bound, it is printed in small, but very readable black type on good quality opaque white paper. The dictionary is printed in two columns with ample white space and presents a very attractive format to the user.

III. Quality and Currency of Entries

Main entry words appear in alphabetical order in boldface type and indented for easy recognition. They are followed immediately by the complete etymological information; no definitions or pronunciations appear unless they have a bearing on word origins. Entries may contain many abbreviations (which the reader would do well to master in advance) and references—indicated by "see" or "cf"—to prefixes, suffixes, compound-forming elements, and other entries and sub-entries.

Some entries are quite brief. For example:

> **gaucho**, a Sp-Amerindian cowboy of the pampas, is a S Am Sp. word, app from Arouchan *cauchu*, a wanderer.

Or, somewhat longer:

> **brogue** (1), stout shoe: an Irishism: Ir *brōg*, EIr *brōc*, a shoe, a hoof, prob from ON *brōk*, hose; cf, therefore, BREECHES.

> **brogue** (2), a dial pron, esp the Ir pron of E; Ir *barrōg*, a hold or bond, e.g. on the tongue, hence a defective pron, hence the E sense: a mdfn of It *barra*, a bar, a hindrance: cf, therefore, BAR.

A word like **light**, however, takes up more than three columns, including five derivatives under the heading *Germanic and Indo-European*, nine under *Latin*, five under *Latin compounds*, and two under *Greek*, plus six additional forms of the word, including **lighten**, **lighter**, and **lighting**. Within an entry there are innumerable cross-references to other parts of the same entry, but more disconcerting, many of Partridge's entries are in fact just cross-references themselves. In this respect, it is interesting to compare Partridge with the OXFORD DICTIONARY OF ENGLISH ETYMOLOGY (*ODEE*). Between **sequin** and **series**, *ODEE* has 17 full entries, while Partridge has 9 full entries and 8 cross-references; between **mackerel** and **madeira**, ODEE has 14 complete entries, while Partridge has 6 full entries and 3 cross-references. Searching becomes a far more laborious process if one has to track down a word rather than finding it in its alphabetical position.

Since the latest revision of this work was made in 1966, the dictionary cannot be counted upon to include words taken into the language after that date. However, because Partridge was concerned with a *core* English vocabulary, the dictionary should remain authoritative and useful for years to come.

IV. Accessibility

Main entries are accessible through the alphabetical order of the words. No indexes are provided. Guide words at the top of every page indicate first and last words on the page, and page numbers appear prominently in the center position above the two columns of text. A table of contents helpfully lists the main sections of the book, and a brief section entitled "How to Use This Dictionary" follows. There is no thumb indexing.

V. Summary

Eric Partridge's *Origins: A Short Etymological Dictionary of Modern English* is a very erudite and yet readable dictionary that all librarians will want to include in their reference collections. Though its entries are longer and more thorough, *Origins* lacks the pronunciation and dating features of the OXFORD DICTIONARY OF ENGLISH ETYMOLOGY. Furthermore, it only includes meanings where confusion could arise, while ODEE provides definitions for every entry. Librarians may wish to include both works, leaving room also for Klein's COMPREHENSIVE ETYMOLOGICAL DICTIONARY OF THE ENGLISH LANGUAGE at the more demanding end of the scholarly shelf, and such selective works as THE FACTS ON FILE ENCYCLOPEDIA OF WORD AND PHRASE ORIGINS at the more popular end of the shelf.

Oxford Dictionary of English Etymology

Facts at a Glance

Full Title: **Oxford Dictionary of English Etymology.**
Publisher: Oxford University Press.
Editor: C. T. Onions.
Edition Reviewed: © 1966; 1983 printing.

Number of Entries: 24,000.
Number of Pages: 1,040.
Trim Size: 6" × 9".
Binding: cloth.

Price: $45.95.
Sold in bookstores; also sold to libraries and other educational institutions.
ISBN 0-19-861112-9.

I. Introduction and Scope

For more than 20 years, this etymological classic has been the ultimate authority on the history of English words. Each of its 24,000 main entries (38,000 words are treated overall) traces the origin, formation, and development of a word. As the introduction states: "The forms from which English words are derived, whether by descent or adoption, are traced to their ultimate source, so far as this is known or reasonably to be presumed."

It is principally a dictionary for those engaged in etymological and linguistic research and teaching, or for writers who need accurate and detailed information about word origins and derivatives.

A concise edition of the *Oxford Dictionary of English Etymology (ODEE)* was published in 1986 and retains the form and more than three quarters of the contents of the work under review here.

II. Format

This is a chunky, single-volume work of over 1,000 pages. There are 20 to 30 entries per double-column page, varying in length from 3 to 20 lines. The word heading each entry is printed in boldface, for instance, **mule** and related words that may be grouped with it are printed in the same type; if any of these end in a suffix that is treated in a separate article, this is printed in small capitals as: **mul**ETEER. Complete etymologies of prefixes and suffixes like **re-**, **-aster**, **-eer** are fully dealt with in the text and there is considerable cross-referencing to link seemingly disparate words such as **mulch** . . . cf MOLLIFY.

Pronunciation (omitted from the concise edition, incidentally) follows the main entry and then there occurs a listing of senses of the word and the century in which each sense first appeared.

> **Frank** †free XIII; †of superior quality XIV; candid XVI.
> †signifies obsolescence.

Neither the dating nor the chronological order appears in ORIGINS: A SHORT ETYMOLOGICAL DICTIONARY OF MODERN ENGLISH, edited by Eric Partridge, the chief etymological dictionary alternative to the *ODEE*. Since Partridge goes from current use to original, readers cannot follow the evolution of meaning that accompanies the changing form of a word.

III. Quality and Currency of Entries

Assiduous scholarship is the hallmark of every entry in this dictionary. The *ODEE*'s Editor-in-Chief, C. T. Onions, is "genetic" in his approach to etymology, rarely accepting folk etymologies and instead tracing each component to its familial origins. Moreover, Onions (unlike Partridge) accepts the inherent integrity of a word and opts for separate entries rather than subsuming them: *ODEE* gives **mulatto** and **mullein** individual treatment, while Partridge refers the reader to "mule" for the first, and "meal" for the second.

American readers will not have to defer to British spellings because the *ODEE* includes U.S. spelling (**program**, **center**) alongside the British. However, it excludes the etymology of most slang (*reefer*, for example) and, more importantly, it excludes the etymology of personal names and scientific vocabulary. For *Catherine* and *Mozarab*, *podophyllum*, and *sipylite*, readers must turn to Klein's A COMPREHENSIVE ETYMOLOGICAL DICTIONARY OF THE ENGLISH LANGUAGE, although, like Partridge, Klein gives neither date nor pronunciation.

IV. Accessibility

The sheer magnitude of detail in the *ODEE* might be considered overwhelming, but Onions and his co-editors did not intend this to be a popular work. An introductory essay on the history and sources of the English language, a pronunciation guide, and an abbreviation list in clear type combine to allow the

Oxford Dictionary of English Etymology

❶ Roman numerals indicate century in which word first appeared in English

❷ Cross-references are set in small capitals

❸ Etymologies of related words are given

❹ Cognates are listed and identified by language

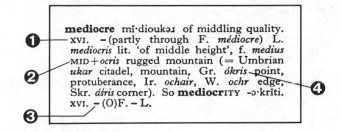

mediocre mi·dioukəɹ of middling quality. XVI. – (partly through F. *médiocre*) L. *mediocris* lit. 'of middle height', f. *medius* MID + *ocris* rugged mountain (= Umbrian *ukar* citadel, mountain, Gr. *ókris* point, protuberance, Ir. *ochair*, W. *ochr* edge, Skr. *áśris* corner). So **mediocrity** -ɔ·kriti. XVI. – (O)F. – L.

interested reader full access to the given etymologies. While Klein's work leaves the original Greek roots in Greek, the *ODEE* transliterates them into English.

Alternative spellings (**manoevre**, U.S. **maneuver**; **Muslim**, **Moslem**) and generous cross-referencing also aid the reader considerably. This cross-referencing is an additional bonus to etymological research as cognate words are often of such different meanings that no one would guess they were descended from the same root.

V. Summary

Readers can accept with confidence the publisher's claim that the *ODEE* is the most complete and reliable etymological dictionary of the English language ever published. Browsers may enjoy the slightly less intellectual style of Partridge, and others who require historical and literary examples of usage may turn to the OXFORD ENGLISH DICTIONARY.

But neither of these works contains anything like the body of etymological information of the Oxford. It stands alone and belongs in the general reference collections of all but the smallest public libraries, which may prefer either the concise edition or the Partridge.

Word for Word

Facts at a Glance

Full Title: **Word for Word**.
Publisher: Verbatim Books; distributed by Gale Research.
Compiler: Edward C. Pinkerton.
Edition Reviewed: © 1982.

Number of Topics: 60.
Number of Pages: 454.
Number of Indexes: 1.
Trim Size: 6″ × 9″.
Binding: cloth.

Price: $60.00.
Sold to libraries and by direct mail.
ISBN 0-930454-06-5.

I. Introduction and Scope

Word for Word, treating etymological cognates, is written on the concept of controlled dictionary rambling. Edward Pinkerton, a linguist, relays his interest in etymology in a most enjoyable style. The introduction provides a brief history of Indo-European studies, explaining the startling late-eighteenth-century discovery that there were regular language similarities between the Western and Near Eastern world.

Pinkerton explains that ". . . cognate words are often of such disparate form and meaning that no one looking at them in alphabetical order would imagine that they were descended from the same root. It was the existence of these sometimes striking—not to say bizarre—disparities . . ." that prompted him to write a series of short essays that later lengthened into this book.

II. Format

Preliminary text of *Word for Word* begins with an introduction containing a brief history of Proto-Indo-European languages, an authoritative bibliography, and a section titled, "How to Use This Book." The main body of the book contains 60 chapters in which a great amount of information is tightly condensed. The chapters are short and interdependent. Each chapter is given a title comprised of the words that will be discussed, for example, "Vasty Vacuous Wastes, Wanton Vanity." The first paragraph begins, "A VACUUM is a VOID is a VACUITY, and the whole nothingness sounds like a terrible WASTE, which in one sense it is, since one of the earliest meanings of the word WASTE is 'uninhabited, uncultivated land.' "

In the succeeding paragraphs, each word is explained, and the ways in which one relates to another

Word for Word

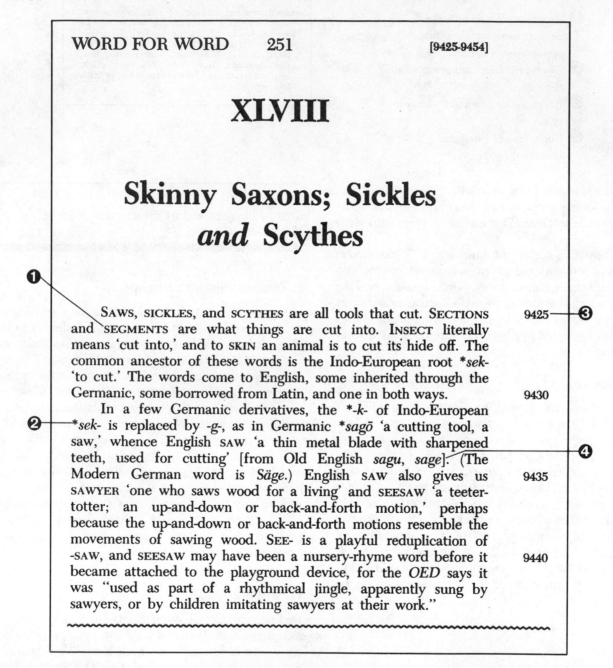

WORD FOR WORD   251   [9425-9454]

XLVIII

Skinny Saxons; Sickles *and* Scythes

❶

SAWS, SICKLES, and SCYTHES are all tools that cut. SECTIONS   9425   ❸
and SEGMENTS are what things are cut into. INSECT literally
means 'cut into,' and to SKIN an animal is to cut its hide off. The
common ancestor of these words is the Indo-European root *sek-
'to cut.' The words come to English, some inherited through the
Germanic, some borrowed from Latin, and one in both ways.   9430

❷ In a few Germanic derivatives, the *-k- of Indo-European
*sek- is replaced by -g-, as in Germanic *sagō 'a cutting tool, a
saw,' whence English SAW 'a thin metal blade with sharpened
teeth, used for cutting' [from Old English *sagu, sage*]. (The   ❹
Modern German word is *Säge*.) English SAW also gives us   9435
SAWYER 'one who saws wood for a living' and SEESAW 'a teeter-
totter; an up-and-down or back-and-forth motion,' perhaps
because the up-and-down or back-and-forth motions resemble the
movements of sawing wood. SEE- is a playful reduplication of
-SAW, and SEESAW may have been a nursery-rhyme word before it   9440
became attached to the playground device, for the *OED* says it
was "used as part of a rhythmical jingle, apparently sung by
sawyers, or by children imitating sawyers at their work."

❶ Words under discussion are set in small capitals

❸ Lines are numbered to permit precise indexing

❹ Brief etymologies are enclosed in brackets

❷ An asterisk indicates a hypothetical form

are discussed in detail. As the author traces the words back to their sources, the original language form is given in italics. If the word is non-Roman (Sanskrit, Russian, Greek, etc.), it has been transliterated, and all languages are clearly identified. Italicized words preceded by an asterisk refer to a form that linguists believe may, or should have, existed at one time during the development of the language, but for which there is no written evidence. Definitions are in single quotes, for example: VACUUM, 'empty space.'

Each fifth line of the text is numbered and noted in the margin, providing convenient access from the 104-page index.

III. Quality and Currency of Entries

The quality of this work is commendable. The author follows standard authorities, specifies disagreements when they seem important, and indicates what is speculative. He also outlines technical evidence which links languages.

Pinkerton is current both in his awareness of etymology as well as in his perception of contemporary society. Chapter 39 is titled "The Mannerly Amanuensis Maneuvers Manure," and begins,

> Women's liberationists are seeking EMANCIPATION; they want to cast off their MANACLES and be free to MAN-AGE, MANEUVER, MANIPULATE, and MAINTAIN their own affairs in their own MANNER with their own well-MANICURED hands, and COMMAND their own not-so-MANIFEST destinies.

A distinct aspect of this work, and one that the examples typify, is a sense of humor in the writing. The whole subject becomes alive and readable. The book itself is a size that is easy to handle. Its print is very legible and its binding sturdy.

IV. Accessibility

Due to the meticulously compiled index, access to this book's contents is outstanding. Using the text's line numbering system, the index provides access to the exact line in the text on which the word appears. In addition to including almost every citation for every word printed in small capitals and italics in the text (for example, the words being discussed and their roots), the index contains listings for all of the meanings included in the book. The index entries are written in the same type style as they appear in the text.

The book's table of contents and guide to use are also very helpful. The table of contents provides the page on which the chapter begins as well as beginning and ending line numbers in each section.

V. Summary

Word for Word does not pretend to be a complete etymological dictionary. Like other compilers of popular works of etymology—the American Heritage Editors' WORD MYSTERIES AND HISTORIES and William and Mary Morris' *Morris Dictionary of Word and Phrase Origins*—Pinkerton has included some words and left out others. We can find **fuel**, **fugue** and **fusillade**, but we can't find *fumble*, *fuss* and *fuzzy*. Those words we can find are examined closely enough to satisfy the needs of most users. However, the serious linguist must still turn to Klein's COMPREHENSIVE ETYMOLOGICAL DICTIONARY OF THE ENGLISH LANGUAGE or the OXFORD DICTIONARY OF ENGLISH ETYMOLOGY (both reviewed in this Buying

Guide) for state-of-the-art etymological scholarship. Reference collections will still need one of these standard etymological dictionaries. But as a fascinating guide to the historical by-ways of our language, Pinkerton's work is a fine choice for any library. As Donald J. Lehman wrote in his review of *Word for Word* (RQ, Fall, 1982), "The book is written to be read and enjoyed as much as it is to be a source of valuable etymological information."

Word Mysteries & Histories

Facts at a Glance

Full Title: **Word Mysteries & Histories: From Quiche to Humble Pie**.
Publisher: Houghton Mifflin.
Compilers: Editors of The American Heritage Dictionaries.
Illustrator: Barry Moser.
Edition Reviewed: © 1986.

Number of Entries: over 500.
Number of Pages: 320.
Number of Indexes: 1.
Number of Illustrations: 34 black-and-white illustrations.
Trim Size: 6″ × 9″.
Binding: cloth.

Price: $16.95.
Sold in bookstores; also sold to libraries.
ISBN 0-395-4-265-4.

I. Introduction and Scope

Word Mysteries & Histories, described in the preface as "a soupçon of lexical history," is a handsomely illustrated volume prepared by the editors of the American Heritage Dictionaries as a response to the many reader queries on "lexical genealogies."

In its preface, Executive Editor Anne H. Soukhanov gives special acknowledgment to Editor Marion Severynse whose word history paragraphs in WEBSTER'S II NEW RIVERSIDE UNIVERSITY DICTIONARY "provided a foundation for this book." Foreword author Robert Claiborne's statement "language is people" is said to be the inspiration for this word appreciation book, whose emphasis is the "human dynamics affecting the language over the centuries."

Words, many of them "animate nouns," that are examples of semantic shifts, revivals of moribund words, foreign adoptions, eponyms (words named after people), and semantic extensions of trademark names make up most of the entries. "Mysteries" are

Word Mysteries & Histories: From Quiche to
Humble Pie

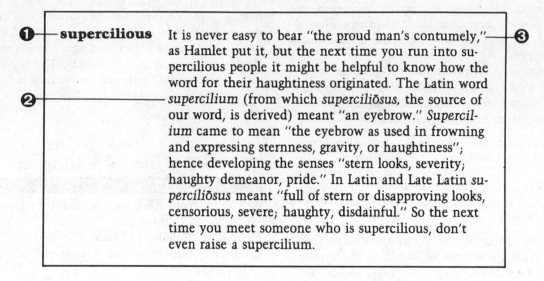

❶ Main entry words are listed
    alphabetically
❷ Etymologies are discussed
❸ Examples of usage are given

words such as **jazz** and **posh** whose origins are "obscure or disputed."

The entries are described in the preface as self-contained articles. The table of contents is followed by artist Barry Moser's list of illustrations and his comments on the origin of their inspiration. A short essay by David A. Jost, "The Last Word," follows the text and provides "a brief encapsulation of the history of English," the titles of sources referred to in the preparation of the text, and the "linguistic processes examined" in the book.

II. Format

Word Mysteries & Histories is a thoughtfully designed volume. Full-page wood-cuts by Barry Moser illustrate 34 of the articles. **Namby-pamby**, for example, is illustrated by a woodcut of a boy in an ill-fitting suit "suggested by figures of indecisiveness, such as film character 'Alfalfa' "; **humble pie**, by a rendering of Uriah Heep; and **yahoo** by a Ku Klux Klannish masked character. The word **Teflon** is represented by a portrait of the fortieth president of the United States.

The text pages are aesthetically pleasing. Main entry words in red are in dictionary format and overhang the text. The volume is bound in a full cloth hard cover and has an attractive dust jacket.

III. Quality and Currency of Entries

Currency of entries is not a particular emphasis in this book. **Latchkey child**, a term that would appear

to be a recent phenomenon, was used as early as 1944 in an NBC radio program. The trademark entry **Teflon** is given more than four pages of narrative. U.S. Representative Patricia Schroeder is credited as "the first to use *Teflon* in connection with Ronald Reagan." This same entry discusses how the Lucasfilm Ltd. registered trademark STAR WARS came to be used as "a synonym for, or as an adjective modifying, the SDI" (Reagan's Strategic Defense Initiative). General comments on the legal ramifications of using "proprietary names" complete this article.

Some foreign adoptions included are **paparazzo** (from the name of a character in Fellini's film *La Dolce Vita* inspired by photo reporter Ron Galella); **mayday** ("a spelling that represents the pronunciation of French *m'aider*, 'help me' "); **eunuch** (derived from the Greek word meaning "a castrated person employed to take charge of the women and act as chamberlain").

Remacadamize, a word made up of elements of five different languages, is a fascinating entry that examines prefixation, suffixation, eponymous words, and proper name derivation. Other eponyms included as entries are **boycott** and **silhouette**.

The article under **hussy** explains how the word developed phonetically from the Middle English compound *huswif*, also ancestor to *housewife*. Under **tawdry**, an alteration of the name of Saint Audry, an Anglo-Saxon princess who died of a throat ailment, the editors explain how the word came to mean "gaudy and cheap."

Mystery words, in addition to **jazz** and **posh**, are **shyster** and **hooker** (not derived, the editors claim, from Civil War general Joseph Hooker).

The narrative entries are easy reading, and linguistic terms are defined as they appear in the various articles. The choice of entries is whimsical and is not directed at any particular group of reader.

IV. Accessibility

There are no guide words or cross-references in the body of the text. A thorough index refers to the illustrations in the text, the main entry words, and words and proper names mentioned in the various articles. All separate features including the index are listed in the table of contents.

V. Summary

Word Mysteries & Histories is an attractive trade book that contains informative entries on the development of more than 500 words. Designed for the word-lover rather than the general reader, it will make a welcome addition to the circulating collection in public libraries where there is a frequent demand for witty, stylish, and sophisticated books on various aspects of the English language. *Word Mysteries & Histories* is well suited for browsing or for bedtime reading. However, it is simply not sufficiently comprehensive to be considered a major ready-reference resource.

Chapter 12
Evaluations of
Synonym and Antonym Dictionaries

Allen's Synonyms and Antonyms

Facts at a Glance

Full Title: **Allen's Synonyms and Antonyms**.
Publisher: Barnes & Noble Books.
Compiler: F. Sturges Allen.
Editor: T. H. Vail Motter.
Edition Reviewed: © 1949; 1985, 14th printing of 1972 paperback edition.

Number of Entries: approximately 12,000.
Number of Pages: 427.
Number of Cross-references: 5,000.
Trim Size: 5⅛″ × 8″.
Binding: paperback.

Price: $4.95.
Sold in bookstores and also through direct mail.
ISBN 0-064-63328-4.

I. Introduction and Scope

The late F. Sturges Allen, general editor of WEB-STER'S THIRD NEW INTERNATIONAL DICTIONARY, prepared the text for the original 1921 edition of *Allen's Synonyms and Antonyms*, published by Harper & Row. The book was revised by T. H. Vail Motter in 1949, who increased the number of main entries by about one third. Motter included words that, he explained, "have not appeared in dictionaries in general use" and he also added "sense discriminations" and the context in which many of the words might be most appropriately used. The edition reviewed here is the 14th printing of the 1972 paperback edition, which is essentially a reprint of the Harper & Row edition. Only this paperback edition is still in print.

The work contains approximately 12,000 main entries and 5,000 cross-references. The publisher claims that *Allen's* "supplies all the synonyms, antonyms, and related words that a thesaurus does, but goes beyond a thesaurus; it tells just how the words differ, makes clear their various shades of meanings, explains their distinctions, and suggests nuances that the writer and reader need to know." This claim, however, is no longer valid.

Allen's lexicon encompasses English language words and terms from the Victorian era through the first half of the twentieth century. The text is intended for an American audience, but the words and terms identified include British, Scottish, Irish, North American, Canadian, Anglo-Indian, slang, rare, colloquial, poetic, affected, and obsolete items. Words that derive from the sciences and technology have such dated synonyms that their chief merit now is to charm or surprise the reader. For example, under the main entry **engineer**, the synonyms listed are: **machinist . . . driver . . . hydraulician, mechanician, pioneer**.

II. Format

This volume is printed in rather small, but readable type. The paper quality is unusually good for an inexpensive paperback and has little show-through. Moreover, it is sturdily bound and should be able to survive frequent use.

A preface, explanatory remarks entitled "How Shall I Say It?" and lists of explanatory terms and abbreviations, for example, (*A*) for archaic and (*R*) for rare, introduce the book. The main vocabulary is ordered alphabetically. For the main entries, which appear in boldface, parts of speech are given, followed by numbered lists of related synonyms with the "sense discrimination" or advice on meaning and usage given in parentheses. Often a "see" cross-reference for at least one of the clusters of meaning is given, referring the reader to another main entry word or words where possible synonyms may be found. For example:

> **dependence**, *n*. 1. hanging, suspension.
> 2. hinging, turning, hanging, resting.
> 3. *See* RELIANCE, SUPPORT.

Antonyms or other cross-references, when provided, follow the numbered section of each entry according to the sense of the word grouping that the editor deems most acceptable.

A condensed, supplementary word list appears at the foot of each page in smaller type. Each main entry in this list has one or more cross-references to entries in the main text. For example: **noiseless**: *silent*. The reader can look up the word **silent** in the main vocabulary, where **noiseless** appears among a more extensive list of synonyms. This device, according to the editor, "eliminate[s] space-consuming duplication of word-groups under separate entries for each component of a group. A maximum amount of space is therefore devoted to non-recurring items, and unavoidable duplications are minimized." Despite this explanation, the system appears cumbersome, and readers could be confused by it.

III. Quality and Currency of Entries

The book contains a large and relatively complicated primary word list, and its synonyms are varied and often voluminous. However, the discrimination of meanings is nearly 40 years out of date. For example, under **entertainer**, the synonyms are

> **hospitator** (*R*) **harborer** (*A*) **host**, **hostess**

with no mention of *actor, singer, dancer, raconteur,* or *comedian*.

In addition, many entries are either insufficiently broad for today's reader or idiosyncratic. For example, Allen and Motter provide ominous warnings about the noun **enthusiast** in their comments following that noun's synonyms:

> fanatic (*although an enthusiast is often carried beyond reason,* a fanatic *is most extreme, esp. in religion*), bigot (*one filled not only with enthusiasm, esp. in the realm of religion, but obstinately inaccessible to other views*), zealot (*a* fanatical *partisan*); booster (*C* [colloquial] *U.S.*), fan (*S* [slang], *U.S.*).

Although the discriminations are well done, the main entry no longer has the general connotation implied. In contrast with this entry, THE DOUBLEDAY ROGET'S THESAURUS IN DICTIONARY FORM simply lists with no discrimination of meanings the following synonyms:

> fan, afficionado, devotee, supporter, buff, booster, faddist, fanatic, follower, disciple, amateur, freak (slang), nut (slang).

This list would be easier for many readers to use with the aid of a dictionary.

IV. Accessibility

The double columns, the boldface guide words in the top margins, and the boldface main entry words overhanging the text are helpful to the reader. Finding main entries in this alphabetical thesaurus is a straightforward procedure. However, because so many cross-references are used both after the main entry words and at the foot of the page, the user must search back and forth many times. Furthermore, the complicated instructions in the prefatory pages must be read and followed before the contents of the book can be fully explored and appreciated. As the editor states in the preface, "One cannot push a button and produce the desired word."

Because this work includes many rare, archaic, and obsolete words, a contemporary user will find *Allen's Synonyms and Antonyms* hopelessly out of date. Those who do not have a special literary research project in mind will probably end up exasperated by its rather cumbersome format and lack of currency.

V. Summary

Allen's Synonyms and Antonyms has historical interest and could be a useful adjunct to serious language and literary study. However, it is no longer useful as a current source of synonyms. The mazelike arrangement of the book and its numerous cross-references will discourage most readers, who will need a dictionary of synonyms and antonyms or a more recent thesaurus—one such as WEBSTER'S COLLEGIATE THESAURUS.

The Basic Book of Synonyms and Antonyms

Facts at a Glance

Full Title: **The Basic Book of Synonyms and Antonyms: New Revised Edition.**
Publisher: New American Library.
Editor: Laurence Urdang.
Edition Reviewed: © 1985; 1986 printing.

Number of Entries: 4,000.
Number of Pages: 413.
Trim Size: 4¼" × 7".
Binding: paperback.

Price: $3.95.
Sold in bookstores and other outlets; also sold to libraries and other educational institutions.
ISBN 0-451-14064-8.

I. Introduction and Scope

The Basic Book of Synonyms and Antonyms contains approximately 4,000 entry words, each with at least one example sentence. According to the preface, "it is intended as a guide to commonly used words in English, and those are almost always the most expressive," as opposed to rare, complicated, or archaic synonyms. This new revised edition expands the 1978 edition by 20 percent and updates the previous entries where relevant.

Laurence Urdang is well known in the field of language and lexicography. He is the editor of *Verbatim, The Language Quarterly*, and has written many highly acclaimed reference books including *The Facts on File Dictionary of Numerical Allusions* (1986) and *–Ologies & –Isms: A Thematic Dictionary* (1986), reviewed in this Buying Guide. His works are known for concision and clarity, and this book is no exception. It continues with the same format and same concept as the earlier edition but contains more entries. Urdang's introductory remarks contain three important pieces of information about using the volume. He first states that there are no true synonyms—"there are words that can be substituted for other words, but they almost never have exactly the same meaning in the same context." He also explains the differences between denotation and connotation; the fact that language functions at formal and informal levels; and the need to select the synonym with the right sense for the context. For example, **discharge** has several common meanings: "*vb.* **1.** relieve, unload, unburden . . . **2.** fire, shoot . . . **3.** let go, dismiss. . . ." Example sentences, therefore, help the reader determine the sense of the context and use the word more effectively.

II. Format

This small, compact volume uses easy-to-read type in a conveniently readable format: The paper is adequate, with little show-through. However, the pages, through repeated use, separate from the unsturdy binding—a distinct drawback. Entry words are set in bold type, overhanging the text. The part of speech

(*n.*, *adj.*, *vb.*) is abbreviated in italics, followed by the synonyms in lightface, an example sentence in italics, and, where appropriate, antonyms (indicated by **ant.**).

Clusters of common synonyms for a main entry word are followed by an illustrative sentence; when different *senses* of a main entry word have synonym lists, these are numbered in boldface:

> **illustration** *n.* **1.** picture, photograph: *This book contains hundreds of illustrations.* **2.** example, explanation: *At least one illustration has been provided for each entry in this dictionary.*

Within a numbered group of synonyms, words belonging to the group that have slightly different characteristics, "as to the level of usage, appropriateness, or the grammatical or syntactic contexts in which they are found," are separated by a semicolon. For example:

> **disciple** *n.* follower, supporter; student; pupil.
> **inn** *n.* hotel, lodge; motel.

There is a guide word in capital letters at the top of each page—the left shows the first word on the page, the right the last—which allows the reader to see the opening and closing entries on a double-page spread. Pages are numbered at the top inner margin.

III. Quality and Currency of Entries

Slang words are not included, nor are some words in current vogue such as *preppy* or *yuppie*, but these are not an important omission for a work that emphasizes *basic* vocabulary. More importantly, many words in common current use, for instance, *compute* and *program* in their computer technology context, are absent from this book. Newly added words in this revised edition include many that are variations of words used previously. For example: in the 1978 edition the words **accident, adore, advertisement, aim,** and **ill** were included. This revised edition includes, in addition, **accidental, adoration, advertise, aimless, ill-advised, ill-at-ease, ill-natured,** and **ill-treated.** Totally new words included are: **abound, all-out, dote, forestall, foretell, mandatory, nebulous, prerequisite, revel in, snappy, surly, torrid, yellow** (cowardly), **zenith, zip,** and so forth. The additions make this the preferable edition to own and help to round out the vocabulary that is useful, according to the editor, "in simple, straightforward writing."

IV. Accessibility

The material in this thesaurus is easily accessible because the boldface entry words and the substantially indented entries make skimming the pages easy. Thumb indexing is absent as is usual in paperbacks. The complete entry is also easy to read with its elements so clearly indicated: bold type is used for numbering the different meanings and for identifying the antonyms and example sentences in italics. The antonyms correspond to the common meaning groups. If there is no antonym for the first set of words, but there is for the second set, the first set of antonyms is marked "**2.**" to correspond to the proper set of synonyms:

> **launch** *vb*. **1**. fire, drive, propel: *The rocket was launched to the moon at dawn.* **2**. initiate, originate, start, begin: *The senator launched his campaign for president early in February.* **ant**. **2**. stop, finish, terminate.

Although the main entry word appears in an inflected form (**launched**) here, that is not usual in the illustrative sentences.

V. Summary

The Basic Book of Synonyms and Antonyms is a handy desk reference that will be useful in homes and in college and public libraries. While it lacks the complexity and number of words found in many large thesauruses, its very simplicity makes it a good source for quick reference. It is concise and easy to use. Although the book lacks many contemporary words and usages, its usefulness lies in its concentration on the words that are common in the English language as well as in its provision of helpful example sentences that place the words in context.

Choose the Right Word

Facts at a Glance

Full Title: **Choose the Right Word: A Modern Guide to Synonyms**.
Former Title: Modern Guide to Synonyms.
Publisher: Harper & Row.
Editor: S. I. Hayakawa.
Edition Reviewed: © 1968; 1987 Perennial Library edition.

Number of Pages: 736.
Number of Entries: 6,000.
Number of Indexes: 1.
Trim Size: 7⅜″ × 9½″.
Binding: paperback.

Price: $12.95.
Sold in bookstores and through direct mail and other outlets; also sold to libraries and other educational institutions.
ISBN 0-06-091393-2.

I. Introduction and Scope

This guide to synonyms was the "collective effort of S. I. Hayakawa . . . and the Funk & Wagnalls Dictionary Staff." It was first published in 1968 as *Modern Guide to Synonyms and Related Words*. The 1987 paperback edition is a reprint rather than a revision. The purpose of the guide is to help the reader or writer choose between words of "similar, but not identical, meaning." It does not, as does Roget's International Thesaurus, intend to provide a list of alternatives for particular words or concepts, but rather to distinguish nuances of meaning and encourage exactness in the use of language. Hayakawa's introduction points to the need for such a reference. It describes the influences of other cultures on Anglo-Saxon, a language particularly receptive to the adoption of foreign words that has left Modern English rich in synonyms.

The essays in this volume cover the use of, and relation between, over 6,000 words. Antonyms are acknowledged for some but not all entries, and there are ample cross-references to related words.

II. Format

All main entry words, regardless of semantic category, are arranged in alphabetical sequence in the generous outer margins of each page of this guide. Under each main entry, related words discussed in an essay are listed in alphabetical order, which is not necessarily the order in which they appear in the text of the individual essay. The main entry words are in lowercase bold, and the related words, or near synonyms, are in lightface. In the body of each essay the first mention of each word appears in boldface type; subsequent appearances are in italic type. This makes for easy location of the word the reader is looking for in the essay.

Cross-references are in small capitals and appear at the ends of the essays. Antonyms, when appropriate, follow the cross-references and are set in italic type, or in small capitals if these words also appear as main entries elsewhere in the text.

When an essay is carried over to another page, the main entry word is repeated on that page with the notation *(continued)* printed beneath. The pages are attractively designed, with a large amount of white space in the outer margins. The inner margins and the spacing between entries are adequate. The paperback volume examined had smooth paper and was sturdily bound.

III. Quality and Currency of Entries

This book's strong point is its thoughtful and intelligent textual essays, which describe subtle differences between near synonyms and related words. Illustrative sentences are given in brackets within the text as examples of proper usage. Under the entry **vindictive**, eight other related words are compared and contrasted, for example:

Spiteful and **rancorous** emphasize the bitterness that attends feelings of malice and hate. *Rancorous* suggests a festering ill will, perhaps stemming from resentment over some real or fancied wrong. It does not, however, like *vindictive* and *spiteful*, necessarily imply a desire to hurt—only a deep-rooted malice.

The total essay covers about one page and closes with cross-references to **enmity** and **resentment**. A separate paragraph that lists eight antonyms (*benevolent*, *friendly*, **generous**, etc.) completes the entry.

Choose the Right Word is weak in currency. As noted, this is a reprint of the 1968 edition. No computer terminology is included, and there are no examples of current slang. The words discussed under the main entry **hippie** are *beatnik, bohemian, dropout, head, hipster, provo,* and *teenybopper.* This is historically interesting but will not help one find the right word for today's counterculturalists. The cross-references lead the reader to **artist, bum,** and **wanderer.**

IV. Accessibility

"How to Use This Book" (p. viii–x) clearly details this synonym guide's special features and the use of its excellent index.

An index entry printed in small capitals in the index signifies that it is a main entry. Index entries in lowercase are followed by the main entry, again in small capitals, under which the word is discussed. Some words, because of their many important meanings, are covered in more than one essay: "virtuous CHASTE" and "virtuous MORAL" are two examples from the index. The indexed main entry words are followed by a part-of-speech marker if there is potential for ambiguity. The same word can appear as a main entry word for more than one essay. In such cases they are distinguished by a part-of-speech marker [good MORAL (adj) 387] or, if they are the same part of speech, "by the alphabetically-first word discussed in each essay": "STOP (arrest)"; "STOP (cease)."

Guide words are not provided, but the prominence of the bold main entry words in the generous margins makes them unnecessary.

V. Summary

In spite of its lack of current slang and technical terms, *Choose the Right Word* is a very useful reference source. The writing is refreshingly straightforward and readable, and its treatment of words that are commonly confused in speech or writing is superlative. It fulfills its aim to strive for precision in the use of the English language.

As a synonym guide it is not as inclusive as WEBSTER'S NEW DICTIONARY OF SYNONYMS, and its related words and antonyms are not identical to those of *Webster's,* but this kind of variety is desirable in a good reference collection. Libraries will want to have a more current synonym guide to supplement this title. The previously mentioned WEBSTER'S NEW DICTIONARY OF SYNONYMS is the best of these works available. Those libraries or individuals who own *Choose the Right Word* under its original title will not need to purchase this reprint.

A Dictionary of Synonyms and Antonyms

Facts at a Glance

Full Title: **A Dictionary of Synonyms and Antonyms**.
Publisher: Warner Books.
Compiler: Joseph Devlin.
Editor: Jerome Fried.
Edition Reviewed: © 1961; 1982 printing.

Number of Words: over 3,000.
Number of Pages: 384.
Trim Size: 4¼" × 7".
Binding: paperback.

Price: $2.95.
Sold in bookstores and other outlets; also sold to
libraries and other educational institutions.
ISBN 0-446-31310-6.

I. Introduction and Scope

A Dictionary of Synonyms and Antonyms is intended to help readers in "finding the exact words they need to express their written and spoken thoughts, with a minimum expenditure of time and effort, and a maximum reward in efficiency and accuracy." The book lists over 3,000 frequently used English words along with many of their synonyms and antonyms. It also includes an article entitled "Word Formation," which briefly introduces etymology and lists and defines the main Latin, Greek, and Old English roots and derivatives, as well as Latin and Greek prefixes and suffixes. Appended at the back of the book is a listing of 5,000 words that Americans frequently mispronounce.

First published in 1938, it was most recently revised in 1961. The potential buyer should be aware that the publisher's claim on the back cover that the word listings are "the most up-to-date . . . available" is no longer valid. Compiler Joseph Devlin is the author of *How to Speak and Write Correctly* and *Development of the English Language.* Editor Jerome Fried compiled *The Bantam Crossword Dictionary* and coedited *Funk & Wagnalls Standard Dictionary of Folklore, Mythology, and Legends.*

II. Format

Entries are arranged alphabetically. Main entry words in boldface overhang the text on double-column pages. The abbreviations *Syn.* and *Ant.* introduce listings of synonyms and antonyms. The following is a representative entry:

> **draw**—*Syn.* pull, haul, drag, attract, inhale, sketch, describe, move, bring, convey, lure, tow, tug, allure, induce, entice, trail. *Ant.* repel, repulse, alienate, estrange, rebuff, reject, leave, abandon.

The print size is adequate for most readers, although non-native English speakers may find it too small. The book's good-quality newsprint paper permits little show-through and the physical design allows generous margins for the text. Like most paperbacks, its spine must be cracked in order for a page to be fully and clearly visible. Pages may, therefore, begin to separate from the binding under frequent use.

III. Quality and Currency of Entries

Nouns, verbs, and adjectives appear as main entries. Entries list from 1 to 50 synonyms and, for most entries, antonyms. Ordering within the listings appears to have no rationale. No definitions or illustrative examples are provided to differentiate among the listings, but the compiler's prefatory comments urge the user to consult a dictionary before using unfamiliar words gleaned from the listings. Parenthetical italicized usage labels helpfully identify slang, colloquialisms, and British and Australian terms.

Italicized part-of-speech labels follow main entry words in some cases, but not in others, with no apparent pattern. Coverage is uneven in other ways as well. For example, the entry term **beauty** is followed by 11 synonyms and no antonyms, while **ugly** has 35 synonyms and 43 antonyms, among them **beauty**. These inconsistencies are likely to prove confusing and misleading.

The inclusion of slang and colloquialisms in the listings lends some currency to the work, although many of the words and phrases labeled *slang* are outdated clichés, such as "hit the hay" under **sleep** and "play the ponies" under **venture**. The volume lacks more than 25 years' worth of new idioms and terms, including the languages of astronautics and computer science.

IV. Accessibility

Two guide words in boldface capitals appear on each page, indicating the first and last entries on the page. No key to abbreviations is provided; however, since only a few easily deciphered abbreviations are used to identify parts of speech and restricted usage, this is not a serious drawback. No table of contents is provided to alert the user to the existence of the work's special features. The absence of cross-references is also an impediment to the volume's usefulness.

V. Summary

A Dictionary of Synonyms and Antonyms cannot be recommended as a first choice for home or library use. For those with a reasonably large vocabulary, it often meets its aim of offering a useful—and quickly used—basis for appropriate word choice. However, its lack of new words and idioms that have entered the language in the past 25 years is a major drawback. For non-native English speakers, the print may be too small, and these users will also lack the vocabulary to discriminate effectively among the synonyms and antonyms offered. An alternative for individuals who need a compact thesaurus is Laurence Urdang's THE BASIC BOOK OF SYNONYMS AND ANTONYMS: NEW REVISED EDITION. This more up-to-date reference work includes illustrative sentences that aid the user in selecting appropriate synonyms.

Funk & Wagnalls Standard Handbook of Synonyms, Antonyms, and Prepositions

Facts at a Glance

Full Title: **Funk & Wagnalls Standard Handbook of Synonyms, Antonyms, and Prepositions.**
Former Title: English Synonyms and Antonyms.
Publisher: Harper & Row (Thomas Y. Crowell).
Editor: James C. Fernald.
Edition Reviewed: © 1947; 1984 printing.

Number of Entries: approximately 1,700.
Number of Pages: 515.
Number of Indexes: 2.
Trim Size: 8½″ × 11″.
Binding: cloth.

Price: $13.95.
Sold in bookstores and other outlets; also sold to libraries and other educational institutions.
ISBN 0-308-40024-9.

I. Introduction and Scope

The original version of this well-known work, prepared by Dr. James Champlain Fernald, was first published in 1896; a revised and enlarged second

Funk & Wagnalls Standard Handbook of Synonyms,
Antonyms, and Prepositions

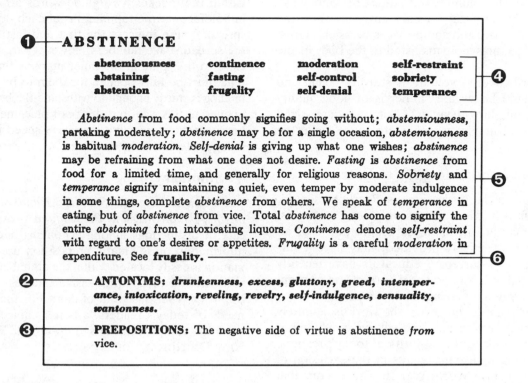

❶ Keywords are set in boldface capitals

❷ Antonyms, in boldface italics, are listed alphabetically

❸ The correct preposition or prepositions to be used with the keyword are italicized in an illustrative sentence

❹ Synonyms are listed alphabetically in boldface type

❺ Distinctions of meaning among synonyms, which are italicized, are discussed

❻ Cross-references appear in boldface type

edition was published in 1914. The present edition was updated and enlarged by the Funk & Wagnalls editorial staff in 1947; the work has not been revised since that date.

There are approximately 1,700 main entries, and over 8,000 synonyms and 3,000 antonyms are accessible through the indexes. Words listed as main entries include nouns, verbs, adjectives, adverbs, and prepositions. Each entry lists synonyms and provides a detailed discussion differentiating among them both denotatively and connotatively. Many entries also list antonyms; for some the idiomatic use of prepositions with the main entry word is also described. For example, under **make**, preposition use is clarified as follows:

Make *of*, *out of*, or *from* certain materials, *into* a certain form, *for* a certain purpose or person; made *with* hands, *by* hand, made *by* a prisoner, *with* a jackknife.

Foreign words and phrases, slang, and colloquialisms are not included among the entries.

II. Format

Within the body of the text, main entry words (termed "key-words") appear in large boldface capitals heading their entries. Part-of-speech is indicated only when the same word is entered as two different parts of speech; **reason**, for example, is entered both as a noun and as a verb. Beneath the heading, also in boldface, appears the list of synonyms, set in three or four short columns. A discussion follows, of one or more paragraphs' length, distinguishing among the synonyms. The proper use of each synonym is explained and illustrated in phrases or sentences. After the discussion antonyms appear in boldface for selected entries and clarifications of correct preposition use with the main entry word are also included.

The "Index of Synonyms" appears in triple-column format. Each index term and, for selected terms, each indented secondary entry, is followed by a page number indicating the location of the term under the appropriate main entry word. The columns are divided by vertical lines; dotted lines connect terms with page numbers.

Also in triple-columns, the "Index of Antonyms" lists one or more pages for each entry on which the antonyms are discussed and provides occasional cross-references to the synonyms listed in the body of the text.

The hard-covered volume is sturdily bound and will withstand heavy use. Paper is of good quality with minimal show-through. Clear, adequate-sized typefaces and ample use of white space make the entries easy to read.

III. Quality and Currency of Entries

Information in the discussions is clearly presented, and careful distinctions are drawn among synonyms. The information on idiomatic preposition use, although only selectively provided, may have a surprising renewed currency: educators have recently noted a decline in the grasp of correct use of prepositions among native English speakers.

In other regards, however, the work is definitely not current in most areas, and will have only minor historical interest to the majority of today's readers. The 1947 copyright date results in the exclusion of terms coined since World War II. Those terms that are included are themselves still in current use, but examples cited in the discussions are in many cases out of date. For example, under **beneath** the following sentence appears, with a meaning that will strike people today as obsolete, at best:

> *Beneath* or *below* may signify occupying a lower plane, as we speak of one marrying *below* or *beneath* his station.

Under **love**, we are told that

> *Love* is used specifically for personal *affection* between the sexes in the highest sense, the *love* that normally leads to marriage, and subsists throughout all happy wedded life.

The discussion of **feminine** and its synonyms is similarly inappropriate for a contemporary audience:

> We apply *female* to the sex, *feminine* to the qualities, especially the finer physical or mental qualities that distinguish the *female* sex in the human family, or to the objects appropriate for or especially employed by them . . . *Womanish* denotes the undesirable; *womanly*, the admirable or lovely qualities of woman. *Womanly* tears would suggest respect and sympathy, *womanish* tears a touch of contempt. . . . *Womanlike* suggests *feminine* frailties or faults of character; *ladylike*, the characteristics of a lady.

IV. Accessibility

The volume combines the convenience of an alphabetical listing for its contents with copious indexing.

A "Special Note: Use the Index" section clarifies the use of the index. Within the main text as well as within the indexes, two guide words are provided, in boldface, at the top margins of each double-page spread. These indicate the first and last entries on the spread. Page numbers, however, are located so close to the spine in the inner margins that the volume must be fully opened for them to be seen. The binding is sturdy enough to withstand the book's being opened in this way, but this poor placement of page numbers interferes with the user's speed in locating a page referred to in the index.

V. Summary

The *Funk & Wagnalls Standard Handbook of Synonyms, Antonyms, and Prepositions* provides clear, careful distinctions among synonyms and valuable information on idiomatic preposition use; its information is easily located within the alphabetical listing with the aid of comprehensive indexes. However, the work is seriously out-of-date. For the reference needs of today's readers, a better choice would be the more comprehensive and up-to-date WEBSTER'S NEW DICTIONARY OF SYNONYMS.

The Merriam-Webster Pocket Dictionary of Synonyms

Facts at a Glance

Full Title: **The Merriam-Webster Pocket Dictionary of Synonyms.**
Publisher: Pocket Books.
Edition Reviewed: © 1972.

Number of Pages: 441.
Number of Entries: 4,244.
Trim Size: 4¼″ × 6¾″.
Binding: paperback.

Price: $3.95.
Sold in bookstores and other outlets; also sold to libraries and other educational institutions.
ISBN 0-671-50445-2.

I. Introduction and Scope

According to its preface, the purpose of the compact paperback edition of *The Merriam-Webster Pocket Dictionary of Synonyms* is "not to provide mere word-finding lists for consultants with a vague notion of the sort of word they seek." Rather, it is intended to help readers make clear distinctions among words of similar denotation. In addition to the alphabetically arranged main entry paragraphs, this dictionary also includes numerous cross-reference entries. Antonyms are listed when they exist. This paperback

The Merriam-Webster Pocket
Dictionary of Synonyms

❶ Synonyms to be discriminated
are set in boldface type

❷ Examples of usage are enclosed
in angle brackets

❸ The shared meaning of each
group of synonyms is
summarized

> **fate, destiny, lot, portion, doom** *shared meaning* : a predetermined state or
> end. Fate implies an inevitable and often an adverse outcome, condition,
> or end <let us, then, be up and doing, with a heart for any *fate* — H.
> W. Longfellow> <the *fate* of all language is change — David Mellinkoff>
> **Destiny** implies something foreordained and inescapable and is more likely
> to suggest a great or noble course or end than one to be feared or resisted
> <the symbol of the *destiny* of the Jewish people, whom no earthly power
> has ever been able to defeat — Bruno Bettelheim> *Lot* and *portion* imply
> a distribution by fate or destiny, **lot** distinctively imputing the action of
> blind chance and **portion** the apportionment of good and evil elements
> <whenever one of the people curses you ... or otherwise mistreats you,
> as is the usual *lot* of a clown — Jack Altman> <her own misery for taking
> from the small sum of peace they had in the world, adding to the *portion*
> of their unhappiness — Bernard Malamud> <poverty was his *portion* all
> his days — Kemp Malone> **Doom** stresses finality and usually implies an
> unhappy or calamitous fate <involution is as much a law of nature as
> evolution. There is no escape from this *doom* — W. R. Inge> <lured
> unsuspecting ships to their *doom* on the rocks on dark and stormy nights
> — Richard Joseph>

edition is based on WEBSTER'S NEW DICTIONARY
OF SYNONYMS, originally published in 1968, and there
is no indication that it has been revised since 1972.

II. Format

Entries appear in two forms: the discriminating article and the cross-reference entry. Each article begins with a boldface main entry word and a boldface
listing of words to be discriminated. A part-of-speech
abbreviation follows the main entry word only when
that word is entered more than once as different parts
of speech. For example, the main entry word **abandon** is identified as a verb (*vb*) and followed by the
list **abandon**, **desert**, **forsake**. (A cross-reference entry for **abandon** as a noun follows.) The main entry
word is usually the most central in meaning or the
one most typically used. Each list is followed by a
statement of the meaning shared among the synonyms. For **abandon**, this appears as:

shared meaning: to give up completely.

Each word is then discussed and illustrated in the
order that the synonyms appear at the opening of
the entry:

Abandon can suggest complete disinterest in the future
of what is given up <the picnickers *abandoned* their
lunch to the ants> <no decent man *abandons* his family>

Desert implies a relationship (as of occupancy or guard-
ianship); it can suggest desolation <*deserted* farms growing up to brush>. . . .

Frequently quotations from well-known writers are
used to illustrate a synonym's meaning:

Forsake implies a breaking of a close association by
repudiation or renunciation <all his knights and cour-
tiers had *forsaken* him; not one came to his help—
Matthew Arnold>. . . .

When the first word in the synonym list has one or

more antonyms, these are listed at the end of the
entry, where they are introduced by the abbreviation
ant. Antonyms for other words from the synonym
list appear in the cross-reference entries for those
words.

Cross-references are provided within some of the
discriminating articles, for senses other than the one
discriminated. Cross-references also appear as separate entries that refer the reader to the appropriate
discriminating article. In both cases, the word "see"
introduces the cross-reference, and the word(s) to
which the reader is referred appear in small capital
letters.

Although the text is printed full page, readability
is impaired by the small size of the print and the
apparent crowding of as many words as possible on
a page. The paper is of standard quality for mass-
market paperbacks. Although it is thin, it permits
only minimal show-through of text. The pages do not
separate easily from the binding of this adequately
sturdy paperback.

III. Quality and Currency of Entries

The work's discriminating articles are carefully detailed, clearly and interestingly illustrated, and useful
to the reader. They provide valuable guidance in the
use of many standard American English words and
their synonyms and antonyms. However, the dictionary's 1972 date results in limited currency. Under
gay, for example, the reader is referred only to **lively**;
nowhere is the homosexual connotation of the word
described. Neither *compute* nor *computer* is entered,
and terms relating to space technology are also not
included. The dictionary excludes slang and colloquialisms, which further limits its currency.

IV. Accessibility

The entries are alphabetized letter by letter. Pairs of
guide words appear at the top of each page, indi-

cating the first and last words entered on the page. These guide words are usefully printed in type larger than that used in the entries.

V. Summary

The Merriam-Webster Pocket Dictionary of Synonyms contains careful and well-illustrated articles which discriminate synonyms for many standard American English words. Its use of quotations from well-known writers provides both interest and useful clarifications of synonyms. However, prospective buyers who are exasperated by frequent cross-referencing will be frustrated by the book's extensive reliance on this technique. The work is not sufficiently current to meet the needs of some readers, and its print is small and cramped. Laurence Urdang's more recent THE BASIC BOOK OF SYNONYMS AND ANTONYMS, which is clear, concise, and easy to read, is a preferable alternative.

The Random House Basic Dictionary of Synonyms & Antonyms

Facts at a Glance

Full Title: **The Random House Basic Dictionary of Synonyms & Antonyms**.
Former Titles: The Random House Vest Pocket Dictionary of Synonyms and Antonyms and *The Random House Dictionary of Synonyms and Antonyms*.
Publisher: Ballantine/Del Rey/Fawcett Books.
Editor: Laurence Urdang.
Edition Reviewed: © 1960; 1984 printing.

Number of Entries: approximately 4,000.
Number of Words: 80,000.
Number of Pages: 137.
Trim Size: 4¼″ × 6⅞″.
Binding: paperback.

Price: $1.50.
Sold in bookstores and through direct mail.
ISBN 0-345-29712-1.

I. Introduction and Scope

The Random House Basic Dictionary of Synonyms & Antonyms was copyrighted in 1960 and previously published as *The Random House Vest Pocket Dictionary of Synonyms and Antonyms* and *The Random House Dictionary of Synonyms and Antonyms*. The paperback edition was first published by Ballantine Books in 1981.

Of the 80,000 synonyms and antonyms included, about 4,000 are main entries. Laurence Urdang, the editor, states that "judicious use of this book will more than treble the average person's . . . vocabulary." Although the book is no longer current, the publisher claims on the cover that it is "comprehensive" and that it offers "everything for writers, speakers, students."

The word list is composed of standard English language words, and its main entries are ample for the vast majority of American users to refer to when searching for a synonym or antonym. The editor's brief introductory remarks will help readers access the vocabulary, although it does not cover new words or acquired meanings that have emerged in the last quarter of a century.

II. Format

The 127 pages that make up this book's synonym and antonym section are printed in double columns in type so small that it is difficult to consult it without the use of a magnifying glass. In addition, margins are narrow, which also detracts from the book's readability. While there is little show-through in the pages, the paper is little better than newsprint and cannot be expected to stand up to hard use. The same may be said for the poorly glued binding that allows the pages to separate from the binding with minimal use. However, the extremely inexpensive price should certainly allow users to replace it frequently.

Many entries are listed in alphabetical order. Each entry appears in boldface type overhanging the text. Main entry words are followed by a list of synonyms, often subgrouped by numbers, and sometimes concluded by a short list of antonyms, all in lightface type.

In the four-paragraph introduction, the editor explains that synonyms are grouped according to the sense most commonly used and numbered from most common, or "strongest," to least common, or "weakest," usage and meaning. The editor advises looking up the few antonyms in the main entry word list to find additional possibilities. The sections preceding the main body of entries contain "A Word of Caution" and a key to the seven "Abbreviations Used in This Book." In the cautionary section, the user is reminded that "there is no true synonym for any word in the English language," that context must be considered, and that a good dictionary must be consulted for any word unknown to the user.

III. Quality and Currency of Entries

The selection of words, including main entries, their parts of speech, and their synonyms and antonyms, represents a fairly broad spectrum of basic English usage. If the user reads the directions for using the book, he or she can easily take advantage of its possibilities with very little effort.

However, that the copyright date is 1960 is quite evident in the book's entries. Because its word list appears not to have been expanded since that date, the book's contemporary vocabulary is virtually nonexistent. Obviously, this is a severe limitation.

IV. Accessibility

The dictionary arrangement, with boldface, lowercase guide words near the top margin of each page, above the outer column, simplifies locating a word in this small paperback book. The abbreviations used in the text are listed in the prefatory pages only. There is no thumb index, which is not a crucial drawback in such a small book, but the absence of cross-referencing does hinder the reader's full access to the book's contents.

There are no definitions, no pronunciations, and, only rarely, examples or explanations of any kind other than the part or parts of speech identified for the main entry word—again, these omissions present serious drawbacks to accessing words in this thesaurus. For example, for the main entry **ill**, 21 words in four numbered sense clusters are listed for the adjective form; 17 words in three numbered clusters for the noun form; and 9 words in four numbered clusters for the adverb form. The seven *antonyms* for **ill** are an unidentified mixture of all three parts of speech; and some of them appear as main entry words in a different form from their listings as antonyms.

The final pages of the book contain three special features: "Common Signs and Symbols" (with listings for **astronomy** and **astrology**, **biology**, **business**, **mathematics**, **medicine**, **money**, and **religion**); "Foreign Alphabets" with transliterations for the Greek, Hebrew, and Russian alphabets; and "Weights and Measures," complete with metric conversion factors. All of these tables may be of some use to the reader, although their inclusion in a thesaurus comes as something of a surprise.

V. Summary

The Random House Basic Dictionary of Synonyms & Antonyms is inexpensive and concise but very outdated. Its print, paper, and binding are all of poor quality. The book cannot be recommended as a good resource for library circulating paperback reference collections or for personal reference.

Reader's Digest Family Word Finder

Facts at a Glance

Full Title: **Reader's Digest Family Word Finder**.
Publisher: The Reader's Digest Association.
Editor: The editors of the Reader's Digest in association with Stuart B. Flexner.
Edition Reviewed: © 1975; 1986 printing.

Number of Entries: 10,000 main entries.
Number of Pages: 896.
Trim Size: 7" × 9³⁄₁₆".
Binding: cloth.

Price: $21.99.
Sold in bookstores and other outlets; also sold to libraries and other educational institutions.
ISBN 0-89577-023-7.

I. Introduction and Scope

Reader's Digest Family Word Finder is a thesaurus with 10,000 main entries and 200,000 associated synonyms and antonyms. Additional treatment may include sample sentences, word histories, pronunciation and spelling tips, and quotations.

Prepared by Reader's Digest editors in association with the well-known lexicographer, Stuart Berg Flexner, the *Family Word Finder* is intended for home use and its key entries include only those words in common use. Hence there are no archaisms, few foreign phrases and technical words, and only a light scattering of (inoffensive) slang.

The popularity of this thesaurus is reflected in the fact that 1986 saw its seventh reprint in ten years. Adults as well as middle and upper grade schoolchildren for whom English is a second language will find the *Family Word Finder* easy to use.

II. Format

This is an attractively printed, sturdily bound volume of 900 pages with 10 to 20 main entries per double-column page. A short introduction first explains the components of the thesaurus—synonyms, antonyms, spelling, usage, and pronunciation tips—and then gives an interesting history of the English language.

The format of the *Family Word Finder* presents the synonym examples for each entry in the first paragraph; the second paragraph lists the antonym examples. For selected words, a third paragraph—outlined in blue and entitled "Exploring the Word"—gives an informal etymology with additional examples. This graphic design is more cluttered than that of ROGET'S II: THE NEW THESAURUS, which divides

Reader's Digest Family Word Finder

❶ Synonyms are listed in decreasing order of use

❷ Antonyms are preceded by the boldface abbreviation *Ant.* and are numbered to match the corresponding synonym list

❸ Spelling tips are preceded by a diamond

❹ Etymologies are preceded by a diamond

❺ Example sentences are italicized

❻ Usage labels are italicized

❼ Cross-references are set in small capitals

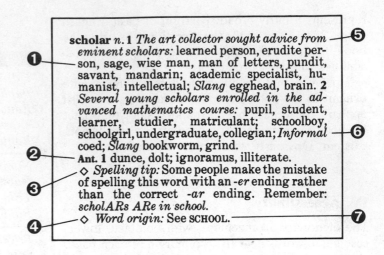

synonyms and antonyms into separate columns and begins each numbered example on a separate line.

Each main entry is followed by its part of speech, an illustrative sentence, and a list of synonyms. Antonyms, quotations, etymologies, and usage notes appear where applicable and sometimes where inapplicable: **girl** has the quote "I want a girl just like the girl that married dear old dad" and though **fiasco** is said to derive from the Italian *fiasco* meaning bottle, the connection is not explained.

III. Quality and Currency of Entries

The mainstay of the work, its synonym lists, are fairly complete, although the lack of slang terms means that some enriching and colorful synonyms are ignored—many of the popular synonyms for **marvelous**, for instance, are slang or informal words. *Family Word Finder* gives just three, while ROGET'S II provides 15 such words:

> **1. Syns:** cool (*Slang*), dandy (*Informal*), divine[1] (*Informal*), dreamy (*Informal*), fabulous (*Informal*), glorious, groovy (*Slang*), heavenly (*Informal*), hot (*Slang*), hunky-dory (*Slang*), keen[1] (*Slang*), neat (*Slang*), nifty (*Slang*), ripping, sensational, splendid, super (*Informal*), superb, swell (*Informal*), terrific, tremendous (*Informal*), wonderful. —*Idiom* out of this world.

Although the jacket promises sample sentences to make meanings clear, most sentences are in fact singularly unenlightening:

> **maroon**[2] *adj. My new winter coat is maroon.*

> **martyrdom** *n. The painting depicts the martyrdom of St. Sebastian.*

> **die** *v. Her husband died in the war.*

Quotations from great writers do help to illustrate the words in action, but this is done to much better effect in WEBSTER'S NEW DICTIONARY OF SYNONYMS. While Webster gives us literary examples for each of the five synonyms for the word **massacre**, the *Family Word Finder* gives just one Twain quotation using **massacre**.

Antonyms are given generous, almost indiscriminate, treatment in the *Family Word Finder*. An entry may have four or five antonyms, but there is no indication as to which is the best one. ROGET'S II ignores opposites, while WEBSTER'S cites just one antonym to the entry word and then lists those associated to the synonyms. **Masculine**, for example, receives ten antonyms in the *Family Word Finder* with its exact antonym, *feminine*, appearing sixth on the list. Webster's may have only six antonyms to **masculine**, but *feminine* pointedly follows the word *Ant* and the others follow the word *Con*.

IV. Accessibility

The major asset of the *Family Word Finder* is its unintimidating and familiar style. "The marshal of the Rose Bowl parade was a movie star," the sample sentence for **marshal**, may lack profundity but it is instantly identifiable. There is a direct one-step approach to finding words, and helpful (though never condescending) guides to usage—"enigmatic rhymes with automatic." This emphasis on "user-friendliness" at all costs is obvious from the first sentence in the introduction where the word "thesaurus" is cushioned by the (incorrect) synonym, "treasury."

V. Summary

The very title, *Family Word Finder*, summarizes the book: it is indeed a place to find family words. Alas, the less familiar words (yes, this volume tells us that family/familiar have the same root)—*ricochet* and *riffraff*, *obsessive* and *obdurate*, *vitreous* and *voodoo*—are not to be found. Slang and idiom are likewise unfindable.

Although the *Family Word Finder* may be an accessible thesaurus for those for whom English is a second language, one of the less circumscribed word finders discussed in this review would be a better choice for libraries.

The Synonym Finder

Facts at a Glance

Full Title: **The Synonym Finder**.
Publisher: Warner Books.
Compiler: J. I. Rodale.
Editor: Laurence Urdang, Editor-in-Chief.
Edition Reviewed: © 1978; 1986 printing.

Number of Entries: 1,500,000 synonyms.
Number of Pages: 1,361.
Trim Size: 6½″ × 9⅜″ (cloth); 6″ × 9″ (paperback).
Binding(s): cloth; paperback.

Price(s): $21.95 (cloth); $12.95 (paperback).
Sold in bookstores and other outlets; also sold to libraries and other educational institutions.
ISBN 0-87857-236-8 (cloth);
ISBN 0-446-370-29 (paperback).

I. Introduction and Scope

The Synonym Finder is a dictionary of synonyms, which, according to its Editor-in-Chief, Laurence Urdang, has "more words than any book of its kind—more than 1,500,000." Its purpose is twofold: to aid users in adding variety to their vocabulary, and to bring back to mind a temporarily lost word or expression.

The prefatory material in the text is emphatic about one limitation of this kind of book: it cannot address the nuances of connotation and tone that sophisticated use of language requires. Users will need to consult a standard dictionary for finer distinctions.

The explanatory material at the beginning of this book gives no indication, however, of what rules or distinctions guided the editors and compilers in selecting or excluding words; a general comparison with ROGET'S INTERNATIONAL THESAURUS, for example, suggests that *The Synonym Finder* is indeed selective (or limited, to put it less charitably) in its entries. Comparing certain sections at random, our reviewers found that ROGET'S invariably has more entries. For example, the following words were included as entries in ROGET'S but not in *The Synonym Finder*:

creamer, *creamery*, *cream puff*, *creaminess*, *gander*, *ganger*, *gangland*, *jailbreak*, *jailhouse*, *jakes*, *jalousie*, *jambon*, *jammed*, *jam-packed*, *jam session*, *jangling*, *Janizary*, *Jansenist*, *Janus*, *Janus-faced*, *Jap*, *Japanese*, *jaquima*, *malt*, *mama*, *mammal*. In fact, many of the entry words that are in Roget's but not in *The Synonym Finder* seem to be odd or slightly obscure. Their omission is not in itself necessarily a defect. It does suggest, however, given the size of the volume (1,361 pages), that it is not the number of entries, but rather the number of synonyms for each entry that accounts for its bulk.

II. Format

Main entry words in *The Synonym Finder* are organized in alphabetical order in dictionary format: double columns, with entries in boldface type overhanging the text. Each page has guide words to its first and last entries that help a reader to locate a word more quickly. The introductory material states that "word listings have been organized numerically according to definitions and major semantic groups; further discriminations are shown within these groups by . . . semicolons," and generally the organization of entries appears logical. A few entries include cross-references to similar, related words.

The paperback version is very thick (about 2½″); the print, though dense, is quite readable. The paper on which it is printed gives an unfortunate impression of cheap, newsprint quality stock, though, to its credit, it makes the pages easy to turn and has very little show-through. In addition, the book is very easy to handle, considering its size and bulk. The gutter margins are narrow. In the middle of the book, entries in the interior columns can be read easily, but to read similarly placed words close to the front or the back of the book, it is necessary to press down and flatten the book's spine.

The paperback stood up to some bending and flattening in the reviewing process, though a frequently used book like this one would have to be exceptionally sturdy to be able to survive the handling and spine-cracking it might typically receive.

III. Quality and Currency of Entries

Subject to the limitations mentioned in this review, this book includes fairly current entries (it was published in 1978). It is not always clear whether entry words are missing because this book is not absolutely current or because some unexplained principle of inclusion or exclusion has been applied to them. For example, you will not find words like *aerobic*; more significantly, the listings for **computer** include the following terms: *adding machine, calculator, calculating machine, analog computer, digital computer,*

The Synonym Finder

❶ Related synonyms are arranged in numbered groups

❷ Field labels are italicized

❸ Usage labels are italicized

❹ Cross-references are set in boldface type

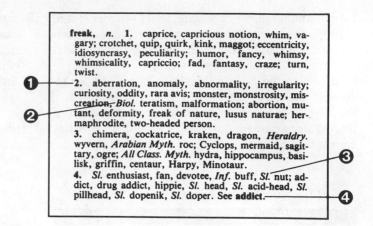

freak, *n.* **1.** caprice, capricious notion, whim, vagary; crotchet, quip, quirk, kink, maggot; eccentricity, idiosyncrasy, peculiarity; humor, fancy, whimsy, whimsicality, capriccio; fad, fantasy, craze; turn, twist.
2. aberration, anomaly, abnormality, irregularity; curiosity, oddity, rara avis; monster, monstrosity, miscreation, *Biol.* teratism, malformation; abortion, mutant, deformity, freak of nature, lusus naturae; hermaphrodite, two-headed person.
3. chimera, cockatrice, kraken, dragon, *Heraldry.* wyvern, *Arabian Myth.* roc; Cyclops, mermaid, sagittary, ogre; *All Class. Myth.* hydra, hippocampus, basilisk, griffin, centaur, Harpy, Minotaur.
4. *Sl.* enthusiast, fan, devotee, *Inf.* buff, *Sl.* nut; addict, drug addict, hippie, *Sl.* head, *Sl.* acid-head, *Sl.* pillhead, *Sl.* dopenik, *Sl.* doper. See **addict.**

and *data processor*, but not *mainframe*, or *mini*, or *micro*. Neither *laser*, nor *radar*, nor *hippy* is included; and synonym categories under the entry for **program** do not include the meaning of "to program a computer," or "to write a computer program."

A comparison of individual entries in ROGET's INTERNATIONAL THESAURUS with those in *The Synonym Finder* suggests that this volume often lists synonyms only vaguely related to the entry, leaving the reader to make crucial distinctions. For example, the entry for **myopic** includes not only the customary literal and figurative meanings having to do with defective sight and narrowness of perspective, but it stretches the point to include *sexist*, and *anti-Semitic*. Similarly, synonyms for **pitiless** include such very tangential words as *obstinate*, *aloof*, *distant*, *apathetic*, *indifferent*, *supine*, and *savage*. Thus, in attempting to be inclusive, the entries sometimes go beyond the useful. In addition, *The Synonym Finder* lacks the conceptual distinctions offered by the index in ROGET's, which not only gives synonyms but also includes a nuanced list of conceptual categories for the meanings of each word. Of course, *The Synonym Finder* is a synonym dictionary and does not claim to be a thesaurus. Nevertheless, the promotional quotes on the cover compare it favorably to ROGET's, and most users of word books will automatically (and often unconsciously) consider ROGET's as a standard.

The Synonym Finder offers the advantage of having all synonyms in one place; ROGET's often requires the user to refer to several widely dispersed sections for different meanings of the same word. On the other hand, ROGET's index allows the user to locate a lost or forgotten word more quickly by having there the nuance of a definition rather than requiring that one read through a long list of specific synonyms.

IV. Accessibility

Given the size of the book, thumb indexes would be useful, though this is not a typical feature of paperback dictionaries or word books. The guide words on each page make locating entries fairly easy; however, the paucity of cross-references limits the reader to synonyms for the one word he or she can remember, thus narrowing rather than expanding the possibilities for finding the mot juste.

V. Summary

A handy reference book with a large number of entries, *The Synonym Finder* suffers somewhat in comparison to ROGET's INTERNATIONAL THESAURUS in lacking any equivalent of the latter's conceptual index. It is also less useful for the general reader than WEBSTER's NEW DICTIONARY OF SYNONYMS, which provides discriminated meanings and quotations from literature. The user's preference for one of these volumes, however, probably depends on habit: many readers are more familiar with a thesaurus than with a synonym dictionary. Someone who depends on word books would probably want a book that provides more guidance for the user. *The Synonym Finder* is fine as a compilation of synonym lists, but it certainly does not go nearly as far as the aforementioned Roget's or Webster's titles in helping the reader to choose the most appropriate synonym for the occasion.

Webster's Compact Dictionary of Synonyms

Facts at a Glance

Full Title: **Webster's Compact Dictionary of Synonyms.**
Publisher: Merriam-Webster.
Editor: Michael G. Belanger.
Edition Reviewed: © 1987.

Number of Entries: more than 700 synonym paragraphs.
Number of Pages: 374.
Trim Size: 4″ × 5½″.
Binding: laminated paper over boards.

Price: $4.95.
Sold in bookstores; also sold to libraries and other educational institutions.
ISBN 0-87779-186-4.

I. Introduction and Scope

Webster's Compact Dictionary of Synonyms was first published in 1987. According to its preface, this hardcover, pocket-size work

> is designed to be a concise guide to the understanding and use of synonyms . . . for people who wish to appreciate the shades of difference that exist among English words that have the same or nearly the same essential meaning and who wish to be able to choose from among synonyms the precisely suitable word for a particular purpose.

Over 700 main entry paragraphs are provided in which groups of synonyms are discussed. Explanations and verbal illustrations serve to clarify the shades of meaning represented by words with the same denotation. All words discussed in the main entry paragraphs appear alphabetically in the word list. As a result, the work contains, according to the preface, "thousands of cross-reference entries."

II. Format

Each main entry paragraph begins with a boldface main entry word, which is printed in larger type than the rest of the entry and overhangs the text. An italicized part-of-speech label follows only when the word has separate entries as more than one part of speech. The entry word is followed by the group of synonyms to be discriminated. These are also in boldface type, and the list may include as few as two or as many as eight synonyms. At the end of the list appears a statement of the words' shared denotation. Then each of the synonyms, again printed in boldface, is explained. Illustrative phrases (with the synonym printed in italic) appear in angle brackets. If the main entry word is discussed as the same part of speech in a different synonym paragraph, the entry ends with the direction "See in addition" and the appropriate main entry word printed in small capitals.

For cross-reference entries, the entry word also appears in large boldface type. Part-of-speech labels are provided only when necessary to distinguish between different part-of-speech applications of the same word. The entry continues with the direction "see" and the appropriate main entry word(s) printed in small capitals.

The typefaces are clear and the print is surprisingly—and pleasingly—large for a pocket-size work.

The good-quality paper permits minimal show-through, and adequate white space also enhances readability. The hardcover work is sturdily bound and will hold up well to heavy use.

III. Quality and Currency of Entries

In the main entries, the list of synonyms is followed by a clear, concise statement of shared meaning. This statement is briefer than most dictionary definitions, but it will be useful to readers in determining whether they have found the entry they need. Then follow the discriminations of the listed synonyms. According to the preface, distinctions drawn among synonyms in the main entry paragraphs

> usually fall into one of three peripheral areas of meaning: implication, connotation, or application. Implications are the usually minor ideas involved in the meaning of the word. Connotations are the ideas which color the meaning of a word. . . . Applications are the restrictions on a word's use established by current idiom.

As this suggests, the work reflects American English as it is currently spoken. However, only standard American English words are discussed; slang, colloquialisms, and regionalisms are excluded.

As the following representative example demonstrates, the entries employ an extended adult vocabulary, and they are clear and detailed:

> **leaning, propensity, proclivity, penchant** means a strong instinct or liking for something. **Leaning** suggests a liking or attraction not strong enough to be decisive or uncontrollable ⟨accused of having socialist *leanings*⟩.
> **Propensity** implies a deeply engrained and usu. irresistible longing ⟨the natural *propensity* of in-laws to offer advice⟩. **Proclivity** suggests a strong natural proneness usu. to something objectionable or evil ⟨movies that reinforce viewers' *proclivities* for violence⟩. **Penchant** implies a strong marked taste in the person or an irresistible attraction in the object ⟨has a *penchant* for overdramatizing his troubles.⟩.

Occasionally, as in the explanation of **penchant**, an additional illustrative phrase would help readers to grasp a shade of meaning. However, those phrases that are provided are frequently concrete and generally useful.

IV. Accessibility

Two boldface guide words appear at the top of each double-page spread, indicating the first and last entries on the page. A table of contents at the beginning of the volume alerts readers to the existence of the preface and the list of abbreviations that precede the main lexicon. Only eight abbreviations are used: these include four part-of-speech labels and the utility abbreviations *esp.* (especially), *occas.* (occasionally), *specif.* (specifically), and *usu.* (usually).

V. Summary

Webster's Compact Dictionary of Synonyms is well designed to serve writers. Although it is necessarily selective and excludes nonstandard usages, this convenient, compact volume enables its users to make careful choices among a large number of standard American English synonym groups.

The work can usefully be compared with both THE BASIC BOOK OF SYNONYMS AND ANTONYMS and THE RIGHT WORD II: A CONCISE THESAURUS. The former is among the most comprehensive synonym dictionaries available; it also lists antonyms, and will meet the needs of the reader seeking extensive vocabulary coverage. However, its entries do not explain distinctions among synonyms; rather, they group closely related synonyms and provide illustrative sentences. THE RIGHT WORD is more directly comparable to *Webster's Compact Dictionary of Synonyms*. Both have paragraphs that present the core meaning of a group of synonyms and carefully explain and illustrate their shades of meanings. The principal difference between the two works is that the former is indexed, while the latter relies on cross-referencing. Prospective buyers should determine which of these two systems of access will better meet their needs. *Webster's Compact Dictionary of Synonyms* is sturdy enough to be recommended for library acquisition, and it merits a place in the home or office reference collection as well.

Webster's New Dictionary of Synonyms

Facts at a Glance

Full Title: **Webster's New Dictionary of Synonyms**.
Publisher: Merriam-Webster.
Editor: Philip B. Gove, Editor-in-Chief.
Edition Reviewed: © 1984.

Number of Entries: 8,733.
Number of Pages: 942.
Trim Size: 6½" × 9½".
Binding: hardcover.

Price: $14.95.
Sold in bookstores and other outlets; also sold to libraries and other educational institutions.
ISBN 0-87779-241-0.

I. Introduction and Scope

Webster's New Dictionary of Synonyms is described by its publisher as "a dictionary of discriminated synonyms and analogous and contrasted words." Brief definitions are included in the main entries. The discriminations carefully distinguish shades of meaning and special applications, and quotations from well-known authors are used to illustrate the meanings discussed. All of the words discriminated also appear in the main alphabetical listing.

Edited and published in 1984, this work is based on *Webster's Dictionary of Synonyms*. The "new" edition is marked by improved discriminations and added articles and quotations. The editorial staff also prepared WEBSTER'S THIRD NEW INTERNATIONAL DICTIONARY.

Four introductory articles precede the lexicon: "Survey of the History of English Synonymy"; "*Synonym*: Analysis and Definition"; "*Antonym*: Analysis and Definition"; and "Analogous and Contrasted Words."

One page of explanatory notes faces the opening page of the lexicon; it consists of a sample column of text with clear, concise numbered descriptions of its features. A useful list of authors quoted in the articles follows the lexicon. This list provides the full names of quoted authors, along with their dates and a brief identification ("Amer. educator," "Eng. satirist," and so forth).

II. Format

Two kinds of entries appear in the work: main entries and secondary entries. Both are introduced by boldface entry words printed in slightly larger type overhanging the text. Entries that are alphabetically close (**acoustic**, **acoustical**) are sometimes listed together. Homographs are listed separately. Italicized part-of-speech abbreviations follow only when a word is entered in more than one part-of-speech application. When an entry is concerned with two or more senses of a word, each is introduced by a boldface numeral.

In the main entry, the entry word is followed by a boldface list of the synonyms to be discriminated and a brief, common definition. Each of the synonyms recurs in boldface within the entry, where its precise meaning is discussed. Each is further clarified by several illustrative phrases. These are easy to spot, appearing within angle brackets with the synonym itself italicized. Some are drawn from the writings of well-known authors, whose names are provided in italics following the quoted phrase.

The entry for **failure** is followed by four synonyms: **neglect**, **default**, **miscarriage**, and **dereliction**, and a short definition. The differences, similarities, and correct use of these five synonyms are then expanded upon in the discriminatory article. A list of 19 analogous words is appended to the article, introduced by the abbreviation *Ana*. Three of these words—**fault**, **lack**, and **imperfection**—receive asterisks di-

Webster's New Dictionary of Synonyms

❶ Main entry words are set in boldface type

❷ The boldface italic abbreviation *Ana* introduces groups of analogous words discussed in other articles

❸ The boldface italic abbreviation *Ant* introduces a list of antonyms

❹ Synonyms to be discriminated are set in boldface type

❺ Examples of usage are enclosed in angle brackets

❻ Cross-references are set in small capitals

❼ An asterisk indicates that a word is a main entry

❽ The boldface italic abbreviation *Con* introduces groups of contrasting words discussed in other articles

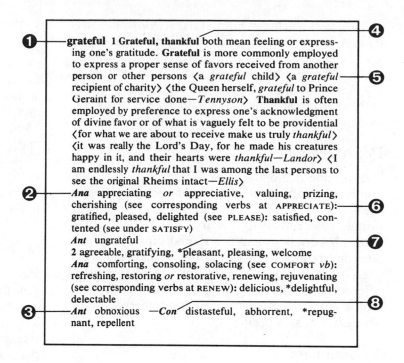

grateful 1 Grateful, thankful both mean feeling or expressing one's gratitude. **Grateful** is more commonly employed to express a proper sense of favors received from another person or other persons ⟨a *grateful* child⟩ ⟨a *grateful* recipient of charity⟩ ⟨the Queen herself, *grateful* to Prince Geraint for service done—*Tennyson*⟩ **Thankful** is often employed by preference to express one's acknowledgment of divine favor or of what is vaguely felt to be providential ⟨for what we are about to receive make us truly *thankful*⟩ ⟨it was really the Lord's Day, for he made his creatures happy in it, and their hearts were *thankful*—*Landor*⟩ ⟨I am endlessly *thankful* that I was among the last persons to see the original Rheims intact—*Ellis*⟩
Ana appreciating *or* appreciative, valuing, prizing, cherishing (see corresponding verbs at APPRECIATE): gratified, pleased, delighted (see PLEASE): satisfied, contented (see under SATISFY)
Ant ungrateful
2 agreeable, gratifying, *pleasant, pleasing, welcome
Ana comforting, consoling, solacing (see COMFORT *vb*): refreshing, restoring *or* restorative, renewing, rejuvenating (see corresponding verbs at RENEW): delicious, *delightful, delectable
Ant obnoxious —*Con* distasteful, abhorrent, *repugnant, repellent

recting the reader to articles where they will receive full treatment. Another two of the words listed—**negligent** and **indifferent**—receive cross-references as, unlike **failure**, they are not nouns.

Antonyms are also listed at the ends of entries, with commas between words that are synonyms of one another and colons separating words that cannot be used synonymously. Under **dissipate**, for example, a colon separates the antonyms *absorb* and *concentrate*. Italic notations follow antonyms as needed to show limited application: "cherish (*hopes, opinions*)."

In secondary entries, the entry word is followed by an alphabetized list of synonyms, and an asterisk or a "SEE" cross-reference directs the reader to the main entry where an article appears. Like main entries, secondary entries also list, as applicable, antonyms, and analogous and contrasted words:

merciful clement, *forbearing, tolerant, lenient, indulgent

Ana compassionate, *tender: benignant, benign, *kind, kindly: forgiving, pardoning, condoning (see EXCUSE vb).

Ant merciless –*Con* *grim, implacable, relentless, unrelenting: cruel, fell, inhuman, *fierce.

The text is printed in two columns divided by a rule. The paper permits only minimal show-through of text. The book is sturdily bound and will hold up well to heavy use.

III. Quality and Currency of Entries

The work's entries are remarkable both for their comprehensiveness and for their detail. The inclusion of antonyms, and analogous and contrasted words, with thorough cross-referencing, provides the reader with a vast amount of information about word relationships. At the main entries, the definitions are clear and concise, and the essays of discrimination are readable and meticulous. The following is representative:

neglect *vb* **Neglect, omit, disregard, ignore, overlook, slight, forget** are comparable when they mean to pass over something without giving it due or sufficient attention. **Neglect** usually implies intentional or unintentional failure to give full or proper attention, especially to something one is doing (as a task) or should do (as a duty) or to someone who has a claim upon one's care or attention ⟨he was changing into his dress clothes. . . . He had *neglected* to hang them up the night before, and for once they were bedraggled—*Mailer*⟩ . . . **Omit** implies a leaving out of something which forms a part of the whole ⟨omit two stanzas of a hymn⟩. . . .
Ant cherish –*Con* *appreciate, value, prize, treasure: *nurse, nurture, foster, cultivate.

The presentation of multiple illustrative phrases is especially useful to the reader, since readers ordinarily derive much of their knowledge of nuances of meaning from context in their reading.

The work excludes nonstandard words, but it is strongly current in its reflection of standard American English. This currency results in part from the editors' incorporation of quotations from more modern authors such as Norman Mailer, Dorothy Parker, and Jack Kerouac, and popular magazines like *Newsweek* and *Life*.

IV. Accessibility

The volume is thumb-indexed, and two large, bold guide words appear at the top of each page within the lexicon. Beneath a rule at the bottom of each double-page spread runs a brief key explaining the three abbreviations and two symbols used in the entries and referring readers to the explanatory notes preceding the lexicon. The use of asterisks for cross-referencing of secondary to main entries saves space and is easy to follow. "See" cross-references show up clearly in small capitals.

V. Summary

Webster's New Dictionary of Synonyms is ideally suitable for the reader or writer who is seeking both a wide scope in vocabulary coverage and careful, detailed discriminating articles. Other synonym dictionaries that provide discriminating articles, like FUNK & WAGNALLS STANDARD HANDBOOK OF SYNONYMS, ANTONYMS, AND PREPOSITIONS or THE RIGHT WORD II: A CONCISE THESAURUS, are less comprehensive. This dictionary is more nearly comparable in size and comprehensiveness to such works as WEBSTER'S COLLEGIATE THESAURUS and THE RANDOM HOUSE THESAURUS: COLLEGE EDITION. It merits a place in the reference collection of all public and academic libraries as well as in many homes.

Webster's New World Dictionary of Synonyms

Facts at a Glance

Full Title: **Webster's New World Dictionary of Synonyms.**
Publisher: Simon & Schuster.
Editor: Ruth Kimball Kent.
Edition Reviewed: © 1984.

Number of Entries: over 4,000 synonyms.
Number of Pages: 255.
Trim Size: 5¼" × 8¼".
Binding: paperback.

Price: $4.95.
Sold in bookstores and directly to libraries.
ISBN 0-671-50403-7.

I. Introduction and Scope

Webster's New World Dictionary of Synonyms is designed, in the publisher's words, "as a handy guide to distinguishing the subtle differences that exist among groups of . . . synonyms." The publisher notes further that "the paragraphs of discrimination, called 'synonymies,' to be found in this book are based upon those prepared for use in WEBSTER'S NEW WORLD DICTIONARY: SECOND COLLEGE EDITION." Altogether, this dictionary explains and differentiates more than 4,000 synonyms; it also lists antonyms.

II. Format

Webster's New World Dictionary of Synonyms is a slim trade paperback. The large typeface with generous space between lines is clear and easy to read. The inner margin is sufficient, although the outer margin is rather narrower than one might wish. The page format is a single column of text.

III. Quality and Currency of Entries

By and large, the entries are functional; by no means are they extensive or exhaustive. They usually provide the reader with sufficient information to distinguish among the synonyms in a particular group, but neither state the shared meaning of these synonymous words nor label their part of speech.

The entries are comparisons of synonymous words that are grouped together as an entry heading, for example: an "entry" may consist of one word followed by a cross-reference, such as

recoup for synonyms see **recover**

or a group such as

recover, regain, retrieve, recoup, reclaim

followed by brief discriminations. The first word in the group is that which, according to the editors, "may generally be considered the most basic or comprehensive for each group." Therefore, we are given entry groups beginning with such basic words as **conspiracy, plot, intrigue, machination, cabal**; or **continual, continuous, constant, incessant, perpetual, eternal**; or **form, figure, outline, shape, configuration**; or **free, release, liberate, emancipate, discharge**; or **inclination, leaning, bent, propensity, proclivity**; and so forth. Note, however, that the first group (**conspiracy**) inexplicably omits *scheme*, which is listed with **plan, design**, and **project**, where it is defined as

a less definite term than the preceding [*project*], often connotes either an impartial, visionary plan or an underhanded intrigue [a *scheme* to embezzle the funds].

Webster's New World Dictionary of Synonyms

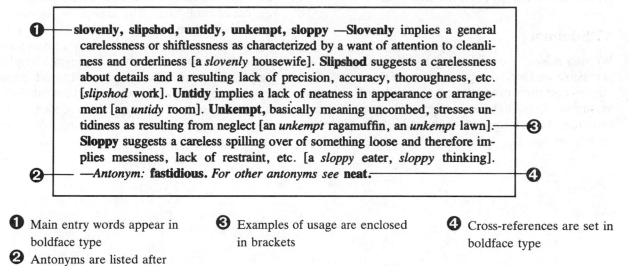

slovenly, slipshod, untidy, unkempt, sloppy —**Slovenly** implies a general carelessness or shiftlessness as characterized by a want of attention to cleanliness and orderliness [a *slovenly* housewife]. **Slipshod** suggests a carelessness about details and a resulting lack of precision, accuracy, thoroughness, etc. [*slipshod* work]. **Untidy** implies a lack of neatness in appearance or arrangement [an *untidy* room]. **Unkempt,** basically meaning uncombed, stresses untidiness as resulting from neglect [an *unkempt* ragamuffin, an *unkempt* lawn]. **Sloppy** suggests a careless spilling over of something loose and therefore implies messiness, lack of restraint, etc. [a *sloppy* eater, *sloppy* thinking]. —*Antonym:* **fastidious.** *For other antonyms see* **neat.**

❶ Main entry words appear in boldface type

❷ Antonyms are listed after synonym entries

❸ Examples of usage are enclosed in brackets

❹ Cross-references are set in boldface type

The entries generally contain a one-sentence definition, noting the particular connotations of each synonym and, sometimes, the context in which the word is used. The following entry for **neglect** and its synonyms illustrates the quality and content of *Webster's New World Dictionary of Synonyms*.

neglect, omit, overlook, disregard, ignore, slight, forget—**Neglect** implies a failure to carry out some expected or required action, either through carelessness or by intention [I *neglected* to wind the clock.] **Omit,** in this connection, implies a neglecting through oversight, absorption, etc. [She should not *omit* to visit the Louvre.] **Overlook** suggests a failure to see or to take action, either inadvertently or indulgently [I'll *overlook* your errors this time.] **Disregard** implies inattention or neglect, usually intentional [She always *disregards* his wishes.] **Ignore** suggests a deliberate disregarding, sometimes through stubborn refusal to see the facts [But you *ignore* the necessity for action.] **Slight** implies a disregarding or neglecting in an indifferent or disdainful way [He seems to *slight* the newer writers.] **Forget,** in this connection, implies an intentional disregarding or omitting [After his election he *forgot* the wishes of the voters.]

While this synonym group includes most if not all the words that one could plausibly use to imply **neglect** in a particular context, the sense discrimination seems superficial and awkward. Moreover, there is an unacceptable reliance on circularity. If neglect "implies a failure to carry out some . . . action," the reader will not be illuminated by the statement that "disregard implies . . . neglect." Such definitions do not go as far as they might in discriminating among related words. Moreover, in many cases the illustrative sentences do not convey the full connotation of

the word they are intended to illustrate. For example, the sentence "He seems to *slight* the newer writers" could be just as easily used to illustrate the words *neglect, omit, overlook, disregard, ignore,* or *forget*.

Although currency is not a major issue in a reference work that emphasizes *basic* vocabulary, reviewers did not encounter a single instance of contemporary or recent slang or neologisms among the entries. For example, under "**compute, calculate, estimate, reckon,**" the discrimination

compute suggests the use of simple mathematics to determine a quantity, amount, etc. and implies a determinable, hence precise, result [to *compute* the volume of a cylinder]

is no longer adequate as the only verb sense of a word commonly used in the electronic age.

IV. Accessibility

Webster's New World Dictionary of Synonyms is adequately accessible. The brief foreword notes that "the paragraphs of discrimination, called 'synonymies' . . . are arranged alphabetically under those words which may generally be considered the most basic or comprehensive for each group." Every word included in the entry groups is also entered separately in the book, in alphabetical order, as a cross-reference entry. This greatly enhances the accessibility and obviates the need for a comprehensive index.

Guide words at the top of each page indicate the first entry on left-hand pages and the last entry on right-hand pages. Entry words are in boldface, and the first entry word overhangs the text by about two characters. Once readers have had a little practice using this book, they will find it easy to locate the synonyms of any word in the dictionary.

V. Summary

Webster's New World Dictionary of Synonyms is an accessible and well-designed synonym dictionary. The entries and their presentation generally follow a conventional style of book design. However, the discriminated meanings are often inadequate due to the circularity of the definitions; the definitions frequently lack the degree of subtlety necessary to enable the reader to choose the desired word with any degree of confidence. The illustrative sentences rarely give a sufficient context for defining the synonym. In short, this synonym dictionary provides only rudimentary information about synonyms. Readers who require a more scholarly, authoritative paperback work of this kind would do well to consult THE MERRIAM-WEBSTER POCKET DICTIONARY OF SYNONYMS or, preferably, THE BASIC BOOK OF SYNONYMS AND ANTONYMS.

Chapter 13
Evaluations of Thesauruses

Chambers 20th Century Thesaurus

Facts at a Glance

Full Title: **Chambers 20th Century Thesaurus: A Comprehensive Word-Finding Dictionary**.
Publisher: W. & R. Chambers Ltd.; published in the United States by Cambridge University Press.
Editors: M. A. Seaton, G. W. Davidson, C. M. Schwarz, and J. Simpson.
Edition Reviewed: © 1986.

Number of Entries: 18,000.
Number of Words: over 350,000 synonyms and antonyms.
Number of Pages: 762.
Trim Size: $5\frac{3}{8}'' \times 8\frac{1}{8}''$.
Binding: cloth.

Price: $14.95.
Sold in bookstores and by direct mail; also sold to libraries and other educational institutions.
ISBN 0-521-60013-8.

I. Introduction and Scope

The *Chambers 20th Century Thesaurus*, prepared by the staff of the respected British publisher W. & R. Chambers, Ltd., has 18,000 entries, with over 350,000 synonyms and antonyms. Listed alphabetically, each entry has "a plentiful supply of alternatives and connected expressions." The thesaurus draws on the CHAMBERS 20TH CENTURY DICTIONARY as well as its database. This is the first edition of this work. The main thesaurus is augmented by two appendixes, one of classified word lists of concrete and technical terms and one of words listed by suffix.

II. Format

The format is as simple and straightforward as its contents. There is a brief preface, the main alphabetical list of entries, and the appendixes. The pages are neatly laid out in two columns, with overhanging entries in boldface. The type is black and clear with plenty of white space. The paper is white and allows some show-through, which does not, however, disturb readability. The binding is sturdy, but it does not allow the pages to lie flat—a disadvantage for a reference book.

III. Quality and Currency of Entries

As the preface points out, the Chambers thesaurus, while rejecting the Roget organization of words around concepts, does acknowledge "the value of Roget's approach by supplying with each entry related vocabulary on a rather broader, more comprehensive basis than that of mere synonymity." The reader will find words listed alphabetically under the entry, following its part of speech. Many of the synonyms have entries of their own, thus providing further opportunities to find the mot juste. Antonyms also often have entries of their own that can be pursued further.

A typical entry reads:

> **fleshy** *adj.* ample, beefy, brawny, carneous, carnose, chubby, chunky, corpulent, fat, flabby, hefty, meaty, obese, overweight, paunchy, plump, podgy, portly, rotund, stout, tubby, well-padded.
> *antonym* thin

All the synonyms for **fleshy** have their own entries with the exception of **carneous**, **carnose**, and **well-padded**. And by seeking the entry for the antonym

Chambers 20th Century Thesaurus

❶ Homographs receive separate, numbered entries

❷ Synonyms are listed alphabetically

❶ ─→ ┌───┐
     │ **nut**[1] *n.* kernel, pip, seed, stone.   │ ←─ ❷
     │ **nut**[2] *n.* brain, crackpot, crank, eccentric, head, │
     │   head-banger, loony, lunatic, madman, man- │
     │   iac, mind, nutcase, nutter, psychopath, │
     │   reason, senses.   │
     └───┘

thin, the user will find a host of opposite meanings for **fleshy**.

The editors recommend that the thesaurus be used in conjunction with a dictionary so that the more obscure words, such as *carneous* and *carnose*, may be found. The emphasis of the thesaurus is on common, everyday language, and many obscure and specialized words, especially in the scientific or technical vocabulary, will not be found here. Even such common, up-to-date terms as *access* and *program* used as verbs in their computer sense will not be found. However, these omissions do not seriously limit the usefulness of this broadly based thesaurus for the general user.

To offset the general, abstract nature of the vocabulary, the editors have provided more concrete and technical terms in the appendixes. They are collected and categorized alphabetically under the headings of "Classified word-lists" and "Words listed by suffix." Under the first group appear **air and space vehicles, alphabets and writing systems, architecture and building, cattle breeds, dances, herbs, spices, languages, minerals, wine-bottle sizes**, and **zodiac signs** among others. And under the second group appear, for example, **-ast, -cracy, -gon, -graph, -iform, -ism, -logy, -meter**, and **-vorous**.

American users should expect some British spellings throughout the thesaurus, for example, **galvanise** for *galvanize* and **licence** for *license*. These do not hamper the understanding of terms, especially with so many available synonyms. Furthermore, although some British meanings appear, a certain attempt at including American terms is apparent; for example, following the entry **jersey**, the term *sweater* has been included, and following the entry **pavement**, *sidewalk* is listed. Still, there are many American thesauruses and books of synonyms that may serve American users more directly.

IV. Accessibility

The alphabetical format makes the thesaurus or, more correctly, book of synonyms, very accessible and is the main advantage of this work over ROGET'S INTERNATIONAL THESAURUS. A contents page clearly locates the main sections of the book, and guide words at the tops of the pages indicate the beginning and ending entries on each page. A thumb index has not been provided; this would have been a helpful aid to the user.

V. Summary

Chambers 20th Century Thesaurus is a useful and straightforward source of alternative terms for the general user. Its format is very accessible, and its vocabulary is basic and broadly based in common, everyday words. It would be useful for the writer, the office worker, and the word game player, if not to the more academically oriented user. It is a sturdy, attractive book that should stand up to library use. WEBSTER'S NEW DICTIONARY OF SYNONYMS and WEBSTER'S NEW WORLD THESAURUS are also arranged alphabetically, but they provide far more analytical word information with numbered entries, cross-references, and discussions of meanings and sources. Chambers, however, is a good alternative choice for quick reference to the similarly formatted THE DOUBLEDAY ROGET'S THESAURUS IN DICTIONARY FORM or to THE RANDOM HOUSE THESAURUS, which also groups synonyms by meanings and has illustrative sentences.

The Doubleday Roget's Thesaurus in Dictionary Form

Facts at a Glance

Full Title: **The Doubleday Roget's Thesaurus in Dictionary Form.**
Publisher: Doubleday & Company.
Editor: Sidney I. Landau, Editor-in-Chief.
Edition Reviewed: © 1977.

Number of Entries: over 17,000.
Number of Words: 250,000 synonyms and antonyms.
Number of Pages: 816.
Trim Size: $5\frac{3}{8}'' \times 8''$.
Binding: cloth.

Price: $12.95.
Sold in bookstores and other outlets; also sold to libraries and other educational institutions.
ISBN 0-385-12379-5.

I. Introduction and Scope

The Doubleday Roget's Thesaurus in Dictionary Form, edited by the respected lexicographer Sidney I. Landau, was first published in 1977 and was not based

The Doubleday Roget's Thesaurus in Dictionary Form

❶ Main entry words are set in boldface type

❷ Antonym lists, introduced by the boldface abbreviation *ant.*, are numbered to correspond with the synonyms above

❸ Synonyms are arranged by parts of speech

❹ Boldface numerals distinguish groups of synonyms that are related in meaning

❺ Cross-references are set in small capitals

❶ **faint** *v.* pass out, black out, collapse, swoon, languish. —*adj.* 1 timid, weak, feeble, irresolute, cowardly, frightened, ineffectual, pusillanimous. 2 indistinct, dim, slight, inconspicuous, soft, tenuous, low, vague, pianissimo. —*n.* blackout, syncope, swoon, collapse. **❸** **❹**

❷ **ant.** *adj.* 1 courageous, firm, resolute, brave, bold, stout, intrepid. 2 strong, clear, bright, sharp, distinct, definite, unequivocal, resonant, resounding.
faint-hearted *adj.* TIMID. **❺**

on any previous thesaurus. Entries were selected from *The Doubleday Dictionary*, published in 1975. This thesaurus is intended for everyday use and is designed to fill the gap between two types of common American thesauruses—the subject-indexed variety and the brief dictionary-style work.

This work contains more than 17,000 entries, with an average of 10 to 15 synonyms per entry. Altogether, more than 250,000 synonyms are listed. As a rule, outdated and trite phrases are omitted, but slang terms have been included.

II. Format

Entry words are alphabetized letter by letter. They appear in boldface type overhanging the text on double-column pages. Homographs—that is, words spelled the same but having different meanings and roots—are entered separately and distinguished by superscript numbers. An italicized part-of-speech abbreviation follows the entry word.

The guide to the use of the thesaurus indicates that "the first few synonyms listed under each meaning are those that best distinguish it from other meanings." Thus common words appear first and are followed by more specialized terms, which are parenthetically labeled. These italicized labels follow the specialized term: for example, "Teddy Boy (*Slang*)" is offered as a synonym for **coxcomb**. Other labels include *Arch.* for archaic and *Brit.* for British. Although most labels are easily deciphered, a key to abbreviations would be of value to the novice users.

Antonyms, when provided, follow the synonyms and are preceded by the abbreviation **ant.** in boldface type. A sample entry appears below.

> **dated** *adj.* old-fashioned, passé, antiquated, outmoded, obsolete, archaic, out of date, stale, tired, antedilu-

vian, moth-eaten, out, old-fogeyish, old hat (*Slang*), démodé. **ant.** new, current, latest, now, fashionable, à la mode, in, hot, *au courant*.

As can be seen in this entry, foreign words are included in the lists for both synonyms and antonyms. The guide to the dictionary does not explain why some are in italics and others are not. Based on the practice in other dictionaries, it may be assumed that italicized foreign words or phrases have not been fully assimilated into the language.

III. Quality and Currency of Entries

For the most part, the entries are words used in everyday language. There are a few less common words included, such as **grandiloquent** (pompous) and **opprobrious** (abusive or offensive). Some archaic words appear among the synonyms: **dray** and **tumbrel** are listed as synonyms for **cart**. Occasionally there is an eponym included among the entries, such as **Cassandra** for **alarmist**. Overall, the entries are only as current as the 1975 dictionary from which they were taken; a number of contemporary terms could doubtlessly be added were the thesaurus revised today, so that *gay* (n.) and *punk*, both found in ROGET'S II: THE NEW THESAURUS, are neither referenced nor cross-referenced.

Many slang synonyms and antonyms are included. Under **kick around** we find **bum** and **rap**; for **roost** we find **pad**; and there is also an entry for the slang term **con** with slang synonyms such as **rip off** and **psych**. These entries effectively reflect modern spoken language, even ten years after the work's latest revision date.

IV. Accessibility

Entries are easily located in this alphabetical thesaurus. The volume is thumb indexed, and there are two guide words at the top of each page indicating the first and last entries on the page. The print is clear, and there is generous white space, and the text is easy to read. Cross-references, in small capitals, are easy to use. For example, "**harum-scarum** *adj.* RECK-LESS" directs users to **reckless**, where they find 27 synonyms, including **harum-scarum**, and six antonyms.

Some entries provide multiple cross-references; for example, "**ego** *n.* **1** SELF. **2** EGOTISM." Cross-referenced entry words are followed by the part-of-speech abbreviation except when other labels are used. For example, the entry "**hatchet job** (*Slang*) CRITICISM," omits the part-of-speech designation.

V. Summary

While the alphabetical arrangement makes this thesaurus a more accessible work than the more comprehensive ROGET'S INTERNATIONAL THESAURUS: FOURTH EDITION, its style and usefulness fall short of the cheaper and more recent ROGET'S II: THE NEW THESAURUS (reviewed in this Buying Guide). ROGET'S II also arranges its entries alphabetically, but it groups its synonyms and idioms by meaning and it uses innumerable illustrations to guide the reader to correct usage. While Doubleday may have 20 synonyms for the verb **neglect**, for instance, ROGET'S II breaks down the verb **neglect** into four meanings with usage examples, and opposite each meaning it presents synonyms or cross-references to further synonyms. Unfortunately, ROGET'S II does not include antonyms.

Most libraries will still want a copy of the distinguished and comprehensive ROGET'S INTERNATIONAL THESAURUS with its traditional classifications. However, for an authoritative, alphabetically arranged thesaurus, it is hard to choose between Doubleday and ROGET'S II. Some users may feel that what Doubleday lacks in style and illustrative examples, it makes up in its important lists of antonyms.

Longman Lexicon of Contemporary English

Facts at a Glance

Full Title: **Longman Lexicon of Contemporary English**.
Publisher: Longman.
Editor: Tom McArthur.
Edition Reviewed: © 1981; 1982 printing.

Number of Entries: 15,000.
Number of Words: 20,000.
Number of Pages: 928.
Number of Indexes: 1.

Number of Illustrations: 700 black-and-white drawings.
Trim Size: 5⅜″ × 8½″.
Binding: paper over boards.

Price: $19.95 (cloth); $15.95 (paper).
Sold in bookstores; also sold to libraries and other educational institutions.
ISBN 0-582-55636-8 (cloth);
ISBN 0-582-55527-2 (paper).

I. Introduction and Scope

The *Longman Lexicon of Contemporary English* is a thesaurus on a new plan. Like the traditional thesaurus, it organizes its contents by subject, not alphabetically like a dictionary. But like a dictionary it includes definitions, illustrations, style labels, examples of usage, and pronunciation.

The resulting vocabulary reference book is not so comprehensive as either a dictionary or a traditional thesaurus. It describes only about 15,000 items from the central vocabulary of English, grouped in 14 "semantic fields" (subject areas). The *Lexicon* meets some dictionary needs, such as a quick guide to pronunciation or usage of common words; but spellings are, of course, British. Although it is more like the traditional thesaurus, the *Longman Lexicon* meets few thesaurus needs, because it lacks the traditional long lists of near-synonyms designed to give advanced writers a lexical nudge.

Instead, the *Lexicon* is designed for those readers who seek to master the central vocabulary of English: the neophyte writer or, even more, the mature student who is learning English as a second language.

II. Format

The *Longman Lexicon* falls into four main sections: 15 pages of introductory matter, including the "List of Sets" (an expanded table of contents), "How to use the Lexicon," and "Guide to the Lexicon"; the 784-page lexicon itself; a 125-page index; and a two-page "Grammar Table."

The lexicon contains 14 subject headings, each designated with an alphabetical letter: For example, **D** is **Buildings, Houses, the Home, Clothes, Belongings, and Personal Care**. Within each section are numbered subsections: the sequence beginning **D20** is **Parts of Houses**.

The sub-subsections are tagged by part of speech (**D29** is *nouns*, **L207** is *adjectives, etc*) and often with a code explained in the Grammatical Table: All the nouns in **D29** are [C] (count nouns), but each item in **L207** receives its own code because not all are in the same grammatical category (some are adjectives compared with "-er," "-est," some with "more," "most"; some are nouns). These tags correspond to the features marked in the lexicon of a modern transformational-generative grammar, which will probably only be of interest to teachers.

More importantly, the same tags provide a clear guide to the grammatical status and combining forms of the items, which will make them far more meaningful and useful. The first sense of **senior** in **L207** is used after a verb and takes no comparative or superlative, the second sense is an ordinary adjective, and the third sense is used before a noun. For example:

> **senior 1** [Wa5;F (*to*)] **a** older: *At age 68 she was senior to everyone in the room.* **b** of higher rank: *His appointment as chairman makes him senior to several older men.* **c** having done longer service in an organization: *He is senior to me; he was in the company when I joined it.*
> **2**[B]**a** old: *He's too senior to try for a young man's job. He is the most senior person in the room.* **b** of high rank: *a meeting of the most senior army officers; a senior government position* **3**[Wa5;*the*A] oldest or highest in rank or time of service: *The senior officer was only a captain.*

Some entries also show how other words can be formed with an affix: **humorously** from **humour** (note the British spelling of *humor*).

Sub-subsection headings often include cross-references to other subsections, marked with a right-hand arrow: for "mature and adult" → the first nine subsections under "People." These major cross-references also appear in the "List of Sets." Further cross-references sometimes appear under the individual items.

Following the sub-subsection heading, the items appear in a series of paragraphs headed by the item in bold sans serif type. Each paragraph includes a definition or definitions with any style and grammatical labels and illustrative quotations. Under "passage and halls," for example, American English usage is labeled:

> **cloakroom** *AmE usu* **checkroom**, a room, as in a theatre, where hats, coats, bags, etc, may be left for a short time, usu under guard: *He asked the cloakroom attendant for his coat.*

Where appropriate, black-and-white illustrations accompany subsections and sub-subsections, like **doors and their parts,** or even constitute the sub-subsection itself, like the illustration **the inside of a room**, with pictured items labeled **radiator**, **sofa**, and so forth.

The lexicon provides a reliable guide to even less concrete terms, distinguishing in one sub-subsection among five meanings of **understand**, three meanings of **appreciate**, and the meanings of **comprehend**, **realize**, **perceive**, **grasp**, **fathom**, **follow**, **see**, **get**, and **dawn on** as degrees of cognitive capacity.

Among the most useful sections are those on words that have no referential meaning: the function of grammatically oriented words such as pronouns, demonstratives, conjunctions, and prepositions. In the same sections are definitions of **grammar, common figures of speech, elements, etc** [!] **of word-formation and word-use,** and other articles that distill the editor's expertise into a mini-grammar and rhetoric. A book of some 15,000 items needs a theoretical framework to give them coherence: here in sections **G230–293** is that framework.

For the treatment of pronunciation, see the discussion of the index under "Accessibility," below.

III. Quality and Currency of Entries

As its title suggests, the *Longman Lexicon* covers the present-day language. It pays no attention to word histories and, although it has style labels for *formal, poetic,* and *pompous,* it has none for *obsolete* or *archaic.* But many current words are ephemeral or marginal, whether slang or scientific, and the *Lexicon* includes only the central vocabulary. So the word *punk* does not appear at all in the book, and the sub-subsection on **spaceships**, with only three items in a scant single column-inch of text, would not give enough help to an earthling who had to write an essay on NASA.

The editor, Tom McArthur, is a British authority on modern English, especially English as an international language. He is the founder-editor of *English Today*, a quarterly journal published by the Cambridge University Press. So he is aware of the stylistic varieties of the language. Several markedly taboo items appear in the **Body, Its Functions and Welfare** section and the **Courting, Sex, and Marriage** subsection. But on some matters of usage that receive wide coverage, the *Longman Lexicon* provides little guidance. It makes no clear distinction between **compare to** and **compare with**, **disinterested** appears but not *uninterested*, **hopeful** but not *hopefully*.

The book does not pretend to give a comprehensive description of British and American varieties of English. Sub-subsection **D29** does not list the Americanism *hallway*, and its definition "**foyer** an entrance hall to a theatre or hotel, where people gather and talk" overlooks the American use that places the entrance hall in a private house.

IV. Accessibility

Some of the accessibility of the *Longman Lexicon* stems from its elaborate and successful system of cross-references. Its preliminary sections "How to

Use the Lexicon" and "Guide to the Lexicon" are lucid. The index, which makes up over an eighth of the book, adds to its accessibility.

Each item in the lexicon is listed alphabetically in the index, with its pronunciation in a version of the International Phonetic Alphabet (IPA) notation, with stress and syllabication where appropriate, and a listing of the place(s) in the lexicon where the word is treated. For example

> **neck** /nek/
>   of the body A51, 53, 54 (pictures), A120, B10
>   (picture)
>   in sex *v* C22
>   meat *n* (pictures)
>   of a guitar *n* K46 (picture)
> . . .
> **news** /nju:z ‖ nu:z/
>   *n* G194
> **news** agency /'.ₗ . . ./
>   *n* G194

The separation of the pronunciation from the definitions is valid: for a spelling or pronunciation, you can search for the item alphabetically; for help with meaning or usage, you need to see the word in the context of other semantically-related (but often alphabetically-remote) terms.

V. Summary

The *Longman Lexicon* will not take the place of a dictionary or thesaurus for most purposes, especially for American students and adult readers, not only because it stresses British usage but also because of British spellings. Instead it supplies a new kind of reference work or textbook, a guide to the central vocabulary of English. It is simple, coherent, and easy to use, yet it is presented in a linguistic framework that will interest advanced students of language.

This book's innovative but rather complicated arrangement, together with its use of British English, will tend to limit its usefulness to all but the most advanced and sophisticated students. Less knowledgeable students will most likely find both aspects of the book more confusing than illuminating, and the American reader will usually possess most of the information the lexicon offers. In fact, both will probably be better served by a standard American thesaurus or dictionary of synonyms.

While the *Longman Lexicon* is a very interesting and well-constructed thesaurus-type reference book, its rather small potential audience will limit its appropriateness in both home and library collections. It will be an intelligent purchase for the home of the advanced student of the English language, and it is also recommended for the larger library that already

has a significant reference collection or the library that serves a large population for whom English is a second language.

Nelson's New Compact Roget's Thesaurus

Facts at a Glance

Full Title: **Nelson's New Compact Roget's Thesaurus.**
Publisher: Thomas Nelson Publishers.
Editor: Laurence Urdang, Editor-in-Chief; Mark Boyer.
Edition Reviewed: © 1978; 1986 printing.

Number of Entries: 1,000.
Number of Pages: 314.
Number of Indexes: 1.
Trim Size: 3½" × 5¼".
Binding: paperback.

Price: $2.45.
Sold in bookstores and other outlets; also sold to educational institutions.
ISBN 0-8407-5634-8.

I. Introduction and Scope

Nelson's New Compact Roget's Thesaurus, published in 1978, is a pocket-sized abridged version of Peter Mark Roget's 1852 work. Laurence Urdang, the work's editor-in-chief, is an authority on lexicography. According to preface, the abridged version serves, like the original, not only as a synonym dictionary, but as "a diverse collection of associated and related words and phrases." Because of Roget's time-tested classification system, when a suitable synonym is not located under a particular entry, the user may find it under one of the nearby entries.

This pocket edition includes a comprehensive index. It retains Roget's general structure and all of the nearly 1,000 main entries of the original. However, antiquated language has been removed and, according to the preface, "the book has been modernized to include the most current usage and the newest developments in language." The work is relatively contemporary, but no longer as current as the preface states. Duplications have been omitted and the user is urged to seek words under associated parts of speech. The preface also contains the valuable caution:

If the word selected is not completely familiar, check its meaning and usage in a good dictionary before risking its use in an incorrect or unidiomatic context.

The work is intended for a general audience, and its compact size makes it convenient for a variety of uses. Its abridgment and emphasis on "everyday" language may render it especially accessible for the high school student to whom a larger work might seem cumbersome or confusing.

II. Format

The thesaurus is organized on the basis of Roget's six broad classes: Abstract Relations, Space, Matter, Intellect, Volition, and Affections. These classes are subdivided to produce 997 numbered main entries, ordered according to relationships of likeness and contrast. A typical sequence of entries, for example, is **friendship**, **enmity**, **friend**, **enemy**, **sociality**, **seclusion**, **exclusion**, **courtesy**, **discourtesy**.

Main entry numbers, in boldface, overhang the text on each page of double-column text. The entry word, also in boldface type, is followed by an italicized, abbreviated part-of-speech, and a list of synonyms. Where more than one part of speech is listed, each is given its own paragraph. Semicolons separate synonym lists, grouped according to shades of meaning. The word *Informal* appears in parentheses after a synonym to indicate informal usage.

Index entries are printed in three columns and appear in boldface type if they are main entry words in the text. All index entries are followed by italicized part-of-speech abbreviations and numbers that refer to the main entries under which they can be located.

The paper is white and allows minimal showthrough. Although the bold main entry words and adequate margins enhance readability, the print within entries is very small and may be difficult for some users to read. Print in the index is, however, adequate in size. The pages do not separate easily from the binding of this sturdy small paperback. The cover is brown vinyl over paper with gold lettering.

III. Quality and Currency of Entries

Entries are thorough and detailed, reflecting a wide range of senses and synonyms. A representative entry is

> **268 traveler** *n* wayfarer, journeyer, rover, rambler, wanderer, free spirit, nomad, vagabond, bohemian, gypsy, itinerant, vagrant, tramp, hobo, straggler, waif; pilgrim, palmer, seeker, quester; voyager, passenger, tourist, sightseer, excursionist, vacationer, globetrotter, jet-setter; immigrant, emigrant, refugee, fugitive; pedestrian, walker, cyclist, biker, rider, horsewoman, horseman, equestrian, driver.

A substantial number of synonyms is included here. Closely related synonyms are placed in groups, which helps a reader to locate a precise word. To be certain of shades of meaning, connotations, and restrictions in usage, the user will require a dictionary, as the work's preface insists.

The work's inclusion of informal words and phrases is a valuable contribution to its currency. For example, **the pits** appears as an informal synonym among adjectives under **badness**. The work's currency is also reflected in its inclusion of such terms as the title **Ms.**, gender neutral terms (**letter carrier**), and female equivalents (**horsewoman**). Although the language of computer technology is not represented in the listings, terms from the fields of astronautics (**cosmonaut, module**) and energy (**nuclear power, solar energy**) are included.

IV. Accessibility

Accessibility is enhanced by the work's prefatory explanation and "Plan of Classification." The "Tabular Synopsis of Categories" permits the user a more detailed overview of the work's organization. Within the main text, boldface guide numbers appear at the top of each double-page spread to indicate the first and last numbered entries on the pages. Bold guide words at the top of each spread in the index serve the same function.

V. Summary

Nelson's New Compact Roget's Thesaurus is a small but thorough reference work. For readers and writers who seek the convenience of a pocket-sized thesaurus, this work provides the advantages of a clear format, comprehensive index, and detailed listings. Although the work is not as up-to-date as many larger thesauruses, its inclusion of informal words and phrases is useful for both a general and a student audience. The work, however, is more current, and thus more useful, than the comparable pocket-sized RANDOM HOUSE THESAURUS: A DICTIONARY OF SYNONYMS AND ANTONYMS, despite the latter's dictionary format. With its careful abridgment and focus on "everyday" language, the volume would be a worthwhile addition to a personal reference collection, and the public library might well make a place for it in a circulating paperback collection, too.

The New American Roget's College Thesaurus in Dictionary Form

Facts at a Glance

Full Title: **The New American Roget's College Thesaurus in Dictionary Form**.
Publisher: Signet/New American Library.

The New American Roget's College Thesaurus in
Dictionary Form

❶ Category headings are set in capital letters

❷ Single-column category entries list synonyms, arranged by parts of speech

❸ Cross-references to antonyms appear at the end of each category

❹ Double-column word list includes a few synonyms and gives cross-references to categories

❺ Cross-references are set in small capitals

❻ Words enclosed in brackets are optional

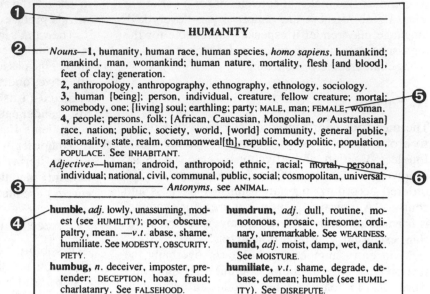

Editor: Philip D. Morehead.
Edition Reviewed: © 1985.

Number of Entries: more than 20,000.
Number of Pages: 649.
Trim Size: 4¼″ × 7″ (paperback); 5¼″ × 8″ (trade paperback).
Binding: paperback.

Price: $3.50 (paperback); $7.95 (trade paperback).
Sold in bookstores and other outlets; also sold to libraries and other educational institutions.
ISBN 0-451-13474-5 (paperback);
ISBN 0-452-000732-1 (trade paperback).

I. Introduction and Scope

The 1985 edition of *The New American Roget's College Thesaurus in Dictionary Form* is a revised, enlarged version of the original, first published in 1958. It combines in one alphabetical list, very much like that in Roget's original thesaurus, categories and a list of words with their close synonyms. If, for instance, we look up the word **golden**, we find seven synonyms and two cross-references, which lead us to the categories **COLOR** and **DEARNESS**. The **COLOR** category is almost a page in length and includes words of related meaning and different parts of speech as well as antonyms. In addition to standard usage, entries reflect nonstandard and specialized vocabularies: colloquialism, slang, dialect, British English, and poetic and archaic usage.

Foreign words and phrases commonly used by speakers of English are not included as main entries within the body of the text, but are gathered in a separate listing at the end of the book, where they are defined and cross-referenced to English terms in the main text.

Excluded from the volume are words with no natural synonyms as well as antonyms formed with prefixes such as *un-*, *in-*, and *dis-*. Words like *unloved* that are "simple negatives" of other words are not listed, but a word like **unbearable** does appear because of the multiple meanings of **bearable**.

II. Format

The thesaurus is organized in dictionary format, which many users will find more accessible than the traditional thesaurus format. A single alphabetical listing incorporates two kinds of listings: one is a word resembling the typical thesaurus's category that shows related terms in an extensive range of parts of speech; and the second is individual words with shorter lists of their close synonyms. The larger category-type listings, headed by a main topic word in bold capitals, are printed across the full width of the page and divided by horizontal rules from the rest of the text on that page. Part-of-speech labels, in italics overhanging the text, introduce groups of related words. Boldface numbers create secondary categories within these groups. At the end of the category antonyms are listed. Entries consisting of close synonyms are printed in a double-column format. Main entry words are in boldface and followed by an abbreviated, italicized part-of-speech label.

In both kinds of entry, cross-references are provided in small capitals. Specialized usages, such as colloquialisms, are introduced by an abbreviated, italicized usage label. Within the listings, secondary groups are demarcated by semicolons.

At the end of the volume appears the alphabetical listing "Foreign Words and Phrases." Entry words are in boldface and overhang the text. Each is followed by an italicized abbreviation indicating the word's language. A translation and cross-references (in small capitals) to the body of the text are also presented.

Print is adequate in size and easy to read; judicious use of white space enhances readability. The mass market edition was examined for review; its pages do not separate easily from the binding and the volume is, for a paperback, acceptably sturdy.

III. Quality and Currency of Entries

Substantial listings, together with copious cross-references, ensure that the user will find a word's extended family in the text. The inclusion of specialized usages also broadens the entries' usefulness, especially for literary and language study.

Currency is reflected in such main entries as **astronautics** (listing, among other terms, **aerospace**, **lunar module**, **L.E.M.**, **space probe**, **escape velocity**, **launch window**, and **reentry corridor**). Although the only synonym given under **computer** is **calculator**, under **numeration**, to which the reader is cross-referred, computer-related terms listed include

cybernetics, computer, electronic computer *or* brain, mainframe [computer], mini-, micro–, *or* personal computer, [micro]processor, punch-card *or* -tape reader.

Under **writing**, the user will also find the terms

printer, dot-matrix *or* daisy-wheel printer, draft- *or* letter-quality printer.

For popular terms, especially slang and colloquialisms, the thesaurus is less up-to-date. For example, in the category labeled **uncomformity**, the terms **hippie** and **yippie** appear, but *punk* is absent. Under **folly** appear **jerk** and **square**, but not *turkey* or *airhead*. While the retention of dated slang terms enhances the work's value as a repository of linguistic history, its omission of more recent (post-1960s) slang somewhat limits its value for today's readers.

IV. Accessibility

The alphabetical format makes the volume readily accessible to readers. Cross-references, in small cap-

itals, stand out clearly. Further, a preface titled "How to Use This Thesaurus" provides a brief but clear guide to the information included in the volume and to techniques for locating it. This feature will be especially valuable for novice thesaurus users.

Also adding to accessibility are the guide words. Two, in boldface type, appear at the top of each page within the body of the text and indicate the first and last words entered on that page. Guide words are not provided within the foreign-word list, but its brevity (five pages) renders them unnecessary.

Alternative spellings are not entered. The authority followed for preferred spellings is THE NEW AMERICAN WEBSTER HANDY COLLEGE DICTIONARY, described in the preface as a "companion volume" to the thesaurus.

V. Summary

The New American Roget's College Thesaurus in Dictionary Form is a compact, thorough reference work, well designed to meet the needs of its wide audience. It is adequately current for most thesaurus users. Further, its dictionary format and its guide to thesaurus use make the volume more accessible than THE PENGUIN POCKET THESAURUS. Its inclusion of poetic and archaic language also enhances its value to those who pursue the study of literature and language. The thesaurus will be useful for personal use, and may also be useful in community and college libraries as well as in libraries with circulating paperback collections.

The Penguin Pocket Thesaurus

Facts at a Glance

Full Title: **The Penguin Pocket Thesaurus.**
Publisher: Penguin Books.
Editors: Faye Carney and Maurice Waite.
Edition Reviewed: © 1985.

Number of Entries: 882.
Number of Pages: 514.
Number of Indexes: 1.
Trim Size: $4\frac{3}{8}'' \times 7\frac{1}{16}''$.
Binding: paperback.

Price: $3.50.
Sold in bookstores and other outlets; also sold to
    libraries and other educational institutions.
ISBN 0-14-051-137-7.

I. Introduction and Scope

Described by its publishers as the "perfect, portable, comprehensive and up-to-date companion to the

English language," *The Penguin Pocket Thesaurus* is an updated paperback version of the classically arranged Roget's thesaurus. Although this 1985 copyright Penguin pocket edition is distributed in the United States, it is prepared in Great Britain for English—not American—readers; it uses British spellings and contains British slang and colloquialisms. Under **vehicle**, for example, words listed include **lorry** but not *flatbed*; under **ingestion** appear **tiffin** and **elevenses**, but not *lunch*. Indeed, the publishers note that "words and phrases current on the other side of the Atlantic are labeled as Americanisms." For American users, the book's usefulness is limited.

As noted in the preface, a paperback thesaurus cannot be as exhaustive as a larger volume; therefore, some terms deemed "rare and obscure" have been omitted. Rearrangement of Roget's sequencing has been undertaken to reflect new priorities in contemporary language and the new fields of knowledge it describes. The editors' goal has been "to cover a comprehensive working vocabulary that takes in all levels of language" and is "sufficiently comprehensive to serve both as a vocabulary builder and as a source of many hours of useful browsing."

II. Format

The pocket-sized volume is alphabetically indexed. The body of its text comprises 882 main topics, consecutively numbered in boldface, grouped according to their meanings. A topic word or phrase is often related synonymically or antonymically to its predecessor. For example, the opening sequence of topic words is **existence**, **nonexistence**, **reality**, **unreality**, **essence**. Under each main topic word and phrase, cross-references (identified by the introductory *See also*, with the topic number in boldface) are followed by paragraphs, one for each part of speech illustrated, listing related words.

When the topic is a concrete term, the paragraphs, according to the preface, "list key words in that semantic area, providing a mini-vocabulary of a subject." For abstract terms, the listings incorporate related words, associations, and figurative and idiomatic usages, with the result that both formal and colloquial equivalents are provided.

Within each paragraph, words with closely related meanings are grouped. The first word in each grouping is italicized, and groups are separated by semicolons. For example, under the topic word **channel** the following paragraph appears:

> **n.** *channel*, conduit, course, canal, waterway; *ditch*, trench, moat, riverbed, gutter, pipeline, aqueduct; *lock*, sluice, floodgate, watergate, weir, barrier; *drain*, gully, overflow, culvert, outfall, waterspout, sewer, downpipe, drainpipe.

However, the main entry for **channel** does not provide an example of its use as a verb or supply a cross-reference to an entry that does contain such an example. The reader must consult the index for further information.

Within the paragraphs, colloquialisms are identified, as are derogatory terms, vulgarisms, and "Americanisms."

The index is a double-column alphabetical listing of words and phrases. Part of speech is identified, and topic numbers refer the reader to the appropriate section within the text.

As in most paperbacks, the print is small, but readability is enhanced by the book's judicious use of white space and boldface type. Pages do not separate easily from the binding, and the book should prove as durable as any paperback of its size.

III. Quality and Currency of Entries

Listings are lengthy, and the editors' goal of reflecting a wide stylistic range of usage is well met. The quality of entries is compromised only by their British slant—for American users.

The thesaurus is up-to-date in its inclusion of terms recently incorporated into the language from such fields as computer science (**CPU**, **disk drive**, **information retrieval**, **machine language**, **word processing**), space technology (**astronaut**, **countdown**, **splashdown**), and contemporary music (**disco**, **new wave**, **punk**). Sexist language has been avoided in some entries (**humankind**, **spaceman/woman**), but not in others (**anchorman**, **chairman**).

IV. Accessibility

As with other thesauruses in the classic format, a user will normally seek a term in the index to be referred to the appropriate section in the main text. Once the reader locates that section, he or she must scan the entire entry to find the desired term. Since some of the paragraphs are lengthy, this can be a frustrating task for a novice to the use of thesauruses.

Accessibility is improved by the inclusion of guide words. On each double-page spread, at the upper right and upper left corners, two guide words appear. These identify the first and last topic entered on the spread. They are printed in boldface block capitals and are preceded by their topic numbers. Two guide words are also provided on each double-page spread within the index.

Minimal instruction in the effective use of the thesaurus is provided. The preface explains the editors' objectives and outlines the volume's format, but there is no explicit guide analogous to that provided, for example, in THE NEW AMERICAN ROGET'S COLLEGIATE THESAURUS IN DICTIONARY FORM. While this omission will not limit the book's accessibility for those familiar with thesaurus use, some users may require a certain amount of guidance, especially if they are unused to classically arranged thesauruses.

V. Summary

The Penguin Pocket Thesaurus is designed to meet the needs of "commuters, crossword addicts, students, journalists, teachers, and all those who work and write on the move." An inexpensive, up-to-date, and compact volume, it probably achieves its goal quite well in Great Britain.

However, despite its currency and convenience, the thesaurus's British slant limits its usefulness, *especially* for those who are not knowledgeable about language use. British spellings would cause them confusion, and they are unlikely to have a need for, or opportunity to use appropriately, many of the British terms and phrases included. In some cases they will be at a loss to substitute appropriate Americanisms. For the college teacher or the librarian seeking an inexpensive, portable thesaurus suitable for the needs of both students and adults, a better choice would be, for example, the comparably priced THE NEW AMERICAN ROGET'S COLLEGE THESAURUS IN DICTIONARY FORM, with its American English focus, its dictionary format, and its guide to thesaurus use.

The Penguin Roget's Thesaurus of English Words and Phrases

Facts at a Glance

Full Title: **The Penguin Roget's Thesaurus of English Words and Phrases**.
Publisher: Penguin Books.
Editor: Susan M. Lloyd.
Edition Reviewed: © 1982; 1985 printing.

Number of Entries: 990.
Number of Pages: 776.
Number of Indexes: 1.
Trim Size: 5″ × 7¾″.
Binding: paperback.

Price: $7.95.
Sold in bookstores and other outlets; also sold to libraries and other educational institutions.
ISBN 0-14-051-155-5.

I. Introduction and Scope

The Penguin Roget's Thesaurus of English Words and Phrases traces its ancestry directly to Peter Mark Roget's original 1852 *Thesaurus of English Words and Phrases* and follows that work's organization.

According to the editor's preface, "In 1952 the copyright passed to the original publishers, now known as Longman. The first Penguin edition appeared in 1953; the second, in 1966, was based by the editor, Robert A. Dutch, on his completely new edition for Longman four years earlier."

The current edition, "completely revised, updated and abridged," was designed to bring the thesaurus up-to-date: to add "the many new words and phrases which had come into circulation over the intervening twenty years as a result of rapid technological change, and the corresponding changes in our lifestyle;" and to delete material that had become outdated or ambiguous. The editor's goal, "to mirror the language and attitudes of our present society," was also met by the inclusion of alternatives to sexist usage. Published in Britain, the work retains British spellings and colloquialisms.

This paperback is an abridgment of the editor's 1982 hardcover edition of Roget's. She notes that she tried to remove wordy and peripheral material and emphasize current over outdated language, general over specific terms. Cross-references in this edition have been checked by computer, and the index is based on a computer listing of the text. The product, "a concise, practical edition which retains all the improvements made to the main edition," is intended for an audience of readers, writers, "word-lovers," and crossword puzzle fans.

II. Format

Like Roget's seminal work, the thesaurus comprises a main text, organized according to an updated version of Roget's classification scheme, and an alphabetical index. The six classes of the taxonomy are "Abstract Relations;" "Space;" "Matter;" "Intellect: the exercise of the mind;" "Volition: the exercise of the will;" and "Emotion, religion and morality." In the double-column main text, each class is divided into sections and subdivided into 990 numbered main entries. This is, according to the editor, "a slight reduction from Roget's original 1,000." Most main entries are usefully grouped in pairs representing the positive and negative aspects of an idea. **Rejoicing**, for example, is followed by **lamentation**; **vanity** by **modesty**.

Main entry words and their numbers are in boldface, as are part-of-speech abbreviations. Entries are subdivided into paragraphs, which are grouped according to part of speech. For example, the entry for **Hatred** comprises three paragraphs of nouns, three of adjectives, and two of verbs. Each paragraph begins with an italicized "keyword," which, according to the editor, "is both the 'key' to the rest of the paragraph, and the 'open sesame' to the whole book, being used to identify the position of other words in the index and cross-references." The keywords are indeed easily seen and useful in locating information throughout the thesaurus. Within the paragraphs, terms are grouped according to meaning or level of diction (formal, colloquial, and so forth). Cross-references are identified by entry numbers and by italicized keywords, enabling the user to locate them quickly without the index.

The index, in four columns, shows alphabetized entries in boldface overhanging the text. Listed below the entry term are italicized keywords followed by entry numbers and part-of-speech abbreviations: A representative index entry appears as follows:

primitive
primal 127 adj.
artist 556 n.
artless 699 adj.

This format is clear and easy to use.

The newsprint-type paper used in the work is smooth and allows some show-through of text; it is also thin and may tear easily as the book ages. The print is clear and readable and use of white space on the pages is generous. Pages do not separate easily from the volume's binding.

III. Quality and Currency of Entries

The entries are extensive, with some numbered main entries comprising several columns. However, the inclusion of British words and senses may prove confusing to some American readers. For example, the first paragraph under **School** contains several terms that may be unfamiliar to some Americans:

> *academy*, institute, institution; conservatoire, ballet school, art s.; academy of dramatic art; charm school, finishing school; college, university, varsity, Open University; redbrick university, Oxbridge; college of further *or* higher education; polytechnic, poly; Academy, Lyceum, Stoa; alma mater, groves of academe.

Further, although words are grouped according to diction level, no usage labels (such as "slang" or "offensive") are provided. Thus, under the entry **Female** in the paragraph headed by the keyword *woman*, the user will find, among others, the terms **feminist**, **women's libber**, **wench**, **crumpet**, and **virago**, with no indications given as to their connotations or appropriate contexts. The absence of discrimination among such synonyms and related terms will be a disadvantage to the less sophisticated user.

The work's currency is strong in its inclusion of both scientific and popular terms recently incorporated into the language. Among these are **floppy disk**, **output**, **sitcom**, **telecommunication**, **teletext**, **space-time continuum**, **spacewoman**, **spaced-out**, and **cybernetics**.

IV. Accessibility

Any thesaurus in the classic thesaurus format, such as this one, will be initially more difficult to use than one in dictionary form such as THE NEW AMERICAN ROGET'S COLLEGE THESAURUS. However, readers who are willing to familiarize themselves with this Roget's will find it easy to use. A brief section titled "How to Use This Book" clearly explains the organization of the text and the use of the index. It is followed by an outline, "Plan of Classification," that provides the user with a helpful overview of the work's structure.

At the top of the main text pages, italicized running heads on left-hand pages show the taxonomic class [695 *Volition* (1)] and, on right-hand pages, the section and head numbers [*Voluntary action* 696]. In the index, each column is headed by a three-letter guide in block capitals, for example:

RAP RAT RAW REA.

Although unusual, these guides make the index extremely useful.

V. Summary

The most valuable feature of *The Penguin Roget's Thesaurus of English Words and Phrases* is its up-to-date vocabulary. However, the work's British focus will present difficulties for the typical American user. This expensive paperback is also not sufficiently sturdy to hold up well to heavy library use. A less expensive American work, such as WEBSTER'S NEW WORLD THESAURUS or THE NEW AMERICAN ROGET'S COLLEGE THESAURUS IN DICTIONARY FORM, might be a better investment for a reference desk or circulating paperback collection.

The Random House Thesaurus: A Dictionary of Synonyms and Antonyms

Facts at a Glance

Full Title: **The Random House Thesaurus: A Dictionary of Synonyms and Antonyms**.
Publisher: Random House.
Editor: Laurence Urdang.
Edition Reviewed: © 1960; 1985 printing.

Number of Entries: 4,500.
Number of Pages: 261.
Trim Size: $2\frac{7}{8}'' \times 5\frac{3}{8}''$.
Binding: paperback with flexible vinyl cover.

Price: $2.95.

Sold in bookstores and office supply stores; also sold to libraries and other educational institutions.
ISBN 0-394-51933-7.

I. Introduction and Scope

The Random House Thesaurus: A Dictionary of Synonyms and Antonyms, published in 1960, is a vest pocket-sized thesaurus in dictionary form. It contains about 4,500 main entries comprising over 80,000 words. The preface claims that "judicious use of this book will more than treble the average person's . . . vocabulary." It also reminds the user that "there is no true synonym for any word in English," that each word has its own distinct set of meanings, and that the use of the word "must always be appropriate to the context in which it appears." The reader is urged to look up unfamiliar synonyms in a good dictionary before using them. Laurence Urdang, an authority on lexicography and author of THE BASIC BOOK OF SYNONYMS AND ANTONYMS, NEW REVISED EDITION, is the editor of this Random House thesaurus. The work serves as a companion to THE RANDOM HOUSE AMERICAN DICTIONARY, NEW REVISED EDITION.

II. Format

Entries are alphabetically arranged, a feature that many users will appreciate. Main entry words are in boldface type overhanging the text. An italicized part-of-speech abbreviation follows, with synonyms listed thereafter. In instances where synonyms are provided for more than one sense of a word, the senses are numbered in boldface and listed in the order of their frequency in usage. Words with more than one part-of-speech application are separated from each other by dashes. Antonyms are provided, as appropriate, at the end of the entry, following the abbreviation *Ant.* There are no sentences to illustrate the application of the words or to demonstrate shades of meaning.

The very small type size makes the entries difficult to read, but the typeface is clear and the white paper permits minimal show-through. The pocket-sized volume has a flexible, washable vinyl cover that enables the reader to open the pages fully. The sturdy binding should stand up well to heavy use.

III. Quality and Currency of Entries

Entries are thorough in their coverage of a wide range of senses and synonyms for many words in standard English. Synonyms are ordered within their lists according to one of two principles, as the preface states:

if the entry word is a 'strong' one, synonyms will be entered in order of decreasing intensity . . . [;] and if 'weak,' in order of increasing strength. Also, informal words have their synonyms given in the order of increasing formality . . . while formal word synonyms go in the opposite direction.

This format will aid users in selecting a synonym with appropriate force or diction level. A representative entry, for **rich**, reads as follows:

1. well-to-do, wealthy, moneyed, opulent, affluent. **2.** abounding, abundant, bounteous, bountiful, fertile, plenteous, plentiful, copious, ample, luxuriant, productive, fruitful, prolific. **3.** valuable, valued, precious, costly, estimable, sumptuous. **4.** dear, expensive, high-priced, elegant. **5.** deep, strong, vivid, bright, gay. **6.** full, mellow, pear-shaped, harmonious, sweet. **7.** fragrant, aromatic.

Ant. poor, impoverished; scarce, barren, sterile; cheap; weak; dull; flat; noisome.

Although the latest printing of this thesaurus occurred in 1985, it was originally published in 1960. The deliberate exclusion of slang from the listings helps to minimize the work's datedness; however, recent popular coinages that have become standard are omitted, as are words that relate to astronautics, artificial intelligence, and other newly developed fields. For example, a word in such common current usage as *statistics* is not found as a main entry. Although the word **data** is listed as a synonym for **information**, it is not given the main entry status its current usage might warrant. This lack of currency could be a drawback for those who wish to be precise in their use of the most contemporary terms.

IV. Accessibility

Although the work's small print impedes accessibility, its alphabetical arrangement enables readers unfamiliar with the more traditional thesaurus format to locate entries easily. Guide words in boldface appear at the top of each double-page spread indicating the first and last words entered on the spread. These, together with the work's flexible cover, enable users to flip quickly to the alphabetic section they are seeking.

V. Summary

The English language is not static; it is fluid. For optimal understanding and use of current language, users require good reference materials with relatively recent publication or revision dates. *The Random House Thesaurus: A Dictionary of Synonyms and Antonyms* was a useful book at its first appearance in 1960, but in the 1980s it is in need of revision and should not be a first choice for purchase. Those in need of a small, concise thesaurus should examine

Urdang's THE BASIC BOOK OF SYNONYMS AND ANTONYMS, NEW REVISED EDITION. Although the latter contains a shorter list of main entries, it is more up-to-date, and it includes illustrative sentences to differentiate synonyms and place them in context.

The Random House Thesaurus: College Edition

Facts at a Glance

Full Title: **The Random House Thesaurus: College Edition**.
Publisher: Random House.
Editors: Jess Stein and Stuart Berg Flexner.
Edition Reviewed: © 1984.

Number of Entries: 11,000.
Number of Pages: 812.
Trim Size: 6⁹⁄₁₆″ × 9⁵⁄₈″.
Binding: cloth.

Price: $14.95.
Sold in bookstores and other outlets; also sold to libraries and other educational institutions.
ISBN 0-394-52949-9.

I. Introduction and Scope

Based on the READER'S DIGEST FAMILY WORD FINDER (© 1975), *The Random House Thesaurus: College Edition* contains 11,000 main entries and is intended for adult as well as college audiences. Although the editors suggest that THE RANDOM HOUSE COLLEGE DICTIONARY would be a useful companion to the thesaurus, only a larger unabridged dictionary is comprehensive enough to include the many thousands of synonyms and antonyms listed under this thesaurus's main entries. The editors rightly point out that the thesaurus is most effective when users "have a particular meaning or thought in mind but do not know, or cannot recall, the most effective word to express it."

II. Format

The thesaurus is arranged alphabetically with main entries in bold type. The book is bound sturdily and clearly printed on good quality ivory stock. The narrow margins are wide enough to prevent eyestrain during typical brief consultations. Some readers, however, might find the print too small if they used this book for a prolonged period.

III. Quality and Currency of Entries

Entries are thorough and well organized. Following the main entry is a standard abbreviation for the part of speech; if a word is given with more than one part of speech, each application is listed separately. When a word has more than one meaning, each is given a boldface number and a separate list of synonyms. Each meaning is introduced by at least one illustrative sentence. For example, "she gets bad grades" is one of the sample sentences for **bad** (in the sense of **not good**, **poor**, **inferior**, **wretched**), while "lying is a bad thing to do" is the sentence illustrating such words as **immoral**, **unethical**, **sinful**, **evil** and **wicked**.

Another helpful feature is that the most common synonyms and those closest in meaning (given the vagaries of usage, however, these aren't always the same) come first in the list of synonyms, so that **baneful**—quite appropriately, given its rather restricted sense—is the last in a long list of synonyms for **bad** in the sense of **not good**. (**Heinous**, curiously, does not appear as a synonym in this thesaurus under any of the 12 senses of **bad**, but it is a separate main entry.)

Italicized labels are another useful feature: users are informed, for example, that **jam** in the sense of **mess** or **trouble** is an *informal* sense of a word that can also mean **crowd**, **tie-up**, **throng**, and other related synonyms. Sometimes the editors warn the reader to be very selective about highly specialized synonyms, which they label with the word *variously*, so that the reader does not assume, for instance, that **howitzer** is a general synonym for **gun**. Although most people use thesauruses for synonyms, a list of antonyms follows many of the synonym entries. Where it is difficult or impossible to assign an antonym, as with **Holy Ghost**, none is provided. Nor do the editors enter into semantic debate about the nature of antonymy, so that, for instance, **hate** is provided as an antonym for **love**, while the less obvious but still quite defensible word, *indifference*, is not.

One does not expect a necessarily selective thesaurus with only 11,000 main entries to include a great many new and trendy words, although the editors do regard the word **trendy** as popular enough to deserve a main entry. *Pop*, on the other hand, as an adjective meaning popular is not listed either as a main entry or as a synonym for **trendy**. One might assume that the editors are conservative about admitting new words: we find **parent** as a noun, but not in its newer sense as a verb; **program** is here in the sense of schedule but not in the sense of programming a computer; **psyche** is here as a noun meaning soul or mind, but not as a verb meaning to anticipate or analyze, a currently familiar sense. Many other newer words and meanings are also excluded, although some old-fashioned words (**balderdash** and **poppycock**) are entered. However, without additional descriptive information, some users might misapply these older terms. It seems fair to conclude that some of the most solidly established new words

The Random House Thesaurus: College Edition

❶ Main entry words are set in
   boldface type

❷ Antonym lists, introduced by the
   boldface italic abbreviation *Ant.*,
   are numbered to correspond with
   the numbered groups of
   synonyms above

❸ Synonyms are grouped by shades
   of meaning, each preceded by
   a boldface numeral

❹ An italicized example sentence
   introduces each group of
   synonyms

❶ **immodest** *adj.* **1** *Clothing once thought immodest is acceptable today:* indecorous, overly revealing, indecent, indelicate, shameless; lewd, loose, suggestive, indecent, risqué; coarse, gross, wanton, unchaste. **2** *The actor made immodest claims about his talent:* vain, exaggerated, inflated, pompous, conceited, high-sounding, brazen, self-centered, self-aggrandizing, braggart, bombastic, boastful, pretentious, peacockish.

❷ **Ant. 1** modest, decent, delicate, decorous, pure, chaste. **2** modest, humble, genteel, restrained.

(including slang) have been recognized as synonyms here, although relatively few of them are included as main entries.

IV. Accessibility

Alternative spellings of words are indicated in boldface at the beginning of the main entry word; for example, "**jail** Also British **gaol**." Each page with two columns of text has a boldface guide word indicating the first word at the top of the left column and the last word at the bottom of the right column.

V. Summary

Because of its alphabetical arrangement, many users will find *The Random House Thesaurus* more accessible than its most familiar competitor, ROGET'S INTERNATIONAL THESAURUS (1984). The most obvious difference between the two is that ROGET'S synoptic arrangement of words into categories of related meanings requires the reader to look up a word in the index before lists of synonyms can be found. ROGET'S includes more words and phrases, as well as numbered categories that clearly distinguish separate senses of a word, but *The Random House Thesaurus* uses sentence examples that may be of real help to some readers. Although ROGET'S offers a greater number of choices, many college and community libraries will still want to offer their readers a choice, especially because many users may find *The Random House Thesaurus* quicker and easier to use.

The Right Word II: A Concise Thesaurus

Facts at a Glance

Full Title: **The Right Word II: A Concise Thesaurus**.
Publisher: Houghton Mifflin.

Editor: Mark H. Boyer, Project Editor.
Edition Reviewed: © 1983.

Number of Entries: approximately 647.
Number of Pages: 288.
Number of Indexes: 1.
Trim Size: 4" × 5½".
Binding: laminated paper over boards.

Price: $3.95.
Sold in bookstores; also sold to libraries and other educational institutions.
ISBN 0-395-34808-0.

I. Introduction and Scope

The Right Word II: A Concise Thesaurus is based on Houghton Mifflin's *American Heritage Dictionary* and replaces the publisher's *The Right Word* (© 1978). That work's space-consuming cross-references have been replaced by an index in *The Right Word II*; contents are also substantially expanded in all categories.

According to the preface, this unique work differs from a traditional thesaurus "that prints exhaustive undifferentiated synonym lists." Instead, it "provides synonym analyses on the most important meanings and ideas and discriminates among many of the most frequently used—and misused—words in the English language." The work especially serves the needs of writers, whether they are seeking a synonym to avoid repetition of a given term or looking for the "precise word to express a specific thought."

In addition to its alphabetized (and indexed) listing of words for which synonyms are provided or differentiated, the work contains four special features. The first, a prefatory article titled "How to Use This Book," defines the term *synonym*, describes the work's two kinds of synonym analyses—

The Right Word II

❶ Synonym paragraphs discriminate terms

❷ Core-meaning studies summarize shared meaning of synonyms and give examples of usage

❸ Usage labels are italicized

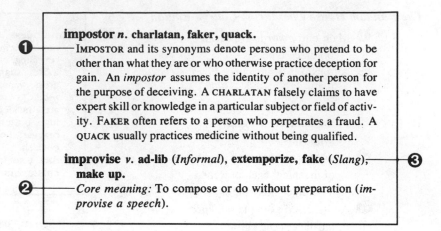

impostor *n.* **charlatan, faker, quack.**
IMPOSTOR and its synonyms denote persons who pretend to be other than what they are or who otherwise practice deception for gain. An *impostor* assumes the identity of another person for the purpose of deceiving. A CHARLATAN falsely claims to have expert skill or knowledge in a particular subject or field of activity. FAKER often refers to a person who perpetrates a fraud. A QUACK usually practices medicine without being qualified.

improvise *v.* **ad-lib** (*Informal*)**, extemporize, fake** (*Slang*)**, make up.**
Core meaning: To compose or do without preparation (*improvise a speech*).

"relatively long paragraphs that discuss the synonyms in detail and short studies that focus on one central meaning of a number of common terms"—and discusses the use of the index.

At the end of the volume appear three supplemental lists. "Collective Nouns" includes nouns applied to groups of animals or people. Seven basic terms appear at the beginning of the list; the first, for example, is

brood—young offspring under the care of the same mother; especially, birds (fowl) or fish having a common birth. Or the word can be applied to the children of a single family.

Also listed are more specialized terms, such as

shrewdness—a company of apes.

There follows a list of collateral adjectives; that is, adjectives that do not resemble the nouns to which they correspond. All nouns are listed alphabetically by category and followed by their collateral adjectives: for example, **laugh, risible.** Categories reflected are zoology, points of the compass, parts of the body, time, seasons, celestial bodies, family, and general. Finally, a section titled "Sciences and Technology" lists major sciences and technological specialties, with field of study and activities indicated for each.

II. Format

Within the body of the text, entry words and phrases are in bold type and overhang the text. Boldface type is also used for synonyms—which are listed alphabetically, following part-of-speech abbreviation, after the entry word. Antonyms are listed at the end of the entry. Small capitals are used for the main entry word and its synonyms when these recur within a synonym analysis; illustrative phrases and sentences are italicized. Typefaces are clear and easy to read, and their variety enables the user to locate information quickly.

The index, in double-column format, also uses type styles to advantage. Entries for which synonym analyses are given appear in small capitals; synonyms appear in roman type with their italicized main entry words following a colon. A typical sequence is:

PASSION
passive: *submissive*
paste: *hit*
PATIENT

Adequate margins and white space add to the work's readability, both in the main text and in the special features. The good-quality, off-white paper permits minimal show-through. The book is sturdily bound and will hold up well to heavy use.

III. Quality and Currency of Entries

Clarity and precision characterize the work's synonym analyses. Two kinds of entries, both frequently including antonyms at the end, appear in the main text. The shorter synonym analyses point out the common denominator of meaning among a group of terms. For example, the user seeking an alternative to the word *provoke* would find the following entry useful:

Provoke *v.* **arouse, excite, goad, impel, incite, inflame, kindle, motivate, move, rouse, spur, stimulate.** *Core meaning*: To stir to action or feeling (*carelessness that provoked anger*).

The second type of entry, the discriminated synonym analyses, distinguishes among synonyms in terms of their appropriate contexts of usage:

hard *adj.* **firm.** Hard and **firm** are often used interchangeably when they refer to what is resistant to pressure (*a hard surface; firm ground*). *Hard* can also suggest that something is physically toughened (*a hard palm with calluses*), while *firm* describes what shows the tone and resiliency characteristic of healthy tissue (*firm muscles*).

Also distinguished, when appropriate, are the varying connotations of the synonyms under discussion:

> Both COWARDLY and CRAVEN suggest a shameful show of fear, but *craven* implies an especially high degree of cowardice: *a cowardly lion; a craven liar.*

It is not the purpose of *The Right Word II* to provide a comprehensive overview of the English language. Therefore, its omission of terms from the field of computer science, for example, does not reflect negatively upon it, since these terms seldom have any significant range of synonyms. The work is current, however, in its careful reflection of the way words are used and distinguished in American English today, and slang and informal usage are provided as appropriate. For example, synonyms listed for **hit** include

> **bash** (*Informal*), **belt** (*Informal*), **clip** (*Informal*), **clobber** (*Slang*), **paste** (*Slang*), **slam**, **slug** (*Slang*), **smack**, **smash**, **sock** (*Slang*), **strike**, **swat**, **wallop** (*Informal*), **whack**.

Although a writer may not find in *The Right Word II* the full range of synonyms available in larger thesauruses, this work's careful groupings and distinctions make it valuable to a wide range of users. Entries are clearly and simply stated, and subtle shades of meanings are elucidated so that appropriate word choices are easily made. Its conciseness and clarity make it particularly useful to non-native speakers and novice writers, who might be overwhelmed by a larger work lacking discriminated synonym analyses.

IV. Accessibility

Entries are easily located with the aid of boldface guide words. Two are located at the top of each double-page spread, indicating the first and last entries on the spread. The compact size of the volume makes it especially easy for the user to flip through quickly in search of an entry that has been located in the index. A contents listing at the front of the volume ensures that the work's special features will not be overlooked.

V. Summary

The Right Word II: A Concise Thesaurus is a valuable work whose only comparable competitor is the MERRIAM-WEBSTER COMPACT DICTIONARY OF SYNONYMS. While another thesaurus, THE NEW AMERICAN ROGET'S COLLEGE THESAURUS IN DICTIONARY FORM, is similar in its accessibility to users of a wide range of age and experience, *The Right Word II* is entirely different in focus. Rather than emphasizing quantity in the numbers of entries and undifferen-

tiated synonyms, the work both provides synonyms for its selected entries and makes careful distinctions among a great number of them. This concise thesaurus can be easily used and is suitable for reference use whenever comprehensive coverage is not required. It is recommended for public library collections and may be especially helpful in community and junior college libraries. It is also suitable for general home use and will be particularly useful in households where English is a second language.

Roget's International Thesaurus: Fourth Edition

Facts at a Glance

Full Title: **Roget's International Thesaurus: Fourth Edition.**
Publisher: Harper & Row.
Editors: Peter Mark Roget, revised by Robert L. Chapman.
Edition Reviewed: © 1977; 4th edition, 1984.

Number of Entries: 256,000.
Number of Pages: 1,318.
Number of Indexes: 1.
Trim Size: 8½" × 11".
Binding: cloth; thumb-indexed cloth; paperback.

Price: $11.45 (cloth); $12.45 (thumb-indexed); $9.95 (paperback).
Sold in bookstores and by direct mail; also sold to libraries and other educational institutions.
ISBN 0-690-00010-3 (cloth);
ISBN 0-690-00011-1 (thumb-indexed);
ISBN 0-06-091169-7 (paperback).

I. Introduction and Scope

The latest edition of *Roget's International Thesaurus*, this 1984 work contains approximately 256,000 words and phrases. It follows the format developed by Peter Mark Roget in his original 1852 thesaurus: entries are grouped in categories according to their meanings, and specific words are located through a comprehensive index.

The original Roget's thesaurus went through 29 editions and printings before being acquired by Thomas Y. Crowell, who published his editions in 1886 and 1911. The first *Roget's International Thesaurus*, which appeared in 1922, was the product of revisions by Crowell's son, T. Irving Crowell. His grandson, Robert L. Crowell, produced a second edition in 1946 and a third edition in 1962. In the course of these several revisions, many expansions

Roget's International Thesaurus

❶ Both main entries and subentries are numbered

❷ Cross-references refer to main entries or subentries by number

❸ Main entry words are set in boldface capitals

❹ Words in boldface type are those which are most commonly used

❺ Usage labels are enclosed in brackets

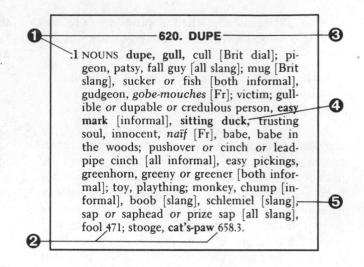

inconstant 141.7
ugly 899.8
unordered 62.12
vague 514.18

were made: Americanisms, foreign expressions, quotations, slang, and vernacular expressions were added. Moreover, the work was reformatted to make it easier to use. Harper & Row is its current publisher.

The fourth edition, revised by Professor Chapman, is still further improved and modernized. Combining forms, such as prefixes and suffixes, have been added, as have many words and phrases from the 1970s. This work is the definitive unabridged English-language thesaurus. According to its publishers, it contains at least 100,000 more words and phrases than any other thesaurus of the English language. Chapman states in his foreword that this edition was "published in the hope and conviction that it will be more useful than its predecessors" for "writers of all sorts."

The revision was based on the "newest and best" general dictionaries of English and of specialized subjects, new specialized encyclopedias, and reverse-indexes of English. New words and phrases were "carefully collected for inclusion," and the "broadest possible range of levels and styles . . . has been encompassed." Computer technology was applied to ensure the accuracy of the index.

II. Format

Both index and the main text are carefully formatted for optimal clarity and use. The thesaurus's alphabetical index is printed in a four-column format. Boldface entry words overhang listings of secondary entries that reflect various senses of the entry word. Each secondary entry is followed by numbers referring the user to the appropriate category and paragraph within that category. For example, looking up **shapeless** in the index, the reader finds the following:

shapeless
 abnormal 85.9
 formless 247.4

If the reader selects "formless" as the synonym closest to the meaning desired, he or she will then turn to the main text, category 247 (**FORMLESSNESS**), where the fourth paragraph enters **formless** with its synonyms. This precise decimal finding system helps readers quickly locate appropriate words and phrases. Lest the system's unfamiliarity render it confusing, an introductory guide, "How to Use This Book," clearly explains the word-finding process and provides illustrative excerpts from both the index and the main text.

The main text is organized into eight broad conceptual classes: **Abstract Relations**, **Space**, **Physics**, **Matter**, **Sensation**, **Intellect**, **Volition**, and **Affections**. These are divided and subdivided—according to an outline reproduced at the front of the volume for quick reference—to produce 1,042 numbered paragraph entries. Main entry words are printed in boldface block capitals and are grouped according to their relationships with one another. For example, the sequence of categories **HEARING**, **DEAFNESS**, **SOUND**, **SILENCE**, **FAINTNESS OF SOUND**, **LOUDNESS** is "a procession of similar, contrasting, and opposing concepts, all dealing with the perception and quality of sounds." Each numbered entry is subdivided by decimal numbered sections (.1, .2, .3, and so on), that are grouped by part of speech. Terms of greatest frequency within each sense group are in boldface for quick location. Ordering within entries is determined by the listed words' relationship to the main entry word: terms closest in meaning are listed first. Semicolons set off each subsequent cluster of terms, with each semicolon signaling a slight change in meaning or usage. Bracketed labels identify foreign words, slang terms, informal usage, and technical language. Numbered cross-references lead readers to related categories, eliminating additional searches in the index.

The paper is white and permits minimal showthrough. The print is clear and easily read, and ample white space further enhances readability. The book is sturdily bound and will hold up well to heavy use.

III. Quality and Currency of Entries

Entries are thorough and detailed. Their principles of ordering and bracketed labels facilitate the reader's choice of an appropriate word, although the editor stresses in the introductory guide that the work should be used in conjunction with a dictionary. Quotations that themselves serve as synonyms enhance the work's range and usefulness. For example, under **patriotism** is listed " 'the last refuge of a scoundrel' [Samuel Johnson]." Some entries are also valuably embellished with lists (often extensive) of specific terms related to the more general entry term. For example, under the main entry **SPACE TRAVEL** the subsection beginning with the term **spacecraft** includes a list of 76 names of spacecraft, including both American and Soviet vessels. Under **airplane parts** appears a list of over 200 items. These additions make the thesaurus a more comprehensive reference work without compromising its primary function as a repository of synonyms and related words.

As its listing of **spacecraft** suggests, the work has been carefully and successfully updated. Included, for example, are many terms relating to space travel (**reaction propulsion**, **velocity peak**), telecommunications (**information theory**, **quadruplex telegraphy**), computer systems and related technologies (**digital graph plotter**, **phase discriminator**), and nuclear energy (**fusion reaction**, **reactor pile**).

IV. Accessibility

Although the classic thesaurus format of *Roget's International Thesaurus* requires a two-step process, the decimal finding system (with two decimal guide numbers at the top of each main text page), and alphabetical index (with two boldface guide words on each index page) facilitates word finding. Readers who find a dictionary format more immediately accessible, will easily learn to appreciate this system's comprehensive groupings of related words. For the few abbreviations that are used, a key is provided at the back of the volume.

V. Summary

In comparison with WEBSTER'S COLLEGIATE THESAURUS and ROGET'S II: THE NEW THESAURUS, *Roget's International Thesaurus* contains more main entries and more synonyms and is widely considered to be the authoritative thesaurus of the English language. Its comprehensiveness, wide usefulness, and reasonable price warrant its inclusion in the general reference collection of all public and college libraries; it is also an excellent choice for individuals and families for their home collections. However, those readers who prefer an alphabetical arrangement of entries might select either WEBSTER'S COLLEGIATE or ROGET'S II instead of *Roget's International Thesaurus*.

Roget's Pocket Thesaurus

Facts at a Glance

Full Title: **Roget's Pocket Thesaurus**.
Publisher: Pocket Books.
Editors: C. O. Sylvester Mawson and Katherine Aldrich Whiting.
Edition Reviewed: © 1946; 124th printing.

Number of Entries: 1,000.
Number of Pages: 479.
Number of Indexes: 1.
Trim size: $4\frac{1}{4}'' \times 6\frac{11}{16}''$.
Binding: paperback.

Price: $3.95.
Sold in bookstores and other outlets; also sold to libraries and other educational institutions.
ISBN 0-671-53090-9.

I. Introduction and Scope

Roget's Pocket Thesaurus, which appeared in 1946, is an abridged version of ROGET'S INTERNATIONAL THESAURUS, first published in 1922 by Thomas Y. Crowell Company, which issued a second edition in 1942. Both works, according to a note at the end of the volume, "derive their extraordinary usefulness from the fidelity with which they adhere to Peter Mark Roget's original concept." Both thesauruses are expansions of Roget's work, with added divisions of knowledge, American colloquialisms, and slang. There is no indication, however, of the principles by which this abridgment was prepared, nor is there any indication that it has been updated since its original appearance in the mid-1940s.

The work begins with a brief, but still engaging introduction, written many years ago by the renowned literary critic I. A. Richards, describing the purpose and value of Roget's *Thesaurus* and cautioning against its misuse. Also included at the front of the volume are a list of abbreviations used in the work; a brief guide, "How to Use the Book"; an outline "Plan of Classification"; and a "Tabular Synopsis of Categories."

Following the thesaurus and its index are two additional special features. A 16-page alphabetized listing of "Foreign Words and Phrases" includes French, German, Italian, and Latin entries. Abbreviations indicating their language are given, and the entries are defined. The foreign words and phrases are not cross-referenced to entries in the thesaurus. Finally, the book includes a 23-page alphabetized list of "Abbreviations Used in Writing and Printing." Useful common abbreviations are clarified, as are abbreviations for, among other categories, associations, titles, languages, and countries.

II. Format

The volume is organized in classical thesaurus format. Large conceptual classes, such as "Abstract Relations" and "Space," are subdivided into numbered, titled sections. For example:

CLASS VI
Words Relating to the SENTIENT AND MORAL
POWERS
I. AFFECTIONS IN GENERAL

820. AFFECTIONS. . . .
821. FEELING. . . .
822. SENSITIVENESS. . . .
823. INSENSITIVENESS. . . .
824. EXCITEMENT. . . .
825. [Excess of Sensitiveness] EXCITABILITY. . . .
826. INEXCITABILITY. . . .
II. PERSONAL AFFECTIONS[1]. . . .

Within these sections, boldface arabic numbers demarcate main entry words printed in bold capitals. Within entries, synonyms and related words are grouped according to part of speech, with the first word in each category in bold type for easier location. Italicized words and phrases in parentheses are provided occasionally to refer users to other lists, which they must locate through the index. Colloquialisms, slang, and foreign language words and phrases are identified with bracketed italicized abbreviations. Occasionally, a bracketed italicized phrase is used to clarify a specialized usage; for example, under **merchant**, the term **bull** is followed by: [*Stock Exchange*].

The index, which is printed in three columns, shows main entry words in bold capital letters. Other index entries are in boldface lowercase letters, followed by part-of-speech abbreviations, used to distinguish multiple uses of a word, and, in many cases, a listing of italicized related words. Each entry or secondary entry is followed by a number referring to the section of the vocabulary where that word can be found. Section numbers are in bold type when the indexed word is a main entry or a secondary entry in boldface.

The type size is generally adequate; however, both within the introductory guide and within the thesaurus, some sections appear in a significantly smaller typeface. There is no clear rationale for this, and these sections are hard to read. Minimal use of white space also makes the work more difficult to read. Paper is of customary paperback quality, and the pages do not separate easily from the spine, so the work should hold up well to repeated use.

III. Quality and Currency of Entries

Entries are thorough and detailed in their presentations of semantic families. Under the main entry **drama** (noun), for example, a typical secondary entry reads as follows:

> **play**, drama, piece, tragedy, comedy, opera, vaudeville, curtain raiser, interlude, afterpiece, farce, extravaganza, harlequinade, pantomime, burlesque, ballet, spectacle, masque, melodrama; comedy of manners; charade, mystery, miracle play, morality play.

Separate secondary entries are given for **act**, **performance**, **theater**, **cast**, **actor**, **buffoon**, **company**, **dramatist**, and **audience**.

On the other hand, the work is markedly dated. No entries are provided for words related to astronautics or computer science. Slang and colloquialisms are frequently outdated. For example, the entry for **fool** (noun) begins with the following listing:

> idiot, tomfool, wiseacre, simpleton, Simple Simon; donkey, ass, owl, goose, dolt, booby, noodle, imbecile, nincompoop [*colloq.*], oaf, lout, blockhead, bonehead [*slang*], calf [*colloq.*], colt, numbskull [*colloq.*], clod, clodhopper; soft or softy [*colloq. or slang*], mooncalf, saphead [*slang*], gawk, rube [*slang*].

Not only are many of these terms no longer current in standard, colloquial, or slang usage, but others—such as *jerk*, *turkey*, and *nerd*—are excluded. Under **place of amusement**, the dated **moving-picture theater** is listed, with the now-standard **movies** listed as a colloquialism. The book appears not to have been updated since its original appearance; and its lack of currency will limit its usefulness.

IV. Accessibility

Accessibility is enhanced by the inclusion of page numbers, section numbers, and categories and subcategories in the running heads of the vocabulary. An example for a double-page spread is:

Left-hand page
| 269a–272 | SPACE | 76 |

Right-hand page
| 77 | MOTION | 272–274 |

Within the index, boldface guide words in capital letters reflect the first and last entries on each spread. A table of contents helpfully lists all special features:

but its placement, after the introduction rather than at the beginning of the volume, may result in its being overlooked.

The index is the primary means of access to the information in the volume. While it is not unduly difficult to use, the explanation provided in the introductory guide may hinder more than it helps the user, and many readers would benefit from a clearer explanation.

V. Summary

Although *Roget's Pocket Thesaurus* is a wide-ranging and detailed reference work—especially for a paperback—it is more than 40 years out of date. Other pocket works, such as THE NEW AMERICAN ROGET'S COLLEGE THESAURUS IN DICTIONARY FORM, provide more up-to-date listings and a more readable format. On the other hand, the *Roget's Pocket Thesaurus* has features that cannot be found in comparable works; for example, the thorough outlines clarifying its organization. Unfortunately, these do not compensate for its 1940s vocabulary. Thus, while this work will be useful for some readers, libraries will need to supplement it with more current paperback thesauruses.

Roget's II: The New Thesaurus

Facts at a Glance

Full Title: **Roget's II: The New Thesaurus**.
Publisher: Houghton Mifflin Company.
Editors: Fernando de Mello Vianna, Editorial Director, and Anne D. Steinhardt, Supervising Editor.
Edition Reviewed: © 1980.

Number of Words: 250,000.
Number of Pages: 1,088.
Trim Size: 6¾" × 9⁹/₁₆".
Binding: cloth.

Price: $11.95.
Sold in bookstores and other outlets; also sold to libraries and other educational institutions.
ISBN 0-395-29605-6.

I. Introduction and Scope

Roget's II: The New Thesaurus, published in 1980, represents a departure from traditional thesaurus presentation, providing not only synonyms, but also definitions and illustrative examples. According to its preface, this work "has been carefully prepared to provide rapid access to synonyms, which are grouped by precise meanings, facilitating the choice of appropriate words to express thoughts." The reader is thus spared from having to cope with cumbersome indexes and the indiscriminate grouping of words with vaguely related meanings.

Arranged alphabetically, *Roget's II* contains 250,000 terms. It is intended to function as "a source of appropriate words to express thoughts or ideas, guiding the user away from the common pitfalls of selecting an unsuitable word." Definitions obviate the need to use a dictionary; usage labels identify specialized and controversial synonyms. Excluded, "for reasons of clarity and accuracy," according to the editors, are related words, antonyms, and contrasting words. This may well make the work more immediately useful, but it also limits its range.

The preparation of this volume involved five years of research. Independent lexicographers aided the publisher's permanent lexicographic staff, who were also responsible for compiling the highly regarded American Heritage dictionaries. Computer technology was applied to ensure the work's accuracy.

II. Format

In a double-column format, the thesaurus presents five kinds of entries, all introduced by boldface main entry words: (1) main entries with synonym lists; (2) indented subentries in smaller type that show words closely related to or derived from the main entry word; (3) secondary entries that refer the user to main-entry lists; (4) cross-references directing the user from secondary to primary variant spellings: as well as (5) cross-references from secondary entries to synonymized subentries.

Entries are listed alphabetically. In the left-hand column, each main entry word is identified by an italicized part-of-speech label. It is followed by a definition and, often, an italicized sentence or phrase using the word in context. Entries for words with multiple meanings list numbered definitions and, in many instances, multiple illustrative sentences or phrases. In the right-hand column appear the synonyms, each alphabetized group preceded by the boldface italicized abbreviation *Syns*. When necessary, synonyms are identified with temporal labels (*Archaic*, *Obsolete*) usage labels (*Informal*, *Slang*, *Poetic*), dialect labels (*Regional*, *Chiefly Regional*), language labels (*French*, *British*), field labels (*Law*, *Motion Pictures*, and *T.V.*), or status labels (*Rare*). It should be noted that *Roget's II* is fairly liberal in its application of labels. Idioms, when applicable, are listed after the synonyms. A representative entry shows the following definition in the left-hand column:

Roget's II: The New Thesaurus

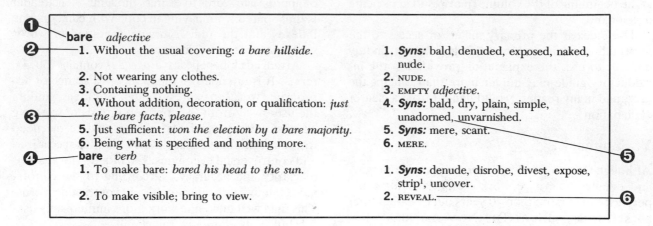

❶ Main entries are set in boldface type

❷ Left column gives numbered senses of the main entry for which synonyms will be listed under the corresponding numbers in the right column

❸ Examples of usage are italicized

❹ Related words are listed as boldface subentries

❺ Synonyms are listed after the boldface italic abbreviation *Syns*.

❻ Cross-references are set in small capitals

destroy *verb*
   1. To cause the complete ruin or wreckage of: *paintings destroyed by fire; drugs that destroyed her health; news that destroyed his hopes.*

Opposite the definition, in the right-hand column, appear the synonyms:

   1. *Syns*: demolish, destruct, dynamite, finish, ruin, ruinate (*Regional*), shatter, sink, smash, total, torpedo, undo, wrack, wreck.—*Idiom* put the kibosh on.

Secondary entries contain main entry words, italicized part-of-speech labels, definition(s), and cross-references to main entries. Cross-references to subentries and to variant spellings are identified by the word SEE.

   aeon *noun*   SEE **eon.**

Cross-references to main entries are printed in small capitals:

   ghoul *noun*   FIEND.
      A perversely bad, cruel, or wicked person.

Turning to **FIEND**, the user would find it listed as a main entry with seven synonyms—**archfiend, beast, ghoul, monster, ogre, tiger, vampire**—and the synonymous idiom **devil incarnate.**
   The work's white paper permits some show-through but not enough to impede readability. Print is clear and adequate in size; white space is used advanta-

geously. The sturdily bound volume will hold up well to heavy use.

III. Quality and Currency of Entries

Definitions are clearly and concisely written, and multiple senses receive appropriate coverage. Illustrative sentences and phrases complement definitions usefully. For example, the entry for **humanitarian** includes the following:

   1. Concerned with human welfare and the alleviation of suffering: *The governor spared the prisoner out of humanitarian considerations.*
   2. Characterized by kindness and concern for others.

The separate listing of synonyms for each sense of the word helps to ensure that users will select a denotatively valid synonym, and the many restrictive labels provided facilitate the selection of a word with the appropriate connotative value.
   The inclusion of slang and informal language brings currency to the work. **Hang around**, for example, is offered as an informal synonym for **frequent; freebie** appears as a main entry. Excluded are many contemporary terms such as *anchorperson, computer, ecology, meltdown, nuclear, program* (in its computer science application), *spacecraft,* and *telecommunications,* although such terms do not have a significant range of synonyms. Although this work falls short of ROGET'S INTERNATIONAL THESAURUS, FOURTH EDITION, which includes all these words,

most readers will find *Roget's II* sufficiently comprehensive to meet a majority of their needs.

IV. Accessibility

An introductory guide, "How to Use This Book," makes good use of illustrative excerpts and examples. A clearly labeled sample page on the back of the dust jacket also provides useful information. Users who do not read the introductory guide may not readily recognize cross-references that are not introduced with SEE. However, this is not a major flaw, since its other features make the thesaurus easy to use without formal instruction.

Boldface guide words at the top of each page identify the first entry on the left-hand page and the last on the right-hand page. A thumb index, with shiny gold-on-blue letter tabs, makes the location of alphabet sections easy. The few abbreviations used in the work are explained in the introductory guide. Variant spellings are easily located through the cross-referencing system.

V. Summary

Roget's II: The New Thesaurus would be a good addition to the college or public library reference collection. Lacking the comprehensiveness and currency of ROGET'S INTERNATIONAL THESAURUS, FOURTH EDITION, it will not replace this standard. Further, users may be disappointed to discover that, unlike most thesauruses, *Roget's II* does not include antonyms. However, its alphabetical arrangement, dictionary-style definitions with illustrative sentences and phrases, and its easily read double-column format make it accessible to a wide variety of readers.

Roget's University Thesaurus

Facts at a Glance

Full Title: **Roget's University Thesaurus.**
Publisher: Barnes & Noble.
Editor: C. O. Sylvester Mawson.
Edition Reviewed: © 1963; 1986 printing.

Number of Entries: 80,000.
Number of Pages: 741.
Number of Indexes: 1.
Trim Size: 5⅛" × 8".
Binding: paperback.

Price: $8.95.
Sold in bookstores and other outlets; also sold to libraries.
ISBN 0-06-46537-6.

I. Introduction and Scope

The date for this paperback volume appears as 1963 on the copyright page which also bears the statement: "This work was originally published under the title *Roget's International Thesaurus of English Words and Phrases.*" For the latest hardcover edition of that title, see the complete review for ROGET'S INTERNATIONAL THESAURUS, FOURTH EDITION in this guide. ROGET'S INTERNATIONAL, however, appears in a different format.

The *University Thesaurus* has somewhat less than one third the number of entries in the hardcover edition. Aside from having a somewhat different form and content, the entries in the paperback volume also have been configured so that an antonym, instead of following the original key word, now appears side by side in the adjoining column. This ingenious arrangement results in an unorthodox page design that includes rules to divide and limit entries—both one-column entries and entries (without opposite meanings) that run across the entire page.

This system is logical and useful, but upon first opening the book, the reader may be confused. The undated preface by C. O. Sylvester Mawson is not particularly helpful in explaining the layout, although the page of instructions entitled "How to Use the Book" includes the fact that antonyms appear in parallel columns, but not the use of rules. A fuller description of the system would have been a distinct aid to the reader.

Aside from the inclusion of P. M. Roget's "Preface to the First Edition (1852)," the frontmatter in the two editions differs. There is no mention in the *University Thesaurus* of its being an abridgment or any explanation of its choice of entries.

A different page design and the inclusion of more current words distinguish ROGET'S INTERNATIONAL from the *University Thesaurus*. Both have an index guiding the reader to synonyms arranged in the first section of the book by categories. This section carries paragraph numbers at the top of each page, and as an added advantage, in this paperback edition, the title of the category at the top of the left-hand page and the subdivision of the category at the top of the right-hand page.

Although the cover states that this is the "largest true thesaurus available in a paperback edition . . . invaluable as ever to all writers and speakers," most readers and all libraries would be better served by the more recent ROGET'S INTERNATIONAL THESAURUS, FOURTH EDITION.

Roget's University Thesaurus

1 Synonyms and antonyms are listed in parallel columns

2 Synonym and antonym main entry words are numbered and set in boldface type

3 Subentries are set in small capitals

4 Subentries are grouped by parts of speech, which are indicated by boldface abbreviations

5 Dashes indicate repetition of a common term

6 Cross-references to other main entry words are italicized and enclosed in parentheses

7 Numbers indicate cross-references to other main entry words

8 Usage labels are italicized and enclosed in brackets

9 The abbreviation *&c.* followed by a part of speech indicates that synonyms of the same part of speech may be used to form words similar to the preceding term

10 Bracketed italic abbreviations identify foreign words and phrases

Webster's Collegiate Thesaurus

Facts at a Glance

Full Title: **Webster's Collegiate Thesaurus**.
Publisher: Merriam-Webster.
Editor: Mairé Weir Kay.
Edition Reviewed: © 1976.

Number of Entries: 23,000.
Number of Pages: 976.
Trim Size: 6½″ × 9½″.
Binding: cloth.

Price: $12.95 (cloth); $13.95 (deluxe).
Sold in bookstores and other outlets; also sold to libraries and other educational institutions.
ISBN 0-87779-069-8 (cloth);
ISBN 0-8779-070-1 (deluxe).

I. Introduction and Scope

Webster's Collegiate Thesaurus was first published in 1976. The material in the book was drawn primarily from WEBSTER'S THIRD NEW INTERNATIONAL DICTIONARY, and the editors also consulted other thesauruses, *Webster's New Collegiate Dictionary*, and the publisher's file of over 12 million citations of English usage. According to its preface, it is "an improved thesaurus," unmarred by the defects that characterize many works of this category.

This thesaurus incorporates uncommon features that are designed to remedy those defects. At each main entry appears a statement reflecting the core meaning shared by the listed synonyms. The organization of the book is strictly alphabetical, and each word presented as a synonym has its own entry within the alphabetical listing. In addition to synonyms, the

Webster's Collegiate Thesaurus

❶ Synonyms are preceded by a boldface italic *syn*.

❷ Related words, introduced by the boldface italic abbreviation *rel.*, are listed separately from synonyms

❸ Cross-references appear in small capitals

❹ Examples of usage are enclosed in angle brackets

❺ Vertical lines indicate limited use

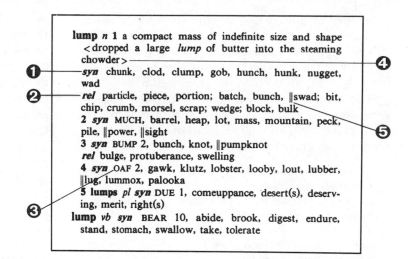

lump *n* **1** a compact mass of indefinite size and shape <dropped a large *lump* of butter into the steaming chowder>
syn chunk, clod, clump, gob, hunch, hunk, nugget, wad
rel particle, piece, portion; batch, bunch, ‖swad; bit, chip, crumb, morsel, scrap; wedge; block, bulk
2 *syn* MUCH, barrel, heap, lot, mass, mountain, peck, pile, ‖power, ‖sight
3 *syn* BUMP 2, bunch, knot, ‖pumpknot
rel bulge, protuberance, swelling
4 *syn* OAF 2, gawk, klutz, lobster, looby, lout, lubber, ‖lug, lummox, palooka
5 lumps *pl syn* DUE 1, comeuppance, desert(s), deserving, merit, right(s)
lump *vb syn* BEAR 10, abide, brook, digest, endure, stand, stomach, swallow, take, tolerate

volume includes idiomatic equivalents, antonyms, and both related and contrasted words. The words listed embrace a wide range of diction levels, including vulgarisms and regionalisms. However, the book excludes terms that are obsolete, archaic, or extremely rare, as well as specialized or technical jargon.

The volume includes two valuable prefatory articles. The detailed and readable introduction discusses the "evolution" of thesauruses. It also provides extended definitions of the terms *synonym*, *antonym*, *related word*, *contrasted word*, and *idiomatic equivalent*. There follows a well-annotated sample double-page spread, which is keyed to the 13 pages of "Explanatory Notes." Although rather daunting in length and detail, and occasionally repetitive, the notes clearly explain all aspects of the entries. They also insist *"that the thesaurus be used in conjunction with an adequate dictionary."*

II. Format

The work includes both main and secondary entries, alphabetized letter by letter. Each is introduced by the entry word, in boldface type overhanging the text. Homographs are entered separately, in the historical order of their appearance in the language.

In the main entry, the entry word is followed by an italicized part-of-speech label. Where multiple senses of the word are presented, each is introduced by a boldface numeral. For each sense, a concise statement is given of the core of meaning shared by the synonyms. An illustrative phrase or sentence, with the entry word italicized, appears in angle brackets. Beneath this are listed synonyms and, as relevant, related words, idiomatic equivalents, contrasted words, and antonyms. Each of these lists is introduced by a bold italic abbreviation, and the words within the lists appear in alphabetical groupings. A cross-reference is sometimes given at the end of the synonym list, with the cross-referenced word printed in small capitals.

In the secondary entry, the core meaning statement and illustration are omitted. Under *syn* a cross-reference will sometimes be given, printed in small capitals, to the main entry in whose synonym list the secondary entry word appears. There follows a list of up to nine of the synonyms listed at that main entry. This is a convenient feature, enabling readers in many cases to forgo following up the cross-reference. Secondary entries may also include lists of related words, idiomatic equivalents, contrasted words, and antonyms. These features are included in the following entry.

> **indestructible** *adj* incapable of being destroyed <*indestructible* idealism>
> *syn* imperishable, incorruptible, inexterminable, inextinguishable, inextirpable, irrefragable, irrefrangible, quenchless, undestroyable, unperishable
> *rel* changeless, immutable, unalterable, unchangeable; deathless, immortal, perpetual, undying; durable, enduring, lasting, permanent; indelible, ineradicable; unextinguishable, unquenchable
> *con* alterable, changeable, corruptible, impermanent, temporary, transient, unlasting; mortal, temporal; evanescent
> *ant* destroyable, destructible, perishable

In both main and secondary entries, one "arbitrary rule" has been followed: *"No word may appear in more than one list at a main or secondary entry."* This rule eliminates potential confusion for readers, since otherwise a word might be listed as, for example, both an antonym and a contrasted word in a single entry.

III. Quality and Currency of Entries

Among the thesaurus's unusual and useful features is its presentation of precise core meanings in main entries. For **coax**, the core meaning is "to influence or persuade by artful ingratiation." This is usually clarified with a well-chosen illustration: "<*coaxed* her friend to help her with her work.>" As necessary, core meanings also include brief usage notes, "subject guide phrases" ("**set** . . . *of a fowl* to incubate eggs . . .") and a description of a word's object of reference (**express** . . . to give expression to [as a thought, an opinion, or an emotion]).

The listings that follow provide a wide range of words related in various ways to the entry word, yet the lists are brief enough to avoid overwhelming the reader. The entry for **coax** continues:

> *syn* ‖barter, blandish, blarney, cajole, con, soft-soap, sweet-talk, wheedle
> *rel* pester, plague, tease; importune, press, urge; get, induce, persuade, prevail; entice, inveigle, lure, tempt; butter (up)
> *con* coerce, compel, constrain, force, oblige; browbeat, bulldoze, cow, intimidate
> *ant* bully

Usage labels are not provided; however, two useful symbols alert the reader to usage restrictions. In front of the word *barter* in the entry just quoted, the double bar indicates that the reader should consult a dictionary to ensure correct use of a term that may be colloquial, slang, regional, or in some other way restricted. And an asterisk precedes terms that are considered vulgar.

Entries also inform readers when words are conventionally capitalized or generally used in the plural in a given sense. Usage alternatives for idiomatic expressions are sometimes provided: "the yoke (*or* chains) of slavery."

The thesaurus is as current as WEBSTER'S THIRD upon which it is based. Although coinages of the late 1970s and 1980s are excluded, the volume reflects a wide range of vocabulary and diction levels and cannot be said to be out-of-date.

IV. Accessibility

The thesaurus is thumb-indexed, and two large, boldface guide words appear at the top of each double-page spread. At the bottom corner of each page within the lexicon appears a key to the abbreviations and symbols used in the entries. Cross-references show up clearly in small capitals, and the volume's cross-referencing system is easy to use. Variant spellings appear in parentheses throughout the entries. When a spelling variant is provided for an entry word, it is also in boldface: **encrust** (*or* **incrust**).

V. Summary

Webster's Collegiate Thesaurus is a comprehensive, easy-to-use thesaurus and a worthy companion volume to WEBSTER'S THIRD NEW INTERNATIONAL DICTIONARY. Particularly valuable is its inclusion of core meanings and verbal illustrations. ROGET'S II: THE NEW THESAURUS is comparable in scope and

also includes definitions and illustrative examples. However, that volume's unusual format is likely to be more difficult for readers to use, and it includes only synonyms and idioms in its entries. *Webster's Collegiate Thesaurus* is significantly more comprehensive in its inclusion of not only synonyms and idiomatic equivalents, but also antonyms and contrasted and related words. The adult writer will find this work a rich source of vocabulary and will appreciate the organization within entries that quickly establishes listed words' relationships to the entry term. Although the volume does not supersede the definitive ROGET'S INTERNATIONAL THESAURUS, it will meet most of the needs of a wide range of adult thesaurus users. This thesaurus is highly recommended for library acquisition and for the home libraries of individuals who wish to refine their writing skills.

Webster's New World Thesaurus (hardcover)

Facts at a Glance

Full Title: **Webster's New World Thesaurus**.
Publisher: Simon & Schuster.
Editor: Charlton Laird; updated by William D. Lutz.
Edition Reviewed: © 1985.

Number of Entries: more than 30,000.
Number of Pages: 854.
Trim Size: 6½″ × 9½″.
Binding: laminated paper over boards.

Price: $14.95 (thumb-indexed); $13.95 (plain).
Sold in bookstores and other outlets; also sold to libraries and other educational institutions.
ISBN 0-671-60437-6 (thumb-indexed);
ISBN 0-671-60738-3 (plain).

I. Introduction and Scope

Webster's New World Thesaurus, first published in 1971, was revised and updated in 1985 to include 7,000 additional new entries. Charlton Laird, who prepared the original work, is the author of *The Miracle of Language*, *Language in America*, and *Modern English Handbook*. In his words, this book "is intended to help writers and speakers in search of a better way to say what they want to." This alphabetically arranged thesaurus lists synonyms and antonyms, and differs both from Roget's original and from recastings of Roget's work in dictionary form. The differences are based on its adherence to the principle that a thesaurus should not be a book about

Webster's New World Thesaurus (hardcover)

❶ Main entry words are set in boldface type

❷ Different senses of the main entry word are given boldface numbers and described in brackets

❸ The symbol *D*, for *diction*, indicates that the following term may be of nonstandard or limited usage

❹ Synonyms are preceded by the italicized abbreviation *Syn.*

❺ Cross-references are set in boldface type

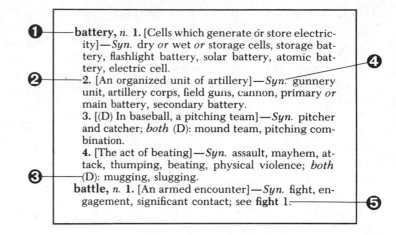

the classification of words; rather, it should be a practical book designed to satisfy the needs of writers and speakers. The editor stresses that the words that "send" readers to a thesaurus are the everyday locutions that come readily to mind. As a result, this thesaurus is "organized on the basis of the commonest words in the language, whatever their standing in respectability, the words that most readily occur to a user of the book."

To put this principle into practice, the editors selected approximately 30,000 main entries that reflected what they deemed to be the most common groupings of synonyms in the language. To check word frequency, they made use of Henry Kučera and W. Nelson Francis's *Computational Analysis of Present-Day American English* (1967), a computer-based study of Brown University's Standard Corpus of the Present-Day American English. Modern American usage is therefore more comprehensively covered in this volume than in its predecessors. The editors have also recognized the value to the writer of specific equivalents (such as **biceps** for **muscle**) of words for which there are no true synonyms, where an earlier thesaurus editor would have excluded the word.

Appended at the back of the work is an 11-page alphabetized listing of discriminated synonym analyses, selected and adapted from WEBSTER'S NEW WORLD DICTIONARY: SECOND COLLEGE EDITION. These paragraphs discuss and illustrate "the subtle differences that distinguish . . . synonyms." This is a useful feature to supplement the main text. Under each word, italicized, discriminated terms refer to main entries in the thesaurus's vocabulary.

II. Format

The alphabetized main entry words are in boldface and overhang the text printed in two columns. An italicized part-of-speech abbreviation follows the main entry word. Numbers in boldface introduce separate uses of the entry word, and a bracketed word or phrase identifies the use under consideration. Synonyms are listed for each use. For the briefer entries of less common words, boldface cross-references are introduced by the word "see" and are followed by a number identifying the relevant part of the entry referred to. "See also" cross-references within the longer entries suggest other meanings of the word that the reader should consider in the search for a synonym. Where applicable, antonyms follow synonyms, are identified with an asterisk, and have their own main entries. (D) identifies words whose diction level restricts use. A representative entry is the following:

> **shown**, *mod.* **1.** [Put on display]—*Syn.* displayed, demonstrated, advertised, exposed, set out, presented, exhibited, delineated, laid out, put up for sale; *both* (D): put up, put on the block.—*Ant.* withdrawn*, concealed, held back.
> **2.** [Proved]—*Syn.* demonstrated, determined, made clear; see **established** 3. **obvious** 2.

At the conclusions of some entries, idioms incorporating the main entry word are alphabetically listed. For example, under **mind** are listed such idioms as **be in one's right mind**, **have half a mind to**, and **take one's mind off**. These appear in boldface type; synonyms and cross-references are provided for each.

The type is clear and its size in the main text is readable, although the type used in the appended discriminated synonym analyses is too small to be read easily. The paper permits minimal show-through, and there is adequate white space with good margins. The volume is sturdily bound and will hold up well to heavy use.

III. Quality and Currency of Entries

The entries are selected and designed to make the volume quick and easy to use. According to the foreword, "usually the commonest set of synonyms carries the main entry; uses of a word are arranged roughly by frequency of use, from common to uncommon." The same principle determines ordering within the lists of synonyms.

The detailed entries include useful features not found in most thesauruses. One of these is the appearance of bracketed phrases identifying separate uses of an entry word. Although these are not—and are not intended to be—definitions, they will assist readers in quickly finding the secondary entry they need.

Another valuable feature is the inclusion of many idioms; those incorporating a main entry word are listed at the conclusions of entries (under **corner**, for example, **around the corner** is one of several idiomatic phrases). Idioms sharing the same first word receive separate main entries (**hit it off**, **hit on**, **hit or miss**, **hit the jackpot**, **hit the hay**). The inclusion of idioms as main entries serves the editors' purpose of listing common words for which readers are most likely to seek synonyms.

The editors' desire to provide specific equivalents for general terms results in some extensive entries. For example, under **Europe** appears an entry of over half a column listing the countries of Europe. Shorter listings of specific equivalents also appear. The entry for **tool** includes:

> common tools include the following—can opener, hammer, knife, jack, crank, pulley, wheel, bar, crowbar, lever, sledge, winch, cam, loom, shuttle, chisel, plane, screw, brace, bit, file, saw, screwdriver, wrench, pliers, ax, hatcher, corkscrew, jimmy.

Such lists are not found in most thesauruses, and they expand the work's application as a reference source. They enable readers to locate specific names and terms for both factual and descriptive purposes.

The work's currency is also strong, in keeping with its editors' concern with making the volume practically useful. Under **computer**, for example, the following appears:

> *Syn.* electronic *or* electric brain, electrocomputer, thinking machine, IBM (trademark), microcomputer, minicomputer, mainframe, personal computer, calculator, master control, high-speed data processor, electronic circuit, number cruncher (D), cybernetic organism, analog computer, digital computer.

There follows a list of computer brand names. Space technology receives good coverage under the entries **space**, **space-age**, **spacecraft**, and **space platform**.

Some aspects of the entries are less specific than the reader may need or expect. For example, the abbreviation *mod.* (for modifier) is used to identify adjectives, adverbs, and articles: this is a drawback, especially for non-native readers and those unsure of grammatical usage. Only one usage label (D) is provided in the work. This identifies the diction level of words that may be slang, colloquial, or vulgar, and alerts a reader to consult a dictionary. The editorial decision to employ a single label was made on the sound basis that usage of these kinds can be only loosely and temporarily defined in more specific ways. However, some readers will prefer a thesaurus that offers more specific usage labels before sending its readers to the dictionary.

IV. Accessibility

Because the volume lacks a table of contents, the appended discriminated synonym analyses are likely to be overlooked. Cross-references are usefully provided to refer readers from one entry to others within the main text. The absence of a key to abbreviations is an irritating omission and may cause difficulties for the user because of the unusual part-of-speech abbreviation *mod.* and the (D) label, for example, although these are explained in the volume's foreword.

Two guide words in boldface appear at the top of each page in both sections, indicating the first and last entries on the page. The volume is available in both thumb-indexed and plain editions.

V. Summary

Webster's New World Thesaurus is a valuable, up-to-date reference source. It is more current and comprehensive than either THE DOUBLEDAY ROGET'S THESAURUS IN DICTIONARY FORM or THE RANDOM HOUSE THESAURUS: COLLEGE EDITION. Although not as extensively detailed as the definitive ROGET'S INTERNATIONAL THESAURUS, it is also less overwhelming and easier to use than that work. Its organization on the basis of the most common words in the language will also enhance its usefulness. The work's minor drawbacks are its blanket use of the part-of-speech abbreviation *mod.* and the diction label (D). *Webster's New World Thesaurus* would be a worthy addition to most public and college library collections and useful for the home reference library of many readers.

Webster's New World Thesaurus (paperback)

Facts at a Glance

Full Title: **Webster's New World Thesaurus.**
Publisher: Warner Books.
Editor: Charlton Laird.
Edition Reviewed: © 1974; 1984 printing.

Number of Entries: 30,000.

Number of Pages: 530.

Trim Size: 4 × 6⅞″ (paper); 5½″ × 8″ (trade paperback).

Binding: paperback.

Price: $3.50 (paper); $8.95 (trade paperback).

Sold in bookstores and other outlets; also sold to libraries and other educational institutions.

ISBN 0-446-31418-8 (paper);

ISBN 0-446-31203-7 (trade paperback).

I. Introduction and Scope

This 1974 thesaurus is the Warner paperback edition of the 1971 *Webster's New World Thesaurus*. The 1985 updating of that hardcover work, published by Simon and Schuster, is reviewed in this Buying Guide. The Warner paperback does not reflect that updating, yet it does incorporate many new words from such fields as computer science and space technology. The introduction has been simplified in the paper editions, and it provides a step-by-step guide to the use of the book.

The very small print of the mass market edition will be a drawback for many readers. However, the work is easy to use, comprehensive, and fairly up-to-date. Relatively inexpensive, it is appropriate for the personal reference library, as well as for the circulating paperback collection of the public library.

Chapter 14
Evaluations of
Usage Dictionaries and Word Books

American Usage and Style: The Consensus

Facts at a Glance

Full Title: **American Usage and Style: The Consensus.**
Publisher: Van Nostrand Reinhold.
Compiler: Roy H. Copperud.
Edition Reviewed: © 1980.

Number of Entries: 3,145.
Number of Pages: 433.
Trim Size: 5⅞″ × 9″.
Binding: paperback.

Price: $12.95.
Sold in bookstores; also sold to libraries and other educational institutions.
ISBN 0-442-24906-3.

I. Introduction and Scope

American Usage and Style: The Consensus, compiled by Roy H. Copperud, a professor of journalism at the University of Southern California, is an updating and consolidation of two of his earlier works: *A Dictionary of Usage and Style* (1964) and *American Usage: The Consensus* (1970). It is Copperud's belief that "dictionaries of usage, including my own, reflect presumption above all": their compilers prescribe "correct usage" as though it were "a matter of revealed truth," when it in fact "oftener than not reflects taste or opinion." Copperud set out to reveal "the spread of opinion and the consensus of authorities" in order to provide a source that will aid users in making their own intelligent choices in usage matters.

First published in 1980, the volume compares the views on disputed points of usage prior to this decade as expressed in nine authoritative works (several now in much updated and revised editions from those consulted by the author) and gives the consensus. The works include, among others, Follett et al., MODERN AMERICAN USAGE, Fowler's A DICTIONARY OF MODERN ENGLISH USAGE, and the HARPER DICTIONARY OF CONTEMPORARY USAGE. The authorities are cited in entries by name "when it appears to serve a useful purpose." In addition to the synthesis of views, Copperud presents his own views on points that have not been addressed elsewhere.

In compiling this usage dictionary, Copperud also consulted a number of highly reputed general dictionaries, since the editors of such dictionaries "have access to voluminous files on current practice . . . and also take a more impersonal attitude toward disputed points." Among the general dictionaries consulted are WEBSTER'S THIRD NEW INTERNATIONAL DICTIONARY, the first edition of the unabridged *Random House Dictionary of the English Language*, and the AMERICAN HERITAGE DICTIONARY: SECOND COLLEGE EDITION. Also consulted were specialized dictionaries and works on grammar, many considerably dated; these titles are listed in a bibliography following the lexicon.

II. Format

The entries are arranged alphabetically with the text printed in a single column. Main entry words and phrases are printed in boldface. Entry words and phrases that refer to a category of grammar or usage are distinguished by initial capitals; for example, there are entries for **Capitalization** and **Sequence of Tenses**. Entry words or phrases that are themselves the usage at issue (**bring**, **take**; **can't hardly**) appear with a lowercase initial unless they are proper nouns.

The discussion of controversy and consensus, in run-in style, follows the entry word or phrase. Within the discussion, when entry words recur, they are printed in italic, as are illustrative phrases containing the entry words and also suggested alternative terms. Longer entries, such as those for **Comma** and **Subject-Verb Agreement**, are divided into numbered paragraphs. Cross-references are provided as needed, for example: **student**. See *pupil, student*. Where appropriate, cross-references also indicate a paragraph number within the entry to which they refer. "See also" cross-references appear occasionally at the ends of entries: **sir** . . . See also *dame*.

The type is clear and adequate in size. Although the boldface entry words do not overhang the text, they remain easy to spot on the page. The good-quality white paper permits minimal show-through, and sufficient white space enhances readability. This sturdy paperback can be opened flat without its pages separating from the spine.

III. Quality and Currency of Entries

Copperud clearly presents both consensus and dissent on many disputed points. A representative entry is the following:

> **among, amongst, amid.** *Among* is generally used with three or more countable things: *among my friends*, *among the audience*, *among the trees*. With singular nouns that are not collectives, *amid* is preferable: *amid the wreckage*, *amid the confusion*. This is the consensus of five authorities, except that Harper also accepts *among* with a singular. Two critics call *amongst* quaint or overrefined, though it is standard in Britain. Bernstein disapproves of *among the news* ("Among the news was a small item about the abdication") though *amid the news* sounds strange.

The longer entries dealing with categories of usage, grammar, and so forth are clear and detailed. Among the entries treated at length are **Dictionaries**, **Ellipsis**, **Hyphens**, **Infinitives**, **Misquotation**, **Modifiers**, and **who, whom**; **whoever, whomever**. For these kinds of articles, the book can serve not only as a quick reference source, but also as a thorough handbook.

Although Copperud makes it clear that all commentary on usage, including his own, is largely opinion, there is obvious conflict in this volume between opinion and the objective synthesis of authorities. For example, when entries provide a single opinion, there is no way for the reader to know whether this is the consensus "of all the authorities that took up the point at hand" (and, if so, how many these were) or the author's "own views concerning points that have not been taken up elsewhere." For example, the entry for **parenting** reads as following:

> For "acting as a parent," a neologism straight from the mildewed halls of sociology, and repugnant for that reason alone. Sentences containing it should be recast to substitute *parenthood, being a parent*. "Parenting grows more difficult each day." *bringing up children*.

Readers should be told whether this strong opinion is a consensus, that of a single authority, or the author's personal preference.

In the case of the entry for **Feminism**, there is similar potential confusion. Copperud cites WEBSTER'S THIRD and the AMERICAN HERITAGE DICTIONARY on the use of *he* as an indefinite personal pronoun. However, the entry as a whole is facetious and heavily biased. It begins: "Feminists appear to be getting more and more worked up . . ." Copperud states further, "It seems inevitable that some pretentious ass will suggest displacing *mankind* with *personkind* . . ." The article's final paragraph begins, "We are on dangerous ground, for William Congreve recorded truly three centuries ago that hell has no fury like a woman scorned, and as is well known this is no less true if she only *thinks* she has been scorned or even slighted." It seems unlikely that this shrewish polemic is a consensus of the best judgments on usage and style, and no serious student of language or literature would summon Congreve as support for such a crude dismissal of a contemporary area of concern.

IV. Accessibility

Two guide words are provided on each double-page spread, indicating the first and last word or phrase entered on the spread. The guide words are suitably placed adjacent to the page numbers, which are flush with the outer margins. However, their italic type makes them hard to focus on; boldface type would be preferable. Because the volume has no table of contents, readers are likely to overlook the bibliography that follows the lexicon.

V. Summary

American Usage and Style: The Consensus is a potentially useful guide to current usage and style. Its greatest strength is its presentation of a range of views that are generally still prevalent on disputed points and of authoritative consensus. While another usage dictionary of merit, WORDS ON WORDS, often cites other authorities, Copperud's is unique in its focus on those authorities in their agreements and disagreements. The reader will also benefit from the handbooklike qualities of this volume. On the other hand, the book blurs the distinction that should be kept clear between consensus and Copperud's personal views, the views of one authority among many. In these instances, the reader would do well to refer to some of Copperud's sources, especially the ENCYCLOPEDIC DICTIONARY OF ENGLISH USAGE and the HARPER DICTIONARY OF CONTEMPORARY USAGE. The well-equipped library reference collection will contain these works, and Copperud's merits a place among them as well.

Beginner's Dictionary of American English Usage

Facts at a Glance

Full Title: **Beginner's Dictionary of American English Usage**.
Publisher: National Textbook Company.
Editors: P. H. Collin, Miriam Lowi, and Carol Weiland.
Illustrator: Erasmo Hernandez.
Edition Reviewed: © 1986.

Number of Entries: 4,000.
Number of Pages: 280.
Number of Illustrations: 11 pages of black-and-white drawings.
Trim Size: 5¼″ × 7″.
Binding: cloth; paperback.

Price: $7.95 (cloth); $4.95 (paperback).
Sold in bookstores; also sold to libraries and other educational institutions.
ISBN 0-8325-0440-8 (cloth);
ISBN 0-8325-0439-4 (paperback).

I. Introduction and Scope

The *Beginner's Dictionary of American English Usage*, first published in 1986, is designed for use by English-language learners of all ages. All its features reflect a focus on this audience. According to its preface, the work "contains the 4,000 most commonly used words in English." All entries contain sample sentences showing typical everyday use of the entry words, and the vocabulary used in definitions is limited to words entered in the dictionary. Information on more difficult points of usage, such as irregular plurals and principal parts of verbs, is provided in shaded boxes throughout the work. Line drawings show places and items frequently encountered in daily life and aid in defining the vocabulary associated with them.

II. Authority

The National Textbook Company is a recognized and respected publisher of books used in English-Spanish bilingual programs. However, no information is provided about the credentials of the book's editors or about their criteria for selecting the words entered in the dictionary.

III. Comprehensiveness

The dictionary is comprehensive in its inclusion of a basic vocabulary of standard American English. The terms included will be helpful in enabling the English-language learner to understand texts used in English as a Second Language (ESL) classes. However, the book is of limited value outside the classroom, since it excludes terms and definitions that would be needed by an individual attempting to negotiate everyday experiences independently. The exclusion of slang and colloquialisms constitutes part of this limitation. For example, the definition of **education** as "teaching" (besides being incorrect), is apt to confuse the user attempting to fill out an application form on which a space is provided for "education."

As is appropriate in an ESL dictionary, the focus is on definitions and illustrations, and therefore this does not meet the usual definition of a usage dictionary. The work excludes etymologies, synonyms, antonyms, and biographical and geographic terms. However, several shaded boxes on each page enclose the kinds of supplemental information that will be most useful to the English-language learner. For example, under **bad** appears a box showing the comparative and superlative of the word: **bad—worse—worst**. For verbs, shaded boxes show principal parts. Irregular noun plurals are shown (**foot . . . feet**), as is the information that a noun such as **plenty** has no plural. Longer notes are provided on more complex points. For example, under **second** a box contains this clarification:

> *Note*: in dates **second** *is usually written* **2: April 2, 1973; November 2, 1980**; *with names of kings and queens* **second** *is usually written* **II: Queen Elizabeth II.**

In some cases, shaded boxes provide information on idiomatic usage. Under **fill**, for example, appears the following:

> *Note*: **fill the glass up** *or* **fill up the glass** *but only* **fill it up.**

The dictionary user may initially require an instructor's help in deciphering the point that "fill up it" is

Beginner's Dictionary of American English Usage

❶ Pronunciations are enclosed in brackets

❷ Simple definitions are given for each meaning

❸ Parts of speech are spelled out in italic type

❹ Examples of usage are set in boldface type

❺ Inflected forms and other usage notes appear in shaded boxes

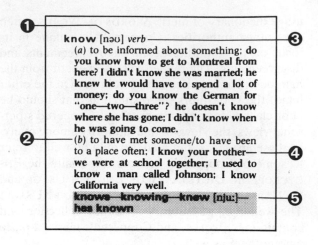

know [nəʊ] *verb*
(*a*) to be informed about something; **do you know how to get to Montreal from here? I didn't know she was married; he knew he would have to spend a lot of money; do you know the German for "one—two—three"? he doesn't know where she has gone; I didn't know when he was going to come.**
(*b*) to have met someone/to have been to a place often; **I know your brother— we were at school together; I used to know a man called Johnson; I know California very well.**
knows—knowing—knew [nju:]— **has known**

unidiomatic; however, with minimal guidance, non-native English speakers will gain access in this volume to a wealth of information about standard usage.

IV. Quality and Currency of Entries

In each entry, the boldface entry word is followed by pronunciation in brackets and the italicized part-of-speech label. The intended audience will find the avoidance of abbreviations for parts of speech helpful. Where multiple part-of-speech applications are presented, each is introduced by a boldface numeral. Separate senses within one part of speech are distinguished by italic lowercase letters in parentheses.

Entries are characterized by their simply stated definitions and by a wealth of illustrative examples in full-sentence format. In most cases, the definitions are both simple and clear. For example, **empty** is defined as "with nothing inside"; **orchard** is "a group of planted fruit trees"; **think** is

(*a*) to use your mind . . . (*b*) to believe/to have an opinion . . . (*c*) to expect . . . (*d*) to plan.

However, in some cases the effort to simplify is likely to cause confusion. For example, the noun **search** is defined as "trying to find something." If this participial phrase is plugged into a sample sentence in place of **search**, the result is incoherent. The editors would have been better advised to define **search** as an "attempt to find something." The noun **attempt** is included in the lexicon, but it may have been overlooked according to the belief that a form of the shorter word **try** would produce a simpler definition.

The illustrative sentences make careful use of a controlled vocabulary to reflect a wide range of contexts in which a word may be applied. For example, the noun **seat**, defined as "something which [*sic*] you sit on," is further clarified by the following illustrations:

sit in the front seat of the car; I want two seats in the front row; I couldn't find a seat on the bus, so I had to

stand; this chair isn't very comfortable—it has a wooden seat; why is your bicycle seat so narrow? take a seat please, the doctor will see you in a few minutes.

In this typical grouping, the reader is shown how the word might be used in a variety of everyday situations: travel, entertainment, health care, and so forth.

V. Syllabication and Pronunciation

Syllabication is shown in the entry word by centered dots. It is not shown elsewhere in the entry, and the absence of syllabication in inflected forms is an inconvenience to users. For example, under **teach**, the English-language learner would benefit from seeing the form **teaches** syllabified. Pronunciation is based on the International Phonetic Alphabet (IPA). The key to pronunciation appears only at the front of the volume; there are no abbreviated keys within the lexicon. This is also inconvenient for the user, especially a novice dictionary user. Within the key, symbols are followed by sample words (j yes), and it is indicated that "the pronunciation shown in the dictionary is that which is most common in the U.S.A." However, no further guidance on pronunciation is provided, and there are no exercises to help familiarize the user with the system.

VI. Special Features

In addition to its shaded boxes of information about usage, the dictionary contains two special features. Preceding the lexicon is a table of the English alphabet. The letters are shown in boldface, in both uppercase and lowercase; they are followed by their pronunciation in IPA symbols (**Ff** ef). Within the lexicon, page numbers are provided at the bottom of pages in both numerals and words.

VII. Accessibility

Two boldface guide words appear at the top of each page, indicating the first and last words on the page.

No list of illustrations is provided at the front of the volume: this omission impedes accessibility to the 11 full-page drawings.

VIII. Graphics and Format

The dictionary's line drawings are among its most valuable features. The 11 pages of drawings are usefully detailed; they are simple and clear without condescending to the audience. These illustrate the bathroom, bedroom, parts of the body, clothes, the country, kitchen, living room, office, restaurant, street, and travel; and they are inserted into the text alphabetically according to these topics. In each, individual parts or items are numerically keyed to labels listed at the bottom of the drawing. For example, the office scene has 23 labeled components, including a calculator, a computer, a magazine, a telephone, a typewriter, and so forth. These graphic illustrations, like the entries' verbal illustrations, will aid users in understanding how words apply in specific contexts.

The dictionary's type is large enough for easy reading, and the typefaces are clear; boldface main entry words overhang the text. The light shading used to box the notes on grammar and usage make these clearly visible. White space is advantageously used, and the heavy paper permits minimal showthrough. The hardcover edition is exceptionally sturdy; the paperback will also stand up well and may be opened flat without its pages separating from the binding.

IX. Summary

The *Beginner's Dictionary of American English Usage* will serve the needs of beginning English-language students, who will find it most useful in the language classroom itself. Students will benefit from its generally clear and simple definitions, its copious verbal illustrations, and its helpful line drawings. The boxed notes on difficult points in the language are another valuable feature, but one that will sometimes require further elaboration by an instructor. Although beginning English-language learners will find the dictionary valuable in the classroom and in related home study, they will find it limited in value as a "survival" dictionary for everyday experiences.

This dictionary may be compared with the EVERYDAY AMERICAN ENGLISH DICTIONARY. That volume is larger (5,500 entries), contains a useful appendix, and has a 40-page comparison workbook, well designed for classroom use. It is suitable for use at beginning and early intermediate levels. On the other hand, the *Beginner's Dictionary* contains many more illustrative sentences, and its absence of special features might make it less intimidating for English-

language learners at the beginning of their studies. In any case, however, once the student has reached a solid intermediate level of English-language skills, he or she will require a larger and more advanced dictionary, such as the LONGMAN DICTIONARY OF AMERICAN ENGLISH, with its 38,000 entries.

British/American Language Dictionary

Facts at a Glance

Full Title: **British/American Language Dictionary**.
Publisher: National Textbook Company (Passport Books).
Compiler: Norman Moss.
Edition Reviewed: © 1984.

Number of Entries: 3,200.
Number of Pages: 192.
Number of Indexes: 2.
Trim Size: 5¼″ × 8¼″.
Binding: paperback.

Price: $7.95.
Sold in bookstores and other outlets; also sold to libraries and other educational institutions.
ISBN 0-8442-9104-8.

I. Introduction and Scope

The *British/American Language Dictionary* is a "bilingual" [*sic*] dictionary of everyday English spoken in America and the United Kingdom. Compiler Norman Moss writes in the introduction that this work is "intended to help Britons and Americans understand one another better and communicate with one another more easily." Moss is a British journalist and author of several popularly oriented works. As a general reference work, it will increase readers' appreciation of the richness of the English language, and it will also help American readers clarify those areas where the language diverges on either side of the Atlantic. Moss notes that "some words in one language are unknown in the other," while others that are used in both nations "have different meanings that can cause misunderstandings." A third group have opposite meanings in America and the United Kingdom. "Words in the first category cause incomprehension," he remarks; "those in the last two may cause trouble, because the difference can create situations in which people think they understand one another when they don't."

This dictionary presents a wide range of words and expressions used in common speech, business, government, and journalism. It includes approximately 1,600 American entries and an equal number of British entries. Brand names, company and political organization names or nicknames, acronyms, and initials are included when they have become part of the common language (**BVDs**, **GOP**, **jap**, **Alliance**, **CID**, **MI5** and **MI6**). Also included are many words that have particularly risque or vulgar connotations in one country but that mean something entirely different in the other, such as **fag**, **fanny**, **hump**, **pecker**, and **rubber**.

However, the *British/American Language Dictionary* does not attempt to be comprehensive. For example, it does not include words that are spelled differently in the two countries but have identical meanings (such as **color** and **colour**). Sports terms are included only when they have acquired a colloquial meaning outside the sport (such as **curve ball**, **home run**, **quarterback**, and **hit for six**) and are part of either country's national lexicon. The compiler notes additional usage areas that are not covered in his introduction.

II. Format

The format of the *British/American Language Dictionary* is similar to that of any standard bilingual, American–foreign language dictionary. The entries in the first section, "American/British," include words that are used only in the United States or that are used in both countries but may have a special connotation in the United States. The definitions are written in British English or in terms that will be readily understandable to the typical British reader.

The entries in the "British/American" section include words that are only used in the United Kingdom or that are used in both nations but may have a specific connotation for the British. The definitions are given in American English to make the meaning clear to the American reader.

In both sections, the main entry word is printed in boldface type and overhangs the text.

III. Quality and Currency of Entries

Main entry words are defined only in the sense in which they differ from the way the word is used in the other country. The part of speech is noted. The only usage label is *col*, for *colloquial*. Within the definition, the context in which the word might be used is sometimes given. The definition may also note when the word is restricted to a certain social class, age group, or region.

Entry length varies according to the complexity of the definition and whether the same word has a different meaning on the other side of the Atlantic. For example, the key entry word for **expressway** in the American/British section of the dictionary reads

in its entirety: **expressway**, *n*—motorway. A more involved definition is given for

> **excise laws**, *n*—the laws governing the sale of drink, when and how it may be sold as well as its manufacture, areas which in Britain are covered by licensing laws.

Unlike those in BRITISH ENGLISH: A TO ZED, entries in the *British/American Language Dictionary* rarely include a comment on usage or etymology. However, the following entry in the "British/American" section of the dictionary illustrates an instance in which a more extensive explanation *is* given:

> **bomb**, *n* (col)—1. a great success, the exact opposite of its meaning in American. 'It was a bomb!' means it was a hit (if a play) or a ball (if a party). It is also used, in a curious grammatical construction, with the verb 'to go': 'It went a bomb' means it worked out great. The word is newish and used in the modern-minded occupations; it is more likely to be heard among advertising men or movie people than doctors or lawyers, at the Dorchester Bar rather than the Reform Club. 2. a lot of money, e.g., 'It cost a bomb.'

The *British/American Language Dictionary* includes a number of British and American terms that have gained currency in the 1980s. Among the British words in this category are the political terms **dry** and **wet**; the name of the telephone company **British Telecom**; and the verb **suss** and the allied expression **suss out**, both of which have entered the common vocabulary from the underworld. Contemporary American words listed include **glitch** and **nerd**, and Mexican food names such as **taco**. The dictionary also has entries for **Trojan** and **Durex**, respective American and British brand names synonymous with condoms.

Some of the listed American words are obsolete, regional, or ethnic, such as **ash can**, **automat**, **beltway**, **buckboard**, **bushwhack**, **butter-and-eggs man**, and **schmuck**. Among British words in this category (including Cockney rhyming slang) are **almoner**, **brass**, **charabanc**, **dicky bird**, and **rotter**. Such words will rarely be encountered in everyday conversation, but are real words that demonstrate the colorfulness of the English language in both the United States and the United Kingdom.

IV. Accessibility

The *British/American Language Dictionary* is a simple, straightforward reference book that is highly accessible. Entries within each section are arranged alphabetically, letter-by-letter. A running head at the top of the left-hand page indicates whether the reader is in the "American/British" section or the "British/American" section. A guide word at the top of the right-hand page indicates the last main entry word on that page.

Idiomatic or derivative phrases, and variant forms, such as the **Buckeye State** and **funk hole**, are not arranged as separate entries, but are included in boldface type within the definition of the main entry words to which they are related, **buckeye** and **funk**, respectively.

Cross-references, printed in small caps, are occasionally provided when the British and American definitions of the same word contrast. For example, following the definition of **dormitory** in the "American/British" section, the reader is advised to "see DORMITORY in the British/American section." In some instances, the cross-reference can also refer the reader to another main word entry within the same section for further information. Following the definition of **high roller**, the reader is directed to "see CRAPS."

Cross-referencing is not consistent, unfortunately, and does not occur every time the same word is defined in the other section; in such cases (**college**, for example), readers can often infer from the definition that the word has another meaning in the other country.

The dictionary is enhanced by two "Useful subject lists" at the end of the book. Each list arranges selected American or British words included in the book by the following subject categories: accommodation, household, food, school and campus, on the road, business and finance, and politics. These lists enable the reader to determine quickly what words related to these subjects are included in the dictionary. While these lists do not contain all the words in the dictionary, they will provide travelers or businesspersons with a vocabulary that is adequate to obtain everyday services.

V. Summary

In its format and purpose, the *British/American Language Dictionary* resembles an English–foreign language dictionary. While this book may have practical value for the tourist and businessperson, it provides only minimal coverage of idiom, and less of grammar and etymology. American readers seeking more and better-documented information on these aspects of the English language in Britain will be better served by BRITISH ENGLISH, A TO ZED. Note, however, that the *British/American Language Dictionary* is more accessible, especially for British (and American) users wishing to learn more about the American language. Librarians may find this book an ideal recommendation for Americans planning to travel in the U.K. and for recent British arrivals who will be living in the United States.

British English, A to Zed

Facts at a Glance

Full Title: **British English, A to Zed**.
Former Title: *English English*.
Publisher: Facts on File.
Author: Norman W. Schur.
Edition Reviewed: © 1987.

Number of Entries: 5,000.
Number of Pages: 496.
Number of Indexes: 1.
Trim Size: $5\frac{3}{4}'' \times 9''$.
Binding: cloth.

Price: $35.00.
Sold in bookstores and other outlets; also sold to libraries and other educational institutions.
ISBN 0-8160-1635-6.

I. Introduction and Scope

The English and the Americans, as Sir Winston Churchill once observed, are two peoples separated by a common language. The extent to which the English and American branches of the language have diverged is documented in *British English, A to Zed*, by the American scholar, philologist, and word lover Norman Schur, whose previous credits include 1000 MOST CHALLENGING WORDS, 1000 MOST IMPORTANT WORDS, and 1000 MOST PRACTICAL WORDS. The jacket copy describes the book as "A rigorously researched, wickedly witty, and eminently useful collection of nearly 5,000 Briticisms (and Americanisms) for English speakers on both sides of the Atlantic."

In his introduction, Schur (who divides his time between England and America) notes that the work is "a comprehensive glossary of Briticisms for Americans, rather than a dictionary of British English in general." He distinguishes among three types of Briticisms:

1. Words that are used in both countries but mean different things in each, such as **holiday**. In America, the word means "a day of religious or national significance" such as Christmas, Memorial Day, or Washington's Birthday; in Britain, the word means "vacation."
2. Expressions that are never or rarely used in America, such as **trunk call** ("long distance telephone call") or **dustman** ("garbage man" or "refuse collector").
3. Expressions that have no direct American equivalent or are not applicable to any situation in America, such as **A-levels** and **O-levels**

(courses and exams taken by 17- or 18-year-olds and 15- or 16-year-olds, respectively) or **Inns of Court** ("the four legal societies which alone may admit persons . . . to practice as barristers").

The Briticisms recorded in *British English* include idioms, eponyms, acronyms, and slang and informal expressions, as well as "ordinary" words. Words and phrases that are no longer current in British speech but might be encountered in older novels and films (and in contemporary "period" works), such as **San Fairy Ann** ("it doesn't matter"—a "British anglicization [World War I] of *ça ne fait rien*") are also included.

While the entries of Briticisms occupy some 400 pages and make up the bulk of the book, *British English* is greatly enhanced by two extensive appendixes. The first provides fairly comprehensive coverage of "General Differences Between British and American English." Here Schur explains the conventions that govern syntax, pronunciation, spoken usage and figures of speech, punctuation and style, and spelling. In every instance he provides copious examples from literature, journalism, and everyday conversation. For example, one learns that "*different from* is heard in Britain but *different to* is more commonly heard"; that *Tuesday week* means "a week from Tuesday"; and that in Britain "a singular noun that describes an institution . . . is followed by a verb . . . in the third person plural." Thus, Harvard *plays* Yale (U.S.) but Oxford *play* Cambridge (Brit.).

Eccentricities of British spelling and pronunciation are clarified in helpful lists of unusual place names and family names, in which such hitherto unfathomable puzzles as **Caius** (KEEZ), **Cholmondeley** (CHUMLEY), and **Featherstonehaugh** (FANSHAW) are demystified. British pronunciations of common words, such as **clerk**, **lieutenant**, and **vitamin**, are also noted.

The second appendix, "Glossaries and Tables," explains British currency (both pre-decimalization and decimal), financial terms, units of measure, numbers (for example, the American "one billion" is expressed as *one thousand million* in Britain), automotive terms (virtually every part of the car has a different name), and musical notation. In addition, Schur also explicates slang (including cant terms, London slang, rhyming slang, and poker slang), betting terms, food names ("there are a good many that would baffle an American shopper," he remarks), botanical and zoological names, and cricket terms. He explains the proper use of **Britain**, **Briton**, **British**, **English**, **Scottish**, **Scotch**, **Scots**, and so forth, and gives glossaries of connotative place names and connotative names of periodicals.

In short, with approximately 5,000 entries and wide-ranging appendix matter, *British English* is a reference work of remarkable scope.

II. Format

As noted, the main entries occupy the greatest part of *British English*. Entries are arranged alphabetically and appear in a format well-suited to the general reader. The main entry word—always a Briticism—is set in boldface on the left hand side of the page, just above the entry. American equivalents are set in boldface on the right, opposite the British headword. When there is no American equivalent, the words SEE COMMENT refer the reader to the comment under the headword. The comment, or definition, is printed directly beneath the British and American headwords. Both the main body of the book and the appendixes are printed in one column per page. The typeface is fairly small (9 point) but clear and easy to read. The binding and paper quality are adequate, and the red-white-and-blue jacket is attractive.

III. Quality and Currency of Entries

As described above, entries are listed under British headwords. Parts of speech are set in italics, immediately following the headword. Usage labels are also given for slang, informal, old-fashioned, and rarely-used terms. When the American equivalent is only an approximation of its British counterpart, it is preceded by the abbreviation *approx*. A simple phonetic pronunciation is given for Briticisms with idiosyncratic pronunciations—for example, SINK PORT for **Cinque Port**.

Comments and definitions are concise but as comprehensive as one would wish, and usually provide a context for the Briticism. The entry for the noun **cutting** reads as follows:

> Meaning 'newspaper clipping.' One resorts to a *cutting service* in Britain, in America to a *clipping bureau*. Sometimes the sense is clarified by amplifying the term to *press cutting*, and *press cutting agency* is synonymous with *cutting service*.

In more complex entries, Schur often quotes from fiction, memoirs, essays, and letters to the London *Times* to illustrate the Briticism in question. As in conventional dictionaries, sense discrimination is indicated by numbers; where necessary, more than one American headword is given to indicate the different senses of the British word. For example, the American headwords opposite the British entry phrase **not on** are: **1. impracticable** and **2.** *Inf*. **bad form**. The comment reads:

1. *Inf.* An employee asks to have his salary doubled. Answer: "It simply isn't on."

2. *Inf.* Denoting impropriety. Synonymous with **off, 1**.

As an indication of the Briticisms and their American equivalents included in *British English*, the reader will encounter (among many others) the following words and expressions: **Asdic** (sonar), **bang** (absolutely), **except for access** (approx. "no through trucks"), **faceglove** (a particular type of washrag or facecloth), **go to the country** (have a general election), **grasp the nettle** (take the bull by the horns), **open the bowling** (set the ball rolling), **Sloane Rangers** (no American equivalent), **West End** ("the shopping and theater center of London" as well as the figurative equivalent of "Broadway"), and **Z car** (pronounced ZED-CAR), a police car.

For this 1987 edition, Schur has added many examples of contemporary usage. He gives us the entry word **Chunnel**, a neologism for *English Channel tunnel*, and notes that "now (1986) . . . agreement has been reached between the affected countries to go ahead with the project. . . ." (He adds the timely comment that "The inhabitants of the Dover area are horrified. So are all the Englishmen this author has spoken to.") He is alert to social and political changes and to new trends affecting both language and culture. All in all, *British English* is admirably up to the moment.

IV. Accessibility

British English is arranged to provide the greatest accessibility to British words and expressions for American readers. Briticisms are entered alphabetically, letter by letter, and each letter of the alphabet has its own section. Entry words, printed in boldface, are easy to see, as are their American equivalents. Unlike conventional dictionaries, *British English* does not have guide words printed at the top of each page, but this is a minor inconvenience. Cross-references within the explanatory comments or definitions are highlighted in boldface, and cross-reference entries are also provided where necessary.

The 45-page index is designed to help users who are searching for British equivalents of particular American words. The American equivalents given in the main, A–Z section of the book are listed alphabetically in the index, together with the equivalent Briticism, which the reader will find treated in full in the main section. Page numbers are given only for items included in the appendix, since subjects discussed there are grouped by category, not alphabetically as are those in the main section.

The table of contents is clear and simple, and the author also provides a page of explanatory notes in the frontmatter. Once the reader has mastered the system by which entries are arranged, finding individual Briticisms or Americanisms should be easy.

V. Summary

British English, A to Zed, is a well-researched, well-written, and well-organized reference book that explains many of the specific differences between British and American English. Needless to say, the utility of this work is limited; the general reader and the typical library patron will probably find little occasion to consult this book. On the other hand, for those who require a glossary of Briticisms, *British English* could hardly be bettered. This work will be most useful—perhaps indispensable—to the serious student of English culture and literature, to devotees of English detective fiction, and to Americans who plan to spend any length of time in Britain. For readers of such quintessentially English writers as Anthony Burgess, Agatha Christie, Anthony Powell, Evelyn Waugh, Dorothy Sayers, P. D. James, Iris Murdoch, and Margaret Drabble, *British English* will help decode nuances and shades of meaning hidden within the language. American businesspeople who have day-to-day dealings with Britons may also find that *British English* will help prevent embarrassing (and possibly costly) misunderstandings. It is a more useful and comprehensive work than the BRITISH/AMERICAN LANGUAGE DICTIONARY. In explaining the language that is written and spoken in the United Kingdom today, Norman Schur has also gone a long way toward illuminating British culture and society in general.

A Browser's Dictionary

Facts at a Glance

Full Title: **A Browser's Dictionary and Native's Guide to the Unknown American Language**.
Publisher: Harper & Row.
Author: John Ciardi.
Edition Reviewed: © 1980.

Number of Entries: 1,275.
Number of Pages: 429.
Trim Size: 6⅛″ × 9⅛″.
Binding: cloth.

Price: $18.45.
Sold in bookstores; also sold to libraries.
ISBN 0-06-010766-9.

I. Introduction and Scope

In the foreword to *A Browser's Dictionary*, the late John Ciardi, who was well-known as a poet, translator, editor, and lecturer, stated that "this book is for browsers, for those who will be pleased to ramble beyond the standard dictionaries to a more intimate conversation with words and phrases and their origins and shifting histories." Ciardi went on to explain that he had made no attempt to be comprehensive: "By limiting the number of entries, I have tried to discuss more fully those terms that are most interesting, and I have been flatly subjective in my choices. A term is interesting if it interests me, for only out of my own interest can I make these word histories interesting to a reader—and informative, and *readable*."

According to Ciardi, the book is the result of a ten-year search through a variety of reference sources. Many of these are well known to librarians; they include *The American Heritage Dictionary*, Brewer's *Dictionary of Phrase and Fable*, Mathews' *A Dictionary of Americanisms on Historical Principles*, Partridge's *A Dictionary of Slang and Unconventional English*, and the *Oxford English Dictionary*. Other sources are *A Classical Dictionary of the Vulgar Tongue* by Captain Francis Grose, *Jamieson's Dictionary of the Scottish Language*, the Old Testament, and Samuel Johnson's dictionary.

At times, Ciardi has disagreed with the derivations found in standard dictionaries and, after noting his disagreement, has suggested his own etymologies. Examples of such etymologies can be found at **cheapskate**, **galleywest**, **ghetto**, **honeymoon**, **kangaroo court**, **lead pipe cinch**, **nincompoop**, **posh**, **sycophant**, and **Yankee**.

II. Format

Entry words and phrases, in boldface type overhanging the text, are arranged in alphabetical order. No pronunciation is given in most cases, but sometimes the author does see a need for explanation. For example, there is a note after **harass** in parentheses that it is "commonly pronounced with accent on the second syllable, and that pronunciation seems to have become American standard, but properly with the accent on the first syllable." Definitions follow, with different meanings numbered and sometimes given italic labels. For example, the entry for **ham-and-egger** reads:

> 1. *Boxing*. A fighter who has never advanced beyond preliminary bouts, or a has-been who continues to fight for "eating money." 2. *Show biz*. A plod-along performer who has never risen to prominent billing. 3. *Ext*. any plod-along person.

The abbreviation *ext*., which can be located in the list of abbreviations in the frontmatter, means "(sense) extension from one meaning of the word to another."

Most entries include a discussion of the word's history. The entry for **demijohn** reads:

> A large bottle covered with wickerwork and equipped with a wicker handle. There is no established size, but the fact that a gallon of water weights [*sic*] 8 pounds imposes a top limit of about 12 gallons as a manageable weight, with perhaps a lower limit of about 2 gallons if the thing is to qualify for the root sense: "an imposing personage of a bottle." [Not <Fr. *demi*, half. These bottles first appeared in XVI France and were given the whimsical name *Dame Jeanne*, Dame Jane, as if in tribute to some robustly slab-sided proprietress of a country inn. Into XVII Brit. as a mangled translation of the Fr. And note It. *damigiana*, Sp. *damajuana*, and Arabic *dāmājāna*. The old dame got around.]

Although the emphasis is etymological, there are some notes about correct grammatical usage. Under **imply** is a note reminding the reader that *imply* and *infer* are not synonyms and that to suggest that they are "is a mark of illiteracy." The difference between the terms is perhaps not as clearly stated as it might be, and most readers who are seriously interested in how to use each term correctly would be better served by a dictionary with good usage notes.

III. Quality and Currency of Entries

This book contains fewer current terms than its 1980 copyright date would suggest. The author's admittedly subjective selection criteria have led him to focus on terms with interesting—and often long—histories rather than terms of recent origin. Few if any entries are of more recent coinage than **brinkmanship**, **bikini**, and **wetback**, all from the 1940s and 1950s.

IV. Accessibility

The base or root word is easy to locate in this dictionary. Variations on the word are not given separate entries but are defined within the paragraph. They are indented and are in boldface type. Under **holy** we find **Holy of Holies**, **holy mackerel**, and **holystone**. **Holy smoke** is found under **holy mackerel** and so might be missed if the reader did not search carefully. The most serious access problem is an occasional blind "see" reference. For instance, under **cheap**, there is a reference "See **shit**," which leads the reader nowhere since *shit* is not included in this dictionary. Signs, abbreviations, and works frequently cited are listed at the front of the book for easy reference, and the guide words at the top of each page are helpful.

V. Summary

A Browser's Dictionary is aptly named. It is amusing to page through it, to read the colorful word histories, and even to chuckle over some of Ciardi's comments. As a reference work, the book is limited in its usefulness. A large library would have most or all of the tools the author consulted, and small libraries use their reference money and space for more basic works. This book will be more suitable for the circulating collection and for home shelves of language lovers, whose browsing will tell them whom the **Murphy bed** was named after and who in the Sam Hill **Sam Hill** was. However, it in no way replaces the NEW DICTIONARY OF AMERICAN SLANG by Wentworth and Flexner or a good historical dictionary.

Chambers Idioms

Facts at a Glance

Full Title: **Chambers Idioms**.
Publisher: W. & R. Chambers, Ltd., published in the United States by Cambridge University Press.
Editors: E. M. Kirkpatrick and C. M. Schwarz.
Compiler: Susan E. Hunter.
Edition Reviewed: © 1982.

Number of Entries: 2,500.
Number of Pages: 440.
Trim Size: 4½″ × 7″.
Binding: paperback.

Price: $7.95.
Sold in bookstores, through other outlets, and by direct mail; also sold directly to libraries and other educational institutions.
ISBN 0-521-60010-3.

I. Introduction and Scope

Chambers Idioms is a concise dictionary that lists more than 2,500 idioms and their meanings. The editors claim the book "will be of immense value to all users of English whether they are learners of English as a foreign language or whether English is their mother tongue." The preface points out that *Chambers Idioms* "not only gives the meanings of idiomatic expressions . . . but includes example sentences or phrases showing the idioms in actual use."

Most of the idioms included in the book are fairly common and will be encountered in everyday conversation as well as in the print and broadcast media. The reader will find such familiar phrases as **that's the way the cookie crumbles; early bird; easy come, easy go; play (something) by ear; the kiss of death; red tape; fall apart at the seams**; and so forth. *Chambers Idioms* is produced in the United Kingdom and distributed in the United States; the British origin is evident: some of the idioms are restricted to English

as spoken in the United Kingdom—for example, **go to the country** (meaning "to call a general election"), **get one's knickers in a twist**, **turn King's/Queen's evidence** (rather than "state's evidence"), and **have a good innings**.

Specifically American idioms are noted as such. For example, the entry for **bum steer** concludes with the note that "literally, in America, a *bum steer* was originally a poor or worthless young bullock." The note at the conclusion of **give (someone) the bum's rush** remarks "originally US, presumably from throwing tramps—bums—out of bars *etc.*"

II. Format

The format of *Chambers Idioms* is a simple one and the book is well designed. The trim size is convenient for shelf, briefcase, or tote bag. The plum-red laminated cover is durable and attractive; the book's durability is enhanced by the binding, which is both sewn and glued. The paper is a good quality heavy stock, the printing is clear and properly inked, and the spacing between lines is generous, increasing the readability of the entries. The margins are more than sufficient, and the one-half inch inner margin ensures that no text is lost in the gutter.

III. Quality and Currency of Entries

Most of the entries are concise and give at least the minimum amount of information necessary for the reader to understand the idiom. All the idiomatic phrases include a clear and simple definition, and many include an illustrative sentence using the idiom in context. Where necessary, 22 abbreviated usage labels identify the idioms as formal, informal, slang, facetious, derogatory, and so forth, or a combination, such as **what's the damage** (*inf facet*), meaning that the phrase is both informal and facetious.

The following examples typify the idiomatic entries in *Chambers Idioms*:

> **give (someone) heart failure** (*inf*) to give someone a very bad shock: *When I looked up and saw my little boy at the top of the tree, it gave me heart failure!*

> **Rome was not built in a day** a saying, meaning that a difficult or important aim cannot be achieved quickly or all at once.

Etymologies are given for selected idioms, though they are the exception rather than the rule. As the editors state in their preface, "sometimes knowing the origin of a phrase adds to one's understanding of the expression itself. For example, **one man's meat is another man's poison** is described as "a Latin proverb from Lucretius' *De Rerum Naturae* [*sic*]." The expression **a merry-go-round**, *Chambers* notes, is derived "from the fairground amusement."

Chambers Idioms

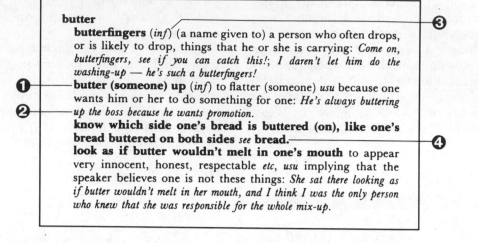

butter
    butterfingers (*inf*) (a name given to) a person who often drops, or is likely to drop, things that he or she is carrying: *Come on, butterfingers, see if you can catch this!*; *I daren't let him do the washing-up — he's such a butterfingers!*
    butter (someone) up (*inf*) to flatter (someone) *usu* because one wants him or her to do something for one: *He's always buttering up the boss because he wants promotion.*
    know which side one's bread is buttered (on), like one's bread buttered on both sides *see* **bread.**
    look as if butter wouldn't melt in one's mouth to appear very innocent, honest, respectable *etc*, *usu* implying that the speaker believes one is not these things: *She sat there looking as if butter wouldn't melt in her mouth, and I think I was the only person who knew that she was responsible for the whole mix-up.*

❶ Each idiom is set in boldface type   **❸** Italicized usage labels are   **❹** Cross-references are set in
❷ Examples of usage are italicized   enclosed in parentheses   boldface type

IV. Accessibility

Although *Chambers Idioms* is described as suitable for those who are learning the English language, the format is more accessible to the reader who wants to know the definition of a particular idiom than to the reader who wishes to learn idiomatic expressions per se.

The main entry words are key words from idioms rather than complete idiomatic phrases. The main entry words are printed in boldface type and overhang the text; they are arranged alphabetically. Idiomatic phrases related to the main entry word are indented under the main entry word and follow in alphabetical order. They are also printed in boldface type. For example, under the main entry word **carpet** are grouped the idioms **on the carpet**, **the red carpet treatment**, and **sweep (something) under the carpet**. The reader looking for such diverse idioms as **be thrown in at the deep end**, **go off the deep end**, and **in deep water** will find them all under the main entry word **deep**.

Because it is not always obvious to the reader which word in an idiomatic phrase is the "key" word, *Chambers Idioms* contains extensive cross-reference entries. For example, suppose one wants to know the definition of the expression **drive (someone) up the wall**. The reader looking this up under **drive** will find **drive (someone) up the wall** *see* **wall**. The expression with its complete definition is listed under **wall**.

Although extensive and based on common sense, the cross-reference entries are not exhaustive. The reader who is unfamiliar with a particular idiom may have to look it up under several main entry words before finding it. For example, neither **of one accord** nor **with one accord** are included as cross-reference entries under **one**; it is up to the reader to seek them out under **accord**, where their definitions are found. With a little persistence and practice, however, the reader will be able to locate any idiom included in *Chambers Idioms*.

The brief preface provides only cursory information on how to use this book; readers are left on their own to figure out how the book is arranged. There is no table of contents or index.

V. Summary

Chambers Idioms provides basic definitions of idiomatic phrases. Once the reader masters the system by which the idioms are arranged, the book is easy to use. Although its scope is fairly wide, the treatment of individual idioms is for the most part superficial. Readers desiring more background and etymological information about idioms will be better served by such works as the NEW DICTIONARY OF AMERICAN SLANG and THE FACTS ON FILE DICTIONARY OF WORD AND PHRASE ORIGINS. Readers should also note that its orientation and spellings are British. *Chambers Idioms* is a handy pocket work for ready reference idioms, but it will not be the first choice for most library or individual reference collections.

Chambers Pocket Guide to Good English

Facts at a Glance

Full Title: **Chambers Pocket Guide to Good English**.
Publisher: W. & R. Chambers Ltd.; published in the United States by Cambridge University Press.
Editor: George W. Davidson.
Edition Reviewed: © 1985; 1986 printing.

Number of Entries: 660.
Number of Pages: 140.
Trim Size: 4½" × 7".
Binding: paperback.

Price: $4.95.
Sold in bookstores; also sold to libraries and other educational institutions.
ISBN 0-521-60017-0.

I. Introduction and Scope

Chambers Pocket Guide to Good English, says its editor, is intended to serve as "a concise and easy-to-use manual of modern English usage," providing a wide range of readers with "guidelines on grammar, vocabulary, spelling, pronunciation and punctuation." It gives answers to commonly asked questions about such subjects as these: the difference between **lend** and **loan**, how to use quotation marks correctly, rules for **shall** and **will**, **may** and **can**, **infer** and **imply**, the possessive of **it**, and more. It assumes some sophistication on the part of its users, however, and would not be appropriate for people who do not know basic rules of grammar, spelling, and punctuation.

Though the emphasis in *Chambers Pocket Guide* is on English as spoken in the United Kingdom, American variants are often noted. With a few obvious exceptions (English spellings such as **aeroplane** or **sceptic**) the English slant of this guide does not diminish its usefulness; however, occasional inaccuracies about American spelling and usage suggest that American readers should be a bit wary. For example, *Chambers Pocket Guide* in its entry for **American spelling** asserts that the American spelling of **catalogue** is **catalog** and that **kidnapped** is **kidnaped** in American English. In both of these cases, the latter spellings are acceptable in American English but are not the only or even the most usual ones.

The small size of *Chambers Pocket Guide*, as well as its title, might lead American readers to assume that it is an English equivalent of Strunk and White's *The Elements of Style*; but while the latter treats general subjects of composition in essay format, *Chambers Pocket Guide* is organized like a dictionary, with key words arranged in alphabetical order. Its main purpose is to provide guidance (and quick answers) for the most common problems and errors found in written English.

II. Format

Entries are organized in alphabetical order; main entry words appear in boldface type overhanging the text. When entries contain more than one word ("**adverse, averse**") the words being compared are discussed in alphabetical order within the entry. Where pronunciation is an issue, as in the distinction between **corps** and **corpse**, phonetic spellings appear in square brackets. Readers can then refer to the chart of phonetic symbols at the front of the book. Pronunciations use the most common and easily recognized symbols, such as:

ā as in fate
o͞o as in moon
oi as in boy

The book's pocket size and sturdy binding (sewn and glued) make it appropriate for the heavy use it will probably get. The paper stock is good quality with little show-through, and both the outside and gutter margins are ample.

III. Quality and Currency of Entries

A pocket guide to good English needs to meet two contradictory needs: conciseness and comprehensiveness. *Chambers Pocket Guide* treads this fine line effectively; the entries, though selective, seem to cover, as promised, "the most common and troublesome points" of English grammar and usage. The style of the entries combines clarity with nuance.

The editor has had to exercise a great deal of judgment to cover such a broad subject in 140 pages, but a quick leaf through the book suggests that he has been effective. His stated goal is to "steer a middle course between a too conservative clinging to outdated usage and an uncritical approval of innovations whose acceptability has not yet been ascertained." For example, the entry **split infinitive** defines the term, notes the dispute sometimes generated on the subject, and argues persuasively that splitting infinitives is not only acceptable, but sometimes necessary.

Chambers Pocket Guide makes no attempt to include new terms for technology, science, or jargon, but given its size limitations, this is probably a good editorial decision.

IV. Accessibility

The dictionary format, the boldface type of major entries, and frequent cross-references in *Chambers Pocket Guide* make it easy to find the entry one wants and almost make up for the lack of an index. The only guide to the book's organization and the philosophy behind its entries is to be found in its introduction, but a glance at any page will key the reader to the book's organizational principles. Readers who become familiar with the book will probably follow the editor's advice and use it not just for quick reference but also as a book to be browsed through at leisure, thus allowing them to "spot errors in their own usage that they would otherwise not even be aware of making." Some entries, in fact, are so odd that only a browser would find them, as for example, the entry "a, an *after* no," which discusses the error in the sentence "I can think of no worse a fate than that" (the *a* should be omitted).

V. Summary

A small, handy, and easy-to-use guide to grammar, spelling, and punctuation of English (with some minor limitations for American users), *Chambers Pocket Guide to Good English* is concise, and clearly and elegantly written. It provides reasonable, unpedantic guidelines for writing clearly and correctly. It takes for granted that its users have some sophistication. This book would not be appropriate for those who have not mastered basic grammar.

A Concise Dictionary of Correct English

Facts at a Glance

Full Title: **A Concise Dictionary of Correct English**.
Publisher: Littlefield, Adams.
Editor: B. A. Phythian.
Edition Reviewed: © 1979.

Number of Entries: approximately 940.
Number of Pages: 166.
Trim Size: 5½" × 8⁷⁄₁₆".
Binding: paperback.

Price: $1.50.
Sold in bookstores and to libraries and other educational institutions.
ISBN 0-822-60349-7.

I. Introduction and Scope

According to its preface, this 1979 reference work "is intended for those who would like to brush up

their English grammar and be guided round some of the more common pitfalls in the use of English." Entries guide the user in grammatical correctness and stylistic conciseness and clarity. Many entries "require the reader to have a working knowledge of the principal parts of speech," and users lacking this knowledge are encouraged to study the work's entries under individual part-of-speech labels before looking at other entries.

The book's British editor, B. A. Phythian, has also edited *A Concise Dictionary of English Slang and Colloquialisms* and *A Concise Dictionary of English Idioms*. In the preface to *A Concise Dictionary of Correct English*, he acknowledges his indebtedness to other works on English usage, including Eric Partridge's USAGE AND ABUSAGE, Fowler's A DICTIONARY OF MODERN ENGLISH USAGE, and Gowers's *Complete Plain Words*. Phythian's volume is admirably up-to-date in its understanding of the constantly shifting nature of English usage. However, its focus is on British usage, and minimal attention is given to "Americanisms." The book is, therefore, of little real value to most American readers.

II. Format

Entries are arranged alphabetically. Boldface main entry words overhang the text. When any form of the entry word or phrase recurs within the entry, it is italicized. Also italicized are phrases containing the entry word, incorrect alternatives to the entry word, and words or phrases presented as correct alternatives for misused main entries. Words used within entries that have their own main entries appear in boldface, and cross-references, beginning with "see," are usefully provided in some cases. For some entries, illustrative sentences are provided. These are printed in roman type and indented from the left margin. A representative entry is the following:

> **degree**. The common phrase *to a less degree* should be used when two things are being referred to, because *less* is the comparative form (see **adjective 1, 3**):
> > Male cosmetics are widely used in America, and to a less degree in England.
> *Lesser* means *less than less*, and *to a lesser degree* should not be used unless this is the intended sense. See **less, lesser**.
> > The expression *to a more or less degree* is bad English because, though *a less degree* makes sense, *a more degree* does not.

The print is clear and adequate in size, with minimal show-through. White space is used advantageously to make pages easy to read. The volume does not open flat, but the pages do not separate easily from the binding of this sturdy paperback.

III. Quality and Currency of Entries

This usage guide provides solutions to many problems that writers encounter. For example, users are shown the distinction between **e.g.** and **i.e.**, **counsel** and **council**, **infer** and **imply**, **militate** and **mitigate**. Users are taught how to form the plurals of such words as **hero**, **crisis**, and **criterion**; how to apply rules of grammar and syntax; how to distinguish **active** from **passive** voice; and how to recognize a **cliché**, a **euphemism**, and figurative language such as a **simile**, a **metaphor**, and **onomatopoeia**.

The work is not intended for the novice in English grammar and usage. Although illustrative examples are often provided, some entries exclude or underemphasize concrete examples. For instance, after a brief definition of **mixed metaphor** ("a ludicrous mixture" of metaphors), the user is merely warned:

> Do not fall into the sort of error committed by the local politician who wrote to tell *The Times* that, at a recent event which had ended in a riot, the police had leaned over backwards to maintain a low profile!

It is left for the reader to identify and analyze the mixed metaphor. Another entry appears as follows:

> **officious** (meddlesome, over–zealous, interfering) should not be confused with **official** (properly authorised).

Without illustrative sentences, the entry may not provide sufficient distinguishing information to the reader.

Most importantly, the American user should be aware that what the entries present is British usage. Some American users could be confused and misled by many of the entries. British spelling is retained. For example, under **gram**, **gramme** the user is told that "either spelling is acceptable"; under **humour**, **humourous**, only the British spellings are provided. The British slant also appears, for example, in the entry for **pound**, which stresses the term's application in British currency, and in the following entry:

> **Mr** and **Mrs** do not need full stops after them.

Not only does this provide the American reader with incorrect usage information, it also uses the unfamiliar "full stop" for "period."

"Americanisms" receive minimal treatment in the book. For example, under **raise** the user is told

> An increase in wages is a *rise*. The use of *raise* in this sense is an Americanism.

Another entry begins:

> **stop off**, **stop over** are Americanisms which have established themselves firmly. *Stop off* means no more than *stop*, and the redundant *off* should be avoided. *Stop over* is slightly more useful, but if *over* means *overnight*, as it usually does, why not say so?

The most obvious strength of this 1979 work rests in its reflection of current trends in usage. The tendency toward dropping the hyphen when "words are taken into common usage (coeducation, hypermarket, cooperation)" is noted. Under **verb** the user is told that it is permissible to split an infinitive for the sake of fluency or clarity of expression.

IV. Accessibility

Information is easily located in this alphabetized and cross-referenced book. Boldface guide words at the top of each spread indicate the first and last entries on the spread.

V. Summary

A Concise Dictionary of Correct English is an informative, clearly written, and easy-to-use guide to usage. However, the book's British slant seriously limits its usefulness for American readers, who would be better served by MODERN AMERICAN USAGE or the HARPER DICTIONARY OF CONTEMPORARY USAGE.

A Dictionary of American Idioms

Facts at a Glance

Full Title: **A Dictionary of American Idioms: Second Edition**.
Publisher: Barron's.
Editor: Adam Makkai.
Edition Reviewed: © 1987.

Number of Volumes: 1.
Number of Entries: over 5,000.
Number of Pages: 480.
Trim Size: 6" × 9".
Binding: paperback.

Price: $11.95.
Sold in bookstores and through direct mail.
ISBN 0-8120-3899-1.

I. Introduction and Scope

This is an expanded and updated edition of the *Dictionary of Idioms* first published by Barron's Educational Series in 1975. That first edition, based upon *A Dictionary of Idioms for the Deaf* (1969), was translated into Japanese and Chinese, and other translations are in progress.

The dictionary defines more than 5,000 American idiomatic words and phrases currently in use. These include CB radio jargon—for example, **that's a ten-**

four—and computer and drug culture expressions that have found their way into common parlance, such as **get a fix**.

Adam Makkai, professor of linguistics at the University of Illinois, has edited both editions of *The Dictionary of Idioms*.

II. Format

Main entries are in boldface type overhanging the text. The pages are set in two columns and are well designed, with plenty of white space for legibility. The paper is of adequate quality with only minor show-through. The paperback edition is useful for the home or office but would not stand up to heavy library use without rebinding.

III. Quality and Currency of Entries

The main entry is followed by its part of speech and a restrictive usage label where applicable. As well as the more common *formal, informal, slang, vulgar,* and *archaic* labels, there are labels such as *substandard* for **in bad** (out of favor) and *Space English* for **chicken switch** (ejection button).

The definition of the idiom is illustrated by an example sentence in italics, followed by a "translation" into simple, clear English in parentheses. Here is a typical entry:

> **fall flat** *v.*, *informal* To be a failure; fail. *The party fell flat because of the rain.* (The party was a failure because of the rain.) *His joke fell flat because no one understood it.* (His joke failed because no one understood it.)

Entries are frequently cross-referenced: **get on the bandwagon** refers the reader to **jump on the bandwagon**; and many entries contain key reference or index words only, such as

> **wear** See IF THE SHOE FITS—WEAR IT, WASH AND WEAR, WORSE FOR WEAR.

In his introduction, Professor Makkai recognizes that there are more idioms than he has listed in the book: "only the most frequently occurring in American English are included. British English or the English spoken in Australia certainly has many idiomatic expressions that are not part of American English." However, there are many less common idioms used in America which also cannot be found in this dictionary, for example, *cross the Rubicon, log in, gilt-edged,* and *hands-on experience,* to mention just a few.

The dictionary lives up to its editor's promise of keeping up with the usage of the seventies and eighties. **Haircut place** (CB jargon for a tight-clearance overpass), **all strung out**, and **main squeeze**, all of which are included, are relative newcomers to the language.

IV. Accessibility

Ease of access is vital for any idioms dictionary since it may be of primary use to students whose first language is not English. Although *A Dictionary of American Idioms* is fairly easy to use, the recently published NTC's AMERICAN IDIOMS DICTIONARY (reviewed elsewhere in this Buying Guide) has a phrase-finder index that gives the user many more access points to an idiomatic phrase. For example, in the latter work **tide over** can be found under either word, while in this dictionary it appears only under **tide**.

The introduction includes an essay "What Is an Idiom?" and explanations on the use of the dictionary. Its two-page "Guide to the Parts of an Entry" is a model of clarity and is followed by a key to abbreviations.

A table of contents lists the main sections of the dictionary, and guide words at the top of each page help to locate idioms.

V. Summary

A Dictionary of American Idioms is an excellent tool to aid comprehension by students whose first language is not English and to improve usage by native speakers. The book compares favorably with the similarly priced NTC's AMERICAN IDIOMS DICTIONARY. However, neither work fulfills a library's need for an authoritative guide to idioms used in other English-speaking countries or idioms found in literary or historical writing. For these purposes a library needs the OXFORD DICTIONARY OF CURRENT IDIOMATIC ENGLISH or the learned predecessor of the present volume, *The Dictionary of Idioms for the Deaf.*

Dictionary of American Regional English

Facts at a Glance

Full Title: **Dictionary of American Regional English: Volume I, Introduction and A–C.**
Publisher: The Belknap Press of Harvard University Press.
Editor: Frederic G. Cassidy, Chief Editor.
Edition Reviewed: © 1985.

Number of Entries: approximately 14,500 plus cross-references.
Number of Pages: 903.
Number of Maps: 17.
Trim Size: 8½" × 11".
Binding: cloth.

Price: $60.00.

Sold in bookstores and other outlets; also sold to libraries and other educational institutions. ISBN 0-674-20511-1.

I. Introduction and Scope

The *Dictionary of American Regional English* (DARE) is a scholarly project sponsored by the American Dialect Society (ADS). It has a history of almost a hundred years of dedicated work by many scholars. DARE's present form has been under the guidance of Frederic G. Cassidy, professor emeritus of English at the University of Wisconsin, where the DARE office is located. The dictionary is projected to be in five volumes with the final volume to include a detailed bibliography of the quoted sources and a complete list of the DARE staff members. Volume II is scheduled for publication in the spring of 1990.

DARE's purpose was to capture and document, as comprehensively as possible, a record of regional American English in 1,000 selected communities. This project is a race against time as our population moves about the country, with its older members dying and the mass media fostering a uniformity of speech.

DARE's editors "have sought to produce a work of useful scholarship, one that will testify to the wondrous variety and creativeness of human language. . . . "

DARE developed a questionnaire that covers 41 categories with a total of 1,847 questions. These questions were phrased without using any words that the informant could use as his answer. The field workers were mostly graduate students trained in English language and linguistics with the ability to handle phonetic transcriptions. The 1,000 communities and 2,777 individual informants were chosen so that the aggregate would reflect the native population of the United States in its diversity. There was, however, a deliberate weighting towards older people since they remember and use language with which younger people are no longer familiar.

DARE excluded technical, scientific, or other learned words or phrases—"or anything else that could be considered standard." With this as the general exclusion policy, the editors were guided by two criteria for inclusion:

> (1) Any word or phrase whose form or meaning is not used generally throughout the United States but only in part (or parts) of it, or by a particular social group.

> (2) Any word or phrase whose form or meaning is distinctively a folk usage. . . .

DARE has defined folk usage as language that is learned at home or in the community, not from schooling, books, or other sources of communication. Artificial forms of speech or any speech whose purpose is to exclude an outsider, such as criminal jargon, are also excluded unless words or phrases from these in-groups have come into wider use. This policy also extends to professional or occupational jargon that is only understood by its users. An example of an "in" word now in general use is the jazz musician's **cool**. Vocabularies of highly specialized or esoteric occupations have also been excluded. DARE has included the vocabularies of widespread occupations such as farming, cattle raising, housework, lumbering, and mining. These occupations involve entire communities and even entire areas and regions.

The language that comes from children's games is included since it is usually of folk origin and has been preserved orally. Children's games also show great regional differences. Some examples in this first volume are **andy-over** with quotations from 1905–67; **base** with quotations from 1845–1980; **battleships** and **bombardment**.

The language collected by DARE "is any form of American English as spoken in the various regions of the United States."

DARE uses computer-generated maps that can look distorted because they are enlarged or diminished according to linguistic groups. Approximately four percent of the entries have explanatory maps which aid the reader's visualization of the region of use of the word or phrase. The final volume will contain a "map section" with interpretive social and contrastive maps.

II. Format

DARE has been printed on acid-free paper with bindings chosen for strength and durability. While the volume is large, it is not too heavy for easy handling. The book lies flat and has a well-designed layout. There are two columns per page with good margins on all sides. The use of different typefaces makes the various elements easy to distinguish. When used, the maps are placed next to or near the word or phrase that is being illustrated.

The first volume contains a lengthy introduction, giving the history of the project and the methodology of data collection. Other sections include an explanation of the DARE maps, the full text of the questionnaire, a list of the informants with tabular information about them, two essays (Cassidy's "Language Changes" and James H. Hartman's "Guide to Pronunciation," both essential for understanding the DARE entries, and also a five-page list of abbreviations.

Entries are arranged in strict alphabetical sequence, letter by letter. WEBSTER'S THIRD NEW INTERNATIONAL DICTIONARY was used as the standard for the spelling of established words. While most entries are single words, phrases and compounds are also entered. Variant forms are used as main entry words, if their frequency warrants it. For example, entries include,

> **briggle** v [Prob obs Scots *breeghle* to fiddle, make little progress despite much bustling]
> To fuss about ineffectively; see quot 1912.
> **1889** *Jrl. Amer. Folkl.* 2.155 **OH**, *Briggle* . . . To be in an uneasy mental condition, to shift attention from one thing to another. "Don't briggle so." **1912** *DN* 3.572 **wIN**, *Briggle* . . . To busy oneself without purpose; to potter. "He never stops brigglin' around." **1930s** in 1944 *ADD* **eWV**, 'Stop brigglin' with that.' Common. **1967** *DARE* (Qu. A10, . . . *Somebody asks*, "*What are you doing?*" *and you answer*, "*Nothing in particular. I'm just____*") Inf **IA8**, Briggling around. [Inf old]

> **chophouse** n [*OED* 1690 →]
> A restaurant, esp one of poor quality.
> **1806** (1970) Webster *Compendious Dict.*, *Chophouse* . . . a house to eat provisions at. **1840** Bird *Robin Day* 31 (*DAE*), I summoned courage enough to enter a little tavern or chophouse. **1873** Miller *Modocs* 340 **CA**, The food was cold refuse of some low chophouse. **1907** Field *Six-Cylinder* 74 **NYC**, A moment later we drew up in front of a well-known chophouse. **1950** *WELS* (*Nicknames . . . a small eating place*) 1 Inf, **ceWI**, Chophouse. **1967–70** *DARE* (Qu. D39, . . . *A small eating place where the food is not especially good*) Inf **CA19**, Chophouse—very bad; **CA** 194, Chophouse.

These entries illustrate the DARE format. After parts of speech, pronunciation, etymology, geographic and usage labels, and cross-references, dated quotations and DARE research are presented to expand and illustrate the word's usage. Original sources were preferred, as were quotations that defined the word or phrase rather than just mentioning it. The bibliography in the final volume will list every source quoted in DARE, giving the reader all the facts necessary to track it down.

III. Quality and Currency of Entries

It must be remembered that DARE concentrates on words and phrases that cannot be found elsewhere. About 45 percent of its entries fall into this category. There are, for instance, 176 names in DARE for dust balls under the bed. Reviewers have had unanimous praise for DARE's quality of entries. *Choice* (January 1986, p. 728) stated, "Cassidy's first volume provides unequaled coverage of words and phrases, with an emphasis on still current colloquialisms. In scope and fieldwork execution, this surpasses all of its predecessors (e.g. *A Dictionary of American English on Historical Principles*, 1936–44) and *American Dialect Dictionary*, 1944)." *Wilson Library Bulletin*

(November 1985, p. 61) stated, "Much more, all of it good, can be said about the dictionary; let it suffice, however, to say that DARE is as essential as the OED."

IV. Accessibility

Though DARE reflects the fine scholarship that has gone into its preparation, its concise definitions are accessible to the general reader. Stumped by the noun **bobbasheely**, the reader easily comprehends DARE's meaning—a very close friend. The subsequent historical evidence in the entry requires greater stamina, but this also becomes accessible with perseverance.

A lengthy "Treatment of Entries" section explains the entries' components. However, this section does not use illustrative examples from the text, nor is there a graphic explanatory guide for easy reference. A fully comprehensive five-page list of abbreviations immediately precedes the text.

Pronunciation is a crucial component of a dictionary of regional English, which perhaps explains why there is a seven-page pronunciation key rather than the quick-access keys usually found in dictionaries.

V. Summary

DARE makes a unique contribution to American lexicography for regional and folk language. *Reference Books Bulletin* (1 April 1986, p. 1126) in its summary and evaluation says "In its presentation, depth of scholarship and unique database, DARE is a stellar addition to existing sources. Because of its sociolinguistic importance, it has cross-disciplinary applications. The information it contains on folklore, natural history, and children's games gives it both scholarly and popular appeal. It will be of interest to anyone who is fascinated by folk language and the vernacular."

DARE should be in all academic and large public libraries. It is a major reference source for lexicographers, linguists, social scientists, and social historians, as well as folklorists and interested lay persons.

Dictionary of Collective Nouns and Group Terms

Facts at a Glance

Full Title: **Dictionary of Collective Nouns and Group Terms. Being a Compendium of More Than 1800 Collective Nouns, Group Terms, and Phrases That from Medieval to Modern Times Have Described Companies of Persons, Birds, Insects, Animals, Professions, and Objects.**
Publisher: Gale Research Company.
Editor: Ivan G. Sparkes.
Edition Reviewed: © 1985.

Number of Entries: over 1,800.
Number of Pages: 288.
Number of Indexes: 1.
Trim Size: 5¼″ × 8½″.
Binding: cloth.

Price: $65.00.
Sold in academic bookstores; also sold to libraries and other educational institutions.
ISBN 0-8103-2188-2.

I. Introduction and Scope

The *Dictionary of Collective Nouns and Group Terms* is a scholarly reference work, now in its second edition, containing entries for more than 1,800 words that function as plurals. These include a number of terms encountered in the press, in general literature, and in everyday conversation, such as **bunch**, **cabal**, **canon**, **caucus**, **heap**, **rabbinate**, **race**, and **squadron**. The majority of the entry words in this book, however, will be unfamiliar to the general reader. Terms in this category may include such obscure words as **ammullock** ("piled untidily in a confused heap"), **briggandage** ("brigands or robbers *collectively*"), **bullary**, **bullarium** ("a collection of papal bulls or documents"), and **cateran** ("common people of the Highlands in a band; brigands, freebooters, or marauders *collectively*"). The editor notes that "most of the terms have been selected because they are unusual, or interesting, or fun."

The contents of the dictionary fall into several groups, including ancient phrases; general terms applied to people, animals, or objects; words made collective by the addition of a *-y* or *-age* ending; modern punning terms; and terms of quantity, number, or capacity.

II. Format

Entries in the *Dictionary of Collective Nouns and Group Terms* are set up in dictionary form. Boldface entry words appear in alphabetical order and overhang the text, which is set one column per page. Guide words indicate the first entry on the left-hand page and the last entry on the right-hand page. There is ample white space in the margins and between entries. The typeface is clear and legible, there is virtually no show-through, and the binding is adequate.

III. Quality and Currency of Entries

Entries are simple, consisting at the most of the entry word, its definition or the context in which it is applied, cross-references to related terms, examples of its use, and the earliest known use of the word or phrase. The following exemplifies an entry containing all these elements:

> **faction** a company of people acting together, often a contentious group; a set or class of people. See also **cabal**, **clique**, **junta**.
> *Examples:* factions of collegians, monks, and canons, 1530; of evil, 1614; of fools, 1606.

Many entries, however, are even briefer and provide little or no information about the term's origin: "**factory** a body of factors, or workers, 1702" or "**schemozzle** of monkeys."

The frontmatter provides a bibliography of sources; for the most part these are antiquarian books, and many are out of print. The editor notes that many group terms date from the medieval period; others are taken from the Elizabethan and Jacobean-Stuart periods, while another large group have their origin in the Victorian period. Only a handful of entry words, such as **strut** (as in the phrase a strut of junior executives), are of recent vintage.

IV. Accessibility

Entries are arranged alphabetically, letter by letter, and the graphic features already mentioned make them easy to locate. The reader is aided further by a 68-page index that lists all the items for which a collective term in this dictionary is used. A brief explanatory note is printed at the head of the index for readers who are unfamiliar with this sort of specialized index. For example, the reader who wants to find out what collective nouns in this dictionary can be used in tandem with the word **abuse** will find the following index entry: "abuse: **school**; **stream**, **torrent**."

V. Summary

This book will have little if any practical utility for the general reader, though people interested in words will like it, and it may be of some interest to writers. It may find a place in academic collections with concentrations in linguistics, etymology, and lexicology, rather than in general reference collections.

Dictionary of Confusing Words and Meanings

Facts at a Glance

Full Title: **Dictionary of Confusing Words and Meanings**.
Publisher: Routledge, Chapman & Hall.
Compiler: Adrian Room.

Edition Reviewed: © 1985; 1986 printing.

Number of Entries: 3,000.
Number of Pages: 267.
Trim Size: 6″ × 9″.
Binding: cloth.

Price: $22.50.
Sold in bookstores; also sold to libraries and other educational institutions.
ISBN 0-7102-0661-5.

I. Introduction and Scope

The introduction to this dictionary states that it is "a revised and enlarged blend, in a single volume, of two earlier books: *Room's Dictionary of Confusibles* (first published in 1979) and *Room's Dictionary of Distinguishables* (1981)." It attempts "to sort out a selection of words [presented usually in pairs] that are annoyingly similar in sound or meaning." The words are drawn from several areas that the compiler describes in the introduction: 1) "hard" words from our passive vocabulary not used daily to express ourselves, such as **abrogate/abdicate** and **assiduous/sedulous**; 2) technical words with which we may not be familiar, such as **apogee/perigee** and **genus/species**; 3) words with known meanings but whose endings cause doubts, such as **luxurious/luxuriant** and **chlorine/chloride**; 4) foreign words, such as **au fait/au courant**; 5) words with sounds matching their meanings, such as **sleigh/sled/sledge**.

Adrian Room is a well-known British linguist and compiler of reference books. The volume contains some words that will have reference value only to British readers, but most words will be familiar to American readers, even when spelled in the British fashion.

II. Format

The words are presented in alphabetical order, two columns per page, with entry words in boldface, followed by the definition or "sense link" that ties the words together in parentheses, above the actual entry, such as

atheist/agnostic (one not inclined to believe in God).

The second word of the entry pair will also have its own entry at the proper alphabetical position—**agnostic** see **atheist**. The overlapping confusion between the words is then discussed, but *all* meanings of the words discussed are not always given. As Room says in the introduction, "Readers who wish for more detailed information on the various sense of a word or would like more examples of usage than are given

here, should consult a good, up-to-date dictionary. . . ."

This volume, in fact, omits most elements of the usual dictionary entry, including pronunciation, etymology, part of speech, and usage label, as well as illustrative phrases or sentences and synonyms. With its spacious, easy-to-read page and its study binding, this is an attractive word book.

III. Quality and Currency of Entries

Word buffs and amateur linguists will find this book of great interest, but its usefulness will really depend on the word knowledge the reader already has. If readers already understand the difference between *astronaut* and *cosmonaut*—and in this case the difference does seem to be an extraordinarily obvious one—they may well wonder why the words have been included in the vocabulary. Other examples of this type of entry include **African elephant/Indian elephant**, **butter/margarine**, **solfeggio/arpeggio** and **software/hardware**.

More examples of pairs (or more) of confusing words include: **equable/equitable**, **cavil/carp**, **censor/censure**, **eruption/irruption**, **decidedly/decisively**, **cartoon/caricature**, **apprehension/anxiety**, **era/epoch/aeon**, **Muslim/Moslem/Mohammedan/Musselman**, **Gestapo/SS**, **prejudice/bias**, and **sortie/sally**.

A sample of entries, reproduced in their entirety, may prove most helpful in clearing up confusion—some recognizedly thorny or technically out-of-reach, some embarassingly simple—for the reader:

envy/jealousy (feeling of resentment caused by someone else having something that one does not have oneself) 'Envy', one of the seven deadly sins, does not necessarily imply a feeling of ill will, but often simply a longing for something that someone else has, even if it is theirs by right. 'Jealousy' is a much more personal thing, a feeling that the other person's right to what he has is not as great as one's own, with a consequent sense of rivalry, as a tussle of love or a contest for promotion at work; you have the prior claim, you know you have!

imply/infer (deduce — or mean)
Two fairly hoary confusibles: the diarist of *The Times* [of London] once . . . used 'inferred' for 'implied' and caused an excited flutter among his readers. (He subsequently, but not too convincingly, referred readers to the *OED* in his defence.) In fact the two are indeed often used interchangeably, but strictly speaking: 'imply' means 'express indirectly' — almost 'mean' — and 'infer' means 'derive by reasoning', 'deduce'. For some reason 'infer' is frequently used where many would prefer 'imply', but 'imply' hardly ever used instead of 'infer'. So if I 'imply' that you are deceitful, I say so indirectly; if I 'infer' that you are deceitful, I gather that you are from what you say or do, or from what I hear about you.

engraving/etching (drawing or picture made by cutting into stone or metal)

An 'engraving' is done by cutting words, a pattern or a drawing in metal, stone, wood, glass, or other incisable substance. An 'etching' is a form of 'engraving' in which the cutting is done not with a cutting tool but with acids or corrosives, and moreover on metal only. The metal plate to be etched is first coated with a thin layer of gums, waxes and resins (the ' "etching"-ground') through which the drawing or pattern is scratched. The plate is then placed in an acid bath and the acid bites or 'eats' (which is the origin of the word 'etch') into the lines traced. The actual etching has to be executed in mirror form, back to front, so that the positive print it produces is the right way round on paper. The 'etching' originated from the custom of etching designs on armour: those responsible for doing this, either enterprisingly or lazily, found it easier to etch this way instead of cutting.

The detail and clarity of the explanation of **engraving/etching** seem unexceptionable, and the reader may infer from the length of this entry the compiler's interest in the subject. Other entries may seem idiosyncratic to many readers, but since the limited selection is clearly that of one compiler, it also may be deemed acceptable, especially when it supplies so many excellent definitions and distinctions.

Nevertheless, what is one man's meat is another man's poison, and this book will doubtless invite many different opinions of its usefulness. When it is good, it is very, very good, and when it seems obvious, it may tend to appear padded or extraneous.

Owing to the nature of the exercise, it is not necessary for the entries to be up-to-date, although a few of them (for example, woofer/tweeter) come close.

IV. Accessibility

The *Dictionary of Confusing Words and Meanings* is very simple to use. The alphabetical listing of words takes up the whole book except for the few pages of the introduction. As noted above, the entry words appear in boldface; guide words appear at the outer top corners of each two-page spread, with folios at the bottom outside corner of each page.

V. Summary

This is another interesting word book by Adrian Room that will appeal to word lovers, although it may have a more limited audience than some of the other books he has compiled. (See elsewhere in this guide for reviews of A DICTIONARY OF TRUE ETYMOLOGIES and DICTIONARY OF CHANGES IN MEANING.) Despite the excellent explanations to clear up confusions, readers may find many of the "confusibles" quite simple and obvious from the outset or idiosyncratic in the extreme and, therefore, not the material

for a general reference book. (This will depend on each reader's knowledge or background.) The book, however, does provide many excellent explanations of word usage and may prove desirable for some large, specialized, or well-endowed collections.

Dictionary of Contemporary American English Contrasted with British English

Facts at a Glance

Full Title: **Dictionary of Contemporary American English Contrasted with British English**.

Former Title: A Dictionary of Modern American and British English on a Contrastive Basis.

Publisher: Arnold-Heinemann; distributed by Humanities Press.

Compiler: Givi Zviadadze.

Edition Reviewed: © 1983.

Number of Entries: over 1,000.
Number of Pages: 404.
Number of Indexes: 1.
Trim Size: $5\frac{1}{2}'' \times 8\frac{3}{4}''$.
Binding: cloth.

Price: $35.00.
ISBN 0-391-02593-7.

I. Introduction and Scope

The *Dictionary of Contemporary American English Contrasted with British English*, published in 1983, replaces a 1972 work, *A Dictionary of Modern American and British English on a Contrastive Basis*, which contrasted British and American English in terms of word meanings, grammar, spelling, and pronunciation. The current volume is a revised, enlarged version of its predecessor.

The book's compiler, Givi Zviadadze, is a professor in the Department of West European Languages and Literature at Tbilisi State University in Georgia, USSR. According to the preface, the compiler has "not only tried to indicate the differences that separate American English from British English in words, phrases, meanings, and grammar but also often fixed attention on similarities." The volume is not intended to prescribe usage to native speakers of either form of English, but rather "to help teachers and students of English, who have it as a foreign language, to use their English more correctly." Members of this audience have often learned British usage in their language classes, but they have a strong interest in American English—an international language—and require a basis for distinguishing British and American variants. In addition to this intended audience, the book will be of interest to both British and American students of linguistics and literature.

Along with contrasted pairs of words and phrases, the volume contains definitions, commentary, synonyms, and verbal illustrations. It also includes a four-page bibliography and a comprehensive index of the words and phrases discussed in the entries.

This book is based in part on contemporary American and British dictionaries. These are listed at the front of the volume and include such works as WEBSTER'S THIRD NEW INTERNATIONAL DICTIONARY and THE SHORTER OXFORD DICTIONARY. The compiler also made use of materials he collected from British and American books and periodicals during his 20 years of lexicographic research.

II. Format

The alphabetically arranged text is full-page width, and each entry is headed by the boldface American entry word or phrase flush left, with its boldface British variant flush right. An asterisk preceding an entry word indicates that it is *chiefly* British or *chiefly* American. Beneath the entry words, slightly indented, appears a definition. This is sometimes preceded by a part-of-speech abbreviation, though no indication is given as to why a part of speech is indicated in some cases but not in others. Following the definition, most entries provide a brief discussion of the variants and other synonyms. The illustrative phrases and sentences appear below, in smaller type and farther indented.

Although this book is distributed by Humanities Press, it is produced in India. A slip inserted in the volume by Humanities Press states that "the Indian publications are not of the high standards of our books." Indeed, the paper quality is poor, and there is considerable bleed-through in the frontmatter. Though there is also show-through of text within the lexicon, it does not impede readability. The typefaces are large and clear, and adequate white space is used. The double-column index pages are also easy to read. The cover is sturdy, but the signatures are poorly sewn and tend to pull apart.

III. Quality and Currency of Entries

The definitions provided are clear and concise. For ***hood . . . bonnet**, for example, the definition given is "movable metal cover of the engine of a car." For **major in . . . read**, the definition is "to specialize; pursue a principal subject or course of study." The discussions that follow are interesting and informa-

tive. For example, under **chow, chuck . . . tuck, chuff, nosh** appears the following discussion:

> 'Chow' is also known in Britain but has never been as widely used as has it in the United States. Synonymous with 'grub,' 'eats,' 'scoff' (all slang; Amer. & Brit.).
>
> The following terms are extended to denote: 'chow' (mealtime), 'chuck' (provisions; a meal or meals), 'tuck' (a hearty meal, esp. of delicacies), 'eats' (meals), 'scoff' (meals).

This entry provides a valuable range of terms and makes some useful distinctions between American and British usage. However, the relegation of **nosh** to British usage will surprise many Americans. Further, the first paragraph appears to suggest that the three synonyms listed are equally frequent in both usages, when most younger Americans are unlikely to be familiar with **scoff**. Other minor drawbacks appear in the entry: the British use of single quotation marks; an unidiomatic inversion (". . . as has it in the United States"); the awkward syntax of the second paragraph. Although the book is strong in its broad distinctions, there are some distracting flaws in its details.

Perhaps the volume's greatest strength is its rich use of illustrative phrases and sentences quoted from the works of well-known twentieth-century popular writers. These quotations are helpfully identified by author and title. In the entry just discussed, the authors quoted include Mickey Spillane, Stephen Crane, and Eugene O'Neill. Quotations from American authors predominate, in keeping with the book's primary intent to focus on American usage. Other authors quoted include, for example, Jack Kerouac, Upton Sinclair, Shirley Jackson, Thomas Wolfe, William Gass, F. Scott Fitzgerald, John Updike, and Truman Capote. For the intended audience, these many examples of the words used in context will be valuable aids to the distinction between British and American usage. However, in a few cases, the compiler's reliance on literary citations results in questionable generalizations. For example, under **fresh-water college . . . small college**, he asserts that "in the United States 'fresh-water college' is a common name for 'small college.' " Although he provides one supporting illustrative phrase, most American readers would take issue with the assertion.

IV. Accessibility

The pages within the lexicon present no guide words to aid users in locating alphabet sections. However, the large, boldface entry word pairs, of which there are seldom more than three on a page, make it easy for readers to find the section they are seeking. The page numbers are centered at the tops of pages, which is useful for tracking down an index reference. The index provides a comprehensive listing not only of entry words, but also of other variants and synonyms discussed within the entries. However, main entry terms are not distinguished from other entries in the index, which is a small inconvenience to the reader. A table of contents is provided at the front of the volume.

V. Summary

The *Dictionary of Contemporary American English Contrasted with British English* will help its intended audience distinguish between British and American usage and will provide them with a wealth of illustrative material from popular writers. Occasionally it will lead them astray, however, by providing insufficient differentiations between the two usages or unwarranted generalizations. The book will also be of interest to native speakers of English who are interested in British and American literature and linguistics.

The volume is more expensive than its low-quality production warrants, and many libraries will not have sufficient call for such a book to overlook flaws in printing and binding. But in public libraries whose patrons include immigrants, as well as in college and university libraries, the dictionary merits a place.

A Dictionary of Modern English Usage

Facts at a Glance

Full Title: **A Dictionary of Modern English Usage: Second Edition.**
Alternative Title: Fowler's Modern English Usage: Second Edition.
Publisher: Oxford University Press.
Compiler: H. W. Fowler.
Editor: Sir Ernest Gowers.
Edition Reviewed: © 1965; 1986 reprinting in the Oxford Paperback Reference series.

Number of Entries: more than 4,350.
Number of Pages: 748.
Trim Size: 4⅞″ × 7¼″.
Binding: cloth; paperback.

Price: $17.95 (cloth); $9.95 (paperback).
Sold in bookstores and through direct mail and other outlets; also sold to libraries and other educational institutions.
ISBN 0-19-869115-7 (cloth);
ISBN 0-19-281389-7 (paperback).

I. Introduction and Scope

In his preface to the revised edition of H. W. Fowler's *A Dictionary of Modern English Usage*, Sir Ernest Gowers presents a loving portrait of Fowler and a brief history of Fowler's collaboration (with his brother Francis) in the highly touted publication of *The King's English* (1906). Even more impressive, however, was Fowler's first edition of *Modern English Usage* (1926). Gowers calls it an "epoch-making book in the strict sense of that overworked phrase," and ponders the huge success of the book, which is not a traditional dictionary but a series of lucid and often meditative general articles (as well as word entries) whose author's wit and personality shine through each page.

Fowler, a strong proponent of simple diction, found "all kinds of affectation and humbug" offensive. Finding the right word is a major emphasis of his dictionary; grammar is secondary. He was a debunker of grammatical "superstitions" and "fetishes" that were, he felt, "invented by pedagogues for no other apparent purpose than to make writing more difficult." Nevertheless, Fowler was criticized by his contemporary, the scholar Otto Jespersen, for being a "prescriptive grammarian." In his revised edition, Gowers makes no attempt to convert Fowler, "the instinctive grammatical moralizer," into anything more or less.

Gowers's alterations in the text are based on a desire to bring the book up to date without sacrificing the "Fowleresque flavour." A significant change is the omission in this edition of the thirty-page article on "Technical Terms" (definitions of terms from rhetoric, grammar, logic, prosody, diplomacy, literature, and other fields). These terms, if relevant to modern usage, can now be found within the running alphabetical text of the dictionary or in other Oxford publications. Gowers also omits the eight-page list of French words included for their pronunciation; he does retain a revised article on the use of **French words** that includes information on pronunciation. A few new entries have been added.

The scope of the title words explored in this volume is enormous. The areas covered include appropriate usage, style, linguistic concepts, grammatical and syntactical terms, the formation of words, their spellings and inflections, pronunciation and typography, the nuances of their meanings or idiomatic usages, and their etymology.

II. Format

General articles and entries on individual words are included in the same alphabetical dictionary format. Title words are printed in lowercase bold type on two-column pages flush with the text of each column. Cross-references are provided in small capital letters.

A Dictionary of Modern English Usage

❶ Main entries are set in boldface type and are arranged alphabetically

❷ Cross-references are set in small capitals

❸ Examples of standard and nonstandard usage are given

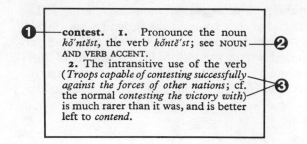

contest. **1.** Pronounce the noun *kŏ'ntĕst*, the verb *kŏntĕ'st*; see NOUN AND VERB ACCENT. **2.** The intransitive use of the verb (*Troops capable of contesting successfully against the forces of other nations*; cf. the normal *contesting the victory with*) is much rarer than it was, and is better left to *contend*.

For long articles the contents are numbered and listed beginning immediately after and on the same line as the entry word. When referred to in the text, the entry word(s) are abbreviated. Under the entry for **split infinitive**, the contents of the article are divided into (1) those who neither know nor care what a split infinitive is; (2) those who do not know, but care very much; (3) those who know and condemn; (4) those who know and approve; and (5) those who know and distinguish. These categories are expanded in detail for several pages.

The paperback edition examined was sturdily bound. The outer margins of each page were quite narrow and the spacing between entries varied with some adequately spaced and others cramped together.

III. Quality and Currency of Entries

As noted above, Gowers's revised edition of Fowler is an update of the 1926 edition. Although published in 1965, and no longer new, the book is still fresh and still a *must* for all writers and students of the language.

Received pronunciation is one completely new addition, an essay that defines and describes the standard of pronunciation "used by only a minority of the people in Britain but heard, since the invention of broadcasting, constantly by almost all of them." This is the same received standard used as the guide to pronunciation in the *OED*. Gowers's article on the subject cites arguments for and against the "R.P." which, he concludes, "goes its own way, regardless of admonition."

Revisions of existing entries are prevalent. Under **popularized technicalities**, for example, Gowers expands and gives a special section to those words gleaned from Medicine and Psychology, notably "Freudian English," a "jargon . . . that employs with greater freedom than accuracy [quasi-scientific] terms such as *ambivalent*, . . . *fixation*, . . . *id*, . . . *phobia*, . . . *psychopath*, . . . [and] *repression* . . ." It is unfortunate that neither Fowler nor Gowers is available for input on the infusion of computer terminology into the language. It is also important to note

that the work's date precludes discussion of other linguistic questions now considered vital, such as the avoidance of sexist language. For such discussions, Fowler must be supplemented by the use of other, more contemporary dictionaries.

Retained unaltered is the useful table on types of **humour** (humor, wit, satire, sarcasm, invective, irony, cynicism, the sardonic) giving motive or aim, province, method or means, and audience for each.

IV. Accessibility

Replacing Fowler's "List of General Articles" and greatly enhancing accessibility in the revised edition is the "Classified Guide to the Dictionary." The guide is divided into four sections: Usage ("points of grammar, syntax, style, and the choice of words"); the formation of words, and their spelling and inflections (further subdivided in the guide); pronunciation; and punctuation and typography. Not included in the classified guide are entries that are "concerned only with the meaning or idiomatic use of the title-words, or their spelling, pronunciation, etymology, or inflexions."

There is a separate key to pronunciation and a list of abbreviations and symbols immediately before the body of the text.

Two guide words, in lowercase boldface type, appear at the top outer margins of each page. This is helpful, of course, but Fowler's has never been known for its ease of access. As Gowers notes in the preface:

What reporter, seeking guidance about the propriety of saying that the reception was held "at the bride's aunt's," would think of looking for it in an article with the title "Out of the Frying-Pan"?

V. Summary

While Gowers's second edition of Fowler's *Modern English Usage* is a successful revision (it updates much of the information in the first edition), both libraries and individuals will want to hold onto their original edition.

A Dictionary of Modern English Usage is indispensable. It should be included in the collections of all types of libraries and a great variety of individuals will want to have it in their personal collections. For its straightforward approach to plain language it is unmatched in the field of usage dictionaries.

Dictionary of Problem Words and Expressions

Facts at a Glance

Full Title: **Dictionary of Problem Words and Expressions**.
Publisher: Washington Square Press.
Author: Harry Shaw.
Edition Reviewed: © 1975; 1985 printing.

Number of Entries: over 1,500.
Number of Pages: 369.
Trim Size: 4⅛″ × 6¾″.
Binding: paperback.

Price: $4.95.
Sold in bookstores.
ISBN 0-671-54558-2.

I. Introduction and Scope

Harry Shaw, editor, teacher, and writer, has published extensively on English composition and literature; his books include *Concise Dictionary of Literary Terms, Errors in English,* and *The Joy of Words.* His *Dictionary of Problem Words and Expressions* is designed to ". . . alert you to faulty speech and writing habits you may have acquired and to confirm and strengthen you in good ones." The volume "singles out, defines, explains, and illustrates some 1,500 of the more common mistakes in word use made by speakers and writers of our language." Dissociating himself from "outmoded notions about 'grammar' and 'correctness,' " Shaw focuses on the effectiveness and appropriateness of diction that is "in *national, present,* and *reputable* use."

In addition to the alphabetical listing of problem words and phrases, the volume contains a prefatory article offering sections titled "Wordiness," "Triteness," "Troublesome Verbs," "Idiomatic Usage," "Euphemisms," and "Slang." Discussions are amplified by illustrative lists of wordy phrases (such as **at the present time** and **in this day and age**) and linguistically economical alternatives (**now, today**); trite expressions (**add insult to injury** and **in the long run**); principal parts of 150 troublesome verbs; idiomatic usages (especially helpful to non-native English speakers); euphemisms (**previously owned car**); and slang (**teenybopper** and **wacky**). Also included

is a discussion, "You and the Way You Talk and Write," highlighting the so-called four commandments of effective communication: "Be concise. . . . Be original. . . . Be specific. . . . Vary the approach."

II. Format

Within the prefatory section, topics are indicated in large boldface type. Illustrative lists appear in double- or triple-column format. Within the alphabetical listing, main entry words and phrases are boldface and overhang the text. When these words and phrases recur within the entry, they are italicized. Also italicized are synonyms and related words and solecisms (as in the indication that **more better** is unacceptable). Cross-references are introduced by *See* or *See also* with the word reference printed in small capitals.

Clear typefaces and ample white space make the work easy to read. Text shows through the pages but does not impede readability. The pages do not separate easily from the binding of this acceptably sturdy paperback.

III. Quality and Currency of Entries

Entries are particularly strong in their clear distinctions between commonly confused words and phrases. For example, the user seeking the correct use of "that" and "which" will find the triad **that, which, who** in proper alphabetical order with a clear explanation of usage. The discussion's definition of *restrictive clauses* ("those that define and limit what precedes by providing information necessary to full understanding") is noteworthily clear. Under **which**, a cross-reference directs the user to the entry for **that**.

Entries are also enhanced by the inclusion of illustrative sentences. For example, **complement** and **compliment** are distinguished in the following entry:

> *Complement* implies something which completes: "This jewelry will *complement* your dress." A *compliment* is flattery or praise: "Beulah enjoyed the *compliment* paid to her."

Similarly, **imply** and **infer** are clearly distinguished and illustrated:

> To *imply* is to suggest a meaning only hinted at, not explicitly stated. To *infer* is to draw a conclusion from statements, evidence, or circumstances. "Your remark *implies* that Bill was untruthful." "The officer *inferred* from the fingerprints that the killer was left-handed."

Entries are in some cases also enhanced by the inclusion of etymological information. In the case of **résumé, synopsis, summary**, for example, etymology usefully clarifies distinctions.

The work is up-to-date in its appropriate inclusion of colloquialisms in current English usage. For example, the list includes **being as**, **being as how**, **being that**:

> Each of these phrases borders on illiteracy; all are vague, wordy, and illogical. Say "*Because* (not *being as*, *being as how*, or *being that*) I am already here, I'll help."

In addition to providing alternatives for unacceptable usages, the work also discusses the use of acceptable colloquialisms, such as **uh-huh**, **huh-uh**, and **O.K.**

However, the work's 1975 date inevitably results in some omissions. Excluded from the list of slang terms are, for example, *nerd*, *punk*, and *yuppie*, while outmoded terms such as **beatnik**, **hepcat**, and **she-bang** do appear. Current euphemisms—such as *funeral director*, *hearing impaired*, and *visually handicapped*—are also omitted. More substantively, the work does not reflect current emphasis on avoiding sexist language. For example, under **everybody**, **everyone**, the reader is told:

> Both pronouns, when used as subjects, require singular verbs; accompanying pronouns should also be singular: "everyone *has* (not *have*) an obligation to cast *his* (not *their*) vote."

In contrast, current works, advising against the use of *he*, *his*, and *him* as indefinite personal pronouns, help their users to avoid offense to portions of their audiences.

IV. Accessibility

The work begins with a contents listing detailing the sections of the prefatory article and ensuring they will not be overlooked. Illustrative lists within this part of the work are alphabetized for easy access. Within the main body of the text, entries are also alphabetized; cross-references clearly direct the user to alternative forms.

In the prefatory article, boldface type underlined running heads on each page repeat the topic titles. Guide words, also in boldface and underlined, appear at the top of each page within the main text; these indicate the first and last terms entered on each double-page spread.

V. Summary

The *Dictionary of Problem Words and Expressions* is intelligent and engaging, and it is an informative, clear, and well-organized reference wordbook. It admirably fulfills its intention of addressing usage and problems in current spoken English. However, it excludes some more recent terms and trends in usage, such as avoiding sexist pronoun use. Despite these omissions, the book's clarity and relative comprehensiveness—given its compact size and reasonable price—earn it commendation. Readers concerned with honing their use of the language will find this a useful and usable source. The work should prove a valuable addition to the circulating paperback collection of the college or public library, and should also be useful in the general home reference collection.

Dictionary of Pronunciation

Facts at a Glance

Full Title: **Dictionary of Pronunciation: Guide to English Spelling and Speech, Fourth Edition.**
Publisher: Cornwall Books.
Author: Samuel Noory.
Edition Reviewed: © 1981.

Number of Entries: 58,000.
Number of Pages: 584.
Trim Size: 6⅛″ × 9¼″.
Binding: cloth.

Price: $19.95.
Sold to libraries and other educational institutions.
ISBN 0-8453-4722-5.

I. Introduction and Scope

First published in 1965, Samuel Noory's *Dictionary of Pronunciation* is now in its fourth edition. Undertaken "to answer the demand left open by the absence today of a comprehensible handbook on spelling and pronunciation, and ultimately to serve as a guide for a thoroughly phonetic spelling for English," according to the author's opening article, "The Way We Spell," the book also serves as a handy spelling–pronunciation reference for ordinary words and names. Based on 37 basic sounds in English—a smaller number than in any other recognized phonetic approach—Noory has abandoned the idea of "devising an orderly precise alphabet" for the principle of reducing speech sounds into "a number of symbols as would suffice to avoid ambiguities." And his new alphabet conforms "as far as practicable with the reading and writing habits of English speakers," that is, based on existing letters.

The book contains lists of 58,000 words and names, and the spelling in Noory's reformed phonetic system. A 57-page introductory section explains the systems and gives a brief history of alphabets since ancient time. The book closes with a brief article by the author rendered into *Broad Transcription*, Noory's proposed system of spelling reform.

II. Format

The main part of the book contains lists of words with their phonctic spellings adjacent, set in two columns per page, with thin rules separating the columns. The paper is off-white and of good quality with minimal show-through. The binding is sturdy, but if heavy use is expected, librarians may wish to rebind.

III. Quality and Currency of Entries

Boldface entry words are presented in alphabetical order, followed by parts of speech in italic, except when a brief definition is given; for example: **dunce**, *fool*. Entries are divided into syllables "according to the printer's method of dividing unfinished words at the end of a line." Variant spellings are given, with an asterisk (*) denoting the preferred spelling, such as **labor***, **labour**. Homonyms are indicated, along with definitions of the original entry word, to facilitate cross-references. The phonetic spellings adjacent to the entry words appear in roman type and are syllabized phonetically. Stress is indicated with an accent mark ('). Where two or more phonetic spellings occur, the first is the preferred and is the one considered in grouping homonyms.

The dictionary is divided into two parts, the first containing common words, the second containing "names of persons and places, and names from the Bible, literature and legend," including some rare words.

Here are some examples of the common words:

knave, *rogue; the jack in cards* Hom, **nave**	nayv
knav-er-y, *n*	nay've-ri
scheme, *n, v*	skēm
sci-at-i-ca, *neuralgia*	sy-a'ti-ke
sell, *vend* Hom, **cell**	sɛl
wretch-ed, *a*	rɛ'ched

From the names section:

Guin-e-vere, *l*	Gwin'ne-vēr
Ha-gar, *b*	Hay'ger
Haver-hill, *g*	Hayv'ɾil
Iph-i-ge-ni-a, *m*	I-fi-je-ny'e
Ja-net, *French philosopher*	Zhaw-ney'
U-dall, *p*	Yū'dawl

In the names section, the letters following the name stand for: **a** = ancient place; **b** = biblical name; **g** = geographical name; **l** = name in legend or literature; **m** = name in mythology; **p** = personal name.

Currency may not be the most important consideration in this book, but **Reagan** and **Zimbabwe**, for example, do appear in the list of names and show that some attempt has been made to update the section.

Following the lists of words, an example of the author's suggested spelling reform in *Broad Transcription* appears in the form of an article, with the phonetic transcription on the facing page. The transcription begins as follows:

> The folōing artikel, renderd intu Brawd Transkripshen, was riten by the awther sum yērz bak on a trip tu the Midel Ēst.

IV. Accessibility

Each page has guide words at the top showing first and last words in the two-column lists below. The page number is centered at the top above a thin rule that crosses the page above the word lists.

The pronunciation key consists of a mere 15 symbols and these are printed in a single line at the bottom of every page. The phonetic alphabets appear at the beginning and end of the book. A table of contents indicates the main sections of the book, and a four-page section entitled "Explanatory Notes" gives information on how to use the book and on the *Broad Transcription* system. There are many cross-references within the word lists, but because of the alphabetical arrangement of words, there is no index.

V. Summary

This is a fascinating and useful guide to the spelling and pronunciation of English that will have wide appeal to anyone interested in or bewildered by the inconsistencies of English pronunciation. The *Wilson Library Bulletin* called it "distinguished for its readable pronouncing alphabet" (October, 1979, p. 133). The book is very accessible to any reader and provides interesting and useful background information on the language in brief. It does not, however, like the Merriam-Webster A PRONOUNCING DICTIONARY OF AMERICAN ENGLISH, attempt to record regional American pronunciations. It presents only one pronunciation for each word which it presumably considers standard.

Large public and academic libraries will want to include this work in their collections, but it may seem too specialized for smaller libraries where up-to-date pronunciations and spellings appear in many reputable dictionaries already in the collections, and questions of phonetic and spelling reform may not be appropriate.

Encyclopedic Dictionary of English Usage

Facts at a Glance

Full Title: **Encyclopedic Dictionary of English Usage**.
Publisher: Prentice Hall Press.

Encyclopedic Dictionary of English Usage

❶ Pronunciations are enclosed in brackets
❷ Related words with which the main entry might be confused appear in small capitals
❸ Main entries are set in boldface type
❹ Inflected forms are given when their spelling might be doubtful

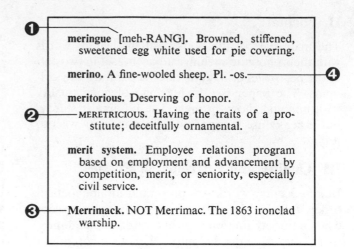

❶
meringue [meh-RANG]. Browned, stiffened, sweetened egg white used for pie covering.

merino. A fine-wooled sheep. Pl. -os. ──── ❹

meritorious. Deserving of honor.

❷ ──MERETRICIOUS. Having the traits of a prostitute; deceitfully ornamental.

merit system. Employee relations program based on employment and advancement by competition, merit, or seniority, especially civil service.

❸ ──**Merrimack.** NOT Merrimac. The 1863 ironclad warship.

Compilers: N. H. Mager and S. K. Mager.
Edition Reviewed: © 1974; 1987 printing.

Number of Entries: over 15,000.
Number of Pages: 342.
Trim Size: 6⅛″ × 9¼″.
Binding: cloth.

Price: $19.95.
Sold in bookstores and other outlets; also sold to libraries and other educational institutions.
ISBN 0-13-275792-3.

I. Introduction and Scope

The *Encyclopedic Dictionary of English Usage* is described as "a composite tool to help you speak and write more correctly and more specifically, to understand more completely the terms you commonly use or read, to resolve your doubts about what is incorrect and what is best usage, and to suggest a uniform style in matters where good usage permits a choice of several alternatives." Its intended audience is "business executives, teachers, speakers, authors, journalists," or anyone who wishes to improve his or her use of spoken or written English.

The *Encyclopedic Dictionary* lists 15,000 definitions; 1,000 common grammatical errors; punctuation problems and their solutions; rules of capitalization; new words, idioms, and names of nations and people in the news; unclear abbreviations; units of measure; and frequently used business terms. The work is intended as a quick reference guide and the compilers admit it is limited to the most current or accepted usages. Since the book has not been revised since its publication in 1974, some of its listings are somewhat dated.

The Magers selected their entries from other reference texts, "from clippings, and from original inquiry." Their authorities on style are: (1) the style manual of the Government Printing Office; (2) *The Chicago Manual of Style*; (3) the style book of the *New York Times*; and (4) other unspecified style manuals and texts on spelling, pronunciation, and common errors. No bibliography of these sources is included.

The last two pages of the book are a list of proofreader's marks and the corrected proof of a sample manuscript.

II. Format

The *Encyclopedic Dictionary* begins with the authors' introduction, which includes the Webster Phonetic Guide to pronunciation, an explanation of the rationale for including entries in the text, and the procedure for using the book: to "1) determine the word or subject that presents a problem, and 2) seek it out in alphabetical order."

There follow 340 pages of reference material in a double-column format with running heads in bold capital letters. Main entries are in bold type, capitalized if they are proper nouns. Most are followed by a pronunciation, definition, other parts of speech from the same root, samples of usage, and cross-references. Many entries, though, have only some of this information, and some entries, for example, **cornetist**, **implausible**, and **twelfth**, have none at all. The compilers have provided the information they believe is most wanted by the user.

Geographical entries include cities, with pronunciation if necessary, and location; states, with abbreviation, native's name, nickname, and capital; and countries, with native's name, adjectival form, capital, and currency. Examples are:

Tennessee [tehn-eh-SEE]. (abbr. Tenn.) Native and adj., Tennessean. Webster's accepts Tennesseean.

Uruguay [OO-ruh-gwie,—gwae]. Native, Uruguayan(s); adj. Uruguayan. Cap., Montevideo. Currency, peso (Ur.$) centesimo.

Grammar rules are in the alphabetical listing of entries in capital letters (**COMMA, THE**), illustrated with italicized examples, and cross-referenced to related material.

III. Quality and Currency of Entries

The *Encyclopedic Dictionary* has not been revised since 1974, so some listings are out of date. This is particularly true of biographical entries that lack dates of death and/or are obscure (for people like **Anwar el-Sadat, Indira Gandhi, Thomas Johnson Agulyi-Ironsi, and Moshoeshoe II**). Some geographical listings likewise are no longer timely (**Quemoy, Ryukyu Islands**), and newsworthy ones like Managua and Soweto are not to be found. And both the preferred spelling and the information for Vietnam are not correct here.

Abbreviations are also dated. **Bvt.** (for *brevet*) is included but not *NRC, AIDS,* or *VCR.* **Twad.** (for *Twaddell*) is obscure and not listed in *Funk and Wagnalls Encyclopedic Dictionary*, 1968 edition.

The book omits computer terminology and current medical terms and abbreviations (for example, *Alzheimer's disease, triage, affect* [n.], *SIDS, ICU*).

The *Encyclopedic Dictionary* does not recognize common usage such as "aggravate—to annoy" (second meaning, THE OXFORD GUIDE TO THE ENGLISH LANGUAGE, 1984) but states "**aggravate**. Worsen. NOT annoy or irritate." Similarly, it advises against the use of *orientate*, but THE OXFORD GUIDE states that it is interchangeable with *orient*. The *Encyclopedic Dictionary*'s citation, "**casket**. A box. A corpse lies in a coffin," insists on a distinction between two terms that current American usage interchanges.

The *Encyclopedic Dictionary*'s footnote format advises the use of *loc. cit.* and *op. cit.*, which the current *MLA Style Sheet* and *A Manual of Style: 13th Edition* reject. The book does not include formats for scientific documentation or inclusion of references within a text.

IV. Accessibility

Information for some entries can be confusing because its relationship to the entry itself is not always clear, particularly if the term is an unfamiliar one. For example, the citation "**Apostles' Creed**. Augsburg Confession, the Twelve Apostles, the Apostle Thomas" seems designed to illustrate a rule of capitalization rather than to supply information about the original entry; the intent of the information is puzzling.

Sections on grammar and usage are generally thorough, but the double columns of rules and examples are often hard to follow because of their brevity, the narrow line spacing, and the number of rules included (*Capitalization* has 39, almost three full columns).

Alphabetizing is sometimes incorrect: **belly** follows **belowstairs**. Inverting proper nouns—**Tunnel, Lincoln** and **Canaveral, Cape**—makes these entries harder to locate and, in the second case, is not consistent with the *Encyclopedic Dictionary*'s own cross-referencing: "**Cape Kennedy**. See Cape Canaveral."

Definitions of words are not always consistent with the most common usage of them. For example, "**Pharisee**. Ancient orthodox Jewish sect" gives no indication of the generic use of the word or its adjectival form.

The authors' choice of information to give for terms sometimes selects the obvious and omits the less familiar. Two common definitions for **acceptance** are provided, but **acclimate** has only two alternative pronunciations and no definition or example of usage.

V. Summary

The *Encyclopedic Dictionary of English Usage* is an adequate supplemental reference text for users looking for spelling or pronunciation of the entries included. Less helpful as a dictionary, it does not distinguish between synonyms and antonyms; it also has dated information, particularly in its biographical and geographical entries. It does not meet its claim of currency in idiomatic usage of words as it is almost 15 years out of date, and it includes some material (abbreviations, weights, and measures) that is archaic.

As a manual of style its strength is in clarifying points for someone well versed in formal grammar and able to follow its abbreviated discussion of rules. The *Encyclopedic Dictionary* would not be a good choice for reference use in libraries, although it could augment dictionaries, thesauruses, and style manuals. While it might be helpful to users who need to be reminded of basic information, no prospective purchaser could overlook the inaccuracies in information it contains.

The Facts on File Dictionary of Troublesome Words

Facts at a Glance

Full Title: **The Facts on File Dictionary of Troublesome Words.**
Publisher: Facts on File.

The Facts on File Dictionary of Troublesome Words

> **❶ crescendo.** 'David English, whose career seemed to be reaching a crescendo this month when he took over editorship of the stumbling Mail on Sunday . . .' (*Sunday Times*). *Crescendo* is frequently misused, **❸** though only rarely trampled on in quite the way it has been here. **❷** It does not mean reaching a milestone, as was apparently intended in the quotation, or signify a loud or explosive noise, as it is more commonly misused. Properly, it should be used to describe a gradual increase in volume or intensity.
>
> **criteria, criterion.** One criterion, two criteria. See also D A T A. **❹**

❶ Main entry words are set in boldface type

❷ Points of usage are discussed

❸ Examples of usage are followed by source citations, in parentheses

❹ Cross-references appear in small capitals

Editor: Bill Bryson.
Edition Reviewed: © 1984.

Number of Articles: 826.
Number of Entries: 1,093.
Number of Pages: 173.
Trim Size: 5½″ × 8½″.
Binding: cloth.

Price: $17.95.
Sold in bookstores and by direct mail; also sold to libraries and other educational institutions.
ISBN 0-87196-889-4.

I. Introduction and Scope

This work was originally published in England as THE PENGUIN DICTIONARY OF TROUBLESOME WORDS. A complete review of the content of this work can be found in the review in this guide of the aforementioned title, which is a paperback edition of the work. Its author, Bill Bryson, is an editor with the London *Times*, but the many contemporary examples he cites of usage and abusage are drawn from both England and the United States. Along with discussions of split infinitives, dangling modifiers, and split compound verbs, Bryson also has witty and instructive entries on the distinctions to be drawn between such familiar pairs as **imply/infer**, **flaunt/flout**, **who/whom**, **historic/historical**, **partly/partially**, and numerous other near twins that often provide pitfalls for the careless writer. In addition, the author also presents a brief guide to punctuation and a glossary of the more common grammatical terms.

The strongest virtues of Bryson's book are its wit, authority, currency, and accessibility. The entries are succinct and easy to understand. Its principal drawback is the limited number of entries, making this volume no rival for such fuller discussions as those provided by Theodore Bernstein or H. W. Fowler. Librarians wishing to purchase this helpful guide for their reference collections will probably prefer the hardback American edition to the less durable Penguin paperback edition.

A Handy Book of Commonly Used American Idioms

Facts at a Glance

Full Title: **A Handy Book of Commonly Used American Idioms**.
Publisher: Prentice Hall Press.
Compiler: Solomon Wiener.
Edition Reviewed: © 1981; 1985 printing.

Number of Entries: over 1,200.
Number of Pages: 112.
Trim Size: 4″ × 6″.
Binding: paperback.

Price: $4.67.
Sold in bookstores; also sold to libraries and other educational institutions.
ISBN 0-88345-061-5.

I. Introduction and Scope

This handy little volume of idioms was first published in 1958 and revised in 1981. It was formerly published by the Regents Publishing Company, Inc., since acquired by Prentice-Hall. The book is limited to American idioms and does not include those of gen-

A Handy Book of Commonly Used American Idioms

❶ Main entries are set in boldface capitals and are arranged alphabetically

❷ Each meaning is followed by an example of usage

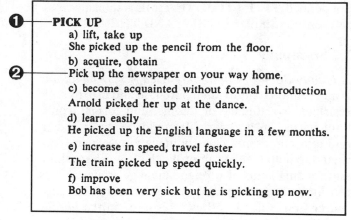

PICK UP
a) lift, take up
She picked up the pencil from the floor.
b) acquire, obtain
Pick up the newspaper on your way home.
c) become acquainted without formal introduction
Arnold picked her up at the dance.
d) learn easily
He picked up the English language in a few months.
e) increase in speed, travel faster
The train picked up speed quickly.
f) improve
Bob has been very sick but he is picking up now.

eral English origin. The simplicity of the book would make it most suitable for individuals whose first language is not English, but who have a basic grasp of the language. The entries are all phrases with which proficient English speakers would be familiar, such as **How do you do?**, **lead by the nose**, **on the tip of one's tongue**, **set free**, and **take with a grain of salt**. Slang phrases are not included.

The editor responsible for this dictionary, Solomon Wiener, has also compiled a number of other publications, including the *Handy Guide to Irregular Verbs and the Use and Formation of Tenses*, published by Handy Book Press in 1959.

II. Format

Words and phrases appear in alphabetical order in boldface capitals overhanging the text. Two lines follow the entry; the first is the definition and the second is a sentence illustrating the use of the idiom. A typical example is as follows:

GO ON!

expression of disbelief
Did you say that you won all that money?
Go on!

When an idiomatic expression has more than one possible meaning, illustrative sentences show how the idiom is used; for example:

GO OVER

a) examine, look at carefully
Let us go over the problem slowly.

b) do again, repeat
Shall we go over the lesson once more?

c) succeed
The designer hoped that the style would go over.

III. Quality and Currency of Entries

Variations in idioms are handled in one of two ways. One type of entry is followed by a similar idiomatic

phrase in parentheses with essentially the same meaning. For example:

BURST INTO TEARS (BURST OUT CRYING)

suddenly begin to cry
She burst out crying when she heard the news.

Variations in longer similar idioms are handled somewhat differently using dashes. See the samples below.

LAUGH IN ONE'S SLEEVE (—— UP —— ——)

be secretly amused
We laughed up our sleeves when she began to sing.

GET AWAY WITH (—— —— —— MURDER)

escape punishment
That careless worker manages to get away with murder.

The sentences used to illustrate meaning are easy to understand and to interpret. The definitions of the idioms are sufficient for an individual who is just beginning to grasp the use of idioms in American English. It is unfortunate, however, that many newer phrases are not included, such as *get with it*, *trashed*, *couch potato*, *let's do lunch*, or *space cadet*. Whatever revision has been done since the original 1958 edition appears to be very slight, a drawback that limits the book's usefulness.

IV. Accessibility

There are no guide words at the top of the page, but idioms are entered in alphabetical order and easily located in this brief dictionary. Bold capital letters help entry words and phrases to stand out clearly. There is good contrast between the print on the page and the white of the paper.

Some entries are cross-referenced to other similar entries with no additional information given. For example, **FLY OFF THE HANDLE** is cross-referenced with the note, **Similar to BLOW ONE'S TOP**, but not defined; **FROM TIME TO TIME** is similarly cross-referenced, **Similar to NOW AND THEN**.

V. Summary

A Handy Book of Commonly Used American Idioms is most suited to individual purchase and use. Its size, restricted vocabulary of idioms, and format would limit its use in a library. It could be purchased in multiple copies for classroom use in a course designed to help teach or improve the English speaking and reading skills of foreign language students. It is too limited in scope to serve as a library reference source and is not listed as a resource in the *Idioms and Phrases Index* by Laurence Urdang and Frank R. Abate (Gale, 1983).

A preferable source for libraries that need information about idioms in the English language would be the LONGMAN DICTIONARY OF ENGLISH IDIOMS. It is more expensive in the hardbound edition at $19.95, and it was last published in 1979, so it is not particularly current, but it is still in print. The comprehensiveness of the two works can be illustrated by examining the word *back*. Many idiomatic phrases start with this word, such as **back and forth** or **back number**. *A Handy Book of Commonly Used American Idioms* lists four phrases for *back* while the *Longman Dictionary* devotes over one page to them. THE RANDOM HOUSE DICTIONARY is another good source for American idioms. Both the Longman and Random House works are referred to in the *Idioms and Phrases Index*.

Harper Dictionary of Contemporary Usage

Facts at a Glance

Full Title: **Harper Dictionary of Contemporary Usage: Second Edition**.
Publisher: Harper & Row.
Editors: William and Mary Morris.
Edition Reviewed: © 1985.

Number of Entries: 2,675.
Number of Pages: 672.
Trim Size: 6″ × 9¼″.
Binding: cloth.

Price: $19.45.
Sold in bookstores. Also sold to libraries and other educational institutions.
ISBN 0-06-181606-X.

I. Introduction and Scope

William Morris, the original editor of the *American Heritage Dictionary of the English Language*, co-edited with Mary Morris the *Harper Dictionary of Contemporary Usage* (1975). Their second edition was published in 1985, and follows the practice established by the first of using a panel of language experts to comment on some of the more egregious or controversial questions of usage. This usage handbook, therefore, "reflects the collaborative efforts of some 165 writers, editors, and public speakers chosen for their demonstrated ability to use the language carefully and effectively." These experts—29 more than in the first edition—range "from Jane Alexander and Isaac Asimov to Barbara Tuchman and William Zinsser."

The existence of the panel results from the idea that the day when one person (such as H. W. Fowler, for example) could mandate "the rights and wrongs of language is long past." The editors see the role of their volume as important in "recording the standards of usage respected by today's foremost writers."

A stated purpose of this dictionary is to call attention to usages regarded as "improper or substandard by careful users of the language," with the intent of correcting or eliminating such usages. A second purpose is "to show by discussion and example the standards of linguistic usage adhered to by those who use the language well." The authors do not believe in being dictatorial, and the questions posed by the usage panel record a healthy disagreement among experts "proving how unstatic the language is." At the end of the introduction, 68 of the panelists give their brief opinions on the current state of the language. A "Glossary of Terms Used in Evaluating Levels of Usage" precedes the body of the text.

II. Format

The text is in dictionary format with a single alphabetical listing for all types of entries. Main topic words are in lowercase boldface type overhanging the text; definitions or comments begin on the same line as the topic words. Many entries are followed by the label "Usage Panel Question" in large boldface capital letters. This label is flush left for the left side of a two-page spread and begins in the center of the page and continues flush right if on the right side of a spread. It is set off from the rest of the text by bold horizontal lines that cross the full width of the page. The label signals comments on the preceding entry. After the entry **bad/badly**, for example, the usage panel question is:

"When referring to your mental or physical state, do you say, 'I feel bad'?" Yes: 77%. No: 23%. "I feel badly"? Yes: 26%. No: 74%.

This information is boxed in by a light horizontal line that crosses the full width of the page.

Following the percentages is a list of, in this case, over 20 responses from the usage panel members.

Harper Dictionary of Contemporary Usage

❶ **me/I/myself** Because countless schoolteachers have campaigned against the expression *It's me* (which see), many Americans have developed a fear of grammatical error in the choice of *I* or *me*. The result has been that they have come to believe that any expression with *me* in it is wrong or, as "Red" Smith so succinctly puts it, that "me" is a dirty word.

One area in which this is all too obvious is in prepositional phrases. Three examples of misuse were reported in one evening's conversation with two college seniors and a college dean: "With Tony and *I* splitting everything right down the middle," "The idea of him and *I* sharing a steak is like old times," and "Remember that this must be kept a secret between you and *I*." We can only hope against long odds to convince such people that "between you and *I*" is wrong and that "between you and *me*" is right.

This fear of the objective case, coupled with a fondness for spurious elegance, has led to the use of *myself* when *me* is called for, as in "He wants to entertain you and *myself*" or "It was a pleasure for Mrs. Grant and *myself*." While there may be nothing grammatically wrong with such usage, the results are awkward and pretentious. *See also* IT'S ME. ❸

---

❷ ## USAGE PANEL QUESTION

Myself as a reflexive or intensive pronoun is completely established in such expressions as "I hurt *myself*" or "I'll do it *myself*." Other often-heard uses of *myself* include such sentences as "The chairlady and *myself* were the chief speakers" and "The captain invited my roommate and *myself* to dinner." Do you approve of these uses of *myself*?

In speech   Yes: 16%. No: 84%.
In writing   Yes: 12%. No: 88%.

Of the small minority which approved the use of *myself* in the examples given, no one really tried to defend it. A panelist wrote (voting "no"): "Once in a while you have to use it when 'me' seems too egocentric." Those who refused to accept *myself* as a substitute for *me* or *I* were more vehement.

SHANA ALEXANDER: "No! No reason—A change in grammar that does not strengthen, weakens."

HAL BORLAND: "All such attempts at 'flossy' talk should be damned. 'I' and 'me' are still in the language and should be used."

HEYWOOD HALE BROUN: "Its principal value would seem to be as a shorer-up of weak identities."

ROBERT CRICHTON: "Whenever you use 'myself' when 'I' or 'me' will do, you are getting delicate and getting delicate is dangerous business."

❶ Main entries are set in boldface type

❷ Some entries include results of a usage panel poll and quotations from selected responses

❸ Cross-references appear in boldface small capitals

The panelists' names appear alphabetically in light-face caps flush left overhanging the text of their comments, which begin on the same line as the names (Robert Cromie: "I avoid the issue by saying, 'I feel lousy' "; Jessica Mitford: "No to both: I should say 'I feel ill' or 'depressed' ").

See and see also references are in small boldface capitals. Entries are separated by a double space. Margins are adequate but not generous; gutters are somewhat narrow. The volume has a cloth cover and a strong adhesive binding.

III. Quality and Currency of Entries

One of the attractions of this interesting dictionary is its currency, and the second edition contains many new entries. **Awesome** is one. The usage panel was asked if it approved of the word's current extension of meaning given the example "Gossage's fast ball has been good this season but it hasn't been awesome." Forty-six percent of the panel approved of its current use in speech and 44 percent for its use in writing. The comments are various: " 'awesome' here is loathsome" (Ben Lucien Burman); "Already established" (Karl V. Teeter); and, "This has become a cliché of awesome proportions" (Wade Mosby).

Burn-out, **lucked out**, **gay** (in the sense of male homosexual), **prioritize**, and **ground zero**, are a few other new entries given full usage panel treatment in the text.

Under the entry **hopefully** is a question on its use as an adverb meaning " 'we hope' in such sentences as 'Hopefully, the war will soon be ended.' " The second edition gives the usage panel opinions for the first edition as well as for this one. Defenders of the language lamented this usage more in 1985 than they did in 1975. Where there has been a relatively significant adjustment of opinion, as in the case of **hopefully**, the percentages and panelists' comments are given for both editions.

Any more as a synonym for "nowadays" or "at this time" is another example where the opinions for both editions are given. Since the use of **chaise lounge** (John Ciardi: "It is taking over with people who sell bedroom suits [*sic*]") for *chaise longue* is as deplored now as it was then (by the usage panelists, that is), the first edition percentages are not repeated, though several new voices have been added to the comments section.

Entries on punctuation and grammar in general are not as fully developed as in comparable older titles such as Wilson Follett's MODERN AMERICAN USAGE, Bergen Evans' and Cornelia Evans' *Dictionary of Contemporary American Usage*, and Fowler's A DICTIONARY OF MODERN ENGLISH USAGE

or the more current WORDS ON WORDS, by John Bremner. This dictionary's strength lies in its diverse panel's witty and vigorous approach to current usage.

IV. Accessibility

The entry and guide words are in lower case boldface type. One guide word for each page of a two-page spread indicates the first and last entry of that spread. The guide words are highlighted by a bold line extending from the outer margin almost to the edge of each page. *See also* and cross-references are in small boldface caps. Large initial letters, flush with the outer margins, indicate the beginning of alphabetical sections and provide a cordon of white space between the sections.

Following the text is a brief epilogue and a two and a half page bibliography. It is a "selective listing of books referred to in the course of writing and editing this dictionary." One purpose of the bibliography is to "give the student of language specific titles and publishing information on works that are somewhat casually referred to in the text." With this in mind, it is curious that publication dates are not given for the majority of listed titles.

V. Summary

The second edition of the *Harper Dictionary of Contemporary Usage* is a welcome update of the first. Not only is it one of the newer of the usage manuals currently in print, but its method of presentation and the many quotations from members of the usage panel in particular, help make this a fascinating and absorbing volume for word enthusiasts. It is difficult to resist reading all the participants' comments under those entries that include usage panel questions. The responses are lively and witty as they duly record the opinions (often acerbic) of the many language experts involved with this dictionary's production.

This book is recommended for a wide variety of readers. All libraries will want to have this comprehensive and up-to-date usage dictionary in their collections. Finally, hats off to William and Mary Morris for their entry **library/librarians**, "The initial 'r' should not be slurred or omitted in pronouncing these words. Say LY-brer-ee, not LY-ber-ee, and ly-BRAIR-ee-un, not ly-BAIR-ee-un."

Homophones and Homographs: An American Dictionary

Facts at a Glance

Full Title: **Homophones and Homographs: An American Dictionary**.
Publisher: McFarland & Company.

Compiler: James B. Hobbs.
Edition Reviewed: © 1986.

Number of Entries: 3,600 homophones; 600 homographs.
Number of Pages: 272.
Trim Size: 5⅜″ × 8½″.
Binding: cloth.

Price: $29.95.
Sold in bookstores; also sold to libraries and other educational institutions.
ISBN 0-89950-182-6.

I. Introduction and Scope

This fascinating dictionary contains 3,600 homophones and 600 homographs, and is one of the most comprehensive works available on these word categories. Homophones are words that sound alike but are spelled differently and have separate meanings such as *dear* and *deer*. Homographs are words that look alike but have different meanings such as *bow* meaning to bend from the waist and *bow* as in bow and arrow.

The editor notes in the foreword that the source for the words listed is primarily WEBSTER'S THIRD NEW INTERNATIONAL DICTIONARY, which was searched twice, plus 41 other word books and articles. The compiler makes no claim that the sources used is a complete list and invites readers to submit additional words for possible inclusion.

The criteria for inclusion for homophones is that:

At least one pronunciation must be common to two or more homophonic candidates.

For homographs that

At least one pronunciation of homographic candidates must be dissimilar.

For example, if two identically spelled words with different meanings could be pronounced in the same way, the word would not be included. Therefore the word **love** was omitted, as **love** (meaning affection) is pronounced the same as **love** (zero score in tennis). Although variations in pronunciation might make a homophone such as *caw* for *car* to rhyme with *caw*, they are not included. The following list of words are excluded:

- Obsolete and archaic words.
  Regional dialects, especially English, Scottish and southern United States.
- Slang and colloquialisms.
- Proper names, such as Claude (clawed), Jim (gym), and Mary (merry).

- Foreign countries, nationalities, provinces, and cities (except familiar ones such as Finn, Greece, Lapp, Lima, Polish, and Rome).
- Foreign units of money and weights (except familiar ones such as the French franc and the Italian lira).

Normally, suffixes were not added to homophones . . . such as **sew** (then sewed, sewing, sews).

II. Format

This dictionary is divided into two main parts with alphabetized homophones appearing in the first section and alphabetized homographs in the second. These two sections are preceded by a nine-page introduction entitled "The Framework of Homophones and Homographs." The "Framework" contains, among other notes, the list of phonetic symbols used in the book that are adapted from WEBSTER'S THIRD NEW INTERNATIONAL DICTIONARY. In addition there are two appendixes. Appendix I contains lists of unusual groupings. These include four or more one-syllable words—right, rite, wright, write—four- and five-syllable words like stationery and stationary, and homographs of three or more words like grave, ′grāv, ′grävē, ′gräv.

Appendix II contains the annotated bibliography of books and articles used in addition to WEBSTER'S THIRD INTERNATIONAL in compiling this dictionary.

The main entry for both homophones and homographs gives a brief definition for each one. A typical homophones entry is as follows:

bold fearless in meeting danger or difficulty
boled having a cylindrical shape or mass
bolled having or producing pods or capsules, as in a plant
bowled played the game of bowls or tenpins

At the end of each letter in the compilation of homophones and homographs there are groups of words unacceptable to the main listing. Group I words were rejected because their roots were too close—residence–residents—and group II words were not included because of perceptibly different pronunciations.

meridian mə′ridēan
meridienne mə:ride:en
meridion mə′ride.än

Definitions appear in the main entry words only. Some homonyms (and homophones) are underlined. This indicates that the word is both a homophone and a homograph.

There are far fewer homographs than homophones. Entries are very similar to those in the homophone section, with the exception that all words are pronounced.

III. Quality and Currency of Entries

Currency was not a consideration in compiling this dictionary. Entries include words from everyday speech as well as some technical and other unusual words, such as the homophones **crotin** which is a "mixture of poisonous proteins found in seeds of a small Asiatic tree," and **Croton** which is a "genus of herbs and shrubs, as spurges." Definitions are brief but adequate for the purpose of this dictionary. Parts of speech and etymologies are not given.

IV. Accessibility

Entries appear in boldface type and are very easy to see. Paired guide words appear at the top of each page, and cross-references are plentiful and easy to locate.

V. Summary

Homophones and Homographs is a comprehensive word book that would be useful in most libraries. It can be compared to *The Encyclopedia of Homonyms* by Dora Newhouse (Los Angeles, CA: Newhouse Press, 1977), which, however, contains no homographs. Newhouse's homonym list is approximately the same length as Hobbs' though less inclusive of the obscure and vernacular words like **boled** and **boo-boo** found in Hobbs.

Homographs and homophones, like palindromes and idioms, are a fascinating part of language structure. As such, this book will be an enriching addition to a library's reference collection.

Longman Dictionary of English Idioms

Facts at a Glance

Full Title: **Longman Dictionary of English Idioms**.
Publisher: Longman.
Editor: Thomas Hill Long, Editorial Director.
Edition Reviewed: © 1979; 1985 printing.

Number of Entries: 5,000.
Number of Pages: 387.
Trim Size: 6″ × 9″.
Binding: cloth.

Price: $19.95.
Sold in bookstores and other outlets; also sold to libraries and other educational institutions.
ISBN 0-582-55524-8.

I. Introduction and Scope

In the publisher's words: "the aim of this dictionary is to provide the student of English with a thorough coverage of the most common idiomatic phrases in use." Potential users should also know that this dictionary is intended for students of *British* English and that some of the idioms and illustrative citations will, therefore, be unfamiliar to an American audience. Since the intended audience is foreign students learning English, the definitions have been written in a controlled vocabulary of approximately 2,000 words. Consequently, more sophisticated readers, expecting nuanced definitions, should seek other sources.

The 5,000 idioms and their derivatives in this source have two major characteristics: they are metaphorical, rather than literal, and their form is fixed, if not invariable. For example, a non-native English speaker might think that the phrase **lose face** refers to the literal loss of skin from the face, while native speakers probably don't need a dictionary like this to tell them the term means "to lose the respect or good opinion that others have of one." And since this term has a relatively fixed form in English, one cannot say "they lost their faces" or "face was lost by them."

II. Format

This book is sturdily bound, with the main word of each idiomatic phrase printed in large boldface and capital letters. Each word or phrase containing the main idiom is printed in smaller, but still quite distinct boldface, so, for example, **FACE** is set in capitals and larger type than **lose face**. While the print size of the definitions and examples may be too small for some readers, the type is clear, with citations that are used as examples of the idioms printed in italics and clearly distinguished from the definitions.

Premium
at a premium   valued highly, esp. because of being in short supply; much desired; in demand: *skilled workers are at a premium in this town. 'The working wife wants the quicker-cooking joints. Time is at a premium.'* (*New Society* 10 Oct 74) [Adj 1] <See at put° a PREMIUM on℗
put° a premium on℗   to make or regard (doing something, a manner of behaviour, etc.) as important, attractive, or advantageous: *there will be only enough food at the party for half the guests—this puts a premium on arriving early—my uncle puts a premium on politeness, so if you want to impress him favourably, make sure you speak politely* [V] <A PREMIUM is a reward

A list of the controlled vocabulary used in the definitions is provided at the end of the book. Helpful explanations of the sequence of information and the numerous abbreviations used in the entries are provided in the endpapers.

III. Quality and Currency of Entries

As well as common idiomatic phrases found in other sources like A DICTIONARY OF AMERICAN IDIOMS, *Longman* has included allusions like **Catch 22**, sayings such as **a rolling stone gathers no moss**, and similes such as **dead as a doornail**. Phrase origin is provided, where known, so that for instance **Catch 22** is attributed to Heller's 1961 book of the same name.

One cannot expect a dictionary like this to contain newly minted words and phrases: while different readers have different perceptions of what constitutes a current word, idioms, by definition, are expressions that have become embedded in the language, so much so that a native speaker seldom pauses to think about when they originated.

IV. Accessibility

Definitions and examples of idioms are written in unambiguous language. If the user is at first overwhelmed by the abbreviations and symbols, there is an easy-to-use guide on the inside cover and a more detailed explanation of the components of each entry in the 13-page introduction.

Much information about usage is presented compactly in symbols and notes. In a typical entry, such as **lose face**, different meanings of the phrase, or variations on it, are noted in separately numbered definitions, so that **save (one's) face**, for example, is distinguished from **lose face**. A superscript circle is placed above a word in an idiom that may inflect or change in form. Other special symbols indicate where the direct or indirect object occurs when used outside the idiom, and whether a word in the idiom may occur either before or after the object. Numerous other grammatical and usage notes are similarly designated by symbols. A generous number of usage labels is used, which sometimes can be critically important to the beginning student, including: formal, not formal, colloquial, slang, derogatory, euphemistic, humorous, literary, old-fashioned, pompous, rhetorical, taboo, and American (unlabeled entries indicate all-purpose usage).

V. Summary

While the OXFORD DICTIONARY OF CURRENT IDIOMATIC ENGLISH also covers British and American Usage, *Longman's* scope is somewhat wider because of its sayings and allusions. However, since Longman's does not include many Americanisms or CB, computer and drug jargon that have become common expressions, a librarian should still consider purchase of NTC's AMERICAN IDIOMS DICTIONARY or Barron's DICTIONARY OF AMERICAN IDIOMS, both reviewed in this Buying Guide.

Considering its primary audience, this should be a very much used dictionary for foreign students trying to make sense of the most common idioms in English, and, incidentally, will also be useful to native speakers curious about expressions that often are not found in other dictionaries.

Longman Dictionary of Phrasal Verbs

Facts at a Glance

Full Title: **Longman Dictionary of Phrasal Verbs**.
Publisher: Longman.
Compiler: Rosemary Courtney.
Edition Reviewed: © 1983; 1986 printing.

Number of Volumes: 1.
Number of Entries: over 12,000.
Number of Pages: 752.
Trim Size: 5¼" × 8½".
Binding: cloth.

Price: $18.95.
Sold in bookstores and other outlets; also sold to
   libraries and other educational institutions.
ISBN: 0-582-55530-2.

I. Introduction and Scope

Phrasal verbs are described by this dictionary as "idiomatic combinations of a verb and adverb, or a verb and preposition (or verb with both adverb and preposition)." These idiomatic expressions cause problems for both English speakers and learners of English. This thorough guide to meaning and usage is published by the British firm Longman Group Limited, a highly respected publisher of reference works. The compiler, Rosemary Courtney, is described on the jacket as having extensive English-language teaching experience in both Canada and Great Britain. She currently teaches English as a Second Language at the University of Toronto. Acknowledgments are given to a number of other individuals, including Professor Randolph Quirk of University College, London, for permission to use his Survey of English Usage.

The *Longman Dictionary of Phrasal Verbs* is called by the publisher the most comprehensive, detailed, and up-to-date guide to phrasal verbs available. More than 12,000 phrasal verbs are included, each one presented simply and clearly with the help of the

2,000-word defining vocabulary used in the LONGMAN DICTIONARY OF CONTEMPORARY ENGLISH. Entries include both British and American English and formal and informal usage. The dictionary defines standard idioms such as "The police broke the door down" and also more colloquial ones such as "let the cat out of the bag."

II. Format

Verbs are entered in alphabetical order followed by an adverb, a preposition, or both. Some examples of entries are **fall between** (verb, preposition), **glance back** (verb, adverb), and **give up to** (verb, adverb, preposition). Entries appear in boldface type and slightly overhang the paragraph that follows. Immediately following each entry the parts of speech are identified in abbreviated format, for example: ***leave out of** *v adv prep.* The asterisk indicates that the entry is an idiomatic phrasal verb as opposed to a literal verb combination.

A brief definition then follows. If there is more than one definition, each is numbered. Idiomatic definitions also are starred. Usage labels such as *sl* (slang), *derog* (derogatory), and *taboo* are included when appropriate. Each definition is given a two-part "grammar code" consisting of a letter (*D* for a transitive verb with both a direct object and an indirect object, *T* for a transitive verb followed by a direct object, *I* for an intransitive verb, and so on) and a number (*Ø* when the verb is not followed by another word, *1* when the verb is followed by a noun or pronoun, and so on). Every definition is illustrated with at least one complete sentence. Cross-references are indicated by an arrow pointing to a boldface term and, if necessary, the number of a definition. Thus, a typical entry reads:

> **roll over** *v adv* →**turn over** (1), **turn up** (2)
> to (cause to) turn over, as moving to another place in bed: [IØ + OVER] *The car hit a lamppost and rolled over twice before coming to a stop. Every time I rolled over, I woke up because I put my weight on my wounded knee.* [T1 + OVER] *The policeman rolled the body over to look for the missing gun.* —**rollover** *n, adj*

III. Quality and Currency of Entries

A wide range of verbal phrases can be found in *Phrasal Verbs*. For the modern vernacular we can find entries such as **zonk out** and **lay into**. Other entries such as **sally forth/out**, may be found in literary works but are not used frequently in American English speech. Definitions are brief but adequate, and the sentence illustrations are quite helpful. Frequently more than one sentence is used to illustrate a single entry, as for **pop over**. Illustrative sentences used for this main entry are *Pop over to your grandmother's and see if*

she's all right. Why don't you pop over and see us one weekend? I'll pop your book over as soon as I've finished reading it. The British character of this dictionary can be seen in entries such as **posh up**, but American slang is also included in such entries as **gussy up**.

IV. Accessibility

The phrasal verbs appear in alphabetical order—if necessary, down to the last word of the phrase, as in *do about, do badly, do by, do down, do for,* and so on through *do without.* Guide words appear at the top of each page of double-column text. A boldface arrow refers the reader to other entries that are either similar or the same in meaning. The introduction to the book points out that cross-references can be used to help a reader find a word he or she is not sure of.

> For example, if you know the expression **come in** but you do not know how to say "to make somebody come in," then you will find at the entry for **come in** an expression you can use: **bring in, take in,** or **wheel in**.

The introduction also explains how to use the book and gives a list of grammar codes for the phrasal verbs.

There is also an excellent sample page with highlighted words or codes and call-out explanations in the margin.

V. Summary

The *Longman Dictionary of Phrasal Verbs* provides an authoritative and comprehensive list of verb phrases and English idioms. At first glance the grammatical codes may make the material look difficult to use, although this is not so. Still, some readers may prefer A HANDY BOOK OF COMMONLY USED AMERICAN IDIOMS. However the latter is far less comprehensive in both number of entries and number of definitions given for an entry. Certainly, *Phrasal Verbs* is a must for college and university libraries; larger public libraries will also want to consider it for their reference shelves.

Modern American Usage

Facts at a Glance

Full Title: **Modern American Usage.**
Publisher: Hill & Wang.
Compiler: Wilson Follett.
Editor: Jacques Barzun in collaboration with Carlos Baker, Frederick W. Dupee, Dudley Fitts, James D. Hart, Phyllis McGinley, and Lionel Trilling.

Modern American Usage

❶ Main entries are set in boldface type

❷ Cross-references appear in small capitals

❸ Standard and nonstandard uses are discussed

❶ —**sanguinary, sanguine.** A biographer of Walt Whitman's remarks: *By New Year's 1857 even the sanguinary Whitman could hardly have avoided realizing the seriousness of his failures.* The writer never dreamed that he was— ❸ calling Whitman either bloodstained or bloodthirsty; his intention was to say that Whitman had a hopeful, confident—what is popularly called an optimistic—disposition. That is, he was *sanguine.*

See also ALTERNATE, ALTERNATIVE; ❷ —FELICITOUS, FORTUITOUS; DANGEROUS PAIRS; MALAPROPS.

Edition Reviewed: © 1966; 1986 printing.

Number of Entries: approximately 340.
Number of Pages: 436.
Trim Size: 5½″ × 8¼″.
Binding: paperback.

Price: $10.95.
Sold in bookstores; also sold to libraries and other educational institutions.
ISBN 0-8090-6950-4.

I. Introduction and Scope

For over 20 years and through 13 printings, *Modern American Usage* has vigorously withstood the test of time. Wilson Follett's philosophy of language and his principles of correct speech and prose are as sensible and sound today as they were on publication in 1966. Follett died in 1963, after finishing more than two-thirds of the first draft. The task of completing the work was taken on by a colleague of Follett's, Jacques Barzun, with the assistance of six other writers and teachers, each of whom, in turn, gave the work "the benefit of his literary skill and educated judgment."

Modern American Usage has three sections: an introduction, the lexicon, and appendixes.

The introductory essays serve as a preview of the aim and purpose of the guide. Stress is placed on choosing in writing and in speech "the fittest among all possible words, idioms, and construction." Errors and ambiguities in current expressions are analyzed, and certain standards are established—that asserted jargon can be revolting and that purism equates with pedantry. Because Follett believed grammar was indispensable, he stoutly advocated "a resumption in our schools of teaching of grammar and the reading of books."

The lexicon makes up the main body of the book. Alphabetically arranged, it is designed as a guide to troublesome words, phrases, constructions, and styles. Also found in the lexicon are grammatical words, such as **adverbs**, **antecedents**, and **subjunctives** with discussions of their principal difficulties. The front-matter of the volume contains an "Inventory of Main Entries" arranged under the headings *Diction*, *Idiom*, *Syntax*, and *Style*. Owing to the complexity governing the usage of *shall* and *will*, *should* and *would*, these words, like the conventions of punctuation, are taken up in separate appendixes at the end of the book.

II. Format

The essays are printed on full pages of clear, readable type. The lexicon is set in two columns in a smaller but equally readable typeface. The main subject entries are indented and in lowercase, boldface type. *See* and *see also* references are in small capitals. Some entries consist of a few words, others are lengthy discussions divided into numbered sections. Quoted references and examples are set in italics. The 13th printing of this well-known and highly respected guide to usage is in paperback, firmly glued, but with gutter margins too narrow for rebinding.

III. Quality and Currency of Entries

The definitions and descriptive accounts in the lexicon are eloquent, scholarly, terse, pithy, enlightening, and entertaining. Sample quotations range from the Old Testament to a nursery rhyme. References for accepted and rejected forms are taken from, among others, political speeches, literature, classical and modern authors, history, newspapers, and journals. Here is a sketchy summary of one of the complex entries (the entry for **that, which**, relative pronoun), which takes up almost two full pages of text. It begins with a memorable schoolboy riddle, goes on to quote the Fowler brothers, then Kittredge and Greenough, enumerates reasons for and against usages, and finally concludes that the conflicting arguments lie deep in the structure of the language and may never find a satisfactory resolution.

To sum up a few entries:

due to runs into trouble when it is converted into a prepositional phrase used to introduce adverbial elements—substitute *because of, owing to*;

eager is often confused with *anxious*;

exciting is ubiquitous, overworked, and intolerable;

exodus cannot refer to the departure of one person;

ology, **ologies** refers to reason and theory about a thing or activity; *technology* should mean the theory of our mechanized world, not the machinery itself. It may be too late to correct that error, but not too late for *methodology* (*method*), *sociological* (*social*), or the vain-glorious *proximology*;

put, as a past participle, calls for vigilance when it stands for *phrased*—the cure is *in other words, that is to say*;

togetherness may have succumbed to its own popularity, "at least in the minds of sensible men";

we, editorial should not be used by a single person, who should "resolve to take the great leap and say *I* . . . a mask is more conspicuous than a face."

Choosing an entry at random can lead to unexpected connections and rewarding reading. No new words have been added since 1966, but most of the basic principles of usage do not change with the passing of time.

IV. Accessibility

The text is arranged alphabetically, and guide words appear at the top of each page, making the entries very accessible. At the beginning of the volume, the editors suggest that it is not necessary to read the introductory chapter before using the guide. It may well work that way. If you use the guide first, then the information in the introduction will be more meaningful and the discursive writing more easily understood.

V. Summary

Modern American Usage is a valuable reference work for every library. The paperback edition should allow for the purchase of duplicate copies for circulation.

The work will be useful for colleges, English and language courses as well as libraries; for business and industrial offices, secretaries, and writers of newspapers, journals, and books.

Mrs. Byrne's Dictionary of Unusual, Obscure, and Preposterous Words

Facts at a Glance

Full Title: **Mrs. Byrne's Dictionary of Unusual, Obscure, and Preposterous Words**.
Publisher: Washington Square Press.
Compiler: Josefa Heifetz Byrne.
Editor: Robert Byrne.
Edition Reviewed: © 1974; 1984 printing.

Number of Entries: 6,000.
Number of Pages: 237.
Trim Size: 4″ × 6¾″.
Binding: paperback.

Price: $3.50.
Sold in bookstores.
ISBN 0-671-49782-0.

I. Introduction and Scope

Mrs. Byrne's Dictionary of Unusual, Obscure, and Preposterous Words contains six thousand main entries of the "weirdest words in the English language," according to the introduction. Many of the words are obscure, others are obsolete, very few are familiar. This is not an ordinary dictionary. The idea is to present words seldom used, the kind that are just right for Scrabble® and other word games.

Mrs. Byrne is Josefa Heifetz Byrne, the daughter of the late violinist, Jascha Heifetz. She is a pianist and composer whose hobby is collecting strange and unique words. She spent ten years researching the material for this dictionary. Every word listed, according to the editor's introduction, "has been accepted as a formal or legitimate English word by at least one major dictionary."

The selection was subjective and not intended to be in any way comprehensive. To be included, a word had to strike Mrs. Byrne "as unusual, obscure, difficult, unfamiliar, amusing, or preposterous."

II. Format

Each page of this paperback is divided into two columns. Bold black lines separate the columns as well as the quick pronunciation key from the columns. Main entries are in bold type overhanging the definitions in regular type. A guide word appears at the top of each column, the one on the left is the first word on the page, the one on the right is the last. This book is an easy-to-read and handy **vade mecum** (favorite object to carry everywhere).

III. Quality and Currency of Entries

Definitions are to the point and not much is left to the imagination. They are not only down to earth, but also sometimes earthy. For example:

> **hunkerousness** *n*. opposition to progress; old-fogyism.
> **pouze** *n*. refuse from cider-making.
> **proctalgia** *n*. a pain in the ass. Also *rectalgia*.

Sometimes several definitions are given, often containing a word that indicates a bit of its etymology. For example:

> **bubbybush** *n*. the Carolina allspice.
> **clavis** *n*. a clue in deciphering, or translating foreign writings; a glossary or key (Latin *clavis* = key).
> **zzxyoanw** *n*. a Maori drum.

Parts of speech are identified in every main entry. Syllabication is not given, pronunciation is. With its 1,913 letters, the longest word included, **methionyl-glutaminylarginy** . . . ("the chemical name for tryptophan synthetase A protein . . .") is the only word where no pronunciation is provided.

Mrs. Byrne provides only one pronunciation per word. A pronunciation key is placed at the beginning of the dictionary; an abbreviated form is printed at the bottom of each page.

Special features of the dictionary are the main entry words themselves and the bibliography of source books that were used for verification of words and definitions. Many of these sources have been revised or updated since *Mrs. Byrne's Dictionary* was first published.

IV. Accessibility

Access is strictly alphabetical. Each entry includes the main entry word, pronunciation, word form, and a brief definition. Clarification or a tidbit of information sometimes follows the definition in parentheses. For example:

> **peckerwood** *n*. a poor southern ASP or Anglo-Saxon Protestant (the woodpecker symbolizing whites in the South).

V. Summary

Mrs. Byrne's Dictionary is great fun for those with **lexiphanic** (using pretentious language) interests. While browsing through this dictionary, one is **motatorious** (constantly active), taking **oblectation** (delight, pleasure) in each new word.

While it is best used by those who play word games or by those who enjoy browsing through words, the editor and author readily recognize that it could fall into the wrong hands and rather charmingly "apologize for the ammunition this book provides to bad writers"! *Mrs. Byrne's* might be purchased as a supplement to a library's circulating reference collection, but its paperback binding will neither stand up to extensive use nor lend itself to rebinding.

New Dictionary of American Slang

Facts at a Glance

Full Title: **New Dictionary of American Slang**.
Former Title: Dictionary of American Slang.
Publisher: Harper & Row.
Editor: Robert L. Chapman.
Edition Reviewed: © 1986.

Number of Entries: 15,000.
Number of Pages: 650.
Number of Indexes: 1.
Trim Size: $7\frac{3}{8}'' \times 9\frac{1}{4}''$.
Binding: cloth.

Price: $21.45.
Sold in bookstores; also sold to libraries and other educational institutions.
ISBN 0-06-181157-2.

I. Introduction and Scope

The *New Dictionary of American Slang*, first published in 1986, is based on the *Dictionary of American Slang* (1960), edited by Harold Wentworth and Stuart Berg Flexner. The current, completely revised work is a comprehensive, up-to-date compilation of American slang words and phrases. It includes definitions, dating labels, pronunciation (as needed), word origins, and usage examples, many of which are quoted from published sources.

Editor Robert L. Chapman is recently retired from Drew University as professor of English. He was an editor of both ROGET'S INTERNATIONAL THESAURUS and the FUNK & WAGNALLS STANDARD COLLEGE DICTIONARY. In the preface to the *New Dictionary of American Slang*, Chapman justifies the compilation of a slang dictionary, discusses the history and practice of slang lexicography, and provides a readable and informative extended definition of the term slang. Also included in the volume are Flexner's preface to the *Dictionary of American Slang* and a four-page "Guide to the Dictionary."

New Dictionary of American Slang

❶ Variant forms, like main entries, are set in boldface type

❷ Dating labels are italicized

❸ Field labels are italicized

❹ Cross-references are set in small capitals

❺ Slang synonyms are preceded by an equals sign

❻ Examples of usage appear in italics

❼ Etymology is enclosed in brackets

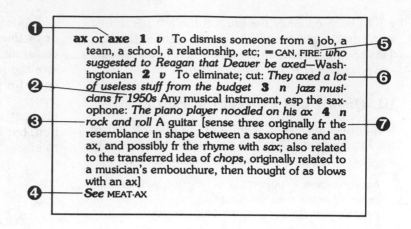

II. Format

The main entry words and phrases are printed in boldface overhanging the text. Some main entries are distinguished by "impact symbols" that indicate terms the editors consider vulgar or taboo. For example, the notation ◁**deadass**▷ indicates that this term should be used only when the speaker or writer is aware of and desires its strong effect. The notation ◀**coon**▶ means that this term should never be used as a synonym for "black person."

Pronunciations follow the main entry only when the editors feel they are necessary. Phonetic respelling is provided, for example, for **sysop** (SISS ahp), meaning computer operator, from system operator. Then follows a part-of-speech abbreviation in bold italic. Most entries next provide a dating label, an italic phrase indicating the period of the term's origin (dating phrases are not provided for terms originating in the 1970s and 1980s). In some cases a provenance label is also supplied, an italic phrase indicating the group responsible for the coinage, such as *WW2 armed forces* or *outdated underworld*.

Definitions follow, identified with bold numerals when more than one is provided. Then come slang synonyms, where provided, preceded by an equal sign. When an editorial note is needed, it appears following a large bold dot.

For example, after the three definitions of **cool it** are listed, there appears the following editorial note:

● In all three senses often an exhortation or irritated command.

Usage examples are printed in italic, and their sources appear in roman type after a dash. For some entries, derivations are provided in square brackets. Finally, any cross-references are listed. They follow the boldface italic word *See* and are printed in small capitals.

The dictionary is well designed and attractive. Its typefaces are large and clear, and white space is advantageously used. The good-quality paper permits almost no show-through of text. The volume is sturdily bound and will hold up well to heavy use.

III. Quality and Currency of Entries

The entries are clear and informative, and multiple senses of a word or phrase are especially well covered. For example, the term **pickup** has seven senses:

1 *n* A person accosted and made a companion, esp in a bar, on the street, etc., for sexual purposes: *His next girlfriend was a pickup he made at Rod's* **2** *n* An arrest **3** *n* (also **pickup truck**). A small truck having a cab, and cargo space with low sidewalls **4** *n* The ability of a car to accelerate rapidly, esp from a halt **5** *n* The act of getting or acquiring something: *He made the pickup at the post office* **6** *adj* Impromptu; unceremonious: *We'll have a pickup lunch in the kitchen* **7** *adj* For one occasion; temporary; ad hoc: *a pickup band/ a pickup corps of waiters*

For the verb phrase **pick up**, five additional definitions are presented.

The entries are enhanced by the plentiful descriptive examples that show the words in contemporary context. The reader will also benefit from the considerable amount of usage information provided as well as from information on variants, synonyms, and origins. Although, as the editor points out, "slang etymology is less certain and precise than standard etymology," the derivations supplied are carefully researched and interesting. For example, under **pussyfoot**, the following derivation is presented:

[fr the nickname of WE Johnson, given because of his catlike stealth as a law-enforcement officer in the Indian Territory (Oklahoma); Johnson became a famous advocate of Prohibition, and the term briefly meant "prohibitionist"].

The work's currency is excellent, an exceptionally important criterion for a dictionary of slang. Among the inclusions are such contemporary terms as **Barbie Doll**, **designer drug**, **ditz**, **greenmail**, **Joe Six-pack**, **rad**, and **Trekkie**. However, the work is equally strong in its coverage of still-current slang terms that entered the language long ago (**dude** . . . *fr late 1800s*) and terms that are now out-of-date (**dutch** . . . *outdated horseracing*).

IV. Accessibility

Two boldface guide words are provided on each double-page spread, indicating the first and last words thereon. Accessibility is also enhanced by comprehensive cross-referencing, with cross-reference terms in small capitals. Alternative spellings are provided in boldface after main entry terms (**hoodang** or **houdang**).

V. Summary

The *New Dictionary of American Slang* is unique and excellent. Its coverage of slang words and phrases is comprehensive; its definitions are clear and thorough; and it provides a wealth of information on usage and word origins. The work will be of value to scholars in the fields of linguistics and literature, but it is by no means limited to this audience. All readers with an interest in slang coinages will find this dictionary informative and entertaining. The work is highly recommended for public and college and university libraries.

The New York Times Everyday Reader's Dictionary of Misunderstood, Misused, and Mispronounced Words

Facts at a Glance

Full Title: **The New York Times Everyday Reader's Dictionary of Misunderstood, Misused, and Mispronounced Words: Revised Edition**.
Publisher: Times Books.
Editor: Laurence Urdang.
Edition Reviewed: © 1985.

Number of Entries: approximately 14,000.
Number of Pages: 410.
Trim Size: 5½″ × 8³⁄₁₆″.
Binding: cloth.

Price: $18.95.
Sold in bookstores and other outlets; also sold to libraries and other educational institutions.
ISBN 0-8129-1181-4.

I. Introduction and Scope

The description on the dust jacket's fly leaf touts this book as "a treasury of fancy five-dollar words for language lovers, word buffs, and polysyllabic people everywhere." The 1985 edition of the work is a revision of an edition published in 1972. According to the foreword, the words that appear here have been selected on the basis of the personal choice of the editor, Laurence Urdang. They also include some uncommon words, such as **obsecrate**, **nugatory**, and **flagitious**, that have appeared in popular newspapers and magazines. Some are words that can be readily applied in ordinary writing and speaking yet are rarely used, such as **lestobiosis**, **renifleur**, and **nimiety**. Urdang closes the foreword to the book with this pithy comment:

> This is not a succedaneum for satisfying the nympholepsy of nullifidians. Rather it is hoped that the haeccecity of this enchiridion of arcane and recondite sesquipedalian terms will appeal to the oniomania of an eximious Gemeinschaft whose legerity and sophrosyne, whose Sprachgefühl and orexis will find more than fugacious fulfillment among its felicific pages.

This book is not for the "everyday reader" but will be fun for those who love words. Its editor is a professional lexicographer who has been responsible for a large number of books on language. He was the managing editor of the first edition of the unabridged RANDOM HOUSE DICTIONARY OF THE ENGLISH LANGUAGE, was the editorial director of *The Collins English Dictionary*, and founder of two language journals.

II. Format

Words are arranged alphabetically, beginning with **aardvark** and ending with **zymurgy**. Entries are in boldface type, and syllabication is shown in the entry word by the use of centered black dots. Pronunciation follows the entry word and is in parentheses. The pronunciation key is located at the beginning of the book only. The part of speech is noted in abbreviated form, followed by a short definition. For the most part, only one definition is given, but a few entries rate two or more. Other forms of a word are not given separate entries but appear at the end of the entry paragraph. A typical entry is shown below:

> **coun′ten ance** (koun′tənəns), *n.* **1.** face; mien; appearance. --*v.* **coun′ten anced**, **coun′ten anc ing**. **2.** to allow or tolerate.

III. Quality and Currency of Entries

If readers are looking for a dictionary that will be an aid to understanding "misunderstood, misused, and mispronounced words," they will be sorely disappointed; the title of this word book is very misleading. Rather, it is a dictionary of assorted words, most of which can be found in any good dictionary. Furthermore, there is nothing significant about the pronunciation or the definitions that would clarify usage beyond that found in other sources. An individual wanting to do some vocabulary building might find this word book useful, but only up to a point. Although the foreword states that "by and large, technical and scientific words have been omitted with the two exceptions of anatomical terms and diseases . . . ," many of the words included are indeed technical. For instance, we find words such as

> **micropyrometer** . . . an adaptation of an optical pyrometer to deal with minute objects, by means of which temperatures above 550° C are measured according to their degree of incandescence;

> **microsiemens** . . . a unit of measurement of electrical conductance equal to one millionth of a siemens.

These terms are followed by such words as **milk-sop**, **milk-toast**, and **Milky Way**; it is difficult to believe that these words are generally misused or misunderstood. Words that are often misused, however, such as *infer* and *imply* or *further* and *farther*, are not to be found. Although to be fair to the editor's choice, comparatively obscure words such as **aliquant** and **aliquot** are included. Abbreviations are noted for certain words, for example, **mb** for **millibar**, "a unit used in measuring atmospheric pressure, equal to one thousandth of a bar" and *millibarn*, "a unit used in measuring a nuclear cross-section, equal to one thousandth of a barn," and "μs" for *microsiemen*.

Currency does not seem to be a major issue in a dictionary as idiosyncratic as this one. Words are included because there is something about them that interested the editor. There is no doubt some appeal in being able to say "I'm fazed" the next time you are embarrassed or to tell a guest that he or she has "ingurgitated" rather than eaten greedily.

IV. Accessibility

There is no guide to using this dictionary, but one is not really needed. Guide words appear at the tops of pages. Alternative spellings are given, such as **pepsin** and **pepsine**. There is also an occasional cross-reference, such as under the entry for **eugenic** where we find "See also **dysgenic**."

V. Summary

An earlier reviewer observed that this word book was "like having all the answers to a linguistic Trivial Pursuit® game" (*ARBA*, 1986, p. 413). It is probably

the ideal gift for someone who wants to sound like William F. Buckley, Jr., but as a reference tool there are other sources that will, in fact, help the reader to understand "misunderstood, misused, and mispronounced words." Copperud's A DICTIONARY OF USAGE AND STYLE, revised in 1980, is an excellent source, and that old standby H. W. Fowler's A DICTIONARY OF MODERN ENGLISH USAGE remains useful to a degree. A random comparison suggests that most if not all of the words in *The New York Times Everyday Reader's Dictionary of Misunderstood, Misused, and Mispronounced Words* can be found in the unabridged RANDOM HOUSE DICTIONARY OF THE ENGLISH LANGUAGE. However, this dictionary does present a varied selection of often unusual words. It seeks to be interesting and entertaining rather than comprehensive and, as such, it is suggested that libraries purchasing the volume include it in their circulating rather than their reference collection.

No Uncertain Terms

Facts at a Glance

Full Title: **No Uncertain Terms**.
Publisher: Facts on File.
Compilers: Mark Dittrick and Diane Kender Dittrick.
Illustrator: Tom Bloom.
Edition Reviewed: © 1984.

Number of Entries: 132.
Number of Pages: 128.
Trim Size: 5½" × 8½".
Binding: paperback.

Price: $6.95.
Sold in bookstores; also sold to libraries and other educational institutions.
ISBN 0-87196-217-9.

I. Introduction and Scope

In his "foreword" (a preface usually written by someone other than the author of the work in hand), Stuart B. Flexner, editor-in-chief of the Random House dictionaries, calls *No Uncertain Terms* a "very entertaining book." The authors, Mark Dittrick and Diane Kender Dittrick, in a "preface," claim to have written this 128-page paperback word book for two reasons: their "personal and professional interest in nailing down the names of things" and the "megabuck" rent on their New York apartment. In the "introduction," we are told that *No Uncertain Terms* is about familiar names of things that people regularly confuse with similar, familiar terms, such as

No Uncertain Terms

❶

A Shlemiel, A Schlimazl

"Shlemiel" has won some currency in the English language; however, "schlimazl," as luck would have it, hasn't.

A SHLEMIEL:

Also spelled schlemiel, schlemihl, or shlemihl, a Yiddish term—from a Hebrew word meaning "good-for-nothing"—for a butter-fingered bungler, an unfortunate misfit, an inept fool, or simply a simpleton.

❷

A SCHLIMAZL:

Also spelled schlimazel or schlemazel, a Yiddish term—from a German word for bad, *schlimm*, and the Hebrew word for luck, *mazel*—for a person plagued with chronic lack of luck. A born loser.

"The classic attempt to discriminate between the two types," explains Leo Rosten's *The Joys of Yiddish*, "runs: 'A *shlemiel* is a man who is always spilling hot soup—down the neck of a *shlimazl*.'" But *The New York Times Everyday Reader's Dictionary of Misunderstood, Misused, Mispronounced Words*, which offers: "schlemiel . . . a poor fool who is always the victim of others" and "schlemazel . . . a particularly stupid and awkward person," seems to have gotten its definitions reversed. The editor wasn't a shlemiel, since he must have known better; at worst he was a schlimazl. The shlemiel was probably the typesetter.

❸

❹

❶ Main entries name groups of confusable terms

❷ Each term is defined separately

❸ Some articles contain a further discussion of the difference between the terms

❹ Examples of usage are often given

pier/dock; *gorge/canyon*; *sweet potato/yam* and *preface*, *foreword*, and *introduction*.

Although few sources are given for their humorously written, apparently accurate definitions/descriptions of familiar words (and some not-so-familiar, e.g., *cyclotron/synchrocyclotron/synchrotron*) "we all *think* we know," the authors' credentials (they are both professional writers and editors; she was a contributor to THE CONCISE COLUMBIA ENCYCLOPEDIA; both are contributors to the latest revised edition of the unabridged RANDOM HOUSE DICTIONARY OF THE ENGLISH LANGUAGE) ensure that their entertaining "distinctions" are also enlightening.

II. Format

Fifty-seven groups of terms are listed in this slim paperback, each group introduced by an amusing statement:

A Monk, a Friar
One of them begs to differ.

Compost, Mulch
To appreciate the difference takes a
good sense of humus.

A Marsh, a Bog, a Swamp
Squish, squush, squash.

Following each heading are humorous, informative paragraphs explaining the distinctions among the several terms in each group. Many of the word groups are accompanied by witty full-page cartoons by Tom Bloom. The range of terms used is very selective, from **cement/concrete**; **optician/optometrist/ophthalmologist**; and **cougar/mountain lion/puma** to **shlemiel/schlimazl**; and **snowstorm/blizzard**. The reader is not told how the terms were chosen or why others (such as **alligator/crocodile**; **dolphin/porpoise**; and **daffodil/jonquil**) are not included.

III. Summary

No Uncertain Terms is a delightful word book that cleverly explains the differences (or "distinctions") among a collection of frequently confused (although not all familiar) words, in a style that is both funny and informative. Tom Bloom's "irreverently illuminating illustrations" fill the pages, and although this is not an essential purchase for all libraries, it would be a popular choice among library users who are curious about the oddities of the English language.

NTC's American Idioms Dictionary

Facts at a Glance

Full Title: **NTC's American Idioms Dictionary**.
Publisher: National Textbook Company.
Author: Richard A. Spears.
Edition Reviewed: © 1987; 1988 printing.

Number of Entries: more than 8,000.
Number of Pages: 480.
Trim Size: 6″ × 9″.
Binding: paperback.

Price: $9.95.
Sold in bookstores; also sold to libraries and other
educational institutions.
ISBN 0-8442-5450-9.

I. Introduction and Scope

NTC's American Idioms Dictionary is a guide to more than 8,000 idiomatic expressions of contemporary American English. The phrases come from many sources, including newspapers, magazines, dictionaries, and an ongoing collection of expressions found difficult by Northwestern University students of English as a foreign language.

The author, Richard A. Spears, and the associate editor, Linda Schinke-Llano, are both linguistics professors specializing in second-language acquisition at Northwestern. Their dictionary is intended for "people who are learning how to understand idiomatic English, the hearing impaired, and for all speakers of English who want to know more about the language."

II. Format

Entries are in boldface type, listed alphabetically by the whole phrase, and overhang the text. There are two columns per page, set in very readable type and surrounded by ample white space. The print is black on white, nearly opaque paper. The large-size paperback format is adequate for home and office use but would not withstand heavy library wear without rebinding.

III. Quality and Currency of Entries

The style, content, and organization of the entries provide a clear approach to idiomatic meaning and usage. The compilers have incorporated slang, clichés, proverbs, and other formal and informal expressions in current American English, although the selection is not exhaustive. We could find entries for **monkey around** and **iron something out**, for example, but *monkey business*, *iron fist*, and *iron in the fire* do not appear.

The main entry phrase is followed by one or more alternate forms, if they occur; the meaning; and then two examples of usage in italic type. If an entry has more than one meaning, they are numbered, each with its own illustrative examples. Here is a typical entry:

draw a blank* (Informal.) **1.** to get no response; to find nothing. *I asked him about Tom's financial problems, and I just drew a blank. We looked in the files for an* *hour, but we drew a blank.* **2.** to fail to remember (something). *I tried to remember her telephone number, but I could only draw a blank.* *It was a very hard test with only one question to answer, and I drew a blank.*

Note the asterisk and usage label following the entry phrase. They indicate that caution should be used in the context of formal writing. Other usage labels include *slang*, *folksy*, and *cliché*; usage labels may include a brief explanation or comparison.

Many entries also include cross-references to related idioms. Hence, **up North** includes references to **back East**, **down South**, and **out West**. Considerable care has also been taken to define and illustrate variant forms of the same idiom—for example, **know one's stuff** AND **know one's onions**, **well and good** AND **all well and good**.

IV. Accessibility

NTC's American Idioms Dictionary is unintimidating and easy to use. Its comprehensive alphabetical "Phrase-Finder Index" at the end of the book allows access to any idiomatic phrase even though the reader may know only one part of it. **Path of least resistance** is indexed three times, and **live from hand to mouth** is indexed under every word except *to*. The "Phrase-Finder Index" avoids the cumbersome cross-referencing within the text that is found in the OXFORD DICTIONARY OF CURRENT IDIOMATIC ENGLISH.

A six-page "How to Use This Dictionary" is an exemplary guide to every aspect of the entries. There is minimal use of abbreviations, and all terms and symbols appear in a list immediately preceding the dictionary. This list has the unusual feature of defining the usage labels, for example:

> **informal**   refers to a very casual expression that is most likely to be spoken and not written.

It is a pity, however, that the ubiquitous asterisk, explained in the dictionary guide, is not repeated in the terms and symbols list.

Finally, a table of contents lists the main sections of the dictionary, and guide words at the top of each page help to locate the idioms.

V. Summary

NTC's American Idioms Dictionary lives up to its cover's promise of providing "practical reference to everyday expressions of contemporary American English." Students and home users will find the dictionary a convenient, accessible, and up-to-date guide to the correct usage and meaning of a large number of modern idiomatic expressions. Libraries, however, will require a dictionary that includes the literary and historical sources of idioms, such as *A*

Concise Dictionary of English Idioms by William Freeman or the OXFORD DICTIONARY OF CURRENT IDIOMATIC ENGLISH.

-Ologies and -Isms

Facts at a Glance

Full Title: **-Ologies and -Isms: A Thematic Dictionary: Third Edition.**
Publisher: Gale Research Company.
Editors: Laurence Urdang, Editor-in-Chief; Anne Ryle, Editor, and Tanya H. Lee, Associate Editor.
Edition Reviewed: © 1986.

Number of Entries: over 17,000.
Number of Pages: 795.
Number of Indexes: 1.
Trim Size: 6″ × 9″.
Binding: cloth.

Price: $90.00.
Sold to libraries and other educational institutions. ISBN 0-8103-1196-8.

I. Introduction and Scope

-Ologies and -Isms bears a resemblance to both a dictionary and a thesaurus. Like the former, it provides short definitions for each of its noun entries and shows "where such forms are unusual or various, [and where] other parts of speech developed from the entry word." Like a thesaurus, it groups terms in thematic categories so that the relationships among entries and different shades of meaning can be quickly identified. This grouping by concept allows the user access to terms and definitions without prior knowledge of their existence or spelling. The third edition is an expanded version of its predecessors, having increased its coverage by about 75 percent from the second edition and added a "Table of Thematic Categories" and numerous cross-references to make entries more accessible.

Part of the lengthy subtitle of the volume explains the principles of selection for entries:

> A Unique Lexicon of More Than 15,000 English Words Used of and about Theories, Concepts, Doctrines, Systems, Attitudes, Practices, States of Mind, and Branches of Science, Focusing Especially on Words Containing the Suffixes *-ology*, *-ism*, *-ics*, *-graphy*, *-metry*, *-archy*, *-cide*, *-philia*, *-phobia*, *-mancy*, *-latry*, et al., Including Derivative Forms of These Words, . . .

The forewords of the first and third editions stress the usefulness of *-Ologies and -Isms* for researchers

-Ologies and -Isms

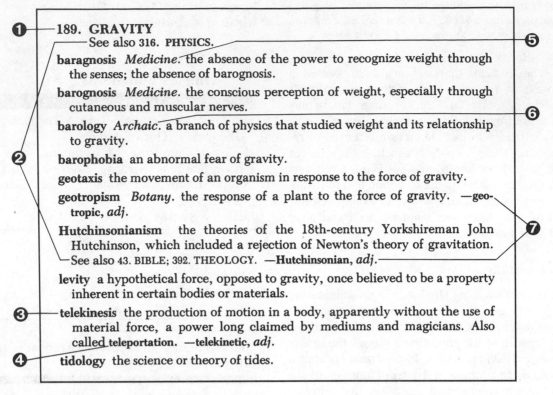

189. GRAVITY
See also 316. PHYSICS.

baragnosis *Medicine.* the absence of the power to recognize weight through the senses; the absence of barognosis.

barognosis *Medicine.* the conscious perception of weight, especially through cutaneous and muscular nerves.

barology *Archaic.* a branch of physics that studied weight and its relationship to gravity.

barophobia an abnormal fear of gravity.

geotaxis the movement of an organism in response to the force of gravity.

geotropism *Botany.* the response of a plant to the force of gravity. —**geotropic**, *adj.*

Hutchinsonianism the theories of the 18th-century Yorkshireman John Hutchinson, which included a rejection of Newton's theory of gravitation. See also 43. BIBLE; 392. THEOLOGY. —**Hutchinsonian**, *adj.*

levity a hypothetical force, opposed to gravity, once believed to be a property inherent in certain bodies or materials.

telekinesis the production of motion in a body, apparently without the use of material force, a power long claimed by mediums and magicians. Also called **teleportation**. —**telekinetic**, *adj.*

tidology the science or theory of tides.

❶ Thematic categories, set in capital letters, are both alphabetized and numbered

❷ *See also* cross-references suggest other appropriate thematic categories, which appear in small capitals

❸ Headwords are set in boldface type

❹ Synonyms of headwords are given

❺ Italicized field labels identify specialized usage

❻ Italicized usage labels identify archaic, obsolete, rare, or facetious usage

❼ Related forms of headwords are listed

who need quick reference to lists of subject-related terms that may be necessary in researching material in indexes and bibliographies, as well as to "those who seek assistance from libraries." Cross-referencing an entry to two or more categories reminds the user that a word's meaning may change, depending upon the context in which it is used (**pluralism** in philosophy and politics, for example). Entries flagged as archaic, obsolete, or rare, and alternative spellings also facilitate a user's search for material that may no longer be current but is still appropriately included in the text.

Howard G. Zettler points out in the foreword to the 1977 edition that *-Ologies and -Isms* was the first reference of its kind to group words according to suffixes, providing the user with an alternative to searching a dictionary for a term with an unusual prefix. For example, **313. PHOBIAS** lists eleven pages of aversions, from **acarophobia** (a fear of skin infestation by mites or ticks) to **zoophobia** (an abnormal fear or dislike of animals), making all these terms readily available to a user who does not know the correct prefix for the term he or she wishes to use.

In some cases entries are so obscure that they do not appear in the standard desktop dictionary (**laclabphily** the collecting of cheese labels), making the text an interesting reference for word enthusiasts.

II. Format

-Ologies and -Isms is prefaced by the forewords of all three editions and a newly added section on "How to Use This Book" that provides concise information about what the user can expect to find and how best to go about it. These are followed by the "Table of Thematic Categories," which functions as a table of contents. The main text contains 430 thematic categories, listed alphabetically and numbered consecutively. Categories are in bold capital letters; running heads appear at the tops of pages. Cross-referencing is by number and name of category.

Each category is followed by two or more noun entries, listed alphabetically and briefly defined. There are no guides to pronunciation and few derivations of words, but occasionally an unusual adjectival or noun form of the entry is also included. These appear in the index and are referred to as "run-ons."

Some entries may be synonymous with the category (**PROVERB** and **maxim**), some may be subcategories, and some may be opposites of each other. For example, under **8. ALCOHOL** one finds both **abstinence** and **insobriety**. All 33 entries in the category and the cross-references **39. BEER**; **158. FERMENTATION**; and **421. WINE** make it clear that this category is concerned with potable alcohol.

A user tracing a specific entry may find it included in several categories but defined the same way in each (**Hermeticism** under **ALCHEMY, LITERARY STYLE, MYSTICISM,** and **PHILOSOPHY**). The entry **ustulation**, however, illustrates the thoroughness with which differences in meaning have been preserved when it is appropriate to do so. Under **162. FIRE** the citation is:

> **ustulation** *Rare.* the act or process of burning or searing. —ustorious, ustulate, adj.;

under **350. REMEDIES**:

> **ustulation** *Pharmacy.* the process of heating moist substances so that they can be pulverized;

and under **364. SEX**:

> **ustulation** *Obsolete.* a burning sexual desire; a lustful passion.

Notes on usage explain the specificity of each term, and unusual variants are supplied under the denotation for which they are appropriate.

III. Quality and Currency of Entries

The enlarged edition of *-Ologies and -Isms* generally keeps pace with evolving terminology. One notable exception is under **HOMOSEXUALITY**, whose eight entries contain no form of the word *gay*. Likewise, **feminism**, included under **ATTITUDES**, is defined as "an attitude favoring the movement to eliminate political, social, and professional discrimination against women," a definition too limited for the term's diverse contemporary meaning and not cross-referenced to **WOMEN** or **POLITICS**, to which it is closely related.

The text has been more successful in keeping up with newly coined terms in current affairs, including **Khomeinism** (**POLITICS**, but not **ISLAM**), and **Reaganomics** (**ECONOMICS**).

IV. Accessibility

The combination of the "Table of Thematic Categories" and the 207-page index at the end of the text make *-Ologies and -Isms* convenient for quick reference. The categories list allows the user to identify broad topics and more specific related terms. This table is an alphabetized list of the categories (numbered and in boldfaced capitals) and entries synonymous with the categories (in boldface type with the initial letter capitalized). Page numbers for categories are given as are relevant cross-references to other categories. Synonyms are referenced to the category(ies) in which they appear.

The index is a double-column alphabetized listing of "all the headwords, variant forms of headwords, and run-on entries from the text." Headwords and variants appear in lowercase boldface type, and run-ons are in lightface type. Proper nouns in both classes are capitalized. Headwords and variants are identified by the number and name (in small lightface capitals) of their categories, and run-ons have the additional reference of the headword that they supplement. For example:

> **abolitionism** [headword] **371. SLAVERY**

> **abolitionist** [run-on] 371. **SLAVERY, abolitionism**.

V. Summary

-Ologies and -Isms accomplishes its announced purpose of collecting terms by important suffixes and grouping them thematically so that the user can find an accurate term for a concept when one does exist, even without knowing it beforehand. The editors admit that the book is not comprehensive, but the third edition's coverage has been expanded (amounting to more than 17,000 entries in total). Lists under some categories, like **CANCER** and **PHOBIAS**, provide basic glossaries for directing a layman's research into the topic. The definitions of entries are generally adequate for a brief reference or reminder of a term already known, and the inclusion of obscure entries is of interest in itself. Careful cross-referencing keeps occasional idiosyncratic classification of entries from being confusing (**Zwinglianism** under **CHRISTIANITY, Calvinism** under **PROTESTANTISM**).

-Ologies and -Isms would be a good addition to a reference collection for students of college level (or even high school) to help them refine and research broad topics, and would also be helpful to the general reader. The more specialized advanced researcher will appreciate its convenient format for rapid reference to specific terms. Those interested in "lexicons and wordhoards" will enjoy consulting it for archaic and obscure terms. Even though neither pronunciation nor etymology is within its scope, the book fulfills its goal of gathering together terms by suffix and making them readily available to users of diverse interests and levels of expertise.

1000 Most Challenging Words

Facts at a Glance

Full Title: **1000 Most Challenging Words.**
Publisher: Facts on File.
Author: Norman W. Schur.
Edition Reviewed: © 1987.

Number of Entries: 1,000.
Number of Pages: 334.
Number of Indexes: 1.
Trim Size: 6″ × 9″.
Binding: cloth.

Price: $18.95.
Sold in bookstores; also sold to libraries and other
educational institutions.
ISBN 0-8160-1196-6.

I. Introduction and Scope

1000 Most Challenging Words is the latest in a series
of books published by Facts on File and written by
Norman W. Schur. Other volumes in the series are
1000 MOST PRACTICAL WORDS and 1000 MOST IM-
PORTANT WORDS. Their author is a graduate of Harvard, a lawyer, and an authority on the English language. The volumes, although in dictionary format,
are essentially vocabulary builders. In contrast to the
two earlier volumes, many of the words in the present
work will be familiar to only the more knowledgeable
students of the English language. As the author points
out in his preface, this is clearly not a book for those
suffering from **sesquipedalophobia**, or the fear of long
words. Such individuals may find a ring of familiarity
in **apocalyptic**, **bifurcate**, **holograph**, **leitmotif**, and
sanguinary, but they are likely (along with others of
us) to be puzzled by **agrestic**, **catachresis**, **dendro-
chronology**, **hamartia**, and **postliminy**.

The emphasis in *1000 Most Challenging Words* is
on words that are forgotten or unusual as well as
colorful, useful, and enticing to those who wish to
stretch their vocabularies. Figurative as well as literal
meanings are given, the etymology of words is provided, and the correct pronunciation is indicated in
a way that will help the reader to avoid **cacoepy**.

II. Format

Main word entries are in boldface and the text of
the entry is in a clear, readable typeface. The page
layout has a somewhat crowded appearance as the
gutter margins are narrow and the text typically runs
close to the bottom edge of the page. The binding
appears to be more than adequate and should stand
up under normal use; however, it is unfortunate that
the book does not lie flat on a surface.

III. Quality and Currency of Entries

In tracing the origin of words, the author includes
those based on fictional characters such as **pecksnif-
fian**, others based on real people, such as **Lucullan**,
and a good number based on geographical locations
both real and imaginary, such as **brummagem** and
lilliputian. As Schur notes, the vast majority of the
entries come from classical Latin and Greek and "are
perfectly good English words that might lurk around
any corner of literature."

The entry for **fanfaronade** is a good example of
Schur's approach. The pronunciation in respelled syllables in parentheses follows the boldface entry word,
along with the part of speech. Then a brief definition
is provided:

> This is a lovely word for arrogant bluster, boastful,
> ostentatious talk or behavior, bragging, bravado.

The etymology of the word is traced to its various
French, Spanish, and Arabic origins. Then the author cites a speech by Gratiano from *The Merchant
of Venice* as a splendid example of **fanfaronade**:

> Gratiano describes the kind of man who strives to give
> an impression of ". . . wisdom, gravity, profound con-
> ceit;/As who should say 'I am Sir Oracle,/And when I
> ope my lips let no dog bark!' "

Finally, the reader is referred to related words also
included in the dictionary: **braggadocio**, **gasconade**,
rodomontade, and **thrasonical**.

Schur's entries are always informed, sometimes
humorous, and often provocative in the sense that
they will tempt readers to explore other entries.

IV. Accessibility

The text of the book is easily accessible and written
in clear, straightforward English, though the words
chosen for discussion are by their very nature often
obscure as well as challenging. There are numerous
cross-references, plus a detailed pronunciation guide
in the author's preface.

V. Summary

It may be a moot point whether these are indeed the
"most" challenging words in the English language,
but there is little doubt that this is the most entertaining of Schur's dictionaries of words. It has the
merits of his earlier volumes (authority, wit, and a
wealth of illuminating examples drawn from world
literature), but the more challenging nature of the
entries seems to have called forth an even greater
piquancy of style. This is a book not simply to be
consulted but to be read with pleasure. As such, it
belongs in the circulating collections of public and
academic libraries.

1000 Most Important Words

Facts at a Glance

Full Title: **1000 Most Important Words**.
Publisher: Facts on File.
Editor: Norman W. Schur.
Edition Reviewed: © 1982.

Number of Entries: 1,000.
Number of Pages: 193.
Trim Size: 6″ × 9″.
Binding: cloth.

Price: $16.95.
Sold in bookstores; also sold to libraries and other educational institutions.
ISBN 0-87196-869-X.

I. Introduction and Scope

1000 Most Important Words is one of a series of books published by Facts on File and authored by Norman W. Schur. Other volumes in the series are 1000 MOST PRACTICAL WORDS and 1000 MOST CHALLENGING WORDS. Their author is a summa cum laude graduate of Harvard, a lawyer, and an authority on the English language. The volumes, although in dictionary format, are essentially vocabulary builders. Schur notes in the preface to his book

> The purpose of this book is to enrich your life by enriching your vocabulary. . . . The usual practice in dictionaries is to present a number, sometimes a large and confusing number, of meanings for each entry. In this volume, I have attempted to choose the one or few most significant and useful meanings in contemporary usage.

In the attempt to show how the selected words may be used most effectively, Schur gives for each entry the following: pronunciation, part of speech represented by the word, varying shades of meaning, derivation and, perhaps most useful of all, quotations or statements demonstrating the word's actual use. Thus, for the word **mien**, Alexander Pope is quoted: "Vice is a monster of so frightful mien,/As to be hated needs but to be seen." At other times, the author simply uses the word in a context that will illustrate its meaning. For the word **apt**: "Adlai Stevenson pleased his audiences with his **apt** remarks on the state of the world." In choosing his quotations or examples, Schur is careful to illustrate figurative as well as literal meanings of the chosen words.

II. Format

Main word entries are in bold type and the text of the entry is in a clear, readable typeface. The page layout has a somewhat crowded appearance as the gutter margins are narrow and the book's text runs almost to the bottom edge of the page. The binding appears to be more than adequate and should stand up under normal wear, which is fortunate since rebinding may be a problem for the librarian.

III. Quality and Currency of Entries

The three Schur books mentioned above actually differ very little in the types of words selected, and the designation "Most" that appears in each title is simply a bit of hyperbole on the part of the publisher. Faced with a given word from any of the three volumes, a reader would be hard pressed to know from which of the volumes it had been selected. Is the word **mnemonic**, for example, practical, important, or challenging? Perhaps the audience for which the 1,000 important words series is intended (the general educated reader) will find it all three.

The author's style is chatty, informal and often humorous. He loves a good story even if he is not sure of the exact setting. For example, for **repartee** he writes:

> A good example of **repartee** is contained in a conversation between Winston Churchill and Lady Astor. Seated next to Winston at a dinner party, Lady Astor said to him, "If I were married to you, I'd put poison in your coffee." Came the **repartee**: "If I were married to you, I'd drink it."

The same story is told elsewhere in the book to illustrate the meaning of an **apposite** reply, but there the butt of Sir Winston's humor is identified as Margot Asquith, without her title.

IV. Accessibility

The text of the book is written in clear, easy-to-understand English. There are occasional cross-references and the few abbreviations used are obvious without having to resort to a list of abbreviations. The only special phonetic symbol used for the pronunciations is the schwa or upside down e [ə] and its use and pronunciation are clearly explained in the preface to the volume.

V. Summary

As with the other Schur books on language, *1000 Most Important Words* is both entertaining and instructive. Some perhaps will quibble that among its "Most Important" words one will not find **beauty**, **liberty**, **equality**, or **justice**. They will, however, find **sacrosanct**, **salacious**, **salubrious**, and **sanctimonious**. Despite its reference format, this work will probably receive more use if assigned to the circulating collection. In short, Schur's book is less a dictionary than a vocabulary builder and in the latter function it should prove valuable to the patrons of high school, public and academic libraries.

1000 Most Practical Words

Facts at a Glance

Full Title: **1000 Most Practical Words**.
Former Title: Practical English: 1000 Most Effective Words.
Publisher: Facts on File.
Editor: Norman W. Schur.
Edition Reviewed: © 1983.

Number of Entries: 1,000.
Number of Pages: 272.
Trim Size: 6" × 9".
Binding: cloth.

Price: $16.95.
Sold in bookstores; also sold to libraries and other educational institutions.
ISBN 0-87196-868-1.

I. Introduction and Scope

1000 Most Practical Words is a hardcover reprint of the paperback title originally appearing as PRACTICAL ENGLISH: 1000 MOST EFFECTIVE WORDS, which is reviewed in-depth elsewhere in this Buying Guide. Its author, Norman W. Schur, a summa cum laude graduate of Harvard, has had a long career as a lawyer and author of numerous works on the English language, including two volumes similar to this: 1000 MOST IMPORTANT WORDS and 1000 MOST CHALLENGING WORDS (both reviewed in this Buying Guide).

On its dust jacket, *1000 Most Practical Words* is described as "a fundamental, quick reference vocabulary builder and dictionary for speakers and students of English." Since the coverage is obviously a highly selective one, the emphasis should be on "vocabulary builder" as opposed to "dictionary." In the former capacity, this is an entertaining and reliable volume, giving the reader information on derivation, pronunciation, shades of meaning, and quotations illustrating the use of the selected words. The entry for **alienate**, for instance, includes its pronunciation, a three-sentence explanation of its use and meaning, and a discussion of the related words **alienable, inalienable, unalienable**, and **alienation**, each with illustrations. This treatment is also followed in Schur's 1000 MOST IMPORTANT WORDS.

The unabbreviated style, usage comments, and extensive illustrations combine to make Schur's *1000 Most . . .* series an entertaining, if not entirely indispensable, guide to the language. Public and academic libraries that add the book to their collections will prefer the sturdier binding of this hardcover edition to the cheaper but flimsier PRACTICAL ENGLISH paperback edition.

Oxford Dictionary of Current Idiomatic English

Facts at a Glance

Full Title: **Oxford Dictionary of Current Idiomatic English**.
Publisher: Oxford University Press.
Compilers: A. P. Cowie, R. Mackin (Volumes 1 and 2); I. R. McCaig (Volume 2).
Edition Reviewed: Vol. 1: © 1975; sixth printing 1984. Vol. 2: © 1983.

Number of Entries: 15,000 idioms.
Number of Pages: 1,225; 2 volumes.
Number of Indexes: 4.
Trim Size: 5⅜" × 8½".
Binding: cloth.

Price: $18.95 (per volume).
Sold in bookstores; also sold to libraries and other educational institutions.
ISBN 0-19-431145-7 (Vol. 1);
ISBN 0-19-431150-3 (Vol. 2).

I. Introduction and Scope

The *Oxford Dictionary of Current Idiomatic English* is a two-volume work compiled and edited by A. P. Cowie, R. Mackin, and I. R. McCaig. Volume 1 is subtitled *Verbs with Prepositions & Particles*; volume 2, *Phrase, Clause & Sentence Idioms*. The basic requirement for inclusion in the dictionary is that the expression be idiomatic according to the terms set down by the editors and that it fit certain grammatical patterns described in the introduction. The 15,000 entries included are supported by citations, both written and spoken, from contemporary sources collected specifically for use in the dictionary. This archive consists of over 30,000 excerpts from works of history, biography, and fiction, including as well quotations from newspapers, periodicals, radio, and television.

According to the foreword, the dictionary was written primarily for the use of foreign-language learners of English "whose control of idiom is not yet sure." Most American English speakers will find few idioms with which they are not already familiar even though this is a British publication.

1000 Most Practical Words

① **impediment** (im ped´ ə mənt) *n.* To *impede* (im peed´) is to hinder. An *impedi-*
② *ment* is a hindrance or obstacle. A lack of education is an *impediment* to advancement in one's work. In *The Book of Common Prayer*, the marriage banns contain
the familiar language: "If any of you know cause, or just *impediment*, why these
two persons should not be joined together in holy Matrimony. . . ." *Impediment*
has a special meaning with regard to speech: a speech defect or disorder is known
as a speech *impediment*, or simply as an *impediment*. The great Greek orator
Demosthenes (384–322 B.C.) overcame a speech *impediment* by practicing speaking with his mouth full of pebbles as he walked along the seashore.

① Pronunciation is enclosed in **③** Quotations from literary works **⑤** Examples of usage illustrate
parentheses and examples from history different senses of the word
② A basic definition is given illustrate usage
④ Related forms are defined and
pronounced

Both volumes include long introductory remarks and explanations to explain the entry words (here termed headphrases), cross-references, grammar, illustrations, and symbols used in the entries, as well as the sources and abbreviations used. Both volumes are indexed; details are explained below under *Accessibility*.

II. Format

The dictionary's division into two volumes works well conceptually and lightens the load physically. Volume 1 is shorter; its simpler headphrases cover single verbs with their different prepositions and the particles that change meanings of idioms. Volume 2 covers more complicated idiomatic sentences. The sturdily bound books lie flat comfortably and are easy to hold. The double-columned pages are somewhat crowded and short of white space, but the type is black and the entries are rationally designed and easy to follow. The paper is lightweight and allows for a good deal of show-through, which is especially noticeable in the introductions and the indexes. The paper in volume 2 is less white and the columns are even longer than those in volume 1.

III. Quality and Currency of Entries

The format of the entries differs somewhat in each volume, although entries in both volumes are in alphabetical order, are in boldface type, and are hung slightly to the left of the paragraph that follows.

In the second volume (described here first for expedience), which covers phrase, clause, and sentence idioms, the main entry phrase (called headphrase) is designed to make clear to foreign-language speakers

that some idiomatic phrases are fixed and others may be filled in with substitute words. Three different styles of entry phrases are used to deal with variability in idiomatic phrases. The first covers minimal optional choices, such as in **day breaks** or **dawn breaks**. These are shown in the headphrase by the use of a slash, for example **dawn/day breaks**, or **in the best/worst of taste** and **in days of old/yore**. The second type of entry occurs when there is either very limited or very open variability in the idiom and is indicated by the placement of the abbreviation **etc** in the headphrase. A phrase with limited variability is entered as follows: **why the hell etc?** After the brief definition a "danger sign" △, follows, which signals limited choice, and a short list of acceptable words that can be substituted—"devil, blazes, heck, dickens." The danger sign does not appear when alternatives are more open: **French etc without tears** indicates that many other nouns are acceptable in place of *French*. Two illustrations are given to make the point, **slimming without tears** and **spinach without tears**.

The third type of entry phrase indicates a minimal lexical or a grammatical choice and is shown by the use of parentheses in the entry, such as **be too little (and) too late** or **(one/another of) life's little ironies**, or

can't do s[ome]th[ing] for love (n) or money . . . modal:
can't, couldn't; won't, wouldn't.

Further abbreviations are sometimes used in the headphrase, such as **sb** and **sth**, which stand for *somebody* and *something*. For example: **in sb's day/time** and **an open sesame (to sth)**. Entries having more than one meaning are given separate listings and are numbered, for example: **give sb etc a break**[1], which means to give somebody a rest or change from work, and **give sb etc a break**[2], which means to provide an opening for a person's talent or ability.

Following the headphrase the parts of speech for words in the phrase are identified and appear in brackets using abbreviations. Labels such as (ironic), (US), and so on follow as appropriate in parentheses. Next comes the definition, which is very brief, and any further refinements of the phrase, including cross-references to synonyms, which are indicated by the abbreviation **qv** in parentheses following the synonymous phrase (*qv* stands for "which may be referred to"). All phrases are used in italic illustrative sentences preceded by a square □. At the end of the illustrative sentence or sentences, there is usually a set of letter symbols that refer the reader to the list of print references used in compiling the dictionary. Following the paragraph are several variations of the entry phrase, each defined by an illustrative sentence. Finally, an arrow may refer the user to the previous or the following entry as a cross-reference. A typical but shorter than usual entry is presented below:

> **have (got)/with the ring of truth etc** seem likely, either by what is said or by the way it is presented, to be true etc; ring true etc (qv) **S**: story, report, account; testimony. **o**: truth, △ sincerity, authenticity; folly, madness □ *His account conflicted with that of other witnesses and yet his story* **had** *for me,* **the ring of truth**. □ *'We should feel wonder at nothing at all in nature except the Incarnation of Christ.' In the seventeenth century, the phrase seemed to make sense. To-day it* **has the ring of madness**. DOP □ distinct from with a ring of merriment, scorn, incredulity etc in his voice indicating a quality of sound.

Note that the parts of speech are not given in this entry immediately following it, but are indicated by the capital **S** and small **o** in boldface type followed by a colon. They stand for subject and object of preposition. Another entry such as **catch one's breath** is followed by: [V + O], which indicates that this is a verb phrase with a direct object. Many such abbreviations and symbols are explained in the introduction. Until users are fully familiar with them, they will have to search for the explanation. The information in the second volume of the *Oxford Dictionary of Current Idiomatic English* is quite complicated to follow.

Volume 1 is somewhat easier to use than volume 2. There are slashes and parentheses in the entry words—for example, **flying/into** or **foist (off) on**—but they are fewer in number, and the entries are shorter. Entry formation is essentially the same as for volume 2, but with more grammatical information

given for the entry word. A typical entry from volume 1 appears below:

> **fork out** [A1 B1iii pass] (informal) pay, usu unwillingly. **S**: public, tax-payer. **o**: cash, money□*'That will be another half-crown.' Brownsworth* **forked out**. RM□ *It would be laughable if we weren't always having to* **fork out** *money for the police which ought to be spent on roads*. RM

In order to interpret the grammatical codes that appear in brackets following the entry, it is necessary to turn to the front of the book where they are explained in some detail over a number of pages. *A1* stands for an intransitive pattern with a particle, and *B1iii* means a transitive pattern with a particle and, when combined with *pass*, a passive transform. Although the information is undoubtedly useful to English teachers, for the learner digging out the codes and understanding them would take a considerable amount of time.

There is little evidence that currency was of concern in compiling this work although magazines and newspapers were used as sources for the idioms. The references consulted for this dictionary appeared in the 1950s or 1960s, which suggests that there has been little if any revision carried out since the dictionary was first published. The "current" in the title may, therefore, be somewhat misleading.

IV. Accessibility

Guide words appear at the top of each page indicating the first and last entries on that page. Each volume has two indexes. Volume 1 has an index of "nouns, etc. used in headphrases" and one of nominalized forms. Volume 2 has an index of headphrases and another of variant and derived forms. Users should take care to read the explanatory remarks at the beginning of each index to avoid confusion. The two volumes are not cross-indexed.

Because each volume has an index of headphrases it may be necessary to consult the indexes for both volumes if the reader is uncertain of the grammatical structure of an idiom. In these key word indexes, which do not indicate pagination, it is often not clear which is the correct word to search for in the dictionary. Take the word *skin*, for instance, as an index entry in volume 1:

> **skin**
>   get under sb's ~
>   reduce to[5] [~and bones]
>   soak to the ~

Each indented entry is the correct one under which to search. There is no entry in volume 1 for *skin*.

While there is an entry for **skin and bone** in volume 2, there is no cross-reference to that volume. **Reduce to skin and bones** can be located under the fifth entry under **reduce to** ~. Note that the tilde is used in place of the key word **skin**.

The second index in volume 1 of nominalized forms includes words that were originally derived from verbs and now nouns, plus particles and/or prepositions. The common forms, such as adding *ing* to a word, are omitted. When the word is a main entry, this information is noted in parentheses; otherwise, the entry is indicated. Many of the words listed are hyphenated. A sampling of a few index items is given below:

> **build-up** build up[1,4]; build up (to)[1,2]
> **hangover/hung over** (*main entry*)
> **(a) see-through (blouse)** see through[1]
> **walkabout** (*main entry*)

The second index in volume 2 lists variant and derived forms of headphrases and noun, adjective, and adverb compounds from which they are derived. Each variant and derived compound is followed by the headphrase(s) of the entry (or entries) in which it appears in the lexicon. Hyphenation is given according to the most accepted form in British usage. A sample listing can be seen below.

> **bugger all** damn all
> **by moonlight** by the light of sth
> **a muck-raker** rake muck
> **you've never had it so good** have it good

These four indexes are useful in locating an idiomatic phrase but complicate the use of the dictionary. An idiomatic dictionary arranged by key word is somewhat easier to use than this rather complicated set of two indexes per volume that are necessary to locate a first entry word.

As previously noted, cross-references indicated by the letters (*qv*) in parentheses refer the reader to synonymous idioms. There are also two other types of cross-references. One type appears at the end of the entry and is marked with a line arrow →. For example, **a stag party . . . a hen party**. In both cases there usually is a cross-reference from that entry to another to which the user is directed for further information. The arrow combined with an exclamation mark surrounded by a triangle often indicates that the entry is either the previous one or the next entry. For instance, **ebb and flow**, meaning to fluctuate, has a reference △ **next entry** and **the ebb and flow (of sth)** directs the reader to the previous entry. Another example is **like a cat on hot bricks . . .** △ **(as) nervous as a cat/kitten**. These references are useful but could be simplified by the use of fewer symbols; the directions themselves would be sufficient.

V. Summary

The two-volume *Oxford Dictionary of Current Idiomatic English* is a comprehensive work, although it is about 20 years out of date. It covers most of the common everyday idioms found in English speech in either Great Britain or the United States. It is not listed as a resource in the *Idioms and Phrases Index* by Laurence Urdang and Frank R. Abate (Gale) since both carry a 1983 imprint date. The Oxford work can be compared to the LONGMAN DICTIONARY OF ENGLISH IDIOMS. Neither could be termed to be up-to-date on current idiom. The Oxford is much more comprehensive than Longman's. For instance, Longman's has six entries and five cross-references for phrases starting with *far*; Oxford has 12. Longman's is arranged under key words, which makes it easier to locate idioms. For example under **duck**, we find **a dead duck**, **a lame duck**, and so on. In the Oxford, **lame duck** is under *l* and **dead duck** under *d*, which means a great deal more searching and use of the indexes to both volumes is required than in Longman's. The latter work also provides the parts of speech, but the key is repeated on the bottom of the pages, so that one does not have to turn to the front of the book to locate abbreviations each time.

The two-volume *Oxford Dictionary of Current Idiomatic English* is a very scholarly work. It provides a great deal of information about idioms and how they are formed. This information is more likely to be of interest to a teacher of English to foreign-language students than to the ESL students themselves.

Given what is basically a very excellent dictionary, it is unfortunate that the publishers did not attempt to simplify its use or to update the entries. Nevertheless, it deserves a place in the circulating collections of large public libraries and in college and university libraries.

The Oxford Guide to English Usage

Facts at a Glance

Full Title: **The Oxford Guide to English Usage.**
Publisher: Oxford University Press.
Compiler: E. S. C. Weiner.
Edition Reviewed: © 1983; 1985 printing.

Number of Entries: approximately 4,581.
Number of Pages: 256.
Number of Indexes: 2.
Trim Size: 5½″ × 8½″.
Binding: cloth.

Price: $14.95.

Sold in bookstores; also sold to libraries and other educational institutions.
ISBN 0-19-869128-9.

I. Introduction and Scope

The Oxford Guide to English Usage was first published in 1983. The preface states that "It is intended for anyone who needs simple and direct guidance about the formation and use of English words . . ." The book covers four areas, including rules of spelling, pronunciation, vocabulary, and grammar. Many of the examples are drawn from the words of well-known twentieth century writers, an unusual feature for a short usage guide. Distinctive features of American English are pointed out wherever possible, but the basic standard is British English.

This work was compiled by E. S. C. Weiner and is based largely on the archives, experience, and resources of the Oxford English Dictionary Department of the Oxford University Press. The preface states that it "has the authority of the Oxford family of dictionaries behind its recommendations."

II. Format

The *Oxford Guide* is divided into the four sections noted above. There is also a brief introduction, a list of grammatical terms used in the book, and a short list of abbreviations. Each section has its own alphabetical arrangement of entries. Each is headed by a title in boldface type. Section II on pronunciation is in two parts, with Part A covering general points of pronunciation and Part B dealing with preference in pronunciation.

The introduction states that the explanations which are given for each entry "are intended to be simple and straightforward." This holds true for the pronunciation and vocabulary sections, but explanations for word formation and grammar are necessarily more detailed and complex. Two symbols are used to indicate recommended use. One is the bullet (•), which indicates a warning or restriction; the second is an open square (□) where no restriction needs to be enforced—the emphasis is on the degree of acceptability in standard English use.

The *Oxford Guide* makes no dogmatic distinctions between right and wrong. Rather words on usage are described as formal and informal, or standard, regional, and non-standard and the like. Technical symbols and the phonetic alphabet are not used, and abbreviations are limited to *Amer.* for "American" and seven book references. Other sources from which examples are drawn are spelled out, such as *Daily Telegraph*, Henry Kissinger, and Evelyn Waugh. Brief examples for each section are explained in the extracts in the following paragraph.

The section on word formation is primarily concerned with how the written forms of English words change or vary. Coverage of hyphenated words or capitals is limited. American spelling is indicated when it differs from the British, but in cases where there is a great deal of variation, the preferred form is that recommended by the Oxford University Press. Much of the explanation is carried out by way of examples. An interesting note can be found in describing the change from *f* to *v* for plurals: "*dwarf*: plural *dwarfs*. •*Dwarves* only in J.R.R. Tolkien's writings." Others include noun endings for **-erous** or **-rous**:

> The ending *-erous* is normal in adjectives related to nouns ending in *-er*, e.g. *murderous*, *slanderous*, *thunderous*. The exceptions are:
>
> | | | |
> |---|---|---|
> | *ambidextrous* | *disastrous* | *monstrous* |
> | *cumbrous* | *leprous* | *slumbrous* |
> | *dextrous* | *meandrous* | *wondrous* |

The section on pronunciation will appeal to many readers as it does not make use of the phonetic alphabet, which many users find difficult to employ, but relies on respelling or the use of words that sound alike. In Part A, for example:

> 2. Note that the final *th* is like *th* in *bathe*, *father* in:
>
> | | |
> |---|---|
> | *bequeath* | *booth* |
> | *betroth* | *mouth* (verb) |

In Part B, which is mainly a list of words with their preferred pronunciations, there is an example of a variation in stress and an American usage under the word **cervical**. Note the box in the entry:

> **cervical:** □ stress either on 1st syllable (with last two syllables as in *vertical*) or on 2nd (rhyming with *cycle*: both pronunciations have been common for at least a century and a half (Amer. only the first pronunciation).

The vocabulary section of the book is concerned with individual words that pose problems in meaning, construction, derivation, and diction. The recommendations are for formal speaking and serious writing, although some attention is paid to American usage and the informal use of words.

For example, and note the use of the bullet:

> **farther, farthest:** though originally interchangeable with *further, furthest*, these words are now only used where the sense of 'distance' is involved, e.g. *One whose actual dwelling lay presumably amid the farther mysteries of the cosmos* (J.I.M. Stewart).
> •Even in this sense many people prefer *further, furthest*.

The grammar section deals only with specific problems of grammar arranged alphabetically; it is not in any sense a "grammar book." Some entries present sets of troublesome words, and others some aspect of grammar, such as auxiliary verbs, double passive, reflexive pronouns, and relative clauses. An example of how entries in this section are handled follows:

none (**pronoun**)

The pronoun *none* can be followed either by singular verb and singular pronouns, or by plural ones. Either is acceptable, although the plural tends to be more common.

Singular: *None of them* was *allowed to forget for a moment* (Anthony Powell)

Plural: *None of the fountains ever* play (Evelyn Waugh) *None of the authors expected* their *books to become bestsellers* (Cyril Connolly)

In addition to these four sections of the *Oxford Guide*, there are three appendixes. Appendix I deals with principles of punctuation and is quite brief. Appendix II presents a list of clichés, including some words that are covered in the vocabulary section as well. Appendix III covers some basic differences of English spoken in the United States, Canada, Australia, New Zealand, and South Africa.

III. Quality and Currency of Entries

The words included in this usage guide are those of everyday speech, but in the four main sections there is no effort to deal with words that have recently entered the English language. Appendix II does cover what the Oxford University Press terms clichés and modish and inflated diction and lists a few more recent words. Some examples are **escalate**, **overkill**, and **simplistic**.

IV. Accessibility

Within each of the four sections of the book, word listings are alphabetized. Although that is helpful, to find a word one must use either the subject index or the word index to the book. There are no guide words at the top of the pages. Cross-references are indicated in boldface type, but not always; many appear as simple **see** references.

V. Summary

The Oxford Guide to English Usage is a useful reference source for speakers of English and may also be of use to foreign students of English. It can be compared to PRACTICAL ENGLISH USAGE in that both serve as practical guides to dealing with problems regularly encountered in the English language. The latter, however, is geared specifically to common er-

rors that foreign students of English make. Both books are based on British English but make an effort to include the differences in American English as well.

The vocabulary section of the *Oxford Guide* can be compared to A DICTIONARY OF MODERN ENGLISH USAGE (last revised in 1965) and to DICTIONARY OF PROBLEM WORDS AND EXPRESSIONS by Harry Shaw.

However, while correct vocabulary use is Fowler's main concern, it occupies less than a quarter of the *Oxford Guide*'s text. Fowler does not include any articles that are concerned only with idiomatic use, spelling, etymology, pronunciation, or inflexion. These latter two aspects of usage are covered very thoroughly in the *Oxford Guide*.

The *Guide* is a useful reference tool for libraries, homes, or for foreign students' collections.

Oxford Guide to the English Language

Facts at a Glance

Full Title: **Oxford Guide to the English Language**.
Publisher: Oxford University Press.
Editors: E. S. C. Weiner and Joyce Hawkins.
Edition Reviewed: © 1984; 1985 printing.

Number of Entries: approximately 30,000.
Number of Pages: 574.
Trim Size: 5" × 7¾".
Binding: paperback.

Price: $9.95.
Sold through newspaper and magazine advertising; also sold in bookstores.
ISBN 0-19-281499-0.

I. Introduction and Scope

This paperback reference book combines E. S. C. Weiner's OXFORD GUIDE TO ENGLISH USAGE with the text of THE OXFORD MINIDICTIONARY compiled by Joyce M. Hawkins. The handbook is designed for anyone concerned with the proper usage of the English language.

The usage guide presents clear solutions to a variety of lexical and grammatical problems. Simple and straightforward explanations are given in each entry, and example sentences (especially in Sections III and IV) are "drawn from the works of some of the best [essentially British] twentieth century writers" to illustrate the point being discussed. For instance, the artificial rule that the split infinitive must always be avoided is easily clarified, and sample sentences are provided to demonstrate both the rule and the exception to the rule:

Good writers usually avoid splitting the infinitive by placing the adverb before the infinitive:

> *I am not able, and I do not want,* completely to abandon *the worldview that I acquired in childhood* (George Orwell)
> *One meets people who have learned* actually to prefer *the tinned fruit to the fresh* (C. S. Lewis)

On the other hand, it is quite natural in speech, and permissible in writing, to say:

> *What could it be like* to actually live *in France?*
> To really let *the fact that these mothers were mothers sink in* (Both examples from Kingsley Amis)

II. Format

The usage guide is divided into four sections: word formation, pronunciation, vocabulary, and grammar. Each section is arranged alphabetically according to entry headings printed in boldface type, and subject and word indexes are provided for easy cross-reference. Three appendixes outline the principles of punctuation, list clichés and overworked diction, and discuss the "five major varieties of foreign English," including the American idiom. The dictionary, which offers definitions "of nearly 30,000 words and phrases," comprises more than half of the book.

Features of *The Oxford Guide to the English Language* include guidelines on distinguishing word endings (e.g., **-ant** or **-ent**, **-able** or **-ible**), on forming the irregular plurals of such words as *echoes* and *tomatoes*, and on determining when to double consonants in words like *bedding* and *heading*, *occurred* and *offered*. The handbook "lists about 600 words that are likely to be misused or confused with other words" (such as *connote* and *denote*, *imply* and *infer*), and advises on the pronunciation of words that often cause difficulty ("**lugubrious**; loo-goo-brious"; "**machination**; *ch* as in mechanical, not as in machine").

III. Quality and Currency of Entries

Overall, most users will find the dictionary section sufficient—it is especially comparable to other dictionary handbooks of its size. However, the dictionary represents the most uniquely British feature of *The Oxford Guide*—American spelling and pronunciation guidelines are completely excluded. Its usefulness for American users will be limited. In addition to its British orientation, other factors to consider when determining whether to buy this handbook include the dictionary's omission of word syllabication and its exclusion of plural formations. Although plural and irregular plural rules are included in the usage section on word formation, the handbook omits any treatment of word syllabication. The 1984 edition

assures a fairly up-to-date application of language usage.

IV. Accessibility

The prospective buyer should be warned that although the handbook occasionally notes American English usage and diction, the guide is designed with British users in mind. The American spellings of many words in the usage guide section are omitted. Uniquely British grammatical constructions also appear in the usage guide—for example, the negative contractions *oughtn't* and *usedn't to* are very much British formations. However, when "formal" usage sounds particularly stilted a note informs the user that this is the case. Generally, the experienced user will seldom have trouble recognizing these usage idiosyncrasies and overly formal constructions.

The section on pronunciation most faithfully acknowledges the distinctions between British and American English. For instance, *February* and *forte* are clearly delineated and include both British and American pronunciation:

> **February**: do not drop the 1st r:
> feb-roor-y, not *feb*-yoor-y or *feb*-wa-ry or *feb*-yoo-erry (Amer. *feb*-roo-erry).
> **Forte** (one's strong point): originally (and Amer.) like *fort* but now usually like the musical term *forte*.

V. Summary

The Oxford Guide has many distinguishing features to recommend it, especially for users who want one handy reference book which combines both a dictionary and a usage guide; the format is easy to follow, the explanations are clear, the examples are well highlighted. However, its British orientation and noninclusive dictionary may make it less useful than comparable works designed for American readers, such as MODERN AMERICAN USAGE.

The Penguin Dictionary of Troublesome Words

Facts at a Glance

Full Title: **The Penguin Dictionary of Troublesome Words**.
Publisher: Viking Penguin Inc.
Editor: Bill Bryson.
Edition Reviewed: © 1984; 1986 printing.

Number of Articles: 826.
Number of Entries: 1,093.
Number of Pages: 173.
Trim Size: 5⅛" × 7¾".
Binding: paperback.

Price: $7.95.
Sold in bookstores and by direct mail; also sold to libraries and other educational institutions.
ISBN 0-14-051130-X.

I. Introduction and Scope

The author of this book notes that it might more accurately have been titled *A Guide to Everything in English Usage That the Author Wasn't Entirely Clear About Until Quite Recently*. This alternate title indicates the humorous and light touch that Bill Bryson brings to his discussion of some of the thorniest issues in the English language: Are split infinitives ever justified? What distinctions should we observe between lie and lay, flaunt and flout, gourmet and gourmand, imply and infer, shall and will?

Bill Bryson, though born in the United States, is now living in England where he is deputy chief sub-editor of London's most prestigious newspaper, *The Times*. A purist might insist that the use of the word prestigious in the preceding sentence is incorrect since the word originally described that which was deceptive or illusory, coming as it did from the Latin *praestigeae*, meaning "juggler's tricks." Bryson, however, is no purist, and he steers a happy course between the prescriptive school and the structural linguists, the latter being those who, as he puts it, "regard the conventions of English usage as intrusive and anachronistic and elitist, the domain of pedants and old men."

II. Format

The Penguin Dictionary of Troublesome Words is a paperback edition of a volume that has since been published in the United States under the title THE FACTS ON FILE DICTIONARY OF TROUBLESOME WORDS. The paperback edition is handy and has a clear, readable typeface and margins wide enough to permit rebinding. The main entry headings are set off in boldface type, but within entries words discussed are italicized or quoted only when this is required to avoid ambiguity.

III. Quality and Currency of Entries

Although many of Bryson's examples are drawn from *The Times*, his work does not have that distinctly English tone that one associates with H. W. Fowler's A DICTIONARY OF MODERN ENGLISH USAGE or even Eric Partridge's USAGE AND ABUSAGE. Bryson also draws on many American speakers and publications. Thus he notes that when the *Washington Post* refers to "the pungent aroma of a cattleyard" an error has

been committed as **aroma** refers properly only to pleasant smells. President Carter's misuse of the word **flaunt** is also cited: "The Government of Iran must realize that it cannot flaunt, with impunity, the expressed will and law of the world community." The word needed here was **flout**.

In a lengthy analysis of the much-discussed word **hopefully**, Bryson describes both sides of the argument and indeed makes a good case that those who condemn the looser use of the word often employ many similar words (sadly, mercifully, happily, etc.) in much the same casual manner. Still, he finally endorses THE AMERICAN HERITAGE DICTIONARY conclusion that the loose usage is "now such a bugbear to traditionalists that it is best avoided on grounds of civility, if not logic." As for split infinitives, he considers the fault, if a fault at all, to be rhetorical, not grammatical. He gives sound advice on how to avoid split infinitives, but also makes it clear that split infinitives are to be preferred to the more grotesque circumlocutions that purists often employ in avoiding their use.

IV. Accessibility

One of the strongest virtues of Bryson's guide is its accessibility. The novice will often find Fowler or even Partridge a bit intimidating. Bryson notes in his introduction that "in correlative conjunctions in the subjunctive mood there should be parity between protasis and apodosis." He says it, but only as an example of an approach that is the polar opposite of his own. Bryson's own writing is succinct and easily understood. Making the guide even more accessible is a short but excellent glossary of the parts of speech and some of the more common grammatical terms such as **mood**, **gerund**, **predicate**, and **substantive**. A nine-page guide to and explanation of the more important rules of punctuation is another useful bonus. Finally, a bibliography gives publication information on many of the authorities (Theodore Bernstein, Bergen Evans, Edwin Newman, William Safire, etc.) that Bryson has cited.

V. Summary

There are too few entries in *The Penguin Dictionary of Troublesome Words* for it to be thought of as a rival, let alone a replacement, for its better known counterparts such as Theodore Bernstein's *The Careful Writer* or Fowler's MODERN ENGLISH USAGE. It has, however, many virtues, including accessibility as well as the authority of an editor who is keenly aware of the pitfalls awaiting those writing today. At its best it represents the kind of personal statement that has made *The Elements of Style* by Strunk and

White a continuing favorite. As such it is recommended for the reference collections of public and academic libraries and personal collections. Libraries may prefer to purchase the hardbound edition, the FACTS ON FILE DICTIONARY OF TROUBLESOME WORDS, which will stand up to greater use.

Practical English: 1000 Most Effective Words

Facts at a Glance

Full Title: **Practical English: 1000 Most Effective Words.**
Publisher: Ballantine Books.
Editor: Norman W. Schur.
Edition Reviewed: © 1983.

Number of Entries: 1,000.
Number of Pages: 343.
Trim Size: 4¼" × 6⅞".
Binding: paperback.

Price: $2.95.
Sold in bookstores; also sold to libraries and other educational institutions.
ISBN 0-345-31038-1.

I. Introduction and Scope

Practical English: 1000 Most Effective Words is advertised on its paperback cover as belonging to the Ballantine Reference Library and as being suitable for "college freshmen," "people learning English as a second language," and "everyone who wants to use everyday words correctly." It is for this diverse readership that the 1,000 words have been selected by Norman W. Schur, a graduate of Harvard. Schur has had a long career as a lawyer and author of numerous works on the English language including *British Self-Taught: With Comments in American*, BRITISH ENGLISH: A TO ZED, and most recently 1000 MOST CHALLENGING WORDS.

Although virtually all of the words discussed by Schur will be at least superficially familiar to an educated reader, Schur is adept at bringing out shades of meaning and at pointing out the pitfalls awaiting the careless user of words. On the surface, the book appears to be a highly selective dictionary, but in essense it is an entertaining aid to developing and sharpening one's vocabulary.

A typical entry runs 15 to 25 lines and describes a word's derivation, its various meanings (with focus on its current meanings), and its pronunciation. Schur then provides either a quotation illustrating the use of the word in literature or an original example, as with the word **memorable**:

> Lincoln's Gettysburg Address is one of the most **memorable** speeches in history.

II. Format

Practical English: 1000 Most Effective Words is a paperback with a binding no sturdier than those of most mass market paperbacks. Libraries purchasing the volume will want to acquire the hardcover reprint, which bears a slightly different title: 1000 MOST PRACTICAL WORDS (Facts on File, 1983).

Main entries are in bold type, and the text of the entry is in a clear, readable typeface. The gutter margins are narrow and not suitable for rebinding.

III. Quality and Currency of Entries

An objection that may be raised is the use of the word *most* in the title. One need not deny that these are "practical" words that, if used correctly, may be "effective." The suggestion, however, that these are the 1,000 *most* effective or practical words is nothing more than a bit of hyperbole from the publisher.

The words chosen for discussion are largely of Latin origin; there is an absence of slang, new words, and vogue words. The author's style is chatty, informal, and often humorous. An occasional lapse of taste occurs, as in the example for **scanty**:

> A **scanty** bathing suit on a well-proportioned young lady stirs up a lot of interest at the beach or swimming pool.

Generally, however, his quotations and examples are witty and well chosen.

IV. Accessibility

The text of the book is quite accessible, written as it is in clear, easy-to-understand English. There are occasional cross-references, and the few abbreviations used are obvious without requiring a list of abbreviations. The only special phonetic symbol used for the pronunciations is the schwa or upside-down *e* [ə], whose use and pronunciation are clearly explained in the preface to the book.

V. Summary

This is an entertaining book and one that will be useful to all who wish to improve their vocabularies. It is in no sense a replacement for a dictionary; any standard college dictionary will cover far more words, and the OXFORD ENGLISH DICTIONARY will clearly be the choice of those with a serious interest in derivations. As a vocabulary builder, Schur's book probably belongs in the circulating rather than the reference collections of libraries. It is recommended for high school, public, and academic libraries.

Practical English Usage

Facts at a Glance

Full Title: **Practical English Usage.**
Publisher: Oxford University Press.
Compiler: Michael Swan.
Edition Reviewed: © 1980; 1985 printing.

Number of Entries: 639.
Number of Pages: 708.
Number of Indexes: 1.
Trim Size: 5½″ × 8½″.
Binding: paperback.

Price: $10.95.
Sold in bookstores; also sold to libraries and other educational institutions.
ISBN 0-19-431185-6.

I. Introduction

Practical English Usage is designed to help intermediate and advanced students of English who are foreign-language speakers clarify some of the fine points of English vocabulary. "It deals with over 600 points which regularly cause difficulty to foreign students of English," the introduction states. Although most of the questions treated are grammatical, explanations are also given for some common vocabulary problems.

The usage manual is published by the Oxford University Press, which is a highly reputable dictionary and reference work publisher. Acknowledgment is given to *A Grammar of Contemporary English*, by Quirk, Greenbaum, Leech, and Svartvik (Longman, 1972).

II. Format

As the book is organized in alphabetical order by word or grammatical form, it is more of a dictionary than a conventional grammar book. Some word entries are single words, such as **do**, **what**, or **ever**; others are pairs or sets of words that are used interchangeably—and sometimes incorrectly. An example of the latter type of entry includes **ever**, **already**, and **yet** and **excuse me**, **pardon**, and **sorry**. Examples of grammatical entries are: past perfect tense, verbs with two objects, and nationality words. Some entries for spelling and punctuation are quite detailed and seem a little more like those in a conventional grammar book than in a dictionary.

Some, but not all, entries are pronounced using a special phonetic alphabet. Stress is indicated by an accent mark. Pronunciation appears immediately following the entry word between slash marks. Most word entries include a *typical mistake*, which appears between horizontal rules. Here is an example for the word **often**, followed by an explanation of the mistake.

often /ˈofn, ˈoftən/   **437**

Typical mistake: **I often fell yesterday when I was skiing.*

Often is used to mean 'frequently on different occasions'. If we want to say 'frequently on the same occasion', we generally use a different expression (like *a lot of times*, *several times*, *frequently*), or the structure *keep (on) -ing*. Compare:

I fell several times yesterday when I was skiing.
I kept falling yesterday when I was skiing.
I often fell in love when I was younger.

For the position of *often* (and other adverbs of frequency), see 24.

An asterisk (*) indicates an incorrect form. It may occur only in the English of foreigners, or it may be used by British or American people but is considered by many to be wrong or substandard. The compiler does not try to indicate the correct form in cases of the latter type, but in other instances states when usage is substandard, such as in the case of **ain't**:

Ain't is not used in standard ('correct') English, but it is a very common word in dialects and 'uneducated' forms of British and American English. It is used as a contracted form of *am not*, *are not*, *is not*, *have not* and *has not*.

The above illustration is not the only place where Swan refers to both British and American English. A five-page section, divided into grammar, vocabulary, spelling, and pronunciation, is devoted to the differences between British and American English. Such information is useful not only to foreign students of English but also to Britishers or Americans traveling to the other's country.

Grammatical entries are somewhat different in format than word entries. Only occasionally do they indicate the "typical mistake," and they frequently are several pages in length. An example of the grammatical entry is:

double genitive   **264**
Note the special construction: *of + genitive (possessive)*

He's a friend of my father's. (= *one of my father's friends*) *He turned up wearing an old coat of Pa-*

trick's. Where's that stupid brother of yours? She's supposed to be a distant cousin of the Queen's.

In the front of this dictionary is an alphabetical listing of the language terminology used. It ranges from **abstract noun** to **zero plural**, which is usually referred to in the United States as an irregular plural form or one that is the same in either the singular or plural such as **fish**, **sheep**, and **aircraft**.

III. Quality and Currency of Entries

The entries are clearly stated and easy to understand. The differences between British and American English are frequently noted. Take the words **further** and **farther** as an example.

1 In British English, both words are used to refer to distance, with no difference of meaning.

>   *Inverness is **farther/further** away than Glasgow.*

>   In American English, only *farther* is used in this sense.

2 *Further* (but not *farther*) can also be used to mean 'additional', 'extra', 'more advanced'.

>   *College of **Further** Education. For **further** information, see page 283.*

Practical English Usage contains current expressions as well as taboo words (so labeled). For example, under *exclamations* are examples such as "***Am I** hungry!*" and "***Did he** look annoyed!*" Under the heading *taboo words* are such exclamations as *Hell! God! Fuck* (*it!*), and *Bugger me!* and since this is a British publication also *bloody well* and *pissed* meaning drunk.

IV. Accessibility

Guide words at the top of each page aid the reader in locating entries. Each entry is numbered, and the index refers to these numbers. Pages are not numbered. Entries may have more than one reference in the index: for example, **asleep** and **sleeping** both appear in the index and refer the reader to the main entry (86) **asleep**. The index refers the reader not only to entry words but to certain terms used within an entry, such as those found under grammatical entries. Although words can be found using the alphabetical arrangement of the dictionary, it is more efficient to use the index. (At least one page of the index in the reviewer's copy was out of alphabetical order, or misbound.)

V. Summary

An excellent and useful reference source for libraries that serve foreign-language students of English,

Practical English Usage provides the reader with clear and comprehensive explanations of both British and American English. It is superior to A Handy Book of Commonly Used American Idioms, which is also intended for students of English. It is somewhat easier to use than the Oxford Dictionary of Current Idiomatic English and goes well beyond idiomatic English-language dictionaries in its coverage of usage and grammatical notes. The English speaker may also find this work helpful to a degree, but it does not replace usage books such as Fowler's A Dictionary of Modern English Usage or the more up-to-date Dictionary of Problem Words and Expressions by Harry Shaw.

Prefixes and Other Word-Initial Elements of English

Facts at a Glance

Full Title: **Prefixes and Other Word-Initial Elements of English**.
Publisher: Gale Research Company.
Editor: Laurence Urdang, Editorial Director; Alexander Humez.
Edition Reviewed: © 1984.

Number of Entries: nearly 3,000.
Number of Pages: 533.
Number of Indexes: 1.
Trim Size: 6″ × 9″.
Binding: cloth.

Price: $78.00.
Sold in bookstores and by direct mail; also sold to libraries and other educational institutions.
ISBN 0-8103-1548-3.

I. Introduction and Scope

Prefixes and Other Word-Initial Elements of English, a companion volume to Urdang's 1982 Suffixes and Other Word-Final Elements of English, contains around 3,000 entries, called "word-initial elements" to make it clear that the list comprises both true prefixes (which cannot stand on their own) and forms that can also function as independent words. Each prefix has been included in this work on the basis of its having occurred in at least five examples in English, except for some prefixes that occur less frequently but are homographs (forms spelled identically but with different etymologies) of those that do occur more frequently or occur in words of high frequency. Thus **col-**[1] of *collate, collect,* and *collo-*

Prefixes and Other Word-Initial Elements of English

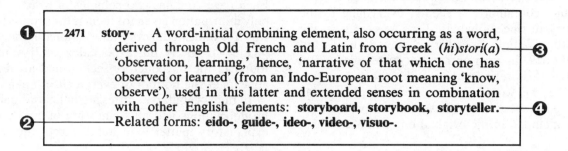

❶ Main entries are numbered sequentially and set in boldface type

❷ Related forms, set in boldface type, are also listed as main entries

❸ Etymology and current meaning of the combining form are given

❹ Examples of use in words are set in boldface type

cation is included along with the more frequent **col-**[2] of *colagia*, *colitis*, and the like. Also, because many prefixes are themselves combinations of elements, they are given cross-references to the main entries of their component parts whenever the meaning is reasonably clear. For example, the meaning of **dinitro** ("having two [NO₂] groups") is obvious from **di-**[1] and **nitro-**. Of course, where the meanings are not obvious such prefixes are given full entries. The Introduction cites **cholecyst-** as an example of a prefix receiving a full entry because its meaning is not immediately evident from **chole-** and **cyst-**.

II. Format

Each full entry contains (1) a sequential number for each prefix in bold type (the final entry, **zymo-**, is number **2860**); (2) the prefix itself in bold type; (3) a description including the etymology in italics, the meaning or meanings in single quotation marks, and its uses; (4) examples in bold type of actual words in which the prefix appears; (5) variant spellings or forms in bold type under the heading "also"; (6) closely related forms in bold type under the heading "compare"; and (7) cognate forms in bold type under the heading "related forms." For example:

> **629 cornu-** A word-initial combining element, derived from Latin *cornū* 'horn,' used in its etymological sense in Neo-Latin combinations: **cornulite, cornupete, Cornuspira.** Also, **corni-** : **corniform.** Compare **corneo-, corner-.** Related forms: **caroten-, cerebello-, cerebro-, cervi-**[2], **cervico-, cranio-, ginger-, hart's-, horn-, keratin-, kerato-.**

III. Quality and Currency of Entries

As one can see from the sample entry, not much seems left to include; the entry certainly seems com-

plete and accurate. In fact, a reader might even become sidetracked by following up interesting related forms. Under **cornu** in an unabridged dictionary, for example, *The Random House Dictionary of the English Language, First Edition, Unabridged*, of which Urdang was the managing editor, we find after the pronunciation and a definition declaring that the word means "a horn, esp. a bony part that resembles a horn" that the word is derived from the Latin for *horn*.

If on the other hand, out of curiosity, we follow up a cognate form noted in the entry, say, **ginger**, we note in entry **1095** that the word is derived from the Sanskrit *srngavera* spicy root of genus *Zingibar*, literally, 'horn-body' (from *srnga* 'horn' plus *vera* 'body'). In Urdang's Random House unabridged, however, there is no mention of Sanskrit in the derivation, only Middle English, Old French, Late Latin, Latin, and Greek. Consequently, we might be moved to look in still another dictionary, this time the college edition of *The American Heritage Dictionary*, and find that to the list of derivative languages are added Prakrit and Sanskrit and some advice to see **ker-**[1] in an appendix.

And then if we do indeed go to that appendix, we find a long list of derivations and cognates much more conveniently set forth than in *Prefixes*, where we would need to look up each one individually. Such a trail might be sniffed at eagerly by word lovers with plenty of time for interesting side tracks, but it is a long way around for the reader who may merely be curious about the derivation of a word like *cornucopia*.

IV. Accessibility

If one knows the prefix to look up one obviously goes to the entry in the main listing and finds as little or as much as one wishes. But, perhaps to improve accessibility, the editors have also included a separate index containing, it seems, everything in the dictionary in one alphabetic list. At **cornu-** in the index, for example, is a list of eleven entries not including **629**, its own entry, that have some information on this prefix. Although this thoroughness is admirable, we would have to be very persevering indeed to follow up all of these, most of which were already included in the original entry at **629**.

V. Summary

Prefixes, although it is thorough and informative, is a book for linguists and other language specialists and belongs only in large collections or academic, research libraries. Patrons of small libraries will find the information they need about prefixes in a good general dictionary of English.

A Pronouncing Dictionary of American English

Facts at a Glance

Full Title: **A Pronouncing Dictionary of American English**.
Publisher: Merriam-Webster.
Compilers: John Samuel Kenyon and Thomas Albert Knott.
Edition Reviewed: © 1953.

Number of Words: over 42,000.
Number of Pages: 542.
Trim Size: 6″ × 8¼″.
Binding: cloth.

Price: $12.95.
Sold in bookstores and other outlets; also sold to libraries and other educational institutions.
ISBN 0-87779-047-7.

I. Introduction and Scope

This dictionary is a guide to the pronunciation of conversational English, and its vocabulary covers common words in use in America. Special treatment has been given to American proper names like Stuyvesant and Weehawken, and other proper names like Fujiyama and Edinburgh which are of traditional interest to Americans.

A Pronouncing Dictionary attempts to document standard, colloquial speech based on actual usage. It does not attempt to represent formal platform speech, as do other Webster dictionaries, nor does it attempt to be a sourcebook for dialects, as does the *Linguistic Atlas of the United States and Canada*.

II. Format

Each page contains two columns of words, and the only information given for them is the pronunciation, which is indicated by the International Phonetic Alphabet (IPA). A full explanation of IPA may be found in the introductory section and an IPA key appears at the bottom of every pair of open pages.

In the vocabulary, entries are in light roman type, pronunciations and all sounds are in boldface, and explanatory matter is in italic, except the regional labels E, S, N, W.

III. Quality and Currency of Entries

As this book is 35 years old, it is not surprising that it omits pronunciation of some new additions to the language. For **byte**, **cryogenics** and **ultrasound**, the user would find an up-to-date dictionary more helpful.

Variant pronunciations are not listed in order of correctness. They represent only differences of colloquial style; these differences are frequently explained in an extended entry:

Massachusetts **mæsaˈtʃusits, -ˈtʃuz-, -ats** *L.A. of N Engd shows that about 28 per cent of the cultured informants pronounce* **z**.

IV. Accessibility

A lengthy introduction provides useful information on such subjects as the phonetic alphabet, variants, and anglicizing, as well as helpful suggestions for using the dictionary. There is, however, no itemized list of contents for this 124-entry introduction.

The format of the dictionary, its guide words, and its well-spaced three-page list of abbreviations combine to make this an accessible work.

V. Summary

Although mainly of interest to scholars and teachers, this reference book belongs in all medium- and large-sized collections. If many of its standard pronunciations can be found in dictionaries, it is nonetheless valuable for its variant pronunciations and their explanations, as well as for its fine introductory essay on the subject.

The Quintessential Dictionary

Facts at a Glance

Full Title: **The Quintessential Dictionary**.
Publisher: Warner Books.
Compiler: I. Moyer Hunsberger.
Edition Reviewed: © 1978; 1984 printing.

Number of Entries: over 1,200.
Number of Pages: 422.
Trim Size: 4⅛″ × 6¾″.
Binding: paperback.

Price: $3.95.
Sold in bookstores and other outlets; also sold to
  libraries and other educational institutions.
ISBN 0-446-32443-4.

I. Introduction and Scope

The compiler of this dictionary has indicated that its
purpose is to: a) increase vocabulary and "self-
expression," b) improve reading comprehension, and
c) enhance pleasure derived from reading and speaking. He has chosen well over 1,200 main entries, to
which he has added some 1,700 secondary entries
(related adjectives, adverbs, nouns), and has culled
illustrations of the main words from such popular
sources as novels, newspapers, and magazines. The
foreword states:

> The Quintessential Dictionary is like no other dictionary
> or word book, because it alone emphasizes *actual* ex-
> amples of *current* word usage, and its scope is limited
> to 'less familiar' words . . . found in newspapers, mag-
> azines, and books of recent vintage.

Zeitgeist, **shamus**, **plebeian**, **nymphomania**, **mantra**,
mesomorph, **homoeroticism**, **holism**, **hedonism**, **gaffe**,
fellatio, **eremite**, and **casuistry** are a few of the words
chosen for inclusion. It is a curious compilation, but
probably no more curious than popular culture in the
United States. It appears that the author might have
chosen the obscure (e.g., **septentrional**) and the trite
(e.g., **narcissistic**) from his personal reading, then
compiled this book to illustrate how "unusual" words
are used in context. In other words, this is an abridged
dictionary of highly personal, often quixotic selections. The compiler states that the book is designed
for "intelligent readers, writers, and students of all
ages," but it is likely to be of primarily entertainment
value.

II. Format

The original publication date of *The Quintessential
Dictionary*, in hardcover format, was 1978. The paperback is an unrevised reprint of the 1978 edition.
While the paperback binding is strong and secure,
the typeface is exceptionally small, and the print appears faint on heavy, but low-grade paper. The very
narrow margins make the book exceedingly difficult
to read. Indeed, this reviewer used the hardcover

copy with larger print for review purposes rather than
this paperback edition. A magnifying glass would be
helpful to some, obligatory for others.

III. Quality and Currency of Entries

The entries seem to have been selected at random
from various popular sources, and herein lie both the
book's strengths and its weaknesses. As a book to
skim for pleasure, or as a vocabulary builder for word
lovers, it may provide considerable entertainment.
As a dictionary for those actually seeking definitions
and correct usage, its use is limited. The compiler
states that he consulted several standard dictionaries
for definitions: WEBSTER'S NEW WORLD DICTION-
ARY: SECOND COLLEGE EDITION, THE RANDOM
HOUSE COLLEGE DICTIONARY and the OXFORD
ENGLISH DICTIONARY among others. The quotations further defining the words, however, are taken
from sources such as *Newsweek*, *Time*, the *New York
Times*, the *Wall Street Journal*, and popular fiction.
Some works of fiction are cited with mystifying frequency. Irving Wallace's *The Fan* and Thomas Berger's *Who is Teddy Villanova?* are heavily used
sources, as is *Centennial* by James Michener. In the
foreword the author justifies his use of these writers
(but not the specific books quoted) by calling them
"recognized, best-selling authors." And William F.
Buckley, Jr., is also cited as, the compiler writes,
"an incomparably rich source of the vivid use of less-
familiar words." Unfortunately, magazines, newspapers, and popular fiction are not noted for their
precision in the use of words, so the sources may
already be of dubious value to someone in search of
accuracy. Sources cited are also ten years old, most
of them being from publications of the mid- to late-
seventies. So, this is "actual," "current" usage of a
decade ago, and no doubt a revised or new compilation would result in a different set of examples from
contemporary writing.

Many of the selections from such popular sources
are misleading, inaccurate, or useless, albeit amusing. For example, "He was a short and slight-built
man—a figure very common among SATYRS" (Thomas
Berger, *Who is Teddy Villanova?*); or "He . . . is
. . . a social ZIRCON with a diamond morality" (from
a film review by J. Kroll in *Newsweek*). "Régine has
wonderful PANACHE" (Linda Bird Francke in *Newsweek*); "He was the ZEITGEIST personified" (C. R.
Hatch in *Harper's*); and ". . . the whimsical, delightfully FEY personality of cats" (Mary Daniels, *Chicago Tribune*) are not phrases that would necessarily
lead to a useful understanding of the words cited.
One of the quotes illustrating the word **voyeur** is so
obscure as to have little relation to the definition:

. . . events will have moved so as to confirm that we have come up from liberalism, and that only historical VOYEURS will want to study the reasons why. (W. F. Buckley, Jr., *Up From Liberalism*)

The definition given for **VOYEUR** is

a person who compulsively engages in the practice of obtaining sexual gratification by looking at sexual organs, acts, or objects, especially secretively.

And though **PURDAH** is defined as

a screen, curtain, or veil, used for hiding women from the sight of men or strangers; seclusion in this manner or the practice of such seclusion,

one of the five illustrative quotes is "Dutch officials were hinting at a reprimand and official purdah for the Prince."

The *Choice* reviewer of this book (January 1979) cites the words **lapidary** and **ontology** as words that do not have clear or correct examples in the sources used. Try these: "Political exchanges are not LAPIDARY models of the SYLLOGISTIC art" and "he is a rogue and (such was the LAPIDARY insinuation) should be impeached" (W. F. Buckley, Jr.). "Peter Singer rejects an ontology of rights" (C. G. Luckhardt in the *New York Times*) and "They are the real flower children of the seventies: their ontology is clear and crisp" (M. Kaplan in *Change*). These are surely not phrases which would help an unsophisticated reader gain an understanding of the meaning of the words. The fact that a word was once seen in print does not mean that its use was accurate or that the meaning of the context is true. This does not seem to trouble the editor, however, for he has apparently had great fun in compiling this dictionary, and that is the spirit in which it should be viewed. The hardcover edition's dust-jacket informs us that Mr. Hunsberger is a chemist and "word maven;" the paperback edition gives no information about the author.

IV. Accessibility

The main entries are easily found in boldface capital letters, arranged in alphabetical order. Each main entry is followed by a pronunciation guide and definition, and then by from one to twelve quotations, arranged with no apparent system, illustrating the main entry word. The author states that only initials and surnames are given for male authors of quotes and that female authors are given their full names in order "to highlight the extent to which women authored the quotations used in this book." This is not the format followed, however, as Thomas Berger is cited as Thomas throughout the book.

V. Summary

Compared with another recent guide to usage and "vocabulary builder," *The Superior Person's Book of Words* by Peter Bowler (first U.S. edition published by Godine in 1985), *The Quintessential Dictionary* is much too pompous and self-congratulatory to be a good source for word definitions. An "aren't we clever," "aren't we intellectual" viewpoint generally seems to pervade the text, whereas *The Superior Person's Book of Words*, while using a much smaller base (500 main words) manages to be wry, witty, and blatantly entertaining with no pretense to current relevance. Bowler wrote his own examples and admits that there may be unintended errors, but it's all in fun. Of **nescience** (lack of knowledge; ignorance), *The Quintessential Dictionary* cites G. Lowes Dickinson (who happens to have the same publisher as the hardcover edition of *The Quintessential Dictionary*—Hart Publishing Co.): "And if I . . . am to tell you my inmost thought I must confess on what a flood of nescience we, who seem to direct the affairs of nations, are borne along together with those whom we appear to control." Bowler's example is his own: A word of which—unlike "prescience" (foreknowledge)—most people are nescient. Hence useful for the "Insult Concealed." "My dear, I can only marvel at the extent of your nescience."

While the quotations in *The Quintessential Dictionary* may still be current enough to be entertaining and understood, nothing becomes dated or quaint faster than popular journalism. However, as a brief overview of the concerns and literary style of the seventies, this dictionary may be of historical use in coming years (but that was not the stated purpose of the book and, similarly, while many dictionaries become relics of a bygone age, that was not their original intention). This paperback edition is not recommended because of the difficulty in reading its very small print. For the general reader or browser among word books, the hardcover edition may still be useful, so libraries may wish to retain it—but it does not properly belong in a reference collection.

Suffixes and Other Word-Final Elements of English

Facts at a Glance

Full Title: **Suffixes and Other Word-Final Elements of English.**
Publisher: Gale Research Company.
Editors: Laurence Urdang, Editorial Director; Alexander Humez, Editor; Howard G. Zettler, Associate Editor.

Edition Reviewed: © 1982.

Number of Entries: 1,545.
Number of Pages: 363.
Trim Size: 6″ × 9″.
Binding: cloth.

Price: $85.00.
Sold in bookstores and by direct mail; sold to libraries and other educational institutions.
ISBN 0-8103-1123-2.

I. Introduction and Scope

Suffixes and Other Word-Final Elements of English, edited by Laurence Urdang, Alexander Humez, and Howard G. Zettler, is one of two volumes designed to list and describe word-final and word-initial elements, the common and technical suffixes and prefixes and similar elements occurring at the ends and beginnings of English words. The other volume, PREFIXES AND OTHER WORD-INITIAL ELEMENTS OF ENGLISH, has the same introduction as this one, with appropriate changes in wording and examples, though, curiously, it is signed by Humez while this one is signed by Urdang. Possibly they collaborated on the introduction to keep the volumes uniform. *Suffixes* contains 1,545 "word-final elements," a term used that includes both true suffixes (which cannot stand on their own) and forms that can also function as independent words.

Though generally each suffix was included on the basis of occurrence in at least five examples in English, some were included on the basis of the high frequency of the words in which they occurred as suffixes; **-mare,** for example, appears only in *nightmare* and the rare *daymare* but is included. The suffix in *seamstress* is another variation, a combining of **-ster** and **-ess,** but the editors felt it more convenient to treat it in its own entry. Usually such combinations are given cross-references to the main entries where their components are described. From **-ically,** for example, we are directed to **-ical** and **-ly.** It is not clear in this instance why we are not directed to **-ic** and **-al** for **-ical,** but we are thankful for whatever blessings we receive; the fewer the cross-references the more convenient for the reader. In fact, a great number of the forms containing **-ic,** happily, receive their own full entries.

II. Format

The format here is essentially the same as that in PREFIXES. Each full entry contains (1) a sequential number in bold type (actually every entry, full or not, has a number); (2) the suffix itself in bold type; (3) its description including its etymology in italics, its meaning or meanings in single quotation marks, and its uses; (4) examples in bold type of actual words in which the suffix appears; (5) variant spellings or forms in bold type under the heading "also"; (6) closely related forms in bold type under the heading "compare"; and (7) cognate forms in bold type under the heading "related forms." For example:

> **849 -cule** A word-final element, derived through French from the common Latin noun- and adjective-forming diminutive suffix *-culus, -cula, -culum,* used in English to form nouns with a diminutive sense, physical or metaphoric, of the combining root: **molecule, animalcule, ridicule.** Also, **-cle.** Compare **-ule.** Related forms: **-culus, -cula, culum** (masculine, feminine, neuter *singulars*); **-culi, -culae, -cula** (masculine, feminine, neuter *plurals*); **-cular, -cularly, -culate** (i.e., **-cule** and **-ate**[3]); **-cules** (*plural*).

III. Quality and Currency of Entries

As with the entries in PREFIXES, one can hardly fault the editors for their achievement of accuracy and completeness. Here there seems less incentive to chase down cognates; and the entries themselves have more interest, probably inherent in the nature of suffixes rather than in any differences in the writing skills of the editors. For whatever reason, it seems to be more fun to browse among the suffixes than the prefixes. At the same time, a user ought to note that a general dictionary gives a good bit of information about suffixes. The entry in the college edition of *The American Heritage Dictionary,* for instance, reads:

> **-cule** . . . Indicates smallness; for example, molecule. [French from New Latin *-cula,* diminutive suffix from Latin *-culus, -cula, -culum.* See also **-cle.**

The Random House Dictionary (first abridged edition), for which Urdang was the managing editor, states:

> **-cule,** a suffix with the meaning 'small,' occurring in loan words from Latin (*ridicule*); used as a diminutive in the formation of compound words: *animalcule.* Also, **-cle, -culum, culus.** [repr. L. *-culus, -cula, -culum* dim. suffix].

Also, **-culum** and **-culus** are in the unabridged dictionary but not in the collegiate dictionary.

Obviously, the dictionary one chooses depends on how thorough one wishes to be in the search.

IV. Accessibility

Here is an example of the need for reading introductions in reference books, for a user of *Suffixes* would be utterly confused by the arrangement of the entries without reading the introduction. Entries are alphabetized backwards, i.e., from the right to the left. And it is a good idea because, as Urdang says, many users of the book may not know where a suffix begins. A word like *turbulent*, for example, unless one relates it to words like *turbid*, *turbine*, and the like, does not immediately yield up its division of root and suffix; and since one does not always think of everything, it is very handy to start at the end. For those who do know, however, the index lists all the boldface forms alphabetized from left to right in the normal way.

Instead of guide words (or elements) at the tops of the pages, there are entry numbers, useful if one is approaching the main list from the index, which does use guide words. The index seems particularly useful for readers who know a definition but cannot think of the suffix for it. For example, suppose a user wanted to know a suffix for "belief in god." They could look it up in the index under *belief* or *god* and be directed to number 1159, **-theism**.

V. Summary

Suffixes is a well-made, sturdy, even handsome book, very easy to handle, and expensive. Its editors have done a thorough and accurate job and should be proud. Its usefulness, however, is somewhat curtailed by the availability of most of this information in other dictionaries that are less costly, some much less, and just as easy to use.

While *Suffixes* may offer some very interesting browsing for linguists, it does not belong on the priority list of necessary purchases for most libraries. Some large research libraries, perhaps those who have found money in their budget for PREFIXES, might wish to own both volumes; and both would find users in those libraries. But small general libraries probably do not need either of these dictionaries and should wait until they have something left over in their budgets and wish to buy themselves a gift.

Usage and Abusage: A Guide to Good English

Facts at a Glance

Full Title: **Usage and Abusage: A Guide to Good English**.
Publisher: Penguin Books in association with Hamish Hamilton.
Editor: Eric Partridge.
Edition Reviewed: ©1973; 1985 printing.

Number of Entries: 3,822.
Number of Pages: 381.
Trim Size: 5⅛" × 7¹³⁄₁₆".
Binding: paperback.

Price: $7.95.
Sold in bookstores and other outlets; also sold to libraries and other educational institutions.
ISBN 0-14-051024-9.

I. Introduction and Scope

Eric Partridge's *Usage and Abusage* is a guide to good English patterned after H. W. Fowler's classic A DICTIONARY OF MODERN ENGLISH USAGE. Partridge's intent was not to compete with Fowler, "but to write a book that should be less Olympian and less austere." The audience aimed at by Partridge is a broad one. He put it well in a passage that reveals both his wit and aim: "My aim has been to conceal erudition and to be readable to students and general public alike, and to humanize the subjects treated by not forgetting that one's readers are—most of them—human beings."

The entries in *Usage and Abusage* range in length from a line or two to articles of five pages or more. A typical brief entry is as follows:

> *evacuate the wounded*
> [This] is a horrible variation of the dignified *remove the wounded*. Beginning as military officialese, it has become journalese—and far too general. I won't swear that I haven't used it myself.

A reader seeking further examples of journalese will be referred from that term to officialese where he will find four columns devoted to horrendous examples of officialese, journalese, and commercialese as well as Partridge's erudite advice on avoiding such terms.

Among the many longer articles in Partridge's guide are alliteration, euphemisms, fused participles, grammar and logic, negation, order of words, puns, standard English, and vogue words. Each of the longer articles is richly illustrated with quotations from the author's own wide reading as well as excerpts from other grammarians.

One of the more entertaining and useful features of the book is Partridge's inclusion of long lists of words illustrating such linguistic concepts as anarchisms or antiques, elegancies, literalisms, and sports technicalities. The amount of information in the latter article is indeed impressive. Where else will a reader go to learn that at rutting time, a badger *shrieks*, a boar *freams*, a goat *rattles*, a hare *taps*, an otter *whines*, a roe *bellows*, and on and on?

II. Format

Each page of the book is divided into two columns. The typeface is readable but quite small. This is un-

Usage and Abusage

❶ Main entries are set in boldface type and are arranged in alphabetical order

❷ Examples of both preferred and nonstandard usage are given

❸ Cross-references are set in small capitals

❶ **worst,** misused for *most,* as in 'What I need worst is a haircut'. A thoroughly idiomatic usage of *worst* is that with verbs of liking or loving, allowing, pleasing, ❷ as in 'This pleased them worst of all', where *worst* = 'least'. (*The O.E.D.*)
worst two is incorrect for *two worst* in, e.g., 'The worst two pupils were sent down to the class below'. Cf. FIRST TWO (for *two first*). ❸

fortunate for as with most first rate reference books the reader is often tempted to "read" as well as "consult." The typeface is not too daunting in the shorter articles or in the lists of words, but it is likely to discourage a reader who starts on the eight plus columns devoted to the "vagaries of the genitive." Indentation is used appropriately, but paragraphs in the extended articles are often longer than those to which most American readers are accustomed.

The paperback binding is sturdy but flexible. Since inner margins are narrow, it is doubtful whether libraries will find this edition suitable for rebinding. There is minimal show-through of the text.

III. Quality and Currency of Entries

Eric Partridge, who died in 1979, was a prolific writer and *Usage and Abusage* is one of his best known works. Published originally in 1942 in the United States, it was adapted for an American audience by Professor W. Cabell Greet, whose helpful additions and modifications appear in brackets at the end of individual entries. Thus, on the usage of the word *data* Partridge notes that it is wrong when used for the correct singular, *datum*. In brackets Cabell Greet has added: "[In American English, *data* may be singular or plural. *Webster's*, Krapp, Perrin.]."

Usage and Abusage has been revised and expanded several times over the years, with the last major revision in 1973. Minor corrections and additions have been made through several printings, including this 1985 reprint.

Partridge's article on officialese does not include examples of the vast array of words and phrases spawned by the computer industry, but the article on vogue words now includes such examples as *charisma*, *shortfall*, *image*, and the *wise* endings of Madison Avenue such as *publicity-wise* and *policy-wise* all of which Partridge condemns.

IV. Accessibility

The volume has running heads, one per page in small capitals. A list of abbreviations is presented at the beginning of the book and cross-references are used

generously. Longer articles are often broken into smaller sections. When appropriate long illustrative lists of words are provided. Thus the article on archaisms presents the reader with five pages of antiques and their modern equivalents, e.g., *betimes* (early), *durst* (dared), *ken* (knowledge), *varlet* (rogue), *yclept* (named), etc.

V. Summary

The long publishing history of *Usage and Abusage* is a testimonial not only to the continuing merit of the volume but to Eric Partridge's standing as a writer and scholar. The man Edmund Wilson once called the "word king" was, according to a 1963 article in *Current Biography*, "probably the foremost British authority on good English."

There is no dearth of manuals and handbooks on the usage of the English language. Among the best are two that are clearly patterned after H. W. Fowler's famous A DICTIONARY OF MODERN ENGLISH USAGE. One is Margaret Nicholson's *A Dictionary of American-English Usage* and the other is Eric Partridge's *Usage and Abusage*. Although Nicholson is authoritative and more geared to an American audience, Partridge's volume remains notable for its wit, the wealth of its illustrative quotations, and the unmatched scholarship of its author. It belongs in most public and high school libraries as well as in every academic library.

Words on Words

Facts at a Glance

Full Title: **Words on Words: A Dictionary for Writers and Others Who Care About Words.**
Publisher: Columbia University Press.
Compiler: John B. Bremner.
Edition Reviewed: © 1980; 5th printing.

Number of Entries: 2,500.
Number of Pages: 406.
Trim Size: 6⅛″ × 9¼″ (cloth); 5¾″ × 9″ (paperback).
Binding: cloth; paperback.

Price: $34.00 (cloth); $12.00 (paperback).
Sold in bookstores and other outlets; also sold to
   libraries.
ISBN 0-231-04492-5 (cloth);
ISBN 0-231-04493-3 (paperback).

I. Introduction and Scope

In his introduction to *Words on Words*, John Bremner, journalist, professor of journalism, and newspaper consultant, deplores "the steady growth of literary ignorance" and "surge of literary barbarism"
that he has witnessed over his long career. The purpose of his book is to "teach words and to foster a
love of them." Traditional dictionary meanings, parts
of speech, spelling, and why a word is "called what
it is called," are combined with Bremner's discussions of "good and bad writing, some verbal games-
manship and excursions into mythology and literary
allusions" (from the Introduction).

The author proposes to stress the parts of speech,
"the grammatic sol-fa [defined in the text] whose
harmony produces the polyphony of syntax;" grammar, not for the sake of rules but for "order, logic
and common sense;" and etymology, mentioned in
the introduction as a major emphasis.

Journalists, students of journalism and "all others
who seek to intensify their love affair with the English language" are the author's intended audience.

A bibliography of the most frequently cited authorities is included in the introduction.

II. Format

This word book is organized in dictionary format
using boldface capitals for main entry words. The
main entry (word, word phrase, or pair of words)
appears on a line by itself flush left followed by the
entry paragraph, also flush left. A double space separates the individual entries. Cross-references are
printed in small boldface block capitals.

The volume examined for review was the trade
paperback. Generous margins and line spacings make
the pages attractive and readable. It was sturdily con-
tructed with a good flexible spine.

III. Quality and Currency of Entries

Many of the entries are pleasantly anecdotal. Under
gobbledygook, for example, the reader is told that
the word was coined by a Texas congressman, Maury
Maverick, to "describe bureaucratic jargon." Several abhorrent examples are given and the entry ends
with a *see* reference to **bureaucratese**, another lengthy

and amusing entry. For more in this genre the reader
can turn to **Pentagonese**.

Under **hopefully** ("a knee-jerk word like **yunno**")
Bremner laments its use to mean "I hope," quotes
Strunk and White, as well as Bernstein on usage, and
ends his entry, "So hopefully, the silly, offensive,
ambiguous . . . use of **hopefully** will diminish."

The length of entries varies from one word, "Ugh!"
for **prioritize**, to almost a full page for **headlinese**.
Careful attention is given to journalism terms and to
common examples of confused usage: **farther/fur-
ther**, for example. Many entries are included simply
because they are commonly misspelled or mispronounced.

Purely etymological entries are apparently chosen
for the fascination the words hold for the author:
crepuscular, **cretin**, and **checkmate**, are a few in this
rich category. A particular advantage is the many
Latin words and phrases and classical allusions included in the body of the text. Parts of speech are
well represented. Under **sequence of tenses**, for example, two pages of text define and illustrate the
"three speeches" used by reporters: **direct**, **parenthetical**, and **reported**.

The currency of entries is rarely an issue in this
type of volume. Under **Coke**, for example, the slang
meaning of *cocaine* is not noted, but since this volume does not purport to be a dictionary of current
slang, a reader would not necessarily expect to find
this meaning here.

IV. Accessibility

The entries and guide words are in clear boldface
block capitals. One guide word for each page of a
two-page spread indicates the first and last entry of
that spread. Cross-references are in boldface block
capitals and *see also* references are in small boldface
block capitals.

An ample bibliography is included at the end of
the introduction. The publisher notes that "Works
quoted more than once in the text are usually referred to by an abbreviated title or name;" these
abbreviations are listed alphabetically in the introduction with the complete bibliographic record given
alongside of each.

V. Summary

Words on Words is an insightful and delightfully idiosyncratic addition to the genre of usage and style
books. Bremner's writing style is engaging and well-
informed. Since he frequently cites the opinions of
other usage authorities, further searching on a particular point is usually unnecessary.

Other recent dictionaries of usage that provide a more comprehensive and scholarly approach are THE HARPER DICTIONARY OF CONTEMPORARY USAGE (William and Mary Morris) and Roy H. Copperud's AMERICAN USAGE AND STYLE.

Words on Words is the sort of volume that interested readers would want to read from cover to cover. It can be recommended for reference as well as for circulating collections and for readers' personal libraries.

PART FIVE

Large-Print General Reference Books

Chapter 15
Evaluations of Large-Print Reference Books

LARGE-PRINT DICTIONARIES

The Large Print Version of The Little Oxford Dictionary of Current English

Facts at a Glance

Full Title: **The Large Print Version of The Little Oxford Dictionary of Current English: Fourth Edition.**
Publisher: Oxford University Press.
Edition Reviewed: © 1969.

Number of Entries: approximately 25,000.
Trim Size: 5½" × 8¾".
Binding: hardcover.

Price: $18.95.
ISBN 0-8161-6459-2.
Available from Ulverscroft Large Print Books.

I. Introduction and Scope

This version of *The Little Oxford Dictionary of Current English* is reprinted from the fourth edition (1969) of the dictionary. This edition, first compiled by George Ostler and edited by Jessie Coulson, has been photographically enlarged to 16- and 18-point type.

This dictionary is a British publication, published by Oxford University Press, and available from a British large-print supplier, from whom further de-

tails can be obtained. Thus the spelling, pronunciation guides, use of words, and specialized meanings reflect their British origins. It can serve, however, as a concise reference source for those requiring basic definitions.

Multiple meanings are preceded by clear boldface numbers. Compound words, run-in entries, and guide words at the top of each page are also printed in boldface type. These are helpful features for the visually impaired.

Despite the dictionary's relatively small size and narrow margins, the strong, clear typeface gives the pages the visual clarity necessary for the large-print user. For further information about the content, see the review of THE LITTLE OXFORD DICTIONARY OF CURRENT ENGLISH that appears elsewhere in this Buying Guide.

The Large Type American Heritage Basic Dictionary

Facts at a Glance

Full Title: **The Large Type American Heritage Basic Dictionary.**
Publisher: Houghton Mifflin.
Editors: Fernando de Mello Vianna, Editor-in-Chief; Anne D. Steinhardt and Pamela DeVinne.

Edition Reviewed: © 1981.

Number of Definitions: over 35,000.
Number of Pages: 312.
Trim Size: 8½″ × 10¹⁵⁄₁₆″.
Binding: paperback.

Price: $7.95.
Approved by the National Association of the
   Visually Handicapped for use by the partially
   seeing.
Sold in bookstores; also sold to libraries and other
   educational institutions.
ISBN 0-395-31673-1.

I. Introduction

This dictionary, part of the American Heritage family, is especially designed "for those who need or prefer large type." The cover states that "the Production Review Committee of National Aid to Visually Handicapped has found this publication to meet its criteria for use by the partially seeing."

There are over 35,000 highly condensed definitions of basic vocabulary words, which appear to be well selected for contemporary dictionary users. All main entries include pronunciations and parts of speech, and most have numbered, multiple meanings. Examples, guidance on usage (except for the guide to punctuation), and all etymologies are omitted, but a large-type, simplified style guide as well as several tables are included.

II. Authority

Houghton Mifflin's American Heritage dictionaries are respected and popular works, especially known for providing guidance on contemporary, educated use of language. This large-type dictionary was prepared by the publisher's American Heritage staff editors, under Fernando de Mello Vianna, who was also Editor-in Chief of THE AMERICAN HERITAGE DESK DICTIONARY and a special consultant to the AMERICAN HERITAGE DICTIONARY: SECOND COLLEGE EDITION. Supervising Editor Anne D. Steinhardt and Associate Editor Pamela DeVinne are also staff editors for other American Heritage dictionaries.

III. Comprehensiveness

The dictionary includes, according to the publisher, over 35,000 definitions. This is between 5,000 and 25,000 fewer than typical pocket-size or paperback dictionaries. Considering the special purpose of this dictionary—for readers who are visually impaired—this quantity is acceptable for spelling or basic use but may be too limited for college students.

The omission of all etymologies, or word sources, and of usage examples is sensible here; ordinarily, these make entries more visually complex and difficult to read, because different typefaces, sizes, and symbols are required to distinguish this information from basic definitions.

A comparison of two segments of entries with those in the CONCISE AMERICAN HERITAGE DICTIONARY illustrates the reduced selection of entries for the large-type edition, and may help buyers to judge whether that version is too limited for readers' use. The CONCISE includes this eight-entry sequence: **lariat, lark¹, lark², larkspur, larrup, larva, laryngitis, larynx.** The large-type edition reduces this to three entries: **lar·i·at, lark, lar·ynx** (under this last entry, both editions include "—la·ryn′ge·al *adj.*"). In a second sample segment, the CONCISE offers **par, par., para-, parable, paraclete, parabola, par·a·chute, pa·rade, paradigm, par·a·dise, par·a·dox, par·af·fin, par·a·gon,** and **par·a·graph.** The *Large Type American Heritage Basic Dictionary* includes nine entries: **par, parable, par·a·chute, pa·rade, par·a·dise, par·a·dox, par·af·fin, par·a·gon,** and **par·a·graph.**

The large-type edition excludes variations of words and combining forms as well as more difficult scientific or technical terms as main entries; however, occasional chemical and medical terms are entered, for example, **epinephrine** and **penicillin.** A considerable number of variant forms of words are included under main entries. For example, under the entry for **discipline,** the following also appear: —*v.* -**plined,** -**plining** [and] —**dis′ci·pli·nar′i·an** *n.*—**dis′ci·pli·nar′y** *adj.*

IV. Quality and Currency of Entries

All definitions are condensed to short phrases or single words. They are generally clear and serviceable. The publisher states that definitions begin with "the current, central meaning" in cases where multiple meanings are listed.

The entries are organized in the following sequence: main entry divided into syllables; pronunciation with some alternatives; parts of speech; inflected forms or, in rare cases, idiomatic usage if the word usually appears in a phrase; definitions (numbered when necessary); and variant forms. An example is:

   var·y (vâr′ē), *v.* -**ied,** -**ying.** 1. To cause or undergo
      change. 2. To give variety to; diversify. 3. To differ.
      —**var′i·ance** *n.* —**var′i·ant** *adj. & n.*

Definitions are usually unambiguous, although they do not attempt to encompass the range of nuances in words. For example, **evangelism** is defined as "The preaching of the Gospel," which omits such customary defining characteristics as *zealous* or *missionary.*

The absence of usage examples makes occasional definitions seem cryptic, as in the third definition provided for **sea**: "A vast amount or extent." Only rarely do homographs appear, but they are included as separate entries with superscript numbers: **pale**[1], **pale**[2].

V. Syllabication and Pronunciation

Main entries and their variant forms are divided into syllables by bold centered dots, and follow the breaks normally used in printing. Inflected forms of verbs are not syllabified. When variant forms of words are included, the part appearing in the main entry is not syllabified, but stress is indicated:

Eve·ry *adj*. . . . **eve′ry·bod′y, eve′ry·one′**.

Pronunciation is based on the symbols used in other American Heritage dictionaries. The publisher indicates that all pronunciations included "are acceptable in all circumstances." The criterion for acceptable pronunciation in American Heritage dictionaries is that of "educated speech" with regional variations. A list of spellings representing the full range of pronunciation symbols appears in the front of the dictionary for easy reference. The accompanying short explanation of the symbols indicates that variation in the pronunciation of the letter *y* is shown by: /y/. The dictionary includes typical variant pronunciations; **es·teem** (ĕ-stēm′, ĭ-stēm′) and **mem·oir** (mĕm′wär′, -wôr′). Bold primary stress marks ′ and lighter secondary stress marks ′ are shown as for **mem′·oir** above.

VI. Special Features

There is a contents list at the front of the dictionary that is rather hard to find, since it is printed above the extensive copyright information. The two-and-one-half page "How to Use This Dictionary" guide is divided into five very short but lucid sections that explain main entries, variants, inflected forms, labels (only for parts of speech and word forms), and pronunciations with a spelling and symbol list that includes the schwa ə, unidentified by name, but with samples of its use for vowel sounds, for example: item and circus.

At the back of the dictionary is a five-page guide to the use of punctuation marks with short explanations (including preferred printing style for dashes) and with usage examples set off in italic print, numbered rules (three for the period and 21 for the comma). There is a two-page guide to the metric system and three pages of metric conversions, plus a handy list of U.S. states with their capital cities, date of joining the Union, and population (based on the 1980 census). All these features are printed in large type with a generous amount of white space that makes reading them easier.

VII. Accessibility

The design of this dictionary ensures that the entries and definitions are as visually accessible as possible. The main entry words are printed in large, readable, bold type which overhangs the text. They are arranged in simple, letter-by-letter alphabetical sequence. The text is printed in two wide columns separated by a bold vertical rule. Page numbers are centered at the top of each text page; variant spellings, inflected verb forms, and words associated with the main entry are printed in smaller boldface type.

The system of guide words is visually simplified to indicate first and last entries on each double-page spread. A single bold word appears near the outside margin at the top of each page: on the left, the guide word indicates the first entry to appear on the left-hand page; on the right, the guide word indicates the last word to appear on the right-hand page.

Within entries, numbered definitions are clearly visible, as are the inflected verb forms and variant forms of words.

VIII. Graphics and Format

The graphic design of this basic dictionary is simple and attractive. There are no pictures or other illustrations. The text is printed in 14-point type with entry words in bold 14-point. There is enough white space between lines to facilitate reading. The text columns are approximately 3¼ inches wide, which means that a reader can use a rectangular magnifying glass as small as 3½ to 4 inches wide without seeing any text distortion.

The guide to the dictionary is in larger type and so are the metric charts, with columns of unit names and measurements generously spaced. Although the punctuation rules are printed in a similar large type, they appear very dense on the page in a single wide-column format. The usage examples are in italic and can be distinguished with ease from the numbered rules.

IX. Summary

The *Large Type American Heritage Basic Dictionary* is visually accessible, attractive, and easy to read. Its definitions, although *very* basic, are reliable. There are few frills beyond the basic meanings in this dictionary, but it is a solid work, clearly related to its respected larger companions in the American Heritage family and a good value for its modest price.

The Merriam-Webster Dictionary for Large Print Users

Facts at a Glance

Full Title: **The Merriam-Webster Dictionary for Large Print Users**.
Publisher: G. K. Hall.
Editor: Henry Bosley Woolf, Editor-in-Chief.
Edition Reviewed: © 1977.

Number of Entries: 57,000.
Number of Pages: 1,120.
Trim Size: 8¾″ × 11″.
Binding: hardcover.

Price: $29.50.
Available directly from the publisher.
ISBN 0-816-16459-2.

I. Introduction

The Merriam-Webster Dictionary for Large Print Users is a descendant of WEBSTER'S THIRD NEW INTERNATIONAL DICTIONARY. It contains over 57,000 entries covering the core of contemporary English vocabulary. The definitions are based on nearly 12 million examples of use entered in the Merriam-Webster citation files. Geographical and biographical information is excluded.

Originally published in 1975, the dictionary is most appropriate for public libraries serving senior citizens or libraries housing special collections for the visually handicapped. Its appreciably smaller vocabulary, however, could limit its usefulness for college students.

II. Authority

The Merriam-Webster Dictionary for Large Print Users is a combined effort of G. K. Hall, a leading U.S. publisher of large-print books, and the G. & C. Merriam Company, long recognized as a highly respected publisher of dictionaries. The staff of dictionary specialists was headed by Merriam-Webster Editor-in-Chief Henry Bosley Woolf.

WEBSTER'S THIRD NEW INTERNATIONAL DICTIONARY, upon which the G. K. Hall large-print version is based, favors contemporary words and usage. Merriam-Webster's authority derives from a dedication to accuracy, clarity, and comprehensiveness.

III. Comprehensiveness

WEBSTER'S THIRD NEW INTERNATIONAL DICTIONARY contains close to 460,000 entries; *The Merriam-Webster Dictionary for Large Print Users* includes approximately 57,000. The bulk of the eliminated matter falls into scientific and technical categories. With its 1975 copyright date, the work excludes a number of terms such as *meltdown*, *modem*, and *robotics* that have gained current usage.

Etymologies in the dictionary appear in boldface brackets preceding the definition. The etymology gives the language from which words assimilated into English have come. Synonyms are indicated by a boldface **syn** near the end of the entry.

Four types of cross-references are used: directional, synonymous, cognate, and inflectional. In each case the cross-reference appears in small capitals. A directional cross-reference follows a light dash and directs the user to look elsewhere for additional information. A synonymous cross-reference follows a boldface colon and indicates that the definition referred to can be used as a substitute. A cognate cross-reference follows an italic *var of* and indicates a variant. An inflectional cross-reference follows an italic label and identifies an entry as an inflected form.

IV. Quality and Currency of Entries

The Merriam-Webster Dictionary for Large Print Users is designed for a general readership and is sufficient to meet the vocabulary needs of many readers. College students, however, may find the relatively small number of entries inadequate for reference purposes.

Definitions are introduced by a boldface colon, which also is used to separate two or more clarifications of a single sense. Definitions of a word that has more than a single sense are separated by boldface Arabic numerals. Multiple senses of a word are presented in historical order. The first known English language sense is entered first. For example: **Master** . . . n. **1 :** a male teacher . . . **2 :** one highly skilled.

Editors have attempted to make the definitions as readable as possible. Although the definitions are brief and verbal illustrations rare, there is little need to consult additional entries for clarification.

V. Syllabication and Pronunciation

Pronunciation is indicated between reversed virgules following the main entry word (for example, **dis·like** \dis-′lik\ vb). A pronunciation key is located in the front of the volume. However, it is not repeated on individual pages. A hyphen is used in the pronunciation to indicate the division of syllables. A high-set mark shows primary stress or accent while a low-set mark indicates secondary stress (for example, **jack·knife** \′jak-ˌnif\ n). Syllables with neither a high-set mark nor a low-set mark are unstressed. An italic label following the pronunciation indicates a part of speech or another functional classification. Alternative pronunciations are included, although no preference is indicated.

VI. Special Features

The *A* to *Z* vocabulary in the *Merriam-Webster Dictionary for Large Print Users* is followed by several special feature sections. Included are population tables of the United States and Canada; a section on widely used signs and symbols; and tables covering the metric system, weights and measures, money, and the planets. While this type of information is occasionally useful, the population figures are out-of-date.

VII. Accessibility

Main entry words are in boldface type set flush with the left-hand margin of each column. They follow one another in letter-by-letter alphabetical order. A pair of guide words appears at the top of each page. When a main entry is followed by the word **or** and an alternative spelling, the two spellings are considered equal variants (**disk** or **disc**). When a variant spelling is joined to the main entry by the word **also** it indicates the second entry occurs less frequently (**surprise** also **sur·prize**. . . vb).

VIII. Graphics and Format

The outstanding characteristic of the Merriam-Webster enlarged print edition is the typography. The *A* to *Z* vocabulary features 18-point type guide words, 14-point type word entries, and 12-point type definitions. The special sections appear in 16-point type. The preface states that this conforms to the accepted standards for reference books for large print users as established by the National Association of the Visually Handicapped. A brief perusal will verify the value of this work to the visually handicapped individual.

The dictionary is in a single volume and is durably bound. Its size prevents it from being easily transported, but the binding does permit it to lie flat on an open surface. The paper is of good quality, sufficiently opaque, and heavy enough to withstand frequent use.

IX. Summary

The Merriam-Webster Dictionary for Large Print Users is an authoritative and highly readable work well designed to meet the needs of a general audience, particularly the visually impaired. In graphics and format the Merriam/G. K. Hall version is superior to the WEBSTER'S NEW WORLD LARGE PRINT DICTIONARY OF THE AMERICAN LANGAGE: SECOND CONCISE EDITION. However, it is less comprehensive, containing about one half the entries incorporated into the latter. Readers involved in extensive reference work may find this a significant shortcoming.

The dictionary is current only through the mid-1970s, but its general vocabulary is still suitable for public library holdings or any special collection serving the visually impaired.

The Random House Dictionary: Classic Edition (Large Print Edition)

Facts at a Glance

Full Title: **The Random House Dictionary: Classic Edition (Large Print Edition).**
Publisher: Random House.
Edition Reviewed: © 1983.

Number of Entries: 75,000.
Number of Pages: 1,082; 2 volumes.
Trim Size: 9" × 14".
Binding: paperback.

Price: One set $140.00; two or more sets $129.00 each.
Available from Library Reproduction Service. Order No. LRS 14244.

I. Introduction and Scope

The 1983 *Random House Dictionary: Classic Edition*, is the most recent reprinting of a large-print dictionary available from Library Reproduction Service. It has been specially selected and recommended by the LRS as an "adult level dictionary that would be excellent for high school and college." The dictionary has been enlarged to 16-point (main entries) and 14-point (definitions).

The boldface entry words are divided into syllables with centered dots. Pronunciations and variants follow. Parts of speech are abbreviated and set in italics. Multiple meanings are numbered in boldface.

The pages are set up in two columns with a center column of white space. While more white space between entries and definitions might be helpful for the visually impaired user, the bold entry word that overhangs the column provides some guidance for the eye.

Usage labels, synonyms, and illustrative phrases are all set in italic. Usage notes are preceded by a bold dash and the word "Usage" printed in boldface.

Among the advertised features of this large-print dictionary are its "encyclopedic" entries, which include brief biographical and geographical entries. A "Manual of Style" deals with punctuation and capitalization, and includes a list of commonly misspelled words. These special features make the dictionary especially convenient for the visually handicapped, as all material is contained within two volumes.

The definitions in this dictionary tend to be basic and even cursory. However, *The Random House Dictionary: Classic Edition* is currently the most up-to-date of all large-print dictionaries, and for this reason will make a valuable addition to all large-print reference collections.

Webster's Concise Family Dictionary: Large Print Edition

Facts at a Glance

Full Title: **Webster's Concise Family Dictionary: Large Print Edition**.
Publisher: Merriam-Webster.
Edition Reviewed: © 1975.

Number of Entries: 57,000.
Number of Pages: 856; 5 volumes.
Trim Size: 11" × 13½".
Binding: hardcover.

Price: $214.00.
Available from Library Reproduction Service.
Order No. LRS 04452.

I. Introduction and Scope

Since the regular-print edition of WEBSTER'S CONCISE FAMILY DICTIONARY was originally set in larger-than-standard adult dictionary print, this large print version includes several features especially helpful for the visually impaired: syllable breaks of boldface entries are marked with extrabold centered dots; high-set and low-set marks indicate primary or secondary stress or accents; a boldface colon introduces a definition; and boldface numerals mark multiple senses of an entry word.

In this large-print edition of WEBSTER'S CONCISE FAMILY DICTIONARY, type sizes range from 14-point definitions to 20-point guide words. For those large print dictionary users who prefer a single volume and who are able to work with 12-point definitions, THE MERRIAM-WEBSTER DICTIONARY FOR LARGE PRINT USERS can be a satisfactory and less expensive alternative reference. The concise definitions and text format are essentially the same for both of these dictionaries.

While this large-print dictionary has been reprinted from the 1975 regular-print edition its "generally authoritative approach to the lexicon" makes it useful for those visually impaired readers who may not require a more extensive current vocabulary.

For a complete analysis, see the review of THE MERRIAM-WEBSTER DICTIONARY for an evaluation of the contents, and the review of WEBSTER'S CONCISE FAMILY DICTIONARY for comments on the reg-ular-size type edition. See also the summary review of THE MERRIAM-WEBSTER DICTIONARY FOR LARGE PRINT USERS. All appear elsewhere in this Buying Guide.

Webster's New Collegiate Dictionary: Large Print Edition

Facts at a Glance

Full Title: **Webster's New Collegiate Dictionary: Large Print Edition**.
Publisher: Merriam-Webster.
Edition Reviewed: © 1976.

Number of Entries: 150,000.
Number of Illustrations: 500.
Trim Size: 11" × 13½".
Binding: hardcover, 9 volumes.

Price: $313.00.
Available from Library Reproduction Service.
LRS No. 04505.

I. Introduction and Scope

Webster's New Collegiate Dictionary is available from Library Reproduction Service in 14-point type, considered the minimum size for large-print material.

This dictionary is a comprehensive, abridged work based on an extensive citation file and list of authoritative historical sources from the venerable publisher. The edition is that preceding WEBSTER'S NINTH COLLEGIATE DICTIONARY, reviewed elsewhere in this Buying Guide.

Occupying nine volumes, it contains complete etymologies, extensive labels, synonyms, usage notes, cross-references, and numbered multiple meanings. Guide words in boldface type are printed at the top of each page. A bold rule draws the eye to the short pronunciation key conveniently placed at the lower right corner of each double-page spread. Various other elements, such as the use of the tilde to stand for the entry word in illustrative sentences, also help attract the eye.

This *Webster's New Collegiate Dictionary*, while lacking somewhat in currency, would be a useful tool for the visually handicapped reader.

Webster's New World Large Print Dictionary of the American Language: Second Concise Edition

Facts at a Glance

Full Title: **Webster's New World Large Print Dictionary of the American Language: Second Concise Edition**.

Publisher: Prentice Hall Press.
Editor: David B. Guralnik, General Editor.
Edition Reviewed: © 1979.

Number of Entries: over 105,000.
Number of Pages: 882.
Number of Illustrations: 612 black-and-white drawings.
Trim Size: 9¾″ × 13¾″.
Binding: cloth.

Price: $29.95.
Sold in bookstores; also sold to libraries.
ISBN 0-671-41818-1.

I. Introduction

Webster's New World Large Print Dictionary is a larger typeface version of *Webster's New World Dictionary of the American Language: Second Concise Edition.* The latter, an abridgment of the 158,000-entry WEBSTER'S NEW WORLD DICTIONARY: SECOND COLLEGE EDITION (1970), was first published in 1975 and updated in 1979.

The version retains many of the features of the *Second College Edition*, including clear and reliable definitions. However, the etymologies are less extensive, and highly technical, and arcane terms as well as synonyms have been eliminated.

In the foreword, the publisher states that this dictionary in its original format was especially prepared for a wide range of general readers, including learners of English as a Second Language (ESL).

II. Authority

Of all the Webster's dictionaries on the market, the *Webster's New World* volumes (originally published by World + Collins) and the Merriam-Webster volumes are among the most reputable. This work was prepared by David B. Guralnik along with the same permanent lexicographical staff that produced the WEBSTER'S NEW WORLD DICTIONARY: SECOND COLLEGE EDITION, using the same database.

The entries were selected on the basis of their frequency of appearance in general interest publications. Only those terms that had gained stability in form and meaning by the late 1970s and that have demonstrated a potential for survival in the language were selected for inclusion.

III. Comprehensiveness

Over 105,000 vocabulary entries are included in the large-print volume. Since the copyright date is 1979, however, a number of terms that are now current are not included. For example, a perusal indicates no entries for *Alzheimer's disease, arbitrage, triathlon,* or *wind shear.*

Obsolete and archaic terms that are often found in standard works of literature or in biblical works have been included. Common technical terms encountered in general writings have been entered, prefaced by an abbreviated field label. A list of abbreviations immediately precedes the first page of the dictionary.

Numerous prefixes, suffixes, and combined forms have been entered, enabling the reader to determine the meanings of thousands of additional words too specialized for inclusion. To conserve space, words that are derived from main entries, such as nouns ending in **-tion**, adjectives ending in **-like**, or adverbs ending in **-ly** are run in to the end of the entry for the base word. Derivatives that have significant meanings not readily identifiable from the main term's separate parts are given in separate entries.

IV. Quality and Currency of Entries

The definitions in this large-print work are uniformly clear and accurate as well as being reasonably thorough. For example, **barter** is defined as "to trade by exchanging goods or services without using money." This precise approach is accommodating to a broad readership, especially students. The definitions of longer entries have been arranged in an order that indicates how the word developed from its etymology and earliest meanings. For example, **Jupiter** is first defined as "the chief Roman god" and secondly as "planet of the solar system." Colloquial, slang, archaic, obsolete, or similar senses follow the general definitions. Occasionally, an obsolete sense may be given first to serve as a link between the etymology and the current senses. Where a primary sense of a word can easily be subdivided into several closely related meanings, this has been done. The words "especially" or "specifically" are frequently used to introduce such groupings or related senses. This procedure for listing definitions could be confusing for readers who might expect to have the most common definition listed first.

V. Syllabication and Pronunciation

All syllables are divided by bold centered dots: **e·lec·tron·ic, pudg·y**. The editors note, however, that it is not customary in written or printed material to break a word after the first syllable or before the last, if that syllable consists of only a single letter or, in the case of lengthy words, two letters.

Pronunciations are given inside parentheses, immediately following the boldface entry. A single space is used between pronounced syllables. Primary and secondary stress are indicated by bold and lighter stress marks.

The editors state that pronunciations are "for the most part those found in the normal relaxed conversation of educated speakers." Common variants are also shown, as well as native pronunciations of foreign words and proper names. A "Guide to the Dictionary" includes a key to pronunciation; an abbreviated key appears at the bottom of every right-hand page of the vocabulary. The symbols in the key can be easily understood from the key words in which they are shown.

VI. Special Features

Several pages preceding and following the lexicon include tables of weights and measures, time zones, and a guide to the mechanics of writing that briefly covers marks of punctuation, numbers, capitalization, abbreviations, and spelling. Also added is a table of alphabets providing the sounds of letters in Arabic, Hebrew, Greek, Russian, and German. This sort of information is readily available in various general almanacs and encyclopedias—often in more complete form. In general, these features add little value to the text.

VII. Accessibility

To increase accessibility in this dictionary, all entries—including proper names of persons and places, abbreviations, affixes, and unnaturalized foreign terms found within English contexts—have been arranged in one alphabetical listing. This eliminates the need to browse through various appendixes in order to pinpoint lexical information.

When variant spellings of a word fall some distance apart in the alphabetical listing, the definition appears with the spelling most frequently used in the U.S. Other spellings of the word are cross-referenced to the form most widely used. Cross-references often indicate that the variant is *British*, *dialectal*, *slang*, *obsolete*, or the like. For example, for **centre** we are given "*Brit. sp.* of **center**."

When two variant spellings appear close to each other in alphabetical order and are used with nearly equal frequency, they are placed together at the head of the entry. In this case, neither spelling is considered to be more accurate, even though the first one listed may be the most often used (for example, **theater, theatre**).

VIII. Graphics and Format

Over 600 black-and-white line drawings contribute to the reader's understanding of the vocabulary. They are used on a very selective basis when the editors felt that an illustration would help to expand or sharpen a definition. The actual sizes of animals have been given in feet or inches, and tools and instruments are shown in use in order to make clearer their function and relative size.

One cautionary note is in order concerning the graphics of this large-print edition. Compared to the diminutive size of typeface found in most dictionaries, the print used in this work can rightly be termed "extra-large." The volume has 16-point type guide words, 11-point type word entries, and 11-point type definitions. However, when measured against the standard 16-point type for the main entry word found in most large-print books, this version comes up short. In consequence, the visually impaired reader may find the text size unacceptable. THE MERRIAM-WEBSTER DICTIONARY FOR LARGE PRINT USERS, for instance, published by G. K. Hall, features 18-point type guide words, 14-point type word entries, and 12-point type definitions.

Generally, the main entry words in this *Webster's New World* are easily spotted and clearly divided into syllables. The opaque paper is of sufficient quality to eliminate reflections and firm enough to avoid crumplings of pages. Thumb indexing facilitates access to the text.

Physically, this is a sturdy book with a binding that should withstand heavy and sustained use and still allow the book to lie flat. Because of its large-size format, the dictionary is not easily transportable or stored, and handling it could be awkward for some readers. Its most appropriate location would be on a separate stand or table.

IX. Summary

The *Webster's New World Large Print Dictionary: Second Concise Edition* is a highly reputable dictionary that retains many of the outstanding features of WEBSTER'S NEW WORLD DICTIONARY: SECOND COLLEGE EDITION, upon which it is based.

In comparing this volume to G. K. Hall's MERRIAM-WEBSTER DICTIONARY FOR LARGE PRINT USERS, the prospective buyer should note two considerations. The graphics, in particular the size of the typeface in the G. K. Hall large-print dictionary, are of sufficient size to accommodate the visually impaired person, while the Prentice Hall *Webster's New World* edition has significantly smaller type; and although it causes less strain on the eye than most dictionaries, it is not likely to satisfy the majority of large-print users who are visually impaired. On the other hand, the Prentice Hall *New World* vocabulary is more comprehensive; it includes nearly twice the number of entries to be found in the G. K. Hall volume.

The *Webster's New World Large Print Dictionary*, while current only through the 1970s, is a useful tool for general vocabulary. In content and format, it is appropriate for public libraries and offices as well as for individual collections where there is need for a large-print dictionary.

LARGE-PRINT THESAURUSES

The Merriam-Webster Thesaurus for Large Print Users

Facts at a Glance

Full Title: **The Merriam-Webster Thesaurus for Large Print Users.**
Publisher: G. K. Hall.
Editors: E. Ward Gilman, Senior Editor; and Kathleen M. Doherty.
Edition Reviewed: © 1978.

Number of Entries: more than 50,000.
Number of Pages: 1,032.
Trim Size: 8⅜" × 10¾".
Binding: cloth.

Price: $35.00.
Available direct from the publisher.
ISBN 0-816-16617-X.

I. Introduction and Scope

Based on the *Webster's Collegiate Thesaurus*, *The Merriam-Webster Thesaurus for Large Print Users* includes 50,000 entries and "is designed to meet the day-to-day requirements of those who need or prefer large type and who want a compact and handy thesaurus," as the preface states. While retaining the basic features of the parent book, the large-print edition simplifies and reorganizes the synonym list to include cross-references. It also eliminates unnecessary elements such as "specialized or abstruse entries" or "synonyms not likely to be of general interest." Ultimately, the book's authority lies in WEBSTER'S THIRD NEW INTERNATIONAL DICTIONARY and the Merriam-Webster research file of nearly 13 million words. Originally published in an attractive format by G. K. Hall, the book conforms to the standards for reference books of the National Association for Visually Handicapped.

II. Format

In addition to the preface, the book includes a 20-page "Explanatory Notes" section, which—with its examples—is necessary for the reader to understand the elements presented in the entries. It includes explanations of labels, punctuation, and symbols. A brief key to some of the abbreviations and symbols also appears on every left-hand page in the book.

The main portion of the book contains 1,000 pages of entries presented in large print in two-column format. The main entry words are in 14-point type, with 12-point type definitions. The columns are clearly separated from 18-point folios and guide words at the top of each page by a vertical black rule. The type (ranging from 12- to 18-point) is printed very black on good quality paper with minimal show-through. This is a page made to order for the visually handicapped or for those who simply prefer larger print. Many other readers may also find it a pleasure to use this thesaurus.

The large-page format is well bound: the pages open easily and lie flat on a desk top.

III. Quality and Currency of Entries

Unlike *Roget's Thesaurus*, which is organized by large concepts, *The Merriam-Webster Thesaurus for Large Print Users* is organized alphabetically, like a dictionary. It is extremely well written and easy to use. Readers will find its list of synonyms, related words, and cross-references helpful and rational, as well as instructive about the fine meanings of words. And far from limiting the browser, this more tightly constructed organization can send the reader on a most gratifying spree of page-turning in search of other words.

Here is an example of a representative main entry:

> **essentially** *adv* **1** in regard to the essential points <essentially the problem is this: he is unreliable>
> *syn* au fond, basically, fundamentally, in essence
> *rel* actually, really
> *idiom* at bottom
> **2** *syn* see ALMOST 2
> *rel* substantially, virtually
> *idiom* in the main

The entry consists of a main entry word, part-of-speech label, a sense number, a core meaning with brief, verbal illustration, and a list of synonyms (*syn*). Synonyms are followed by related words (*rel*), idiomatic equivalents (*idiom*), contrasted words (*con*), and antonyms (*ant*), where applicable.

A core meaning may be supplemented by a usage note and by two verbal illustrations if it is broad enough to cause confusion.

Secondary entries include main entry word, part-of-speech label, sense number when needed, and a "see" reference to the main entry where a list of synonyms that includes the secondary entry is given.

The editors state in the "Explanatory Notes" that *"No word may appear in more than one list at* [sic] *a main or secondary entry*." Users will be grateful for the special thought and care that has gone into this simplifying rule.

Because this thesaurus was published in 1978, it omits some words or idioms in current usage. Verbs such as *access* and *program* are not used in their computer-related senses, for example. Because the book is concerned with the general vocabulary of the language, more technological, scientific, and other specialized words are also not found here.

However, because the established—as well as the new—meanings of words in the English language include so many senses and nuances, the editors state that "it is essential that the thesaurus be used in conjunction with an adequate dictionary."

IV. Accessibility

The "Explanatory Notes" make the thesaurus completely accessible to any reader. A simple key to some of the abbreviations and symbols used appears on the bottom of every left-hand page. Guide words in 18-point type appear at the top of every page. There is no thumb index, but because of the larger print, generous use of white space, and bold main entry words overhanging the text, the alphabet is easy to follow.

V. Summary

The Merriam-Webster Thesaurus for Large Print Users contains a good compact vocabulary of the language in general use. The large-print format is excellent, with the dictionarylike organization providing a rich trove of synonyms and cross-references. Access is simple; the volume fulfills its purpose in making information easily readable for the visually handicapped. This thesaurus is highly recommended for library collections serving readers who require large print and will find the format pleasing and exceptionally accessible.

Roget's International Thesaurus

Facts at a Glance

Full Title: **Roget's International Thesaurus: Third Edition**.
Publisher: Lippincott.
Edition Reviewed: © 1962.

Number of Categories: 1,040.
Number of Pages: 1,258; 7 volumes.
Number of Indexes: 1.
Trim Size: 8½″ × 11″.
Binding: hardcover.

Price: $390.00.

Available from Library Reproduction Service.
  Order No. LRS 03160.

I. Introduction and Scope

This large-print edition of Roget's International Thesaurus is photoenlarged from the third edition of the thesaurus which appeared in 1960. There have been no cuts or changes made for this large-print version, and its quality and comprehensiveness make it suitable for the visually impaired student or home user.

Words are arranged into 1,040 categories with an alphabetical index referring to the categories. There has been a considerable expansion in the number of words and categories since the 1946 edition, but the more recent ROGET'S INTERNATIONAL THESAURUS: FOURTH EDITION (reviewed in this Buying Guide), only available in regular print, has expanded even further.

II. Format

To allow for the larger print size, the thesaurus is printed on its side with just 28 lines per double-column page. Page numbering follows the third edition pagination, with each original page spread over two large-print pages. This will be useful in integrated group study situations. Type is considerably larger than many other large-type reference books with headings in 24-point type and entries in 20-point type. The text columns are four-and-a-half inches wide with only one-half inch between the two columns and this minimal white space detracts somewhat from the clarity.

The Roget biography, contents, preface and text of the How-to-Use section are spread across a double (nine inch) column. The synopsis of categories appears in three (two and a half inch) columns.

Entries are arranged in numbered categories with parts of speech designated in both text and index. The most commonly used words are printed in heavy type and extensive cross-referencing in text and index leads the user to more synonyms:

ADJS. 3. **original**, sulphitic *or* sulphidic [slang]; **novel**, fresh, unique; underived, **firsthand**; **authentic** 515.3.

III. Quality and Currency of Entries

The publisher's preface emphasizes the new words and idiomatic phrases added since the 1946 edition. In turn, however, this edition does not reflect the slang and technical terms included in the 1977 fourth edition, unavailable in large print.

Colloquial (**dead and done for**), slang (**dud**) and dialect (**nary one**) synonyms are generously distributed, but there are no usage illustrations. Two-column alphabetical word lists are inserted where appropriate. Under quantities, for example, there are 40 synonyms from armful and bag(ful) to teacup(ful) and teaspoon(ful).

There are no antonyms within individual entries, but these may be found in nearby categories. Shade (337) follows light (334) and luminary (335).

IV. Accessibility

The large-print, large-page design of this thesaurus ensures ease of use by the sight impaired. Many features of the original thesaurus add to this accessibility. There is a clear step-by-step guide to use written in an unintimidating style and explaining each part of the thesaurus and every type of entry. The text itself features distinguishing print types: categories are centered in large capitals, parts of speech are in small capitals, most common words are in bold type, and foreign phrases and conjunctions are in italics. The 600-page index includes distinctions for each meaning of a word and index entries are in bold type overhanging the lists associated with them.

V. Summary

The large-print edition of *Roget's International Thesaurus: Third Edition* is easy to use and visually accessible. It retains the traditional format and scholarship of the earlier Roget thesauruses and will be useful to students and writers who require larger type than usually found in language reference works. For a more up-to-date thesaurus, the user may want to examine WEBSTER'S NEW WORLD THESAURUS: LARGE PRINT EDITION, which is based on the thesaurus of the same name (published in 1971) and reviewed elsewhere in this Buying Guide.

Webster's New World Thesaurus: Large Print Edition

Facts at a Glance

Full Title: **Webster's New World Thesaurus: Large Print Edition**.
Publisher: World.
Editor: Charlton G. Laird.
Edition Reviewed: © 1974.

Number of Entries: 30,000.
Number of Pages: 544; 4 volumes.
Trim Size: 8″ × 10″.
Binding: hardcover.

Price: $136.00.
Available from Library Reproduction Service.
 Order No. LRS 08536.

I. Introduction and Scope

The large-print edition of *Webster's New World Thesaurus* is based on a work of the same title, originally published in 1971. Its type has been enlarged to 18-point size.

The volume includes a guide to the use of the thesaurus, and its entries are alphabetically arranged. Among its features are some that will be especially helpful to visually impaired readers. Main entry words are printed in boldface and overhang the text; pairs of bold guide words appear at the top of each page. The entries contain no illustrative phrases or sentences. Although this in some cases makes it more difficult for a reader to grasp nuances of meaning, the omission does visually simplify the entries. Librarians serving readers who prefer or require large print will be interested in the fact that the Library Reproduction Service has decreased many of their prices (this volume was decreased from $168.00 to $136.00) to make their offerings more widely available.

A review of the 1985 updating of the regular-print WEBSTER'S NEW WORLD THESAURUS appears elsewhere in this Buying Guide.

LARGE-PRINT ATLAS

Hammond Large Type World Atlas

Facts at a Glance

Full Title: **Hammond Large Type World Atlas**.
Publisher: Hammond.
Edition Reviewed: © 1986.

Number of Pages: 144.
Number of Maps: 52.
Number of Indexes: 1.
Number of Index Entries: 3,100.
Trim Size: 9¾″ × 12¼″.
Binding: cloth.

Price: $24.95.
Sold in bookstores; also sold to libraries and other educational institutions.
ISBN 0-843-71246-5.
No scheduled revision.

I. Introduction

Described on its dust jacket as "the only large type atlas on the market today," the *Hammond Large Type World Atlas* fills a significant gap for the visually impaired. First published in 1969 by Franklin Watts, this work features entirely different cartography from that used in other Hammond atlases in deference to its special format. It is 9¾″ by 12¼″ in size, with a sturdy, sewn hardcover binding and an attractive, easily readable two-color dust jacket. The editors claim that this atlas "makes it easy for the reader to grasp the essential details of today's world." It contains 52 maps in its 144 pages, and carries a 1986 copyright.

II. Format

The *Hammond Large Type Atlas* contains 100 pages of political maps, each of which occupies two pages. The book is a manageable size and weight. It is bound in an attractive, sturdy hard cover; the heavy, nonglossy pages lie flat when open.

No legend is provided for map symbols, which include significant spot elevations (given in both feet and meters), various types of boundaries, large cities and capitals, scientific research stations, permanent and seasonal rivers and lakes, reefs, salt pans, canals, cataracts, and waterfalls. Natural features, such as mountain ranges, are indicated on the maps by name but not a symbol, nor is relief depicted. Most of these symbols are self-explanatory to the experienced atlas user but may present a stumbling block for the neophyte.

Although the publisher claims "the editors have succeeded brilliantly in assembling a vast amount of essential . . . information," in keeping with the needs of the visually impaired, this work in fact presents only the most basic geographic information. As a result, the *Hammond Large Type World Atlas* necessarily lacks much of the detail one would expect in an atlas designed for normally sighted people or experienced atlas users.

III. Special Features

An eight-page gazetteer-index of the world lists countries, states, and other major geographic units; their area in square miles; population (based on "latest reliable figures obtainable"); capital or chief town; and map page and grid coordinate reference. Membership in the United Nations is also indicated. This easy-to-read table is useful for basic reference.

IV. Geographical Balance

With eight maps, the United States receives by far the most extensive coverage, compared, for example, to one map each for Canada and one for the Soviet Union. Many countries are grouped on a single page. As an example of the *Hammond Large Type World Atlas*'s geographic bias, Europe has twelve maps in all, whereas Africa has only five.

V. Scale and Projections

Scales are presented only as bar scales, calibrated in miles and kilometers, making comparison of different areas difficult. In addition, a wide variety of scales is used. As a result, the inexperienced or inattentive user might suppose that the areas shown on various maps are similar in size. The average scale (excluding the world map) is about one inch to 150 miles, or 1:9,500,000. The smallest scale is that used for the world map, around one inch to 1,500 miles, or 1:95,000,000. The largest scale is approximately one inch to 14 miles, or 1:887,000.

Projections are not named (except for the map of Antarctica), but those used represent the mapped areas without unacceptable distortion.

VI. Accuracy

Conventional anglicized spellings are used as much as possible, a convenience for the average American reader. The index, however, provides no cross-references from vernacular spellings to anglicized ones. Thus, the reader searching for Braunschweig, West Germany, for example, may not realize that it has a rarely used anglicized form, *Brunswick*, which is used in this atlas. Alternative names are rare, so that *Islas Malvinas*, for example, does not appear on the map in parentheses following *Falkland Islands*. Likewise, the Pinyin spelling *Beijing* is ignored in favor of the traditional *Peking*.

The maps of France and Spain delineate and label the nation of Andorra but do not outline its borders in red as is done for Monaco. As a result, the reader might wonder whether Andorra is in fact a separate country. Curiously, both maps outline a small unlabeled area just to the east of Andorra, where no country exists. This is probably a cartographic error.

Official names of countries are not always used on the maps but are listed in the gazetteer-index, a convenient feature for reference. Placement of names of natural features is generally accurate. The Seychelles islands, in the Indian Ocean east of Africa, are only partially represented on the map by one of its island groups, Aldabra. Because *Seychelles* appears in parentheses after *Aldabra Islands* to indicate ownership, the reader might assume incorrectly that it is an alternative name for the Aldabra Islands. On the whole, however, the *Hammond Large Type* atlas is accurate and will serve readers well within the scope of its inherent limitations.

VII. Currency

The *Hammond Large Type* atlas accurately reflects the current world political situation, up to its 1986 copyright date, although, as is still the practice in many recent atlases, *Cambodia* is used rather than *Kampuchea*. Brunei became a member of the United Nations in 1984 but is not indicated as such in the gazetteer-index.

VIII. Legibility

Legibility is, of course, the principal goal of this atlas, and the editors have succeeded in achieving this objective. Print is dark, typefaces are sufficiently differentiated for the level of detail shown, and the pages are uncluttered. Colors are limited to blue, yellow, red, white, and black, a scheme that preserves clarity and consistency. Overall, the maps are visually pleasing. They are not contained by neat lines, and they fill the whole page; a half-inch margin on the inner edge of each page insures that nothing is lost in the gutter, but the margin is unnecessarily wide and the maps lose their continuity. Place names are often divided inconveniently (for example, *Norma* on the left page and *n, Oklahoma* on the right page), and borders and rivers sometimes appear disjointed. In most cases, however, a good match can be achieved by bunching the two pages of the map together. It should be noted, however, that frequent handling of this type can damage the pages.

National (and—for the United States and Canada—state and provincial) borders are clearly marked. Natural features are indicated, although only by name; no shading or symbols are used except for spot elevations.

IX. Accessibility

The gazetteer-index includes some 315 entries arranged conveniently for ready reference. It includes countries and other areas of the world, such as U.S. states. The number of actual unique entries is somewhat smaller, since alternative names are entries rather than cross-references. For example, information entered for Vanuatu is duplicated in an entry for its previous name, New Hebrides, which is followed by the new name in parentheses.

The master index, located at the end of the atlas, contains approximately 2,700 entries listing all features that appear in the atlas except those included in the gazetteer-index. Most entries are indexed to the map having the largest scale; occasionally more than one reference is given. Entries usually include the name or abbreviation of the political unit or continent in which they are located. Many are modified by a word or abbreviation describing the type of feature, for example, "sea," "pen.," or "cap." There is no key to the abbreviations, but most of them will be obvious to experienced atlas users.

Index entries cite page number and alphanumeric grid coordinates but not latitude and longitude coordinates. Three inset maps, at the same scale as their main maps, are included.

The editors' failure to provide cross-references from vernacular to anglicized versions of place names in the index (see *Accuracy*) is a major drawback and seriously limits accessibility if the reader is familiar only with the vernacular spelling.

X. Summary

The *Hammond Large Type World Atlas* is a large-format, large-type atlas designed for use by the visually impaired. Attractive, highly legible, and uncluttered in appearance, it serves its intended readers admirably within the limits imposed by its purpose. What would be a serious omission of detail in a more comprehensive atlas is a virtue in this volume.

Of necessity, maps in this atlas provide only the most general information. Prospective purchasers must decide whether simplicity and clarity outweigh detail and completeness, depending upon the needs of their patrons. Visually impaired readers might prefer to use a more detailed atlas with a magnifying lens. However, this title provides convenient ready reference while doubling as an excellent source of outline or base maps for other uses.

The lack of map legends and the absence of index references from vernacular to anglicized place names are the two principal drawbacks of this volume. It has been executed carefully, with close attention to the needs of its primary users, and represents good value.

Bibliography

General

American Reference Books Annual (ARBA). Edited by Bohdan S. Wynar. Littleton, Colo.: Libraries Unlimited, 1970–. Contains reviews of reference books.

ARBA Guide to Subject Encyclopedias and Dictionaries. Edited by Bohdan S. Wynar. Littleton, Colo.: Libraries Unlimited, 1986.

Booklist: Including Reference Books Bulletin (Formerly, *Booklist and Reference and Subscription Books Reviews*). Chicago: American Library Association, 1905–. Semimonthly. Contains reviews of reference books.

Choice. Middletown, Conn.: Association of College and Research Libraries, a division of the American Library Association, 1964–. Monthly. Contains reviews of reference books.

College and Research Libraries. Chicago: Association of College and Research Libraries, a division of the American Library Association, 1939–. Bimonthly. Contains reviews of reference books.

Horowitz, Lois. "Judging Books by More Than Covers." *Consumer's Digest*, October 1985, 46.

Katz, William A. *Introduction to Reference Work*. Vol. 1. Basic Information Sources. 5th ed. New York: McGraw-Hill, 1987.

Library Journal. New York: R. R. Bowker, 1876–. Semimonthly. Contains reviews of reference books. "Reference Books of [year]" published annually in April issue.

Partridge, Eric. *From Sanskrit to Brazil*. Freeport, N.Y.: Books for Libraries Press, 1952. Contains short essays on the etymology of words and their use—for the general and interested reader rather than for academics.

Reference Services Review. Ann Arbor, Mich.: Pierian Press, 1973–. Quarterly. Contains information of interest about reference books.

RQ. Chicago: Reference and Adult Services Division of the American Library Association, 1960–. Quarterly. Contains reviews of reference books.

Sheehy, Eugene P., comp. *Guide to Reference Books*. 10th ed. Chicago: American Library Association, 1986.

Walford, Albert J. *Guide to Reference Material*. 3 vols. 4th ed. London: The Library Association, 1980.

Wilson Library Bulletin. New York: H. W. Wilson, 1914–. Ten issues per year. Contains reviews of reference books.

Wynar, Bohdan S., ed. *Recommended Reference Books for Small and Medium-sized Libraries and Media Centers 1987*. Littleton, Colo.: Libraries Unlimited, 1987.

Encyclopedias

"Acquisition and Use of General Encyclopedias in Small Academic Libraries." *RQ* 25 (Winter 1985): 218–22.

Bennion, Bruce. "Performance Testing of a Book and Its Index as an Information Retrieval System." *Journal of the American Society for Information Science* (July 1980): 264–70.

Bunge, Charles A. "Illustrated Reference Books: Technological, Intellectual and Economic Developments." *Reference Services Review* (Spring 1983): 89–98.

Collison, Robert L. "Encyclopaedias." In *The New Encyclopaedia Britannica: Macropaedia* 6: 779–99. Chicago: Encyclopaedia Britannica, 1980.

———. *Encyclopedias: Their History Throughout the Ages*. 2d ed. New York: Hafner, 1966.

Darnton, Robert. *The Business of Enlightenment: A Publishing History of the Encyclopédie, 1775–1800*. Cambridge: Harvard University Press, 1979.

Denenberg, Herbert S. "Consumers' Guide to Buying an Encyclopedia." *Caveat Emptor*, August–September 1979, 19–20.

Einbinder, Harvey. "Encyclopedias: Some Foreign and Domestic Developments." *Wilson Library Bulletin* (December 1980): 257–61.

"Encyclopedia Sales Frauds." *Consumer Reports*, March 1971, 172–74.

Engle, June L., and Elizabeth Futas. "Sexism in Adult Encyclopedias." *RQ* (Fall 1983): 29–39.

Grieves, Robert T. "Short Circuiting Reference Books." *Time*, 13 June 1983, 96.

Hellemans, Alexander. "New Directions for Encyclopedias." *Publishers Weekly*, 2 October 1987, 40–44.

Johnston, W. T., and Joy B. Trulock. "Buying an Encyclopedia." *Consumers' Research Magazine*, February 1975, 12–16.

Kister, Kenneth. *Encyclopedia Buying Guide: A Consumer Guide to the Best Encyclopedias for Adults and Children*. 3rd ed. New York: R. R. Bowker, 1981.

Mathisen, Tyler. "All about Encyclopedias." *Money*, October 1983, 209–12.

Miller, Jerome K. "Popular Encyclopedias as a Source of Information about Copyright: A Critical Comparison." *RQ* (Summer 1983): 388–92.

Purchasing an Encyclopedia: 12 Points to Consider. Chicago: American Library Association, 1979.

"Six Multivolume Adult Encyclopedias." *Booklist* (1 December 1982): 515–32.

Walsh, S. Padraig. *Anglo-American General Encyclopedias: A Historical Bibliography, 1703–1967.* New York: R. R. Bowker, 1968.

Whitelock, Otto V. St. "On the Making and Survival of Encyclopedias." *Choice* (June 1967): 381–89.

Atlases

Alexander, G. L. *Guide to Atlases: World, Regional, National, Thematic: An International Listing of Atlases Published Since 1950.* Metuchen, N.J.: Scarecrow Press, 1971.

———. *Supplement: An International Listing of Atlases Published 1971 through 1975 with Comprehensive Indexes.* Metuchen, N.J.: Scarecrow Press, 1977.

American Cartographer. Falls Church, Va.: American Cartographic Association, 1974–. Semiannual. Contains reviews of atlases.

Base Line: A Newsletter of the Map and Geography Round Table. Chicago: American Library Association, 1980–. Six issues per year. Contains news and reviews of new atlases.

Cartographic Journal. London: British Cartographic Society, 1964–. Semiannual. Contains reviews of atlases.

Geography and Map Division Bulletin. Special Libraries Association. 1947–. Quarterly. Contains reviews of atlases.

Kister, K[enneth] F. *Kister's Atlas Buying Guide: General English-language World Atlases Available in North America.* Phoenix, Ariz.: Oryx Press, 1984.

Porter, Roy E. "How to Select an Atlas." *Library Journal* (1 November 1961): 3747–50.

Schorr, Alan Edward. "General World Atlases." *Booklist* (15 December 1981): 564–67.

Western Association of Map Libraries Information Bulletin. Santa Cruz, Calif.: Western Association of Map Libraries, 1968–. Three issues per year. Contains reviews of atlases.

Dictionaries and Word Books

Bailey, Richard W. "Research Dictionaries." *American Speech* (Fall 1969): 166–72.

———, ed. *Dictionaries of English: Prospects for the Record of Our Language.* Ann Arbor: University of Michigan Press, 1987.

Barnhart, Clarence L. "General Dictionaries." *American Speech* (Fall 1969): 173–78.

Brewer, Annie M., ed. *Dictionaries, Encyclopedias, and Other Word-Related Books.* 3 vols. 4th ed. Detroit, Mich.: Gale Research Company, 1987.

Burchfield, Robert W. "The End of an Innings but Not the End of the Game" (Threlford Memorial Lecture, 1984). *The Incorporated Linguist* (Summer 1984): 114–19.

Carter, Robert A. "The War of Words." *Publishers Weekly*, 2 October 1987, 27–36.

Chadbourne, Robert. "Keeping Up with Conversation: Merriam-Webster Is on the Job." *Wilson Library Bulletin* (September 1987): 41–44.

Chapman, Robert L. "A Working Lexicographer Appraises *Webster's Third New International Dictionary*." *American Speech* 42 (1967): 202–10.

Chapman R. W. *Lexicography.* London: Oxford University Press, 1948.

Chomsky, Noam. *Reflections on Language.* New York: Pantheon, 1976.

Collison, Robert L. "Dictionaries before 1800." In *Encyclopedia of Library and Information Science*, edited by Allen Kent and Harold Lancour, 7: 170–91. New York: Marcel Dekker, 1972.

———. *Dictionaries of English and Foreign Languages: A Bibliographical Guide to Both General and Technical Dictionaries with Historical and Explanatory Notes and References.* 2d ed. New York: Hafner, 1971.

Dillard, Joey Lee. *American Talk: Where Our Words Came From.* New York: Random House, 1976.

Douglas, George H. "What's Happened to the Thesaurus?" *RQ* (Winter 1976): 149–55.

Fillmore, C. J. "Types of Lexical Information." In *Semantics: An Interdisciplinary Reader in Philosophy, Linguistics, and Psychology*, edited by D. D. Steinberg and L. A. Jakobovits. London: Cambridge University Press, 1971.

Gimson, A. C. *An Introduction to the Pronunciation of English.* London: The English Language Book Society/Edward Arnold, 1980.

Guralnik, David B. "The Making of a Dictionary." *The Bulletin of the Cleveland Medical Library* (January 1977): 5–23.

Hartmann, R. R. K. "Dictionaries of English: The User's Perspective." In *Dictionaries of English: Prospects for the Record of Our Language*, edited by Richard W. Bailey. Ann Arbor: University of Michigan Press, 1987.

Hartmann, R. R. K., and F. C. Stork. *Dictionary of Language and Linguistics.* New York: Halsted/Wiley, 1972.

Herbert, Rosemary. "The Building of a Dictionary." *Publishers Weekly*, 2 October 1987, 38–39.

Hindmarsh, R. *Cambridge English Lexicon.* Cambridge: Cambridge University Press, 1980.

"Historical Introduction." In the *Oxford English*

Dictionary, edited by James A. H. Murray, et al., vii–xxvi. Oxford: Clarendon Press, 1933.

Hulbert, James R. *Dictionaries: British and American*. Rev. ed. London: Andre Deutsch, 1968.

Ilson, Robert, ed. *Lexicography: An Emerging International Profession*. Manchester: Manchester University Press, 1986.

Katzner, Kenneth. *The Languages of the World*. New York: Funk & Wagnalls, 1975.

Kister, Kenneth. *Dictionary Buying Guide*. New York: R. R. Bowker, 1977.

Kučera, Henry. "Computers in Language Analysis and in Lexicography." In *The American Heritage Dictionary*: New College Edition, xxxviii–xl. Edited by William Morris. Boston: Houghton Mifflin, 1976.

———. "The Mathematics of Language." In *The American Heritage Dictionary*: Second College Edition, 37–41. Boston: Houghton Mifflin, 1982.

Kučera, H[enry], and W. Francis. *Computational Analysis of Present-Day American English*. Providence, R.I.: Brown University Press, 1967.

Laird, Charlton Grant. *Language in America*. New York: World Publishing Company, 1970.

Landau, Sidney I. *Dictionaries: The Art and Craft of Lexicography*. New York: Scribners, 1984.

———. "The Numbers' Game: Dictionary Entry Count." *RQ* (September 1964): 6, 13–15.

Miller, Casey, and Kate Swift. *Words and Women: New Language in New Times*. New York: Anchor/Doubleday, 1976.

Newman, Edwin. *A Civil Tongue*. New York: Bobbs-Merrill, 1976.

———. *Strictly Speaking: Will America Be the Death of English?* New York: Bobbs-Merrill, 1974.

Pei, Mario. *Words in Sheep's Clothing*. New York: Hawthorn, 1969.

Pierson, Robert M. *Desk Dic·tio·nar·ies: A Consumer's Guide*. Chicago and London: American Library Association, 1986.

———. "Offensive Epithets in Six Dictionaries." *Reference Services Review* (Fall 1984): 41–48.

Read, Allen Walker. "Approaches to Lexicography and Semantics." In *Current Trends in Linguistics* 10: 145–205. The Hague: Mouton, 1972.

———. "Dictionary." In *Encyclopaedia Britannica: Macropaedia* 5: 713–22. Chicago: Encyclopaedia Britannica, 1977.

Rogers, Byron. "Eric Partridge and the Underworld of Language." *Horizon* (Winter 1976): 49–53.

Shipley, Joseph T. *In Praise of English: The Growth and Use of Language*. New York: Times Books, 1977.

Sledd, James, and Wilma R. Edditt. *Dictionaries and That Dictionary*. Chicago: Scott, Foresman, 1962.

Smitherman, Geneva. *Talkin and Testifyin: The Language of Black America*. Boston: Houghton Mifflin, 1977.

Stubbs, K. L. "Dictionaries after 1800." In *Encyclopedia of Library and Information Science*, edited by Allen Kent and Harold Lancour, 7: 191–207. New York: Marcel Dekker, 1972.

U.S. General Services Administration. Federal Supply Service. *Federal Specification: Dictionaries, English*. Washington, D.C.: Government Printing Office, 28 June 1974. (Superintendent of Documents Number: GS 2.8: G-D-331D.)

Wells, Ronald A. *Dictionaries and the Authoritarian Tradition: A Study in English Usage and Lexicography*. The Hague: Mouton, 1973.

West, M. *A General Service List of English Words*. London: Longman, 1953.

Whittaker, Kenneth. *Dictionaries*. New York: Philosophical Library, 1966.

List of Publishers

American Map Corporation
Subsidiary of Langenscheidt Publishers, Inc.
46–35 54th Road
Maspeth, NY 11378
(718) 784-0055
The Great World Atlas

Avon Books
A Division of The Hearst Corp.
105 Madison Avenue
New York, NY 10016
(212) 481-5600
The Concise Columbia Encyclopedia
Oxford American Dictionary

The Ayer Company, Publishers, Inc.
382 Main Street
Box 958
Salem, NH 03079
(603) 898-1200
A Dictionary of the English Language

Ballantine/Del Rey/Fawcett Books
A Division of Random House, Inc.
201 East 50th Street
New York, NY 10022
(212) 751-2600
New Words Dictionary
Practical English: 1000 Most Effective Words
The Random House Basic Dictionary of
  Synonyms and Antonyms
The Random House Dictionary
Webster's New School & Office Dictionary

Bantam Books
A Division of Bantam Doubleday Dell Publishing
  Group, Inc.
666 Fifth Avenue
New York, NY 10103
(212) 765-6500
The Scribner-Bantam English Dictionary
The Thorndike Barnhart Handy Pocket
  Dictionary

Barnes & Noble Books
Division of Harper & Row, Publishers, Inc.
10 East 53rd Street
New York, NY 10022
(212) 207-7000
Allen's Synonyms and Antonyms
Webster's Dictionary for Everyday Use
Roget's University Thesaurus

Barron's Educational Series Inc.
250 Wireless Blvd.
Hauppauge, NY 11788
(516) 434-3311
A Dictionary of American Idioms: 2nd
  Revised Edition

John Bartholomew & Son, Ltd
Duncan Street
Edinburgh Scotland
EH91TA
The Bartholomew Mini World Atlas
(See also Hammond, Inc.)

The Belknap Press
(See Harvard University Press)

Berkley Publishing Group
Subsidiary of The Putnam Publishing Group
200 Madison Avenue
New York, NY 10016
(212) 686-9820
Webster's II New Riverside Dictionary

Cambridge University Press
32 East 57th Street
New York, NY 10022
(212) 688-8885
Chambers Concise 20th Century Dictionary
Chambers Idioms
Chambers Mini Dictionary
Chambers Pocket Guide to Good English
Chambers Pocket 20th Century Dictionary
Chambers 20th Century Dictionary
Chambers 20th Century Thesaurus
Chambers Universal Learner's Dictionary
Chambers Wordlore

Clarendon Press
(See Oxford University Press)

Columbia University Press
562 West 113th Street
New York, NY 10025
(212) 316-7100
The Concise Columbia Encyclopedia
Words on Words

Cornwall Books
440 Forsgate Drive
Cranbury, NJ 08512
(609) 655-4770
A Dictionary of Pronunciation

591

Dell Publishing Co., Inc.
A Division of Bantam Doubleday Dell Publishing
    Group, Inc.
1 Dag Hammarskjold Plaza
New York, NY 10017
(212) 605-3000
    The American Heritage Dictionary

J. M. Dent & Sons, Ltd.
33 Welbeck Street
London W1M 8LX
England
    Everyman's Encyclopedia (on-line)

Doubleday & Company
A Division of Bantam Doubleday Dell Publishing
    Group, Inc.
666 Fifth Avenue
New York, NY 10103
(212) 984-7561
    *The Doubleday Dictionary for Home, School,
        and Office*
    *The Doubleday Roget's Thesaurus in
        Dictionary Form*

Dover Publications, Inc.
31 East Second Street
Mineola, NY 11501
(516) 294-7000
    *An Etymological Dictionary of Modern
        English*

Elsevier Publishing Company, Inc.
Subsidiary of Elsevier NDU NV
52 Vanderbilt Avenue
New York, NY 10017
(212) 370-5520
    *Comprehensive Etymological Dictionary of
        the English Language*

Encyclopaedia Britannica, Inc.
310 South Michigan Avenue
Chicago, IL 60604
(312) 347-7000
    Britannica Atlas
    The New Encyclopaedia Britannica

Facts on File, Inc.
Subsidiary of Commerce Clearing House
460 Park Avenue South
New York, NY 10016
(212) 683-2244
    British English, A to Zed
    *The Facts on File Dictionary of Troublesome
        Words*

    *The Facts on File Encyclopedia of Word and
        Phrase Origins*
    The Facts on File Visual Dictionary
    No Uncertain Terms
    1000 Most Challenging Words
    1000 Most Important Words
    1000 Most Practical Words

Fawcett Books
(See Ballantine)

J. G. Ferguson Publishing Company
111 East Wacker Drive
Chicago, IL 60601
(312) 861-0666
    *Webster Comprehensive Dictionary:
        Encyclopedic Edition*
    *Webster Comprehensive Dictionary:
        International Edition*
    Webster Illustrated Contemporary Dictionary

The Frontier Press Company
P.O. Box 1098
Columbus, OH 43216
(614) 864-3737
    The Lincoln Library of Essential Information

Funk & Wagnalls, Inc.
70 Hilltop Road
Ramsey, NJ 07446
(201) 934-7500
    Funk & Wagnalls New Encyclopedia
    Funk & Wagnalls Standard Desk Dictionary
    (See also Harper & Row, Publishers, Inc.)

Gale Research Company
Subsidiary of International Thomson Library
    Services
Book Tower
Detroit, MI 48226
(313) 961-2242
    *Dictionary of Collective Nouns and Group
        Terms*
    —Ologies and —Isms: A Thematic Dictionary
    *Prefixes and Other Word-Initial Elements of
        English*
    *Suffixes and Other Word-Final Elements of
        English*

General Videotex Corporation
3 Blackstone Street
Cambridge, MA 02139
(617) 491-3393
    Kussmaul Encyclopedia (on-line)

Graphic Learning International
One Galleria Tower
Suite 1425
Dallas, TX 75240
    Concise Earthbook
    Earthbook

Grolier Inc.
Sherman Turnpike
Danbury, CT 06816
(203) 797-3500
    Academic American Encyclopedia
    Academic American Encyclopedia
      (CD-ROM)
    Academic American Encyclopedia (on-line)
    Encyclopedia Americana

G. K. Hall & Company
A Division of Macmillan Publishing Company
70 Lincoln Street
Boston, MA 02111
(617) 423-3990
    The Merriam-Webster Dictionary for Large
      Print Users
    The Merriam-Webster Thesaurus for Large
      Print Users

Halstead Press
(See Wiley)

Hammond, Inc.
515 Valley Street
Maplewood, NJ 07040
(201) 763-6000
    Ambassador World Atlas
    Bartholomew Mini World Atlas
    Citation World Atlas
    Gold Medallion World Atlas
    Hammond Large Type World Atlas
    International World Atlas
    The Whole Earth Atlas

Harper & Row, Publishers, Inc.
Subsidiary of News America Holdings, Inc.
10 East 53rd Street
New York, NY 10022
(212) 207-7000
    A Browser's Dictionary
    Choose the Right Word
    Funk & Wagnalls Standard Desk Dictionary
    Funk & Wagnalls Standard Handbook of
      Synonyms, Antonyms, and Prepositions
    Harper Dictionary of Contemporary Usage,
      2nd Edition
    New Dictionary of American Slang
    Roget's International Thesaurus, Fourth
      Edition

Harvard University Press
79 Garden Street
Cambridge, MA 02138
(617) 495-2600
    The Dictionary of American Regional English

Hill & Wang
A Division of Farrar, Straus & Giroux, Inc.
19 Union Square West
New York, NY 10003
(212) 741-6900
    Modern American Usage

Houghton Mifflin Company
One Beacon Street
Boston, MA 02108
(617) 725-5000
    The American Heritage Desk Dictionary
    The American Heritage Dictionary of Indo-
      European Roots
    The American Heritage Dictionary: Second
      College Edition
    The American Heritage Illustrated
      Encyclopedic Dictionary
    The Concise American Heritage Dictionary
    The Right Word II: A Concise Thesaurus
    Roget's II: The New Thesaurus
    Webster's II New Riverside Pocket Dictionary
    Webster's II New Riverside University
      Dictionary
    Word Mysteries & Histories

Hugo's Language Books Ltd.
(Distributed by Littlefield, Adams & Co.)
81 Adams Drive
Totowa, NJ 07512
    Hugo English Dictionary

Humanities Press International, Inc.
171 First Avenue
Atlantic Highlands, NJ 07716-1289
(201) 872-1441
    Dictionary of Contemporary American
      English Contrasted with British English

The Johns Hopkins University Press
701 West 40th Street, Suite 275
Baltimore, MD 21211
(301) 338-6900
    The Origins of English Words

Langenscheidt Publishers, Inc.
46–35 54th Road
Maspeth, NY 11378
(718) 784-0055
    The Little Webster
    The Universal Webster

Lexik House
P.O. Box 247
75 Main Street
Cold Spring, NY 10516
(914) 265-2822
   The Barnhart Dictionary Companion

The Library Reproduction Service of the
   Microfilm Company of California
1977 South Los Angeles Street
Los Angeles, CA 90011
(213) 749-2463
   The Random House Dictionary: Classic
      Edition ·
   Roget's International Thesaurus: Third
      Edition
   Webster's New Collegiate Dictionary
   Webster's New World Thesaurus

Littlefield, Adams & Company
81 Adams Drive
Totowa, NJ 07512
(201) 256-8600
   A Concise Dictionary of Correct English
   A Dictionary of Word Origins

Longman, Inc.
Subsidiary of Longman Group USA, Inc.
Longman Building
95 Church Street
White Plains, NY 10601
(914) 993-5000
   Longman Dictionary of American English
   Longman Dictionary of Contemporary
      English
   Longman Dictionary of English Idioms
   Longman Dictionary of Phrasal Verbs
   Longman Lexicon of Contemporary English
   Longman Photo Dictionary

McFarland & Company, Inc. Publishers
Box 611
Jefferson, NC 28640
(919) 246-4460
   Homophones and Homographs: An American
      Dictionary
   McGraw-Hill Pictorial Atlas of the World

Macmillan Publishing Co., Inc.
A Division of Macmillan, Inc.
866 Third Avenue
New York, NY 10022
(212) 702-2000
   Collier's Encyclopedia

   Origins: A Short Etymological Dictionary of
      Modern English

Merriam-Webster Inc.
Subsidiary of Encyclopaedia Britannica, Inc.
47 Federal Street
Springfield, MA 01102
(413) 734-3134
   A Pronouncing Dictionary of American
      English
   Webster's Collegiate Thesaurus
   Webster's Compact Dictionary of Synonyms
   Webster's Concise Family Dictionary
   Webster's Concise Family Dictionary: Large
      Print Edition
   Webster's New Dictionary of Synonyms
   Webster's New Collegiate Dictionary: Large
      Print Edition
   Webster's New Ideal Dictionary
   Webster's Ninth New Collegiate Dictionary
   Webster's Third New International Dictionary
   Webster's Vest Pocket Dictionary
   12,000 Words

Methuen, Inc.
(See Routledge, Chapman & Hall)

Microsoft Corporation
16011 NE 36th Way
Box 97017
Redmond, WA 98073-9717
(206) 882-8080
   Microsoft Bookshelf CD-ROM Reference
      Library (on-line)

National Geographic Society
17 & "M" Sts. NW
Washington, DC 20036
(202) 857-7000
   National Geographic Atlas of the World

National Library Service for the Blind and
   Physically Handicapped
The Library of Congress
Washington, DC 20542
   (Write for list of titles currently available.)

National Textbook Company
A Division of NTC Publishing Group
4255 W. Touhy Avenue
Lincolnwood, IL 60646-1975
(312) 679-5500
   Beginner's Dictionary of American English
      Usage
   British/American Language Dictionary

Everyday American English Dictionary
NTC's American Idioms Dictionary

Thomas Nelson, Inc.
Nelson Place at Elm Hill Pike
Nashville, TN 37214
(615) 889-9000
 Nelson's New Compact Webster's Dictionary
 Nelson's New Compact Roget's Thesaurus
 Webster's New Compact Dictionary for
  School and Office
 Webster's New Dictionary and Roget's
  Thesaurus
 Webster's Vest Pocket Dictionary

New American Library
1633 Broadway
New York, NY 10019
(212) 397-8000
 The Basic Book of Synonyms and Antonyms
 Funk & Wagnalls Standard Dictionary
 The New American Desk Encyclopedia
 The New American Roget's College Thesaurus
  in Dictionary Form
 New American Webster Handy College
  Dictionary
 Webster's New World Dictionary: The
  Concise Edition

New Century Publishers, Inc.
A Division of New Century Education
 Corporation
220 Old New Brunswick Road
Piscataway, NJ 08854
(201) 981-0820
 The New Century Vest-Pocket Webster
  Dictionary

Oxford University Press, Inc.
200 Madison Avenue
New York, NY 10016
(212) 679-7300
 The Compact Edition of the Oxford English
  Dictionary
 The Concise Oxford Dictionary of Current
  English
 The Concise Oxford Dictionary of English
  Etymology
 A Dictionary of Modern English Usage
 An English-Reader's Dictionary
 The Large Print Version of The Little Oxford
  Dictionary of Current English
 The Little Oxford Dictionary of Current
  English
 Oxford Advanced Learner's Dictionary of
  Current English
 Oxford American Dictionary

Oxford Dictionary of Current Idiomatic
 English
Oxford Dictionary of English Etymology
Oxford-Duden Pictorial English Dictionary
The Oxford English Dictionary and
 Supplement
The Oxford English Dictionary on Compact
 Disc
The Oxford Guide to the English Language
The Oxford Guide to English Usage
The Oxford Minidictionary
Oxford Student's Dictionary of American
 English
Oxford Student's Dictionary of Current
 English
The Pocket Oxford Dictionary of Current
 English
Practical English Usage
Shorter Oxford English Dictionary on
 Historical Principles

Passport Books
(See National Textbook Company)

Penguin
(See Viking Penguin Inc.)

Philosophical Library, Inc.
200 West 57th Street, Suite 510
New York, NY 10019
(212) 265-6050
 Dictionary of Word Origins

Pocket Books
A Division of Simon & Schuster, Inc.
The Simon & Schuster Building
1230 Avenue of the Americas
New York, NY 10020
(212) 698-7000
 Dictionary of Problem Words and
  Expressions
 The Merriam-Webster Dictionary
 The Merriam-Webster Pocket Dictionary of
  Synonyms
 Mrs. Byrne's Dictionary of Unusual, Obscure,
  and Preposterous Words
 Roget's Pocket Thesaurus

Prentice Hall Press
A Division of Simon & Schuster, Inc.
Sylvan Avenue
Englewood Cliffs, NJ 07632
(201) 592-2000
 Basic Dictionary of English
 Encyclopedic Dictionary of English Usage
 A Handy Book of Commonly Used American
  Idioms
 The Prentice-Hall New World Atlas

The Prentice-Hall Pocket Atlas of the World
The Prentice-Hall Universal Atlas
The Prentice-Hall University Atlas
Webster's New Twentieth Century Dictionary:
   Unabridged, Second Edition
Webster's New World Compact Dictionary of
   American English
Webster's New World Dictionary: Second
   College Edition
Webster's New World Compact School &
   Office Dictionary
Webster's New World Pocket Dictionary
Webster's New World Large Print Dictionary
   of the American Language: Second Concise
   Edition
Webster's New World Thesaurus

Rand McNally & Company
8255 Central Park Avenue
Skokie, IL 60076
(312) 673-9100
   The New International Atlas
   Rand McNally Contemporary World Atlas
   Rand McNally Cosmopolitan World Atlas
   The Rand McNally Desk Reference World
      Atlas
   Rand McNally Family World Atlas
   Rand McNally Goode's World Atlas
   Rand McNally Images of the World
   Rand McNally Quick Reference World Atlas

Random House, Inc.
201 East 50th Street
New York, NY 10022
(212) 751-2600
   The Random House American Dictionary:
      New Revised Edition
   The Random House College Dictionary:
      Revised Edition
   The Random House Concise World Atlas
   The Random House Dictionary: Concise
      Edition
   The Random House Dictionary of the English
      Language: Second Edition, Unabridged
   The Random House Mini World Atlas
   The Random House Thesaurus: College
      Edition
   The Random House Thesaurus: A Dictionary
      of Synonyms and Antonyms

The Reader's Digest Association
Reader's Digest Road
Pleasantville, NY 10570
(914) 769-7000

Reader's Digest Family Word Finder
Reader's Digest Illustrated Encyclopedic
   Dictionary
Reader's Digest Wide World Atlas

Routledge, Chapman & Hall
29 West 35th Street
New York, NY 10001
(212) 244-3336
   Dictionary of Changes in Meaning
   Dictionary of Confusing Words and Meanings
   Dictionary of True Etymologies

Rowman & Littlefield
(See Littlefield, Adams & Company)

Salem House Publishers Ltd.
Subsidiary of News America Holdings, Inc.
462 Boston Street
Topsfield, MA 01983
(617) 887-2440
   The American Encyclopedic Dictionary

Simon & Schuster, Inc.
Subsidiary of Gulf & Western, Inc.
The Simon & Schuster Building
1230 Avenue of the Americas
New York, NY 10020
(212) 698-7000
   Webster's New World Dictionary of Synonyms
   Webster's New World Vest Pocket Dictionary

The Southwestern Company
P.O. Box 820
Nashville, TN 37202
(615) 790-4000
   The Volume Library

Standard Educational Corporation
200 West Monroe
Chicago, IL 60606
(312) 346-7440
   New Standard Encyclopedia

Stein & Day Publishers
Scarborough House
Briarcliff Manor, NY 10510
(914) 762-2151
   The Dictionary of Eponyms: Names That
      Became Words

Times Books
Subsidiary of Random House, Inc.
201 East 50th Street
New York, NY 10022
(212) 751-2600
  The New York Times Atlas of the World
  New York Times Everyday Reader's
    Dictionary of Misunderstood, Misused, and
    Mispronounced Words
  The Times Atlas of the World

Times Books
(See also Ayer)

Tri Star Publishing
Subsidiary of Reed Telepublishing
475 Virginia Drive
Fort Washington, PA 19034
(215) 641-6000
  The Oxford English Dictionary on Compact
    Disc

U.S. Department of State
Distributed by the Superintendent of Documents
U.S. Government Printing Office
Washington, DC 20402
  Background Notes on the Countries of the
    World

Van Nostrand Reinhold Company, Inc.
A Division of International Thomson
  Organization, Inc.
115 Fifth Avenue
New York, NY 10003
(212) 254-3232
  American Usage and Style: The Consensus
  VNR Pocket Atlas

Verbatim Books
Subsidiary of Verbatim, The Language Quarterly
Affiliate of Laurence Urdang, Inc.
4 Laurel Heights
Old Lyme, CT 06371
(203) 434-2104
  Word for Word

Viking-Penguin Inc.
40 W. 23 Street
New York, NY 10010
(212) 337-5200
  The New Penguin World Atlas
  The Penguin Dictionary of Troublesome
    Words
  The Penguin Pocket Thesaurus
  The Penguin Roget's Thesaurus of English
    Words and Phrases
  Usage and Abusage

Warner Books, Inc.
Subsidiary of Warner Publishing, Inc.
666 Fifth Avenue
New York, NY 10103
(212) 484-2900
  A Dictionary of Synonyms and Antonyms
  The Quintessential Dictionary
  The Synonym Finder
  Webster's New World Dictionary of the
    American Language
  Webster's New World Thesaurus

Washington Square Press
(See Pocket Books)

John Wiley & Sons, Inc.
605 Third Avenue
New York, NY 10158
(212) 850-6000
  A Concept Dictionary of English

The H. W. Wilson Company
950 University Avenue
Bronx, NY 10452
(212) 588-8400
  The Barnhart Dictionary of Etymology

World Book, Inc.
Subsidiary of the Scott Fetzer Company
Merchandise Mart Plaza
Chicago, IL 60654
(312) 245-3456
  The World Book Dictionary
  The World Book Encyclopedia

Acknowledgments

Page numbers are followed by titles listed in alphabetical order.

Page 64 from volume 9, page 248 in *Academic American Encyclopedia.* Copyright © 1988 by Grolier Incorporated. Reprinted by permission of Grolier Incorporated.

Page 240 from *The American Encyclopedic Dictionary,* page 286. Copyright © 1987 by Text Bay Books Pty Ltd. derived from the Oxford Illustrated Dictionary © Oxford University Press; © Illustrations and captions: Bay Books Pty Ltd. Reprinted by permission of Salem House Publishers.

Page 243 from *The American Heritage Desk Dictionary,* page 269. Copyright © 1981 by Houghton Mifflin Company. Reprinted by permission of Houghton Mifflin Company.

Page 416 from *The American Heritage Dictionary of Indo-European Roots,* page 37, ed. Calvert Watkins. Copyright © 1985 by Houghton Mifflin Company. Reprinted by permission of Houghton Mifflin Company.

Page 251 from *The American Heritage Dictionary: Second College Edition,* page 1309. Copyright © 1985 by Houghton Mifflin Company. Reprinted by permission of Houghton Mifflin Company.

Page 256 from *The American Heritage Illustrated Encyclopedic Dictionary,* page 1216. Copyright © 1987 by Houghton Mifflin Company. Reprinted by permission of Houghton Mifflin Company.

Page 418 from *The Barnhart Dictionary Companion,* volume III, no. 4, Winter 1984, page 110. Copyright © 1987 by Lexik House Publishers. Reprinted by permission of Lexik House Publishers.

Page 420 from Robert K. Barnhart, *The Barnhart Dictionary of Etymology,* page 50, ed. Sol Steinmetz. Copyright © 1987 by the H. W. Wilson Company. Reprinted by permission of the H. W. Wilson Company.

Page 260 from *The Basic Dictionary of English,* page 112, ed. G. Capelle. Copyright © 1983 by Regents Publishing Company, Inc. Reprinted by permission of Regents Publishing Company, Inc.

Page 504 from *Beginner's Dictionary of American English Usage,* page 121, eds. P. H. Collin, Miriam Lowi, and Carol Weiland. Copyright © 1986 by Voluntad Publishers, Inc., a subsidiary of National Textbook Company. Reprinted by permission of National Textbook Company.

Page 262 from *Chambers Concise 20th Century Dictionary,* page 648, eds. G. W. Davidson, M. A. Seaton and J. Simpson. Copyright © 1985 by W. & R. Chambers, Ltd., Edinburgh. Reprinted by permission of W. & R. Chambers, Ltd.

Page 512 from *Chambers Idioms,* page 46, eds. E. M. Kirkpatrick and C. M. Schwarz. Copyright © 1982 by W. & R. Chambers, Ltd., Edinburgh. Reprinted by permission of W. & R. Chambers, Ltd.

Page 264 from *Chambers Mini Dictionary: New Edition,* page 671, ed. E. M. Kirkpatrick. Copyright © 1983 by W. & R. Chambers, Ltd., Edinburgh. Reprinted by permission of W. & R. Chambers, Ltd.

Page 267 from *Chambers 20th Century Dictionary,* page 671, ed. E. M. Kirkpatrick. Copyright © 1983 by W. & R. Chambers, Ltd., Edinburgh. Reprinted by permission of W. & R. Chambers, Ltd.

Page 472 from *Chambers 20th Century Thesaurus,* page 431, eds. M. A. Seaton, G. W. Davidson, C. M. Schwarz and J. Simpson. Copyright © 1986 by W. & R. Chambers, Ltd., Edinburgh. Reprinted by permission of W. & R. Chambers, Ltd.

Page 75 from volume 12, page 409 in *Collier's Encyclopedia.* Copyright © 1986 by Macmillan Educational Company. Reprinted by permission of Macmillan Educational Company.

Page 423 from Ernest Klein, *Comprehensive Etymological Dictionary of the English Language,* page 125. Copyright © 1971 by Elsevier Science Publishers, The Netherlands. Reprinted by permission of Elsevier Science Publishers.

Page 82 from page 481 in *The Concise Columbia Encyclopedia.* Copyright © 1983 by Columbia University Press. Reprinted by permission of Columbia University Press.

Page 426 from *The Concise Oxford Dictionary of English Etymology,* page 144, ed. T. F. Hoad. Copyright © 1986 by Oxford University Press. Reprinted by permission of Oxford University Press.

Page 426 from Adrian Room, *Dictionary of Changes in Meaning,* page 169. Copyright © 1986 by Adrian Room. Reprinted by permission of Routledge, Chapman and Hall.

Page 524 from H. W. Fowler, *A Dictionary of Modern English Usage: Second Edition,* page 109, ed. Sir Ernest Gowers. Copyright © 1965 by Oxford University Press.

Page 429 from Samuel Johnson, *A Dictionary of the English Language.* Reprinted by permission of Times Books.

Page 432 from Robert Hendrickson, *The Dictionary of Eponyms: Names That Became Words,* page 37. Copyright © 1972 by Robert Hendrickson. Reprinted by permission of Stein & Day Publishers.

Page 316 from Eugene Ehrlich, Stuart Berg Flexner, Gorton Carruth, and Joyce M. Hawkins, *Oxford American Dictionary*, page 314. Copyright © 1980 by Oxford University Press, Inc. Reprinted by permission of Oxford University Press, Inc.

Page 445 from *The Oxford Dictionary of English Etymology*, page 566, ed. C. T. Onions. Copyright © 1966 by Oxford University Press, Inc. Reprinted by permission of Oxford University Press, Inc.

Page 320 from *The Oxford English Dictionary*, page 491, eds. James A. H. Murray, Henry Bradley, W. A. Craigie, and C. T. Onions. Copyright © 1933 by Oxford University Press. Reprinted by Oxford University Press.

Page 329 from A. S. Hornby, *Oxford Student's Dictionary of American English*, page 67, eds. Dolores Harris and William A. Stewart. Copyright © 1986 by Oxford University Press. Reprinted by permission of Oxford University Press.

Page 563 from *Prefixes and Other Word-Initial Elements of English*, page 345, eds. Laurence Urdang and Alexander Humez. Copyright © 1984 by Gale Research Company. Reprinted by permission of Gale Research Company.

Page 336 from *The Random House College Dictionary: Revised Edition*, page 691. Copyright © 1984 by Random House, Inc. Reprinted by permission of Random House, Inc.

Page 341 from *The Random House Dictionary of the English Language: Second Edition, Unabridged*, page 223, ed. Stuart Berg Flexner. Copyright © 1987 by Random House, Inc. Reprinted by permission of Random House, Inc.

Page 485 from *The Random House Thesaurus: College Edition*, page 362, eds. Jess Stein and Stuart Berg Flexner. Copyright © 1984 by Random House, Inc. Reprinted by permission of Random House, Inc.

Page 462 from *Reader's Digest Family Word Finder*, page 695. Copyright © 1975 by The Reader's Digest Association. Reprinted by permission of the Reader's Digest Association.

Page 486 from *The Right Word II*, page 106. Copyright © 1983 by Houghton Mifflin Company. Reprinted by permission of Houghton Mifflin Company.

Page 488 from *Roget's International Thesaurus: Fourth Edition*, page 478, revised by Robert L. Chapman. Copyright © 1977 by Harper & Row, Publishers, Inc. Reprinted by permission of Harper & Row, Publishers, Inc.

Page 492 from *Roget's II: The New Thesaurus*, page 75, ed. Fernando de Mello Vianno. Copyright © 1980 by Houghton Mifflin Company. Reprinted by permission of Houghton Mifflin Company.

Page 494 from *Roget's University Thesaurus*, page 189, ed. C. O. Sylvester Mawson. Copyright © 1963 by Harper & Row, Publishers, Inc. Reprinted by permission of Barnes & Noble Books, a Division of Harper & Row, Publishers, Inc.

Page 462 from J. I. Rodale, *The Synonym Finder*, page 437, eds. Laurence Urdang and Nancy LaRoche. Copyright © 1978 by Rodale Press, Inc. Reprinted by permission of Rodale Press, Inc.

Page 354 by permission. From *12,000 Words*, page 119. Copyright © 1986 by Merriam-Webster Inc., publisher of the Merriam-Webster® dictionaries.

Page 569 from Eric Partridge, *Usage and Abusage*, page 375. Copyright © 1973 by the Estate of Eric Partridge. Reprinted by permission of Viking-Penguin, Inc.

Page 495 by permission. From *Webster's Collegiate Thesaurus*, page 498. Copyright © 1976 by Merriam-Webster Inc., publisher of the Merriam-Webster® dictionaries.

Page 361 from *Webster's Comprehensive Dictionary: International Edition*, volume one, page 336. Copyright © 1986 by J. G. Ferguson Publishing Company. Reprinted by permission of J. G. Ferguson Publishing Company.

Page 368 from *Webster's New Dictionary and Roget's Thesaurus*, pages 53–54. Copyright © 1984 by Thomas Nelson, Inc. Reprinted by permission of Thomas Nelson, Inc.

Page 467 by permission. From *Webster's New Dictionary of Synonyms*, page 382. Copyright © 1984 by Merriam-Webster Inc., publisher of the Merriam-Webster® dictionaries.

Page 370 by permission. From *Webster's New Ideal Dictionary*, page 389. Copyright © 1984 by Merriam-Webster Inc., publisher of the Merriam-Webster® dictionaries.

Page 375 from *Webster's New Twentieth Century Dictionary of the English Language: Unabridged, Second Edition*, page 258, ed. Jean L. McKechnie. Copyright © 1983 by Simon & Schuster. Reprinted by permission of Simon & Schuster, Inc.

Page 469 from *Webster's New World Dictionary of Synonyms*, page 209, eds. Ruth Kimball Kent and David B. Guralnik. Copyright © 1984 by Simon & Schuster, Inc. Reprinted by permission of Simon & Schuster, Inc.

Page 386 from *Webster's New World Dictionary of the American Language: Second College Edition*, page 4, ed. David B. Guralnik. Copyright © 1986 by Simon & Schuster, Inc. Reprinted by permission of Simon & Schuster, Inc.

Page 497 from *Webster's New World Thesaurus*, page 59, ed. Charlton G. Laird. Copyright © 1974 by Charlton G. Laird. Reprinted by permission of Simon & Schuster, Inc.

Index

Titles with full reviews in this Buying Guide appear below in small capital letters. Inclusive page numbers for full reviews are in boldface type. All other titles are in italics. Abbreviations of titles are fully cross-referenced (for example, "AHD. See *American Heritage Dictionary, The*"). Italic page numbers indicate facsimiles and other illustrations.